From the original design by J. Fouracre.

THE SIEGE OF PLYMOUTH, 1643-1645.

THE GOOD WOMEN COURAGEOUSLY BRING STRONG WATERS TO THE MEN.

(From a memorial window erected at the Plymouth Club, testifying the enduring regard of the members for and their admiration of their Chairman, F. B. Westlake, 1895).

PLYMOUTH AND DEVONPORT:

IN TIMES OF WAR AND PEACE.

BY

· HENRY FRANCIS WHITFELD.

Author of " Overcrowded Plymouth," &c.

BLESS'D is the ideal charm attach'd to PLACE
That thus throws round it an illusive grace,
The LOCAL LOVE that with resistless force
Wings the plum'd bird, and nerves the noble horse ;
O'er sky-wrapt crags the eagle's pinions wave,
The monarch lion loves his forest cave ;
Each has a sympathy for den or nest ;
Some dear retreat--the scene of play or rest ;
And humbler names with anxious care provide
One spot—preferr'd to all the world beside.
There is no charm in this our pilgrimage,
More dear—aye, even to the heart of age,
Than when the fond Remembrancer displays
The fair localities of early days :
Delightful are her visions—at her calls
They rise—of youths the hopes and pleasures all ;
The entrancing joys, the griefs, the groundless fears
That brighten'd, darken'd, all our infant years.—*Carrington.*

PLYMOUTH: E. CHAPPLE, GEORGE STREET.

DEVONPORT: HIORNS & MILLER, FORE STREET.

[*All Rights Reserved.*]

1900.

PRINTED AT
" YE CAXTON PRESS,"
DEVONPORT.

PREFACE.

TAMAR rolls
His sinuous course 'mid foliage, flowers, and songs,
Until he mingles with the azure Sound,
The reservoir of rivers. Silvery bays
Are seen where commerce lifts the peaceful sail,
Or where the war-barks rise; the indented coast
Frowns with wave-breasting rocks, nor does the eye
Forget the proud display of bustling towns
And busy arsenals, and cliffs high crown'd
With pealing batteries, and flags that wave
In the fresh ocean gale.
—*Carrington.*

THE present work represents the first attempt that has been made to blend the histories of Plymouth and Devonport. Originally the intention of the author was to supply the romance of their development during the century which is now rapidly closing in. When, however, he thought that his task was approaching completion, he discovered that it was in reality beginning. There had been a desire—strongly expressed for some years—that the past of the Three Towns should be realistically recalled, and the author had to some extent anticipated this wish by devoting himself to the collection of more picturesque material than had presumably hitherto been gathered. A vein of a new order was thus struck, and, with the perception of its interest, it became a fascination to pursue it until it was apparently exhausted.

Rich in romantic and legendary lore, and wealthier still in the achievements of her many maritime heroes, "Plymouth, Mother Plymouth sitting by the Sea," has reflected, through the panoramic roll of centuries, with a versatility that scarcely any other great town in the kingdom can claim, the pulsating hopes and fears of the nation. The enthusiasm for the place of his birth which every Plymothian feels, springs from the consciousness that his ancestors were primarily concerned in laying the foundations of the mightiest Empire for beneficence that the world has known. "The town," wrote Camden, three centuries ago, "is not large, but its reputation is very great among all nations, and that not so much for the convenience of the harbour as for the excellence of the natives." In thus consecrating to the purpose of Civilization an overspreading Commerce, strange lands were explored with a courage not unworthy of the racial home of the early Britons and the Danish settlers who transmitted their sturdy Viking strain in peaceful Wessex marriages. If, in the course of the story, the gruesome occasionally stands in forbidding contrast with the gay, the appalling with the inspiriting, the sombre with the light, it must be remembered that it has been the object to impart to the present picture of local Life and Customs a simple, unimpassioned, though vivid and truthful colouring. At a time of crisis, when the national emotions are profoundly stirred by the greatest war in which our forces have been engaged for many years, the work may be useful in showing how often similar difficulties, arising from departmental mismangement, have by patience and patriotism been splendidly surmounted.

Instead of re-traversing archæological, geological, biological, and heraldic bye-ways, an effort has been made to pourtray the old Plymothians and "Dockers" in successive periods, under kaleidoscopic movements and transitions—to reproduce their habits in times of war; the excitement to which plagues, privateering, piracy and smuggling gave rise; to discuss local customs and pursuits in times of peace ; to show the forefathers at their devotions and their sports; to indicate their speculative or scientific proclivities; to deal with social conditions and criminal characteristics when capital punishment was indiscriminate ; to convey some idea of the superstitions of the weak and the lawlessness of the brutal ; to depict, for the strengthening of the faithful, the unbending integrity of champions of public right like Sir John Eliot, and the turpitude of such traitors to the common welfare as "The Bottomless Bagg."

It has been the aim of the author to present the story in chronological sequence, and to trace the effect of changing circumstances, in each essentially epoch-making era, upon high art, popular education, religious evolution, dramatic development, and general culture. The task has necessitated innumerable references to the State papers which, in recent years, have been rendered available, and the author has thus been enabled to bridge over many hitherto abandoned historic gaps. Files of newspapers, dating back to the eighteenth century, have been systematically explored ; and municipal archives have been searched with the eager interest of another standpoint. The task has been no light one. It has been conducted in the intervals of an anxious journalistic experience, and the author has produced his own work, and acted as his own publisher, in order that he might attain completeness without incurring personal loss.

The spelling of proper names and places has in general been that of the time, and every effort has been .made to ensure conciseness and compactness by reducing each event to its proper proportion. There has also been an endeavour to associate at successive stages in Plymouth and Devonport history the worthies with their deeds and spheres of influence. In other hands the material production of the volume would have · been less open to criticism, but it is hoped that its comprehensiveness may be accepted as in some degree compensatory. Among those to whom the author is especially indebted for pictorial assistance are Mr. W. H. Pike and Mr. J. Fouracre, who have contributed original drawings. The warmest acknowledgments are also due to Mr. J. Kinton Bond, for revising the proofs, and to Mr. W. H. K. Wright for the loan of his own collection of interesting topographical data. Every facility has also been offered by the Proprietary, Athenæum and Free Libraries ; and Mr. Charles Williams and Mr. J. Keys have placed several old playbills at the author's disposal, and thus supplemented the series from which he has been able to make his own representative selection.

January, 1900.

CONTENTS.

ILLUSTRATIONS.

IN APPENDIX.

PLYMOUTH AND DEVONPORT:

IN TIMES OF WAR AND PEACE.

CHAPTER I.—EARLY HISTORY.

Traditionary and Romantic. In the dimmest past, Brutus, the grandson of Æneas, wandered to the Devonshire Coast, and made discovery of a new country. Having kissed "the blessed shore," he penetrated to the place "where Totnes now doth stand," thence he pressed on to Plymouth, and there his companions solemnized their arrival with appropriate rites. Suddenly the worshippers were disturbed by the ribald jests and boastful challenges of Goemagot and his monstrous companions. The Trojans accepted the gage, but the achievements of Goemagot filled them with dismay, for his strength, alike the glory and protection of the Western barbarians, was so majestic that, with one wrench, he could upheave an oak and wield the trunk as though it were a hazel wand. Thus he wrought a mighty havoc, many of the invaders were slain, others were hewn and maimed, and the annihilation of the remainder was imminent when Brutus entreated the gods for deliverance. Using their superior weapons with inspired effect, the survivors charged in a body, killed all the giants except Goemagot, and only spared him to match his prowess against the science of Coronæus in the games that followed the victory. To quote Michael Drayton:

> Upon that lofty place at Plinmouth called the Hoe,
> Those mighty wrastlers met, with many an ireful looke,
> Who threatened as the one the other tooke.

Standing face to face, panting for breath, the rivals held each other fiercely in their arms, and, in that first-recorded Cornish "hug," Goemagot so crushed the Trojan that he fractured three of his ribs. Pain and mortification incensed and nerved Coronæus to a supreme effort, lusty sinews swelled like cables, fire glowed in the eyes of the combatants, and trampling feet sent thunder out of earth:

> Then Corin up did take
> The Giant 'twixt the graynes and voyding of his hold,
> Before his cumbrous feet he well recover could,
> Pitched headlong from the hill.

Goemagot fell with a crash upon the rocks, the coast was bespattered with his blood, the ocean "feasted on his wasted gore," and, when the tide returned, the soul of the victim had "flitted to the infernal dead," and the waters overspread a corpse twelve cubits long. From century to century was transmitted this tradition, the place where the giant fell was called "Goemagot's Leap," and, for generations, there remained engraven upon the native granite of the Hoe, the "portrayture" of two men, the one more massive than the other, "with clubbes in their hands." Through the obscure to the Middle Ages the old Plymothians pointed out to their children the cave in which the giants dwelt, and when the cliffs of Wynrigge—or the Hoe—were excavated, in the reign of Charles II., to give place to the Citadel, and the fossils of mammoths were discovered, the wondering workmen were assured, as they believed, that the great teeth and jaws were those of Goemagot. More recent excavations at Mount Batten and Cattedown prove that, if there were no giants in the earlier days, the district was infested with lions, rhinoceros, wolves, hyænas and foxes, and that horses and oxen of huge proportions were not unknown.

As soon as the student emerges from the mists of mythology he is confronted by a nebulous and impenetrable interval, in which fable is blended with fact and imagination plays its lively part. The discovery of kistvaens and urns in Union and Stillman Streets afford incontestable evidence of occupation in the Stone Age, and the unearthing of a skeleton at Mount Batten, buried with its face to the sun, is proof of a prehistoric population. The merchants came from afar in their ornate sloops to purchase tin and fish and other commodities, and the island at the mouth of the Tamar was one of the chief emporia of enterprise. Industriously working in metals and clays at Batten and Cawsand, the natives fashioned daggers, knives and spearheads for their warriors; bracelets, rings, brooches and scissors for their wives and daughters; and, in the mirrors of bronze which they polished, the swarthy heathen beauties admired their comely persons. The potters calcined in black and yellow, and produced in abundance bowls and jars, vases, drinking cups, and cooking pots—evolving from nature's law the ingenious promptings of necessity and offering to the traders their superfluous wares. The scattered hamlets by the Tamar and the Plym rose and fell with the degrees of importance thus attained; but as their fame went forth so was their doom encompassed, and the foreign pirates were only surpassed in their greed by British Princes, who regained their fastnesses after each descent on horses mightily ridden.

The scene may be conjectured without much violence to the antiquarian imagination. First burying their gold and silver in the ground, the primitive Plymothians withstood the rude hordes who either plunged through the waters to the land or burst from the clearings of the forests round about. Driven from their thatched hovels, the assailed made for the common stronghold; there they defied attack, with the aid of those who dwelt further inland; and then, responding to the weird invocations of the Druids, and supplicating their accustomed idols, the despoiled menaced the shaggy invaders. From their earthworks they crept, unkempt and unclad save with skins, through the thick vegetation; and, encouraged by the shrill cries of their women, whose long hair flew gustily over sombre and scanty garments, the defenders sallied forth at dusk, flaming torches leading the way, and, amid the shrieking of horns, the brandishing of clubs, the shooting of arrows, the thud of hammers, and the flashing of spears, the intruders were swept to their boats. With bellying sails and bending oars they made for the open, carrying such prizes as they had secured, and Tamarwoerth delved for another generation and dealt in peace with the merchants of Carthage and Phœnicia.

In Anglo-Saxon Times.   Cornwall grew more Celtic, and the Angles increasingly settled in Devon, during the epochs of ravage which preceded the incursions of the Danes, and for many generations the warfare was maintained between the antagonistic races. Early in the fifth century there appeared in the West the pioneers of a new dispensation, holy men, who were tall of stature and robed in the vestments of a merciful message — priests who preached the doctrine of a Saviour, their sure and certain faith in the resurrection of the dead, and an inspiring confidence in the life to come. But the sword was so often flashing from its scabbard that the efforts of the missionaries made slow progress. Ambrosius landed at Totnes with ten thousand Armoricans early in the fifth century, and thus saved the Britons from the subjugation that threatened them at the hands of the Saxons. In the sixth century, Cerdic, at the head of the Western Saxons, engaged the Western Britons in many battles, chiefly fought on Cornish territory. It was at Camelford that King Arthur and his knights fought Mordred in 542, and it is said that the former received there the fatal wound of which he died at Glastonbury.

In the seventh century the Saxon sword was irresistible, and the Britons scattered at its approach. The "Western Welsh," however, remained unsubdued in their inacessible mountain recesses, and thus preserved their uncontaminated strain until defeat and disaster overtook them, and they submitted their heads to the Saxon yoke. A desultory warfare was nevertheless maintained amid the hills until 692, and then Geraint was expelled from his kingdom of Cornwall after a sanguinary encounter with Ina, the Wessex chieftain. Attracted by the increasing prosperity and repute of the West, the Danes made their appearance, and landing near Cotehele, passed through the glen to which the name of Danescombe has ever since been given. Laying waste the country and subjecting the natives to frightful tortures, they continued without check until Egbert assembled the Saxons on Hingston Down. The invaders had been reinforced by vast hordes of the unconverted Cornish, but Egbert put the allies to rout, and completing the reverse at Camelford, pursued them to the banks of the Tamar, where the survivors recovered their ships and fled the coast. Before Egbert could claim the undisputed sovereignty of the district, however, he had to dispose of the Mercians, and, after a bloody encounter at Callington, he was confirmed in his previous sway.

A few years later another grisly horde from the North landed at the mouth of the River Yealm, and the Alderman Coerl, massing the warriors of the West, marched forth "against the heathen men at Wembury, made great slaughter there and gained the victory." Returning in 877, the Danes "sailed west about," and burnt and hewed their way through Devon ; but a mighty hurricane arose during their absence in the interior, many of their ships were dashed against the frowning rocks of Rame and Batten, and 120 vessels foundered with all hands. Their escape thus cut off, King Alfred so hemmed in the Vikings that they were compelled to submit for want of supplies, and giving him as "many hostages as he would have," they vehemently vowed "to hold good peace." The respite was only temporary, for the Danes collected a fresh fleet, and after harrying "the West Saxon's land," carried the more wealthy into captivity "across the seas," and only restored them on the payment of large ransoms. "The men of Wessex in Devonshire' were next worried by the brother of Ingvar and Halfden, who landed on the coast and plied torch and sword until the famous fight in which the standard "which the Danes call The Raven" was captured, and 840 of their men lay dead or dying on the field. The remnants of the force were pursued to a fastnesse, and encircled for fourteen nights, when, having spent their arrows and stones and exhausted their reserves of food, they swore more loudly than ever that they would depart from the kingdom.

During the tenth century the Britons held a quasi independence on the border line between Devon and Cornwall, and, growing formidable with impunity, penetrated as far as Exeter and conducted a disastrous guerilla warfare. Athelstan faced them on Haldon, and drove them to the banks of the Tamar, where he exacted the fealty of their princes and forbade them to transgress the Cornish boundary again. It was not until 980 that the West was thrown into renewed commotion, and then the Danes ravaged Padstow "and other struggling ports" with comparatively discouraging results. It was in 977 that they effected their most successful raid. Rumour had coloured the monastic wealth at Tavistock, and it spoke with alluring tongue of the golden hoards that lay in the mint at Lydford. A fleet of irresistible dimensions worked its way from the Land's End to Plymouth, the crews visiting each port to obtain supplies of corn and cattle, and wreaking everywhere "great evil" in burning as well as in mutilations and "man-slaying." Entering the Sound, they sailed up the Tamar—then a vast river which was navigable for many miles—plundered the miners of their accumulations of silver, tin and copper, stripped Ordulph's Abbey and set it on fire, and sacked the mint of its wealth. Indescribable horrors were inflicted on the natives, and the Danes retired with "unspeakable booty."

Gorged but not glutted, the Norsemen returned in 1,001, and sailing up the Exe, overcame the defence of the city, plundered it with the same thoroughness, and, "as was their wont, slew and burned." The natives were collected from the remotest parts of

TAVISTOCK ABBEY.
(From the Engraving by Buck.)

Devon, but they gave ground in the crash of the conflict at Pinhoe, and were decimated. "Ever," to quote the Saxon chronicles, "was their last incursion worse than the preceding one, and it was in every wise sad because the Danes never ceased from their evil." Their arrogance and cruelty were withstood until massacre almost threatened extermination, and they burnt "Teignton and many other good vills which we cannot name." Not only along the coast, but the summits of the Devonshire hills are yet crowned by entrenchments, varying in interest and importance, and adapted by successive generations to their own aggressive and defensive tactics—the forts from which the tribes of Devon sallied forth to the defeat of the Britons and from which the predatory bands from the North were from time to time expelled in their turn.

Romans and Normans in the West.   When the Romans first appeared, it is said that Britain was a cold and watery desert, with masses of vegetation that held and condensed the rain. It is not difficult to believe that that was the impression which the visitors from sunny Italy formed on their first acquaintance with "Plymouth weather." That they overran the two counties is beyond dispute. Tin, with which to harden their bronze, for purposes of war as well as of commerce, was the article of which they were ever in quest ; and Dartmoor presents countless memorials of their mining activities—in burrowing and smelting, in rude appliances for separating the metal from the stone, and granite moulds for receiving the liquid ore. In sturdy flat-bottomed boats, with sails of tanned skin, the foreigners darted in and about the western harbours, and then departed, deeply laden with those ingots which were so essential to the success of their sword and their world-spreading commerce. One of their popular resorts was the ancient Tamara, or Tamerton Foliott, which stood at the junction of the Tavy and the Tamar, and formed a convenient port from which minerals could be despatched as they were brought in from the moorland workings.

Any doubt as to the presence of the Romans in Plymouth has long since been dispelled. The coins of many Emperors have been discovered embedded in its foreshore ; an extensive burial place in Stonehouse Creek strongly presumed the contiguity of a stately Roman villa ; a jar of brass Roman coins has been excavated at Compton ; Mount Batten has yielded not only coins, but pottery and sculpture of unquestioned authenticity ; the snug harbour of Hooe has given up the god of a Roman mariner who probably moored his ship there; a skiff of the period of the Cæsars has been unearthed at Newnham Park, and contemporaneous coins have been excavated in the same vicinity. So that we may assume that, whatever of civilization existed before, was stimulated by this intercourse. Clad in cloaks of black, with tunics that reached to the waist, these bearded Britons of the west wandered from point to point, taking their cattle with them, and bartering metals and fish for salt and brazen vessels.

Before the Norman set foot on English soil, the rays of real religion were piercing the darkness. Briton and Saxon and Dane were embracing the golden solaces of Christianity, and the missionary presented to the hardy blend of population arising a fascinating and impressive ideal. Dartmoor has been defined as a natural Druidical temple—one mass of logan stones and idols of solar type, and many a monumental pillar and cairn must have been raised to the worship of Belius or others of the heathen deities. Distributed over the expanse were the consecrated rocks, such as those at Wembury, Brent Tor and Bowerman's Nose, whilst at Shaugh, Sheepstor, Yealmpton, and, it may be, Plymouth, existed those pagan piles that grateful navigators raised, and before which they and their fellow mariners paused to supplicate the divinities of the ocean. In an old coast map of Plymouth, which is still to be seen in the British Museum, a tolmen, so suggestive of the mysteries of primæval superstition, is shown standing upon the Hoe with a cross erected in close proximity to a little church. A kistvaen at Sheepstor, and a cromlech at Shaugh, also testify to the practice of the sepulchral and other rites of aboriginal mankind. The pagan edifices were converted to the purposes of Christian worship, and if there was no longer that homage of the sun, moon and heathen deities that had obtained, fearsome superstitions appealed to the craving for the mysterious and the dread of the supernatural which the new faith did not extinguish. Dartmoor was haunted by the disembodied spirits of children who died without baptism ; the Wish Hounds swept through the valleys at night, with hideous howls, to forewarn those who did evil on the Sabbath ; charms were muttered to ward off the enchantments of the fairies who "piskey-laid" the wayfarers ; and the devil, dressed in black, roamed amid the bogs and the forests with a long tree on his shoulder. Mothers prayed that the saints might keep the hags away as their children slept ; good fairies reposed on beds of violets ; and, whilst sprites turned luxuriant forests into barren wastes, others no less evil led the travellers astray with flickering torches.

Not once, nor twice, but a third time the natives of the west rose in resistance to the Normans ; and bearing the banner of liberty to Exeter, desolated the towns, villages and farmsteads which had acknowledged the invader. After they were subdued, their demeanour remained sullen and menacing ; and so, to give permanence to the Norman rule, the victors reared their castles on the more conspicuous heights of Devon and Cornwall. As time went on the priests exercised more power, and local administration was placed in their hands. Not many glimpses into the domestic economy of Plymouth are to be obtained, but such as there are exhibit, as in a misty vision, the movements of the Plympton Priors —" those good men who cemented rich and poor," and so consolidated their privileges that they eventually controlled two-thirds of the manor of which Sutton formed the most valuable part. Romance and superstition mingled with their system of order, for Ancients sat at the mouths of caves as the sea rolled into Deadman's Bay ; fishers, like Roger Reepe, were condemned by the evil spirits to the eternal task of spinning rope from strands of sand ; and the rocks of Catwater, on being rent by the golden wand of the Saints, "threw out the head of Bear, in stone to scowl controul without laborious share." The Bear rock animated these legends until the birth of the nineteenth century, when it was defaced beyond recognition.

Thus sang Carrington :

> They are flown,
> Beautiful fictions of our fathers, wove
> In superstition's web, when time was young,
> And fondly loved and cherished, they are flown
> Before the wand of science ! Hills and vales,
> Mountains and moors of Devon, ye have lost
> The enchantments, the delights, the visions all,
> The elfin visions that so blessed the sight,
> In the old days romantic.

Rule of the Priors in Sutton. Stately sanctuaries slowly took shape in the twilight, and civiliza tion dawned its softer discipline upon the community. "The chief glorie of Plymptoune was the Priory there builded and richly endowed with lands." Its first settlement of monks is attributed to Æthelwulf, whose palace was at Yealmpton, in contact with a temple of prehistoric and probably pagan authority. In those ascetic times the monks wore neither skins nor shirts ; they touched not meat, unless in grievous sickness ; and they consumed neither fish, eggs, milk nor cheese, save upon extraordinary occasions. They drank no wine ; their lonely couch consisted of uncharitable straw ; their sole protection from the cold was their cowls and tunics ; and, as till dusk they laboured in silence, so from midnight till the day dawned they sang and praised the Giver of All Good.

Plympton attained real importance when Warelwast, the nephew and chaplain of William the Conqueror, enhanced its scope. His priests and prebendaries at Exeter had refused to obey Anselm's injunction to "leve their concubines," and he retaliated by transferring to Plympton his college of "black canons regular" and lavishing on the establishment the means that his princely wealth permitted. Bowing with reverence to his ecclesiastical yoke, the parishioners, as a mark of subjection, walked in procession on Palm Sunday, carrying in their hands the consecrated emblems of the festival. After the death of Warelwast, the custom fell into disuse, but Bishop Lacy discovered the omission on visiting this part of the diocese ; and, displaying sore displeasure, caused the palms to be once more held aloft by a long line of reverent laymen. With increased power, the priests

PLYMPTON CASTLE AND CHURCH TOWER.
(*From an old Sketch.*)

exacted the privileges that were formerly vouchsafed from sentiment and devotion, but, in the reign of Henry I., their right to the benefice of Sutton was challenged by John de Valletorta. The Prior proved prescriptive usage and the King refused to interfere with its exercise.

Baldwin de Redvers took the field against King Stephen when he refused to extend the privileges of the nobles, and strongly entrenching himself at Exeter, left the "castelle" at Plympton to the defence of his retainers. These, however, were surprised by the Royal archers : the stronghold was stormed, the garrison overwhelmed, the country laid bare for miles around, the cattle were forced in droves to Exeter for the support of the Royal army, and Baldwin himself was banished. Domestic convulsions subsequently restored the de Redvers family to the enjoyment of their dignities, and Plympton Castle was rebuilt. "A fair large structure," the apartments furnished all the accommodation and comfort necessary for the knights and their bowmen, and grim and ruthless warriors paced the ballium wall, and sternly resisted every attempt to surprise and storm the frowning battlements.

As the pretensions of the prelates grew more exacting, and A'Beckett's sway became intolerable, Henry II. solicited the assistance of Gilbert Foliott, the Devonshire worthy who was born at Tamerton. Gilbert, albeit a Bishop himself, supported the throne against the Church, and journeyed to Rome to impress the Pope with the arrogance that his brethren were displaying. He could hardly have failed to notice the evidence of their assumptions in his native district, where, to quote the humour of Baron :

> We may smile, but the Plympton Prior
> Held his head a great deal higher
> Than Valletort or Vautort.

Trematon Castle was raised in 1086 to protect the Cornish from the incursions of the

Saxons, and it was used as the residence of the Valletorts, until it was surrendered to Henry III., with the Vill of Ayshe (Saltash) and the rights and profits of Sutton Pool. Walter de Valletorta made over "the Isle of St. Nicholas, lying at the mouths of the Tamar and the Plym Rivers," to the Priory of Plympton, other generous nobles and knights enriched its resources, a branch of the monastery was set up in the Vill of Sutton, and rights of milling, rabbiting and fishing were ceded to secure the "perpetual repose" of the souls of the donors for all generations. In conjunction with the manorial lords, a form of local government was evolved, the methods of defence suggested more of skill, the weapons of war assumed a finer finish, the barbarian retreated into the background, and the knight and his retainers paced the stage in picturesque panoply. A prefect or prepositus was elected in Sutton "and sworne into office, and the markets, the instruments of punishment and the assize of bread and beer belonged to him." The parish also comprised St. Budox and East Stonehouse, the tythings of Weston Peverell and Compton, and the chapels of the two former, together with that at Pennycross, were supplied with services by the Vicar of Plymouth. All baptisms and burials took place, however, at the mother church of St. Andrew's, and when the district was inundated, as often happened from the want of drainage, the rites were observed at the peril of many lives.

CHURCH OF THE CARMELITES, OR WHITE FRIARS, PLYMOUTH.
(*Site of S.W.R. Friary Station.*)

Whenever criminals were hanged, their goods passed to the priests, but there were sharp controversies as to jurisdiction. The lands of Nicholas de Smale, for example, were seized by the Cathedral authorities at Exeter, and very resolutely detained, until the King gave "seisin of the same" to the Prior of Plympton and issued his writ that the trespassers "answered for it." The papal records teem with priestly petitions craving the advantages of pluralism, so that the dignities of their priories might be enhanced, and the Abbot of the Cistercian Convent at "Plimeut" was in 1257 confirmed in his various holdings "as a fit portion," notwithstanding the opposition raised by the Bishop and Chapter of Exeter. Plymouth increased in importance as the centre of the metal industry, and the adventurers were authorised, at their own request, to weigh their tin at Plympton, "black as well as white," instead of carrying it to Tavistock and "Chaggeford," in accordance with ancient custom. The Carmelite Friars of "Suthen upon Plimuth" also evaded the Statute requiring Church lands to render feudal service, and Johel de Pollard bequeathed them a messuage that adjoined their sanctuary "for their enjoyment thereof." Thus was the Statute of Mortmain astutely disregarded in the West and the ire of the older settlements aroused.

Between the Crown and Nicholas de Plimpton association grew intimate, as also between the Pope and that illustrious Prior. Nicholas was the papal sub-dean in 1255, and he was granted several benefices with which to "enlarge the hospitalities of the monastery," so that there should be an ever-open door for wayfarers and wealthy alike. The priests took their meals in the refectory, and the meanest fare consisted of "one white loaf called Trequartes, a dish called General, a mess of fish or flesh called Pittance, and three pottles of beer daily." There were teetotalers in those days, and these received as the reward of their self-denial a daily allowance of "three silver halfpence." Devotion to their sacred calling did not subdue the instinctive resolve to safeguard existing privileges, and after the Crusades and the dispersal of the Carmelites, a few of the brethren found their way to Plymouth. Here they preached in the open air to knots of impressionable people; and they attended the victims of the sweating and leprous diseases with such holy heroism that their growing popularity enabled them to start the house at Tothill, which eventually became known as the Home of the Gray Friars, and Master Michael Sergeaux, the Vicar of Sutton, applied in the Roman Court for powers to limit their operations. The Carmelite priests had to live as well as their more favoured fellows; but, whilst they were permitted to continue their good works, they were inhibited from encroaching upon the revenues of the brethren in possession.

Amicia, Countess of Devon, instituted Buckland Abbey in 1278, and a colony of Cistercian monks from the Isle of Wight arranged to furnish its ministrations. As soon as they entered into residence, they celebrated Mass and other solemn ordinances, but Bishop Branscombe was so displeased at their failure to present their credentials that he forbade them to conduct further services, and it was only on the intercession of Queen Eleanor that the interdict was removed. The difficulties of these monks were not at an end, for, setting up a large branch monastery at East Stonehouse, they erected there a tumbril and pillory and held a court of frank pledge. William Rolph was ordered by the Crown to remove the tumbril and the pillory and assure John Derneford, the complainant, that the trespass would not be repeated. Nor were the relations with Rome of unvarying cordiality, as a dispute between Matthew the Prior and the Pope evidenced in 1326. Matthew was formally instructed to admit John de Holim as one of his canons, but he tore up the mandate, flung the pieces in the face of the messenger, and was cited to Rome to answer for this insubordination. As passionate a contention raged between the Prior of Plympton and the Vicar of St. Peter and Paul of Sutton in 1347, and as there was no other method of reconciling the conflicting interests, one of the contestants was preferred to the treasurership of Exeter Cathedral, which, fortunately, fell vacant when the acrimony had most sharply developed.

About the third year of the reign of Edward II. disputes arose between the Prior of Plympton and the King respecting certain privileges and immunities claimed by the latter; and a jury having been empannelled it was decreed that the former should still pay a fee-farm rent of £29 6s. 8d. into the exchequer for the use of his Majesty, and continue to nominate to the Vicarage of St. Andrew's Church. He was also confirmed in the right to grant leases of houses as lord of the fee, to hold a manor court of frank pledge, an assize of bread and beer, a ducking stool and pillory, and to monopolise the fishing from the entrance of Catwater to the head of the Plym. In the reign of Edward III. the manor came into the hands of John de Eltham, Earl of Cornwall, and he

BUCKLAND PRIORY.
(From the Engraving by Buck.)

challenged the rights of the prior to the fishery of the waters. But another special jury decided that the latter had exercised these privileges for fifteen years, and the court confirmed him in their exercise.

In 1318 the inhabitants invoked an enquiry to determine "what prejudice to the King or others would result if the town were made a corporation." Plymouth had been empowered by Edward I. to elect "two men of sufficient probity and discretion, who are alike cognisant of mercantile affairs and the interests of the neighbourhood, to come to Westminster;" but the claim to interference in local affairs provoked strenuous resistance, and the King refused the petition of the merchants. The port and water in "Suthon" were decreed, however, to pertain to the manor and honor of Trematon, then held by Queen Isabella, and they were so regarded until 1337, when the possessions and privileges were included within the Duchy of Cornwall, then first created to the glory and profit of the Black Prince.

Meanwhile the Abbey at Tavistock was esteemed the most imposing sacred retreat in Devonshire. In course of time it mournfully fell from grace, and John de Courtenaye signalised his regime by unaccustomed indulgences in 1334. Passionately addicted to hunting and hawking, the stately hall was ever strewn with the spoils of the chase, and his reverence feasted sumptuously. To add to his manifold vanities, he attired himself in costly raiment, and thus won the reputation of an "incurable spendthrift." Luxury similarly vitiated the ministrations of his canons, and instead of resorting to the refectory as of old, so that their moderation might be observed of all men, they retired to their private apartments and there led the lives of epicures. Thomas Cullyng, the next abbot, was no less improvident than Courtenaye, for he wore fine linen and buttoned boots, walked abroad with beaked hoods after the manner of knights, allowed his monks to roam at pleasure, to dine in each other's rooms, and enjoy to the full the pleasures of secret feastings. Prior Jocelyn was also severely censured for ecclesiastical defaults at Totnes, and his successor, Robert, was suspended for personal imprudence and neglect in allowing the church to decay. At "Modbyri" there existed a house of monks, "aliens of the French Order," but the founder was "scant knowen," and its temporalities were periodically seized in pursuance of the custom which visited the sins of the enemy on compatriot priests who remained to preach the Gospel.

The devotional temperament of Plymouth is quaintly illumined by a record in 1337. "Miracles were wrought by the Saviour at the chapel dedicated to him at Suthen in Plimeut," and multitudes flocked to participate in the cures and join their praises with those who had gained relief. When the circumstances were submitted to the Pope he granted relaxation of penance to all who visited "the said church and image" on the Nativity of the Blessed Virgin. At this period withering diseases were prevalent in the town, and in 1374 a Leper House was erected on the site of North Hill by the Franciscan Friars, who had also ingratiated themselves with the poorer populace by their medical skill. As in the case of the Carmelites, only a few of these priests appeared at first; but by the dawn of the fourteenth century they had erected by the waterside, on the site of Woolster Street, a range of buildings which afforded hospitality to scores of pilgrims. A noble pile in Southside Street, surmounted by a massive stone cross, constituted the settlement of the Dominicans, or Black Friars, with a magnificent doorway, which still exists, leading to the court, and another no less spacious to the cellar. The edifice covered the length of the site of the still familiar Blackfriars Lane, and large numbers of guests were entertained in a spacious room that extended over the area of the court. Superbly designed and carved was the interior of the roof, and for dignity and elaboration there was no such architecture to be witnessed in the district.

Civil and Ecclesiastical Enquiries: 1292-1409. Piracy became the trade mark of the port after Plymouth had been harshly educated, and the blood of the Dane and the Norman was animating its Wessex veins. Water thieves, smugglers and cut-throats prowled and pounced as they listed, and anarchy was rife in Sutton. In the reign of Edward I. each town was held responsible for its better order and the disposition of its malefactors. Conservators of the peace reported to the Court any criminal acts, and their vigilance is attested by various State reports. The gates of "Suthon" were barred and locked at nightfall, the mouth of the harbour was chained over, the fortifications were watched by pacing sentinels, the approaches to the town were cleared of brushwood to prevent surprises, and strangers were cast in prison in default of a satisfactory explanation. In 1292 Henry de Raleye and Andrew de Trelosk investigated the complaint of John, son of Truda, citizen and merchant of Zealand, "touching certain persons who entered his ship at Suthon in Plumuth and beat his men and carried off his goods." Again, in 1312, two of the King's yeomen, richly attired, galloped into "Plommothe" with one thousand marks in their possession, and, suspicious of the honest holding of so much wealth, the authorities sought to extort the object with which they were journeying. Thereby hung a tale, and when the travellers referred the inquisitors to the King, the Governor committed them to the Castle of "Suthon" until a mounted messenger had been despatched to the Court. When he returned it transpired that affairs in Gascony were in a parlous state, and that Bertrand Assailat and Berduces de Marsan had been authorised to embark for France and to use this money on behalf of the King "for certain purposes of his own enjoined." Sir William Martyn released his prisoners, and the yeomen resumed their journey. In 1313 the same alert Governor confiscated 129 ingots of tin at "Suthen near Plympue," the cargo having been concealed under less suspicious material in La Grace Due de Fawey. An official enquiry was held, and the certificate that Sir William was justified in his action was attested by "Robert, Abbot of Tavistok, and Matthias, Prior of Plymptoune, because their seals are unknown to many"—a precaution due to the fact that the forgery of seals was one of the most troublesome crimes of the age. The shores of

"Plimmouth" were strewn with the wreckage of several craft in 1362, and, like so many ghouls, the inhabitants settled on the Tarrit and its companion ships in misfortune, and carried off their contents. Hugh de Courtenaye held an investigation in the town, and the offenders were imprisoned and restitution made.

Imposing enquiries were conducted at the various religious settlements. Depositions for that remarkable trial known as the Scrope and Grosvenor controversy, touching the right to the arms—Azure a Bend or—were taken in June, 1386, in the Palace of John of Gaunt, at the Carmelite Friary, Plymouth, before Lord Fitzwalter, Sir John Marmion and Sir John Kentwood, as Royal Commissioners. John of Gaunt, who was then on his way to claim the Spanish throne, asserted that when the English lay under the walls of Paris, in 1360, one Carminow, a Cornish knight, challenged Scrope's title to use the arms which the former's ancestors claimed to have borne in the time of King Arthur and Scrope's progenitor at the Conquest. The trial itself lasted four years, and amongst the witnesses called were one sovereign prince, one duke, three earls, three barons, three mitred abbots, two priors, eleven bannerets, and more than 150 knights, esquires, gentlemen and others —an array such as no other case has ever witnessed before or since.

The Church of St. Germans pursued its course without jar until the relations between the convent and the burgesses of Saltash became strained, and the latter consented to the annual payment of a candle weighing one whole pound of pure wax as an admission of certain wrongs they had done the priors. On the occasion of a ceremonial visit, in 1404, Bishop Stafford was shocked to discover that some of the canons were living in flagrant violation of the celibate code, and the chief offender was condemned to sit in the centre of the refectory during the public meal and to exist on bread and water for seven days. Periodical fasts were also imposed for twelve months, the strictest enclosure was enforced, the culprit was denied admission to the nave, and one noble was deducted from his annual salary. Two other canons who were similarly convicted of unchastity were sent to sleep in the common dormitory, and a fourth was denied the use of wine on Fridays, and restricted to "bread, legumes, and small beer" for the rest of the week.

In 1409 investigation was held into a tragedy that had disturbed the quiet of Sutton Priory. The chief cook was a passionate man, and in an outburst, either of insanity or drunken delirium, he assailed the Superior with scurrilous epithets and tried to plunge a dagger in his chest. Thomas Cryer, the Prior, laid him senseless with a blow from his staff, and when he recovered consciousness the wounded man refused all ministrations, medical and otherwise, and expired in three days. Horrified at having taken human life, Cryer abdicated his claim to officiate, but Bishop Stafford relieved him of censure and restored him forthwith to the full discharge of his duties.

Plymouth as a Naval Centre: 1287-1403.   As soon as order had been created out of chaos in England, Edward I. resolved to visit his foreign possessions, and a national navy was for the first time brought together. It assembled at Plymouth under the command of the Earl of Lancaster, and the treasure for the payment and hire of the various "men-at-war, hobblers, archers, and seamen" was sent from London on the backs of pack-horses, and every custodian was protected by guards armed with bows and battleaxes. Safe passage of the commissariat was also provided for, together with every item of the calculated expenditure; and the arrangements displayed remarkable administrative foresight. During their stay at Plymouth, whither they journeyed to join the fleet, the King and his Ministers were the guests of the Prior of Plympton, and Edward issued from the monastery several state writs. After his return from France domestic troubles thickened, and Robert Bruce placed himself at the head of the Scottish Rebellion. In 1302 orders were despatched to the "Mayors and Bailiffs of Plimue, Dertamue, and Teyngnmue to prepare and equip immediately, with all the armaments and appurtenances, and to chose and arm with suitable weapons, one ship and 42 of the strongest and most able-bodied men of each port, of whom one is to be master and one to be constable, to assist in repressing the rebellion of Robert de Brus in Scotland, the King having decreed that a fleet shall quickly sail from various ports in the kingdom to Carlisle to reinforce his army." Twenty marks were set aside for the crew of each ship, "and the King will cause them to be satisfied for their wages whilst in his service." This fleet also concentrated at Plymouth, and the Prior of Plympton contributed, "by way of loan" for the expedition, large stores of wheat, malt, sheep and other provisions. Although the revolt was suppressed with great carnage, the embers glowed afresh in 1308, and the same ports were required to supply ships and men to sail against "Robert de Brus and his accomplices, rebels in Scotland." Every source of strength was consolidated, and no waste in idle sports was countenanced; and when the King learnt in 1309 that certain persons intended to leave "Plummuthe to do tourney and other feats of arms in parts beyond the seas," no earls, barons, knights, or other men-at-arms were allowed to quit the port without his sanction, and the bailiffs were authorised to prevent the exportation of either horses, armour or precious metal. The houses of individuals suspected of smuggling out such goods were searched at pleasure, and transgressors were committed to the Castle and their goods forfeited.

The mandates to the minor ports to supply ships, crews and stores at their own expense were not always agreeable to the inhabitants; and in June, 1324, a portion of the fleet, wearied of waiting, sailed from the harbour in contempt of the King's commands. As the expedition to Guienne was thus seriously jeopardised, Sir John Deverye, a faithful priest, was deputed to consult "with the good people" as to the best means of manning and fitting out the ships, and Plympton, Modbury, Newton Ferrers and "Yealme-mouth" were constrained to assist the inhabitants of Sutton in achieving this indispensable purpose. In 1330 the local authorities assembled forty of the most powerful ships that could be obtained - varying from 160 to 180 tons—"for the passage of John de Eltham, Earl of Cornwall, and other magnates in his company, sent by the King to restore order in the Duchy of Aquitaine." Edward III. brought the relations with France to a crisis by assuming a common sovereignty, and Plymouth assisted for some years to supply the sinews of war, and its waters witnessed the departure of many fleets. Meanwhile the French "pyratts" were not idle, and their galleys and pinnaces, entering the Sound without warning in May, 1339, set several merchant ships on fire. An attempt to land was foiled with heavy loss to the townsfolk in killed and wounded; but the foreigners returned to the attack in a few days, fired the ships that were sheltering in Catwater, and applied the torch to the houses which fringed the foreshore. Hugh de Courtenaye, a veteran of fourscore years, rode from Plympton at the head of his retainers, and hewing their way through the invaders, the warriors slew five hundred of them and "chaced the residue" to their ships, which, as usual, were moored at a convenient point up the harbour.

To the siege of Calais, Plymouth forwarded more ships and mariners than London itself, and reluctance on the part of its seamen to volunteer for the war was met by stern impressment. Another important squadron gathered in Catwater to escort the King's daughter, Joan of Gascony, to Bordeaux, where she wedded the eldest son of the King of Castille. It was in 1356, however, that the Sound witnessed the most glittering display of naval might, for "the never enough commended Black Prince," attended by the puissant nobles, arrived with the army that was to deliver the crushing blow in France. For several weeks this proud and hopeful host was detained by contrary winds, and princes, knights, retainers and mariners were munificently refreshed at the Priory of Plympton, as well as by the monks of Sutton. To quote Baron :

> The date was many years ago,
> . Full many years ago,
> When Princely Edward and his peers
>   Paraded on the Hoe.
> 'Twas in the age when bow and lance
> Clashed home with sturdy foe in France,
>   As local records show !

After the storm had moderated, the Black Prince, " committed himself to the sea for the purpose of mayntayning his father's rights in France." There were in all 300 bottoms, and the local contribution was 25 vessels and 203 warriors. Radiant with the flush of victory, this mighty fleet returned in 1357, and amongst the prisoners landed were King John, " Philip the Hardy," James de Bourbon, and other nobles taken at " the glorious battel of Poictiers." Hitherto some doubt has been cast on the statement that it was from Plymouth that the captive monarch set out on his white charger to take part in the triumphal procession in London, but the old chronicles fully confirm the story, and include the instructions to Dabernoun, Sheriff of Exeter, who rode to the port and furnished the Royal party with the necessary provisions for the journey. In 1362 the Black Prince was granted the Duchy of Aquitaine, and he left Plymouth for Gascony in company with his consort and Richard, their son, the future King of England. When the hero returned it was with a constitution enfeebled with consumption, and he was affectionately carried to the capital to await the end and watch the intrigues which his impending death occasioned.

Plymouth recovered with such amazing vigour from the last French descent that it contained 7,000 inhabitants in 1377, and there were only three centres in the kingdom that could boast of larger populations. It was when it was the scene of so much prosperity, and the wool and metal industries were enriching its traders, that a large force of Bretons landed at the east end, ravaged and set it in flames. Thereupon the royal writ was issued to the authorities to " circumvallate the town and fortify it " ; but the enemy returned in greater force within two years, and entering Plymouth by the " bak haf " swept the inhabitants before them, scaled the Castle and battered down the Old Town Gate. At Plympton a younger Courtenay marshalled the knights and their vassals, and into the town dashed an army of succour—the nobles bright in steel, and mounted on richly caparisoned horses. Companies of bowmen followed, and, amid lusty shouts, they assailed the invaders with lance and arrow, hammer and battleaxe, and drove them back to their ships. But the reprisals were by no means at an end and the inhabitants were rarely free from apprehensions of a fresh descent. In 1400 James Bourbon, Earl of March, was sent by the French to the aid of Owen Glendower in Wales, but his squadron was driven by gales to Plymouth, where he found several fighting ships at anchor. These his superior strength enabled him to burn, and after firing the houses he put the leading merchants to the sword. He was setting sail to avoid chastisement, when a hurricane overtook him at the mouth of the harbour. and his vessels being thrown into confusion, many of them foundered within view of the inhabitants and hundreds of bodies were washed ashore.

Upon St. Lawrence's Day, in 1403, the gravest calamity of all befell the town. The lord of Castelle landed within a mile of Plymouth " with a greate companie of Normans and Brytons," waited outside the walls through the night, and at daybreak " spoyled and robbed the sayd towne and caryed away all that was therein and returned again to the shippes." Hundreds of dwellings were destroyed and the people diabolically tortured. The "western navie" was at once collected to exact reprisals. Repairing to the coast of Brittany, it burnt several towns, lordships and mills, and William Wreford cheered the Plymothians by returning with forty sail of prizes. Retaliation was loudly threatened in 1405, and armed "shippes and crayers" were sent from the Severn to safeguard the port, and the Priors of Plympton received the Royal summons to repair with their tenants to Sutton "whenever that coast is threatened by the French." De Rieux set out from Spain with one fleet and De Hangest from France with another, and they united their forces in the Channel. The confederates were at first dispersed by a hurricane, but persisting in the attempt they reached the Cornish coast, snapped up several fishing boats and made the crews informers as well as captives. At Shuta, near Looe, resistance was offered by the inhabitants, but the majority were put to the sword. No opposition was raised to their landing at Falmouth, and after revictualling, the allies sailed for Plymouth in the hope of a rich haul. Here their arrival was anticipated by a bridge of boats that spanned the mouth of the harbour from the Barbican to Batten, and as the decoys fell back from the boom, the pursuing enemy were so heavily bombarded from the Castle that they retired in disorder.

Incorporation   Plymouth flourished during the peaceful periods.   There were
Granted: 1440.   markets for the sale of fish and agricultural produce, a court leet was held every Monday and an overseer chosen to watch the farming. A reeve directed the affairs of one part of the manor and a guild of traders shaped the fortunes of the other. After the French visitations, Sutton lapsed into "a mene inhabitation of fischars," the residents were as men without faith in the future, the roads were neglected, and access to the town from the country was almost out of the question. It was upon the initiative of the priests that the citizens depended for redress, and indulgences were granted to the faithful who improved the approaches to Tamerton, Plympton, Ivybridge and Fowey. The Chapel of St. Katherine "on the Hawe, built for God's honour," and the cross that stood beside it, fell in ruins, and as the edifice was "commonly attended by large masses of people," ecclesiastical concessions were vouchsafed those who rebuilt it. So, too, when

THE FAIR CHAPEL OF ST. CATHERINE AND CROSS, ON THE HOE.
(From an old Sketch in the British Museum.)

the towers of the Castle and its causeway were demolished by the invaders, the people effected the more urgent repairs on the same conditions.   But there was nevertheless a want of clear authority, and the resources of the port were so freely taxed that the merchants clamoured for a Mayor.   They had made one or two unauthorised appointments which had been unwittingly recognised ; but their presumption in 1385 was rebuked by the Priors, the manorial lords, and the Crown.   "One Humphrey Passour cunningly usurped the powers of the King, and did make himself Mayor of Suthen Prior by the name of Suthen Pleymuth, and took the profits which belonged to the Prior and converted them to his own use."   Passour's dignity was shortlived, and, at an enquiry which was held at Egg Buckland, it was declared that it had not been usual for a Mayor to govern in the town of Sutton Prior, "and that by right there ought to be no Mayor there, and therefore it was adjudged that Passour was no longer Mayor of the town."

Still the agitation for independence was sturdily kept alive, and the Crown itself challenged the authority of the priests in granting leases as lords of the fee, in exercising an assize of bread and beer, in sentencing offenders to the ducking stool and pillory, and in prosecuting the rights of fishing in Catwater and the Plym.   Periodical losses undermined the submissive humour of the people, and "The Commons of Plummouthe," and other persons specified, again prayed the King for larger self-government in 1412.   "The Prior of Sutton, fearing the diminution of his power, did still obstruct" the concession, and the Court hesitated to offend him.   National events were fast making, however, for the recognition of civil rights.   Strip by strip the territory gained in France was lost, Joan of Arc inspired her countrymen to holy zeal, and with every fresh victory that she obtained, discontent asserted 'itself in England.   The poor agitated against the rich, the inviolability of Church property was denied by the bishops, and communities under ecclesiastical rule openly repudiated the old traditions.   Unceasing was the drain upon Plymouth, and the town was required with every fresh calamity to recruit the naval and military resources of the nation.   "Forasmoche"—ran the usual proclamation—"as we from tyme to tyme, as well by ourselves as by reports of credible informacions, know that our adversarie of France is fully appointed and disposed to come in his own person into our own dominions we, with all diligence possible, doe ordeyne as many shippes and vessels as do belong to our ports of Plymmothe, Dertemouthe, Fowy and Falmouthe, to withstand the malicious purposes of our adversaries and enemyes to the plesire of God and worshipe and welfare of this our land."   In obedience to these commands the new levies repaired to Plymouth, where all concerned were "straightely charged on our behalfe to exerte, stire, moeve and endure all owners and mastres of the shippes belonging to our porte of Plymmouthe" to set sail with every despatch.   The inhabitants were also forbidden to molest friendly foreigners.

The courage of the Crown was at a low ebb, the clergy were relaxing their temporal powers, and an insistent spirit was abroad, when the inhabitants more fearlessly recited the evils that afflicted the town of Sutton "Pryor," the tything of Sutton Raf, the parcel of the hamlet of Sutton Vautort and the parcel of the tything of Compton—"which town, tything and parcels are commonly called the town of Plymouth."   Situate so near the shore and being a common resort "as well of enemies as others," the town had "in the times of your famous progenitors been very often burnt and destroyed in many parts thereof by reason of a defect in the enclosure or walling of the same."   Thus the residents had been "dayly and nyghtly spoyled of their goods and chattels," many were carried to distant parts and there "cruelly imprisoned" until they submitted to "evil losses and great discommodities" to secure their ransoms.   Divers troubles were feared unless measures were adopted "for resisting at Plymouth the malice of the King's enemys there dayly arising," and reliefs, fortifications and "better things" were advocated, coupled with a request that the people might choose their own officers and levy their own dues. When Bishop Lacy held his enquiry in the nave of the Priory of Plympton in January, 1440, the monks were conscious of the eclipse of their cause. The popular pulse was beating high, laymen of light and leading entered the sanctuary with a firmer tread than hitherto, and the gates of the church were open thrown so that the meanest might enter and listen to all that was urged. On the part of the prepositus and his colleagues, compensation was offered to the priors for the use of the lands, tenements, fairs, markets and mills, and by the jurors the terms were adjudged to be equitable. Resistance was waived by the ecclesiastics, and the King willed "that it be as is desired by this petition." Special exemption was made of the rights in Sutton Pool enjoyed by the Manor of Trematon, and the burgh of "Saltayshe" was left to the monopoly of the waters of the Tamar. A yearly rent charge of £41 was guaranteed in return for the manorial priviliges that were ceded to the town, with power of distress to the Prior in the event of non-punctual payment, and three messuages and a garden were reserved as a "sanctuary," together with the advowson of the Church of Plymouth and the "tythes, oblations, obventions, emoluments, rights and profits thereof."

Under the eagerly-desired designation of "Mayor and Commonalty" the various sections were thus incorporated, and the Old Towne, Higher Vintre, Lower Vintre and

REMAINS OF PLYMPTON PRIORY.
(From the Sketch by Samuel Prout.)

B

Looe Street wardes were created. The walls were extended to enclose the east end, a blockhouse was placed on the west side of the harbour, the "greate castle quadrate" which stood on the rocky hill adjacent was rendered impregnable, and the inhabitants breathed anew and retrieved their losses. As the east end recovered its importance, the merchants of the higher part of the town evinced jealousies that for centuries took the form of faction fights ; and the youths at Briton Side became the Breton or Burton Boys, and assisted by the 'prentice lads who lived in French and Catch-French Lanes, attacked the Old Town Boys with clubs and fists. On such recognised festivals as Freedom Day, when the metes and bounds were perambulated in state, the opposing forces were matched and the successful party regaled with beer and the Aldermen and Councillors with wine.

The powers exercised by the Mayor and his brethren were considerable. They passed bye-laws regulating the sale of priestly garments and expelled disagreeable persons. Nicholas Lane and his wife, for example, were forbidden, under a penalty of £20, to return and remain in the town for more than three days. If any person disobeyed the Mayor or disturbed him in the execution of justice, drew knife, sword or hanger upon him, or threatened his person with a billaxe or other instrument of war, he was punished as his worship directed. Anyone revealing the designs of the town to spies or traitors was imprisoned or executed at the Mayor's discretion, and those who conspired with lords, knights or persons of degree, to diminish the civic authority were sent into perpetual exile. As time went on the powers exercised "for the good gyding of the towne" assumed still larger scope. The farmers were restrained from fixing excessive charges and the townsfolk forbidden to commence marketing before 9 a.m. A drinking feast was held on Corpus Christi Day for the benefit of St. Andrew's Church, and taverns were required to refrain from selling "wynes or ale" during the ordinary "dyner" and "soper" hours. His Worship "commandith in the King's name that all maner of bakers make good brede and of good corn and holsome for mannys bodye and that they make a loffe for a peny" ; and, in the event of default, there was "payne of the pillorye," forfeiture of "brede and bodye," and heavy fines "att the Mayre's will." Similar regulations were applied to the sale of liquor and none was tapped until "the ale taster have tasted it, so that it be found good, holsome and able for mannys bodye." Brewers and hoggesters were under similar threats of "forfeyture," imprisonment, "fynes and ransome" at the Mayre's discretion, and traffic in "corrupt," "reboyled" and "mellid" wines was forbidden.

Bye-laws as to the butchers were no less stringent, and they were prohibited from selling Bull's flesh, Ramme's flesh, "Cowe flesh that be in calfe and the calfe be quicke." They were also expected to expose the kidneys in the carcases of sheep and to bring the skins of all manner of flesh to market. Ostlers "and vagabonds" were not permitted to loiter about the town, and workmen were forbidden to frequent taverns unless they were in regular occupation. Nor were suspicious persons allowed to "ly to ryott in the hostelries," casual couples were refused lodging unless the landlord "knowe verily that it be a man and his wyfe," and harlotts and strumpets were to be turned to doors "on payne of a grevous amercyment." To forestall the general body of farmers by selling before the hour for business, or to regrate "before the town was well served," were offences specially vetoed ; the liberties and privileges of all craftsmen were specifically safeguarded ; and the name of every freeman was entered in the "town ligger." The sons of freemen, or those who had served their apprenticeship with a freeman, were required to pay eighteenpence "and no more" on being made free ; but outsiders were charged 10s. on admission. Those who damaged hedges or fences within the "liberty" were placed in the stocks on three market days ; persons who gutted fish on the "Kays" were visited with severe "paynes" ; and the penalty for taking any "stingkyng thyng" to the water's edge, such as "ffyshe, flesh, deadd beasts, or Dogges, Cattes and Swyne," was dispossession of stock. Beer could not be carried through the streets on the Sabbath, but strange ships might be supplied.   The artifice with which the sanitary regulations were evaded may be judged from efforts to check the practice of leaving heaps of filth in public places; to prevent the inhabitants from placing foul refuse under the walls of their neighbours, to stop the washing of clothes in the public water supplies; and to clear dung, mixen and slaughter-house offal from the streets within twenty-four hours.

In the Borough Court the aggrieved found redress, and the pleas in a breach of promise action instituted in the reign of Henry VII. throw some light on the scope of its powers.   John Mayow, of Plympton, was "attached by his bodye" to answer Johanna Colleyn, of Bykley, an "honest mayden" replete with many womanly qualities, "as well of the gifts of nature as of grace and fortune able and mete to have bene the match in marriage of any honest man's son of this country, not beyng above the state, decree and condicion of a yeoman." Her complaint was that John Mayow, "being unmindful of the laws of Almighty God, as well as of this most noble realme of England, and blinded by inordynatt concupiscence, did fraudulently, falsely and damnably promise marriage and intyse her to the synne of incontynancy."   After effecting her ruin, "agaynst all law and common honesty, he refused to take her to his wyff," and thus Johanna Colleyn was "denied such honest marriage and sayeth she is the wurse and adamaged, and thereof bryngith this sute."   The result does not transpire.   There is another record in the Corporate muniments of an inquest held at Stonehouse in 1501 to discuss the death of Robert Mathew, a fisherman, who was "stabbed in his belly" by John Croste, of Lipson, with the connivance of the deceased's wife—evidently a domestic tragedy of an equally familiar character.

Early Plymouth Mayors: 1440-1466.   To a pen and ink artist of no mean faculty, who extenuated nothing, and it may be set down some things in malice, we owe a realistic presentment of the early Plymouth Mayors.   If the portraits are not always flattering, the author must be accredited with too unkindly reflecting personal failings. Their worships were chosen, it is true, from amongst the more "honest and discreet," but their eccentricities never escaped the sardonic humour of irreverent observation.   To those who were endowed with the social attributes homage was rendered with a generous hand, but the critics knew no pity for the men of foibles.   The first Mayor to swear under the Charter was William Kethriche, "a little squat man," prone to flouts and sneers, with a facility for "pulling the long-bow" that was eagerly testified of his colleagues.   He was not barren of the graces of hospitality, and the conglomeration of fish, flesh and fowl— cooked in a vessel of tremendous dimensions—with which he entertained the community, was known to subsequent generations as "Kethriche's Pie."   His successor, Walter Clovelly (1441), lost his wife during his term of office, and on vowing that he would never more trim his beard, was rewarded for his excess of conjugal devotion by the suggestive nickname of "Goat's Face."   William Pollard, another mighty "archer," was just as derisively designated "Pull hard," but his counterpart was found in John Schepley, whose "meaknesse and mildnesse" won for him the epithet of "Sheeply."   "Worship Facey" (1446) was so inflated with the dignity of his office that he slapped the Town Clerk in the face for failing to address him as "Your Worship," and he was harried ever afterwards by the "Whorson boys," as he described them.   The choleric little man would run the length of the street to thrash his tormentors.

The chief characteristic of John Page (1449) was his piety, and never "absent from mattins or vespers" himself, he darted furtive glances around the church so that he might reproach the truants. "Very mean in his origin" was Stephen Chapman, "a notorious trafficker," and a miserly hoarder of wealth; but, after the worst had been said of his greed, he was "just as a magistrate." Rosy to contemplate is the picture of Thomas Greyle (1451), for he was a lover of "good cheer" who delighted in "feasting his neighbours." "A right gallant man in his home, with a goodly train, and abundant means for the support thereof."

Happy the citizen to whom so pleasant a tribute could be paid four centuries ago! Greyle's recall to the chair was inevitable and, eclipsing his excellent prestige, he gave "a most noble feast," and induced the nobility to attend a tournament on the Hoe, where fair ladies betrayed their loves to gallant knights. A Mayor without gastronomic capacity commanded little enduring respect. James Derneford (1455) had the misfortune to fall in a fit on the day he was sworn in, but he made "shift with a fine Michaelmas goose" in the evening, and boasted that his illness had given him "a passing good stomach."

Affecting the custom of his betters, John Carynnick (1457) excited no small diversion by walking to church in a laced bonnet and with silver buckles on his shoes. The stingy proclivities of William Yogge (1459) supplied the antithesis, and he was described as "a close, thrifty

THE ABBEY IN FINEWELL STREET.

man, proud of no exterior show, but much bent on amassing wealth." Yet it was Yogge's beneficence that contributed to St. Andrew's Church the tower which still survives—the oldest part of the existing edifice, and in all probability the first effort made towards the general reconstruction. Yogge's was a period of much religious activity, for the Abbey was commenced about this time and connected, by means of a subterranean crypt, with the chancel of St. Andrew's Church, for the better convenience of the priests. As to the part Yogge played in rearing the tower there is not much doubt, for he was Mayor so often that his redeeming qualities must have been unmistakable. He did not disdain to carry home his little Sunday joint from the Market, and, when he was twitted with degrading his office, sourly retorted that it was a poor horse that was ashamed to bear its provender to the stable. The stigma of pride, on the other hand, did attach to John Pollard (1460), but only amongst those "who knew him not." Close and reserved he was, but "his word did fast bind," and heartier tribute than that could no Mayor desire. "A plain simple man" was the most that could be said of Richard Bovey (1466). He was without offence in his manners and easy in his office;

"something less of the stork than the log." Whilst he was Mayor no one found fault with him, and nobody missed him when he was gone. Ruthless verdict this, but, as that fifteenth century chronicler added: "Well would it be if the same could be written of all other chief magistrates."

During Wars of the   Disaster abroad, distress at home, and the disgrace visited upon
Roses: 1462-1483.   the fleet which the western ports helped to form, supplied the
Lollards with a happy hunting ground in Devon and Cornwall. Wat Tyler counted a host of adherents in the western counties, and, when his revolt was suppressed, Tresilian and other Cornish knights were executed at Tyburn, and their estates and lordships apportioned amongst the faithful. Plymouth joyously acquiesced in the revolution that called Henry of Lancaster to the throne, and, during his reign, it was frequently requisitioned for arms and archers "for the King's service beyond the seas," and more than once expelled the French intruders. But it found time to cultivate the woollen industry, the means by which the poorer classes were kept honest; and search was made in the local mines for gold and silver, as well as the baser metals. There is a record that the Marquis of Suffolk received his fifteenth of one mass of seventeen pounds of pure silver, raised on the banks of the Tamar, and that he sold it at 3s. per pound.

The reign of Henry IV. was not without local significance, and when his relations with the Archbishop of Canterbury stood in need of readjustment, the Prior of Plympton left with a lordly retinue to promote a better understanding. The help of the district was also invoked when the resolve to regain the French possessions rendered necessary a widespread system of loans; and Alexander Champernowne, the Mayor of Plymouth, and Robert Gray, the Prior of Plympton, were amongst those from whom Henry V. borrowed the sinews of war and with whom he deposited jewels by way of security. Death claimed the King in the zenith of his splendour, and he left as heir to the throne —in the person of Henry VI.—a merely infantile survivor of the dynasty. Thereupon ensued those intrigues in the interest of the House of York which gave rise to the Wars of the Roses. Plymouth rarely exceeded the bounds of political prejudice, although the sword played freely enough in its neighbourhood; and as its advocacy was regulated by the trend of circumstance, the apparent mood of the moment did not pledge the Commonalty to unswerving fidelity.

Whilst Henry VI. was confined in the Tower, Warwick and the Queen were thrown into the hands of France, and attempts were made to land on the Cornish coast. The most serious was the incursion at Fowey in 1457, when the wife of Thomas Treffry, of Place House, rallied retainers and servants in the absence of her husband and successfully repulsed the foe. In view of these attacks, commissions were issued in 1461 to Plymouth and the "port of Ayshe and river Tamar to supply several ships, well equipped with men, victuals, munitions and all the habiliments of war," for the defence of the western coast "after the example of his Majesty's subjects in other places." The instructions were most comprehensive. "Soldiers, smiths, carpenters, and other workmen ; bows, bowstrings, arrows, lances, cannons and powder ; cables, cords, wheat, beans, peas, cheese, ale, bread, and other victuals" were to be supplied, and the Charter of Saltash, which was originally granted by Reginald de Valla Torta, was fully confirmed by way of compensation. Acknowledgment was also made to the Mayor and Commonalty of Plymouth, who were allowed for ten years to draw £20 per annum from the customs levied in the neighbouring ports "for the relief and safeguard of the defence of the borough."

At times there were violent altercations, but the fervour was always amenable to discreet modifications, as when the Mayor and the Vicar of St. Andrew's quarrelled in

1462. It was not that the rose by any other name was less sweet to the smell, but it was the throne rather than the occupant for which his worship demanded reverence, and he asked that prayers should be offered for the success of Henry's arms against the rebellious Yorkists. "Not unwisely but stubbornly" the sagacious priest declined to commit himself, and when the Mayor threatened to report him, he set his Worship at defiance, as though the pretender of to-day might be the sovereign of to-morrow. John Page, who was called to the civic chair in 1468, was no bigoted Lancastrian; and after the rout of Henry and the flight of his Queen, Margaret of Anjou, his Worship munificently entertained the Duke of Clarence on landing at the port, and drank in a bumper long life and a prosperous reign to Edward of York. So that there was always a fair reserve of loyalty for the successful claimant of the throne. For years the chief magistrate and his brethren wore red roses in their hats as they walked to church, but, after the collapse at Towton and the beheading of the Earl of Devonshire, the preference was discarded. "More from fear and awe than reverence and love," John Rowland, "a man of great interest and closely attached to the House of York," was chosen as Mayor three years in succession.

A side-light was thrown upon the ingenuity with which chance was turned to account in the interest of the Crown. William Briton, and other persons of importance, belonging to Brittany, were captured by a Fowey privateer and cast into prison. One hundred marks was the price fixed for the release of Briton, and thirty tuns of wine were sent by his friends into Catwater to be converted into cash. On the arrival of the ransom a sinister report was made to the King; and John Hill, Henry Drewe, John Carnewek, Thomas Gale and Geoffrey Veale were appointed "to enquire whether any wines had been brought into the port of Plymmouthe contrary to the late ordinance of the King that no one should bring in any wine of the growth of Bordeaux, Bayonne, or any other place in the Duchy of Aquitaine, under colour of safeguard or otherwise, except such as might be taken by His Majesty's subjects at sea." As authority had been given to confiscate such liquors, the cargo intended for the release of the prisoners at Fowey was seized under the pretence that "it belongs to the King as being the wine of the Duchy of Aquitaine, to the great loss of the prisoners and the petitioners," who were prepared to prove that it was of the approved growth of Brittany. The Abbot of Tavistock, Walter Ralegh, Thomas Clemens and Alfred Cornburgh were appointed to settle the controversy, and it is not too late to hope that they took a humane view of their functions.

Many apparently respectable persons were more concerned with their material aggrandisement than in settling dynastic disputes, and, empowered to spoil any enemy who fell in their way, they occupied their spare moments in plundering their neighbours. Richard Dabernoun, "merchant" of Plymouth, was outlawed in 1467 "for taking eight silver cups, two silver covers, sixteen silver spoons, sixteen ounces of broken silver, and a purse containing £36," the property of Thomas Tregarthen, a fellow-adventurer; but he surrendered and purged himself of his crime to the content of the Crown. Within a few months a hulk laden with merchandise, and belonging to Bernard de la Borde, was driven ashore near the town of Plymouth. "Certain of the goods came into the hands of the King's lieges" in the borough, and they stripped the vessel of the gear as well as of the cargo. The wreckers usually avoided punishment by returning the spoils after they were ordered to do so, and their offences were the more tenderly regarded because the evils that they inflicted did not compensate for those that they experienced. It was decreed by the King in 1466 that, as Plymouth, Stonehouse, Cremyll Passage, "Woreston" Passage, "Yalam," and other places, from "Ramhede" on the west to "Gorneforth" on the east, lay open to the buccaneers who burnt and spoiled those towns, carried away the residents as prisoners, and stripped the various churches of chalices, jewels and other ornaments, their inhabitants might "sue before the Pope for the excommunication of any such pirates who may do the like, which will give them greater security."

Accompanied by Richard, the new Duke of Clarence, Warwick landed at Plymouth in 1470, and, dining with the Mayor at the Guildhall, there proclaimed Henry VI. as the monarch of the British Isles. His army rapidly gained adherents in the course of his march to Exeter, and the forces of Edward IV. crumbled before the earl who had substituted the Red Rose for the White. Inspired by this success, Margaret of Anjou consented to her son's marriage with Warwick's daughter, and, after a stormy voyage, she disembarked with the young Lancastrian heir at the Barbican. Sympathy for the beautiful Queen ran high, and a crowd of auxiliaries responded to her impassioned appeal for help to consummate the restoration. But, during a lavish display of homage and hospitality, a messenger hurriedly entered the town with the news that the tide had already turned, that the army of Warwick had been defeated at Barnet, and the King-Maker killed on the battlefield. The hitherto undaunted lady was crushed with grief when she learnt the worst, and her impulse was to return to the ships and seek safety in flight. Her cause excited so much compassion, however, that hundreds of West-countrymen rallied to her flag, and she left Plymouth at the head of an enthusiastic host. In spite of the ardour with which she inspired the nobles and their retainers by her eloquent harangues, the hapless Queen was outgeneralled at Tewkesbury, and, in the slaughter that followed the panic, her son was slain and she surrendered her person into the hands of the Yorkists. Her imprisonment was followed by the strange death of her husband, and thus the direct Lancastrian line was brought to an end.

Henry Tudor next interposed his lineage between Richard III. and the throne, and he hovered about the coast of Cawsand in the hope of effecting a favourable landing. Such strict watch was kept "for his coming to Plymouth," however, that he was obliged to "refresh himself by stealth." One of his warmest adherents was Sir Richard Edgecombe, who lived at Cotehele, an embattled and embosomed mansion on the bank of the Tamar, whose grey masonries were already clustered with romantic memories. Hidden amid the stately oaks and the spread-

THE HALL AT COTEHELE.
(After the Drawing by N. Condy.)

ing chestnuts, the house had witnessed many a secret approach, momentous negociations had been conducted within its walls, and triumphant assaults as often insidiously encompassed. Again and again had the cheerful strains of "carrolying and daunsyng" that filled its hall changed to the discord of clanging armour, the rustle of coats of mail, the clatter of halberd and pike, bill and cross-bill, as the retainers repelled the enemies at the gate. Within a park at Beer Ferris, where the deer gently browsed, stood a mansion in which the wassail had been imbibed from cups of countless forms, and "the boar's head with mustarde" oft cheered and "pleased at Christmasse." Here de Broke undertook the championship of the White Rose, and, from a hall which also scintillated with armour and corselets, and where wardour's horns and heads of deer testified to the rewards of the chase, he set out at the head of his retainers, in "form of war arrayed," and made "great affrays" with intent to "morder" his opponents. Thus Cotehele House was repeatedly assailed and stripped of its valuables, and its defenders were carried across the Tamar and thrown into the enemy's dungeons. There now remains not a stone to define the site or a tree to suggest the park of Willoughby de Broke's demesne.

The most truculent adherent of Richard III. was Henry Trenoweth, of Bodrugan, who assumed the prerogative of committing in various parts of Cornwall "robberies, despoyleries, murthers as well by water as land, entrees with force and wrongful imprisonments." Sir Henry Bodrugan, for he was thus dignified as the reward of his many vices, "regarded not God nor the dredeful censures of the Church," and "damnably" changing the wills of other knights, converted their properties to his personal use. Might was right and confiscation the natural reward of the champion of the King. Sir Richard Edgecombe was deeply involved in the plot to put Henry Tudor on the throne in 1483, and, as the Bishop of Exeter and other members of the Courtenay family were at the source of the conspiracy in Devon, the overtures between the Cathedral and Cotehele pointed to simultaneous movement. But a check was administered to Henry when he and his fleet were driven back by storms to the French coast, Sir Richard fled to Cotehele with the dispersion of Buckingham's Welsh allies, and Bodrugan undertook to unearth him. It was the coveted opportunity of Richard the Third's most trusted Cornish courtier. By repute, no less than by personal knowledge, he was familiar with the approach to the quadrangular court, knew well the janitor who paced "the gateway to and fro," and was confident that he could dare the fire of the arrows, storm the hall and chapel, and bear the hunted Sir Richard to the riverside!

All did not happen as the King's henchman anticipated. The sentinel was surprised at his post when Bodrugan's supporters stole from the glades, and, his battleaxe being snatched from his hand, his skull was cleft, and the stones bespattered as he dropped with a dying groan. Seizing the key the party entered the quadrangle, but the moment that their presence was discovered, gleaming swords flashed from the hands of sentinels, and, from embattlement and embrasure, from guests lingering at the table and inmates about to retire, a tempest of warning pierced the early morning air. As Sir Richard required no interpreter, "extremity taught him a sudden policy," and, whilst his pursuers were hunting high and low, he escaped at the rear. Vainly they raised the ornate tapestries to see that no culprit was concealed, irreverently they trespassed the aisle of the chapel, as through its "panes of storied glass scarce could the light of morning pass," and they ransacked the hall, so that no knight should breathe under headpiece or skull cap, corselet or armour. Realising that Edgecombe had gained the woods, the pursuers raised the hue and cry, and the sorely pressed fugitive placed a stone in his cap and threw it in the river. The stratagem was successful, and Bodrugan's retainers were ruefully contemplating the eddy caused by the splash as Edgecombe penetrated the recesses of a secret cave.   Polwhele has lent poetic animation to the episode:

> They heard the plunge and his floating cap
> Sure signal of immersion gave—
> The inscription of his watery tomb!
> And when fierce swords again were sheathed,
> And with the peaceful olive wreath'd,
> He reared, at the cavern rock,
> A fabric that his praises spoke,
> Nor shall to ages speak in vain—
> He rear'd the monumental fane!

So it fell with the lapse of time, for the field of Bosworth brought security to Henry Tudor, and, on his accession, the blending of the Roses was consummated.   Then Sir Richard Edgecombe, who was supposed to have "desperately drouned" himself, was welcomed home from Brittany, and the estates of his foeman were bestowed upon the knight who had been so venomously pursued.   Justice was even more complete when the writ was issued to "Sir Richard Edgecombe to arrest Sir Henry Bodrugan, John Bimont and others, who have withdrawn themselves into private places within the counties of Devon and Cornwall to stir up sedition and rebellion."   Bodrugan was hunted to his domain, and there in detail history repeated itself, for he was chased from his backdoor to a neighbouring cliff, and constrained to take "Harry Bodrugan's Leap"—a descent of one hundred feet to the sands, where a friendly boat was in waiting.   Unable to render Sir Richard too much honour, Henry VII. conferred on him a variety of offices, gave him the castle of Totnes, and made him constable of Launceston.   He also entrusted him

SACRED WELL AT MOUNT EDGCUMBE.
(From an old Engraving.)

with the duty of reducing the authors of the Lambert Simnel revolt, and Sir Richard left Mount's Bay in 1488 with four warships and 500 men, and meeting with contrary winds, sunk a few of the "rovers" who were scourging the coast between Plymouth and the Land's End. Then, making for Kinsale, he extorted oaths of fealty from various Irish chieftains, and respited their necks and restored their estates. As an expression of his gratitude for the mercies vouchsafed him, Sir Richard erected near the spot at Cotehele where he cast his cap into the water, and not far from the sacred well over which he had often so reverently bent, the little chapel that bespoke his devotion to a'Beckett, his patron saint. He passed away at Morlaix whilst completing the treaty that brought to a close the dreary chapter of the French wars.

Perkin Warbeck, the most plausible and persistent of the pretenders who dogged the peace of Henry Tudor, landed on the Cornish coast in 1497. Driven from pillar to post, derided and deserted, the "Duke of York" expected to find in Cornwall a sympathy with his cause which its people had not hitherto avowed. Two months previously, resenting the attempt to impose on them a part of the cost of the Scottish war, they had marched in their thousands to Blackheath, where they were attacked by the Royal troops and pitilessly mown down. Back to their homes the survivors tramped, but if their hate had deepened, their sufferings were too recent to admit of much sympathy for Perkin Warbeck. A few hundred miners and fishermen flocked to his standard, and the pretender made for Bodmin in the expectation that the hundreds would swell into thousands. The Corporation of Plymouth called up their trained bands, and clothing them in green jerseys, sent them in pursuit of Warbeck's followers. They sadly harassed the pretender in the rear, until Henry intercepted his progress and made him prisoner.

CATHERINE OF ARAGON AT PALACE COURT:

As depicted in the Skardon window, Plymouth.

(From the original Drawing by J. Foutacre.)

CHAPTER II.—SPAIN: AS FRIEND AND FOE.

Through the Spanish   Events conspired to draw England and Spain together. The
Alliance: 1501-1534.   Breton ports involved the mastery of the Channel and France aimed
at their supremacy. In her alarm, Spain negociated the union of Ferdinand of Aragon
and Isabella of Castille, and when their daughter Catherine ripened into girlhood, they
proposed her marriage to Henry VII.'s eldest son, Arthur. The King originally humoured
the idea, then his hesitation caused a dreary time to be spent in preliminaries, and, if
Ferdinand had not been insistent, the marriage would have been abandoned. It was not,
however, until Warbeck had been executed, so that no doubt as to the succession should
arise, that Catherine bade farewell to her home. No benevolent ray was bestowed by the elements, and as the Spanish fleet approached the harbour it was tossed by "a most furious
vendabal, thunderstorms and east winds, and it was impossible not to be frightened." On
the 2nd October, 1501, the Princess landed at Plymouth, "the first port in England," and
she was as joyously received as "if she had been the Saviour of the World." She went in
procession to St. Andrew's Church, where, as Isabella's private secretary wrote, "it is to be
hoped that God gave her the possession of all these realms for such a period as will be
long enough to enable her to enjoy existence and leave heirs to the throne." The citizens
proffered the bride-elect many a tribute of exultant homage, "country sports and pastimes"
were held for her amusement, the minstrels of Spain sang alternately with those of England, and, at the request of the Mayor, Catherine's own almoner converted into Spanish
"oure supplicacion," or municipal address of welcome. Prelates and dignitaries of every
rank flocked to the house of Master Paynter, the stately and picturesque group so long
known as Palace Court, and from the residential nobles and gentry there flowed in presents
of oxen and sheep, hogsheads of "Gaston wyne" and mellow "clarett," and pipes of
"Meskedell." To the crowd the Princess was not allowed by her duenna to unveil, but
her beauty was "much admired in private, as well as her gracious and dignified demeanour." A brilliant equipage escorted her out of the town, and Catherine broke her journey
at Exeter, to the joy of the Cathedral clergy and the country gentry, whose hospitality was
unstinted. Overwrought, however, by the unceasing salutations of the populace, the
Princess was unable to sleep for the noise of a neighbouring weathercock, and this was
taken down "for her greater content."

On arriving at the capital, Catherine was wedded to Arthur in the "most royal wise,"
but, within three months, the wife was a widow, and in Plymouth, instead of joyful peals
and grateful services, there were solemn "dyrges and masses for my lord prynce." The
diplomatic fabric so skilfully woven was thus imperilled ; and Catherine's alliance with
Henry's next surviving son was suggested. The marriage was not encouraged by the
Pope, and his antagonism caused much irritation, until the union of Philip of Austria with
the Princess Juana fortified the waning Spanish influence, and the Prince and his consort
sailed for England to bring the arrangement to a definite issue. Memorable was the
voyage, for a dead calm was suddenly broken by a storm so terrible as to alarm the oldest
mariners. The sky was dark and hazardous the Channel when the roar of the hurricane
was first heard, and knights and ladies knelt in prayer as the sails were lowered. Towards
the sullen dawn the fleet was dispersed, and only here and there was a sail perceptible.

Then a temporary lull filled all hands with a sense of relief, redoubled exertions were made to reach the nearest harbour, and the vessels were once more drawing together when a pall as of night overspread the sky, the sea was lashed to fiercer fury, and all sought shelter "as best they could." Some ships stood out for safety, others bore direct for Plymouth, and, "through the marvellous agency of the Almighty, to whom the crews and officers had addressed vows and prayers, despairing of any succour," several vessels reached Catwater and the remainder ran for Falmouth in the most distressful state that the hardiest veterans had witnessed. During that awful crisis, when more than one battleship foundered in their sight, Philip and Juana prostrated themselves in appeals to the Almighty for deliverance, and the Prince was swept along the deck with such force that everyone feared he was killed. His ship was blown up the Channel and eventually rounded Portland with bare poles.

Philip despatched messengers in every direction to learn the fate of the other vessels. Those which made Plymouth had sailed for Falmouth, and in the condition of the ships and the state of the roads, there was no escape from that port. Thus the courtiers who had been anticipating a whirl of gaieties in the famous English capital suffered the disappointment of inevitable exclusion. "We are at the extremity of the island," one of Philip's nobles pathetically complained, "in a wild spot where no human being ever comes save a few boors who inhabit there." Philip and Juana were meanwhile receiving stately welcomes throughout the metropolis, and when their courtiers pictured the vortex into which the royal couple had plunged, they fretted that they could not even forward their letters to London "at any price." At length the sacred compact between the "kings of peace and confederation" was concluded, and Philip and Juana rejoined their suite at Falmouth. Their departure, however, was delayed by vexatious difficulties ; the ships were in want of extensive repairs, replenishment of stores was indispensable, and refitting could only be effected at "enormous expense on account of the incredible cost of everything." The stay at Falmouth made common scandal the strained relations between the Archduke and his bride, for Juana was consumed with unreasoning jealousy of her Flemish attendants, and Philip was compelled, "if he would live in peace," to despatch the women to their homes in Flanders in a ship chartered for the purpose.

The betrothal of Henry VIII. with Catherine paved the way for an aggressive alliance, and in 1509 an imposing array of knights and warriors assembled at Plymouth "in four royal ships." They departed for Cadiz to assist the King of Aragon against the Moors, but the differences were composed before their interposition was needed. In 1511 the Marquis of Dorset and other noblemen were despatched to Spain at the head of an expedition which embarked at " Pasage," and returned to Plymouth after destroying "two goodly French shippes." The sword of France was apparently invincible when the marriage with Catherine was celebrated, and Henry settled with Ferdinand the conditions of the offensive and defensive Holy League. The English fleet was concentrated at Plymouth, and Henry asked "my father," as he designated the Spanish King, to despatch a supplementary squadron to the Sound "well provisioned with all the engines of war." He modestly demanded "ten galleys in all, six of which are to be swift and four heavy ones," and 5,000 men so armed as to "fight on shore." Henry fired the fervour of the country by landing at the head of the allied force in the north of France, and Edward Howard, the Lord High Admiral, hourly and daily awaited the enemy's movements in Plymouth Road or Catwater. "I trust in God and St. George to have a fair day with them," he wrote, and, after some delay, fifteen French sail of the line approached. They "fled like cowards" when Howard spread his sails in pursuit, and he chased them towards Brest until another squadron joined the foe and compelled him to fall back upon Plymouth. Still, he was confident that he should soon take them at the greatest "disadvantage that ever men had."

The next news from Plymouth, however, was so "dolorous" that it could "hardly be written for sorrow." Dashing upon the English line, the French broke and cut it in twain, "sank the ship that was Master Crampton's, and strake through one of the King's new barks so badly that she was with difficulty kept above water." In an outburst of exasperation, Howard pursued a galley that "laye in a baye between the rocks," but there issued from the guns and crossbows a flight of arrows as blinding as a storm of "haylestones." Howard knew no fear, and recklessly jumping into one of the enemy's galleys, as it was slipping its cable, he was left in the lurch by his deserting countrymen. "And so this poore Admirall," after vainly shouting "Comme aboarde agayn," took his familiar whistle from around his neck, "wrapped it together," and mournfully cast it into the sea. As he did so, the enemy "thrast" him over the side with their Morris pikes, and with flags at half-mast, his fleet returned to the Sound. Whatever of faith existed before now evaporated, and, in their shame and dread, one-half of the seamen concealed themselves in and about the town, "and the remainder is stolen away." Disease smote many of the soldiers, so that "when they felt the earth they dropped down dede," pillage was rife, and there was wanton waste and embezzlement of stores "by some persons that would not have the King's navy continue any longer on the seas." Terror of the French naval prowess filled the men, and the officers were no less wanting in courage, so that "if the King's noble grace will have his galleys and row barges to do any harm to the Frenchmen he must put in them some gentilman that is of good corage and the rowers must be tied with chaynes and the boats well manned with archers." So little did the sailors disguise their misgivings that they vowed that they would "as lief go to purgatory" as face the enemy again.

Thomas Howard succeeded his brother, and asserted the full weight of his responsibility as soon as he put foot in the town. Soundly rating officers and men on their want of pluck, he set them working so that the shores should be "well bulwarked," and, erecting a gallows on the Hoe, hanged the "knaves who have been robbing and stealing on land and doing much hurt." Confidence was reasserting itself when the Brittany squadron abandoned its post of observation and made for Plymouth with a cargo of excuses. A council of war was held in the Sound on board the Mary Rose, and Howard demanded the reason for the flight. "Default of provisions" was the plausible pretence, but it was the "marvellous" French ordnance—"capable of sinking the English navy in a calm"—of which the sailors stood in awe. Howard's impatience was so dimmed by distrust that he impressed Wolsey with the conviction that it was hazardous to take further risk of Channel warfare, and the one consolation he cherished was a belief that "the French dare not come to the western parte of this realme." Unconscious of this discreditable naval scuttle, Henry scattered the enemy at the Battle of Spurs, and England was restored as the arbiter of European affairs. There was a lull until 1522, when another Breton squadron entered the Sound, and glowing with a prouder faith, Howard moved out to give them battle, and his arrows fell in showers so thick that the enemy erected "beddes stuffed with straw" to protect their bodies. This humiliation did not stop piratical incursions, and the Channel swarmed with privateers who did such "hurt to the Englishmen at sea" that the Plymouth merchants were afraid to despatch their traders without convoys. There is no reason to doubt, however, that they fought the enemy with their own weapons by fitting out "armed pyratts," and the interchanges continued until 1537, when Sir John Dudley victualled a squadron at Plymouth and visited with crushing reverses those "that be dayly spoylers of His Majesty's subjects."

The peaceful interval that ensued was occupied with the prosecution of mercantile projects, tin streaming was so vigorously promoted that Catwater was impossible of navigation, and it was with difficulty that a ship of 100 tons could sail through the Laira.   Instructions were sent to the Corporation to prohibit all such works unless hatches were raised to prevent the escape of the silt ; but remonstrance was provoked by this check upon local enterprise, and, "in consideration of the great charges the town has been called on to bear for the maintenance of the port which is the key of the country," it was absolved from the payment of various farm fee-rents in the Vicarages of Ugborough and Blackawton.   Still, the Commonalty remained indifferent to the Royal mandate, and, as ships were growing too large to anchor, a measure was passed in 1535 whose premises declared that, as "the people of Plymouth have little respect, regard, love or affection for their own interests or those of posterity," as shown by their failure to prevent the silt from accumulating, any person might recover rewards for instituting prosecutions, even though he did not reside in the borough.   This reproach possessed no terrors for the townsfolk, nor did it excite their compunctions.   They felt, and not unnaturally, that they could not fairly be held responsible for the obstruction, and that the fault lay with the tinners on Dartmoor, who flooded the rivers with sand and mud and choked the havens with the unceasing discharge.   This was the view expressed in no unmeasured terms by Henry Strode, the member for Plympton, and when the wild miners learnt that he had reported their conduct to the King, their heathen instincts gave play.   Unkempt and unclothed for the most part, these moormen, of whom it was said that Cæsar could not tame them : who lawless lived, with manners rude, "all savage in their dens," and who, to quote the old poet, William Brown, "no knowledge have of law or God," at once called upon their stannators to exact vengeance. From time immemorial the tinners had held their Court at Crockern Tor, where the Lord Warden sat in a throne carved out of the solid granite, with an embowelled chamber to which he and his brethren resorted for refreshment.   These Home Rulers met to consider Strode's intervention; and, having formally sentenced him to the payment of a heavy fine, discounted his readiness to satisfy the demand by arresting and confining him for three weeks in a dungeon at Lydford Castle, which was described at the time as "one of the most hainous, contagious and detestable places in this realm."   Hence Brown's interesting reminiscences :

> I oft have heard of Lydford law,
> How in the morn they hang and draw,
>   And sit in judgment after :
> They have a castle on a hill
> I took it for some old wind-mill :
>   The vanes blown off by weather.
> To lie therein one night 'tis guessed
> 'Twere better to be stoned or pressed
>   Or hang'd 'ere you come hither :
> Two men less room within its cave
> Than five mice in a lantern have,
>   The keepers too are sly ones :
> When I beheld it, Lord, thought I,
> What justice and what clemency
>   Hath Lydford's Castle high hall !

Suppression of the Monasteries : 1535-1539.   When Henry put away Catherine and married Anne Boleyn, the priests at Plymouth shared the horror with which that transaction filled the ecclesiastical community.   They talked freely and their words were communicated to the Court by James Horswell, a former Mayor, who stood by the King in the hope of reward. " There be knave friars here," he cautioned Secretary Cromwell, "that play their parts and move sedition in all their communications." There were similar symptoms at Saltash, where disloyal incitements were uttered by Nicholas Kempe, "now prisoner in that town, the Mayor of which has been much troubled and concerned at the occurrence." In reporting this business, Horswell was very discreet, and set down nought in exaggeration. " Kempe denies the words, and it is doubtful whether Agas, the informant, accused him of malice or not." So undisguised was the indignation that repressive measures were inevitable, and Sir Piers Edgecombe arrested Father Gawden, Sir Thomas Dorssed, and Sir Thomas Fleet—three of the friars who were loudest in their criticisms of the conduct of the King. The credit for these prosecutions was attributed to Horswell, and he was "sore spoken to" by the Prior of Plympton for interfering. The three priests were rigorously examined in private and apart, and, as their statements were not strictly consistent with veneration for the King, they

CHURCH AND CONVENT OF THE FRANCISCANS. (*Site*, Woolster Street.)
(*From an old Map in the British Museum.*)

were committed to the seclusion of Launceston Castle to "await His Majesty's pleasure." Persons of "minor degree" who spoke "opprobrious words of the Queen" were dragged to the market-place in Old Town, and exposed "in the pillory and the stocks" to jeers and insults. Still, the voice of remonstrance was not stifled, and in 1535 the "town of Plymouth" implored Richard Cromwell to "give credence to John Elyott, our Mayor, and to James Horswell," whom they appointed to wait upon him. It transpired that the Commonalty had been "much troubled by divers treasonable persons, viz., John Pollard, Will Sommaster, Thomas Fowle and Peter Gryslyng, who are people without substance and unfit to rule our town." Gryslyng had openly denounced Horswell "as a naughty heretic knave" and urged one Bull "to go and tell him so," but, when the disturber was laid by the heels, his persecutors relented and explained that they took his remarks "for malicious, not treasonable words, spoken in his fury and his drink." This modification of attitude may be ascribed to the conduct of Will Sommaster, a powerful man capable of much violence, who swaggered about the ale houses and threatened the witnesses with brute force. There was an impression that he would be as good as his word.

c

When Henry declared war on the monasteries, Plymouth's eye was directed to the main chance, and there was "much talk" of the advantage that would accrue to the municipality. Even the villagers agitated against the priests, the Prior of Plympton was accused of habitual default, and there were complaints from Wembury, "Plymstocke," Brixton and "Schaffe" that sacred wants were not regularly met. Unless the inhabitants sent many miles, it was impossible to procure a priest, numbers died "without shrift, housel or other sacrament, such as christening, burying or nayling"; there were no ministrations save on Sundays, and then the "canon comes from Plympton and says mass, matins and evensong before noon and goes back to take his dinner." This was not the worst, for the Prior refused to send a monk to bury a corpse "for less than sevenpence," and when the tenants hired a substitute, he threatened to confiscate their holdings.

Sir Piers Edgecombe revisited Plymouth as the King's intermediary in 1536. This time the Mayor, Will Hawkyns and John Elyott were the principal dissentients, but after an earnest appeal, the trio agreed "to waive their differences and live together in peace, according to the good old custom of the town." About the time that Anne Boleyn was divorced another outburst occurred; and summary measures were recommended against Nicholas Horswell and his brother, James, as the active fomentors of the discord. "If their conduct has been for the detriment of Plymouth, I hope," urged Edgecombe, "that you will provide the remedy, for the borough was never so poor." James Horswell was "commanded to avoyde the towne," but matters were not composed by his banishment, "for William Hawkyns, John Elyott, and others of the confederate band troubled the inhabitants in divers ways" and loudly agitated for his return. "This will be to Plymouth's destruction," wrote Edgecombe, and he advised that the disturbers should be replaced on the Council by three other burgesses, "so that they may no more meddle" with the affairs of the Commonalty. There was a further exercise of the diplomatic arts and Thomas Bull, the Mayor, conveyed an assurance that the townsfolk were "all agreed and dissension clearly extinguished." James Horswell, it was true, had been denied the right to resume his residence, but this was all for the best, and there would be no more trouble if his banishment remained in force, since he was the head and front of all offending. "Men," vowed Bull, "despair of his amendment, for he is a man of a marvellous nature, disposed naturally to malice, loving to keep a great port divers ways, which cannot be maintained without souking the poor people, for he has nothing to live upon save a little office, which, speaking truly, cannot be worth twenty nobles a year and he is greatly indebted." This fine scorn did not damage Horswell, for, when the religious houses were doomed, he was conciliated by an appointment to value their effects for the King.

If the suppression of the monasteries was popular in the town, there were a few adherents of the Church who had the courage to uphold their hands at the sacrilege. Amongst these were Mr. Harford and a "money washer" of the name of Hewer, and the recusants were hanged in company. Bending to the storm, some of the priests submitted to the oath of supremacy, but this did not save their establishments. Plymouth being "poor and in dekaye," actively petitioned for some of the spoils as the reward of its loyalty, and, in the end, was relieved of the necessity of paying the friars even a reduced rental for the manorial lands and privileges. Thus the powers and revenues of the Commonalty were enlarged and the Mayor and his brethren rejoiced; and if the incidents of expulsion were pathetic, they were relieved by a flicker of worldly humour. The house of the Grey Friars was handed over "by warden and convent" to the Lord Visitor and formally transferred by him to Thomas Cloutinge, the Mayor. Reverend hands had not been sluggish, and there only remained at the high altar "an alabaster table" in addition

RUINS OF ARCHWAY, FRANCISCAN CONVENT
(Woolster Street, Plymouth.)

to the "pore stalls." A lectern stood in the choir, "and two bells and a clock in the steeple," but "the rest of the stuffe was like to have been brybed away." Every cranny in the edifice was explored, and "a chalice of eight ounces" was discovered and seized for the royal confiscator. Vestments, copes and altar cloths were yielded up by the White Friars, but, in this case also, the sacramental silver had been removed. High and low the Lord Visitor hunted, through the church and in the houses of friends close at hand, and he recovered 211 ounces. In March, 1539, the iconoclastic waters reached the monastery of Plympton, and the Prior and eighteen of the friars submitted at discretion. Thus were transferred to the possession of Plymouth the "lordship of the house, and all its privileges in Devon, Cornwall, Somerset and Dorset, together with the patronage of St. Andrew's Church and the other religious establishments." Included in the deed of capitulation was a convent in "Katt" Street, a Cistercian abbey near the mother church and a convent in Catherine Street. On the site of the latter the Corporation established a school in 1561 "for all the children native and inhabitant within the towne," the master being enjoined to "teache no other but gramer and writinge." By way of compensation for the unhallowed disturbance, the Prior of Plympton was allowed a pension of £120 a year, his colleagues were granted means to preserve them from starvation, the advowsons of Ugborough and Blackawton were set apart for their residence, and there they eked out an obscure existence until the hour of reaction arrived.

"Commocion Time":   As soon as the boy Edward was called to the throne, Somerset
1547-1548.   accentuated by his rigour the existing differences. Many of the Abbey lands fell into the hands of Protestant landlords, who proved more usurious than the indulgent priests, and throughout the West the farmers confessed that they had jumped from the frying pan into the fire. Somerset instituted a system of congregational worship, in which the laity were admitted to the same sacramental rights as the priests, and this depreciation of the holy office excited a torrent of protest. Cornwall led the way in 1547, by satirising the Protector's Communion Service as "a Christmas game," and its people, who had been accustomed to listen to "our old service of Latin," and of whom "certain of us understand no English," utterly refused this "new language." In defence of the Mass an uprising occurred, but it was easily suppressed and only "one bodye was slayne"

in the fight. Harsh sentences were passed on the ringleaders and several distinguished Cornishmen were "hanged, drawen and quartered." But the hatred of the innovations increased with their enforcement, and the revolt against the Book of Common Prayer burst into general conflagration in 1548. The houses of leading Protestants in Devon and Cornwall were besieged, the families fled to the woods and the caves, and the reactionaries declared in their manifesto: "We will have the Bible and all Books of Scripture to be called in again. For, we are informed that otherwise the clergy shall not for long confound the heretics." It was now indeed "Commocion Time," to use the phrase in the borough records; and, mustering in thousands, the Catholics hammered at the gates of the town. The "Castell of Plymmothe was valyently defended and kept from the rebelles" — but the Mayor soon capitulated, and the refugees took shelter in St. Nicholas Island until Lord Russell, at the head of a large army, raised the relief of the town. "Numbers were slain, several were put to execuyon out of hande, one rebell was burnt, and others hanged at Tyborne." It was during this insurrection that "our steepell was burnt with all the towne's evidence in the same," but to what particular building this refers no one has yet been able to suggest. In all probability, with the confiscation of the friary in Southside Side, its use as a municipal establishment commenced, and the disaster that consumed the early Plymouth records was there enacted. Still, the "obstinacy" of the Western Catholics was not exhausted, and they made another attempt upon Plymouth—only to find the garrison so powerful that their dispersion was inevitable.

Reaction increased in intensity with the recklessness of Somerset. Then the young King died, the Protector was brought to the block, Mary ascended the throne despite the intrigues to supplant her, and with her resolve to wed the heir to the Spanish throne, the overthrow of Protestantism was complete. In 1553 the Earl of Bedford and Lord Fitzwalters, "with sundry other men of honour and also of worshippe, tooke shippinge at Plymmothe in the Queen's Majestie's shippes and sayled unto Spayne to Phillyppe's eldest son, he being determyned to come into England." This was the courtly record made in the Plymouth chronicles, but the facts were less complimentary. Resentment of the approaching nuptials was so strongly evinced by the seamen, that the fleet was dispersed by mutinous risings and Philip anchored in the Sound without any escort. After some delay, he sailed for Southampton and was there married to "our most drade sovereigne ladye at Winchester." After this, the relations with Spain grew more cordial and several nobles who arrived "with much treasor" for Mary in 1554 were shown profuse hospitality at Mount Edgcumbe. The joint attack upon France followed, and the absence of the Navy "so far off" from Plymouth occasioned much alarm at the outset of the campaign, for the Castle and Island were "poorly furnished" with men and munitions and the town was "in manifest danger." When Philip arrived and the English fleet joined the Spanish, the relief was so keen that the Mayor and Corporation spent £300 in entertaining him and his suite. The war did not last long, but, whenever the allies entered the harbour, the French battleships awaited them outside—only to retire towards the Lizard as soon as a responsive movement was made. They opened fire "without doing much hurt" and then scudded away in the direction of Brest.

Plymouth was a passive spectator in the war of religions, and subordinated sentiment to interest whilst the stake tested the staunchness of Latimer and Ridley. The substitution of the Mass for the Prayer Book evoked no remonstrance in the town, and it was not until the accession of Elizabeth that the Protestant bias of the population was avowed. Trevanion, a Cornish knight, was thrown into prison for his "hainous" religious opinions, but as he was popular with the county families, an effort was made to secure his

THE OLD TOWN GATE.

(From an old Drawing.)

release.   It fell to the lot of his consistent foe, Sir Richard Edgecombe, to report to Mary upon his character and proceedings.   That delightful raconteur, Carew, tells how Sir Richard served his enemy by recording so much to his honour that he was restored to his freedom and the friendship of Edgecombe himself.   When Trevanion learnt how nobly Sir Richard had acted he was profoundly affected, and the method in which he exhibited his gratitude throws a vivid light on the mirth and hospitality of which the stately home of Cotehele was then the theatre.   The time was the gladsome season, and " 'twas merry in the hall " as Sir Richard entertained his kinsfolk, neighbours and friends. Yule logs blazed on the hearth, flagons and cups sparkled with mead and wines, and Half-Cup was being daintily spiced when the Master of Misrule intimated tidings of grave concernment.   The harper ceased to sound his harp, the fool left his jests unfinished, and Sir Richard restored his cup untasted on the board when it was reported that a company of armed men had crossed from Plymouth and were advancing towards the house. Knowing that Trevanion was in the neighbourhood, Sir Richard apprehended that his old foe was coming to him with "dire and hostile intent," but, unwilling to withhold the graces of courtesy, he threw the· gates wide open, taking the precaution to place his servants, armed with sword and buckler, on either side of the hall, so as to form an avenue through which the strangers should pass.   Doubts and fears, however, gave place to delight, for the visitors were a company of Christmas maskers, with armour and weapons of painted paper, and instead of trying their force with blows, they " made proof of the skill of the ladies in dancing."   Sir Richard showed the way to the feast, and Trevanion, gaily removing his vizard, disclosed himself to his host, and, in token of his true meaning, presented him his nephew, disguised in a nymph's attire, as a match for one of his daughters. And the marriage came to pass, the damsel being the fruit of the Edgecombe alliance with Joan, daughter and heiress of Stephen Dernford, of East Stonehouse.

View of Elizabethan   How much Elizabeth owed to the men of Plymouth, or the men
   Plymouth.   of Plymouth to Elizabeth, it would be hard to determine.   Did Elizabeth create the position, or was it created in the main by those restless sailors who made the western port the scene of their operations, and blended with unflinching courage and scant remorse an artless profession and a rigid piety which never doubted that the Heavens were on the side of a hardy Protestant impunity?   When the virgin Queen wrested the throne from the designs of Marie Stuart, the fortunes of the country were desperate indeed, and Philip clung to England for the preservation of his own existence. Spain had become the mother of many colonies with the discovery of the New World, and the riches yielded by hitherto unexplored countries filled the minds of Plymouth mariners with haunting dreams of gold and silver mines and fields of dazzling gems.   It was when so many were distracted by the marriages of Henry that " Old Master William Hawkyns," the principal sea captain of the town, and a man esteemed by the King for "his wisdome, valure, experience and skill," not content with making short voyages to familiar coasts, armed "a tall and goodlie shippe of his own "—the Paule of Plimmouth —and made his way to the Brazils.   There he trafficked in negroes and ivory and other commodities, and so won the confidence of the natives that he prevailed upon their dusky chief to accompany him to London.   He presented this strange object at Court, to the dismay and astonishment of the nobles, who contemplated his ebonized ears and cheeks with wonder, pierced as they were with jewels and flashing with diamonds.   The luckless barbarian was killed by the attentions of his hosts and his people knew him no more.

   Captivated by the prospect of remunerative discoveries, the modest content of the locality was infused as with the thrilling of a new desire.   Elizabeth was yet young when her mariners of Devon were carving their barques through the waters to the El Dorados of which they heard with ever-increasing amazement. Little they recked of trespassing on neutral or friendly territory, for scruples neither burdened nor forebodings oppressed them. Their aim was to reach the untold wealth that lay beyond the waters, and it was their pursuit of this ideal that made for England's maritime supremacy. Some of these pioneers had passed through the fire of civil and religious warfare, and having witnessed the persecutions to which their fathers were condemned, and shared in the sacrifices and sufferings of their families, they felt, with the accession of Elizabeth, and if they did not feel all they professed, the plea was sufficient to the justification, that they had a divine commission to harass, perplex and impeach the Catholic claim to universal empire. And so Plymouth yielded an inspiration that placed the country in the foremost rank for contempt of peril and sternness of purpose. Francis Drake had watched from his unpretending home at Tavistock, where his father quietly ministered till he was expatriated, the intercourse of his hale, bluff and indifferent uncle Hawkins, with that hale, bluff and unscrupulous monarch who gloried in the defiance with which he hewed his own rude ways to his own rough ends. Whilst he was yet aflame with the ardour of imaginative youth, Drake was introduced by his kinsman to the sea—and around this apostle of self-sufficiency, this assertive, bull-necked, firmly-set lad, there gathered such a company of lusty young gallants—the unflinching striplings of the staunchest Devonshire stocks—that there was a passionate competition to accompany the pioneers, share their perils and divide the spoils.

Thus the little town, with its seven thousand inhabitants and its fifteen hundred houses, whose gables encircled the waters of Sutton Pool as with a warm fringe of mellow thatch, the smoke of whose chimneys curled in irregular clouds to the sanctuary of St. Andrew's and thence to the Old Town Gate, to dissolve without in the expanse of pasture and of marsh, of arable and isolated farmstead—was peopled by a busy, robust and dauntless generation. Well may the visitor, on exploring the historic bye-ways of Old Plymouth, be invited to pause with the reminder: "Stop, traveller, for here you are treading on the dust of heroes!" If the resident population was small, albeit not insignificant for the age, there were thousands of men and lads coming and going—the hardiest making for sea and returning with unhallowed wealth, and the aged resorting to church to pray that success might favour the brave. The merchants were always fitting out fresh ships, and if the town ever stood aghast at its

"Rose and Crown," Old Town Street.
(From a Photo. by R. Rugg Monk, 1895.)

own temerity and wondered whether the mills of time would grind out some bitter retribution, the reserve and caution of Hawkins blended with the arrogance and boasting of Drake, and faith sprang green afresh.

With the easy accession of riches, and familiarity with bloodshed the social habit of Plymouth degenerated. In the mansions of the merchant princes the Morris dancers burlesqued the lavish toilettes and dainty affectations of their superiors, made sport of the Romish priests, and jested loudly of the times. Ostentation grew the rule and simplicity the exception, the sports became more brutal, and the dainty daughters of hitherto austere citizens witnessed the baiting of bulls and revelled in the masquerades which were the fashion of the period. In those old taverns with spreading areas, where mine hosts had been aforetime privileged by the priors of Plympton to entertain pilgrims, doughty adventurers dined in state : exciting awe as they ate the wonderful potato, sampled the delicious fruits, drank the rare wines, and smoked in pipes of precious metals the newly-discovered tobacco. Richly apparelled in silk, laces and velvets were these gentlemen, and armed with delicately tempered rapiers that bore the stain of many a confident and fatal thrust. They drank as heavily as devoutly they prayed, and swaggered as hilariously as fervently they toasted their maiden Queen : old John Hawkins—manly, frank and a bit of a beau, according to some, crafty and grasping in the estimation of others, Father of the English Navy in the judgment of posterity ; young Francis Drake—masterful, merci-less, but no niggard ; Richard Hawkins, the "perfect seaman" who was to receive in captivity the addresses of a Spanish beauty ; Raleigh—exquisite, scholarly and generous ; Gilbert—polished, sensitive and scrupulous ; Frobisher—frothy, fierce and unheeding ; Richard Grenville—blue of blood and unquestioned of courage ; Thomas Fenner—a fear-less warrior in a fearless age ; Edward Wynter—heir to splendid traditions ; Borough—as vehement and doubtful of valour as John Oxenham was impetuously brave on shore and on ship ; and others no less adroit as corsairs than loyal as subjects. And so, from an epoch of enterprise that began in doubt, and which the Queen long regarded with scruples of uncertainty, these Plymouth speculators fashioned a situation which appealed to an instinct that was rarely above the suspicion of miserly mistrust when its perception of opportunity was most alert. And as each company went forth to its weal or its woe, and drank confusion and discomfiture to the emissaries of Spain, the town was alive with joustings and merrymakings, and there were joustings and merrymakings when the survivors returned with the rich stuffs, spices and treasure they had seized. The evolu-tion of commercial adventure—from the period of halting piracy to that of chartered free-booting—may be traced in no shadowy lines through the history of the port which was destined to play so remarkable a part in shaping the national course.

John Hawkins as Adventurer: 1564. John Hawkins followed in the track of his father, and opened up the Canaries by a policy calculated to gain the favour of the people and win large profits. Henry Strangeways and William Wreford, who were among his earlier imitators, exploited Madeira in two vessels of 140 tons, each carrying fifty Devon-shire gentlemen and their servants, with mercenaries to conduct the fighting. Thus pleasurable excitement was associated with grim business and the popularity of these excursions increased. John Hawkins next arranged a trip to Guinea, and Sir Lionel Ducket, Sir Thomas Lodge and Sir William Winter were amongst the modish gallants who bore him company. Landing at Sierra Leone, Hawkins, "partly by the sworde and partly by other meanes," secured 300 negroes ; and, as God had given the heathen to the "elect for an inheritance," he made himself responsible for the inauguration of the slave trade. He cooly sent his chief ship to Cadiz, and, treating it as a pirate, the officers of that port seized the cargo and imprisoned the crew. Hawkins stormed and threatened ; but Philip had been passing patient, and if he had no particular wish to break with Eliza-beth, he was not inclined to tolerate any further abridgement of his monopolies. Planting his spies in Plymouth and other western ports, he was able, without loss of time, to remonstrate with the Queen on the ill faith of her subjects. Elizabeth was no less wary, and as sure as the adventurers unduly prolonged their preparations, she vetoed their departure. As the voyages increased in number the Queen's sympathies were less disguised, and when she augmented "the defensive armament of Pleve"—the designation is Spanish—and issued her fiat to render impregnable its four forts, Philip was convinced that her heart was with her sailors and that the heart of her sailors was with Elizabeth. In 1564 Hawkins lay in the Sound with seven armed ships—one of them the Jesus of Lubeck, a vessel of 800 tons belonging to the Queen. His intention was to still further develop the traffic in negroes, and in the prosecution of this holy aim, he instructed his seamen to serve God daily, love one another, preserve their victuals, beware of fire and keep good company. Guzman de Silva, the Spanish Ambassador, waxed exceeding wroth at this

increasing audacity. "He is said to be going to Guinea," he wrote Philip, "in a ship of 800 tons, with 24 pieces of artillery large, mostly of bronze but some of iron." As other vessels were being held in readiness to reinforce this fleet, de Silva proceeded to Elizabeth, and, driven in a corner, she made Hawkins promise that "he will not plunder your Majesty's subjects."

Hawkins did not keep his word, but, with the true instinct of a free trader, went to San Domingo, "where they say, by leave of the Governor, he treated with the Spaniards." On his return to Plymouth, he was hailed with the utmost joy, and encouraged Winter to start with another party. "These people must be waxing fat on the spoils of the Indies," de Silva ejaculated, "and their greed is such that they may usurp the trade of those who traffic under your Majesty's license. I don't believe," he added, "that any ship would be safe if they were strong enough to take it." The gossip as to Hawkins's achievements overwhelmed de Silva; "but," he assured his master, "the full truth cannot be long concealed, as steps are being taken to ascertain the facts." Dissembling annoyance and assuming an absorbing curiosity, he tried to draw the offender over a glass of wine; but, alive to the intent of his hospitality, Hawkins toyed with him in return. He

Notte Street.
(*From a Drawing by H. J. Snell, prior to its reconstruction.*)

admitted, with a suggestion of weariness, that the voyage had been long, pretended that "he was very tired," and confessed having treated "with many of your Majesty's subjects." As he artlessly explained that he had only done this after certificates were granted him, nothing could apparently have been fairer; and, when de Silva hinted that he should like to glance at these documents, Hawkins genially promised to bring them the next time that he passed that way.

From other sources the ambassador soon discovered with what address Hawkins had extorted these concessions to trade. On landing he was met with the objection that the merchants could only deal on peril of their lives; whereupon, pointing to his ships, he hinted that they contained armed men, for whose passions he could not answer if facilities to barter were withheld. As a diplomatic preliminary, he suggested that the crews ought to be allowed to land, that there might be some firing to lend an appearance of invasion to the visit, and that the Governor should then agree to trade if the lives of the inhabitants were respected. This adroitness completely won the respect of the colonists, and the merchants showed studious courtesy instead of replying with their muskets. Hawkins landed his men and cannon, the farce of firing and fighting was rehearsed, the Governor duly implored him to spare the people, the mariner yielded to the importunity, commercial intercourse ensued, and the adventurers received "a testimonial of good behaviour" when they took their departure.

When de Silva learnt that this expedition yielded a profit of 60 per cent., he was more than ever anxious, and turned over in his mind the use to which its organiser might be turned in the interest of Spain. His artless confession of his attempts to undermine the loyal Plymothian is embodied in the account of the overtures he sent to Philip. "Hawkins is considered a good sailor and he is a clever man. I have told him that he is not a fit man for this country, and that he would be much better off if he went and served your Majesty, where he could find plenty to occupy him, as other Englishmen have done." The Spaniard did not over-estimate Hawkins's power and skill, but he failed to appreciate his reserve of patriotism when he imagined that he was available to the highest bidder. The admiral dissembled his fidelity to the Queen, and de Silva thought that he was moulding at will a creature of clay. "It is advisable to get him out of the country, so that he may not teach others in that port, for they have good ships there and are greedy folks, and enjoy more liberty than is good for them." The exchange of duplicity was more or less skilfully sustained, and Hawkins frankly exposed the certificates he had received, "from which it appears that there are grounds for addressing the Queen and letting her know the excesses which have been committed." De Silva begged him to continue his calls, and so answered him that he might "learn more of his business and keep him in play that he might not return, as they want him to do, on a similar voyage to his former one." Early in 1566, Hawkins enquired if there were any instructions "from your Majesty respecting his offer of services." De Silva temporised and said he expected a letter shortly: "I am keeping him in hand because there are so many people urging him to take charge of other voyages. This Hawkins assures me that he has ten or twelve men who understand the navigation of those parts as well as himself. There is great need to be on the alert if we are to prevent these people from trading."

During this palaver Hawkins was arranging for another expedition, and Elizabeth's ministers were abetting him to befool de Silva. When further concealment was scarcely possible, the ambassador feared that he was the victim of subterfuge; but, as soon as Hawkins offered to go against the Turkish pirates on behalf of the King of Spain, he repented of his misgivings. "I believe now I did him an injustice," he wrote; but his worst fears returned as the admiral hastened to Plymouth to command the gathering fleet. When de Silva remonstrated with Elizabeth on this bad faith, she minimised present apprehensions, and extenuated previous occurrences, by asserting that Hawkins fully intended to keep within his bargain and not touch the prohibited countries. "But he was forced by winds to some places which were forbidden and traded by the licence of the governors only." Although the Queen was obliged to inhibit her subject, his friends at Court made no effort to arrest his fleet. "They have dallied longer than I like," hinted de Silva, "notwithstanding that I have hurried them all I could, as I am afraid that they delay advising him so that he may have time to despatch his ships before the order arrives. This is the sort of thing," he suggestively added, "that the people are in the habit of doing at Plymouth." In this instance the mandate did not miscarry, the admiral was checkmated, and de Silva was complimented by Philip upon his alertness. "Your action in preventing Hawkins and others from going to the East Indies was very opportune, and you will thank the Queen for complying with my request." Hurt by the imputation that he meant to violate Philip's rights, the sea-dog sought and was admitted to the presence of Elizabeth. "I know," he said, "that the Spaniards hate me," but he only desired "to lade negroes in Guinea and sell them in truck in the West Indies for golde, perles and emeraldes." This modest design found favour with the Court, and, learning that the expedition was being reorganised, de Silva wrote: "The matter is being kept secret. Some of the ships are said to belong to the Queen herself. I have spoken to her Majesty, and she says she has had the merchants in her presence and made them swear that they are not going to call at any place belonging to your Majesty. I have requested her not to allow it, seeing the trouble that it may cause." To seal the compact, Hawkins personally assured de Silva that he would not travel anywhere "to offend your Majesty, and I thanked him, saying I was sure he would keep his word."

Philip's energy in limiting the operations of the western adventurers excited much resentment, and Spanish ships were so molested in and about the harbour that de Silva insisted that the Queen should punish the authors of all "such daring acts." Elizabeth promised to exercise closer control; but there was no amendment, and a Biscayan trader with a cargo of whale oil was arrested and spoiled in the Sound in 1566. "As soon as these things look better," he protested, "the pirates begin their labours again no doubt for the purpose of keeping their hands in." The Queen's penitence was only accounted to be skin-deep: "Some of the robbers have been hanged, but none with influential friends, although there are some of these in the Plymouth prison condemned to death." It was at this period that reference first seems to have been made to the existence of Martin Frobisher, who was at Saltash in charge of a vessel with which he had been playing the buccaneer. Instructions were sent to the Mayor to impound his ship, but the hint to clear was not lost, and the mariner roamed about less guarded parts of the coasts.

Firing on the Spanish Flag in Catwater: 1567.   The break between Elizabeth and Philip was not yet at hand, and she commanded every deference to be shown the officers of Spain.

Hawkins had no respect for hollow friendships, and chafed at the interference which had so often restrained him. His effrontery was exhibited in September, 1567, when a Spanish fleet sailed into Plymouth under the command of de Watchen and entered between the island and the main, to the number of fifty vessels, "without vayling their topsayles or taking in of their flags." Hawkins was "ryding in Cattwater" at the time, and affecting a feeling of outrage and alarm· outrage at the failure to salute the English flag and fear at the presence of so many foreign battleships –he fired across de Watchen's bows. Notwithstanding the warning, the visitors continued "arrogantly to keepe" their flags flying; and, hotly embracing the challenge, as he was pleased to construe this behaviour, Hawkins "lact the admyrall through and through, whereby the Spanyards, finding that the matter begann to grow to earnest, promptly took in their flags and top-sayles and so ranne to an anchor." According to de Watchen, the Englishmen gave him no time to show his good faith. "As I was entering the port of Plymouth," he explained, "and before I had time to cast anchor, a certain Mr. John Hawkins, who calls himself a commander of six large vessels and four smaller ones, which he has fitted out with all speed here, although he says he does not know their destination, as the Queen has not yet told him, opened fire upon us from the tower and also from the ships, and discharged six

or seven cannon, and so on until one shot went into my ship. I was obliged to haul down your Majesty's flag—a thing that has never happened to me before in England."

Expostulation was met in a cavalier spirit, and, when de Watchen sent one of his officers to ascertain the cause of the assault, his assailant would neither receive him on board nor listen to his message. In high dudgeon he leant over the side of the Jesus of Lubeck and told the emissary to inform de Watchen, with his compliments, that "as in the Queene's port and chamber he had neglected to do the acknowledgment and reverence which all owe unto her Majestie, especially her ships being present, and comming with so great a navie, he could not but give suspicion of malicious intention." He therefore ordered the Spanish to leave the port in twelve hours "upon paine" of

ST. ANDREW'S STREET.
(*From a Drawing by H. J. Snell, 1899.*)

being treated as a common enemy ; and, when de Watchen insisted upon holding an interview with Hawkins, it was only after repeated entreaties that the sea-dog would consent to parley. Loud words were exchanged, and Hawkins retorted that just as much anger would have been shown if an English fleet had entered a Spanish port carrying "their flags in the toppes." The abashed and crestfallen de Watchen admitted his fault, disclaimed any malicious intention, and begged that there might be no "jarre" between Philip and Elizabeth. Hawkins maintained the appearance of the injured party for some time, "but in the end all was shut up by his acknowledgment, and the ancient amities were renewed by feasting each other aboard and ashore."

Hawkins and Drake   All differences having been composed, de Watchen's fleet resumed
Entrapped: 1568.   its voyage, and Hawkins departed to furrow hitherto unknown seas with two vessels that belonged to the Queen, four that were run in his own name, and young Francis Drake in charge of the Judith. The African Coast was scoured for negroes with little success, then the Gold Coast was explored and the company did a little fighting on behalf of a black chief who was "oppressed by other kings." From this point Hawkins sailed to the West Indies, but at San Juan de Ulloa he was entrapped. He had taken refuge from a hurricane, with three vessels that had struck their flags to his little fleet, when seventeen Spanish ships hove in sight, and he prepared to make terms with the foe or sell the lives of his sailors dearly. He had the choice of preventing them from approaching the port, and thus condemning them to "shipwracke"; or of suffering them to enter "with their accustomed treason." As San Juan de Ulloa was a foreign port, and a hostile attack there would be a cause of war, Hawkins closed with the Spanish admiral and allowed his fleet to anchor.

The opportunity was too inviting for the new arrivals, and they concerted to annihilate the English adventurers. Hawkins awoke to a sense of the danger when an officer whom he was feasting drew his dagger and attempted to slay him. After this the Spanish plans quickly developed, their forces were summoned by trumpet blast, and Englishmen loitering on shore, "stricken with sudden fear, ran to recover succour of the ships." Most of them were hacked or shot down as they raced, and the Spaniards surrounded the ensnared vessels as the officers on board were trying to unmoor them. The fight was carried to the water's side, then the guns of the fort were brought into action, and the despatch of two fireships almost completed the destruction of those that were getting under weigh. Only two barques escaped, Drake in the confusion getting clear in the Judith, and Hawkins gaining the mutilated Minion by pulling from the shore in a small boat. Calling for a stoup of beer to wash the powder from his throat, he waved his silver cup, and bade the men stand firmly to their guns. He then drank the liquor with infinite relish, placed the cup by his side, and it was forthwith knocked overboard by a small shot. The crew were aghast at the narrow escape of the admiral, but Hawkins allowed them no time for panic: "Fear nothing," he shouted, "for the God who hath preserved me from that shot will deliver us all from these traitors and villains." The Spaniards made repeated efforts to storm the Minion; but, as they swarmed over her side, the gallant crew stood on their defence, slashing and hewing and contesting every inch. "God and St. George," panted Hawkins, as he laid about with his sword in the foremost rank; "out upon these traitorous villains and let us rescue our vessel. Trust in God and the victory shall be ours." The foemen fell back, the Minion ran up such sails as remained on such poles as stood, and having gained the open, the exhausted and begrimed survivors reverently committed their dead to the deep and bore away for a safer haven. After many privations, in which the men subsisted upon rats, cats and mice, Hawkins and Drake put into Penzance to lament that the whole business had been visited by "infelicity, misfortune and unhappy end." The Spaniards repaid themselves for a good many slights by exposing the prisoners to the whip and the rack, and those who outlived these tortures were thrown to the flames of a grand auto da fe.

Piratical Plymouth: The lusty lad whose indomitable spirit was destined to inspire
1568-1572.   the spirit of our Imperial system, was already attracting attention.
"Mr. Fraunces Drake" soon developed remarkable force of character, speaking "arrogantly

but well," and reaping " vengeance and wealth " by his voyages in his sturdy little barque.
It was inevitable that he should attract other spirits as intrepid as his own ; and if the
lives of some boon companions, like Oxenham, were cut short by the pressure of the
Spanish rope, the principal grief was that they were so indiscreet as to be caught. " To
the elect of God " the future hero appealed, and ancient mariners whose skins had been
tanned in other climes soon regarded him with wondering and suggestive reverence :

> At Plymouthe speedilye they took shippe valiantlye,
> Braver men never were seen under sayle,
> With fair colours spread and streamers o'er their heads,
> Now bragging Spaniards take heed of your tayle.
> Dub a dub, dub a dub, thus strike your drums,
> Tintara, Tintara, the Englishman comes.

Not only was Plymouth prosecuting these enterprises on her own account, but the
port formed the market for piratical cargoes taken elsewhere. In November, 1568, the
Rochellers seized sixteen French traders "and carried them into Plymouth to dispose of
the cargoes in safety." Elizabeth was urged by Louis " not to permit such injustice to be
committed in her kingdom," but she was able to offer little redress. A month later the
Marseilles was stripped within the limits of the harbour, and an empty undertaking was
tendered that the offence should be "remedied." Early in January, 1569, "certain
English pirates took into Plymouth three Flemish and one Spanish vessel, very rich, and
divided and sold the wares." Don Gereau d'Espes made no secret of his belief that "the
marauders were in the haven of Plymouth are favoured by friendship at the Court," and the
Queen's demeanour confirmed these suspicions. "She showed very great incontinence
by declaring that she had been informed that the treasure did not belong to the King of
Spain but to certain merchants, and therefore she was minded to keep it and pay the
owners." This was the frankest avowal that Elizabeth had yet made, and justly appraising
its moral, the Don retaliated by arresting the goods and persons of Englishmen resident
in Spanish ports. In March a Plymouth pirate, with a crew of 200, robbed a Flemish
ship of every farthing it contained. The vessel was taken into Catwater and, as the men
were turned adrift on the Barbican, they heard their captors saying what a fine vessel the
Brielle would make for Admiral Hawkins. The stranded mariners were so destitute that
they begged at the doors of St. Andrew's Church, but charity was cold indeed. "They
never got a penny and would have starved if it had not been for a country woman dwelling
in the town, who kept them for several days and collected money for them."

Light and airy views were held as to international etiquette. The ship Pelican, of
Normandy, was plundered by John Granger, and three of its crew were slain as they
reposed in Catwater. Barnard Grave, of St. Maloes, was imprisoned in his own ship by
the Plymouth pirate Johnaman; and William Hawkins, who was ordered to rescue the
vessel, kept her for his own pleasure after doing so. Alert as were the officials to their own
opportunities, there was amongst the commercial classes a hearty desire to excel in less
ostentatious forms. Their aspirations were not encouraged; and, when smuggling grew
too open, no one "with cloake, bag or malle, which did smell of prizes, for they could
well be smelled on account of the musk or amber," was allowed to pass without search.

When Hawkins and Drake harrowed Plymouth with the sensational details of the
massacre at San Juan de Ulloa, there was a mighty outburst ; and the former begged the
Queen, if she would not declare war herself, to allow the West-countrymen to exact
vengeance in their characteristic fashion against "God's enemies." Drake was no less
insistent, and three Spanish treasure ships were pounced upon as they reposed by the

waterside at "Saltayshe" and "Foy." Remonstrances followed, and the Spaniards retaliated that Hawkins had only received his just deserts, because he had either stripped every ship he had hailed, or compelled the masters to sell their cargoes under threat or practice of torture. They moreover drew scathing and realistic portraits of the freebooter, as he paced his deck showily attired in velvets and silks, and flashing with buttons of gold and pearl.

Drake stalks from the group in 1572 as the great assertive figure, with a quenchless faith in his own mission and the destiny of his country. He implored Elizabeth to let him grip the Dons single-handed, and the Queen was so fascinated by his lion-hearted daring that she gave her consent to the first real exploit identified with his name. Leaving for Nombre de Dios, in the Bay of Darien, he conciliated the natives who were groaning under the oppressions of the Spanish; and marching inland, overtook several mules that were laden with gold and jewels, and confiscated the treasure intended for Vera Cruz. On the summit of a mountain in the Isthmus of Panama there stood a lofty tree, and a flight of rude steps carved around the trunk led to its upper branches. From this dizzy height could be commanded, on one side, the sapphire-like waters of the Spanish Main, and, on the other, the unknown expanse of the Pacific. With imagination quickened, Drake resolved to explore those seas, and John Oxenham vowed by God's grace to follow him— only to fall, alas, into the hands of the enemy and to hang from a gibbet at Lima. The risk was an element of the attraction, and, after deploring the fate of his comrade, Drake continued his course and returned to Plymouth with the treasure of a hundred Spanish ships.

Whilst he had been burning, smiting and stripping every foreigner that strayed across his course, exacting revenge for "treachery" and acquiring "additional glory," his uncle had once more subtly inveigled the King of Spain. Pretending that the Queen had treated him scurvily, he offered to put his own fleet at Philip's service and assist in placing Mary, Queen of Scots, on the English throne. It was a dangerous game to play, but Hawkins disclosed every stage of the negociations, so that Elizabeth could not afterwards complain that his diplomacy was too profound. Philip was as easily wheedled as de Silva, and he awarded Hawkins special dignity as a mark of his confidence, released those of his friends who were rotting in Spanish prisons, and sent him sufficient money to man sixteen ships with two thousand men. "Large enough is the pardon," laughed the recipent, "with great titles and honours from the King, from which may God deliver me!" He emphasized his good faith by spending the money on the fortifications of Plymouth!

BULL HILL—TOP OF HIGH STREET.
(As still existing.)

Voyage of Circum-
navigation : 1577-80.
"I would be revenged on the King of Spain for divers injuries that I have received, and you are the man that might do this exploit." Taking into confidence his "fellow adventurers" as they surrounded him on the deck of the Pelican, Drake repeated the words of Elizabeth, and then set out on what proved to be the first voyage of circumnavigation. Making successful cruises on the coasts of Chili, Peru, and California, he depleted Spanish and Portuguese traders of their precious metals, stones and jewels ; despoiled rich cities and departed from them with boatloads of silver ; and succeeded so well that he doubted the wisdom of prolonging his voyage. Learning by chance that the Spaniards had fitted out a fleet of overpowering strength to intercept him, he endeavoured to discover a north-west passage to Europe ; but, after the first cold snap, his crews refused to continue that course. Suspecting—and with good cause—that the avengers were hovering near the Straits of Magellan, he steered south and remained for months in the Indian Seas. Here Drake encountered many thrilling adventures, and he restored to freedom the owner of one rich trader who presented him with a falcon of solid gold, whose eyes gleamed with emeralds of surpassing size.

If the party were savagely attacked by the natives in some parts, in others they were as ceremoniously received, and they danced in many a sylvan glade with princesses arrayed in petticoats of palm leaves. Having gained Java, Drake was inspired with new greed ; but his men objected to another voyage, and they were encouraged in this attitude by the chaplain. In his irritation and omniscience, the Admiral accordingly ruled Fletcher "from out of the Church of God, and all the benefits and graces thereof," and finally renounced him "to the devil and all his angels as the falseth knave that liveth." Compelled by the discontent to return, Drake doubled the Cape of Good Hope, and returned to the port one Sunday morning in 1573, his fleet ponderous with treasure and his crews reconciled by the home-coming. The momentous whisper electrified the congregation of St. Andrew's, and "the news of our captain's return did so speedily pass all over those in church and surpasse their mindes with delight and desire to see him that very few or none remained with the preacher, all hastening to see the evidence of God's love and blessing towards our gratious Queen and countrey by the fruite of our captain's labour and success." With "shouts and congratulations" they ran to the quay ; and, by worshippers and wayfarers alike, Drake was lustily acclaimed for securing such "greate store of golde and sylver in blockes, and perles and emeraldes and diamonds."

Elizabeth's first emotion was one of misgiving as to whether Drake had violated the instincts of honour, and, professing to be shocked by these "robberies," she summoned the author to London. Depositing the bullion and the precious stones in Saltash Castle, "the master thief"—to use the terse if expressive Spanish expletive—proceeded to the Court, and there so bewitched the Queen by the glamour of his adventures that she commanded him to bring the spoils to the Tower. In gaping amazement the burgesses of Saltash witnessed the departure of that picturesque procession of oxen and horses ; and, amid frantic shouts, the hero brought up the rear of a train of mariners, rich in gorgeous capes and bright with woven scarves. Of unrefined silver there was nearly six tons, of fine silver about five hundredweight, and over one hundred pounds of gold—the metal in slabs of the dimensions of bricks, in which form it had displaced the shingle originally used as ballast. The spectacle shook the last remnant of Elizabeth's prejudice, and she was so gratified at Drake's service "in that behalfe," that she commanded his presence at Deptford "where he was done knighted" on the deck of his favourite ship, the Pelican. The Spanish Ambassador had complained that he had ravaged his master's possessions, and the Queen affected to rate him soundly until he pleaded that it was always war beyond the line. "Upon that," wrote Drake, "she did call me malapert and saucy knave, and,

D

QUEEN ELIZABETH KNIGHTING DRAKE.
(From the Fresco by W. Brewer, as exhibited at the Royal Academy, and destroyed by fire at the Plymouth Palace of Varieties, 1898.)

when His Excellency was gone, did bid me kneel, and borrowing Cecil's sword did say, 'Arise, Sir Francis, and I wish, Sir Knight, I had more such saucy knaves.'" To which the favourite made reply : "Your Majesty has a thousand of such in Plymouth ! " Eliza beth did not confine herself to ceremonial observances, for she gave instructions that Drake should receive £10,000, craftily enjoining that the present was to be kept "most secret and for himself alone."

In a little while the incident leaked out which, more than any other, bedims the viking's memory. The execution of Doughty his fellow mariner, has found its apologists, but the deed did not seem capable of justification at the time, and the chief question is whether political plotting or personal dislike was responsible for the act. The original excuse for " this bloudie tragedy " was found in expressions dropped in Drake's garden at Plymouth when the expedition was about to sail—"weighty and dangerous words." Soon after getting afloat, Thomas Drake cultivated a habit of dipping too freely into the treasure chest, "diving suddenly into the same," and he was discovered at these riflings by Doughty. When Sir Francis learnt that his brother's peccadilloes had been exciting the reproaches of his fellow officer, his once "good and esteemed friend " led a miserable existence. "Grudges did grow between them from day to day, to the no small admiration of the company," and, as the offender's retorts were unpleasantly flavoured, he was transferred to the Swan fly-boat. This vessel was soon afterwards separated from the fleet by a storm, an incident that induced Drake to assert that the wind must have come out of Master Doughty's "cap-case." So that the imputation that the victim exercised the powers of witchcraft was introduced to deepen the prejudice of crews easily enough terrorised by any reference to the supernatural arts. Doughty was brought back to the Pelican when the fleet anchored in the River Plate, and there some of the seamen deserted because they would not witness any more of the persecution to which the prisoner had been subjected. Near a barren island, in St. Julian's Bay, the admiral "being set in a place of judgment," caused Doughty to be brought before him, "more like a thief than an honest gentleman," and impeached him for discrediting his authority. Doughty demanded to be tried upon his return to England, but Drake empannelled a jury on the deck. " I hope you will see that your commission is good ! " was the significant challenge, but the cynic retaliated : " I'll warrant you my commission is good enough ! " After being bound, so that Drake should be in no " fear of his life," Doughty was charged with saying to Edward Blight at Plymouth, that the Queen's advisers were open to corruption. The prisoner retorted that the only pretence for this imputation was a casual remark that, if the expedition returned with gold, " we should be the better welcome." Recognising that that there was little hope for him, Doughty pleaded that he might be tried at home, but Sir Francis refused to discuss the point; and, when Leonard Vicary exclaimed " Master Drake, this is not law or justice," he adroitly threatened to return before any more plunder had been secured. This was a certain stroke, for the gentlemen aboard were " a company of desperate bankrupts who could not live in their own country," and, with a deprecating chorus of " God forbid, good general," they acquiesced in the sentence. Two days and nights Doughty spent in prayer and in arranging his affairs, and, when his time was at hand, he asked that he might receive the sacrament. Drake offered to join him, and so, in incomprehensible juxtaposition, the two knelt side by side at the Lord's table, Fletcher officiating. Doughty was then asked to choose the manner of his death, and, in a mood of condescension that still more complicates the psychological problem, Drake told him that, " if he would be shotten with a piece," he would do him that service himself, " so that he should die by the hands of a gentleman ! " Sir Francis claimed that in private conversation on the eve of the execution, Doughty fully confessed his treason. Certain it is that he prayed for himself, the Queen and the success of the voyage, and that he embraced " my good general "—Drake himself. Then he placed his neck upon the block and the axe descended—only to bungle in its horrid work. When the head eventually fell and it was held aloft by the executioner, the admiral exclaimed : " See, all of ye, this is the end of traitors ! " The Doughtys were frenzied when they learnt the facts, and urged that the author should be tried for the murder. Unable to obtain redress, the anger of the victim's brother found relief in scathing taunts. " When," he said, " the Queen did knight Drake she did then knight the arrantest knave, the vilest villain, the falsest thief, and the cruellest murderer that ever was born." For uttering this " slander," he was arrested on suspicion of conspiring with the Spaniards ; and, his petitions for release being disregarded, he lingered in prison until death released him.

Raleigh, Gilbert, Gren- Clustered as the port ever was with an " infinite swarme of single
ville and Frobisher : ships and pettie fleets," either " cutting sayle" or returning with
1578-1586. " spoyle and honour," it was periodically the medium of intro-
ducing the Black Death and of communicating the pestilence to the country round about. The first visitation occurred in 1571, when a cargo of cotton wool from Smyrna was unloaded before it had been exposed to the air, and the disease made such ravages that the church bells were always tolling for funerals, and every street was rendered doleful with the blue crosses that testified to infected homes. In a few months 600 victims were claimed, and lamentation and panic were so general that the Commonalty elected their Mayor " under the canopy of Heaven "—in other words, in the open air at Catdown. His Worship, Mr. Hollowaye, also postponed the usual feast until " it had pleased God to avert this heavy calamity." Comparative immunity was enjoyed until 1581, and then the plague laid its death-dealing hand more heavily than ever on the population, herded as it was within narrow thoroughfares and in dwellings which were innocent of all sanitary precautions. Disastrous epidemics, however, had no seriously deterrent influence on the commercial development and collective daring of Plymouth. Small was

the town as to dimensions; but its fame encompassed the globe, and its mariners won their way to the confidence of the Court. Young Walter Raleigh, albeit he spoke with a Devonshire accent, was the most elegant and cultured of all that wonderful generation of adventurers. As a lad he was distinguished for his oratory and knowledge of philosophy, and showed his passionate sympathy by fighting under the banner of the persecuted Hugenots. On returning he was appointed to the command of the Royal forces in Ireland; and, desiring to compose some differences with his fellow officers, went straight to Elizabeth, "whose ear he caught in a trice, with his bold and plausible tongue." Indeed the Queen was so charmed with the youth that there were few favours she would deny him. "She was taken with his elocution, loved to hear his reasons, and regarded him as a kind of oracle."

Raleigh soon entered the lists as a colonial speculator, adopting as the standard of his ethics the prevailing sentiment that "good success admits of no examination;" and few of the bravest brought richer spoils into the harbour than he, or were more generous in supporting similar endeavours on the part of their kinsmen. At his suggestion, Humphrey Gilbert, of Compton, his half brother, submitted to the Queen an undertaking "by gentlemen of the West conceived, and, with the help of God, reserved for England," which was designed to open up "remote and barbarous lands not possessed by any Christian princes or people, and to hold and enjoy the same with all commodities." Elizabeth not only gave her consent, but endowed the adventurer with an anchor of solid gold, which he wore on his breast as a mark of the Royal favour. The omens were inauspicious. Gilbert counted upon the redoubtable Knowles to co-operate with him; but a quarrel occurred at the eleventh hour, and the latter organised a voyage of his own "with a notorious store of evil men." The Mayor of Plymouth was called upon to investigate the dispute, and Knowles alleged that he had been slanderously accused of being "proud, factious, seditious and vain." Gilbert denied using the words in public or with intent; but, on being invited to swear that he meant no malice, pleaded that "oaths were made for judges." His first attempt to discover "a new navigation" was abortive, and the ships returned to Plymouth no less crippled than the crews were disaffected. The second voyage was even more disastrous; and, a few days after the squadron left, the Raleigh, a ship which Sir Walter had elaborately fitted out as his personal contribution to the scheme, returned to the port, some of the crew reduced by sickness and the rest mutinous. Full of faith, Gilbert persevered with his perilous undertaking and planted the English flag on Newfoundland—only to meet his fate in the hour of his success. Overtaken by a tempest that momentarily threatened to engulf his trembling barque, he exclaimed in a phrase of undying serenity: "Fear not, for we are as near heaven by sea as by land." When the thick clouds broke there was no sign of his ship, and her heroic commander was sleeping at the bottom of the ocean.

Whilst his contemporaries thirsted for gold and silver and precious stones, Raleigh directed an eye to commercial intercourse, and his calculation that sugar, tobacco, hides, ginger, and other products, contained the germs of as much wealth as ore, led to the opening up of "sundry rich and unknown lands," to which he gave the name of Virginia in honour of the maiden Queen. Encouraged by the luxurious soil and valuable products, "with knightly courage countervailable to his double desire and honour," he furnished another squadron towards a similar adventure. These assembled in the Sound in 1585, and the command was given to Sir Richard Grenville: "a gentleman esteemed both for his parentage and sundry good virtues as lieutenant." On its return to England, a Spanish galleon, the Cacafuego, fell in the way of the expedition; and, as this was fair game in the unofficial war which was the fashion of the time, Grenville carried her with a "boate made of boards of chests which fell asunder and sunke at the ship's side as soon as he and his men were out of it." The crew dropped before the English charges; and the vessel, with its gold and silver bullion, was anchored in Catwater amid "tremendous joy, not only with great ordnance then shot off, but with the willing hearts of all the people of the town and country, who were not sparing of ordnance to requite and answer him again." Raleigh sold his patent rights of colonization in Virginia to a number of merchants, but they lacked the energy to complete his original scheme and abandoned the settlers to the mercy of the natives.

Every inducement was offered those who took part in these expeditions; but there were a few men of leading who avowed doubts as to the morality of the traffic, and Major Sedgwick sent from Plymouth a remarkable protest. "I am much averse," he declared, "to this marooning, cruising, plundering and burning of towns; though it has long been practised in these parts, yet it is not honourable for a princely navy." The remonstrance did not avail as against the lust for gold and glory which had set in, and Gilbert's failure to penetrate to the North West threw Martin Frobisher into contact with Michael Lok, the son of a London merchant. Frobisher was a rugged sailor, with ideas and no visible means of subsistence, who made Lok's house his home. "My purse was at his need, my credit his credit, my friends his friends; when he was utterly destitute of money, credit and friends." An expedition was despatched to Meta Incognita, but controversies as to direction disturbed the harmony of Frobisher and his financiers. The captain was "very headily sure" as to the route; and grew "into such a monstrous mind that the whole kingdom could not contain him, but already by discovery of a New World he fancied himself a second Columbus." Frobisher more than satisfied the Queen on his return, and she appointed him admiral of all such seas as he had traversed—a concession that resulted in the formation of the Company of Cathay.

Within six months Frobisher applied for authority to undertake a second voyage, and Sir William Wynter assured the Queen that he approved the enterprise as "a thing worthy to be encouraged." Minerals, which Frobisher claimed to contain large percentages of gold, were flourished in the face of investors without serious attempts at analysis, and Lok attracted another coterie of capitalists. According to the custom which set prisoners at liberty if they were ready to risk their lives, Frobisher scoured the gaols for seamen, and he was surrounded by as rough and ready a gang as ever revelled on the waters. But the offices of religion were strictly enjoined; "swearing, dice, cards and filthy talk" were completely banished; hymns took the place of coarse and ribald songs; and the men were amongst the mildest mannered saints who were ever engaged to cut throats. Each sailor was required to serve God twice a day, and "to clear glasses every night, according to the old worship of England." These observances, however, did not prevent Frobisher and Lok from quarrelling, and, when the cruisers returned to Plymouth, the latter stigmatised the admiral as "a false accountant, a cozener, no venturer at all, and a bankrupt knave." Frobisher did not quietly submit to these reproaches, but lashed himself into "great storms and rages, and raised shameful reports and false slanders." The cause of it all was the failure to extract gold either from the mariner's samples or bulk metals, and Lok's fortune melted in the depths of the ocean when Frobisher's ore was pronounced to be worthless. He appealed to Elizabeth from a debtor's prison for an allowance to keep him alive, and attributed all his misfortunes to the admiral whom he had maintained free of cost. "He has eat most of the meat at my table freely and gladly." Frobisher's ardour won new supporters, and he sailed in 1583 to the Coast of Brazil. But Drake had been too successful; Philip was offering ten thousand ducats for his head, and Spaniards were everywhere forbidden to afford the slightest assistance to any Englishman. "The spoils and robberies committed by Sir Francis Drake in the South Seas" were a fatal bar to the success of Frobisher's mission; and, if the Brazilians had not relieved the destitution of his fleet, all hands must have perished. The expedition was a failure, and the admiral's supporters were once more utterly undone.

Drake Gives Philip "a   The fame of Drake suffered no passing eclipse; and, if he rested
Cooling": 1585.   awhile at Plymouth, he knew no rest. In 1582 his townsmen elected him as Mayor, and he set "the mariner's compass upon the Hoe" the better to secure that eminence as a post of observation. Two years later, on the petition of his successor, he was nominated as captain of St. Nicholas Island and the Fort of Plymouth; and what there was to be said was conclusively submitted. "He is one of the brethren of the town, sworn, and a gentleman most fit for that purpose." Alive to its opportunity, the Corporation emphasized its right to propose, and insisted that the town should be relieved of the responsibility of defence if this were not conceded. The argument was apparently decisive, although there is no actual evidence that Drake held the office; for, in a few months, Elizabeth had need of her great enthusiast. Philip was asserting an intolerable maritime supremacy; but those fire-eating freebooters of Plymouth, who measured their own strength by Spanish incapacity, contemplated his pretensions with amused contempt. Accustomed to sweep the seas whenever they chose to go afloat, they only required the royal authority to move, and their chief regret was that it was a point of etiquette to wait for that. Philip invited the punishment that was in store for him by luring English corn ships to Bilbao and there detaining them. This was just the provocation that Elizabeth required, and when she looked to Drake to exact retribution, he was as promptly at her bidding as though he had been awaiting a preconcerted signal. Around him clustered the flower of the English nobility; Plymouth was selected as the rendezvous; and, "with great jollity," all concerned repaired to the port. Here were gathered twenty-five sail "of merchaunte shippes and other small barks and pinnaces," each vessel in charge of men with a just claim to lion-heartedness:

> The Bonaventure, a shippe royall
>   Chief admyrall of the fleete,
> Sir Frauncis Drake chief generalle,
>   As by desertes he was most meete:
> Most worthy captayns of hande and hert
>   In this boon voyage they took hys parte.
>
> The Primrose next wise admirall
>   Appointed by their best desire,
> Captain Frobisher, wise generall,
>   A valyant captayn ware and wise:
> Captain Carellel they did ordayne
>   Lieutenant Generall on the mayne.
>
> At Plimmouthe they remained a space
>   Till all their shippes were furnished.
> Their government, good fame, and grace,
>   Through all the land is published.
> In countreys strange beyond the sea:
>   If God permit who can say nay?

Drake's especial mission was to rescue the vessels on which Philip had laid an embargo; but the order was too small for his appetite. He steered direct for Vigo; and

DEFEAT OF THE ARMADA, OFF PLYMOUTH.
(From an old Print.)

when he demanded the prisoners, the Spaniards hinted that, if he remained there much longer, they would wash their hands in his blood. Determined to chasten the authors of these threats, Drake set about burning and sinking their ships; and then, after much parley, " we received back our men." Having despatched his business, Drake steered for the Canaries, where he extorted oil, wine and water; and then made for San Domingo, where "he runneth through the country like a conqueror." As the inhabitants buried their treasure, and fled to the bushes and the woods, Drake fired the town; and, amid a chorus of wailing "which we may very well hear," bearers of a flag of truce advanced, the flames were extinguished, and occupation was peacefully conceded. The customary expedient of torturing the prisoners revealed the places where the wealth was concealed, and the stately silver bier was disclosed on which, "with a very rich canopy over his head," the Catholic Bishop had been usually borne to his sacred throne. Burning, hanging and slaying as he went, Sir Francis passed from island to island until he reached Tierra Firma, the golden goal of the pirates who subsequently sacked the Spanish main. Here the resistance was so hot "that it was almost impossible by man's reason for us to win," and the ships could not approach the fortified harbour because of the shallowness of the waters. "Yet God fought for us," wrote Drake, and the soldiers plied their pikes with such deadly effect that the Spaniards withdrew to their inland fortresses. After the houses were in flames, the customary flag of truce hove in sight; but, as soon as the heralds saw their temple in a blaze, they refused to discuss terms, "for they esteemed their church more than their town." Drake brought them to their knees by applying the torch with still less compunction: "We began to burn more, so that at last they compounded and ransomed the same." Towards the end the only structure that yet resisted was "a little friary without the town" which was held by 200 Spaniards; and it was not until "we had laid wood to it and were ready to fire it" that the Prior came forth "and ransomed the same." After sacking and destroying at pleasure, Drake made for Plymouth with the spoils and brass cannon, and he boasted on his arrival that he had given Philip "such a cooling as never happened to him since he was King of Spain."

> When tidings came unto the courte
>   Sir Fraunces Drake was newe come home.
> Her highnesse hearing this reporte
>   Her grace was glad that he was come,
> And all her lords with one accord
>   For his safe returne praysed the lord.

Singeing Philip's Beard: 1587. "All these and various woorthy and valyante exploytes performed and doone," filled Philip with such anger that he demanded the delivery of Drake's person; but Elizabeth quietly informed his ambassador that she would fling him in a dungeon if ever he spoke to her in a similar strain. Spoiled and scorned the world over, his coasting centres destroyed and his treasure escorted in state to the Bank of England, the Spanish King prepared for war in downright earnest. Squadrons of ships and provisions by hundreds of tons were collected at Lisbon, "with intent to employ the same in some attempt either against this realm or the coast of Ireland." In this design Philip had the sympathy of all European countries, for the name of the Devonshire daredevil had inspired every trading nation with fear and trembling:

> Both Pope and Turk and all our foes
> Do dread this Drake where'er he goes.

A woman of quick resolves, Elizabeth decided to let Sir Francis once more loose amongst her competitors, with open orders " to prevent or withstand any enterprise that may be attempted against the Queen's dominions." Drake waited for no second bidding. In a few days he was at work in his beloved Plymouth ; and, with such unsleeping energy did he apply himself to the task of fitting, that the fleet was ready to sail within a week. None better appreciated than he the dilemma that delay might occasion—there were, in fact, influences at work to undermine Elizabeth's resolve. Howard, the Lord High Admiral, warned the Queen that " this going out of Sir Francis will cause grave peril" ; and, discounting his own influence the more surely to win her confidence, he added : " I fear me ere it be long, Her Majesty will be sorry she hath believed some so much as she hath, but it will be very late." Duly impressed, Elizabeth despatched a mounted messenger to inform Drake that Philip's forces were being disbanded. " Forbear," she wrote, " for the King of Spain intendeth no harm " ; and it was therefore her " express will and pleasure " that the Vice-Admiral should not invade " any of the King's ports or havens or offer violence to any of his towns or shipping within harbouring." The countermand reached Plymouth too late, and when the courier dashed to the waterside, Drake's fleet was dissolving into shadows beyond the horizon. His intuition had stood him in good stead, and although a pinnace was sent in pursuit with strict injunctions to deliver the Queen's recall, young Hawkins, who was in charge of it, returned to assure the royal courier that the winds were so adverse that he was unable to overtake the fleet.

Drake had had some trouble in getting away, for several of his sailors deserted at the last moment, and it was only by impressing soldiers that he could fill the vacancies. He stood not on the order of " any charge," so that he might the better do " our gracious mistress such service as may be to the honour of God, the safety and contentment of her Majesty and realm, and a satisfaction of your honourable expectation." He was eager to be at large, and his words certainly read as though he had no intention of being baulked : " If your honour did now see the fleet under sail, and knew with what resolution men's minds do enter into this action, as your honour would rejoice to see them, so you would judge a small force would not divide them." Interposing a prescient protest against those who usually kept " their finger out of the fire," he waved the Queen this picturesque farewell : " The wind now commands me away. Our ship is under sail. God grant that we may so live in his fear as the enemy may have cause to say that God doth fight for her Majesty as well abroad as at home. Haste ! From aboard her Majesty's good ship the Bonaventure, this 2nd April, 1587." So that Drake cleared with unabridged instructions, and he was fortunately relieved from observing the " milder course " enjoined for his guidance. Making direct for Cadiz, he found in its harbour " sundry great ships laden with provisions to support the invasion of England " ; so that, at the outset, he was more than justified, and his critics confounded. Although his flagship was only 550 tons, he fell upon a Biscayan of more than twice its size, and burnt another vessel from Vera Cruz which was even larger than that. The Spanish galleys made a show of resistance ; but the descent was so smart and unexpected that Drake, moving as he pleased, destroyed some thirty vessels, appropriated all the provisions he could stow away, and left with " as much honour as we could wish." Realising that Phillip's preparations were far advanced, he passed from port to port, pounced upon the store ships with the same celerity, and disturbed the Spanish commissariat arrangements by setting a hundred transports on fire. The daring sea-dog was thus engaged in " singeing the King of Spain's beard " when his fleet was blown out of Lisbon, and its only safety lay in a run to England. He could not resign himself, however, to the idea of saluting Plymouth Castle until he had been blessed with a little of the " comfortable dew of

Heaven "—his euphemistic way of describing treasure ;—and, as his good luck availed
him, he made an unprecedented haul. Off St. Vincent a Portuguese carrack bore down
upon the Buonaventure, whose identity had been disguised by hanging out flags, streamers,
and pendants. All unconscious, the San Felipe continued its course ; and, as soon as she
was within range, Drake opened fire and "made short work of her." Her gold, silver and
precious stones were valued at a million pounds sterling, and the spoils were landed at
Plymouth, to quote the Black Book, "to the great comforte of her Majestie and her
subjects."

Defeat of the Armada :   During the absence of its protector the suspense in Plymouth was
1588.   acute, broken by panic. It was Drake's presence that restored
confidence and his contempt of the enemy revived the courage of his townsmen. Having
tested the quality of the vessels that were to form the Armada, he airily declared that
they were not "the bugs" that should create alarm. But, whilst he thus moderated
apprehension, he took care to stiffen the backs of the local authorities, who had positively
permitted five Spanish treasure ships to take temporary shelter in the harbour without the
slightest attempt to confiscate their contents. After a sharp letter had been sent from the
Court, roundly rating the authorities on their "insufficience," bye-laws were published
warning the craven that their goods and chattels would be seized if they left the town in
the event of attack, and threatening the freemen with perpetual banishment if they were
absent from their posts when wanted. Philip was stunned when he learnt the havoc that
Drake had wrought at the various ports and he could only account for his success by
inferring that he was in league with "a familiar spirit." Recovering from his discomfiture,
however, he caused "a direful host of floating citadels" to assemble at Corunna in the
spring of 1588 ; "puissant and mighty vessels," as Drake informed the Queen, " for a
vast army by seas to come out of Spain and Portugal to effect the full conquest of
England." Dwelling in the port to which the merchantmen were daily resorting, the ears
of Sir Francis were open to every rumour ; and, without delay, he communicated with the
court the reports brought by the mariners from France as they heard them from Spanish
overland travellers. The one fear that haunted him was that the Armada might catch the
English fleet in a trap, and again and again he urged the impolicy of keeping it at
Plymouth, instead of assuming the aggressive. Waxing bold "in discharge of my
conscience and being burdened to signify unto your Highness the imminent dangers, that
in my simple opinion, do hang over us," he advocated the despatch of the forces "somewhat off and near their own coast." This course he commended as "better cheap for
your Majesty and people, and much the dearer for the enemy."

    Knowing by experience that she might rely upon Drake in a perilous hour, Elizabeth
wrote to ask him how the Spanish "now at Lisbon might be best distressed." To tender
explanations as to detail when Drake trusted to dash was most difficult. Truly, he
observed by way of reply, "the point is hardly to be answered as yet ; but if your Highness
will give present order for our proceeding to sea, and send to the strengthening of the fleet
at Plymouth four more of your Majesty's good ships, and those sixteen sail of ships, with
their pinnaces, which are preparing in London, then shall your Majesty stand assured, with
God's assistance, that, if the fleet come out of Lisbon, as long as we have victuals to live
withal upon that coast, they shall be fought with, and I hope, through the goodness of our
merciful God, in such sort as shall hinder their quiet passage into England. I assure your
Majesty I have not in my lifetime known better men, and possessed with gallanter minds,
than your Majesty's people are for the most part which are gathered here together." The
advantage of time and place he persuasively continued, "is half a victory, which being

lost is irrecoverable. Wherefore command me away with those ships which are in Plymouth already, and the rest to follow with all possible expedition." This, "in my poor opinion, is the best and surest course." Drake's views were not shared by ministers, and so he repeatedly begged them to believe that "with fifty sail of line we shall do more good upon the Spanish coast than a great many more will do here at Plymouth." But Walsingham and Howard were not convinced, and so the preparations were pushed in Catwater, and the tatterdemalions of Spain sang in their sunny streets :

> My brother Don Juan
> To England has gone ;
> To kill the Drake
> And the Queen to take,
> And the heretics all to destroy !

Those were momentous days at Plymouth, for the shipwrights were at work by night as well as by day with the aid of torchlights and cressets ; and, as the boisterous winds extinguished this form of illumination, pitch, tallows and firs were "consumed abundantly." William Hawkins proudly reported to the Queen that the ships "sit strongly and are as staunch as if they were made of a whole tree " ; John Hawkins cheered the inhabitants with his conviction that the "only way to gain a solid peace is to wage a resolute and determined war " ; and Drake counselled a supreme effort in the pregnant phrase : " Stop him now and you shall stop him ever." As the ruddy glare served as a beacon, suspense gave way to exhilaration ; amid beating drums and waving flags, seventeen thousand soldiers marched into Plymouth and encamped on the Hoe ; and eleven thousand more continued the journey to Falmouth to resist the attack if it fell there. Drake kept the artillerymen alert by constant practice, and a gun explosion supplied Howard with the excuse for drawing Walsingham's attention to his "wasteful firing." The failure to convey a direct hint to the vice-admiral illustrated the general hesitation to repress the exercise of his judgment. " If you would write a word to him to spare his powder it would be well." But Drake had no intention of being caught napping. There were only eleven "lasts " in the Castle, and, "if we should want the powder when we have most need thereof, it will be too late to send to the Tower for it." The supply of powder was not the extent of his demand, for the local equipment was lacking in other respects. " Forget not 500 muskets, and at least 1,000 arrows ; and such other munition as by the particulars you shall find most wanting and best to be procured."

Howard set sail from the Downs in May, and approached Plymouth with "a pleasant gale." Drake sailed out to meet him with sixty vessels " very well appointed " ; and after exchanging courtesies, the Lord High Admiral took the first fair wind for the Spanish coast. After aimlessly beating about the Channel, he returned for fresh stores, and "an extreme continual storm " prevented him from resuming his observations for some days. As the Catwater was now crowded with the smaller vessels, Howard rode out the gale in the Sound "with four or five of the greatest ships," and Drake took refuge between the island and the main with others of equal dimensions. Meanwhile "the Heaven threatening host " was reported by small coasters making their way to Plymouth, to whom the enemy had given chase "and made shot." Drake in reporting to the Queen the approach of the Armada "never doubted that the enemy should be so sought out and encountered withal in such sort as I hope shall qualify their malicious and long intended practices. Pray continually for our good success in this action," he pleaded, "to the performance of which we have resolutely vowed the adventure of our lives." The Lord High Admiral advanced to meet the foe in the open, but their ships had been dispersed by a hurricane, and, after a futile attempt at search, he returned to Plymouth to refresh and re-victual. The English admirals were engaged in a game of bowls upon the Hoe when one of the barques that had been "left in the Sleeve for discovery" sailed into the harbour with the alarming intelligence that the Armada was off the coast "in greate companies." In one of their dramas the Spaniards argue that their commanders carried the business with England "so cunningly and secretly as to bring the Armada to its shores whilst the captains were at play upon the Hoe. Had only my lord Alonzo Guzman, the Duke of Medina Sidonia, possessed the resolution, but in truth his commission was otherwise, he might have surprised them whilst their ships lay at anchor and the like." The accepted legend ascribes to the officers an impulse to rush to their ships, when their nerves were steadied by the man of iron. "There is plenty of time," said Drake, "to finish the game and lick the Spaniards afterwards." A hoary tradition in vogue at Buckland Monachorum invests the knight with the added halo of a miracle worker; for the simple villagers were wont to declare that, as soon as the game was finished, he threw a bowl in the pool and it came up a ship, and that when the remainder were cast into Catwater, the fleet was largely reinforced!

Some of Drake's stolidity may have been due to the fact that the wind made it hard for the ships to be "gotten out of harbour"; but the industry and goodwill of the men were so exerted that they eventually emerged as with "a fair wind." The Armada stretched from the "Idyestone" to Fowey as Howard plied out of the Sound; towering argosies, carracks with stately sterns, and huge hulks—all of them bearing the names of saints and grand dames, and consecrated by the priests at the respective ports of departure. Medina Sidonia eschewed the tactics that had oppressed Drake with apprehension; and, instead of attempting to force the English fleet within the neck of the bottle, he perpetrated the irreparable mistake of leaving the port untouched and pressing up Channel. Perceiving this folly, Howard and Drake swiftly seized the advantage; and two leagues to the west of the Eddystone recovered the wind of the Spaniards. Howard sent his

THE GAME OF BOWLS: "THE ARMADA IS IN SIGHT!"

(After Seymour Lucas, A.R.A.; reproduced by permission from the Engraving published by Arthur Lucas, London.)

pinnace, the Disdain, to give Medina Sidonia defiance; and bearing up in the Ark, so fought his antagonist that he summoned several of his ships to the rescue. Drake, Hawkins and Frobisher devoted their attention to a Portuguese galleon; and prosecuting the attack fouled Don Pedro's battleship with such disastrous effect that, "being with great dishonour" abandoned, it fell, with all hands, into Drake's possession. Night closed in as a Biscayan blew up, and Howard held a council of war in the offing. Forty sail of ships were yet due from Plymouth; and having decided to await their arrival "before hazarding the rest too far," the Lord High Admiral "dismissed each man to go aboard his own ship," and Drake set the watch for the night.

At daybreak the Armada was as far leeward as Berry Head, and rowing by the side of the devastated Biscayan, Howard witnessed a "pitiful sight"—the deck destroyed, the stern blown out, and fifty poor creatures "burnt with powder in most miserable sort." The Spanish now gained the wind of the English; and, driving them towards the shore, endeavoured to board. The fight was resumed in earnest; but the defenders "abode the coming" of the enemy, and "seeing us able to abide them," they fell astern of the rearmost vessel. Howard then assaulted hotly; broadside answered to broadside "very nobly"; and never was seen "a more terrible value of great shot nor sharper conflict." The Spanish were yielding, and flocking together "like sheep," when the English ammunition gave out; and Howard despatched "divers barks and pinnaces" into Plymouth for fresh supplies. Upon their return, the Lord High Admiral divided the fleet and invested Drake, Hawkins and Frobisher with individual commands. A calm led to an enforced suspension of hostilities; but, with the return of the gale, the divisions drew near to each other, powder and shot were again "well wasted," and the despatch of eight fireships into the midst of the Armada caused its officers "to let slip or cut cables at half." With each lull in the fighting, and the despatch of reports to the shore, Drake forwarded messages of rejoicing to the Queen. "God has given us so good a day in forcing the enemy so far to leeward as I hope in God the Prince of Parma and the Duke of Sidonia shall not shake hands these few days; and, when they meet, I believe neither of them will rejoice over this day's service." Again he wrote: "We have the army of Philip before us and mean with the grace of God to wrestle a pull with him." Then he grimly anticipated that Medina Sidonia would "wish himself at St. Mary's Port amongst his orange trees. May God so give us grace to depend on him: so we shall not doubt victory, for our cause is good."

After this the Spaniards were scarcely able to live upon the seas; and, retorting upon a scornful remark of Mendoza, Howard told him that Elizabeth's "rotten ships" had dared to meet "his master's sound ships," and, in spite of their superiority in size and numbers, "we have shortened them by sixteen, whereof there is three a fishing at the bottom of the seas." The conquest was similarly glorified in the Plymouth archives: "God be praised, the enemye never hadd power to land so mouche as one man on any territorie of ours." By acclamation the honour was given to Drake; and, in Spain, the name of no other English warrior was held in similar detestation. It was at first reported at Madrid that Plymouth had been stormed, and that "the greate dog, Francis Drake, is in chains and fetters." Upon this the dons pranced about on horseback, richly apparalled, burnt bonfires all over the city and pierced the palace with their cheers. But, when the truth was known, they hung down their faces "like cur dogs and are shamed of all they did." The disposition to glorify Drake at the expense of his colleagues created the jealousy, especially of Frobisher; and, when the land was ringing with the fame of Sir Francis, he indulged in more than one angry outburst. "Drake reporteth," he exclaimed, "that no one hath done any good service save he. But he shall well understand that others hath done as good service as he, and better too. He came bragging up at the first indeed and gave the Spaniards his prow and his broadside.   Then he kept his luff and was glad he was gone again, like a cowardly knave or traitor—I rest doubtful, but the one I will swear."   It was the apprehension of an inequitable distribution of prize money that instigated this robustious outburst.   Drake laid claim to the capture of the Don Pedro, "for, after he hath seen her in the evening, that she had spent her masts, then, like a coward, he kept by her all night, because he would have the spoil.   He thinketh," Frobisher protested, "to cozen us of our shares of fifteen thousand ducats, but we will have our shares, or I will make him spend the best blood in his belly, for we have had enough of those cozening cheats already.   He hath used certain speeches of me, which I will make him eat again."   To sum up his estimate of Drake's iniquity, Frobisher declared that "Sir Francis was the cause of all these troubles and in this action he showed himself the most coward."

Not only were there quarrels between the admirals, but the Queen's officers had no little difficulty in clearing the coast of "pilling knaves in quest of valuable wreckage." Cary visited Plymouth, and warned the Mayor that "such brass pieces as were taken out of the Spanish carrack whereof Don Pedro had charge should be laid on shore and put in safe keeping for her Majestie's use."   For "the better satisfying" of the Councillors, he read the Royal warrant, and with wry faces they promised to disgorge.   Other Spanish battleships were cast ashore at Salcombe and Bigbury, and "great pilfering and spoils being made by the country people," Cary rode to those villages and "took order for the restoring and rehaving" of the ducats and plate that had been rifled before his arrival.

THE ARMADA OFF PLYMOUTH.
(From the Fresco by W. Brewer. as exhibited at the Royal Academy, destroyed by fire at the Plymouth Palace of Varieties. 1898.)

Drake Bringing in the   To the growth of Plymouth, the international importance it had
Water: 1591.   attained, and its increased popularity as a place for shipping, must be attributed that improvement of its water supply with which the name of Drake will ever be identified.   The inhabitants were dependent upon the wells, and of these the more

important were Jacob's Well, in Southside Street; St. Andrew's Well, near the Lary; Catdown Well, and Maudlin Well, at the north of the town.   Holy Well, Fine Well, West Well, Buck Well and others suggest how general was this form of service.   The first conduit was erected by William Hawkins, and there is little doubt that this existed on the New Quay.   In 1585 a bill was promoted to bring the water from Dartmoor, and the chief reason urged was the difficulty of an adequate yield in the town in the summer.   So many ships traded from "forren parts" to this "very pleasaunte and safe harbouroughe" that the supplies gave out in the event of drought; and so urgent were the necessities of the fleets, that "divers good wyndes" and opportunities were lost when the "enemye" was upon the coasts.   A town which had been so often fired also considered that it was entitled to larger facilities for coping with similar outbreaks, and the more so since no "greate prejudice or damage" could befall the owners through whose estates the water was to be brought, as the "lande is either barren and heathie or else hillye and drye ground which will be bettered and amended by the water that shall be brought through the same."

After the bill received the royal assent, Drake was entrusted by the municipality with the execution of the work.   A man of indomitable courage, he was best qualified to settle difficult points with reluctant owners; and, as he was also wealthy, the Corporation gladly allowed him to finance the scheme.   His familiarity with the systems of older civilizations also rendered him a conspicuous authority, and so events combined to distinguish Drake as the indispensable man.   He did not disappoint the expectations which were formed, and the story of his construction of the leat reads like one of his own resistless dashes to the Spanish coast.   In December, 1590, he cut the first sod; and, by the ensuing April, amid the rejoicings of the populace, the water was flowing into Plymouth through a circuitous channel of twenty-five miles (old style).   The Mayor and the gownsmen went out to meet Sir Francis and the water, and ushered the stream and its pioneer into the town in state, "but whether the water was dammed back, to keep pace with their worships, or whether their worships galloped along to keep pace with the water, neither tradition nor legend hands down to us."   As the stream ran past the door of his own house, Sir Francis dipped his scarlet cloak therein "in exultation that he had obtained his desired end."   For his "great care and diligence" in prosecuting this conception, Drake was paid £352 16s. in tardy instalments, and the right to use certain mills for seven years was also conceded.   The cost of the labour was £200, and the judges of Assize assessed at £100 the value of the land.

Stormy rhetoric has raged over the attempt to delimit the value of Drake's services. That he gave the water to the town is a comparatively modern misconception, for which neither he nor his contemporaries are to blame.   That he brought the water to the town, and that his passionate energy and personal resource rendered possjble a benefaction which would otherwise have continued in abeyance, is an historical fact that academic shredding can never impair.   Controversialists may grope for stray entries in musty records to support their favourite theories, but the Councillors who sat with Drake, and were conscious of his strength and their weakness, knew how and where to bestow the credit when they inscribed these lines beneath the portrait of their dauntless fellow citizen :—

> Who with fresh streams refresht this town that first
> Though kist with waters yet did pine with thirst,
> Who bothe a pilot and a magistrate
> Steered in his turne the ship of Plymouth state.

DRAKE BRINGING IN THE WATER BY BURRATOR FALLS:

Now submerged. The site of the Burrator Reservoir.

(From a Panel by Samuel Cook, at Cann House, reproduced by permission of Mr. H. Grigg. Photo. by R. R. Monk, 1899.)

Watching and Fortifying Plymouth: 1590-1595. Philip did not conceal the exasperation which the ruin of the Armada occasioned him, and his shipbuilding yards were occupied in the equipment of a more formidable fleet. The idea was to keep Elizabeth in feverish alarm, so that she might be dissuaded from allowing merchant ships to leave her own shores; but the expedient did not prevent the Earl of Cumberland from setting out with a strong fleet to the coast of Spain, and Howard of Effingham left for the Azores to intercept the Spanish traders on the homeward journey. As soon as the latter found another and overpowering Armada in his pursuit, however, he gave directions for a general retreat, and it was in passionate resentment of this withdrawal that Sir Richard Grenville, regardless of odds and orders, dashed at two squadrons of the foe in his little barque "The Revenge." For fifteen hours did he sustain the flag against the blazing guns of those fifteen Spanish battleships, either of them big enough to blow him off the face of the waters, and the unengaged officers looked on in amazement and admiration as Grenville thus valiantly contended with the huge galleons, dodging them here and evading them there, until the hold of his shattered vessel could only be compared to a slaughter-house, so "marvellous unsavoury" was it with the decomposing fragments of the dead and dying. And then, force of numbers prevailing, the Revenge was stormed, and Grenville, pathetically perishing of innumerable wounds, swooned as he was transported into the presence of the courtly Spanish admiral. There was no faltering in the resolve of Spain to crush an enemy that bred such heroes as Grenville, who, to quote Bacon, rose to the height "of heroical fable," and there was also the anxiety to wipe out a reproach and convince the Spanish people that the Lord of Hosts was with the Catholic King.

Elizabeth collected a no less imposing navy than that which had dispersed the first Armada; and in Plymouth, as elsewhere, every available man was armed, and there were frequent reviews of troops. The inhabitants were on tenter hooks, as stories came that the town was in the hands of the priests, that the Castle was held by a confederate who had been bought with fifty thousand crowns, and that 8,000 men were to be landed, at peep o' day, westward of the harbour, on a date that the traitors would decide. The doubts thus generated were fostered by Andrew Facey, "of Stonehouse, near Plymouth," who, on escaping from the prison at Madrid, deposed that he was tortured into a promise to serve the King of Spain—"whose throat I would have cut if it had lain in my power"— and that he gathered sufficient knowledge of the foul work in progress to assert that "all were not the Queen's good subjects that dwelt in Plymouth," and that Thomas Griffin was amongst the faithless. The imputations were received with wholesome scepticism: "As they are subtle and have missed their stroke," the Mayor observed, "they may give these things out to put the place in confusion." All this time his worship and his brethren were alert to the presence of suspicious personages, and several priests were laid by the heels on being found with copies of the bull of excommunication pronounced against Elizabeth. The spies so multiplied that some were sent to Trematon Castle and others to Plymstocke, as the prison accommodation in Plymouth was unequal to the demand. In reporting his difficulty, his worship suggested a short way out: "They had better be hanged at once, as the cost of keeping them is greate." An instance of over zeal occurred in the case of Thomas Wharton, a courier of the Privy Council, who was leaving the port when the dis-covery of State papers led to his arrest. Wharton was taken before the assembled Council and an indiscriminate crowd of spectators, in whose presence some of the documents were read aloud and commented upon. "Some did not stick to say that they well knew your Honour would not send me over to Spain"; and the Mayor opened sealed letters in the presence of one Goddard, a Portuguese, and quoted portions "which may tend to my overthrow." His worship was peremptorily bidden to release Wharton as soon as the report and remonstrance were received, and everything in atonement was done to facilitate his mission.

With each threat "to burn the town next summer" there was a return of the uneasiness, and many of the inhabitants could not be persuaded to "stay for the defence thereof as is wished." Thereupon the north west tower of the Castle was covered with lead; seven brass pieces were hoisted in position; the gate at "Cocksyde" was "shutte every night"; the "greate platforme by the gate at the Hawe" was completed and iron cannon were mounted on the Barbican and the bulwarks. But these measures were only regarded as an inadequate instalment; and, "being neither worthy of that most princely love and gracious care your Majesty hath had of the good preservation of our toune and ourselves," the Mayor and Commonalty petitioned the Queen to methodise the fortifications, perfect the fort and instal a sufficient garrison. These measures, they pointed out, would induce "the countrie forces" to rally to their succour, "on which (next under God and your Majesty) depends the preservation and defence of our towne and ourselves from

TREMATON CASTLE.
(From the Engraving by Buck.)

the force and violence of an obstinate enemy against whom the fort can defend but itself and not our towne." The memorial was supported by Richard Adams, who described Plymouth harbour as "peerless and without an equal"; but too vast for the citizens to defend since they possessed "small means," and there was only hope of "a cold charity" on the part of the country gentry. Drake, who was also consulted, said that millions would be required to environ Plymouth with "a royal strength, as Nature itself hath commandment of it"; but, with £5,000, he thought it might be fortified against surprise. Block houses and platforms were accordingly added, and consolidated under the name of "the Fort on the Hoe Cliffs." The Mayor had promised that the municipality would do its part "if fish is as plentiful as it has been of late years"; and, recognising that the "island" was "the natural life of the harbour," the Commonalty spent £1,000 in providing it with "artillerie, furniture and munitions." Special duties were levied to meet this expenditure, which was "verie requisite and needful for the better defence of these western parts against any attempt to be made by the enemy."

The Spanish were not indulging in empty boasts, nor were the English adventurers deterred from going forth by reason of their menaces. In February, 1595, enflamed with the desire to explore the El Dorado of which he had read in the literature of the Dons, Sir Walter Raleigh left the Sound in five small barques, manned in the ordinary way by mariners and spendthrift gentlemen "who had no roofs to cover them." His destination was Manao, the capital of Guiana, a city where the houses were reported to be mainly built of gold, and whose roofs glistened in the sunshine. Here the priests indulged in the dazzling worship of Montezuma; and travellers who penetrated its mysterious boundaries were escorted blindfold to its further limits. Within a few months of Raleigh's departure in quest of this fairyland, an attempt was made to realise the boast of the generalissimo at Madrid, who had exasperated a Plymouth captive by telling him that with "eight galleys he could sweep the coast of Devon and Cornwall." With half that number of boats, the "Spanyards" entered Penzance, Newlyn, Mousehole, and other Cornish ports; and, much "to their disgrace," to quote Hannibal Vivyan, the governor of St. Mawes Castle, the inhabitants offered no resistance and allowed their homes to be burnt. A few weeks later, a Spanish pinnace, carrying 25 armed men, entered Cawsham (Cawsand) Bay; and, rolling ashore several barrels of powder, caused explosions in various parts of the village and fired the houses. The scouts thereupon ran from their posts on the hilltops, firing their weapons as they went, and the visitors took to their boat. As there were other galleys in the distance messengers crossed over to Plymouth, and the scare was general. The drums beat to arms; the soldiers donned their armour; the Hoe was held by the trained bands; bells were rung to advise sailors to repair to their ships; and barricades were thrown up. Although the alarm passed, there was hardly a month when the foe were not expected, or during which the more intrepid did not remind the inhabitants of their proximity. Meanwhile Raleigh was threading the labyrinthine mazes of the Orinoco in a few small boats; only to find, after weeks spent amid torrential rains and tropical heats, that the one escape from the rapidly rising stream was a hasty flight to the anchorage in which his barques were reposing two hundred miles away. When he returned to Plymouth and told strange tales of unfamiliar tribes and hideous Amazons, to compensate for the lack of the promised treasures, the weary townsfolk, who were evidently in need of substantial encouragement, indulged in exasperating cynicism.

Death of Hawkins, Preparations for delivering and meeting the second blow were ripe
Drake, and Frobisher: in 1595, and both sides were never better prepared. In June, Essex,
1596 Howard and Raleigh left Plymouth with the idea of anticipating the departure of the Spanish fleet for the English shores, and although there was a want of enthusiasm among the admirals at the outset of the voyage, Sir Walter fired his colleagues by his vigorous proposal to run his small vessels by the side of the galleons reposing in Cadiz harbour, thus escaping the fire of their guns and exposing them to easy shot and boarding parties. Vowing that he would be "revenged for The Revenge," Raleigh carried the fight against the majestic Philip with such valour and persistence that, after laying a fuse to the magazine to prevent the monster from falling into English hands, the crew went over the sides and avoided the explosion that followed. Sir Walter was not to be denied his reward, however, and, tackling the Saint Andrew and the Saint Matthew in the same fashion, he boarded each in turn and took possession. These were the only two prizes that could be trusted to float, so mutilated were the other Spanish galleons which had been jammed within the harbour. To avoid the possibility of their rescue, Raleigh sent them forward, and they were anchored in Catwater in triumph. The subsequent attempt to carry Lisbon was a failure, although, to quote the local archives, Essex knocked at the

gate "with such instrument as he hadd in his hand." He obtained no response ; and, as a pestilence now broke out and decimated his crews, the fleet returned to Plymouth, and the inhabitants were again scourged by the odious infection. In spite of the surprise upon Cadiz, and the havoc thus occasioned, the wealth of Spain enabled her to recruit by purchasing ships from other countries. The extent to which the influence of Philip was thereupon asserted in France led to Frobisher's despatch to Brest ; where, in an encounter otherwise satisfactory, he received his fatal wound. He reached Plymouth alive, but surgical skill could not save him ; and, after his " bowells " had been solemnly interred in St. Andrew's Church, his embalmed body was carried to London. Thus passed not the least rugged of the Elizabethan race of warriors—a man with no fear and scant remorse ; and who, if he did not reap the highest fruits of discovery, ploughed and prepared the way for others.

Drake and Hawkins were invited by the Queen to renew their triumphs at the expense of the Spanish marine. The former had settled in the peaceful hollow at Buckland Monachorum, partly by grant from the Queen and partly by the exercise of his own wealth. His uncle was fast failing in health and "more like to provide for my grave than encumber myself with worldly affairs." Still the kinsmen were as ready as ever " to spend our lives and abilities in your Majesty's service " ; and Drake went to London to take charge, jointly with Hawkins, of a fleet of six ships of the Royal Navy and a cluster of smaller craft—the expedition as a whole well found and manned with excellent troops. After destroying Cadiz, the fleet proceeded to the Indies ; Havana was captured, and Porto Rico was attacked. Here every preparation had been made to give the Englishmen a warm reception, and they were repulsed with heavy loss. The discomfiture precipitated the death of Hawkins. There had been many " sharp debates " between the two admirals. Naturally impatient of suggestion, and "rude in behaviour," the old man's temper had betrayed intolerable developments and frequent fits presaged a speedy constitutional collapse. No less "deep in conceit" than haughty in conference, Drake retorted upon his uncle with "unkind speeches." These Hawkins never forgave and " being unable to bear his grief, he sickened." In the words of the memorial erected at Deptford :

> The sea his body keeps,
> Where, for a while, as Jonas now he sleeps,
> Till He, which said to Lazarus, " Come Forth "
> Awakes this Knight and gives to him his worth.

On arriving at Nombre de Dios, Drake marched to Panama to intercept five millions of gold which Don Alonzo de Sottomayor was only awaiting the Spanish fleet to deport. Learning that the English were advancing across the isthmus, he laid in ambush in a narrow pass and fell upon Drake's force with such energy that they fled from the scene, leaving 150 dead in the defile. Don Bernardin del Aviglianeda's fifty ships were daily expected from Spain, and Don Alonzo anticipated that certain rout awaited Drake's squadron "already crushed and exhausted by seven months' service on the open seas." The reinforcements, fresh and in good trim, encountered this miserable remnant, consisting of fourteen vessels, in the open Channel. Every artifice to confuse and ram the larger Spanish galleons was attempted by the Englishmen and D'Aviglianeda was evidently astonished by their smartness. But the fates were against them ; and after losing one ship, Drake carried the remainder to Nombre de Dios to refit. "There he died," to quote the Spanish despatch. Dysentery decimated the survivors of the doomed expedition, and crushed by reverse, Drake fell a victim to the epidemic himself. "Sickness did not so much untie his cloaths as sorrow did rend at once the robe of his mortality asunder." After days of suffering he grew delirious, " muttering speeches at a little or before his death, and rising and apparrellinge himself. Being brought to bed within one hour, he died—yielding up his spirit, like a Christian, to his Creator, quietly in his cabin." Henry Newbolt has given thrilling expression to the retrospective dreamings of the dying hero :

> Drake he's in his hammock an' a thousand miles away,
>   (Capten art tha sleepin' there below ?)
> Slung atween the round shot in Nombre de Dios Bay,
>   An' dreamin' arl the time of Piymouth Hoe.
> Yarnder lumes the island, yarnder lie the ships
>   Wi' sailor lads a dancin' heel an' toe,
> An' the shore lights flashin', and the night tide dashin',
>   He sees et arl so plainly as he saw et long ago,
>
> Drake he was a Devon man, an' ruled the Devon seas,
>   (Capten, art tha sleepin' there below ?)
> Rovin' tho' his death fell, he went wi' heart at ease
>   An' dreamin' arl the time of Plymouth Hoe.
> " Take my drum to England, hang et by the shore,
>   Strike et when your powder's running low,
> If the Dons sight Devon, I'll quit the port o' Heaven
>   An' drum them up the Channel as we drummed them long ago.
>
> Drake he's in his hammock till the great Armada come,
>   (Capten, art tha sleepin' there below ?)
> Slung atween the round shot, listenin' for the drum,
>   An' dreamin' arl the time of Plymouth Hoe.
> Call him on the deep sea, call him up the Sound,
>   Call him when ye sail to meet the foe ;
> Where the old trade's plyin' an' the old flag flyin'
>   You shall find him ware an' wakin', as you found him long ago.

Bedimmed veterans clustered the rails as the waves became Drake's "winding sheet," and to his home were carried the relics that had been his inseparable companions the wide world over, and especially the drum that had summoned his crew to unequal conflicts and rewards beyond the dreams of avarice. Mournfully the remnant of the fleet entered Falmouth Harbour, lamenting the loss of the chieftains and deploring the discredit that enshrouded their end. When the extent of the calamity was revealed, men spoke to each other in fearsome whispers and the consternation was profound : " Drake and Hawkins and many worthies are dead." In Spain, however, the news caused the liveliest satisfaction and the dying King vowed that he would now recover from his illness. " Everyone is saying that the Lord God has undertaken the protection of his Catholic Majesty," and D'Aviglianeda boasted : " I cannot believe, after the shame of this expedition, the English will ever return to the Indies." If the end was inglorious, the grief in Plymouth was no less genuine ; and all other figures stood in relief as that of Drake loomed majestic—the pride of his own generation ; if, in some respects, the controversial heritage of posterity.

Failùre of the Second   Philip was not slow to follow up his advantage, and he requested
Armada : 1597-99.   harbourage for his ships in French waters. At the suggestion of
Elizabeth, this privilege was denied and she collected sixty vessels, " chiefly Dutch," and

stationed them "at the extremity of the island, near Plymouth." In November, 1597, the second Armada, consisting of 120 ships, sailed from Corunna ; and, thirty leagues out, instructions were sent to the various commanders, "in the name of God and St. James" to press on for Plymouth. "A cheer of joy went up and even the sick forgot their ailments." Off Falmouth, however, the fleet was overtaken by heavy downpours and withering gales, "and each thought of his own safety." Rudders were unshipped, yards were carried away, and the majority gave themselves up for lost. But precisely the same experience befell Sir Walter Raleigh, who was on the look-out for the invaders, and was at his "wit's ends" to avenge their presumptions. It was impossible, he wrote, to imagine a fleet so weakly or so wretchedly manned as that with which he had endeavoured to discover the enemy, and he attributed his success in making the port at all to "God's Extraordinary Blessing." Three leagues off Rame Head, he was overtaken by a violent storm. "The night was extremely dark, save for the flashes of lightning, and the strength of the hurricane drove the ships towards the lee shore." His own vessel was in peril of sinking, many of the masts cracked, the sails were reduced to rags, and the water poured through gaping timbers. "We are dismayed unto death by these misfortunes because God has turned the Heavens against us"; but Sir Walter begged the Queen to believe that the state of "our storm-beaten fleet is as unpleasant to us who have endured the danger as it must be to your Majesty whom we had hoped to serve."

The knowledge that the Spaniards were in force upon the coast had created much unrest in Plymouth, but the town was held by three hundred horse and ten thousand infantry, who were disposed around St. Budeaux and along the banks of the Tamar, to prevent an overland attack from the Cornish side. Whilst the disconcerted Spaniards were making the best of their return to Corunna, Essex's fleet arrived from another voyage, "and not only comforted but reassured everyone." In his complacency he even wrote to assure Elizabeth that "with us in Plymouth the fear of the Spanish fleet has passed, which maketh us glad, hoping we shall be the sooner removed hence." Thomas Howard asked, at the same time, that the troops who were compensating for their lack of pay by the usual alternative of plundering the inhabitants, might be removed from the town. This counsel was acted upon, but the Commonalty prayed for their return at any price as the alarms redoubled. Apprehension was intense with every fresh cry of "wolf" until familiarity bred the customary contempt, and Thomas Stallenge, the Commissioner of the port, vowed in a report "that the Spanish are more afraid of us than we are of them, and I would to God that they had more cause to fear us than as yet they have."

There was a pause of two years during which the inhabitants took heart, but they gave way to undignified panic in 1599, when a cloud of canvas covered the horizon and there were no means of defence at the disposal of the authorities. "Haste, post haste for life," a messenger was despatched to the Queen to beg than an army should be sent for the town's defence ; but, when the fleet anchored, there was an anti-climax, for the visitors were none other than friendly Flemish traders. The alarm, however, had done its work, and the Earl of Bath marched into Plymouth with 4,000 men and some cornets of horse. They entered the town, to find that the enemies were friends ; but, as the nerves of the inhabitants had been unsettled, the troops decided to remain and extract as much enjoyment from the visit as local liberality would afford. Thus for weeks the army was "well lodged and entertained to the greate comfort and encouragement both of the towne and the country, who, if itt pleased God that the enemy should come were then readye and willinge to fight."

The revival of the might of France became manifest in spite of the incursions of Philip. The energies of Spain waxed feeble the threats to invade England appreciably

waned, and Elizabeth was left to the undisturbed enjoyment of her throne.   That something survived of the saucy initiative of Drake, however, was testified by William Parker,
of Plymouth, who left the port with a small squadron in 1601, and plundered Puerto Pello
without resistance.   An insolent expedition this, for Parker landed with a force so small
that the Spaniards could have swept his mercenaries off their legs if they had not stood
aghast instead of running for their arms.   When the Governor of Cartagena heard the
story, and learnt how Parker had extorted ransoms in pearls and precious stones, he vowed
that he would give a mule's load of silver to see the impudent freebooter.   After the little
band returned to the port to jest of the ease with which they bedazed the Spaniards,
the love of the impudent was kindled anew and the old longings possessed the mariners.
Parker was not the only pirate of audacious courage.   Stephen Piers, with a crew of eighty
Plymouth men, fifty of them armed, laid in wait for Venetian ships ; and, when he seized
the Veniera in 1603, took counsel with his officers as to whether he should kill the whole
of the prisoners "to hide the traces of his guilt."   He eventually adopted the humaner
device of turning the captives adrift, some hundreds of miles away.   Stephen Infold, another
Plymouth captain, was reported for "scandalous excesses" at Zante.   When his conduct
was communicated to Elizabeth's ambassador at Constantinople, "he shrugged his
shoulders, shewed great uneasiness, and said the Queen would make a stern example."
There is no record that she did.

CHAPTER III.—"THE MERCHANT OF PLYMOUTH."

The Merchant of Ply-   Romance was for the first time associated with tragedy in Ply-
mouth; or, Murder of   mouth in 1590. Ulalia Glandfield, the fair daughter of a Tavistock
Master Page: 1590.   tradesman, was wooed by an eager and stalwart youth, George
Strangwidge. His attentions were reciprocated, and a happy marriage would probably
have resulted if the plans and pledges of the lovers had not been frustrated by the parents
of the maiden. The story is of intrinsic interest, inasmuch as the tragedy occurred when
the printing press was coming into fashion; and every heinous crime, superstitious
portent, or event that appealed to the morbid, the curious and the hero worshippers was
put into verse and type, and sung and sold in towns and villages. There was no printing
machine in Plymouth at this time, of course. In only three cities in England, including
London, were licenses granted; so that the strange, the weird and the wonderful "narrations"
circulated were in the main travellers' tales that could hardly have failed to gain in the
telling. To this category the various versions of the Page story evidently belong, for
his violent death was the means of producing in ballads, tract and play the earliest
known essentially local literature. Although these effusions are of contemporaneous
date, they are naturally unreliable, the circumstances put on record are the obvious
result of rumour rather than of authentic information, and in parts the stories are inconsistent. According to "The True Discourse," Ulalia's father was so proud of his
daughter's choice that he decided to make over to him the whole of his business, and
Strangwidge went to London to gain more experience of the method of conducting it.
Possessed of large means himself there was no sordid necessity for Glandfield to arrange
an unequal marriage for his favourite child, and it was only the intervention of "Sathan"
that disturbed his confidence in his daughter's sweetheart. In the ballad which purposed
to contain her "confession" on the eve of execution, Ulalia pleaded that she was driven
to wed Master Page, a widower approaching dotage, because of his wealth and the miserly
instincts of her father. The suggestion by no means harmonises with the story that the
latter had generously given Strangwidge his "wares, shops and dealings." No copy of the
tragedy written by Ben Jonson and Thomas Deeker, "called Pagge of Plimothe," is
apparently in existence—all that serves to testify that it was written is an entry in Hens-
lowe's Diary, republished in the Shakespeare Papers, that the collaborateurs were advanced
money "in earnest of their booke they are writinge" with the title quoted above. The
play, which was composed by Lyne Brett, early in the eighteenth century, "The Merchant
of Plymouth," blends the leading features of "The True Discourse" and "Mistress Page's
Lamentation," and presents what is probably the real as well as the poetic rendering of the
transaction.

Young Strangwidge leaves with one of the expeditions for Spain—an idea that may be
easily reconciled with his temporary stay in the house of a London merchant, since peril
is appealing to patriotism,—and it is during his absence that the parents of Ulalia put
pressure upon their daughter to marry aged Master Page, whose mansion in Woolster
street, subsequently the residence of the Mayors, represents position if it brings no solace.
The inability of Strangwidge to communicate with Ulalia, or the interception of any letters
if he was able to send them, rendered it all the easier to convince her that her lover had

fallen in the campaign which Essex was conducting. She was evidently not the type of girl who would have submitted, even under compulsion, to wed a tottering widower for the mere sake of his money, and the return of her lover from the expedition, and his passionate importunities, distracted her with the consciousness that she had been persuaded to take an irreparable step. As to the manner of the murder "The True Discourse" speaks of repeated attempts on the part of Ulalia to poison her husband, and then as to her desperate device in bribing two men to strangle him. As the old man battles fiercely for life the desperadoes break his neck against the bedstead. This version does not agree with the theory which Lyne Brett adopted, that Strangwidge was his own avenger and the maid servant and her mistress were only indirectly accessories. According to his view, the women were rather hanged for their share in the intrigue than by reason of their knowledge that it was likely to end in tragedy. This is a reasonable exercise of the author's discretion that would naturally intensify the sympathy for the forlorn and despairing wife. The tracts do agree that Ulalia and Strangwidge were hanged for "consenting" to the crime, but the one testifies to the execution of Robert Priddis and Tom Stone, in company with the lover and his mistress ; and the other speaks of Harriet, the confidential intermediary, as sharing their fate. As eighteen persons were gibbetted on the same day as the result of these assizes, which were held at Barnstaple on account of the virulence with which the plague was raging in Exeter, it is possible that in all five persons were hanged for the part they played in the conspiracy. The final touch of art is embodied in the tradition that Judge Glanville, who sentenced the prisoners to death, was connected by ties of blood with Ulalia, and that he was so overcome with grief that he never sat upon the bench again and led thereafter the life of a recluse. The similarity of name is no doubt responsible for the added glamour with which the tragedy has been thus invested. There were Plymothians living in Lyne Brett's days who carried forward, from ancestors of remarkable longevity, interesting family traditions, and it may be that, as he has transmitted the least disagreeable form of the romance, he has given us that which is most to be relied upon. In any case, as examples of early literature affecting the history of the town, and illuminating the manners of its inhabitants at the period, the reproduction of the tract and the ballads will enable readers to give play to their own fancies.

The second attempt to dramatise the story was made in the earlier years of the 18th century by Lyne Brett, a man of letters who was a prominent figure of the social circle which assembled at the Otter Club. He so much distrusted his work, however, that he intimated on his death-bed his intention of committing the manuscript to the flames. Upon this a lady acquaintance craved the favour of perusing the work before it was destroyed ; and, Brett yielding to this request, she sat up through the night and made a transcript, which had the disadvantage of being hasty and incomplete. Lyne Brett laid the scene of the tragedy in Master Page's house in Woolster Street, and the dramatis personæ were : Page, a rich merchant, the husband of Ulalia ; Glandfield, her father ; Strangwidge, her lover ; Martin, a friend of Strangwidge ; Ulalia, the wife of Page ; Isabella, the daughter of Page by a former wife ; and Harriet, the maid servant and confidante of Ulalia.

It is the morning of Martin's marriage with Isabella, and the former is urging Strangwidge to act as his best man. The latter represents the difficulty of his position—he will be thrown across the path of Ulalia, whom he still adores, but whose affection for him has cooled ; and Page will naturally resent his appearance under his roof. Martin leaves the hall half convinced, and Ulalia enters and is at once addressed in impassioned terms by her lover. As she melts Strangwidge vows that she is more beautiful in tears than in smiles ; and, seeing that the unholy fires are being rekindled, she implores her lover to desist, by addressing an appeal to his manhood that stings him to reproach.

Strangwidge : Your love is false and you would still deceive me with a passion only feign'd.   What else could mean your letter unaccompanied by one kind word and your greeting with scarce a look ?   But, oh, too clearly now I see the painful change, and truly believe what I as much feared—that charmed and dazzled by the wealth of your old dotard you willingly yielded and were not forced, as you have falsely said, by the many arts of a cruel father, to this curst marriage.

Ulalia : How ?   Did not Martin, when first you arrived in England, assure you of the truth ?   Did not he tell you, your faithful friend inform you, that neither prayers nor threatenings could prevail, till by their successful casuistry they made me believe you died in Spain.   Then all conditions were to me alike, and I consented to the unequal match—

Strangwidge : Forgive me, then, Ulalia, if my passion hurried me beyond the bounds of reason, and kindly tell me why yesterday you sent that cruel message ?

Ulalia : If you ever had for me the least regard, or if you do desire my future quiet, I pray you will enquire no further.

Strangwidge : And if you ever loved or had the least regard for me, or if you do desire my further quiet, I beg on my knees that you will let me know the cruel cause of this so strange, this dark, this different behaviour.

Ulalia : Rise, Strangwidge, and be satisfied that the cause is tenderest affection.

Isabella appears as the lovers are once more reconciled and, never having disguised her hostility to her father's marriage, she sympathetically takes in the situation.   Strangwidge is still lingering, reluctant to enter the house, when Page greets him with an invitation to do so, and jocosely hints that he is not afflicted by jealousies.   Ulalia does not accompany the wedding party to church, but remains behind to complete the arrangements for the feast.   A company of players and musicians arrive in the meanwhile, and she induces one of the vocalists to sing a song that Strangwidge has composed for the occasion :

> Sure we deny our heavenly birth
> When we debase our souls to earth ;
> And prize its trifles and its joys
> Of foolish pleasures make our choice :
> Which soon must end in Death !

Touched by the sentiment Ulalia exclaims : " Ah, Strangwidge, if you had always kept those doctrines I had not been the guilty wretch I am ; and though it is possible I could never have been happy, I still should have been innocent."   The maid servant overhears the reproach of her young mistress and meets them with the protestation that it is no sin to love, to which Ulalia responds that it is Harriet's innocence that prevents her from realising that she is so guilty as she is.

Ulalia : There is but one I can love without crime and he I never can love.   Oh, hard, hard fate.   Thou saiest I am not guilty.   Alas !   Thy unsuspecting innocence and love do hinder thee from thinking I am so wicked as I am.

Taking Harriet into confidence, Ulalia recalls the dangerous illness into which Strangwidge fell, on his return, when he learnt of her marriage.   Upon his convalescence he sought her out; and, in the summer house of Page's garden, threatened to fall upon his sword if his overtures were unrequited.   " Terrified, I caught him in my arms ; then fainted away in his."   But the maid, so far from reprobating her weakness, extenuated it, " for never was woman more tried or tempted than you have been."   Ulalia resolves, however, to resist all further advances, but, with each invocation to "ye chaste and holy powers," her evil genius reappears, and her resolution ebbs away. Master Page and Glandfield are garrulously recalling their respective pasts, and illustrating many a human foible with personal reminiscences, when Strangwidge and Ulalia are seen by the senile pair carrying on a tearful and earnest discussion in the garden. Strangwidge is sophistically appealing to Ulalia to discard the idea that all crimes are necessarily criminal, and he argues that it is absurd to suppose that the Almighty gives us " desires and then dams our every enjoyment of them." The effort to claim the divine sanction for sin inspires Ulalia with new nerve, and she bravely answers : " It is true we have our passions given us, but our reason should always govern them." The lovers have been perceived in the course of this colloquy. Page's distrust is for the first time aroused by their impassioned demeanour, and he communicates to Glandfield his awakening that an intrigue is in progress. A mask with a moral is now performed within the house, to which all the guests are summoned, and the circumstances of young and blighted affections, such as those of Strangwidge and Ulalia, are reproduced. Alive to the application of the plot, Page watches his girlish wife ; notices her flushes and tremors ; and takes note of her deathly paleness, approaching to faintness, when the more serious developments of the unequal alliance are unfolded. The doubts of her husband are confirmed, his sluggish blood is aflame with the desire of revenge, and he warns Glandfield that he will visit his wife with exposure and punishment. He is raving that he will poison the villain Strangwidge, lock up his wife and "tell the world she is a whore"—when Glandfield steals to the garden and intercepts Ulalia, as she is hurrying to the gate.

Glandfield : Stay, stay, Ulalia ; I would speak to you. I have something to say to you in private.

Ulalia : To me, sir ?

Glandfield : Yes, my child. I have observed your behaviour, and I desire you will not in future converse so freely with Mr. Strangwidge.

Ulalia : Not so freely ? I do not understand you, sir.

Glandfield : You need not be so moved. I am not angry, nor do I suspect your virtue. All I would is to let you know your husband is jealous. He has as good as hinted it to me. I saw him watch your eyes whilst the mask was performing, and he even turned pale when you just now asked the unlucky question if interest was never the cause of unhappiness in the marriage state.

Ulalia : Well, sir, can I prevent these wrong suspicions ? How may you counsel me ?

Glandfield : You cannot help what has just passed, but must take more than common care for the time to come. Be careful to do nothing which may increase his jealousy and all else within your power to convince him of your innocence. This, I know, will be a hard task. We cannot see into other's souls or know what passes there, and therefore our suspicions have full liberty to range. All you can do to cure his jealousy is, by an open behaviour, to throw a light upon your sentiments and let him see, if possible, the springs of your most indifferent actions. You must look to it and take all imaginable care that neither by indecent welcome of others, nor coldness towards himself, nor by affected fondness or other weaknesses, you give him reason to suspect you aught. If other you do, you must expect a miserable life.

Ulalia : More miserable than I am, I cannot be.

As the night falls the lovers are again together in the garden, Ulalia resenting and resisting, until Strangwidge spurns her with the remark that her love is all affectation. Unable to bear this reproach, she is saluting her lover's cheek as Page emerges from the house, and, with an appalling shriek, she falls into the arms of her paramour. Rudely tearing them apart, Page drives his wife before him with savage cries: "Heaven protect thee! No; Hell will sooner have thee!" Strangwidge is dismayed when he finds himself alone, and he contemplates suicide until he reflects that if he forsakes Ulalia the world will "applaud the tyrant's treatment." With so many visitors within engaged in celebrating the marriage of Isabella, Page is reluctant to proclaim his shame, and so Ulalia and Strangwidge once more contrive to meet and concert measures by which they may yet extricate themselves from the dilemma in which they are involved.

Ulalia : Had not the tyrant been unwilling to disturb the family to-night—

Strangwidge : I had never seen thee more, and since fortune has been so good as to give us this opportunity, let us use it to the best advantage.

Ulalia : Alas, all the advantage it can be, and all the use, is to take one last embrace, and bid each other an eternal adieu. That, that is all !

Strangwidge : I hope not. Suppose that you disguise yourself in man's apparel and with me go on board one of our ships now in Catwater, bound for our new plantations in Virginia. My fortune is sufficient for both and there we may live in peace and joy, and you will never feel the eternal fury of your tyrant husband.

Ulalia : What, leave my father's friends and native country, and, still worse, leave a bad name of lasting infamy behind me ? What would the world and my friends say of me if I should go?

Strangwidge : The very same that you shall hear ten thousand times repeated if you stay. Sure, then, it is better not to hear it, and it will grieve you less, whatever it be, than to have it always sounding in your ears, like the alarm, to awake you to a painful sense of shame.

Ulalia : Wheresoever thou carriest me I should have that painful sense of shame— adulteress ! Oh, impossible ! Will not the busy world so call me?

Strangwidge : Yet, if thou will be wife, that, too, shall be avoided, and the mistaken world shall never brand thee with that odious name.

Ulalia : As how, good Strangwidge, prethie tell me, and I'll forgive thee all those words ; and, for the future, do whatsoever you will have me.

Strangwidge : You know that Page has sworn that he would publish all your faults, and I believe his rage will permit him to add even falsehood to increase your guilt and deceive his own barbarities, but (he pauses)—

Ulalia : But what ?

Strangwidge : All in the grave are silent !

Ulalia : Ha ! Art thou a villain. Surely this, this will cure my love. Oh, I shall hate thee with a virtuous hatred. Oh, that my foolish heart should be fond of thee again and I will call but this to mind and hate thee more. There is no other way to be safe but to fly from thee. (Exit.)

Strangwidge : That you shall not do. Yet murder is the vilest and most black of all the deeds of darkness. What then? This is not murder. Who calls so thus the execution of a thief, a robber? No one. Well, then, this Page has been to me a thief and robber. So, if he dies, this is justice—not murder.

> Yes, nought the purpose of my soul shall move,
> His life shall answer for my much wrong'd love.

Ulalia is left to herself for the night, in the solitude of her own chamber, and she wonders, since she cannot sleep, what is to be her fate. Now she prays that Strangwidge will come and take her away. Then she implores the saints to protect her. Whilst she is thus distracted, she hears a movement—a sharp cry—a fleeting footstep from Page's bedroom—and then all is still. The deed has been wrought. Maddened by ill-intent, Strangwidge has clapsed him horridly by the throat until he has ceased to breathe. In leaving, however, the strangler has dropped one of his gloves ; and when, with the break of day, the crime is discovered, Strangwidge is sent for and confronted with the evidence of his guilt. "It must be so," he says, "for I would scorn to play the hypocrite and to keep you any longer in suspense. I do confess and glory in the action, since by his death I have not only revenged the wrongs he did my life, but have prevented the unhappiness of one who is far dearer to me than existence." Challenged as to whether he committed the tragedy alone or if Ulalia had any hand in it, he scouts the alternative and remarks that she would have forbidden "the noble deed." Overwhelmed by his impending fate, he bemoans that he did not fall in Spain when "the noble Essex, our brave general, prais'd and loved" his officers for the prizes they took. "Then," he adds, "I had left the world with honour. Now I leave it on worse terms than slaves and robbers, I shall be remembered for my infamy, and my sad story told to children's children yet unborn."

The silence that followed the crime had caused Ulalia to fall into a fitful slumber, and she left the house at dawn to walk abroad with Harriet. She returns to hear the worst and to find Strangwidge under arrest.

"Pardon me, Ulalia," he says, "the black deed I have done, rashly done. Indeed, it was very rashly done. But it was done for you, to preserve you from the fate which the miser and tyrant designed for you." "What wouldst thou ?" is her reply, for she now resolved to die in his company ; "are we not guilty both ?" In his dismay her lover asks : "Why do you madly thus accuse yourself ?" Ulalia rejoins : "Didst thou imagine that I could be so mean and base or lost that I could ever let thee bear it singly all ? If I could have done this I should be viler than I am." Stricken with remorse, old Glandfield rails against his own "cursed avarice" as the curtain falls :

> Ye rigid parents learn from her sad fate
> Never to wed your children where they hate ;
> But if chaste passion their young hearts inspire
> With kind indulgence feed the kindled fire !
> For, if by force the bride a bridegroom led,
> Eternal discord waits the nuptial bed.
> Love should be free : it cannot be constrained,
> Nor ever bought or sold : it must be gained.

"*A true discourse of a cruel and inhumane murder, committed upon M. Padge, of Plimouth, the* 11 *day of February last,* 1591, *by the consent of his own wife and sundry other.*

"In the town of Testock, 10 miles or thereabouts from Plimouth, there dwelled one M. Glandfeeld, a man of as good wealth and account as any occupier in that cuntrie. This M. Glandfeeld favoured a young man named George Strangwidge, who was of such great credit with him, that he turned over all his wares, shop, and dealings, into his handes, and tooke so good a liking of him, being a proper young man, that it was supposed he should have had his daughter in marriage ; and the rather for that he had learned the full perfection and knowledge of his trade in London, in the service of a worshipful cittizen called M. Powell, in Bred Street. He grew so painfulle, and seemed so good a husband as the said M. Glandfeeld's daughter did wholye resolve that the said George Strangwidge should be her husband, and no other : whereto in troth her parents never did condescend. But Sathan, who is the author of evill, crept so farre into the dealings of these persons, that he procured the parentes to mislike Strangwidge, and to perswade their daughter to refraine his company, shewing her that they had found out a more meeter match for her, and mocioned unto her that it was their pleasure shee should marrye one M. Padge, of Plimouth, who was a widower, and one of the cheefest inhabitants of that towne : and by reason that the sayde M. Glandfeeld did mean to abide at Plimouth, he thought it a more sufficient matche to marrye her in Plimouth, where she might be hard by him, than to marry her to Strangwidge, who dwelt farre from him.

"In the end, such was the success, that although she had settled her affections altogether upon Strangwidge, yet, through the perswasions of her friends, though sore against her will, she was married to M. Padge, of Plimouth, notwithstanding that she had protested never to love the man with her heart, nor never to remove her affection, settled upon the saide Strangwidge, and he to her at his coming to Plimouth ; whereby the divell so wrought in the harts of them both, that they practised day and night how to bring her husband to his end : and thereupon the saide Mistris Padge, as appeareth since by her own confession, did, within the space of one yeere and lesse, attempt sundry times to poison her husband ; for it was not full a yeere but that she had procured him to be murthered as you shall hear immediately.

"But God who preserveth many persons from such perils and dangers, defended still the said M. Padge from the secret snares and practises of present death, which his wife had laid for him, yet not without great hurt unto his body, for still the poison wanted force to kill him, so wonderfully did almighty God worke for him ; yet was he compelled to vomit blood and much corruption, which doubtless in the end would have killed him, and that shortlye. But to prosecute, and that with great speed to perform, this wicked and inhumain act, the saide Mistris Padge and Strangwidge ommitted no opportunitie. They wanted no meanes nor freends to performe it for their mony, whereof they had good store and more than they knew how to imploy, except it had beene to better uses ; for she on the one side practised with one of her servants, named Robert Priddis, whom as she thought, nothing would more sooner make him pretend the murdering of his maister then silver and gold, wherewith she so corrupted him, with promise of seven score poundes more, that he solemnly undertook and vowed to performe the task to her contentment.

" On the other side Strangwidge hired one Tom Stone to be an actor in this tragical action ; and promised him a great summe of mony for performing the same, who by a . solemne vow had graunted the effecting thereof, though to the hazard of his own life.

"These two instruments wickedly prepared themselves to effect this desperate and villanous deed upon the 11th of February, being Wednesday, on which night following the act was committed : but it is to be remembered that this Mistris Padge lay not then with her husband, by reason of the untimely birth of a child, whereof she was newly delivered, the same being dead borne : upon which cause she then kept her chamber, having before sworn that she would never beare child of his getting that should prosper ; which argued a most ungodlye minde in the woman, for in that sort she had been the death of two of her own children.

" About ten of the clock at night, M. Padge being in his bed slumbring, could not happen upon a sound sleepe, and lying musing to himselfe, Tom Stone came softlye and knocked at the doore, whereupon Priddis, his companion, did let him in, who was made privie to this deed ; and by reason that Mistris Padge, gave them straight charge to dispatche it that night, whatsoever came of it, they drew towards the bed, intending immediately to go about it.   M. Padge being not asleep, as is aforsaid, asked who came in, whereat Priddis leapt upon his maister, being in his bed, who roused himself and got upon his feete and had been hard enough for his man, but that Stone flew upon him, and tooke the kercher from his head, and knitting the same about his neck they immediately stifled him ; and, as it appeereth, even in the anguish of death the said M. Padge greatly laboured to put the kercher from about his neck, by reason of the marks and skratches which he had made with his nails upon his throat, but therewith he could not prevail, for they would not let slip their hold until he was full dead.   This doon, they laid him overthwart the bed, and against the bedside broke his neck ; and when they sawe he was surely dead, they stretched him and laid him on his bed again, spreading the clothes in ordinary sort, as though no such act had been attempted, but that he had died on Gods hand.

Whereupon Priddis immediately went to Mistris Padge's chamber and tolde her that all was dispatcht ; and about one hower after he came again to his Mistris chamber doore, and called aloud, Mistresse, quoth he, let somebody look unto my Maister's chamber, me thinks I heard him grone. With that she called her maide, who was not privie to anything, and had her light a candle, whereupon she slipt on her petticote and went thither likewise sending her maid first into the chamber, where she herselfe stood at the doore, as one whose conscience would not permit her to come and behold the detestable deed which she had procured.   The maid simply felt on her Maister's face and found him cold and stiffe, and so tolde her Mistress ; whereat she bade the maid to warme a cloth and wrap it about his feete, which she did, and when she felt his legges, they were as colde as claye ; wherat she cried out, saying her Maister was dead.

" Whereupon her Mistris got her to bed, and caused her man Priddis to goe call her father, M. Glandfeeld, then dwelling at Plimouth, and sent for one of her husband's sisters likewise, willing her to make haste if ever she would see her brother alive, for he was taken with the disease called the Pull, as they tearme it in that country : these persons being sent for, they came immediately ; wherat Mistris Padge arose, and in counterfeit manner sounded ; whereby there was no suspition a long time concerning any murder perfourmed upon him until Mistris Harris his sister, spied blood about his bosome, which he had with his nails procured by scratching for the kerchief when it was about his throate : they then moved his head, and found his neck broken, and on both kness the skin was beaten off, by striving with them to save his life.   Mistris Harris hereupon perceiving how he was made away, went to the Mayor and the worshipful of the towne, desiring them of justice, and entreated them to come and beholde this lamentable spectacle, which they immediately perfourmed, and by searching him found that he was murdered the same night.

" Upon this the Mayor committed Priddis to prison, who, being examined, did impeach Tom Stone, shewing that he was a chiefe actor in the same.   This Thomas Stone was married upon the next day after the murder was committed, and being in the midst of his jollity suddenly he was attacked and committed to prison to beare his fellow company.

" Thus did the Lord unfold this wretched deed, whereby immediately the said Mistris Padge attached upon the murther, and examined before Sir Francis Drake, Knight, with the Mayor and other Magistrates of Plimouth ; who denied not the same, but said she had rather dye with Strangwidge than to live with Padge.

" At the same time also the said George Strangwide was newly come to Plimouth, being very heavy and doubtfull by reason he had given consent to the saide murder : who being in company with some of London, was apprehended and called before the justices

F

for the same, whereupon at his coming before them, he confessed the trueth of all and offered to prove that he had written a letter to Plimouth before his coming thither, that at any hand they should not perfourm the act: nevertheless M. Padge was murdered before the comming of this letter, and therefore he was sent to prison with the rest unto Exeter: and at the assizes holden this last Lent the said George Strangwidge, Mistris Padge, Priddis, and Tom Stone, were condemed and adjudged to dye for the saide fact, and were all executed accordinglye upon Satterdaye, being the twentith day of Februarye last, 1591."

Lamentation of Master Page's wife, of Plimmouth, who, being enforced by her parents to wed him against her will, did most wickedly consent to his murther, for which fact she suffered death at Barnstaple in Devonshire.

Unhappy she whom fortune hath forslayne,
Despised of grace that suffered grace with scorn;
My lawlesse love that lucklesse brought my woe,
My discontent content did overthrow.

My loathed life too late I doe lament,
My hateful deed with heart I doe repent,
A wife I was that wilful went awry,
And for that fault am here prepared to die.

In blooming years my father's greedy mind
Against my will a match for me did find,
Great wealth there was, yea gold and mony store,
But yet my heart had chosen long before.

My eye mislikt my father's liking quite,
My heart did loath my parent's fond delight;
My grieved mind and fancy told to me
That with his age my youth could not agree.

On knees I craved they would not me constrain,
With tears I cride their purpose to restrain;
With sighs and sobs I bid them often move
I might not wed whereas I could not love.

But all in vain: my speeches still I spent,
My father's will my wishes did prevent.
Though wealthy, Page possessed no outward part,
George Strangwidge still was lodged in my heart.

I wedded was, but wrapped all in woe,
That such disdain within my mind should grow,
I loathed to live, yet liv'd in deadly strife,
Because, perforce, I was made Page's wife.

My chosen eyes could not his sight abide,
My tender youth did scorn his aged side,
Scant could I taste the meat whereon he fed,
My legs did loath to lodge within his bed.

Cause knew I none I should despise him so,
That such disdain within my mind should grow,
Save only this, that fancy did me move,
And told me still George Strangwidge was my love.

But here began my downfall and decay,
In mind I mus'd to make him straight away,
I that became his discontented wife,
Contented was he should be rid of life.

Methinks that Heaven cries vengeance for my fact,
Methinks the world condemns my monstrous act;
Methinks within my conscience tells me true,
That for that deed hell fire is my due.

My pensive life doth sorrow for my sin,
For this offence my soul does bleed within;
Yet mercy, Lord, for mercy do I cry,
Save Thou my soul and let my body die.

Well could I wish that Page enjoyed his life,
So that he had some other to his wife;
But never would I wish of low or lie
A longer life and see sweet Strangwidge die.

Ah! woe is me that had no better grace
To stay till he had run out Nature's race.
My deed I rue, but more I doe lament,
That to the same my Strangwidge gave consent.

Wronged he was through fond desire of gain;
Wronged he was even through my parents plain;
If faith and troth a perfect pledge might be,
I had been wife unto no man but he.

You parents fond that greedy minded be,
And seek to grafte upon a golden tree,
Consider well and rightful judges be,   .
And give your doom 'twixt parents love and me.

You Devonshire dames and courteous Cornwall
That here are come to visit woeful wights,
Regard my griefe and marke my woeful end,
And to your children be a better friend.

Ulalia, thy friend, doth take her last farewell,
Whose soul with thine in Heaven shall ever dwell,
Sweet Saviour Christ doth Thou my soul receive,
The world I doe with all my heart forgive.

And Plimmouth proud, I bid thee eke farewell,
Take heed you wives, let not your hands rebel;
And farewell life wherein such sorrow shows,
And welcome grave which must my corpse enclose.

Lord blesse our Queen with long and happy life,
And send true love betwixt each man and wife ;
And give all parents wisdome to forsee
The match is marred where minds do not agree.

Lament of George Strangwidge, who, for consenting to the murther of Master Page at
Plimmouth, suffered death at Barnstaple.

Ulalia fair, more bright than summer's sun,
Whose beauty hath my heart for ever won,
My soule most sobs to think of thy disgrace
Than to behold my own untimely race.

The deed late done in heart I doe lament,
But that I lov'd I cannot yet repent ;
Thy seemly sight was ever sweet to me,
Would God my death would thy excuse be.

It was for me (alas !) thou didst the same,
On me of right they ought to lay the blame ;
My worthlesse love has brought my soul to scorne,
Now woe is me that ever I was borne.

Farewell, my love, whose loyal hearte was seen,
Would God Thou hadst not half so constant been ;
Farewell, my love, the pride of Plimmouth Towne,
Farewell the flower whose beauty is cut downe.

Wretch that I am that I consent did give,
Had I denied Ulalia still should live ;
Blind fancy said her suite do not deny,
Live thou in blisse or else in sorrow die.

CHAPTER IV.—THROUGH THE CIVIL WARS.

James I. and Plymouth. The wars with Spain had assumed a religious aspect so far as Plymouth was concerned. It was the possible sway of a Roman Catholic power that had so often filled it with alarm, and the men who were ever in the forefront of the fight carried in their veins the early instincts of Puritanism. When Elizabeth joined the procession of heroes who had made her reign memorable, and James of Scotland was "proclaymed to be Kinge at ye Market Crosse here in Plymouth," demonstrative was the "triumphe with bonfires, gunnes, ringing of bells and other kindes of music." There was evidently an impression that the King intended to adopt the policy of his predecessor, and that the distrust of Papist forms and ceremonies would be as emphatically shown. For years the inhabitants had watched upon the Hoe the harrying of the animals that were awaiting the knife of the butchers, and had grouped around the strolling players who recited with impressive gestures the plays of the great living dramatists. Now their thoughts were turning to the emancipated Bible and a sour spirit of controversy was abroad. The Council sent actors about their business, suppressed disorderly and superfluous ale-houses, scrupulously controlled the strength of liquor, set watches upon suspected wives, and tied termagants to the ducking stool and dipped them in Sutton Pool. The more incorrigible were banished so that the peace of the town should be secured ; and when Lady Hawkins slapped the face of the Mayoress, Mrs Downame, whom she had formerly employed as one of her maids, because, in the resolve to live up to her privileges, the latter refused to surrender the civic pew in St. Andrew's Church, the Corporation were only conciliated by the gift to the town of a house which Sir Richard owned in the Market Place.

At the commencement of the reign all went as Plymouth wished. The Castle was crowded with Catholic prisoners, every ship was searched for Papist spies, and the authorities sternly enforced the law compelling recusants who entered the port to take the oath of allegiance or "straightway return into exile at their own expense." James relaxed these restrictions to please Spain, and the Mayor and his brethren were astounded on being ordered to release a ship from St. Malo, which had been driven into the port, and was found to contain "an Agnus Dei and sacred pictures intended for Romish ladies." The belief gained ground that the King was at heart a Catholic until his vacillation provoked the Gunpowder Plot, and then Plymouth repented of its misgiving. In order that none of the accomplices should escape by way of the neighbouring ports, the Mayor made "staye of all manner of shippes within this harbourough" and sent pinnaces along the coast "to lie in wayte." The solicitude was unnecessary, as every accomplice in these "most horrid treasons" was secured, and an intimation was sent to his worship to that effect. The deliverance of the King and Parliament "from the treason of Pircie and others" was commemorated on the following fifth of November by the "shooting of ordynance."

James was not long in disclosing the fatal flaw in the Stuart character—its fatuity as well as its cleverness. He met the growing desire for religious toleration by insisting upon Conformity ; and the parishioners of St. Andrew's were paternally admonished not to wander to other preachers "with better gifts," but to rest content with "the word of God read and homilies." But, whilst he provoked a sullen murmur of discontent on the one hand, he ingratiated himself with the moneyed classes on the other by bestowing many favours upon the town, which proved the avenues to its commercial prosperity. The legitimate trader entered into competition with the pirate, and the Plymouth Company owed its existence to a patent from the King which enabled it to levy duties in New England and set up a mint there. A hundred adventurers sailed from the port in 1607 in the Richard of Plymouth, and landed at the mouth of the Kewnebeck, on the North East Coast of America. They chose Parker's Island for a settlement, and raised Fort Saint George ; but, severe winters, the destruction of their stores by fire, and the death of their president, Popham, caused many to return.

The primary object of these concessions was to supplement James's scanty means. Borrowing in every direction, he included several Plymouth merchants in the list of those whom he invited to make "free gifts" to himself and his daughter. Not content with extorting money in his own interest the King sought to obtain similar favours for his dissolute associates ; and Sir William Ravie presented himself to the Mayor with a letter in which James requested that he should be granted "free passage" of whatever merchandise he wished to take back to France, and that "no difficulty" should be thrown in the way of his raising "a loan of £400" from the merchants of the town. "He has hunted me all the summer," he explained. James granted the town a new charter, in which some new privileges were embodied, and by authorising Plymouth to continue the colonization of America, indelibly associated its name with the Greater Britain beyond the seas. The intercourse proved so lucrative that Sir Ferdinando Gorges and Lord Chief Justice Popham equipped expeditions on their own account, and the superiority of the port over London as a point of departure rendered easy the command of any capital that the pioneers required. Of the mariners one of the more famous was Captain John Smith, who, after a series of hairbreadth escapes and love passages, triumphed over misfortune and mutiny in all parts of the world, and finally achieved conspicuous successes on American soil. Sir Richard Hawkins was another of the group ; and although constant feuds among the North American Indians, and between the Indians and the settlers, led to heavy loss of life and interruption of business, he assisted to make Plymouth the centre of restless and profitable activity. By the authority of the company the colonists were empowered to set up a constitution of their own, and as female society was at a premium, women were sent out and selected as wives by the bachelors on payment of about £20 a piece. Tobacco at three shillings per pound was accepted in lieu of cash.

As the Old Guildhall in Southside Street was much in want of repair, vacant land at the top of Looe Street was selected as a site for a more commodious building. After the manner of the times, this was raised upon arches, so that the public business might be conducted above, and the butter and poultry markets carried on beneath. The sale of corn and vegetables was transacted in the adjacent streets, much to the annoyance of the ordinary citizens, who were unable to make their way through the throng of bargaining farmers and lusty retailers ; and still more to the exasperation of the shopkeepers in the vicinity, who could not make themselves heard amid the clamour and confusion. The main hall was ascended by a forbidding flight and it was the custom to say that any person suspected of malpractice would soon ascend those "seventeen steps." The open staircase of the tower projected into the street and rendered it especially narrow at this point ; and, at the end of the Council Chamber, there were rooms for the confinement of debtors. Dungeons at the basement were reserved for criminals, and this section of the establishment was known as "The Clink." After the excitement of the Saturday trading, the open space was thoroughly cleansed and it served the purpose of a Sunday morning promenade. Here the begowned members of the Corporation assembled prior to the ringing of the bells of St. Andrew's; and, having conversed on affairs of state and little consequence, in the presence of a respectful fringe of less important gossips, they marched to church, escorted by the halberdiers, who bore aloft the town flags as their insignia of office. The increasing resources of the borough enabled the Commonalty to rebuild the Barbican Pier and improve the approaches to the various quays; and preliminary measures were taken to provide for the education of the children of the town.

THE JACOBEAN GUILDHALL. West View, showing the Shambles underneath.
(From the Original Drawing by W. Whitfeld. 1800.)

Raleigh's Last Voyage and Execution. With the accession of James, attempts were made to convince him that Sir Walter Raleigh was disloyal, and that his dislike of a Scotch king had taken the form of a conspiracy to set up a Commonwealth. As the air grew rife with rumours of "dangerous undertakings," James committed to the Tower one of the bravest spirits of the age. It was in vain that Raleigh declared his innocence and vowed that he would never ask for mercy if a shred of proof were adduced to his discredit. "I protest before the Everlasting God," he exclaimed, "that I never invented treason, consented to treason, nor performed treason." In spite of every remonstrance, a charge of having intrigued to place Lady Arabella Stuart on the throne was concocted, and Sir Edward Coke denounced the prisoner as "a spider of hell with a Spanish heart." Sir Walter retorted by pointing out that he had only just published a pamphlet to demonstrate the best method of humbling the peninsular enemy; but his eloquence and courage did not avail, and he was sentenced to be executed. He demeaned himself with such surprising restraint and dignity, however, merely asking that the manner of his death might not be ignominious, that the revulsion in his favour was universal. He was respited, to pass long years in those literary pursuits of which his "History of the World" is the most enduring example. Wearying of his imprisonment and aware of the destitution of James, Raleigh hinted at the existence of a gold mine along the banks of the Orinoco, of whose wealth none knew save himself, and he assured the King that he would prefer not to live if he returned with less than half a ton of slate gold ore. James signed the order for his release; and Sir Walter organised at Plymouth a fleet of such power, and armed with cannon of dimensions so unusual, that the concern of the ambassadors was excited, and they journeyed to the port to inspect the ships, of which the Destiny, by reason of its proportions and equipment, was the most conspicuous. The representative of France was amongst the visitors, and Raleigh was subsequently declared to have intimated his resolve to abandon his own country, and give this ambassador the first offer of his services: statements wholly inconsistent with Sir Walter's own letters.

Raleigh and his fellow adventurers were profusely entertained by the municipality, who rejoiced rather in the freedom of Drake's companion in arms than in the promise of abundant bullion. Rules were formulated by the knight himself enjoining the religious exercises that were to be observed on each ship, and the code of tactics to be pursued in the event of attack. A carvel and two flyboats joined the "little fleet" in the Sound— one of the crews under the thumb of a scoundrel named Bazley: "a deserter, a false witness, and a rascal of the worst kind." Whether the disaster that ensued was compassed by his instrumentality or the treachery of the King is not quite clear. James was probably the instigator, and Bazley his tool. Raleigh's crews were summoned from their merry-makings by the municipal drummer, and amidst the fanfare of trumpets, the psalm singing of waits, the shouting of numberless voices and the interchange of cannon between Castle and fleet, "ten good ships of war, and three pinnaces extremely well manned, munitioned and victualled," buoyantly left the harbour. On arriving at his destination, Raleigh found a force of Spanish soldiers lying in ambush; and, taken by surprise, the exploiters were swept away, Sir Walter's son was felled by the butt end of a musket, and the survivors were compelled to run for the ships. Sick at heart, with fleet shattered, and men distracted by disaffection and doubts, Raleigh returned to Plymouth; and there, as the Destiny lay in Hamoaze, his unhappy lady learnt the worst, and united in the distress of her husband over the death of their son and the failure of their expectations. In the hope of exciting compassion at Court, they set out for London; but an officer of the King overtook them at Ashburton with words that were the premonition of death. "I have orders," said he, "to arrest you and your ship." In the anguish of despondency, Raleigh and his wife turned back, and Sir Walter was importuned at Cornwood by relatives and friends alike to make good his escape. All had been prepared to make this easy—a barque lay in Catwater ready to sail, and the coast of France would appear in sight with the break of the morning. Raleigh yielded to these appeals, and proceeding to Plymouth he embarked, and, with a fair wind, his vessel made for the Channel. But his courage revived when the cliffs of England faded from the view, and refusing to sacrifice his dignity for the sake of his head, he ordered the boat to be put about, and returned to the Barbican to face whatever accusations there might be in store.

Stukeley, his own base relative, who had recommended him to fly, was busily occupied in appropriating the cargo of the Destiny to his own use when an imperative summons, "all delays set apart to safely and speedily bring hither the person of Sir Walter Raleigh," recalled him to an appreciation of his own risk. Then he quoted the escape at which he had connived as confirmatory evidence of the prisoner's guilt, and insinuated that his cousin surrendered "in discharge of his conscience" a document he had concealed at

Cornwood.   As the methods of Stukeley were suggestive of embezzlement, Sir Ferdinando Gorges, the Governor, checked the inventory of the Destiny, its "furniture and goods," and the official record showed one watch of fine gold, a slob of coarser gold, a Guinea blob of gold and copper, gold ore in packages, 63 gold buttons with sparks of diamonds, and a sprig jewel and gold chain set with soft stones—an aggregate of melancholy insignificance. Sir Walter was accused by his enemies of having invented the mine so that he might engage in a freebooting enterprise.   Indeed, it was sworn that he proposed to seize the Mexican fleet "if the mine failed," and one of the informers asserted that, when he was told that it would be playing the pirate thus to compensate for the failure of the original scheme, he replied that adventurers who aimed at millions were not pirates—the name was only suitable to those who schemed and worked for small things !   As against these hearsay remarks, retailed by men who were conniving at Raleigh's death, and the fact that James was desirous of conciliating Spain by negociating the marriage of Charles with the Infanta, we have Sir Walter's consciousness that his return to Plymouth involved his certain death.   In that hour, as the headsman stood by his side with the glistening axe, his composure and serenity were sublime ; and when the executioner paused, he met him with the remonstrance : "Strike, man, strike—why dost thou hesitate ?"   And thus passed the noblest embodiment of Elizabethan chivalry.

Sir John Eliot and the   Sympathy with Raleigh caused Stukeley to cower with shame, and
Western Pirates :   he was deprived of his position at the port.   Sir John Eliot was
1615-1624.   appointed to succeed him, although, unknown to the Court, there
was already implanted within his breast a distrust of the royal methods and a stern resolve to be heard in freedom's cause.   Eliot was as yet a comparative youth, with his career unopened and a glorious reputation to mould ; and, when he was drawn from St. Germans to exercise unchallenged authority at Plymouth, the emoluments were pretty much what the admirals determined.   No officer of the time was free from suspicion, and even Sir Richard Hawkins had been charged with dealing in piratical cargoes.   The coast was infested by corsairs, who dogged the merchantmen as they made for Plymouth, and roamed at large from Scilly to Torbay, manned by upwards of 2,000 mercenaries.   "A Jew," fitted out by the King of Morocco, was cut off outside the harbour as it was convoying Spanish treasure ships, and the whole of the prizes were brought into Catwater.   This unwonted vigour so alarmed the authorities that they hesitated to renew the attack, and they were the more alarmed because the score or so of ships which constituted the navy could not be trusted to give pursuit.   Meanwhile the status of the town rapidly deteriorated, and as the defence of its commerce was thrown upon the merchants, and only a score of these could contribute, they pleaded that the west should be taxed as a whole.   Truro, for instance, "one of the wealthiest ports, and far abler than Plymouth to pay, sent only £10" towards the cost of the last attempt to wipe out these pests.   The dread of a landing was so general that trained bands were raised to defend the accessible points, but there was "so much neglect and disobedience of orders" that no real protection was afforded, trade further languished, and such mariners as resisted the fascinations of piracy sailed for Newfoundland.   It may have been in the hope of bargaining with Providence for the protection of his cargo that William Laurence, who carried on business in "Foxhole," bequeathed £100 to establish an almhouse for the education of poor children and orphans—the money to be paid "on the return of the good shippe Jonathan of Plymouth from her now intended voyage to the Straits."

With a Court that was profligate, prodigal and without scruple, it is not surprising to find corruption the rule and public virtue the exception.   At Plymouth, the officials pursued their dishonest way with unblushing audacity, sequestering foreign ships on slight pretence, pillaging the wares, and meeting all complaints with mendacious boldness. Accused of winking at these practices, Sir Thomas Wise pleaded that he only yielded to " the importunities of distressed and noble persons," and, as these aspirations to play the pirate in genteel fashion were accepted as sufficient, the knight was only admonished to be more careful. " My punishment is light" he candidly confessed. Left to their own devices, with no means of earning a livelihood, and fearless of results, the local robbers grew no less formidable than the

foreigners. It was not that their tendencies were evil, but that there was so little employment. "We western lads respect not such things as these so we may have wars and be in action." Many of the sturdiest joined the banner of Captain Nutt, the pirate chief of Devon, whose payments were so generous that sailors of the Royal Navy deserted to his flag. His retreat was a cove in Torbay, so fortified that he set the authorities at defiance ; and as no real attempt was for three years made to disconcert him, he made valuable seizures, and clothed his men in the uniforms of their prisoners. The one expedient that occurred to James was the offer of a pardon that left this bully in undisputed possession of his spoils.

Eliot went to Torbay, on learning that Nutt's fleet lay there at anchor, in the hope of alluring him by the promise of the King. Letters having passed, the pirate professed his readiness to abandon the traffic on receiving an ample assurance. Eliot invited him ashore to discuss the details; but, at the eleventh hour, Nutt

Doorway leading to Orphans' Aid Almshouse
(1615).

warily pleaded that "his company would not suffer him " to put his head in the lion's mouth. Eliot rowed out to the pirate's "man of war"; and, over a bottle of wine in the state cabin, the proposal was discussed. When Eliot hinted that the surrender of recent captures must take precedence of the pardon, Nutt snapped his fingers at the proposition, and the admiral was glad to escape with a sound skin from the outlaw's society. Although he made up his mind to incur no second risk, Eliot did not relinquish his project. Addressing the pirate a disarming letter, he induced him to pull ashore ; and, arresting him and his crew, impounded the ship. Having seized by

stratagem the man whom he "despaired to take by fighting," Eliot asked the Council:
"What am I to do with him?" Nutt had shown no redeeming graces, for the men
now in irons had even strutted about Dartmouth wearing the uniforms of which
they had just stripped the seamen of a local trader; and, in Sir John's judgment, his
Majesty should resent these insolences "as his owne wrongs." Eliot was commanded to
communicate the full details of the capture, and he was vouchsafed at Court "the favour
of kissing the King's hands." As the result of Sir John's report, Nutt and his colleagues
were impeached "to answer for their cruelties and unjust curses"; but, prompted by the
ruffians in high places, the pirate accused Eliot of inciting him to further acts of piracy,
and suggested that his object in interfering was to convert ship and cargo to his own use.
Subterranean influences were at work, sinister slanders were circulated, and the Court
restored Nutt to liberty and imprisoned his captor in the Marshalsea! "The poore man,"
the disingenuous judge declared of the pirate, "is able to doe the King service, if he were
employed; and I doe assure myselfe he doth soe detest his former course of life as he will
never enter into it againe." Nutt was released to become a more unscrupulous pillager
than ever.

Eliot's career at Plymouth was conceived in the broadest standard of statesmanship.
Turkish, Moorish and Dutch pirates had previously entered the harbour without resistance,
sent the inhabitants into captivity, and sold the cargoes in the vicinity. Sternly resolved
to curb these truculent knaves, Sir John prosecuted the local confederates who supplied
them with stores and provisions. He also put "several Turks and Renegadoes upon their
trial, both those that this year came into Plymouth and some others that have been
auncientlie in the gaol and upon former tryalls neglected." Twenty red-handed rascals he
hanged in one day, but, with the fine sense of equity that marked all his actions, he
pardoned the wretches who had been rotting in the gaol without trial for over eight years.
Thus, without waiting upon the whim of the judges, he set the humane precedent of not
allowing malefactors to linger for an age in filthy dungeons. Another instance of his
alertness is forthcoming in the controversy that distracted Plymouth and Saltash, over a
sunken vessel that obstructed the navigation of the harbour. When the legal owners of
the Tamar and the Plym were ordered to remove it the Mayor was aghast, and urged that
whilst the cost would be ruinous, the advantage must be mainly for Plymouth. Cynically
retorting upon her neighbour, Plymouth replied that, as Saltash insisted upon exacting the
dues for the shipping, it should keep Catwater free. Eliot drily summarised the contentions: "Plymouth envies Saltash the privilege of the harbour, and will undertake to be
the Prince's tenants therein. Saltash fearing to refuse the charge apprehends that the
precedent will trench upon the interests of the Prince." Plymouth pushed its advantage,
and, as Eliot was unable to find a basis of agreement that would not injure his old friends,
he raised the ship himself at a cost of £300.

Plague, Plunder and   Eliot was detained some months in prison, and, upon his release,
Mutiny at Plymouth : he wrote the Duke of Buckingham, as High Lord Admiral, demand-
1625.   ing reparation for the outrage. But all domestic concerns were
subordinated to the intrigues to secure a Spanish bride for Charles, Sir John received no
satisfaction, and the Plymouth traders complained in vain of continued piracy. The
Huguenots, on the other hand, ran from Rochelle to escape the persecution of the French,
and their ships took refuge in the port. As member for St. Germans, Eliot gave expression to the resentment with which this misgovernment was filling the country, and, from
that time forward, he earned the ever-deepening animosity of the Sovereign. He had
warned the Duke against "tale-bearers" and the King against mere seekers after "place,"

so that he was evidently alive to the conspiracies at his expense.   James Bagg, a man of
Westcountry birth, who was as infamous as Buckingham was incapable, insinuated that Eliot
was an indifferent steward of his grace's "tenths" in Devon and Cornwall, and assured
him that, if he were appointed to the office, the change "will not only be profitable to you,
but make me greate in your grace's esteem for an honest man."   Thus stealing his way to
favour, Bagg was appointed Vice Admiral of Cornwall, and invested with the victualling of
the port of Plymouth.   From that time he fawned as the courtier, secretly disparaged
contemporaries whom he had professed to hold in esteem, and was guilty of such flagrant
embezzlements that Archbishop Laud denounced him for his frauds and hypocrisies.   A
knowledge of Bagg's villainies is necessary to a full grasp of the horrors in which Plymouth
was plunged as the result of the Spanish expedition.

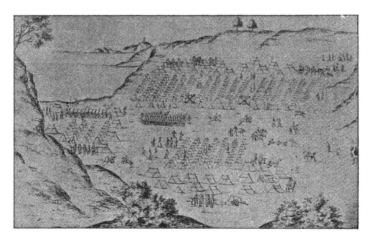

TROOPS ENCAMPED ON PLYMOUTH HOE.

(From an old Sketch in the British Museum.)

The last shred of the scheme for allying the Prince of Wales with the Infanta was
broken as soon as Eliot denounced its impolicy, and the popular hatred of the Spanish
supplied the young King with an excuse for raiding their treasure ships and filling the
purse that James had left empty.   Meanwhile the navy was degenerate and pirates
plundered as they listed.   Hundreds of west countrymen were torn from their village
homes, this man bewailing his son, that his father, another his brother, and a fourth his
servant.   Although "noe former times have been exampled with the like," not a vessel
was despatched to the "sacrifice of these monsters."   Charles had other plans ; and, in
1625, ninety battleships were collected in the Sound, and 10,000 soldiers were encamped
upon the Hoe.   The destination of the force was not revealed, but it was surmised that
the King expected, by a sudden descent, to fill his exchequer.   Distressed, drained and
destitute, the maintenance of this army fell upon Plymouth with crushing weight.   There
was some pretence of paying for the board of the soldiers, but the amount nominally

allowed for each man—2s. 6d. per week—was "not enough to find them in meat and drink." Dismay was added to dejection, for the only clothing served out was a cassock apiece, and the soldiers had neither stockings, shirts nor breeches to wear. There were no officers to hold them in check ; and, to accentuate the terror, the plague broke out in the town, and was "like to overthrow the English arms before they see the enemy." Squeezing his tonnage and poundage dues, Charles eventually raised sufficient money to supply the expedition with hose, shoes, and shirts, and a proportion of the men were granted trousers. But the finances were soon exhausted, and the authorities warned Buckingham that it was impossible "to satisfy with words the hungry bellies of the soldiers and the empty pockets of their hosts." Spasmodic risings rendered life in the town a torture, traffic was paralyzed, and there was a dearth of commodities. As these appeals were unheeded, the officers on the spot posed as "importunate solicitors for a second supply of money." They were weeks in arrears to the billeters, the general health was impaired by foul diet, and the whole army was despondent. The "Mayor and his brethren" also remonstrated with the Privy Council, depicting the penury caused by the pirates, the impossibility of exterminating them because their ships were so fleet, and demanding relief for the billeters "who are at their last resources."

A more ragged, ribald and rebellious horde never gathered on the eve of an important expedition. Mutiny was common in the town, and the ringleaders were tried at drum-head and shot in the nearest open space. Sir John Ogle vowed in his despair that "he was neither in mind nor body qualified for action," and implored leave to retire from Plymouth and then "from the world." Incensed at the disregard of their appeals, the publicans thrust the soldiers to doors ; and the outcasts, turning highwaymen, stole cattle and sheep with impunity, slew the animals and cooked the joints "in the open eye of the world," and sullenly vowed that they would have "meat rather than famish." By means of forced loans the privations of the troops were at length assuaged, and Charles visited Plymouth, attended by "his whole Courte." The scene was gay indeed as the monarch, with plumes waving over his beaver cap, rode into the town with a suite of gallants in gleaming helmets and cuirasses, and guarded by troopers armed with pikes, halberds and other weapons. Mr. Nicholas Blake, the Mayor, craved the King's acceptance of a purse containing one thousand marks, and Charles passed, with his richly-apparelled courtiers, and amid the silvery trumpetings of the heralds, through a myriad of acclaiming subjects. He was sumptuously feasted by the municipality, and jesters of repute gratified his evening humours. Early next morning he marched at the head of the troops to Roborough, and a series of successful evolutions confirmed the belief that, with more generous fare and warmer clothing, the men had forgotten their recent miseries. A Council of War was held on the return of the army to the Hoe. Buckingham gave the assurance that general sickness no longer afflicted the army ; the soldiers embarked in the presence of the King ; and the canvas of every ship was soon distended with a favourable wind.

Charles had taken his departure, the decorations were laid aside, and the inhabitants were rejoicing at their respite, when the fleet re-entered the Sound in indescribable dis-order. Seized by unaccountable panic, several ships had turned about, their example was followed by others, and many forced their way into Catwater "with such haste and fear that divers of them came into collision with each other." A week elapsed before con-fidence was restored, and then the fleet left the port so deficient in ammunition, stores and cables that several vessels faltered in the offing. It was only the signal to weigh anchor "on pain of death" that induced the captains to resume the voyage. In the interval the appearance of every fresh sail off Plymouth was an incitement to disgraceful misgiving, and the West was a prey to alarms. Several Royalist Frenchmen chased a squadron of

Rochelle revolutionists towards Fowey, and a conflict would have occurred if the volunteers had not protected the refugees by manning the forts and covering the pursuers. Inglorious was the fate of the expedition to Cadiz. Warned in time, the Spaniards had concealed their treasure and removed the ships; and wasted by want and disease, the English soldiers converted the invasion into a drunken orgie. They refused to march whilst their comrades dying from starvation and plague, and a retreat was ordered before the enemy had even been seen.

When the fleet slunk back to Plymouth the regiments were thinned as by battle, and putrid corpses were thrown by hundreds into the harbour. As sick and wounded were carried on shore, the streets grew fœtid with the stench of desperate wretches who could not even clothe their famished bodies. Scarcely less destitution afflicted the officers, whose misery was aggravated by the feeling "that so chargeable a business has foully miscarried." The condition of the rank and file was abject. "They stink as they go, and their poor rags are rotten and ready to fall if touched." The vessels were ricketty and pestiferous, there was "scarcely a man left to trim the sails," and Captain John Pennington could only find a score that would float, and these were "poor, miserable, rotten things." There was neither "meat nor drink" available, the plague became general within a month and the victims were thrown into open graves, often, it is feared, before the last throe had been experienced. As the winter hardened, the majority were obliged to keep their beds for want of clothes. More than one captain sold his stores to feed the sick, and others abandoned their frigates and left the prizes to drift.

Throughout those awful winter months the squalor of the garrison passed all endurance, and Captain Pennington, now Vice-Admiral at Plymouth, could obtain neither remittances nor replies to his supplications. Apart from his daily encounter with "mortality and sickness" he was so worried by the pertinacious that he was weary of his life. It was useless to serve out the unused victuals, for these were decomposed and the "men die after eating them." So, by turns, Pennington insisted on his recall, pleaded for redress, threatened to dismiss the soldiers and sailors, "and let the battleships ride destitute." Again and again he begged : "Send the money or it will break my heart, for I am so followed about and called upon that I know not what to do." The wail remained unheeded, the town became a charnel house, the air was heavy with death, and fearsome faces and appalling silence told of desolation and dread. From Plymouth the plague spread to Plympton and the villages round about, and the consternation of all classes was terrible. Magistrates deserted their posts, "the common people of the better sort" fled to other towns, even the constables disappeared, and there was no pretence of public safety. Hundreds of soldiers and sailors left their posts to beg or bully their way to their homes, and a regiment of the most destitute threatened to march in a body to London "to show his Majesty our nakedness." Eventually the disease exhausted its virulence, the troops who escaped infection were distributed through inland towns, and, for a time, "this small corner breathed again," and prayed to be preserved from all future visitations.

Renewed Horrors at　　Eliot had witnessed at Plymouth the disgrace in which the nation
Plymouth : 1627.　　was involved, and he knew that Bagg, as the instrument of Buckingham, had furnished the meat that stank, embezzled the stores so that the men went about naked, and caused such famine that many could hardly stand for weakness. "Our honour is ruined, our ships are sunk, our men perished ; not by the sword, not by the enemy, not by chance, but by those we trust." From his place in Parliament, Sir John demanded that "not only the money but the service" should be accounted for, and he insisted that all who were responsible for these nefarious transactions skould "receive such punish-

ment as in the judgment of Parliament they may merit." Bagg tried to stay the vote by affecting to possess some confidences of the Duke which it would be impolitic to reveal, but Parliament held his grace personally responsible. His impeachment followed, broadened to admit the bad faith illustrated in the seizure of the St. Peter, of Newhaven, a French vessel which had been plundered at Plymouth of its gold and silver and precious stones. Stitched within leather bags, the money was sent direct to Buckingham, and the pearls and emeralds were conveyed to him with similar care. When the ship was ordered to be restored it was impudently detained, and no second thought was devoted to the restitution of the treasure. As to the Cadiz expedition, Eliot was equally fearless. Not only had the national strength and safety been impaired by that miscarriage, but the "inestimable jewel of honour" tarnished. By whom? The Duke of Buckingham! "Well done, Sir John Eliot," was the cry that rang through a house unaccustomed to the denunciation of a favourite or to criticism of the King himself. In his passion, Charles committed Eliot to the Tower, but the Parliament "was never quiett till the King released him." Charles dissolved the Commons to shunt the impeachment; but the thunder rolled and volleyed through the west. Hampden at Grampound, Pym at Tavistock, Glanville at Plymouth, Strode at Beeralston, Bevil Granville at Launceston, William Coryton at Liskeard, Edward Giles at Totnes—all these giants denounced the assumptions of the King, the dishonesty of his instruments, and the sordid barter in judicial appointments. Glanville was sent on foreign service, so that his scathing catalogue of the royal abuses should be stifled, but Plymouth adopted him again as soon as he returned. The persecution of Eliot now started in downright earnest. "Divers foul abuses and misdemeanours" were alleged to have marked the discharge of his duties at Plymouth, and, "the scandal and dishonour" being assumed, Buckingham forbade him "from all further meddling" with the office of Vice-Admiral of Devon. Bagg was appointed in his place, and with opportunities for revenge thus enlarged, he converted St. Germans into a barracks for the mutinous, and insinuated his surprise that it had been so long exempted from the "taking of souldiers."

The quarrel with France in 1627 was the outcome of mysterious personal disappointments. Two years before, Buckingham sold a portion of the English fleet to enable Richelieu to crush the Huguenots; but now, in the hour of wounded vanity, arising from the rejection of his addresses by the French Queen, he posed as the Protestant champion. As Rhé was hard pressed, Buckingham decided to attempt its relief in person, and another forced loan was sanctioned. Cornwall rose in revolt, Eliot was re-committed to the Tower, and it was not until his means had been adjusted that he could meet the demands it was the pleasure of Bagg to levy. "I hope," this miscreant wrote to his master, "that events will tende to his utter ruine; for my heart desires nothing more than to have that traitor's base ingratitude appeare to the worlde." A shudder passed through Plymouth with the report of another war. Its fortifications were in ruins, new ports and drawbridges were necessary, "as no doubt the King will recollect," and more guards were required "or the French will soon be practising how they may be quittance with us." Privation was the rule on land, mutiny was rife ashore and afloat, pirates were taking "the air off the port and your Spanish rabbits," and the supplies were menaced with extinction as there were so few husbandmen to attend the crops. Indignation was universal when the soldiers staggered into the town, and swelled into thousands the hundreds who constituted the garrison. As they could not be billeted for want of money, or encamped for lack of canvas, they "mastered the people and disturbed the peace with frequent robberies, burglaries, rapes, rapines, murders and barbarous cruelties." The highways were so dangerous that the markets were abandoned and the troops "a danger to all and the undoing of many." Officers grievously complained "of their necessities," and, so far from the prospect of another brush being viewed with composure, it was declared that the enemy might advance without fear upon Plymouth and deliver "his great blow at last." When Lord Holland hoisted his flag, the confusion was bewildering. No creature could tell what provisions were stored in the ships, and several of these were Dutch "with no Englishmen in charge." The fleet was nothing more than a bedraggled and dishevelled phantom.

Bagg compensated for his infamies by tracking the steps of his predecessor, setting spies upon his friends, and insinuating doubts as to the loyalty of everyone with whom Eliot conversed. Lord Warwick lodged at the house of one Jennens, a personal friend of Eliot's, and Bagg, in communicating the details of his "restinge place," proved to his complete contentment that the treachery of this officer was also beyond question. "As soone as ever he put foot ashore his invited familiars have been that pattern of ingratitude, Eliot, the malicious Coryton, and a man no less true to his friend, Sir Ferdinando Gorges." Bagg entreated the Duke to "make those that thus disaffectionately disserve you examples for all tyme to come." Persistent in his tattle bearing, he hinted that the association of Eliot and Warwick bred "much wonder in these partes," and the fact that "they were still together and walk in the way they entered" filled his reptilious mind with sore concern. Bagg was equally sure that Coryton's conduct would be found "foul to his ruin." However blind the King and Buckingham may have been to the servility of their "slave," the Cornish gentry had formed their own estimate of him, and the "insufferable pride of the

PLYMOUTH, WITH THE WALL ENCLOSURE, AND CASTLE.

TROOPS EMBARKING FOR THE WARS.

(From an old Sketch in the British Museum.)

fellow" filled Sir Robert Killigrew with such loathing that he expressed for Bagg the utmost "scorne."

Unable to extract any money from Bagg, Holland distributed £1,000 of his own amongst the officers, and these summoned the tradesmen by beat of drums and paid off "their old scores." But the soldiers dared not show themselves lest they should be molested, and discipline was impossible. There were no means of housing, feeding, or clothing them ; the new arrivals wandered aimlessly about, and threatened a general uprising. Again drawing upon his resources, Holland bought 300 sheep "for the sick men who die for want of fresh meat." "Most despair here," he wrote, and the distress was so acute that the Mayor raised the standard of revolt. The losses of the town had been calamitous, first at the hands of the pirates, next by collapse of trade, and, finally, by the billeting. Nicholas Blake had been ruined and some merchants "turned out of their lives, others out of their means, and all out of their trade and employment." Haunted by "the cries of my soldiers," Gorges, the Governor, applied to their relief a cargo of oil that had been seized outside the harbour. "Oil to an army," he cheerfully testified, "is as cheap and more useful and as healthy as butter." Thus were the troops sustained on the eve of the campaign.

"Such miserable rotten ships" as Holland had made ready, "no man ever saw, and our enemies seeing them may well scoff at our nation." Still, contemptible as they were, he could not tarry, for Buckingham had sailed for Rhé. In fine weather and, with the fairest wind, the reinforcements set out ; but the want of pikes, corselets, match and swords was so ridiculously manifest that the admiral was compelled to put back. The dismayed townsfolk refused to give the soldiers house room, expelled from their premises those who had been left for the defence of the port, and martial law was proclaimed. Bagg was meanwhile praying and believing that Buckingham would return a hero ; but just as Holland was ready to leave with the deficiencies repaired, his grace crawled into Plymouth ! He had been bandying puerile courtesies, and the enemy surprised and cut his force to pieces. All this was of inferior concern to Bagg. He was only too grateful for any chance that brought Buckingham's despised retinue into Catwater, since it enabled him to entertain the Duke "at my house at Saltram." Every sense of shame was forgotten in the exultation which filled the parasite when he breathed under his own roof the atmosphere of His Grace, who thus conferred on him an honour which "is more to me than children, wife or life."

The Duke's first care was to send tidings of the disaster to the King, and the postboy was "sworn and conjured on his head" to disclose the secret to no one on the way. A few hours revealed the overwhelming nature of the English reverse. Buckingham's ships, as they lay in Catwater, were seen to have been riddled, and the crews were suffering torments from plague and wounds combined. Anarchy stalked hideous through the streets after the survivors gained the shore. The soldiers stole from the inhabitants, the sailors robbed the soldiers, furies of one branch of the service fought with gangs of the other, and the victors sold for food the weapons that fell to them as spoils. "So noisome and ill favouring" were the ships that the officers dared not use their berths, and the Navy would have been abandoned if it were not "to oblige the Duke." Frost accentuated the terrors of the garrison, and Sir Henry Mervyn predicted that the winter would "eat out more than the enemy." The sailors had neither stockings nor rags to cover their nakedness ; and, so many of them were stricken with disease, that the officers declared there would "soon be more ships than men." Buckingham still hugged the hope of raising the relief of Rhé ; and, in the spring of 1628, stores were collected at Plymouth for another dash. But the bread, beer and cheese were worthless, and the officers protested that to use the

G

ships in their unclean state, with tons of barnacles clustering their keels, must be "to send them into the jaws of death." Previous lessons were lost on the Duke; and, as the levies poured in, fearful mortality arose from want of clothing, numbers fell dead with exhaustion and scurvy, the shoeless soldiers were frostbitten, and their "rotting toes fall away piece-meal." At the "dock of Plymouth," as well as at Saltash, there was not a vessel which was fit for sea, and the commanders were so insubordinate that some were suspended and others discharged.

There was a rising of especial gravity in March, and Captain Sydenham removed a hundred newly-impressed men to the Guildhall for safety. Here there were supplies of pikes awaiting distribution, and, seizing these, the men refused to obey their officers. During a temporary hesitation, they were bidden to throw down their weapons, but a marine named Kirby rallied them with the challenge: "Let us die, one and all." After the mutiny was quelled, Kirby and a companion were tried by drum-head court-martial, and sentenced to be hanged on the Hoe in the morning. At daybreak, however, a crowd of rebellious soldiers, sailors and townsmen assembled around the gallows, demolished the structure, and tossed the timbers into the sea amid shouts of defiance. Then they repaired to the prison to set the captives at liberty; but the army, responding to bugle and drum, proved faithful to the Crown, and fired a volley on the crowd. The fall of the more reckless daunted the remainder, and, with black looks and sullen threats, they with-drew. Insubordination commanded so much sympathy, however, that the execution of Kirby was abandoned. "On more deliberate advisement," wrote Lord Denbigh, the general of the forces at Plymouth, "I find that this poor Kirby has been a very honest and careful man, and, if he be pardoned, it may lead the sailors to the opinion that they have forced a way to their own ends." The astute commander wanted, however, a less popular victim. "With the pardon of the one I would join the execution of the other." Thus Kirby was spared and his comrade sacrificed to overawe the mutineers.

The outbreak led to enquiry touching this "heartburning and grief." Simple enough was the explanation. The sailors "say they are used like dogs and not permitted to come ashore: they have no means to put clothes on their backs or relieve the wants of their wives and families; when they fall ill they have no allowance of fresh meat; the sick, when put on shore, are suffered to perish for want of attendance; the provisions generally are neither fit nor wholesome; and the men would as lief be hanged as be where they are." Such was the morale of the second expedition destined for the relief of Rochelle. The ships were delayed for weeks by "the high and mighty difficulty" of procuring men and stores, and they were so meanly furnished that it was "a thing pitiful to be observed." The defences were in ruins, the magazines empty, and the officers "out of countenance and discouraged." In sooth the ships were "in equipage scarce fit for a merchant's voyage," there was nothing to "avert the common stratagems of artful enemies," and the soldiers were rather disposed "to run into mutiny than obey orders." It was "neither counsellable nor honourable," asserted the King's advisers on the spot, to put to sea with this apology for a fleet, and all experienced men were against the venture. Amid "grudging and murmuring" the soldiers were sent to their ships, and, by "fair words or ill language," compelled to proceed. But even then there was further delay. Messengers had to be sent to the Tower for ammunition, and waggons loaded with powder were despatched to Plymouth over "hard ways" that had to be traversed with teams of oxen.

The expedition was foredoomed to disaster. Sir John Eliot watched the jobbery that was being enacted at Plymouth, and Sir Francis Seymour vowed that the public funds were being emptied into "a Bottomless Bagg." The "base fellow," as Laud subsequently termed him, was untouched by criticisms: his only concern was to implore his grace not to jeopardise his sacred person or prestige by resuming the command. Buckingham had more confidence in his capacity, and left Portsmouth with one portion of the expedition, as Denbigh sailed from Plymouth to co-operate—only to witness and be smothered with the Duke in another emphatic and humiliating discomfiture. Soon the news reached Plymouth of dire disaster, of ships destroyed by fire, of others blown up by blundering—of another English abasement. In their exultation the French chased their assailants and fired into them until they were within hail of Plymouth. When the survivors landed, "foul and scandalous aspersions" were passed on Denbigh for running away, anger was intensified by the losses sustained by merchants whose ships had been seized, and Gorges, as Governor of the port, offered to take charge of an avenging expedition. Bagg discounted all this declamatory sentiment, and called himself friend "to such as only love the Duke."

The time-server's opportunity of lavishing adulations upon Buckingham from "my house at Saltram" was not destined to be repeated, for his grace was stabbed to the heart by Felton. Scarcely a whisper of sympathy was heard save from Bagg, and he was faithful even in death to the Duke—and himself! He could not sleep for thinking of the damnable act of the assassin, and, if it were not for the sake of the monarch, he feared to sin against Heaven by holding any future converse with mankind. "Nothing shall comfort me but the King's commands, and nothing shall delight my spirits but to use them in his service." His master was gone, but the master's patron remained. "Not for myne own sake, but for my dead lord's sake, retain mee in your favour ; I know the world sees me lost by my losse, and without markes of his Majestie's favour I shall be much disabled for his service." Bagg was not forgotten by the King, but Charles could not avert the rising of the tide. In Plymouth his prerogative was scouted, discredit was thrown on the services, and his Majestie was "no longer awesome." The civil authorities requested him to remove from their midst the demoralised rabble. They reminded him that the Cadiz expedition resulted in 1,600 deaths by plague, and that, after the disaster at Rhé, their ablest citizens were swept away by the contaminations of billeting. Diplomacy came to the rescue, the dreaded nightmare vanished, and soldiers and sailors alike hastened to their homes.

Rising Hatred of the Stuarts: 1633-1642.   Relieved of external difficulties, Charles entered on his struggle with Parliament; the authority of the Star Chamber was supreme, and "insolencies" uttered within the house were visited with pains and penalties without. In the evil-smelling cell to which he had again been committed for arraigning the Sovereign, Eliot's indomitable spirit took its flight in 1632. Plymouth sullenly watched the conflict, and, when Charles arrogated to himself increased ecclesiastical powers, "sundry refractory persons" urged the Mayor to raise the civil and religious standard. Dread of the Roman Catholics was all pervading. In November, 1633, John Jenkyn, a native of Penzance, was found in possession of "crucifixes, pictures and other superstitious things"; and, as he had lived in Spain for 25 years, as a member of the Society of Jesuits, he was sent to prison, and his Popish books were burnt in the market-place. Another such prosecution occurred in 1635, when Derby O'Callaghan, an Irishman, was convicted of making proselytes to the Church of Rome. He had wandered about the streets in rags, but a trunk found at his lodgings was full of good clothing, and "Popish books, beads, crucifixes and indulgences" were concealed underneath. O'Callaghan had a companion whose manners created suspicion; but, as soon as the search was instituted, he made his escape and was not overtaken, although "the hue and cry" was raised.

In the same year the Corporation came into conflict with the Crown   The Star Chamber insisted that the gift of St. Andrew's was conditional, and that the local

authorities had forfeited their rights by infringement.   Dr. Aaron Wilson, who had commended himself to Bagg as a good hater of Presbyterianism, was appointed as vicar by the
King, "in defiance of all law and custom."   He inaugurated the strife by charging the Mayor
and his brethren with trespassing upon the churchyard by erecting on the west side a
hospital for the poor, and thus interfering with his rights of burial ; and a row of shambles
and houses on the east side, and thus absorbing the space where the vicar had "anciently
a dwelling."   He also disputed the claim of the Councillors to pews in the church and
seats in the chancel, questioned his worship's right to appoint a churchwarden, and
charged the latter with not accounting for the offerings.   In a mood of hesitation, subsequently to be avenged, the Corporation assigned their right of presentation to the King,
"as they were unwilling to dispute the matter with him."   They prayed, however, that the

HOSPITAL OF POOR'S PORTION.   Erected 1630.   (St. Andrew's Churchyard, Catherine Street).
(From a Photograph in the possession of Mr. W. Waterman.)

Grammar School should have "some maintenance set upon it" in any fresh arrangement.
The Star Chamber compromised the issues by waiving the accusation of encroachment,
other points were left to the Bishop, the readjustment of the pews was reserved to the
churchwardens, the money for the poor was distributed as hitherto, and the fees for
marriages and burials were allocated to the Archbishop of Canterbury.   The Corporation
were by no means complaisant in transferring their patronage to the Crown ; and, the
spirit of caution intervening, his majesty restored the power, and sought to conciliate the
Corporation by dividing the parish and sanctioning the building of "Charles Church"—
subsequently styled the church of "St. Charles Ye Martyr" by a too sympathetic parish
clerk.   But this concession, which enabled the Presbyterian section of the worshippers at
St. Andrew's to remove to the scene of less pretentious ritual, did not mitigate the irritation
the King's interference had caused.   The incident rankled and festered; and, when the

torch was laid to the explosives, Plymouth threw in its lot with representative rule, it cast Aaron Wilson into prison, and wreaked revenge on all who had contrived to emasculate its charter.

Charles was too concerned in humbling the Parliament to devote much attention to law and order. "Egypt was never more infested with caterpillars" than were the coves and bays of the west with Turks, Dutchmen, Dunkirkers and Biscayans. When the pirates were driven hard they ran amongst the shoals; and, as they could not be followed, awaited their own time for putting out to sea. Captain Nutt had resumed his depredations, and his brother joined him in his "devilish enterprise" after being asked to wean him by the promise of another pardon. Loathing of the King was associated with contempt of his officers, and there was no heed paid to his representatives in Plymouth. "No ships are more unwilling to give his Majesty's vessels respect than those of our own merchants in this town." Bagg was aghast at the scorn of the populace. "Here they hate all gentlemen, especially such as serve the King at sea." Cawsand and Yealm yielded a fleet of "picking rascals, who set out without any provisions, and are forced to rob every man they meet, and are no better than pirates themselves." Captain Pennington employed every art to catch them, but the corsairs dodged him in Whitsand Bay, and as Plymouth confederates revealed his plans to these "slippery rogues," they were able to "make shift" just as he was encircling them. Then, when the coast was clear, they swarmed out anew and "packed on sail" with such alacrity that the swiftest frigates failed to catch them. In 1635 two Turkish men-of-war, lying in wait for the Newfoundland oil ships, pursued them towards Plymouth, but they received more than they bargained for on attempting to board, and forty of the Ottomans were slain.

Abroad, the prowess of England was held in fast diminishing esteem. One Plymouth crew was massacred because the national good faith was distrusted, and scores of sailors reached the Sound stripped of all their effects—so naked and destitute that they had to be clothed and fed by the wealthier inhabitants and forwarded to their homes. Even in the town the same contempt was shown by foreigners, and the crew of the Amersfoot, an Amsterdam vessel, were reported for "barbarous cruelty." Observing a body of shipwrights quitting "the dock in Catwater" they followed them with swords; and, when the workmen stood on their defence with axes and addices (adzes), drove them to the Friary Gate. One apprentice was stabbed in the shoulder, another was beaten with staves, and a third defended himself with a halberd. Dutch reinforcements hurried up, and made free use of pistols, cutlasses and petronels. An artisan who was wielding a hammer with deadly effect was knocked over a clump of furze and sent crashing down a precipice. Others took refuge in a cottage, and were there besieged with shouts of "Upsteaken, Upsteaken the English." The assailants fired repeatedly, an onlooker was stabbed to death, and the knife went into his stomach "as softly as into a cabbage cole." Eight of the assassins were arrested by the soldiery; and, when they were challenged by the Mayor, asserted that the cause of the riot was the failure of Charles to keep his word with Holland. "They were poor beggarly malefactors with not enough to maintain them in prison."

In 1636 a party of Turkish pirates overhauled the Plymouth fishing fleet, and after taking out thirty hands, sent the boats adrift. In dread of being sent into slavery in the same way, many English captains ran their ships ashore as soon as the foreigners hove in sight, and the robbers appropriated the cargoes whilst the crews made their way across country. Wembury, Cawsand and other bays were strewn in 1640 with vessels thus abandoned, and freebooting resumed the dimensions of a national menace. The Corporation demanded munitions to fortify St. Nicholas Island, where the ordnance was unserviceable, the carriages decayed, the stores exhausted, and the "powder so much waste."

In a confiding moment, Charles forwarded the supplies, and they were afterwards employed against himself. Tumult was lifting its head throughout the country, the long gathering storm was ready to burst, and as one good turn deserved another, Charles called upon the Mayor to assist in quelling the rebellions in the north. He was reminded in return that the town had been too impoverished by his exactions to help him, and that not a man could be spared from the protection of the port. This was substantially true, although John Bussureau was imprisoned for circulating disquieting hints of a French descent upon Plymouth. He was justified in his prediction, however, for a squadron from Brest entered the port, and seized the provisions which were stored along the cliffs. Charles remained deaf to the appeals of the local merchants ; and the Mayor's alarmist statement that the French Admiral's vessels were of enormous dimensions evoked no reply—the English ship of state itself was fast drifting towards the rocks ! The enemy stood off Rame Head for some hours, then the cloud of canvas swept seawards, and the invaders left as peacefully as they came, unaware of the ease with which they might have taken the town.

Pilgrim Fathers and Commercial Development: 1620-1642. There is more than a sentimental survival of the picturesque theory that the Pilgrim Fathers were associated with the life of Plymouth. Those who departed in 1620 were in the main, if not wholly, strangers to the town, but they supplemented the blood and sinew that the port had already contributed to the conversion of Virginia and other choice tracts. Many of the townsmen had long sympathised with the demand of the Brownists for freedom of congregational worship, and there was a keen sympathy with the community who crossed to Holland in search of a freer atmosphere. Disappointed with the environment of Leyden, the Pilgrim Fathers were enchanted with Raleigh's account of America's natural resources ; and well weaned, to use their own language, from the milk of their Mother Country, the prospect of distant emigration did not appal them. Industrious and frugal by temperament, they were knit together by "a most sacred covenant of the Lord, of the violation whereof we make great conscience, and by virtue whereof we hold ourselves straitly tied to all care of each other's goods and of the whole. It is not with us as with men whom small things can discourage." Such was the sturdy pride of the pilgrims who left Leyden in the Speedwell and the Mayflower, only to be buffeted by the storms until Dartmouth haven made its welcome appearance. Thus far the "viage" had been "as full of crosses" as the passengers were "full of crookedness," and the prospect was ominous. Fairly taut and well trimmed when she first set out, the Speedwell's timber opened like a sieve, and the sea rushed in as through "a mole hole." From the bluff captain who, unlike Miles Standish, had little reverence for the advocates of a conscience clause, the emigrants received scant sympathy ; and, repeatedly rebuking the more frail complainants as "froward, waspish, and discontented," he addressed them with "as much scorne and contempte as though they were not good enough to wipe his shoes."

Having refitted, the Speedwell and the Mayflower resumed the voyage, but, after quitting Dartmouth, the distressing experiences were renewed, days of torture and suspense ensued, and the wretched vessels made for Plymouth. Here they were thoroughly overhauled, and the Speedwell having been condemned as unfit for sea was despatched to London with the exhausted creatures who preferred persecution on land to the torments of the ocean. Amongst the sympathizers who dwelt by the Barbican the voyagers found spiritual consolation and homely hospitality, and the relations were most affectionate. "All troubles being blown over," the undaunted were "compacted together in the one ship," and then they departed in their frail barque. Amid the devoutest of salutations from their newly found friends, and the fluttering of kindly emblems from the

DEPARTURE OF THE PILGRIM FATHERS FROM THE OLD BARBICAN, PLYMOUTH.

(*Specially drawn by W. H. Pike.*)

rugged sailors who watched as the vessel worked her way to the Sound, the Mayflower sped from the port to found the desired habitation. "According to the usual manner" many were afflicted with sea sickness, and their sufferings were aggravated by brutal jibes. But, wrote Bradford in a spirit of sacred satisfaction, "there was a special worke of God's providence." Amongst the crew was a "proud and profane" young mariner of "lustie body" who was always ridiculing the misery of the passengers, and assailing them with "greeveous execrations." He did not shrink from saying that he hoped it would be his lot to cast half of the pilgrims overboard and make merry with their money and effects. If he were by any gently reproved, he would curse and swear most bitterly. "But," the chronicler continued, "it pleased God before we came half seas over to smite this young man with a greeevous disease, of which he died in a desperate manner, and it was himself the first that was thrown overboard. Thus his curses light on his own head, and it was an astonishment to all his fellows, for they noted it to be the just hand of God upon him." Fair winds were followed by fierce storms, and the Mayflower was "shroudly shaken." Nine weary weeks of buffeting elapsed before Cape Cod was sighted, and christening their landing place as Plymouth Rock and their settlement as New Plymouth, in honour of the town whose memory they held so fragrant, the pilgrims set up their historic habitation.

Plymouth and other merchants were meanwhile steadily exploiting the new country. In 1622 Samuel Jennens fitted out the Abraham of Plymouth, and the Nightingale of Portsmouth, with useful stores for the natives and colonists; and bear skins, oil, fish and pipe staves were received in exchange. At Richmond Island, close to the south-eastern part of Port Elizabeth, was established the nucleus of a trading station, and in 1631 a contract was completed between the President and Council on the one part, and Robert Trelawney and Moses Goodyear (the son-in-law of Abraham Jennens), to develop the resources of New England "from sea to sea throughout the Main Land." Sir Ferdinando Gorges, then Governor of Plymouth, accepted the administration of the area, and enforced his own laws until Charles required his military genius at home for the defence of the Crown. Robert Trelawney appointed "John Winter, of Plymouth, marryner—a very grave and discreet man," to superintend this enterprise at the head of sixty employees, and there were many others who went forth to become the personal friends of those whom the desire for "purity of conscience and liberty of worship" had driven forth. It was by the merest chance that Thomas Cammock, a relative of the Earl of Warwick, did not join Trelawney in the partnership. The arrangements were discussed in the latter's house at Plymouth, but Cammock met with an accident shortly after his arrival, and Winter took possession as Trelawney's agent.

"Strong waters" were sent to Winter to gratify the ardent throats of the Indians, and the savages rushed to the beach with welcomes and beaver skins whenever a fresh ship hailed in sight. Trelawney was not without competitors, and, in the person of George Cleeve, a fellow Plymothian, he found an unscrupulous rival who slandered Winter's wife as the most drunken wanton in the town, where she remained for some time after his departure. The plantation was large enough, however; and attracted by the freedom and the products, west-country and other folks flocked there in "heaps." In his alarm at the possible depopulation of Devon and Cornwall, the King inhibited the departure of emigrants without his written license. "A most heavenly and comfortable sight it is to observe with what power and purity the religious ordinances at Richmond Island are administered, so that no one place in the world comes neer it." Thus wrote Edward Trelawney in a letter to his brother Robert. "There is such a holy walking, such a sweet communion and fellowshippe on all sides, that I am persuaded, unless a man were all paste and grace, it would convince the veriest reprobate alive. Oh, that Old England were Newe, then would the Lord certainly bee better pleased with it." The sweet communion and fellowship were disturbed in a few years by sectional controversies, and the natural disposition of men to differ resulted in the institution of a penal code, not less disagreeable than that which the pilgrims had escaped. And the most bigoted found consolation in the consciousness that it was "impious to tolerate error," and "blasphemy" to suggest an unorthodox view of any portion of the Scriptures. Heresies, especially those preached by the Baptists, were visited with fines and flogging, and the more obstinate and self-opiniated were banished from the colony.

Commencement   Commercial interest, political faith, personal loss and religious
of the   conviction alike made for the part that Plymouth played in the Civil
Struggle : 1642-1643. Wars. Its resources had been wasted in insensate wars, its families
thinned by the attendant plagues, and its hero statesmen martyred. If the national indictment of the Stuart dynasty was heavy, on no town had the evils of their mismanagement fallen with more accumulative cruelty than Plymouth itself. It was full ripe for the Revolution before the Revolution was ripe, and its citizens were only awaiting the signal that was to light the torch. And yet, despite this discontent, Plymouth sent to Parliament, in the person of Robert Trelawney, one of the most consistent champions of the King. Extremely difficult it must have been to discard that gentle and generous merchant. The son of a distinguished Cornishman who was thrice chosen as the Mayor of Plymouth, and whose many benefactions endeared him to the poor, Robert Trelawney had secured for the town the advantages of a continuous commercial intercourse which, in times of dread and disaster, had been its sustenance, and, it may be, its salvation.

Robert Trelawney was not disposed to submit in silence to arbitrary methods for limiting the pretensions of Charles, and he was actuated as much by fear of the Revolution as by his instinctive loyalty. According to Clarendon, the Roundhead demeanour was "notorious and terrible," and spies carried casual observations that fell from those who disagreed with the Commons. Robert Trelawney was arrested for expressing his opinion that the Commoners were guilty of treason in appointing a guard for their protection without the consent of the King. Two informations were filed against the member for Plymouth—one by Mr. Fletcher and another by Captain Andrews, "subscribed with their own hands." Andrews admitted that Trelawney did not force the conversation, but rather expressed his view of public opinion. Fletcher confessed that the meeting was accidental, and that Trelawney, on being asked "What news?" deprecated the action of Parliament as unconstitutional. That the member was entrapped is manifest. The House forthwith resolved upon his expulsion, and a writ was issued for another burgess to sit in his place. Trelawney was committed to Winchester Gaol, and was there confined until the eve of the outbreak, when he was restored to his counting house in Looe Street.

Plymouth was admittedly the key to the west country. Its fortifications were extensive, and it possessed a constant source of recuperation in its seaboard. On the one side the sea flowed as far as Tothill ; and, on the other, by way of Sourpool and Deadlake, to Lipson. So that the geographical formation of the town was a peninsula. Between Lipson and Tothill there was a marshy tract, over which the tide flowed and formed a bay, and vessels sailed through the space now occupied by Union Street and moored on the site of the Octagon. The town was almost completely surrounded by a trench, across which drawbridges were thrown ; and the wall enclosure was over six feet in width, with gates at various points, through which alone was admission possible. The circumvallation commenced at the Coxside Gate, and traversing to the north-east included, within formidable ramparts, the Friary Court and Gardens. It then ran along Tothill to the sites of

PLYMOUTH AND DISTRICT DURING THE SIEGE.

Gascoyne Street, Ham Street, Park Street, across Old Town Street, through the rear of Drake Street, the Market and Cornwall Street, intercepting the Frankfort Gate at the north of the land on which the Globe Hotel so long remained. Curving away towards the coast, it passed through the site of Princess Square and reached the Hoe Gate, and thence deflected its course to the Barbican and terminated at a point near the Castle on Lambhay Hill. There were other gates than those already mentioned—the Western Gate, at Briton Side; the Gasking Gate, with Resolution Fort adjacent; the Old Town Gate, with Terrour Drawbridge and a moat, and Charles Fort near at hand; St. George Drawbridge, to the north of Bedford Street; and the South Gate, commanding the steps that led from Sutton Pool to the Barbican. Whilst the town was thus fortified within, there were several works thrown up on the outskirts—a mound at Eldad, another at the top of York Street, and a third at Pennycomequick, all agricultural land at this period. There were important defences of the same class at Maudlin, now North Hill; Holiwell, a field west of Woodside; and at Lipson and its mill the country was commanded by a fort. At Leerie Point, or Little Saltram, as well as at Catdown, there were earthworks with breastwork connections, all of them liable to be washed away by heavy rains. Every point of access to the harbours was commanded by towers of great strength, with walls of tremendous thickness, and embrasures to admit of small cannon. Some of these block-houses were square, a few octagonal, and one seven-sided to fit the zigzag conformation of the ground. The granite entrances with oaken doors were opened by the removal of sliding bars, and underground were the dungeons to which prisoners were condemned. Similar defences existed at Western King, Devil's Point, Eastern King and Fisher's Nose. A tower of contemporaneous architecture in Fire-stone Bay commanded the narrowest point of the entrance to Hamoaze, and a bulwark of exceptional resistance crowned the summit of Drake's Island, or the Island of St. Nicholas or St. Michael's, as from time to time it was described. Half a dozen farm huts could be seen near Stoke Church. Keame House lay by Hamoaze, and " Sir Thomas Wise hee hath builded upon an advanced ground a new mansion for his own pleasure and named it Mount Wise." There were a few irregular streets on the north side of Fore Street, Stonehouse, and these sloped towards the water between the site of the Naval Hospital and the bridge, where there yet existed the ruins of the old town which was fired by the French. The site of the Naval Hospital was occupied by the remains of an exten-sive quadrangular group that presented the lineaments of an abandoned abbey; and on Stonehall, near the site of the existing St. George's Church, was the manorial house of the Durnford's—a massive struc-ture with embattlements, approached by

HOEGATE.

(Taken down in 1863.)

CHURCH OF ST. LAWRENCE, DEVIL'S POINT, STONEHOUSE.

(From a Sketch by W. Payne.)

a gateway of bold design, with a tower of imposing dimensions overshadowing "a small forte" adjacent. By the waterside at Devil's Point, now covered by the Victualling Yard, was the little edifice of St. Lawrance, another of the survivals of an age when peril rendered mariners especially devout.

On the eve of the crash, Slanning was summoned to the Court, with injunctions to dissemble as to the cause of his departure. There he learnt that Charles wanted money to meet the threatened assault, and, on returning to Plymouth, he prevailed upon Robert Trelawney to lend 681 ounces of silver, 999 gold links, and other valuables which could be pledged. These transactions were detected by the watchdogs of the Parliament, and Trelawney was taken from his mansion at Ham, and again committed to the prison at Winchester—there to write in his foul cell a last will and testament which showed his rare affection for the town. He bequeathed, "according to a former promise made in the Guildhall of Plymouth," £200 towards the proposed Charles Church, and a sum of £600 to be distributed in various benevolent forms. The vicar of St. Andrew's and the vicar of the new church "that is ordained to be built" were to receive 40s. a-piece each year for preaching exhortations to "works of piety and charity." Every third year the sum of £20 was to be paid "to a maid servant that is of spotless life and hath served in one house five years : but only maids are hereof capable"—an interesting comment on Cleeve's assertion that "there are not four honest women in the whole town." Five pounds were to be awarded every third year to a young sailor "that hath served five yeares or more of his apprenticeship in the towne or parish of Plymouth aforesaid"—the choice to be made by "lott," with the names "putt into a hatt all rold up alike." Trelawney's generosity did not rest here, for he left £150 to the Rev. Thomas Bedford, who had also suffered at the hands of the Parliament. Bedford was curate to Aaron Wilson ; and, upon the death of the vicar, he was presented by the King to the living of St. Andrew's. "But the faction put him by because he had preached an honest sermon, and were not content to throw him out of his undoubted right, but also cast him into a nasty jail." The municipality despatched him by sea to London, and he was not only imprisoned by order of the Commons, but discharged of being "lecturer in the town of Plymouth." He, too, poured coals of fire upon the inhabitants by willing the sum of ten pounds to the New Church "as a testimony of my thankfulness to God for that legacy which by the last will and testament of mine ever honoured friend, Mr. Robert Trelawney, was bequeathed to me." The money was spent in sacramental plate, which is still used in the sacred edifice, and bears the name of the donor and the date.

As soon as Charles set up his standard at Nottingham, many of the old Cornish families declared for him, and Sir Ralph Hopton put himself at their head. An attempt was made to hold the field for the Roundheads, but the influence of the Royalists was predominant. The martyrdom of Eliot was forgotten, the name of the Parliament ceased to intimidate, and one stronghold after another was abandoned, until Saltash threw open its gates. At this juncture, the Mayor of Plymouth, Thomas Ceely, declared for the Parliament, and seized the Castle and the Island to check the advance of Hopton's army of "malignants" into Devon. Crossing the Tamar without much resistance, the Cavaliers threatened Plymouth from Tavistock, and, while the trained bands of the town held the gates and the drawbridges, Colonel Ruthven took possession of Stamford Fort, near Oreston, as well as several villages and hamlets. Hopton's army was so strong, however, that Ruthven recalled his outposts the same day ; and, as he put it, retired within the wall for fear his men would damage "one another in the darke." At daybreak he dashed towards Plympton, with several companies of dragoons, to ascertain the disposition of the enemy. They were under such excellent cover, however, that they declined to give "a charge upon faire ground," and fled from the scene after repeated attempts to lead the Roundheads into ambush. Hopton now made Modbury his headquarters, and he had no sooner settled there than Ruthven led his forces over Roborough Down (Ruberdowne), and, stealing along the lanes, rushed into the town without a note of warning. There was no time to summon the Royalist troops, for the men were billeted in the houses, and the officers were taking their ease in Master Champernowne's mansion. Sir Ralph Hopton and Sir Nicholas Slanning did their best to stay the panic, but the "soudain coming" of the Roundheads so surprised them that they mounted their horses and ran. As for their "souldiers," they were utterly demoralised, and after a feeble resistance, abandoned the other officers to their fate. They resisted capture until the buildings and the outhouses were in flames, and then came forth in a body and made their submission. This success so inspirited Ruthven that he resolved to clear Cornwall of the "malignants," and distributed his army around Stoke, Plympton and Roborough, in order to prevent the passage of the Tamar. The limits were nevertheless forded daily, and foraging parties of Cavaliers experienced no difficulty in procuring without payment whatever supplies they required. "Some of the theeves" were taken by the artifice of a farmer who plied them with liquor until they "became drunk withal" and fell easy victims, but Master Blight—the most notorious ringleader of these incursionists—afterwards escaped out of Plymouth with the connivance of his gaolers.

Some remarkable stories were told as the campaign went on, but none eclipsed that of Major-General Chudley, who penetrated a vast multitude of Cavaliers at Launceston with a mere handful of horse, and created such confusion in their ranks that they fell upon each other. To add to the picturesque horror of the occasion, a thunderstorm ensued, the lightning set fire to the "bondeleroes" of the Cavaliers and caused such injuries "that many of the wounded and scall'd men dyed daily." In May of the same year, 1643,

Ruthven consolidated his forces within two miles of Saltash, and charged the Royalists with such "good courage" that their cavalry took refuge in flight, and left 400 dead on the field. This victory stimulated Ruthven to press on to Bodmin, only to discover his fatal error in abandoning his base. The Cavaliers pitched their tents for the night within the lovely park at Boconnoc, and as the main body slept by "good fires," the sentinels watched by the hedges. At daybreak, the refreshed loyalists marched to the "fair heath" near Braddick Church, and from the opposing knolls the rivals saluted each other with showers of bullets. Neither was disposed to budge, and, weary of the desultory firing, Hopton resolved to leave "all to the mercy of God and the valour of our side." Solemn prayers were first offered; and then, Sir Richard Grenville, leading the van, made his way "down one hill and up the other" with such intrepidity that the Roundheads fled in disorder. If they had not been well mounted, Ruthven and his officers must have fallen into Hopton's hands. As it was, they dashed across country and entered Plymouth under cover of night. This humiliation rendered inevitable the rout at Stratton. The battle began with the customary invocations, the Roundheads "snuffling psalms" and the Cavaliers shouting aloud for "God and the King." So stubborn was the conflict that the Royalist ammunition gave out, but, without alarming their men by saying so, the officers ordered them to charge with "their full bodies and without making any more shot." Chudley jumped into the thick of the fight "with a good stand of pikes," but a rush of reinforcements isolated his heroic group and decided the fate of the day. As their opponents yielded, the Cavaliers advanced in four parties to the crest of the hill, where they embraced "with unspeakable joy, each congratulating the other's success, and acknowledging the wonderful blessing of God." Then they turned the captured cannon on the flying Roundheads, and advanced with ringing cheers to the perfect victory.

Charles was overcome with delight on learning of these triumphs, and in a letter, preserved in the parish church of Landulph, he professed himself "highly sensible of the merit of our county of Cornwall, of its zeal for the defence of our person, and the just rights of our Crown in a time when we could contribute so little to our own defence or to their assistance; in a time when not only no reward appeared, but great and probable dangers threatened obedience and loyalty; of its great and eminent courage and patience in the indefatigable prosecution of our work against so potent an enemy, backed with so strong, rich and populous cities, and plentifully furnished, and supplied with men, arms, money, ammunition and provisions of all kinds." The King rejoiced over the success with which loyalty and patience were rewarded "in dispight of all human probability and all imaginable disadvantages," and he published to the world, so that it may perpetuate to all time, the memory of these, their merits, and of our acceptance of them, and to that end we do hereby render our royal thanks to that our county in the most publick and lasting manner we can devise, commanding copies hereof to be printed and published, and one of them to be read in every church and chapel therein, and to be kept for ever as a record in the same, that, as long as the history of these times and of this nation shall continue, the memory of how much that county hath merited of us and our Crown may be derived with it to posterity."

Early Miseries of the Siege: 1643.   Distressed was Plymouth, but not dismayed; and, as soon as the Royalists went towards Bristol, there to lose the "wain" of their Cornish chivalry on the battlefield, the defenders set to work to renew the wall "for better safetie against those enemys that dayly and nyghtly threaten our said burrow." There were enemies not only without, but within; and the officers put in charge of the town by the Parliament were none other than a set of military marauders, who, under one specious pretence or another, made the best use of their opportunity. Large sums were sent down by water for the support of the soldiery in Devon ; but embezzlement was general and fearless, especially on the part of Master Charles Vaughan and Thomas Gewen, his brother-in-law, the latter an impudent scoundrel who refused to supply even his colleagues with any account of the sums received for wages or in prisage. There was a prevailing suspicion that Vaughan and Gewen "transported the money beyond the sea," and the want resulting from their misappropriations rendered it necessary to tax the inhabitants as a whole. Apart from this there was wholesale plunder at the expense of those who were suspected of being Royalists. Gewen was the autocrat of these impositions, and he demeaned himself "peremptorily and partially," easing his friends and laying "immoderate rates upon others." Those who could not or would not pay he committed to prison, where "divers wretchedly ended their days " ; and he demanded outrageous ransoms from gentlemen who were brought in from the country districts. The prisoners were condemned to the filthiest dungeons to compel them to come to terms without loss of time ; but, when the "calenture" became epidemic, the more wealthy and influential were removed to wholesome confinement because their lives were too precious to be sacrificed. Gewen's conduct was intolerable even to his colleagues, for "he would pay whom he list, and when he list, and what he list," and grew to such "a heighte of pride" that he treated the commands of the Commonwealth with the utmost disdain.

The end of these "oppressions, vexations and abuses" was hastened by the conduct of some of the conspirators in tampering with a cabinet of pearls of exceptional value, which had been seized from a Plymouth merchant. After it had been overhauled by the Commissioners, the Mayor took charge of the treasure for the Parliament ; and he was called upon by Gewen to surrender it. Francis refused to do so without the direct authority of the Speaker, and he was thereupon incarcerated in the Castle for two months. In the meantime Gewen and Vaughan obtained possession of the cabinet ; and Peter Kekewich, a confederate, conveyed it to London "in close and secret manner." After it had remained concealed there for ten weeks, the ropes of pearls were deprived of their most splendid specimens, and there was not a chain or bracelet that was not thus impoverished. The rest of the property was then valued in a small sum for Gewen, Vaughan and the others ; and if Francis, immediately on his release, had not ridden to town to expose the plotters to the Parliament, the cheat would never have been discovered. Before a committee of both houses Vaughan was arraigned ; and he boldly urged that, as the official sequestrator, he had the right to enter any dwelling in Plymouth and confiscate money and plate "if the owners would not part with it otherwise." He contended that he had endeavoured to make the best price of the pearls and insinuated that the Mayor was a traitor to the cause ; but when Francis proved there had been "juggling therein, but by whom he cannot say," and that the articles did not correspond to the original inventory, Vaughan stood convicted. "Therefore," admonished the Speaker, "blush if you can, Master Vaughan, to charge the said Francis, so innocent herein, with so false and scandalous an aspersion."

The siege did not commence in earnest until September, 1643, when Exeter opened its gates to the Prince. Realising that the fall of Plymouth must represent a catastrophe, Colonel Wardlow was sent from Portsmouth in command of a company of Roundheads, with instructions to maintain the defence. At the outset, however, St. Nicholas Island was nearly betrayed by Sir Alexander Carew, whose honesty was suspected by Philip Francis, the Mayor. Taking Richard Evans, the caterer of the island, into his confidence, his Worship induced John Hancock, then a sergeant, Benjamin Fuge, and other stalwarts to watch the movements of their chief. Doubts as to Carew's good faith increased, but the evidence did not justify an immediate interference. Apart from this, Hancock feared that, if Sir

H

Alexander were arrested without proof, the rank and file might join the enemy, "then lying very near, viz., at Mount Edgcombe." Carew was soon detected making nocturnal visits to the mainland, and he accentuated misgivings by refusing to cross to Plymouth to receive his pay and balance his accounts. Confirmed in his suspicions, Francis sent Master Wills and Master Randall, two ministers who had been accustomed to preach on the Island, to urge the sergeants to adopt summary measures. They found to their relief that Hancock and the soldiers had already seized Carew, and were awaiting a strong guard to convey him to Plymouth gaol. Setting out from Sutton Pool with a flotilla of forty boats, well manned and armed, the Mayor made for the Island, received Carew into custody, and promoted Hancock to a captaincy. The Speaker, in thanking Francis, acknowledged the "industry and circumspection" with which Plymouth had been preserved from "the greedy and violent attempts" of its open enemies, and especially "from the secret and mischievous treachery of Sir Alexander Carew, by whose perfidious endeavours to betray his trust your toune in special was in apparent danger to have suffered much injury." So odious was this treachery "unto the women" of Plymouth that they nearly hanged the author on the spot. He was spared this indignity to be sent to the Tower, where his head was severed with the same axe that decapitated Strafford, a distinction he had once jocosely professed to crave.

Gewen and his friends were actively treating with the enemy as Maurice approached Plymouth with a formidable army. After these traitors had been punished, confidence was restored, the defenders rallied more vigorously than ever to the side of the Parliament, and, in the end, "the poor Prince was frustrated in his design." At the outset, however, Maurice hemmed in the town and no provisions entered it for several weeks. An attempt was then made to raise the relief, and the Roundheads, outflanking the enemy at Plympton and Hooe, seized several of the "malignants." Colonel Wardlow made a similar dash upon a heavy guard of Cavalier horse at "Knockers Hole," with an insignificant force of musketeers, and the besiegers fled towards "Roborow" Down. The Roundheads, in their exuberance, continued the pursuit "too farre," and narrowly escaped annihilation.

Fall of Mount Stam-   The pang of suffering was keen when Maurice again surrounded
ford and Sabbath   the town, and there were frequent sorties to restore confidence
Day Fight: 1643.   within. The Prince made Widey his head-quarters, and threw a
powerful force of cavalry and infantry from the Yealm towards Pomphlete. It was the impression in Plymouth that he intended to land at Prince Rock, but the objective was Mount Stamford, about which the Cavaliers threw up mounds. They were dislodged with the utmost difficulty, but neglect or treachery enabled them to recover the entrenchments before even a trumpet had been sounded, a failure of precaution which cost the Round-head captain his life on his flight to the fort. Determined to recover the position, the defenders sallied out, and, despite resistance of horse and foot, regained the advantage. The loss was heavy on both sides, but the Roundheads could ill afford any diminution of their numbers. In other words, the retention of Mount Stamford was already impossible. Making their way by inches, the besiegers planted cannon within reach of the embrasures, and, as their aim was accurate, they dismounted many guns, clogged others with earth, and "performed what the hellish plot of the Gunpowder Treason should have accomplished." Advancing with all their foot and horse, on a concerted signal, the Cavaliers drove the defenders within their breastworks. Although wearied by long and anxious vigils and incessant attacks, they frequently forced their assailants to retreat in disorder, and if they could have procured "indifferent relief from over the watere," they would have persevered. But when the beleaguered captain intimated, by "hanging out a wift," that he was at the

end of his resources, and no response was forthcoming, his only alternative was to make the best terms possible. He had comparatively few men left, his ammunition was nigh spent, and his provisions were exhausted, but he contracted to march out with the honours of war—colours flying, match lighted, bullets in mouth and a demi-culverine cannon. The vanquished were "not anxious" to let the world know by whose treachery or neglect the fort was lost, but they attributed the blame to John Cawse, the Mayor.

Hope sprang eternal in the breasts of the defenders, and the optimism of Plymouth immediately discovered that the reverse was "a wonderful proof of the providence of God." Mount Stamford, it was urged, had been a burden instead of a help, because its defence absorbed so much of the vitality of the town, and the release of its garrison enabled the forts and the island to be turned to practical account. Thus a blow that might have depressed the inhabitants caused their spirits to rise, and they resolved to burn the town rather than capitulate "to the enemys of God and his cause." Every adult accordingly subscribed to "a solemn vow and covenant" to defend Plymouth against the forces "now raised against it," to resist its surrender until the consent of Parliament had been given, and to accept no pardon from the enemy "So help me God." Little realising what was transpiring within, and "accounting all to be their own," the Royalists sent forth a herald to summon the town to surrender "so that you may see our hearty desires for a just peace." It was a conciliatory message that was delivered, guaranteeing pardon and protection from violence and plunder, but there was the usual sting in the tail: "We have now acquitted ourselves on our parts, and let the blood that shall be spilt in obtaining these just demands if denied by you be your guilt." The defenders were in no humour to listen to negociations, and the trumpeter was told that there was no answer for his master.

Supplies now entered the gates without interruption, and Maurice issued a manifesto in which he threatened to visit on the farmers of South Hams, "and all abettors of this horrid rebellion," penal consequences in body and estate. Incensed at the cool contempt with which his menaces were received, the Prince attacked the Roundhead positions, but his battalions were repulsed with heavy losses at Thornhill and Knackersknowle. He next concentrated his forces at Lipson, and the valley scintillated with uniforms and glowed with banners. The presence of the Royalists was viewed with composure by the defenders, until a cry of alarm rang through the town one day in December that the foe were gaining the Laira position. "Two notorious malignants" had corrupted the guards, and with the retreat of the tide, the Cavaliers crept along the bank and surprised the Maudlin Fort. In a trice the besieged hurried to the scene and the earthwork was regained, but persistent

SABRATH-DAY FIGHT IN FREEDOM FIELDS.

(From a Window by J. Fouracre.)

attempts to re-enter the town resulted in the Sabbath Day Fight. Under cover of their ordnance, the attacking force made such deadly work in the open that they again sent forth a trumpeter to offer terms to the town. He was "ordered to depart," and the battle was resumed with so much fury that the Cavaliers fell back upon Lipson. "The town is ours!" they had been shouting. Now, with exclamations of "God with us!", the Round-heads swept all before them like a roaring torrent. At this crisis the trained bands were hurled against the disorganised rabble, the retreat became an utter rout, and the bewildered Royalists floundered into the treacherous foreshore of the river, where their distracted horses plunged in the mud and their riders fell beside them, riddled with shot. The fleet of the Parliament had done little as yet to justify its adhesion, for the ships lay listlessly in the stream, officers and crews surveying the scene and making no attempt to influence the issue. But, when the Cavaliers and their steeds struggled in the mire, without the hope of extrica-tion, the frigates "became honest again," and directed their guns against those who dashed towards Plympton. Crowds of prisoners and much heavy ordnance fell into the hands of the besieged, and the Mayor complacently reported that "the Lord showed himself wonderfully in our deliverance."

Thus cowed, the assailants followed their "usual course" of remaining quiet for a few weeks, and the sentries anxiously paced the drawbridges and the outworks, pausing anon to warm their hands at dim fires, and piercing the gloom by the aid of flickering candles. Then the enemy retrieved something of their disgrace by assaulting "Peny-Corn-Quick." The position, however, was so bombarded in return that their artillery were obliged to evacuate the fort. Faith was again firm until, one dark and stormy night, the Cavaliers attempted the communications between Pennycomequick and Maudlin. Sharply turning the attack, the besieged fell upon them with unexpected vigour, and the slaughter so dis-heartened Maurice that his courage waned faint and his confidence evaporated. He had more than once promised his troops that they should eat their dinner in Plymouth on Christmas Day. When the festival was at hand, he fell back upon Tavistock, and the waits·within sang in a twofold sense their carols of deliverance. Prolonged environment had tested the best qualities of the inhabitants—their courage, self-denial and patience— and they emerged from the ordeal without blemish. There were periods when they were hard pressed, even for ammunition, and, in one critical emergency, there was a solitary charge of powder left. Loaded with this and scrap iron, a cannon was placed in the lane through which the Cavaliers were advancing and a hero volunteered to fire it. Concealing himself in the hedge, until the road teemed with soldiers, he leapt out, applied the match, and scattered death "in so many shapes," that the foe retreated in a panic. The warrior fell dead beside his charge, struck by the shot of a retreating Cavalier, and for generations his deed was perpetuated on the pavement of the Barbican Gate, where there was engraven the representation of a man in the act of firing a cannon. As a rule the townsfolk had been able to obtain their supplies from the agricultural districts, but there was one occasion when the roads were blocked and "the poor people greevously punished" for the want of victuals. Then was wrought a miracle of relief, for the harbour swarmed "with an infinite number of pilchards," and the people dipped out the fish in baskets from the quickened pool. Thus were they not only "refreshed," but a vast harvest was preserved for future consumption. In the patriotism of its "good women," the town was also favoured, and when the fighting was at its fiercest, they carried out solid refreshments to husbands and sweethearts, and "strong waters" with which to inspirit them. More than one of these Amazons lived to exhibit to their children, and children's children, the garments that were rent by the Cavalier bullets in the days of their fearless youth.

Unharassed for the time, the inhabitants repaired the walls, pulled down hedges, built new mounds, and ran up breastworks. Although the siege was suspended, a strict blockade was maintained by Colonel Digby, who held Mount Stamford and controlled the supplies from South Devon, "the richest part of this countrie, whence most of the provisions and victuals do come." Sir Richard Grenville was entrusted with the duty of resuming the siege, and, as he was an uncompromising anti-Puritan, who only saw in the "odious and pernicious" practices of sectaries a cloak for rebellion, the task was most congenial. "Skellam," as the townsfolk hatefully designated Sir Richard, boasted that he would soon enter the town, and although "garrison and Plymouth will not believe him," his tactics were so irritating that the besieged did duty for nights together, and they were worn out with dismal watches during the winter of 1643. To terrify the defenders, Grenville threatened to execute all who fell into his hands. He hanged one of his own nephews who was instructed to deliver a message, and sent back the servant to intimate that this was the fate in store for all rebels. His despatch of a Plymouth attorney was almost more heartless and discreditable, for he hanged the man for having vanquished him in a law suit, rather than for any complicity in the rebellion. "Skellam" cynically met remonstrances by declaring that the lawyer was a "traitor"; but he readily admitted that, as he had played the knave in court, he was content to find "a just occasion for punishing him." These exasperating deeds led to reprisals, and the temper on both sides became morose and revengeful.

With the opening of 1644, there were several exciting "bickerings" at Treniman's or Treliman's Jump and Tamerton; but to their minor successes the Roundheads gave no especial prominence, as their commanders were more desirous to serve their God and country than "gaggle like hens on the laying of every egg"—an insinuation that Grenville was overmuch vaunting of his triumphs. In March, Colonel Gould "was called to Jesus to have a crown set upon his head for his golden activity and indefatigable patience in the defence of the town," and the command of St. Nicholas Island was bestowed on Henry Hatsell, a soldier of such known integrity that, "although envious stomachs may rail against him, yet they cannot draw off the affections of the well-disposed from a high esteem of his approved vigour and fidelity." Providence continued to watch over the destinies of Plymouth, and the presence in the Sound of the powerful Parliamentary fleet emboldened its inhabitants to disregard the heavy shot "liberally spent" which were hurled within the wall. "So far from being affrighted, they slighted them, being hardened." Meanwhile the sense of responsibility of the authorities was not diminished. The town was purged of evil-livers, swearers, and drunkards, and the inhabitants observed with scrupulous care the Lord's Day and the Days of Humiliation, and attended the Sacraments as frequently as possible. So that the resistance was maintained with a devotional fervour that reverse could not shake or privation disturb.

Charles Before Ply-   A demeanour so reposeful upset the calculations of the Cavaliers;
mouth: 1644.   and, irritated at observing that the inhabitants plied their avocations, sustained their religious consistency, and promenaded the heights, Grenville attempted to wheedle those amongst whom he had lived. It was his affection that prompted his overtures—"my anxiety to regaine my lost friends by love rather than to subject them to ruine." Experience of "Skellam," had not enhanced respect for his word, and the Roundheads poured "highest contempt and scorne" on the proposition, so that the world might know in what esteem they held the man who was so notorious for his "apostacy and treachery." Scathingly rebuking his dissimulation, the Mayor and his brethren rejoiced that he was an avowed enemy outside the wall "instead of a pretended friend at home," since they were persuaded that his principles "could not afford cordial endeavours for an honest cause."

Several hundred Royalists next quartered near St. Budeaux, but Colonel Martin's musketeers, skilfully moving under cover, scattered the garrison, and compelled the prisoners to take the covenant. Another body of Roundheads dashed upon Plympton, "a grand quarter of the enemy," and beat them from hedge to hedge. Then, their ammunition giving out, they retreated—"fairly and without the loss of a man." Another body rushed from Prince Rock to Pomphlete, and the Royalist garrison "fled like hares." So that the besieged were "neither idle and successless on land, nor lotterless at sea"; and, with fortune invariably on their side, "you may see how the Lord doth alwaies work for this poor and distressed garnson." These victories were of comparative insignificance and the West faltered with the approach of the King. Plymouth was in sore straits, and its distress so acute that a message was sent to Essex, who was then at Tiverton, to assure

KING CHARLES'S BEDROOM AT COTEHELE.
(After the Drawing by N. Condy.)

him that "the people of these parts" could no longer be safely abandoned to their own resources. Essex was hesitating as to whether he should hasten to Bath and intercept the advance of Charles, or move upon Plymouth and clear the country between Tavistock and that town. The importunities from the port were too loud to be disregarded, and, leaving the King's road open, he marched to Tavistock, and drove the beleaguers across the Tamar.

Having relieved Plymouth, Essex perpetrated the irretrievable blunder of pouring his troops into Cornwall "to clear that county." Charles anticipated this manœuvre, and followed swiftly upon the Roundhead general. He slept one night at Cotehele on the way, and concentrated in the neighbourhood of Boconnoc, within sight of the moor where Ruthven's army met its fate. Conscious that he had walked into a trap, Essex resolved to sell "our lives as dear and as hard as can be." He did not draw upon his imagination for his fears, for he was encircled by three armies, and escape was out of the question

From a design by Fouracre.

KING CHARLES THE FIRST
SUMMONETH THE TOWN OF PLYMOUTH TO SURRENDER.

(From a window in commemoration of the distinguished services rendered to the Plymouth Club by Francis Beer Westlake, as Chairman and Member, 1892-3).

Charles slept in his coach through the night, the park in repose covered with tents, and the outposts alert with the knowledge that the Roundheads were encamped near Lost-withiel. At sunrise the combatants approached each other in undulating masses, but Essex's companies were soon overpowered. For awhile they fought with the courage of despair, but, as the survivors saw their comrades falling thick around them, they broke and scattered—making for the highway and the fishing hamlets, and thence by boats for Plymouth. The Cromwellian fleet was thundering "the rigour of warre" against Mount Edgcumbe when Essex's remnant sailed into the Sound; but the officials were struck with dismay as Charles re-crossed the Tamar, drums beating and flags flying, and encamped at Lipson and flaunting salvoes of artillery. Frenzied appeals were forwarded to the Parliament for the necessary help: "If this town be lost, all the West will be in danger," wrote Warwick, and Essex prayed his chiefs to be careful of Plymouth, "knowing it to be a place of the greatest concernment next to London." When the Royal regiments lined the hedges and threatened the outworks, Lord Robartes apprehended the worst. He was evidently a pessimist, "a sour and surly man," according to the Royalists, but one whom the Roundheads revered for the nobility of his character. The town, as he found it, was in no condition to withstand a formidable attack. Its best troops had left to reinforce the main army, and the soldiers in charge were "low in courage and loud in complaint." Some of the inhabitants, in their weariness of the two years' siege, were "cold and indifferent," the ammunition was scant, and there was a deadness of spirit "which I doubt not indicates a disaffected party within."

Such was the morale of the garrison in September, when Charles commenced the bombardment of the town. In his despair, Robartes despatched what he imagined would be his last warning of the inevitable catastrophe. "This day, upon the return of the trumpets, it is probable that the enemy will storm the works." Spirited enough was the cannonade, but its echoes aroused the wonted sturdiness of the population, and, so far from indicating any disposition to surrender, they playfully applied the epithet of "Vapouring Hill" to the eminence from which the Royal forces breathed smoke and fury every morning. Robartes still trembled, for he knew better than the inhabitants that their resources were nearly spent. "You well understand the importance of this place,",he urged, "and how much better it is to defend than regain." Charles grew impatient of the empty monotony of his attack, and he sent a female messenger with a formal demand for the surrender of the town, assuring the people, on "my royal honour," that the past would be forgiven, and that they should enjoy their accustomed privileges. The woman returned with the reply that Plymouth would resist to the last gasp. Sir Richard Grenville was then entrusted with a similar document, but, "being a fugitive, he received no answer." The result was in the nature of an anti-climax. After further exchange of great and small shot, the King abandoned all hope of securing the surrender of the town, either by fighting or pleading, and he drew off the main body of his troops, to the profound relief of the besieged. General Digby was left in charge of the district, and, attacking Saltash, which the army of the Parliament had for some time occupied, he expelled the garrison and put five hundred men to the sword.

For months the conflict was conducted with contending savageries, and, early in 1645, the forts at Pennycomequick and Maudlin witnessed strenuous encounters. The latter was at length carried, but the Roundhead commander loaded a cannon with case shot, and the ground was covered with the mangled remains of the trespassers. The battle became general, and Grenville, entering the town at North Hill, a hand-to-hand fight ensued with pike and butt end. The Cavaliers yielded before the ever increasing multitude of armed inhabitants; they were hurled down the hill at Mutley, and chased towards Lipson, leaving 600 killed and wounded on the ground, and as many prisoners in the hands of the townsfolk. After this disaster, the "blockeering" of Plymouth was entrusted to Berkeley, and the Royalist hopes rode buoyantly, until, in another fit of impatience, Digby attempted to bribe Colonel Ker. "On my honour and the faith of a gentleman, I promise you £10,000 and the command of a regiment if you will render the very eminent service of delivering up Plymouth to your native King and country." The overture was repudiated as "a temptation from hell and worthy of all detestation." Thus to the end the town remained true to the cause of the Parliament. It fared not well with Charles elsewhere, the Ironsides were victorious at Naseby, the Cavaliers capitulated at Truro in March, and "the King has now no force in the West." The monarch was a hunted fugitive whilst the flag of Plymouth yet waved from the tower of the Castle; her people unbroken, unbent and incorruptible when the disaster that overthrew the dynasty caused their assailants to melt in the mist of "Vapouring Hill."

CHAPTER V.—FROM COMMONWEALTH TO RESTORATION.

First Dutch War: The condition of Plymouth was now "very sad;" distress and
Battles off Plymouth: suffering were poignant, the town swarmed with destitute soldiers
1650-1656.   and sailors, the meanest necessaries commanded prohibitive rates,
and civil discord was aggravated by mutinous uprisings.   Cromwell and his colleagues
professed no little concern when the state of affairs was represented, and promised to
forward "a bountiful and speedy supply" of food and clothing.   But the relief was forthcoming in such tardy instalments that the seamen abandoned the port, and in genuine
alarm the Protector enjoined "the necessity of all our forces in the west-country remaining
there, for though there is no enemye in the field in these parts now, yet we know that it is
only the presence of our forces that prevent it.   If our troops are called away the party
will not only be forthcoming, but Plymouth and other places will soon be in the enemye's
power."   The retort assumed the inevitable hint that men would not famish without the
prospect of relief, and Colonel Weldon, the governor of the garrison, thereupon received
another temporising epistle from Cromwell: "As soon as we have again acquainted the
House with their condition, we may be able to give your soldiers forthwith such means of
subsistence that they will be content to continue and stop there."   Two grants—one of
£10,000 and a second of £6,000—were forwarded, the stress of the crisis was relaxed,
and the angry voice of the billeters was stilled.

The last word was not spoken with the execution of Charles.   Prince Rupert took to
the water with several frigates, and the Scilly Islands, strong in their isolation, withstood all
importunities to surrender.   Blake was given a roving commission to hunt the Royalists
from the Channel, and, assembling his fleet at Plymouth, and draining every village of its
able-bodied, he set out to "sink, burn, or destroy" the Stuart squadron.   Every precaution
for the safety of Plymouth was adopted until Scilly came to terms.   There were no serious
grounds for doubting the fidelity of the Corporation to the new regime, for the arms of the
Commonwealth were set up in the Guildhall, and every reference to Royalty was eliminated
from the seal.   It was the tendencies of the Cornish that were feared, and the continued
depletion of seamen.   "Exercise the most special care of the town, as there is a dangerous
design against it."   The precise nature of the conspiracy did not transpire, but the commands of the Secretary of State were peremptory.   "You are therefore to order that no
more sailors or others shall be shipped aboard" the traders who were daily leaving the
port.   It is possible that the attitude of the Mayor towards the prisoners generated some
misgiving.   The town resented the burden of their maintenance, and his worship first
released several Cavaliers and then asked leave to set them at liberty.   When the Protector
heard of this unconditional amnesty he soundly rated the authorities.   The least the
Mayor could have done was to hold these gentlemen as hostages for the "better usage of
ours"; and, severely using the lash, his secretary added: "The Commonwealth has
therefore been done great disservice."   Unmoved by the rebuke, his worship serenely
enquired how the prisoners were to be maintained; and, duly impressed, Cromwell and
the Council decided that, out of the yield of cargoes captured within the jurisdiction of
the port, the Commonalty might henceforth deduct eightpence per day for each man.

With the fall of Scilly disappeared the last abiding place of the Stuarts, and Cromwell
sought to recover the commercial ground of which the Dutch had taken possession.   For

some time their vessels had been allowed to enter English ports with goods gathered from all parts of the world, but the Navigation Act soon rendered it impossible for any foreign trader to introduce products which it had not brought from its own country. This abrogation of the open-door doctrine was little to the liking of the Dutch, who saw in the expedient an attack on their profitable monopoly, and they prepared a fleet to protect their traders from interference on the open ocean. This was the more necessary, as the disposition of the west country ports was to give revengeful effect to the new legislation. There was no eagerness to proceed to hostilities so far as either of the Republics was concerned; but the exchanges between the opposing sailors were in disregard of international etiquette, and the competing governments were busily engaged in reproving and repressing rival manifestations. In March, 1652, Vice-Admiral Evertsen was admonished to refrain from acts and speeches tending to excite contempt and disdain for the English; and, by way of reply, he assured the States-General that he had enjoined increased courtesy, and insisted upon more careful abstinence from offence than hitherto. The English, on the contrary, were thirsting for a cause of difference. Evertsen hauled his ship ashore at Falmouth, for the purpose of refitting her, and upon his accidentally grazing a local trader, the offended captain discharged a fusillade of abusive words and threats. A few weeks later another Dutch captain cleaned his ship in the same port; and, as he left, it was twice fired at from the fort. On sending his launch ashore to enquire the cause of this outrage he was told that he had refrained from saluting; and, when he replied that he had dipped his flag, the complaint was made that he had not sufficiently lowered his topsails. In some instances the Dutch sailors were tortured into confessing that they were seconding the efforts of the French privateers, then preying upon English commerce; so that the popular readiness for an outbreak was more ripe than the design of either Commonwealth.

As soon as the Dutch increased their fleet to safeguard their commerce, friendly amenities were at an end. Cromwell responded with the institution of a national navy, and the Dutch construed the retort into an early intent to wage war. "As they brew so shall they bake" was the sentiment on each side. The ships were more easily constructed than manned, and press gangs accordingly scoured the county of Devon. Their operations were resisted in several ports, but the Council of the State peremptorily ordered the local justices "to impress and cause to be impressed,' the number of 300 sailors, and the same to be sent to Plymouth, where they shall be received on board and entered into the States' pay." Constables, tithing men and others were directed to assist in carrying out the instructions; and, if they failed, the commanders of the various ships were empowered to seize them as substitutes. This dread alternative was tempered by the payment of fees to officials who re-arrested good hands that made their escape from the various captains. As these raw levies flowed into Plymouth, the excesses of the military gave rise to widespread discontent. Their duty was difficult, for, at dusk, the impressed men ran from the dwellings in which they were confined, and, candle in hand, the sentinels spent the dark hours of the night in searching suspected outhouses. Recurring turbulence and excitement kept the inhabitants in feverish fears, mutinies in the streets were of common occurrence, mutterings of the drums mustered the guards and musketeers, and refractory sailors were flogged in public. Doubt as to the capacity of the port to resist an invasion increased, and was repeatedly expressed: "Plymouth being a town of consequence we again put you in mind that we have an early return of the state the place is in." By way of answer, the defences were strengthened, and Colonel Popham's Militia were embodied. The victualling of the ships made tardy progress however, and, as "beef, pork and poor jack" could not be obtained in sufficient quantities, supplies were despatched from

London. One merchant, Anthony Praunce, was arrested for debt as he was on the eve of sailing, but the emergency was so acute that the Commonwealth set aside the legal obstacles.

It was on the western coast, where the Dutch enforced the closest precautions against the surprise of their merchantmen, that the earliest interchanges occurred. A young trumpeter's mate of the Triumph, named Heaton, whose name was destined to be prominent in the history of Plymouth, behaved "so wisely and stout" in one of these fights that he was appointed to the command of the Sapphire. He secured so many prizes that "on a festival day" he hung her yards, stays, backstays and shrouds with Dutch, French, Spanish and Burgundian colours and pendants, "variously intermixed with the English colours and pendants spread"; and in this way made "a beautiful show that raised the courage of all who belonged to her." After thus parading his prowess, Heaton was tallowing the Sapphire in Catwater—to prevent boarding parties from securing too sure a grip—when he was ordered to remove her with all promptitude to another station. The vessel was without ballast, and her rotten mainmast had just been removed. To cap the difficulty, one-third of the crew were enjoying a brief respite with their wives and families on shore. Every officer and sailor responded to Heaton's summons; and "so eager and regular" was his command, and so proud every man in its performance, that, by changing the watches every two hours, "himself being always on deck," he received the necessary ballast, carriages, guns, victuals and cables; set his new mainmast, shrouds and rattles; rigged his yards to the masts and his anchors to the bow—and in two days was standing out to sea. "During those 48 hours you could not have told whether the captain was on board unless you had known him." Patriotic vigour was similarly evidenced by Captain Anthony Young in May, 1652. He was in command of the "Westguard," when he came across a dozen Hollanders off the Start. Sending his master aboard the admiral's ship, he counselled him to haul down his ensign. The latter replied that he would lose his head if he surrendered, and retorted that Young had better come aboard and strike the flag himself. Broadsides and volleys ensued; and then the enemy, having had "a bellyful of it . . . did strike, which makes me conceive that he had enough of it." The Dutch captain had more pluck than his vice-admiral, for he refused to haul down the flag; and the rear-admiral apologised for this conduct by asserting that his subordinate must be drunk! There was only one way of settling this point of authority. Young "handsomely banged" away again until both officers gave up their swords and "fawned like spaniels." They commemorated their capitulation with a drinking bout at Plymouth.

Blake and Van Tromp were watching each other in the Downs, when the latter's polite salute caused the former to open fire. It was a useful misunderstanding on the part of Blake, and conceived at the auspicious moment. After five hours' cannonading at close quarters, Van Tromp withdrew in disorder, and Blake enflamed his countrymen by the story of his success. The next meeting was not so encouraging. Van Tromp sailed from Texel with a hundred ships, and nearly wiped out Ayscue under the Dover Cliffs. In August, whilst Blake was giving his personal attention to Van Tromp, Ayscue fell in with De Ruyter off Plymouth harbour. There was little difference in the strength of the fleets, each was composite in character, and several Indiamen were brought into play. Fierce and devastating was the fire; sullen and stubborn the conflict; and, in the end, the deck of every vessel was strewn with dead and dying, and the sea presented a vista of shreds and patches. Both admirals claimed the victory, but neither had much to boast of. The English ships were so crippled that Ayscue took refuge under the Plymouth forts, and De Ruyter's were too battered to pursue them. The wounded were landed by hundreds, and as the inhabitants refused to provide beds, General Brown converted the

Castle into a hospital. Contiguous dwelling-houses were also seized, and wretched men suffering the torments of gangrened wounds, were dragged to attics, where a lingering fate awaited them. The sound in limb indulged in riot and pillage ; and, for want of a better specific, the Mayor and his brethren dispensed liquor as the one expedient for " appeasinge of the men in a mutinie." The municipal accounts testify that this was the fashion in which the authorities held the candle to the devil.

About the next battle there was less room for controversy. The outward bound Dutch commerce was being convoyed off the port when Ayscue dashed out of Plymouth in the Rainbow, and with his refreshed and refitted fleet engaged and defeated the enemy. As the Hollanders had constructed a new and stronger class of ship, the prizes were immediately available for service in the English Navy. Thus reinforced, Ayscue sailed to join Blake, and off the Kentish Knock helped to administer the most disastrous discomfiture the enemy's arms had yet suffered. Along the coast, and away to the Lizard, the frigates stretched to signal the coming of foreigners, and brushes were thus frequent : not only with the Dutch, but with the French, who were no less eager to impair the English prestige. In October, 1654, Captain Heaton rejoiced the hearts of Plymouth by the welcome cry of prize-money : the one stimulant that answered when all others failed. Mooring his captures in Catwater, he fell on his knees, and wrote : " I thank God in His mercy that not only has He delivered me from the French fleet, who were men-of-war as well as merchantmen, but that He has given me a happy and financial victory for the Commonwealth." This was well said, for Cromwell required victories that brought funds as well as honour. Another decisive encounter covered the same officer with congratulations in August, 1655. The enemy did not appreciate the numerical inferiority of the English, and being dealt with in detail, suffered defeat. As each ship struck her flag, the crew were stowed below, and the prisoners soon surpassed in numbers their wily conquerors. On entering the Sound, they were called up to make the various ships fast, and when they saw that they had been entrapped by a small force, " they were ready to tear their hair to see their strength and our weakness—I had so few men to spare."

Plymouth During the   Prisoners of war were confined in the Castle, and numbers of
Commonwealth.   sympathisers with the Stuarts were herded in its loathsome dungeons in 1655. Existence in the now decaying fortress was intolerable. The chambers reeked with the odours of overcrowding and decomposition, the light only chanced through the chinks of the mouldering masonry, and wind and rain penetrated so freely that the inmates were "cold and wet by day and night." Death rather than durance, rheumatism, fever and kindred horrors rendered the captives morose and desperate ; and, during a prolonged hurricane, forty of them burrowed through the walls of one of the towers, and clinging to the clustering ivy, descended unheard and undiscerned by the sentinel. Huddled beneath the shadow of a friendly porch, the wretched men knew not where to turn ; and in ignorance of the bearings of the neighbourhood, they dispersed in various directions, some striking out for Dartmoor and others making towards Plympton. A few slunk into the courts and alleys and kindled sympathy by the promise of rewards. Lanes and fields, farms and outhouses, hamlets and villages were scoured by the soldiery, but the refugees travelled "so fiercely," with the crack of the musket at their heels, that they bounded over hedges and waded across rivers in their frenzy. Some dropped " dead or nearly so " from sheer exhaustion and were picked up near Plympton. Of the remainder, a few made good their escape, and others perished in the rivers. Captain Hatsell, the custodian of the Castle, was intensely chagrined at this outbreak ; and, as there were large numbers of " these wild Irish " remaining in the town, he asked that he might transfer them to the

merchant ships. "I do not know what to do with them," he said. Nor did the captains of these vessels, for with their shrill Celtic tongues and dishevelled hair, the captives filled the ordinary seamen with dread. "They should be shipped to the West Indies," urged Hatsell, in despair; "there they might be made hewers of stone and drawers of water." It was a suggestive recommendation, but there is no evidence that it was acted upon. A subsequent attempt to escape from the Castle was less successful, although the watch was small and the temptation hard to resist. One "dark and stormy night," some months after the previous escapade, Captain Jordain organised the Biscayan prisoners. They removed some of the masonry, crept by the ivy to the ground, and were moving noiselessly and with bare feet, in order to avoid the guard, when one of them stumbled and aroused a sleeping sentinel at the gate. The firing of the muskets brought forth the other custodians, the refugees held their hands aloft in token of surrender, and were restored to their cells heavily chained. "I have caused," the gaoler reported, "stronger irons to be forged whereby the more unruly may be hampered."

As the national difficulty was the want of men to wage the war, every effort was made to induce lads to migrate to the seaside; drinking propensities were discouraged as responsible for sterility; and the prevailing tendency to celibacy in Plymouth was checked by conferring the freedom of the borough on "unfree Protestants," who married the daughters of freemen. The bankruptcy laws were also suspended, so that the muscular might not be imprisoned when they could be more usefully employed in fighting. A charming discourse, unearthed by Professor Gardiner, between an English sea captain and a Dutch skipper, who exchanged confidences "over a bottle and a pipe" in Plymouth, illumines the characteristics of the town at the period. Whilst the inland centres decayed, Plymouth and other ports flourished by "their sea conduct and courage." The more seamen they bred the greater prosperity attended them, "by getting food out of the ocean and work for the poor." "The carriage" of the men was "joyful" in the battlefield, and even condemned criminals showed "no fear of death" on the gallows. The Dutch skipper sententiously attributed the English naval successes to the fact that, whilst the States-General put "gentlemen creatures" in command of their frigates, the Commonwealth promoted seamen to the supreme charge. Of these democratic Admirals, Blake was the most conspicuous example and he waved the English banner over every Spanish and French possession.

Recalled to England in August, 1657, he was seized with illness, and his life was ebbing away when the hills of Dartmoor rose to view. Plymouth, all unconscious of his condition, was belching its welcomes from the forts, and church bells pealed across the waters. Clinging to life the expiring warrior begged to be carried on shore. But the desire could not be gratified, and Blake breathed his last, "to the great loss of the State and of the nation," before the vessel had anchored in Cawsand Bay. The passing of the warrior was most impressive. Upon his heart reposed the little jewel with which Cromwell had decorated him, and around him were gathered his most faithful colleagues in many a stubborn fight. "He was," reported Captain Hatsell, "very desirous to be ashore, and, if God saw it good, to add some days to his life for the settling of his estate. But his course was finished, and his memorial shall be blessed. As he lived, so he continued to the death—faithful. The Lord grant that a supply of his great loss may be made up for the good of his poor people." To quote Henry Newbold's beautiful lines:

> So he was silently praying, till now, when his strength was ebbing faster,
>   The Lizard lay before him faintly blue;
> Now on the gleaming horizon the white cliffs laughed along the coast-line,
>   And now the forelands took the shapes they knew.

There lay the Sound and the Island with green leaves down beside the water,
  The town, the Hoe, the masts, with sunset fired—
Dreams! ay, dreams of the dead! for the great heart faltered on the threshold ;
  And darkness took the land his soul desired.

"I suppose," wrote Captain Hatsell, "that he will have a very honourable interment, befitting a person of his worth, who, indeed, setting some human frailties aside, from which the best of men are not free, may be ranked with the best that have gone before." At Plymouth the body was embalmed, pending the receipt of definite instructions. "His bowells were buried here by the Mayor's seat door," and the frame, enclosed within a shell, was conveyed in state to London, the frigates flying their flags at half-mast.

During the Civil Wars the local authorities had exercised powers which were not embodied in the original charters, marrying by civil contract, and paying their representatives in Parliament. After enjoying these privileges, the aldermen and freemen wanted to continue in their own course. The more masterful claimed a share of the general plunder, and the Mayor and his brethren were as prone as others to "undue practises to defraud the Excise and the Commonwealth." Extremely unpleasant was the position of the collectors, as they could not hope for convictions when members of the Commonalty reaped a rich harvest themselves, or connived at the malpractices of their relatives by adopting quaint municipal devices for silencing the emissaries of the Revenue. When the duty was demanded, the claim was resisted as extortionate, blows followed words, and, as the collectors were always the aggressors, the Mayor confined them in the cells until the goods had been disposed of. "These affronts and abuses" provoked indignant remonstrances, but his worship was invariably unmoved and immovable. A cargo of pipe staves was brought into the Barbican, and the offending Councillor—one Peter—on being asked to pay the duty, was so outraged by the indignity offered to his office and his person that he threatened to throw the official from his door. Formal application was made that Peter should "be brought up and punished as a stubborn knave, and thus strike terror into such malignant fellows ;" but there are no depositions with which to point the moral and supply the sequel. More successful supervision was exercised when Captain Stokes reached the port with a cargo of treasure taken from the Dutch, and fit guards escorted the chests of gold from Plymouth to London, so that they should be "neither violated nor embezzled." The official estimate of local honour did not err on the side of implicit confidence.

There were "rogues" afloat as well as on shore. A new pirate chief arose in the person of Captain Beach ; and, as the adventurer found a reliable ally in Captain Ensem, the traders would not stir out of Catwater without a convoy, and commercial operations were paralysed. At length the pair were laid by the heels and carried to Exeter, where the one was as submissive as the other was violent. Ensem, indeed, was "such a notorious fellow that no one could hold him," and he was manacled over the arms and legs. Beach was wise in his generation, and his behaviour so won the authorities that they allowed his wife to console him in his solitude. The lady rewarded this indulgence by smuggling a suit of sober black and a stately periwig into the gaol ; and, discarding his histrionic guise as a buccaneer for these unsuspecting habiliments, Beach walked out unchallenged from his enforced retreat. Rejoining his merry associates at Plymouth, he embarked on other expeditions, and increased his notoriety and resources whilst his confederate miserably languished. His career, however, suffered another pathetic interruption. He was visited again with confinement, and this time with chains ; and, to complete the indignity, was denied the condolences of his wife.

Drunkenness was the all-pervading local vice. There was a free sale of beer, wine and "strong waters" in the town; the passion for tobacco was scarcely less irresistible than its companion; and workmen grew so "deboish," especially on Sundays, that they would neither agree to "labour on shore nor sail upon the seas." Of the liquor supplied, Captain Hatsell reported to the Commonwealth in language of scathing condemnation. "The abominable strong drink brewed in this town is of more prejudice to the State and the borough than the heads of all the brewers and ale-house keepers are worth." As an instance of its maddening effect, it was mentioned that two Dutchmen, "deep in liquor," were strolling towards their ship in Sutton Pool, when a band of apprentices who were at their sports "outside the Friary Gate" saucily shouted "Butter Boxes." The epithet provoked an outbreak of hostilities on the spot. The Dutchmen drew knives, and the apprentices brandished staves; and, in the struggle, one of the lads was stabbed to death. "This strong drink is supplied at from 26s. to 27s. a hogshead. It is stronger than sack, and when a sailor has drunk half a bowl it makes him out of his wits. I want a letter," continued Captain Hatsell, "to be sent the Mayor and the magistrates concerning this abominable strong liquor brewed here. The Mayor and his brethren protest that they cannot hinder the brewers, fencing with us most stoutly. If it were not against the law," he added, with righteous heat, "I would have all the brewers pressed and sent in the Great Charity"—a vessel which was unable to leave Catwater for want of sailors. "It would be no sin against God, for by such means is His name profaned, His creatures abused, and much evil committed here." The strangest medley of sanctimonious protest and sleek assumption was revealed at a court-martial held in the Sound on Lieutenant Henry Barrow, of the Gift. It was alleged that he landed at Plymouth without leave, returned on board hopelessly drunk, behaved alike brutally and boisterously, and preached sedition against captain and Commonwealth. Barrow's defence consisted of canting retaliations

SPARKE'S GATE, AT FRIARY.

against Dickinson, the commander, for profanely causing the trumpets to be sounded on the Sabbath Day, discharging forty pieces of cannon on the same occasion, and giving utterance in his cabin to the roystering sentiment: "I shall drink and be merry!"

Irreconcilable as were the relations between the Presbyterian and the Episcopalian sections of the Church, they united in hatred of the Quakers, whose idiosyncrasies were too uncanny to be tolerated by either Republican or Royalist. When the pioneers of the new faith first arrived, the district was oppressed by the direst omens. Clouds of ravens darkened and agitated the air, and the witches mournfully croaked of coming disasters. "Some of the oldest people saith that, for some several years past, when there was a great plague, that they hath always seen the like. So that it doth much trouble them for fearing the like plague may fall upon them, which God forbid." Perplexed by symptoms so weird, the people were indisposed to humour the prophets of the early coming of the Lord, and visited them with every mark of obloquy. The authorities cast them in prison when they attempted religious disputations, and flogged them at the cart's tail if their indignation got the better of their judgment in places of public worship. In May, 1655, a few of the missionaries dawned upon the outskirts of the town, and "made discovery of new lights" to a gaping crowd. If they awed and impressed the more susceptible, they moved the orthodox to anger and abuse, and the Mayor issued warrants for their arrest, with a hint that they might fly. These proposals the Quakers received with supreme calm, and, advancing towards the Court-house, entered the hall with their hats on and saluted his worship with the enquiry: "What wilt thou have of us?" This quaint challenge "much amused" the onlookers; but, after arguments and threats had been bandied, two of the visitors promised amendment. As the "third stood stiff in his folly," he was committed to prison, where "he neither considered God by prayers, craved a blessing on what he received, nor even returned thanks." The racalcitrant was joined by converts as "stiff" as himself. "Our quiet country folk," Captain Hatsell affectedly explained, "judge them to be men of strange humour, but the more I behold the workings of Satan in this manner the more I acknowledge God's goodness." Imprisonment and torture induced no regretful recantations, the apostles assembled in private, and not even the invasion of their meetings, or the imprisonment of their leaders, dissuaded them from their propaganda. "A sickly maid," on emerging from a forbidden service, was cast into a cell, left for nights without straw to lie upon, and publicly whipped. Thus were harrased the Plymouth Quakers in their early struggle for civil and religious liberty.

The "Happy Restauration": 1661. The Commonwealth crumbled, and Plymouth counted the cost of another pronouncement. Anticipation of this faltering was forthcoming in 1659, when Booth and other "rebells and traytors" were outlawed. A copy of the manifesto was sent to the Constable of Plymouth, and delivered to him on a Sunday; and, in doubt as to his course, he went to the church in which the Mayor was at prayers. Whisperings were exchanged, and his worship told the officer that, as the declaration was addressed to him, he must perform his duty. This vacillation involved the Mayor in the penalty he desired to avoid, and he was arrested for remaining on his knees instead of promulgating the decree. It would have fared ill with Mr. Northcote if the leading Republicans in Devon had not certified that he was "a goodly honest man and an old Puritan." Soreness being thus mitigated, he was restored to his office, and skilfully temporised in very trying circumstances. Plymouth watched with feverish doubts the futile efforts of Lambert to avert the Restoration; and, when the tide turned, joined in acclaiming the Stuarts. Henry Woollcombe insists that the inhabitants were tired of the cant and hypocrisy of the Puritans, both in civil and religious concerns, and that their only quarrel was with the unconstitutional arrogance of Charles I. This view gracefully extenuates Plymouth's surrender to the inevitable, and its welcome of "the happy restauration" was followed by "gratious pardons" wherever the offenders prostrated their persons with becoming alacrity. When Lambert's army in the North had "mouldered away," to quote the language of the Plymouth Black Book, the path was prepared "for the coming of our gracious sovereign Charles II," and then, "by God's grace and merçye and to the greate joye of the nation," the King recovered "his crowne and dignities." How could Plymouth resist the recall? The monarch was "proclaimed in this towne with greate triumph, the cunditts running two days with wyne, and shortly after a curious gift of rare plate was presented to his Majesty by this Corporation." For the two "royal pieces of gold" thus voted "the summe of foure hundred pounds" was paid to Aldermen

Vyner, of London, and Sir William Morice and Samuel Trelawney were sent to Court to attest thus substantially the desire of the burgesses to be spared the price of independence.

Peace between England and Spain was formally declared in Plymouth; and the Ambassador who brought the ratification from Madrid was banquetted at the town's expense. Everything was done to drug the lurking resentment of the King, and Northcote, among others, "laid on and accepted," in the public presence, the proffered forgiveness. Charles was thus spared the necessity of multiplying the victims of the cell and the block. Several, however, had too aggressively identified their fortunes with the Commonwealth, and General Lambert, "that old rebel"—the contempt is his crown—was condemned to spend his declining days in the Island of St. Nicholas, and Mr. Lilburne, one of the judges, was sent to the same exile. A more drastic end was reserved for John Alward, whose fate is grimly explained in the patent despatched to the Plymouth authorities :—" Devon : Peter Prideaux, Baronet, Sheriff of the County of Devon aforesaid, to Roger Andrews, junr., John Andrews, and George Good, and to every and either

of you greeting; whereas, John Alward, late of Stokenhead, within this county, hath, at the Assizes and General Gaol delivery held for this County of Devon, the 13th March instant, been convicted of high treason and sentence of law hath been accordingly pronounced against him, and execution of the said sentence hath been performed by me accordingly and likewise his quarters have been disposed of according to the order of the Judge, J. Terrill, that did pronounce the said sentence against the said Alward. And whereas I have order and direction likewise to cause his head to be put and set up at the most publique and convenient place within the town of Plymouth. Therefore these are in his Majesty's name to require you and every and either of you that you forthwith cause the head of the said John Alward to be put upon a spike of iron fixed to a strong pole and that you cause it to be put and strongly fixed upon the highest and most visible place of the Guildhall at Plymouth aforesaid. And all officers and souldiers are hereby required to be aiding and assisting you in the doing thereof, and hereof fail not at your perill. Given under my seal of office the 24th day of March in the yeare of our Lord 1661."

Alward's head accordingly frowned upon the authors of the barbarous retaliations which caused so many Puritans to shrink from the consequences. The friends of the Protectorate having been displaced, the Council craved the power of levying dues, and assured the King

I

they would always be ready "with our lives and fortunes to serve your Majesty." To complete the contrast, the reconstituted Commonalty vowed that "we doe abominate and detest the rebellious and factious proceedings of the former Corporation," and professed their readiness to "discharge our duty to your most sacred Majesty as you in your great wisdom shall see fitt." This was the natural voice of Episcopalian, and not Puritan Plymouth; but it was for the town that the memorial professed to speak. Meanwhile, Charles's more especial care was the compensation of the faithful. Samuel Trelawney was one of the more importunate, and with good reason, for his fine old father, Robert, was the lealest of all the local Cavaliers. As member for Plymouth, he maintained with such courage the doctrine of the royal prerogative that he was expelled from the House; he lent "The Martyr" £2,000 worth of plate on the eve of the Revolution, and despatched ships to Cornwall with supplies; his mansion at Ham was partly burnt; he was twice sent to Winchester Prison; and his estate was appropriated by the Long Parliament. Such was the story of ruin that his destitute son recited in his memorial for redress; but the young monarch could only recommend the Corporation to appoint "Samuel Trelawney, fitly qualified, as Town Clerk of Plymouth." As there was no vacancy, Charles again confirmed this behest, "notwithstanding any letters that may have been obtained from me to the contrary, having expressly forbidden any other nomination to the same place." Eventually a more lucrative appointment was found for the dispossessed Cavalier, and Thomas Preston, "who has suffered much for loyalty and conformity," and who was the first before the Restoration "to crave the Divine blessing on his Majesty's person in the presence of a large auditory at Plymouth," also obtained preferment. Joseph Glanville, most charming of authors and the son of a local merchant, was appointed chaplain-in-ordinary to the King on making his submission.

The Ejeoted   The social habit of Plymouth grew more austere and forbidding,
Ministers: 1861-1867. and the religious exercises which absorbed the inhabitants were utilised for revolutionary intercourse. The persecution to which the Quakers had been subjected in the declining days of the Commonwealth was extended to the Church Puritans; and Baptists, Brownists and other sectaries were drawn more closely in sympathy. Bernard Gomme, the engineer who prepared the plans for the Citadel, was sorely bored by his experiences of "this wilderness town, almost out of the world, where the Presbyterian is in his most Puritanical seat, and "—thus the genus—"there is neither company nor woman fit for a gentleman to pass his time with." It was this sympathetic soul who induced the Merry Monarch to remonstrate with the Mayor and magistrates touching "the increase of unlawful meetings, under the pretence of religious worship, contrary to the law, and in affront of the Government." Orders were despatched to break up and disperse such meetings as soon as they were formed, and to proceed against the ringleaders, "as much danger is to be apprehended from such within any of the garrisons and places of strength." This interference with freedom of worship, aggravated by limitations of civil liberty, generated universal protest. At the Archdeacon's Court, held at Plympton in 1663, the churchwardens of St. Andrew's presented the names of several Anabaptists and Quakers, whose children were not christened, and who "have separated themselves from church and ordinances." "The people will not believe in the King's goodness, and spread seducing pamphlets everywhere." George Hughes, vicar of St. Andrew's, whose mildness of aspect was increased by his clean-shaven face, nevertheless most resolutely adhered to Presbyterian methods, and the old sea captains declared that "the Common Prayer shall not come into Mr. Hughes's Church." The same feeling existed along the coast, and Hughes was deprived of his living and consigned to St. Nicholas Island. He was then 60 years of

age, and confinement in a damp dungeon so impaired his health that he was offered his freedom on furnishing heavy securities not to live within twenty miles of Plymouth. He retired to Kingsbridge, and there, in spite of infirmities and weakness, studied hard and encouraged his friends to remain steadfast in the faith. "The cross is the way of the crown," he told them. "If we suffer with Christ, we shall rise with him. This dead cause of Reformation for which we suffer shall rise again and revive, and salvation shall come to the churches. I die, but you shall live to see freedom. The very means these men take to suppress and destroy it shall most effectively promote it." The mantle of George Hughes fell upon his son, Obadiah, his verisimilitude in personal appearance ; grave, gentle, but inflexible. He was ejected from College at Oxford as he was about to take his degree, and was seized and imprisoned on reaching Plymouth. After his release he was privately ordained to the Nonconformist ministry with several of his colleagues.

Although it has been suggested that George Hughes paid clandestine visits to Plymouth and held unauthorised services, the organisation of avowed Dissent in the town is accredited to Nicholas Sherwill, M.A., a native whose ancestors were people of means and influence. Sherwill ministered at " The Old Marshall's " in Southside Street—and conducted irregular services there, to the risk of all concerned. The various "conventicles" were watched by the soldiery, the lowest type of spies followed the suspects, and the enrolled were admitted by passwords through obscure entrances. "When any of the said persons came to the dore there was one that stood by the said dore and opened itt to lett them in, and as soon as they were gott in the dore was presently shut." Craning their necks, the soldiers listened intently, and, as soon as the praying commenced, they rushed to the nearest magistrate. Their own movements being as closely watched, the signal was given for the worshippers to disperse. From house to house they migrated, changing their hours to upset the plans of the authorities, but the prosecutions were frequent and the sufferings of the leaders poignant. In October, 1665, Mr. Sherwill was bidden by an officer of the garrison to repair to a tavern to speak with the Governor, and. as soon as he entered, he was surrounded by soldiers and taken to the Townhall, where he was detained for three months.

Previous to the Act of Uniformity the Rev. Thomas Martyn, brother-in-law of George Hughes, was lecturer at St. Andrew's Church. He also was apprehended, and his wife and children suffered "much grief and his estate much loss." Martyn petitioned for his removal from the island upon the outbreak of an epidemic, and he was restored to freedom on the same conditions as Hughes. The Rev. Nathaniel Jacob, another of the Ejected Ministers, held the vicarage of Ugborough until he was silenced. When he could no longer instruct his converts in public, he taught them in private, and rode once a fortnight to Plymouth to preach to " Mr. Thomas Martyn's people." Mr. Jacob took charge of the congregation after his friend's death, and was sent to Exeter Gaol for six months. Thomas Ford, of Brixton, was cited for assailing the "superstitious observances then gaining ground under the patronage of Laud." After his imprisonment, he was selected by the Plymouth magistrates as their preacher, but they were forbidden to complete the appointment, and Ford was driven from the town. John Quicke, the most famous divine of the district, was another of the persecuted, and he was expelled from his living and imprisoned at Plymouth.

The Baptists had suffered no molestation under the Commonwealth, and their ministrations were prosperous. Some two hundred of them regularly worshipped in a small building near the Pig Market until symptoms of disquiet disturbed their sanctuary. Then its precincts were invaded, and fifty members of the congregation were arrested for refusing to subscribe to the oath of allegiance. Abraham Cheare, a man of humble birth who was elected pastor of the Plymouth Baptists, was imprisoned for his unbending Nonconformity. He was restored to freedom after three years, through the intervention of his sister, and her importunities induced him to revisit Plymouth. The local loyalists were so much incensed when they saw him at liberty in the town, that they ordered his re-arrest and threw him in a dungeon for another month. Here he wrote some verses, descriptive of his sufferings and "displaying the fortitude and resignation of his mind," and affixed them to the wall of his cell:

> Nigh four years since, sent out from hence
>   To Exon gaol was I ;
> But special grace, in three months space,
>   Wrought out my liberty.

> Till Bartholomew, in sixty-two,
>   That freedom did remain :
> When, without bail, to Exon gaol
>   I hurried was again.

> Where having lain as do the slain,
>   'Mong dead men wholly free,
> Full three years space, my native place
>   By leave I come to see.

> And thought not then I here again
>   A month's restraint should find ;
> Since to my den, cast out from men,
>   I'm during life designed.

> But since my lines the Lord assigns,
>   In such a lot to be,
> I kiss the rod, confess my God
>   Deals faithfully with me.

> My charged crime, in his due time,
>   He fully will decide,
> And until then, forgiving men,
>   In peace with him I bide.

Banished to St. Nicholas Island, where he was watched by military guards, Cheare was seized by a violent sickness, the outcome of the surrounding filth and neglect. On his unexpected recovery, "this poor prisoner of hope, whose life, upon all occasions, hath been marvellously preserved, and delivered with a great salvation from the pit of corruption," composed an affecting poem of gratitude "to his truly eternal Majesty, the High and Mighty Potentate, King of Kings, Prince of Life and Peace, Heir of all Things, Head Over All to the Church." During this illness, and that which followed, his concern was for his congregation, now harassed by "every species of cruelty, in body and estate." Cheare's mind was serene to the end. "To suffer with Christ is honourable," he declared upon his death-bed. "God will not put this honour upon everyone. He gives grace to a man, forming him into a vessel of silver or of gold, and then throws him into the fire to melt or suffer for His name." "Is all well within?" he was asked as his heart-throbs grew fainter. "All is well there, blessed be God, my God, the high rock of my salvation. My soul hath trusted in Him and shall not be disappointed." "They looked unto the Lord and were not frightened," observed a friend, tenderly pressing his hand. "Yes," he said, "and their faces were not ashamed!" And so passed this indomitable spirit. For nineteen years his flock were without regular ministrations; but they were loyal to his standard, abstained from the recognised services in St. Andrew's Church, communed together in their own fashion, and thus exposed "their goods and bodies to be spoiled."

Meanwhile the "Solemn League and Covenant" was at a discount with those who preferred personal safety to qualms of conscience, and, on being brought to the sticking point, magistrates and councillors compounded for their safety by subscribing their repudiations. "I doe declare," they wrote "that their lies upon me or any other person noe obligation" to that Protestant Manifesto. "The same was in itself an unlawful oathe and impressed upon the subjects of this realme against the knowne laws and liberties of the Kingdom." The disclaimer was attested by John Harris, as chief magistrate, "at the time when he was sworne Mayor for the yeare then next following," and witnessed by William Jennens, the Ex-Mayor, with this superlative flout: "Let the proclaiming Rcihard Cromwell be accounted as an instance of his rebellious affection to God, the King, and the country, by advancing the continuance of succession to horrid rebels." Jennens, indeed, was "a most furious" justice, who was invariably "verie busie" in breaking up meetings and "making sport for soldiers and officers." Numbers of women and men were sent for trial to the assizes, and one grieved commentator of the period wrote that "the men in power are strangely set against the servants and service of God." Thus passed the local Puritans under the yoke; but, when Colonel Ludlow fanned the slumbering and silent fires in the West, the enemies of the King boasted that they could count on Tough Old Puritan, and the then Mayor and his brethren showed their true bent by permitting all save known Cavalier prisoners to regain their liberty. On one mean wretch "who looks rather like a rogue than a traitor," the officers of the Crown laid hands for shouting that Charles was doomed to an early death, and that his bastard would only survive a little longer than himself. Major Cawborne directed a conspiracy whose headquarters were at Plymouth and whose password was "Tumbledown Dick"; and Francis Buller was reported because his servant said at Saltash that "if his master were tried in Parliament, he doubted not that he would find friends enough to take his part, and that it might cost the King as much as the five members did his father."

Fights with the Dutch off Plymouth: 1665.   Whilst the King enacted these oppressions at the expense of his subjects, every courtesy was ensured to foreigners visiting the port. Spanish battleships were refitted in Catwater with ostentatious attention, and French crews were permitted to land in such numbers as would occasion no "jealousy." As their presence infected the town with a foul disease, the warmth of the welcome soon waned, although the general toleration of foreigners was maintained. The international quiet was disturbed in 1665, when the Dutch fumed to wipe out Blake's splendid record; and as Charles was not prepared for their descent, he pleaded with the Plymouth victuallers to supply the fleet with provisions. The old spirit blazed out forthwith, and the bakers vowed that they would not "heat their ovens without gold." On went the preparations, however, and hundreds of recruits were lured into the town under false pretences. The King had authorised his officers to assure them they were only required for the defence of the district; but, on finding vessels waiting to deport them, they denounced "the trick" so vehemently that the Governor declared the credit of the Crown was lessened, and that so flagrant a subterfuge could "only be acted once." Hundreds of tradesmen were also torn from industrious pursuits—an outrage the more gratuitous since the villages teemed with "idle fellows."

The Dutch were scouring the Channel, and running so close to the harbour that their firing was heard and clouds of smoke were seen from the Hoe. Misfortune unsettled the English plans at the outset. The ships were tossed in a storm, and the Admiral's levies lay so helpless on the decks that he described them as sad fools of all trades, "only fit to settle a plantation." Loudly the Hollanders laughed at these untrained antagonists ; and, in their caricature of John Skinner, the Plymouth dwarf, made sport of the local spirit of braggadocio. In swaggering fashion this oddity was accustomed to challenge all who " by a thousand boasts defy my sword, as yet firmly sheathed. By and by may I draw it. Oh you may tremble, my bravados, I pierce even at one blow when I am enraged." Such were the lines written in Dutch under the portrait, and the Governor of Plymouth plaintively

THE PLYMOUTH DWARF, JOHN SKINNER. (1663.)

(From an old Dutch Engraving.)

remarked : "It is like them to speak high when no enemy is near." It was some solace to know that the enemy had also to depend upon undrilled boys and weak men, and that they could claim no special advantage. In a few weeks Plymouth was again presenting evidence of shameful neglect, many of the sailors perished "miserably for want, which cannot be helped, and also malignant fevers and fluxes," and hundreds stole ashore and robbed the inhabitants, "having no other means to relieve their perishing wives and children." Despite destitution and alarm, the flag was not discredited, and men fought the more wolfishly in the hope of securing money to purchase food. It was little the Government contributed to these successes beyond despatching powder and shot, and the stores were hurried "with trotting crash over a rugged country." There was as little thought for the officers as the men, and Sir John Skelton rebuked his superiors for compelling him to sustain hospitalities at his own cost, "which I must do or be accounted a clown." Sir Jeremiah Smith reinforced the defence with twelve frigates, and as the enemy decamped, Plymothians flattered themselves that "the Dutch have lost all interest in the west country." There were frequent interchanges in the Channel, however, and prisoners of war so rapidly accumulated that the authorities protested against the over-crowding of the Castle and forts, and hundreds were removed to other centres. A curious glimpse of custom was afforded when the under-keeper desired "the old witch of Plymouth to show the prisoners some of her tricks," and the hag went through her elfish programme to the delight of the foreigners.

Cowardice afloat received no encouragement, and glaring examples were punished with death. In 1665, Captain Nixon, of the Elizabeth, and Captain Stanesby, of the Eagle, were attacked on the Cornish Coast by a pair of Dutch battleships; and, after fighting for two hours, went their several ways. According to the crews the conduct of the commanders was "very foul," in extinguishing lights to disguise their whereabouts, and making away under cover of night. It was true the wind was boisterous, but "there were no sufficient reasons for running from the Dutch." A worthier account of the enemy was rendered by Captain Jonathan, of the Sorlings, who tackled two frigates off Scilly and "would have secured" both if assistance had been forthcoming. The number of the wounded who were landed testified that this encounter was no pretentious promenade. It was not long before the enemy developed more daring, the dream of immunity was dispelled, captains hesitated to leave the port, and shipowners were racked with suspense. In May, 1667, hostile guns roared off the coast, and shot were hurled into the villages, "which much frightened the country people, but did no hurt." The worst fears, however, dominated the authorities, and Charles warned the Earl of Bath, as the Governor of Plymouth, that the enemy were boasting of their intention to "spoil, burn and sackage" the western coast. It was not only the Dutch that had to be reckoned with, and the Drake frigate returned with a forlorn account of her "long dispute" with a French rival, which she was on the point of capturing when the opposing fleet stood in two squadrons "and made her forbear." She was chased into Plymouth, but sought refuge in Hamoaze—now coming into fashion as "a very safe harbour."

Because the local bakers and butchers refused to supply food unless their accounts were paid upon delivery, the Royalists accused Plymothians of wishing well to the Dutch. This was a libel on their patriotism, for their relief was overwhelming when it was reported that De Ruyter had been humiliated. It is by no means certain that the English squadrons triumphed, but no doubt was admitted in Plymouth, and the news was hailed with the ringing of bells and the firing of guns. "All the new Fort-street was covered with bonfires, and there were in all public places the greatest demonstrations of joy ever seen in this town." Transient were these emotions and in June, 1667, the local ports were plundered with impunity, "and the enemy's success dismays the people very much." Then Scilly fell into the hands of the French, the county of Cornwall was enraged, hostile frigates and fireships skimmed the Channel, and "the whole coast lies in fear of invasion and poor England is in miserable lot." Plymouth was aroused by these reports, further fortifications were thrown up, troops of horse poured in, and battleships belted the mouth of the harbour. From every part of the west the Militia were rallied, guns were planted on the

Hoe, the army of tinners marched from Cornwall, St. Nicholas Island was victualled for a month's siege, and cannons were hauled on its exposed parts "in case the enemy should attempt to land." De Ruyter, however, had more ambitious aims, and sweeping away under cover of the night, he forced the Channel, and "the news that the Dutch lie in the Thames makes Plymouth men look sadly." Their faces lengthened still further when sixty hostile battleships ran for Falmouth, and there was much murmuring because resistance had not been provided for. De Ruyter returned to Plymouth and anchored in Bigbury Bay. There he held a council of war; and, whilst the officers were thus engaged, his seamen landed to "steal sheep." They were repulsed by the soldiery and the militia reserves of all sorts, who sprang to the protection of the coast. From cliff to cliff the defenders raced, hand to hand were the fights, and the prospect of spoil was so poor that the Dutch took to their boats "and durst land" no more. De Ruyter sailed for Torquay, stripping and burning the coasters as he went, with the object of intercepting a crowd of merchantmen who were making for Plymouth. Warned by urgent signals, they eluded his vigilance and danced into the waters of the Sound. The Dutch were thus hugging the coast when Charles negociated his inglorious peace, the enemy dipped the horizon and disappeared, and the sense of shame was only mitigated by release from a profitless strain.

Charles II. Opens the Citadel 1671.　　It was the impression of Plymouth—pardonable enough in the circumstances—that Charles erected the Citadel "to hold in check the rebellious spirits in the neighbourhood." In the original patent no encouragement was accorded this theory, and the provision of "a new Citadel upon the Hoe" was claimed as an indispensible safeguard against foreign invasion. Cosmo the Third, however, noted

PLYMOUTH CITADEL.

(From the Engraving by Daniell in 1825.)

that the site commanded the other defences, and, drawing his own inference, he concluded that the King intended the fortress as a check upon the inhabitants who showed themselves, "on a former occasion, prone to sedition." The wealth created by a flourishing commerce rendered them "the reasonable objects of suspicion," and as the Citadel was placed "on the top of a mountain," it was in a position to batter or defend the town as emergency required. Amongst the fortifications thus covered was "an entrenchment of earth, well supplied with artillery; a similar one defends the dock, towards the city; and others are disposed on a rock, which protects, in front, the whole length of the bay." The foundation stone of the Citadel was laid by the Earl of Bath, the governor, in the presence of Sir John Skelton, his deputy, and Sir Bernard Gomme, the chief engineer. "Wholly irregular" in its general design, the structure, with its breastwork of granite boulders, was nevertheless very formidable; but it is only of late, when the Citadel has been partially rebuilt and extensive excavations have taken place, that the existence of a considerable range of underground apartments has been revealed. What the purpose of these rooms was, or whether they were originally associated with the subterranean passage that extends from St. Andrew's Church Tower to a point near Tinside, is not known, and may prove beyond elucidation. The excavators in 1899 have also opened up a subterranean reservoir of unfailing natural supply, which was intended to be used for filling the ditch. Five companies of officers and soldiers were told off for duty whilst the Citadel was being erected—the men "handsome, and in excellent order: four companies wearing red jackets faced with yellow, and the Duke of Cornwall's yellow jackets with red linings." Within the old fort the victualling office had stood for many years, and this, with Sir George Carteret's yard and houses, was appropriated. "A just value of £100 per house" was fixed, but the money was only paid after repeated pressure, and the town received no allowance for the land abstracted from the Hoe. Lord Howard travelled from the metropolis to view the Citadel as it was approaching completion, and cannon from fort, island and ships proclaimed his welcome. Then Charles paid a flying visit, and he was loudly cheered by the hundreds of artizans who were engaged in facing and placing the stone. Miserable epidemics were raging, as the result of prolonged drought and the impurity of the wells on which the inhabitants were again dependent, and heavy mortality intensified the common superstition. The vision of a man was seen near the Citadel by one of the guard: "it went away as it were by the sea."

Charles bestowed his blessing on the work in his own impulsive fashion. It was by chance that Lord Bath learnt one Sunday morning in July, 1671, that he was making for the port in his pleasure boat. Taking horse, the Governor rode from his seat with four of his servants, and reached the town the same afternoon. As the winds had been perverse, the King was still at sea, so the Earl made "all possible preparation," and the soldiers were bidden to respond on "the sound of drum." When the squadron hove in sight a vast concourse of courtiers assembled to "wait upon the King;" Lord Bath rowed out in company with the Mayor and his dissembling brethren; and the whole were presented to his Majesty and his brother James. On landing the Mayor essayed to salve the past by presenting Charles with a purse of gold, and Lord Bath, respectfully kneeling, begged his acceptance of a silver key. The King retained the gold, but returned the open sesame with the assurance that he could not entrust it to better keeping—a pretty compliment he would have modified if he had lived sufficiently long. On entering "the house by the citadel," he was saluted with "a peal of all the ordnance," and the frigates detonated their approval of the welcome. At night "there were many fires of joy in the several parts of this town."

Lord Bath entertained the King "at his own cost," and "kept a table at the house of Captain Philip Lanyon, where he had for his guests the Duke of York, the Duke of Monmouth, the Marquess of Blanquefort, and many others of the nobility, having provided all things in very great plenty, besides giving money to his Majesty's inferior officers." Charles was more than satisfied with his day's visit, and "so well pleased indeed with this place that he will be ready to grant it anything to promote its trade, and he will have the Mayor think on anything to cleanse and preserve the harbour." At four the next morning his Majesty explored the harbour of "Hammos" as far as Saltash, and, having visited "Osen," landed at the Lambhey Stairs. After dinner he strolled through the thronging streets and "touched many for the evill." Protesting his loyalty overmuch, the Mayor consulted with his brethren as to how they "might further treat the King;" and, waiting on him to learn "his next resolve," suggested that Charles should survey the outworks that existed "in the time of the late war." No proposal could have been less adroit, and "on a sudden" the King walked towards the steps, entered his pinnace, and made for Mount Edgcumbe. His worship and the be-robed aldermen followed at a distance— surprised, bewildered and apologetic; but, procuring a wherry, they started in pursuit, disembarked at Barnpool, obtained access to the grounds, and "accosted his Majesty in the Bowling Green." Charles had recovered his self-possession, and no trace of vexation remained. He assured the Mayor that he was proud of the harbour "beyond any in the whole of his dominions," and soon restored the confidence of the civic authorities by his complaisance. The panorama threw him into rhapsodies, he testified to the beauties of "the river of Saltash," and promised that he would henceforth be no stranger to Plymouth. He set sail the same night, and the big guns accorded the frigates and pleasure boats "a very loud farewell." It was a tedious voyage to Torbay, but this did not disturb the King, "who takes great pleasure in being upon the sea." A deal of "alarm"—or rather chagrin—followed this precipitate flight of the Court, for the gentry were still flocking into the town, so that "they might be in a posture to kiss the royal hands," when the fleet was beating up the Devon coast.

The impregnability of the port was a part of Charles's design for crushing Holland; and, when war was declared in 1672, the proclamation was recited by the Mayor in all the public places of Plymouth. "The ceremony had the maidenhead of three very large fair maces, and was performed with drums and trumpets. The Mayor afterwards treated the better sort of citizens at his house." Plymouth, after all, was free from menace. The brunt of the campaign was largely left to the French, with whom Charles had intrigued to this end, and England was rather the market for the spoils. But the prizes brought into the harbour did not compensate the Plymouth merchants for the losses in which they were involved when the London bankers stopped payment. Many of the old families were involved in ruin, and only a few retained agreeable recollections.

Emasculating Plymouth's Charter: 1683.   Charles was true to his word. He made Plymouth the scene of frequent visits, built a house within the Fort, and his attentions to the ladies were gracious, if not affectionate. John Allen, one of the local mercers, testifies, in his diary, that the King frequently visited his young bride and himself. "I saw his Majesty oftentimes, and my wife had the honour of being kissed both by the King and his brother James." Charles returned in 1676, in company with the Duke of York, and under an imposing canopy "touched for the King's Evil in our great church of St. Andrew's." At a special meeting of the Corporation the Duke of Albemarle and forty gentlemen in his retinue were granted the freedom of the borough; and a whirl of gaieties temporarily dispelled a deal of the accustomed gloom. As, with the years of repression, the hatred of the Stuarts deepened, so the revolutionary spirit re-asserted itself;

and when "the damn'd fanatical plott" to assassinate the King and place the Duke of Monmouth upon the throne was discovered in 1683, Lord and Lady Lansdown found in Plymouth a convenient refuge from the vengeance of the Court. Then a visit by the Bishop of Exeter to the town "sett us anew in a flame," and all was disorder within the Council. William Martin was made a magistrate, and "the fopp" so freely criticised the King's interference in a local excise prosecution that he was reprimanded by the Privy Council. Convinced that Martin was not without friends, Charles directed an enquiry to be held into the fidelity of the Corporation, and the town was ordered by "the loyal judge," Jeffreys, to expiate its transgressions by surrendering its charter. "Knowing that it were quite in vain to dispute about a Government that would not exist long," the majority of the Aldermen and Councillors agreed, "beseeching your royal favour that what is not useful to your Majesty's service, but of great benefit and advantage to the said town, may be preserved." The objects of Charles were twofold—to obtain the funds which the grant of the new charter would bring to the exchequer, and to dismiss distrusted citizens from public service. The inhabitants rejoiced, however, to have their privileges revived in any form, and the news that the amended document was on its way to the town excited much enthusiasm. At Ridgway the coach was met by the Mayor, Governor and thirty horsemen, and the charter was carried aloft to the Plymouth Townhall, where its provisions were declared to the townsfolk. A treat was provided at the Mayor's house, the guns of the fort were fired for an hour, the ships in harbour were dressed, and, after the patent had been deposited with the other muniments, there was an "abundance of bonfires." All existing charters were surrendered in exchange for these curtailed liberties, and the public were admonished that the object of the amendment was to keep the peace, "so that the said borough from henceforth for ever may be and remain a burrough of quietness, to the terror of evildoers and for the reward of good men."

Charles died the year after he had thus emasculated the Plymouth Charter, and James II. restored some of the privileges. But his concessions did not prevent the outflow of sympathy to Monmouth, and many who went forth up from Plymouth and the western counties to ally their fortunes with the Dukes, reaped their reward in the Bloody Assize of the infamous Jeffreys, whose ruthless sentences were long commemorated in the ballad "Widows of the West":

> Good people, I pray, attend to my muse,
> I'll sing of a villain I cannot abuse,
> The halter and axe no such men will refuse,
>   Sing hey, brave Chancellor!
>   Oh, fine Chancellor! delicate Chancellor, oh!
>
> The next to the west he hurried with speed,
> To murther poor men, a very good deed!
> He made many honest men's hearts for to bleed.
>   Sing hey, brave Chancellor, etc.
>
> The prisoners to plead to his lordship did cry,
> But still he made answer, and thus did reply—
> We'll hang you up first and then after we'll try.
>   Sing hey, brave Chancellor!

CHAPTER VI.—LIFE AND CUSTOMS IN THE 17TH CENTURY.

Plymouth during the   At the Restoration, Plymouth depended upon its navigation. Cod,
Revolution.   tin, and merchandise were carried to every part of the world "at an
immense profit "; and, so extensive was the general commerce, that, except in times of
war, only women, boys and decayed old men were seen in the streets—the able-bodied were
invariably afloat or abroad.   The necessaries of life were on sale in the town, and the only
duty was imposed upon wine.   Cloth and linen could be purchased without difficulty, and
articles that ministered to luxury.   Silversmiths, jewellers and watchmakers plied profitable
undertakings; and there were extensive dealings in exquisitely polished marbles.   Within a
short distance of the town the mines produced eighty per cent. of tin, and ore was
successfully crushed for gold and silver.   Oysters were yielded in abundance, the rivers
flashed with fine salmon, and fishing and hunting were the pastimes of the gentry.   In
" the Old Church Twelves," which stood to the north of St. Andrew's and partly enclosed
the burial ground, the deserving poor were housed, and the edifice was almost surrounded by
other cottages erected by charitable Plymothians—Fownes, Miller and Pryn.   Emulating
this good feeling, John Lanyon endowed a similar group in juxtaposition to Charles Church.

INTERIOR OF LANYON'S ALMS HOUSES (corner of Ham and Green Streets).
Founded 1674—Demolished 1868.
(From a photograph on eve of reconstruction.)

The contemporary description of Plymouth, as written by Stroud in the Devonshire dialect, suggests the enthusiasm with which the town inspired visitors from the rural districts :

> Zich streets, zich men, zich hugeous seas,
> Zich things and guns there rumbling,
> Thyself, like me, would bless to zee
> Zuch bomination grumbling,
> The streets be pight of shindle stone
> Doe glisten like the sky-a.
> The zhops stan ope and all yeere long
> I'ze think a faire there bee-a.

The houses were lofty and narrow, with rich pannellings that spoke of cultured taste and wisely-ordered wealth. The pointed roofs were thick with thatch, and diamond panes were used with such prodigality that interiors could be surveyed without the imputation of curiosity. Magnificent were the staircases of these dwellings, with walls of stately wainscotting and elegant ceilings, whilst heraldic shields within and without formed leading features in the schemes of decoration. With gable ends in juxtaposition, so close that in some streets they almost touched, the good wives gossiped as they knitted, and reciprocated attentions by balancing their clothes-lines from their own window sills to those of their neighbours. Off Briton side was a mansion with a tablet adorned with the arms of Spain, Castile and Leon quarterly, with an escutcheon of pretence, and fleur de lis surrounded by the collar of the Golden Fleece. Respect for antiquities was so high that,

PIN'S LANE : demolished in 1898.

(Drawn by H. Martin. Photo. by H. Scrine Hill.)

upon the building of the Alms Houses in the Pig Market, the oldest architectural relic Plymouth then possessed was worked into the group—a door of the early 12th century, of round arch, bold mouldings and superb pillars and capitals—evidently derived from some old monastic ruin in the locality and still preserved at the Athenæum. At the corner of Pin's Lane was an imposing house, and over its handsome entrance were the arms of Captain Cockes of Plymouth—the "cock of the game" who lost his life during the Armada, bravely contending in his own little ship. Though the approaches of the town were narrow, neglected, and dangerous, the taverns were excellent. They were bountifully stored with commodities, and the capacity of some was so great that scores of travellers could be lodged. In Southside Street stood the Mitre, historic among the hostelries, in which the wealthy cemented their regard for the famous. This inn extended as far back as Seven Stars Lane ; its substantial elevation relieved by majestic Gothic approaches and arched doorways. There was a cloistered court within, with bedrooms built upon elaborate colonnades, to which the town yielded no parallel. On one side of the enclosure was an ancient chapel, whose entrance consisted of two piers of square stone, similar to the buttresses of Old Church, with carved effigies occupying the niches. Venerable was the appearance of this edifice, with arches of solid oak, and compartments of saints and prophets arrayed in curious costumes, and "in strange and ridiculous postures." A label from the mouth of each figure bore a name and inscription, and the series extended from angle to angle of the building. Much to the scandal of the Puritans, Adam and Eve were depicted in "a perfect state of nudity," and with the serpent and tree between them. Several human figures were pourtrayed throughout the ornate cornice, and shields with fleur de lis and legends alternated.

Amid the palatial edifices in Looe Street, with their bulging storeys and quaint projections, and splendid scrolls of seasoned oak, was the town residence of the Trelawneys. The arms of the family were carved on the mantlepiece, and brackets of rampant lions and other grotesque conceits were distributed through the mansion. Close at hand stood the Pope's Head—an inn that remained the leading hostelry until the eighteenth century. In the north-west corner of Higher Lane nestled the Turk's Head, formerly known as the

LOOE STREET IN 1830.
(From a Drawing by Samuel Cook.)

Abbot's House, a small building with a Gothic doorway—a memorial of the days when the Crusaders sailed from the port. The Rose and Crown, in Old Town Street; and the Old Four Castles, close at hand, told their own stories; and the White Hart and the Lion were no less mellowed with ripe traditions. Near the juncture of Looe Street and Vauxhall Street a piece of carving, exposed as a signboard, testified to the salacious wit of the artist rather than to his respect for the proprieties. The pacific ideal intended to be presented in this work was expressed in the couplet written underneath: "The time shall be when a lyon and a lamb will agree." At the Sun Tavern lion and lamb more decently consorted, and, when Sir Gilbert Talbot was elected member in 1666, he returned thanks in this guileless and genial fashion: "Gentlemen, I desire your company at 3 of the clock at the Sun Tavern. Hereat have a glass of wine at your service." That the landlords did not fail to charge those who listened to their stories and enjoyed their hospitality, is quaintly illustrated in "Davenant's Newes from Plimouth," where an old mariner is made to exclaim: "This town is dearer than Jerusalem after a year's siege; they would make us pay for the daylight if they knew how to measure the sunbeams by the yard; nay, sell the very air, too, if they could serve it out in fine china bottles; if you walk three times in the High Street they will ask for money for wearing out the pebbles." Through the centres of these narrow and crooked thoroughfares, the gutters carried so much filth that the Corporation were more than once ordered by Charles II. to cleanse them.

Drinking customs were common enough amongst the aristocratic classes; and Harris's account of the fatal duel at the Higher Mills, in 1665, testifies to the noisy brawls witnessed in the taverns. Francis, the second son of Pierce Edgcumbe, of Mount Edgcumbe, and John, the second son of Sir John Skelton, Deputy Governor of the Fort, were engaged in an archery match at "Esqr. Sparkes," when they quarrelled over a punctilio of honour. There was an exchange of bloody noses, and then the party adjourned to the Three Cranes, where Sir Richard Edgcumbe, young Sparkes, John Vowel and John Webb, one of the new magistrates, were loudest of the company. A furious controversy raged over the "sack pots," and the disputants, heated with drink and anger, fell from words to blows. Skelton had "well pillaged Edgcumbe's head, by pealing off a considerable quantity of his hair," when Sir Richard upbraided him with cowardice in attacking one who was "upsighted and suffered from palsy." Drawing his rapier, Skelton demanded satisfaction, and Sir Richard jumped to reach a sword which was lying in the window. The interposition of the spectators prevented any serious conflict, so that the orgie thus far only resulted in a gross display of "ill manners." The disputants quaffed on more agreeable terms until 3 a.m., "when it may be that, having lost their wits," they retired to bed, "peaceably as well as their legs would carry them." The Edgcumbes shared the same room; but, rising in a drunken stupor, Francis stole to Skelton's apartment with a fresh challenge. The two men crept shoeless from the house, and walked to the higher part of the town, where, in a field from which the houses of the combatants could be seen, they fell "to their fatal and dismal sport." Edgcumbe received sundry thrusts and dropped dead, and Skelton fled the scene and was never more heard of.

Visitors of distinction were received with elaborate ceremonial. The Mayor, in his robes of scarlet and ermine, walked to the Barbican, with the twenty-four aldermen attired in trailing gowns of black cloth. The garments were enriched with stripes of velvet, and the collars trimmed with sable—so that if the composition was sombre, the cost was heavy. Bearing them company was the Governor, who paid his respects in the name of the King; or, if the visitor happened to be the King, on behalf of the garrison. Between the knights and their armed tenants, who came from all parts of the county, walked the guest—the procession protected by double lines of soldiery—colours flying, trumpets sounding, and drums beating—the population festive and enthusiastic, as "for want of room in the streets" they clustered the gables or manned the yards in Sutton Pool. From their country seats the knights rode into Plymouth to pay their respects, and every "gentleman of consideration" did the same. These picturesque ceremonies were observed when the Duke of Tuscany, Cosmo the Third, visited the port in 1669. Forty elegantly costumed nobles followed in his wake, and prince and suite were greeted "with all respect imaginable." Largesses were distributed with the generosity of abounding wealth, golden tokens with the Duke's portrait being given to some, exquisite necklets to others, whilst crowns and pistoles were showered with the utmost prodigality. A pleasure visit to Saltash, "a small town where formerly flourished the same commerce which is now transferred to Plymouth," constituted a part of the programme, and discharges of artillery pealed from the forts at the mouth of Hamoaze. During the troublous times of the Commonwealth, Plymouth was reckoned "amongst the best cities of England." It contained about fifteen thousand inhabitants when the merchant fleet was at home, and its leading adventurers were possessed of princely means. The River Tamar was navigable for six miles by the largest men-of-war and for ten miles by traders of all kinds; and, as its serpentine course was protected by hills, it afforded an unrivalled retreat. Vessels were able in the early Tudor days to sail four miles up the Laira, but the narrowness of the channel and frequent landslips so filled the bottom that little more than a mile was available to the larger frigates at the time of the Restoration.

Although the Calvinistic fervour of Plymouth was intense, the morality of many was at a low ebb. Not even the terrors of the stake, the gallows, or of branding, intimidated from acts of sin and criminality "the multitudes of devils that walk in temples ahd congregations, in streets and houses, in chambers and closets, in ships and shops, upon keys and exchange." That rigid and gloomy old Puritan—John Quicke—is witness to the profanity and uncleanness that prevailed, and to the roaring of oaths and curses in the streets; and he passionately prayed that the town of his birth should never be a Sodom, but a Jerusalem for Gospel privileges, rich as Tyre for traffic and a Zoar for divine safety. It was not for want of warnings that the wicked went their way, for the ministers preached of a Lord who would come with myriads of angels to execute vengeance upon the ungodly, and to convince them of their fault "in flames of fire and brimstone and horrible tempests." Yet were these vivid pictures of the future discounted, and the unregenerate were "stupid and judgment proof." Malefactors were hanged in chains in the public view, the evil were visited by plagues as a token of "great wrath," but they preferred to "create unto themselves their owne bane, temporal and eternal." The prison adjoining the Townhall was accessible to ministers at all times; and, where curiosity was excited, the general public as easily obtained admission to the dungeons in which the accused were confined—stinking dens that were the scenes of flagrant and boasted immoralities. Here the Puritan pastors instructed, exhorted, wept, prayed, held forth the torments that awaited the damned, promised gracious forgiveness in the event of confession—only to find they were "beating the air and plowing the rock." When the sinful were asked if they wished to be rescued from the clutches of "the devils and of the Damned Spirits," or whether they preferred to be flung into hell for their sins, the more hardened only "shrugg'd up their shoulders."

Thrown together as the accused were, regardless of age and sex, the prisons were the common sinks "wherein all impiety is soonest learnt and attained." What the female offenders did not confess, the ministers were not slow to suggest—they hinted the names of persons with whom, according to rumour, the women had been "unclean," and those of their employers they mentioned as freely as others of less importance. The male criminals were amenable at times to the ministerial harangues, and one prisoner, John Codmore, who was executed for burglary, admitted twenty-eight offences, including his marriage without his father's consent, and the sale of his wife to a miller for five pounds—one half of the money to be paid on Easter Monday and the other half on Whit Monday —the transaction duly covered by so-called "bills." Horse stealing, cattle stealing, poultry stealing, and jewel robberies at Tamerton were included in this prisoner's catalogue and Plymouth was his favourite market. Coiners received scant mercy, for it was "a sin against the whole nation to invade the prerogatives" of the King. Before the condemned were "turned off," each received the benefit of intercessions of frenzied energy and remarkable duration. As the ministers prayed, the convicts either wept and entreated that their torture on the gallows might not be prolonged, or cursed and repelled the advances of those who pleaded in their behalf. The invocations of the pastors were followed by the singing of psalms by the spectators; and as the crowd chorussed, the "incarnate fiends," who were awaiting their doom, often howled and yelled in contempt. The redeeming feature of local character was its fearlessness even in villainy, a characteristic which is most tersely testified by the simple Devonian who visited London and recorded in rhyme his joy at returning:

> E'en to Devonshire again
> Where honest men are honest men,
> And rogues are hanged for rogues.

Some West-country Ballads. John Quicke supplies the most squalid view of life and customs in Plymouth and the west, but the old ballads are no less significant, although obviously intended to appeal as much to our humour as our sympathies. In "The West-country Jigg" we have the story of "A longing maid" who had a mind to marry and was at length spied by a brisk young lad, who, liking her well, "resolved to try her." As soon as he courted her and vowed to be constant, a bargain was "clapt up" in an instant. In the "West-country Wooing or the Verry Conceited Couple" (sung to the tune of "My Merry Little Rogue") is given the sequel:

> In pleasant terms he lets her know his mind,
> And fairly woos her, for to make her kind.
> At first she seemed coy to his persuasion,
> And put him off with many a sly evasion;
> But finding at the last his love was constant,
> Her heart she did resign from that same instant.

Without disguise or delicacy the curtain is lifted on domestic life in "The West-country Dialogue or a Pleasant Ditty between Aniseed Robin the Miller and his brother Jack the Ploughman, concerning Joan, poor Robin's unkind lover." This ballad was not inappropriately set to the tune of "O folly, desperate folly." Robin has been told by his mother that he is big enough to marry; but in the truly economic spirit of the times, he exclaims: "O charges, family charges, make me afraid to wed." Jack's philosophy is admirable. It is when times are hard, he points out, that a man should marry, for if he can live when everything's dear, "in times of full plenty much money you'll clear." But this excuse of Robin's is only a subterfuge. He has been showing Joan some attentions, and once or twice endeavoured to kiss her. But his reception was too warm:

> And then with her fists she battered my snout,
> Till blood from the same came trickling out.

K

Jack is ready with an explanation. Robin evidently went about his courting like some clownish booby, with his hat hanging over his eyes, and shoes and stockings muddy. No, this was not so. Robin protested that he wooed Joan in style, wearing his grandfather's hat and calve leather clothes, "and made her a congee right down to my toes." Jack encourages Robin to make another effort to win the maiden by more demonstrative arts and delicate bribes, of which presents of fairing are to be the least commendable. Robin promises that he will comply, and treat the girl to custards, cakes and ale :

> I'll spend a whole shilling, and when it is done,
> If she will not love me, as sure as a gun
> I'll call her young wench and away I will run,
> To leave her, utterly leave her, never come there again.

In " The Witty Westerne Lasse," which was sung to the tune of " The Beggar Boy," we have the lament of a beauty who expects to be the victim of her own incontinence, and whose cleverness consists in a candid admission that she intends to deceive some tradesman by " my modesty and carriage," and so behave " as by some trick to get a marriage." If the husband she thus wins proves to be true and kind she will be faithful. " If he crabb'd be and crosse," a secret friend she will " keep in store," and now and then in the tavern roar, " with joviall gallants, men of fashion." " The West-country Weaver " (1685) set out " his sorrowful lamentation for the hardship to which he is subjected by his proud, imperious wife, together with his resolution to reclaim her by the well-appointed Oil of Holly." The lot of this " Peel garlic" was sad enough. In freedom's days he often played at stone-ball or cricket, and even rode to Plymouth market with Margery. Now he has to rise in the winter and light the fire, and, if he permits the porridge to burn, she hurls the ladle at his head and leaves him at home to play the nurse whilst she walks abroad " with her gallant." She does not even scruple to bring home her lover, and the latter is so secure of his footing that he threatens to throw the weaver over the stairs if he attempts to interrupt the interview :

> With courage I told him I fear'd not his blows,
> I would peep through the keyhole in spite of his nose ;
> Then the spark in a passion his rapier he drew,
> Straight away from the door òf the chamber I flew ;
> I know that young gallants are desperate men,
> And thought I, should he kill me, faith where am I then?
>
> I took her to task when the gallant was gone,
> And I said " Love, consider, but what have you done ?"
> It was all that I said, when she flew with disdain,
> Ay, and call'd me poor wittal and cuckold in grain ;
> A three-legged stool at my noddle she sends,
> So you see what it is to be marry'd, my friends.

" William the Miller " also lived in the west, and was in the habit of " learing at the pretty-faced Nancy—a sweet, charming lass and " one wonderful witty." The coquette, recognising in the miller a knave, beguiled him to make love to her, and arranged to meet him at the mill. Thereupon she told Robin, the ploughman, her sweetheart, all that had been passed, and he was carried in a sack of grist on the back of the maiden's horse, in order that he might be present at the intrigue and witness her unflinching constancy. When the miller's importunities became effusive, Robin emerged from the sack and administered so stout a cudgelling that he cried out for mercy, and compromised the affair by paying a sum sufficient to enable the designing pair to marry in comfort. "The Witty Maid of the West" was sung to the tune of "The Ladies of London," and virtue was no less poetically rewarded by "The West-country Lawyer." He endeavoured to seduce a young damsel of low degree, but she resisted his bribes and importunities with such resolution that he determined to marry her:

> And now she's a lawyer's wife, her husband does dearly love her,
> So that she leads a happy life: there's few in the town above her.

Memorials and Epitaphs in St. Andrew's Church. Reverence for the departed was evidenced during the Stuart period in the multichrome monuments erected in St. Andrew's Church, with their accompaniments of cherubim, archangels and skulls. To what extent the art of the Norman and Plantagenet days was banished from the edifice during the Cromwellian era, or whether it was ever represented there, is now unknown; but there were many statuaries and sculptures of the Charles's, very brilliantly painted, and with the inscriptions written instead of chiselled. A tablet to John Sparke and his wife Deborah, daughter of John Rashleigh, of Foy, was thus dedicated to them and their children (1633-1640):

> A father, mother and two daughters deere,
> In silent earth are sweetly lodged heere;
> Two still of age and two in infancye
> Denotes to all both old and young must die.
> A vertuous life they lived amongst friends,
> And crownes of glory now for them attends.

A monument in juxtaposition testified to the tendency of the age to jest with death, and it bore another tribute to a member of the same family, evidently people of means and position:

> Life is but a sparke, a weak uncertain breathe,
> No sooner kindled but put out by death;
> Sparke was my name, my fame, my fate, yet I
> Am still a living Sparke though thus I dye,
> And shine in heaven's orbe a star most bright
> Though death on earth soon eclipst my light.

The same propensity to play upon the name was evidenced in a monument bearing the crest of the Wills family, who subsequently migrated to Saltash:

> His parents' chieftest joy and grief here lies
> Their only child like Abram's sacrifice,
> Whom the Almighty's fatal marshall rules
> To God's will then they did resign their wills;
> Like Noah's dove in the tempestuous seas,
> Of a distracted state he found noe ease;
> His soule then mounted like the early larke
> To find a resting place in Heaven his arke.

The most imposing memorial in St. Andrew's was erected in honour of Sir John Skelton, the Governor of Plymouth, and the fact that his official residence was within the fort, caused it to be afterwards known as the Citadel Monument. The structure, which was of the elaborate and highly coloured style of the period, was surmounted by a knight's helmet; and Sir John and his wife—Dame Bridget Prideaux—were represented as kneeling on either side of a lectern. The inscription testified that the departed worthy "loyally served his prince both in his exile and since his restoration." Grotesque enough was a monument erected to the memory of the wife of Moses Goodyear, showing the woman in full dress and near her a tiny infant, with another child toddling towards the recumbent mother and gleefully exposing a skull in its right hand:

> I being delivered of a dead-borne soune,
> My soule's delivered and my labour's done ;
> His birthday wrought my death to sweeten this,
> Death is to me the birthday of my blisse.

Dr. Aaron Wilson was commemorated with a long and handsome "altar" stone in which he was described as "Right Worshipful" and his accomplishments were set forth in a Latin inscription. A plain tablet—"Rebekah's tombstone"—marked the burial place of the wife of the Rev. George Hughes, one of the evicted clergy:

> My God I have, Now in the Grave,
> Death is no pain, Christ made it gain ;
> Arise I shall, when God doth call,
> Look upon me and godly be ;
> Next her another, lieth a mother—Frances Hughes.

Hughes himself, as we have seen, passed the remainder of his days at Kingsbridge, and there a Latin inscription in his memory was written by Mr. Duncombe, the master of the Grammar School in that town. It was thus translated:

To the Redolent, Immortal, and Ever to be Respected Memory of that most excellent man, George Hughes, B.D., late of Plymouth ; Highly Vigilant to unfold the Hidden Truths of the Holy Scriptures, to incline Mankind by his Preaching, the Almighty by his Prayers, Being particularly Learned: Who (Like the Luminary of Day), Auspiciously commencing his career in the East, (Having received his Birth in London), Thence beamed a Star in the West for a long time, Diffusing light on every side by his Life and wailing by his Death. His early course (Truly Useful), having been extended to 64 years, Contributing Good and Enduring Ill, He at length found pure rest For His Soul in the Skies, His Body in the Grave beneath, on the 9th of July, in the year of Grace 1667, with his Fellow pastor long most dear, George Geffery, A.M., Whose remains, thrice nine years before, were deposited in the same place, And being first turned to dust, Are now to mingle with fresh ashes:

> Urn that contains such holy dust
> Fulfil with faith and truth thy trust ;
> Those sacred ashes in the tomb
> Will fertilize thy barren womb ;
> Auspicious matrice thence shall spring
> Famed Twins, reborn from Death's dire sting.

* This monument was erected at the cost of the Rev. Thomas Martyn, brother-in-law of Hughes ; but a no less noble eulogy, and one as deserving to live, was that pronounced upon Martyn himself from the pulpit of St. Andrew's by Canon Gilbert, the then vicar: "I have said more of this worthy man than I dare say of myself or deserve that any person should ever say of me."

Natural Phenomena   Superstition was deeply rooted in the Devonian mind in these
and Superstition.   glimmering ages, and the old tract and ballad literature presents
abounding fascinations.   Birds with white breasts hovered over the sick as the harbingers
of death; and four of the Oxenham family died at Zeal Monachorum "with the like
apparition."   "The Wonder of this age or God's Miraculous Revenge Against Murder"
professed to yield a narrative of "Undoubted Truth Out of the West."   The print
explained with becoming awe how the skull of a person murdered at an inn "was found
with a linnen cap on still whole."   A ghost thereupon urged the incoming tenant to reveal
the discovery, promised that God would provide witnesses for the prosecution, and that
the apparition should appear at the trial.   Suspicion fell on an old servant, and when she
repudiated all knowledge of the crime, "and was suddenly smitten and dyed," the coincidence was regarded as conclusive.

   "The true and strange relation of a boy at Crediton" was another appeal to the
credulous which found ready acceptance in town and in country.   It set forth the nefarious
career of a lad who "was entertayned by the Devill to be servant to him with the consent
of his father."   Retribution was swift, for "the Devill carried him up in the aire and there
showed him the torments of hell."   At Totnes "a blazing starr" was seen as a boy of
gentle birth was engaged in committing a heinous offence.·   "Att that instant a fearful
comett appeared to the terrour and amazement of all the people thereabouts," and the
author of this "damnable attempt" was struck with a flaming sword, "so that he died a
fearful example."   No less "strange and wonderfull" was "the dreadful apparition" seen
by Mr. Jacob Seley, who gave "the full account to the judges" then travelling on the
Western Circuit, and testified to several visitations of "the monster" at Sampford Courtenay.
The doings of the demon of Spreyton, in which the spectrum of an ancient gentleman of
Devon often terrified his son's servant; and the weird freaks of "the demon of an ancient
woman, wife of the gentleman aforesaid," tended to keep alive the shrinking dreads of the
simpler folk, as well as of many of the educated.

   The fate of the Bideford witches occasioned as much joy as a national victory.
Temperance Floyd apparently believed that she had been in league with the Devil, and
boasted that she had even cohabited with him.   She and her companions caused the cows
of one farmer to give blood instead of milk, and the hags cackled over other Satanic arts.
"Tryal and condemnation" of the incantating trio took place at Exeter, and they were
hanged for their "hellish practices" in the presence of a crowd, by whom their "strange
and much to be lamented impudence is never to be forgotten."   Ballads were sold containing the "confessions," and in these the witches joyfully claimed in their last hours that
they squeezed one Hannah Thomas in their arms till she was suffocated, cast several ships
away, caused a youngster to fall from a mainmast into the sea, destroyed many "cattel on
land," and did other "wonderful things well worth your reading."

   "In the county of Devon and in the parish of the famous towne of Plimmouth there
is a village called Stonehouse, a pretty little fisher towne, for it consisteth mostly of men
who live by the sea and gaine their livelihood by the water."   Here was told "A True
and Certain Relation of a Strange Birth" in 1635, together with a report of the sermon
preached in "the Church of Plimmouth at the interring of the said birth."   The wife of
John Parsons, a fisherman, was delivered "from head to heels, so farre as I could discerne,
of two complete bodies, but concorporate and joined together from breast to belly, two in
one."   There were two heads and necks, two backs, two sets of ribs, four hands and arms,
four thighs and legs.   "Soone is the fame thereof spread round about, and the eye is not
satisfied with seeing and admiring, and towne and countrie cometh in to see, so that they
may say hereafter 'at such a time in such a place I saw the strangest birth in all respects
that ever I did witness.'"

A Cotehele legend testified to the remarkable resurrection from the tomb of Lady Edgcumbe after her solemn interment. At nightfall, the sexton, who had learnt that she had been buried in the vault with jewellery of value, opened the cavity and forced the coffin. There was a gold ring upon her ladyship's finger; and, as it was difficult of removal, he pressed the joint with the utmost violence. The body thereupon moved in the coffin, and the man ran away, leaving his lantern behind him. Astonished at finding herself in shrouds, Lady Edgcumbe made her way to the mansion, where rejoicings soon succeeded the terror which her return at first occasioned. Polwhele vouched for the authenticity of this story of a trance, and declared that the lady subsequently bore the member of the house, Sir Richard, who was created a baron.

The ease with which an apparently mysterious disappearance was attributed to the play of the supernatural was illustrated in the art with which the ballad-mongers adapted an otherwise common-place occurrence : " A Warning for Married Women, being an example of Mrs. Jane Reynolds, a west country woman born neer unto Plimouth, who, having plighted her troth to a seaman, was afterwards married to a carpenter, and at last carried away by a spirit, the manner whereof shall be presently recited." The lady evidently gave up her lover for dead, but he returned at the end of seven years, and, unlike Enoch Arden, persuaded her to abandon her home and family. That is the prosaic inference to be drawn from the narration, but, as the sailor apparently took no one into confidence, and Mrs. Reynolds left without communicating her intentions to her neighbours, the trustful folk could only account for the phenomenon by other than materialistic agencies. The ballad was sung to the west-country tune called "The Fair Maid of Bristol :"

> There dwelt a fair maiden in the West, of worthy birth and fame,
> Neer unto Plymouth's stately town, Jane Reynolds was her name ;
> This damsel dearly was beloved by many a proper youth,
> And what of her is to be said is known for very truth.

> Among the rest, a seaman brave unto her a wooing came,
> A comely proper youth he was, James Harris call'd by name ;
> The man and young maid was agreed, as time did them allow,
> And to each other secretly they made a solemn vow :

> That they would ever faithful be, whilst Heaven afforded life,
> He was to be her husband kind, and she his faithful wife.
> A day appointed was, also, when they were to be married ;
> But, before these things were brought to pass, matters were strangely carried.

> All you that faithful lovers be, give ear and hearken well,
> And what of them became at last, I will directly tell.
> The young man he was pressed to sea and forced was to go,
> His sweetheart she must stay behind, whether she would or no.

> And after he from her was gone, she three years for him staid
> Expecting of his coming home and kept herself a maid.
> At last news came that he was dead, within a foreign land,
> And how that he was buried, she well did understand.

> For whose sweet sake, the maiden, she lamented many a day,
> And never was she known to all the wanton for to play.

A carpenter that lived hard by, when he heard of the same,
Like as the other had done before, to her a wooing came.

But when that he had gained her love, they married were with speed,
And four years space (being man and wife) they lovingly agreed.
Three pretty children in this time, this loving couple had,
Which made the father's heart rejoyce and mother wondrous glad.

But, as occasion served, one time the good man took his way
Some three days' journey from his home, intending not to stay.
But whilst that he was gone away, a spirit in the night,
Came to the window to his wife and did her sorely fright.

Which spirit spake like to a man and unto her did say
"My dear and only love," quoth he, "prepare and come away."
"James Harris is my name," quoth he, "whom thou didst love so dear,
"And I have travell'd for thy sake, at least this seven year."

"And now I am returned again, to take thee to my wife;
"And thou with me shalt go to sea, to end all further strife."
"O tempt me not, sweet James," quoth she, "with thee away to go!
"If I should leave my children small, alas, what would they do?

"My husband is a carpenter, a carpenter of great fame,
"I would not for five hundred pounds that he should know the same."
"I might have had a King's daughter and she would have married me;
·"But I forsook her golden crown even for the love of thee."

"Therefore, if thou'll thy husband forsake and thy children three also,
"I will forgive thee what is past, if thou wilt with me go."
"If I forsake my husband and my little children three,
"What means hast thou to bring me to, if I should go with thee?"

"I have seven ships upon the sea; when they are come to land,
"Both mariners and merchandize shall be at thy command;
"The ship wherein my love shall sail is glorious to behold,
"The sails shall be of finest silk and the mast of shining gold."

When he had told her these fair tales, to love him she began,
Because he was in human shape, much like unto a man.
And so together away they went from off the English shore,
And since that time the woman kind was never seen no more.

But when her husband he came home and found his wife was gone
And left three sweet pretty babes within the house alone,
He beat his breast and tore his hair, the tears fell from his eyes,
And to the open streets he runs, with heavy doleful cries.

And in this sad distracted case he hanged himself for woe
Upon a tree near to the place, the truth of all is so.
The children now are fatherless, and left without a guide,
But yet no doubt the heavenly powers will for them well provide.

In August, 1675, the wife of William Weeks, a dyer of Plymouth, "departed this life" after "many and frequent vomitings." Her husband and daughter were seized with the same extraordinary motions, varied by "grievous pains and swellings in their stomacks," cold sweats and faintings, and "great and unquenchable drought." At the outset the physician suspected that they were "poysoned," and he was more than confirmed in his judgment when a neighbour of these "afflicted and murthered persons" found "crude arsenick" in a pot of oatmeal in the kitchen. "The child of Mistress Pengelley, daughter of the said Master Weeks," was also affected with the same symptoms. Philippa Cary, the nurse, together with the servant, first excited suspicion by counterfeiting sickness and vomiting, but the general prostration and agony were lacking in their case. The administration of emetics led to the recovery of the child and grandfather, but Mistress Pengelley, having laboured for some days under "exquisite tortures, without any remission (Physick and Physitians being disabled by God's Holy Wise Providence from affording any relief or succor), she also yielded up the Ghost."

When the news of "this horrid accident" spread abroad, the nurse and the girl were arrested. The first brought before the Mayor was Anne Evans, "apprentice of the said Mistress Weeks, a poor child whose mother being dead, had been bound out in the Mayoralty of Mr. Peter Schaggel, Anno 1672, by the churchwardens and overseers of Charles Parish, being then about twelve or thirteen years old." To elucidate "this hellish and crying sin" Anne Evans admitted that she bought "a pottle of girts" in the market, that when they were cooked, she found "some yellow thing in the girts," and the family were afflicted with incessant tortures after they had partaken. Between the nurse and Mrs. Weeks there had been a dispute, and the former asked Evans "where she should have any Rats' bane." Cary alleged that the quarrel arose during the frying of some pilchards, and that Mrs. Weeks accused her of committing adultery. She added that Evans was also on bad terms with her mistress and that the girl had threatened to join "the mountebanks." Upon being told of the nurse's bad faith, Evans spoke more freely. She was gathering herbs when she found a packet of Rat's Bane, and on showing it to Cary she said it was just the thing "to fit" Mrs. Weeks, and that a little of it would soon "make work." Drawing the rope more tightly, the girl mentioned that Cary abused her for removing "a great spider" from some beer of which Mrs. Weeks was about to drink, adding "Thou shouldst have let it alone thou Fool and not have taken it out, but shouldst have squatted it amongst the beer." When she was taxed with this superstitious admonition, Cary retorted that she had "no such discourse with the girl, nor spake any such thing," but that she heard Evans threaten to do away with her mistress on account of a difference "on Saturday week was fortnight."

The Mayor continued playing the one witness against the other, and when Evans was informed what the nurse had stated, she improved upon her story by asserting that she saw Cary breaking the poison into powder between two tiles, and that when she asked what she was going to do with the stuff, she replied that she meant to "fit a medicine for the old woman, meaning the said Mistress Weeks." Having placed the powder in a cloam dish, she added small beer and allowed it to steep for the night. She then gave some of the poison to the girl to put into the "Old Woman's Dish" of porridge, adding "You shall see what sport we shall have with her to-morrow." This was merely to cause the victim premonitory discomfort, but the nurse declared that she meant the fatal dose to cause death in half-an-hour. After Mrs. Weeks was gone, she jauntily predicted, "we shall live so merry as the days are long." She further reminded the girl that if she held her tongue nothing would come to light, but that if she supplied any information, "she would lay it

DOUBLE EXECUTION AT CATDOWN, 1679.
(*From the original Engraving.*)

all upon this examinant." In due time Mrs. Weeks asked for her porridge, and the girl put the arsenic into the bowl, "according as the nurse had ordered, thinking no hurt." Later on Cary drank from a jug; and, after pouring in the poisoned liquor, delivered it to Mr. Weeks, by whom it was enquiringly passed from mouth to mouth. The decoction was promptly discarded as having a "keamy" taste; but, small though the amount was, all who tasted were soon in convulsions. In sore concern at seeing her master and mistress in such anguish, the girl exclaimed : "Alas! nurse, what have you done that our master and mistress are so very ill?" She replied that in so acting "she had done God good service in it to rid her out of the way, and that she had done no sin in it." When she was challenged with this damning confession, Cary denied every detail, "but saith that she doth believe that they shall both die for it, because she hath concealed the Counsel of the saith Anne Evans."

The two women were held "in safe custody in the prison joyning the Town Hall in Plymouth," where they had "time and leisure to ruminate upon their foul and odious crime, to consider of the horrible danger to which their pretious souls are now exposed, and to make their peace with God, if the time be well husbanded and improved." The witnesses having been bound over to prosecute at the Assizes, Cary and Evans found themselves "in the very suburbs of Hell," for the local prison was none other than "a seminary of all villainies, prophaneness and impieties"; and those confined there were "destitute of good company, of good books, of the good means of grace, and of all helps saving their affliction that might lead them Heavenwards." After months of waiting, the prisoners were carried to Exeter, and there, as the trumpets sounded, they were summoned to the bar. They responded "with heavy hearts though with undejected countenances," adding "lying and impudent denials" to their sin, until the verdict of the jury had been delivered. "They are cast, sentence is pronounced, and, now, being dead in law, they petition for a transportation." Here was the last refuge of miserable murderers, but justice dispensed no favours. "They may be transported to another world : not to another land. Blood cries for blood. Innocent Blood demandeth vengeance. God hath said it, and the Righteous Law of England confirms it."

The girl was sentenced "to be drawn on a hurdle to a place where she shall be executed and there burnt to death." "Methinks," said Quicke, "the very sentence should have struck her dead : an emblem and lively picture of Hell's torments. Drawn as if dragged by devils. Burnt alive as if in the Lake of Fire and Brimstone already." The nurse was ordered to hang until she was dead : "a too gentle death for such a prodigy of ungodliness. She pleads stiffly her innocence, disowns her guilt, takes no shame, her brow is of brass, she is impudent and hath an whore's forehead. If ever there were a very daughter of Hell, this was one in her proper colours. No evidence shall convince her. 'Confess,' saith she, 'then I shall hang indeed. I deny the fact, none saw, none knew it but the girl; it may be that vile person, my husband, had a hand in it, but he is gone. Some will pitty me, though none will believe me, none can help me.'" And now the Devil helps Cary to "an expedient that may help her life." "My Lord," she exclaims, "I am with child. Do not kill two Innocents. If I must die, let my child live." Being "too righteous to destroy the child for the mother's fault," the judge ordered a jury of matrons to be empannelled, but they found Cary "a lyar, to have troubled the Court needlessly," and so both women returned to their prison "in sight of Hell."

As Plymouth had been the scene of the tragedy, the Judge had little difficulty in consenting to the petition of the relatives that it might also be appointed as the place of execution : "Provided that the magistrates of the towne, or Mr. Weeks, whose wife was by the malefactors above named poysoned, shall defray the extraordinary charges thereof, and shall undertake for the same before Easter Day, being Sunday next. The day of execution is to bee on Thursday in Easter weeke, but if you, the magistrate of the said towne, or Mr. Weeks, shall fail to undertake before Easter Day to defray the extraordinary charges thereof, then the execution on these malefactors is to be done at the common place of execution for this countie." The local authorities undertook the arrangements for carrying out Lord Chief Justice North's sentence, and the execution was anticipated as a rare spectacle, for such a sight had never been seen since the foundation of Plymouth. "Oh! that it might be the last." Every endeavour was made to persuade Cary to confess, but she laid the crime upon the girl, and distressed the ministers by refusing to admit to man when she could reveal to God. Of the would-be confessors who haunted her dungeon, John Quicke was the most importunate, and he warned her that "she had sworn a bargain with the Devil for secrecy to her own destruction, that all would come out at last, as cunningly and closely as she did carry it before men and angels ; and, said I, you are one of the most bloody women that ever came into this gaol ; you are guilty of two murthers, one of your master, another of your mistress, and a third in having drawn in this poor girl like a Devil, as you are, to joyn with you to ruin them and herself also." Quicke further assured her that he did "as verily believe she would be in hell unless there were a very wonderful change wrought upon her as that old Murderer, her Father, the Devil, was." These words extorted tears, but no confession ; and, when Cary implored the minister to think of her with more indulgence, he declined to tone his invectives till he knew "her stony heart was riven and shivered to pieces and her bones broken under her Hellish wickedness."

Waiting without the cell door during this appalling altercation was "a crowd of vulgar persons" who were desirous of obtaining admission. "It is sad, too sad, a truth that the covetous keepers, for love of a piece of money, let them in, who, by their loose, idle, and impertinent discourses, obstruct the success of ministerial labours." During a subsequent visit, influenced by apparent relenting, Quicke assured "the two penitents" that it was quite as "easie going to Heaven from the stake and the gallows as it was from their beds." He was mistaken as to any real yielding on the part of Cary, for, pulling him aside, she wheedled him to ask the girl "who set it upon her to accuse her." Beside himself with passion, Quicke upbraided the condemned creature as "a brazen impudent hypocrite thus to dissemble with God and man" ; and warning her that, as she kept the Devil's counsel, to the Devil she would go, he added that he saw no promise of a good issue in spending further time in her company. "Look to it, woman," he shouted in her ears at parting, "that this do not make thy Hell hotter than ordinary."

As the prisoners were brought from Exeter on horseback, the nurse exchanged ribald and obscene jests with the spectators, and at the entrance to Plymouth, the procession was met by thousands. Persons of all ages and quality crowded to the outskirts, and Cary and Evans were gazed at "as so many monsters." Everyone passed his censure, and, although many had "bowels of pitty on the poor girl," none "hath charity for the nurse." On being conducted to their cells, various ministers attended them ; but the crush of the morbid was so great that intercessions were impossible. Late at night, when all was still in the town, the divines returned, "but the flinty rock will sooner gush out with waters and the adamant be broken to pieces with the hammer" than the Nurse persuaded to "one syllable of guilt." The maid "owneth and confesseth all," and was besought not to fear the fire. "God will carry thee through it—it can only hurt thy Body ; it shall not singe thy Soul."

On the appointed day the women were escorted to gallows erected on the heights of Prince Rock. "The streets are crowded ; the Mayor, magistrates, and Under Sheriff can hardly pass for the throng. The poor maid was drawn on the hurdle. The posture she lay in was on her left side, her face in her bosom, her Bible under her arm, seeming like one dead rather than alive. At length we come, though slowly, to the place of execution. Plimmouth was then naked of inhabitants, the towne was easy to be taken, and the houses to be plundered, if an enemie had been at hand to have done it. Cat-downe, the Lambhay, the Citadel, and Catwater are pressed with a multitude of twenty thousand persons. But commanders, who have lived in wars and seen great armies, and are therefore the most competent judges in this case, estimate them at one-half. I write within compass. The maid being nailed to the stake, and the iron hoop about her, and the nurse mounted on the ladder, she desires that this Relator may pray with her." With passionate invocations to the Deity, Mr. Quicke complied, the crowd were invited at the close to join in the singing of a psalm, and in this part of the ceremony the voice of Evans was clearly heard. Then prayers of inordinate length were offered, and attempts made by the contending zealots to urge the maid to an avowal of her pet dogmas. But the persecutors were summarily waived aside. "'Tis unseasonable now to catechise in doctrinals," stormed Quicke, in stern reproach to his fellow ministers. "She stands in need of some sovereign cordials to revive and support her drooping spirit in these her last agonies with Death and conflicts with the Devil."

The rope was now drawn close to the girl's neck, "and the hangman would have set fire unto the furze before she was strangled; but some, more charitable and tenderhearted, cryed to him to take away the block from under her feet, which, having been done, she soon fell down and expired in a trice." The executioner could cause neither powder, wood nor fuel to catch fire till the girl had been dead a quarter of an hour; and then, as the flames kindled, the wind blew the smoke into the face of the nurse, "as if God had spoken to her: 'the smoke of My Fury and flames of My Fiery Vengeance are now riding upon the wings of the wind towards thee.'" For two hours Cary was compelled to feed her eyes and feast her thoughts on the spectacle of the maid burning, and then there were renewed attempts to wring the desired confession. Threats of eternal damnation and promises of life eternal were alike unavailing. When the word went forth to despatch her, the executioner could not be discovered. He had run off with the halter under the cliffs; and, on being found, was carried by the exploring party to the scene and cast intoxicated at the foot of the gallows, there to slumber whilst expedients were exhausted to win the nurse to repentance. But the last words she uttered before being swung into the air were: "Judge and revenge my cause, O God." "A sure proof," concluded Quicke, "that she went into a lake of brimstone and fire, there to be tormented for ever and ever."

CHAPTER VII.—THE DAWN OF DEVELOPMENT.

Naval Panic and Disasters off Plymouth: 1688-1692. The persecution of the Huguenots by Louis XIV. sent them in shoals to Plymouth. First came the ministers, famished and chilled, and many who braved the Channel in small boats were sodden to the skin with the spray. Then followed their wives and children and members of their congregations ; a settlement was formed and a chapel raised. James hesitated to withhold the protection that Elizabeth had extended to the refugees, and they were received with such kindness that they abused the privileges of hospitality. Protection of home industries, and especially of individual citizens, was scrupulously regarded in the town ; foreign goods were rigidly excluded if local manufacturers were prejudiced ; and no one could trade who had not acquired the borough freedom—a measure that guaranteed the interests of masters and apprentices. Nathaniel Dowrish, "owner and lader" of the barque Agnes, contravened alike local custom and the Navigation Laws by manning a vessel with several Huguenots "who inhabit about Plymouth at a place called Stonehouse." The settlers had enjoyed such immunity that they thought they might be "accounted freemen" ; but ship, officers and crew were arrested, and the voyage was prohibited. The repugnance, however, in which James held the Puritans averted real jealousies, and the renewed barbarities inflicted upon the Huguenots created no less pity than indignation. James filled the cup to overflowing by calling Jesuit priests to his side, and when he suggested the expediency of similar persecutions, the Stuart dynasty was doomed. In their terror and unrest, nobility and people appealed to William, Prince of Orange. Associated by ties of heredity to the English throne, and imbued with Protestant instincts, there was everything in his favour, and with a fleet of 500 sail, he left Maasluis "to help our poor England." France trembled as this array passed within sight of her coast, but the hearts of thousands bounded at Plymouth when it appeared at the mouth of the Sound. Whatever the design of the Prince, his course was shaped by the weather, for the Armada of Deliverance put about with the shifting of the wind; and multitudes darkened the slopes, and acclaimed the coming King, as Torbay spread its heights to the sunshine.

James Yonge described the joy that obtained in Plymouth : "In the Mayoralty of William Symons, God wrought a wonderful deliverance in these kingdomes in rescuing us from Popery and slavery by bringing over the Prince of Orange with a fleet of ships and some land forces who went ashore at Torbay, the 5th day of November, 1688, without any opposition, and so marched for Exon, where the gentry and country flocked unto him. Soon after all the tounes and garrisons in England declared for him, Plymouth being the first." So fell the Stuarts ; and it was from Devon, and especially from its most Puritan port, that the earliest answer was supplied to the plot to restore the Catholic dispensation. William received from the Earl of Bath his heartiest encouragement—that nobleman into whose custody Charles II. so confidently committed the key of the Citadel—for he dispatched Lieutenant Carter to assure him that he might rely upon the soldiery in Plymouth to hold in check any hostile Cornish movement. The sentiment amongst the regiments in garrison was not unanimous, for a strong Jacobite feeling animated Lord Huntingdon's Regiment, and several of his subordinates were arrested in the fort, and the Earl was sent to the Tower for protesting against James's deposition. Huntingdon was

ARRIVAL OF THE HUGUENOTS AT PLYMOUTH.

(From a Window by J. Fouracre.)

subsequently excluded from the benefits of the Act of Indemnity, but was nevertheless restored to his liberty when the danger of a restoration had passed. The Dutch fleet wintered in Catwater, and it was from thence that operations were directed in the spring against the disaffected Irish and their French allies. Something like delirium prevailed as the ships swarmed, regiment upon regiment marched into Plymouth for embarkation, and when William left to win the Battle of the Boyne, Catwater was clustered with the traders of all nations—seeking shelter or treatment. "Great infection happened"; disease spread with appalling rapidity; the air was noisom with repulsive odours; and there were a thousand burials within three months. Meanwhile the emissaries of James industriously circulated "the late King's proclamation"; and, tracking them into Cornwall, Colonel Henry Trelawney freely enforced the penalties of belated loyalty.

Engagements were waged off Plymouth within sight of the villagers as they ran to the cliffs. Numerous prizes were seized on either side, but the French privateers had the worst of the exchanges. One Plymouth vessel fought till her mainmast went by the board; and, as she stood out to sea, her antagonist sank in the foam. A French frigate drove ashore at a point where the population was sparse, and the crew held the beach "standing upon their defence to make better terms with the Cornish." Another frigate of the same nationality reached Rame Head; and, after a ding-dong contest, in which her decks coursed with blood, she struck her flag to the St. Albans. Two French second-raters were escorting sixteen traders when the Nonsuch challenged them; and, after a conflict in which the enemy lost heavily in men and officers, in succession they struck their colours. The merchantmen vanished in the dusk, but the convoys were escorted into Hamoaze with their sails in shreds, and their decks coursed by the blood of the dying. "Customer" Warren was sorely disgraced for his negligent watch over the two com-manders. He confined them in the cabin of a small yawl lying in Catwater, whose windows were barred with iron; but, obtaining possession of a file, the prisoners overcame these obstacles, and, with the assistance of a waterman, effected their escape. Warren could not avert suspicion of connivance as the responsible officer, and he was dismissed from the service as a warning to others.

The Jacobite plot of 1690 involved the English arms in signal disgrace. It was arranged that a French fleet should force the Thames, and the Queen and her Ministers were to be seized by confederates in the city. A flotilla of transports were to land eight thousand troops in Torbay and weapons for sympathisers in the neighbourhood were to be distributed from French frigates. This was the programme, but it fell somewhat short of execution. In June the white squadron, under De Tourville, and the blue squadron, under Damfreville, appeared off Plymouth—a fleet of nearly one hundred frigates, gun-boats and fire ships, carrying five thousand pieces of cannon. After surveying the port, the enemy sailed in search of the defenders, and, off the Lizard, seized several fishermen; but, on learning how unprepared the English were, the Admiral sent the informants adrift. Lord Torrington was aghast when he heard at St. Helens that de Tourville was hunting for his fleet. As his own force was small, and he had no idea of Killigrew's whereabouts, he was relying upon Dutch reinforcements. He was reflecting upon this dire dilemma when de Tourville hove in sight off Beachy Head, and inflicted a crushing defeat.

In expectation of the enemy's return, new forts were thrown up at Plymouth, the reserves were "kept in arms with good watching," and huge waggons, drawn by teams of oxen, lumbered into the town with stores and provisions. Mounted messengers told of the disastrous blow that had fallen elsewhere; and, when the extent of the calamity was revealed, Killigrew, in his alarm, resolved to gain the estuary of the Tamar whilst the tide suited, instead of waiting until the victorious French were at hand—tactics all the more necessary because want of stores would have prevented him from following up a successful encounter. Killigrew's judgment was approved at a council of war which was held near Saltash after Cloudesley Shovel arrived with his own squadron. Admirals Allemande and Evertzen sought the same shelter with the Dutch detachments, and the allies united in strengthening the defences of the harbour. Batteries of cannon were thrown up, the heights were restless with troops and volunteers, and the inhabitants caught the ardour of the soldiery. With a clear course, de Tourville's ships sailed for Plymouth, but they were swept in the direction of Berry Head. There the wind took them short, and they put about for Teignmouth, which they burnt after a desperate resistance; and four ships of war and eight merchantmen fell into their hands. A contemporary ballad tells the rest of the story :

> Brave Devonshire boys made haste away,
> When news did come from Tinmouth Bay ;
> The French were landed in that town
> And treacherously had burnt it down.
>
> When to the town they did draw near,
> The French did streightway disappear :
> Because that they had then beat down,
> And basely burnt poor Tinmouth town.
>
> On Halden Hill they did design,
> To draw their men up in a line ;
> But Devonshire boys did make them run,
> When once they did discharge a gun.

Hostilities were resumed in the spring of 1691, and the French lay in wait in the Channel. Plymouth merchantmen sailed with the battleship Kent as their protector; but the Superbe, the finest sailer in the enemy's navy, overhauled them, and a desperate conflict ensued. Excessive service had rendered the Superbe so defective that she struck her flag. Fifty of her sailors were killed and wounded, and 400 survivors were landed at Plymouth as prisoners. Admiral Russell intercepted a convoy which was laden with fresh provisions for the French fleet, and, learning from the officers that de Tourville was instructed to refrain from further fighting, he returned for amended orders. He was driven towards the "dangerous port of Plymouth"; and, in the violent weather and thick haze, he could not distinguish many of his vessels on anchoring in the Sound. A clearing in the sky showed one of the second-raters, the Coronation, at anchor off the Rame Head, with nothing standing but her ensign staff; and, amid the shrieks of spectators, she went down by the head, carrying Captain Skelton and all hands. Many of the first-raters failed to weather the eastermost point of the Sound, and they there took sanctuary in the confusion which a lee shore, thick weather, and a hard gale necessarily occasioned. The Harwich, a third-rater, ran on shore and broke up near Mount Edgcumbe House. and the Royal Oak and the Northumberland tailed on the ground, but were "luckily gotten off." A Dutch frigate foundered with all hands, and others only escaped the dangers of the reef "called the Edistone" by cutting away their masts and dropping anchors. The fleet was refitted but the year's naval operations ended with little profit or honour to the nation.

Thrilling was the experience of a squadron that left the port in the spring, under Captain Martin, to convoy several East Indiamen and Virginia traders. A gale arose in the Channel that was "enough to devour a ship," and, during the lurches, several of the guns were swept overboard, others broke loose and were regained at infinite peril, and the majority of the sailors "stole into holes and corners." During "that dismal and wonderful night" Martin remained at his post, animating the courageous to deeds of heroism. The storm raged for seven days; and, as the distress guns belched their appeals for help, foreign privateers blazed away at the distressed flotilla. Battleships and traders finally returned to Plymouth to rejoice and refit.

William had his domestic trials as well as his foreign difficulties, and, of the former, the revolt of the Western miners was the most serious. The stannary laws had been hitherto reformed by delegates at the various streaming centres, and attempts to abridge their privileges led to much commotion. In October, 1691, "the four Cornish Mayors" were invited to attend the parliament of tinners at Lostwithiel. After a stormy debate, the sittings were resumed at Saltash, where it was hoped that menaces would be waived and the new arrangements ratified. The "influence of the tymes" had so wrought, however, on the tempers of those interested that "some were grown peevish and suspicious and started new jealousies and difficulties." Lord Bath sought to smooth over matters by inviting the Cornishmen to Plymouth to celebrate the King's birthday. They enjoyed his hospitality, but the overnight orgie brought no milder reflections in the morning, and "they were still in the same heats." In the end the proposals were accepted with modifications, and Bath then summoned the Devonshire tinners, only to find that, if their interests, were small as compared with those of their neighbours, "their concern for their privileges is just as great." As an uprising was feared, the defences of Exeter were secured, but the disputes were eventually accommodated.

Construction of Plymouth-Dock. As the King's military prejudices led him to forget that the navy was the right arm of the national defence, the fleet rapidly went from bad to worse, and English maritime prestige sunk to a deplorable ebb. The extent to which dock accommodation existed at Plymouth is not quite clear, although the state papers raise more presumptions than controversialists may dismiss. In the earlier days there was

PLYMOUTH IN THE REIGN OF WILLIAM III.

a dock at Saltash, and it is said a naval board sat there.   Tradition is maintained to this date by the designation of " Dock Beach," and the name of " Battery Yard," which is applied to the space adjoining, points to some measure of armed protection.   According to Henry Woollcombe the navy was fitted out in Catwater and at Turnchapel, and frequent reference is made to " His Majesty's dock at Plymouth " in the reign of Charles II.   So late as 1677 there were establishments at Turnchapel and Teat's Hill for breaming and repairing the King's ships.   These operations, and the increasing dimensions of vessels, rendered essential the construction of graving slips and dry docks; and Edward Dummer, the naval officer at Teat's Hill, wrote to the Surveyor of the Navy concerning the capacity of the barton at Mount Wise, and the foreshore at Point Froward.   It was at first intended to excavate the low inside field of Teat's Hill; and a proposal was made to utilize the foreshore of Saltash until the fishermen urged that the construction of a dock would destroy their industry.   Eventually the superiority of the existing site for the purpose was recognised; and there was deposited a "plan of that place in Hamoaze which is proposed to be purchased for a dockyard."   It comprised a field in the occupation of Mr. Doidge, containing the well to which his name was given a little later on, a field in the occupation of Sir N. Morice, and a third within the barton of Mount Wise itself.   A contract with Robert Waters, mason, for carrying out the work, was signed in December 1690; and on Dummer's advice, it was agreed to construct a second basin at the first opportunity.

The discovery of Hamoaze was due to Sir Walter Raleigh, who, in his famous pamphlet, proclaimed in a spirit of prescient patriotism that "he who rules the sea, rules the commerce of the world, and to him that rules the commerce of the world belong all the treasures of the world, indeed the world itself."   Among other notable suggestions he urged the worth of Hamoaze as a national safeguard, showed how Point Froward was qualified for "a great design in a little space," and indicated with remarkable foresight the peril to which England would be exposed if a foreign fleet entered the Thames.   Charles II. and his brother James were excellent sailors, and, impatient to witness the evolution of a floating citadel of formidable dimensions, the former suggested a vessel of 124 feet by the keel, with a draught of 24 feet of water.   The loyal Master of Trinity House started in amazement, and asked if the King did not remember that on his last visit to Plymouth, the Sound itself could not be used as a place of harbourage, so foul was the weather?   They begged him to understand that the wild seas could be the only port of such a floating fortress, and anchors and cables its one source of safety.   Neither the wit nor the mind of man, they protested, could rear a war machine with three tiers of ordnance; but, if either were equal to the task, the loss of such a structure must involve the deaths of hundreds of brave fellows at one time.   If history justified the foresight of the King, the sorrowings of Devonport have too often palliated the timidity of Charles's advisers.

Plymouth-Dock was geographically identical with the Manor of Stoke Damerel, as it was originally held by the Damerells, who gave their name to the parish.   The barton of 1,600 acres passed to Sir Edward Wise, and, in order to raise the funds for building Sydenham House, near Launceston, he sold the property to Sir William Morice for £11,000.   Charles II. granted the advowson of Stoke Church to the new owner, and the manor was thus held until 1725, when it descended to the present family by the marriage of Sir John St. Aubyn with Catherine, the eldest surviving child of Sir William Morice.   The estate was covered with brake and abounded in partridges; no roads or thoroughfares intersected it; and the approaches were merely beaten tracks.   The mansion at Mount Wise was surrounded by a few fields which yielded food for the family in possession, but the foreshore from Plymouth was still unreclaimed when William and Mary inspected the site of the Dock.   There were no dwellings, with the exception of a few low-built huts at Stonehouse, and those were occupied by fishermen. The site selected was admirably adapted to the scheme, for the seaboard extended several miles, and the tidal harbour was capable of floating battleships ponderous beyond imagination. A belt of hills protected the anchorage from heavy winds, and it was fortified by natural barriers in the form of shoals, that forbade the entrance of foreigners without the assistance of local pilots.

In 1692 the want of reliable ships gave the French a maritime superiority that evoked the complaints of English merchants and mutterings of the people. William inspected the site of the proposed dock at Plymouth before leaving for Ireland; but little was done beyond clearing it. The plight of successive fleets when they ran before the wind or the enemy, admitted of no further delay and Parliament voted a sum of two millions sterling "for finishing forthwith their Majestie's naval yard at Hamoaze." This departure was viewed with suspicion by the old town, whose merchants foresaw that the creation of shipbuilding yards so far removed from Plymouth, must cost them a portion of their population, and divert the normal channel of expenditure. But their scruples were allayed, the Mayor and his brethren visited the dockyard in state, and distributed silver amongst the artisans which they scrupulously charged to the borough accounts. They were destined to be justified of their jealousy, for, around this scene of activity arose a community which, for generations, outstripped the mother town in numbers, surpassed it in pleasures, and rivalled it in profits.

Henry Greenhill held office as the First Commissioner until 1696; and, during his appointment, the artificers were berthed in a battleship. As the genius of the constructor became manifest, and State necessities increased, the shipwrights could not all be accommodated at night in the frigate which was set apart for the purpose. Dock was divided from Plymouth by the creek now spanned by the Stonehouse Bridge. A ferry-boat conveyed the employees across, and as the men had to splash through marshes, they were fatigued and filthy when they reached the scene of their work. The avenues between Plymouth and Dock were the more "rotten and troublesome" in the winter months by reason of the heavy traffic, and the officers memorialised the Government that "the persons who are employed here may have liberty to build habitations near their business." Thereupon was disclosed the prelude to that manorial system which has been periodically impeached by State officials and local authorities. After the peace many of the ships were berthed in Hamoaze; and, as others arrived, the need of dwellings for the wives and families of sailors and shipwrights became insistent. "What shall these poor men do?" was the reiterated interrogation of the officers. If there was no accommodation for those employed in ship construction, what was to happen to the disorderly train of servants, hucksters and loafers? Unless there were houses there would be a vagrant population, and the safety of the service would thus be imperilled and its comfort prejudiced. Overtures had been made to the manor, with no result, and the officers sent the Admiralty, a warmly-worded remonstrance, accusing the owner and the trustees of "obstinacy" and "ill-treatment." Before the King determined to use the land in the public service it was worth but £80 a year. Now his Majesty was paying £100 a year for a part of the foreshore, and the rest, by virtue of the use to which this portion was put, was still realising the original rental. Before the dock was resolved upon, the whole barton was not worth eighteen years' purchase at £80, but the change enhanced its value to thirty years at £100, exclusive of the appropriated section. "We humbly hope," Dummer and his colleagues wrote, "so great wilfulness will be considered by the wisdom of the nation, which may prevent by all means the further demands which they, by this stubbornness, seem to aim at, when the present lease shall terminate; so that we think it a matter very particular, and hope it will be taken care of, and not that the public shall pay for the price of its own expenses, wherein the proprietor hath had no share, yet seems hereafter to expect great emoluments."

The manor authorities set their precedent, since slavishly followed, of tardily yielding. The first hut was constructed of wood at the bottom of Cornwall Street, and the name of North Corner was given to the point. There the original dock was built, and it extended towards the camber that survives. The cottage was the first of a series facing west, isolated buildings became rows, and irregular streets were fashioned. The waterside was rented from the Manor by the Government until 1718, and then a lease of forty years was granted. As shipbuilding operations increased, sites for houses were grudgingly accorded, and rough ways were hewn to admit of access. How insignificant the town remained! In 1727 the total amount of the poor rates was £122; in 1729 the sum stood at £147; and it rose to £205 in 1735. Then £180 was spent in erecting almshouses, and the parish surgeon

PLYMOUTH-DOCK, SHOWING NORTH CORNER.
(*From an old Print.*)

was paid £8 a year. There were now scattered indications of a Fore Street, but the town to the south had no existence. Princess Street, King Street and Queen Street followed. There were no symptoms of Cherry Garden Street, or Marlborough Street, and a few scattered cottages stood on the site of Granby Street. Morice Square was a hamlet with meadow land around it, only recently reclaimed, and away to the north, and from Fore Street to Mount Wise, the moor was laid down to pasture. Back Street (Cherry Garden Street) emerged in a few years, and extended to the east end of St. Aubyn Street; and, by gradual stages, Catherine Street, Stafford's Hill and Dockwall Street, with the cross lanes known as the site of " The Cribs." Duke Street started from the Ponds, and the Market was erected on the filled-in space. There were no symptoms of James Street, and the way to the waterside was open and unbroken as far as Stonehouse. From 1726 to 1737 the unappropriated manor land was rented for £60 a year by Sir Nicholas Trevanion, who was the Commissioner during that period. The Prince of Wales subsequently claimed the lands below high water mark in the whole of the Tamar, and it was held by the Courts that the " the honour and manor of Trematon " excluded the foreshore from private ownership. The deed of gift to the Black Prince was quoted to prove that it was inalienable, indissoluble, and inseparable from the Duchy of Cornwall, at any time and in any shape or manner, either by the Crown or by any force whatsoever.

When Anne was   With the peace of Ryswick the Stuart cause was lost. From that
Queen.   time the popularity of William waned, and his hold upon his restless subjects had nearly disappeared, at the time of his death, in consequence of his unwearying attempts to effect entangling alliances. Still, it was impossible to avert another European war when Louis hailed as heir to the British throne the son of James II. In 1702, to quote the Plymouth Black Book, " our glorious Queen ' Anne was proclaymed and crowned, whom God long preserve to reign over us." The hour was very critical; but Churchill, Duke of Marlborough, the son of a Devonshire cavalier, alike a masterful soldier and a rare diplomatic genius, nobly sustained the national flag. Plymouth throbbed with sensations and surprises throughout this struggle. The artificers were urged to keener industry with Anne's declaration against France and Spain, and forests were depleted of their noblest oaks to increase the efficiency of the navy. Rollicking was the life and breezy were the habits of the port during those feverish and fighting generations, with intervals of suffering that filled the minds of peaceful men with pain and loathing. The arrival and sales of captures, the punishment of defaulters, the loss of familiar ships, and the perishing of intimate acquaintances—these formed the absorbing topics, varied by the recital of conspicuous deeds by Honest Benbow, Cloudesley Shovel, Leake and Rooke ; or by distractions arising out of wanton mismanagement, inconceivable cowardice, or malfeasance on the part of subordinates. Embezzlement and smuggling were practised with impunity by naval officers and leading merchants, and even battleships were so laden with contraband goods that it was dangerous to take them into action. The captain of the Stirling Castle frigate, trafficked with such disregard of the safety of his crew that he was arrested as his ship lay top heavy in Plymouth Sound. Fleets were despatched with provisions below the contract standard, and stores intended to last months gave out in as many weeks. Bounteous as was the local harvest, the merchants waxed selfish with success ; entering into combinations to restrict the bidding at auctions, and sharing in private the gains that accrued from impudent conspiracies. Irritated and incensed, the Admiralty Commissioners advised that ships and cargoes alike should be forwarded to London, " as it is the number of bidders that makes the market." The plan was approved by the Queen as " the best for her service," but the change was opposed by the Mayor and Commonalty of Plymouth as closing the avenues of compensation for previous losses. They had reaped too plenteously, however, to secure redress, and, after experimental sales in the metropolis, the prize agencies were transferred. " There is much better value in London than at any other port." Thither captures and merchandise were accordingly transported, until emergency reconciled the authorities to the proclivities of the local dealers.

The first movement from Plymouth was made in July, 1702, when Captain John Leake, having gained the best intelligence as to the state " of our own affairs and those of the enemy," set out in charge of a small squadron, and returned to the port with 27 prizes, two of which he destroyed. When the " pretended Prince of Wales," with thirty ships of war, sailed from France in the faith that the Scotchmen would join him, the rebels were frustrated " by the comeing of Sir George Byng, a member of Parliament for this borough and Admiral of the Blew." On being confronted, the French fled, " and being clean ships made their escape, except one of their men of war, which was taken, and in her a good quantity of money, several persons of quality, 213 souldiers and 250 seamen." Such is the record in the Plymouth archives; but this did not exhaust the pride of the port. The fall of Ghent was followed by the capture of Minorca and Majorca by Admiral John Leake, " who, on first coming to this town after his many successes in Spain, was by this Mayor, Robert Hewer, presented with his freedom."

"Honest Benbow" conceived the idea of destroying the French forces and seizing the Spanish galleons, and hearing that Du Casse was at Carthagena, he sailed in 1702 with a squadron of seven vessels.   Ten line of tall ships were at length encountered steering along shore under topsails, and fighting commenced before the disposition of the English force was complete.   Benbow was left to withstand almost alone the withering fire of the enemy.   With only one companion he pursued the French fleet, and, from day to day, although he kept the signal for battle flying, the subordinate commanders remained out of fighting range.   Uttering expletives of disgust, Benbow went on his course and administered a series of broadsides to the sternmost vessel of Du Casse's squadron. Three times did he board the French flagship, and in the conflict first his arm and then his face was slashed.   But he fought on like a maimed lion until his right leg was shattered by a chain shot, and then he was taken below.   After his wound had been dressed, he insisted on being carried aloft, and directed the fight until a French frigate of seventy guns was in ruins.   When Du Casse saw that the other vessels had left the Breda to its fate, he bore down, poured in a tremendous volley, and tore its rigging to shreds,   Guns were repeatedly fired to remind Captain Wade and Captain Kirby of their cowardice, but they only approached to advise the Admiral to withdraw from the action.   The other officers had as little stomach for the fight; and, filled with impatience and feverish with his wounds, Benbow put about for the nearest port.   The only explanation of Wade's conduct was that he was drunk during the engagement; but he and Kirby were sentenced to death, and their colleagues cashiered.   If aught were wanting to confirm the justice of the verdict it was supplied in the letter Du Casse sent Benbow before he withdrew from further action : " I had hoped to have supped in your cabin to-night.   But it pleased God to order it otherwise.   I am glad.   As for those captains who deserted you, hang them up, for, by God, they deserve it."   The rugged old sailor's brave words to a lieutenant who saw his leg shot away constituted as sublime a tribute to his gallantry : " I had rather have lost them both than have seen this dishonour brought upon the English nation.   But, do you hear, if another shot should carry me off, behave like men, and fight it out."   Benbow did not live to witness the expiation of the infidelity which he laid so much to heart ; and, in less than a month, he fell a prey to his melancholy and his wounds.   In April, 1703, Kirby and Wade reached Plymouth, where the Port Admiral held "dead warrants" for their immediate execution.   On the deck of the Bristol, as it lay in Cawsand Bay, the condemned officers knelt awhile in prayer, and then fell riddled with bullets.   They showed at their death "a courage and constancy which made it evident that their behaviour did not flow from any infirmity of nature, but from the corruption of their minds."   The popular interpretation of their conduct was that they conspired to prevent Benbow from taking his squadron into action because he had reprimanded them for some oversight.

Heavy as was the loss of Benbow, the death of Cloudesley Shovel was a national calamity.   From a shoemaker's apprentice this gallant sailor had attained the highest honours it was in the power of his Sovereign to bestow.   Beloved by the seamen for his sailorly qualities, his name inspired the enemy with terror, and it was after exhausting the strength of Spain that he sailed to meet his tragic end.   Off the Scilly Islands a fatal miscalculation was made by the navigating officers—drunk with joy, it is said, at witnessing

HOUSES NEAR THE ABBEY.

(From a Drawing by Samuel Prout, in the possession of Mrs. Skardon.)

their native land—and from every ship in the fleet signals of distress were flown as their commanders realised that they were in the maze of the dreaded rocks. The Royal Anne and other frigates were saved, but Cloudesley Shovel's flagship and several vessels were dashed ashore. The corpse of the Admiral was thrown up the next day, lying upon a hatch, with his dog beside him, and the fishermen, after stripping the veteran of his uniform, and tearing an emerald ring from his finger, buried the body in the sands. In a cave between two tolmens this valiant sea captain lay "naked and not to be distinguished from the most ordinary sailor," and, after being reverently covered, the remains were taken to Plymouth, where the heart was buried in St. Andrew's Church. The body was embalmed and carried in State to Westminster where they were interred amid the tears of the Queen and her subjects.

Severe losses were sustained in consequence of the indifference of the commanding officers, and Sir Thomas Hardy was charged with allowing a French squadron to escape off the Cornish Coast. "We do beseech you," the traders urged the government "that our sea affairs may always be your first and most peculiar care." The master of a Canary trader complained that Hardy refused to convoy him out of Plymyuth; but the Admiral's instructions were accepted as absolving him from censure. Despite all explanations, the peers, in an address to the Queen, attributed the seizure of ships and cargoes to the "brutish obstinacy" of the officers; the treachery, corruption and carelessness of their dependants; the haughty airs of the commanders and their saucy contempt of remonstrances. This castigation had the desired result. Hardy revictualled his squadron at Plymouth, and throwing the required protection over the coast, exterminated many privateers who had operated with impunity.

In February, 1709, Captain Tollett sailed with three battleships, and off the Lizard four sail, which had been standing after him, hoisted the French colours. Broadsides having been exchanged, the foreigners were joined by five others, and the Assurance, Tollet's flagship, was shot through and through, her shrouds and backstays being cut to pieces, and her bower anchor driven through her timbers. The foreigners were nevertheless so mauled that they were obliged to wear off, and they were sighted in retreat by Lord Dursley, who set out from the Sound in pursuit with four sail of the line. Owing to the thickness of the weather he missed them; but Tollet's daring was on every lip when his riddled flagship entered the port with her scarcely less damaged companions. There was equal pleasure over the exploit of Captain Ryddel, of the Falmouth, who was overhauled off Scilly as he was convoying timber ships. The enemy found the reception much too cordial, and after cutting the Falmouth's lanyards to prevent her from going to the rescue of her convoys, went in pursuit of them herself. Although his vessel was crippled, Ryddell's seamanship was equal to the emergency, and he safely moored the traders in Catwater. Whilst this engagement was in progress, the Plymouth ran down, and engaged off the Deadman the L'Adriad, a French frigate mounted with forty guns, and brought her into port with the rescued merchantmen.

Thus the Channel was tremulous with warlike movements, the grey coastline resounded with the volleys, and the smoke of many an encounter was seen from afar. In 1712 Hardy overtook a squadron, blew up one ship with all hands, and sent the other three into Plymouth. The Chevalier Dare was one of hundreds of prisoners, and his ship, the Griffin, contained goods to the value of £80,000. Stimulated by this activity, the merchants fitted out privateers, and these were despatched from every western port manned by loud swearing smugglers, who were as ready to strip a countryman as scuttle a foreigner. Of these gentlemen, Stephen Woon and Benjamin Cruse were fearless types. They rewarded the intervention of Mr. Pike, the tide surveyor, when they were running a consignment of brandy, by killing him in the fight; and, in a lane near Plymouth, they afterwards slew the chief witness to their guilt. They were hanged in chains on the site of their crime at Crabtree. On the eve of their departure such hardy roughs as these revelled in feasts and orgies, and the unblemished reprobates of the Barbican were welcomed to their dances and dissipations. In the villages all such enterprises were regarded as of communal concern, the bells rang out as the hospitalities were dispensed, and the beaches were crowded when the adventurers took to the deep:

> The anchor is up and the harbour chain down,
>   And the bells ring merrily out from the town;
> We shall soon find a Spaniard or Frenchman, they say,
>   And bring something back to this snug little bay.
> To take from such prowlers it can be no crime,
>   We've no letters of marque, but can get them next time;
> So away! and at last we are out on the sea
>   And the cliffs of old Cornwall fade fast on the lee.

Despite this lionising, the local adventurers did not necessarily get the best of the deal even in home waters. No less shaggy desperadoes manned the foreign privateers, and hand-to-hand encounters eventuated in occasional surprises. Stokes has pleasantly testified to the over-confidence that occasionally betrayed the most alert:

> "A sail, boys, to windward, which soon we'll overhaul,
>   "Let royals and spankers and studding sails all;
> "She sees us and seems in no haste to escape,
>   "A fine Spanish galleon in size and in shape!"

> But our captain looks ugly the moment we come,
>   He whistles and swears—then grows awfully glum;
> A shot from her stern port comes bowling along—
>   "She'll take us and keep us, I'll bet you a song!"

> "And where do you come from and where are you bound?"
>   "From Fowey, sir, I come, and must make Plymouth Sound;
> "And thence to the Scheldt for a cargo of cheese,
>   "And here are my papers to see, if you please."

> "I see," said the foreigner, with a queer smile,
>   "But I think you'll be safer with us for awhile;
> "Your pikes, guns and swivels, and shot so well ranged,
>   "No doubt were to be for Dutch cheeses exchanged."

> 'Twill be many a month before I shout "Ship ahoy!"
>   A long, long good-bye to the sweethearts of Fowey!

Now and again Plymouth swarmed with sick and wounded seamen. Many perished for want of food and attention, and the privations of prisoners were especially harrowing. Unable to keep them in health, the agents asked how the enemy could be expected to regard the comfort of the English when their countrymen rotted at Plymouth. Mr. Slaughter, the responsible official, sold his personal effects in 1711, and borrowed "a little of everyone" who would lend to him. How to sustain his charges he knew not, but he promised his best, "if I sell the bed I lay upon." These assurances rendered Ministers the less anxious; and, adopting a minatory tone, Slaughter threatened to open the prison doors and let the occupants "shift for themselves." So pestered was he that he dared not "leave my door open"; and, bestripped of all credit, the merchants would not advance him loans at any rate of interest. "Send someone in my place," he said, "for I am an undone man." He required £20 a day to obtain the necessaries of life, and the Mayor threatened to throw his marshals into prison and give the foreigners their freedom. "Never were the people reduced to such extremities as now, and the soldiers starve in the streets." In accordance with ancient custom, the Government came to the rescue when every hope of succour was abandoned.

PLYMOUTH IN THE REIGN OF ANNE.

Jacobite Symptoms & Service Customs at Plymouth: 1714-1770. "Our Gracious Queen Anne dyed in August, 1714, and King George was proclaimed in this town." The succession had been secured to the "illustrious House of Hanover," but the Pretender was in evidence with an army and a fleet; and, as the new monarch had not reached England, Sir Charles Hardy was sent from Plymouth to secure the Channel. Only one man in the borough declared himself a Jacobite, and he was placed in the pillory. "Ye hangman stood by him all the tyme, being one hour at noon." With the Highland rising, loyalty to the new regime was not so complete in Plymouth as had been imagined, and Lieutenant Nickleson was arrested for exclaiming, in the heat of a furious altercation, "God damn the King." His punishment was sufficiently humiliating. He was seated in the pillory from eleven to one o'clock: "One houre with his face towards the Guildhall, the other houre towards the church style." To complete his discomfiture, the seditious phrase was printed and "fasned to his hatt." Similar words were uttered by Lieutenant Butler in the course of a tavern brawl, and Captain Dawson drew his sword and stabbed him "a little above ye right pap." The Jacobite immediately expired.

When George guaranteed the Orleans line in France, and Louis promised to uphold the House of Hanover, the Spaniards prepared for war, and Plymouth was strengthened with additional regiments in view of a threatened invasion. The various powers took sides, and a general conflagration was only avoided by the Treaty of Seville, which restored the popular confidence.   Plymouth was particularly festive : "Martin's cundict, New Quay cundict, Pope's Head cundict, and Old Town cundict ran with wine, 21 guns were fired at ye forte, with several bonfires and candles in a great many houses, and much ringing of bells."   The rejoicing was due to escape from a state of affairs which enormously enhanced prices, for a halfpenny roll only weighed a crown-piece, two turnips sold for a penny, and coals were 40s. a quarter.   Although everything was "soe dear," goods were "very bad in kinde," and the distress had been aggravated by a storm which stopped all intercourse for weeks.   The lightning tore down St. Andrew's Church wall, and "some with the surprise was struck down backward to ye ground."   Joy over the peace was superseded by mourning at the death of the King ; and, when the express galloped into Plymouth at midnight to inform the Mayor that George I. was no more, guns were fired "minitly" to arouse the townsfolk, and "ye bell struck ye same at ye church."   Three days later, George II. was proclaimed ; first at the Guildhall, where the Town Clerk stood on a stool and read the patent ; next, from the cross at the shambles in Old Town Street ; then, at the New Quay ; and, finally, at Martin's Gate.   A band of fifes and drums headed the municipal party, and "several played on music."   But, as the new King was rather detested than beloved in the borough, the demonstrations were confined to one bonfire, and there were "no appearants of any gentlemen, nor one spoonful of drink given.   Ye bells rung and ye forts fired"—and this was the extent of popular exuberance.

Fellowship with France was an evanescent sentiment, and the real feeling found a form of expression in 1742 that recalled the daring of Hawkins.   Lieutenant Smith, "Tom of Ten Thousand," or, in other words, the one man in ten thousand equal to the act, was in charge of the Gosport frigate in Cawsand Bay, when a French battleship, passing out of the harbour, omitted to lower her sails.   The young officer avenged the discourtesy by firing a broadside into the visitor, and he was reduced in rank for acting without instructions.   His plea, however, that he had only insisted upon the honour of the flag, was noised from port to port ; and the Admiralty promptly reinstated the offender, and made him a captain, "without insisting on the intermediate grades."   Claims to maritime search brought about another rupture with Spain in 1745, and France dipped her finger in the pie.   A British expedition was sent to the West Indies, and, the troops having fallen a prey to the climate, the ague-stricken survivors landed at Plymouth.   Devon and Cornwall were requisitioned for substitutes, but no sooner had the Tiger left the port with hundreds of recruits than a hurricane overtook her, and the vessel was driven upon the rocks off Berry Head.   Soldiers and sailors jumped overboard in scores, and the coast was strewn with their mangled bodies.   Those who escaped made for Plymouth, where placards were posted offering a reward of one pound for every soldier caught and sixpence a day for his subsistence.   Admiral Medlen's fleet was also driven out of Torbay, every ship slipped its cable, and the state of danger is "not to be described."   Merchantmen ran foul of each other ; one foundered, and another joined the Tiger on the rocks ; battleships ran into traders, and traders into battleships ; and the squadron reached Plymouth no less crippled than if it had emerged from a fight.   Compensation was found in 1746, when Admirals Anson and Warren, after lying in wait at Plymouth dashed across the Channel as the French cleared Brest, and returned to Catwater with a procession of prizes and 1,000 prisoners.   They pursued precisely the same tactics in 1747, cutting off four East India-men and their convoy battleships, and the trophies were moored in Hamoaze, with acclaiming tributes thundering from every battery.   Anson was appointed Lord High Steward of the borough in recognition of his splendid services.

Officers and men were alike licentious, and naval demoralization passed all credence. Women joined as sailors in order to be near the object of their affections, and fought with the intrepidity of veterans. Discovery only followed conviction for breaches of discipline or in the event of illness. In 1761 a young woman in male attire was seized by a press-gang, and sent, with others, to Dock. She had served as a marine, and it was only to avoid flogging that Hannah Whitney revealed her sex. She had passed through various engagements, and left the navy whenever she pleased by resuming her proper attire. The toleration of women of ill-character was notorious, and dissipations on deck were encouraged in port as the least of possible evils. To drunkenness all classes were no less prone, and the superiors quarrelled on slight provocation. The officers of the Sampson, 64, invited some friends to dine with them as she lay in the Sound, and a dispute arose between Mr. Walter, the master, and Captain Douglas, of the marines. Insults mingled with threats, and Walter struck Douglas a blow in the face. Smarting under this indignity, the captain flew to his cabin, procured his bayonet, and stabbed Walter to the heart. The assassin was carried to Saltash on a charge of murder, but the Judge at the Cornwall Assizes took the provocation into account, and a nominal sentence was imposed.

Dreadful punishments were inflicted in the presence of thousands of the inhabitants for grave naval and military misdemeanours. In the mayoralty of John Facey, a young grenadier was sentenced to 500 lashes for desertion, and a general court-martial, to whom he had appealed, ordered him to be shot. He was taken out upon the Hoe before the assembled garrison, "and suffered death with great fortitude, having done nothing," he said, "to offend his Saviour." More humanity was evinced when extenuation was established and the post did not miscarry. Ordinarily, the King's pardon was withheld till the last moment: the troops were massed, the firing party was at the ready, and the criminal received on his knees the consolations of the chaplain. Then his Majesty's clemency was announced, and suspense was dissipated by ringing cheers. In 1750 a captain of the Royal Marines overplayed his part. Pardon was confidently expected, although there was nothing wanting to complete the solemnity of the arrangements. Suddenly the condemned man rose from the ground, hope suffusing his face as he detected symptoms of a coming intimation. But the officer's lips remained impassive, he waved to the prisoner to resume his kneeling posture, and the unfortunate marine dropped his handkerchief. Before the officer could interpose, the victim fell pierced with bullets, and the pardon was withdrawn from the pocket in which it had too long been detained for dramatic effect. So smitten was the Colonel with remorse that he resigned his command and left the neighbourhood.

Military and Commercial Expansion: Early 18th Century. Plymouth and Dock made huge strides during the Seven Years' War. Dock was prismatic with colour as troops sailed amid the waving of flags, the playing of bands, the shouting of crowds, and the compliment of plenteous powder. The chief concern of Plymouth was the fitting out of letters of marque and the sales of prizes, so that the profits were divided between the two towns. There was little provision for the soldiers in Plymouth, and the facilities offered by the tavern keepers were always at a premium. At Dock, a series of huts of low elevation were scattered over Mount Wise and the site occupied by the Raglan Barracks. Encampments were established in the villages, and drains upon food supplies periodically menaced the populace with starvation. There were no hospitals for the wounded, but rude accommodation was made in malt-houses and empty sheds. Of nursing there was little idea; the lofts in which the patients were laid reeked with the odours of mortification, and the repose for which the victims longed was broken by the bellowing of cattle, the squealing of pigs, the neighing of horses, and the shrill cries of the chanticleers. Animals and poultry roamed at pleasure about the streets, grovelling amid the garbage as though the town was a straggling farmyard; and, to aggravate the want of a solacing night, tattoo was beaten at every point by parties authorised to arrest intoxicated stragglers and prevent murderous conflicts. To meet the wants of sufferers and the requirements of the army, ever growing more numerous and regular in its constitution, the Royal Naval Hospital was started at Stonehouse in 1761, and the Marine Barracks were projected to accommodate troops who, up to that time, had been billeted near the Barbican. The site selected was the neck of land which divided Millbay from Stonehouse Pool; and the view was clear to the water on either side, as Durnford Street had not yet been commenced.

MARINE BARRACKS, STONEHOUSE, BEFORE THE CONSTRUCTION OF DURNFORD STREET.

The Hoe, more spacious than at present, extended to the site of the Royal Hotel and Princess Square, but a deal of the land was in the hands of private proprietors. Apart from the billeting, regimental affairs were ordered in taverns, and the Mitre and Prince George Inn were commonly used for the purposes of courts-martial.

Plymouth did not neglect the commercial arts whilst the nations warred. Its staple was pilchard curing, and the Pollexfens, Rogers, Trelawneys, Hewers and others amassed huge fortunes out of this industry. There was a flourishing intercourse with the Straits, Newfoundland and West Indies, and the exports were "beyond computation." Extensive quays existed in Whitsand Bay, Lugger's Cove and Port Wrinkle, and trawling and deep sea fishing were an unfailing nursery for pilots. All transactions, however, were hampered by Customs restrictions, and coils of rope, slings of net, and bulky casks were smuggled overland to Borough Island to defeat the vigilance afloat. In an abandoned nunnery at Coxside linseed oil was produced; and refining was carried on in Sugar House at the east end of Sutton Pool. About a mile from the town, on the Exeter road, canes were ground in a disused fort by an apparatus worked by a horizontal wheel. The yarn market was "kept weekly in St. Andrew's Churchyard," and the woollen industry was so prosperous that Mr. William Shepherd employed over 4,000 hands in the reign of George II. An exemplary character, he divided one tenth of his profits among the poor, and obliged "small tradesmen of good character with loans," As the world thickened with smoke, the industry languished until one small factory in Old Town-street alone remained. Fell-mongering was also conducted by Mr. Shepherd ; at Marrow Bone Slip foot-oil was extracted ; and salt was refined at the Sawyer's Arms in Lower-street, where a spring existed. Plymouth's fame was gloriously enhanced by William Cookworthy, whose mother, on being impoverished by the South Sea speculation, left Kingsbridge, the home of the family, and set up a dressmaking business in "Nut"-street. The son, a clever chemist, discovered that china as fine as Sevres could be made with Cornish clay, "a white, unctuous and vitrifiable earth"; and he produced at Coxside such exquisitely transparent vases and figures that there was an insatiable and world-wide demand for them. In 1757 the secret of manufacturing the ware was sold to a Bristol firm, and Cookworthy's young apprentice, Bone, left the town to become the most famous of the British enamellers. The foundations of China House were then hollowed out for the building of battleships.

The Eddystone   Amid whirling eddies, to the west of Plymouth, lay the insidious
Lighthouses: Eddystone reef. Concealed beneath the waves it had been prolific
1696-1759.   in disaster and death, and countless treasure had sunk in its vicinity.
The first suggestion to place a lighthouse on the site emanated from Mr. Walter Whitfeld in 1691, who offered to do the work at his own expense if certain patent rights were granted in return. These proposals were apparently not agreeable to the Crown ; and recurring wrecks were little heeded until 1696, when the Snowdrop disappeared with sixty men, and the brig Content was cast away on Christmas Eve of the same year. According to Miss Ingelow, this vessel belonged to Henry Winstanley, a mercer of London ; and he was merrymaking with some of his fellow aldermen, when two seamen, survivors of the disaster who had tramped from Plymouth, claimed admittance. They told in simple language the story of the calamity, how the Constant drove on the rock with sternsail set, and, staggering with the impact, leapt at it again—only to collapse and the water to swarm with seamen's heads. Winstanley had previously lost one ship on the same ridge, and he registered on the moment a vow that no vessel of his should again cross the Channel whilst this menace to life and property remained without a beacon. Winstanley was a man of whimsical genius, and he was fond of mechanical experiments which testified rather to his ingenuity than his stolidity. One of his contemporaries declared that, if you touched a hidden spring in his house, you were confronted by a ghost ; and that, if you sat in his elbow chair, you found the arms encircling you. Winstanley, however, was convinced that he could rear a structure on the Eddystone that should resist the wind and waves ; and riding to Plymouth, through sleet and snow, he sought out the Mayor and communicated his intention of constructing a lantern tower. When he asked that he might be furnished with the loan of a lighter to convey men and material to the scene, the old functionary mournfully smiled at Winstanley's enthusiasm, assured him that artisans could never live on the reef, told him that he had lost two sons there, and that the project was hopeless. Winstanley, whatever his other failings may have been, was not wanting in courage ; and, when he refused to relinquish the project, the Mayor, with a fervent "Have thy will, Mr. Mercer," consented to render whatever assistance was at the disposal of the Corporation.

Winstanley prepared the parts of his fantastic lighthouse on shore ; and his men bore holes in the reef to receive the twelve massive bars of iron by which the structure was to be held. Deep down into the solid rock the piles were driven, but continuous tempests swept away by night the solid beams that were deposited by day. After months of weary toil the difficulties were conquered ; an edifice radiant in colours and gay with decorations

M

rose to the height of a hundred feet ; and the lantern shed from the summit its sacred glow
of warning.   The townsfolk were so excited, partly by pleasure and more by fear, that
they watched every night from the Hoe to see that the building remained ; and Winstanley
was so transported with congratulations that, in an ecstatic moment, he expressed his
wish to watch in the lighthouse on the stormiest night that ever blew.   Three years afterwards, lured on by the destiny he had invoked, he paid Plymouth a visit—to find that his
ideal was apparently more sound and staunch than ever after the assaults of many a
hurricane.   He remained in the tower the eventful night of his visit, and the devastating

FIRST EDDYSTONE LIGHTHOUSE :
Erected by Henry Winstanley.   Destroyed in the storm of 1703.
From an old Engraving.)

gale that broke without warning swept the lighthouse, its keepers, and the devoted architect into the ocean. Ships in distress that were plunging madly towards the port, by the
aid of the light, saw signals of distress flying—and then the edifice rocked and creaked
and suddenly collapsed in the surf. In the town the concern was universal whilst the gale
raged thus fiercely, and the people who had remembered Winstanley's fatal wish were in
terror at the prospect of its consummation. All through that night "the great mad waves
were rolling graves"; the shores were strewn with wrecks; and, with the dull dawn of morning,
the anxious realised to their horror that the lighthouse had crumbled away. Great was the
havoc wrought during those frightful hours. The beacon had scarcely disappeared when
the Winchelsea drove on to the reef, and the moans of the dying harrowed those who
were tossing despairingly on the wreckage. In Plymouth, the devastation was widespread.
The Friary Green, Old Tree Slip and other points were strewn with wreckage, and two
sons of Mr. Collier met a tragic fate as they watched the mountainous waves rolling into
the harbour. They had stationed themselves behind the Old Fish House, the whilom
military store on the Barbican which had so long served to break the rush of the waters
into Sutton Pool. A huge bore suddenly swept towards the ruins, carried them away with
the two victims, and the lads were last seen on the crest of the surf beyond the possibility
of rescue. In the absence of the light the old scenes were soon re-enacted. To quote
Gay :

> So when famed Edystone's far shooting ray,
> That led the sailor through the stormy way,
> Was from its rocky roots by billows torn,
> And the high turret in the whirlwind borne,
> Fleets bulged their sides against the craggy land,
> And pitchy ruins blackened all the strand.

Rudyerd, another London mercer, made the next attempt to rear a lighthouse three
years later, and he adopted as his ideal a plain circular form, shorn of elaborate galleries

RUDYERD'S LIGHTHOUSE.
(From an old Engraving.)

and projections, with the smallest possible apertures to prevent the play of the wind. To steady the building he introduced 270 tons of stone as ballast, and he adopted wood to admit of elasticity in roaring gusts. The work was being prosecuted when war was declared, and the artisans employed were taken off in a body by a French privateer. As soon as he learnt that they had been made prisoners, Louis XIV. ordered their immediate restoration with their tools. "Although I am at war with England," he grandly said, "I am not so with mankind." Rudyerd's structure lasted for fifty years, and then the element which was most to be dreaded, but as to which there had been the least suspicion, involved it in destruction. One night in December, 1756, the keeper rose to trim his lamp, but he was too late, for the lantern was already ablaze. Admiral West was lying at anchor in the Sound at the time that the flames shot up, and he manned two or three boats and sailed to the rock. This he found impossible to approach; although, in the meantime, the keepers were hanging to the outskirts of the reef, their bodies immersed in the sea as the only protection from the raging furnace. Coils of ropes were thrown by the rescuers to each man in turn, and so the whole were drawn to the boats. Twelve hundred tons of timber were destroyed by the time the fabric was burnt to the water's edge, and smouldering embers alone survived to mark the site. When the keepers were taken ashore one of them declared that, as he looked up towards the lantern, the molten lead poured in a stream down his throat. As he seemed no worse for the experience, his story was discredited. Twelve days later he was taken seriously ill; and, after his death, a wedge of metal, seven ounces in weight, was removed from his stomach.

No delay elapsed in replacing with stone the wooden erection thus destroyed, Smeaton was the architect, and he adopted as his design the base of a spreading oak as being the best calculated by natural laws to withstand the tempest. The masses of granite were so dovetailed into each other and into the rock that they formed a part of it. The cement was carried to the scene in cider casks; and, with jointed rocks and cramps of wrought iron, Smeaton thus triumphantly contended with Neptune, and completed a column in 1759 against which the most memorable storms beat in vain. When, in truth. within modern memory, the structure was abandoned to give place to the design of Sir James Douglass, it was the action of the water on the ridge, and not the decay of the building, that led to the supersession of Smeaton's monument.

Of the earlier custodians quaint incidents are told. It was customary for two men to watch by turns. One was taken ill and died, but the survivor was afraid to throw his body in the sea lest suspicion should arise. Gales raged, and a month elapsed before the attendance boat drew near. Then the corpse was so decomposed that the crew refused to carry it ashore, and it was thrown in the water. On another occasion a visitor suggested to one of the keepers that their lives must be pleasant in spite of the apparent solitude. "Yes," was the reply, "we might be very comfortable indeed if we had the use of our tongues. But it is more than a month since my partner and I addressed each other." A third story is told of a shoemaker who wanted to act as keeper of the light. When he was pressed as to why he desired an existence so lonely, he ingenuously replied that he disliked the confinement of his trade, and sighed for a little more freedom!

The Halfpenny Gate and Locomotion: 1760-1767. Approach to the Three Towns, for three towns were in course of formation, was so difficult that it is hard to realise how Plymouth could have been the centre of such kaleidoscopic restlessness. The original line of communication was by way of Tavistock and Okehampton, and thence to Exeter; and a main road through Lydford permitted access from Devon into Cornwall. Ten to twelve feet was the extreme width of the frequented ways; the hedges were lofty;

and natural bowers of overhanging branches supplied alike a protection from the sun and the rain. There were few means of travelling or conveyance. Heavy burdens were placed on pack horses, and carriers regularly traded between Plymouth and Dock with treasure and merchandise, each man supplied with a case of pistols to confront irrepressible highwaymen. A track for pedestrians, along the marsh to the ferry at Stonehouse, continued to Stoke, and thence to the scene of naval industry. This difficulty occasioned the erection of the bridge across the Stonehouse Creek. The preamble of the Act obtained in 1767 by George, Lord Edgcumbe, on the one side, and Sir John St. Aubyn, on the other, as owners and proprietors, and tenants in common of the ferry, explains the circumstances with sufficient perspicacity. This ferry was the "nearest and most direct way from the town of Plymouth to the said Dock," and, on account of the "narrowness of the avenues and approaches to and from the said ferry, and other obstructions," it could only be used by those who went on foot. The building of a substantial bridge "over the said creek, as well for the safe and commodious passage of persons on foot, as of carts, waggons, and other carriages, and the opening of proper and convenient avenues and roads to such bridge from the said town and Dock of Plymouth," would afford a shorter and easier means of communication. Thus the provision of a carriage thoroughfare over the creek, and convenient roads to the same, were commended as conferring great advantages upon the public; but, as "the said good purposes" could not be effected without the aid of Parliament, leave was asked to build the bridge, to widen and deepen the creek for the purpose, and to compensate all owners whom it might be necessary to expropriate. Powers were reserved to local authorities or others to treat for the rental or purchase of the same; and, by virtue of "the great charges" incurred in erecting, repairing and supporting the bridge, it was vested in equal moieties in Lord Edgcumbe and Sir John St. Aubyn, their heirs and assigns, "for ever." They were empowered to demand as tolls—"before any passage over the said bridge shall be permitted"—for every chaise, chair, or calash drawn by one horse the sum of twopence; for every cart, dray, car, sledge, or other carriage drawn by one horse, mule, or ass, the same amount; for every coach or chariot drawn by two horses, the sum of threepence; for every coach or chariot drawn by more than two horses, the sum of sixpence; and so on, the toll for pedestrians being fixed at a halfpenny. The owners were authorised to deny passage to those who refused to pay the pontage, and they or their agents were empowered to distrain "any horse, cattle, or anything upon or in respect of which such tolls or duties shall be payable, or any other of the goods and chattels of such person or persons who ought to pay the same." No person who paid toll was to be subject to another demand on the return journey, the condition being the delivery of a ticket, which the collector was required to supply when payment was made. The owners could reduce the tolls at pleasure, or raise them to the point stated in the Act; and the bridge was absolved from every "public or parochial rate or tax whatsoever."

The powers were large, but the Act was granted at a time when the view of a carriage was phenomenal, and even a jolting waggon was an unusual spectacle in the town. Mounted travellers, bound for Plymouth, or journeying to the metropolis, forded the shallow waters of the rivers, and entered fields through opportune gateways to avoid collision with horses carrying the extended crooks from which produce and merchandise were alike suspended. At Longbridge a beaten track, which was subject to inundations and other impediments, traversed the tidal marshes. It communicated on one side with the road leading from Leigham Gate to Knackersknowle Village, and with Plympton by means of a bridge across the river. When the landowners were constituted a highway board, they were authorised to collect tolls and improve and widen the almost impassable highways; and the

New Bridge—as distinguished from Plymbridge—was erected at a right angle across the river, and its width of ten feet was considered ample.   There was a road across the sands that stretched from Crabtree to Blaxton, under Saltram ; but, as its use depended on the tide, it was inconvenient and dangerous.   After the new road to Exeter became necessary, vehement altercation arose as to whether it should run from Crabtree over a bridge to be built at Blaxton, and thence through Underwood and Plymouth to Ivybridge, or over the New Bridge and so towards Ridgeway.   Sir John Rogers led the successful party, and Mr. Parker, of Saltram, espoused the defeated route.   Not content with the conflicts arising out of turnpike oratory, lampoons and squibs were circulated, and their humours were recalled for many years.

THE STAGE COACH PROCEEDING OVER THE OLD LONGBRIDGE.

(From an old Painting.)

When the highest surgical treatment was required the patient was sent to London in a carriage which was forwarded from the metropolis for the purpose. So little regarded was the journey on foot that James Northcote relates, in a matter of fact way, the story of his tramp from Plymouth to the capital, when, as a young artist, with ten guineas in his pocket, he left to sit at the feet of Sir Joshua Reynolds, who was then in the zenith of his fame. The era of the stage coach had not been inaugurated in the West, and the Rogers family were the only Plymothians who used a carriage. This was a primitive suggestion of a modern baker's cart—a covered vehicle, moving on roughly-made wheels, and it excited lively interest whenever it entered the town. The people ran to their doors as its approach was heralded ; and, drawn by four long-tailed horses, it was regarded as a weird example of man's

The London and Exeter

STAGE-COACHES

In Th...

SET out from the New-Inn, Exon, from the *Saracen's Head, Friday-Street*, LONDON, every *Monday* and *Thursday* Morning at Five o'Clock; carry in Paffengers at at 45 s each, Out-fide Paffengers and Children on Lap Half Fare; each infide Paffenger to be allowed 16 lb. weight of Luggage, all above to pay Two-pence *per* Pound.

ALSO

A MACHINE,

Sets out after the arrival of the *London Coaches* at the New-Inn, Exon, for Plymouth, every *Monday* and *Thurfday* Morning, and return every *Wednefday* and *Saturday* at Exeter, carrying Paffengers at 15 s each. The MACHINE fets up at Mr. *Nathaniel* .... *White-Hart* in Old-Town, Plymouth, ... and Others may have Places for London, and be fupply'd with good Chaifes at NINE-PENCE *per* Mile to Exeter, and Saddle Horfes on the leaft Notice.

Plymouth: Printed by O. ADAMS, in *South-fide-ftreet*, 1760.

[Reproduced from an original Handbill enumerating the engagements and route of the first Stage Coach that travelled between Plymouth, Exeter, and London.]

ingenuity in an age of evolution. As the eighteenth century approached its concluding decade, and the necessities for transport were more exacting, a turnpike road was made from Totnes to Gasking Gate, and the occasional coach entered, with radiant driver and cheery horn.

VIEW OF PLYMOUTH FROM THE OLD LONDON ROAD, SHOWING A PORTION OF THE "SEVEN TREES."

(From a Sketch in possession of Sir George Birdwood.)

Municipal and Parliamentary Episodes: 1696-1784. The reign of George II. was marked by momentous departures. So great was "the cure of souls" in Plymouth that parish clerks took deacons' orders, and married, christened, buried, read "both lessons and administered the cup at the sacrament." There was such a consuming thirst for information that "two printing offices were allowed to advertise of matters and subsisted chiefly by the printing of newspapers." The number of inhabitants in 1740 was only 8,400, but the drift to Dock more than accounted for the difference. The Prince George Inn, the half-way house between the two communities, attained distinction when Mr. Bignall, the proprietor, introduced in 1760 the first carriage used between the two towns by the general public. In 1772, under the style of Barings, Lee, Sellons, and Tingcombe, the earliest bank was established in Plymouth; and the "Naval" was next constituted by Harris, Harris, Tanner and Herbert. Plymouth also witnessed some notable maritime triumphs, and Captain Wallis, in the Dolphin, and Captain Carteret, in the Swallow, set out from its harbour to achieve their voyages of circumnavigation. Captain Cook sailed in the Endeavour in 1769; and, although England was at war the French issued a general order to preserve the explorer from molestation, as his services were for the benefit of humanity—not the only tribute on record to the magnanimity of the "hereditary foe."

In 1772, Captain Cook once more left the port in the Resolution and met his death at the hands of the savages whom he endeavoured to win to commercial enterprises.

The conduits at Foxhole, and other survivals of the Elizabethan era, were removed " to the lasting infamy " of Joseph Collier and Robert Philip, who were fond of demolishing " archæological remains and substituting for them insignificant maggots of their own." There was evidently little love lost between Plymouth Utilitarians and Antiquarians in the Georgian era ! Without the Frankfort Gate a horsepond had existed from time immemorial; and after this eyesore was filled in, the space was planted with trees. The expansion of the traffic compelled the abolition of the picturesque gate, and a tablet was inserted in the wall of the Globe Tavern some years later, which bore this inscription : " Near this place formerly stood Frankfort Gate which, with others, formed the principal entrance into the town then enclosed by a wall erected for the greater protection thereof by the Mayor and Commonalty under the authority of the Charter of Henry VI. But, in course of years, this mode of defence ceasing to be of any effect, the gate was taken down in 1783 and the street and avenues adjoining were considerably widened and improved. This tablet was put up by order of the Mayor and Commonalty 4th of June, 1813."

Rails with gates and turnstiles were erected around the Hoe and down to the water-side as an assertion of public right; the "Old Fish Cage," or Market, with its festering offal, was removed to improve Whimple-street ; and St. Martin's Gate, which stood between Briton's Side and Lower Broad-street, was demolished on the representation of one of the princes, whose servant was killed by knocking his head against its masonry when riding on the roof of the royal coach ! The barrier gates at Stonehouse—the one at Emma Place and the other on the site of the Naval Hospital—were also taken down and reconstructed at Mount Edgcumbe ; so that the Vandals were abroad with the dawn of development. Serious attention was also paid to the paving of the streets, lamps were set up at the expense of the Commonalty ; and to avoid the levy of a rate, the authorities mis-appropriated Joan Bennett's charitable bequest. Similar malversations continued for years, and the Corporation of 1824 were compelled by the courts to disgorge £2,000. But it was the rulers in 1740 who set them the example.

Freedom Day at Plymouth was observed with turbulent affection for custom ; and the Mayor-elect was formally shown around the boundaries by his predecessor, unless, as in 1744, the high tide curtailed the programme. On that occasion boats floated about the streets ; the Fish House was undermined ; and the quays collapsed. The leading citizens were borne to their homes on the shoulders of brawny fishermen and more than once they were maliciously dipped. The observance was never wanting in excitement ; as, mounted on horseback and wearing the insignia of their office, the aldermen and councillors encouraged the charity lads at their mischievous pranks. At Catdown the boys were "taken out of the boat" by the Mayor himself, and a box upon the ears impressed on their memories the boundaries of the borough. By way of solatium the common law was waived for the day; and the youngsters not only stole victuals without fear of punishment, but pelted magistrates and councillors alike with dung and filth as they assembled in the Freedom Feld. Beer was distributed at the close of the perambulation, and the use of fists and sticks was encouraged as inspiring the rising generation with a proper degree of personal daring.

Over the municipal and parliamentary elections there were violent altercations. In 1697 the "tricks" of the Presbyterians were so "exposed" that the credit of their party was broken, and the leaders were so "mortifyed" that they abstained for some time from interfering in the town's affairs. The Mayor for this year, John Neal, was so dense and ignorant that things went "very uneasy"; beggars multiplied ; the streets were filthy ; and the Corporation fell into contempt. In 1699 John Opie refused to abet "the arbitrary, sinnister, Whiggish designs" of his predecessors, and the balance of power was thus overthrown by a Mayor whom Sir Francis Drake, the Whig-leader, had given his opportunity. In profound disgust, "Drake abdicated the town and came not near the Chamber for several years, doing us all the spite he could, without regard to his oath or the interest of his friends here, who suffered from his oppressions as did his enemies." It was Joseph Webb, however, who, as Mayor, quite broke the neck of the Whig interest in 1700, and he assisted to secure the representation in Parliament for the Trelawneys, although he was opposed by "all the power and tricks of the Dissenters, Whiggs and enemys of the church."

The election of Thomas Darracott as Mayor in 1704 was a false move on the part of the Tories. They thought him "honest," but he proved a "shuffler" and encouraged Sir Francis Drake to reappear. In the political fight that occurred during his year of office, this "knave and hypocrite," with the help of Berry, the Town Clerk, coalesced with the Whigs, and returned Sir George Byng. "I don't say elected him, for had the good votes of the ones which they refused been admitted and their ill ones refused we had carried it. But they lived not long in their iniquity, both dying the next year." Darracott and Berry were "no great loss to the town, save that they made way for two scablers to be put upon the bench." There was a terrific contest for the office of Town Clerk, and, "as the result of Sir Francis Drake's tricks, the insinuations, cowardice and evil principles of others," Mr. Pengelly, a barrister, was chosen—"less a knave than his colleagues." Samuel Allen, the Mayor for 1706, was "a creature of the Regulators," but he was pardoned much for "the goodness of meat and drinks at his dinners." William Roche, the Mayor in 1710, was a sturdy enough Tory in his way, but he was of a headstrong disposition, and rejecting the advice of "wiser and honester men," allowed himself to be "scandalously baffled" by the enemy. The office fell in 1711 into the hands of Mr. Berry, a Whig without a house of his own, who "lodged and kept the Mayoralty at a place that was common for quartering strangers and selling punch and ale, to the great scandal of the town."

The spirit of contention did not blaze forth again until 1721, and then, at the eleventh hour, Sir John Rogers, declined the contest, and Mr. Patt Byng and Mr. William Chettwin were returned unopposed as M.P.'s. Twenty houses were free for meat and drink—wine and strong liquor being provided for the voters, and two hogsheads of small beer were distributed amongst "the rabble." To the nomination as Mayor of Benjamin Berry, in 1726, there was great opposition, and the dispute was riotously sustained till midnight. In 1727 John Rogers and George Treeby obtained eighteen votes apiece and the contention waxed more than ever uproarious. The exasperating grievance was that time-expired apprentices were not admitted to the freedom; the candidates in their passion brandished their swords at each other; and it was only the superior attraction of a fire in Gasking Street that drew off the crowd and restored the peace. On resuming, agreement was still impossible, and the town remained without a Mayor until the following March, when Rogers was appointed by a mandamus from the Court of Queen's Bench, on the ground that the apprentices were entitled to vote and had already decided against Treeby. The Mayor and Aldermen attempted to elect freemen the following year, but their pretensions were non-suited at the Devon Assizes. Thus the same number of votes were cast for Mr. Allen and Mr. Hewer; and, after a wrangle that lasted several hours, the freemen consented to re-elect the retiring Aldermen. As the result of this compromise, Mr. Allen was granted the chair, but the Aldermen subsequently asserted their privileges more strenuously than ever.

The choice of member occasioned serious dissension in 1738, when the rights of the freemen were raised and determined. Four days were occupied in discussing the claims of faggot voters who travelled from Cornwall in the interest of Mr. John Rogers, and the contest was adjourned from the Guildhall to the Workhouse. There Rogers was declared elected, and a petition was filed by the friends of Mr. Charles Vanbrugh, the defeated candidate. Although Plymouth had returned members prior to the Act of Henry VI., and down to the Restoration, the right of election was monopolised by the Select part of the Corporation—the Mayor, Aldermen, and members of the Common Council. In the reign of Charles II. a double return was made—one by the Select part of the Corporation, and the other by the freemen and freeholders ; but the House deprived the latter of their pretensions until the claim of the community at large was sanctioned, and then freemen and

freeholders voted at seven successive elections. The returns were made in the name of the Mayor and Commonalty, until, in the reign of James II., the Select part of the Corporation again sought to exclude both freemen and freeholders. Although the manœuvre did not prevail, the allies were so aroused at the prospect of disfranchisement that they insisted, at the next contest, that the return should be made not only on behalf of the Mayor and the Commonalty, but the freemen and freeholders as well. A few years afterwards the freemen were precluded from voting, and the franchises of freeholders alone were recognised.

During the contest between Rogers and Vanbrugh, the freemen monopolised the franchise in the interest of the latter, and their action was approved in Parliament to secure the seat for the Ministerial and favourite local candidate. Thus the freemen acquired an exclusive right which they had never previously exercised, and Commonalty was declared to apply only to their privilege—a decision which remained unchallenged. In 1750 James Richardson was chosen Mayor to please the Government party: "Though a man of neither figure nor character, he was readily accepted by the vile scoundrel aldermen and their lacqueys on the Common Council—one-half of both benches having made themselves slaves and dependents on the Board of Admiralty by getting into positions." The battle was revived in 1784, when Admiral Macbride, "the faithful Irishman," who had obtained several favours for Plymouth, defeated Sir Frederick Rogers to the popular rhyme: "Macbride's a man and Sir Frederick's a mouse—Macbride shall sit in the Parliament House." Macbride had obtained much fame by "winging the French gentry in their own harbours," but he earned high repute as M.P. by "exposing the infamous and expensive project" for fortifying the dockyards of Plymouth and Portsmouth.

Reconstruction of Stoke Church: 1730-1750. The rapid increase of Dock rendered necessary the extension of Stoke Church, and this reference to the fabric may be regarded as convenient for discussing its origin. Nothing is known even of its dedication; the State papers contain no reference to its early history; and there is no old chest that supplies any evidence. Two stones preserved from previous restorations, and inserted at the avenue leading to the North Door, contain figures which do not err on the side of the beautiful; but they are of interest, the one as representing the fleur-de-lis, or sign of the Virgin Mary, and the other as being typical of the Cross of St. Andrew. The conjunction possibly indicates the dedication of the church, but no document ascribes to it any other name than that of Stoke Damerel. Although the earliest work is about the twelfth century, there is no entry in the register before the reign of Elizabeth, and then an unpretentious nave, surmounted by a tower, stood on the storm-swept moor, in the midst of a few farms from which the rector drew his scanty tithes. Mr. German Gouldston, apparently a priest with foreign Protestant views, was pastor in 1595, and he variously called himself Goulstone, Gouldestone, Goldston, and Goldstone. The same disregard for uniformity was evidenced in writing the name of the parish, which was severally given as Dameron, Dammerel, Damerel, and Damarel; but Stoke, with more consistency, was invariably rendered as Stoake. Solitude and poverty did not consign Gouldston to an early grave, for he ministered till January, 1660, and his "widdow, Dorothy Gouldestone," was "buryed the 13th day of July" of the same year—a touching picture of an aged couple who in death were not divided. An entry in 1654 contains the appointment of an outsider, Walter Marchant, to administer the parish under the Commonwealth; and there are also records of the baptism of bastards, under the designation of filius or filia populi. "Robert Percy and Barbary Sulke, widdowe, were marryed the second time" in 1678—presumably to rectify a previous and irregular ceremony. In Gouldston's time every page of the register was signed at the bottom; but, as the churchwardens could not always write, they made various distinctive marks, something after the construction of shorthand characters or Greek literals. Originally the church consisted of a simple nave with the oblong tower so characteristic of West-country architecture, which gave access to the sanctuary and caused the ringers to stand in the view of the congregation. In the existing belfry are the remains of the porch which opened up the church, and at the base of the tower is the built-in portion of the staircase.

Before any addition was made to the edifice, a chapel was built within the dockyard, with the object of detaching the artisans and sailors, who taxed the space of the little building. The occasion was the return of the fleets after the peace of Ryswick, and officers and men alike contributed from their prize money to rear the chapel of "St. Lo at the Docke at Plymouth." The addition afforded little relief, and an aisle was erected north of the nave of Stoke Church in 1730, at the instance of Mr. Robert Young, an officer of the dockyard, to whose virtues the memorial now dimmed by decay bore not ungenerous testimony.

"Within these walls lie interred the remains of Mr. Robert Young, who faithfully discharged the duty of an officer in the dockyard, in this parish, nearly 40 years, and departed this life March 12, 1732, aged 70. He was the son of Captain Benjamin Young, commander of, and slain in her Majesty's ship "Advice," A.D. 1670, fighting in defence of his King and country. Unaffected piety and strict justice, compassion to the poor, and benevolence to all were qualities which adorned his character. He was industrious in, and handsomely contributed to, the enlarging and beautifying of this church. The remains of Mrs. Ann Young, who departed this life January 21, 1741, aged 78, lie interred with those of Mr. Robert Young, her husband. She was the daughter of George Woodyeare, of Shorn, in the County of Kent, Esquire. A woman excelled by few or none. They were eminent examples of conjugal affection and fidelity. Of their children a son and daughter were interred here. Six sons and one daughter survived them. In duty and gratitude their children pay this small tribute to the memories of their worthy parents."

In 1750 the pressure of worshippers rendered imperative substantial reconstruction. The only central access to the church was removed bodily south, and its centre carried several feet to the original line as it went through the tower. An attempt was made to induce the Admiralty to contribute to the cost of the rebuilding, but the authorities would only subscribe in the form of material, which was obtained from the dockyard. Thus the roof was constructed on the lines of a battleship, with knees, beams and masts, and fastened with copper bolts. Little of the original building remained, with the exception of the tower; and a reconstruction which contemporary taste and expediency regarded as alike incongruous and inartistic was commended as "beautiful and handsome." Included in the "improvements" was "a spacious gallery," which ran across the width of the church, and this excrescence was not removed until the lapse of over a hundred years.

Arian Controversy at Plymouth: 1710-1780.   Historical events were bridged in the life of John Fox, whose unpublished memoirs are rich in biographical details. His great-grandfather was a major of horse under Oliver Cromwell, and he was so famed for his strength that he boxed to death a noted Cornish wrestler, who came from the adjoining county in order to fight him, in response to a public challenge. On the restoration of the monarchy this old warrior and redoubtable pugilist buried his identity in farming at Aveton Gifford. Fox's grandfather, the son of this stalwart, settled near Beeralston, and married the daughter of Mr. Samuel Brett, a merchant who served his time with Mr. Northcote, of Plymouth, "a very rigid Puritan, who kept a great trade and did much merchandise, but was afterwards sadly reduced by losses at sea." Fox spanned the seventeenth and eighteenth centuries in his acquaintance with Hannah Collier, who told how one of her relatives was carrying the midday refreshment to her husband at the Maudlin fort, when she met the corpse of a man, thrown across a horse like a sack, with the head shot away. The maimed remains were those of her partner. Hannah Collier also recalled the fact that her grown-up relatives, as did all the adults of the time, assisted in carrying the stones for the workmen who were engaged in erecting the Citadel, in order to boast that they helped to rear that structure.

Fox's ancestors were witnesses by "ear and eye" to the cruelties James inflicted on the survivors of "Monmouth's foolish rebellion," and his mother was so affected by the persecutions that her mind was weaned to democratic sympathies, and she designed her son for the Puritan ministry. His religious tendencies were broader than those of his parents, and, when the Arian controversy arose to disturb his faith in the Trinity, he assured his distressed father that he could not subscribe to the Articles. At this time the Rev. Isaac Gilling, of Newton, was indicted for keeping a school in defiance of the Schism Act; and, to avoid prosecution, he disguised himself in a long wig and lay habit and made his escape to Plymouth, where his appearance much amused those who had been accustomed to see him in ministerial attire. As Fox's father acted as the offender's host, he took him into confidence concerning his son, and it was arranged that the lad should leave the town in Gilling's company, so that he might receive the benefit of his counsel and the advice of other ministers. "Skulking through the bye-paths and crossways" of Devonshire, Gilling and his charge made their way to London, and there Fox saw Queen Anne at State worship with the Duke of Marlborough; witnessed the great fire, and walked over the Thames during the no less famous frost; attended the Coronation of George I., the trial of rebel lords, and the beheading of Derwentwater and Kenmure on Tower Hill. The while that he studied for the ministry the more he was prejudiced in favour of the Unitarian argument, and, upon his return, his parents were more than ever concerned at his heresies. The Rev. Edmund Calamy was at this time staying "at the great inn at Plymouth for the ministers which was kept by Mrs. Vinson"; and this shining light added little to Fox's respect for the cloth by assuring him that it was the custom for ministers to hide their doubts from their brethren, and that "if he kept himself to himself" no one need ever suspect that he was haunted by any difficulties.

The Arian controversy marched too rapidly for Mr. Fox; and, as suspicion and mistrust gained ground in Plymouth, the Calvinists made the pamphleteering pace hot for their doubting brethren. In 1716 the orthodox issued a test declaration of faith, and compelled all ministers who were amenable to pressure to subscribe to the Thirty-Nine Articles. "Everybody believed them," but Fox refused to submit himself to the intimidation of the Presbyterian Assembly; because, exercising their power "in a crafty and arbitrary manner," the members elicited the private opinions of candidates and "tricked" the congregations out of their right of appointment. The young minister formed a very low opinion of the Plymouth preachers, especially of those who assumed "the canting way of speaking peculiar to the Puritans." To avert professional ruin many dependent young ministers, with freethought tendencies, issued a manifesto in which they protested that they were "no Arians, and that they believed in the Scriptures"—an ambiguity that caused everyone to laugh and say that they had not only admitted the charge, but "set their hands to it." Cast adrift they were left with "broken congregations," and the rage, aspersions and violence of their Trinitarian pursuers involved the more needy dissidents in sheer ruin. Passionately attached to religious liberty of thought, Mr. Fox accordingly transmitted to posterity his impressions of the teachers of the Gospel with whom he was brought into contact, "to show how very difficult it is for men to be interested in any party of religion as a party, and how few can be said to deserve that title of which such party is composed." Arianism reasserted itself in Plymouth in the form of Unitarian doctrine some years later on, when an avowedly Unitarian congregation appointed its own ministers.

A generous discount must be taken off Fox's estimate of the ministers by whom he was surrounded, and whose assumptions filled him with so rare a scorn and merciless a contempt. Still his portraitures assist to illuminate the period which was so heavily overcast by the stormy and unscrupulous polemics of the Calvinistic devotees. Nathaniel

Harding's presence in Plymouth was the result of an accident.   He left Ireland, where his father was a well-known Dissenting minister, and, by chance, the ship in which he was bound for London put into Catwater.   During the delay, Harding preached at a chapel which had just been bereaved of its minister, the congregation fell in love with his gifts upon the spot, and elected him pastor.   Harding discoursed incessantly of the mysteries of Christianity, of Election, Adoption and Sanctification ; and his behaviour in the pulpit was suitable to his way of thinking, for he made a "most monstrous noise," especially when he grew angry, as he did whenever he happened to confute an opponent in public. Upon one occasion he nearly threw a quarto Bible at the head of a brother minister, who was sitting at the desk underneath the pulpit ; and, in the course of another controversial heat, he jerked his wig off his head in the violence of his agitation, and with difficulty recovered and replaced it.   He was much "more disagreeable in prayer" than in sermon ; but, as he committed every word to heart, and never faltered in expression, his delivery was peculiarly impressive.   In the midst of all this "holyness," he was "very inquisitive after other people's secrets" ; encouraged gossips to visit him ; and listened with smug contentment to their "stories and scandals."   Impatient of contradiction, he governed his family with positive harshness ; but he was otherwise pious, and when he could no longer speak, his hands were clasped in prayer.

James Sandercock was contemporary with Harding in Plymouth, and his mother was "so holy and so nasty, and stank so much of tobacco" that Fox "always hated her." Sandercock had in him a deal of the wisdom of the serpent, and was so familiar with the temper of his people that he knew how "to govern them absolutely and to please them at the same time."   His sermons were not disfigured by nonsense, but were so delivered as to lull his listeners to sleep, for he was "a most dull, drowsy, and disagreeable man in the pulpit."   As his party sway was potent, he directed the votes of most of his hearers at election times" ; and, through the influence of "the old Sir Francis Drake, he hath often provided for such of his friends as wanted places."

George Brett was another minister of note—a native of Liskeard, who, after learning grammar at Plymouth, set up in the town as a schoolmaster, "and whipt some children into learning and others out of their senses."   After existing more or less on the bounty of his friends, he became chaplain to an old Dissenting lady in the South Hams, and frequently figured in the local pulpits.   "A man of no learning, of much bigotry, some cruelty, and a little cracked," it was hard to determine whether he was the more regarded for his good qualities or hated for his bad ones.   John Enty was educated at the expense of a Dissenting lady in Cornwall, and afterwards elected to a congregation at Plymouth, in the room of Mr. Byfield, "who had best sense and parts of any Dissenter who ever lived in the town."   On losing his first wife, Enty's grief was immoderate, and Mrs. Vinson, fearing that his health would be impaired, proposed a new match, and persuaded the Shilston family to bestow their eldest daughter on her friend.   She was a fine young woman, and at first was averse to the match ; but domestic persuasions and the play of such arts as the bereaved was able to exercise at last prevailed, and, in less than a month, Enty's distress for his first wife had ceased, and he was "in eager pursuit of his second." Having by these means added wealth to ability, Enty exercised considerable influence in the controversial arena.

Whitefield and   With James's declaration in favour of liberty of conscience, the
Wesley at Plymouth: Baptists once more worshipped in their own way, but the dis-
1744-1787.   couragements which were experienced in the absence of a "stated
ministry" prevented the formation of a strong following.   Nonconformist thought in

PLYMOUTH IN THE 18TH CENTURY, FROM THE FOOTPATH OVER STONEHOUSE HILL, SHOWING UNION STREET AS A MARSH.

(*From an old Sketch in the possession of Sir George Birdwood.*)

Plymouth was at its dreariest ebb, "low and afflicted," when George Whitefield and the Wesleys stirred its dormant embers. The town was first visited by Whitefield and his companion in thought, Cennick, and they kindled such interest by their appeals that, after their departure, and the consequent re-action, an old lady encouraged a convert by exclaiming: "Though Mr. Whitefield and Mr. Cennick are gone, the Gospel is not gone: it is still preached at our meetings by Mr. Crispin Curtis, our pastor; and, whilst there is a great difference between his public gifts and theirs, yet you will hear the same truths." Young Gibbs, the convert in question, became a candidate for the ministry, but he was impressed at these services rather by "the love which I saw amongst the people than by Mr. Curtis's preaching." It remained necessary for the aspirant to be "called," and the simplicity of the method surprised him. The congregation held their hands aloft after hearing his professions of faith, and Mr. Curtis "without much form" observed: "Brother Gibbs, the Church calls on you to exercise your gifts among us." At the next service Gibbs preached with extraordinary effect, and, penetrating to the country districts, created "a great stir" and achieved a reputation that outlived his death.

The Wesleys were for a time indisposed to compete with Whitefield's followers, since they held so much in common as Revivalists; and leaving Plymouth untouched, the former penetrated Cornwall, where Charles took the field with a noble fervour that contumely and insult failed to moderate. He was preaching at St. Ives when the news arrived that Admiral Matthews had beaten the Spaniards, and, in their wantonness, the crowd destroyed the chapel in which the Methodists were assembled. "Such," he remarked, "is the Cornish method of offering thanksgiving. I suppose," he added, "if Admiral Lestock had also fought they would also have knocked all the worshippers on the head."

Exasperated at the persistence of the missioners, the county gentlemen conspired with the magistrates to imprison them on the plea that they possessed no visible means of existence: and, when the justices declined to push this farce to the extreme, they urged the lieutenants of pressgangs to seize them as eligible seamen. One strenuous disciple, of the name of Maxwell, was taken in charge at St. Ives and offered to the master of a ship lying in Mount's Bay. He shrewdly declined the recruit, however, for fear his crew would be persuaded to pray when they ought to be trimming the sails. Charles Wesley was also apprehended for preaching in the open air; but, finding that he had on his hands a gentleman by birth and education, the magistrate found a convenient excuse for restoring him to liberty. Charles was again in danger of his life at Falmouth, for a horde of privateering seamen besieged the house in which he was lodging and terrorised the inmates with their shouts of "Bring forth the Cannorum"—the nickname which was locally applied to the Methodists. Walking bareheaded into the midst of these bullies, Charles bravely raised his voice with the challenge: "Here I am; what have you to say to me?" and, as the abashed and disconcerted mob fell back, a clergyman, taking Wesley by the arm, conducted him to the waterside, whence he escaped in a boat to Penryn.

John Wesley traversed the ground in 1746; and, although he was regarded as "mazed" by those who differed from his tenets, he addressed a multitude of Cornishmen in Gwennap Pit, and his ringing notes ascended the slopes with such effect, as the sun was setting in a glow behind him, that the majority of those present received ineffaceable impressions. Meanwhile colonies of Methodists were created in Plymouth and Dock, and the Tabernacle was erected in the former town, with the assistance of the Baptists, who alternately shared its facilities. John Wesley harangued the West-country folk with heroic persistence, despite petty persecutions and recurring discouragements, overcoming weariness and faintness, and even feverish exhaustion, in the resolve to impress the people. On the occasion of his first visit to Plymouth the meeting place was crowded, and he was importuned to call on his way back from Cornwall. The Revivalist favoured his adherents at Dock instead and addressed them at night, as well as at five o'clock the following morning. On journeying to the district a few months subsequently--June, 1747--a hostile demonstration had been organised. "All the Dock was in an uproar ; " the house of Mr. Hide, his host, was besieged by thousands of people ; and a constable was severely mauled and beaten in the struggle. Messengers were despatched to inform Wesley that his life was in peril, and to suggest the postponement of the proposed service. He replied by pushing his way into the town and penetrating the midst of the rioters, by whom he was immediately cheered in recognition of his courage. As soon as he entered his lodgings, however, the crowd "recovered its spirits and fought valiantly with the doors and windows" until "they were weary." Then, the night being far advanced, "every man went to his own home." The following day the Revivalist conferred with the members of the society ; and, in the evening, he endeavoured to hold a service in the open air' Whilst the worshippers were rendering the opening hymn, an officer, "a famous man," swaggered towards them with a retinue of "soldiers, drummers and mob." As soon as the drums ceased, "a gentleman barber" made an attempt to speak, but his voice was drowned in the shouts of the multitude, growing "fiercer and fiercer" with increase of numbers. Menacing as was the crowd, Wesley advanced in its direction with serene confidence, and heartily grasped the lieutenant by the hand. The sublime assurance thus displayed immediately won the officer, and he escorted the evangelist to Mr. Hide's door, from which, as the mob grew better humoured, he discoursed without further attempts at outrage. On the following day—Sunday—he preached in the Brickfields— "the Common"—to an earnest and well-behaved congregation, and took his departure with the consciousness that his advocacy had not been barren of excellent consequences.

John Wesley returned to the west after the lapse of four years, and found even the people of Dock more reconciled to his programme. The night was far advanced when he rode into the town, "but the moon gave us all the light we wanted." At the outset "one poor man bawled out for the Church, but he soon went away ashamed." Multitudes assembled at the various services in Plymouth,— "but no scoffer ; no inattentive person. The time for this is past, till God shall see good to let Satan loose again." Dock was more often visited than Plymouth, as it was a kind of half-way house into Cornwall. Its Methodists, however, were nearly always distracted by polemical differences ; and, with a view of teaching the more bigoted a lesson, Wesley "willingly accepted the offer to preach in the chapel lately built for Mr. Whitefield." The enrolled united in 1754 to erect a hall three or four times as large as that in which they had been accustomed to assemble ; but even this was too small to accommodate those who desired to hear the Revivalist on the occasion of his next pilgrimage. "Is the time come," he joyously asked, "when even this barren soil of Dock shall bring forth fruits of righteousness ?" But, in 1757, the Methodists were again rended by disputes and their numbers much reduced. Despite John Wesley's pleading, reconciliation was impossible, and the tension was so acute when he revisited the town, in 1760, that he described the state of the settle- ment as "melancholy." Reproaching the controversialists with much effect, he at last healed the breach ; "many were convinced afresh ; " backsliders were "cut to the heart " ; and the society was restored to its normal strength before he passed into Cornwall. The peace was only patched, however ; disputes ran high concerning "a worthless man " ; and, in 1765, the membership was in a more "miserable" condition than ever. Wesley again brought the malcontents to promise that on no pretence whatever would they reproach each other with anything that had been said or done on either side ; and the advice was so respected that, when he came down in 1766, "a calm " had taken the place of "the great storms." After preaching in the Tabernacle at Plymouth, Wesley pleaded with a crowded congregation at Dock. At the close of the sermon a large stone was hurled through one of the windows and fell at the preacher's feet—" the best place that could have been found for it."

The fearlessness of the divine was evinced in October, 1768, when he was making post haste from Cornwall to fulfil an engagement at Plymouth. At Cremyll the watermen at first declined to take the risk of the passage, because a heavy storm was raging; but Wesley prevailed upon them to venture across, "and we did not ship one sea till we got over." He held forth almost immediately upon the quay at Plymouth; where, in spite of heavy rain, the listeners remained uncovered to the end. One "silly man," however, insisted upon interrupting "till I desired the people to open right and left, and let me look in his face." When the avenue was formed the disturber pulled off his hat and quietly stole from the scene. The same afternoon Wesley preached " in the square at the Dock ": and, throughout a downpour, the congregation were steadfast. The old distractions were revived after Wesley's departure, however, and he abstained from further attempts to reconstitute the society until 1774. Then, "after a long interval of deadness," the membership at Dock doubled. During his next visit, in 1775, Wesley found revolutionary sentiments abroad, and many of his adherents were "deeply prejudiced against the King and his Ministers." He spoke with freedom as to their disloyalty at the private meeting of the dockyard members, "and I think there is not one of them now who does not see things in another light." A few months later he occupied a spare hour in attending the service at St. Andrew's Church, and admired "the seriousness and decency" of the congregation. "None bowed or curtsied or looked about them." He was even more agreeably surprised to find that there were 300 communicants. In the course of his own sermon, however, which he delivered on the Barbican, Wesley was "shocked at the stupidity and ill-breeding" of several officers, who walked about and talked "with the utmost unconcern." Marked improvement in the behaviour of the military was exhibited at Dock in 1782. A regiment entered the Square as the Revivalist was exhorting a large crowd; and, appreciating the situation, the commanding officer immediately stopped the band, drew up his men in line, and thus they remained—"still as night, nor did any of them stir till I had pronounced the blessing."

There was another ferment at Dock in 1785, when William Moore renounced the Methodists, hired a place to preach in, and, drawing away forty of the members, formed a society of his own. The stewards and leaders immediately communicated with John Wesley, who was then at Spitalfields; and, "seeing there was no time to be lost," he took a seat in "the Exeter Diligence," to find on his arrival that a serious cleavage had been effected. He at once assured the congregation that they were "better without William Moore, as his heart is not with God"; and, after giving "a plain statement of the case, with regard to the deed of declaration, which William Moore had so wonderfully misrepresented," he entirely reassured the faltering brethren. Begging them to put away all bitterness, wrath, anger and clamour, John Wesley left with the advice " not to talk about Mr. Moore at all, but to give him up to God." The separation did "little hurt"; a few turbulent men withdrew from the society, but their places were taken by others of a more pacific spirit. So rapidly did Methodism progress at Dock that Wesley could not pass through the throng that filled the new chapel in 1787; and strong men lifted him over the seats so that he might gain the entrance to the pulpit. Peace and unanimity made very pleasant the path of the Methodists, both at Plymouth and Dock, until 1789; and then "a senseless quarrel" broke out, "wherein I could not but blame both sides, and knew not which to blame most." The astute divine accordingly refused to hear either representation, and shut himself in his lodgings until the hour of service arrived.   As the new edifice in Ker Street was inadequate to hold a proportion of the worshippers and the curious, he adjourned to the open space to the south and preached to a great throng, of whom hundreds sat on the ridge of the rocks "which ran along at my left hand."   It was the veteran's last journey to the west.   His figure was fragile, his voice less robust, his capacity for enforcing discipline far from strenuous.   By the time he returned from Cornwall, however, "the jars" at Plymouth and Dock had been adjusted, "and the contending parties are willing to live in peace."   And so he left them at his last farewell.

Men and Manners :   Art was represented in Plymouth by William. Gandy, the gifted
Early 18th Century.   son of a more gifted father.   Of the latter, James, little is known save that he was born at Exeter, and shewed such talent that Vandyck engaged him to paint his draperies.   William was a man of remarkable gifts ; and, when he settled in Plymouth in 1744, he was known for the splendour of his work, and his disinclination to remain at his easel.   The little he did for his patrons was executed in a short time ; and, though slight and sketchy, was the obvious result of real genius.   Sir Joshua Reynolds compared some paintings by Gandy to those of Rembrandt ; and, when Sir Godfrey Kneller inspected a masterpiece, and was told the author was in poverty, he exclaimed "Let the man come to London at once."   Great rewards were not desired by William Gandy, who, in his unbounded pride, would receive no suggestions, and preferred idle dissipations to a distinguished career.   The anecdotes told of him might be expected of such a Bohemian.   On one occasion he was employed to paint a portrait of Mr. Vallack, a wealthy Plymouth apothecary, who lived in considerable state.   Gandy attended his patron in his own house, and the while that he worked he thought of the recherché dinner that awaited him.   It was the old gentleman's custom to feast his friends once a week, but he ordinarily dined in a simple fashion; and, much to his disgust and disappointment, Gandy was consequently invited to partake of a humble, if savoury, dish of pork and peas. Smothering his rage until he reached his lodgings, he astonished his landlady by showering curses on the head of his patron, and vowing that he would avenge himself upon the portrait, delivered it to Vallack in an unfinished condition.   Subsequently he was invited to Antony House, to paint Sir William Carew, and Nathaniel Northcote was asked to accompany him.   The mansion was so full of visitors that Gandy and Northcote were asked to occupy the same room.   Gandy exploded with passion at the indignity, and the more Northcote tried to assuage him by pointing out the difficulty of the host, the more his friend stormed and cursed.   It was when this victim of wounded dignity undressed that the explanation was forthcoming.   He was wearing two shirts, "each equally ruinous and tattered, such a mere bundle of rags that, out of the two, it would have been impossible to make a decent garment."   In the judgment of Northcote, William Gandy might have been the greatest painter of his time "if he he had not been his own greatest enemy."

In a canvas crowded with famous men, Sir Joshua Reynolds stands out pre-eminent. Born and educated at Plympton, he developed such artistic precocity that he was put under Hudson.   His relations continued friendly until the master included one of his pupil's pictures in an exhibition to show the effect of his training, and he was deeply wounded to hear the critics declaring, as with one voice, that it was the lad who was the genius. Hudson promptly sent Reynolds adrift, and the youth returned to the west.   His sisters took a shop at Dock, and there carried on a millinery business whilst their brother painted portraits on the first floor.   Young Joshua forthwith attracted a bevy of lady patrons because, for the first time within their experience, justice was done to their loveliness in a town where foreign impostors had hitherto only marred it by their ineffective treatment. Securing the Edgcumbes as his patrons, Reynolds painted each member of the family in turn, and then Admiral Lord Keppel enabled him to study the masters at Rome by inviting him to take a voyage up the Mediterranean. On his return to Plymouth, Lord Edgcumbe urged Reynolds to spend no more time in a "country town"; and he at once moved to London, where his commissions increased so rapidly that he raised his fees from twenty to thirty-five guineas for a head, and thus achieved his desire to spend more time upon each portrait.

The master of his own genius, Sir Joshua could not communicate it to others, and, of all his pupils, James Northcote "alone succeeded in escaping starvation." Reynolds did nothing for the young men beyond setting them to copy his own paintings, and he seemed incapable of impressing his methods upon others. He had a poor opinion of his native town as an art centre; and, when Northcote painted his portrait to send to Plymouth, he observed "You are greatly mistaken if you think you will get a customer there for the work." But Reynolds was wrong, for the Recorder of the borough became the purchaser at £20. On another occasion, when Northcote bemoaned the lack of sitters at Plymouth, Sir Joshua consoled him with the reply "You should have remained there until you had painted them all out." Asked how it was that, viewing so many beauties, he did not fall in love, this disciple of Plato answered "Because I am like the grave-digger in Shakespeare's 'Hamlet'—grown callous." His social table was frequented by men of all talents and politics; but party was never introduced, literary and artistic subjects alone were discussed, and premeditated bon mots and studied witticisms were "never tolerated for a moment." Of all his visitors, Boswell was first favourite, and he induced Reynolds to attend the execution at the Old Bailey of a man whom they had known as the butler of a mutual friend. When the criminal saw Sir Joshua, he attracted the attention of the spectators by bowing to him, and the criticisms in the papers were far from pleasant. "Such conduct might have been expected," they said, "from Mr. Boswell, but not from the elegant and graceful Sir Joshua." Reynolds's treatment of his patrons was a little abrupt, and he especially mortified a lady who desired a special sitting, so that justice should be done her hands, by assuring her that he always painted the hands from his servants! On another occasion, when a gentleman suggested that he had not finished his ruffles so that the pattern of the lace might be distinguished, Reynolds waspishly replied: "That's my manner—that's my manner." A ruder criticism caused him lasting mortification; when, on being asked to paint Admiral Boscawen, he produced that familiar inclination of the head which was due either to habit or muscular contraction. Lord Falmouth called in time to inspect the portrait; and, flying in a passion, he accused Sir Joshua of having satirised his brother, and, swinging his cane about, told him that he deserved to be flogged. Reynolds was so amazed that he withdrew from the room to consider his course. He was at first tempted to challenge the author of this "disgusting transaction," but eventually ignored the incident "as the best means of hiding it from a gossiping world." The happiest instance of his consciousness of power occurred when he painted a portrait of Fox for Lord Holland. "You get your money very easily," laughed his lordship, "how long did you take to paint it?" "All my life," was the terse reply.

Foremost among the clergy was Zachariah Mudge, who, when the vicarage of St. Andrew's fell vacant, was urged by a strong competitor to enter the lists, in order that he might dislodge by dividing the vote for the most formidable of many potent competitors. His test sermon, however, so completely outshone all who had gone before, that the contest lay between him and Dr. Burnett, the Government candidate. For Mudge, fifteen votes were cast, and Burnett fourteen, and the result so astonished the Mayor that he spoke of adjourning the poll to take the franchise of two bed-ridden supporters of the latter. This "base trick" was warmly contested ; and when the Black Book was consulted, and it was made clear that the qualified must be present to vote, Mr. Mudge was declared elected. Upon taking possession, he entered the edifice alone, locked the door from within, offered a prayer, and repeatedly tolled one of the bells. He then reappeared at the entrance to the church, his appointment was signed by the officials in waiting, and Mudge invited them to join him in a glass of wine "at Morgan's," as he had "no place of his own." According to Reynolds, Johnson and Burke, the divine would have attained higher distinction at the Bar than in the Church ; and his judgment upon his contemporaries was the more readily accepted, because he admitted their honesty but regretted that they "only saw a little way." So that Dr. Mudge evidently shared Reynolds's opinion that he was "the wisest man in the whole world." If a theological discussion was started in Sir Joshua's presence, and a difficult point arose, he would airily dispose of it by reminding his guests: "Dr. Mudge has answered that." This interposition was always accepted as final. The divine, according to Hazlitt, was gifted and eloquent, but it was his High Church predilections that rendered Johnson and Reynolds so warm in his advocacy. He was not prodigal of his gifts, and rarely delivered more than one sermon a month, although he was chosen for his oratory. An exemplary pastor, an excellent companion, and a man of unaffected and cheerful temperament, Mudge remained vicar for thirty-eight years. His monument in St. Andrew's testified that "in private life he was amiable and benevolent ; in his ministry faithful, eloquent and persuasive ; distinguished for knowledge among the learned, and for talent among men of science." A hundred years later the vault which contained this old worthy was opened, and, for one moment, the churchwarden, Mr. Bone, caught a perfect glimpse of Mudge's face and head, the latter covered with a scarlet nightcap. Then, in an instant, the whole crumbled to dust !

Of the merchants of the period the quaintest picture is drawn of Benjamin Smithurst, "Honest Ben," as he was designated. His father left London to escape the plague, and, after settling awhile at Saltash, removed to Plymouth, where Ben started as a bookseller and draper. Having no competitors in the literary department of his business, Smithurst never sent for any volume that was not ordered, and invariably returned publications that were forwarded on approval. He was always excessively jealous lest new works should be seen by his customers ; and, if by chance he left one exposed and a patron took it up to look at, he apologetically placed it out of reach. An excellent binder, and in a good way of business, he nevertheless accepted no invitations and received no visitors. He would occasionally spend threepence on ale at a neighbouring tavern, and there exercise his wit by relating droll tales concerning "matrimony and women." John Elford, chief attorney of the town, was not only "a furious bigot to the Church," but "a bear in every shape, always raving against respectable people who had more sense and modesty than himself." "Impudent and petulant" abroad, he was "worse than a Bashaw" in his own domestic circle. Matt Batt was another character of interest. He was the son of a carpenter, familiarly known as "Timber'n Will." who, from small beginnings, accumulated a fortune as a tobacco merchant and distiller. Mark, the favourite son, had a taste for cock-fighting and other sports, and a no less emphatic prejudice against Christianity and marriage. His natural son, John, enjoyed life with the same freedom, and no one was surprised when his fair daughter, Jane, walked to church with an officer, and then eloped in a post chaise. After some months, Ensign Gilbert and his wife returned to Plymouth and took rooms at "Bellman's lodgings," where they gave themselves "uncommon airs, suffing up their noses and wondering at the presumption of those who visited them." When their first son arrived, however, the young officer turned out to be a bit of an

Drawn by E. Phillips, from an old print

ENTRANCE TO ST. ANDREW'S CHURCH, WITH THE HOUSES IN BEDFORD STREET THAT
FACED THE GRAVEYARD (site of Pig Market, 18th Century).

adventurer, and Mark Grigg, the joint heir of Matt Batt's fortune, came to the rescue of the disinherited lady.

Medical skill had not attained much distinction, but the locality produced practitioners of widespread repute. Of these the most famous was Dr. Huxham, who was born near Staverton, where his father owned a small farm. Mrs. Whitfeld, the first mistress of the Plymouth Public School, and a direct descendant of the doctor, attributed his career to a gentleman of the same name, who, with his wife, was snowbound, and remained some days as the guests of the Huxhams. They were so interested in the child's precocity that they offered to adopt him as their heir; and, when the parents would not spare their son, the visitors insisted upon paying the cost of his education. Thus the lad took his degrees; and upon the death of Mr. Hunkyn -"a thick-headed physician of Plymouth "--Huxham tried to collect the threads of his practice. Dr. Seymour, the surviving practitioner, secured the best of the patronage; and, in his anger, Huxham described Plymouth as "a damned quacking place, where the inhabitants would rather trust themselves in the hands of an old apothecary than in those of a young physician whom they did not know." He employed every device to make people believe he was busy; booted and spurred himself when he had no place to ride to; galloped from his front door and returned by his back garden to maintain the fiction of an active career; and rarely went to church unless he was called out, "though he had nothing in the world to do." Seymour so far took leave of his senses as to plunge into ecclesiastical disputes; and, adopting the fashionable side, Huxham abandoned Dissent for the Church. From that time his practice grew daily, and he was gradually accepted as the leading authority on fevers. A realistic presentment recalls his figure, as, conspicuous in a scarlet cloak, flowing wig and velvet dress, ruffled shirt and golden snuff-box, he moved with affected strut and simulated gravity from house to house; or was carried in his sedan chair, with linkboys in attendance, when the nights were dreary. No one was more conscious of these elaborate impositions than Huxham himself, and he confessed that, although he laughed when he indulged in them, they largely contributed to his prosperity.

Huxham's skill was unquestioned; he was moderate in his fees, and especially compassionate to the poor. His most distinguished successor was Dr. John Mudge, the son of Zachariah Mudge, whose professional success was hampered by unfortunate marriages. After his first wife's death, the famous Plymouth beauty, Mrs. Horneck—Goldsmith's "Jessamy Bride"—recommended Mudge to engage her companion as his housekeeper. Won by her handsome presence, he married her, and then experienced less comfort than he enjoyed with his first wife. She did not live long, and Mudge contracted a third ill-assorted alliance. The doctor was a universal favourite, an instructive companion and charitable citizen; but, as nearly all his children died young, he had no circumstance in life to make him happy, for all his wives troubled him by "their ill humours," and his only solace was the entertainment of his friends. For fifty years he was the leading host at the Otter Club, whose members regularly bathed under the Hoe and periodically met to enjoy each other's society. Literary and artistic "lions" like Dr. Johnson and Sir Joshua Reynolds were welcomed to the tea-bouts, and the twelve principal members wore silver medals chastely designed to symbolise their purpose, on one side of which was depicted a hearty handclasp and on the other a lusty matron suspending her son by one foot, preparatory to dipping him into the sea. The hospitalities were not confined, however, to the consumption of tea, for this was merely the preliminary course; and the card of invitation was a snare and a delusion to such guests as imagined that an early escape was in store for them: "The gentlemen of the Otter Club present their compliments to Mr ——, and request the honour of his company on —— next, to drink tea and spend the evening.'

Tea was accompanied by the consumption of two huge cakes, and amongst the liquors provided during the intermediate entertainment were punch, brandy, port and sherry. Porter and cider were taken with the supper, and the room was illuminated by wax candles, the cost of this one item amounting to fifteen shillings at a single sitting. Extravagance was not the badge of the members, however, and the inclusive charge for each person present did not usually exceed ten shillings. Polemics and bantering personalities were banished from the club; the object was literary and scientific interchange, associated with the primary aim of good health, which gave rise to the origin of the institution. The best idea of the intentions of the founders may be gathered from the song which Lyne Brett composed in its honour—

> Now all ye merry Otters, obey the merry call,
> Without delay, come haste away, away to Otter Hall.
> > And a bathing we will go, etc.
>
> In bed while drowsy mortals waste the sweet time of day,
> We rise to bread the dewy mead and midst y' waters play.
> > And a bathing we will go, etc.
>
> Cold bathing health procures us, new strings each slackened nerve,
> And makes each Otter better his friend or mistress serve.
> > And a bathing we will go, etc.
>
> Within this social cavern, now fill the flowing bowl,
> And while we drink and laugh and sing no Otter dare be dull.
> > And a bathing we will go, etc.
>
> Of Church nor State disputing, one moment let us spend,
> Nor for the sake of joking, let any risk a friend.
> > And a bathing we will go, etc.
>
> But sing with good Will Wiseman, how joyful 'tis to see
> Brethren together first to hold the bond of amity.
> > And a bathing we will go, etc.
>
> While here with us rejoicing, gay mirth and pleasure dwell,
> See Neptune leave his coral court, the Tritons tune their shell.
> > And a bathing we will go, etc.
>
> All Nature joy expressing, drink to the Otter king,
> And with a loud huzza, boys, make Otter Hall to ring.
> > And a bathing we will go, etc.
>
> Then Vernon, bravest Otter, we fill the glass to thee,
> And every loyal brother drink off that glass with glee.
> > And a bathing we will go, etc.
>
> And when our mirth is ended, as sober as we came,
> We all go home in hopes again next month to do the same
> > And a bathing we will go, etc

•

CHAPTER VI.—WHEN GEORGE III. WAS KING.

Attempts to Fire the   Personally disliked for his sullen and selfish temperament,
Dockyard: 1762-1785.   George II. nevertheless left England stronger than he found it; and,
at the time of his death, the British flag waved over Canada and India, and France was
cut off from fresh effective alliances.   There were 7,000 prisoners at Plymouth in 1762,
and the Mayor was in continual unrest lest they should rise and overpower the guards.
In spite of the general sense of insecurity, the garrison did not number 2,500 men in all;
and, importuned by frequent memorials, the Government reduced the menace by drafting
batches of the captives to inland towns.   France added to the unrest by plotting to burn
the English dockyards, and preparations for their destruction were ripe in 1764, when Lord
Halifax learnt from secret sources that a newly-invented kind of fire was to be employed.
Supplies of the explosive were traced to various ports, and two foreigners, who spoke the
English tongue, were known to be the organising conspirators.   Closely watched from
harbour to harbour, they set sail for France; but they returned to Plymouth in disguise
and bribed to their assistance "proper persons in the dockyard."   The Port Admiral was
admonished to act in this crisis with the closest prudence, and to refrain from taking even
his "chief subordinates into confidence without absolute necessity."   A Frenchman named
Dumesnil, upon arriving in the Henriette Victorie, was detained by Admiral Pye; and
Peter Gony, his servant, who had lived in Plymouth for several months, was also placed
under arrest.   Dumesnil was taken on board a battleship; and there the supervision was so
lax that he easily deceived the guard by filling his bed with an effigy.   Dropping through
a porthole, he escaped in a friendly yawl; and, as the cheat was not discovered until the
morning, he was then on a fair way to France.

This wholesale use of spies induced "the learned but unfortunate" Dr. Musgrave, of
Plymouth, to enter the lists as a pamphleteer.   He was in Paris when the unpopular
peace of 1765 was negociated, and professed to know that the interests of England had
been sold by members of the Privy Council, and that the Chevalier D'Eon held many
incriminating letters.   The impeachment rendered obligatory some reply, and D'Eon
called upon Musgrave to reveal the name "of the audacious person who has made use of
mine to cover his own odious offers."   Musgrave deposited his papers with the Speaker,
and charged the Chevalier with having dined with boon companions at the Beefsteak Club.
When Musgrave was heard at the bar of the Commons, his statement was condemned as
"frivolous and unworthy of credit"; but he considered himself avenged upon his critics
when it was asserted that D'Eon was a woman with a genius for diplomacy who was
masquerading as a man to attain the ends of the French.   She suddenly disappeared from
London; and, to add to the romance, was said to have been kidnapped by her own
countrymen.   Doubt as to her sex had long existed, and wagers were made; and, when
claims to recover were instituted, sworn testimony was tendered that the Chevalier betrayed
her sex to an English nobleman and made equivalent admissions to other persons.

Another emissary was run to earth in 1771.   Having failed in business at Brittany,
and discredited himself by acts of fraud, Mathuren Danet volunteered to act as a spy.   As
Mons. Thebaud he haunted Plymouth and Dock; lived in style, and liberally treated the
officers.   His intention was to burn the dockyards; and after firing that at Portsmouth,

he took coach for Plymouth, where his presence was discovered by means of letters which he indiscreetly trusted to the post. He was lodging at the time at "Beckford's Punch House, Butcher's Lane," and was pounced upon at Mutton Cove as he was busily making suggestive enquiries. A third attempt upon Plymouth Dockyard was made in 1776 by James Aitken, an American, who entered the establishment as an artisan, and was known to his comrades as "John the Painter." On two occasions he scaled the wall after dusk, but the watchman was so vigilant that he abandoned the attempt. Annoyed at his failure, he went to Portsmouth ; and, seizing the first opportunity, threw explosives into the Rope House and destroyed the stores. This "most abandoned miscreant" made a clean breast before he was "thrown off," and he assured the authorities that their supervision was so lax that a desperate man might easily wreak havoc at any of their docks. A similar endeavour was made at Dock one Saturday night, in January, 1779. As the shouts of the revellers were growing faint, a man scaled the wall by throwing over a large fish hook, which was attached to a stout piece of cord, and hauled himself to the summit by the attachment thus obtained. The moving figure was seen near the Hemp House and the watchman fired at the intruder. He slid to the street and dived into one of the alleys adjacent ; but, in his haste, left behind a basket containing a dark lantern, a bottle of explosives, and a long piece of fuse. One of the windows of the adjacent department had been left ajar, so that the liquid fire might ignite inflammable stores. The authorities were convinced that the author's ally occupied no mean position in the establishment.

An extensive conspiracy was unravelled the following year, when a gentleman, of the name of De la Motte, dropped documents, in one of the public offices, which led to his arrest. He was a spy who undertook to supply details of English defence, the resources of the dockyards, the extent to which ships were undermanned, and the number of sailors available. He had a confederate at Plymouth—an official called Ryder, and this man was admitted as informer at the enquiry although he had betrayed the English code of signals. De la Motte was sentenced by Judge Willes "to be hanged by the neck but not till dead ; then to be cut down and his bowels taken out and burnt before him ; his head to be taken off and his body cut into four quarters." The prisoner received his "awful doom with great composure," and was removed to the Tower for execution. The same year Jose Seyling, a Spaniard, engaged two boatmen to row him round the harbour at Plymouth. He asked so many questions of sinister intent that he was given into custody ; and, when his lodgings were searched, his trunk contained maps of the coast, the dock, the magazine and other points. Seyling also received the reward of his curiosity in London. Some months afterwards two officers of the Plymouth garrison, Donaldson and Basely, were visited with terrible punishment for conniving at the escape of prisoners of distinction. After being sentenced, the culprits broke out of their cells and ran towards Dartmoor. Hundreds of soldiers joined in the pursuit, and the officers were driven to earth in one of the bogs, whence they were brought back to the town in a condition of abject filth and exhaustion. Donaldson was shot on Mount Wise, and Basely was subjected to the less humane ordeal of one thousand lashes inflicted in the presence of a vast crowd of soldiers and civilians.

Hostile Fleets in   The English Navy occasionally sustained as much damage from
Cawsand Bay : 1779. the elements as from the French, and the calamities that befell Boscawen's fleet on leaving for the Channel were as devastating as a naval engagement. Thunder, lightning and hail alternated in 1760 ; houses in Plymouth were unroofed by hundreds ; trees were blown up by the roots ; and scores of cottages were swept away. The Conqueror battleship, which had only just been launched, was dashed against Drake's

Island, and the vessel went to pieces after the crew had been saved and the guns removed. Inexpressible grief prevailed over the loss of the Ramillies, which was sailing from the port, in company with other three-deckers, when a westerly wind dispersed the squadron. In the thick and hazy weather, the Ramillies mistook the Bolt Tail for the Rame Head ; and, when the error was discovered, it was too late to avert disaster. The best bower anchor hung for a few minutes ; the cables ran out and crossed each other ; and the masts were cut away and thrown overboard. All efforts were fruitless to prevent the vessel from going ashore, for the cables parted ; and, as the Ramillies bumped, volumes of water rushed through the apertures, the ship was swept by mountainous waves, the men were washed away in groups, and seven hundred soldiers and sailors were drowned. A series of misfortunes overtook Sir James Douglas's fleet as it was leaving Plymouth Sound in 1774. The Egmont and the Lennox sprung their foremasts ; the Dublin was reduced to bare poles ; the Albion and the Raisonnable lost their yards ; and the Cerberus ran on Penlee Point. This was not the end of Sir James's disasters, for the Torbay frigate caught fire a few months later, and was burnt to the water's edge ; and the Kent blew up in Plymouth Sound whilst a salute was being fired in honour of the Admiral. Some sparks fell into an ammunition chest and a drummer who was sitting on the lid was blown in the air, and dropped uninjured into the water. The catastrophe was "otherwise too dreadful and shocking" to be conceived ; for over fifty brave fellows were maimed and flayed by the crashing splinters, and many were scorched and blinded.

When the standard of Independence was raised in America, the news reached Plymouth in disagreeable forms. The Charming Nancy and other transports brought hundreds of wounded soldiers and fugitives—some without arms and others without legs. Their clothes hung about them "like mourning garments," and the widows and orphans were hollow-eyed with starvation and misery. Surprised by the incensed colonials, the survivors took to the ships without sufficient stores ; and, as there were no means of alleviating their sufferings, insufferable odours filled the ships, and the famished and mutilated lay herded in the cabin like so many helpless animals. The revolt was the opportunity of France and Spain ; and it was at this crisis that an ambitious adventurer and accomplished linguist, in the person of Count de Parades, resolved to visit this country, and, by obtaining a knowledge of its defences, "lay the foundation of my future advancement." His recital savours rather of romance than reality, but it coincides with circumstances beyond dispute. "The negligence of some in office and the corruption of others" cast no discredit on these remarkable memoirs, because in so many instances the treachery of highly-placed servants was indisputable. Liberally supplied with funds, the Count devoted to the dockyards "the most scrupulous attention," and so acquired the information that the French desired. Parades discovered someone at Dock who promised to supply him with the confidential orders for £100 a month ; and, having secured the confederate, he proceeded by coach to London—a journey which was "infinitely more dangerous" than crossing the Channel in war-time.

Parades returned to Plymouth with letters of introduction to the chiefs of departments, and he readily obtained admission to the dockyard. The information he secured was sent across the Channel by a trusty smuggler ; but the Count was anxious above all else to make a personal inspection of the Citadel, as he was unable to gather in conversation the detailed knowledge that he required. Rising one morning at daybreak, he asked a labourer to escort him to the Hoe, and there he awaited the opening of the gate. No objection to his entrance was raised by the sentinel ; and, ascending the ramparts, Parades surveyed the country from the land as well as the sea, hastily made such sketches as he required, and strolled towards the left of the fort. There he was observed, and the guard being turned out by bugle, a soldier approached. Parades was descending as though his walk were at end, when he was taken to task for trespassing about the forbidden bastions. Profuse in his apologies, he mentioned that he was unaware of the regulation, and regretted that his guide had not given him the hint. "Seize the rascal," shouted the sergeant, pointing to the labourer, "and convey him to the guard house." The soldiers were hustling the man away, when Parades presented a few guineas to the sergeant, and begged him to "let the poor fellow go; he has done no harm to be sure; it is all through ignorance." Pocketing the money the traitor shouted to the guard: "drive that rascal out, and take care he comes here no more." In a softened tone, he asked the Count: "Perhaps your Honour would wish to see the fortress. If so, I will take you over it. I will leave my firelock in the house, and be with you in a moment." Parades thrust his tell-tale papers in the mouth of a cannon, but there was no reason for excessive concern. "My friend, the sergeant" showed him the ramparts, descended to the battery that commanded the harbour entrance, and explained "the most complete works of the kind I ever saw." Parades recovered his papers at a convenient moment; and, urging the sergeant to accompany him to his inn, presented him with two guineas more.

As Parades could not remain in Plymouth without ostensible pretence, he made the acquaintance of a mariner, "unemployed, dissatisfied with Government, and loaded with debts." The man consented to run a privateer on condition that the American prizes remained his personal property, that he was paid £80 a month, and that his crew of seventy hands were maintained by the French. The business being hazardous, the Count acquiesced in the terms, and he embarked upon limited smuggling operations the more readily to enlist the service of officers along the coast. Supplied with their wines, spirits and tobacco free of duty, responsible men waxed communicative, and Parades more than once was the means of checkmating the intentions of his hosts. It was only the incredulity of Orvilliers that prevented the entrapping of the fleet with which Byron left for America. Parades crossed to France to assure him that the English ships were badly equipped and insufficiently manned, but the admiral would not act on his information. The Count then returned to Plymouth, and anchored in the Sound, under pretence that he wanted provisions. His object was to renew his acquaintance with the sergeant, and he strolled about unmolested until he met him. "He seemed very glad to see me," and readily accepted an invitation to visit the Count's ship. Having paved the way with guineas and brandy, Parades offered to make his fortune, and the sergeant confessed to a desire to "change his condition for the better." Parades then explained that he was contriving to throw Plymouth into the hands of the enemy. The man "trembled at the greatness of the danger"; but, when the Count put in his hand "a solemn pledge, in writing, in the name of the French King, for £10,000," he banished any lingering emotions of fear. The porter and flag-keepers were to be "bought over to my interest"; it was arranged that the cannon should be spiked in the event of a landing, and the gate was to be left unlocked, so that the troops might defile from the bottom of the cliffs.

Not content with this scheme, Parades assisted in the escape of a compatriot who was also on a mission of espionage. In spite of his disguise, the officer was recognised as he was walking through the streets, and the cry was raised: "He's a French spy—an officer of marine who used to be a prisoner at Millbay." He ran to his inn for refuge, but the mob pursued him with shouts of "He's a spy, we will take him and have him hanged." The landlord came to the rescue of the visitor; and, as he refused to surrender him, a magistrate was sent for. Parades, who had witnessed all this hubbub, hastened to the rear of the hostelry; and, after muffling his countryman in a cloak, hurried him to the waterside and despatched him in a boat.

When the Count revealed his arrangements for surprising Plymouth, M. Sartine was indisposed to believe that the defence was so lax, and deputed M. Berthois, "an officer of genius," to ascertain how far Parades was justified in his assumption. The Count's crew were intoxicated when his vessel anchored in the Sound; and as the master insolently answered the challenge of a frigate, arrangements were thereupon made to board the visitor. Overcome by surprise, Parades and Berthois jumped into smocks and mingled with the seamen to escape cross-examination. They were betrayed at the first enquiry. "To whom does this vessel belong?" asked the lieutenant, and the master, pointing to his employers, replied "To these gentlemen." The spies were placed under arrest and sent on shore, where the resource of Parades availed him. He enquired for an examining officer who was in his pay, drew a draft for £1,500 on his bankers, and once more placed his charmed life beyond peril. Adopting the profession of prize-agents, the emissaries moved about at will, until one evening they saw from their window that six soldiers had mounted guard over the entrance to the hotel. "This was no pleasing sight," and their alarm was only allayed when "an officer of rank stationed at Dock," mentioned that he had called to renew his acquaintance with the Count. Parades was begged to bring his friend to the barracks; the invitation was embraced; and, over the walnuts and wine, the foolish host admitted that the port was undermanned; complained that the ammunition was at its lowest ebb; and that the defence was practically dependent upon the militia. Parades was more than justified.

It was by the merest chance that the Count and Berthois were enabled to return to France, for their crew and officers were seized by a press-gang, and the privateer must have lain in the Sound if they had not been able to employ the usual arts. Arranging to join the ship at Portsmouth, the Count attended a sale of prizes at Dock and purchased nine traders for £4,600, and resold them at a profit of £7,000. Before leaving, the spies took cordial farewell of the prisoners at Millbay; and, engaging a stylish coach, they passed through Tavistock, "a small town, which was made a place of confinement for French officers on parole." Here the Count exerted his influence to obtain greater freedom of exercise for the captives, and the walking limit was extended to three miles. On reaching French soil, Berthois confirmed Parades, and it was agreed to make an early attempt. The Count urged that 4,000 men should embark at Brest; and, feigning that their destination was America, sail direct for Plymouth, where there was not "the slightest idea of the danger that threatened." When the project was discussed by the French Cabinet, however, the ministers resolved "to make a great affair of it"—much to the chagrin of Parades, who was convinced that success lay in small numbers.

An army of 30,000 having been collected, the magnitude of the arrangements awoke the English to a sense of insecurity and Parades was incensed at the blunder that threatened his expedient with ridicule. "If they had done as I suggested, England would have been reduced in a very awkward fashion, for she had not, at the time, fifteen men-of-war to set out." He nevertheless slipped across to Plymouth, to engage the pilots to take the combined fleets into the port, and arrange for the storming of the Citadel. The French and Spanish sailed in August to seize Plymouth "without striking a blow"; and, on the 16th, "we came within sight of the Sound and anchored at the distance of four leagues from the town." As the invaders had left without sufficient provisions, however, they were already without heart; and the officers argued that it would be prudent to return to Brest unless they "fell in with the victuallers." Parades then offered, "under the penalty of losing my head," to anchor the allies in the Sound, and supply them with all the food of which they stood in need; and, as the wind blew the battleships towards the harbour, he endeavoured to encourage the admiral by insisting that the batteries were unfit for use. In reply, the

9

officers pointed to the militia encampments along the coast, and one officer protested that his men could only land at unreasonable hazard to their lives.

The combined fleets dropped anchor in Cawsand Bay, "to the great dismay" of the inhabitants ; and there, to the number of 66 sail, they remained.   Every point along the coast was at once fortified ; old cannon were wheeled out and placed in position ; booms were thrown across the entrance to Catwater ; ships were sunk in the narrow channels ; French prisoners were marched by hundreds across country to prevent their escape ; and so grave was the fear at Dock that the Commissioner seriously contemplated firing the establishment to prevent the seizure of its stores.   On the heights of Rame and Staddon hundreds assembled to judge for themselves if the ships were really hostile, and then they scattered with the woeful news to the remotest rural districts.   On the fifth day a storm drove the allies out to sea, and the Ardent, bearing down with a friendly salute, received shot and shell in answer to her compliment.   The commander discreetly yielded, and the traders he was convoying cleverly slipped up Channel.   All this time Sir Charles Hardy was cruising in the Soundings ; and he showed no eagerness for close quarters, when he sighted the enemy because his fleet could hardly ride the waves, and his men had no fight within them.   He drew up in order of battle, and the enemy followed suit; but the same considerations were influencing both admirals.   Neither felt sufficient confidence to go into action ; and, at sunset, the foreigners made for their own coast "with no other advantage save that of not having been defeated," and Hardy returned to Plymouth without a pang.

"Plymouth in an   This "insult" caused widespread alarm and terror; sequestered
Uproar": 1779.   hamlets and villages along the coasts were agitated by the dread of invasion ; and the cry that the French had landed caused such consternation in one church that males and females leapt over the pews, and rushed out shouting and shrieking. They left the sacred edifice deserted by all save the parson—for the clerk had fled—and the soldiers, who were curtly commanded by their officer to remain.   A well-worn legend attributes the departure of the enemy to an artifice of the women of Plymouth.   Arraying themselves in red petticoats, and brandishing broomsticks, they presented the aspect of an armed host, and the astounded allies set sail the moment that they marched across the Hoe.   In the comedy of "Plymouth in an Uproar," to which Dibdin supplied the songs and music, this weather-beaten explanation finds no place.   The scene was laid in an inn near the Barbican, where fishermen, travellers, cowards and press-gangs were singing in patriotic chorus :

> We on the present hour relying
> Think not of future or of past,
> But pall each moment as 'tis flying
> The next, mayhap, may be our last.

"Go it, my hearties," exclaimed Boniface, " here's plenty of work cutting out for us. The French fleet all ahigh!   The town in confusion.   Britons flocking in.   Here's the Devil to pay, and no pitch hot ! "   " How many sail ? " the landlord is asked.   " Seven or eight at most, which fear had increased to a thousand at least."

Pipes : " Let 'em come.   I'll be bound they wont approach within reach of our bulldogs, landlord ! "

Landlord : " No, no ; they know a trick worth two on't."

Pipes : " How many sail do they see ? "

Landlord : " Seven or eight at the utmost, which fear has increased to a thousand at least.   However, it brings grist to my mill."

" Plague on the French fleet," ejaculates Ben, the boatswain.   " They have filled the streets so full of blockheads that there's no such thing as keeping one's feet, unless one carries about a stout pair of fists.   Streets," he adds, in a scornful aside, " they're no more than alleys—what a plague do they make them so narrow for ? "

Whilst this excitement is reigning the young heroine of the comedy is kidnapped by a coarse lover, and rescued by the lieutenant of a press-gang.   The second act discovers a panic-stricken crowd, some armed with pokers and others shouldering broomsticks, and the majority carrying luggage of various descriptions.   Coaches are being hired at fabulous rates to send the women and children across country, and the cravens are much in evidence.   " Ostler, ostler, you ostler? "   " Yes, sir."   " You ostler ; where on earth is the scoundrel? "   The din is distracting, but the landlord remains cool.   " Are you from Maker Tower? " he blandly asks a new arrival.

Landlord : " And what news?   How many sail in sight, sir ?"

Traveller : " Not less than seventy sail, sir—you ostler ? "

Ostler : " Yes, sir."

Second Traveller : " Seventy sail of the line !   Mercy on me !   Have you any kind of carriage left ? "

Landlord : " Nothing, sir, but an old one-horse chaise, with the wheels tied on and an old blind horse to draw it."

The conveyance will suffice, though twenty guineas have to be paid for it ; but it is only intended for the transport of a timid wife and children.

" Why, sir, do you mean to stay behind, then? " asks Boniface, with growing good opinion.

" Stay, sir ! most certainly ; or how should I deserve the name of an Englishman if I deserted my country in the hour of danger? "

Coward : " Gad, you're right ; and I've a good mind to stay, too ! "

Landlord : " Good mind to stay !   Why you'll never be able to wipe out the disgrace of having intended to run away but by killing the first Frenchman who shall set his foot on shore ! "

How the inebriated sailors and soldiers who swarmed the galleries of the Plymouth and Dock theatres in later days were accustomed to cheer these patriotic sentiments. The crowning touch of contempt was supplied by Mr. Snip, one of the local tailors.

Tailor : " Ostler ! landlord ! ostler !   What is to become of me ? "

" What's the news, sir ? "   Boniface placidly asks : " How many sail of the line now ?"

Tailor : " A hundred sail of the line, sir, and two thousand transports ; the whole beach covered with French troops as thick as fleas ; a bridge of boats begun that's to reach from Plymouth to France, and we shall all be killed in less than an hour ! "

The prospect is too dreadful for Snip, and, turning to the ostler, he wails : " Pray, Mr. Ostler, can you stuff me into a boot or a basket?   I shan't take up much room—I'm but a tailor ! "

Ostler : " Stand out of the way and make use of your feet."

Tailor : " I can't, I've got the palsy all over me ; oh, dear, here come some of the French."

Alas, for the glory of Mr. Snip, the new arrivals are Jack Buckram and his fellow tailors—members of the same profession, with another standard of courage, who are ready to fight for Old England and accordingly offer their services.

"O, damme!" shouts Ben, "if that's the case there's no doubt of your being English—men I wont call you. But you'll be of some service, for, though a tailor is but the ninth part of a man, yet a Frenchman is not above the ninth part of an English tailor!"

After her previous experience, Sally, the heroine, has assumed male attire to throw her pursuers off the scent. "Charming sweet lips, egad," says Ben, with admiration, "but they'd be sweeter in petticoats. To kiss a woman in trousers is like drinking grog from a tar bucket!" An alarming rush through the streets culminates the excitement, and a waiter pants into the bar of the tavern with the outcry: "Mercy on us, save yourselves. Three thousand Frenchman coming up the garden killing all they meet." The tension is at once relieved, for the invaders are Cornish miners, of whom crowds are marching to the relief of Plymouth.

Lieutenant: "What's your pleasure, gentlemen?"

Miner: "To do our duty to our King and Master, sleep soundly of nights—and now and then see daylight."

Lieutenant: "What are you?"

Miner: "Miners."

Ben: "Minors you are; darn my old shoes; you'll be sweet creatures by the time you are of age, then!"

Lieutenant: "And what is your design in thus appearing in a body?"

Miner: "We come to offer our assistance to our country."

Ben: "That's hearty. That's my beauties; fight like what you look and you'll fight like devils."

Lieutenant: "How many are there of you?"

Miner: "Two hundred of us, and a thousand or two more coming—all determined upon death or victory."

Lieutenant: "And where would you wish to serve!"

Miner: "Where there's most danger and least fun."

Ben: "Afraid of tanning your skins, may be; perhaps you best fight as you work—by candle light!"

"They're fine fellows," apostrophised the lieutenant, "and I fancy that the French will have reason to repent of their rashness if they presume to land!" And so the audiences dispersed to the chorus:

> While you can boast such hearts as these,
> Your foes in vain may brave ye;
> Let French and Spaniards vainly boast,
> No dangers shall annoy our coast
> Whilst you've a British navy.

Growth of Plymouth Dock: 1770-1780. Dock gradually shaped itself in the form of a trapezium, the longest side of which measured 3,000 feet from north to south. Its breadth from east to west, at the south end, was about 1,000 feet, and, at the north end, a little more. Only a portion of St. Aubyn Street was built up to 1770; there were a few irregular cottages in Chapel Street; ropewalks existed on the site of Pembroke and Clowance Streets; and the Liberty Fields was the popular meeting place. In 1770 a special Act sanctioned the raising of fortifications and trenches around Dock, and the plans were prepared by Mr. Smelt, who was in charge of the Engineers' Department. After the combined fleets entered Cawsand Bay, General Dixon hastened the completion of the defences, and Mr. Francis Bassett marched from Tehidy at the head of a thousand miners to supply the necessary labour. As the population increased, unreclaimed land was cultivated ; fields were mapped into streets ; and unpretending shops were opened with the barest necessities of life for sale. Capital slowly accumulated, and consisted mainly of the earnings of thrifty mechanics. House speculation became a fever, and Liberty Street, Clowance Street, Mount Street and the intersecting thoroughfares were created. Morice, or the Town Square, supplied the residences of the salaried classes ; and the construction of St. Aubyn Chapel was sanctioned in 1771. Wooden shambles were erected in Fore Street ; and, after the pond at the bottom of Tavistock Street had been filled in, rude stalls were provided for the sale of farmers' produce. The way to the Market was known as Pond Lane.

The demand for houses was insatiable in 1780, and every space within the lines was utilised. Only the Windmill Field was held sacred, and this because the lives of the tenants continued in "good health." Land and houses were held on leases of 99 years, subject to three lives ; and, "in order to encourage a more durable mode of building than at present prevails," the right of perpetual renewal was temporarily granted. The tenant was required to keep his premises long-lived, to pay an additional conventionary rent, and a fine equivalent to two years' value of the premises. Sir John St. Aubyn lived to regret this liberality, he even refused to renew leases on lives, and, as other houses and lands fell in hand, they were let for seven years only. At the end of the eighteenth century, the income from the Manor was about £6,000 ; "but there can be no doubt," wrote a contemporary critic, "that the annual value will increase to £80,000 when the whole falls in hand." Sir John St. Aubyn considerably improved the market accommodation, and it was freely supplied with every article, "corn only excepted." Amongst other fish on sale, the John Dories were considered the finest in the world for delicacy and sweetness of taste, "as epicures may learn from Quin, who came to this place to obtain them in perfection." In season the quantities of mackerel and pilchards landed "exceed all description short of ocular demonstration."

There were three gates within the lines : the North Barrier, leading to Newpassage ; the Stoke Barrier, leading to Tavistock ; the Stonehouse Barrier, leading to Plymouth. A redoubt and block-house on Mount Pleasant commanded the lines, so that Dock was practically surrounded by defences. It is uncertain when it was first used as an arsenal, but its shipbuilding facilities were the finest in the country. The yard itself, and the stores of munitions, were enclosed within an area of over seventy acres, but only a small portion of the estate had been acquired by the Government. It was held on a lease of 21 years, subject to a rental of 50s. per acre and a fine of £534, or three years' value, on every seven years renewal, a sum that had to be paid on penalty of forfeiture. Sir William Morice granted the first lease in 1728, and the remaining portion of the site was enclosed in 1768. The yard was entered from Fore Street, on the land side, and the military sentinels suffered no one to pass the gate who was not in uniform or authenticated by a ticket. In 1799, St. John's Church was the outcome of another public subscription, and although the presentation was vested in the rector of the parish, the first appointment was made by the contributors. The stipulated stipend of the curate was £60 a year, and the sum was increased to £200 by the voluntary offerings of the proprietors, "if the person appointed meets with their approval."

Dock was only partially supplied with water, and the poor earned a livelihood by fetching supplies from springs at some distance from the town. Rain was much used by the laundresses, who collected vast quantities by means of contrivances for conveying it from the roofs to underground cisterns. When the supplies failed, as they did in dry or frosty weather, the water was fetched in carts, at a distance of many miles, and sold at a shilling per hogshead. Thus the proverbial allusion to a local downpour gave rise to the eighteenth century adage: "A Plymouth Rain is a Dock Fair." There were times when the Dockers were reduced to the greatest straits by drought; and, during the American War, the difficulty of supplying the military was so great that the commanding engineer applied to the Plymouth Corporation to permit Dock to participate in their plentitude, on condition that compensation were made. The controversy that ensued was acrimonious, and its humour is illustrated in the story that Boswell tells of Dr. Johnson, who was then on a visit to Sir Joshua Reynolds. According to his biographer, Johnson assumed that, if a man hates at all, he hates his neighbour, and he concluded that the new and rising town had excited the envy and jealousy of the Plymothians. Confirmed in this conjecture, he set himself on the side of the old town; professed to regard the Dockers as upstarts and aliens; and, half laughing at himself for his pretended zeal, where he had no concern, exclaimed: "No, no, I am against the Dockers: I am a Plymouth man. Rogues! Let them die of thirst. They shall not have a drop of our water." Still the proposal would have been sanctioned if it had not been for the obstinacy of Mr. White, the Mayor in 1779, who refused to affix the Corporate seal to the contract on the ground that the yield of the leat was not adequate to the wants of both boroughs. General Dixon thereupon took the levels of the river Walkham, near Walkhampton, and recommended that an independent supply should be brought into Dock at a cost of over £18,000. The expense alarmed the authorities, and successive proposals were abandoned until Messrs Jones and Bryer offered to construct another channel and dispose of the water at the same charge as that imposed at Plymouth, on condition that they were guaranteed the right to serve the soldiers and the ships. The programme was welcomed by the Government; and the moment the Plymouth Corporation perceived that a rival system was being officially encouraged, they altered their tune, vowed that their leat could be enlarged to meet the circumstances of both towns, and offered to deepen it if they were conceded the privilege of supplying the army and navy on the same terms. Repentance had come too late, for ministers supported the bill that Messrs. Jones and Bryer promoted; and, in spite of all opposition, it passed through Parliament and received the royal assent.

The War Panorama: In the estimation of one of its literary students, Dock was not
1700-1784.   adapted to the "cultivation of intellect," for wealth was the idol "and science scarcely vegetates." It was impossible to realise any more incongruous rigid picture than the town presented. Undisguised profanity was associated with the most sanctity. The indecent revels of the drunken and dissolute were heard by worshippers at their devotions; and sanctuaries of religion were often built by the side of notorious temples of profligacy. Prostitution walked the streets, shameless and unabashed, and levity and extortion were the rule. In the lulls of peace, the preternatural animation of Dock was annihilated. Shops were shut up and streets were silent. With every fresh declaration of war, the scene was changed—a new spirit predominated; the town teemed with the industrious; and sharpers started business one week and decamped the next, after selling at any sacrifice the goods they had obtained on credit from merchants at a distance. Amid the excitement of marching and counter-marching, the growth of intellect, as Mr. Jacobson felicitously pointed out, was almost impossible. No sooner did the student open his book than there was a shout in the street, and the servant rushed in to announce that the enemy had landed and that the Volunteers were going out to Crabtree to meet them! "Phoo!" remarked the disgusted student, and he resumed his translation. Then the

strains of a soul-stirring march, with abundant drum, were borne on the air, and the servant again bounded into the room to proclaim the return of the —th Regiment, "with only 200 returned out of 600, sir, colours shot through and through, poor fellows, all looking terribly tanned—here they are, sir, just passing the door." The pageant is witnessed by the student; and, as the tumult subsides, he resumes his scholarly pursuits. Soon a great gun shakes every window in the house! "What can this mean?" Enter Sam once more. "I beg your pardon, sir, but they say a man-of-war's in the Sound, bringing in two ships of the line, French prizes, all the people are running to the Hoe, sir; I hope you'll let me go." Down goes the book once more, and the student is as mad as his neighbours, as the victorious ship and her prizes, with the Jack flying triumphantly over the tricoloured flag, sails majestically into the harbour amid deafening cheers. Work is now out of the question, the healths of the brave fellows who have fought and bled must be toasted, and every enquiry instituted as to the particulars of the action. Such was the average Plymouth day, and intellectual advancement was almost impossible in the circumstances.

The panorama was continually changing, and the glitter of heroism was ever dazzling the imaginative townsfolk. How could the career of the Hon. George Edgcumbe be followed with other than neighbourly pride?—the story of his capture of the Jason, as she was trying to clear the Cornish Coast, with her rich consignment of silver; the knowledge that his gallantry at Minorca did so much to retrieve the discredit of Byng's expedition; his arrival at Dock with the first news of the fall of Louisberg, for which the King presented him with five hundred guineas; and, above all, the sacrifice of several of his plantations at Mount Edgcumbe because their removal was indispensable to effective defence—gratuitous acts for which the grateful old King raised him to the peerage. Then there was young Pole, Edgcumbe's contemporary and the friend of Nelson, who was born at Stoke and educated at Plympton. He headed the party who effected the destruction of Pondicherry, and the town rang with the applause that Nelson showered upon him when he caused the Santa Catalina to haul down her flag, and then blew her up to prevent the cargo from falling into the hands of an apparently hostile force that loomed upon the horizon. "In his seamanship," Nelson declared, "he showed himself as superior to the Don as in his gallantry, and no man in the world was ever so modest in his account of it."

And the anecdotes told of Keppel and Rodney! In 1760 the former was commanding the Plymouth Division of Marines, and he sailed from the port to prevent the French from seizing the English trading fleet—only to find the enemy so strong that he had to fall back for reinforcements. Strengthened by accessions, he renewed the voyage; and, after thwarting the French, he was only prevented from completing their discomfiture by Sir Hugh Palliser's deliberate refusal to co-operate. Acute was the interest with which Keppel's trial for mismanagement was followed; and, when Palliser's insinuations were dismissed as ill-founded and malicious, the shipwrights carried their bundles of chips to the Liberty Fields, and there raised a monster bonfire of rejoicing. "Is it not said in the book of Jasher that the men of the place gathered themselves in the fields between Mount Billing's O! (Billing's Row, since Mount Street), and Mount Wisdom (Mount Wise), over against the Mount of the Lord (Edgcumbe), and that those fields are called Liberty Fields unto this day?"

Rodney and Kempenfeldt were frequently in evidence during the unsatisfactory exchanges with De Grasse in 1781. Kempenfeldt left Plymouth to prevent the junction of two French fleets, but their numbers and weight prevented him from hazarding a general action. He thereupon laid in wait to cut off the convoy; and, as the van and the centre of the ·enemy shot ahead, and the convoy fell to leeward, he bore up in line-of-battle ahead, engaged the rear with his van, cut off fifteen sail of merchantmen, and so battered the four battleships which were protecting them that they sank with hundreds of brave fellows. As the wind was blowing from the English coast, Kempenfeldt formed his fleet in divisions, the first taking the prizes in tow, and the other maintaining a running fire with the enemy. He thus shaped his course for Plymouth under a full press of sail, and brought his captures into port in the very teeth of the enemy, and in spite of their resolute manœuvres to thwart him. This success was most valuable, for the prizes were deep in the water with naval and military stores, and the transports were carrying a thousand troops. These were consigned to the guardships without so much as striking a blow ! One cartel missed stays in clearing Mount Batten, and drove upon the eastern reef, where the frenzied Frenchmen shrieked and wrung their hands in despair. In the heavy gale the majority of the boats that put off to the rescue were dashed against the rocks. Some reached the cartel, only to be swamped, and they were tossed upon the shore by the return waves. Those who clung to the wreck fared the best, and were taken off in cutters before the vessel broke up. Kempenfeldt's victory, and the pleasure excited by his procession of prizes, found expression in the gay pealing of the bells of St. Andrew's and other popular ebullitions—rejoicings and congratulations to be sadly dimmed, in a few months, by the loss of the Royal George, off Spithead, with the intrepid admiral as one of the 900 victims.

Shortly afterwards Rodney engaged De Grasse ; and, although the latter had the worst of the encounter, the English victory was incomplete. Rodney reached Cawsand Bay with a sinking flagship that testified to the terrific tenacity of the combatants, and the Sound swarmed with boats and barges and crowds of spectators, pride universal at the knowledge that there had at any rate been a partial checkmate administered. On shore the admiral was hailed by acclaiming tars ; the streets were impassable as he left in a coach to give the King the details of his success ; and, when he returned to Plymouth in command of a squadron that was intended to bring De Grasse to a decisive encounter, there were anticipatory episodes of exultation. Paul Ourry, the Commissioner of Dock, entertained the sea-dog before his departure, and extracted from him a promise that, if he were successful in the coming conflict, he would make his friend, Hancock Kelly, a captain. Four months later Ourry received from Rodney the news of the French defeat and the capture of the Ville de Paris, with De Grasse as a prisoner. " My dear Paul," the victor laconically wrote, " 'tis done, the battle's past, the British flag's victorious, and I have made your friend Kelly a captain. My compliments to the amiable Caroline, and I remain your old friend, G. B. Rodney."

Breezy were the relations between some of the officers and men, and the former were welcomed at every country house, with the exception of that at Antony, where the Carews treated all navy men with " uncommon rudeness." Having a pretty wit, Captain Edward Thompson retaliated with a lampoon that made the squire the butt of the countryside, and from that moment he became as polite as he was formerly insulting. When the crew of the Hyæna were paid off, Thompson merrily asked them how long they would require to spend their money ; and, upon the majority saying they would be satisfied with four days, he rejoined : " I will give you six, and then I shall expect every man to be at his post." One of the dockyard officials ventured to warn Thompson that he would never see his crew again, but he laughed at these fears. " I know them all so well," he said, " that I will take upon myself every consequence that shall arise from this indulgence." On the following day " The Fair Quaker of Deal " was staged at Plymouth Theatre : and, as Thompson's name was set forth on the bills as author and patron, his crew resolved to witness the play. At nightfall they hammered at the entrance and claimed to be admitted without charge, on the ground that they were welcome to whatever belonged to their captain. There was a tremendous hubbub as the door was shut in their faces, and when the captain was told that his crew were storming the gallery, he replied : "Let them in ; I will pay for all hands." The men, however, had already surmounted every obstacle ; and, on recognising their captain in the stage box, they cheered again and again, exclaiming : "There's his honour, God bless him ! He's got as good and tight a frigate as ever was manned in his Majesty's navy." Then these jolly tars rendered in unison "The Topsail Shivers in the Wind !" a song "full of heroism and tenderness" which the captain had composed and taught them. At the end of the six days, not one of the crew was missing.

Social Life and Customs : 1750-1780. Sharp lines of social division were drawn by the officers of the service. At the London Hotel, Wheatley's Hotel and the Fountain Inn the county beauties met England's most famous naval captains in the mazes of the "country dance or the slow and stately figures of the minuet." It was the rule at these functions to "draw for a queen" from amongst the married patronesses, and it was her privilege to appoint two gentlemen "to assist her in receiving the compliments of the company." In the event of dispute her decision was final, and unauthenticated ladies were on no account received. Similar rigidity was not observed at the Fountain, no masters of ceremonies were appointed, nor any stewards to introduce partners to strangers. The hotels were approached by stone stairs descending to spacious halls, and these were relieved by the chastened glow of leaded windows. As the noble corridors were traversed by fascinating women and brave men, crowds of wistful faces surveyed the sheen and the shimmer of the gaieties from the oil-lit gloom of Fore Street. The guests dispersed with the rising sun, and the posthorn never failed to gather an expectant and bustling throng.

Balls, routs, plays and effrontery were pursued with as much warmth in Plymouth and Dock as on the spacious quarter-decks, and leading tradesmen emulated the excess of fashion which was observed at the various country seats. The princes were little scrupulous in the selection of their lodgings, and the existence of the royal arms over an obscure house led to the discovery that every young prince of the Guelph family had honoured Dock with "distinguishing attention." "A charming trait" in the early character of the Duke of Cumberland was related. Observing the royal arms in a "very shabby street," near the yard, he enquired who had lodged there ; and, on being told the late Duke of York, he replied, "Then so will I." "Your Highness will surely not lodge in so disagreeable a place as that ?" asked his companion. "And why not ?" rejoined the Prince ; "if it was pleasant enough for my uncle, it is good enough for me." Patriotic fervour indeed was frequently stimulated by visits of the princes, and they entered with light hearts into the pleasures of the people without regard to class. Pentillie, Cothele, Mount Edgcumbe and Saltram were the centres of brilliant hospitalities. At the outer gates of these mansions, porters, who were dressed in the quaint habits of another age, announced the guests by sounding a horn, and gentlemen-in-waiting escorted them into the presence of their hosts with "an attention truly flattering." The company assembled "very fast," the apartments were speedily crowded, dancing was sustained to a late hour, and an "elegant supper" was followed by "superior singing and other fashionable productions." At six in the morning an appetising breakfast was served ; and, after final shafts of raillery had been despatched, the visitors dispersed. By the young princes and officers the compliment was returned on board ships of the line, and their entertainments were "splendid." What a wonderful spectacle did the interiors of those old wooden walls present ! You could not imagine "to yourself more neatness, precision and regularity" ; the cabins were draped with the ship's colours and festooned with variegated lamps ; and dancing was sustained till daylight paled the glow. Then cold collations with choice wines were served, and songs and badinage exchanged. One gentleman, who united "the elegance of a man of fashion with the abilities of a scholar and the skill of a commander," found that his attentions to a lady at a Longroom dance involved him in the satire of a titled guest.   On entering the hall, surrounded by "a group of petty wits and retailers of her ladyships's bonmots," she exclaimed : "What ! is Mr. —— tied up to Miss —— again ?   I protest that the girl puts me in mind of the Indefatigable !"   At this the crowding "beaux and belles laughed immoderately," but Miss —— smilingly retorted that, "whenever she saw Lady ——, she viewed her with as much surprise and admiration as she did the Commerce de Marseilles "—the biggest ship in the world.   The Indefatigable was a seventy-four "cut down," and Miss ——, albeit low of stature, was endowed "with the face of a Hebe," a mouth that was "perfectly beautiful," and cheeks that were sweetly dimpled.   Lady —— was tall in stature, with the movement of a queen and the air of a goddess.

Prince William Henry was an immense favourite in the locality.   Under Lieutenant Williams, a Devonshire man, who had served before the mast, and Lieutenant Goodwin Neats, another seadog from Tiverton, he learnt the principles of common seamanship on board the Prince George.   He was with Hardy when the allied fleets anchored in Cawsand Bay ; and, after the foemen had escaped each other's attentions, he put ashore at Plymouth and travelled to Windsor on a visit to his parents.   As another middy had been denied permission to land, this exception in favour of the prince excited the disdain of the cockpit, and he incurred no little ridicule.   His popularity grew among his mates, and they swore by the "Royal William" instead of using coarser oaths.   When on a visit to the mines near Truro, he partook of beefsteak dressed upon the white hot ingots as they were drawn from the furnaces—a device that was esteemed the perfection of grilling ; and, on being reminded that every block paid a duty to the King, he replied that "this tin money" would be very acceptable to his father.   The Prince repaired to Plymouth on receiving his appointment as lieutenant to the Pegasus, and was presented with the freedom of the borough enclosed in a golden casket.   Much to his chagrin his fellow lieutenants were not invited to attend his levee, and he organised a special evening for their pleasure, with the intimation : "A jolly night, my boys, we will make of it."

After an eighteen-months' cruise, he returned to the port, and occasioned the watchmen grave disquiet by the skylarking in which he and his colleagues indulged.   Armed with lanterns, these young bucks awoke the echoes of George Street with their merriment ; and, on one occasion, they proceeded after midnight to Mount Wise, where, with a troop of instrumentalists and a big drum, they aroused the general in command by the strains of "Rule Britannia"—to the scandal and indignation of that loyal but outraged officer.   The duke received his punishment in the form of a sharp reprimand for leaving his ship whilst she was under repairs ; but a keener trial of his complacency awaited him after he had arranged to visit London.   Informed of his peccadilloes, his father ordered that he should act like other officers, and forbade him to quit the Pegasus without express permission. The Prince chafed under this rigour and his brothers, the Prince of Wales and the Duke of York, resolved to solace him by a visit.   As they drove through Plymouth in their magnificent equipage, drawn by six horses, the concourse that greeted them was "truly astonishing."   Illuminations were general, "the expressions of joy on every face most pleasing," and Dock was the scene of rollicking adventures.   The caricature representing the fight between Big Bess and the Prig Major typifies the hilarity which prevailed in the streets—"Fought at Plymouth, to the amusement of their Royal Highnesses the Prince of Wales, the Duke of York and Prince William Henry.   This battle lasted but five minutes, being decided on the first onset by a knockdown blow which completely did up the Prig Major.   N.B.—Big Bess was carried in triumph around the town exclaiming : ' I have done the Major ! ' "

The BATTLE ROYAL between the PRIG-MAJOR and BIG BEN

The kindliness of heart of Prince William was illustrated in the nocturnal expedition which he undertook with the object of observing the habits of the seamen and the treatment they received at the hands of the officers when a royal lieutenant was not upon the scene.   The story is told in the crude Dock ballad of the period :

Prince William and a nobleman, the rose of England's nation,
Went one day at Plymouth Dock to seek for recreation,
Into the suburbs they did go, in sailor's dress from top to toe,
Prince William wanted for to know, what usage had bold sailors.

All in a sailor's dress so trim, straightway they hastened to an inn,
The landlord would not let them in, but their good words prevailed,
Walk in my lads, be not afraid ; have you a private room ? they said ;
Walk in my lads, be not afraid, we love the jolly sailors.

Then up the stairs the Prince did go, into a private room, sir,
Prince William said, now landlord see, you bring both white and red, sir ;
Before the wine they had drunk out, the pressgang came both bold & stout,
The lower rooms did search about, for jolly warlike sailors.

Go upstairs the landlord said, if sailors you are seeking,
There's one so fat, I dare to say that you can scarcely ship him,
O never mind the gang did say, and upstairs they went straightaway,
What ship, brother? tell us pray, for we are jolly sailors.

We belong to George, Prince William said ; they said where's your protection ;
We've none at all the Prince replies, don't cast on us reflection,
With that the officer did say, come with me without delay,
Avast you must not make a stay, my warrant is for sailors.

Then to a tender they were brought where many more were sitting,
Prince William said, kind gentlemen, take care of our shipping,
With that the captain he did swear, I am your pilot I declare,
I'll let you know you saucy are, here's none but jolly sailors.

The nobleman he did go down, Prince William he refused,
The officer on him did frown, and on his soul abused ;
Where must I lie, Prince William said, must I not have a feather bed ?
You're fat enough, the captain said, peg down among the sailors.

Then down below the Prince did go, among his comrades dear, sir,
How he did stare to see the fate of many a British tar, sir ;
Going down below his trousers tore, aloud for a tailor he did roar,
The captain said, you saucy are, there's none but ragged sailors.

Now for your saucy language here, you surely shall be flogg'd, sir,
Then up the gangway he was brought, to be whipp'd like a dog, sir,
Come strip ! they cried, the Prince replied, I do not like your law, sir,
I'll never strip to be whipt, so touch me if you dare, sir.

The boatswain's mate began with speed to get the Prince undress'd, sir,
And presently he did espy a star all on his breast, sir,
Then all upon their knees did fall, and loud for mercy they did call,
Prince William said, you villains, for using thus poor sailors.

No wonder my father cannot get men for his shipping,
When you so cruelly use and always them are whipping,
But for the future, sailors shall have good usage great and small,
To hear the news, they all did cry, Heaven bless Prince William.

He made them all new officers that stood in need of wealth, sir,
He gave the hearty crew some gold, all for to drink his health, sir ;
And when his Highness went away, the sailors with a loud huzza,
Cried ever blessed be the day on which we pressed Prince William.

Launching the Wooden   During one of the visits of the princes, the Royal Sovereign was
Walls : 1760-1787.   launched with all the pomp and circumstance worthy of a first-
rater carrying 100 guns.   One mass of seasoned British oak, her contour appealed to the
imagination, and the noble figure of George III. was beautifully carved.   She took the
water in view of the Temeraire, the French 74 that Boscawen had presented as an addition
to the British Navy, and which, after splendid service in many a battle, now reposed in
Hamoaze as a floating battery.   In honour of the launch, the royal brothers attended a

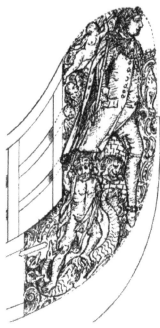

FIGURE-HEAD OF ROYAL SOVEREIGN.

(From the original sketch by Dickerson, in the
possession of Mr. Sydenham.)

ball at the Longroom, and the Sailor Prince,
frank, bold and handsome, "and as impetuous
and volatile as youth and fortune could render
him," was the hero of that festivity.   When the
three princes entered arm-in-arm, the eldest in
the centre, they received the welcomes of the
entire company ; and, returning the compliment
"with affability, ease and dignity," danced with
the reigning beauties of Plymouth.   On the
following morning, they drove to Maker Heights
to inspect the fortifications and returned to Dock
to dine.   At a later hour they attended another
ball at the Longroom, the most popular rendezvous for social functions, as its velvety lawn
stretched to the waterside, and the situation
afforded scope for fantastic displays of oil lamps
and wax candles.   Here the brothers "frisked
light in frolic measure."   Plymouth possessed
in the bloom of health many charming women,
and envy and calumny were naturally at work.
"But there was nothing more than a little flirta-
tion."   The princes enjoyed the ball exceedingly,
and their "condescension" made many ladies
happy in selecting them for partners.   Prince
William's extravagance, and his more serious sin
of making love to the daughter of a Plymouth
merchant, caused the Admiralty, at the request
of the King, to cut short this agreeable sojourn ;
and, on finding himself inveigled into a dreary
voyage to Antigua, his Highness muttered a
prayer or two "with more energy than devotion"
for the first Lord who had deceived him as to
the destination of the new ship.

All the stories about Prince William are not unredeemed, and the incident that occurred with James Northcote supplies a pleasanter moral. He was watching him in his studio as he was at work upon a portrait, when he began to quiz the appearance of the Academician, who was attired in shreds and patches. Although a lady of title was present, the royal visitor twitched the collar of his gown, and Northcote resented the insult by turning and frowning upon him. Nothing daunted, the prince smoothed his scanty locks with the remark that the artist did not devote much time to his hair. Assuming a demeanour of great sternness, Northcote replied : " Sir, I never allow anyone to take personal liberties with me. You are the first that ever presumed to do so, and I beg your Highness to remember that I am in my own house." Resuming his work he addressed himself solely to the lady, and Prince William stole from the room a little ashamed. " Dear Mr. Northcote," said the Countess, " I am afraid you have annoyed his Highness." " Madame," replied the painter, " I am the offended party." The next day the Prince called to express his sorrow that he had taken so unbecoming a liberty. " And what did you say ?" asked a friend to whom Northcote related the interview. " Say, why nothing. I only bowed, and he could easily see what I felt. I could at that moment have sacrificed my life for him. Such a prince is worthy to be a king."

The launch of the Royal Sovereign, with its bright social accessories, was preceded by that of the Glory, almost as fine a vessel, with 98 guns, and the Cæsar, a superb third-rater, with 74 guns. The last-named carried the head of Julius at the fore, the warrior grasping his sword and advancing his shield on his nervous right arm, his eye darting lightning upon the foe : confidence and victory in his attitude. Then came the turn of the Foudroyant to take the water, a magnificent third-rater of 80 guns, whose trophy name perpetuated the capture of the French first-rater of the same dimensions by the little Monmouth line-of-battleship. At this period the vessels were not "housed" preparatory to being launched, and the spectators beheld at once the superb object of the slip. The three-deckers were painted with black and yellow alternations, and the heads were fancifully treated in appropriate colours. The structures did not present, as they did later on, billet heads and round sterns—one blaze of economical yellow, fore and aft. They had glorious figure heads and such symmetry that "no one could forget their beauty or their grandeur." The carved work was exquisite, and the eye reposed with delight on the mythological devices that graced the quarter gallery and the full stern. These decorations, in less than a generation, were to be no more ! This elaboration of carving may be imagined from the work bestowed at Dock upon the Narcissus, a six-rater that only carried 21 guns. In the

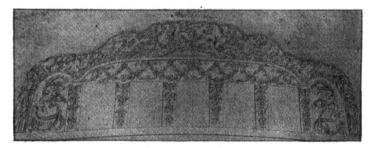

STERN OF H.M.S. NARCISSUS.
(From the original Sketch by Dickerson, in the possession of Mr. Sydenham.)

middle of the taffrail was the figure of Narcissus, in a reclining attitude, admiring himself in a brook. He was attended by two young Pans, diverting him with their musical reeds, and radiant in garlands of flowers. On the larboard side of the taffrail was a rabbit, as being native 'of the woods; and, on the starboard, a dog was depicted by way of contrast. Trees, flowers, plants and shrubs were introduced to complete the picture. At the upper end of the larboard quarter piece was a fawn; and, opposite to this, on the corresponding part of the starboard quarter piece, a pair of doves. On the larboard quarter piece was the figure of Diana, "goddess of the woods, standing upon a pedestal, and attired in light drapery, and holding in her hand a bow; in the other she extends an arrow." The principal figure in the starboard quarter piece was the figure of "Echo," who died for Narcissus. She was "cloathed in light drapery, holding in one hand the flower Daffodil, the flower into which Narcissus was supposed to have been converted after death. The other hand is applied to the drapery, and the whole is compleated with an introduction of contrasts." This description is taken from the explanatory notes of Mr. Dickerson, the dockyard sculptor, as written upon the original design, and from which the accompanying sketch is photographed.

The latest three-decker was the eternal theme for weeks in advance, and it was no inconsiderable part of the pleasure of the townsfolk to visit, in the breakfast-hour, the advance of the preparations, as these daily assumed additional importance. Every morning the new warship was surrounded by anxious hundreds, many of whom, allured by the trumpetings of fame, journeyed from the adjacent country side. It was a continual source of delight to witness the progress of the shipwrights and the painters, and to notice the gradual disappearance of the scaffolding until the form of the vessel rose upon the view in all its symmetry, magnificence and strength. The eve of the launch was observed as a carnival, and parties were made up for the following day. Cousins from distant villages and towns were constantly arriving, and bustle and anticipation prevailed. In a hundred festive nooks the connoisseurs discussed the dimensions and capacities of the new floating wonder, and veterans renewed old stories of old vessels, with lion heads and lion-hearted crews, and many an anecdote of personal touch with the heroes who had made enthralling some chapter or other of the national history. On the eventful afternoon the gates were opened to a multitude of happy countenances; and the stream poured through the streets in deep and dense masses, until, at last, the flow accumulated in one closely compacted concourse around the slip. Impressive was the picture, for there reposed the vessel—the sublime result of so many combinations, charming in all her proportions, painted, gilded, ornamented, towering above the throng, with her Union and Ensign and Standard, "the unconquered and unconquerable flags of Old England" floating in the breeze of evening. On either side clustered the booths, ascending step over step, and filled with the beauty and fashion of the day. Nor was the panorama afloat less interesting, as yachts, pleasure boats and barques pursued different tacks or arranged their disposition in lines. As the tide flowed silently to its height, the artisans removed some of the supports, the bands playing popular and national tunes the while; and soon an intense and breathless interest was excited as the blocks split out, the dog-shores cleared, and the screw was applied. The cry: "She creeps!" was raised, and the air was thick with waving hats and handkerchiefs as, rapidly and majestically, the vessel plunged into the waters that claimed her.

Visit of George III.   The recovery of George III. to health was followed, in 1789, by a
1789.   visit to Plymouth which evoked the warmest loyalty and patriotism.
Accompanying the King were the Queen, the three eldest Princesses and an imposing suite. Travelling in coaches, drawn by prancing teams of six horses, the party reached Saltram

THE ROYAL DOCKYARD AT PLYMOUTH.

Taken from a point on the western beach of the River Tamar, on the occasion of the visit of George III. in August, 1789.

(After a Drawing by R. Dodd, in the possession of Mr. E. Parkhouse. Photo: W. H. Lamb.)

House in the afternoon; and, after their Majesties had been welcomed by the Mayor under an arch at the entrance to the borough, they were escorted to the end of Stonehouse Lane. They "drove thence to the Dock," where the troops were massed, and, at Commissioner Lafore's house, within the yard, the Earls of Chesterfield, Howe, and Chatham awaited them. George, spent an hour on board the Impregnable, the ships in harbour saluting the while; and, on taking his leave, the Standard and Admiralty flags were hauled down, and the vessel was in one magical moment arrayed in variegated hues. As the royal barge was pulled to the shore, it was accompanied by a decorated cutter, "rowed by six fine young women and steered by a seventh." The girls were habited in loose white gowns, "with nankeen safeguards and black bonnets," and the shoulders of each were resplendent with sashes of purple bearing the inscription in gold : "Long Live their Majesties." The progress to Saltram was attended by a flotilla of sloops and boats; ship followed ship with salutes; and the guns boomed from Mount Edgcumbe Park. A naval review was held the following morning, and the King surveyed the operations from a point of vantage near the Mewstone. One hundred battleships emerged from different parts of the harbour; and, as they formed into distinct groups, a thunderous display was maintained for several minutes. Then the squadrons sailed westward, where the first line gave way and was so hotly bombarded that the spectators thought the conflict had terminated. They were mistaken, for the enemy wore upon the larboard tack, and resumed the battle with murderous energy. Still there could only be one end to the engagement, seeing that the foe were Frenchmen, and the invaders eventually struck their colours to the strains of " Rule Britannia."

Recruited by a rest, George visited the Lambhay Victualling Yard to examine the provisions, and a piece of "junk" was sent to Saltram "for his own tasting." The Mayor was "most graciously received, and aldermen and councillors had the honour of kissing hands." Monarch and Queen crossed to Mount Edgcumbe in the afternoon, and sixteen maidens dressed in white strewed the path with roses, carnations and myrtles. Triumphal cars, drawn by white ponies, conveyed the party to Cotehele; and Maristow was viewed on the Sunday in various enchanting moods. The original peal at Stoke Church numbered four bells up to the period of this visit,.and a new peal of eight were first rung as George passed on his way to Dock. An inscription in the belfry thus commemorated the event :

> Let awful Silence first among us Reign,
> Then let this useful Law each one maintain :
> We ring the Quick to church, the Dead to grave,
> Our use is good, such usage let us have ;
> Who Swear or Curse, or yet in Angry Mood
> Quarrel or Strike (although he draws no blood),
> Wears Hat, Boot, Spur, or overturn a Bell,
> Or by unskilful handling Mars a Peal,
> Let him pay Six-Pence for each single crime
> To make him cautious at another Time.
> When 'tis the Sexton's fault to cause delay
> We call from him a Double Penalty.
> May Concord Reign Among Us as we Ring,
> Pray God Preserve our Country, Church, and King,
> On whose account these Bells were first rung Here
> When George our King did in the West appear.

.

CHAPTER IX.—THROUGH THE NAPOLEONIC WARS.

The Glorious First of   The growth of the military power of France was met in England
June: 1794.   by steady naval preparations. As the imperial armies marched
triumphantly through Europe, huge stores were accumulated at Dock and the other
arsenals, and glorious battleships were added to the fleet, so that, when the emergency
arose, the response should be unmistakeable. Then the peril seemed to pass, as the
subjects of Louis XVI., crushed and famished, rose in revolt, and the Reign of Terror
presented to the watching world the appalling spectacle of a ruthless retribution. When
the Revolution had exhausted its agonies and annihilated its leaders, the Girondists
challenged England to a death struggle, oblivious of the fact that France was not only
inferior upon the sea, so far the number of her ships were concerned, but that her officers
and sailors had been too concerned with the internal struggle to confront a people who had
been resolutely preparing for years. Dock was the scene of tremendous excitement as the
ships were commissioned and traders were stripped of their crews. The Fencibles and the
Militia were called out in unparalleled numbers, until it seemed as though the available
supply of the able-bodied had been exhausted in defending the district and completing
the national equipment. In May it became known that the French had gathered a fleet
of 26 sail of the line at Brest ; and, as they were on the point of setting out to secure the
safety of a mighty cloud of merchantmen due from America, Lord Howe left Plymouth
with a force of corresponding strength to defeat their purpose. There prevailed in the town
the utmost enthusiasm as majestic three-deckers and frigates sailed in the full splendour
of the summer sun and confidence in the outcome of the struggle was hardly displaced by
the carking sense of expectancy. That faith was superbly justified, for, upon the first of June,
Howe came across the enemy, and achieved a victory that gave to England the maritime
supremacy at which it had been consistently aiming.

It was Howe himself who brought the news of this memorable engagement. His
stately fleet, flying the banners of victory and mightily booming their return, arrived in
the Sound, with six dismasted and riddled French battleships; their decks blackened
with powder and coursed by the blood of the victims who were stretched there. The
victors anchored amid such tumults of joy as Plymouth and Dock had rarely witnessed—
of salutes, of bell ringing, of bands playing and of universal illumination. In each house
a candle was burnt in every pane, and rows of lights were similarly ranged in perforated
boards in every window of the various barracks—a spectacular effect which was regarded at
the time as a triumph of ingenuity.

Loss of the Dutton and   Naval disasters failed to affect the military ardour of France and
the Amphion : 1796.   her armed hosts continued their triumphant tramp throughout
Europe, crushing the allies wherever they were met, in spite of all the subsidies which were
poured into the combined money chest by English ministers. In 1796 there were rumours
of the contemplated invasion of Ireland, and Plymouth was the scene of continuous
embarkations of troops with which to supplement the garrisons in that country. It was

at this crisis that heavy calamities befell the service within the limits of the harbour.   In January, 1796, a gale of incredible fury raged at Plymouth.   Monster breakers burst against the rocks and shot over the glacis of the Citadel, carrying away the sentry box, although it had been riveted to the ground with iron clamps, and gullying up the ground in their progress.   So terrific was the force of the waves that the Cobbler Buoy was driven from its moorings, and, at the height of the hurricane, the Dutton, an East Indiaman which was serving as a transport, was driven into Plymouth, and dashed against the rocks under the Citadel.   There she tossed with five hundred souls on board, the seas breaking over, until the masts went by the board and fell in-shore, and the ship heeled towards the sea.   Her wave-swept deck was crowded with soldiers, seamen, women and children— so closely huddled that there seemed to be no room for any more if they were below.

WRECK OF THE DUTTON INDIAMAN, UNDER PLYMOUTH CITADEL, 1796.
(From the original Painting by Luny.)

Some there were who leapt to battle with the breakers, and the guns of the Citadel boomed overhead their sullen summons to rescue.   A rope was cast from the shore to the ship, one end of it attached to a bolt and the other held by the fishermen on shore ; and, as the ship yielded now and again to the action of the sea, one passenger after another clasped the iron ring and was drawn through the surf more dead than alive.

Small headway was being made ; the mountainous seas were threatening to finish the wreck ; and there were symptoms of cowardly demoralisation when Captain Edward Pellew, who had been shouting suggestions from the rocks through his speaking trumpet, asked for volunteers to board the doomed vessel.   Of all those men, accustomed to the perils of the deep, there was only one who responded, Mr. Edgell, the Admiral's signal midshipman ; and the two heroes, fastened together, were drawn through the sea towards the Dutton, now raised high in the air, now struggling deep in the water, until, amid the frantic huzzas of those who lined shores and s'opes, and the pent-up cheers of hundreds awaiting death, they jumped upon the deck. Pellew immediately assumed the command and stood with his bared sword to secure the first passage for the women and children. More ropes with rings were thrown out; and, as stout boats were rowed from the dockyard, the hero stilled by his sternness of demeanour all disposition to selfish rush and panic, and struck some drunken soldiers with the blunt end of his weapon when their conduct threatened anarchy. One of the sailors was so impressed by this bravery that he exclaimed: "They are thundering good fellows, and I'll not leave the ship till I see them safely ashore." Pellew and Edgell remained at their post till the last, and the deck was under water as they were received on the rocks amid the cheers of saved and spectators. So highly did the Plymouth Corporation estimate this gallantry that they presented Sir Edward Pellew with the freedom of the town, and Eastlake's special eulogy was read at the function:

> While o'er the reeling wreck the savage storm
>   Poured all its lightnings, thunders, blasts and hail;
> And every horror, in its wildest form,
>   Smote the firm heart that never knew to fail;
> 'Twas thine, Pellew, sublimely great and good,
>   For man, thy brother in distress, to dare
> The dreadful passage of the raging flood,
>   And join the frantic children of despair;
> There it was thine, in comfort's balmy tone,
>   To soothe their sorrows, mid the tempest's roar;
> To hush the mother's shriek, the sick man's groan,
>   And bear the sufferers trembling to the shore.

By September the plans of the French were apparently ripe for the threatened descent, and ships were despatched from Plymouth with incredible celerity. It was on the 22nd of this month that the most deplorable disaster ever known in the port occurred. The Amphion, frigate, had received directions to proceed on a special mission; and, as she was being victualled, farewell dinner parties were given by the officers, and wives and sweethearts exchanged their boisterous pleasures with the sailors on deck. In a moment festivity was turned to terror; the masts lifted as though they were forced upwards, and the hull immediately sunk. There followed an upheaval as of a mighty earthquake, the sky reddened, the air was thick with bleeding limbs and lifeless trunks, and heads blackened by gunpowder dropped into the water and floated on the surface. The Amphion rose until her keel showed; then her masts flew into the air; and the waters boiled and hissed as the mass of flames subsided. Captain Israel Pellew was thrown off his seat and partially stunned; but, darting to his cabin window, he seized a hawser and cleared the ship "with an amazing leap." Captain Swaffield, who had been sitting by his side, was crushed to death in the wreckage. Some men in the tops were uplifted with them, and dropped into the water unhurt. One of the sentinels was looking at his watch when it flew from his hands, and he remembered no more until he discovered himself floating. Swept from the cathead, the boatswain was entangled in the mesh of rigging, but he cleared his arms by exercising phenomenal presence of mind, and cut his way through with his pocket knife. The wife of a sailor was blown up with her child, and her arms were locked around the still living infant when her body was picked up. Miraculous as were the escapes, they were few in number, and 300 persons perished:

REPRESENTATION OF THE DREADFUL EXPLOSION OF HIS MAJESTY'S FRIGATE AMPHION, OF 32 GUNS, AS SHE LAY ALONGSIDE THE PRINCESS, A HULK, IN HAMOAZE, PLYMOUTH, ON THE 22ND SEPTEMBER, 1796.

Amphion's noble sons, no longer now,
Shall weave fresh garlands for Britannia's brow ;
Your pointed thunder shall no long roar,
And carry terror to each hostile shore.
We mourn such honest zeal and service lost,
When Britain's roused and needs such service most.

Consternation prevailed throughout the Three Towns when the explosion was heard. The heavens glowed as with a sudden sunset and the truth spread with electrical rapidity. Appalling cries passed from mouth to mouth, and distracted relatives invested the gate to witness the removal of sackloads of limbs and the agonies of mangled survivors.   As the wreck came to the surface, portions of bodies floated between the timbers, and limbs were washed ashore with every tide.   Many were the conjectures as to the origin of the explosion, but the discovery of a sack of powder, with a thick layer of biscuits on the top, confirmed the theory that a light was dropped by a gunner who was stealing the ship's ammunition.   A few weeks later, commercial Plymouth was imperilled by a devastating fire ; an extensive sail loft in Southside Street, which was stored with inflammable materials, spontaneously bursting into flames.   These spread to other establishments in which prize cargoes had been deposited pending their disposal by auction, and the blaze stript several ships in Sutton Pool of their masts and rigging.   It was not until the tide returned that the burning vessels could be taken out of reach, and the havoc was only stayed by demolishing threatened premises.

The Fleet in Mutiny at   Meanwhile the navy of England swept the seas, and the French
   Plymouth: 1797.   admitted its prowess. So many of their squadrons had been shattered
and destroyed that admirals dared not emerge from harbours, and there was an insistent demand that the magnificent triumphs which the young Napoleon was achieving on land should receive a corresponding vindication afloat.   There was no diminution in the ship-building activity of the enemy, and scores of transports waited at the various ports to pour a hundred thousand seasoned warriors upon the English shores.   That project was thwarted by a friendly tempest ; and, for the time, the scare passed which this massive congregation of soldiers occasioned.   The war had involved depressing consequences in England, and fear, famine and want were aggravated by widespread naval disaffection.   The short shrift which Robespierre had vouchsafed the French aristocracy occasioned revolutionary sentiments on the lower deck of every British battleship ; and, at Plymouth, six Irish sailors, who had been fomenting agitation, were run up at the yard-arm of their frigate after a brief but conclusive trial.   In 1797 the officials had to deal with a more potential factor than United Irishmen, for the navy was honeycombed with discontent, and a conspiracy was directed by an executive acting in concert with committees all over the world.   The chief grievances were the failure to increase the pay of the sailors, the disparity of the prize allowances, and the punishments inflicted for insignificant offences.   It was at Spithead that the mutiny found its first expression ; but, as soon as the news reached Plymouth and Dock, the red flag was run to the mainmast of every battleship amid a hurricane of cheers. The outburst was stayed by the concession of a shilling a day increase and the promise to refrain from making examples of the ringleaders.

With the arrival of the next Portsmouth coach it was known that the Admiralty had violated their pledge to refrain from arrests, that the leaders had been fired upon, and had responded by deposing the admiral at the Nore and hoisting anew the emblems of defiance.   Irritation developed into insanity at Dock, as a courier from Torquay announced that the squadron there had also revolted, and sent the officers ashore. The epidemic spread like a prairie fire, and the officers were summarily evicted from their commands. Wooden gratings were improvised as rafts, and captains and lieutenants were towed to North Corner and Mutton Cove, and thrown on shore more dead than alive. Notorious martinets were not allowed to escape so easily, for ropes were slung under their arms, and they were hoisted to the yards amid yells of delight, and dipped until they shouted for mercy. There was only one vessel in the harbour containing ammunition—the Powerful—and the dare-devils selected this as their head-quarters. Popular sympathy ran with the men, and the town was given over to riot. Obnoxious officers were paraded under bodyguards of sailors, and consigned for the night to the Black Hole in Fore Street. Known friends of the official classes, who barricaded their houses, were hotly besieged. Their doors were battered ; and bedsteads, bedding, chairs and tables were thrown from the windows, piled upon waggons, and paraded in triumph. Loud were the jubilations as hilarious seamen mounted the trophies, and toasted the crowd in tankards of foaming ale, drawn from the barrels that they defiantly carried.

The rigour of Ministers caused the movement to collapse at Spithead, and the courage of the rioters evaporated at Dock. Then Lord Keith—accompanied by launches of armed sailors who had made their peace—boarded the Saturn ; and, addressing the assembled crew on deck, denounced them for encouraging the enemies of England, and demanded instant capitulation as the price of forgiveness. He had in his possession, he said, the names of fifty active mutineers, and these must be surrendered if the others were to escape. Angry threats were shouted in response ; and, vowing that they would not be betrayed, those who had the liveliest reason to fear rushed upon the admiral with drawn bayonets. Standing upon the defence with his naked sword, Keith threatened to run through the first man who approached him, and the leaders fell back abashed. Fourteen men were condemned to death, and many others to hundreds of lashes apiece ; and, for days, the harbour was made hideous by the spectacle of dangling corpses and the cease-less whish of the "cat" around the fleet. One amusing incident redeems the horror of the period. It was the custom at the Black Hole to leave the prisoners under the care of an old woman, who kept the keys of the various cells. One of the imprisoned officers begged her to fetch him some brandy ; and, when she entered the cell to obtain the money, he overpowered her, secured the keys, locked her in his cell, and threw open the apartments in which his colleagues were confined.

There had been no suspicion that the land forces were also ill-affected ; but a conspiracy of a dangerous character was discovered through the medium of a drummer. The lad was sleeping under a furze bush at the crest of Stonehouse Hill when he was aroused by an earnest conversation, in which he heard a marine named Lee administering an oath to a comrade, pledging him to a treasonable uprising on a date to be fixed. Hastening to the barracks, the lad told a sergeant what had passed, and the latter went to the commandant to reveal the news. Colonel Bowater, the officer in question, under the impression that his ease was being lightly disturbed, told his servant that he did not wish to be interrupted. The sergeant thereupon declared that, if the colonel would not see him, he would force his way into his presence. Bowater appreciated the gravity of the disclosure as soon as the drummer told his story ; and, entering the mess, where the officers were at dinner, he directed them to accompany him with loaded pistols, and to take care that the gates were securely locked. Then the assembly was sounded, and the various companies swarmed on parade, marvelling at the unusual perturbation. The command to ground arms was obeyed without a murmur ; every man was deprived of his ammunition by the non-commissioned officers ; and the muskets were deposited in the guard-room until the extent of the conspiracy had been ascertained. Lee and his companions were tried at drum-head court-martial, and it was then elicited that they had addressed secret meetings, with the intention of seizing the barracks. They had also administered oaths pledging the enrolled "to be true and faithful to each other, to free themselves and the French prisoners, and not to rest until they had overturned the Government." The Hoe was appointed as the place of execution, and an old soldier, John McGennip, who had encouraged Lee's designs, was mercilessly flogged there in the presence of a vast multitude. Then the doomed men emerged from the west sally-port of the Citadel—Lee attended by the Rev. Robert Hawker, and Coffee and Braning by a priest of the Church of Rome. The march to the plateau was of "the most awful kind ever witnessed." The Marine Band, with instruments and drums clothed in crape, went on in front playing the Dead March, and the shells intended for the reception of the bodies were carried aloft, in sight of those who were to occupy them. Having knelt in prayer with the prisoners upon the coffins, the clergymen withdrew from the scene, weeping bitterly. Then the firing party approached ; and, at the first volley, Coffee and Braning rolled over and fell dead. Lee remained untouched, however, even after the reserves had exhausted their ammunition. Then one of the number walked up to his side with a loaded revolver ; and, placing the muzzle at his ear, blew off the top of his head. During this tragic scene the troops paraded around the condemned in a serried mass, and thus only the sounds of the intermittent firing reached the harrowed crowd without. When the last shot had been fired the bodies were placed in the coffins, and thousands followed the procession to the Citadel.

Despite this disaffection, the navy soon performed prodigies of valour. An attempt of the Spaniards to relieve Brest, so that the French fleet might make their escape, led Admiral Jervis to engage an overwhelming force of the allies off Cape St. Vincent—the point that gave the name to the peerage with which he was rewarded. It was on this occasion that Nelson and Collingwood covered themselves with undying lustre by the fury with which they faced and fought the San Josef and the Salvador del Mundo—the noblest battleships in the Spanish fleet—and compelled the captains to haul down their colours as they menaced them upon their own decks. Whilst Jervis chased the flying Spaniards to Cadiz, Nelson brought the San Josef and Salvador del Mundo into Plymouth, where their arrival, with hundreds of prisoners, occasioned transports of joy. There had been a lingering suspense, but the anxiety that pervaded every class was broken by the pæans of victory.

At first there were palpitating rumours, and then the convoys trumpeted the tidings of joy. Frenzied were the salutations as the royal messengers sped through the town in gaily-arrayed coaches to acquaint the King and his Ministers, and the enthusiasm of the crowd could not be controlled when the prizes rolled in. The town was alive with the record of Nelson's daring as the San Josef shadowed the waters of the Sound, and the officers in charge described the genius with which he broke the line of leading Spanish battleships and boarded one vessel after another until the crowning feat of the day was achieved ! How the authorities at Dock laughed and rubbed their hands when the huge San Josef was towed in, with sails in rags and masts blown away, so strangely exemplified was the fortune of war in its fate ! When the Spanish Admiral visited Plymouth a few years before, his attention was drawn to the works then approaching completion. "Is not that the most capacious basin you have ever seen ?" Gravini was confidently asked, and grievous was the chagrin of the superintendent when he critically replied : "The dock, although very large, would not hold the San Josef, our finest man-of-war." Yet here was Gravini's leviathan berthed in the space he had disparaged with faint praise, and tons of copper rivettings were being driven into her timbers.

It was customary for each power to bear the cost of maintaining the other's prisoners, but the French allowance was inadequate even to the provision of necessaries. To kill dull care or to add to their means, many of the captives resorted to gambling. Thus their destitution was aggravated, sickness ravaged their ranks, and the more famished pledged the clothes in which they stood in order to sustain life. During the severe frosts captives were to be seen nude at the Millbay Prison, and their only protection on board the guardships was rotten straw. So weak with privation and suffering did "these walking skeletons" become that some of them fell out of their hammocks and broke their necks. By the more calculating of the prisoners harsh and degrading usury was practised. They "cornered" the supplies as these were doled out; and, by carrying on daily "markets," received the bedding or clothing of the distressed in exchange. These infamies were so openly practised that some of the usurers were sent to the Black Hole, and the incurable were punished by forfeiting their opportunity of transfer. Repeated attempts were made at escape, and the preparations were on the most laborious scale. The wall which ran under the eastern end of the Millbay Barracks was again burrowed by the captives in 1799 whilst the sentinels slept at their posts, and after months of patient excavation, an opening was effected. Acting upon a given signal, several hundred men gained their freedom, but the garrison was alarmed by trumpet and drum, the hue and cry rang through the west, and haystacks and outhouses were searched for weary fugitives. Scores were found famished and footsore in the neighbourhood, and many were concealed in the holds of merchant ships, whose presence in the harbour was not the mere result of coincidence. So systematic was the search that there were few absentees by the end of the week, and the remainder surrendered in a very forlorn condition. The officers were able to effect their escape without the same risk or effort, and they found plenty of people ready to receive their bribes Citoyen Nicholas and Citoyen Delasses were not so fortunate after escaping from their guardship as some of their colleagues. A boat had been engaged to carry them ashore, and a post chaise, for which seventeen guineas was paid, was in waiting near the landing stage at Mutton Cove. There was no hitch in the local arrangements, for the prisoners dropped into their boat, reached their coach, and drove as far as Honiton without being challenged. There the suspicions of the hotel-keeper were aroused and he caused his guests to be apprehended. The driver was transported for conniving at the plot, and the officers were subjected to a closer supervision.

If the French allowance for prisoners was small, the character of the English supplies was deplorable. Contracts were placed with political favourites, and the provisions were scarcely examined by the corrupt officials. In 1799 the prisoners, in spite of their hunger, threw their cheese overboard, and refused to eat their bread. Overwhelmed with virtuous indignation, the contractors invited the leading officers and citizens to taste their samples at the Plymouth Guildhall, and after these had been pronounced "sound and sweet" the surplus was distributed among the poor, "who thankfully received what the insolence of the prisoners so wantonly refused." This manœuvre did not redress the grievance, and urgent appeals were made for a more generous dietary. The French Government replied in response that they humanely treated Englishmen so far as food and clothing were concerned, and that it was the duty of the Britannic King to do the same. It was in vain that the advisers of George III. urged that there was no comparison in the number of prisoners. The excuse was not accepted, and the English ministers were told that they must accept with the pleasures the penalties of success. To this conclusion they submitted, and the prisoners were supplied with warmer clothing and a more liberal allowance of food.

Naval and Other Disasters: 1798-1799. In April, 1798, the frigate Pallas had just anchored, after a cruise to the French coast, when a heavy gale arose. Through the night her decks were swept by tremendous seas ; and having lost an anchor at daybreak, she drove upon the rocks. Although her crew cut away her masts to prevent her from holding so much wind, it was impossible to bring her up, and the waves made free break until the cables parted, when she hove broadside round and the swirls of spray hid her from view. Every hope of saving the crew was abandoned as each surf forced her bow nearer the land, and numbers were drowned in making precipitate jumps. When the Pallas was nearly end on, the tide ebbed and she heeled towards the shore ; and sheltered from the beat of the sea, the survivors reached the mainland.

A fire broke out in the gunroom of the French prize, La Coquelle, in December of the same year, as she reposed in Millbrook lake. Her quarter-deck was blown up and the mizzen fell over the side, the flames ran along the main deck to the upper mast and the standing rigging ; and, in half an hour, the ship was a furnace from stem to stern. The thick weather and fierce north-east wind lent horror to the sight ; mutilated bodies were scattered broadcast ; women jumped through flaming portholes ; and seamen, to whom no help could be given, despairingly thrust their arms through the scuttles. A Guernsey brig, the Endeavour, was also destroyed, and other vessels were only spared a similar fate by being towed to the centre of the stream.

Early in 1799 Plymouth was cut from the rest of the country by snow drifts, and the Naiad and Bon Ardre frigates were driven ashore at Catdown. The fall of a stack into the Ladywell School buried the mistress and thirty children. In December the coast was largely preserved from invasion by similar tempests. At Plymouth the tide rose several feet, battleships fouled each other in Cawsand Bay, the new Ramillies was driven to sea without a rag of sail, and a smuggler sank off Rame Head with all hands. The lightning played so vividly that several seamen were injured, and one was struck deaf, dumb and blind.

During the same year, Mr. Day constructed a vessel in which he claimed that a man might live under water and restore himself to the surface—the original conception of the diving bell. The inventor's views arrested attention, and public demonstrations attracted large crowds of spectators. It was a curious ship that was on view, with a false bottom that contained the ballast and enabled the vessel to stand like a butcher's block. The first experiment was conducted in the comparatively shallow Catwater ; where, after retiring to a cabin and lowering the structure, Day lay six hours during the flow of the tide and six hours during the ebb. After he unscrewed the pins and left the false bottom behind, his vessel righted and ascended without mishap. Scientists gathered from all parts of the country to witness the second experiment, which was conducted under the Hoe. Proceeding below the deck, Day let in the water, retired to his cabin with the utmost composure, and shut up the valve. The undertaking this time was to remain in over twenty fathoms, and to send up occasional buoys to intimate that all was well. No signals appeared, however, and the crew of the Orpheus sought in vain to discover the sunken vessel. The dockyard riggers were also engaged for days in creeping and sweeping at the bed of the sea, but no trace even of timbers could be found, and it was urged by hydrostatic experts that any air-tight machine lowered in 28 fathoms of water would experience such pressure that it must have been crushed before it reached the bottom, and the inmate killed in an instant.

Escorting Treasure from Plymouth: 1798-1800. "All's well !" So exclaimed the sentinel as he marked each ship bell of the national watch. The might of Britain was exerted with dramatic effect, the land was ringing with the fame of Nelson, Cawsand Bay was sheltering many of the hero's prizes, and faith pervaded every class as the eighteenth century was closing in. Then the French were vanquished by General Suwarrow, and the troops were reviewed at Plymouth in honour of that event. Letters from the Success bore tribute to the gallantry of Lieutenant Facey, a native of Dock, and Mr. Sampson Peter, a Cornish midshipman, in their fight with a Spanish polacre. Lieutenant Newton, the regulating officer of the port, frequently exercised the Sea Fencibles on the Hoe in big gun drill, and exhorted them as to their duty in the event of invasion. There was witnessed, whilst the pulse was thus feverishly throbbing, more than one illustration of French audacity. A privateer intercepted a brig in Whitsand Bay; and, having despatched her across Channel, sailed to Looe Island, and appropriated cattle and corn—"the property of a man who lives there." A gunboat was despatched from the dockyard in pursuit, but the blithesome buccaneer vanished in the mist. Other foreigners were less successful, although they threw away their guns and spread their sweeps as soon as an English frigate hove in sight. The Clyde frigate sailed into Catwater with La Vestale, 30, after an interchange of broadsides for fifteen minutes, at the end of which the French colours were struck. Disapproving of such a contemptible surrender, La Vestale's seamen continued firing; and, in their rage, the crew of the Clyde gave them "a proper dose" and the survivors shrieked for mercy. The Mars, a frigate of 74 guns, came into Dock with her prize, L'Hercule, a frigate of the same dimensions, which had been vanquished in a fight of such ferocity that the portholes of both vessels were seen to have been pounded. Captain Hood and other officers and men of the Mars died of their wounds at the Royal Naval Hospital, and a memorial in their honour was erected in Stoke Church by the survivors.

The victories in Holland again moved the Three Towns to imposing demonstrations. Six thousand troops were massed in the Brickfields, Orange favours were worn by the soldiers, and festoons of flowers and ribbons of similar hue were suspended from house to house. Thus glowed the emotions when Sir Thomas Paisley assumed the command of the port. He had shared in the exploits of Howe, and lost a leg in the hottest of the fire; and, when he hoisted his flag, every battleship in Hamoaze changed its ensign from white to red, and shouts rang from the manned yards. Paisley had not been installed a week when exultation gave way to chagrin, and signals were flashed from the Lizard that the fleet at Brest had slipped Bridport in a dense fog. Not a moment was to be lost, for the enemy might be landing troops on the coast; and so every tavern in the Three Towns was ransacked by the officers, men on leave were recalled by drum and bugle, and courts and alleys were aroused to life and motion. There was no holding back, unless faculties had been deadened by drugs or drink, and responding with alacrity to the summons, the sailors worked through the night, getting in powder and shot, and guns as well—"an astonishing proof of British endurance and energy." The signal that the French were menacing the west was hoisted at Maker; and, amid fluttering farewells from hundreds of craft, and cheers from thousands of throats, the fleet set forth to rendezvous off Cape Clear, if the enemy were not encountered nearer home.

In Whitsand Bay a French decoy was picked up, with bogus despatches in her cabin. In a day or two their contents were discounted, for the enemy was known to be steering south. There was now only one three-decker in Cawsand Bay, and the flagship was alone in Hamoaze—"a circumstance never remembered before." In a few weeks, Bridport returned for reinforcements, and dreadful casualties testified to the hurry. Sailors pacing the deck were killed by falling blocks, others were mutilated by the explosion of priming horns; some crashed from the maintop, and one man was transfixed on the bayonet of a patrol and his head pierced. The Gunwharf narrowly escaped destruction by the hasty handling of live six-inch shells, and the Three Towns were convulsed as by an earthquake as the fuses lit. The establishment was wrecked, and the survivors witnessed a horrid nightmare of flying limbs and maimed corpses—all so sudden and terrible, that the number of the victims was never ascertained.

Another fleet having been mobilised, eighteen sail of the line and four frigates moved from Hamoaze in majestic combination. They were leaving amid martial strains when Nereide brought in La Vengeance, most active of the privateers, and resailed to rescue a merchantman, who had been observed in the toils. Fresh ships were duly victualled and despatched, but the Centaur was riddled with shot and shell on reconnoitring the enemy's fleet, and one of the handsomest vessels in the service was thus reduced to wreck within a few days of leaving Dock. The only consolation was her record, for in two years she had destroyed four French frigates and seized several merchantmen and privateers. Her return as a cripple was insufficient to damp local ardour, for ten chasse marees, deep in the water with food and spirits, were escorted into Catwater a few hours after her arrival.

Crowds gathered on the Hoe to witness Indiamen convoyed past the port, and the horizon flashed with the white wings of a world-wide commerce as the traders stretched in retreating splendour from Penlee Point to Bolt Head. In August, these "floating emblems of Albion's proud Isles," to the number of five hundred sail, emerged from a dense fog into the effulgence of a noonday sun ; and, as they stood towards the Eddystone, the townsfolk contemplated a spectacle "picturesque, grand and interesting to every lover of his country's welfare. Two French frigates presumed to harass this noble flotilla whilst it was yet in view, but they were silenced by a towering battleship, whose cannons roared as the trespassers were steered into Hamoaze. The record, indeed, of the engagements that crowded the harbour with prizes would fill many volumes, but the arrival of the Thetis and the San Brigida, after their reduction in a running fight, created exceptional interest. Sixty-three waggons were required to transport the treasure from the Dockyard for temporary deposit in the Citadel dungeons ; and, when it was removed to the Bank of England, it was escorted through the Pig Market "in great style" :

A trumpeter of the Surrey Dragoons, sounding a charge.

Two artillery conductors.

An Officer of the Surrey Dragoons.

Surrey Dragoons, two and two, with drawn swords.

Music. Drums and Fifes

Playing Rule Britannia and God Save the King.

Sixty-three waggons with dollars in nine divisions of seven waggons.

On the First Waggon a Seaman

Carrying the British over the Spanish Jack.

Two Officers of Marines, Armed.

On the Centre Waggon

A Seaman with the British Ensign over the Spanish Ensign.

Midshipmen Armed with Cutlasses.

On the Last Waggon

A Seaman Carrying the British Pennant over the Spanish Pennant.

Armed Marines and Seamen, two and two.

Music, Drums, and Fifes, playing "Britons Strike Home."

Armed Seamen with Cutlasses.

An Artillery officer.

Two Officers of Marines, Armed.

Surrey Dragoons, two and two, with drawn sabres.

Two Trumpeters of the Surrey Dragoons Sounding a Charge.

Great was the delight that "so much treasure, once the property of the enemy, was soon to be in the pockets of our jolly tars." As the ladies waved their handkerchiefs, the "honest seamen" reciprocated by cheering. One gentleman, who wanted to know how the dollars were packed, was asked if he would like to smell them ; and, upon his naive retort that he would rather taste them, the ready-witted salt pulled a small Spanish coin and a quid of tobacco from his mouth, and, placing both in the civilian's palm, exclaimed : "By Davy Jones, tasting is better than smelling, so your honour's welcome." The heroes were welcomed by the civic authorities in London, and hospitality was profusely accorded. Similar ceremonies were observed when the Doris conducted two treasure ships to port. Armed sailors sat on the flags that covered the chests, and the Plymouth Volunteer Band played the waggons towards the Exeter Road. The procession was met in London by the Grenadier Guards, and the Lord Mayor pledged the captors in "a golden cup."

Remorse moderated the glee with which four treasure ships were hailed when they were escorted by the Indefatigable. A desperate battle had preceded the surrender, and La Mercedes, one of the Spanish flotilla, blew up with all hands. Nearly a million dollars sank with her—the total savings of a grandee who was returning from South America with his wife, four daughters and five sons. The father had crossed to one of the larger vessels to dine with the officers, when the English came upon the scene ; and, unable to return, he witnessed the foundering of his family and his wealth. This victim of "almost unheard of calamities" was shown exceptional sympathy in Plymouth, and the successful officers and seamen were moved to generous contributions.

A severe blow was given to French confidence when L'Engageante, La Pomone and La Babet were brought to close action in seeking to recover the Channel. Two hundred men were killed, two frigates struck, a third lay unmanageable, and three splendid prizes, with a thousand prisoners, were carried into Hamoaze. As much satisfaction was caused by the adventures of a Plymouth brigantine, The Sisters, as by more imposing conquests. Driven upon the enemy's coast, Captain Hood received an armed deputation of French Custom House officers, and "very politely, and as became a well-bred man," invited them to accept refreshment. Having produced the best liquors at his disposal, he left his cabin to fetch a corkscrew, turned the key from without, and thus held his visitors as prisoners. The cable was slipped with the change of wind, and the party emerged from confinement to enjoy a larger breathing space aboard one of the prison hulks in Hamoaze. Of the French privateers, the Morgan's energy was the envy of English rivals, and it was reserved for Captain Tomlinson to terminate her career. Learning at Plymouth that she had captured several East Indiamen, he set out in La Suffliante ; and, getting within hail, poured in a decimating volley. The merchantmen were recovered and taken into Plymouth.

A heavy storm was raging when the Cerberus anchored with some prizes, and one of them was driven into Firestone Bay. Captain Drew entered a yawl to reach the shore ; but heavy seas were shipped, the boat settled down, and, with the exception of two sailors, all hands were drowned. The survivors clung to a floating oak, and were flung upon the rocks. A severe action off the Eddystone resulted in the capitulation of the Robust, an American ; and, placing some of her men in charge, the Spitfire sailed in search of fresh adventures. Whilst the Englishmen were trimming the sails, the "parricides" placed the steersman and master in chains, and threatened to pick off the others with their muskets if they did not quit the ship. They descended one by one, dropped over the side and pulled into Salcombe Harbour. Off Scilly the sloop Scourge fell in with "a complete naval curiosity"—a privateer without tar, pitch or paint, and wholly uncaulked. "Single-found" in every respect, the poverty-stricken visitor nevertheless resisted boarding her for over four hours. The Scourge then chased and vanquished a French merchantman, and made for Plymouth with so many prisoners that each man of her crew had to carry "a brace of pistols." A Spanish register ship, with a million dollars in gold, was taken near the Lizard by the Phaëton. There was an impression that the bars were base metal, until the pewter film was removed at Plymouth, and the value of the cargo established. The Ambuscade frigate left the port in a gay humour, only to be challenged outside by a French corvette. Early in the encounter Captain Jenkin received a musket ball in the groin; the master was killed outright; a lieutenant was shattered in the shoulder whilst supporting his dying friend; and the second officer fell dead beside him. The men were being rallied on the main deck when a gun burst; and, in the panic, the French soldiers swarmed over the bowsprit and drove all below. The prisoners were transferred to a passing cartel, and sent into Plymouth in a pitiable plight.

ACTION BETWEEN THE CLÉOPATRA AND THE NYMPHE.
(From an old line engraving.)

Cornwall shone in the capture of the Cléopatra by the Nymphe. The foreign frigate was bigger and more heavily manned, but the Nymphe knew no misgiving. All was silent till the vessels were within hail, and then, at the bidding of Edward Pellew, his crew sprang to the shrouds, and the air rang with cheers for King George! Immediate was the response—the French manned their yards, their captain stood in the gangway and waved his hat, and yard-arm jostled yard-arm amid shouts of "Vive La Nation." Sails and rigging were so intermixed that the Englishmen boarded and cut the foreigners from their quarters. Then the Nymphe received some unlucky shots, away went her mizzen-mast, the steering wheel was disabled, and the Cléopatra fell aboard. The contending ships were now enveloped in fire and smoke, and the crew of the Nymphe stood on the defensive, until, taking advantage of the enemy's temporary hesitation, Pellew swept her decks, hauled down her colours, and hoisted the English flag. Over one hundred men were killed in the engagement, and the list of wounded was much heavier.

The Invasion Scare: In view of the preparations in France, every device was adopted
       1799-1800.   that prudence could suggest for defending the coast.   The wildest
turmoil prevailed in Plymouth and civilians were impressed in spite of privilege and
protest.   The gangs acted like madmen, and stripped and spoiled many ships of liquor as well
as of crews.   In their delirium these ruffians set some of the officers on top of one buoy and
the seamen on others—leaving them exposed to the wash.   The victims remained in this
plight for hours, and were taken off benumbed and starving.   Prison-ships, slop-ships,
privateers and traders were alike depleted of men ; hundreds of impressed victims were
brought from other ports under escorts of marines ; the dockyard was alive and alight by
night as well as by day, and every available coasting tub was fitted for service.   The saucy
corvette, La Bourdelais, which had beaten the fastest of English cruisers, and had seized
one hundred and sixty prizes in four years, was brought in by a frigate and classed for
active service.   Each battleship was provisioned for five months and sent with all speed
to checkmate " our inveterate enemy."

Twenty-six vessels of all rates, including the Saucy Arethusa, set sail for Torbay, to
prepare for the dash.   The prisoners were much excited by the rumours and scurry ;
and, so formidable were their numbers, that the authorities could neither control nor
watch them.   Undeterred by previous failures and rigorous examples, they renewed their
efforts to escape and burrowed under walls and intersected sewers.   As the barracks

The Arethusa Frigate scudding under Foresail in a STORM with a View of PLYMOUTH and Maker Church at a distance

at Millbay were required for the troops, additional ships were set apart for their reception ;
and five thousand were relegated to the cold comfort of Hamoaze, the soldiers standing
alongside with loaded muskets as they embarked in the gunboats.   In spite of the
alarms which inspired the prisoners with so much audacity, the invaders only arrived in
limited detachments, and then to join their countrymen in irksome confinement.

Cyrus Redding drew an animated picture of the old Market Street at this time of
perturbation.   Outside Haydon's shop congregated gossipers of all grades—civil, military
and naval.   The mild and gallant Sir Israel Pellew might be heard deprecating the

imperious methods of his brother, Sir Edward. Old Captain Wynne would buttonhole a friend to repeat his familiar anecdote concerning the glorious First of June—how, when Sir Roger Curtis told the Admiral that the line was complete, Howe replied "Then up with the helm in the name of God!" In close contiguity was Admiral Manley, of whom it was insinuated that he mistook a cloud for a ship, and fired volleys at it, until the sky cleared and there was not a sail to be seen. One-armed Sir Michael Seymour chatted with "that huge hill of flesh, General England"; and, anon, "little Sir Manasseh Lopez, of Maristow, would show his smiling face there, or Sir W. Elford his bluff one; and the stiff and stately Admiral Young would bow to another of the group—old Herbert, the banker, one of Pharaoh's lean kine." Of this cadaverous gentleman it was told that two sailors rambled one evening into the garden of his house in Frankfort Place, as he was nodding before his fire in the twilight. One of the seamen, struck by his lank form and anæmic face, exclaimed: "Jim, Jim, did'st thou ever see 'Death?' Come look in here—here, here, heave a-head." And the banker was designated for the rest of his life by that disagreeable sobriquet.

Nelson at Plymouth: 1800-1801. Tumultuous welcomes awaited Nelson at Plymouth when he arrived towards the end of 1800 to take up the command of the San Josef. The huge masts destroyed in battle had been replaced by others of imposing dimensions and fitted "in the most complete style ever seen at Dock." As the hero passed through the fleet, the yards were manned, bands played on shore as well as afloat, and volleys of cheering mingled with reports of cannon. When his flag was run up, further salutes were fired in his honour, vociferous shouts arose, and the waters were clustered with small craft, from which ladies waved pretty bannerets and handkerchiefs. Nelson was received with magnificent hospitality, and he was greeted with almost reverent affection in the streets. His step-brother and his friend, Captain Hardy, were his invariable companions, and the figures of the trio became more familiar than ever to the grateful populace. No time was lost by the Corporation in asking Nelson to receive the freedom of the borough; and, on the day fixed for the function, the streets were resplendent with uniforms, and he drove through delirious crowds, in the full uniform of his office, blazing stars and golden medals on his breast. Cannon boomed, the air was rent with acclamations, and sailors maimed and others sound in limb—his companions in many a fight—threw their caps aloft and struggled through the white and scarlet lines to clasp his remaining hand. Cries of "God Bless Your Honour" were raised from a thousand throats as the hero passed into the Mayoralty House in Notte Street; and, within and without, the cheering was thunderous. After silence had been commanded, Sir William Elford, the Recorder, read the authority of the Corporation:

"To all to whom these presents shall come Know ye that We, the Mayor and Commonalty of the Borough of Plymouth, in the County of Devon, considering the many and meritorious services rendered to this Country by that truly Great and Illustrious Hero, the Right Honorable Horatio Lord Nelson, Baron Nelson of the Nile; Vice-Admiral of the Blue in His Majesty's Navy; and particularly his gallant, spirited, and magnanimous conduct at the Battle with the French Fleet off the mouth of the Nile, on the first and second days of August, one thousand seven hundred and ninety-eight; Have conferred and by these presents Do confer on the said Right Honorable Horatio Lord Nelson, Baron Nelson of the Nile, All the rights and privileges of a Freeman of this ancient borough, In Testimony of such highly meritorious conduct and services. Given at the Mayoralty House of the said borough, under our Common Seal, this twenty-second day of January, one thousand eight hundred and one,"

The patent was written on parchment, and enclosed in a silver casket; and, in presenting it, the Recorder emphasized the renown the guest had gained by his victories over an " unprincipled and implacable foe." Brief, but modest, was the reply of Nelson. It was to the experience of his officers, and the devotion of his sailors, that he ascribed the glory, and he protested that, with God on the side of England, and with comrades so true and faithful, the future of the country was assured. On emerging from the building, the hero's carriage was borne away by a hoarse and surging throng, and from every window fluttered flags and devices, winsome faces beaming the while, and receiving gallant acknowledgments in return.

There was hardly a day on which Nelson was not in evidence, and every night the theatres were filled—officers in boxes, sailors swarming galleries, and naval dramas and patriotic songs in constant request. At a dinner which was held at the Fountain Inn, in Fore Street, Nelson was supported by Sir Edward Pellew and the fire-eating Jeremiah Coghlan, the authors of as many daring deeds as any contemporaries. A model of a French frigate was on view in Plymouth—every part of it blown in glass—and this curiosity the hero closely scrutinized. A special day was set apart for the inspection of the Citadel; and, as Nelson drove up, the main guard was turned out. But the Admiral " politely desired the officer to turn them in again "—a request which was complied with. Nelson subsequently cruised with his fleet around the Devon coast, awaiting the signal for departure. In a few weeks, too precipitate signalling threw Plymouth into consternation. The look-out frigates stationed near the Dodman were misled by signals from the British fleet off Brest, and from one station to another, it was represented that the enemy's forces were moving across the Channel. Haste was urged to give the foe a warm reception, but the message had been misunderstood and so little cause was there for panic that cutters, privateers, smugglers, and other prizes continued to accumulate under the guns of the Citadel. A French gunboat was cut out off the harbour; and, when she struck her flag, she was full of soldiers. The Dick, a Guineaman, was challenged on leaving Plymouth by La Grand Decide, a French privateer; and, after losing her captain and several seamen, lowered her colours. As she was being carried off, the Fisgard frigate hove in sight, and La Grand Decide took to her heels. At this juncture a French frigate covered the flight, whereupon the Indefatigable came to the assistance of the Fisgard, and the new comer—La Venus—was captured and taken into Plymouth. The reverse of the story was experienced by the Duke of Clarence, an Oreston privateer, which was challenged off the Start, and obliged to strike her flag to a foeman of much heavier capacity. Battered and leaky, the French abandoned her to the mercy of the waves after pouring in three farewell broadsides; yet she succeeded in struggling into port and landed one body in fragments and several wounded men. A section of the Channel Fleet brought other complements of wounded men, amongst them a number who had been mutilated by the bursting of a gun on board the Triton. During an engagement her deck was ripped open, bodies were scattered through the air, and limbs were separated from the trunks of poor fellows already slain The survivors were conveyed to the Royal Naval Hospital, where hundreds of beds were already filled with patients experiencing the worst results of hurried amputation.

Famine Riots   Food was approaching famine prices, and the sufferings of the poor
at Plymouth : 1801.   were acute. Crowds paraded the streets, clamouring for relief, and
balladmongers fanned the flames by singing seditious songs. In March disturbances broke out in the market, where the populace were dispersed by the police. Receiving accessions, the mob marched about with crowbars and bludgeons, attacked the shambles, and retailed the meat to the bystanders "at very small prices." They also stormed the

bakers' shops, carried away the loaves, and threw about bags of flour and joints of beef and mutton. One tradesman who had made himself peculiarly obnoxious was escorted to the old place of execution at Catdown with a rope around his neck, but he was rescued by a friend, who laid about him with the flat of a sword. The military were called out to suppress the disturbances, and many persons were injured in the bayonet charges. A manifesto was issued by the authorities in these terms :

BOROUGH OF PLYMOUTH.

The magistrates have seen with much concern the riotous and outrageous behaviour of the populace in the market and streets of this borough, on Monday last, to the grave disturbance of the public peace and serious injury of the inhabitants.

At the present time of scarcity and dearth such disorderly conduct, instead of lessening, cannot fail to enhance the price of every article of provisions and prevent a regular supply from reaching the market. Every exertion is already being used to relieve the distresses of the poor in the town and neighbourhood by procuring a sufficient quantity of food for the consumption of the inhabitants, and the necessary measures are being taken to secure a continuance thereof.

At the same time, the magistrates have determined to protect the farmers, bakers, butchers and others in the disposal of their property, and to suppress all riotous conduct in future. Notice is therefore hereby given to farmers, bakers, butchers and others that, on Thursday next, and succeeding market days, a strong patrol of peace officers will attend the Plymouth markets in order to protect everyone in the peaceable sale and disposal of their property. And all persons who shall be guilty of any disorderly conduct tending to disturb the public tranquillity will be immediately apprehended and prosecuted with the utmost severity of the law.

P. LANGMEAD, Mayor.

Mayoralty House, Plymouth, March 31, 1801.

The manifesto failed to calm the public, and the riots were resumed. The markets were stormed, purveyors of food were threatened, and cavalry corps scoured the country lanes to prevent unpopular farmers from being waylaid on their way to town. Explanatory statements were issued by butchers, bakers and corn factors in order to assuage the exasperation of the populace. The butchers, in an address "To the Public," protested that "designing people, who are the enemies of the community at large," had been enflaming the minds of the poor and "injuring the characters of the butchers of Plymouth, Plymouth-Dock and Stonehouse" by insinuating that "the enormous price of meat" was due to their selfish conduct. In order to convince "the impartial public, on whose liberality the butchers rest the justice of their case, the undersigned, being impressed with the necessities of the poor, are willing to exert every effort in their power to lower the high price of provisions." To emphasize their good faith, they held a meeting at the house of Mr. Jeans, "known by the sign of the London Inn, Plymouth-Dock, Devon," and resolved to supply mutton at 7d. per lb. ; and, if the farmers would not come to reasonable terms, "we solemnly declare not to purchase any cattle of them in future." After "this liberal and impartial conduct," the butchers presumed that no blame could attach to them, and appealed to "a generous public to exert every effort in their power to enable them to fulfil their resolutions." "Plain Words" were disseminated by the farmers, who pointed out in their defence that the Three Towns were, in years of ordinary plenty, supplied with flour from Hampshire, Sussex and remoter counties, and that only a small portion was raised for sale in the immediate locality. Of recent months, however, the quantity stored in the neighbourhood had been very small by reason of abnormal demands. The price of flour in the Three Towns could not be reduced until there was a general fall, and there was reason to hope that this "will gradually happen to a certain extent, in consequence of the large importations of corn arriving and expected from foreign counties if tranquillity and good order be preserved and trade be permitted to go in the ordinary channels."

Explanations did not satisfy stomachs; and, as the excitement continued, the Mayor declared that the object of the authorities had been "scandalously misrepresented, and the legal protection afforded to the farmers, bakers, butchers and others in the peaceable disposition of their property" attributed to a desire to encourage them "in keeping up the present high prices of provisions." The magistrates, in a manifesto, held it to be their duty "to declare that nothing could be so far from their intentions," and they therefore "most earnestly" cautioned the public against "such poisonous and inflammable nonsense, hatched by evil-minded persons, with the wicked view of misleading the poorer classes, and of stirring them up to further acts of outrage and violence; tending in their consequences to aggravate the distress which it is the object of all good and well-disposed persons to alleviate by every means in their power. The magistrates therefore declare it to be their fixed determination to apprehend all persons who shall be guilty of disorderly conduct by word or deed, and repeat their promise of protection to the farmers who bring their products to the market." The crisis arising from the absolute dearth of stores in the district was nevertheless most pressing, and the Mayor assured the Government that the only way of preventing absolute famine was to authorise contractors to sell in the Three Towns the army and navy supplies. Compliance with this suggestion was followed by immediate relief, special constables were dismissed to their homes, military patrols were withdrawn, ringleaders were restored to liberty, and assistance was given the poor.

Celebrating the Peace   England's naval existence now depended upon a succession of
of Amiens: 1802.   blows. "We must brace up," Nelson observed; "these are not times for nervous systems." As one stately squadron left Plymouth to join his mighty fleet at Yarmouth, the harbour resounded with the strains of "Come Cheer Up My Lads, 'Tis to Glory We Steer," and hilarious crowds ashore and afloat united in the chorus of "Britons, Strike Home!" An embargo was laid upon a flotilla of thirty Danish timber ships, which had unsuspectingly entered the port, and the seizure of their stores of oak, masts and hemp was the prelude to the surprise of Copenhagen. Prizes poured into Plymouth until Catwater presented the aspect of a naval wood of countless masts:

> Of ships under sail here you shall meet
> Of every rate and size; frigates, galleons,
> The nimble ketches, and small pickeroons;
> Some bound to this port, some where wind and weather
> Will drive them—they are bound they know not whither.
> Some steer to Heaven—some for Hell:
> To which some steer themselves can hardly tell!

Captain O'Connor was lionised for his intrepidity in the Channel. His ship, the Beaver, parted from her convoy in a gale and fell an easy prey to the foe. A prize master and crew were put in possession; and, with the exception of O'Connor and his son, the Englishmen were transferred to the hold of the victor. Inviting the prize master to his cabin, O'Connor overpowered him and tied his hands behind his back; and, after depriving him of his pistol, locked him in, and furnished the boy with a crowbar. The pair dared the French sailors who were manning the yards to descend on peril of their lives; and, with the enemy secured below and fixed aloft, O'Connor steered his ship into the Sound, where the submission of the intimidated seamen was complete. Good humour was heightened when Cornwallis crossed over from Brest in the Fisgard. Whilst surveying the position of the enemy he approached so near to their batteries that shot upon shot fell over him; and, grimly relating his experience to his Plymouth friends, the old admiral observed: "If their 24 sail of the line and 10 frigates had only come out, I would have beaten them with my 14 three-deckers and left the 74's to see fair play." French spirits were dimmed by the reverses in Egypt that heralded their expulsion. In the meantime, Sir John Saumarez left Plymouth with his fateful expedition, and another wistful period of suspense ensued. Then with pride and joy, the populace hailed the report that he had prevented the junction of the Spanish and French fleets off Algeciras; and, with an inferior force of riddled ships, thwarted the intended combination under the forts of Cadiz. The mail coach that announced this successful strategy entered Plymouth flying the Royal Standard and Union Jack; and blue flags, with embroidered devices, were suspended from the hotel windows bearing the boast: "Saumarez and Victory."

France was energetically prosecuting her plans for invasion, and England was responding to the challenge with astonishing resource, when peace pourparlers reached an attainable basis. Towards the end of 1801 the mail coach dashed into Plymouth, the horses decorated with laurels, and the driver, guard and passengers resplendent with gold and blue favours. Joy pervaded every class when the news was promulgated. Traders of all nations displayed their colours in Sutton Pool and Catwater; the "Extraordinary Gazette" was read to teeming audiences at the theatres; civilians embraced each other in the pit; and females danced with sailors and soldiers in the galleries. On learning of their approaching release the prisoners were thrown into transports of delight, and the sick left their berths to participate in breakdowns on the decks. Transparencies testified to the exhilaration at Stonehouse, the Naval Hospital and the Marine Barracks; and 800 barrels of tar, oil and pitch were consumed in a monster bonfire upon the Hoe. In Cawsand Bay the battleships showed their toplights, and their rockets and showers of signals were answered from Mount Wise, the Citadel and Mount Edgcumbe.

In a few days the peace was sufficiently confirmed from other sources to admit of popular commemorations. The coaches were adorned with laurels and flags, and they were surrounded by the populace from the Exeter Road to the Dockyard Gates. Four thousand yardsmen marched in procession, the shipwrights carrying models of English sails of the line—"symbols of those floating bulwarks which hurl their thunders at old England's enemies and surprise the world." Musicians in scarlet and gold, and banners, "sublime and beautiful," constituted the grandest spectacle "ever seen in the world." Artificers and shipwrights formed a circle at Morice Square, and sang "God Save the King," "Rule Britannia," and "Fame Let thy Trumpet Sound." From the balcony of the Crown Hotel royal salutes were discharged, and "mirth, hilarity, and goodwill everywhere prevailed." The Plymouth hostelries were resplendent with the portraits of heroes yet alive—Nelson, Saumarez and others, and Britannia held a weeping willow over the remains of Abercromby, Parker "and the illustrious dead."

Not forgotten were the devotion of the reserve and volunteer regiments. The Royal Invalids took charge of the batteries at the Citadel, the Artillery held the fort at Eastern King, the Artificers that at Western King, and the Cawsand Artillery commanded the bastions on Maker Heights. The remainder were massed within the lines at Dock—the Plymouth Blues, the Plymouth Volunteers, Langmead's Volunteers, Julian's Rangers, the Dock Volunteers, the Dock Association, Scobell's Artillery, and the Stonehouse Volunteers —and in every man's cap a cockade was fixed, with a sprig of laurel. At dusk a rocket was flashed from the main guard, and there blazed from 200 cannon a mighty discharge of combined salutes. Each feu-de-joie evoked a roar of stentorian responses from the prisoners who swarmed the decks and riggings of the guard ships. Especial distinction was in store for the Marines, and "a most gracious warrant," constituting them his Majesty's Royal Corps, was received by Major-General Bowater and announced to the men on parade. The officers entertained their colleagues of the garrison at dinner and "on the tap of the drum" volleys were fired, and the barracks burst into colours with "truly electrical" effect. When the Marines assumed their new uniforms for the first time, the Barrack Square was thronged and the windows were radiant with toilettes. Salutes having been fired, the battalion presented arms, and the veteran, Colonel Eliot, exclaimed in a loud voice: "Royal Marines, here's God Save the King, and long life to him." The sentiment ran through the lines like lightning, and heartier cheers than those raised within and without the barracks were "rarely heard." Always regarded as "a family and constitutional corps," the Marines were surrounded on this occasion by the aristocracy of the West, and "a most brilliant ball" was held in honour of the event at Pridham's Long Rooms.

General thanksgiving was offered in June 1802, and the ratification of the Peace of Amiens was welcomed "with every mark of loyalty and respect." By way of intensifying patriotic fervour, the anniversary of "the defeat of the great Spanish Armada by two Plymothians" was seized as the occasion for another gala day. International courtesies were already being resumed, French battleships and transports anchored in the Sound without interference, Admiral Villaret sent Admiral Cornwallis presents of fruit, and this "flag of truce" was acknowledged by Mdme. Villaret's present of a silver bust of Napoleon. Prisoners roamed at large by hundreds, and British seamen fraternised with their former foes. One sailor, meeting a group of Frenchmen in Frankfort Place, identified a man whose life he had saved from La Vengeur as it was foundering on the 1st of June. Congratulations passed, and "the honest British tar," flush of funds, treated the whole of the foreigners, to the number of twenty, and they pledged each other in prosperity to England and France! As the captives left the port their joy mingled with tears, and the sensation of relief was overpowering to those who had been detained for over nine years. Many only returned to their homes to mourn the loss of their dearest and nearest friends, victims either of the war or of its revolutions, whilst hundreds more lay buried in the embowered prison cemetery. To quote Carrington once more:

> Age had sank to the tomb, ere peace her trump,
> Exulting blew; and still upon the eye
> In dread monotony, at morn, noon, eve,
> Arose the moor, the moor, the moor!

Effervescing recklessness characterised the paying off scenes, and a popular dementia obtained. Raw spirits were heedlessly consumed, many seamen drank themselves to death, and others were plundered by crimps as they lay helpless and unconscious. Afloat, the sailors made merry, heedless of their officers, and a seaman of the Royal Sovereign, who sat astride the King's head as she was steered up the harbour, vociferously saluted other crews, and was cheered in return. It was not every commander who tolerated licence, as two men found who staggered to the pay table of the Impetueux, and created uproarious laughter by dancing a jig. Having threatened to punish those who resorted to excesses before the pennant was down, the Admiral ordered a dozen lashes apiece to be inflicted. The charm of the story lies in the assurance that the culprits called upon the martinet at his lodgings at Dock, and "departed in high good humour" after they had obtained his forgiveness. Fate was tempted with utter disregard as the men jumped into the overcrowded boats; and hustled, larked and danced in the stern sheets. In some instances, the occupants were suddenly immersed, and many exultant and hazardous spirits were drowned in this way. A man entangled in the steering gear was unable to make his cries for rescue heard above the din, and when his remains were extricated they were so mutilated that it was useless to remove them to the hospital.

A flood of reminiscences swept the town—anecdotes of heroes, like Admiral Lord Graves, of Thanckes, who participated in Howe's victory, Graves, indeed, played one of the proudest parts; for, with the Royal Sovereign at the head of eleven battleships, he was the first to enter the battle and the last to quit the pursuit of the flying enemy. Many there were who told how Lord St. Vincent won his action in the ensuing February, and others who assisted Nelson in the fight of the following August. Then there was Hugh Downam, the plucky Plymothian, who was shipwrecked on the coast of France and held prisoner until a few months before the Peace. Resuming his command, he crippled several hostile privateers, saved the Oporto fleet, rescued the priceless Florentine gems, and gave the protection of his flag to the King and Queen of Sardinia just as the French were about to make them prisoners. Downam brought a rich harvest of presents from his royal guests and the grateful merchants of Oporto. It was not only of the gently born that memorable services were related. One lad was the darling of Dock for his intrepidity at Algeciras, where the Hannibal ran ashore in the course of the battle, and it was imperative for intelligence of the disaster to be conveyed to the Venerable? The youngster swam from the Cæsar with the message in his mouth, and returned with the reply under a fierce fire from the French fleet and batteries.

Romance mingled with tragedy. Lieutenant Cartel, of the Argus frigate, returned after long imprisonment in France; and, unable to advise his aged parents of his release, entered his home at Cawsand without warning. His mother was so affected that "she expired of excessive joy." Another officer, whose wife lived at Dock, resolved on the pleasure of an unannounced visit; and, delaying his journey until the night was far spent, scaled his garden wall and climbed by the clinging ivy to the bedroom window. The noise aroused the sleeper; and, in the belief that the house was being attempted by a burglar, she armed herself with a sword and crouched behind the curtain until the head appeared. In the moonlight the officer saw the flash of the steel; and, just as his wife was about to cut him down, he shouted her name. At the sound of his voice the weapon fell to the floor, and husband and wife were locked in each other's arms.

Whilst officers and men were kindling five pound notes to light their pipes, and "scattering their guineas" in heedless bounties, there was a monster auction at Plymouth. Merchants travelled from London, Bristol and Exeter to participate in the harvest, and ships and stores alike fetched "extravagant prices." A wide field for commerce was opening up in the Mediterranean, and prize ships and goods were purchased to develop that trade. The window of one famous hostelry bore an inscription that testified to the vivid play of colour that was witnessed by the landlord during this Napoleonic lull: "I have seen the specious vain Frenchman; the truckling, scrub Dutchman; the tame, low Dane; the sturdy, self-righting Swede; the barbarous German; the pay-fighting Swiss; the subtle, splendid Italian; the salacious Turk; the ever lounging warring Maltese; the piratical Moor; the proud, cruel Spaniard; the bigoted, base Portuguese; and hail again, Old England, my native land!"

CHAPTER X.—THROUGH THE SUPREME STRUGGLE.

Press-gangs at Work in Plymouth: 1803. Every effort was made to convince Napoleon that England intended to give the peace a fair trial. Warships were "hogged" and their masts carefully laid aside. Night signals were discontinued, the militia were disbanded, and dockyard artisans were restricted to normal hours. Petty officers were empowered to resume their rank in the event of another outbreak, sailors were restored by thousands to their freedom, and the press-gangs were deprived of their warrants. Lord St. Vincent gave elaborate entertainments at his official residence in George-street, during a visit of enquiry, and received the freedom of Plymouth in a silver casket. As soon as he returned to town, wholesale discharges were ordered, and shipwrights and others were cast adrift by hundreds, and their places filled by sailors. Arising out of the retrenchments, one seaman used seditious expressions "almost too bad to repeat"; and, after receiving five hundred lashes, he was sent to prison for two years. Confidence in the peace was very thin, and, as soon as Napoleon had been enthroned, preparations were made for that invasion which was the absorbing passion of his life. The English response was no less resolute; battleships sailed from port to port with sealed orders, and signalling was again brisk from Maker to the Lizard. Sailors rejoined the fleet and soldiers the army; naval trophies were surveyed at Dock for active service; discarded battleships were encased in one-inch oak—"a new expedient"—and the artificers worked long after nightfall. The navy was victualled for six months, and ships were recommissioned with their old crews. Vigorously did Bidlake pourtray the activity in his native town:

> Haste to the busy docks, where noisy toil
> Its task laborious plies, and sturdy strokes
> Re-echo round the astonish'd shores. Whilst some
> The massive anchor forge, the cable coil,
> And all the instruments of naval pride:
> There, cloth'd in majesty, Britannia's guard
> With ribs of natal oak and lightning wing'd,
> With painted streamers, gay and proud and large,
> The warlike vessel over the billows rides,
> A floating world and arbitress of fate:
> Shaking with rival thunder's voice the skies.

The presence of an immense concourse of gunboats and armed transports at Boulogne and other ports proved the reality of the peril, and when stormy words passed between the Emperor and the English Ambassador, George III. responded with increased preparations. One afternoon, in May, 1803, a messenger galloped into Plymouth with instructions that were intended for the eyes of the Commander-in-Chief alone. War was to be waged forthwith against the "insolent upstart" who declared that England could not fight without an ally; and, within an hour, Admiral Dacres confined the soldiery to barracks, the various gates were bolted, and no one could leave either town without a written permit. As soon as the lamps were lit, the streets were paced by armed parties of marines; the avenues to the Barbican, Mutton Cove and North Corner were surrounded;

"IN CAWSAND BAY."

gin shops and vessels by the quays were invaded, every prime seaman was claimed and lusty landlubbers as well. Each impressor carried "stretchers"—pieces of wood that were ordinarily fixed at the bottoms of boats—"things just as well in their proper place as flourishing about a man's head, especially if he hadn't his hat on." Grim were the scruples of the officers: "Take care you don't use any violence, my lads, but, if the fellows won't stop their nonsense, knock them down." As the inns were rushed, the lights were as suddenly "doused." Fierce struggles followed, the use of stretchers was met by hurling pewter pots, and the raising of bumps found its retaliation in the cracking of skulls. As the mauled and maimed were thrown through the windows into the streets, shrieking women and children clung to the legs of the officer in charge. His reply to their appeals admitted of little controversy: "Who the devil's to man the ships?" Imprecations and resistance were rewarded with savage punishments. The bodies of the refractory were bared as soon as they were hauled to the deck, and, after the men had been tied to the gratings, they were lashed until the doctrine of submission had been sufficiently enforced. Then, excoriated and bleeding, they were flung below, to keep company with half-suffocated wretches writhing as the result of similar flagellations. Plymouth was thus condemned to a state of siege, and the agitation was intense as the impressment continued.

As it was clear this was no spasmodic effort, attempts were made to penetrate to the country districts; but these tactics were frustrated by soldiers who patrolled through Plympton, Modbury and Yealmpton on the one side, and away to Saltash, St. Germans and Liskeard on the other. Thence the detachments overspread the western counties; and hundreds of useful recruits limped footsore through the streets and passed within the gates of the yard with many a wistful look. Coasting seamen, with no anxiety for honourable mention, stowed themselves in haunts of ill repute, when their Delilahs betrayed them for the sake of the rewards. After desperate struggles, they were bundled out, bruised and bloodstained, and hurried to the vessels that required their services. There was no security for any business, and working men enlisted in the volunteer regiments as the only means of protection. The order of release seldom came in any form, much less in the romantic guise of the old ballad:

> In Cawsand Bay lying, with the blue Peter flying,
> And all hands on deck for the anchor to weigh,
> There came a young lady, as fresh as a daisy,
> And, modestly hailing, this damsel did say:
>
> "Ship ahoy! bear a hand there! I want a young man there,
> So heave us a rope man or send him to me;
> His name's Henry Grady, and I am a lady
> Just come to prevent him from going to sea!"
>
> Now the Captain, His Honour, when he looked upon her,
> He ran down the ship's side to help her aboard,
> Said he with emotion, "What son of the ocean
> Can thus be looked after by Helena Ford?"
>
> Then the lady made answer, "That there is my man, sir,
> And I'll make him as free and as fine as a lord."
> "Now that," says the cap'en, "can't very well happen
> I've got sailing orders, you, sir, stay on board."
>
> Then up spoke the lady, "Don't mind him, Hal Grady,
> He once was your cap'en but now you're at large,
> You shan't stop on board her for all that chap's order,"
> And out of her bosom she hauled his discharge!

Hundreds were torn from pleasures and occupations, and places of amusement were not privileged. The theatres were thrown into riotous confusion as the performances were in progress; and, amid the shrieks of women and the curses of men, the galleries were cleared of the physically fit, and the way to the water's edge was a prolonged free fight, the press-gangs cleaving their course through the seething mass, with their bleeding victims bound by the wrists. Terrorism was so general that watermen would not ply for hire between the Three Towns, Cremyll and Batten; traffic by these routes was suspended; and apprentices went into hiding, although they could not legally be seized. But they were torn from their places of concealment, and the harshness of their fate was deplored in many a home:

SWEET POLL OF PLYMOUTH.
(After the Engraving by Stothard.)

Sweet Poll of Plymouth was my dear
  When forced from her to go ;
Adown her cheek ran many a tear,
  Her heart was fraught with woe.

And have they torn my love away,
  And is he gone ? she cry'd,
My love, the sweetest flower in May,
  Then languished, drooped and died.

Quarrymen at work at Oreston were deported to the flagship, and any apology for a uniform sufficed to clothe the recruits—a stained sailor's smock or an old soldier's tunic, the fit was of little account. After a lull, parties were again "judiciously placed" on the turnpike roads and the escape of fugitives checked. Towns, villages and hamlets were regularly visited, and stout rustics and sturdy fishermen passed daily through Fore Street amid the cheers of seasoned salts and pleasantries of the maimed. "Amazing" was the activity with the arsenal. Teams of horses conveyed the wheat from the granaries to the King's mills without the Old Town Gate, so that flour for biscuits might be ground; the revenue cutters abandoned smuggling service and went on secret missions; and a majestic fleet of observation was fitted out by Lord Keith. Traders intensified the fever by reporting that seventeen sail of the line were at Brest, ready for a rush across the Channel, and as "hot presses" continued, worn-out uniforms were in vain affected to throw officers off the scent. East and West Indiamen, with no idea that the peace was in peril, found themselves besieged in the Sound by service boats in search of sturdy mariners. Fishermen from remote Cornish villages, plying their avocations off the Eddystone, were overtaken by armed gangs, and over forty trawlers were left with a third of their crews in one day. As the battleships in Hamoaze were provisioned and stored, Plymouth and Dock looked "as gay as in time of fighting." The wary local pilots steered many an unconscious merchantman into the Sound, and gained large rewards by enabling lieutenants on the pounce to make "fair sweeps" of their crews. Country bumpkins who journeyed to Plymouth to witness local festivities were found "good enough" to serve the King. There were rough and tumble battles and much blood-letting, but pickets of soldiers protected the press-gangs "from molestation and insult."

Hostilities began in an unofficial way. Le Frontier mistook the disguised Doris for an East Indiaman, and the latter remained passive until the French captain assumed that she intended to capitulate. Then a body of marines leapt to her decks, and the foreigners were mowed by a hail of musketry. Le Frontier lowered her flag and was taken into Plymouth, where the details of the first brush excited prodigious mirth. A French frigate, returning from a voyage of discovery, entered the harbour in ignorance of the situation, and was permitted to go on her way. The error of Le Frontier was repeated by a fine corvette, the Atalante, who chased the Plantagenet, 74 guns, in the belief that her business was commerce. Captain Hammond poured in a deadly broadside when the stranger came within pistol shot, and the prize was towed into Hamoaze in a sinking condition. A French privateer, which was rigged as a smuggler, sailed into Cawsand Bay, and escaped suspicion until the morning, when the usual signals were made from Maker to which all vessels were required to respond. Perceiving the danger of her situation, the privateer stood out to sea before the cheat was discovered, and being swift of sail, scudded beyond the reach of the English cutters that were sent in pursuit.

Napoleon had been postponing the inevitable until his East and West Indian fleets returned, but the advisers of George III. decided that it was in the highest degree impolitic to wait upon his pleasure. Thus the declaration of war followed the event, and, as the Channel was swarming with the enemy's traders, it rained prizes on the Plymouth cruisers. Brigs, corvettes, galliots, schooners and frigates congregated so rapidly that the agents could scarcely thread their way through the cluster; and in three weeks spoil to the value of over two millions sterling was moored in Catwater—a mass of captures never previously witnessed in so short a time. The French merchantmen had left with these costly freights when there was every appearance of an enduring peace; and, as few of them had effected risk insurances, their losses were "peculiarly distressing." Frigates, sloops and schooners, "fitted Channel over," were stationed along the coast with instructions to fall back when the enemy appeared, so that the telegraph might communicate east and west without delay. Soldiers poured into Plymouth from every part of the kingdom, and volunteers were now so plentiful that Admiral Dacres paid £4,000 in bounties in less than a week. A powerful guardship was stationed off the Yealm, and the redoubts at that point were restored to reliable defence. A battery of 32-pounders was erected at Staddon with the Dock Artillery and South Devon Militia in charge. 1,500 service artificers were embodied under Colonel Fanshaw, and there was no branch of the public service which did not contribute to the defence of the district. "Pressed men badly wanted" arrived in battleships from other ports, the barracks were soon filled to overflowing, and prisoners of war were removed to the prison ships. "It is your turn to guard us now," they spluttered in their anger, "but it will be our turn to guard you before very long." Their confidence was not strengthened as their numbers increased and the individual ratio of comfort was diminished.

Anticipation of a descent was keen and surmise active when the Sound was lashed by hurricanes that drove several prizes ashore, and threatened peril to the battleships awaiting orders. The horror of one memorable night was intensified by the "awful spectacle" of a merchantman in flames in Wembury Bay. No help could be afforded, for mighty seas swept over Drake's Island, and the spray smothered the topmost fort of the Citadel. A gang of water pirates settled upon an East Indiaman which stranded under the Hoe, and Langmead's Volunteers passed the night on the cliffs firing rounds of ball cartridge over the wreck in order to intimidate the thieves. Meanwhile the battleships in Cawsand Bay rode at anchor, and their numbers were increased by the San Josef, the Impetueux, the Royal Sovereign, the Doris, and other three-deckers, which had been nearly engulfed in running from Torbay. For days the storms raged, and the Foudroyant was despaired of; but, one after another, the noble vessels arrived, and, as they took up their accustomed stations, the relief was inexpressible. The work of refitting was prosecuted day and night, in view of the threatened descent; and, whilst it was in progress, the Sound was stirred more furiously than ever to foam. Before those hollow and rolling seas the fleet could not stand. Yards and topmasts were struck, frigates fouled line-of-battle-ships, and the heads of several vessels ominously dipped. In a few hours a "a melancholy and frightful spectacle" was presented. Masts, bowsprits, yards, topmasts and wreckage tossed in bewildering confusion; gunboats crashed upon the rocks; and brigs sunk in sight of harrowed spectators. The wind thundered as though the horizon were the mouth of a monster weapon, emitting a roar that stunned those afloat and lent indescribable terrors to the devastation ashore. "A boiling pot" seethed between Drake's Island and the main, and a pinnace was swallowed up there before any aid could be given to some thirty doomed officers and men. Smart's Quay, New Quay, Grey's Quay, and Foxhole Quay were inundated; lower Plymouth was flooded; the waves swept the Barbican to the height of several feet, and even parlours were immersed to the depth of several inches.

Spain was suspected of supplying France with cash, and war was declared that her treasure ships might be surprised in the British interest. The hum of industrial effort forthwith deepened, and the liveliest energy was displayed from the highest officer to the lowest "oakum boy." Shipwrights, house carpenters, labourers, and sawyers were freely entered at the yard and there was ever some kaleidoscopic variation. Now the Polyphemus entered Cawsand Bay with a frigate and a letter of marque, which struck their flags outside; then the Naiad's prize with her cargo of silks and spices, drove ashore in Jennycliff Bay; the Santa Maria was brought in with several hundred ounces of gold dust; and the Santa Gertruda, with a million and a half of dollars for the use of the Spanish King, was safely anchored in Catwater. Then confidence was dispelled by a vision of blue lights from the westward. The flashes travelled from point to point until they reached Maker, guns boomed from and Citadel, and townsfolk left their beds and hurried to the Hoe—only to learn that a friendly squadron had been chased by Cornwallis under a misapprehension. Gallooners, deep in water with spoils, came every other week ; but Spanish officers were treated as foes who might soon be allies, and "hospitable, polite and friendly receptions" were organised in their honour. They were not condemned to "noisome dungeons," like the French, but allowed to roam at will. With innumerable press-gangs on the prowl, the lame, the halt, and, it is said, the blind in at least the one eye, were included amongst the conscripts, and the small proportion who failed to pass a medical examination proved how the West was ransacked. A rollicking idea of the thrill of the movement is supplied in the old song :

> When I cum up to Plymouth town,
> Along with a gurt chap a 'ostling ;
> I sailed over to Cremyll Green
> For to have a turn to wrastling.

Assembled in picturesque medley were the patrons of the sport : aristocratic backers, villagers, champions from far and near, Devonian matched against Cornish—sheer strength against pure science, with the traditional pair of breeches exhibited as a chief inducement to the winner. Just as the spectators were immersed in the first throw, "up came a passel of ugly chaps," armed with "zwords and zticks," and, needless to say, their interference "perfectly spiled the games." Cool and overbearing in his manner was a "veller with a gurt cocked hat who zeemed for to be the King," and the brutality of his myrmidons so incensed the simple visitors that the bravest of them issued a challenge : "If you've any consait will 'ee plaze to step into the ring ?" But the visitors had no desire to excel in wrestling ; and, dragging combatants, bottle holders, and spectators to the waterside, they threw them into the cutters, without superlative ceremony, and pulled towards the Sound :

> They halled us out to a gurt big ship
> And through a hole in the zide,
> Lor' a massy, I was so sick
> I thawt I should av' died !

> At last they spied a gurt French ship
> And towards us 'er was a commin
> Zo they kelled up all the hands to fight,
> With a feller who went round drummin'.

> Zo I stepped up to the maister's side
> I zim to zee the zword o'rn ;
> Darn 'ee, zes 'ee, if you'll voller me,
> I warn 'ee us'll zoon be board o'rn.

Boarding ensued in the nature of things ; and, during the scramble, "a nasty French toad" endeavoured to slay "maister" (the lieutenant) by "going for to skiver 'un " :

> But when we had vairly beat mun all,
> And drove the French blackguards below ;
> Maister he halled their colours down,
> And we all of us gave a loud Worroh !
> With a Ri-too-rall-loo-rall, etc.

Fresh orders were promulgated as to the measures to be adopted in the event of alarm. If the warning were made during the day three guns were to be fired from Mount

R

Wise and answered by the same number from the Island and the Citadel.   If the alarm were raised at night the firing of rockets was to supplement the report of cannon, and the officer at Maker was to set fire to the beacon.   " But he is to be very careful not to do this unless he is perfectly sure that there is good ground for doing so."   Throughout the garrison regulars and volunteers alike were to drum to arms and repair to their respective parades.   The " sentinels are to be very watchful and attentive, both by day and night, to these orders, and upon the first signalling they are to call out the guard and to acquaint the commander of such a circumstance having taken place."

Up to this time instructions had been conveyed by colours burnt from batttleship to battleship and station to station, but the system was now improved upon.   There were two sets of " telegraphs "—one fixed within the Higher Lines at Dock, the other upon the heights above Saltram ; and, from lodges erected for the operators, messages were sent to the Admiralty and answers received in thirty minutes.   Intimations were conveyed with such celerity to London that replies were flashed back in ten or twelve minutes : " a rapidity of conveying intelligence hitherto unknown in this part of the country," and one that represented a " great saving in expresses."   Night telegraphs were also evolved by the manipulation of various shades, simple and compound.   A plane of convex or double convex lens formed hollow, and filled with transparent coloured liquids, was placed before the centre lamp, and a neck or tube admitted of the contraction or expansion of each lens.   The process was capable of 63 changes, without varying the line of direction, and 252 signals in all were possible.

The Alien Laws were enjoined with traditional rigour, and the town was posted with proclamations warning foreigners that they must disclose their presence under pain of imprisonment : " All such aliens as are now residing without the borough of Plymouth are hereby required to attend at the Guildhall, and there to produce their respective passports and licenses.   And those who neglect to attend at the time and place mentioned will be immediately apprehended and prosecuted according to law."   In October, 1804, concern was occasioned by the apparent flight from the town of a distinguished-looking foreigner. After staying at Murch's Hotel he inspected the dockyard, and subsequently took coach for Tavistock.   As he had neglected to produce his passport, " as required by the Alien Act," the Mayor sent officers in pursuit with a letter explaining certain circumstances that had created suspicion at the tavern, where the servant had refused to give any clue to the identity of his master or to explain the nature of his business.   The sergeants-of-mace tracked the visitor to Launceston, where he took a suite of rooms at the King's Arms Hotel, Thither magistrates and officers repaired, to find that the gentleman was the Duke de Montpensier, and that he held a letter from the Home Office testifying that he was one of the " persons of distinction " to whom the Alien Act was not intended to apply in con-sequence of his " being of the royal blood of France."

Cochrane's Triumphs   Kissing went by favour at the Admiralty, and political opponents
and Nelson's Death : were almost regarded with aversion.   Incensed at being repeatedly
1804-1805.   passed over, young Cochrane called upon Lord St. Vincent, and told him that, as the country had no need of his services, he should quit the navy and pursue another profession.   Stung by this disdain, the admiral replied : " Well, you shall have a ship ; go down to Plymouth and there await orders."   The grapes turned to ashes as Cochrane found himself appointed to a collier-looking craft that sailed " like a haystack," and yielded neither profit, honour nor adventure.   The Duke of Hamilton, Lord Vincent's successor and " my excellent friend," emancipated Cochrane from this " penal hulk," and appointed him to the Pallas, a fir-built frigate of 32 guns.   Cochrane's adventure in his

THE PRESS GANG AT THE MAKER GAMES.

old tub had given him such a poor reputation amongst seamen that his efforts to procure a crew resulted in an ugly brush with the local authorities. The mission of the Pallas was urgent and her prompt equipment imperative ; so, placing himself at the head of his own press-gang, Cochrane went to work in no tender fashion. The town was almost given over to anarchy by the brutality practised ; and, hot with indignation, the Mayor mustered the watchmen and called upon the disturbers to desist.   Blows passed between Cochrane and his Worship, two constables were wounded by Lieutenant Crawley, the sailors were attacked by the crowd, and swords and staves were freely exchanged.   On the following day Cochrane was served with a summons for assaulting the peace officers, but he disdained to appear at the court, and sent " Mr. Eliott, Plymouth," the Mayor, this curt and scornful note : "Sir,—I received your letter of yesterday's date this day at 12 o'clock.   If anyone has cause of complaint let the due course of law be followed. Sir, your most obedient servant, Cochrane." A warrant for his arrest was issued, but the young lord set sail before it could be executed, and the proceedings were transferred by writ of certiorari to the Court of the King's Bench, where a verdict was given in the defendant's favour. The disdainful officer plumed himself that this was "the only time I ever found it necessary to impress men." As dashing as Nelson in his methods, he reached the Bay of Biscay in time to intercept three treasure ships, conveying diamonds, gold and dollars in unprecedented values.   Putting prize crews on board, he forwarded the captures to Plymouth ; and in his defiant enthusiasm, sent his friends in the town a letter, in which he claimed that he had fulfilled the promise contained in the advertisements which he posted about Catwater on the eve of his departure, promising those who joined him "pewter and cobs"—the nicknames for ingots and dollars.

It was just a chance the Pallas was not sent to the bottom in returning to Plymouth, for a French squadron started in chase, and Cochrane's only hope was superior seaman-ship. Having secured the masts, he gave the order to clew and haul down the sails on the instant. The manœuvre was executed with the utmost precision—the helm was put hard a-weather, the ship wore, and the Pallas was promptly brought up. From stem to stern she trembled as she crossed the trough of the sea, but her pursuers shot past at full speed, and ran for miles before they could shorten sail or trim. As night was setting in, Cochrane threw over a ballasted cask to mislead the enemy ; and, when morning dawned, the foreigners were out of sight. Cochrane received his compensation in the overwhelming reception which he was accorded when the Pallas sailed into Catwater, with three towering candlesticks of chased gold jauntily exposed at the mastheads. These exquisite ornaments had been intended to adorn a Spanish church ; and, as they appealed to Cochrane's luxurious tastes, he arranged to retain personal possession of them. The Custom-house officers, however, thwarted this design by demanding the customary duty for articles of plate ; and, although the candlesticks were of the rarest workmanship, Cochrane was so enraged that he destroyed them upon the spot in order that they might pass for old gold :

> The Gunroom and the Reefer's berth
> Were now the strangest scenes on earth,
> The prisoners scarcely seemed to be
> Behind their conquerors in glee ;
> On their own stock they fed and laughed,
> And their own Claret gaily quaffed,
> Nor e'er looked sulky till the day
> They were all landed in Mill-Bay.

When in the Sound our ship appeared,
By all the others she was cheered ;
And visitors from morn till night
Flocked off to ask about the fight ;
And Girls and Jews came off to try
For Sailors' Love, and Agency.

Our Hero often had a job
To keep the ship clear of the mob,
And found it not a trifling bore,
When sent on duty to the shore,
To seek the Boats' Crews out, and fag
Through Mutton Cove, or Castle-Rag.
For ere long (we may well suppose)
The ships were order'd up Hamoaze.

There was a sense of hush as men waited for the blow that was to determine England's fate. Nelson was steering after the French, as he assured a friend in Plymouth by letter, "with every sail set," confident that he would eventually overtake them. The loss of the Magnificent, a noble frigate, which had been manned in the main by mariners from Stonehouse, of whom more than eighty perished on the rocks off Brest, accentuated the anxiety. Then the thunders of Trafalgar burst the clouds and the tidings flashed like a morning radiance. The anguish that underlay the joy was evidenced by the scene at one of the local theatres where, as the "Poor Gentleman" was being performed, an artiste rushed on the stage with the news of the victory, and a tumult arose "such as shrouds make in a stiff tempest." Hats, cloaks and doublets flew up, "Rule Britannia" was sung by "every true and loyal son," and the play was resumed. Fervour again overflowed when the Corporal exclaimed in the third act: "Victory and Old England for Ever," and the audience uprose to cheer as the lieutenant rejoined: "Against the World in Arms, Old England for Ever." "He will never fight for Old England again," one of the performers added in a pathetic aside; and, at this allusion to the death of the hero, there was not a dry eye in the house, the farce was abandoned, and the audience dispersed to mournful music. The sorrow intensified as the prizes followed in the wake of the news, the battle-ships with their flags at half-masts. The Sound presented a wonderfully diversified picture with the belching of smoke; and responding orchestral effects of gun and drum reverberated with every important variation of the spectacle—privateers escorting their captures, Indiamen that the returning fleet had seized, and a few of the foreign line-of-battleships to testify to the completeness of the French defeat. From the remotest towns of the west visitors made for Plymouth so that they might hail the victors and inspect their trophies. The harbour swarmed with rowing and sailing craft, and the honeycombed sides and devastated riggings of English, French and Spanish battleships exercised a weird and sustained fascination. The more curious visitors climbed to the decks to inspect the blood-stained evidences of the carnage, and as they heard the moans of wounded and inhaled the stenches that arose from the charnel-houses below, they turned shuddering and pained as from loathsome spectacles. Connoisseurs held an indifferent opinion as to the quality of the prizes. "They are fine men-of-war, but not to be compared with our 74's." Britannia sat sad and pale in the hour of her triumph ; but the congregation at St. Andrew's Church smiled through their tears on the day of thanksgiving and mourning. Reference from the pulpit to the glorious Victory excited the jealousy of two seamen of the Temeraire, who imagined that Nelson's flagship was receiving all the credit. At length one of them

gave audible expression to his irritation : " Listen, Jack, its about the Victory again—
nothing but the Victory.   That chap has never once mentioned the Temeraire, although
she was in the hottest of the fight, and captured two ships."   And, in their disgust, the
comrades rose and walked out, to discuss their grievance with the bystanders in the
porch.

Plymouth was not without its heroic reminiscences.   Dr. Halloran, the chaplain of
the Britannia, stood with a speaking trumpet throughout the storm and fury of the fight,
repeating the orders of the commander to the crew.   His eldest son, Laurence Halloran,
directed the firing during a tremendous bombardment; and, although officers and men were
blown to pieces by a bursting gun, the little midshipman from Tamerton escaped with a
singeing.   An instance of the immortal admiral's kindly nature was elucidated by Colonel
Tyrwhitt, the M.P. for Plymouth.   Hearing a child addressed as "Nelson" by its little
playmates under the Hoe, he made enquiries and found that the father, who was working
at Rusty Anchor, served in the Minotaur with the hero.   His wife was laundress of the
ship when a son was born to her, and Nelson stood sponsor at the christening.   Thereafter
the father lost his leg at the battle of the Nile and returned to Plymouth without informing
his patron of the straits to which he was reduced.   Colonel Tyrwhitt followed up Nelson's
intentions by putting the child to a naval school so as to fit him " for the service of his
country," and a subscription list was also raised for the parents " out of respect to the
memory of an admiral beloved, admired and adored, and whose fame will be entwined
around the heartstrings of every lover of naval virtue and heroism."

Engagements off the   So overflowing was the national pride that the scions of aristo-
Port : 1805-1808.   cratic houses rushed to join the navy ; and, with the arrival of each
noble recruit, the battleships presented brilliant examples of uniforms, and lavish
hospitalities were dispensed on the eve of every fresh departure for the French Coast.   Swiss
and other friendly foreigners were invited to join the service, and they cheerfully co-
operated.   French prisoners were landed at Devil's Point, in batches of hundreds, and
at once drafted to the guardships in Hamoaze or removed inland.   They were " uncommonly
impudent and overbearing " in their demeanour, but the Plymouth Volunteers exercised
an iron discipline ; a drum-head court-martial on the moor and a flogging out of hand
being the expedient the escorts employed to avert open mutiny.   The incidents multiplied,
although the invaders never came.   When Cornwallis ran over from Brest to get the
rudder of his flagship repaired, he was saluted with seventeen guns, but the veteran replied
that there was no necessity for fuss and ceremony, and gruffly declined invitations ashore.
Within forty-eight hours the Ville de Paris was bowling down Channel with a fine wind.
Again Admiral Lord Gardner set off for London in a post-chaise and four to receive
instructions, and there was a fresh outburst of enthusiasm.   Within ten days he returned
to hoist his flag at the mast of the Hibernia ; and, taking advantage of the first spurt of
wind, sailed amid salutes and cheers.   There were disappointments to lament, such as the
surprise of the Swallow, a Plymouth privateer, who closed with a hostile merchantman in
the belief that she was defenceless.   At the trumpet blast, a hundred soldiers sprang from
below, and the Swallow's crew were cut to pieces.   It was only her superior sailing that
enabled her to return to port.

Nelson's old " Agamemnons " in Plymouth turned their " quids very sour " when Sir
John Duckworth was outwitted in his chase of the French fleet in 1807 ; and, to add to
the bitterness, the Americans jeered at England as worn out in strength and jaded in spirit.
A demand arose that the country should more directly interpose to prevent the dominance
of Napoleon ; and, as ministers yielded to this clamour, vigilance was redoubled at

Plymouth, the completion of battleships was insisted upon, and "improper persons" were forbidden to enter the arsenal.   French men-of-war chased home-bound traders along the Cornish coasts, and panic was made familiar by recurring alarms that the hostile fleet was off the port, and there was imminent danger of landing; that the enemy had been out-manœuvred, the English had been cleverly tricked in turn, and the foe was at large.   Amid turmoil the officers were summoned to their ships; women who had been dancing on deck were hurried to the boats; sailors and marines on leave were hunted out of their haunts at North Corner and Mutton Cove; and sentries visited every house and were not over-scrupulous in identification.   Off the men were hurried in a flotilla of cutters, some cheering and others shouting, the impressed bewailing their lot, the salts aglow at the prospect of a brush!   And, as the fleet set forth in stately disposition, the alarm sped to the look-out stations!

Numerous were the displays of gallantry off Plymouth, and endless the adventures. A strange sail was seen off the Lizard with two merchantmen in tow; and, in response to the signal from Maker, the schooner Sealark left the Sound and overtook the Frenchman. "Monsieur" crowded sail and attempted to get away; but Lieutenant Warrand closed and boarded and reboarded several times.   British prowess prevailed and when Le Ville de Caen, 16, struck her flag after a resistance of two hours, there lay lifeless on her deck the captain and fifteen men, and sixteen others were badly wounded.   The prize was moored under Richmond Walk and was there seen to have been so pounded "as to have lost nearly every semblance to a vessel."   The Sealark escaped almost unscathed: "another proof that discomfiture and disgrace must attend every effort of our inveterate enemy to wrest our maritime rights from the stout arms of those who defend them."

The American Wasp was no less aggressive along the western coast, and the experience of the Reindeer, soon after she left Hamoaze, illustrated her alertness and energy.   Perceiving an enemy to leeward, Captain Manners gave the word, and rushed to the side of the Wasp.   He was at once picked off and his body carried to the cabin riddled with shots.   After losing one-half of his crew, the surviving officer capitulated and his vessel was so "irretrievably damaged" that the Americans sunk her.   Upon the arrival of the crew at Plymouth—for the victors contemptuously sent them home in a passing boat, nothing short of the defeat of the Argus could balance the account.   This visitor had fired a local trader, when the Pelican danced towards her with three cheers and fired five broadsides in forty minutes.   The Argus resisted with the utmost gallantry, but her guns were not levelled with precision and the Britishers, "through irritated by braggadocio," remained cool and steady.   The American commander had his leg shot away, his chief officer was killed by a ball from the foretop, and then the Argus was swept with a wild hurrah and her ensign hauled down.   Several officers and men lay dead on her deck, and others were gasping in their last throes, with limbs splintered by grape.   When the sufferers landed at Millbay their injured limbs had gangrened, and the captain succumbed to mortification. The death of this "model of symmetry and manly comeliness" was much deplored, and the victim was buried with full military honours.   Eight officers of the garrison acted as pall-bearers, the survivors of both ships wore crape tied with white ribbons, the naval captains hatbands and scarves, and there was "a respectable retinue of inhabitants."   Over a velvet pall the American ensign was spread, with the sword and hat of the deceased.   The body was interred in the south side of St. Andrew's Church, and the remains of Mr. Dephy, a midshipman of the Argus, who lost both legs in the same action were deposited alongside.

A daring vessel and an amazing fast sailer was the Sans Souci, of St. Malo, which carried a crew of 106 men, "drawn from the dregs of all nations."   She effected surprising captures on the Cornish coast, but her last onslaught cost her dearly.   The Briton came along as she made a fresh conquest ; and, exhausted by a previous struggle, she struck her flag.   Almost within view the Andromache frigate captured the American schooner Leader, and the two Britishers bore up with their prizes for Plymouth.   Returning to the Channel, the Andromache fell in with the Treves, a beautiful frigate of 44 guns.   A desperate wound prostrated her captain, and others fell so rapidly that the surviving officer surrendered with 300 prisoners.   More pleasing is the story of the capture of the Two Friends by the privateer Le Furet.   When the captains met, the Englishman made Masonic signals, and the foreigner returned the ship and cargo "as a token of his respect for the illustrious and ancient order."   The Two Friends resumed her journey, and the local brethren were so touched " by this example of fraternal virtue " that they presented the " enemy " with a silver cup of the value of one hundred guineas !

A league from the Eddystone, the Morning Star was overtaken by a French privateer cutter, carrying forty men.   Having delivered her papers, the Morning Star was told to go on her way ; but a battleship to whom she gave information went in pursuit, and the cutter was compelled to drop anchor in Cawsand Bay.   Mr. David Cow, of Dock, was challenged by a privateer off the Eddystone Lighthouse, but his Chatham gave as good as she received, and the enemy sheered off in "a sadly mutilated state."   Cow was shot through the mouth, his chief mate and a boy were slain, and nine seamen wounded.   Off the Scilly Islands the Hind revenue cutter fell in with a French privateer exhibiting the American colours.   The foreigner crowded on every stitch, but the Intrepide surrendered after receiving several searching broadsides and hails of musketry.   Whilst cruising in the Amethyst frigate, Captain Seymour came across La Thetis.   The shades were falling thickly, but broadsides were exchanged until midnight ; and, after 200 men had been placed hors de combat, La Thetis was convoyed into Plymouth.   The mizzen of the Amethyst was shivered to the stump, her masts and rigging were dishevelled, and eighty of her officers and men lay killed and wounded.   Captain Seymour received the hearty congratulations of his fellow Plymothians on escaping unscathed from this desperate duel.

Captain Zachary Mudge, another local worthy, was inveigled by four foreign sail disguised with English ensigns as he was cruising in thick and hazy weather in the Blanche. Escape was out of the question, and he resolved to fight to the death.   Running up their own flag, the enemy poured in a broadside, and Mudge replied by raking and battering the Commodore's ship.   Warm and steady was the action, the frigates running large under easy sail, and the corvettes blazing astern as opportunity served.   In two hours the Blanche was a wreck—her sails in shreds, her foremast toppling, her mainmast and rigging cut to pieces, and seven of her cannon dismounted.   Then and then only, when his ship would not answer her helm, did Mudge hesitate to further sacrifice "as brave a crew as ever lived."   As his men took to the boats, the Blanche went down by the head, and the explosion of her magazine shredded with splinters this scene of heroic resistance.   Mudge wrote from his French prison to his Plympton home to glory in the fact that the enemy's colours never flew from the mast of his ship ; and, after his exchange, the President of the Court that tried him at Dock returned him his sword, with the assurance that his defence of his vessel " merited the highest degree of approbation."

Tension at Plymouth: The ensuing months witnessed a change in the fortunes of
1808-1809. Napoleon.   Having laid Prussia bleeding on the field of Jena, he was himself overpowered by the Russians at Eylau, and a colossal stroke was necessary to the restoration of his prestige.   England had been dissipating her strength in detached and inglorious operations ; and, when Napoleon resolved on the invasion of Spain, public opinion demanded that the Britannic forces should play a more direct part in crushing

him. A fever of exultation prevailed in Plymouth and Dock in 1808, when regiment upon regiment embarked for the Peninsula, under the command of Sir John Moore and Sir David Baird. From that time forward, the port increasingly witnessed the massing of troops and departure of battleships; privateers brought in merchantmen; and smugglers ran their cargoes into Whitsand Bay under the blazing guns of revenue cutters. Plymouth was a babbling mart—its auction rooms thronged with speculators from all parts of the country, every section of the community making money with ease and just as recklessly spending it. At night the streets were alive with revels, the watchmen were harried, knockers were wrested from doors, the lamps were smashed with impunity, and a laughing disregard of such supervision as existed did dim duty for the observance of social order. Ever throbbing was the local mind with some new rumour, and the spectacle of a mutineer lashed around the fleet, or of a deserter dangling from the yardarm of the flagship, varied many a ghastly recital in murky taprooms. Now a privateer of the enemy pounced upon a trader within the fishing limits of the port, and then, overtaken by a calm, fought till its decks were ensanguined and its hold was filled with dead and dying. The fleets escorting in stately strength the Indiamen; the spectacle of almost unending processions of superb traders moving up Channel with all sail set—these displays of force and wealth thrilled the inhabitants with ecstasy and inspired them with expectation. They were further enthused when officers arrived from London by forced driving, or the Port Admiral entertained distinguished guests at Mount Wise, where the Royal Standard was spread upon the banqueting table "in honour of our glorious naval victories," and "beautiful transparencies" were exhibited to the townsfolk who listened to the band without.

So insatiable was the demand for news that two weekly journals were simultaneously started—the "Plymouth Chronicle" and the "Dock Telegraph"; and, if the relations between these organs were at least as hostile as those of England and France, their records of the campaign, invested as they were with the varying emotions of the services, vividly illustrate the throb and palpitation of the port. As the months rolled on and the despatch boats reached Dock with gloomy forecasts of the campaign in Gallicia, the suspense was afflicting. The first positive gleam of relief was afforded by the naval battle in the Basque Roads, and it is quaint to know that both local papers suspended publication until they could allay the anxiety, and no less instructive to observe the roundabout means by which the knowledge was acquired by the editors: "The London mail which should have reached Dock at nine o'clock this morning did not appear till after three this afternoon. It brought neither papers nor letters, because the Bath coach, which usually delivers them at Exeter, was unable to travel by reason of the inundated state of the roads. The London mail, however, brought a gratifying and welcome announcement. The guard of the coach states that, in coming to Exeter, he met Sir H. Burrard Neale proceeding express for town with despatches from Lord Gambier, containing the important news of the destruction of the French fleet in the Basque Roads. Those ships which were not destroyed lay on their beam ends. THREE SAIL of the LINE, and the Calcutta, taken from us some time since, were BURNT, and SEVEN SAIL of the LINE and FOUR FRIGATES Driven on Shore. This pleasing information, we are happy to add, is confirmed by a letter to a gentleman holding a high official situation at this port. The mail coach and horses were decked with a profusion of laurel."

In June voluminous arrears were delivered in the form of a series of "Madrid Gazettes," with which "we have been favoured by a gentleman who landed at this port." The responsive hum was meanwhile maintained by the local reserves: "On Wednesday, the Loyal Dock Associated Cavalry, commanded by Captain Thomas, paraded on Buckland Down, and performed their various manœuvres in a manner highly creditable both to themselves and their officers. After this they adjourned to the Roborough Inn, where a sumptuous dinner, comprising every delicacy the season could produce, was served up. A number of loyal and appropriate songs and toasts were given by members of the corps, and the utmost mirth and harmony prevailed *till a late hour.* On the following day the above cavalry were inspected by Colonel Farwell, who was pleased to express his approbation of their soldier-like appearance under arms. The fumes of Bacchus, arising from the conviviality of the preceding night, were not entirely evaporated; but the men nevertheless acquitted themselves in a manner perfectly satisfactory." Another paragraph in the same issue told a somewhat less agreeable story : " Mr. Hammond, formerly a pilot of the Saturn (a person well known in the neighbourhood), has been arrested in France, as a spy, and beheaded by order of the French Government. After his execution, his body was dragged around the town—the name of which is not mentioned. He had been sent from the Saturn on board L'Aigle, Captain Wolfe, to reconnoitre the French coast, and landed at a port near L'Orient. He had been on shore 12 days, and was preparing to come off in a boat, when he was arrested by two custom-house officers. He received a pension of £50 per annum from the English authorities for the information he obtained some time since by landing on the enemy's coast. He was a Frenchman by birth, but had been many years in our service, in the course of which he had more than once risked his life, by making incursions into France and returning in an open boat to our ships off the coast."

Public attention was now engrossed with the march of events in the peninsula, and the one question asked was " What is the news from Spain ? " (June 18). " On Tuesday last a Spanish Nobleman landed here from the Statira, and immediately set off for London. He came from the province of Asturias, deputed by the Constituted Authorities to our Government, in order to expedite the assistance which it may be deemed necessary to afford the Spanish Patriots. They are much in want of ammunition, a large quantity of which has already been shipped for their use ; and 40,000 pikes were sent from the Gunwharf at Plymouth-Dock on board two transports, which sailed to-day for the coast of Spain, accompanied by the Temeraire, 98." Affairs were now moving so rapidly that occurrences which would, at other times, have excited no small degree of interest daily transpired unheeded. It was the fight of the " Patriots " that enthralled the public : " We are sorry to state on the authority of a gentleman who landed here yesterday in the Raven gunbrig, that it is generally believed the French have obtained possession of the combined fleets in Cadiz ; and also of the Russian squadron in the Tagus."

Much more encouraging was the pleasantry received during the first week of July : " The Cheerful has brought us a letter from an officer on board the Hibernia, of which the following is an extract :—" We are in hourly expectation of entering Lisbon ; OUR FLEET IS IN CADIZ, and the Spaniards are cutting the Frenchmen's throats. I hope to see you ere long, with the Russian fleet at our sterns ! " Meanwhile every available labourer was enrolled in the reserves. The men liable to duty in the Local Militia were those between the ages of 18 and 30 ; and there was no protection derived by joining subcriptions or clubs. Every volunteer who agreed to transfer his service to the Local Militia received two guineas bounty, and was entitled to the same allowances, exemptions and privileges as he previously enjoyed. The engagement was for four years, the service was the same as that of a volunteer, the man could not be called out of the county, unless in case of invasion, and even then he was not bound to leave the kingdom. He was not (as under the Training Act) liable to be incorporated with a regular regiment, or to be under the command of officers of the line, except Generals and Field Officers. At the expiration of every four years, each person enrolled under this act was to enjoy *further exemption* from ballot for *two years* more. In explanation of the good faith of the authorities, Plymouth and Dock were posted with placards to dispel certain rumours that had been circulated ; and little disposition was evinced to allow militiamen to be perfunctory in the discharge of their duties :

C A U T I O N .

WHEREAS, a scandalous and infamous report has been very industriously circulated, tending to impress on the public mind that the offer of service of the Duke of York's Battalion of Volunteer Royal Artillery Local Militia, had not been accepted by his Majesty, with a view no doubt to prevent persons from enrolling themselves therein :

The Commanding Officer therefore, hereby cautions all such fabricators of falsehood, to refrain from a continuance of such conduct, as prosecutions will be instituted against each and every person who shall be found so offending after this public notice.

N.B.—As the battalion is to consist of 700 persons, there are yet vacancies for young and spirited men—who, on enrolment, will have Protections granted, and a bounty of Two Guineas.

Fourth Devon, or Roborough Regiment of Local Militia.

THE Regiment will ASSEMBLE at Head Quarters, Plymouth, on TUESDAY, the 7th day of May next, at *one o'clock* in the afternoon, to be Trained and Exercised for *fourteen clear days.*

Those men who have never joined to be *trained and exercised*, are ordered to attend for that purpose, for twenty-one clear days, on *Tuesday, the 30th day of April inst.*, at the above place and hour ; if any Non-commissioned Officer, Drummer, or Private should not be present at the time and place appointed, without satisfactory reasons, he or they will be considered as *Deserters.*

MASSEH LOPES,

Lieutenant-Colonel Commandant.

Head-quarters, Plymouth,

April 11, 1809.

Successive English and Spanish successes diffused a spirit of universal exultation ; but the "Dock Telegraph" had an additional cause for joy, "in having (exclusively) communicated the momentous news to our readers, four days prior to its appearance in the London papers." The same week the Bittern brig put in with two Turkish envoys: "They slept at the Fountain Inn, and next morning proceeded for London, accompanied by their attendants, in a post coach, and two chariots and four. They come with pacific proposals from the Porte, and with demands for succour and protection against the machinations of France and her allies. In what a grand and dignified altitude does Great Britain stand at the present moment !—the protector of the injured ! the avenger of the oppressed ! the only nation capable of saving the world ! Captain Usher, of the Bittern, immediately on landing, set off express for town, having brought despatches from Vigo." Despite this little amalgam of fact and hysteria, it was acknowledged that the war could only end with the extermination of the French in Spain, and that Napoleon, unaccustomed to failure, would never confess to defeat. There was the manliest enthusiasm in Plymouth and Dock in August, and hundreds of volunteers and militiamen enlisted for the peninsula. The "Dock Telegraph" apologised to its readers (September 17th) for once more delaying publication, "having deemed it our duty to wait for the official details of the defeat of Junot and the Russian Fleet. The confirmation has not yet reached us, although there can be no doubt as to capitulation having taken place." In a stop-press edition, it was able to announce that Major Dalrymple had landed at Teignmouth and immediately set off express for London. "The contents of his despatches were not suffered to transpire ; but we have pleasure in stating on authority, that they contain the gratifying and long anticipated intelligence of the unconditional surrender of Junot and the Russian Fleet to the British forces in Portugal."

There was now a period of reaction and reproach, due to failures to follow up success, but "the black clouds of disgrace formed by imbecility and misconduct" were at length dispelled "by the bright sunshine of Victory." The Unicorn frigate anchored in the Sound, from off Bilbao, with tidings of considerable importance. General Blake had routed the French with fearful slaughter, and resolved to attack "King Joe and his banditti" at Vittoria. The Unicorn landed hundreds of prisoners at Millbay, and might have brought over as many more if its capacity had permitted. And next week the "Dock Telegraph" crowed more loudly than ever: "The important information, which the arrival of the Unicorn enabled us to lay before our readers last week (four days earlier than most of our contemporaries) has furnished the leading matter in the London papers of the current week—a striking proof of the priority which our situation enables us to command. The Intelligence gun-brig arrived here yesterday from Lisbon, and reports a brilliant victory by the Patriots over the main body of the French army at Vittoria."

The Survivors of Corunna at Plymouth: 1809. During November there were distressing rumours of a "dreadful battle," and its progress and result were awaited with tremulous anxiety. Masses of French troops had been overflowing the Spanish frontier, with Massena and Sebestina, ablest and boldest of Napoleon's generals, in command; and so long an interval had elapsed since characteristic and jaunty intimations had been received that the French were being surrounded that the "Dock Telegraph" now began to discount the infallibility of British arms: "For the first time we are reluctantly compelled to confess that we have very serious apprehensions for the result of this unequal and unnatural contest. We by no means wish to underrate either Spanish valour or Spanish patriotism; but, knowing the character and genius of the French Emperor, and the vast resources which he commands—his revenge—his ambition—his hatred—and his mortified pride at being checked where he least expected it—we are convinced he will leave no means untried to accomplish his diabolical design. Hitherto the advantage has been decisively in favour of the Patriots; and we pray Heaven our fears for the ultimate issue of the contest may prove unfounded. The long continuance of the violent easterly gales has prevented our receiving any details from the scene of action; the next arrivals, we may safely predict, will furnish the result of a conflict, more obstinately contested, and more important in its consequences, than any that has hitherto taken place."

Hearts again bounded when the Mediator arrived with despatches from Santona announcing that the French army there had been "literally cut to pieces." Then followed the Parthian, "after a fortunate escape from three French brigs and a corvette in the Bay of Biscay. The Parthian, being in the middle of the four, fired a musket to bring to one of the brigs, when three boats were perceived alongside intending to board, the crews calling out 'Strike your colours; we are all Frenchmen.' The Parthian immediately made sail. Two brigs on her lee beam, of 18 guns each, and a corvette of 20 guns, on her weather quarter, opened their broadsides, accompanied with volleys of musketry, but the Parthian returned their fire for about a quarter of an hour, and by her superior handling made her escape, and arrived safely with her despatches."

December plunged Plymouth and Dock in irremediable gloom. Castano's army had been routed by the French, and Sir John Moore was hastily retreating upon Corunna. The Sound swarmed with transports about to leave with reinforcements, when it was announced that Moore was recovering his position: "The Cheerful cutter arrived last evening from Corunna, and landed a messenger with despatches, which are said to contain good news,

One important fact is well ascertained, namely, that the troops under GENERAL BAIRD HAVE ADVANCED TO JOIN SIR JOHN MOORE, AND ALL THOUGHTS OF OUR TROOPS BEING RE-EMBARKED HAVE BEEN GIVEN OVER." This short-lived consolation was dispelled in a second edition of the "Dock Telegraph": "Captain Wyndham, aid-de-camp to Sir John Moore, arrived this afternoon and immediately proceeded to town, having brought despatches from the British Commander-in-Chief, which are of an extremely unpleasant nature. It is even said that Generals Moore and Baird were retiring from Astorga to take possession of the heights of Villa Franca, in order to secure a retreat !—Bonaparte, with an immense army, was only three leagues in their rear, having apparently withdrawn his attention from every other object in order to cut them off, or bring them to a general engagement."

Absence of definite information caused the transports to be detained in the Sound, and the Portsmouth contingents put into Plymouth for further orders. Fears for the safety of Moore's army increased every hour, and those who rejoiced a few weeks before were now "content to hope that our brave defenders may safely embark." The worst was known (January, 1809) with the arrival at Plymouth of the remnant of the army itself, and the story of Sir John Moore's heroic death. Within a week the Sound swarmed with the vessels that carried Moore's brave companions ; and as they landed, hollow-eyed and gaunt, ragged and savage with privation, despondency and dismay filled the town, and fears and lamentations were general. Tears sprang unbidden to the eyes even of men as the poor fellows so eagerly sought the shelter of barracks and hospitals. The maimed were numbered by hundreds, arms and legs had been shot from many, portions of limbs had been amputated, and scores exposed wounds that were decomposing from neglect. As the sufferers lay on stretchers awaiting removal, the effluvia caused the spectators to shrink, whilst their flesh crept, and the moans were piteous. Sir David Baird, one arm severed from the socket, was amongst the victims. Many of the officers were destitute of shoes and linen, and in want of almost every necessary. After every bed in the Stoke Military and Stonehouse Naval Hospitals had been filled, there were hundreds unprovided for. Numbers were conveyed to the convalescent ships in Hamoaze, "where they receive every attention their situation requires"; and the inhabitants abandoned their own beds to accommodate the remainder. Scores of gallant fellows died as the transports lay in the Sound ; others expired with fatigue and suffering as they were being landed or conveyed to operating rooms. The women who accompanied their husbands into Spain, and took part in the retreat through the ice-bound defiles, had endured unspeakable privations and hardships, and many perished despite the attentions of doctors who journeyed from every part to give them help. Over 2,000 sick and wounded soldiers were herded in the town in this extraordinary emergency ; and, owing to the deplorable destitution of their families, a meeting was summoned by the Mayor :

BOROUGH OF PLYMOUTH.

AT a very numerous and respectable Meeting of the Inhabitants of this Borough, convened by public advertisement by the Worshipful the Mayor, at the Guildhall thereof, on WEDNESDAY, the 25th day of January instant, to take into consideration the situation of the SOLDIERS' WIVES and FAMILIES that are now landing at this Port from Spain, and to make Provision for affording RELIEF to such as may require it, THE WORSHIPFUL THE MAYOR, in the Chair;

Resolved :—That a subscription be immediately entered into for the above purposes, and that Books be forthwith opened at the Guildhall, and the several Banks in Plymouth, to receive the names of Subscribers and amount of Subscriptions,

Relief was forthwith given to 800 women ; clothing was distributed by the ladies, and Colonel Hawker's Volunteers sacrificed their uniforms so that the regulars might be clad. A general humiliation was proclaimed in Plymouth and Dock, and at services held in the churches and chapels, collections were made in aid of the distressed, £1,800 in all being raised.

Suspense and Rejoicings at Plymouth : 1809-1813. Sir Arthur Wellesley, soon to be Lord Wellington, personally superintended the embarkation at Plymouth of the army with which he was to retrieve the painful chapter of Corunna. In April, 1809, soldiers inundated the town in one apparently unending stream of scarlet ; and artillery, ammunition, and stores of provisions obstructed the approaches to the docks. Faith and hope pervaded every class as Wellington sailed for Lisbon ; and from week to week, with the departure of reinforcements, the streets were radiant with the glittering accoutrements of additional officers. It was the check administered at Talavera that first restored confidence in the capacity of English generalship to out-manœuvre and vanquish the French, and illuminations testified to the spirit of rejoicing that inspired every house and battleship. The subsequent retreat of the English induced corresponding emotions of despondency ; and the dread of another Corunna was not diminished by the knowledge that the transports were once more in waiting to receive the English regiments if Massena drove them to the water. The depression passed, as Captain Stanhope, of the Guards, arrived with documents that presaged a fortunate issue of the campaign in Portugal. Massena's retreat was proclaimed as "Glorious News," and the parade with which it was communicated is not without its humour : "We are truly happy in being able to lay the following glorious intelligence before our readers, with which we have been favoured by a correspondent at Falmouth. For some unaccountable reason it has been delayed on the road, the injury of which to us is considerable, but nothing compared to our disappointment in not being earlier able to relieve the public anxiety on matters so very interesting to every individual who has the love of his country at heart." More "Glorious News" came to hand in July (1810), when the Eagle cutter reported that Sir Charles Cotton, who had not long set out from the port (his residence was at Stoke), had taken five sail of the line and 9,000 troops. In November, 1811, General Renaud was smothered with good wishes when he landed and assured his hosts that the flower of the French army had been annihilated at Ciudad Rodrigo. Chaises, full of officers, who came in the same boat from Spain "have just left Dock for London." It was asserted by Captain Canning, Wellington's aide-de-camp, that in six weeks there would not be a Frenchman left in Spain "unless in the hospitals," and the crowd cheered itself hoarse as he left in a carriage drawn by four greys to explain to the King with what impetuosity Picton scaled the walls of Badajoz. Again the "Dock Telegraph" indulged in its characteristic note of jubilation : "We feel particularly happy in being the *first paper* to communicate the pleasing intelligence, so gratifying to the feelings of every true Englishman, and which is a proof, among many others, of the very extensive and superior sources of intelligence possessed by this paper, to which, in a great measure, it is indebted for the extensive circulation and the great support it experiences, and which it will ever be the pride and care of the Proprietor to merit."

Signals of distress were fired in February, 1811, when the Amethyst frigate drifted from her moorings in the Sound. As she was riding at single anchor, it was impossible to bring her up, and the hurricane was so unintermittent that no assistance could be rendered. The vessel dashed under Mount Batten, where scores of volunteers went to the rescue with ropes, and the survivors were brought ashore. In their anxiety to reach land several men jumped into an already overloaded boat, and thirty more lives were sacrificed in this way.

The gun-brig Growler was also swept into Firestone Bay, and reduced to matchwood in a few hours. At sunrise one morning in June volumes of smoke arose from the Rope House, and the fire spread so rapidly that a flaming mass of two hundred feet emerged from the roof. The clanging of the alarm bell caused a vast crowd to assemble; seamen landed from the ships with buckets at their backs, and engines were towed to the scene on floats. It was only by using hatchets and thus destroying the connections, that the outbreak was eventually quelled. It was the impression that France had bribed some scoundrels in the yard to effect their "infamous purpose," but patriots of a prosaic disposition attributed the disaster to the action of the sun's rays upon one of the windows.

Again and again was the cup filled until Salamanca gave assurance that Marmont's force was in full retreat (1812). Wellington was voted a freeman in his absence, and the patent was enclosed in a silver casket. Every window was a blaze of light on the night of rejoicing, and though the moon was at her full, "her silvery rays were overpowered by the radiance that prevailed in every direction." Over the entrance to the house of the Mayor, Dr. Bellamy, the name of Wellington was presented in luminous characters and his worship's garden glittered with lamps. On the west front of the Guildhall was placed a full length portrait of the hero, with the French flag at his feet and Fame advancing with a crown of laurels. One transparency depicted " Mars discarding his favoured minion " and another showed the God of War conferring upon the general a chaplet of laurel. An elaborate delineation of "the late contest " was shown at the exterior of the Commercial Inn, in Old Town Street. Wellington was seated on a white charger directing the charge of the British cavalry, and the enemy were "flying in all directions." A French standard bearer was falling from his horse, and Marmont was depicted "with a face wrung by agony, pain and discomfiture." Elsewhere a dying warrior was " prostrating the Gallic ensign " in the dust, the English infantry were resorting to the bayonet, and the trumpet sounded "Wellington Victorious." Another view of the battlefield was strewn with the dead, dying and wounded ; French eagles and implements of war were scattered about, and the dogs of Bellona "furiously roamed over the bodies of the slain." This representation "had more the appearance of an historical painting, intended to descend to posterity, than a transparency doomed only to delight for a few hours and then disappear for ever." There was no inclination to tumult, no indecent revellings were to be descried, and every citizen was inspired with " deep-felt joy and gratitude to Providence."

In 1813 the cost of necessaries was so prohibitive that bread could not be purchased by the poorer classes ; and, in this emergency, cargoes of potatoes were imported from Cornwall, and distributed without profit by charitable societies. Then the Mayor discovered that the flour sold by some local millers was impregnated with china clay, and enquires resulted in the discovery that hundreds of tons of the powder had been brought from St. Austell, and used to adulterate even the Peninsular supplies. Indignant multitudes paraded the streets, the houses of local conspirators were attacked, and their effigies burnt in the market place. A miller at Widey offered £100 to those who would prove that he had been guilty of nefarious practices, and threatened anyone "who puts my reputation in peril." Excitement was intensified by Corn Law manœuvres to enhance the price of the loaf ; and, at stirring meetings of the people of Plymouth and Dock, petitions were approved protesting against the device for assisting affluent landlords to mar "the expected return of peace." The halls were insufficient to accommodate one-third of the remonstrants and ministers were told in the petitions that were adopted that the landowners must reduce their rents and approximate their expenditure to the new circumstances. The bill was thrown out and "the mail-coach that brought this pleasing intelligence was decked with laurels and welcomed by the acclamation of the populace."

During the same year the dockyard was again jeopardised by an outbreak on board the Captain, 74 guns, which must also have destroyed the San Josef but for the promptitude with which her lashings were unmoored when the cry rang out. As a light and fanning wind played over the Captain, her interior glowed as with molten metal, and the glare overspread every object at midnight. The Captain then showed signs of drifting amidst the other wooden walls, and large clamps were driven into her bow, and bolts through her stern, to which chains were attached so that the debris might be towed to the opposite shore. Efforts to scuttle the wreckage were thwarted by the intense heat. Two field pieces were thereupon conveyed to the vicinity in launches and 200 shots fired into the incandescent mass, of which the majority went between wind and water. As the hulk increased in buoyancy by the action of the flames, many shot-holes gradually appeared above water. The bombardment aroused the attendant echoes, but the Captain flared until four, when she majestically glided to the bottom, contending as she went with the waves, so that "like the hero who once commanded her, the vessel was glorious in the manner of her exit." The mighty mass of flames created artificial day in Dock, and the reflection was seen at thirty miles distance. Several of the crew were burnt with the vessel—how many the authorities were never able to ascertain.

When Lieutenant Freemantle came in the Sparrow with the despatches from Vittoria enthusiasm attained its zenith, and then the brig Nova Scotia appeared with the "highly agreeable intelligence of a lightning-like action" between the Shannon and Chesapeake, in which, "with an impetuosity that bore down all resistance," the American's deck was swept and cleared by British cutlasses. "Wellington, the Prince of Heroes, scourge of France and England's glory," was the familiar form of thanksgiving ; and a transparency at the John Bull tavern depicted a group of Jack Tars rejoicing with the captain of the Shannon. A local mercer exhibited "this ludicrous inscription":

> When Britons fight and Frenchmen fall ;
> O what delight it gives George Hall.

"The Last Gun" was the most realistic of these expansive pourtrayals. At the top of a carriage from which the weapon had been unlimbered, Frenchmen were fighting with the courage of despair. There was a lurid and vivid idea of Wellington in pursuit of Marshal Jourdan, who was dropping his baton in the act of taking flight. At another hotel "Joe's Carriage" was galloping over cannon, colours and corpses, and the King of Naples was standing in the distance with his crown under his arm—the whole forming "a magnificent coup d'œil." Bands paraded the streets playing martial airs, and the members of "the Wellington Club," in Old Town Street, toasted their hero to the chorus :

> Then raise high the glass, to his health let it pass,
> And soon may victories crown his endeavour :
> For we've now a new boast, as we honour the toast,
> Salamanca, my boys, and Vittoria for Ever.

Wellington entered France in October, 1813, and marched upon Paris ; and, when Sir Thomas Graham, the hero of Barrosa, "honoured this town by remaining awhile at the Fountain Inn," he was presented with the freedom of the borough, and escorted beyond its boundaries by a serenading and cheering multitude. Napoleon's continued reverses caused another outburst, and Plymouth Hoe was "a moving theatre of human countenances" on the night fixed by the Mayor for the rejoicings. At the summit of a monster bonfire stood the figure of Napoleon "or Apollyon, the arch destroyer alluded to in the Scriptures"; and such "uncommon anxiety" was manifested to witness the downfall of

S

the effigy, that shrieks vied with shouts as the figure dropped into the burning mass. The French and American colours followed suit; and, when the British flag flew unscathed overhead, salutes were fired by the big guns, feux-de-joie rattled from the soldiery, blue lights were burnt in the Sound, massed bands rendered hymns of thanksgiving, the church bells rang, and the crowd never wearied of cheering. There were scrambles for cakes and ale, and "wines and other delicacies" were supplied to the visitors. The festivities concluded with a ball at the "New Royal Hotel."

Painful reaction involved distressing doubts until the allied grasp was firmly closing upon "the serpent, so long the bane of Europe." A proclamation was issued by Henry Woollcombe, the Mayor, in which the latest information was accompanied by a few words of encouragement: "The world at length approaches her deliverance, and England may triumphantly look forward to reap, in conjunction with her allies, that glory which her unexampled and steady efforts in the common cause so justly entitle her to receive." It was popularly recalled that, when Lucien Bonaparte visited Plymouth three years before, he predicted that his brother's sun would set in Spain; and, to add to the spirit of recovery, the Prince of Orange landed and drove to the house of the Port Admiral, accompanied by guards of honour and military bands. Plymouth was soon cut off from the rest of the country by a snowfall heavy beyond "the memory of man;" the coaches could not travel for several days; and, although a road was cut from Ivybridge, three weeks elapsed before traffic was resumed. Then it became known that a decisive battle was imminent; but, as day passed day and the crowning triumph appeared as far removed as ever, language was incapable of describing the dismay and despair which the suspense diffused throughout the Three Towns. Hope was bestirred by the arrival of two sturdy French frigates, the Iphigenia and Alemene, which were threatening the Cyana with capture when the Venerable opportunely sailed to its rescue and turned the scale. Within a few hours the Menelaus anchored in Hamoaze with a prize of the value of a quarter of a million. In March the town rang with Captain Phillimore's gallantry in the engagement between the Eurotas and the Clorinde; during which, regardless of a terrible wound in his shoulder, he urged on his men until he fell exhausted upon his arm. On entering the harbour, Phillimore was lowered into the Port Admiral's barge, and officers and men were enjoined not to cheer him on his way through Stonehouse creek. The Hebrus ran down L'Etoile after a fifteen hours' chase; and, upon her surrender, the enemy's deck was strewn with "horribly wounded men," who still lay writhing in tortures when she was brought into Plymouth. L'Etoile had borne a charmed life, and the treasure of which she had relieved seventeen prizes lay in her hold.

It was at Falmouth that the message was first received of Bonaparte's decisive defeat and retreat on Paris. Bonfire responded to bonfire, and rockets carried the news to every village. Plymouth and Dock were overcome with joy; but the prisoners, in their incredulity, refused to hoist white flags in homage and loyalty to the Bourbons until they had received official notice of their restoration. In May was witnessed "the remarkable spectacle of a French squadron entering the Sound in amity with England;" and a thousand prisoners were landed, and as many received in exchange. For weeks similar transfers continued, but hundreds failed to respond to the roll call, whose bones had been laid in the local cemeteries, with a few Plymouth sympathisers as their only mourners. The peace was proclaimed by the Town Clerk, Mr. Whiteford, in the Market and other public places, and 1,200 children partook "with overflowing glee" of a dinner laid in the streets. "Actuated by the gayest and yet most harmonious feelings," multitudes were attracted from afar to witness the illuminations, and the pressure of the crowd was beyond all precedent. Hugh transparencies by Walter Whitfeld were fixed outside the Royal and

Windsor's Hotels. At the former Britannia trampled on the tri-coloured flag, and the Devil was carrying Bonaparte below to an accompaniment of fiddles, drums and bullocks' horns over the portals of Windsor's. Near the Church Inn the Emperor was caricatured with his nose at a grinding-stone, and the handle turned by a Cossack. Elsewhere the "oppressor" was depicted as a miner in chains, engaged in boring a rock, and visited with castigation whenever he relaxed his efforts—the sound of blasting adding realism to the transparency. In "an admirable delineation" of the interior of a bakehouse, Satan tempted the foreman to mix clay with the flour, and two millers were suspended from a gibbet—a satire which occasioned so much offence that it was stolen as soon as the watch-men dozed in their boxes. In front of the Townhall, Britannia held aloft a view of the Eddystone Lighthouse, with the fleet restfully reposing in Hamoaze, and the Eye of Providence shedding a serene ray on the word "Peace!" Humour was in evidence in Broad Street, where the inevitable tailor displayed the philosophical reflection :

> When Britons fought and Frenchmen fell,
> Sailors got rich and slops did sell ;
> But now, alas, the war's no more,
> Poor George must "Cabbage" as before!

Hilarity and fun found devoted votaries at Teat's Hill on the second day of the commemoration, when a rowing match for women was won "by the beauties of Devon." Two hundred "juvenile females" dined in the Market, and walked to the Old Corn Chamber with a trio of fiddlers at their head. Amid boisterous salutations, nonogenarian ladies "merrily tripped it on the light fantastic toe," and then the veterans retired in favour of the young folk, who kept the ball rolling till daybreak. At Dock every child was decorated with white ribbons, and carried a wand tipped with laurel in one hand and a knife and fork in the other. Tables which "groaned under the weight of Old English fare" were laid through St. Aubyn and Fore Streets, and countless spectators clustered at the windows. At the sound of trumpet, hats and caps flew off "as by magic," and the infantile aspirants elevated their voices in melodious grace. Aged, halt, maim and blind assembled in front of the Government House, and marched amid triumphal strains to the Dockyard Gates, where huge joints and plum puddings of four feet in diameter were sliced and the whole washed down "with hogsheads of strong beer." Not a house was devoid of embellishment, and hundreds of variegated lamps and floral festoons produced a fairy-like effect. Plymouth Breakwater was depicted with the Queen Charlotte at anchor—the first ship moored within the bulwark when the earliest section was completed. In Pembroke Street "John Bull" drank to the health of Wellington, and Napoleon sat "in melancholy posture," contemplating "A History of Tyrants." At the façade of the Theatre, Bonaparte was dethroned and in chains, with a scroll proclaiming "A long farewell to all my greatness;" and, over the balcony of the Crown Hotel, "Time" pointed to the guillotine with the remark : "Victory! Victory! Vice is in Chains." Some sailors and marines, and their sweethearts, "imitating their betters," dined gloriously by the waterside at North Corner, to the extraordinary amusement of the public," and nautical and other jokes and jibes "of the most laughable description" saluted the ears of the spectators.

Neither expense nor labour was spared to make the Dockyard procession "one that Emperors, Kings, or Princes might gaze at with satisfactory emotions," and the town was thronged by persons of all ranks, clad in engaging attire. Coaches and conveyances poured in from remote districts and hundreds of belated travellers finished their journey on foot because it was impossible to procure horses. Over four thousand employés assembled in "the King's ground outside the lines," and at nine o'clock the scavelmen and shipwrights entered Fore Street, with St. Catherine habited as a white nun. Britannia followed in a resplendent car, a lion crouching at her feet ; and Neptune sat astride the waves upholding the ship and trident. Noah awaited at the Ark the return of the Dove ; and Peace sat at the summit of an enormous Cornucopia, radiant with real fruit. The figure was represented by a young man, " who, by the peculiar innocence of his face, the modesty of his dress, and the propriety of his attitude, induced every beholder to forget the delusion." Models of battleships, some under a housing, and others with planks left out to indicate the method of framing the side and bottom, were accompanied by ship's mainmasts and brig's mainmasts, showing the yards crossed. The caulkers exhibited an imposing Crown on a Cushion, the Ancients of Gebal were present in classical costume, the foreman of the Oakum boys carried a silver dove, and axe-bearing lads surrounded every group. Tubal Cain and St. Clement were the gods of the smiths, and anchors " in the highest degree of polish" were carried aloft by the hammermen. Solomon was enthroned by the joiners, the carpenters paraded a model of the Dockyard Gates, and one of the party rang out the dreaded and welcome hours at the Bell Post. Minerva, on a white horse, was followed by an elaborate model of the Parthenon ; and Palladio, the architect, pointed to a painting of the Pagan temple in its original proportions. Even the Ratcatcher of the Yard was not omitted, for he exhibited a rodent confined in a cage and flourished a wand to typify his importance. Escorted by regimental bands the procession walked through Dock and Plymouth ; and the festivities concluded with banquets at Goude's, Wheatley's and other hotels.

Torpoint also welcomed the " heavenly stranger." Flowers and laurel were interwoven at every habitation and dancing followed dinners. The ladies wore white bonnets and wreaths of myrtle, oak and fir; and the hats of youngsters were emblazoned with " Peace and Union." Tavistock presented the aspect of a grove, so numerous were the arches and so bright the flowers ; and maidens appeared in the rural procession pastorally clad and leading lambs that were decked with blue ribbons. A sham fight between lusty lads habited as Englishmen, Cossacks and Frenchmen was waged through the town, and Bonaparte and his army were driven into retreat and then escorted in state to Elba, " otherwise the Island of Tavy." Louis XVIII. was enthroned amid coruscations of stars, and the freeholders were entertained at dinner by the members. A silvery fanfare of trumpets heralded the morning of the celebration at Plympton, and the scene was bright at the Castle Green where young and old gambolled in and about the ditch. A free meal was given to the patriarchal folk; wrestling and hurling matches followed ; and at night the ruins were bathed in a ruddy glow and fireworks flashed from the summit. At Ridgway 300 people sat down on hurdles, " a complete if simple method." Dancing was interspersed with " spinning " competitions for groceries, and dramatic transparencies glowed at dusk. Before tea was served to the children they sang an original hymn by way of grace :

> When War smooths his visage and Peace, lovely maid,
> Her head, crowned with olive, again is displayed,
> Joy brightens each cheek and bids us be gay,
> Whilst Love decked with smiles, with her train leads the way.
>
> No longer the drum beats to hostile arms,
> The nation disturbing with fearful alarms ;
> Each swain shall his humble employment pursue,
> Nor shrink at the sight of a press-gang in view.
>
> The sons to their mothers shall come once again,
> Escap'd from the dangers of land and the main,

The lasses their sweethearts once more shall behold,
Their brows crowned with honour, their pockets with gold.

Then let us unite in loud tributes of praise,
To God who alone such great wonders can raise ;
To him let the Voice of Thanksgiving ne'er cease,
For blessings of Victory, crowned by Sweet Peace.

Escapes, Uprisings and Habits of Prisoners: 1809-1818. As it was impossible to accommodate the prisoners in the hulks or barracks, much less to control so vast a crowd, the Prince Regent granted land near Tor Royal to raise a large establishment in which the more effective seclusion of the captives might be guaranteed. Five rectangular buildings were erected, each capable of accommodating fifteen hundred men, and the total cost of the group was over £130,000. Greatly to their relief, many prisoners were employed in useful arts and the monotony of their confinement was not only mitigated, but they received gratuities that permitted their indulgence in little luxuries. Ten thousand Frenchmen and Americans were herded in the buildings ; and five hundred soldiers, who were garrisoned in small barracks, acted as sentinels. The parapets were paraded by sentries, but liberty of the subject was otherwise unfettered. Although the climate was severe, it was extremely healthy ; but the prisoners purchased such rich foods and liquors when they received the money to humour their tastes, that epidemics of low fever were periodically prevalent. As the Americans were in regular receipt of remittances from friends, they lived more luxuriously than the other captives ; and their transfer from foul barracks or rotting prison-ships predisposed them to ailments which the overladen atmosphere of the crowded sleeping apartments at Dartmoor rendered the more malignant. Gently-born Frenchmen and cultured Americans instituted rigid social codes ; and the latter, insisting upon their own standards of exclusion, not only expelled from their society the blacks who fought side-by-side with them, but declined any intercourse with the French—an ostracising assumption that resulted in disputes of honour and gave occasion to savage duelling. In the absence of swords, scissors were fastened to long sticks ; and the weapons thus improvised were sufficiently incisive to satisfy the most embittered antagonist.

The French organised a constitution with a president. Each apartment appointed its own commissary, the choice being by ballot and the suffrage universal. President and commissaries were alike policemen and magistrates, and executed their own decrees. The cook of one ward was sentenced to death for allowing rats to find their way into the soup, and he was only pardoned on pleading that the perfidious British guard left the door open at night. Petty offenders were sent to Coventry, the undesirable were isolated, and otherwise inevitable unpleasantness was thus avoided. The Lords were the prisoners who received remittances—and they traded in small luxuries which were brought and delivered through the gates by the moorland villagers who flocked there once a week with fresh supplies. Those who worked at trades were known as the Labourers, and their industry enabled them to enjoy tobacco and other solaces. The Indifferents did nothing, and were relegated to the tender mercies of the gaolers. Perpetual difficulty was experienced with the gamblers, some of whom—the Minables—sold coats and trousers to gratify their vice. The Kaiserlicks—a still lower grade of speculators—parted with hose and linen to the highest bidder. Most degraded of all were the Romans—so-called because they were relegated to the Capitol, the highest storey in each block. They rarely wore any other article of attire than a blanket, with a hole in the top to admit the head ; and fought like mere hogs for stray bones or chance potato peelings. On one occasion, when the Governor's cart was left unguarded in the yard, they killed the horse, and cooked and consumed the best joints. These "canaille" so disgusted the Americans that they represented their existence in the prison as "revolting," and the most abandoned were deported to the guardships. Intellectual Frenchmen educated their more ignorant countrymen, and their amateur comedians rehearsed standard comedies in the "Theatre." Some were taught straw and hair work, bone and ivory carving appealed to others, and not a few became expert in these arts. Criminal ingenuity also found expression in forging English five-pound notes with remarkable fidelity, and the men who escaped with the "flimsies" easily deceived leading Plymouth, Exeter and other bankers. The material for manufacturing the notes was imported from without; but confederates were rarely betrayed, and thousands of the counterfeits found their way into circulation. The method pursued was revealed at Plymouth in 1809, when two French prisoners, Charles Guiller and Victor Collas, who were berthed on board El Firm, in Hamoaze, made overtures for their transfer to the Genereux, from

VIEW OF THE WAR PRISON, NEAR TOR ROYAL, UPON DARTMOOR.
(Designed for the accommodation of 10,000 men.)

(From a sketch by S. Prout, junr.)

which they could direct their operations with more freedom. They opened negociations with the captain's clerk of the Genereux, candidly telling him that their object was the forging and passing of bank notes, and promising him a share of the spoils. The man affected to entertain the proposal; and, having first taken his captain into confidence, secured the transfers as desired and supplied the prisoners with all the necessary facilities. By means of fine hair pencils and Indian ink they forged to a point of remarkable finish notes on the Bank of England, the Naval and Commercial Bank, and Okehampton one pound notes. To compensate for the deficiency of the official perforated stamps, they set to work with smooth half-pennies and sailmakers' needles, and thus imitation was carried to perfection. When the prisoners had made sufficient progress their trunk was seized with the evidences of their guilt, and they were restored to closer supervision and visited with the usual corporal punishment.

Heavy bribes were offered to facilitate the escape of officers, and the authorities frequently changed the soldiery to disturb intercourse with foreign agents. Plans for escapes were laid with consummate art—covered carts, with emergency doors in front and behind, being used inland, and eight-oared boats of a light build, so painted as to disarm observation, were in waiting at the appointed port. Between 1809 and 1812 five hundred officers violated their paroles and left the country in these conveyances, and a thousand ordinary prisoners scaled the walls instead of returning to their quarters. Confinement was so irksome that in 1809 one Frenchman stabbed himself with a pair of scissors and penetrated his heart to the depth of an inch and a half. The jury returned a verdict of "Delirious." Four soldiers belonging to the Nottingham Militia who were on guard at Dartmoor, were charged at Plymouth in the same year with promoting the escape of two French prisoners after nightfall. The conspiracy was revealed by friendly Americans and the hue-and-cry being raised, one was captured at "Jump" and the other at Kingsbridge. On being apprehended the sentinels confessed that the Frenchmen presented them with eight guineas apiece, and that they left their posts and explained the route by which the coast might be reached. Three gold coins covered with soap were found in the shaving box of one of the accused, and the evidence being regarded as conclusive, both were shot. At this time prisoners-of-war flooded the town and its environs ; and, in one week, 2,700 of them were marched to Dartmoor under armed escorts of militia. The baggage of the crew of the Beinfasant alone occupied 35 carts, "a striking contrast to the treatment vouchsafed to our own countrymen in France, who are not allowed to retain any other property than the clothes they wear." The impossibility of controlling such a mass of captives as 20,000 at Dartmoor alone, led to the issue of this notice :

A CAUTION.

WHEREAS many French Prisoners-of-War have absconded from Plymouth and other towns appointed for the residence, in violation of *their parole of honour,* and there is reason to believe that several of them are now secreted in different parts of the country, bordering on the sea coasts nearest to France and Holland, with the intention of completing their escape, by seizing upon vessels or boats, which may be left not sufficiently guarded ; all owners of such vessels are hereby warned thereof, in order to prevent the loss, which from want of due care they will be subjected to, as no part of any such loss can be made good by Government.

And, whereas there is reason to believe, that some of those persons have been aided in such breach of their parole by British subjects, Notice is Hereby Given, that as every British subject enticing or inducing a prisoner of war to break his parole, is guilty of a misdemeanour, and liable to severe punishment by fine and imprisonment, the Commissioners for the Transport Service, &c., will cause every person so offending to be prosecuted with the utmost rigour of the law.

Millbay Barracks, 23rd August, 1809.

Patience was justified in 1810, when several Frenchmen effected their departure from the hulk in which they were confined. They fashioned a saw from a piece of hoop iron, then they abstracted an auger from the carpenter's chest, and, in the course of six weeks, cut a large hole in the ship's side. Through this they leapt into the water, and, when they reached the shore, the rest was easy. In June the Union powder ship was stacked with shot, shell and powder for a frigate awaiting orders. As the arrangements for transferring the arms were not ripe, the crew resolved on a night ashore near Keyham, leaving one of their number to guard the ship. Solitude induced sleep, and the recreant only awoke to find himself in the toils. Several French prisoners had dropped from the Genereux, boarded the Union, and bound the drowsy sentinel with ropes; and, with wind and fortune in their favour, ran the store-ship out of the harbour and bore merrily away for their own coast. The Gleaner ketch, and the Gambier cutter, were sent in pursuit, but the runaways had secured an unmolested start and a valuable prize in addition to their freedom. In November, 1811, six prisoners made their escape from Dartmoor, and lay concealed in the common near Okehampton until they were conducted by a sympathetic Devonian towards Bovey. At this point the guide failed in his geography, and asked so many suspicious questions that the villagers followed in a body. Three of the Frenchmen were secured, but the remainder took to the bogs, where they were overtaken and driven at bay. The guide plunged a dagger in the breast of the foremost pursuer, and killed him on the spot. Two unarmed moormen who went to the rescue were also stabbed, and in the confusion the assassin got away.

After the Dartmoor prisons were evacuated by the French, the Americans grew impatient, and, having the run of the entire establishment, formulated a plan of escaping, by means of a passage of 250 feet long, that would enable them to reach the outer wall, whence their flight could without difficulty be accomplished. The men were discovered after they had burrowed sixty feet; but there was no idea that similar operations were in progress in the other departments, and, with confidence restored, exertions were redoubled, the American blacksmiths furnishing as many daggers and tools as were necessary to the excavations. When the design was approaching completion, one of the number led the Governor to the passage, then hollowed to within forty feet of the outer wall, and this scheme was also thwarted. Correspondence had been maintained with the American agents outside, and a fleet of friendly fishing boats was hovering about Torbay to receive the prisoners. Before the official confirmation of peace was to hand, the Surprise privateer pursued the Briton transport off the Start, and, in the exchange, her stem and stern boats were smashed to pieces. Unconscious that she was disturbing a hornet's nest, the American continued her broadsides; and, as the Briton's helm was put a-lee, a company sprung from below, her deck swarmed with redcoats, and a deadly volley was discharged from the muskets. The Americans sheered off "in the greatest possible confusion," and the last brush on the coast had taken place.

No sooner had peace been signed with the United States than the prisoners remaining at Dartmoor suspected that they were being detained for service against the Algerines; and, denouncing this as an invasion of their rights, they burnt their Ministers in effigy, tore down the gates, drove the sentries to the guard house, and resisted a bayonet charge of the troops. Captain Shortland, the governor, who was absent in Plymouth, received an imperative request to return forthwith with military reinforcements. At nightfall the rioters pierced the wall of a court in which the reserves of arms were stacked, and, crowding to the main gate, broke the chain by which it was fastened, and poured by hundreds into the Market Square. The clanging of the alarm bell was heard by the governor as he was driving across the moor, and, on reaching the scene, he assured the mutineers that they would soon be free. His appeals were unheeded, and the prisoners, advancing on the soldiery, tried to seize their weapons. The answer was a volley in the air, and the man fell dead. His flowing blood enflamed the crowd, the shooting became general, the mutineers closed in a desperate struggle, and several were killed and seventy wounded before the disturbance was quelled. The rebellious spirit was far from extinguished, and another endeavour was made to get free. When the first head emerged from a hole in the roof, it was riddled; and, with this death, the outbreak was at an end. As soon as the negociations for exchange were completed, five thousand prisoners marched to Plymouth;

and, whilst they embarked in the cartels that awaited them, they held aloft a large white flag as a memento of "the massacre." In the centre, the Goddess of Liberty sorrowed over the tomb of recumbent Americans, and the lament was set forth in large letters; "Columbia weeps and we remember."

Napoleon in Plymouth Sound: 1815. Napoleon repaid the clemency that had been shown him in "sparing his life" by landing in France and marching upon Paris at the head of a warrior host that wildly hailed his daring. Plymouth was again in arms, and the coast of Devon and Cornwall was swarming anew with French privateers. Le Leocade was seized off the port by the Sealark, and the captain cut his throat when he learnt that his destination was Dartmoor. Local incidents multiplied as the Duchess d'Angouleme, daughter of Louis XVII., arrived in the Wanderer sloop of War, with a suite of expelled noblemen, officers, and maids of honour. Crowds of sympathisers witnessed the landing of the visitors ; and, when the "niece of the lawful monarch of France," pallid of countenance and fragile of figure, stood at one of the windows on Mount Wise, the air was filled with mighty shouts of "Vive L'Roi." The Princess left for London the next day, and an unsophisticated yeoman at Ivybridge caused no little amusement by asking her questions about her carriage and making maladroit references to the clumsiness of its construction. "Dreadful in the extreme" was the anxiety that followed the resumption of hostilities, but events marched rapidly, and suspense culminated in frenzied demonstrations when bulletins told the crushing story of Waterloo. On the day the news reached Plymouth, H.M.S. Actæon, disguised as a collier, entrapped a French frigate which was playing the part of a decoy on

NAPOLEON ON BOARD THE BELLEROPHON.

(From the Painting by M. Orance.)

the Cornish coast; and, ten days afterwards, thousands of prisoners landed at Millbay and Stonehouse Pool in a truly "deplorable condition." Only shreds and patches of clothing remained upon them, for the Prussians had appropriated everything portable; and, as the captives were no less famished than filthy, the townsfolk gave them food to sustain them on the rough journey to Dartmoor. In conversation with the bystanders the Frenchmen readily confessed the dash of the British, and avowed that nothing could withstand the sweep of their cavalry. In a few weeks the Princetown settlement was more crowded than ever, and after that the local barracks and guardships. As many thousands were imported in a month as had previously been brought over in a year; food was at a premium; and the ovens of bakehouses were kept ablaze by night as well as day. Cat-water and Hamoaze continuously received accessions, and the agents once more rubbed their hands.

Bonaparte's submission on the deck of the Bellerophon quelled all fears of any recrudescence of his activity. By no means unmindful of the homage to which he had been accustomed, he "manœuvred with such audacity as to usurp an admiral's cabin"; and amongst other methods of "keeping alive his darling title," his practice of intimating that his suite might approach and partake was to announce that the Emperor was at the table. In Torbay distinguished residents offered him presents of fruit; but, as soon as the Bellerophon anchored in Plymouth, the captive was deprived of unusual deferences. "The fascinating monster," was on view for many days, but it was impossible for even distinguished visitors to approach the prison ship, as the Bellerophon was now designated, and no inter-course was sanctioned with the multitude afloat. Blank charges of musketry were fired to intimidate spectators from infringing the defined limits, and their greetings whenever Napoleon could be seen so exasperated the authorities that they rammed many shore boats for pulling within one hundred yards of the ship. The Emperor's feeling were henceforth no more consulted than those of an ordinary prisoner-of-war, and his appeal that he might be treated as England's guest was contemptuously disregarded. At the outset he refused to believe that communication with the land had been denied him, and the severity of the restrictions created quite a revulsion in his favour, indignant yachtsmen cheering "The Corsican" and ladies wearing his floral emblem—the red carnation. Belair—near Plymouth —was at this time the seat of Captain Thomas Elphinstone; and, with a view of distract-ing attention, a Council of War was held in its dining room, at which Lord Keith and Admiral Sir Thomas Duckworth were present. Mr. Alexander Elphinstone, nephew of the captain, kept guard over the door with a drawn sword, now in the possession of Major Elphinstone Holloway, and the Order of State was then divulged that St. Helena was to be the destination of the Emperor. The secret was preserved until the last day in July, when Lord Keith and Sir Henry Bunbury boarded the Bellerophon, and informed Napoleon of the place of his banishment. Protesting, with dignified mien. that he was not a prisoner of war "according to the laws of nations," he urged his captors to remember "what I have been, and how I stood amongst the Sovereigns of Europe. One of them courted my protection. Another gave me his daughter in marriage. All of them sought my friendship." Lord Keith replied that he had no authority to enter into explanations, and then the "little tiger" insisted that St. Helena would mean "sentence of death." Keith declined to discuss the matter, for the local sympathy had exasperated Ministers, and Plymouth was regarded as a hotbed of treason. Napoleon became more retiring in his habits on receiving the ultimatum, but the public still crowded to see the caged lion, and Plymouth presented the appearance of a holiday centre. As the weather was fine, and the surface of the water calm, everything was in favour of the multitude which received daily accessions from all parts of the country; and not only was the Breakwater used as a place of vantage, but thousands surveyed the Bellerophon's deck from the heights of Mount Edgcumbe. Napoleon's indisposition, in a morose moment, to humour the crowd, induced two ladies to approach the ship without an escort ; and, disappointed at the Emperor's seclusion, they stood athwart their boat and waved their handkerchiefs. This compliment Napoleon could not resist ; and, appearing at the stern window of his cabin, he held out his head, inclined it downwards, and so rested his arms on his elbows that a full view of his face was obtained.

During this stay his linen was sent into Plymouth to be washed, and the fact that some of it was marked with an " N " and an imperial crown, and the rest with an " L " and the royal crown, led to the inference that the latter had been "stolen from Louis." This moral reflection did not disturb several residents of the town ; for, with the connivance of a perfidious laundress, they tried on the shirts in order that they might boast they had

ADMIRAL COCKBURN SEARCHING NAPOLEON'S LUGGAGE IN PLYMOUTH SOUND.
(From an old Print.)

worn them ! Agitation in favour of a modification of the sentence was becoming formidable, when the authorities were disturbed by an astute manœuvre to effect Napoleon's removal to the shore. A writ of Habeas Corpus had been obtained requiring his presence in an action for libel that had been instituted by a naval officer, and Keith and Bunbury were at their wits' end to baffle an attorney who was armed with the subpœna, and hourly endeavoured to approach the ship. In view of his pertinacity, Lord Keith ordered the Bellerophon to cruise in the offing ; and, under the impression that the hour of departure was at hand, Napoleon vowed that he would never reach St. Helena alive. Disturbed by this threat, his faithful followers implored him not to end his career after the fashion of a gamester, and reminded him that the fall of a Cabinet or the death of a Prince might restore him to the throne.   Their persuasions prevailed, but Napoleon's gaiety departed ; and, although hundreds of boats kept in the track of the Bellerophon as she rounded Penlee Point, he retired to his cabin and moodily drew the curtains.   As he did so, a too daring waterman was cut down by a gunboat, and some of the passengers were drowned. Off the harbour the Bellerophon was intercepted by the Northumberland, and Sir George Cockburn received charge of the prisoner.   Waiving all punctilio, he deprived his suite of their weapons, and requested the Emperor to surrender his pistols.   He next overhauled Napoleon's effects, and left his valet de chambre—the only retainer who witnessed this degradation—fifteen hundred gold coins to meet his master's immediate wants.   When it came, the parting between Emperor and staff was affecting : some of them weeping and others clinging to his knees.   Again and again Napoleon vehemently asked why he could not pass the rest of his life in rural England ; and, when an officer replied that he might have been surrendered to the Russians, he rejoined, with a shrug of the shoulders : "God save me from them."   As his friends took their departure the Emperor waved them fond farewells until they disappeared in the Eurotas towards Plymouth.   Their final and unfading reminiscence was the familiar picture of their hero in his green coat, with red facings and epaulettes, white waistcoat and breeches, silk stockings, and chapeau bras with tricoloured cockade.   With studied effect, Cockburn turned to Napoleon with the enquiry: " At what hour, General, shall I receive you on board the Northumberland ?"   Napoleon was profoundly agitated on being deprived of his title, and, stamping his foot and furiously taking snuff, he rapped out : " The people who made me a General made me an Emperor, and you can no more deprive me of one designation than the other."   The last scene was the most ignominious of all, for Cockburn refused to allow his charge to distribute a hundred golden coins amongst the crew of the Bellerophon, on the ground that such a sum was too generous for a "general" to disburse.   This hauteur confirmed the local sentiment that unnecessary indignity had been heaped on the fallen warrior.

CHAPTER XI.—LIFE AND CUSTOMS DURING AND AFTER THE AMERICAN AND NAPOLEONIC WARS.

Scenes in Port: Sailing, Paying Off, Etc. Whilst Dock was taking form, with the advantages of new growth, Plymouth presented many structural vices. It had stood still for a century and only Frankfort Row and George Street bore evidences of improvement. The thoroughfares were narrow and crooked, there was no uniformity in house construction, and the ignorance of common rules of form was appalling. A few of the more important streets were paved, but the work was rudely done ; and, as the residents threw refuse into the gutters that ran with water outside their doors, the accretions were revolting. The lines were zigzags, with styles anomalous and incongruous, and the heights of houses so varied as to evoke the derision of many quidnuncs who were already prepared to sacrifice the quaint, historical, and picturesque to comfort, cleanliness and air. The Jacobean Guildhall was taken down in 1800, and it was hoped its successor

TOWN-HALL IN WHIMPLE STREET
(Now the Free Library).

would be placed on a more open site. Private interest induced the Corporation to erect the new building on the old position ; and, "in an evil hour, a man named Eveleigh," a mere clerk of works, was allowed to place there a pile that should supply a Mayoralty House, cooking and dining rooms, cells for rogues and vagabonds, a hall for discussing the day's news, and a market place. Although the contempt of critics was loudly pronounced, no effectual opposition could be offered, and when £7,000 had been spent, the town possessed a structure too small for the market, too contracted for trials, and utterly unfit as a prison. In its irremediable ugliness the building was typical, in fact, of the "ignorance, folly, and presumption of its authors." Neglect and indifference condemned debtors and culprits to apartments that reeked with loathsome smells, misery and dirt ; and the chief pastime of the detained was to beg alms through the bars of cells or receive scraps of food from friends. Herding was indiscriminate, quarrels were frequent, and the peace officers only visited the unfortunates to supply them with such fare as they were entitled to receive :

> Here many a luckless naval wight
> Hath often passed a dreary night.

After dusk "The Clink" was deserted, and remained till the morning without light or heat—a gruesome scene of desolation, the monotony broken by the voice of the watchman as he went his rounds, commenting on the hour of the night or mumbling as to the state of the weather. In the morning prisoners were dragged, regardless of rank and station, and amid the jeers and scoffs of the gamins, to the residence of the magistrate ; and they often revenged themselves on this public parade by knocking down the Charleys and endeavouring to escape. Lawlessness and disorder were aggravated by soldiers and sailors who roamed abroad with their arms ; and the combats between unfriendly regiments, or crews jealous of each other's success, reproduced so much of the ferocity of actual warfare that leading tradesmen erected barricades to prevent the storming of their premises. The authorities were helpless in these emergencies, for the officers dared not interfere. In 1780 a crowd of 300 tars armed with bludgeons, landed from the Medway ; and, after parading Dock, marched to the Liberty Fields to do battle with the crew of the Crown. Similarly armed the latter put ashore at Mutton Cove ; and, after several skulls had been broken on either side, the challenged seamen were reinforced by a cheering crowd that filled the boats of the Vengeance. The hopelessly outnumbered men of the Medway then took to their heels, "a measure of precaution which prevented a deal of bloodshed." At night the pandemonium was indescribable : "nothing but rioting and fighting."

Freedom Day continued in favour as a municipal institution, the glove being set outside the Townhall as a challenge, and the certain result a ferocious encounter. From morn till eve Plymouth was given over to commotion and petty larcency, and respectable persons could not venture into the open without danger of insult, for the Freedom Boys dipped their ducking horns in the gutters and soused every passer-by. The ringleader of the Burton Boys was Nickey Glubb, the champion pugilist of the quays, who lost one eye in a famous combat and was blinded in the other during a no less savage encounter. This calamity did not reduce his pugilistic appetite ; and, when he was insulted by the young bloods his wife would lead him to his antagonists, who then discovered that his fist had lost neither force nor cunning. The impunity with which Freedom Day was commemorated led to an interregnum of the custom, and a painting of Nickey Glubb, distributing the hardly-won beer amongst his adherents, survived as the sign of a tavern in Exeter Street.

Less exciting though of unfailing interest were the proceedings of the Ancient Order of Free and Accepted Masons. The earliest lodge was formed at Plymouth Dock in 1735, at the instigation of Mr. Francis Brownbill, and the place of installation was the Freemasons' Arms. "There was a grand procession on the opening day from the said Dock to Plymouth Town ; a fine band of musick playing before them and the bells ringing at both places. The brethren were all cloathed in white gloves and aprons, and they dined at Prince Eugene's Head, where an elegant entertainment was made and such a number of people flocked together that never was seen in the west before." Another lodge that attained distinction was the "Prince George," instituted in 1748, and Prince William was enrolled a member on the occasion of his visit to Plymouth When the Duke visited the port in the capacity of Lord High Admiral in 1827, he attended a grand gathering of the Masonic lodges of the Three Towns, at which he was presented with a conjoint address, expressing "the pleasure we feel, in common with the country at large, at the satisfaction so universally evinced by the appointment of your Royal Highness to the ancient and most responsible office of Lord High Admiral, but particularly at the benefits which have already resulted from the assiduous and scrupulous attention evinced by your Royal Highness, in the discharge of the several arduous duties attached to this office. We wish more especially to greet your Royal Highness at a member of the loyal and ancient Fraternity of Free-masons, not insensible of the great honour which must ever accompany the local history of this neighbourhood, by its being the first to enjoy the distinguished privilege of enrolling the illustrious name of your Royal Highness among the patrons of our order,

Under a firm conviction that whatever may tend to the advancement of Free-masonry will receive the unqualified approbation of your Royal Highness, we presume to inform you that a few public-spirited brethren are erecting a Masonic Hall, in a central and excellent situation, in the borough of Plymouth, which we fervently hope to complete at an early period, thereby extending the order, and upholding the respectability of our fraternity in these populous, increasing, and loyal towns." Addressing his reply to "Gentlemen and Brethren Masons," the Duke replied : " I cannot forget that nearly two and forty years ago I was received a mason at this place. The family now on the throne of these realms, I am confident, will ever govern this great empire on the true principles of liberty and happiness. I shall contribute, with sincere satisfaction, to the erection of the Masonic Hall, now completing in the borough of Plymouth, and thank you for your good wishes towards myself, who will, by a faithful and diligent discharge of my duty, endeavour to obtain the approbation of God and my fellow subjects." The Hall, in Cornwall Street, was opened with great state the following year.

It was only during the winter that the lamps were lit, and then "very imperfectly"; and the watchmen were supplied with "boxes," to which the inhabitants resorted to give alarm in the event of fire, robbery or housebreaking. Nightfall was the signal for disorder and tumult, and women of abandoned character were always responsible for exciting or promoting riots. As soon as seamen or soldiers became flush of funds, the irresponsible classes indulged in unbridled dissipation, and profligacy, debauchery and incredible waste were unrestrained. "Jack" was a chartered libertine—an honest fellow with whom it was the height of indiscretion to pick a quarrel, who snatched kisses in the taverns where he squandered his money, and embraced in the street damsels to whom his addresses were not always agreeable. He walked abroad with pockets full of guineas if especially fortunate, or carried gold in his cap with a consuming anxiety to dissipate it. At one paying-off a seaman came on deck with a pewter pot brimming over with guineas, and implored his captain's leave to go ashore; and on meeting with a refusal he tossed pot and contents into the sea with the remark : "What's the good of the money if you can't spend it ? "

> The fleet began to victual fast,
> Repairs in quick succession passed ;
> The prizes were put up and sold
> And Valour found reward in gold.

Officers were as prone as seamen to dissolute proclivities ; and, in the desire to show that "a faultless sailor ne'er did live," rowed from Mutton Cove to Devil's Point—"a devilish ragged rocky place projecting into the sea, approached by houses not the most respectable." The admirals publicly admonished them to wear their uniforms and avoid drunken brawls ; and moreover forbade them to enter "the disreputable public-houses which abound," and thus give a wide berth "to profligate and designing characters." Often were these gentlemen obliged to trust to their crews for rescue as, with glittering swords recklessly flourished, they were hauled to prison by the watchmen. But ere the Black Hole was reached, the seamen rallied and :

> With stretchers soon they levelled low
> The constables and every foe ;
> And the middy carried in their arms
> Secure from dangers and alarms,
> To where his boat skimmed o'er the bay
> And bore him safely from the fray.

When the crews went on shore the paroxysm of delight into which they were thrown after years of confinement communicated itself to those by whom they were surrounded, and the recital of their perilous escapes in battle or in shipwreck made the heroes easy victims. The streets of Dock were crowded with officers and sailors at liberty, and in possession of funds which they knew not how to disburse. Carriages were in request at enormous prices, and young officers, who had hundreds of pounds to spend in a week, hired one for themselves, another for their gold laced hats, and a third for their dirks or hangers. As for the sailors, they retained coaches to remain on the Fore Street stand, and danced hornpipes and reels on the roof to the harsh raspings of a violinist seated on the box. At the end of these diversions they engaged in furious races, for ten or twenty guineas a-side, and urged the horses until they were ready to drop. One singular scene in Fore Street on some such occasion may be recalled. Several sailors, just paid off, hired a hackney coach for "a short cruise." The dilly was drawn up to the door of a public-house "to cheer all hearts before starting with a moisture of the wet." Here the idea seemed to strike them instinctively, that their brute companions ought to share in their entertainment. Accordingly the horses were supplied in their turn with beer; and, when their repugnance gradually subsided, men and beasts were seen drinking from buckets. When all was ready, the tars, instead of getting into the hold, mounted the backs of the harnessed cattle, and the coachman, who felt his situation extremely awkward, accelerated the speed of his horses by whipping the shoulders of the sailors; who, communicating the impulse to those under them, thus "made way before the wind." The most rollicking idea of the sense of abandonment is supplied in the "Adventures of Johnny Newcome":

> ————While this was yet in contemplation,
> Paddy, agog for recreation,
> To Ivy-Bridge, a short excursion
> Suggested for a day's diversion.—
>
> Away they rattled, tight and fast—
> The village hove in sight at last—
> "And there!" cried Shaughnessy, "we'll dine!"—
> Just then a hapless herd of swine,
> As Johnny turned a corner sudden,
> Lay wallowing the ruts and mud in;
> And the next moment, grunts and squeals
> Proclaimed them underneath the wheels·—
> Poor John pulled with might and main,
> Till snapped at last the Leader's rein;
> Of course then all command he lost,
> And crash, the gig went 'gainst a post.
>
> The Lady took a mighty pitch,
> And stuck heels upward in a ditch;
> Our Hero quitted too the gig,
> And flew against a great boar pig,
> Whose belly luckily was full
> And soft, or John had cracked his skull.
>
> However, help was soon obtained;
> And daub'd with dirt, the Inn they gained;
> Where tongue and fowls, and lots of Wet,
> Made them their late capsize forget.

GOING TO IVYBRIDGE.
(From the original Sketch by Rowlandson.)

"North Corner is the place for Wilkie!" said Haydon, then in the zenith of his fame, "for there is famous grouping—sailors and their lasses, drunk and sober; bearded Jews, salesmen and soldiers." The observation was made after Wilkie, then on a visit to Plymouth, had astonished his host by evincing no taste for beautiful scenery, and emitting exclamations of real delight at the spectacle of a number of children romping on a dunghill. Inferring that "Daavid" would prefer that "bustling and dissipated landing-place which is always so very crowded and busy in war time," Haydon escorted his friend there to find that the variety quickened the man for whom Mount Edgcumbe had no charms. Captain Marryatt has transmitted vivid impressions of the paying-off and sailing-scenes that rendered North Corner and Mutton Cove proverbial. The traders always knew when the men were to receive their money, and the ships were surrounded from an early hour with wherries conveying Jews and scarcely less-exacting Christians—some desirous of selling goods and others requiring payment for articles supplied on credit. They were not allowed to mount the ladder until business was in full swing, and sentries staved the boats of the importunate with cold shot if they insisted on hanging too close. At eleven o'clock the dockyard launch pulled alongside with the cashier in charge of a chest of gold, and his staff were shown to the cabin, where, in the captain's presence, the men were called in one by one, and as rapidly paid. As they passed out with the cash in their caps, the suitors swarmed up the sides, the deck was soon invaded, and smuggled spirits were distributed. All was confusion and uproar, with "sharks" selling clothes or obtaining the discharge of old debts; bumboat men and women pleading for payment of long arrears, and tradesmen for the settlement of small debts; wives and sweethearts shrewishly challenging every item of extortion, and a monstrous babel of "bawling, threatening, laughing and crying." Now a petty merchant was upset and his hamper tossed into the hold, then a blaspheming sailor ran for the man who had cheated him, and all was squabbling, skylarking and drunkenness, Some were much in the toils—to a Jew

T

for clothes, to a wife for maintenance, and, if the money did not satisfy more than one demand, ladies were invariably accorded the preference. At five o'clock the order went forth to clear the ship, disputants were separated by marines, visitors were dismissed over the side, the intoxicated were put to bed, and peace prevailed to the relief of all on board.

The clothing of sailors did not gratify their paid-off whims, and the finest broadcloths were used; scarlet velvet and lace adorned their waistcoats, perforated guineas were sewn on as buttons, and white trousers were trimmed with gold fringe. Overlapping rows of half-guineas glittered on jackets, and seven shilling gold pieces were worn on gorgeous waist-coats. Captains made no attempt to check this dissipation, for it was their settled conviction that the crews would only return to duty when their money had been spent. Tap-rooms over-flowed with grog and milk punch, and, with the help of favourites and friends, funds were exhausted in three or four days. The steward of a line of-battleship, who amassed £3,000 during one voyage, engaged rooms at the chief hotel, and was fitted out with rich suits of kerseymere, lined with satin and trimmed with gold braid. His hair was dressed and powdered every morning, he drove about in a carriage and four, reserved a stage box at the theatre, invited tradesmen to dine with him before attending the play, and passed several nights in revelries. Tiring of this amusement, he hired a sloop and ran to Ports-mouth with a deck crowded with companions of both sexes. This expedition exhausted his funds; in three weeks the stranded roué pledged what remained of his effects, and penniless and deserted, he was found in a shutter-box, and carried in a dying state to the hospital at Stonehouse. Johnny Newcome's adventure in Plymouth best tells the endless devices of the practical jokers to raise the ire of the tradesmen and exasperate the Charleys:

> ——A window then they chanced to pass,
> And Pat his stick poked through the glass;
> Out from his Box the Watchman started,
> And off Pat like an arrow darted;
> Quoth Johnny: "There's no staying here!"
> Off he, too, bolted like a deer;
> But the alarm was so well sounded,
> That he perceived he was surrounded.
> A Grocer's shop door open stood,
> And seemed to offer shelter good.
> John reached it soon, and in he scamper'd,
> But found himself still further hamper'd,
> For soon as e'r the Owner saw
> Him, he declared against him War;
> And all the Watchman's bellowing crew
> Came puffing, blowing, after, too.
>
> ——John never let his courage drop,
> But like a cat flew round the shop;
> At last he on the counter jump'd,
> And, scrambling down, by chance he plump'd,
> With squash and splash, and dab and splutter,
> Chin-deep into a cask of Butter.
> Down rolled the cask, and forth he sprung
> Directly all the gang among;
> They grappled him, but 'twas not easy
> To hold him now, he was so greasy

Like pig with soapy tail, he slipped
Their fingers through, tho' hard they nipped,
Then by good luck regained the street,
And to such purpose used his feet,
That thinking it a hopeless case,
The Watchmen all gave up the chase.

——As he continued his retreat,
He happed his friend again to meet ;
" We're both shut out, Jack !" t'other roared,
" I vote we therefore go on board ;
I know that Watchman well—the Sluts
Have often told me how he cuts
As many capers—a Spalpeen !
As Reefer o'er a dead Marine !—
They'll follow yet—pull foot, unless
You'd lose the number of your Mess !
Come, bear a fist ! a boat we'll shove
Off, from the steps at Mutton Cove !"—
" I second," Johnny said, " your vote !"
And both soon jumped into a boat.

The day before sailing was unpleasant. All the money was spent, and the crew were
" either half drunk or suffering the effects of intoxication." Here again a lively picture of
the scene was drawn by Captain Marryatt. Disorder reigned supreme as stock and spare
stores were hurried aboard—the first lieutenant cross, the juniors grave, and the midshipmen harassed and " driven about like post horses." " Jump into the cutter, sir, and go to
Mount Wise for the officers ! Be careful that none of your men leave the boat "—an
injunction invariably bred of bitter experience. At Mutton Cove foul oaths escaped the
seamen, as they dashed their hooks into watermen's craft, and cleared a way to the beach.
The steward went in search of provisions, and the midshipman was driven out of his wits.
Seeing his wife on the wharf " with his clothes from the wash," the bowman begged leave
to fetch them. For a time the young officer was implacable, and shouted that the wife
could bring them to her husband. " Now," she would reply, " aren't you a nice lady's
man to go for to axe me to muddle my way through all the dead dogs, cabbage stalks, and
stinking fish, with my brand-new shoes and clean stockings ?" Who could resist this
delicate appeal ? Certainly not the middy, for the spouse was spruce, and the beach
was strewed with offal in the way she had described. " If you please, sir, there's my young
woman come down—mayn't I speak to her ?" During this second importunity, bowman
and wife disappeared, and the " women of the ship " extended noisy greetings and tempted
the crew to land. " One carried an article for Jim ; another clothes for Bill ; some jumped
into the boat and frolicked with the men ; the rest brought tobacco and beer they had been
sent to purchase." Crowd, noise and confusion rendered it impossible to hold the crew,
and one after the other they left the boat and mixed with the crowd. Then a sergeant
of marines was sent in search of the absentees, whom he picked up " roaring drunk " in
one of the neighbouring inns, and tumbled into the boat. Their arrival increased the
difficulty ; since, in looking after the riotous, it was impossible to control those who were
sober. A marine now darted off to Stonehouse to take a last farewell of his wife, and then
the stewards brought baskets of eggs, strings of onions, joints of mutton, parcels of
groceries, and feathered stock ; and not only the stern sheets, but the boat was

crammed full to the thwarts. Three of the smartest men next bolted, and the midship-man ordered the craft to be shoved under the wharf, where it was impossible for others to land. "The men became mutinous, grumbled much, and would hardly obey me," and the air was filled with the invectives of angry women and execrations of watermen. In an hour the defaulters returned, and the boatload of intoxicated sailors pulled off. Plunging in the heavy seas off Devil's Point, the drunken ones staggered to their feet, soft bread and parcels of groceries floated about, and a lurch threw the steward upon the crockery and eggs. Drenched and cramped with the cold, the crew seized a line thrown from their frigate, and were "hauled up by the marines" as the boat plunged bows under, and ruined all the uniforms.

The launches continued a never-failing source of attraction. In 1801 the Armada was buoyantly despatched from Mr. Blackburn's yard at Turnchapel. She was the first of her class raised outside the dockyard ; and in point of workmanship took high rank, with a head of the Elizabethan hero and a stern that bore the Plymouth arms. Mr. Blackburn entertained 300 ladies and gentlemen in his loft, and "The pious memory of Sir Francis Drake" and "Success to H.M.S. Armada" were toasted amid reiterated acclamations. Three months later the Insolent, "a new avenger of her country's wrongs," glided from the stocks, and the dogshores of the Union were also knocked away. "With a majesty impossible to be described," she spurned the receding tide, and bravely saluted the element she was destined to adorn. Electrical was the rapidity of her course, the flags of many nations waved, and over fifty thousand voices combined with the massed bands. The Union was built after the model of the Victory—in point of external form and internal convenience the ideal battleship. Her state cabins were decorated with cedar, and the rose, shamrock and thistle were entwined in exquisite carving in the centre of the stern. 3,000 loads of oak, or 2,000 trees of two tons each, were employed in her construction. The Heir Apparent was present to effect the launch of the Caledonia in 1802—a handsome battleship mounting 120 guns. Her stern was light and elegant, there was no profusion of carved work, and her head bore an emblematic figure, arrayed in plaid and bonnet, with thistle on the one side and bagpipes on the other. Thenceforward until the historic year 1805, launches were phenomenal in the history of the port, and the Hibernia, a first-rater of 130 guns, and the Pallas and Circe frigates took the water. Immense as to fabric was the Hibernia, and the scene of her dedication at once "proud and glorious." Not only did she appeal to the fervour of the population, but the admiration of prisoners was unstinted ; and, as she sailed into Cawsand Bay, they exclaimed, "There goes the coup-de-grace of Bonaparte." When the colossal battleship reached her moorings, she was saluted with cheers from the fleet, and airs played on her deck were answered by anthems from Devil's Point. Soon had the Hibernia's crew cause to lament the elements. The chief cutter was returning to port with stores, when the wind and waves obliged her to put about. In the opaque darkness that prevailed only flashes of lightning revealed her course, and, in their despair, the men made for the Mewstone. The sea ran in mountains ; and, with the capsize of the boat, forty seamen were thrown in the surf, and only the lieutenant and a few seamen survived the disaster. Shortly after Bonaparte's escape from Elba, 60,000 persons assembled at Dock to witness the launch of the Vincent, 120 tons. Her proportions were contemplated with admiration approaching to awe, for she was a sublime specimen of naval architecture "destined to be the pride of the seas," and floated like "some proud tower, menacing to England's foes and promising gallant achievements." Social celebrations took the form of balls on board the Impregnable and other battleships. The Java, too, was also sent on her way, "to become, when wanted, a match for the Yankees ; and thus Old Ocean received another master." The Java was, happily, never wanted ; for she was not a success.

*A Characteristic
Auction Scene.* There is excitement in Plymouth this morning, for Mr. James Slade, "authorised broker," is to sell "at the London Tavern, Foxhole Street," a magnificent array of stores and other prizes of war. Ship-brokers, smugglers, jobbers, fishermen, speculators, form a picturesque and motley throng. Steaming glasses of grog are before them, and there is scarcely a Docker or Plymothian who is not smoking a pipe of contraband tobacco. A roaring, rollicking, devil-may-care crowd, seated around a big table, with a heavy fringe of spectators upstanding. Some are cracking equivocal jokes ; others are debating the latest untoward reverses of Sir John Moore in Spain, and contemptuously dismissing the suggestion that he should meet the difficulties of the campaign by re-embarking his troops. No ; he must tweak and elongate the nose of that "little impostor Napoleon" before he returns to England. And he is never to return ! And what is that sensational scandal which a knot are retailing in whispers. Oh, the lovely Lady ——— is declared by the "Plymouth Chronicle" to have eloped with that chartered seducer, Sir ———, whilst Lord ——— has instituted proceedings for crim. con. and put the damages at £50,000 ! The paper is passed from hand-to-hand and the gossipers read of their beautiful neighbour : "The story has for several days occupied and engrossed the attention of all the circles of fashion, and a thousand versions of it are whispered with the most confidential publicity. It is said that the Noble Lord had a long conversation with his Lady, on the subject of the constant visits of Sir ——, and that he insisted on her forthwith going from London to their mansion near Plymouth. She chose, but seemingly with a heavy heart, to quit the house ; and it is believed that, as soon as the forms of law shall permit, she will become the wife of Sir ——. The lady, who was long the envied object of her own sex, and the toasted belle among the other, first charmed her seducer, by the exhibition of her picture in the midst of a group of portraits of beautiful women, painted on one piece of canvas, expressly for a great Personage, by a celebrated artist. How long the flight was in contemplation is not known, but from the preparatory steps taken by the Lady, it is supposed her mind was long since made up. To give facility to her departure, her waiting woman was discharged three days previously to her going off ; and all her clothes were secretly conveyed away."

The policy of instituting a force of supervisors for Plymouth is here being eagerly condemned, and how far the projected bill will disastrously affect the privileges of merchants by putting them at the mercy of a too potent officialism. And here is another knot discussing a question of good faith as to the payment of prize money, which has excited much discussion and is now settled by a bill posted in the room by Mr. Blewett, the rival auctioneer. Quite a gossipy gathering, bursting with rumour and rum, flushed of face, and full of purse. Ah, here is Mr. Auctioneer. Deprecatory taps with his hammer assert his authority. "Silence, gentlemen, if you please." And a certain approach to order is obtained. "Now, the conditions of the sale are as usual. Shall we read them ?" "No," is roared back in a thumping chorus, and the jingle of tumblers is heard as more drink is taken. "Now, our first lot is the good American ship Sally. You know her dimensions. She is nearly new, is well found in stores, and fit for general purposes. She is square-sterned, and may be sent to sea at a trifling expense. She was captured by her Majesty's frigate Indefatigable, John Tremayne Rodd, Esq., commander, and thank Heaven, gentlemen, we have still a Rodd in pickle for the enemies of our King and country." An outburst of cheering salutes this pun, and the emboldened broker continues : "Reward them for their brilliant services, gentlemen, make your bids substantial, and I'll promise that all the prize money shall be spent in your shops and taverns before the month is over." This witticism excites hilarious incredulity : but no stormy bidding, for these are the early days of the "Forty Thieves," and the real competition is to be witnessed at the "knock-out" in the house of a famous smuggler in Vennel Street a few hours later. So the "good American ship Sally " goes for something like a song, and the auctioneer, who is accustomed to this form of disappointment, passes with a light heart to the next lot—"Le General Laureston," built of oak. "She had been only out 24 hours, gentlemen, when she was captured by his Majesty's ship Hero, on her voyage from L'Orient to the Mauritius, and needs only to be seen to be admired."

The same incidents, and the same result. Patriotism does not trespass on the path of prudence this morning. "Now, gentlemen, we have the daring little French privateer, La Diane, which had the impudence to come right in upon our coast and walk off with one of our merchantmen, when the guns of our good sloop Raleigh bore upon her, and she had to capitulate with her prize." This thrilling narration made very little effect upon the bidding either, for patriotism was not strict business. "Next, gentlemen, we have to offer you the cargoes of two chasse-marées destroyed at sea by the boat of his Majesty's ship Narcissus, Captain Malcolm in command." Now there is something like excitement. " Here we have 438 hogsheads of white wine, 69 quarter casks of Medoc, 600 cases of red and white wine, containing no less than 2,000 dozen bottles, and kegs of olive oil in large numbers. The excellent understanding that prevails amongst the purchasers of ships does not extend to the liquor merchants. As bottle after bottle is opened, the bidding becomes keener and keener. "Try some of this," says the broker, ironically opening a bottle of olive oil. " Ah, here are some tubs of brandy," and the pleasant warnings of the auctioneer not to mix are soon disregarded. "There is history here, gentlemen, so be generous in your bids. The French brig L'Adéle captured two of our Britishers as prisoners-of-war, and, one fine morning, whilst officers and crew were all below, having thoughtlessly left their visitors on deck for a moment, our countrymen actually saw the old flag flying a few miles off. What did they do? Why they instantly put down the hatches, imprisoned officers and crew below, set sail for the good ship Naiad, Captain Cocks, and delivered L'Adéle into his hands." Up bounds the prize money for the daring couple. And, here, too is romance : " One box containing a diamond necklace and bracelets, case of ribbons, and packet of spangled veils and mantles ; another containing silk stockings, gloves and pieces of silk ; a third containing a Bishop's Vestment of scarlet silk, embroidered with gold ; a Bishop's Vestment of purple silk, embroidered with gold and spangles, sent by the King of Spain to the Bishop of Buenos Ayres, accompanied by a letter of thanks for his holy conduct in invoking the assistance of the Almighty to overcome General Whitelock and the British army." An outburst of ironical laughter is followed by admiring glances at the gems ; and Jews and Christians are in sturdy competition. And here are hogsheads of Malaga, and sherry, and Bordeaux,—all going, going, gone—aye, gone indeed, long years ago, together with their roystering purchasers and, no doubt, equally dare-devil consumers ! And so the sale of war spoils went on, and the company became frousier, and the available prize money accumulated, and Jack went ashore a week or two later with more funds than he had ever hoped to possess, and dissipated it more quickly than he had helped his country to win it—as he fell in with Pretty Poll of Plymouth, and those crimps and sharks who had been her companions when Jack was engaged afloat, calling upon the enemy to heave to or be sent to Davy Jones.

Dockyard Abuses and   The employés in the Dockyard—officials and artisans alike—were
Uprisings.   regarded as the happiest section of the salaried and wage-earning
community. They were not only remunerated in the regular way, but their privileges were numerous and understood. In the case of the smiths, custom was carried further than the enjoyment of perquisites, for they received a substantial allowance " on the day

DEVONPORT DOCKYARD.

(From the Water Colour by J. W. M. Turner, R.A.)

of St. Clement" with which to commemorate the festival of their titular saint. Excellent dinners were provided for the men and light refreshments for their wives and children. The spirit of hospitality was profuse, and everything was done to enable all concerned to spend the day "in the greatest harmony and festivity." The artificers were humoured in the same way, their occupation was continuous, overtime was paid at the rate of 7½d. per tide, and each individual was entitled to remain on the books until he was incapable of any further manual exertion. Usage and example accustomed every rank to frauds ånd pilferings, and men of otherwise blameless character instituted important distinctions between the property of the nation and that of individuåls, and excused without severe moral strain the general resort to embezzlement. Heavy bribes were received by those who promoted plunder or shielded the perpetrators, and crime became the rule and abuses multiplied. Attempts to extirpate these abuses were unavailing—there were so many officials who had "always been ill-paid" and who argued that they could not support themselves with decency, if the axe were put to the roots of corruption.

The pillage at Plymouth alone was estimated at half a million a year. Coasters and foreign ships entered the port to purchase cheap stores, and marine-store dealers were chiefly supplied from the yard. When auctions of old or surplus effects took place, articles which had not been submitted to the hammer were removed with the connivance of the officials ; and, as the storehouses were always full, the new articles were smuggled out as old, and the decaying masses were left behind. There was such a struggle to obtain snug positions of impunity that a bribe of £300 was paid for an office which carried a salary of £40 a year ; and, when a Dock justice discovered that wholesale robbery was in progress, and hastened to divulge the conspiracy to the departmental head, he was told, with an oath, to mind his own business, as "such things have always been done, and will continue to be done, in spite of you or me." Artificers were allowed to carry to their homes as firewood a bundle of chips ; but from chips the transition to timber was easy, and the men cut up the best wood in their regular time. Within this supposed waste copper bolts were concealed, and the metal was sold to the Hebrews who infested the lanes near the yard. After the gravest cogitation, the authorities discovered that fragments estimated at sixpence were worth three times the amount, because first-class timber was destroyed to create the requisite supply. Enough wood, in fact, was removed from the yard in one month to build a sloop of war ; and, as the allowance was attended with more loss to the public than advantage to the recipients, the authorities resolved to substitute a small money consideration. Then the storm burst ; and, pleading that they were only the meaner offenders, the ship-wrights protested that theirs was the case of the sailor who was found on his knees in the course of the action : "I am only praying," quoth he, "that the shot may be distributed in the same proportion as the prize money."

Remonstrances were not confined to anecdotes ; for, in May, 1775, when the American people repudiated their allegiance to the English Crown, and strenuous preparations were in progress to avert that humiliation, thousands of artificers quitted the yard and riotously demonstrated through the streets. The Admiralty, however, counselled the King not to yield ; and, incentives being offered carpenters to join the staff, the response was so large that the shipwrights hastened back to their work, and, by the end of September, were all reinstalled. They were exposed after this to such systematic satire, menace and inconvenience by the overseers, that they worked awhile "with the greatest dilligence and alacrity." The spirit of rebellion slumbered, but was not suppressed, and in 1780, upon the introduction of the exacting system of "job and task," it blazed forth anew. In the heat of the agitation an endeavour was made to confine the shipwrights within the yard ; but, marching in a body to the gates, they forced them open, held a tumultuous meeting in the Liberty Fields, and refused to return to their occupations until the obnoxious rule had been abandoned. It was not long before the various classes were again excited by regulations calculated to extort higher results without increased remuneration. Necessaries were at famine prices, and the dockyardsmen joined the public in forcing open the storehouses and distributing the corn. The Dock market was seized and delegates were appointed to ensure that provisions should be sold at fixed prices. Crowds gathered daily in Fore Street, and companies of artillery stood at either end to sweep the populace if violence were attempted against the official residences. If the magistrates had not interceded, the people would have been decimated, for the troops were exasperated beyond endurance by the merciless hurling of missiles. Some of the leaders were seized as prisoners, and the disturbances were not quelled for thirteen weeks.

Recurring wars rendered the dockyardsmen masters of the situation, and, although the chip allowance was prohibited, their inventive genius found other outlets. The use of bumboats was the most popular medium of intercourse, and cordage was removed in such quantities that firms engaged staffs to untwist the portions that contained the King's mark, and to eliminate the coloured strand which was introduced as a check upon fraud. Others beat out the broad arrow from the copper bolts and bar iron on which it was impressed, and depredation raised its head with such indifference that special statutes were passed for the summary punishment of those who were found with stores in their possession. One of the favourite devices was to conceal articles in tall hats—a trick which led to the hateful order that heads should be bared as artisans and labourers passed out. Others rolled canvas around their waists, and the pillage was only resented when the thief's appearance was too Falstaffian. These were only petty exploits, for favouritism was the rule, and the higher the rank, the greater the corruption. Ships were hired from politicians as the price of support, and the fraudulent were often highly placed. Several crews were lost as the result of these "hellish frauds"; contracts for clothing were placed with leading partizans; seamen were charged extravagant sums; gross impositions were practised; and damaged and inferior goods were supplied. The King's casks found their way by hundreds into Plymouth breweries, and inspectors of timber received hampers of wine from incriminated tradesmen. Indeed the dockyards "stank of corruption," and emissaries of copper and rope merchants hovered about the harbour in craft of every class, and found abundant facilities for receiving stores in bulk.

No less revolting were affairs in the victualling departments, and fortunes were made by cheating sick and wounded of their proper allowances. Stonehouse Hospital was in the hands of "a set of villains whose seared consciences were proof against the silent but eloquent pleadings of their fellow creatures"; and "waste, corruption, fraud, extravagance and villainy" prevailed there "to a truly disgusting extent." One surgeon's assistant spent £2,000 a year in entertaining officers on board a hospital hulk in Hamoaze, and the purser shared the surplus. "The most scandalous feature was that, when the wretches in the ward-room were rioting in luxury, they dissipated the allowances of the wounded!" "I hope," protested Lord St. Vincent, "there is sufficient virtue in Parliament to punish and expose these blood-sucking leeches." In the economical fit that followed disclosures, sponge was employed to cleanse the sores, instead of lint, so that it might be used over again! Thus many patients lost limbs and others their lives by blood-poisoning.

It was to punish a blacksmith, who was beating out the broad-arrow, that the pillory was first introduced at Dock. Barrels containing sheeting bolts were found on suspected premises, and a Plymouth merchant committed suicide to avoid the obloquy of trial. A firm of tradesmen at Millbrook were transported for concealing stores in their ropewalk. As the wars progressed, the resort to the pillory became frequent, and delinquents were flogged at the cart's tail amid the derision of their undetected colleagues. In 1808, Daniel Crocker, a sailmaker, stood in Fore Street pillory for two hours, exposed to the insults and missiles of the mob, for stealing a roll of canvas. John Geddy, the master of an Admiralty hoy, was also condemned to the pillory for appropriating stores. A shipwright was in the habit of carrying an umbrella, large of dimensions and no less capacious, which he was never known to use as a protection against rain. During a frost the fellow slipped over the steps as he was leaving his work, and the umbrella rolled to the feet of an official. Courteously stooping to raise it, he was surprised at its weight, and found that the handle was packed with copper nails. The culprit was sentenced to stand in the pillory, with his umbrella beside him, and the presence of his suggestive companion excited many an unpleasant jibe.

An illustration of the all-prevailing faith in corruption was afforded in November, 1802, when a Plymouth tinman, named Hamlyn, attempted to bribe Mr. Addington. The office of landing surveyor at Dock was vacant, and he promised to pay £2,000 for the position, and to enter into bonds to keep the matter secret. The overtures originated in such unaffected simplicity that, when the police confronted Hamlyn with the stamped summons, he imagined that the document embodied the bestowal of the office. The confiding simpleton was sent to the Marshalsea for three months, and fined £100 in addition. The authorities only touched the fringe of the scandal by punishing humble offenders, and the Plymouth Dock Police Act was passed in 1809. Under its provisions the justices had power over the waters of the Sound ; and, as the borough of Plymouth was thus included, its authorities were aflame with indignation and fear. Police surveyors were invested with the right to enter ships or barges by day or night, and the conduct of all on board was open to inference for the purpose of prosecution. As it had been usual for four or five Custom House officers to visit every merchantman on its arrival, this involved more than a hint that the interests of the revenue had been inadequately guarded, and that existing authorities were not reliable. With suspicious warmth, the merchants of Plymouth and Dock condemned these imputations, but unlimited powers were granted the new police, and they overhauled without warrant any cart, boat or ship, within or without the borough. They also challenged or searched tradesmen or artisans in the exercise of casual pursuits, and at the assertion of " their own caprice." Even these measures were doomed to failure, for no King's boat was interfered with if there was a commissioned officer on board ; and, as only service craft could approach the landing steps, devices to prevent plunder necessarily proved futile. Stores were thus transferred to trading cutters, and an active recruiting of accessories was alone necessary to prevent the chief offenders from being incriminated. A force of 120 surveyors was created by the Act, and political influence conferred the appointments on freemen and their friends. The connection of the " Government party " with Plymouth thus became " so close as to be improper "—especially from the standpoint of those who were not freemen, and who believed in free trade at the expense of the taxpayers.

A change in the method of payment adopted in the dockyard led to irritation on the part of tradesmen. It was the custom to calculate the wages of artificers and workmen at the end of each quarter, and the expiration of the ensuing three months was at hand before payments were forthcoming. Thus employés were dependent for subsistence on the shop and tavern-keepers, who only advanced on the authority of notes from the Check Office testifying to the balance that was due. Naturally enough, the majority became involved, and some tradesmen even prohibited them from purchasing elsewhere the articles they did not sell in a regular way. In 1805, this abuse was suppressed by a method of payment under which three-fourths of the wages were supplied every week as " subsistence money," and the balance was delivered at the end of each quarter. In their exasperation, the tradesmen threatened to cut off supplies to thwart the reform, but their menaces were in vain ; and expert shipwrights who had joined private docks now returned to the King's service. The principle of "shoaling" or classifying the artisans was inaugurated by Lord St. Vincent. Every shipwright was paid according to individual ability or exertion ; and ships of the line were thus completed in less than a year by some fifty artificers. The object of the change was to frustrate "the jobbers," and the master shipwrights established prices and regulations for every class of work.

Murder, Mutiny, Executions and the "Cat."   Fear and not regard was the instrument by which seamen were disciplined ; and whip, stick and rope's end were not more familiar to the slave. Revolting tyranny was practised on board many ships, floggings at the gangways were of daily occurrence, and any boy lieutenant could order a man "to be started" by a boatswain's mate. Through the ship pierced the boatswain's whistle, then the wailing cry "All hands" was uttered, the offender was pinioned to the grating, and the instrument descended with swish and thud. As one sailor wearied of wielding the weapon, another was ordered to take his place, and left-handed men were employed in relays so that time should not be lost. Appalling exclamations started from lads at the first rush of blood, varied by agonising appeals for mercy and water, and prayers to God and Mother for deliverance. Hardened offenders placed bullets between their teeth, and only smothered oaths escaped them ; but some of the persecuted jumped overboard to avoid the renewal of the castigation, whilst their wounds were raw, and found in death a welcome release. The greater part of the crews were brought on board against their wills, dragged from their beds at night, or taken from traders to serve at inferior wages—and thus there prevailed a sullen murmur of discontent and a silent brooding for revenge in almost every ship. Repression was the leading thought that animated officers ; and, from the firing of the daylight gun, when all hands were summoned to wash decks, until the signal to repair to hammocks, there was an atmosphere of hoarse blasphemy and muttered mutiny. Sailors were lashed if a gleam of contempt were supposed to lurk in a glance towards an officer, and midshipmen fresh from school realised the true meaning of "a perfect hell upon earth."

> For he who freedom gives to all,
> Must bend at proud oppression's thrall ;
> And British sailor on the wave
> Is but a name for British slave ;
> Oh ! Let impressment meet the ear,
> E'en tyranny must drop the tear ;
> Nor mercy to the black men roam,
> When thousand whites are slaves at home.

When executions were carried out in Barnpool or Hamoaze, boats' crews were sent from every ship in harbour, and the spectacle was often rendered horrifying by blundering or malice. Flogging around the fleet was a no less barbarous institution, and young watermen, seized from their families at dead of night, and who crept ashore at the first chance, were condemned to be shot or hanged, and occasionally reprieved to receive the "milder" punishment of flogging. On the day appointed for the torture, the yellow flag was hoisted at the mainmast ; the boats' crews repaired in melancholy procession from every vessel ; and the victim was towed from east to west to receive at each stage a certain number of lashes. Thus anguish was accentuated as the sufferer stood exposed in the launch, his naked body fastened to a triangle of handspikes, the arms extended outwards or upwards, and wrists bound tightly by cords. The boat was crowded by shipmates, an officer superintended the punishment, and a surgeon saw that excoriation stopped short of death. In close company gathered the other boats, so that the men could witness the fall of lash and hear each awful yell. "Do your duty," was the order, and the cuts fell at intervals of moments that seemed minutes. Blood was drawn at the outset, but the hardy clenched their teeth until the fifth or sixth stroke, when their pent-up feelings found vent in shrieks that were enough to melt a heart of stone. Boy officers fainted at the first contemplation of these tortures, and the sympathetic only rallied after a stout rope's ending. The spectators groaned as the victim's back presented one horrible mass of lacerated flesh and blood, and sickened when a blanket steeped in vinegar and brine was spread over the wounds "to prevent mortification." From ship to ship the dreadful scene was repeated, until the unconscious victim was reported as unfit for further punishment and taken to the Royal Naval Hospital at Stonehouse.

James Silk Buckingham vowed that the first such horror he witnessed at Plymouth resulted in death, and that many lashes must have been inflicted after utter collapse. The impression made upon this young sailor, who had left a home of comfort to join the navy, determined him to desert from this "demoniacal service" the next time he was sent in a jollyboat to Mutton Cove. Whilst the crew were lounging about the quay, he dived into a convenient lane and crossed to Torpoint; where he scrambled over hedges and fields until he reached a hayrick, and soundly slept until the morning. Aroused by the farmer, he made a clean breast; and the man, in his compassion, gave him food and furnished him with a smock frock and fustian trousers, and supplied him with some silver in exchange for his uniform. Lighter of heart and firmer of step, the youngster struck out for his home at Falmouth. He sought the shelter of an obscure inn at Liskeard, and slept with other tramps in a barn until, at midnight, a constable with his staff, a soldier carrying a naked bayonet, and two armed seamen entered in search of deserters. Buckingham was struck dumb with fear, and his heart sunk within him; until, to his intense relief, the men mentioned that they were simply engaged in a regulation hunt, and were not in quest of any particular individual. Gathering courage at this assurance, Buckingham answered enquiries in the broadest Cornish he could command, and the party left satisfied. At the end of the week the lad reached Flushing, and was received by his mother "with all the tenderness of a younger son and favourite."

A story told of Lord Exmouth shows how the atmosphere was quickened by dread of uprisings. Sir Edward Pellew, during one period of agitation, recommended that a ship, manned with officers and sailors who could be trusted, should attack the next vessel that started the mutiny flag in Hamoaze, and bombard her in the presence of the fleet! This proposal, however, was too drastic to meet with the favour of the Port Admiral. Shortly afterwards, as the Indefatigable lay off Falmouth, the crew refused to sail until they had been paid their wages; and, at dead of night, a sailor knocked at Pellew's cabin and informed him of the plot. Sir Edward apparently took no steps to checkmate the movement; but, when the ship got under weigh, and the lieutenant reported that the crew would not go round with the capstan, Pellew walked into their midst with a drawn sword; and, addressing the officers, exclaimed: "You never can die so well as on your own deck quelling a mutiny; and, now, if a man hesitates to obey you, cut him down without a word." The mutineers immediately submitted, and the Indefatigable was making progress when Captain Barlow sent a message from the Phœbe to the effect that his men had also mutinied, and begging Sir Edward to destroy his vessel. Pellew replied that, as this suggestion was discountenanced at Plymouth, he could not enforce it at Falmouth, and

Captain Barlow allowed his insubordinates to steer the Phœbe to the east without further remonstrance.

Lieutenant George Rutherford was put upon trial at Dock for flogging three men to death in 1801 ; and, left to his devices, he leapt from his cabin through the porthole of the Salvador del Mundo, and swam ashore. There his friends were in waiting to complete his escape, and he was never more heard of, although notices of reward were issued.

£300 REWARD !

Whereas it has been humbly represented to the Government that Lieutenant George Rutherford stands charged with the Murder of three Seamen of His Majesty's ship Trident, which said seamen are alleged to have died from excessive punishment inflicted on them by order of the said Lieutenant George Rutherford, commander of His Majesty's ship Trident ; and whereas the said Lieutenant George Rutherford did, on the evening of Wednesday, the 12th day of March instant, jump overboard from His Majesty's ship, the Salvador del Mundo, lying at Plymouth, and is supposed to have effected his escape, His Majesty, for the better providing and bringing to Justice of the said Lieutenant George Rutherford, is hereby pleased to require and command all his loving subjects to discover and bring the said Lieutenant George Rutherford, and to carry him before some of His Majesty's justices of the peace, or the chief magistrate of the county town, or place where he shall be apprehended, who are respectively required to secure him, and to give notice thereof to one of His Majesty's principal Secretaries of State, to the end that he may be forthcoming and dealt with withal and proceeded against according to law.

And, as an encouragement, His Majesty is pleased hereby to offer a reward of £300 to any person who shall discover and apprehend the said Lieutenant George Rutherford, to be paid by the Right Hon. the Lords Commissioners of His Majesty's Treasury.

Lieutenant George Rutherford is about 40 years of age, upwards of five feet ten inches in height, of a dark, swarthy complexion ; of slender person, but well made ; of a long, thin face, with dark eyes and black eyebrows."

"A dark night, a sharp knife, and a bloody blanket !" was the insubordinate toast ; and, if some officers were prone to excesses, not a few seamen were ready for piratical opportunities. The yellow flag was hoisted at Dock in October, 1806, and Woods, one of the ringleaders of the Hermione mutiny, was brought up for judgment. The crime was the most atrocious in naval annals. The captain and his fellow officers were driven to the cabin, hacked with bayonets and cutlasses, and their mutilated bodies thrown out of the stern windows. The runaway crew were pursued, and the ringleaders hanged at Portsmouth. Some years after, Woods, one of the few who escaped, was discovered in hiding in Dock, and sentenced to share the fate of his colleagues. He protested to the last that he was innocent of any part in the massacre, but admitted that he deserved death for his other offences, "which were numerous." A "sincere penitent," he passed away praying and "at peace with all the world." Four sailors were tried at Dock for conspiring to run away with the Montague and massacre her officers, and they were hanged in company at the yardarm. A seaman of the Union, named Abchurch, entered Captain Linzee's cabin, and, mysteriously approaching that officer, whispered : "There's a mutiny in your ship— take that." Linzee started to avoid the unsheathed knife, but the weapon penetrated his left side. It was believed that the assassin was insane, yet he was hanged at Dock in the presence of boatloads of spectators. A desperado of the worst type, named Lake, attempted the life of Lieutenant Kent in 1807. The ship was lying in Hamoaze when the sailor complained that the officer had unnecessarily ordered him to cleanse his berth. When the captain discovered that it was in a filthy state, he told Lake to strip for punishment, and, upon his refusal, directed the sentinels to divest him by force. With the spring of a wild animal the man scattered officers and crew, and seized Kent by the hair. The combatants fell into the lee scuppers, and the fury was not secured until he had broken the lieutenant's nose. He was hanged with the usual ceremony.

A lieutenant of the Hazard experienced even-handed rigour in 1807 ; when, on being convicted of a nameless crime at Dock, he was hanged on board the Salvador del Mundo. Heavy iron shots were tied to his legs, but the knot was clumsily adjusted and he suffered "great convulsions for a quarter of an hour." It was upon the evidence of a female that he was doomed—a girl of fourteen, named Bowden, who entered the service as a sailor boy, and had frequently climbed the masthead to clear the pennant, and even reefed the sails in a gale of wind. After the discovery of her sex, she was retained as a domestic and allowed a separate cabin. On another occasion an officer of noble lineage, the Hon. A—— J———, assaulted his senior lieutenant. The Naiad was at anchor in Hamoaze at the time of the quarrel, and an insulting expression was avenged by a reeling blow. The indignity was returned with interest, and the young aristocrat was sentenced to death. At the end of a week he was called up, apparently to be shot ; but influence had been employed ; and he walked into the presence of the ship's company to learn that he had been pardoned and restored to rank. "When his sword was returned to him, the Hon. A—— J———— was much affected at this fresh instance of his Majesty's magnanimity."

The chief officer of the Cyane was reduced to the bottom of the list for beating a seaman "in the most cruel and dreadful manner," and the master's mate of the Medusa was expelled for robbing seamen of their rum and flogging them to the point of death. An anonymous letter from the seamen of the Diana, whilst she lay in harbour, induced the Admiralty to send down a Special Commissioner. Each sailor was challenged as to the authorship of the document, and one man admitted that he wrote it to stop the captain's brutality. The crew were asked if the letter was written at their request, and they replied that it was. After the memorial of the seamen had been granted, the marines also asked that they might be drafted elsewhere. Their advocates were arrested ; but similar reasoning prevailed, and they were likewise acquitted. The Edgar was at anchor in Cawsand Bay, in 1808, when the crew assembled on the quarter-deck and shouted for "Fresh captain and officers." Some of them added : "An answer and no mutiny." The marines were commanded to fire, and the remonstrants dispersed. Subsequently five ringleaders were put in irons, lashed around the fleet, and visited with imprisonment. Eight petty officers of the Naiad were arraigned for forwarding an anonymous letter to the Admiralty, in which they declared that the crew would not sail under Captain Hill. Three of them were hanged from the yardarm of the Salvador del Mundo, and others were flogged around the fleet. The master's mate of the Crocodile killed a seaman with a marlinspike ; but, upon his trial at Dock for murder, it was held that, although his conduct had been severe, he was not guilty of the capital offence, and he was simply dismissed the service with disgrace.

In January, 1809, a seaman and a carpenter's mate were being rowed from Cawsand Bay to stand their trial for mutiny, when the boat was upset off Mount Edgcumbe. One prisoner and several witnesses were drowned ; and, as the surviving culprit was exhausted by immersion and shock, the court offered to adjourn. The man asked, however, that the case should be finished out of hand, and it then transpired that a "round robin" had been sent to the Admiralty on the subject of the captain's brutality. When the prisoner was asked if he had any grievance, he respectfully answered that punishment had been too common for trifling offences. Producing from his pocket the waterstained paper which contained his defence, he made such an impression that his acquittal was directed. Drunkenness and insubordination were general on board the sloop Orestes in 1809. Lieutenant Harris indulged "in provoking speeches"; Mr. John Callan, the surgeon, varied the use of seditious language with occasional resort to blows; and Mr. Goddard, the purser, challenged his fellow officers to duels, entered into plots against the captain, and secretly disposed of the liquors entrusted to his care. The prisoners had organised several mutinous assemblies and "bred other nuisances," and the Court made a clean sweep of them. It was not so surprising, however, that not a few officers of the Reserves and Volunteers found it difficult to submit to the discipline of active service; and, when Adjutant Jennings, of the 1st Devon Militia, was ordered by Major Rawle to conduct certain evolutions on the Hoe, he exclaimed: "Get away with you; you're an insulting fellow, and I will not obey you." He was put on his trial in March, 1809, "for highly improper and disrespectful language," and suspended from rank and pay for three months. Nothing but the prisoner's belief that he was only amenable to Colonel Elford, could have induced "His Majesty to confirm this clemency." The King trusted that it would make the adjutant more "circumspect and temperate in his future conduct."

The sloop Parthian arrived in June, 1809, with despatches from Collingwood, and the inhabitants were discussing her encounter with three French brigs and a corvette. At a dinner given in his honour by the Port Admiral, Captain Balderston recounted the thrilling story; but he had, alas, only escaped by virtue of his superior seamanship, to fall beneath an assassin's hand. His stay was not intended to be of long duration; and, in a few days, he received from London, by special coach, urgent despatches with which he was to return to Corunna. The Parthian got under weigh and was moving between Drake's Island and the main, with sails set in stately symmetry, when Balderston observed that James Smith, the master's mate, was not on deck. Summoning him from below, he asked why he was absent from his post when the vessel was under weigh. "Because," he replied in a contemptuous tone, "I was not sent for." "Then, sir, you ought to know that it is the duty of every officer to remain on deck when the ship is getting under weigh. You must consider yourself disrated." "You may do as you please," was the surly rejoinder, and returning to his cabin, the reduced officer loaded his pistol with two shots and made his way on deck, exclaiming "I'll be revenged." Balderston, unconscious of the threat, was looking over the larboard gangway, when Smith raised the pistol and discharged both balls in his back. "I am shot," cried the victim, "who has killed me?" There stood the assassin, the smoking weapon in his hand, men and officers holding him by the neck and arms as he struggled. "You need not seize me," he shouted, "let me know what I've been disrated for." Conscious that his wounds were fatal, Balderston directed the ship to be put back, and watched the operations with his head resting on the arms of his colleagues. "Summon all hands on deck," he said, as he felt himself dying, and sailors and marines clustered around, a sad and striking group from which the only absentee was Smith, now confined in irons below. "Men," proceeded Captain Balderston, "I am about to leave you. Before I expire I should like to ask whether I have done anything to merit the enmity or censure of any one of you? If I have, I trust you will forgive me, as I most freely forgive all my enemies, including the unhappy man who has compassed my death." There was not a dry eye, and the bared heads of all hung reverently, as the body of the captain suddenly collapsed in the arms of his compatriots. Then the Parthian returned to Dock, her flag at half-mast and her guns firing every minute until she anchored, and the townsfolk crowded to North Corner and Mutton Cove to learn with grief and horror the cause of the untoward omens.

James Smith was tried for the murder the day after the funeral. Plymouth and Dock contributed sympathetic multitudes to swell the melancholy train, and hundreds of field officers and navy men participated in the ceremony, which took place in St. George's Church. The court-martial assembled within twenty-four hours on board the Salvador del Mundo. There were one or two petty preliminaries to be dispensed. A marine was brought forward for striking a sergeant, and sentenced to 200 lashes. Another poor wretch had caused the death of a fellow seaman whilst skylarking, and the court ordered him to be flogged round the fleet. James Smith was introduced between a file of marines. A young man of 25, he presented in his person undeniable evidences of Creole birth and passionate temperament. He looked sullenly upon the Court, listened indifferently to the evidence, and only regretted that he had not shot the lieutenant as well. Sentence was pronounced by the President : "The Court is of opinion that the charge against you has been fully proved ; and, in consequence thereof, it directs that you be hanged by the neck, until you be dead, from the yardarm of one of his Majesty's ships, and at such time, as the Commissioners of the Admiralty shall direct." And then Admiral Sutton continued in tones of exceeding gravity : "After the solemn and awful sentence just pronounced on you for the foul murder of your captain, manifesting, by the nature of the act, a mind of the most depraved assassin, you cannot expect mercy even from the unremitting humanity of a benevolent sovereign ; therefore, for the remaining period of your existence in this life, lose not an instant in preparing yourself, by every possible means, for the awful tribunal before which you must appear." Within a week, confirmation of the sentence was received from London ; and, at eight o'clock on the following Monday morning, the dreaded flags were hoisted at the forearm of the Salvador del Mundo—blue pierced with white, light yellow with black border, and white and blue. Formerly the yellow flag was the omen of execution, but everyone recognised in this triple display the intimation that Smith was to discharge the penalty of his crime. Immediately the signal was made, the Parthian reciprocated by running up similar flags, and the firing of a gun informed the civil population that the assassin was about to die. Townsfolk thronged the waterside from Devil's Point to Cremyll, and hundreds went afloat to view the awful ceremony. The way around the Parthian was kept clear by ships' boats sent, in accordance with custom, from every man-of-war in port. It was half-past nine, and there was no more grace at the disposal of the condemned man. The chaplain appeared in company with the prisoner ; the master-at-arms, carrying a drawn sword, walked on the other side ; and the procession made its way, from a cell near the gangway, to a platform erected on the forecastle. This was the place of execution, and Smith moved steadily to the spot. No longer sullen or defiant, his eyes were cast upwards, his lips moved in silence, his countenance bespoke the sincere penitent, and firmness mingled with resignation. Smith meant to die like a man in the presence of his assembled comrades ; and, after kneeling in prayer on the platform, he exclaimed : "I hope God will have mercy on my soul." Looking towards his brother tars, he added : "God bless you all and pray take warning by my fate. For days before I shot the captain I had been giving way to intoxication. When he disrated me, my pride was hurt. I did not allow myself time to think, and my frenzy overcame my reason. Forgive me, gracious God, the evil I have done to others, more particularly to the friends and relations of my late captain, whose soul, I hope, O merciful God, thou has received into Thy kingdom. I come, O Lord, with earnest prayers and tears, supplicating Thee, of Thy mercy, to look upon me and forgive me, to spare me, to deliver me." "And now," concluded Smith, "I am ready." Calling forward some of his friends he tapped his body, and said, "Take care of this—see it decently in the ground. And now let me ask," he begged, "that my hands may be tied behind my

U

back, and that two 32-pound shot may be suspended to my feet." The hands were tied and the shot were secured. In a moment the knot was placed under the left ear, the fatal bow gun was fired, and the unhappy man was slung up amidst hushed sensation ashore and afloat.

In June, 1810, three lads attempted to desert from the Defiance to the enemy. They were sentenced to death "with great solemnity," but the Admiralty substituted the long drawn-out agony of 800 lashes apiece. Two seamen of the Abercrombie, who pleaded that they were "rather exposed to the shot," were convicted of cowardice, and flogged around the fleet in Hamoaze. Mutiny with ghastly episodes was investigated at Dock in December, 1811. The Diana frigate had captured a French brig; and the subordinate officers and men who were put in charge of the prize conceived the idea of seizing and selling her in a French port. The ringleaders were three coloured sailors and an Englishman; and two of them approaching Mr. Andrews, the midshipman, killed him with crowbars as he lay asleep on deck. Another attacked the steward with an axe, and brought down the weapon with such force that the steel struck the deck after it had cleft the victim's skull. The bodies were thrown overboard; and, proceeding below, the mutineers invited the rest of the crew to co-operate. A shout of defiance was the response from the barricades behind which the loyal ones had taken refuge; and, upon the cry of "A British sail," some of the insubordinates lowered a boat and hastened away. The stranger proved to be none other than the Diana herself, whose captain had renewed chase in the belief that he was about to make a fresh capture. Upon this, the faithful section of the crew burst their barriers; and, overpowering the remaining mutineers, placed them in chains, and compelled the others to return at pistol-point. The Diana's deck bore evidence of frightful carnage; and, at the court-martial held in Dock, full confession was made. The shrouds of all the frigates in port were manned on the day appointed for the executions, and a multitude of spectators assembled on shore. The condemned men were hoisted up the side of the flagship; and, after spending some time in prayer, were escorted to the platform, two standing on the larboard and two on the starboard side. Those ever-terrible words "Haul the ropes taut" were mistaken for the fatal signal, and one doomed wretch fell fainting to the deck. Upon his recovery, the guns were fired, and the quartette dangled in company at the end of the masts. The bodies remained suspended for an hour, officers and men standing bareheaded the while, and were then sent to the Naval Hospital at Stonehouse for the anatomical purposes of service surgeons.

In November, 1812, Mr. Paul Walker, midshipman of the Sylvia, entered into an altercation with Isaac Smith, a corporal of the Marines; and, being the worse for liquor, he drew his dirk and stabbed the man in several places. Prisoner was sentenced to serve before the mast, and was rowed around the fleet at Plymouth to hear the details of his degradation proclaimed from point to point in the presence of officers and crews. Two days later, by way of contrast to this severity, a private of Marines, Gastano Cajano, who was awaiting death for insubordination, was overwhelmed, on being paraded for execution, to learn that the Prince Regent had forgiven him. "After a suitable admonition," Cajano received the congratulations of his shipmates. Lurid light was thrown upon naval horrors at an inquiry held at Plymouth in August, 1814, when Lieutenant Leaver was charged with causing the death of a lad named Ansdell by inflicting "cruel and excessive punishment, repugnant to the rules of His Majesty's service." The boy was frequently and heavily cobbed; and, after being placed on the sick list, was doused in cold water, and his head scrubbed until his shrieks pierced the ship. The agonies culminated when the dying lad was placed in the black-hole, from which he was only withdrawn a corpse. Leaver denied that he authorised these tortures, but admitted that he had flogged other boys without making the required entries in the Martial's books. His fellow officers evinced their sympathy by acquitting him ; but public opinion was so insistent that the Admiralty directed him to be re-tried, and he was dismissed with disgrace from the service. After the wars oppression was relaxed ; and, although the cat was used with the old freedom, persecution was not so marked a characteristic of some of the officers. In 1827, however, Lieutenant Bowaker, of the Windsor Castle, was indicted at Dock for systematic tyranny and dismissed the service by a court-martial, of which Admiral Sir James Saumarez was the president. As the prisoner had "bled in the service of his country" the sentence was so modified as to permit him to continue with a disadvantage as to promotion.

Smuggling Devices   Extremely lax was public sentiment as to smuggling. The
and Encounters: simple West-country folk could never understand why the King should
1776-1840.   want to tax good liquor, especially when so many could not afford
to indulge in such luxuries if the duty were added ; and, in revenge, these critics of national finance traded in contraband spirits and taxable tea, silks, laces and tobacco. Few inhabitants of the fishing villages appreciated the enormity of dealing in smuggled goods or putting an irrepressible exciseman to death. It was towards the close of the eighteenth century that the traffic assumed its boldest face, and there was some excuse for its popularity. Men had to choose between enforced existence in the battleships, with the prospect of moderate prize-money ; and a life of equal peril and more freedom, with a substantial share of the profits. Courageous and chivalrous were many of these adventurers and their word was not to be despised when they gave it. So associated were their transactions with the life of their havens that the sympathy of every villager went out to them. Often, as the poet vicar of Morwenstow testified, the country folk crowded to the beach to help the cargo ashore, and they received their reward in common access to a staved keg ; and, in the absence of cups and glasses, dipped their shoes in the liquor. As they drank so did they curse and swear, fight and wrestle ; and an astonished visitor who witnessed one such scene exclaimed : "Is there no magistrate to be found in this fearful country ?" "No, thanks be to God," answered a hoarse, gruff voice, "none within eight miles." "Then is there no clergyman ?" asked the stranger, terrified at the drunkenness and bloodshed. "Yes," was the reply, "that's he holding the lanthorn !" "And there," wrote Mr. Hawker, "stood the parson on a rock, pouring the light of other days on a busy congregation."

In every seaside hamlet confederates were found, and in every branch of the service an ally. Coastguardmen were often most active coadjutors ; and, when suspects were dismissed the service for connivance, they turned smugglers themselves, and gave more trouble than experienced offenders. One of these adventurers, after doing as he pleased at Newton and Noss, set up at Plymouth as a "smuggling broker," and defied the authorities with impunity. Held together by the bonds of a fraternal criminality, the smugglers observed their own code of honour. For the brother who dropped a treacherous hint there was certain death, with no witnesses to account for the authors ; and, now and again, no corpse to testify to the crime. Outside the Channel limit armed cutters and luggers hovered about until nightfall, and then steered for their destinations. Stealing after dusk into one or other of the innumerable concealments of Whitsand Bay or the Yealm, they flashed their rockets ; signal fires flared from the headlands in response ; and the rendezvous was reached with accuracy and alertness. Customs' officers were never sure when the privateers took to smuggling, or the smugglers resorted to privateering, for the boats were capable of either branch of service ; and if one device failed, there was little scruple in adopting the other. Heavy penalties were imposed for lighting beacon fires ; and, when the preventive men were scented, the smugglers secured their casks to rafts, left their particular mark of identification, and sank the cargo till the coast was clear.

These devices occasionally went wrong; casks rose before it was possible to "run" them, and the goods were arrested afloat. On other occasions the luggers were chased as they were reaching port; and, with heartfelt pangs, the crews committed contraband cargoes to the deep. Reluctant were the captains to throw away what it had cost so much effort to secure; and, as they postponed the sacrifice until the last moment, the King's servants suddenly sailed into a sea of tobacco stalks, ankers of spirits bobbed serenely around them, and the smugglers looking flushed as with unusual exercise. Their feeble excuse that they had suffered sea-sickness was discounted when their vessels were found to be empty, and the offenders then regretted that they had not stood by their cargoes and raced for the beach. The "Three Friends" was thus overtaken in 1790, and not only refused to surrender, but opened a brisk fire by way of answer. The strength of the revenue cutter had been under-estimated, the smuggler was strewn with corpses, and her survivors were impressed for war service. The Lottery's crew behaved with a callous disregard of life in the same year. Slipping into Cawsand Bay, they received the usual welcome, and the sands soon swarmed with helpers. The revenue cutter Hind marred this happy picture by approaching unperceived, and made for the Lottery as its cargo was being transferred to an adjacent cave. In reply to the demand of Humphrey Glynn, the chief officer, that they should surrender, the desperadoes fired point blank, and blew away the top of his head. The Hind retaliated on the Lottery with bloody effect, and the survivors dodged to the open under cover of the night. Thus the authors of the murder escaped the officials, until a heavy reward induced one of the crew, named Toms, to confess that the fatal shot was fired by Thomas Potter, and that William Searle and Thomas Bentham abetted the tragedy. Toms returned to his cottage after he had been accepted as King's evidence, and was last seen alive on the rocks at Whitsand in altercation with his old companions. It was conjectured that, after slaying him, the gang buried his body in one of the caves, and the absence of actual evidence of death rendered it impossible to carry the case to a conviction.

There was a considerable retreat at Mutton Cove, since excavated into stores; and one of remarkable extent was revealed at Stonehouse in 1776, in the course of blasting operations. A broad, flat stone was displaced from a mass of rubbish which had been used to cover it, and an opening of four feet in diameter was disclosed. The cave within resembled a tent, and stretched pyramidically to an invisible point. Its sides were uncouthly indented, and strengthened with natural ribs suggestive of fluted pillars. Hence to the opposite point was a long road of steep and rugged descent—strongly but rudely arched, and terminating in a Gothic-like arch, from which fantastic stalactites were suspended. An avenue to the left was floored with clay and vaulted with stone; and, in creeping through, Mr. Geach, of Dock, penetrated another tortuous passage—difficult of access and dangerous of investigation. Making his way from cell to cell, the investigator found a well of fathomless depth; and, after descending piles of limestone and surmounting slippery ridges of rocks, a vault some thirty feet high was disclosed, and a road to the south-east that ascended seventy feet to the surface. It may easily be conjectured with what confidence smugglers who mastered the involutions of these encrusted grottoes defied discovery and baffled pursuit.

A murderous affray took place at Torpoint, in 1796, between the crew of the Viper and a party of armed smugglers. The midshipman and two sailors were dangerously wounded, and one smuggler was killed and two seriously injured. The sailors captured twenty large casks of brandy; but the smugglers were soon reinforced, and, after another fight, recovered the booty, and compelled the enemy to retreat. In 1799 there was a ferocious encounter between smugglers and Custom-house officers off Salcombe. The former, who were in strong

RUNNING A CARGO IN WHITSAND BAY.

(*From an old Engraving.*)

force, fired into a revenue cutter, only to find the latter carrying a formidable contingent of soldiery, who peppered the adventurers with such effect that the survivors—fourteen in number—surrendered. They were escorted through Plymouth by a company of the Surrey Cavalry, and carried on board the flagship Cambridge for war service. After the Peace of 1802, the authorities decided to extirpate these hardy pests. Privateers were now available for forbidden traffic, and unemployed sailors, to whom the prospect of bloodshed presented no terrors, were attracted by the promise of reward. From Berry Head to Mount's Bay the coast was infested, but Admiral Thornborough rapidly thinned their craft, and speculators experienced heavy losses. A fleet of armed smugglers, despatched from the Channel Islands, was destroyed off Plymouth ; and the handsome Flora, of Fowey, was run down by the Fisgard, 44, and taken into Hamoaze, with several thousand ankers of brandy and tons of dry goods.

Mons. Carnon bore a charmed life. Introduced to the port as a prisoner, he acted as surgeon to his fellow-countrymen, and his freedom afforded him many commercial advantages. After he received his exchange, he negociated smuggling enterprises, with Falmouth as his favourite landing place. He travelled overland to Plymouth with his wares, was met by confederates on the outskirts of the town, and thence the goods were distributed with a skill that surprised the local authorities. Carnon had a reputation for smuggling on the grand scale that was the envy of his contemporaries, and he slipped through the hands of the authorities in every form of disguise, of which the common dress of a sailor was not unusual. In 1802, contrary to regulations, he took a French cartel into Catwater ; and, after landing his cargo, opened up communications with Mr. Bampfylde, a Falmouth merchant. The authorities intercepted his letters and sought to arrest him. Through every inn and smuggling rendezvous they hunted, but Carnon did not return to his boat, and made for Falmouth by coach. Thither he was pursued, and the merchant was threatened with prosecution if he did not inveigle Carnon on board the cartel, which had meantime arrived from Plymouth. He agreed to do so, but only deluded the authorities by causing them to apprehend a French prisoner, whom he induced to take a passage to Plymouth in the boat. The Mayor was most indignant at the trick, and was concerting measures to punish the captain when Carnon re-embarked, and the smuggler levanted with a fair wind. A gun-boat was sent in pursuit, and fired a dozen shots at the retreating vessel ; but the smuggler's lead was too pronounced, and it safely eluded the pursuit. Carnon, however, had been hard pressed, and he left a bag of gold and a stock of jewellery at his lodgings in Plymouth. The treasure was confiscated to the Crown, together with £350 which Mr. Bampfylde owed Carnon for contraband goods. The reverse did not stale the surgeon's appetite for adventure, and he continued his lucrative journeys without serious molestation.

With the renewal of the wars in 1803, vigilance was relaxed, and good stories were related with gusto by the chief actors. Suspected stores were often examined after hints had been conveyed by subordinates, and opportune and neighbourly transfers were thus effected. There was a general search at Dock in 1808, and in one case the code of honour was amusingly violated. The premises of an old lady in Cherry Garden Street were marked, and she implored her neighbour, a cobbler, to accept storeage until the inspection was over. Silks, tobacco and other stores were transferred to his shop and covered with skins of leather ; the old lady's house was ransacked in vain, and the officers knew that they had been forestalled. The cobbler was asked in the morning to return the goods. In reply he laughed at the owner ; and, when she threatened him, told the virago to do her worst. She at once wrote the Excise authorities to say that they had searched the wrong house, and that the cobbler's premises would yield a harvest. In the afternoon the officers reappeared with smiles, to find the cobbler smiling more broadly, for he had removed the goods to his own haunt in the course of the night.

A Guernsey merchant, who made frequent trips to Plymouth, carried his own bedstead with him, on board and on shore. It was a curious whim, and in time the excisemen suspected that the furniture was not simply used as a sleeping partner. They seized it as it was being drawn to Stonehouse, and found lace and shawls to the value of £3,000 packed in its hollow and cunningly-devised woodwork. The owner had long travelled with his indispensable companion, "for the benefit of his health," and patronised various seaside resorts. The keenness of loyal officials was illustrated in the fate of a Plymouth trawler. Her captain troubled himself very little with catching fish, and remained longer from the port than was necessary to his ostensible profession. Undesirous of too rudely pushing his misgivings, the lieutenant of a revenue cutter took to shooting gulls in Catwater, and the pseudo fisherman joined in the sport, until some birds dropped upon his deck. These the King's officer claimed; and, finding the captain indisposed to surrender them, he clambered up the side of the trawler and demanded his spoils. In the hold he saw that hundreds of tubs of brandy lay concealed beneath masses of nets and fishing gear. Then the impolicy of shooting gulls occurred to the master, for his cargo and craft were impounded, the cargo was sold, the ship sawn into sections, and the utmost penalties were exacted.

Unscrupulous jockeying relieved the "notorious Sarah Dunn" and her son-in-law from the risks to which they were devoted. Anne Gillman, who was as famous as Sarah Dunn herself, smuggled ashore in bulk the daintiest of draperies, and her one difficulty was to find a satisfactory means of distribution. Sarah Dunn, appreciating the dilemma, undertook to dispose of the wares to traders who were endowed with small compunctions. Mrs. Gillman was grateful for the proferred service, but stipulated that the goods should not quit her sight—a reservation which, on reflection, appealed to Mrs. Dunn's sense of fairness. An excursion in the direction of Catdown was accordingly arranged. The road was desolate, and this feature of the expedition Mrs. Gillman appreciated when the pair had walked some distance through the lane. Mrs. Dunn suddenly and excitedly exclaimed: "There is that rogue, Niles, the Custom-house officer." The supposed cause of this terror demanded to know the contents of the parcel; and Mrs. Dunn, who had placed a layer of pilchards across the silks to show her good faith, replied : "Don't you see it is fish ? " The parcel was opened and the wares disclosed ; and, in a moment, " Niles " made off with it. Mrs. Dunn now committed an irreparable error in tactics, and shouted so loudly for the help she did not expect that a horseman galloped to the scene. Then Dunn subdued her voice, and Mrs. Gillman's ascended to a shriek until the alleged Niles was run down. He proved to be Mrs. Dunn's son-in-law, and he had been prevailed upon by that too astute lady to wear a Custom-house uniform for the occasion. In the weak desire to preserve his freedom the young man revealed the conspiracy, and the pair were sent beyond the seas.

After Waterloo, the lack of occupation for sailors, soldiers and dockyardsmen, and the abject state to which merchants were reduced, led to the revival of smuggling on a skilful and ambitious scale. Cawsand fitted out a fleet of cutters, varying from eighty to one hundred and twenty tons each, which trafficked with the Channel Islands and Dutch and French ports. Some of these boats carried over a thousand five-gallon casks of spirits, in addition to general cargo and bales of tobacco. In 1826, several notorious smugglers were absent from Cawsand, and the Harpy sailed to intercept them. The boats kept outside the "hovering" limits ; and, after a deal of "battyfagging," the cargoes were run, amid the thanksgivings of the populace. The experience of the Lively in 1827 was tragic. She was overtaken by the Harpy off Penlee Point; and, several muskets having been discharged at her, consented to lay-to. On being boarded it was found that a small line was hanging from her starboard quarter, with a mark-buoy and sinking-stone attached. Surmising that the tubs were deposited in the neighbourhood, Lieutenant Roche dropped the line, so as to identify the scene later on, and proceeded to examine the smuggler. She smelt strongly of spirits, but there was not a pint on board ; and the only evidence in support of suspicion was the small cordage hanging to the sides by means of which the tubs had been lowered. Seizing this appliance Roche detained the Lively and her crew, and the captain—John Brown—appeared before the Plymouth magistrates on an indictment for carrying cordage adapted for slinging casks under forty gallons. Counsel for the accused—Mr. John Bayly—raised the ingenious plea that the cordage, though adapted, was not prepared for slinging casks, and that the prisoners could not therefore be condemned. The magistrates had no doubt as to the illicit transactions in which accused were engaged, but acquitted them on the technicality. Joy at their release was dimmed by the pertinacity with which Lieutenant Roche worked with creepers and sweep-lines around the spot where the cordage had been deposited ; and he received his compensation by raising 175 casks of rum in one day.

There was grim humour in the prosecution which was instituted in 1827 at the expense of James Coram, a publican, of Higher Stoke. The informer in the proceedings was John Jones, the man who had supplied the spirits to the defendant. Jones had furnished Coram with a considerable quantity of Geneva in exchange for a horse, and when he took the animal home he found that it was blind in one eye and otherwise defective. He at once returned with a demand that the contract should be retracted, and Coram threatened to reveal to the Excise the fact that Jones had been dealing in contraband goods. Overcome at the prospect the latter withdrew ; and, in the resolve that the biter should be bitten, he laid an information against the landlord as a purchaser of smuggled liquor. He thus shifted the responsibility of the offence, and received his share of the penalty of £25 with which Coram was visited. On the same occasion a master-mariner, in charge of one of the Breakwater vessels, was charged with being in possession of rum and wine which had not paid the duty. It was urged that the liquor was served out by the Government ; and that, although it became contraband on being landed, the intention of Ryder was to use it for his own household. It was admitted that the leading officers on the Breakwater were permitted this privilege, but Ryder was fined £25 for aspiring to circumstances of equality.

Through the instrumentality of spies who wandered about the country lanes in smock-frocks, and who kept their ears open in the drinking haunts of the suspects, the revenue officers obtained the necessary information of contemplated expeditions and expected returns. In 1831 a crowd of some forty smugglers, armed with stout sticks, were pursued and overtaken by six preventive men. They had just received a cargo of fifty kegs of brandy from a sloop in Whitsand Bay, and were unloading the tubs at the foot of the cliffs when the officers pounced upon them. A desperate fight ensued, and the preventive men fired ball-cartridge to restrain the marauders from further violence. Several of them were wounded ; but they were carried off by their companions, and the only man who fell into the hands of the officers was Sampson Trevan, who was taken, with a tub on his back, running towards Sheviock. In default of paying the fine of £100 he was sent to prison. A gang of twenty smugglers were clearing a cargo of brandy in Millbrook Lake, in 1832, when they were overtaken on Anderton Beach. Undaunted by superior numbers the preventive officers attempted to seize the leaders ; but they were surrounded, and some were beaten with bludgeons and others wounded with cutlasses. Several excisemen came to the rescue and the battle was continued on fairer conditions, a few on either side being badly bruised and slashed about heads and hips. Robert Barrowford was held tight when the others decamped ; and, although he shouted out "Come back you cowards," he was left to his fate. Whilst one group of officers took Barrowford to the lock-up the smugglers returned in search of their spoil ; and, overwhelming the officers left in charge, carried off the kegs in triumph. Barrowford was convicted in the full penalty of £100 ; and went to prison. Pistols and cutlasses were used on the Elburton Road in 1833, where the preventive men intercepted a waggon loaded with spirits, and guarded by armed men. When the latter were asked to surrender they showed fight ; and, after several had been wounded on either side, the smugglers repulsed the officers, the cargo was saved, and the injured were removed to their homes. A similar struggle occurred at Port Wrinkle, where a revenue officer perceived a body of men watching in a field. They rose as he approached ; and, as he feared an attack, he discharged his pistol. The smugglers surrounded and stoned him ; and, with cutlass in one hand and pistol in the other, the officer stood at bay, slashing and firing at the fugitive crowd. Only one member of the gang was arrested, and the magistrates acquitted him on the ground that the men might have been looking out to sea without an evil intention. An al-fresco party was sorely disconcerted at Wembury on reaching the summit of a cliff with a dozen kegs of brandy. An officer had watched them unloading, and creeping through three fields, jumped over the hedge, and summoned the roysterers to surrender. The next moment he was shouting "Murder !" for the gang beat him with stones and sticks, and threatened instant death. His cries for help, the ringing of shots, and clashing of cutlasses, mingled with loud oaths and deep curses, attracted other officers. With shouts of "Death or Glory" and "Life for Life," the smugglers closed, threw their enemies to the grass, tied their hands and feet with ropes, and poured neat brandy down their throats. The spirit that remained they dashed in their faces ; and, waving bludgeons with menacing taps, threatened that, if they did not kiss the tubs, they should certainly feel the sticks. At length they left the exhausted officers on the ground, and some hours elapsed before they were released by comrades from their ignominious posture. Thus reinforced they proceeded to Down Thomas, where some of the assailants were discovered in female attire. Those who could be identified were severely punished, but the majority escaped the toils of the law. And so the traffic continued well into the 'forties ; but its doom was inevitable, for law-breakers were periodically sent into transportation and their smart craft sawn into separate portions for the edification of the sympathetic. One of the last to be convicted was John Bray, member of a notorious Cawsand brotherhood. He and others were engaged in the early morning, two miles outside the Breakwater, and were spotted by coastguardsmen raising a cargo. They had secured several kegs before they were discovered, and one craft containing liquor pressed on all sail for Cawsand Bay. The Charles Turner, Bray's boat, was boarded ; and creepers, creep-ropes and stones with holes and slings attached, were found at the bottom. Several kegs were also afloat which had been hurriedly cast overboard on the approach of the officers. "It's a fair prize for them," the prisoners bitterly exclaimed on their way to the Stonehouse "Watch-house," and their long imprisonment assisted to wear out their zeal for a hazardous service.

Ben Brace and the   Life and manners in Plymouth and Dock were tenderly pourtrayed
Cawsand Smugglers. by Captain Chamier in his biography of " Ben Brace "—a work in which "the truths were touched by the hand of romance." Born at Cawsand in 1758, the hero stood by the hour watching the sea as it rolled into the Sound, longing to face its dangers and participate in the glories of his country's defence. As his parents refused to grant the desire of his heart, Ben left his home one night, and, crossing from Cremyll to Mutton Cove, managed, by the use of his legs and the help of a waggoner, to reach Portsmouth. Here he joined the Raisonnable, sailed as Nelson's "shipmate" on his first voyage, and the hero made Ben his friend and confidant. The young sailor was ever

PREVENTIVE OFFICERS SEIZING A CONTRABAND CARGO.

(From an old Engraving.)

at hand in the hour of his necessity, and when, after an association of thirteen years, Ben longed to visit his parents, Nelson gave him the means to journey from London. His story of how he was tricked by a land pirate is sufficiently quaint. He stopped at a wayside inn, and a genial-looking customer asked him where he was bound to, "for you don't belong to this place?"

"No, not I" (I wondered how he guessed it); "I am going to Plymouth."

"To Plymouth?" says he.

"Yes," said I, "to Plymouth; the wars are over now, and I am off for home. I am not without a shot in the locker," giving my pocket a bit of a smack.

"I can assist you, my noble-hearted fellow," says my friend; "give me your hand. You sailors are the best men in the world."

"Take a drop out of my jorum, sir," said I. "Here, landlord, another pot of porter."

"Yes, sir," said he, "but who pays for it?"

"I do, you lubber," says I. "Do you think I'm a shark to come swallowing the bait and then shake myself off the hook? No, I never did that; so, here's your pay, and I have enough left to buy a hogshead of porter, and a purser's bread-bag of tobacco; so, stir your stumps, old Blowhard."

A night of hard drinking and vows of eternal friendship ensued, and when Ben rose from his stupor and the inerview in the morning, he started "like a harpooned porpoise" to find that the end of his handkerchief had been cut off, and that he had only eight guineas left in another pocket, which he had taken the precaution to sew up: I made friends with the waggoner, and walked by his side almost all day. Towards evening I got into my straw again, and slept like a weasel with one eye open comfortably enough. In seven days' time we got to Plymouth, and I did not stand long in taking leave of the waggoner, who was contented with four shillings, and told me that he should be returning in a fortnight, which would be quite long enough for me to remain in Cawsand Bay. I told him that I should be steering up to London about that time, and would be with him. Then, giving my trousers a hitch up, I stepped out like a good one for Mutton Cove, got into the ferry, and was soon over at Mount Edgcumbe. I trotted away like a postman, never looking behind me, and carrying a press of sail, until I came to the turn which overlooks the bay and commands a view of the village. Here I stopped. I remember at this moment the feeling which overcame me. I saw before me the cottage in which I was born and reared. I could perceive the door from which I had escaped, and left my poor father and mother in all the agony of uncertainty whether I had been kidnapped or murdered.

Ben casually met his father in the village, and was able to render him good service in a brawl with some drunken scoundrel. He did not disclose his identity, but was asked home to supper. How his heart fluttered to witness the familiar room and no less familiar furniture:

But where was Jane all this time? I was anxious not to discover myself, and therefore did not say a word; but I looked round the cottage in the hope of finding some mark of female dress by which I could guess if she were alive. I saw nothing, however, except a curious old chair which stood up in a corner; and, when I took my eyes off it, I found that both father and mother were looking at me with so inquisitive a stare, that I began to fear I was recognised.

"Ah!" he began, ' a chair reminds us often of our troubles; we keep it that we may not forget those who have forgotten us."

My mother looked like a wax figure in tears as my father went on to speak.

"In that chair we laid our son Ben when he was first born, for we had no cradle in the house; he left us when he was about twelve years of age, and we have never heard of him since! But what is the matter with you, young man? You change colour like a dying dolphin. Lord love you, dame; just see how like he is to our Ben!"

I could not hold on any longer—the tears stood in my eyes. "Stop, father," said I, "you shall be happy again, I hope." My mother, who had never taken her gaze off me, immediately recollected me, and had me in her arms in a moment, exclaiming, "Ben! Ben! God Almighty be praised that I see you before I die!"

The son's joy is dimmed by the disclosure that his sister Jane, the toddling child who developed sweet maidenhood, had succumbed to the designs of Tackle—"as great a scoundrel as ever cursed Cawsand with his company"—and that she had eloped with him to Dock, where all trace of her had been lost. After four or five years, Ben obtained permission to re-visit his parents: I took good care to profit by former experience, and not to talk about gold-dust to any chaps who had not been to the coast of Africa; so I had it all sewed into my neckerchief, excepting the present service store, which I carefully tied up in the corner. Because, do you see, in those times, although we had long tails, we had no pockets, and I thought no pirate should take my cargo without cutting my throat. Away I went "with a light heart and a thin pair of breeches," as the song says; and I fell in with the Plymouth waggon.

"Good day to you, my jolly sailor," said the waggoner, "you must have been in foreign parts, I suppose, for you are as brown as a gipsy?"

"Just so, old Blowhard," says I; "and now, do you see, I am going to moor ship for a full due."

"Nay, sir," said he, "I don't know the place—we don't pass through it. There's Dart-*moor*, but that's on t'other road; and there's Moorfields, but that's t'other side of Lunnun; but Moorship—no, I never heard of it afore; it's nowhere here abouts, and its not near Plymouth."

"Yes, but it is," says I; "it's at Cawsand Bay."

"I say, master sailor," replied the old waggoner, "you bean't very mad, be you? or I can't let you get into the waggon, for there's a poor woman in there with her child."

"What, a sail!" said I; "then here goes, old boy, for an overhaul."

I jumped into the waggon; and there, sure enough, I saw a pretty young creature, with a poor little half-starved infant.

The young woman is stricken with despair and famished with want, and Ben becomes her protector after hearing her story of seduction and desertion. As the waggon approaches Plymouth he gives her good advice and some "shiners":

She looked at the money, and then at the child, as much as to say, "We need not part yet." But I shoved in my oar and said "Take an old sailor's advice; leave the young one with the grandmother, buy the new rigging, and go to service like a Christian, and don't be having a penn'o'rth of steps at Point or Stonehouse—that always leads to evil with you pretty creatures. If you get a place, and are honest and hard-working, you will soon be able to look after the young one again; and although your upper-works may be damaged, I think the steerage of your heart is all right and clear. There, put those in your pocket; and if one sailor has injured you, another has relieved you; so don't abuse us *all* as you did do."

She took my hand, and looking earnestly in my face for the first time, she blessed me. "Tell me," said she, "who you are."

Richards, a labourer, who had been suspected of waylaying and killing a sentry because he refused to admit him to the barracks after nightfall. He drew attention to the serious probability of his complicity in this case by insinuating that he knew the actual author. He was walking through the Five Fields, when he saw a "tailor" lark-nesting with a stick from which one end had been sawed, and he professed his belief that this individual was the murderer. As the relations between the man, his trade, and the crime, were not clear, the police drew their own inference. Richards said he could swear to the stick amongst a thousand; and, one of the constables having noticed that he had been recently consorting with as dissolute and disorderly a ruffian as himself, William Smith, searched and found in the latter's court such a weapon as Richards had described. The informant, when confronted, replied that it was truly the same stick, but that Smith was not the man whom he saw carrying it in the Five Fields. He increased suspicion by assuring different

THE TRAGEDY AT MILLBRIDGE, 1789: MURDERERS HANGING IN CHAINS.

people that he was glad he was not from home "after bell-ringing" on the night of the crime. A publican, who thought that he affirmed his innocence with too much anxiety, thereupon asked him to confirm his statement, and Richards first referred to his landlady, who knew nothing of his movements; and then to his wife, who reproached him for opening his "blab mouth." Richard was arrested, but there were only negative admissions to associate him with the crime. No sooner was he released than he boasted that, if the authorities had not interfered with him, the murder would have been cleared up. Now it should not, "and if I am bound to be hanged, I will hang myself." The hat which was picked up was next identified as Smith's; and he decamped as soon as he heard that an acquaintance had sworn to it. He was tracked to Dartmouth; and, conscious that his flight was fatal, there admitted the whole story. He and Richards met by arrangement under the hospital wall, where the latter said he wanted to be revenged on an official who had discharged him from the yard. Whispering " Here he comes," Richards jumped out, and smote the doomed man a frightful blow across the mouth; and, in the scuffle that

Y

followed, Smith lost his hat and Richards dropped the bludgeon. After this confession the evidence rapidly accumulated. Someone noticed Richards leave by his back door on the night of the murder; a woman recognised him as the man who ran across the Millbridge, with wet blood on his hat; a neighbour testified that he drew attention to stains on his jacket, and that he replied: "That's nothing; don't hang me!" There was confirmatory evidence that Richards uttered threats against Mr. Philip Smith because he had dismissed him. The prisoners had little to urge in their defence. William Smith simply denied that he struck any blows; and Richards whined that the people of Dock only wanted to see him hanged. The miscreants were convicted, and Judge Buller declared that it was a most wonderful providence which had established their guilt. He determined that the usual course of giving their corpses to the surgeons for dissection should not be followed, but that they should be suspended between Heaven and Earth, "as they were fit for neither." Richards and Smith were hanged at Heavitree, and their bodies subsequently conveyed to Stoke, where they where hoisted on a transverse gibbet erected in the shallow opposite the Churchyard. The remains—"to the terror of some and the disgust of many"—loaded the air with putrefaction for months. In seven years the skeleton of Smith dropped with a portion of the gibbet; and the other fell bit by bit into the mud. Then the gibbet yielded to decay, the stump was used as a mooring buoy, and a carpenter of Devonport converted some of the soundest wood into snuff boxes! "By the vulgar and ignorant," the locality was infested with superstitious horror, and, for more than a generation, a stone in the churchyard wall was declared to bear indelible marks of blood. As a matter of fact, the stain received an added impression of red from the brush of every passing painter, until, in 1841, the stone fell out. The legend wore away as the gruesome reminiscence of a barbarous survival passed from observation.

Sensational was the murder of a child at Dodbrook. The deceased was beaten to death in a field, and a labourer named Liscombe was four times examined by the magistrates with a view to the elucidation of the mystery. All was unavailing, and Liscombe was released for want of direct evidence. He forthwith disappeared from the district; and, in four days, an old woman, Sarah Ford, was slain at North Huish, in the absence of her husband at market, her throat being cut with a wind hook and the head covered with a bag. A man answering to Liscombe's appearance had been seen lurking near the house, and his connection with this second crime was confirmed by the discovery of his clothes in the stream that ran at the rear of the linhay. He had appropriated a suit belonging to Mr. Ford; and, after locking the house, tied his own garments in a bundle, and cast them away to throw his pursuers off the scent. This atrocity intensified horror through the county, and the Prince Regent offered a reward of one hundred guineas for the murderer's capture. Liscombe was small of stature, walked with a limp, lisped in his speech, and possessed a prominent nose, so that identification was not difficult. When it was rumoured that such a man had passed through Plymouth and crossed to Torpoint, the entire population thrilled with excitement and alarm. The inducement stimulated hundreds to scour the country on the other side of the Tamar, but Liscombe was run to earth by two Kingsbridge constables to whom his presence was familiar. On being conveyed to the Dartmouth Inn, at Plymouth, he confessed that he committed both the tragedies which, for so many months, had mystified the inhabitants of Devonshire. The prisoner met his doom at Exeter.

In 1804 a miner, Simon Pryor, descended Crown Dale Mine, near Tavistock, by a windlass, in company with John James, the brother-in-law of James Matthews, overseer of the undertaking. After blasting some rock, Pryor was drawn up, and James called upon his comrades to pull him to the surface. In a moment Matthews let go the windlass, and bade

Pryor do the same. Upon his refusal, Matthews struck him with a pick hilt; and, as his grip relaxed, James was precipitated to the bottom, and his body was picked up almost crushed beyond recognition. Pryor revealed the crime to the other workmen, but they imprisoned him in the smith's shop during the inquest lest operations in the mine should be stopped if the manager were hanged. A verdict of "accidental death" was returned, and the secret was not disclosed till sixteen years later. The perils of watchmen were illustrated in December, 1810, when an officer, named Taylor, was proceeding through Higher Street, Plymouth, and observed four men coming from the waterside near Catdown Road, with bags on their backs. Upon accosting them as to what they were carrying, one replied: "Nothing but what belongs to us." Taylor then offered to light them to their houses, and another ruffian exclaimed: "I will do for him," and plunged a knife in the watchman's stomach. Taylor struggled to the Guildhall, where he was able to relate what had occurred, and the following morning he expired. The gang dropped some valuables which they had stolen from a merchantman lying in the harbour, but they were never brought to justice. Alarm prevailed in Clowance Street, in June, of the same year, when Mathurin Dagorn, a French pilot in the British service, shot his wife in a fit of jealousy, and then put a similar end to his own existence. The jury having returned a verdict of felo-de-se, as well as of wilful murder, against Dagorn, his body was conveyed to the Deadlake and buried without service of any sort in the high road, in the presence of thousands of spectators. For years the scene of interment was reputed to be haunted, and few would pass that way after nightfall lest they should see the spectre which floated in the air "just over the unhallowed grave of the murderer and suicide," and glowed "with a phosphoric glare which made it plainly perceptible to the horrified beholder."

A mysterious tragedy was discovered at Fowey in November, 1811, the victim being Isaac Valentine, a young Jew, whose body was found near the quay with jaw broken, head fractured and pockets turned inside out. Valentine, who lived at Dock, was enticed to Fowey by a tavern-keeper named Wyatt, who formerly carried on business at Plymouth. Learning that Valentine was in the habit of carrying a good deal of money about him, he wrote to tell him that he had a number of "old buttons" (guineas) to dispose of. The young Jew jumped at the bait; but, suspicious of the publican's good faith, induced a friend to accompany him. On the fatal night two merchant seamen were sitting smoking on their barque, when they were startled by an agonized cry of "Oh, Mr. Wyatt." There ensued the sound of a splash and then a man jumped from the pier, and apparently held the resisting form under water until the sound of struggles wholly ceased. All was so quiet and normal by the time they reached the pier, that the sailors assumed that only the noise of a drunken frolic had reached them, and they sailed early next morning without making any comment. Valentine's companion had meanwhile grown anxious concerning his friend, whose premonition had never ceased to haunt him, and returning to the inn, he challenged the publican as to the Jew's whereabouts. "What," he replied, "have you not heard that he was drowned to-night?" As this was the first intimation in the town that Valentine had met an ill end, all present started to hear Wyatt say the stranger had met his death in the water. In a few days the corpse of the Jew rose to the surface, and the seamen, on returning to Fowey, disclosed all they had heard and witnessed the night before their departure. Wyatt's incriminating confession of knowledge was then construed as conclusive. In the meantime, he had been observed to pay frequent visits to his stables, and a search at midnight resulted in the discovery beneath the dung of a roll of notes which were saturated with the salt water in which they had been steeped. Plymouth bankers identified, by the numbers, the notes as those they paid to Valentine before his departure for Fowey, and in the pockets of the deceased's clothing were found the letters with which the publican had inveigled his victim to Fowey. Wyatt was sent for trial at the Assizes at Launceston, and there he was charged with the murder, as well as with felony in stealing the property. For fully eleven hours the prisoner exhibited the utmost unconcern, but his agitation overcame him when the jury turned in the box to consider their verdict. Challenged by the Clerk of Arraigns to "Hold up your hand, and say why sentence of death should not be passed upon you?" Wyatt responded with his left, but preserved a sullen silence. After a pause, the Judge told the prisoner that he had violated every instinct of "honour, justice, humanity and friendship" in committing "one of the blackest crimes on record." He then sentenced him to be hanged on the Monday, but soon discovered to his amazement, that he should have directed the execution to take place two days before that date. He accordingly re-summoned Wyatt before him, and once more condemned him to the gallows with the same impressiveness; adding, at the end of his admonition, that the prisoner should nevertheless be allowed to live longer. "But you must not expect any eventual mercy, for that is impossible." Wyatt was carried out in shocking convulsions, and was hanged at Bodmin, three weeks later, in the presence of a multitude which flocked from all the countryside.

Whilst Mr. Metters, a farmer of large means, residing at Whitchurch, was attending Plymouth Market in February, 1813. his wife was murdered by Samuel Norton, a servant man. After mutilating her with a round hook, he conveyed the body to an outhouse, covered it with straw, and plundered the farm. All the other inmates were from home, so that Norton was able to dress himself in his master's clothing. He made off towards Prince-town with a large sum of gold, and there loitered until he was apprehended. The conduct of this "hardened wretch" during his confinement exhibited the "most brutal depravity of mind." He met his fate on the gallows with fear and trembling, and Samuel Summers, for administering poison to his master, Samuel Denning, of Plymouth, with intent to kill him, was hanged at the same time. A murder that occasioned excitement was committed in October, 1817, by a waterman named Green, who attended the boat that conveyed the Cornish mails to Torpoint. A married woman named Smith had eloped with Green to Ireland, and lived with him for eighteen months. After entreating her husband's forgiveness she returned to Dock, and Green followed to persecute her with attentions. The woman was overheard by the neighbours to say: "Jack Green, you mean to murder me," and he replied: "I value not my own life, but I do not wish to hurt you." She begged him to leave her to her husband; but, a few days later, the couple entered the Lion and Anchor Inn, in Cherry Garden Street, where the woman was heard to shriek, and the man hurriedly left the premises. Mrs. Smith was found dying of her wounds, a case knife was discovered under a heap of shavings in the room, and Green admitted that he killed the woman because of her refusal to elope with him again. He was convicted at the Devon Assizes, in March, 1818, and expiated his crime with "more of despair than of hope for the state of his soul in the next world."

Of female executions in public places, those of Mary Woodman and Sarah Polgreen supplied effective contrasts in the behaviour of the condemned, and illustrated the morbid attractions which such scenes possessed for the public. The trial of the former in 1819 was followed with the keenest interest in Plymouth, where the woman and her husband had been in the habit of attending the November fairs, and the woman was notorious for her "handsome appearance and dissolute habits." At Okehampton an intrigue with a gipsy called Smallacombe led to a quarrel; the woman sent a child for a packet of arsenic; and the husband having eaten poisoned bread and butter, died in fearful tortures. The prisoner was sentenced "to be drawn on a hurdle to the place of execution; and, after hanging by the neck until dead, to be delivered over for dissection," The woman evinced the utmost indifference to her fate ; and, as the judge addressed her, she leant her head upon her arm, looked him steadily in the face, and, assuming a daring demeanour as he finished, exclaimed, to the horror of the court : " Well, I will never forgive any of my persecutors —they have sworn false, and the devil will send them into hell and God will forgive me." As Woodman was dragged from the dock she uttered " the vilest imprecations," and no efforts of the clergy could soften her. She manifested the same defiant and violent spirit until the morning of her execution, and her only desire was to bid farewell to her paramour, who was lying under sentence of death for uttering counterfeit coin, and who had tried to secure the woman's release by confessing that he poisoned her husband. On the thongs being removed which bound her to the hurdle, Mary Woodman mounted the steps of the gallows with firmness, and, facing the crowd, met her end with a courage that astonished beholders. Smallacombe was hanged in her presence. Sarah Polgreen was executed at Bodmin in 1820 for poisoning her husband, and the scene was attended by dramatic horrors. After she was sentenced, the woman was so overwhelmed that she had to be supported in the dock, and she was carried to her cell in a state of insensibility. On the day appointed for her hanging, she emerged from the gaol composed of countenance ; and, having taken her seat upon the hurdle without the least hesitation, conversed with the hangman as he drove the horse. After joining in prayer, she arose and sang aloud, in the presence of the crowd, " Come let us anew our journey pursue." Having addressed an appeal to the spectators to take warning by her example and avoid bad company, she implored a young man whom she recognised to come forward ; and, after wishing him an affectionate farewell, begged him to give her love to her female friends. She continued fervently praying whilst the hangman adjusted the rope, and confessed that her aversion to her husband, and his well-founded jealousy, were the cause of the tragedy. At the desire of the hangman, she repeated the Lord's Prayer, and dropped a handkerchief by way of signal. Her body was carried to a linhay and dissected, and the heart was given to the prison surgeon.

A ferocious attempt to murder on the highway at Ridgway, in 1827, led to diverse speculations as to the authorship. James Jeffry, a tributer, engaged at Bottle Hill Mine, went to the Devonshire Inn, Ridgway, to divide joint earnings with some fellow employés. Thomas Helston and William Trethrew overheard the conversation, and knew that Jeffry intended to walk at dusk to his home at Buckfastleigh. Prosecutor and prisoners went to the George Inn, where the latter obtained permission to sleep in the cow-loft, from which they could steal unobserved. Instead of the prisoners overtaking Jeffry, he came up to them when he had walked two miles. Helston was carrying a shovel ; and, after a few words, the implement was brought on the prosecutor's head with great force. As Jeffry tried to recover himself, a second blow was inflicted ; he fell to the ground, and was found unconscious by the driver of the Subscription Coach, whose wheels nearly passed over the body. On recovering, Jeffry at once mentioned the prisoners as being the men who assaulted him ; and, when the police searched the cow-loft, they found them, either asleep or pretending to be so. Prosecutor had been robbed, but the money was not discovered, and Helson and Trethrew pleaded that they never left the inn. Much to the disturbance of the public conscience, they were found guilty ; and, in spite of their dying protestations, were hanged at Exeter. After the executions, a farmer publicly testified that he saw the prisoners in a lane near Chaddlewood ; and that he did not tender himself as a witness because the evidence appeared to him sufficiently strong.

Duels and Duelling :   There are many recorded instances of duelling towards the close
   1769-1837.   of the eighteenth and far into the nineteenth century. In 1769 a lieutenant of marines quarrelled with his captain whilst they were in liquor, and they

adjourned to a hostelry in Stonehouse, where they fought with swords until the younger combatant fell with a mortal thrust. The spectacle of the flowing blood overwhelmed the captain, and he helped to carry his junior to his quarters. The wounded man expired, however, on the doorstep, and the captain surrendered himself to the watchman. He was put upon his trial for murder, but his inconsolable grief so touched the jury that they experienced no difficulty in reducing the offence. Exasperating words passed at a dinner on board the Mermaid in 1799, and the second lieutenant challenged the surgeon. Several pistol charges were fired, and both men fell severely wounded, and were conveyed to their respective lodgings. Lieutenant D., of the Navy, and Lieutenant M., of the Marines, passionate rivals for the same hand, met in a secluded site at Stoke; and, after the pistols had been twice discharged, the former fell with a bullet in his thigh. Faint from loss of blood, he was smuggled to a neighbouring inn, where for weeks his life was despaired of. An American surgeon, during some badinage at mess, maintained that England's conduct towards her colonies had justly stirred his countrymen to resistance. A young lieutenant challenged him across the table, the preliminaries were arranged, and the duel was fought on the outskirts of Dock. The Englishman was shot through the heart, and his assailant was committed for trial, with the master, who acted as his second. The two were sentenced to be hanged, but were eventually pardoned, as the chief object of the prosecution was "to check, if not to entirely put an end to, this barbarous and ever-to-be-lamented custom."

Impromptu dances were the fashion and love feuds often proceeded to extremes. At an improvised entertainment in Pembroke Street, two middies—Mr. Armstrong and Mr. Long—quarrelled and repaired to a field; where, in the presence of friends flushed with the night's dissipation, the hot-heads fought with pistols. Long was hit on the right side, and the ball travelling to his left shoulder, he fell dead upon the spot. All concerned rushed guiltily from the rendezvous. The Resistance was on the point of sailing when the middy's absence was noted; and, parties being sent in search, his body was discovered in a field, his gilt-laced cap on his head and a cane by his side. Armstrong was lodged in irons, and then publicly degraded and imprisoned. "Two young sparks" of the Princess Charlotte, inflamed over a similar episode in 1808, met at the back of St. Nicholas Island and agreed to fire until one dropped fatally wounded. They exchanged three shots at five paces without doing much harm, and were chewing musket balls for another round when the officer of the island placed them under arrest. They were dismissed the service.

Asperities, followed by a hasty blow, caused Lieutenant Paget and Assistant-Surgeon French to meet on the Hoe in June, 1814. The combatants were comparative youngsters, and the cause of their enmity was a girl of great charms. On arriving at a retired spot they fired and Mr. French, on being hit in the groin, collapsed with the cry: "My dear friend, I am killed." Pressing his opponent's hand he added, "The Lord have mercy on my soul," and breathed his last. A crowd of officers and soldiers surveyed the scene with "as much sympathy as they would have shown in a cockpit." An encounter of similar gravity occurred at Ridgeway in March, 1817, between Lieutenant Hines and Lieutenant Cordery. The parties fired on the order, and Hines received a fatal ball in his loins. His wife was summoned from Plymouth, but she only arrived to witness his decease. Cordery and his second left the country.

A duel between Lieutenant Lockyer and a gentleman of the name of Sutton placed the Mayor of Plymouth in a delicate position in 1817. Lockyer had seen active service at Corunna, and the Mayor was his kinsman. In the quarrel he killed Mr. Sutton, and Mr. Edmund Lockyer was informed that he was making his way to his native town, and that "a verdict of wilful murder has been returned against him." His worship stiffly but most loyally replied : " If the person to whom you allude appears in this town his relatives will take no steps to prevent the punishment due to his crime from falling on him who committed it." The ruin in which principals were involved rendered duelling unfashionable, and one of the last interchanges of the kind was in the nature of an anti-climax. A lieutenant of the Genoa, and an officer of the Ocean, met one summer's morning in 1827, in a field near Torpoint. The precaution of admonishing the police to be in attendance had not been overlooked ; and, after the combatants had twice missed each other, the constable made his appearance. One gentleman ran away and the other was taken to Devonport, where he was bound over in recognisances to be of better behaviour. A court-martial assembled on board the San Josef, in Hamoaze, in 1834, for the trial of Mr. John Christie, an assistant-surgeon, who was charged with challenging one after the other of his brother officers. One promising duel with a lieutenant was stopped as the parties were on the field ; in another case Christie drew a knife upon the chief mate and cut his fingers as he was defending himself; and, in a third quarrel, a fellow officer knocked him down. The prisoner was found "partly guilty" and sentenced to lose one year's seniority.

Superstitions and the   There survived a respectful affection for creepy legends, and a
Superstitious.   ready desire to accept as gospel weird reports of unnatural appear-ances ; and so recently as March, 1788, there was a whole population ready to affirm on oath that a great dragon was seen "neer unto Plymouth." The creature was "very terrible to behold," and it "croaked and made a great noise like two cannons, which was very surprising to the town's people," who were glad enough when this atmospheric freak "took its departure." Early in the 19th century Admiral Duckworth was held in awe as a severe disciplinarian ; and, a few nights after he died, the sentry on Mount Wise created alarm by firing his gun into the air. The guard turned out and placed the man under arrest, and he explained that he shot at the ghost of the admiral as it was hurried away by a dark figure. It would have fared ill with the soldier if the butler had not declared that he heard the clock strike thirteen when the sound of the explosion reached him. The explanation that Admiral Duckworth had been fetched by the devil was seriously accepted in the town, and the story was handed down from father to son.

An association of persons chiefly connected with literature and art met at the Bunch of Grapes, in Kinterbury Street, Plymouth, for conviviality; and their staple liquor was white ale --a concoction peculiar to the town, and drunk from silver flagons. The president was Humphrey Tallent, and concerning him a superstition endured for years. One evening there was a too conspicuously vacant chair, for the president was lying at the point of death. An air of gloom pervaded the conversation, when the door flew open, and a spectre, pale and ghastly, and habited in bedgown and nightcap, entered and sat on a footstool. Temporarily rendered speechless, one of the more courageous at last observed : " How do you do, sir. I am glad to see you here again. I hope you are better." The apparition only bowed, raised an empty glass, moved its lips in the toast of death, and withdrew as silently as it had entered. When the shock passed a member walked across to Mr. Tallent's house to enquire how he fared, and learnt to his horror that he had just passed away. The faith of the members that they had witnessed his disembodied spirit remained unshaken until the nurse confessed that she fell asleep whilst attending the dying man, and found on waking that he had left the room. In ten minutes he returned from the club, composed himself to rest, and, exhausted by the effort, breathed his last.

By the water at Coxside a woollen manufactory was kept going by Mr. Sturt ; and, when the industry failed, the authorities rented the premises as a war prison. A French officer disclosed to a compatriot, during an illness, the place where he concealed his money, and implored him, in the event of his death, to send it to his friends.   When he began to recover, his confidant feared he would be deprived of the small fortune within his grasp, and he pushed the convalescent out of window as he was watching the shipping.   Though feeble with weakness, the drowning man struggled hard to reach the shore :

> Vainly he his voice set forth
> To catch a listening ear ;
> And " Boat a-hoy " this minute north
> The next would westward veer.

For years, when stormy winds and billows rose, the spirit voice ranged from shore to shore, exclaiming " Boat a-hoy, a-hoy, a-hoy." The courage of the stoutest waterman quailed as he walked near the spot, as he did with louder than ordinary tread, dreading to hear the reiterated appeal. Those who were not superstitious attributed the sounds to the agency of the wind as it moaned through the rigging of ships at anchor.

In " The Plymouth Tragedy " was presented in illiterate verse " a full and particular account of the appearing of the ghost of Madame E. Johnstone, a beautiful young lady, who fell in love with Mr. John Hunt, a captain of one of the regiments sent into Spain, who forsook her after he had promised her marriage." The maiden was fair to view, but her folly involved soul and body in ruin. Mr. Hunt was ordered to the scene of the war and the girl besought him to grant her the saving grace of wedlock. In her despair at his refusal she smote her breast, tore her hair, and sold herself to the Devil to obtain revenge. One night as she was walking out alone, the Evil One presented himself in the form of a man, and urged her to prick her arm and give him a drop of her blood, as by virtue of its agency he could compel the recreant to appear. Overjoyed at the prospect the girl withdrew to a room, and made the necessary incision, only to find that the blood would not flow, and to realise that the Devil was in possesion of her secret. He vanished from the apartment as the girl shrieked in distress, and she was carried to her home with mind unhinged. Here she was carefully watched, but she procured a penknife and stabbed herself to the heart. The frigate that carried the seducer was speeding to Vigo when it was overtaken by a hurricane, and was "like to have been lost " as a punishment for tolerating a Jonah. When the peril was at its worst one of the sentries saw the young woman through the mist and spray, and, as she advanced, timidly asked what she wanted. Miss Johnson gave her name and revealed her mission, and the deceiver was sent for. Hunt was thus dramatically confronted by the victim of his perfidy, her life's blood even yet staining her snow-white garments, and in his dismay :

> He went to run to hide his face,
> She cried " False man it is too late " ;
> She clasped him in her arms straightway,
> But no man knew his dying day.
> In a flash of fire that many see,
> She dragged him down into the sea,
> The storm it soon abated were
> They all returned thanks by prayer.

Another early version of the " The Plymouth Tragedy " furnished a full account of " Beautiful Susan's overthrow by permission of her unkind parents." It was the familiar story of a lovely maiden who had plighted her troth to a ship's officer ; and during his prolonged absence at sea, was urged by her parents to marry a wealthy young merchant who was captivated by her charms.   Within a few weeks, she learnt that her devoted William was in the Downs, awaiting the next ship to carry him to Plymouth and claim his bride.   In her remorse, Susan was seized in a fatal delirium :

> When darksome night bright Sol had encompassed,
>   And twinkling stars spread the spangled sky ;
> William, who then in his cabin was sleeping
>   Was wak'd by a voice that faintly did cry :
> " William, arise, see thy beautiful Susan,
>   Whose charms were once as bright as the sun ;
> Now in Death's frozen arms is enclosed,
>   William, make haste, to your own lover come."

William awakes and sees the ghost of Susan " more pale than lead " ; and, when he attempts to enfold her, the vision disappears.   In his despair, he hastens to Plymouth ; where, to his grief, he learns that the object of his affections has expired.   Proceeding to the cemetery he induces the sexton to unearth the coffin and falling on it, dies broken-hearted.   The bodies were poetically enclosed in the " same silent tomb."

A curious story is told of Sir George Magrath, an old naval surgeon, who was the friend of Nelson, by whom he was visited in Plymouth.   Sir George lived in a house on the site of Lockyer Hotel—then a gloomy mansion screened by trees.   He was one of the most conspicuous beaux in the town, although his detractors vowed that, in addition to a false eye, the existence of which was perceptible, he wore " false shoulders, false hips, false calves," and that his superb bust consisted of padding.   At the outset of Sir George's fatal illness he was visited by many " old relics of the battle and the breeze," and pious ladies read the Scriptures "and prayed to his great consolation."   The more precise, however, were surprised to notice a charming lady flitting about the hall ; and, when they hinted that her presence was open to conjecture, Sir George requested them to visit him no more.   After this the nocturnal quiet was broken by weird sounds, and crowds gathered to listen.   Excited by rumours the police forced their way through the door, with the Mayor at their head, and accompanied by a well known physician ; and Sir George protested that he was only dying, as he desired, amid the strains of solemn music.   The visitors had no alternative save to quit the house, and the door was closed against future visitors.   Communications were held through the gates of the garden until the old man died ; and, on the day of his funeral, a shouting and yelling mob assembled.   The coffin was received with shrieks of laughter ; " mourners " were hustled ; the service was conducted in dumb show ; and, as the last prayer was uttered by the clergyman, someone grabbed the orders of knighthood which glittered on the pall.   Whilst these desecrations were in progress a member of the family entered the house and removed the family plate.   The author of the robbery was identified and visited with a long term of imprisonment.

The mother of George Canning resided in Plymouth and occupied rooms over a carpenter's shop near the Theatre in which she acted.   The premises were "notoriously haunted," but Mrs. Canning knew no fear.   On the first night of her residence she was disturbed by a perfect pandemonium : the tools became animated ; and planing, sawing, filing, chopping and hammering were in hideous progress.   Ths plucky actress seized a candle, walked downstairs, and entered the workshop.   The sounds immediately ceased, no living soul was visible, and there were no symptoms of disturbance.   The ghosts resumed their operations immediately she closed the door.   On the following night Mrs. Canning invited the landlord to accompany her to the workshop, as soon as the noises were renewed.   He was so alarmed at the experience that he ran into the street, and Mrs. Canning obtained a quieter domicile.

More romantic is the story told of the wife of a naval officer at Dock ; who, on returning from chapel one evening, entered the drawing-room and walked to the window to close it, only to shriek and fall fainting on the stairs.   When she recovered, she stated that her husband had appeared on the outside of the window, and she was positive that something serious had befallen him.   Assured that her nerves were unstrung, the fair young bride sought to forget the apparition until it was reported that the ship was missing. The sloop foundered in the Grecian Archipelago, and the date corresponded with the evening on which the widow saw the spectre. That the dread of witchery was associated with persecution is again and again in evidence.   In 1804, Deborah Tanner, under the impression that her neighbour, Anne Radden, had wished her ill, enticed the poor woman into her house, and stabbed her with a needle to see whether the blood would flow—an apparently infallible test.   Mrs. Radden instituted a persecution, but Tanner published a public apology in which she recanted all imputations, and the proceedings were withdrawn.   Tortures were inflicted upon a suspected fowl, at Hooe, in 1808.   A farmer lost a quantity of poultry, and he concluded that one of the brood, which had been laying dun-coloured eggs, had bewitched the rest.   A servant offered to break the enchantment by burning the bird alive, but her agitation prevented the fire from being effective.   The effort was renewed on three separate days, and the success with which the bird struggled from the embers confirmed the belief in its evil powers. Then the woman deliberately held it over a blazing faggot until it was roasted.   " Just retribution " followed this atrocity, for the perpetrator was seized with fits, and " expired in the greatest agonies."

No less circumstantial were the proceedings of a night-roaming ghost which thrilled the inhabitants of Dock in 1810.   The apparition was known by its saucer eyes ; and, so general was the belief in its appearances, that women and children would not leave their houses after nightfall.   The visitations were attributed to the act of a widow of a deceased waterman in too readily relinquishing her weeds at the request of a baker.   The departed husband caused the oven fire to burn blue with revenge ; uttered fearful shrieks and threw about the tins ; shook and obstructed the customers as they entered the shop ; and cursed the bread so that it was heavy and uneatable.   The apparition hovered near the house till the early hours, and leaving a suffocating atmosphere in its train, skimmed across the fields towards Stoke Church, " where it was several times seen by people proceeding to Dock Market."   A candid confession of witchcraft was made by an old crone, of the name of Redhill, living in Southside Street, who excused the presence of plunder in her house by pleading that she was afflicted with " the evil eye "—a defence that in no way lightened her punishment.   A wizard named Baker, who carried on his operations all over Devon, induced a woman who complained that she was being " overlooked " by a neighbour " to draw blood from the witch."   She did so by going to the dame's house with her daughters, and abominably maiming her.   In order to complete the charm, she wore an amulet around her neck, with directions for using powders and pills with which she was supplied : " Mrs. ———, the Jar of Mixtur is to be Mixt with half a Pint of Gen, and then a table spunfull to be taken Mornings and at Eleven O 'Clock four and Eight; and four of the Pills to be taken every Morning fasting. And the Paper of Powders to be Divided in tew parts and one part to be taken every night going to bed in a little honey.   The Paper of Arbs is to be burnt a Small bet at a time on a few Coals with a little bay and Rosemary, and while it is burning, read the two first Verses of the 68 Psalm and say the Lord's Prayer After. B. BAKER."   Abraham Hart, a no less notorious quack, was much in evidence in the Three Towns, where he was advertised as " the death-killing doctor."   He derived his custom by boldly claiming that he depended upon supernatural agencies for his cures :

With toads calcined, spells, adders bone,
I drive off plague, the gout, and stone ;
Diseases venomous I defy,
And live by what my patients die.

The hardiest ghost in Plymouth went by the name of "Screeching Dolly," and the scene of her mysterious antics was an attic in one of the picturesque old houses in High Street. Irrational movements, and the cries of a figure in white attracted nightly crowds. After some years "Screeching Dolly" vanished from the locality, and reappeared in a detached dwelling facing Notte Street. As this was used by a medical man, materialists attributed the inexplicable phenomena to the fact that the doctor had received an imbecile patient. Uproar prevailed in Devonport in 1822, when a ghost appeared in Fore Street. The thoroughfare was impassable, and the occupants of the house bolted their front and back doors. As the garrison would listen to no terms, a

blockade was instituted, and the premises would have been stormed if admission had been any longer denied. The explanation of the inscrutable was simple enough. An uncouth country girl, who had just been engaged as a servant, took advantage of a few minutes' rest to stand at the window and gaze in the street; and, as it was twilight, "the people took her for an evil spirit." To the arts of a witch were ascribed eccentricities on the part of a girl at Dock. "Impossible as it may seem," she ran up the wall to the ceiling, and remained immovable on her feet for minutes. Her clothes preserved their usual position, as though, by supernatural agency, she possessed the power of changing the centre of gravity. The other children were also influenced by "demons," for they whirled round in their chairs, like tops set in motion, and it was impossible to restrain them. A lad of ten years was afflicted in the same way, and the scientific were unable to account for his frenzies. Thus firmly rooted was

OLD HOUSES IN HIGH STREET, PLYMOUTH.

superstition so late as 1828, that one of a number of imprisoned schoolboys at Dock amused his companions by relating ghost stories, and played upon their feelings, until laughter turned to fear and terrified weeping. Thereupon the young urchin became over-wrought himself, and yelled aloud that he saw a ghost in the room. Terror was universal when the other boys returned to school, and the moment they unlocked the door, those who had been " kept in " escaped with a rush, swept the new arrivals over the stairs, and injured them in the panic. Half the town was thrown into consternation ; the credulous supplemented the story with uncanny details ; and, night after night, the schoolhouse was watched by hundreds of inhabitants.

Lawless Customs and Memorable Crimes : 1800-1899.   At the opening of the 19th century order was maintained by rounders and watchmen, armed with staves, lanterns, and rattles, and each force was controlled by its captain. The Charleys were held in light esteem ; but their occupation was hazardous, and they were the victims at times of murderous assaults. Licensed victuallers kept their houses open the greater part of the night ; and the scenes witnessed within them defied all description. Saturdays were the occasions of disgusting orgies, and tradesmen and workmen alike remained from their homes until an early hour. Tavern keepers, who permitted women of loose character to revel in lewd dances that were characteristic of an Inferno, did not scruple to send cards inviting officers of foreign ships to attend balls held in their honour "by the ladies of Devonport "—and justices of the peace spoke with horror of these wanton saturnalias. Card-playing, drinking, singing, and fighting were varied by daring robberies and outrageous practical joking even in the best conducted of these licensed establishments. Decked in gorgeous red-plaid shawls and beaver bonnets, women of a lower grade robbed Jack whilst he slept ; and were to be seen a few minutes later sitting upon the knees of redcoats. When one of the company became "dead drunk," it was the fashion to hold a kind of Irish wake over "the remains." The body was laid out with ceremony, the breast tattooed with grease and soot, and the whole enclosed in "a sawdust shroud." A "corpse" of this kind was found in the Plymouth Inn on a Sunday afternoon, surrounded by men and women in an advanced state of intoxication ; but, as drinking pots were not in evidence, the defendant was jocosely warned not to occasion the coroner any more alarms.

So mischievous were these "improper and immoral practices," that the Sunday was spent in recovering from or reviving Saturday night's drunkenness, and families were plunged in poverty and distress for the want of money thus spent in debauchery, "to the evil example and destruction of the morals of the working classes." Innkeepers transferred their licenses "without the knowledge of magistrates," and thus defied the laws for the "regulation of victuallers"; and a manifesto by the justices threatened to deprive offenders of further right to sell beer and spirits. Crimps abounded at North Corner ; men were lured into vile dens to ensure the rewards that the press-gangs offered ; sailors were drugged and robbed by flaunting harpies ; and from the purlieus of Dock Wall the victims emerged with scarcely a rag to cover them—their faces battered, not knowing the house from which they had been kicked, or awaking from their stupor in some unfamiliar alley. Property

WHEREAS I, F—— D——, wife of T—— A—— D——, of the parish of East Stone-house, in the county of Devon, did, on Monday, the 26th day of this instant June, unwarrantably and illegally defame the character of A—— B——, of Plymouth-Dock, in the same county, in the public streets of the borough of Plymouth, and charge her with improper acts ; and whereas the said A—— B—— was about to commence a prose-cution against me for such my improper conduct, but hath kindly desisted from it, on my paying to her the sum of Five Pounds, and making a public apology.

Now I do therefore hereby declare, that the said A—— B—— is perfectly innocent of the charges I made against her, that I am sorry that I should have made such charges, humbly beg her pardon for my conduct, and thank her for her lenity towards me.

Witness my hand, this 30th day of June, 1809.

and comfort were alike at the mercy of marauders. Vessels lying off the foreshore were entered for rum ; and, if the invaders met with remonstrance, they thrust their sticks down the throats of men left in charge. One interloper, who roused some sleeping sailors near Mutton Cove, was stripped, tarred, feathered, and sent ashore with his clothes tied in a bundle.

Terrorism prevailed in Chapel Street in 1808, and garden palings were torn down, scrapers pulled up and doors smashed. " W. May, No. 4, Chapel Street, promises for himself a reward of one hundred pounds if those pests of society are prosecuted to conviction. W. May, with all due respect, would ask the gentlemen of Dock whether it would not be desirable to appoint a nightly watch, as we have so many strangers and foreigners about." A number of Spaniards were escorting several lasses to their ship, when a body of bluejackets, resenting this embargo on the " fair and frail cargo," attacked and wounded several men, and carried off the women in triumph. Sacrilege, involving the plundering of the poor box, rarely resulted in arrest ; vagrants and footpads haunted the lanes and environs ; and officers often bribed the watchmen or influenced the superintendent and justices. Several young sparks of the garrison were detected red-handed in the commission of midnight outrages in Fore Street ; but their alibis satisfied the magistrates, and rewards for the discovery of the " actual offenders " were published to conciliate the community. " Respectable females " could not remain at their front doors after dark, and peace officers got drunk and noisy on their own account. The slaying of domestic pets was an unfailing source of amusement, and one officer earned the sobriquet of " The Cat-Killing Colonel." Burglary, highway-robbery, arson, the maiming of cattle, mutilation of individuals, compounding of felonies, thefts of scrapers, knockers, lamps, bell-pulls, and leaden pipes were among the commoner outrages and recreations. Farms were entered at dusk ; country lanes were infested ; and produce, sheep, cattle and horses were boldly carried off. One Sunday night a body of armed servants were protecting an outhouse on a St. Budeaux farm, when a notorious gang from Dock approached. The thieves fell upon the watchers, but one of their number was shot dead, and the rest abandoned their spoils. The jury returned a verdict of " Justifiable Homicide."

Public whipping, the stocks, and the ducking-stool were in vogue for petty offences. Annie Wilcox, a widow living in St. Aubyn Street, was indicted in 1806, at the instance of Mr. Shillabeer, an auctioneer, for being " a common scold," and she was sentenced to be dipped as " a warning to the numerous oratrices in Dock who daily raise their discordant voices to the disturbance of their peaceful and quiet neighbours." As she came up dank and dishevelled, after her third immersion, the termagant shrieked : " And now I won't hold my tongue !" Lieutenant Gibbons, of H.M.S. Alphea, earned a disastrous notoriety by taking the law into his own hands. Mrs. Bentley, the wife of a corporal of marines, was pursuing her avocation as a bumboat woman, when the officer entered upon a chaffing match. The lieutenant showed himself no less familiar than the lady with the language of " the slopseller," and the pair indulged in disgusting retorts to the delight of the sailors. In the war of words, the lieutenant was worsted ; the farce turned to tragedy ; and, irritated at being obviously routed, Gibbons sentenced Bentley as a scold to the bobbing of a mooring-buoy—a piece of brutality for which there was no palliation as the woman was about to give birth to a son. Weather and waves were so rough that she was almost lifeless when she was taken off; and this unauthorised and heartless " ducking " raised such a storm of protest that the lieutenant was tried by court-martial, and after " a full and fair investigation," dismissed from his ship. A few months subsequently, Gibbons was adjudged, at the Quarter Sessions, to pay Mrs. Bentley £500 damages. The same brutal presumption was manifested in Cawsand Bay in 1809, when a marine belonging to the

Defiance shot a waterman through the knee for approaching too close to the ship, and another marine fired at two tradesmen who were waiting permission to sell their "slops."

PLYMOUTH-DOCK ASSOCIATION,
For the Protection of the Persons and Property of Individuals from Vio'ence and Plunder.

A T a respectable Meeting of the Inhabitants of Plymouth-Dock, held at the Town-Hall, on Thursday, the 16th day of January, 1812, the following Resolutions and Articles were unanimously agreed to :—

1st, That the numerous, awful, and alarming crimes which continually occur in this kingdom, forcibly evince the propriety and necessity of the inhabitants uniting together, for the purpose of forming an Association, the objects of which shall be to prevent, as far as possible, the occurrence of crimes in this neighbourhood, at least to operate as some check, and to bring the offenders to discovery and justice, when unfortunately such atrocities may happen.

2nd, That to effectuate such views, each member willing to join this Association, shall subscribe a certain annual sum, not less than 10s. a year ; the amount of the first year's subscription to be paid on entrance ; and to be subject to such calls for extraordinaries as may be approved of by a majority of the members, at any meeting to be called for that purpose.

3rd, That if any member shall neglect to pay his subscription to the treasurer within one month after it becomes due, or if his subscription shall be in arrear at the time of his being injured, within the view of this Institution, such member shall not be entitled to any benefit from the society.

4th, That a committee of safety be chosen from this Association to manage its concerns, and that no prosecution be commenced without the sanction of the majority of such committee, who shall have a power of rejecting such cases as may be by them deemed frivolous.

5th, That any member, being criminally injured in his person or his property, do immediately apply to the solicitor, who shall report the same to the committee, and receive their instructions for adopting all proper means for the pursuing, advertising, apprehending, and prosecuting the offenders.

6th, That the society, by their committee, shall offer and pay such rewards as to them shall seem meet, for the apprehending offenders against the persons or property of the members of this Institution, viz., in cases of burglary, highway robbery, setting fire to any house, grain, hay, &c., stealing, killing, or maiming cattle, stealing money, household goods, shop goods, wearing apparel, provisions, hay, corn, implements of husbandry or trade, poultry, robbing and damaging fences, gardens, plantations, orchards, or vegetables in any enclosed ground, leaden pipes, palisados, scrapers, knockers, lamps, bell-pulls, or any similar offences, obtaining goods under false pretences, assaulting with intent to kill, rob, maim, disfigure, or do any bodily harm, buying or receiving any stolen goods, knowing the same to be stolen, compounding or compromising felonies, giving false characters to servants, and all other offences committed against the person, property, or to the injury, of any member of this Institution.

The ball went through the parcels and the conduct of the captain was freely denounced as "capricious and tyrannical." A case which was shortly afterwards heard at the Dock court showed that bumboat women were not without courage. When the Aurora was paid off the crew ran up a yellow flag as an intimation that they meant to "bilk" their creditors. In the true spirit of her profession, one, Mrs. Grafton, resolved to extort her money's worth out of the face of her chief creditor, and, in the police-court proceedings that followed, the scratches he exhibited formed the most picturesque part of the evidence. In 1812 the "Plymouth and Dock Association" was formed to protect "the lives and persons of individuals from violence and plunder." A Committee of Safety was chosen, and the executive were authorised to adopt measures for "pursuing, advertising, apprehending, and prosecuting offenders." Disorderly houses were prosecuted as "hotbeds of vice"; strangers lurking about "with an apparent intention" to violate the public security were taken into custody ; and movements of vagrants were closely watched, as their presence was the invariable signal for robbery and murder.

Criminality and immorality were never more manifest than in the years following the peace of 1815, when thousands were thrown on their own resources. It was not only among discharged soldiers and sailors that licence prevailed. Gangs of both sexes infested the town from Briton Side to Broad Street; virtuous women were cruelly molested and insulted in the purlieus of the theatre, and obscure districts witnessed most scandalous episodes of profligacy and terror. "That dreadful nuisance, Stonehouse Lane, which has so long disgraced Plymouth," excited the abhorrence of those who were not destitute of moral feeling, for it was " a mass of corruption, offensive and loathsome," and generated appalling consequences. Bullies and thieves, vagrants and youthful depredators, united in the use of signs, marks and slang language, and excited in every honest homestead "a trembling anxiety." A set of miscreants surprised Lieutenant Hayes in the Parsonage Fields, and when he drew his sword, other ruffians rushed to the assistance of the garotters. Hayes thereupon struck one of the gang, and laid his head open, and the rest found refuge in the wooded approaches to Stoke Church. As Lieutenant Pullen, of the Scylla, was descending Manadon Hill, a footpad sprang from the hedge and ordered him to stop. When the officer asked "What for?" his assailant replied : "If you don't do so, I'll fire." Mounted on a good horse, Mr. Pullen gave rein and exclaimed "Then fire, and be hanged to you." The footpad blazed away, and missed his aim. He was a young man "decently dressed in a blue coat and pantaloons," whom poverty must have driven to his dangerous occupation, for "his hand trembled very much in the act of presenting the pistol." One December night in 1820 three desperate assaults were reported. Mr. Thomas Gill, soap manufacturer, on returning from Tavistock, was accosted by a trio at the end of Compton Lane and attacked over the head with bludgeons. The robbers were rifling his pockets when his cries for help were heard, and several young men ran to his rescue. The footpads made off, and the same night Mr. Harris, a butcher of Dock, was overtaken on Manadon Hill, thrown from his horse, robbed of his purse, and left unconscious by a desperado who affected a white smock over his clothes. At dawn, two days later, the body of Captain Worsel, of the Providence Revenue cutter, was found at the bottom of a quarry near Devil's Point, chain and gold seals wrenched from his watch, and his head "dreadfully fractured." On the same night Mr. Marchant, a purser in the navy, was walking in a lane near Pennycross, and a loafer exclaimed: "You're the person I've been waiting for." Blows followed and the officer was hurled in a ditch and his pockets rifled of their contents. All these outrages were supposed to be the work of one formidable gang, whose chiefs were known to rumour, and when the ringleader was captured in a Plymouth slum, he was wearing Mr. Gill's damaged hat, with a cut corresponding to the wound that had been inflicted on his head. The chief miscreant—Bagwell—and his companions were sent to Exeter on various charges, and there they were hanged in company outside the County gaol, hundreds of people travelling by coaches from Plymouth to swell the concourse of spectators. The voice of the social reformer was first raised on this occasion in protest against the inhumanity and inexpediency of hanging for other than actual murder. The argument of the more lenient was that highwaymen would never proceed to extremes of violence but for their dread of hanging, and that they maimed the witnesses as a measure of precaution rather than from truly murderous motives. This sentiment against capital punishment was intensified when the purser of the Spartan, who lived at Stonehouse, was executed for forgery. After the widow and family had taken their distracting farewells, the former was torn from her husband's arms in a raving condition, and the children clung to his feet with affecting caresses. The condemned man committed his wife and little ones to the compassion of the public, and a substantial sum was raised for their relief.

Counterfeit coins were in general circulation in the Three Towns after Waterloo, and the manufacturers were unearthed at Cawsand. Following each distribution, a party of gipsies crossed from Stonehouse to Cawsand, and thither the peace officers one morning directed their way. A woman, who was washing a carpet in the sea, was recognised as one of the group, and, on being asked where her husband could be found, she turned to her son with the word "Tip." The lad dashed away, the officers in pursuit, and, on gaining the door of the cottage, the boy knocked and the door was unbolted. The watchman was close at his heels ; and, on forcing an entrance, found several men lacquering and polishing base coins. Milling and other implements were strewn about, counterfeit coins were piled in cupboards, and genuine guineas lay hoarded in the kitchen. The criminals were hanged at Bodmin. Jack Sheppard's cleverness by assuming clerical attire, and imposing upon the Rev. John Hawker when that famous divine visited London, so inspired the local youth to deeds of emulation that, in 1820, three Stonehouse lads set off on a predatory expedition. They stole a chisel from an outhouse at Falmouth, and were making their way to Truro when an open window at Colonel Williams's house invited their attention. Entering the room they prized a desk containing gold snuff boxes, seals, rings, and a roll of bank-notes; and, having secured this booty, they opened the stable-doors and saddled three excellent horses. On the outskirts of Bodmin they turned the animals adrift, and hired a post-chaise and drove to Dock. Here their generosity surpassed their discretion, for they made various presents to those who sheltered them, and gave the post-boy an ivory snuff-box on procuring suitable disguises. They were all transported from the scene of their exploits. A roll of bank-notes was stolen from the office of Mr. Billing, at Mutton Cove, in 1822. The premises had been forced, and crowbar and lantern were hidden under a pile of stones. Suspicion fell upon an employé; and a trap was laid by Mr. Andrews, the proprietor of the Black Horse Inn, whose house the man was in the habit of visiting. Cheques as well as notes had been abstracted from the chest, and Andrews hinted to Trimble, the suspect, that he was prepared to negociate the former. The man could not resist this appeal to his greed; and, when he brought the cheques, the watchman pounced upon him with the proofs of his guilt in his pocket. After his arrest, Trimble offered to reveal the place where the gold and notes were concealed; and, escorting the peace officers from spot to spot, surrendered several hundred pounds. Whilst they were discussing his ingenuity, and he was pretending to lead them to another rendezvous, he made a bolt in the dark and was seen no more.

The sale of wives was not necessarily associated with destitution, but it was common at this period. In December, 1822, the crier of Plymouth announced that James Brooks intended to dispose of his spouse by public auction. The lady was advertised as young and handsome, and as being likely to succeed to an inheritance of £700. Expectation was whetted by the intimation that she meant to attend the sale of her own free will, and to ride to market on horseback. A curious and babbling crowd assembled to behold "the marvel"; and, precisely at midday, in accordance with the announcement, she rode up, attended by the ostler of the "Lord Exmouth." The husband officiated as the auctioneer; and, from five shillings, the bidding advanced to ten and fifteen. As the competition grew keen on the part of the onlookers, "three pounds" was offered by the ostler. At this point two watchmen interfered, one laying hands on wife and another on husband, and the ill-matched pair were escorted to the Guildhall. When the mayor took them to task, the husband vowed that he did not think they were doing wrong. He and his wife had agreed to the sale, as they had not lived together for a long time. She was not loyal to him, since she had cohabited with others; and, as the ostler was prepared to pay twenty pounds for her—three pounds down and the balance at Christmas—and the woman was quite agreeable, he could not perceive that he had erred. There was nothing "below board" in the transaction; the auction had been "called" three times in Modbury Market; and the wife also thought that she could be sold at a public fair. The Mayor asked the woman the name of the individual who had agreed to buy her. "Mr. K.————," said she, "and I am very much annoyed to find that he has not kept his promise. But I was so determined to be loosed from Mr. Brooks that, when Mr. K———— did not attend, I asked the ostler to buy me with my own money, unless I went for more than twenty pounds." Taking into consideration the ignorance of the parties, the justices bound them over in sureties to be of good behaviour. An army sergeant in residence at Dock tracked his faithless wife to Liskeard, and there engaged the bell-man to intimate that he meant to sell her to the best bidder. Procuring a rope, he placed it around the neck of his spouse, and led her unresistingly to the Higher Cross, opposite the Market, where the offers were taking a spirited turn until the police authorities interfered. In the same year, 1823, William Hodge was indicted at Plymouth for putting up his wife to auction, and William Andrews for purchasing her. It was shown that Hodge had frequently threatened to sell his wife, that the latter had as often welcomed the prospect, and that Andrews had anticipated the transaction by living with the female defendant. At the Quarter Sessions "the auctioneer" was conspicuous by his absence ; the wife pleaded that he had frequently assaulted her ; and Andrews was condemned to prison for a brief period "by way of warning."

The population of the Three Towns learnt with intense relief of the arrest of the Robinson gang in June, 1829. For months daring robberies had been perpetrated in Plymouth, Stonehouse and Devonport ; and attempts were made on more than one of the banks. Similar exploits had been effected in London, whence the group removed west as soon as the city became too warm. For nearly a year, they baffled every effort at identification ; and the public were ever agog with suspicion. · During the absence of the landlord of the India Arms, in Cornwall Street, Devonport, one of the men made his way upstairs, and forcing a wooden box with a jemmy, abstracted a hundred guineas. Suspicion fell upon the ringleader, who had for some time frequented the bar ; and Ellis, the peace officer, quietly dogged his footsteps. He had noticed him loitering about the town with questionable characters, and, proceeding with other officers to the Richmond Inn, found Robinson and his colleagues drinking in a small tap-room. Ellis at once closed every avenue of escape ; and, boldly announcing himself, told the suspects to consider themselves under arrest. Every man was found in possession of abundant gold and silver, and a "lucky shilling" was discovered in the pocket of Robinson, which had been given to the landlord's daughter "by a hardy tar." On the morning that these "dreads of the west" were tried, the Town Hall was thronged to hear the details of the "cunning and notorious Robinson, and his clamorous and insulting harangues." Outside the Town-hall a surging crowd assembled ; and, when the gang were identified as the authors of the London robberies, the crowd attempted to storm the court-house. A servant girl at one of the Plymouth banks told how one of the prisoners made love to her, and walked out with her by appointment. On all these excursions he was ever curious as to the habits of the family, enquired if she was the only domestic employed, whether her mistress regularly attended church, and how long they remained from home. Thus they learnt that the office was always left to itself after dusk and the attempt to force the safe followed. Robinson offered 200 sovereigns to any constable who would make away with the marked shilling, and a warder overheard one man assert in an adjoining cell that, if he had known "it would come to this, he would have murdered all in the old man's house." The prisoners were sentenced to transportation for life. They worked for a few weeks on board the Captivity convict ship at Devonport, and then "took passage for the utmost boundary of this hemisphere."

Police-court humours are worthy of passing reference no less than the periodical public notices, as throwing light upon the times. The happiest instance of repartee is attributed to Dr. Bellamy, on the occasion of the trial of the son of a well-known trades-man for felony in 1828. Dr. Bellamy had testified that certain eccentricities had always characterised the youth, but that he was so far from insane that his parents intended to bring him up to the law. Counsel for the prosecution confused this answer and retorted : And so this weak, half-witted fool you advised to be brought up as an attorney ? Dr. Bellamy deprecated this misconstruction ; but added, amid an outburst from Counsel, "I did not suggest that the prisoner should be trained as an attorney, but I have no doubt, if he had been so trained, he would have made as bright a figure at the bar as yourself." Appren-

w

tices were a perennial source of trouble to employers, but they were not always to blame. A member of the fraternity who met at "The Goose and Cabbage," in Plymouth, charged one of his lads in 1830 with refusing to continue work in the absence of a fire. It seemed that the master was "a rum one" when in drink, and that he threw the irons at the youth. The jury accordingly justified the apprentice for "putting his peepers in mourning and otherwise damaging his beautiful face." In the same year, a sailor breezily described the woman, whom he charged with robbery, as "a raker-rigged vessel, with a figure-head like a moon of fifteen days' growth, and a mouth like the Bawltic." He had just been paid off from the Java when he fell in with "the frigate abaft," and they "set sail for a port in Pembroke Street," where they took in "max" until they were turned adrift. Jack explained that he had "stowed his rhino well away in his hold," and that, after he put himself "under convoy," the cruiser steered for "an unknown coast," where he "ran aground and lost the whole of his freight." The "pirate" charged the amphibious hero with being the

FEMALE IMPOSTER.

WHEREAS J——S——L——, of Fore Street, Dock, did maliciously publish a FALSE STATEMENT, under the head "FEMALE IMPOSTOR," purporting that S—— G——, of this town, milliner, had feloniously conveyed away her Goods and Chattels, with intent to defraud her said landlord of the sum of £15 15s., which said advertisement has greatly injured the character of the said S—— G——, and is likely to deprive her of the means of support; and for which she is on the eve of entering a prosecution. She therefore humbly intreats the attention of the respectable inhabitants of Plymouth-Dock and its vicinity, to a brief, but just statement of the facts, which are these,—"that the said S—— G—— did neither convey nor ever cause to be conveyed away, any part of her own property, the whole having been distrained and sold by public auction, even her wearing apparel. She only sent a bed to Mr. S——, of Plymouth, of whom it had been hired: for this only, has the character of the said S —— G—— been most grossly traduced to the very serious injury of herself and orphan child. She most earnestly, therefore, entreats the continuance of those favors which have been, and will continue to be, her utmost study to deserve."

For the present, orders will be received at No. 1, Granby Row. Dock, 13th Feb., 1812.

A LADY LOST.

SUPPOSED to have gone from her home in a fit of delirium from severe and repeated illness, about noon, on Thursday, the nineteenth of September instant. If she will return to her distracted family, she will be received with joy, and all possible tenderness and affection.

She is a very little woman, young looking, of about thirty years of age, pale complexion, small limbs, rather round-shouldered, nose rather large, dark, hazel eyes, black eye-lashes and eye-brows, long black hair, curled and twisted on her head. She had on a white striped muslin gown, a straw bonnet, with purple ribands and a white feather, and a picture of an infant, set in gold, with a gold chain round her neck.

It is supposed she has some jewels and other valuables about her which, it is requested, may be stopped, if offered by any person for sale, as it may lead to a discovery of her.

Whoever may meet with this unfortunate Lady, is earnestly entreated to secure her, and send immediate information to Mr. Haydon, Printer, No. 75, Market Place, Plymouth, who will send word to her friends.

A handsome Reward will be given, and all expenses paid.

Dated September 20, 1811.

author of all her woes; whereupon, giving a lurch, he shouted "Avast, heave astern there, and don't tell such lies." The population of Devonport were hoaxed in 1832 by the story that two live bullocks were to be removed to Exeter on the top of the coach, and an excited concourse assembled to witness the whimsical sight. After waiting an hour two young men, who were handcuffed to each other, mounted the conveyance, and the driver made arrangements to leave. A general outcry was thereupon raised by the mob: "Where are the bullocks?"; and the knight of the whip, pointing to the prisoners, knowingly replied: "There, you *asses!*" The accused Bullocks had been committed for trial for forcibly entering the Market and robbing a till. The magistrates at Devonport laughed heartily on one occasion when the watchman declared that it took eight of the officers to carry a dapper little tailor to the lock-up. Asked the reason for exerting all this force the witness mentioned that a crowd of several hundred people attempted to rescue the prisoner. "As for me," the Charley exclaimed, drawing himself to his full height, with ineffable scorn, "I should not be afraid of an army of such *things.*" A man trifled with a grave subject to his personal inconvenience in 1838. A body had been washed ashore, and men with an ambulance were sent to the Barbican to effect its removal. The officers left the apparatus on the pier, and proceeded to the other side of the pool to make enquiries. During their absence, a man who had observed their proceedings, deposited himself on the stretcher at full length; and, when the watchmen returned, he lay there motionless. The bearers supposed him to be the corpse of which they were in search, and moved towards the Townhall with measured step and suitable gravity. There a carpenter passed his rule along the body to measure it for a coffin; and, to his horror, the practical-joker sprang off the bier, floored a couple of the officers, and bolted down Looe Street. The author of the frolic was arrested, but the magistrates declined to take a serious view of his offence.

For years the churchyard at Stoke was the happy hunting ground of the Resurrectionists or Body-snatchers, who carried off corpses with impunity and sold them to doctors in need of subjects for dissection. It was a question of acute controversy in the parish as to whether the environs of the sacred edifice should not be lit as a deterrent; but this proposal was not encouraged as the hirelings of the anatomical schools would not be deterred by a few oil lamps from effecting exhumations on dark and dismal nights. It was considered by some that body-snatching was in its way a protection for the community, for Burke and his confederates had murdered to obtain the necessary subjects for wealthy employers, and the dis-interment of the recently buried was the lesser of two evils. This convenient reasoning did not diminish the horror aroused in the Three Towns with every fresh disclosure of rifled graves. Stoke Church was surrounded by a large area of ground, and, as its situation was secluded and it was protected from observation by a high wall, the dread of passing that way at night was general. Thus it afforded exceptional facilities to those who traded in human remains, and the frequency of funerals rendered it a more lucrative centre than any in the district. The arrival of body-snatching reinforcements in 1830 excited alarm and distress amongst the recently-bereaved, and suspicion fell upon the occupiers of a dwelling at Mount Pleasant, within a stone-throw of the Millbridge. The situation was doubly convenient, inasmuch as access to the churchyard and escape from it were equally easy, and boxes of remains were transferred without difficulty to barges that lay in the stream below the Deadlake. The villa at Mount Pleasant was occupied by a man named Gosling, who was understood to possess private means. He was accompanied by a number of confederates of both sexes, and these facilitated their gruesome operations by attending the funerals. They mingled with the mourners and sympathised with them in their grief; and expressed solicitude as to the age of the deceased and causes of death, so that the value of the bodies for anatomical purposes might be ascertained in advance. At night, when all was dark and quiet, the

PETITION.

"To the Right Honourable the Lords Spiritual and Temporal in Parliament assembled.

"The humble petition of the members of the Plymouth Medical Society.

"We, the undersigned, Physicians and Surgeons, Members of the Plymouth Medical Society, respectfully solicit the attention of your Lordships to the difficulties attendant upon the due and necessary study of *Anatomy*, and the great importance of giving a legislative authority to the cultivation of that science.

"The knowledge of the different parts of the human body is essential to the physician or the surgeon, who is called upon to treat the diseases to which it is liable. The want of this knowledge inevitably leads to erroneous practice, and is punishable by the same code which forbids the attainment of it.

"In other countries, the dissection of the dead, so necessary to the well-being of the living, is permitted and protected; and is actually prosecuted, without shocking any existing prejudice, or violating the sanctuaries of the dead.

"It follows either that the professional gentleman of this kingdom must be contended with a very inferior medical education, or that they must resort to the Continent to obtain that information which is denied to them by the laws of Great Britain.

"Your petitioners, therefore, earnestly and respectfully implore the earliest and most serious consideration of this important subject by your Lordships, and the adoption of such measures as your Lordships, in your wisdom, may deem fit.

"And your petitioners will ever pray."
Plymouth, May, 1827.

gang stole forth, armed with shovels and equipped with sacks, and cleared away the layers of earth, which they arranged with the grave diggers should not be too thick. Forcing open the coffins they determined whether the corpse was of use ; and, if it was too decomposed, they contented themselves with drawing the teeth—not the least lucrative branch of their business. Whenever decomposition set in rapidly after removal they buried the bodies in their back garden, and restored them to the cemetery as soon as the coast was clear. The attention of a servant girl who lived in the district was first excited by the constant burning of lights in the neighbourhood. Setting her own watch, she observed in the early morn mysterious movements of shadowy figures, and saw men enter the stable doors carrying sacks on their shoulders. Her misgivings increased when packing-cases were periodically taken away in carts to the creek below, and she mentioned to her master what she had noticed. Thus the police were brought acquainted with the circumstances, and they lay in wait in the burial ground at the close of one day, upon which Gosling had administered many consolations to mourners at various funerals. At midnight the miscreants arrived ; and, after digging and shovelling for several minutes, struck a coffin, forced off the top, removed the corpse and put it in a sack. They then sent their scout to see that no one was about, hoisted the body over the wall, and made towards Mount Pleasant. Hesitating to surprise this stronghold with an inadequate force, the officers returned to Devonport ; and, accompanied by a body of watchmen and special constables, surrounded the building where the criminals were now soundly sleeping. Scaling the wall by means of a ladder, the invaders proceeded in their stockings to the various bedrooms, and four men and two women were gagged and pinioned before concerted resistance was possible. In the kitchen were two sacks, one containing the body of a girl of eighteen, and the other the remains of a man of advanced years. The cupboards were stocked with extracted teeth, and implements of dentistry revealed the revolting business of the inmates. When it was noised in Devonport that a confederacy of these marauders had been captured, there was a distracting ferment, and the churchyard was filled with relatives of the recently buried. Grave after grave was opened, and dishevelled shrouds were the chief remaining evidence of actual burial. The misery of the bereaved was inexpressible, and the mutilation of several bodies added to the universal dismay. Gosling and his confederates admitted their guilt and revelled in their gruesome reminiscences ; grimly recalling one sacrilegious night, when, in a drunken quarrel, they fought by an open grave, under the shadow of the church. After they were transported friends and relatives watched the gravesides by turns, and more than one man who did duty in this dreary way was pounced upon under the impression that he belonged to a new importation. Lieutenant Dewes, of the 89th Regiment, was compelled to compensate a tradesman whom he savagely assaulted in the belief that he was a Burkite ; and another individual, who laid a wager that he would enter the churchyard after midnight, was locked up on suspicion of being a Resurrectionist.

A powerful and determined set of men, ten in number, were landed in chains at Plymouth in 1845, and put upon their trial for mutiny and murder on the high seas. The Wasp had overhauled the Felicitude, a suspicious-looking schooner, which turned out to be a slaver ; and a young midshipman, Mr. Palmer, was put in charge with a party of sailors. He was admonished to be specially vigilant ; but the advice did not avert the catastrophe, for the Brazilians rose in the night ; and, overwhelming the Englishmen, hacked their bodies and threw them overboard. Just as they had gained the vessel and were making-off with her, the Star brig appeared upon the scene, and the blood-coursed decks supplied evidence of a fearful conflict. The Felicitude was taken into Plymouth Sound ; and, before the local magistrates, horrible stories were told by negroes, admitted as Queen's evidence, of toasts drunk in the blood of flayed victims. Several of the malefactors were hanged at Exeter. In 1856 the Runnymead lay in the Sound with a contingent of convicts and pensioners, who were proceeding as colonists to the Swan River settlement. Between Sergeant-Major Robinson, who was in charge of the latter, and a pensioner named Nevin, a quarrel arose. Fixing a cap on his firelock, Nevin fired point blank at the officer; and the ball, shattering the stock of the musket, and entering his breast, caused instantaneous death. The wives and children of the disputants were spectators of the tragedy, and piteously bemoaned the anguish thus mutually entailed. Nevin was sent for trial and executed. A similar tragedy occurred at Millbay Barracks in 1859, when Colour-Sergeant Jones, of the 61st Regiment, reproved Private Hacked for giving shelter to a pensioner. Hacked, who was suffering from delirium tremens, shot him on the spot, and his state of mind did not save him from the gallows. No little mystery surrounded the crime of Private Taylor, of the 57th Regiment, who assassinated Corporal Skullin in 1869. Taylor was doing punishment drill in the Raglan Barracks, when Skullin remonstrated with him for carrying an empty knapsack. He left in order to fill it; but, suddenly returning to the parade ground, levelled his rifle with military precision, and lodged a bullet in Skullin's brain. Taylor was convicted of the murder and executed in due course.

The settlement at Dartmoor, so long used for the confinement of prisoners-of-war, remained " a silent pile," until it occurred to the Home-office during the Russian war that it was an unnecessary expense to deport convicts to distant climes. The pretty dream of occupying the unemployed in reclaiming Dartmoor had failed, and now it was argued that prison labour might be directed to this end. At the outset discipline was lax, owing to the indiscriminate herding of convicts: the settlement was described as little other than a training school for blackguards and robbers ; and at night the noise in the association room resembled that of a low tap-room. In one corner an old hand instructed a youngster to excel in puglistic encounters ; in a quiet recess a greenhorn was taught a few lightfingered experiments ; and a third learnt the approved mode of garrotting. Adventures in house-breaking and pocket-picking were related each night to admiring groups, and the scientific use of the life-preserver or bludgeon on presumptuous policemen was indicated with illustrations. Experience was no less debasing on the moor ; and, as the men were scattered about the farm, and officers were limited, it was not uncommon for two ruffians to strip to the waist and fight a pitched battle for over an hour. They had their backers, betting in tobacco went on briskly, and mob-law was so strong that the warders hesitated to interfere. A stalwart officer named Rose, who informed upon one turbulent ruffian, had his skull laid open with a spade, and he was invalided from the service insane. The author of this offence was spirited away whilst the rest of the convicts were at church, lest his rescue should be attempted by the general body. Another warder named Mason was struck from behind and nearly killed, but the officers so dreaded to make an example that the assailant was let off with two dozen lashes.

One Sunday in December, 1863, as the convicts were proceeding to the prison chapel, a notorious burglar called on his fellows to " down the screws," and he accompanied his attack on the startled warders with a frightful volley of imprecations. He was arrested on the spot, whereupon 200 prisoners rushed to his rescue, and, in the tumult, " the yells were truly demoniacal." Armed warders, and civil guards with fixed bayonets, ran to the scene, and, as the remonstrances of Captain Best were unavailing, the order to charge was given. The mutineers dispersed and the ringleaders were punished with solitary confinement. Shortly afterwards the governor was felled to the ground ; and, encouraged by this success, other convicts rallied to the attack until reinforcements enabled the guard to withstand them. So little effect had these ferocious onslaughts that cell doors were left open on Christmas Day in order that the convicts might amuse themselves ; and they sang and danced, cheered and groaned, in the halls and wards.   Much of this demoralisation was due to the custom of allowing parties from Plymouth to contemplate a visit to Princetown prisons as an indispensable feature of their programme.   The convicts were thus supplied with tobacco and other contraband articles; and, when the scandal could no longer be tolerated, a system of solitude and monotony replaced the former license : visitors were not permitted to enter the establishment without the authority of the Secretary of State, and the dietary scale was modified.   The most sagacious reform resulted in a revised classification of prisoners that did not allow novices in crime to consort with the depraved and hardened, and first-timers were in this way given a chance of recovering their manhood.   Dark stories of criminality within the settlement ceased to be of common report, and murderous conflicts were no longer of weekly occurrence.

Attempts at escape have usually been nipped in the bud.   With their powerful glasses the officials commanded the long lines of valleys and usually detected moving or uniformed objects without difficulty.   Thus there is a tradition that only in one case has a convict ever made his way from the moor, and then with the connivance of a farmer's wife, who was so touched by compassion that she dressed him to represent her own mother.   On one occasion five men left their coats behind a haystack, and asked permission to fetch them as the rain was falling.   By the time the officer in charge was aware of their design, they had bounded over the wall and were nowhere to be seen.   Having been tracked to a neighbouring cow-shed they surrendered quietly.   One tragic attempt to clear took place in 1870, after smouldering discontent amongst the quarrymen, which was attributed to the harshness of the chief warder.   Arrangements for an extensive rising were perfected, and the agreed-on signal was the overpowering of the guard.   The conspiracy was betrayed to the governor, and the officers pursued their usual routine until the preconcerted loud-talking began.   Walking into the midst of the gang, the chief warder bade them cease their noise, and the ringleader replied by striking him upon the head with his crowbar.   For the moment, the officer was stunned ; but, at the second aim, he drew sword and confronted his assailant.   Around the ridges of the quarry the warders and guards followed the exciting scene with arms loaded and pointed at the ready.   Preserving his presence of mind, and perceiving that the convicts were partially cowed, the chief warder ordered them to return to prison.   Sullenly they formed into squad, and the officers closed in and surrounded the insubordinates.   As they were passing through the gate, the chief warder's assailant exclaimed : " Now, then, if you are men, follow me," and dashing from the ranks with a fellow convict, he ran along the highway like a harried hare.   The chief warder shouted to the guard " Ready, present—fire !"   The two men dropped before the volley : the instigator of the outbreak riddled with bullets.   " Forgive me," he said, and expired.   The second man escaped with his life, but his legs bore to the grave the scars of his adventure.

The visit of a professional gang of burglars to Plymouth, in 1872, resulted in several depredations, of which the spoiling of a house in Portland square was the most ambitious.   Mr. Thomas Pollard, the occupant, left his residence at six o'clock on Sunday evening, and immediately afterwards the door was forced by a jemmy, and a chest-of-drawers plundered of valuable contents, including a cash-box containing notes and gold, and silver plate and jewellery to the value of £2,000.   Suspicion fell upon five men, with a Birmingham accent, who had taken lodgings in different parts of the town.   They had been seen in one another's company on various occasions: some of them in a garden at Stoke, where they were evidently meditating another forcible entrance.   When the arrangements of the Plymouth police were ripe, the prisoners were entrapped under one roof, dining off a boiled leg of mutton ; and, although they offered a deal of resistance, they were overpowered, and taken in cabs to the police station.   On the way, one of the men, Jones, butted a detective in the face; another, Fox, drew a knife and endeavoured to stab a second officer ; and a third, Palmer, tried to gouge a constable with his finger. In the excitement of the struggle he put it in his mouth and withdrew it in a lacerated condition. A portmanteau which was seized in the room of the captured men contained jemmies, centre-bits, saws, screw-drivers, chisels, dark lanterns, goloshes, and other paraphernalia ; and each of the men had a purse of sovereigns—the apparent proceeds of "the swag." Alibis were establised in two cases, but the other prisoners were sentenced to penal servitude. Audacious swindling was perpetrated in 1899 by the Western Insurance Society, which was promoted by a financing genius—"Major Walford"—who formed a circle of congenial friends at the various hotel bars. Under the guise of protecting shipping against disasters afloat, and tradesmen against losses by fire, a large capital was subscribed ; tons of illustrated literature were circulated ; a steam fire-engine was presented to the Plymouth municipality and accepted ; a complimentary dinner was given to the Mayor by the directors; and each Councillor was presented with a substantial gold medal in honour of the event. When the crash was imminent, the Major decamped and left a local dupe to suffer penal servitude. The Corporation retained the engine, but the elaborate tokens ceased to hang upon watch chains, and found their way to the local melting pots.

Christmas Eve, 1897, was waning when three convicts at Dartmoor made a dash for liberty under cover of a friendly fog. They were working at the rear of the prison, on the Blackabrook Farm, with some sixty other prisoners, when Ralph Goodwin, William Carter and William Martin conceived the expedient of bolting. Goodwin was entrusted with the signal ; and, on the spur of the moment, the trio dug their fingers in the earth, flung the soil in the face of the guards, and disappeared in the mist. The chief warder exclaimed "Cover them"; then the words "Down with them" were uttered ; and the rifles rang out. As Goodwin cleared the hedge and held to the bush with both hands, before dropping to the bottom, he heard the whizz of a bullet and the cry of a wounded man. This came from Carter, a desperado, who admitted to Goodwin that he took part in the Lewisham masked burglary, which had resulted in the murder of an aged gentleman. He fell on the moor with a shot in his heart, and was quite dead when picked up. Martin, the third man, stood at bay under a tree ; and, on threatening the warder with a piece of granite, was felled by a bludgeon and carried unconscious to his cells. In the meantime Goodwin fled like a hare for miles through torrents of rain, stopping now and again to draw breath, and often plunging to his knees in the bog. At daybreak, the fugitive observed the outlines of houses in the distance, and moved towards them under the impression that he had reached Plymouth. He found to his dismay that he had simply been running around the prison in a circle and that he was within reach of any gun from the posts of observation. Afraid to surrender, lest he might be shot, Goodwin climbed up one side of a tor and rolled down the other ; and then scudded across country : leaping hedges, fording rivers, and clearing brambles. As the day declined he followed the course of the moon, so that he might reach Plymouth ; and, on reaching Post Bridge, broke into two houses to obtain food and clothing. Taking to the moors again, he walked on through the night, until, on the outskirts of Tavistock, he was perishing of cold and hunger. Entering another house, he acquired the remains of a Christmas turkey and resumed his way invigorated. At last he struck the railway, making occasional detours for refreshment and clothing, and in order to thwart his pursuers. This he succeeded in doing ; but gave himself away at the end of several days' chase, by bolting from a policeman, who did not suspect his identity until he made a guilty rush under the impression that he was being followed. Exhausted and foot-sore the author of these remarkable adventures fell to the ground near Camel's Head, and was soon restored to the settlement to finish his term.

CHAPTER XII.—STAGE AND MUSIC.

Plymouth and Dock Theatres: Scenes and Episodes: 1728-1899. In the early days of the stage in Plymouth, strolling players were regarded as dangerous scamps, and they were controlled by drastic regulations. During 1728 the town was suffering acutely from peace depression; vacant premises rapidly multiplied; and the cost of maintaining the paupers became almost intolerable. Under these circumstances it was necessary to discourage all tendencies "to vice and immorality," and the freemen rulers of the Hospital of the Poor's Portion adopted an "inviolable resolution" that, "in case players or actors of inter-ludes, who by statute law are declared rogues and vagabonds, shall presume to act within the borough of Plymouth," they should be "kept in prison to hard labour till the further pleasure of this Corporation herein ; and the Governor and his brother members will indemnifie and defend such constables as may be mulcted or prosecuted for doing their duty." These repressive measures were relaxed when renewed hostilities brought a return of prosperity, and a structure was improvised in Broad Hoe Lane (Hoegate Street), where concerts and dramas were presented. "Nothing under the full price" was ever taken at the doors, and a lurid allegorical scene was drawn up "precisely at half an hour after six o'clock." In order to cheat the act which prohibited stage plays without express legislative sanction, the performance was advertised as a concert ; and, during the interval, standard works were performed "gratis," such as "The Tempest, or Enchanted Island," with "the original musick, songs, dances, machinery and decorations proper to the enter-tainment." A travelling company of comedians who gave "The Beaux Stratagem" in 1749 were said to constitute the famous "Brandy Company," run by Mr. Kennedy, and it was so described because the majority drank themselves to death. In 1758, the makeshift in Broad Hoe Lane was abandoned; and Arthur, a light comedian of eminence, converted three partly-finished houses opposite Frankfort Gate. To economise time, his company performed three nights without a roof—an expedient which was welcomed, as the June evenings were so sultry. On the opening night, £38 was taken at the door ; and, during the ensuing ten weeks, the total reached £1,800. The audiences soon asserted a critical demeanour, and vehemently vented their disappointment in February, 1759, when "Jane Shore" was announced in a playbill of some vaunt :

> To-night, if you have brought your good old taste,
> We'll treat you with a downright English feast ;
> A tale which long since told in humble wise
> Hath never failed of melting eyes !

A poetic prologue was spoken by Mr. Pittard ; a comic dance was rendered by Signora Tereza Calvi and Signor Balbi, in the respective roles of Italian peasant and harlequin ; and there was a farce "Miss In Her Teens," in which an epilogue was delivered on "Everybody, to be Spoken by Somebody in the Character of Nobody." Although there was a hornpipe at the finish, the artistes did not please; and "to make amends for past favours" Pittard travelled to Launceston, and engaged some of the best actors on tour in that town. "I am quite confident that everything attempted next Thursday night will be to the satisfaction of the audience, in playing, dancing and singing. If not, I don't

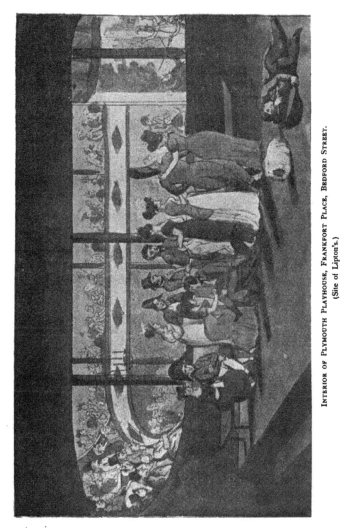

INTERIOR OF PLYMOUTH PLAYHOUSE, FRANKFORT PLACE, BEDFORD STREET.

(Site of Lipton's.)

(*From the original Water Colour by Rowlandson.*)

desire to receive any further favours from my former friends." As a further exercise of the conciliatory arts, Pittard made an earnest appeal for "encouragement from the generous and humane." Arthur disposed of his interest to Madame Deville, an eminent danseuse who had enchanted his patrons, and she appointed Mr. Mattocks as her manager. The latter was taken into partnership in 1761, and Andrew Kerly acquired the remainder of Deville's interest. "'Tis hoped," the playbills ran, "that no gentleman will take it amiss that he cannot possibly be admitted behind the scenes."

The theatre at Frankfort Gate was structurally unreliable, and the beam of the gallery oscillated on the occasion of a benefit given to Shuter. Two uprights were requisitioned before the play proceeded, and these remained in the same position for several years. Of one of the stock actors, Packer, it was suggested that he never moved audiences either to smiles or tears, but could always be depended upon to dress neatly and remember his lines. Mr. Manley next addressed himself with energy to the proprietary; and, in 1770, divided responsibility with Mr. Foote, a butcher of Exeter, and Mr. Wolfe, a gentleman of Pinhoe. This inharmonious association continued till 1784, when Jefferson joined Wolfe and Mr. Hunn, a Plymouth draper, was induced to acquire a share. He sought to escape by sacrificing his deposit, but Wolfe issued a writ and threw him into prison, and refused to release him until the purchase money was paid in full.

Often the plays performed were of the highest class; and, on one occasion, Mrs. Bradshaw delivered "An Address to the Ladies and Gentlemen of Plymouth and Dock, written by David Garrick, Esq." The fair artiste met with a melancholy end, accelerated by the treatment she received in the course of this performance. There was some local scandal because she presented as her adopted daughter her own child, and she was so loudly hissed that she was seized with fits and died insane. Stage morality did not touch high-water mark, and the Plymouth Theatre was said to be the only one in England in which "Grace" and "Virtue" were to be found associated. These were the names rather than characteristics of the performers; and Bernard, who obtained an act to perform dramas at Plymouth, introduced a fresh wife at the commencement of each season. In answer to one blank look of amazement, he whispered: "Don't be angry, my dear sir, this is the real Mrs. Bernard, upon my soul!" There was no lack of advertising audacity either; and Mrs. Sumbell, on the occasion of George III.'s visit in 1789, in the resolve to attract his attention as the Royal Family were rowed to Mount Edgcumbe, sat astride a gun on the deck of a yacht, and declaimed "God Save the King" in clarion-like notes, amid the cheers of the spectators.

Mr. Barrett joined Bernard, and Mrs. Siddons was amongst the "stars" who travelled westward. In 1793, a dispute occurred between the partners; and Barrett built a wooden structure in an open space in George Street. To this he gave the name of the "New Theatre," to distinguish it from the "Old Theatre," by which the other establishment was already known. As Dock was separately catered for, this attempt to run two houses was foredoomed; and, tired of the competition, Bernard opened three times a week at Dock, and Barrett the alternate nights at Frankfort Place. Local favourites never scrupled to take grave familiarities with the programme, and occasioned distinguished artistes distressful episodes. Bernard was a chartered offender; and, when John Kemble called upon him to play the pipes, the scapegrace cried out: "Well, if I must, I must," and rendered "'The Black Joke'—a joke much too black for the occasion." "The Farthing Rushlight" was another suggestive song as noisily in demand, and Incledon—"allow'd to be the first singer in the Three Kingdoms"—was not permitted to resume until Bernard had rendered it. A similar disturbance was organised upon Incledon's second visit in 1804, when the local "want of musical taste" was evinced in an insistent demand that Bernard should sing "that truly ridiculous and unmeaning song, 'Barney Leave the Girls Alone!'" Incledon was compelled to allow Bernard to "wait upon the audience at the end of the first act." The proprietary passed into the hands of Mr. Freeman, who bestowed on the theatre the name of "Royal." On what authority none professed to know: "However, it's a good travelling name, and avoids many troublesome enquiries." Dock Theatre was next closed to stop disastrous competition. The device did not make the two ends meet, and Hughes arranged to run at Dock with Plymouth companies. The establishment speedily developed licentious features, with sailors drinking from their bottles of rum, and passing the liquor to the dissolute women who were penned apart in the hope that they would thus be amenable to some decency. The seamen threw themselves into the spirit of the plays with deadly earnestness; and, during one performance of "Othello," a remarkable scene was witnessed. Rage and sympathy filled every gallant tar. "Is the black brute allowed to cut her life lines?" one asked his friend with bated breath; and, when Desdemona was seized by the throat as she lay in bed, his companion shouted "I'm —— if I can stand it any longer." Throwing himself over the side of the gallery, he called upon his companions to rush to the rescue, and in a minute Desdemona was torn from the grasp of the Moor. Othello bolted into the street, and rushed in terror through the back lanes to his home—dagger in hand, and with war-paint untouched. In the pit respectable tradesmen were the victims of insulting exclamations and showers of nuts and orange peel; and, although the magistrates asserted the right of attending to preserve the peace, "not only for themselves but their friends," they were as impotent as the manager to stop the debauchery in which sailors, soldiers and civilians indulged. Freeman then adopted the name of Foote; and, selling his interest to Messrs. Smith and Winson for six hundred guineas, purchased a commission in the army. Improvements were freely effected; the proscenium was adorned in a "light and elegant manner"; and a career of renewed enterprise was apparently opened. The dimensions of the Plymouth stage prevented spectacular efforts from being properly represented, but the melodrama of "Valentine and Orson" was produced in a style "far superior to anything hitherto witnessed in the town." Still the higher class performances were never remunerative, because the local patrons "preferred buffoonery to the chastest acting." Audience and actors were annoyed by half-priced visitors; and, at Dock, the rioters carried their revelries to a disgusting extent. The invariable prelude to turbulent scenes was the payment of a lucky crew, and a contemporary observer thus describes a typical night :

> The Actors sent to beg, 'that they
> 'Would deign to patronize a Play ;
> 'Since 'twas designed, (with their consent)
> 'To celebrate the late event—
> 'To represent the Achievement high,
> 'An Interlude was cut and dry ;
> 'And an Occasional Address,
> 'All, for the purpose writ express.'—
>
> The Daggerwood's request was granted ;
> For 'twas just what the Reefers wanted.
> ——The Day arrived—In gallant style
> The Tars rolled on in rank and file,
> With Fiddles squeaking loud before them,
> And Colours flying proudly o'er them.
> Their very fame insured a house,
> And filled choke full old Plymouth Play House ;

For the BENEFIT of
Mr. FOLLETT, and Mr. MORGAN.
By His Majesty's Servants, at the

Theatre, Frankfort-Gate,

On MONDAY, Sept. 2, 1771, will be prefented a
Comedy called The
RECRUITING OFFICER.
Capt. Plume by Mr. Jefferson, Juftice Ballance by
Mr. Foote, Worthy by Mr. Wolfe, Sergeant Kite
by Mr. Follett.
Melinda by Mifs Sherry, Rofe by Mifs Bromwich,
Lucy by Mrs. Bradshaw, and Sylvia by Mifs
Burton.
End of Act 2d. [by Defire] *the Farmer's Blunder,*
By Mr. Follett.
End of Act 3d. a Song by Mr. Follett.
End of Act 4th., *Mr. Shuter's Drunken Man,*
By Mr. Morgan.
Between the Play and Farce, an Interlude of
Singing, called
TRUE BLUE:
Or, The Contest of Love and Glory.
(As it was performed upwards of 60 Nights, at the
Theatre Covent-Garden, with additional
Songs by Mr. Arnold).
Trueblue by Mr. Gaudry, Lieut. Dreadnought, Mr.
Humphries; Careful by Mr. Follett, Nancy by
Mrs. Manning.
In which will be introduced the Sailor's Pageant,
the Hornpipe by Mafter Cape.
To which will be added a Farce. called
THE MAYOR OF GARRETT.
Major Sturgeon by Mr. Baddeley, Sir Jacob Jollup
by Mr. Morgan, Bruin by Mr. Foote, Crifpin
Heeltap by Mr. Brunsdon, Lint by Mr.
Humphries, Simon Snuffie by Mr. Bainbridge,
and Jerry Sneak by Mr. Follett, Mrs. Bruin by
Mifs Bromwich, and Mrs. Sneak by Mifs
Burton.
*To Conclude with a Country Dance by the
Characters.*

For the BENEFIT of MRS. MANNING.
By His Majesty's Servants, at the

Theatre, Frankfort-Gate,

On FRIDAY, Sept. 6, 1771, will be prefented a
Comedy called
THE BEGGAR'S OPERA,
Capt. Mackheath by Mr. Gaudry, Locket by Mr.
Morgan, Mat o' th' Mint Mr. Humphries, Ben
Budge by Mr. Brunsdon. Filch by Mr. Follett,
Niming Ned Mr. Bainbridge, Wat Dreary Mr.
Oborne, Crook Finger'd Jack Mr. Wolfe, Drawer
by Mafter Cape, and Peachum by Mr. Baddeley,
Lucy by Mrs. Jefferson, Mrs. Peachum by Mifs
Burton, Dina Trapes by Mrs. Bradshaw, Sucky
Tawdry by Mifs Sherry, Mrs. Coaxer by Mrs.
Egan, Jenny Diver by Mifs Bromwoich, and
Polly by Mrs. Manning,
*To Conclude with a Country Dance by the
Characters.*
In Act 3rd. a HORNPIPE by Mafter CAPE.
Between the Play and Farce, an Interlude of
Singing, called
TRUE BLUE:
Or, the Contest of Love and Glory.
To which will be added a FARCE, called
HIGH LIFE BELOW STAIRS.
Lovel by Mr. Jefferson, Freeman by Mr. Morgan,
Freeman by Mr. Morgan, Lord Duke by Mr.
Follett, Coachman by Mr. Wolfe, Robert by Mr.
Bainbridge, Sir Harry by Mr. Brunsdon, Kingfton
by Mafter Cape, Tom by Mr. Oborne, and
Philip by Mr. Baddeley, Lady Charlotte (with a
Song in Character) by Mrs. Jefferson, Lady Babb
by Mifs Bromwoich, Cook by Mrs. Bradshaw,
Cloe by Mrs. Manning, and Kitty by Mifs Burton.
In Act 2d. a Mock Minuet, by Sir Harry and
Mrs. Kitty.
'Tis hop'd no Gentleman will take it amifs that he
cannot poffibly be admitted behind the Scenes.
To begin at 7 o'clock.
Vivante et Rex Regina.

At the
Theatre, Frankfort-Gate,

On TUESDAY, Sept. 17, 1771, will be performed
The Tragedy of
GEORGE BARNWELL.
*Learn to be Wife from others Harm,
And you shall do full Well.* Lillo.
Barnwell by Mr. JEFFERSON,
Thoroughgood by Mr. GAUDRY,
Uncle by Mr. FOOTE, Blunt by Mr. MORGAN,
And Trueman by Mr. FLEETWOOD.
Maria by Mifs BURTON, Lucy by Mifs BROM-
WOICH, And Millwood by Mrs. JEFFERSON.
To which will be added an Entertainment, called
THE JUBILEE.
The Principal Characters,
By Mr. MORGAN, Mr. AICKIN, Mr. FOOTE,
Mr. JEFFERSON, Mr. WOLFE, Mr. OBORNE,
Mr. WHITTAKER, Mr. BAINBRIDGE,
Mr. BADDELEY, Mr. BRUNSDON,
Mafter CAPE.
Mrs. BRADSHAW, Mifs BURTON, Mifs
SHERRY, Mifs BROMWICH, and Mrs. EGAN.
The Vocal parts,
By Mr. GAUDRY, Mr. HUMPHRIES,
Mr. FLEETWOOD, Mrs. JEFFERSON, and
Mrs. MANNING.
Wanted, an Apprentice, to learn the Art and
Mystery of Printing.

For the BENEFIT of MISS BROWNE.
Theatre, Plymouth.

On WEDNESDAY, May the 20th, 1795, by the
Young Gentlemen of the Grammar School, will be
prefented a new Tragedy, performed but once, called
VIRGINIA;
Or, The Fall of the Decemvirs.
Appius, Mafter GREGG; Icilius, Mafter WILLS;
Claudius, Mafter WHITE; Numitor, Mafter
NASH; Lucius, Mafter FUGE; Publius, Mafter
ST. AUBYN; Lictor. Mafter DUNSTERVILLE;
Numa, Mafter MORICE; and Virginius, Mafter
SHULDHAM. Virginia, Mifs BROWNE.
GUARDS, &c.
*An Orcafional Prologue to be Spoken by Mafter
Shuldham.*
To which will be added a MASQUE, called
ALFRED.
Altered from THOMPSON.
Alfred, Mafter SHULDHAM; Earl of Devon,
Mafter FUGE; Earl of Kent, Mafter NASH;
Corin, Mafter WHITE; Sylvius, Master WILLS;
Hermit, Mafter GREGG; Eltruda, Mifs BROWNE.
SOLDIERS, &c.
The Whole to Conclude with
*An Occasional New Epilogue, to be Spoken by Mifs
Browne.*

HAYDON, CLARENCE PRESS, PLYMOUTH.

THEATRE ROYAL, PLYMOUTH.

FOR THE BENEFIT OF MR. BENNETT.

ON MONDAY, OCTOBER, 28, 1808, will be performed a MELO-DRAMA, in three acts (never performed here), called the
LADY OF THE ROCK,
With new Scenery, Music, Machinery, Dresses, and Decorations.

The Music selected and composed by Mr. J. Bowden ; the Machinery by Mr. Richards ; and the new Scenery painted by Mr. Bennett.

In the course of the evening, Mr. Bennett will sing the following favourite SONGS
(for the last time) .—
THE BOLD DRAGOON.
A NEW COMIC SONG, CALLED
PAUDIEN O'RAFFERTY;
And Long Life to the Petticoat.

An admired COMIC OPERA (in two acts), called
THE BANDITTI;
or, CASTLE OF ANDALUSIA.

The whole to conclude with a new Ballet Dance (composed by Mr. Bennett), called
THE SAILOR'S WEDDING.

Tickets to be had as usual, and of Mr. Bennett, at Mr. Tarret's, No. 6, Frankfort Street, Plymouth.

Dock Theatre.

By desire of the Officers and Gentlemen of His Majesty's Dock-Yard.

FOR THE BENEFIT OF MR. SANDFORD.

ON TUESDAY next, October the 9th, will be presented the favourite Comedy of
LAUGH WHEN YOU CAN ;
OR, THE RIVAL PHILOSOPHERS.

Gossamer, Mr. Sandford ; Delville, Mr. Crookseley ; Mortimer, Mr. Wilson ; Sambo, Mr. Langhorne ; Bonus, Mr. Andrews ; Mrs. Mortimer, Mrs. Noble ; Emily, Miss Foote.

End of the Play, a Comic Epilogue, called
"EVERYONE'S FAULT," by Mr. SANDFORD,
A Comic Song by Mr. Whitfeld.
DRYDEN'S ODE ON ST. CECILIA'S DAY ;
Or, the Feast of Alexander,
WILL BE RECITED BY MR. SANDFORD.

To Conclude with the Pantomime of
HARLEQUIN PILGRIM,
Or, the REGIONS OF FANCY.

Harlequin, Mr. Kendall ; Clown, Mr. Langhorne ; Columbine (with a favourite Pas Seul), Mrs. Noble.

Tickets to be had of Mr. SANDFORD, 41, St. Aubyn Street, where Places in the Boxes may be taken.

Dock Theatre.

The Last THREE NIGHTS of Mr. MUNDEN,
THE FIRST COMEDIAN ON THE ENGLISH STAGE.

THIS present SATURDAY, July 21st, 1810, will be performed the Comedy of
SPEED THE PLOUGH,
To which will be added the Farce of
THE AGREEABLE SURPRISE.
Sir Abel Handy and Lingo by Mr. MUNDEN.

On TUESDAY, July 24th (by very particular desire), the Comedy of
THE BIRTH-DAY.
Captain Bertram, Mr. MUNDEN,
And Emma Bertram by Miss FOOTE, being her first appearance on this Stage ;
With the FARCE of The FARMER.
Jemmy Jumps, Mr. MUNDEN.

On THURSDAY, July 26th, the Comedy of
THE BUSY BODY,
With the Farce of SPRIGS of LAUREL.
Sir Francis Gripe and Nipperkin (with a variety of New Comic Songs), by Mr. MUNDEN,
BEING FOR HIS BENEFIT.

And positively the last night of his performing here.

To prevent confusion and disappointment, early applications are requested for places in the Boxes, on the above nights, particularly for Mr. MUNDEN's Benefit.

Dock Theatre.

Miss Duncan's last Night but Two.

This PRESENT EVENING, June 25, 1810.
THE COMEDY OF
THE BELLE'S STRATAGEM.
Doricourt, Mr. Farren ; Sir George, Mr. Woodley ; Hardy, Mr. White ; Villers, Mr. Hughes ;
Flutter, Mr. Crisp ;
Lady Frances, Mrs. Cummins ;
Mrs. Racket, Mrs. Hughes ;
Letitia Hardy (with Songs), Miss DUNCAN.
After which, the Farce of
THE SULTAN.
The Sultan, Mr. Higgans ; Osmyn, Mr. Crisp ;
Roxalana, Miss DUNCAN ;
Ismena (with Songs), Mrs. Hughes.

On Monday, at the Theatre Royal, Plymouth,
"The Provok'd Husband," and "Wedding-Day."
MISS DUNCAN'S LAST NIGHT BUT ONE.
On TUESDAY, June 28th,
THE COMEDY OF
THE WONDER!
Felix, Mr. Farren ; Colonel Briton, Mr. Wheeler ;
Donna Violante, Miss DUNCAN.
After which THE WEDDING DAY.
Adam Contest, Mr. W. Farren ;
Lady Contest (with Songs), Miss DUNCAN.

PLYMOUTH AND DOCK THEATRE PLAYBILLS: 1808-1810.

> Meanwhile the Luffs and Mids were dining
> At Mother Mac's, and laying Wine in,
> The walls were dancing round the rooms,
> Their heads were making mops and brooms,
> 'Till Sháughnessy the Party rallied
> And out they to their coaches sallied.—
>
> For the Plymothian Poet's fustian
> Set all their fervour in combustion.
> They shouted, stamp'd, hurrah'd, and clapped
> And cudgels on the benches rapped ;
> In short, Sir, much our hearts were eased,
> Could you so easily be pleased.—
>
> ——See ! gaily up into the slips,
> Our Hero 'mong his comrade trips,
> And many a pretty girl is there,
> With sparkling eyes and bosom fair !—

Disgraceful interruptions and riots occurred in the narrow and badly-constructed galleries of both theatres, and rowdyism manifested itself in the dress circles as well. At one performance at Dock, in 1808, a lady was insulted when the lights were lowered ; and the officers indulged in a free fight. Captain Skinner was upbraided by a lieutenant, and the middies subjected him to such offensive epithets that he left the house. Similar scenes of shame and scandal occurred in 1810, when a midshipman of the Tartarus created a disturbance in the upper boxes ; and, on being ordered by his captain to leave the theatre, retaliated with the mutinous observation : "No martial law here !" His fellow officers used their whips and bludgeons upon the police ; but the ringleader was carried bodily to his ship, publicly stripped of the uniform "he had so shamefully disgraced," dismissed the service and sentenced to solitary confinement for two years. The effect of the example was very salutary. Although Jack continued as demonstrative in the pit, officers showed more restraint, and "ladies of the first quality" again patronised the performances. Mr. Sandford succeeded to the control of the Plymouth Theatre ; and, to compensate for his expenditure on embellishments, increased the prices of admission by a shilling to the boxes and sixpence to the pit. Every effort to explain and justify was ridiculed ; and, on the opening night, actors performed in dumb show, and the "O.P.'s" hammered, roared, bellowed, groaned, barked and cock-crowed. Trumpets, whistles, and other discordant instruments were sounded in distracting defiance, and illustrated verses were passed from hand to hand :

> This the house, built very strong :
> Pray God ! The owner's life prolong !
> This is the house, built very fast !
> But pray how long do you think 'twill last ?
> Lock up your Jaws, or shout with Applause,
> O.P.'s for ever, Huzza !

During the excitement a crowd of Jack Tars jumped from the pit to the stage and danced and "cut various capers" ; and one of the most daring helped himself to a chair, and advancing to the footlights, sat there with much composure to the delight of the "gods.', These, in their turn, dangled a huge padlock and keys and sang in lusty chorus:

x

Mr. O.P. and N.P. together sat down,
When N.P. gave O.P. a thump on the crown :
O.P. called his friends, and they thought it meet
To turn the rogue N.P. into the street !

There was no alternative save capitulation ; and, on the promise to restore the old prices, catcalls were drowned by cheering. Throughout these turbulent times, topical plays and songs were most heartily welcomed, and " Plymouth in an Uproar " held the boards. " Naval Revels, or All Alive at Dock," embodied " A British Sailor's Advice to the Volunteers, written expressly for and dedicated to the inhabitants of Dock." Mr. Moore, a favourite comedian, was wont to describe " The Sailor's Hobby, the Soldier's Hobby, the Freemason's Hobby, Bonaparte's Hobby, and the Plymouth Dock Hobby " ; and, when George III. was lying ill, he supplemented his song with the toast : " The noble commander of that glorious First Rater, the Britannia ; Heaven bless him and restore him to his messmates." Advancing to the footlights with glass in hand, Moore called upon the sailors and soldiers to join him in a bumper ; and, " being well provided with liquor as usual," they raised the bottles to their lips with uproarious shouts. At the benefit given to Mrs. Marden, " The British Volunteer " was sung by Mr. Whitfeld, the scenic artist, and " Father Stump's Visit to Dock " caused quite as much hilarity. " The Mail Coach " was another jeu d'esprit that abounded in local illustrations, but " The Launch of the Union "—in which a Plymouth humorist satirised the foibles of Society as witnessed at a dockyard function in 1811—was most successful of all. The drolleries were sustained by Dick and Timothy—the one lout typical of Devon, and the other of Cornwall, and the play of dialects provoked much mirth. " The Sailor's Return, or Dock Alive," was another favourite trifle, in which Miss Edgcumbe, a Plymouth actress, danced a hornpipe and sang " The Cabin Boy." On the occasion of the peace rejoicings in 1813, Mr. Bennett sustained the role of " Tom Grog " in " Hearts of Oak," and sang " Lots of Laughing, or Barney's Monday Trip to the Hoe."

It is to Mr. Jacobson that posterity is indebted for recording some diverting episodes which occurred during the abandon of the war times. " Jack " was always in evidence as a source of mischief ; and, on one occasion, when a shipwrecked hero was buffeting with the waves, a sailor rushed to the rescue with a wild cry of " Man Overboard ! " Scrambling over heads, shoulders, seats and slips, he dropped upon the stage, seized Don Juan by the leg, and triumphantly hauled him to the footlights despite all his struggles. When the acting-manager remonstrated, the interruptor directed a stream of tobacco juice in his face, and protestingly remarked " Why there was a man overboard, and no one shall be in distress so long as I can lend a hand ! " Mr. Hayne, a tragedian, was often the cause of unconscious fun ; and he would interpolate Othello's address to the Senate with a running commentary on the conduct of the disturbers in the upper boxes : " Most potent, grave and reverend seigneurs, my very noble and approved good Masters. (I'll tell you what, young fellows ; I'll have everyone of you in custody before you are aware of it.) That I have taken away this old man's daughter is most true. (That young woman with blue ribbons is as bad as any of you.) True, I have married her. (What, are you at it again ?) She loved me for the dangers I had passed, and I loved her that she did pity them. (Now if there's a constable in the house let him do his duty.") So irritable was this artiste that the temptation was irresistible to play pranks upon him, and two ladies, who were smarting under one of his caustic rebukes, sewed beneath the trailing part of the robe in which he went on as Richard the Third a long and curly tail intended for a demon scene. Advancing to the footlights, Hayne exclaimed " Now are our brows bound with victorious wreaths," and, twitching the robe, the tail stood out much more prominently than his crooked back.

Dock Theatre.

Dock Theatre.

For the Benefit of Mr. BENNETT.

ON MONDAY Evening next, the 26th of March, 1810, will be presented Colman's celebrated Play of The
IRON CHEST.
Mr. BENNETT will sing the following comic Songs, (for that night only)
"The POWER of GOLD," in the character of Samson.
In the course of the evening,
"PAT ROONEY of BALLINAFAD,"
"THE BOLD DRAGOON,"
AND
"PAUDIEN O'RAFFERTY."
After which, the favorite Musical Interlude (by desire) of the
RECRUITING SERJEANT.
To which will be added (for this night only) a New Ballet Dance, composed and got up under the direction of Mr. BENNETT, called
THE SAILOR'S WEDDING;
OR, THE JOVIAL TARS.
To conclude with a GRAND BOWER DANCE.

Tickets to be had of Mr. BENNETT, at the Old Crown Hotel, Cumberland Street; Mr. CONGDON and Mr. HOXLAND, Printers, Fore-street; Mr. ROACH, Bookseller, George-street ; and at Mr. SANDFORD's Circulating Library, St. Aubyn-street, Dock, where Places in the Boxes are to be taken.

For the benefit of Mr. WOODLEY.

ON TUESDAY Evening, March 27th, will be presented the Historical Play of
CORIOLANUS;
Or, the Roman Matron.
In the course of the evening, the following favorite songs :
"SANDY and JENNY," by Miss DRAKE,
"LONG LIFE TO THE PETTICOATS,"
By Mr. LANGHORNE,
And a HORNPIPE by Master FRIMBLEY.
To conclude with the grand Melo-Drama of The BLIND BOY.
Tickets to be had of Mr. Woodley, No. 39, Duke-street, and at the usual places.

For the Benefit of Mr. FRIMBLEY.

ON WEDNESDAY Evening, March 28th, will be performed Shakspeare's Comedy of
AS YOU LIKE IT.
In the course of the evening,
TWO COMIC SONGS and a Scotch PAS SEUL, By Master FRIMBLEY.
To which will be added (for the last time) the grand Romance of
THE CARAVAN;
Or, the Driver and his Dog.
Tickets to be had of Mr. Frimbley, and at the usual places.

Dock Theatre.

MR. HUGHES, the Proprietor, most respectfully begs leave to acquaint the public, that this Theatre will open on Monday next the 19th inst. under the management of Mr. SANDFORD, who takes the liberty to inform his patrons and friends, that the Theatre, at great expence, has been newly painted and decorated, and has undergone a thorough repair, in which the comfort and convenience of the audience have been consulted as much as possible ; he therefore trusts that a moderate advance in the prices, as undermentioned, will be sanctioned by general approbation, more particularly as he has the honour of assuring the friends of the Drama, that no expence is withholden, and the utmost care has been taken to provide a Company whose talents he presumes to hope, will afford the most complete satisfaction.
Mr. SANDFORD likewise takes the liberty to add, that under the gracious auspices of an encouraging and liberal public, it is his intention to bring forward many of the most highly estimated Dramas, in a style of eminence and splendor, which if ever equalled, has never yet been excelled, in any Theatre out of the metropolis.

On Monday, November the 19th, 1810,
Will be performed the Tragedy of
JANE SHORE.
Dumont.........Mr. Campbell,
(His first appearance these six years.)
Lord Hastings, Mr. Sandford. Gloster, Mr. Crooksly.
Jane Shore.. ......Mrs. Moore. ·
(From the Theatre Royal, Dublin, her first appearance on this Stage.)
Between the Play and Farce,
A DANCE by Master Frimbley,
And a COMIC SONG by Mr. Whitfeld.
To which will be added the Musical Entertainment of
LOCK AND KEY.
Ralph, by Mr. Moore, from the Theatre Royal, Dublin, his first appearance on this Stage.

Boxes, 4s.—Pit, 2s. 6d.—Gallery, 1s.
Second account to the Boxes, 2s. 6d.—Pit, 1s. 6d.
Nothing under FULL PRICE to the Gallery.
Tickets to be had at Mr. Sandford's Circulating Library, St. Aubyn-street, where Places in the Boxes are to be taken.

Dock Theatre.

THIS present SATURDAY, January the 12th, 1811, will be performed the Comedy of
THE BATTLE OF HEXHAM
With the Farce of
KILLING NO MURDER!

THE FIRST NIGHT OF BLUEBEARD.
The Manager, with the greatest respect, begs leave to assure the Inhabitants of Dock, that the utmost expence, care, and attention, have been bestowed upon this GRAND and BEAUTIFUL SPECTACLE which can contribute to render it every way *worthy of public patronage ;* and he ventures to assert, that no Drama of *equal splendor* has been produced in this Theatre for many years. On account of the IMMENSE EXPENCE INCURRED, nothing under *full prices* can be received.

DOCK THEATRE PLAYBILLS: 1810-1811,

Theatre Royal, Plymouth.

MR. FARREN begs leave most respectfully to return his grateful acknowledgments to his friends, the inhabitants of Plymouth, and the public in general, for their liberal support of the Plymouth Theatre last season. He fears that the nature of his engagement in Dublin will preclude him the honour of performing in the Plymouth Theatre this season, but assures them it will give him infinite pleasure again to share those plaudits which a candid and generous audience is ever ready to bestow when merited ; and while he remains A PROPRIETOR of the Plymouth Theatre, he shall be happy, and feel it his duty to exert every effort to render the entertainments worthy the approbation of the public.

He also begs leave to return his sincere thanks for their liberal support of MRS. FARREN's Benefit, who will shortly have the honour of again appearing on the Plymouth boards, when every exertion on her part will be used to merit a continuance of that distinguished patronage and approbation which she has ever been so liberally honoured with.

May 20, 1811.

A REPORT having been circulated that Mr. Farren has no longer any share in the Plymouth Theatre, I deem it necessary for the purpose of counteracting any injury likely to result from such a rumour, thus to make known to Mr. Farren's friends, and the public in general, that he holds an equal interest in the Theatre with Mr. Foote, viz.—one-half each, and will resume his part of management at the termination of his present engagement in Dublin. Signed Mary Farren, July 26, 1811, Frankfort-place, Plymouth.

Dock Theatre.

DURING the time Mr. FOOTE has been a Proprietor of the Plymouth Theatre, he has had the honour to present to the Dock Audience, the following very eminent London Performers, viz, Mrs. Siddons, Mr. Kemble, Mr. Cooke, Mr. Elliston, Mr. Bannister, Mr. Munden, Mr. Kelly, Mr. Incledon, Mrs. Mountain, Mrs. Crouch, Miss Duncan, Mr. and Mrs. Pope, Mr. and Mrs. C. Kemble, Mr. Dowton, Mr. Holman, &c. &c. in addition to whom, he has now the pleasure to announce, that he has engaged (FOR A FEW NIGHTS ONLY) Mr. FAWCETT, of the Theatre-Royal, Convent-Garden, who is unquestionably the most favourite Comedian on the London Boards ; in short, his high reputation, in every point of view, is too well known to need any preliminary comment or observation, except to announce, that on TUESDAY next, the 30th July inst. he will appear in two of these very distinguished comic characters, which, in London, have acquired him universal celebrity, and never yet failed to fill all those Country Theatres in which he has occasionally acted ; therefore, in order to prevent disappointments, early application for Tickets, and Places in the Boxes, are most particularly requested.

THE PIECES SELECTED ARE,
The Comedy of JOHN BULL ; or, AN ENGLISH-MAN'S FIRESIDE.
And the Farce of
The REVIEW ; or, Wags at Windsor,
The part of Job Thornbury in the Play, and Caleb Quotum in the Farce, by Mr. FAWCETT, as originally performed by him in the London Theatres. Dock, 26th July, 1811.

WONDERFUL INFANTILE NOVELTIES, Never exhibited in Dock or Plymouth.

THE ROYAL CAMBRIAN ROSCIA

WILL display her wonderful vocal and rhetorical powers in a variety of RECITATIONS and SONGS, as delivered by her by command of his Royal Highness the Prince Regent, at Carlton House. The above child will perform in the Assembly-Room, Fountain Inn, Dock, on Monday evening, April the 29th, and on Tuesday evening, the 30th, 1811.

N. B. The above child will perform in Plymouth on Friday evening, May the 3rd.—Performance to commence at seven o'clock.

Tickets to be had of Mr. CONGDON, Stationer, Fore-street, Dock.

Dock Theatre.

THIS present Saturday Evening, March 30th, 1811, will be performed the favourite Comedy of

WIVES AS THEY WERE,
AND MAIDS AS THEY ARE;
With the musical Farce of
LOVE LAUGHS AT LOCKSMITHS.

─○─

MR. MOORE

MOST respectfully informs his friends and the public in general, that HIS BENEFIT is appointed for Monday next, the 1st of April, 1811, when will be presented (not acted this season) the favourite Comedy of

THE HONEY-MOON.
Duke Aranza, Mr. Sandford ;
Rolando, Mr. Campbell ; Doctor Lampedo, Mr. Moore ; and Juliana, Mrs. Moore ;
In which character she will introduce, by desire,
"HAIL LOVELY ROSE,"
Composed by HOOK.

In the course of the evening Mr. MOORE will sing two new Comic Songs, (first time here),
CHIT! CHAT! or PRETTY LITTLE LADIES ;
And THE HOBBIES OF 1811.

Among the prevailing Hobbies, he will describe the Sailor's Hobby, the Soldier's Hobby, the Freemason's Hobby, Bonaparte's Hobby, his own Hobby, and the Plymouth-Dock Hobby.

BY DESIRE, THE POPULAR SONG OF
PRIME AND BANG-UP!!
(In character) from the musical Entertainment of
"HIT OR MISS."

A VIEW OF MOUNT ETNA, In a STATE of ERUPTION, With an attempt to represent, by the aid of Chymical Preparations and Machinery, the astonishing effects which are produced by an overflowing of the Lava, from that wonderful Volcano, the most awful, grand, and terrific object in the known world.

To which will be added, (by very particular request) the musical Farce of
PAUL AND VIRGINIA,
With new Dresses and Decorations, and a great variety of New Scenery.

Paul, Mrs. Foote ; and Virginia, Miss Foote, being her second performance on this stage.

Tickets to be had of Mr. Moore, 57, Clowance-street, Mr. Goude, King's Arms, and at the usual places.—Places in the boxes to be taken at Mr. Sandford's.

Dock Theatre.

THE EMPEROR OF CONJURORS!!!

THE MANAGER of the Theatre, with the greatest respect, begs leave to acquaint the Public that he has, at an excessive expense, engaged and brought down from Exeter, for the purpose of exhibiting his truly WONDERFUL PERFORM-ANCES at the Theatre this Evening, and MONDAY next, and for three nights only; Mr. INGLEBY has been styled in the Metropolis, and generally known by the Title of EMPEROR OF ALL CON-JURORS.—Mr. INGLEBY has just been exhibit-ing in Exeter to overflowing Houses, sanctioned and patronized by all the Nobility and Gentry in and about that Capital.—The inimitable MISS YOUNG and the unrivalled Master INGLEBY will also display their matchless abilities on the SLACK-WIRE and the SLACK-ROPE!

Mr. INGLEBY forbears from an unnecessary crowd-ing his bills, being well aware that many pretenders to his art have imposed upon the public with swelling bills and large promises, whose real gratifications are unfit to entertain even children.

The Public are respectfully informed, that on the Nights of Mr. INGLEBY's performance nothing under FULL PRICE can be taken.

THIS EVENING will be performed,
THE DRAMATIST;
Or, STOP HIM WHO CAN.
On MONDAY, the Tragedy of DOUGLAS.

Dock Theatre.

MR. HUGHES, the proprietor, begs leave to acquaint his Friends and the Public at large that this THEATRE will OPEN for the winter season on MONDAY next, the 11th instant, under the direction of Mr. SANDFORD, manager. He most respectfully solicits the attention of the Inhabi-tants of Dock, to the anxious care and immense expense he has bestowed, in order to render the Theatre comfortable, commodious, and in every way worthy of public patronage. He flatters himself that the company now engaged, will obtain general approbation; the talents of many of whom have been highly appreciated in Theatres of the first res-pectability throughout the kingdom.

Mr. HUGHES also takes the liberty to add, that during the last six months, machinists and artists have been perpetually. employed in devising and executing improvements.—The chief part of the scenery is entirely new, and the Theatre has been elegantly decorated by Mr. Wheatley, artist.

The following very moderate terms of subscription are submitted to consideration: tickets for every night in the season, (benefits excepted,) transferable, £5. 5s. untransferable, £3. 13s. 6d.

On MONDAY, November the 11th, 1811,
Will be presented the celebrated Play, called
THE HONEY-MOON.
Duke Aranza, by Mr. Sandford, and Rolando, by Mr. Howard, (from the Theatre-Royal, Weymouth, his first appearance on this stage.)

Between the Play and Entertainment, DANCING by Mr. Wollacott and Mrs. Noble.
After which, the Farce of
RAISING THE WIND.

Dock Theatre.

By desire of Capt. THOMAS,
And the OFFICERS and GENTLEMEN of the
DOCK CAVALRY.

For the Benefit of Mrs. MARDIN.

ON WEDNESDAY Evening, May the 1st, will be presented the favourite Comedy of
ADRIAN AND ORILLA.
After which the two following Songs:
"THE BRITISH VOLUNTEER," by Mr. Whitfeld,
And " Farmer Stump's Visit to Dock,"
By Mr. Langhorne.
To which will be added, the musical Farce of
ROBIN HOOD.
Tickets to be had at the usual places.

Dock Theatre.

Last Week of Performing.—Not acted this Season.

BY DESIRE OF THE
Officers and Gentlemen of his Majesty's Dock-Yard.

FOR THE BENEFIT OF MRS. MOORE.

ON Monday next the 13th of May, 1811, will be presented the celebrated Comedy of
THE SCHOOL FOR SCANDAL.
Sir Peter Teazle, Mr. Moore,
Charles Surface, Mr. Sandford,
And Lady Teazle, Mrs. Moore.

End of the second act Mr. Moore will sing (first time here) the popular song of
"THE MAIL-COACH."
And end of the third act, a new comic song called "Mr. and Mrs. BURNE and Mr. MOORE."

From the melo-dramatic performance of "Twenty Years ago," as performed with unbounded applause at the Lyceum Theatre, London.—Copies of these two songs will be delivered gratis to those who may honour the Theatre with their attendance.

At the conclusion of the play, Mr. Moore, (by de-sire) for this night only, will give his popular
IMITATIONS
OF THE FOLLOWING CELEBRATED ACTORS:
Mr. Kemble, Octavan, Mountaineers; Mr. Munden, Nipperkin, Sprigs of Laurel; Mr. Cooke, Richard, King Richard III.; Mr. Mathews, Cypher, Hit or Miss; and Mr. Fawcett, Caleb Quotem, Wags of Windsor.

To which will be added (by desire) last time this season, the musical farce of
TRANSFORMATION;
OR, THE THREE AND DEUCE.
Pertinax Single, Mr. Moore; Peregrine Single, Mrs. Moore; Percival Single, Mr. Moore; and Taffline, Mrs. Campbell.

PREVIOUS TO THE FARCE,
An Introductory Address will be spoken
By Mr. Moore.

Tickets to be had of Mrs. Moore, at No. 57, Clowance-street; of Messrs. Congdon, Hoxland, Roach and Harris, booksellers; at the music-shops; Mr. Goude, King's Arms; and of Mr. Sandford, St. Aubyn-street, Dock.

DOCK THEATRE PLAYBILLS: 1811.

Amid paroxysms of merriment, he ran from the stage with the appendage in his hand, " projecting like a bowsprit." A child of the veteran Jefferson's was trained to take the part of the baby King in Macbeth ; and Little Joe, having successfully emerged from the rehearsals, was held in readiness on the occasion of a visit by Kemble. The contingency that the tragedian would alarm a nervous child on approaching him, stern of aspect and weird of voice, had not been taken into account ; and, when the boy was sent to confront the gloomy monarch, and Kemble, in his forbidding manner, demanded to know what form was this that rose like the issue of a king, and wore upon its baby brow the round and top of sovereignty, poor Little Joe was struck dumb with terror. Kemble glared and muttered madly, " Why the devil don't you speak?" and still more terrified, the child shrieked " Let me down, let me down ! " His request had to be complied with ; and, to Kemble's disgust,

EXTERIOR OF PLYMOUTH THEATRE (SITE OF LIPTONS', IN BEDFORD STREET).

the audience was convulsed with laughter. On another occasion, as Holman was impressively reciting " The Ode to Alexander's Feast," a sailor leant over the gallery, and shouted in a tone " that might have been heard above a whirlwind ": " Hold your jaw, you lubber, and give us a hornpipe instead ! " So greatly did the sailors delight in making this demand at inauspicious moments that Kemble was warned that he might be requested to oblige. " Well," he answered, soured by his previous experience of local irreverence, " if they ask me for a hornpipe I shall dance one."

Spectacular effects were in request in the earlier years of the nineteenth century. The melodrama of " The Wood Demon, or the Clock Has Struck ! " was staged at Plymouth after its production in London, and the " singular beauty " of the cloud scene and drawbridge was considered no less " elegant and appropriate " than the Necromantic Cavern. In " The

Gretna Green Elopement," the harlequin shot "from the back of the gallery head foremost over the pit, and thence to the rear of the stage in a shower of fire." "Timour the Tartar" was the "wonder of admiring crowds," and the skill of the horses was "simply marvellous" in scaling ramparts, leaping waterfalls, and flying through breaches. The spectacle of "Blue Beard, or Female Curiosity," was varied by a procession over the mountains, in which the tyrant sat astride his "noble Hanoverian charger," and was escorted by cavalry, infantry and a military band. Within the Castle the audience viewed the nuptial chamber; then the bridge was stormed and horses and knights were overthrown; the ogre was slain and "new and surprising feats of courage, boldness and sagacity" were presented. The "Woodman's Hut" was long in vogue at both theatres: "During a most interesting scene a tremendous storm is heard, the walls of the cottage are shivered by lightning, the river is violently agitated, and over this Maria and Count Conenburg eventually escape from their enemies." In the final act "the woodman's hut is on fire, the bridge burns, the forest is in flames—the most sublime and awful coup d'œil ever attempted on this or any other stage." "The Forest of Bondy, or the Dog of Montargis," attracted overflowing houses in 1814, and so did the Chinese spectacle, "Aladdin, or the Wonderful Lamp," which was offered with an "Oriental splendour and pomp only to be found in the 'Arabian Nights Entertainment.'" In 1815, Ducrow ascended the Plymouth gallery, standing upon his head at the top of a balloon, with two boys suspended from the car. "Ladoisha" yielded the no less sensational incident of headless horses galloping through flames to the rescue of the Princess, and the Tyrant's Castle was enveloped in a general conflagration.

In 1811, the genius of Foulston conceived one structure that should unite different objects—the Royal Hotel, Assembly Rooms, and Theatre. The foundation-stone was laid by the Mayor, the town colours flew in the procession, and music was supplied by the Royal Marine band. A lovely vase of Plymouth porcelain was deposited in a cavity of the foundation stone, and it contained a commemorative medal giving a view of the classic group, with its Ionic porticos, as well as the current gold and several silver coins. The block of three tons was lowered by means of a windlass, and Mr. Lockyer dedicated the project in these words: "I throw wine, corn and oil on this stone in the hope that it may prove to be the foundation of the Peace, Prosperity and Happiness of Plymouth." Amid salutes from cannon, pealing of bells, and general acclamations, the guests adjourned to the King's Arms Hotel, and dined "with true British conviviality and good humour." With business instinct, the Corporation at once adopted repressive measures against low-class competitors; and, in 1812, John Kelland, a victualler, who permitted a number of young people to assemble in his house, "known as the Fox and Goose," near Frankfort Place, and there witness "theatricals in defiance of the law," was summoned and admonished to be "more circumspect." The actors were also put in the dock, and required to give recognisances for their better behaviour. "The evil tendency of meetings of this description," the magistrates sedately proclaimed, "as affording incentives to vice, is so evident, and their immediate suppression a matter of such imperative necessity, that the Mayor feels it his bounden duty to declare his fixed determination to punish all future offenders, after this public notice, with every severity of the law." A ball was held to dedicate the Assembly Rooms, and a haunch of venison was forwarded by the Prince Regent as a goodwill offering to the Plymouth epicures who commemorated the opening of the hotel with a dinner. As his health was drunk a salute of 21 guns was fired from the Citadel. The toast, "Mr. Lockyer, and may his Indefatigable Exertions in the erection and completion of this building be Conducive to the Gratification and Accommodation of Visitors to and Inhabitants of Plymouth, and of Ultimate Advantage to the Corporation," was hailed with "three times three." His worship's reply was followed by a song "of peculiar fervency—'Britain claims the Martial Strain!'"—a recognition of "the late proud achievements in the Peninsula." A bill was issued in which: "The Public is most respectfully informed that the new Theatre Royal, Plymouth, will open on Monday next (August 23rd, 1813), with 'An Occasional Address.' After which will be acted Shakespeare's Celebrated Play of 'As You Like It.' To which will be added, from the same Author, 'Catherine and Petruchio.'" "Gods" and "pittites" were more interested in hearing "Paudien O'Rafferty," and scenes of disorder continued throughout the week because this disreputable song was forbidden. On the first night the Mayor, Mr. John Arthur, was asked to suppress the disorder, and his use of the constabulary led to the issue of squibs:

> Strive not, great Arthur, to enquire
>   If Mayors in Theatres may reign,
> Nor odious Constables employ
>   The long disputed point to gain.
> Whether the gallery may call,
>   For any tune they like to hear,
> Or thou the orchestra control
>   And suit its musick to thy ear.

The theatre was excessively cold during the winter, and the inconvenience was mitigated by burning large fires in the pit. At the age of eighteen, Miss Feron captivated the musical cognoscenti as Margaretta, in "No Song, No Supper," and Caroline in "The Young Hussar!" Miss Duncan, of Drury Lane, made her appearance as Lady Teazle, and Madame Catalini in "Deh Frenata," which had been composed for this "astonishing genius." Mr. Farren associated himself with Mr. Foote, but financial difficulties led to many differences and disclaimers, and Mr. Hughes acquired the entire interest. Each artiste commanded devoted partisans, and those who were fascinated by Mrs. Billington were no less delighted with Mrs. Mountain—"the sweetest and most scientific songstress on the English stage." Mrs. Kemble went on as Morgiana in the "The Forty Thieves"; but few ladies were more "exquisitely attractive" than Miss O'Neill, with whom no fault could be found in figure, tone or gesture—either in the role of Jane Shore or as Miss Beverley in "The Gamester." Under Mr. Brunton's management, the theatre maintained high character. Miss Paton and Miss Huddart were the tragediennes; and Madame Vestris was the principal attraction during a royal visit in 1828, when her fine acting, attractive person and animated countenance added much to the songs with which she charmed her hearers. In spite of these engagements, the theatre did not draw commensurate receipts, and Mr. Brunton's explanation of his relinquishment of the lesseeship sufficiently suggests the reason: "Whether the want of success may be attributed to the embarrassments of the country, or to the hostility of a presumed moral principle, which is said to have raised its head in society, I am not prepared to say. It is probable that both causes have operated to injure the stage, but the latter is chiefly instrumental, and is somewhat corroborated by the discussions which have recently appeared. It is extraordinary, however, that the question should be raised at this time of day, whether, with reference to the morals of society, the theatre ought not to be discontinued. Much more so is the opinion, which among certain classes appears to gain ground, that the stage is positively injurious to the weal of mankind. Shall we listen to the cant of the day against the drama, because, forsooth, its language is not always precisely what an innocent old maid of three score could wish—because in its pictures of nature, vice sometimes appears by the side of virtue, to fulfil the end of some great argument?"

Born in Plymouth in 1798, Miss Foote made her debut as Juliet in 1810, at the theatre of which her father was lessee, and so successful was her maiden impersonation of the heroine that she secured an immediate engagement at Covent Garden, as Amanthis, in " The Child of Nature." Even as a mere child she was admirable in " Old Minetta " ; and her warbling of " Oh, come my gallant soldier," with dancing accompaniment, was an enchanting achievement.   Her critics were candid in their criticisms, especially those of her native town, who nevertheless wrote nothing that could impair her popularity in any degree. Graceful, elegant, feminine and beautiful, in the piquant arts of girlhood Miss Foote was a profound adept, and her badinage and coquetry were admittedly exquisite. She delighted the fancy and stimulated the imagination, with the power a dainty maiden always possesses ; although, as an actress, everyone was surprised to observe the crowds which flocked to witness her performances. Artistes with higher intellectual powers failed to draw such overflowing houses, and the secret lay in the witchery of her manner, and her peculiar faculty of drawing attention to herself as a budding woman.   As a victim of man's cruelty and tyranny, she arrested the sympathy of audiences, and excited the feeling that she was in her own person warm-hearted, ingenuous and confiding. Her blithesome song of " Buy-a-broom," and the German waltz accompanying

CHARLES MATHEWS AND MISS FOOTE (AS JONATHAN OLDSKIRT AND FANNY)
IN " WHO WANTS A GUINEA ?"

THEATRE-ROYAL, *Plymouth.*

Mr. MACREADY'S
Appearance for this Night only.
THIS EVENING, SATURDAY, Dec. 27th, 1823,
WILL BE PRESENTED

VIRGINIUS;
Or, the Liberation of Rome.
Virginius, Mr. MACREADY.
FOLLOWED BY

HOW TO DIE FOR LOVE.
In the course of the evening, the orchestra will play
a variety of select music.

THEATRE-ROYAL,
PLYMOUTH.

MR. BRUNTON has the honour to inform the public, that the Theatre will OPEN, for a season of three months, on Wednesday, the 1st of September, on the same plan as last year.

The short interval which elapsed last year between Mr. Brunton's taking and opening the Theatre, deprived him of the means of making arrangements with performers of the London Theatres, during the season here, and he was chiefly able to gratify the public by their appearance on extra nights, subsequently to the close of the regular season. He takes the liberty to state that he is differently circumstanced this year, and that there will be no extra performances after the close of the subscription nights.

Mrs. YATES (late Miss BRUNTON) is engaged for the very early part of the season, and will play *Lady Teazle* in the "School for Scandal," on the first night of opening.

Some complaints having been made last season, that the plans of the boxes had occasionally been withheld from general inspection in an undue manner, and had not been exhibited until the boxes were all taken, the public is respectfully informed, that to guard against the possibility of such an occurrence during the approaching season, the box plans for every night of representation will be prepared and exhibited at Rowe's Library, previously to the opening of the Theatre, and continue so during the season. By this course it is clear that no preference, with respect to securing places, can be shewn.

Subscriptions received at ROWE's Library,
No. 7, Whimple-street.
Plymouth, August 17, 1824.

Theatre Royal, Plymouth.

THE FIRST NIGHT OF
MR. MATHEWS' PERFORMANCE.
On *MONDAY, July 18th,* 1825.
THE Public is respectfully informed, that the
justly-celebrated
MR. MATHEWS,
FROM THE ENGLISH OPERA, WILL BE FOUND
AT HOME,
At the Theatre-Royal, Plymouth, on MONDAY, the 18th inst. when he will have the honour of presenting his celebrated entertainment, called

A TRIP TO AMERICA.
Doors open at Seven, and commence at Eight.
ADMISSION AS USUAL.
*Mr. MATHEWS will positively perform
for four nights only.*

Old Theatre, Plymouth.

MESSRS. COLUMBIER & BALL
BEG to return their best thanks to the Gentry and Inhabitants in general of Plymouth, Dock, and Stonehouse, for the kind encouragement afforded them during the
EXHIBITION OF THEIR
French Company of Performers,
IN THE MARKET-PLACE, PLYMOUTH,
And most respectfully announce, that they have obtained permission of the Worshipful the Mayor, and
WILL OPEN THE OLD THEATRE,
(FOR A SHORT SEASON,)
ON MONDAY NEXT, July 20, 1825,
*And hope by the Selection of the most pleasing
Exhibitions, to secure the patronage and
support of the Public generally.*

THE PERFORMANCE WILL COMMENCE WITH
A GRAND COMBINATION OF HYDRAULICS
(FIRE AND WATER);
AFTER WHICH,
THE INFANT SAQUI
Will exhibit her unparalleled Performances on the
SINGLE AND DOUBLE TIGHT ROPE.
MONS. LOUIS
*Will DANCE on the TIGHT ROPE, the GRAND
BRETAGNE, in WOODEN SHOES; and
MONS. RENE, in BASKETS, &c.*
THE WHOLE WILL CONCLUDE WITH
A GRAND SERIOUS PANTOMIME,
IN FOUR ACTS, CALLED
HARADIN, THE CHIEF OF
THE TURKS;
*With other Entertainments as will be expressed in
the bills of the day.*
Boxes, 2s.—Pit, 1s.—Gallery 6d.
Doors to be opened at six, and the exhibition to
begin at seven o'clock.
GOOD FIRES CONSTANTLY KEPT UP.

THEATRICALS.

ON SATURDAY NEXT, the 5th of January, 1828, will be Published, price 2d.,

The Plymouth Theatrical Spy,
OR A PAIR OF SPECTACLES FOR THE MANAGER.
(TO BE CONTINUED WEEKLY.)
Containing a strict and impartial Review of the Performances at the Plymouth Theatre during the preceding week, Hints to the Manager and Performers, and a particular notice of all circumstances behind and before the curtain, which may affect the welfare of the Drama, or the enjoyment of its patrons.

EDITED BY A GREAT UNKNOWN,
With the assistance of Paul Pry, Gentleman.

This work is undertaken with the view of correcting many abuses which the partiality or supineness of the Newspaper Press has hitherto suffered to prevail unnoticed. To effect this object the lash will not be spared, whilst nevertheless, merit shall always meet with due praise. The spirit of the work shall be in strict accordance with its motto.
" Nothing extenuate, nor set down aught in malice."

To be published by W. HAVILAND, 50, Bedford-street, Plymouth, and to be had of all Booksellers in Plymouth, Devonport, and Stonehouse.

Theatre Royal, Plymouth.

THIS Theatre will open for the season 26th December, 1827, with the celebrated
MISS PATON
Of the Theatres-Royal, Covent-garden, and Drury-lane, in the character of ROSETTA, in
LOVE IN A VILLAGE,
In which character she will introduce the following songs :—

"Hope thou Nurse," a Duet with Miss MAYHEW.
"My Heart's my own."
"Gentle Youth."
"How blest the Maid."
"I've been roaming."
"Go, naughty Man."
"The Banks of Allan Water."
"The Soldier tir'd."
"When thy Bosom heaves a Sigh," Duet with Mr. WESTON.
Young Meadows—Mr. WESTON.
Of the Theatres-Royal, Birmingham and Bath.
WHO WILL SING
"O, had I been."
"Still in hopes to get the better."
"Oh, how can I."
"The Bonnie Lass."
TO CONCLUDE WITH
THE YOUNG WIDOW.
Mandeville—Mr. BRUNTON.
Aurelia—Miss HUDDART.
ON THURSDAY,
THE DEVIL'S BRIDGE,
ROSALVINA—MISS PATON.
Count Belino—Mr. WESTON.
Doors will open at half-past Six, and begin at Seven. Tickets for the Boxes 4s. each.

Theatre=Royal, Plymouth.

MR. HAY feels great pleasure in informing his Friends and the Public, that the OFFICERS of the GARRISON and other GENTLEMEN AMATEURS, whose performance was so favourably received on two former occasions, have, in consideration of the great sacrifices he has made to render the Drama effective, kindly consented to perform for his advantage, on MONDAY Evening, when will be presented the Petite Comedia, called
CHARLES II.
After the Play, Mr. HAY will have the honour of singing an ORIGINAL SONG, written expressly for the occasion, called
The Play, the Play's the thing.
THE HIGHLAND FLING, by Miss REEKIE.
To conclude with the Farce of
RAISING THE WIND.
On TUESDAY Evening, Shakspeare's celebrated Play, called the
MERCHANT OF VENICE.
SHYLOCK, ... Mr. PHELPS.
With, for the last time, the splendid Ballet of
CINDERELLA.
In the course of the evening, the following new Comic Songs by Mr. DOBBS :—
"What's Beauty without a Name."
"Dicky Snip and Family's Visit to Plymouth, Devonport, and Stonehouse."
AND
"St. Patrick's Day."

Theatre-Royal, Plymouth.

THE MANAGER feels great pleasure in announcing the engagement of that fascinating and favorite Actress
MISS FOOTE,
FOR FOUR NIGHTS ONLY,
VIZ :—
Monday, Tuesday, Thursday, and Friday, the 1st, 2nd, 4th, and 5th June, 1829.
During the last four years Miss FOOTE has travelled upwards of Eighteen Thousand Miles, and fulfilled more than Two Hundred different Engagements in England, Ireland, Scotland, and France ; and it is now her intention *to relax,* if not *totally to retire,* from such incessant and very great professional exertions ; therefore this will most probably be *the last time* she will have the honour of appearing in Plymouth.

ON MONDAY will be performed the very celebrated Comedy of
WHICH IS THE MAN?
Written by Mrs. COWLEY, Authoress of the "Belle's Stratagem," "Who's the Dupe?" &c.
Lady Bell Bloomer .. by Miss FOOTE.
At the end of the Play Miss FOOTE, assisted by Mesdames NEWMAN, HONEY, and GLIDDON, and Messieurs SELBY, MARTIN, BUTTER, & GARDNER, will dance the fashionable
Polish Mazurka ; also, La Gallopade.
The Evening's Entertainment will conclude, by particular desire, with the new Farce of
Perfection, or The Lady of Munster.
Which was received with such decided approbation and applause on Tuesday last.
Kate O'Brien (the Lady of Munster) by Miss FOOTE, in which character she will sing the Guitar Song of
"TO THE GAY TOURNAMENT."

ON TUESDAY will be performed a new OPERA, written by Mr. POCOCK, the music by Mr. BISHOP, called
HOME, SWEET HOME,
Or, the Rans des Vaches,
Madame Germance.........MISS FOOTE.
In which character she will sing the following Songs:
"Come, my gallant Soldier,"
"Ah no ! First Love is but a name,"
"I well remember that sweet hour."
After which, the Interlude of
HE LIES LIKE TRUTH,
To conclude with the comic musical FARCE of
LITTLE JOCKEY,
Or, Youth, Love, and Folly.
Arinette, the little Jockey...Miss FOOTE.
In which character she will introduce the Dancing Castanet Song of
"Oh, remember the time."
The celebrated Jockey Song of
"The Boy in Yellow wins the Day."
AND
"Why ? Pretty Maiden, why ?"
ON WEDNESDAY,
MUCH ADO ABOUT NOTHING,
Beatrice.........Miss FOOTE.
WITH
THE ROMP.
Priscilla Tomboy.........Miss FOOTE.

PLYMOUTH THEATRE PLAYBILLS : 1827-1829.

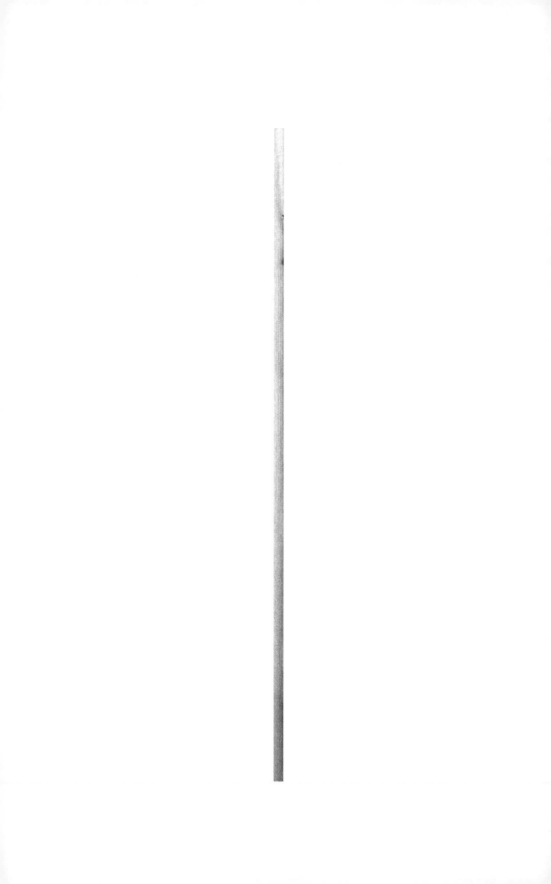

it, always elicited tumults of applause; and "I'd be a Butterfly" was no less sweetly sung. After she had emerged from her 'teens something of the fire of her pourtrayals abated, but she evinced a superior grasp and maturer conception that silenced even the captious. In 1829, Earl Harrington, who had long worshipped at the lady's shrine, made her his wife.

Between Edmund Kean and Macready the local playgoers insisted upon instituting contrasts, although the task was hopeless, because the men possessed minds that ran parallel and never met. Kean gave Shakespeare without his "commentation" and a richer treat was not within the range of intellect. Virginius, Hamlet, William Tell and Werner were the roles in which Macready rejoiced. Kean leant to the romantic, was all passion, and intellect was really the medium of expression. Kean could not render Macready's classic roles, and Macready could make nothing of Kean's; but those who felt deeply with Kean were as affected by Macready, although it was hard to say to whom the locality voted the palm. Just as Shakespeare wrote, so did Macready perform, and the actor was apparently as peerless as the author. Curiosity was great when Charles Mathews fulfilled his first engagement, for every seat was engaged for days in advance, and the performance was voted of "real sterling merit." His volubility, incessant changes of voice, imitations of sounds, and infinite humours left ineffaceable impressions, and he was pronounced "an excellent moral physician against spleen and hypochondria."

Although the theatres were "genteely attended" during the next decade, crushed houses were the exception even at "star" performances—for distress stalked the land and the pulpit fulminated. The "Hunchback," albeit it was written by a gifted Plymothian, Sheridan Knowles, was repeatedly in request with Mr. Sandford as "Master Walter." When Fanny Kemble first appeared she was generally considered to be over-schooled on her father's model, and her manner was described as artificial. She did not overstep the modesty of nature; and, with less of instinct than Miss O'Neill, possessed more of the ornament of art. In course of time, her sweet and musical voice, winsome manner, intellectual countenance and fine perceptions carried all before her. Mr. Kemble was already a patriarch of the old school, little changed by time or circumstance, when Charles Kean advanced to the front, and more nearly approached his father's ideal than any living actor, "especially in the bloody and resolute Richard the Third." In his earliest presentation of Hamlet at the Plymouth Theatre his picture of the Dane was bright, pathetic, intelligent and beautiful: more effective than Macready's, though in classic beauty less perfect. When the guilty King and Queen retire conscience-stricken, and Hamlet exclaims with surpassing energy,

> Why, let the stricken deer go weep
> The hart ungalled play;
> For some must watch while some must sleep—
> Thus runs the world away.

the effect upon the audience was electrical, and several minutes elapsed before the cheering subsided. In the midst of the "bravos" which resounded from every part of the house, a voice in the pit cried out "He's a chip of the old block," and the interruption produced a pause in the performance, so much was the actor affected by this allusion to his father at such a triumphant moment. In 1837 Samuel Phelps made his bow in Devonport. Little honour awaited him in his native town, where his Lear was condemned as "a distorted skeleton," and his Hamlet as "too original." In the provinces the welcome was more generous, although Phelps had to contend with the jealousy of Charles Kean and others. "Kemble," said Kean, "did all he could to prevent me from supplanting him, and I owe it to my family to do all I can to prevent Phelps from supplanting me." Phelps's turn arrived when the two actors appeared in powerful roles in the same cast, and "Punch" cut his rival to the quick by

Y

PHELPS AS RICHELIEU.

announcing that the Devonport artiste had graciously presented him with a " silver extinguisher." From that time Phelps made splendid appearances, and his " Cardinal " in "Henry VIII." was marked by stately reserve and suppressed passion.

One of the most interesting managers of Dock Theatre was Mr. James Dawson, who had travelled through Cornwall performing in barns, hotels, and more or less public places. The competition at Plymouth was deadly, but Dawson boasted a comic triumvirate who always sent his patrons laughing to bed. Apart from Dawson himself, who was preferred to the Infant Roscius, James Doel had only to walk across the stage, if anything went wrong, and ask, " What are you laughing at? " for hilarity to ring through the house. Doel, like Timothy Quaint, never suffered a smile to mantle his countenance; his presence was a certain signal for merriment; and he turned dismal and doubtful moments to sportive account. At Plymouth it was rarely that the laugh came in: at Dock, the fun was ever furious.

A financial crisis in the fortunes of Plymouth Theatre occurred in 1837, when the "ghost would not walk," and the performances were suspended by the refusal of the artistes to perform. Mr. Davenport, the lessee, issued an appeal to the public, but the company replied with a placard that did not err on the side of mercy :

" Upon the representation made by Mr. Davenport as to his property, stating that he was possessed of a large and independent fortune, and that his taste leading him to patronize the Drama, he had taken the Plymouth Theatre : with this plausible tale he induced several ladies and gentlemen to enrol themselves under his banners. Suffice it to say, that the Company had not been more than three weeks in his service before the bubble burst, and exposed the thing of air.

" At the opening of the season, Mr. Davenport commenced the destruction of the Theatre's interest, by attempting the character of ' Virginius,' to the mortification of us all. The audience marked their disapprobation of him strongly on the first night. Instead of this taking its proper effect, and showing him the ruin that he would bring upon the Theatre if he did not desist from obtruding himself before the Public, he still persisted in insulting them by attempting the character of ' Othello '—at least so much of that small portion of the text that he had committed to memory; and, further, to disgust the dramatic supporters in other characters, namely, ' Skirts,' in ' The Man About Town '; Mr. Levison, in ' Hunting a Turtle '; attempting to sing comic songs, &c., &c., even to the last, in defiance of the interests of the Theatre; insisting on obtruding himself in various characters which he proposed undertaking during Madame Celeste's engagement, had she continued. These are truths incontrovertible, and the ground-work of our misfortunes."

To these charges the Lessee replied with no less candour :

"One portion of the hand-bill would induce a belief that I represented myself as possessed of a large and independent fortune, and induced several ladies and gentlemen to enrol themselves under my banners, which assertion goes to prove, if anything, that the motives which actuated them, when they joined to form the company, were not to rest so much on their own merits, and thus qualify themselves, and receive the approbation, patronage and support of a discerning public, as to repose on the contents of my purse, which feeling, it appears, has not ceased to prompt them on to this very hour. Supposing I had so represented myself, which I unequivocally deny having done, for instead of exercising my own judgment in the selection, I reposed that duty with confidence, I will say misplaced, in Mr. Hamerton, my intended stage manager, at the same time showing him the sum of money which I had determined should be the limit of my loss ; if I sustained any, therefore, in the absence of such an opportunity, I could not have misrepresented myself, but for me to say that I have not been misrepresented, would be false indeed."

A similar experience dogged Mr. Hay's efforts as lessee, and Ellen Tree presented her famous roles to a handful of gallery spectators. It was no uncommon experience for companies to perform to twenty-shilling houses by the aid of flickering gas jets that only accentuated the gloom. Charles Mathews himself fell flat, and turned by preference to Devonport, where the audiences more promptly responded to his witticisms. To a select gathering which once received him with unusual cordiality at Plymouth, he severely observed : "I will say I never played before a prettier audience, although there are not many of ye." The Countess of Morley so much enjoyed the rebuke that she went behind the scenes at the close of the performance and shook hands with the artiste. Despite the neglect of the public, Mathews was an honoured guest in private circles, and passed many a merry night with the Blue Friars—a select club whose members dined in monastic garb, and espoused the hospitable phases of local Bohemianism—William Jacobson, a leading solicitor with a capacity for humour ; George Wightwick, a witty and scholarly architect ; William Snow Harris, a man of many parts, who was said to resemble a barrel organ, in that he could be easily set to any tune ; Edwin Lovell, T. D. Newton, and a few others. It was poetic that Charles Mathews should have breathed his last in Plymouth. He landed exhausted after a sea voyage, and passed away at his lodgings in Lockyer Street amid the drolleries which, even on his death-bed, he could not deny his Blue Friar colleagues. His remains were interred in 1835 in the western vestibule of St. Andrew's Church :

> Scarce come back from abroad when that unexpected bourne
> Which permits no return finds "Charles Mathews 'At Home.'"

For presenting "Jack Sheppard," and other doubtful melodrama, Mr. Hay was censured by the Corporation ; and, when he fell in arrears with his rent, the character of his plays was impeached. Mr. Hay claimed a moral tone for "Jack Sheppard" in a farewell apologia that was Hogarthian: "We introduce to you the idle apprentice; we show him to you triumphant in crime; we present him to you at his mother's hearth—repentant and miserable ; and, at length, we lead him to the scaffold." Mr. Hay asserted that it was impossible to make Plymouth theatre pay : "It is too large for the town ; very frequently it is a mere wilderness ; it presents a most melancholy and comfortless sight ; and it is impossible for the actor to dispel the prevailing sadness." The declension of patronage of which Mr. Hay complained was largely due to private theatricals. At the local mansions festivities of this order were given, and the roles were sustained by Lady

Morley, Lady Elizabeth Bulteel, Lady Whitmore, the Hon. Mrs. Edgcumbe, Mrs. Calmady, Sir Henry Blackwood, and Sir George Whitmore. A prologue by Mr. Wightwick, which preceded the rendering of " Perfection " at Saltram, sketched the melancholy fall the drama had locally experienced :

> In Plymouth, vis-a-vis, to George's Place,
> Rising in column'd pride and Attic grace,
> The portal of the Playhouse greeted me
> With hopes of some advancement ; for, you see,
> I'm a poor actor, wand'ring on, to seek
> For bread and fame at one-pound-one a week.
> I batter'd at the door—a hollow sound
> (As from some dark and murky cave profound)
> Cried, " Who comes here, to pierce this fearful gloom !
> " The Drama's Ghost disturbing in its tomb !
> " Away ! Away ! The drop has fallen here ;
> " And Fancy, hopeless, weeps above my bier.
> " Desertion now holds her tyrannic sway ;
> " But even she must yield—alack the day !
> " Tremble ye cobwebs ! Fly each fleeting mouse !
> " They mean to make the Play—a Meeting—House."
>
> Thus spake the Ghost.   I turn'd in grief to go ;
> Wond'ring what next the world—and I—should do ;
> And thinking how—to carry well the farce on—
> I'd fire the playhouse, and get hanged for arson.
> So fix'd these thoughts, I deemed I ne'er should alt'r 'em,—
> When, lo ! the ghostly voice cried : " Go to Saltram."

The public lost all taste for theatricals until Charles Kean, with his established fame " as a fashionable actor," made his annual appearances, and the unaccustomed spectacle was then witnessed of houses crowded night after night.   Although he was the rage, local critics refused to allow him talents of the highest order, and Macready still held the first place in their hearts.   Kean's visits brought little grist to the mill, and the expenses swallowed up the receipts.   1845 found Devonport Theatre under the management of Mr. James Doel ; and, on the occasion of his benefit, the local trifle was presented : " Did You Ever Send Your Wife to Plymouth ?"   After ten years' heart-breaking experience, he retired with a pathetic confession : " I have toiled unceasingly for a reputation," he declared, " and, in my struggles after it, found the path not so flowery as my early fancy painted.   Instead of roses, I realise that it is beset with thorns.   I am not," he added, " one jot less ambitious now than when my theatrical life began, but the claims of my family are more powerful than the calls of ambition."   At Plymouth he received a benefit after his retirement, and appeared as Captain Copp in the comedy of " Charles II," an item which was followed by " Raising the Wind," with Mr. J. R. Newcombe as Jeremy Diddler and Mr. Doel as Sam. From year to year—until, all too prematurely, he imagined that age was creeping upon him—he made his intermittent appearances :

> Once more James Doel ventures to convene
> His worthy patrons to the mimic scene,
> Not in defiance of the public will,
> But in the hope that you'll support him still ;

inimitable and mysterious power of exciting sympathy which always fired her audiences with enthusiasm. A touch of burlesque associated with the 1869 pantomime brought the military authorities into ridicule, as a subsequent incident did the more Puritan members of the Council. An elaborate view of the Royal Marine Barracks was presented ; and, to complete the realism, a sentry box was placed at the entrance, with a guard in military costume of whom the clown made sport. Colonel Penrose, who was in command of the Marines, construed this as a reflection on the corps, and not only issued an instruction prohibiting the regiment from attending the performance, but placed a file at the doors to prevent the men from entering. It was only after a deal of badinage that the order was withdrawn. More serious was the controversy over the engagement of a ballet corps of scanty characteristics, and the caricaturing on the stage of three local celebrities who complained of the tendencies of "the Can-can." The oldest theatrical manager in England experienced no lack of friends in the hour of his difficulty, and tided over the storm which his differences with the authorities created. Indeed, Mr. Newcombe was able at a bumper benefit to indulge in "topical" congratulation : "During the 22 years I have had the management of this theatre I have known what it is to play the principal part in life's devious farce of ' Raising the Wind '; and, if the labour in which I had been engaged had not been a ' Labour of Love ' to me, I should never have appreciated ' Life's Labour Won,' or dreaded the effects of ' Life's Labour Lost.' To recite to you the whole of my difficulties, trials and struggles would indeed prove a tedious ' Winter's Tale,' while to me their contemplation has been the subject of many ' A Midsummer Night's Dream.' Now that ' The Tempest ' is over I have found " A Cure for the Heartache ' in giving satisfaction to ' John Bull,' to whom I find ' Money ' always provides an attraction. When I look around me and see so many smiles it does indeed put me in mind of those ' Faces in the Fire,' where the flames of true friendship light up the flickering rays of admiration in our hearts."

In comparatively recent years the Plymouth Theatre has been the scene of tragic events, the most distressing in 1854, when every device was employed to lend attraction to an amateur dramatic performance. There was a crowded and aristocratic audience, the house was gay and animated, every seat in the circle was occupied, and pit and gallery were filled to overflowing. " Plot and Passion " was presented, and the performers were entering with spirit into their several parts when Mrs. Kirby came on in a light muslin dress as a country belle. Approaching too near the footlights, she was instantly enveloped in flames. For a moment everyone was paralysed with horror ; then several gentlemen rushed to the rescue with overcoats, rugs and cloaks, and the lady was taken to the green room. The audience suffered such acute anguish that many ladies were hysterical ; and the spectators dispersed as soon as the announcement was made that the artiste was terribly injured. The unhappy victim did not survive the accident. During the pantomime season of 1863, and, shortly after the house had emptied, the lessee, Mr. J. R. Newcombe, noticed a suspicious smell, and went through the theatre from the gallery to the stage. As there were no symptoms of fire, he took his departure, but he rose unsatisfied from his bed within an hour, and returned to find the building in flames. The property-room was the scene of the outbreak, and, in order to reach it, a hole was made in the roof. The introduction of air did more injury than the inlet of water did good ; the intrepid firemen were driven from the spot, and vibrating rafters crashed like roars of artillery. The flames shot up, the country was illuminated for miles, and thousands left their homes when the guns from the Citadel boomed. Running from Theatre to Hotel, the conflagration enveloped the western part from foundation to parapets, and a body of engineers saved the rest of the establishment by hacking the roof with hatchets. The floor of the ball-room collapsed into the tea-room with such force as to cause a sinkage of several inches ; but the aperture gave play to the

z

hoses and the firemen obtained the mastery. In 1878, Mr. Joseph Eldred's company had concluded their entertainment when the acting manager, Mr. Albert Newcombe, saw a cloud of smoke issuing from the upper windows. Flames soon followed; and, in a couple of hours, the theatre was once more gutted and nothing remained but the bare walls.

Negociations for the erection in Plymouth of a Theatre of Varieties were completed in 1898, when a site which had hitherto been devoted to a pandemonium known as "The Fancy Fair" was occupied by a structure of elegant design and magnificent proportions, from plans prepared by Mr. W. H. Arber, of London, to which the name of "The Palace" was given. A commanding façade in terra cotta contained panel reproductions in tiles of Sir Oswald Brierly's celebrated Armada pictures. From the principal entrance in Union Street, a handsome Sicilian marble staircase led to the balcony and foyers, and the stalls were reached through avenues of mirrors. In the draping of the proscenium the Union Jack formed the leading feature of a sumptuous expanse of velvet, and the panels in the dome, the friezes and the balcony were filled with paintings of naval and military triumphs, as well as incidents of local and national interest. Over the proscenium arch was a fresco illustrating the knighting of Drake, and the dome contained similar representations of brilliant naval successes, painted by W. H. C. Brewer, of London, and exhibited at the Royal Academy prior to their fixture in this resplendent temple of amusement. The inception of the scheme for thus replacing a nuisance by a stately edifice was due to Mr. Edward Snow Lancaster and Mr. Charles E. Cottier; and the scheme was financed by Mr. Henry Pocock, a London millionaire. Up to this period the stage at St. James's Hall had been used by variety performers. It was now acquired at a cost of £11,000 and closed to prevent damaging competition; and the artistes formerly engaged by the Messrs. Livermore were transferred to the new hall. Upon the death of Mr. J. R. Newcombe, Mr. Henry Reed, his son-in-law, leased the Theatre Royal, but the Corporation, having invited tenders from the general public, the institution was run for several years by Mr. Charles Williams, a native of Plympton, who had long evinced his taste for theatricals by organising amateur evenings in the country villages for purely charitable purposes. Mr. Reed thereupon constructed the Grand Theatre, in Union Street, Stonehouse; but the old establishment continued to command the strong favour of the public, and the proprietor of "The Palace" easily induced Mr. Reed to sell the "Grand" for £17,000. Including the cost of re-erecting the Great Western Hotel as an adjunct of the new group, some £185,000 was thus expended—the largest sum invested on any architectural pile in the West.

"The Palace" had not been opened more than seven months when it was visited by fire, due to the neglect of those precautions which had weighed so seriously with the architect. During the pourtrayal of a mimic battle scene, scraps of burning paper flew to the wings; and, after the audience had dispersed, and the iron curtain had been allowed to remain overhead, the stage became wrapped in flames which completely destroyed the decorations and costly upholstering. "The Palace" was closed for several months during the repairs, and it was found impossible to replace the works of art which had rendered unique the dome and proscenium. Photographs of the more locally attractive appear in the Drake period of this volume. Not the least interesting theatrical revival was that effected by Mr. Arthur Carlton at Devonport; who, in a few years, converted a howling waste, which was little better than "a penny gaff," into a popular and flourishing resort. The ruins of the old theatre had for more than a generation been cleared at the instance of Alderman Anstey, and the area converted into the Cumberland Gardens. In five years from the date of its erection, the "Metropole" in Tavistock Street was almost reconstructed to meet the pressure of play-goers; and a new pit was created under the level of the public road whilst the performances were in progress.

Amongst the amateurs who were introduced to the public was Miss Maggie Grigg, a Plymouth beauty, who subsequently achieved fame on the Lyric stage as " Florence St. John." Mr. John Pardew, then a lad of promise as an instrumentalist, also evinced those varied accomplishments which marked him as the most cosmopolitan virtuoso his native town has produced. Amateur dramatic performances were organised by Major Rendle and Mr. Kinton Bond at the Theatre and the old Volunteer depôt in Catherine Street ; and Captain " Jack " Stevens, Captain " Alf " Dyer, Captain Holmes, Captain " David " Brown, Lovel Dunstan, Fred Dunstan, " Billy " Pike and others constituted a gifted Bohemian band by whom "The Ticket of Leave Man" and other plays were presented, often with side-splitting unrehearsed effects. In the more amusing contretemps the amateurs revelled, and there is more than a suspicion that they sometimes contrived to bring about diverting episodes. During a representation of Macbeth the gentleman who was ascending as an evil spirit, when half-way between Heaven and Earth, came suddenly crashing to the stage, and there he sat disconcerted, amid uproarious laughter. This individual nevertheless clung to Hecate as his favourite rôle, but stipulated for a more reliable apparatus. A trap arrangement was substituted for the sliding beam, but he now allowed his foot to dangle outside the little platform on which he was picturesquely posed. The merry ones in the wings thereupon prompted the mechanical artist to shoot the consequential part of the scene with the utmost velocity ; and, instead of the sombre remark which Hecate was expected to make at this juncture, the agonised cry rang through the stillness, " Oh, my toe, my toe." The Devonshire dialect played sad havoc at times with the composure of the audience. Lagardère was in the act of flight during the performance of the " Duke's Motto," when a gallant artiste suddenly arrested the chief officer in pursuit with the tragic intimation : " Leegurdare is ded. Bind'n with koards and pitch'n overboard. Wunst to the bottom he'll nivvur cum op agaen." A volunteer who acted the soldier in Hamlet, was accustomed to demand with a flavour that was worthy of Widdecombe Fair : " Who cums yur ? " One worthy captain religiously waited from half-past seven until a quarter to ten in order to utter the majestic command : " Make way for the king." Every few minutes he pestered his friends as to when it was his turn to go on ; and, when, at last, he received the cue, he walked with measured stride to the centre of the stage—and there stood speechless ! In his fright he had quite forgotten his one line, and he escaped to the wings amidst bewildering shouts. Excruciating was the scene when " Billy " Pike, entering with profound obeisance, exclaimed : " Here comes the king ! " The king, however, was not in evidence, and Jack Fly repeated the trumpet obligato that heralded his approach. " Billy " repeated the fateful words : " Here comes the King ! " Still, no king, or any indications of his majesty. Fly reiterated the instrumental flourish with prolonged crescendo, and then the monarch painfully shuffled on the stage, holding by his two hands the royal skirts which he had found an insurmountable difficulty in adjusting.

Music and Musicians :   The cold and cheerless Puritanism which characterised Plymouth
    1823-1899.   found its reflex in the distaste for music which was long evidenced in its places of worship, and that excluded the organ from St. Andrew's Church till the 18th century. During the early recollections of Henry Woollcombe, music was not much in vogue in the Three Towns, and the little that was heard in private places was not of a high character. One of the earliest announcements of a concert occurs in 1821, when W. Halls, who "gratefully" acknowledged the favours he had reached from the lovers of music in the Three Towns and neighbourhood, informed them that, with the assistance of a few friends, he proposed holding a concert at the Dock Theatre, with Mr. John Bowden as

leader, Mr. Honey as principal violoncello, Mr. Smale as trumpet, and Miss Nightingale as soloist on the double action pedal harp.   The programme included songs—sentimental and comic—glees, instrumental solos and " catches "—of which " Ah, how Sophia," alias " A house on fire," was distinctly popular.   " When shall we three meet again ? " was one of the glees.   The Dock Harmonic Society gave their first concert at the Philosophical Rooms in 1823, with Mrs. Bennett as chief soprano vocalist.   The Stonehouse Harmonic Society commenced the following year ; and, for some seasons, went through their pro- grammes at the Commercial Inn.   Subscription concerts were established in 1827, at the Royal Hotel, by Messrs. Collins and Honey ; and the artistes were drawn " from the Theatre " and Plymouth regimental bands.   In 1828 Madame Catalani appeared before a brilliant audience in the Assembly Rooms.   It was the last appearance upon the stage of the then "Queen of Song," and she was rapturously received.   Hers was the majesty of singing, in the estimation of Plymothians, by whom the depreciatory comments of London critics could not be understood; and her rendering of " All that's bright must fade " was described as a glorious achievement.   So electrifying was her " Rule Britannia " that the audience rose and joined in the chorus, and, on responding, similar ebullitions were evoked.   Mr. Bowden was the leader on this occasion, and the orchestral arrangements were in the hands of Mr. Honey.

Mount Sinai, a new oratorio, was well presented at the Town Hall, Devonport, in 1831, with band and chorus selected from the professionals and amateurs of the Three Towns. Messrs. Beer, Brown, Gosling, Chegwyn and Code were the leading vocalists.   Mrs. Case gave a concert at the Freemasons' Hall in 1833, and the circular contained a testimonial from the Mayor and several leading citizens to the quality of the glee singing of her sons " whose voices peculiarly and beautifully harmonise with each other.   Their correct taste and style of singing affords a rich treat ; and, under the peculiar circumstances in which this family is placed, we strongly recommend them to public notice and support."   In 1834 the Devonport Choral Society acquitted themselves with distinction in "The Witches," from Macbeth—a chorus composed when Locke was organist of Exeter Cathedral, and first performed when Charles II. entered the " Ever Faithful " city.   Miss Martin was the bright heroine of this reproduction.   Insufficient support and other difficulties were overcome in 1835 : harmony ruled amongst the leading musicians, and the first Devonport Subscription Concert was held.   No " star " appeared upon the horizon, but Mrs. Waye and Miss Lavallin justified the confidence reposed in " home produce."   Mrs. Waye sang with much sweetness " Come where the Jessamine "; and Miss Lavallin a solo from Meyerbeer's " Grovenetto Cavalier."   At one period the latter was disturbed by a lady in hysterics ; and, in her next song, she was left behind by the accompanist—intentionally, it was insinuated, in order to damage a young and rising vocalist.   If some of the comment was generous not a little of it was malicious.   Mr. Locke's mellifluous sweetness with the flute was said to be marred by an offensive treatment of a low note, which he produced " as though in great disgust, and spitting with all his might" into the mouth of his instrument.   Young Mr. Moore selected a fantasia " which was entirely above his strength " ; and substituted a " sawyer-like bowing " for flowing and continuous manipulation.   As the leader, Mr. Moore, senior, was commended for his energy ; but he was admonished without delay to refrain from his "odious glissades up the strings."   The one complaint against Mr. Tom's songs was that he accompanied himself, and thereby suggested "a nice analogy to the man who is his own lawyer."

Much restraint under the lash must have characterised the various performers and vocalists at these Devonport concerts.   Their entertainments were "cheap as dirt," but orchestra and chorus were reminded that they could never expect to be commensurately remunerated for their "dreadfully-hard work in the fortissimo climaxes." They forgot, they were told, that "huge blown blasts of sounds" were not always wanted, and were accused of introducing Vulcan's noisy forge into the Concert-room by clanging, banging and blasting away "like so many Cyclops." In 1836, Mr. P. E. Rowe announced a subscription evening at Plymouth ; and Miss Taylor, from the Colosseum, London, sang delightfully, executed a capriccio upon the harp, and accompanied herself at the piano. At these concerts musical instruments and performers of manifold sorts and conditions were included, "in classes and out of classes, from the pseudo-classic R.A.M. to the camel driver's bells." The rooms engaged were the Freemasons' in Cornwall Street, the New London in Vauxhall Street, the Assembly Rooms at the Royal Hotel, the Lyceum in Westwell Street, and, later on, with the institution of the Devon and Cornwall Philharmonic Society, St. George's Hall, as the only building sufficiently large to allow of choral works. The Assembly Rooms were engaged for a concert by Liszt in 1840—"the first appearance here of this extraordinary pianiste." The artiste performed his grand march "Hongroise" and his gallop "Chromatique."

The principal artistes at the concerts given by the Plymouth Harmonic Society were Mr. and Mrs. Crouch, who made Dock their place of residence, and the west the arena of their professional scope. Crouch was a thriftless genius, with a musical wife and sixteen musical children. According to his daughter, Cora Pearl, who was born in Plymouth in 1842, and earned a most unenviable notoriety as "The English beauty of the French Empire," nothing was ever heard at home but music and musical dialogues. Those who did not appreciate Crouch's "Kathleen Mavourneen" were "fools" in the estimation of the author, and "beasts" in the judgment of his children. Crouch was devoted to his family, but his income melted so rapidly that little of it was expended on the house, and he squandered two fortunes in the course of his life. His manner of singing was "pleasing and touching"; but he lacked the "thunder" necessary for the songs in "The Tempest," and it was jocosely remarked that his voice scarcely amounted to a "squall." Indeed it was more than once hinted that he did not justify the highly favourable criticisms of his own performances which he regularly supplied to the "West of England Conservative," and that he owed most of his success to the indifferent ability of his competitors. Mrs. Crouch possessed an exquisite voice and an accurate ear, and she was especially charming in Swiss melodies and familiar English ballads that required no exercise of the bravura. On one occasion she excited so much emotion in the character song, "Spare Poor Little Gipsy a Halfpenny" that a sailor in the stalls shouted "That I will my dear," and flung on the stage the first coin that he could draw from his pocket. At the Crouch concerts, Miss Clara Novello was a welcome favourite, and the compass of her voice was astonishing and her execution animated. Mr. Patey, a native of Plymouth, was accustomed to render the violin solos. A leading tenor at one of these evenings was reminded that a little less of the trumpet-stop of his nasal organ would be acceptable, and that the air in finding its way through the wrong passage caused a "very disagreeable twang."

Classical music owed much of its local cultivation to Mr. T. E. Weekes, who, for sixty years, presented concertos on the pianoforte, with the assistance of a small orchestra. During his earlier career, Mr. Weekes was accustomed to give performances at his house ; and, as the sitting-room was necessarily limited, the programme was repeated on three successive days—first to the schools, next to the townfolk, and, finally, to visitors from the country. In promoting this taste, Mr. Weekes had to overcome prejudice on the part of parents who preferred more popular compositions. His mantle fell upon the shoulders of his son, Mr. Samuel Weekes, to whom the west is no less indebted for the development of culture. Sir William Snow Harris was a cordial patron of the art in Plymouth ; and, apart from concerts held at his own house in Windsor Villas, with Mr. T. E. Weekes as conductor, he fitted up St. George's Hall as a drawing-room on more than one occasion, Mr. Winterbottom, leader of the Marine Band, wielding the baton.

Lord Graves and Sir William formed the Devon and Cornwall Philharmonic Society in 1848, with Mr. Lancaster, organist of St. John's Chapel, as the moving professional force. Haydn's oratorio, "The Creation," was rendered in 1852, with Mr. Smyth as conductor; and Madame Smyth, Miss E. Phillips, Mr. Carpenter (tenor), Mr. H. Phillips (bass), Mr Constantine (chorus master), Mr. Macdonald (pianist), Mr. Rogers (oboe), and Mr. Henry Reed (leader of the orchestra) were the principal figures on the occasion. The institution existed for a few seasons, and Miss Clara Novello and Miss Anna Bishop alternately appeared as the chief soloists. As the spirit of jealousy ate into the management the influential supporters took their departure and established the Plymouth, Devonport and Stonehouse Choral Society, with Mr. George Hele as the first conductor. The Plymouth Choral Society next enjoyed a brief existence, travelling from one small town to another in the locality. As the use of gas had not spread to the country, the various halls in Plympton, Saltash, Okehampton and Liskeard were lit by candles only.

Jenny Lind was "beholden with rapturous eyes" in 1849, and the beauty and melody of her voice, and its marvellous capacity for expression, filled the audience with delight. Carried away by her own enthusiasm, "The Swedish Nightingale" sang with such fervour that genius was declared in every accent, phrase and impulse. On the Sunday following her concert, St. Andrew's Church was besieged in the belief that Jenny Lind would attend the service; and, to confirm the report, a lady, who bore some resemblance to the cantatrice, entered the edifice as the prayers commenced. She was ostentatiously conducted by the verger to a favoured pew, and her every movement was rhapsodically followed. Her singing was the subject of endless whisperings, and "melodious" and "flute-like" passed from mouth to mouth. After the sermon was over and the worshippers (of Jenny Lind) were dispersing, the lady was mobbed, and she could scarcely reach the door. In her surprise, she enquired and learnt the reason of the smiles and compliments that were being bestowed upon her, and the lady blushingly explained: "You're much mistaken; I came to see Jenny Lind myself." As a matter of fact, the artiste had already left for Exeter.

Music was under lasting obligations to Mr. J. R. Newcombe, through whose efforts Mr. Sims Reeves and Miss Lucombe made occasional appearances in grand opera. The former took the part of Edgar Ravenswood in Lucia de Lammermoor, and Miss Lucombe that of Miss Ashton. Mr. Sims Reeves also impersonated Tom Tug in the Waterman. M. Jullien was regularly engaged, and concerts "a la Jullien" were given by other artistes. "The greatest lyrical artiste of the century," Madame Grisi, took her farewell in Plymouth. "There is something inexpressibly affecting to me in addressing the word 'farewell' to an English audience; for that farewell is an adieu—and for ever—to the land of my adoption as an artiste; to the land in which have been centred all my hopes, in which have been realised my brightest wishes. It is a farewell to a career which, by unexampled generosity and unparalleled kindness, has far surpassed my expectations and exceeded my deserts. To say *adieu*, therefore, to this country, inspires me with the deepest regret. That this regret is shared by the English public I venture to believe; for to think otherwise would be to do violence to a support that has never failed me—to a partiality on which I have had but too often to depend. It is this consciousness that mitigates the pain inseparable from such an occasion, and that will always be a source of pleasure to me in my retirement, enhancing the remembrance of those countless acts of favour, for which the thousands who have bestowed them will have the heartfelt gratitude of GIULIA GRISI."

Thys comelie little Booke wylle, when yᵉ fame fhalle have bene unfolded, defcourfe yᵉ matter yat pertaneth to a

𝕲𝖗𝖆𝖓𝖉𝖊 𝕮𝖔𝖓𝖈𝖊𝖗𝖈𝖊

To be helde in yᵉ buildinge ycleped

yᵉ 𝕹𝖊𝖜 𝕲𝖚𝖎𝖑𝖉𝖊 = 𝕳𝖆𝖑𝖑

in yᵉ Borough of *Plymouthe*, atte viij of yᵉ clocke on yᵉ
XIXth *daie of yᵉ month of Octobere*, MDCCCLXXXI,
And for whyche *Maifters MOON & SONS*, have broughte from yᵉ
great Citie of *London* yᵉ followinge bande of ryghte fkilfulle
mufickianiers ycleped

✛✛ 𝕳𝖊𝖗 𝕸𝖆𝖏𝖊𝖋𝖙𝖎𝖊'𝖘 𝕺𝖕𝖊𝖗𝖆. ✛✛

Mdme. Marie Roze.	*Mdme Enriquez.*
Signor De Monaco.	*Signor Foli.*
Signor Zoboli.	*Mr. Farley Sinkins.*

Signor Papini (Solo *Violinift*).

✶ ✶ ✶ ✶ ✶ ✶ ✶ ✶ ✶ ✶ ✶ ✶ ✶ ✶

𝕐e 𝕸𝖞𝖓𝖋𝖙𝖗𝖆𝖑𝖈𝖞𝖊 wille be ledde by one *Signor ANTONIO MORA*, a verie cunnynge mufickianier, whofe fingers wylle caufe yᵉ grande harpfychorde (or as fomme in yfe dayes doe call it yᵉ pianoe) mayde by Maifters Collard & Collard, toe give forthe fweete and cherefulle muficke.

OF Yᴱ TICKETS

and yᵉ mony to bee payed for yᵉ fame.

For yᵉ Numbered Stalles, V fhillinges.
For yᵉ Seats referved in Blockes, III fhillinges and VI pence.
For yᵉ Balconie and yᵉ Area, II fhillinges.
For yᵉ refte of yᵉ Hall where yᵉ younge menne and maydenes and
divers perfonnes maye either walk or fitte down, I fhillinge.

𝕹ow 𝖑𝖊𝖙𝖙𝖊 𝖆𝖑𝖑𝖊 thatte purpofe toe come toe yis *Concerte*, bothe yᵉ olde and younge—give moft fpecyalle hede untoe yᵉ followynge :
Yᵉ Ticketts may bee hadde off Maifter Moon & Sons, at their figne of
"𝖄𝖊 𝕳𝖆𝖗𝖕𝖋𝖞𝖈𝖍𝖔𝖗𝖉𝖊,"
in yᵉ streete ycleped George, in yᵉ faid Boroughe.
Yᵉ ladyes wyll fynd a Cloke-roome clofe bye yᵉ entraunce doores, where they may leave their clokes and wrappes in fafe charge.

𝕹OWE if their bee any yat doe defyre toe knowe more anent any matter touchynge yis Concerte, lette yem ftrait waie applie to eithere of yᵉ *Maifter Moons*, who wille fayn willynglie expounde fuche matere as appearthe nott hereinne.

Querie I.   What is yᵉ keye note toe good manners?   Anfwere—B natural.
Querie II. Whye is an authore yᵉ ftraungefte animale on yᵉ earthe ?   Anfwere—Becaufe his tayle iffueth out of hys heade.

N.B.—Thys Booke is not for eury rude and unconnynge man to fee/ but for clerkys and uerie gentylmen yat underftande gentylnefs and fcyence.—Willyam Caxton.

Theatre Royal, Plymouth.

FOR THE BENEFIT OF MR. EDMUND KEAN.

ON MONDAY evening, October 11th, 1830, being the last night Mr. KEAN will ever perform in Plymouth, it has been deemed expedient, for the better amusement of his patrons, to follow the plan he adopted in London, of performing his three principal characters, in three acts of different plays, in the following order :—

THE FOURTH ACT OF
THE MERCHANT OF VENICE,
SHYLOCK...... ......Mr. KEAN.

THE FOURTH ACT OF
THE DRAMATIST.
The Second Act of the Iron Chest,
Sir E. Mortimore......Mr. KEAN.

THE FARCE OF
The Day after the Wedding.
THE FIFTH ACT OF
A New Way to Pay Old Debts.
Sir Giles Overreach......Mr. KEAN.

TO CONCLUDE WITH **The Two Gregories.**
On WEDNESDAY—"THE GAMBLERS" and "BLACK-EYED SUSAN."
Nights of Performing this week—MONDAY, WEDNESDAY, THURSDAY, and FRIDAY.
Boxes—First Circle, 4s. ; Second Circle, 3s. ; Third Circle, 2s. Pit, 2s. Gallery 1s.
Tickets may be had, and places for the boxes taken, at Mr. NETTLETON's *Herald-office,* Whimple street.
Doors open at half-past 6 and commence at 7.
Second account at half-past 8.

Theatre Royal, Plymouth.

THE LAST NIGHT OF SARDANAPALUS !!
Mr. Charles Kean as Sardanapalus.

THIS present SATURDAY, JANUARY 10th, 1835, will be presented a New Tragedy, called
SARDANAPALUS!
OR, THE FALL OF NINEVEH !
With New Scenery, Machinery, Dresses, and Decorations.
SARDANAPALUS (King of Assyria) Mr. KEAN.
Principal New Scenery.. PALACE OF SARDANAPALUS ! A View of the EUPHRATES. GRAND HALL of NIMROD. Brilliant and Sumptuous Banquet. Conflagration of the Palace. Destruction of the Assyrian Monarch with his Ionian Maid. Superb and Awful Perspective of the City of Nineveh wrapped in Flames.
The Scenery designed by Mr. STAMPFORD, and executed by him with Assistants under his immediate direction...The Machinery by Mr. SAMPSON... Dresses and other Decorations by Mr. FORDE.
To conclude with PERFECTION.
On MONDAY, JANUARY 12,
FOR THE BENEFIT OF MR. KEAN,
And LAST NIGHT of his performing this Season, the Grand TRAGIC PLAY OF
HAMLET, PRINCE OF DENMARK.
After which the highly-popular and celebrated Musical Entertainment of the
THE HUNTER OF THE ALPS.
The characters of HAMLET in the Play, and FELIX in the Afterpiece, by Mr. KEAN.

Theatre Royal, Devonport.

MR. DAWSON in again having the honor to open the Devonport Theatre, begs to offer the sincere tribute of his thanks for the liberal Patronage with which he was favoured last season. The Recess has been passed in active preparations for the present Campaign, and the arrangements made for the amusement and convenience of the Public, will, he trusts, ensure a continuance of their highly-appreciated favour. He is proud to think that among the new "Corps Dramatique" whom he has engaged, he will have the good fortune to introduce a decided importation of TALENT, which he respectfully recommends to the fostering encouragement of the Public. He pledges himself to produce a succession of Novelties, that for variety, beauty, and pleasing effect, shall not be surpassed ; and which, while evincing his gratitude for the past will likewise secure him future favours.

Mr. Dawson has the honour to announce that he has secured the services of that established favorite, MISS JARMAN, for a LIMITED PERIOD.

The Theatre will open for the Winter Season on MONDAY, October 17th, 1836. On the rising of the Curtain Mrs. DAWSON will have the honour to deliver an OPENING ADDRESS; after which the National Anthem of "God save the King," will be sung by the Company.

Followed by a New Nautical Drama, called
THE OCEAN OF LIFE !
OR EVERY INCH A SAILOR.
Two new scenes have been painted expressly for this piece.
Act 2nd—AN INDIAN VILLAGE.
Act 3rd—A VIEW OF HAMOAZE.
The performances to conclude with the Musical Farce called
The Loan of a Lover.
On TUESDAY Evening, a favourite Nautical Drama, with the new Vaudeville called the WELSH GIRL, in which Miss JARMAN will take the part of JULIA.
On WEDNESDAY Evening, will be presented a new Romantic Melo-Drama, entitled the EDDYSTONE ELF, or the Light-house in 1696 ; followed by the Farce of the £100 NOTE, the Hon. Miss Arlington, by Miss JARMAN.

Theatre Royal, Plymouth.

THE MANAGER feels great pleasure in informing his Patrons that he has prevailed on the very talented and popular Actor
MR. MACREADY,
to accept an engagement at this Theatre, for positively
THREE NIGHTS ONLY,
viz :—MONDAY 26th, TUESDAY 27th, and WEDNESDAY 28th April, being (in consequence of Mr. Macready having become Lessee of the Theatre Royal, Drury Lane) probably the last time he will be seen in Plymouth, for many seasons,
On MONDAY, the 26th of APRIL,
MACBETH,
TUESDAY, 27th—WERNER.
WEDNESDAY, the 28th—RICHELIEU.
Dated April 13th, 1841.

PLYMOUTH AND DEVONPORT THEATRE PLAYBILLS : 1830-1841.

Theatre Royal, Plymouth.

First appearance of Madam CELESTE this season.

ON MONDAY, April 2nd, 1838, will be presented the entire New Piece of
ST. MARY'S EVE,
Or, the Story of the Solway.
Madeline........................Mademciselle CELESTE.
After which Madam Celeste will dance the celebrated
CACHUSA.
To be followed by the laughable farce of
MY FELLOW CLERK.
M. Celeste will also perform a novel description Dance, for the First time here, entitled,
LA CHATTE.
The whole to conclude with the Operata of
THE SENTINEL.
Mr. Davenport has the honor of announcing that he has succeeded in engaging Madam CELESTE, for THREE NIGHTS, and which is POSITIVELY her last appearance in Plymouth.

Her Nights for Performance will be MONDAY, TUESDAY, and THURSDAY.

Boxes, 4s. ; Half-price, 2s.—Upper Circle, 3s. ; Half-price, 1s. 6d—Pit, 2s. ; Half-price, 1s.— Gallery, 1s. ; Half-price, 6d.

Doors open at ½ past 6, commence at 7.

Box Tickets, &c. may be had of Mr. ROWE, Music Seller, Bedford-street, and of Mr. MAY, Printer, Bilbury-street, Plymouth ; also of Mr. BYERS, Printer, Devonport.

LAST WEEK BUT TWO OF THE SEASON.

Theatre Royal, Plymouth.

THE Manager feels great pleasure in informing the Public *REAR-ADMIRAL ROSS, C.B.*, has, with extreme kindness, condescended to honour this Theatre with his FAREWELL PATRONAGE.

On MONDAY, April 17, will be presented the Comedy entitled
THE CLIMBING BOY.
After which a new series of SPLENDID TABLEAUX, the subjects of these beautiful pictorial groupings are taken from the Waverley Novels.
After which the laughable FARCE called
NICHOLAS FLAM.
Nicholas Flam (Attorney-at-Law)...Mr. PHELPS.
Shrimp (his Clerk).................. ..Mr. HAY.
ON TUESDAY PLACE CALLED
OTHELLO.
Othello..Mr. PHELPS. Iago..Mr. SHALDERS.
After which the SPLENDID BALLET called
CINDERELLA.
With the magnificent Ball Room and Dancing, which has nightly been received with shouts of applause, and is universally allowed to be the most splendid production of the provincial stage.

Doors open at Half-past Six, Performance commences at Half-past Seven.

Tickets to be had of Mr. NETTLETON, Printer, &c, Whimple street, Plymouth, where places for the boxes can be taken.

Theatre Royal, Devonport.

POSITIVELY THE LAST NIGHT OF THE SEASON!

UNDER DISTINGUISHED PATRONAGE.
FOR THE BENEFIT OF MR. DOEL.

MR. DOEL takes this opportunity of returning his sincere thanks to the Nobility, Gentry, the Army and Navy and the Public in general, who have kindly honoured him with their support, during a long season of seven months.

Mr. DOEL begs to state that he has been surrounded by Novelties during the whole of his Season, but proud, at the same time, to say that he has redeemed the pledge he made to the public—that if he opened the Theatre, he would rescue it from the state it had fallen. He has fought the battle, but leaves it to the Public to decide whether he has gained it or not. He makes his bow to the Public on MONDAY, March 10th, 1845, for the LAST TIME this Season, and it will be the proudest recollection of his life to keep the feather in his cap that his Patrons have placed there, and they may be assured he will wear it gratefully as well as triumphantly.

On Monday, March 10th, 1845, the performances will commence with the celebrated Domestic Drama called
THE DESERTED VILLAGE!
Or, Who'll Lend me a Shilling ?
Peter Grievous............................ ....Mr. DOEL.
Song—"*The Spirit of the Storm.*"—Mr.Dodsworth.
To be followed, by particular desire, by the favourite Farce of
YOUNG ENGLAND.
Mr. James Pooley ....Mr. Doel.
Mrs. Pooley........ ....Mrs. Hartell.
A New Comic Song—Mr. RORKE.
The whole to conclude with the laughable Farce of the
£100 NOTE.
Billy Black (with a string of conundrums)—Mr. Doel
"*Why is Mr. Doel like a good Parlour Fire?*"
Do you give it up? Come and he'll tell you.

Theatre Royal, Devonport.

FASHIONABLE NIGHT.

By desire and under the immediate Patronage of LADY DICKSON AND LADY LEEKE.

FOR the BENEFIT of MRS. DOEL. On which occasion Mr. Doel solicits the support of the Ladies, Gentlemen, officers of the Navy, Army and the public, and assures them that nothing shall be wanting to render the evening's amusement worthy the above distinguished patronage.

'*Tis not in mortals to command success,*
But we'll do more—deserve it.

On MONDAY, January the 18th, 1847, the entertainments will commence with Tobin's celebrated comedy in five acts, called the
HONEY-MOON!
OR, HOW TO RULE A WIFE.
To be followed with the laughable interlude entitled
THE SECRET; or, A HOLE IN THE WALL
Comic Song..........Mr. T. Reeves.
To conclude with (second time in this Theatre)
THE CAPTAIN IS NOT A MISS.

PLYMOUTH AND DEVONPORT THEATRE PLAYBILLS : 1838-1847.

Theatre Royal, Plymouth.

GREAT SUCCESS OF MRS. WAYLETT
Who has been nightly received with rapturous encores in all her songs by CROWDED and FASHIONABLE HOUSES.

THIS EVENING (SATURDAY), February 24th, 1838, the performance, under the immediate Patronage of

The Ladies and Gentlemen

Of George-street and Terrace, Frankfort and Union-streets, Athenæum-street and Terrace, Buckland and Mount Pleasant Terraces, the Crescent, St. Andrew's Terrace, Princess Square, and Lockyer-street,

Will Commence With

WOOING A WIDOW;

OR,

LOVE UNDER A LAMP POST.

Ellen Bloomly................. ...Mrs. WAYLETT.

In which character she will sing " *Meet Me in the Willow Glen,*" and the Irish Ballad of " *Norah Creina,*" after which,

LOVE AND MYSTERY.

Celeste de Montgomery...............Mrs. WAYLETT,

With the Songs, " *Ah, don't you, dear Harry, remember,*" and " *Those Tinkling Bells.*"

The whole to conclude with,

A DAY WELL SPENT.

Boxes, 4s. ; Half-price, 2s.—Upper Circle, 3s. ; Half-price, 1s. 6d.—Pit, 2s. ; Half-price, 1s.—Gallery, 1s. ; Half-price, 6d.

Doors open at ½ past 6, commence at 7.

CAUTION.

This is to give notice, that any person throwing anything on the stage, or into the pit, will be immediately apprehended, and a Reward of ONE POUND will be given, on such Person or Persons being convicted before a Magistrate.

Theatre Royal, Devonport.

THE Lessee begs most respectfully to inform the Public that the Theatre will be OPENED for the LAST TIME (until the commencement of the Season in October, 1842) on TUESDAY NEXT, in honour of the Launch of the 90-gun Ship from the Dock-yard, at Devonport.

The performances will commence with a Melo-Drama, in Two Acts, entitled

THE WIZARD OF THE MOOR.

After which the Farce of the MUMMY.

A VARIETY OF SINGING AND DANCING.

The whole to conclude with a Farce, called

RAISING THE WIND.

Boxes, 2s. 6d. Slips, 2s. Pit, 1s. Gallery, 6d.

£5 REWARD.

VIOLENT ASSAULT ON MR. OWEN.

Whereas, some Person did on the night of TUESDAY, the 30th of August, 1842, about 9 o'clock, nearly opposite Mr. Reed's, Hair Dresser, Cumberland-street, Devonport, Strike a Violent Blow on the Head of Mr. Owen :—Whoever will give information of the Offender, in order that he may be brought to Justice, shall on conviction, receive the above Reward. This is the Second Assault on Mr. Owen during the last six days.

Theatre Royal, Plymouth.

The last night but Five of the Engagement of Sir WILLIAM and LADY DON.

ON MONDAY, the entertainments will commence with Mr. J. B. BUCKSTONE'S powerful Drama, in Three Acts, entitled the

FLOWERS OF THE FOREST :

A GIPSY STORY.

The Kinchin, a Gipsy, Sir WM. DON, Bart., Starlight Bess, Basket Maker, Fortune Teller, and Ballad Singer, Lady DON.

To conclude with the popular Burletta, in Two Acts, called

NICHOLAS NICKLEBY;

Or, *Doings at Do-The-Boys' Hall.*

John Brodie, a Yorkshire Farmer, Sir WM. DON, Bart. ; Smike, an Orphan, Lady DON.

MR. J. R. NEWCOMBE has the honour to announce that the LAST GRAND MILITARY AMATEUR PERFORMANCE Is fixed for MONDAY, January 31, 1853, when will be presented Tobin's elegant Comedy of

THE HONEY-MOON.

In compliance with a wish expressed by the Gentlemen Amateurs, Mrs. HENRY REED will perform a Grand Fantasia on Airs from " Lucia di Lammermoor."—*E. Prudent.*

Ballad—" The Old Chimney Corner "—*Composed by J. M. Jolly*—Miss F. Young.

To Conclude with the Comedy of

CHARLES II.

Theatre Royal, Plymouth.

LAST NIGHT BUT ONE OF THE ENGAGE-MENT OF MR. AND MRS.

CHARLES KEAN.

THEY WILL BE ASSISTED BY

MISS CHAPMAN, MR. G. EVERETT, AND MR. J. F. CATHCART

(Late Members of the Royal Princess's Company, London).

ON MONDAY, OCTOBER 17TH, 1859, Shakspere's Tragedy,

HAMLET.

Hamlet, son to the former, and nephew to the present King, Mr. CHARLES KEAN ; Gertrude, Queen of Denmark, and mother of Hamlet, Mrs. CHARLES KEAN.

After which,

A GRAND FAIRY BALLET,

In which Madlles. MARIE and COLLINSON will appear, supported by Miss H. Morris, Miss F. Morris, Miss L. Coleman, Miss Hicks, Miss Russell, Miss Osmond, Miss Copeland, Miss Archer, &c., &c.

To conclude with the laughable Farce of

NOTHING TO WEAR.

On TUESDAY.—" Mary Queen of Scots," " Le Corsaire," and " As Like as two Peas."

On WEDNESDAY.—" Much Ado about Nothing," " The Star of the Rhine," and " Raising the Wind "; being for the Benefit of Mr. and Mrs. CHARLES KEAN, and Positively the LAST NIGHT OF THEIR APPEARANCE.

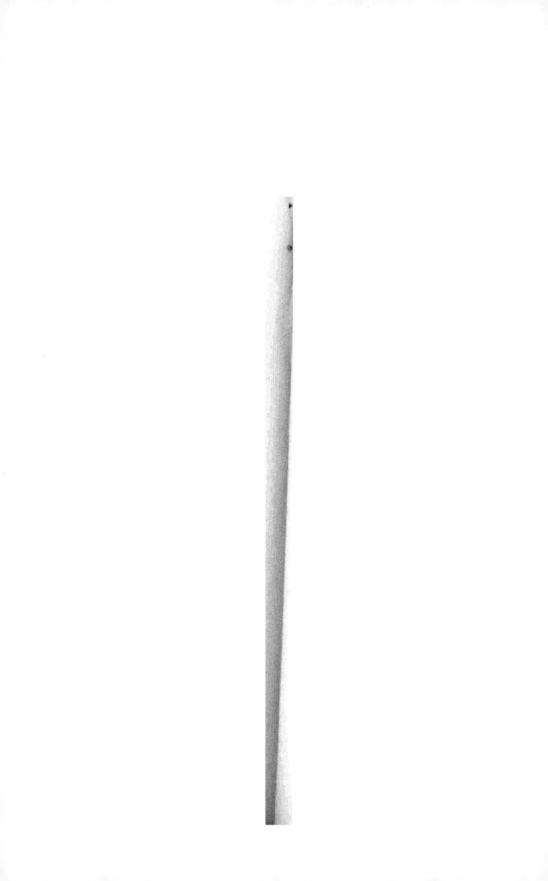

THEATRE ROYAL, PLYMOUTH.
LESSEE AND MANAGER.—MR. J. R. NEWCOMBE.

LAST NIGHT BUT TWO of the Engagement of the popular
Author and Actor, Mr. E. STIRLING.

THE FIVE-FIELDS TRAGEDY, which was received Last Night with the greatest Applause and Approbation, by a House crowded to the Ceiling, will be repeated this Evening.

On TUESDAY, Oct. 29th, 1850,
Will be produced a NEW LOCAL DRAMA,
founded on actual Events that occurred at Stoke, in the year 1787,--written expressly
for this Theatre by **Mr. E. STIRLING,** produced with New Scenery **painted
from Sketches on the Spot,** appropriate Dresses, Music, &c., to be
called The

FIVE - FIELDS TRAGEDY;
Or, The ASSASSIN'S BRIDGE:
A TALE OF STOKE, IN 1787.

☞ **The subject on which this Drama is founded occupied a large
share of public attention at the time; and goes far to prove that,
despite the cunning or ingenuity employed by Man to CONCEAL, a
retributive Providence in its wise dispensation REVEALS, for the fur-
therance of justice and the vindication of outraged humanity.**

CHARACTERS IN DRAMA:—

Master Philip Smith, a Clerk to the Navy Pay-Office, Dock		Mr. J. W. RAY
Charles Grainger } two young farmers—living at Stoke,		Mr. SYDNEY DAVIS
Edward Lawrance } suitors to Lucy.		Mr. LESLIE
Bobby Bobbin, a Somersetshire Lad—wanting a job		Mr. P. EMERY
Jack Richards, the Butcher } the Assassins of the {		Mr. ROBERTS TINDELL
William Smith, a London Tailor } Bridge {		Mr. ANDREWS
Mr. Bone, the Borough Constable .. Mr. PHELPS	Judge of the Assize ..	Mr. FRANCE
James Grill, a Witness .. Mr. DIXON	Wilson Jones, a Jailer .	Mr. STOTHARD
Lucy Smith, Daughter to old Philip Smith	..	Miss FRANCE
Widow Lawrance, Mother of Edward	..	Mrs. HUDSON KIRBY
Nancy Short, a Devonshire Duck .. Miss C. TELLETT	Amy Couch .	Mrs. HARDING
Constables, Dockyard Men, Mob, &c.		

STOKE,—1787.
A Cottage known as the Lovers' Rest.   Distant view of the **RIVER TAMAR**.
The Father and Daughter—DISAPPOINTED SUITORS—A Secret Foe—Harsh Words—Hard
Blows—Lovers' Stratagems—Stolen Meetings—Surprised!—The Blow !
" Forget not he is my Father ! "
ELM LODGE—The Abode of Peace and Plenty.
Brotherhood of Crime—Evil Thoughts will rise—Idleness, the Root of all Evil—A Tailor's Con-
science—Compact of Guilt to ▬▬▬▬▬   A kind word never ill-bestowed—Disappointment—
Blighted Hopes—The Plot !—Successful Villainy—Discharging a Dockyard Reckoning.
The Mill Field, Stoke Church,
AND THE ASSASSIN'S BRIDGE, As they appeared in the year 1787.
Solitary Watcher—"We won't go home till morning." A New Method of telling the hours—It
strikes One !—Dark Clouds—The Victim—Death Struggle !—The Escape and Recognition—A
False Friend—Mistaken Evidence—A Dying Man's Injunction.
The Farmer's Home—Accusation and Exposure—A Chain of Guilt—Presumptive Evidence—
Agony and Remorse—Woman's Love—A Father's Commands—"Wed not the Murderer !
—Exulting Villainy.
**THE DARK CLOUDS GATHER OVER THE INNOCENT,
AND SUCCESSFUL GUILT SEEMS TO PROSPER.**
Act 2.—A LAPSE OF ONE MONTH. THE PRISON—WIDOW AND HER SON—
" Now, before I dare look upon your face or clasp you by the hand, tell me, I conjure you, by your
trust in heaven, are you innocent ?" Sorrow and suffering. A bright Star rises in the DARK
CLOUDS. Woman's influence prevails—A Link in Guilt's Chain Broken !
THE LOVER'S PRAYER—SPARE THE INNOCENT.   Holm Farm.
MYSTERY OF CRIME—Silent Monitor—Influence of the Evil One—The Mother's Appeal—Unwel-
come Guest—Fearful consequences of ▬▬▬▬▬   The cry is up—Justice on the Scent—
Terrors of Evil-Doers—and Flight—Far, far from Home. " Away, away, your Life hangs on
a Thread ! and your Safety."—Misery and Despair !
THE BARBICAN.
Ups and Downs of Fortune's Wheel—Born under a poor Planet—A new System of studying
Geography. Not a Candidate for Matrimonial Honours—Short Acquaintances. News ! News !!
News ! ! ! SINGLE LIFE—A Warning from Below--How to raise the Old Gentleman—Beggars
and Ballad Singers—An Old Song to a New Tune. The Clock strikes Three ! and another Link
in the Chain of Guilt is Broken. The ARREST.
HOPE IS FOR ALL !—THE DARK CLOUDS DISPERSE.
COURT OF ASSIZE prepared for the TRIAL of the FIVE-FIELDS ASSASSIN.
Wrongfully Accused—The last Ray Hope—The VERDICT—All is Lost—Save him ! save him !
SENTENCE OF THE LAW. The Widow's Prayer. New Lights—The DARK CLOUDS
BRIGHTEN—and the Chain of Guilt is Destroyed ! THE ASSASSINS revealed—Crown
Witness—Retributive Justice.
THE ONE ESCAPE FOR PERJURY AND FALSEHOOD !
Past Sorrows end in Present Joys.

PLYMOUTH THEATRE PLAYBILL: 1850.

No small stir was created in musical circles in 1857 by the institution of a choral and instrumental society, of which Mr. James E. Moon accepted the conductorship, and which aspired to loftier flights than its predecessors. Miss Sherrington, Madame Laura Baxter, Miss Annie Hirst, Miss Ellison, Madame Sainton Dolby, Madame Parepa Rosa, Miss Susan Pyne, and Mr. Wilbye Carper were engaged in the production of Judas Maccabeus, Alexander's Feast, Twelfth Mass and other masterpieces. The festivals continued social functions of the highest order, until dissensions as to precedence led to the resignation of Mr. Moon, and the dissolution of the society. Mr. Samuel Weekes returned from London and originated the Plymouth Orchestral Society in 1862. Open and semi-public nights were given at the Athenæum and the Assembly Rooms. When the new Guildhall was opened money was taken at the doors ; and from that time forward, substantial balances were distributed among the local charities. In 1866, a few enthusiasts, Mr. W. H. K. Wright of the number, formed the Plymouth Musical Association, and a concert was given with a hundred performers. The aim was pure choral music, and the conductor, Mr. Mitchell, a gentleman from West Cornwall, succeeded admirably for three seasons. The attempt to sustain the interest of the leading local musicians failed through internal dissensions, and the Plymouth Vocal Association next evolved with a small orchestra and membership. Mr. Frederick Lohr, a native of Norwich, assumed the conductorship, and produced the finest oratorios with conspicuous success. His tact welded the society for several years, and it was his death that proved the irrecoverable blow. His life was commemorated by a window in the great hall that had been the scene of so many triumphs. The Private Orchestra Society owed its prolonged existence to the ability and direction of Mr. Samuel Weekes, on whom the degree of Fellow of the Academy of Music was conferred after the visit to Plymouth in 1898 of the National Society of Musicians. A spirit of abnegation induced the various musical organisations to combine on that occasion, and the festival thus rendered possible was pronounced as of extraordinary merit. The conductors were Mr. Frank Winterbottom (Royal Marine Band), Mr. Binding (Port Admiral's Band), Mr. Faull (Philharmonic Society), Mr. Bradbury (Stoke Musical Union), and Mr. Moreton (St. Andrew's choir). The presentation of Mr. Weekes' "Nehemiah" evoked a furore from the connoisseurs, and was the direct cause of the distinction conferred upon him.

In more recent times Plymouth has welcomed Patti, Albani, Trebelli, Christine Neilson, Titiens, Nikita, Marie Rose, Nordica, and Clara Butt. Patti attracted a great house in 1890, with the Guildhall floor nearly reserved at a guinea a seat, and the Prince of Wales in attendance. Nikita drew the greatest gathering on record from a numerical standpoint, and every ticket was sold in advance. Miss Robertson owed her introduction to Messrs. Moon, and Miss Marian Mackenzie, a rich contralto, first appeared in her native town. Madame Patey took her farewell performance at Plymouth and died a few days afterwards. Sarasaté, on the violin, and Paderewski and Pachmann, on the piano, were also regular visitors. Messrs. Turner and Phillips, Plymouth, brought many of the "star" artistes to the town.

CHAPTER XIII.—SPORTS AND PASTIMES.

Wrestling Encounters : Cann and Polkinghorne: 1815-1870.   Devon and Cornwall were more celebrated for wrestlers than pugilists. Nevertheless Plymouth and Dock were the birthplaces of several famous boxers, and Broughton was knocked-out by Medder, a ropemaker, who journeyed to confront him in London. Pugilism went out as wrestling came into vogue, and the latter was welcomed as a respectable alternative, although cynics declined to admit that there was much moral difference in pounding a face with a pair of fists and lacerating a shin with shoes that had been soaked in bullock's blood and baked hard for kicking purposes. Early in the nineteenth century there were symptoms of comparative refinement, and the authorities prohibited the use of the Hoe for baiting bulls, and repressed various desecrations of the Sabbath. A further guarantee of excellent intentions was forthcoming in 1808, when several young men, who played "Chuck Farthing" during the hours of Divine Service, publicly confessed their iniquity in widely distributed hand-bills. The same year notice was given that " No Bull Baiting will be permitted on the Eastern Hoe, or anywhere within the borough of Plymouth, during the ensuing holidays, Easter and Whitsun, and all persons who shall be found to offend therein will be proceeded against and punished as the law directs." At the same time, every citizen was at liberty to enjoy "all other lawful pastimes on the Eastern Hoe, and other lands of the Mayor and Commonalty of this borough during the holidays, as heretofore accustomed." Of the sports that most appealed to the temperament of the age, wrestling held the foremost place, and it was usually accompanied by bell-ringing matches for purses of guineas, cudgelling, jingling, jumping in bags, and other competitions, including races for women and donkey hunts. In the neighbourhood of Plymouth there were many competitions between the champions of Devon and Cornwall. At the Maker games :

> A pair of leathern breeches was the prize
> A little the wuss for wear ;
> Jan Jordan and I drawed two valls apiece
> And Dick Simmons comed in for a share.

There was a deal of difference between the two styles of play—the Devonshire champions performing with big boots, and the Cornishmen more often than not with bare feet and legs, although they were allowed the use of shoes and padding. Thorne, of Widdecombe-in-the-Moor, a famous Devonshire wrestler, presented to his antagonists so perfect a form and such uncommon strength that his career was marked by a sharp succession of triumphs. Induced to enlist in the Life Guards, he took part in 1815 in the famous charge against the French Cuirassiers at Waterloo. There his superb figure was conspicuous on the battlefield, dealing death and destruction around him, and he was cutting down his tenth victim when a shot from a carbine laid him low. Thus, at the age of 23, passed one of the stateliest of all the Devonshire athletes.

Shortly after Thorne's death, Devon produced two young giants in the persons of Jordan and Flower, each of them six feet in height and weighing a trifle over eighteen stone. Jordan was a mighty kicker, and men who had entered the ring with unflinching courage made the reservation in their challenges, "Jordan alone excepted." Morice Town was the scene of Whitsun revels, and the harsh play of Flower and Jordan was so notorious there that Cornishmen would not participate, and the redoubtable standards were at one meeting matched against each other. This arrangement was ideal, and the betting ruled in favour of Flower. He shrank from Jordan's dreadful foot blows; and, after a supreme resistance lasting seventeen minutes, was seized by the fore hip and so finely thrown that the air was thick with hats and rent by acclamations. In 1816, Flower was confronted by Polkinghorne; and, after a protracted struggle, " Old Jack " was magnificently thrown amid delirious cheering of the Cornishmen. Jackman, another Devonian exponent, confronted Polkinghorne the following day, and the " flying mare" was his portion also. On an appeal the judges disallowed the fall, and Polkinghorne withdrew from the ring. William Wreford, at the age of eighteen, achieved reputation by throwing "the terrible Jordan" with such force that "the crash was similar to that produced by the felling of an oak tree." In company with the equally famous Thomas Balkwill, he vanquished the best Cornish wrestlers at Plymouth, but met his match in James Stone, nick-named "The Little Elephant" by reason of his strength. Simultaneously the men grappled each other "in such a way as to realise an Olympian encounter"; and, although Wreford had the advantage at the outset, he was hurled into the air, and fell with terrific violence on his back. At Southmolton the same champions played the return, but Stone's strength was

the more enduring; and, after repeatedly forcing his opponent on his side, he was declared the victor through Wreford's inability to continue the con test. Wreford remained a prominent figure in the ring, however; and threw the Cornishman, Francis Olver, although several of his ribs had been crushed in an especially deadly " hug."

As the years rolled on a cleverer, if not a greater, than Jordan arose in the person of Abraham Cann, and the encounters attracted multitudes of spectators. At Totnes, in 1825, Jordan threw a fine player named Huxtable in one minute, and the keenest interest was shown in the expected struggle with Cann, whose legs he had boasted he could kick to rags in "vive minutes." When his turn came, and Cann awaited him in the ring, Jordan declined the contest; and, in the general disgust, it was asserted that Jordan's character was gone. He was evidently out of form at this meeting, for two days later he was roughly handled by a young Cornishman named Hook, and too injured to resume the contest. At the Tavistock sports, Parkyn, on whom the hopes of Cornwall were centred, dislocated his

ABRAHAM CANN, THE DEVONSHIRE WRESTLER.

ankle in a fall, and was at once outclassed. Out of 32 standards, 22 were made by
Devonians and 10 by Cornishmen, and Cann was the solitary combatant who emerged
unscathed. He was now elevated as the county idol, and, treading the ring like a
Colossus, challenged the Cornishmen at every festive rural revel. Frequent letters were
exchanged to induce Cann and Polkinghorne to face each other, but bluster so often
ended in excuses that the opinion prevailed that the men were afraid to do so. The
situation was not unfairly summed up in the song which was in vogue with the Cornish
partisans :

> Cann is a man of as good a game
>   As ever yet was born, sir ;
> But he has not the weight or power to tame
>   The strength of Polkinghorne, sir !

The supporters of the champions were equally anxious to remove damaging impressions, and a meeting was arranged in 1826. Tamar Green, Devonport, was chosen for the
purpose ; and the west was alive with speculation when it was known that the backers meant
business. On the evening before the contest the town was inundated, and the resources of
its hotels and inns were taxed to the utmost. Truculent and redoubtable gladiators flocked
to the scene—kickers from Dartmoor, the recruiting ground of the Devonshire system ;
and bear-like huggers from the land of Tre, Pol and Pen —a wonderful company of
tried and stalwart experts. The enclosure consecrated by so many strenuous encounters now
constituted an amphitheatre "worthy of Rome." Ten thousand persons bought tickets
at a premium for the seats, and the hills around swarmed with spectators. Excitement
was at the highest possible pitch, and overwhelming volleys of cheering relieved the
tension as the rivals entered the ring—Polkinghorne in his stockings and Cann with a
monstrous pair of shoes whose toes had been baked like flints. As the men "peeled" for
action, such a shout ascended as awed the nerves of all present. Polkinghorne had been
discounted as fat and unwieldy, but the Devonians were dismayed to realise that, great as
was his girth, his arms were tough and his shoulders immensely powerful. Three stone
lighter in weight, Cann displayed a more sinewy form, and his figure was knit for strength,
and as statuesquely proportioned. His grip, like Polkinghorne's, was well known. No man
had ever shaken off either when once he had clinched—and each enjoyed a reputation for
presence of mind and resource in extremity beyond those of other masters of the art.
The match was for the best of three back falls, the men to catch what hold they could,
and two experts from each county were selected as "sticklers." The betting was in favour
of Cann at the outset ; but it receded as the Cornishman impressed the multitude with
his muscular superiority. Repeatedly shifting their positions, the combatants sought their
favourite "holts." As soon as Cann caught his adversary by the collar, after a contending
display of shifty and evasive form, Polkinghorne released himself by a feint ; and, amid
"terrible shouts from the Cornishmen," he drove his foe to his knees. Nothing daunted,
the Devonian accepted the Cornish hug, and the efforts of the rivals were superb. Cann
depended upon his science to serve him ; but Polkinghorne gathered his head under his
arm, and lifting him from the ground, threw him clean over his shoulder, and planted him
upon his back. "The very earth groaned with the uproar that followed ; the Cornishmen
jumped by hundreds into the ring ; there they embraced their champion till he begged to be
released ; and, amid cheers and execrations, the fall was announced to have complied with
the conditions. Bets to the amount of hundreds of pounds were decided by this event.

Polkinghorne now went to work with caution, and Cann was conscious that he had an
awkward customer to tackle. After heavy kicking and attempted hugging, the Cornishman
tried once more to lift his opponent ; but Cann caught his opponent's leg in his descent, and

threw him to the ground first. In the ensuing rounds both men played for wind. Polkinghorne was the more distressed, his knees quite raw with punishment, and the betting veered round in Cann's favour. Then the play changed, and Cann was apparently at the mercy of his foe, when he upset Polkinghorne's balance by a consummate effort and drove him to his back by sheer strength—the first that the sticklers allowed him. Cann next kicked tremendously; but, although the Cornishman suffered severely, he remained "dead game," and twice saved himself by falling on his chest. Disputes now disturbed the umpires, and their number was reduced to two. In the eighth round Polkinghorne's strength began to fail, and a dispute was improvised which occasioned another hour's delay. With wind regained and strength revived, the tenth round was contested with absolute fury; and, taking the kicking with fine contempt, Polkinghorne gripped Cann with leonine majesty, lifted him from the earth in his arms, turned him over his head, and dashed him to the ground with stunning force. As the Cornishman dropped on his knee, the fall was disputed, and the turn was disallowed. Polkinghorne then left the ring amid a mighty clamour, and by reason of his default the stakes were awarded to Cann. The victor emerged from the terrific hugs of his opponent with a mass of bruises which proved that kicking was only one degree more effective than bruises.

A more unsatisfactory issue could hardly have been conceived, and the rival backers forthwith endeavoured to arrange another encounter. Polkinghorne refused to meet Cann, however, unless he discarded his shoes, and the latter replied in a letter of "bluffing" scorn :

"The amount of all your bragging, and "West Briton" bravado, and abuse, is that you will not play out the match, which you ran away from at Devonport, but you will meet me if I will come into Cornwall, and put on Frenchmen's shoes, and play in the Cornish manner, and promise not to break your skin. This is what I expected —I thought you would be rather *coy*.

"Remember, sir, I do not stand under the same circumstances towards you, as I do towards all other men—*you first challenged me*, a thing I should never have thought of doing to any man alive, and you came voluntarily into Devonshire to throw me; you had, therefore, manifestly, no right to expect any concessions from the Devonshire mode of playing. But I did concede to you the liberty of padding your legs in any way you pleased, and we were to play until the Triers were unanimous as to the winner; and indeed the public had a right to expect this, after all the annoyance it had suffered on the subject. But you chose to set yourself up as your own umpire, and leave the ring and the match undetermined, although it since appears that three Triers out of the four were Cornishmen.

"In consequence of the subsequent conduct of yourself and friends, I now tell you, but for the last time, that I again wish to meet you to play out the match, and, as I have before stated, in order to prevent partiality towards either party, I will meet you in any county in England you may name, unconnected with us both, the Triers to be taken therefrom, and only have our written conditions to be guided by in their decision; and, as a further inducement, I will take off my stockings, and play barelegged with you, whilst you may have two of the hardest and heaviest shoes that can be made of leather in the county of Cornwall; and you shall be allowed to stuff yourself as high as the armpits, to any extent not exceeding the size of a Cornish pack of wool; and I will further engage not to kick you if you will make anything like play, and will kick me. As to any new match, or new conditions, there will be quite time enough for that after we have settled this, but I should think that that will hardly be found necessary; your friends had better employ themselves in getting your Subscription Plate."

Meanwhile Cann indulged in genuine business with " Irish Gaffney," at the Golden Eagle in the Mile End Road, and the event drew such a crowd and resulted in so much excitement that the grand stand collapsed. Hundreds of persons fell with it, but bruises were the extent of the injuries. When the champions grappled, the interest of the crowd was intense, and Gaffney's left hand was grasping Cann's loose jacket when the Devonian firmly fixed his right on the Irishman's waistband. Gaffney assumed the offensive, but the Devonian remain fixed to the earth, his face indicating caution, confidence and self-possession. Gaffney kicked at Cann's knees until the reports rang through the ring. No blood was drawn, however; but, as soon as the champion retaliated, Gaffney's worsted stockings were saturated, and he soon looked as though he had emerged from a shambles. Cann then threw him in his cleanest form; and, after a pause, the men closed for the second round. Gaffney stood wide and front to his man; and, presenting his side, Cann allowed the Irishman to put his left leg around his right. Cann was thwarted in striving for the lock, and Gaffney shortly afterwards twisted his left leg behind Cann's right and lifted him from the earth. Ever resourceful, Cann threw his body erect, in a position of immovable rigidity; and, rapidly disentangling his left leg, fell upon his face and brought his adversary with him. Cann thus displayed such perfect science that all betting was at an end. It was recognised that his presence of mind was perfect, and that, if he could not gain the fall, he could prevent his antagonist from putting him on his back. On resuming, the combatants closed for two minutes; and then Cann caught his man on the shift and threw him a fair back in artistic form. Gaffney was now distressed: with the blood flowing down his shoes through his worsted stockings, whilst Cann's knees were almost unhurt. In the next round the Devonian again landed his opponent square on his back; and, having in the process pulled Gaffney's left shoulder out of its socket, was declared the winner. The injured man was taken to the hospital and Cann was hoisted on the shoulders of his backers.

Cann's next famous encounter was with Frost, a moorman of Aveton Gifford, who was of a thicker build than the champion, a fearless and fine young man, and a severe punisher withal. Cann started by making a bold catch with his left at his opponent's collar, but Frost broke away as he tried to make good with his right. Cautious and wary, Cann looked out for another opportunity, Frost eyeing him as though he would learn the secret of his inmost intentions. The champion's placid face betrayed no proposal, and, Frost's glance wavering, Cann pounced upon him with the velocity of an eagle, seized him with one hand at the nape of the neck, and made good with his favourite hold above the elbow. Frost tried to stand off, but Cann was not to be denied; and, being brought up, Frost put his "hammers" to work with terrific effect, striking Cann on the knee. A bustling rally ensued, and after smart leg work, right and left, Cann again closed and gathered up his opponent until his head was seen projecting from under the champion's arms. Whilst the air was filled with the thunder of the cheering, Cann cautiously brought his man round, fastened his right outer firmly in its position, and, at the end of seventeen minutes, hove away. Breathless silence prevailed during the execution of this masterly effort; but Frost resisted with such strength that the manœuvre was thwarted, and the men fell to the ground in company. Resuming with the same determination on each part, Cann repeated the experiment, but Frost contrived to turn himself by a Herculean effort, and, catching Cann in his arms, lifted him off the ground amid "astounding cheering." Retaining his self-possession, Cann locked each leg firmly in those of his opponent, and Frost released himself by a feint, which again brought both men to the ground. On regaining their legs the combatants stood still, intently watching each other, Frost's "bellows" working at a smart rate, whilst his body presented overspreading symptoms of punishment. The champion did not despise this "crabbed" opponent, and next tried the inner lock, a movement to which Frost replied by catching the champion in his arms and again bodily uplifting him like a flash of lightning. The two men again went heavily to ground. When Frost came up he was "piping," and, rushing in without fear, Cann grappled and once more essayed the outer lock, only to find that his sturdy antagonist was again holding him exultingly aloft. This time Cann would not go to the ground; and, extricating himself by a prodigious effort, planted some tremendous kicks in the course of a most furious rally. Frost looked wildly; but, holding Cann firmly by both hands at the collar, he inflicted several resounding retaliatory kicks. Cann resumed, and then Frost, desperately at bay, struck the champion such "a heavy toe" that Cann was "all but gone." For over thirty minutes these foils were exchanged, and then Frost released himself from a dangerous hold. A quarter of an hour afterwards he made another offer; and Cann, seizing his opportunity, brought him over as flat as a flounder, amid the stentorian cheering with which the suspense was at last relieved.

Cunning devices were made to bring Cann and Polkinghorne again together; and, in 1828, when the former turned up at Tavistock to take part in the wrestling matches, a chaise was despatched to St. Columb, with relays of horses through the night, to induce the Cornishman to travel and face his old opponent. Polkinghorne and Parkyn both returned in the conveyance, the former with no immediate intention of wrestling, but of ascertaining the nature of any definite proposition. Cann was in the ring, preparing to polish off the man with whom he was matched, when Polkinghorne entered and offered his hand in the spirit of a sportsman. One of the committee then asked Polkinghorne if he intended to play, but his reply, "Not for the stakes, but for any sum you like to name," upset their expedient. Parkyn thereon cast his hat in the centre as a challenge to Cann; but the friends of the champion would not allow him to accept it. Parkyn then threw two men so that he might be matched against Jordan, but the committee declined to permit them to play together. Repeated overtures passed between Cann and Polkinghorne, Jordan and Parkyn. Polkinghorne's backers declared that they would entertain nothing but a positive challenge from Cann himself; and Cann replied that he was ready to meet their man forthwith. The shoe, however, was the rock on which the contestants split, no less than Polkinghorne's desire to have the result settled in a single throw. At one time it seemed likely that the meeting would take place, for it was arranged that fair shoes and padding should be provided, and that no restrictions as to the character of the play were to be interposed. At this juncture the strength of "the wrestling pride of Devon" failed so suddenly and completely that the match became out of the question; and Cann visited Polkinghorne at St. Columb to enjoy his hospitality and recruit his health. And, with this redeeming incident, the athletic careers of these Trojans closed.

An old grudge between Oliver and Trewicke, two young Cornishmen, the latter of whom was known as the "Young Russian," by reason of his extraordinary strength, was decided in 1829. Trewicke was thrown in five minutes, and Oliver then gave James Cann, brother of the champion, a beautiful back fall in ten minutes. The hopes of Devon now depended upon the veteran Wreford, but he was thrown by James Rook, a mere youngster. For some time the wrestling matches in Plymouth were held upon the Hoe, where they constituted such an obstruction to business that workmen could not be persuaded to attend to their employment. On these occasions an average of £150 per day was taken at the gate, and the promenade was finally prohibited for the purpose of such meetings. Chelson Meadow then became the arena, but the disposition of some of the Devonshire men to increase the size of the shoes, and the limitation of sport that arose from the refusal of the Cornishmen to appear, led to the issue of this proviso in the announcements:

"Men of all counties' will be allowed to play for the above fifty sovereigns, with the exception of John Jordan, sen., who will also be allowed to play provided he uses a fair single-soled shoe." The umpires were drawn, one from Devon and the other from Cornwall, and the third was determined by ballot, "or what is commonly termed a toss." At Devonport, in 1829, the "great Jordan" played Charles Cock, of Cornwall, who had gained repute by throwing Rogers, of Modbury. "Take off your shoes!" was vociferated by those around the ring, and the Devonshire giant offered to change them for those of any man present. Not a shoe could be found, however, in that muscular crowd, which would admit his expansive sole. A dead silence ensued as the men set to work, Jordan kicking violently when his assailant tried to hold him, and grinning with delight as Cock winced. This so enraged the Cornishman that he offered to fight instead . of wrestle, and Jordan thereupon "smoothed his face." The miner renewed the attack by rushing to close quarters, but Jordan kept his opponent at a distance, and used his shoes with ghastly effect. With blood streaming to his feet, Cock caught the carcase of the giant in his arms, and Jordan replied by casting his full weight upon the Cornishman and bearing him bodily to the ground. Cock again flew at his opponent ; and, lifting him off his feet, hurled him to the earth on his right side with tremendous force. Administering punishment with deadly deliberation, Jordan now baffled every effort of Cock to get close, until the latter, with a spring, locked his arms around his body. Amid breathless suspense, Jordan tried to release himself, and the miner firmly clinching, the rivals again fell. Some move was now necessary to restore the confidence of Jordan's backers, but it was not until the succeeding round that he asserted his supremacy. The men were involved in another iron grip, when Jordan, by an adroit manœuvre, shifted his position, and placed the Cornishman upon his back amid a deafening din. Jordan in his turn was thrown by Frost at Devonport, and his arm was dislocated in the struggle. Subsequently Chappell carried all before him, until Tom Cooper entered the field, and his kicking bore down all William Pollard's Cornish science. Thenceforward interest in wrestling declined, although Sam Rundle and Carkeek—another Hercules in strength—did something to revive the embers.

Regattas, Yachting, Etc. : 1823-1899.   The credit of the earliest known regatta must be accorded to Stonehouse, where rowing and sailing matches were regularly held in the early years of the nineteenth century :

> Success to Stonehouse, her regatta men,
>   And to her maidens ; yes, to all success !
> For public spirit centres there, and when
>   It is called forward shows no bashfulness
>   To vindicate her right or aid distress.
> Who knows her best they most esteem her then ;
>   For spirit stamps a nobleness on all
>   However eminent—however small.
>
> And she is both—both small and eminent,
>   And enviable, but not envious ;
> She knows that Plymouth has assistance lent—
>   Acknowledges the favour without fuss :
>   Then let their motto be in future (Nos)—
> " Ut una vivimus," by which is meant
>   "*As one we flourish.*" Devonport's new name
>   May yet find lustre in Regatta fame.

Not in exclusion of another's name,
For dear to him is every brother's fame.
A feeble plant when nourished by your care
Even in the winter of its age may bear.
Therefore it is your actor keeps the stage
With all the pertinacity of age.
Here, if he fails, and should the night's event
Prove that your favours and his fires be spent,
What on the part of candour can be said
But that his heart was stouter than his head?
And that advancing to a fresh attack
He dropp'd and died with "harness on his back."

When the fortunes of Plymouth Theatre were at their lowest ebb Mr. J. R. Newcombe, who had emerged from one unsuccessful experiment at Bath, made a bid for the management. Season after season passed without profit, the appearance of a patron in the dress circle was phenomenal, and it was considered irreverent and dangerous to enter a place of amusement whenever disease was rife in the town. Intimation of expensive engagements fell upon indifferent ears, and years elapsed before fortune smiled upon his efforts. Although his capital had nearly vanished, Mr. Newcombe never lost heart; and, if the returns were inadequate, his engagements were of the highest class. Regular visits were made by Sim Reeves as Edgar Ravenswood; Mdlle. Taglioni as La Sylphide; Mrs. FitzWilliam as Nelly O'Neill; Helen Faucit as Rosalind; Sir Walter and Lady Amyott; and Kean and Macready to the end of their careers. Prodigal were the "benefits" from lessee even to call-boy; and the performances were usually prolonged until midnight. Every taste was consulted, and a farce or comedietta followed high-class opera, even when the "stars" were of first importance.

The appetite of Mr. Newcombe's patrons was strong for local effects; and, in April, 1849, was presented a legendary drama, founded upon a tale of early Plymouth, and treating of the joys, sorrows, loves and hatreds "of the good old citizens in the days of yore." Driven to despair by the abduction of his sweetheart, Michael Erle walked about a homeless and incurable madman until he encountered the author of his injuries and exacted a terrible revenge. This story was "beautifully illustrated" in the drama of "The Fayre Lasse of Plymouth." "Plymouth Wives, or a Lesson for Husbands," was much in request as the farce. Essentially local was "The Five Fields Tragedy, or the Assassin's Bridge: A Tale of Stoke, in 1787." It treated of the memorable murder at Millbridge; and each party to the event was introduced—Richards and Smith as the assassins, and the daughter of the murdered man as the heroine of touching love episodes. Light to this shade was submitted in the farce "Plymouth Races, or Our New Cook of Plymouth"—with the scene laid at "No. 60, Octagon." An "entirely new local legendary drama" was given in 1851—"Plymouth in 1747, or the Dogs of Cotehele." Near a clearing in the gloomy woods the robber crouched over a small fire, and the canine detective tracked him by scenting his blood-stained apparel. A burlesque "written expressly for this theatre" represented "Richard Cœur de Lion 'taking in' Plymouth on his way to Palestine—an incident not to be found recorded in either Hume, Smollett, Goldsmith or Macaulay!" In this trifle Princess Verynice, attired in bloomer costume, sang "In the Days When We Wore Petticoats—A Long Time Ago." The Mayor and Corporation awaited Richard's arrival at the Plymouth Railway Station, and "the King" addressed his last appeal for funds to a generous public at Gill's Pier. "True to the Core," a nautical drama by Angiolo Slous, opened with a view of "Ye Pelican Inn" and the entrance to "Ye Bow Lynge Greene." Trevanion, Governor of Plymouth Castle, plotted to bring the Armada into the Sound; and the sighting of the Spanish fleet, the game of bowls, the kidnapping of the hero, and the killing of the Spanish Admiral, as his vessel lay wrecked upon the Eddystone rocks, were among the developments depicted. Plymouth Castle constituted "an elaborate piece of stage display," and Queen Elizabeth's pageant was "magnificent."

Mr. George Wightwick's first play of "Valerio" was a failure: vastly complicated in construction although there was ample field for the display of talent. Originally consisting of five acts, the author cut it to three; and it was then more adapted for the drawing-room than the stage, as the pith and marrow of the action had been eviscerated. In the resolve to earn a better reputation, the genial Plymouth architect produced "Richard the First" in 1848, and expectations were entertained that this play would live:

> Shakspere for Richard, Number Two and Three,
> Has done, what none could do save only he;
> And now to make amends for what's undone,
> We come to do our best for Number One.
> The Second Richard oft has moved our tears,
> The tyrant Third has often stirred our fears;
> Our author fills up a gap in the past,
> And the First Richard makes his bow at last.
> Be gentle with him on his opening night,
> For ('tween ourselves) he's in a royal fright,
> Yield but to him his best intentions due,
> And even his Lion Heart shall yield to you.

Mr. J. R. Newcombe took the part of the Duke of Leicester; and, at the close of a performance of "immense interest," the author, "after having been repeatedly called for, presented himself and bowed to the audience amidst great cheering." Wightwick's other historical tragedy, "Henry II.," was well mounted in 1852. It excited and sustained the sympathies; there was chaste poetic expression throughout; "an infusion of much feeling and considerable beauty; and, when requisite, pungency in the dialogue." There were no facilities for the display "either of garish diction or ad captandum sentimentalities," and no attempt at "fine writing." Mr. Paumier's King was "dignified and correct," but Mr. Falconer might have been "a little more oily as the sanctified a Becket." Two beautiful scenes were executed by Mr. Samuel Cook at a few hours' notice that displayed wonderful familiarity with old costumes. In the failure to provide a doorway, however, an actor was compelled to bolt through a hole cut in the canvas. The audience was pleased with the tragedy, and called loudly for the author, a compliment which Mr. Wightwick acknowledged by bowing from the stage box. Discursive dialogue and overcrowded action was fatal, however, to the reproduction of Richard I.

The stage in 1859 boasted no actor of pre-eminent genius. The retirement of Macready left a void, and the only artistes in the front rank were Phelps and Charles Kean, the latter assisted by a wife who was a native of Devon. In 1869 the name of Mrs. Rousby was heard on the Plymouth boards; and this beautiful girl, the daughter of a local officer, leapt into immediate favour. Her genius for histrionic art was so genuine, her personal charms so commanding, and the story of her young life so romantic that a brilliant future awaited her. For a few years she excelled as Rosalind in "As You Like It," and as Elizabeth in "'Twixt Axe and Crown"; and then tragically passed from the scene of her triumphs. It was not her extraordinary ability that had constituted her chief attractions: but an

THE PALACE THEATRE OF VARIETIES, UNION STREET, PLYMOUTH.

(From a Sketch by W. H. Arber, the Architect.)

> But when I say that Plymouth has assisted
> Her little darling, Stonehouse, let me now
> (Lest I should twist—all know what tars term twisted)
> Just hint, that Stonehouse first taught Plymouth how
> To skim the wave with the Regatta prow :
> She first the western mariner enlisted
> To race his little bark for prize and sport ;
> As wings the sea-gull that is seen off port.

In 1823 a meeting was held at Plymouth, and it was determined to establish an annual regatta for the port. Subscriptions were so liberal that a second day's programme was arranged to encourage the construction of sailing vessels of all classes. A further resolution was adopted which explains its own purpose : "That boat racing being not only an elegant amusement, but having a direct tendency to improve the construction of Sailing Vessels, and this port having many decided advantages for this purpose, it is desirable that the Port of Plymouth should stand forward in the promotion of so useful an object ; and it cannot be doubted, but the inhabitants of Plymouth, Dock, Stonehouse, and the neighbourhood, will give every possible support to this regatta." The prizes were a handsome silver vase, for gentlemen's decked or open boats between 20 and 25 tons ; a lady's cup for gentlemen's boats, between ten and twenty tons ; and a silver goblet, for gentlemen's decked or open boats, not exceeding 22 feet aloft, from the stem to the stern post, and not admeasuring more than ten tons. The cups were chaste and the largest was capable of holding three quarts, and weighed seventy ounces. It was supported by a figure of Neptune riding on the ocean in a car composed of dolphins. On the body of the cup was a representation of a boat-race, the handles double-twisted, and silver cables reefed through buoys terminating in true lovers' knots at the top. One of the sensations of the festival itself was the spectacle of Commodore O'Brien sailing about the Sound in his "Lilliputian cutter"—to the astonishment of the multitude.

Never did Plymouth Sound and offing present, in a time of peace, so interesting a spectacle as in August, 1824. Almost every description of vessel, from the rowing boat to the majestic 74-gun ship, was before the eye at once. A Dutch man-of-war presented a fine "wall-sided battery" of cannon in close proximity to the Ocean battleship, and both crews returned the cheers that arose from the passengers on board the Sir Francis Drake and Cambria "steam-vessels," which were plying in all parts of the Sound during the day. The Royal Sovereign yacht contributed considerably to the splendour of the scene, and her embellishments, added to the circumstance of her being dressed in colours, delighted the eyes of the tens of thousands who stretched in a deep mass from the foot to the brow of the promenade, and even clustered the edges of those "most tremendous precipices at the Western Hoe." The Admiralty and Commissioners' yachts were present, and naval brigs and pleasure vessels innumerable glided over the surface of the Sound. Yachtsmen were everywhere in evidence, sauntering over the slopes with their handkerchiefs *a la Belcher*, their blue jackets and flowing trousers giving them a particularly seaman-like air —"a compliment to the immortal tars who have in that dress made the four corners of the world feel their irresistible prowess." In the first race there was an interesting display, the yachts spreading, when necessary, a cloud of canvas and rounding the station boats with precision. At starting, Mr. Maxse's Sabrina cutter, 84 tons, took the lead, but Mr. Joseph Wilde's Arrow, 84 tons, by using an immense gib topsail, gained an advantage which she held to the close of the race. The Arrow arrived many seconds before her antagonists, but, in tacking, ran foul of the Sabrina, and the Ladies' Cup was accordingly

AA

won by Mr. Smith's Jack o' the Lantern yawl, 140 tons.   Fine seamanship was displayed
in the next class, the skill being called forth by the light and variable winds.   Mr. Talbot's
yawl Guila, 42 tons, arrived first, but, on a technical point, yielded the prize to Mr.
Weld's Julia cutter.   There were a variety of other races ; and, on the second day, the
rowing matches drew a scarcely less numerous crowd.   The events for six and four-oared
gigs were abandoned because the other competitors would not compete against the Saltash
men.   In the race for women, eight sovereigns were awarded as prizes, and the Harriet,
of Anderton, rowed by Mary Woolet, Jane Snell, Mary Clatworthy and Nancy Colmer,
and steered by Mary Ann Johns, all of Saltash, came in first.   The Cawsand boat, Flora,
was second ; but the ladies of Oreston abandoned the contest.   The course was from a
moored boat under the Hoe to the Cobbler buoy, thence by way of Millbay to Barnpool,
and back to the starting point.   The distance was accomplished in 29 minutes :

> The world is here—the busy world of fashion,
>   All gay and smiling, while the sun is bright ;
> Around me there are looks that speak of passion,
>   And forms that give the human heart delight ;
> The words of wit—the brilliant thoughts that flash on
>   The mind of man when it doth take its flight ;
> And happy dreams are with the sons of men,
> For "eyes look love, to eyes which shall speak again."—
>
> And merrily the sound of music rises
>   Upon the ear—the signal gun is fired :—
> Yawls, luggers, schooners, barks of various sizes,
>   Are under way with thirst of fame inspired ;—
> There pleasure sits manœuv'ring for the prizes,
>   The helm is guided by a hand not hired ;
> But gentlemen of high and proud degree,
> Who have a *penchant* for the turbulent sea.
>
> And aye ! 'tis beautiful to see them there,
>   Courting the summer breezes as they blow ;
> With streamers floating in the buoyant air,
>   The blue waves parted by each gallant prow ;
> Cheered by the bright eyes of the sweet and fair,
>   And feeling life with a renewed glow ;
> While earth and heaven are smiling in their pride,
> And gentle echoes float along the tide.—*Anon, Plymouth, Aug., 1824.*

The first real impulse to local yachting occurred in 1827, when the Duke of Clarence
visited the port, and brought in his train the "cracks" of the National Yachting Club.
The ladies affected bloomers on this occasion, and it was suggested that they should
attempt an aerial flight to Batten, with their spreading bonnets inflated with gas, as also
their flowing petticoats and muslin trousers !   The contest for "The Clarence Cup" was
thus described by Carrington :

> How every heart the glorious prospect thrills !
> How dwells the glance upon thy hallow'd ground,
> Edgcumbe—dear Edgcumbe—thou soul-stirring spot
> Which once, but once, beheld through life is ne'er forgot !

Their bows with foam-bells sparkling, see they steer—
Those wanton barks to seek the goal; they fly
On the fresh wing of Auster;—near, more near
They come—the victor vessel now is nigh—
The fleet Menai; see how in glad career   .
Parting the surge, she sweeps triumphant by
The goal—'tis won! and hark from rock and pier
And cliff, and hill's green crest, the gratulating cheer!

With increased funds and popularity, the following year witnessed an even finer competition. Amongst the boats in attendance were Mr. Weld's Lulworth, 127 tons; Mr.
Smith's Menai, 189 tons; Lord Belfast's Harriet, 96 tons, and Mr. Corbett's Hebe, 70
tons—all cutter rigged. Lulworth took the lead at starting, with an enormous mainsheet;
but Menai gave her a deal of trouble. Menai was followed by Harriet, and at some
distance by Hebe. Lulworth finished the distance, twelve miles, in 1 hour 13mins.
40secs. on the first round, and Menai was thirty-six seconds later. Lulworth kept her
place on the second round, but one of her men fell overboard, and the delay spent in
picking him up gave Menai the victory Time, 2 hours 32mins. 30secs. Lulworth was
only a few yards behind, and Harriet and Hebe followed. The Clarence Cup, for which
the same boats competed on the second day, was easily won by Lulworth. In one
medallion of this golden trophy of 92 ounces were the full Clarence arms, richly chased in
high relief, with cable handles supported by dead-geld dolphins, and the sides chased with
marine shells and other devices. Lord Clanbrock's Scorpion, 180 tons, was the first vessel
under weigh, but she was soon overtaken by Lulworth, who kept the lead throughout.
The Menai was becalmed. Mr. Heneage's Harriet (Southampton), 60 tons, took the
cup in the other competition, beating Mr. Lyons' Blue-Eyed Maid (Cowes) and Mr.
Corbett's Hebe (Cowes) with several minutes to spare. A gale kept the Cowes yachts at
home in 1830, and the depression caused by their absence, the withdrawal of the Clarence
Cup, and a serious financial modification of the programme, rendered imperative the start
of the Royal Western Yacht Club in 1833. Arrangements were made with the French
Government by which the colours might be flown in their ports, and the regatta management was remodelled. In 1834 there were 1,500 crafts of various rigs in the Sound, and
the yacht of Captain Ross, the commodore, was lavishly decorated as a committee-boat,
and her spacious deck crowded with "fashionables." Mr. Webber's Zaroda cutter, 31 tons
(Southampton), took the cup presented by the Duchess of Kent, with a two minutes' lead
from Mr. Holt's Liberty cutter, 42 tons (Exmouth). The Victoria Cup was won by Mr.
Hare's Ann cutter, 22 tons (Plymouth) in competition with Mr. Burrough's Red Rover
cutter, 12 tons (Southampton). The rowing matches excited exceptional interest, inasmuch
as £20 was offered for boats "manned" by women. The rivals were Ann Stodden, Mary
Glanville, Mary Ann Johns, and Jane Bullen, and they finished in this order. But, at the
dinner at which the prizes were distributed, the competitors so eloquently fought their
battles over again, and stubbornly ignored the President's invitation to withdraw, that a
gallant officer proposed the toast of "the Ladies" and it was drunk amid the waving of
"old caps and new bonnets."

Saltash, Torpoint and Devonport held their first regattas in 1835. Saltash was the
home of the "Nonpariels"—a race of rowers who defied competition. It was said that
the only men who ever thought of challenging them were those at St. Ives, but this temerity
was due to a night's libation and was recanted the moment the authors were sober. At Torpoint, Anthony House, with its fine home-brewed ale, was always thrown open to a number

of veteran watermen, between 60 and 80, whose prowess invariably excited unstinted admiration. The Saltash festival was by no means wholly intended for the encouragement of males—for the "ladies" feathered their oars with such dexterity that few of the opposite sex would enter the lists against them. Before the races for these damsels of uncertain age were started, blue favours were tied around their white caps by members of the committee. The fair rowers were attired in short white bedgowns and blue safeguards, and their gigs shot around the course of five miles "like so many birds." Occasionally the event ended in a free fight between the contestants; and those who sought to pacify them came in for "clouts and scratches." From a sporting point of view, the feature of the first regatta was a life or death competition between Jacky Gould and the Glanvilles. If Jacky's boat, Miller's Daughter, was the "crack," Alarm was scarcely inferior, and Paul Pry was a first-class craft. "Crash!" went the starting gun, and the competitors dashed away with a flood tide and a breeze from the north'ard. When they left on their ten-mile course one vast shout went up, the boats flew as instinct with life, every nerve on the stretch, "like a weather breast backstay in a double reef topsail breeze." The first five miles were covered in thirty minutes; and, as the boats turned the committee vessel, there were deafening shouts of "Bravo, Jacky," "Well done, Granville!" "Britons, Every Man." Then these hearts-of-oak flashed on their second round, and excitement intensified as the telescopes reported progress. When the boats reappeared, the suspense broke into a feverish roar; and calls to the rivals were tossed about "like corks on a sea of voices." Swiftly they drew near, the boats in a line, and interest increased to painful intensity as the race was neck-and-neck. The judge stood by, red-hot poker in hand; and, as the bow of the Alarm, pulled by the Glanvilles, first touched the hawser of the committee vessel, "Bang!" went the signal gun; and "See the Conquering Hero" burst from the band, and hundreds clustered round to congratulate the victors and condole with Jacky Gould, who was only five seconds behind!

It was the tanned and sinewy ladies, after all, who rendered the prowess of Saltash with the oar so historical. The crews of Louisa Moyse and Mrs. Furnace were redoubtable, but Anne Glanville became the heroine of the Hamoaze, and acquired such renown that she crossed the Channel and entered for the international stakes at Havre. Here the health of her crew was toasted in champagne by the municipal authorities, but "chivalrous motives" prevented the French watermen from contending against them. Not to be deprived of their opportunity the Glanvilles matched themselves against a number of their own countrymen; and, in the presence of 20,000 spectators, triumphed with ease. Thus the women of Saltash earned a new trophy on the bosom of the Seine, and the French thought all the better of their politeness in withdrawing from the contest. Upon Anne Glanville's death the band of the Royal Marines were sent by the commandant at Stonehouse to play a funeral march.

In 1834 two of the finest yachts afloat—Waterwitch, a brig of 351 tons, and Galatea, a schooner of 179 tons, sailed from the Isle of Wight around the Eddystone and back to the Nab, for a stake of a thousand guineas. Waterwich only won by 20 minutes. There were 34 yachts in Plymouth in 1835, 29 of them cutters, and Lady Sir Kilda, the property of Sir Thomas Acland, was the largest. There was little individuality of form about the local yachts until 1842, when the sport was revolutionised at Plymouth, under the patronage of the Queen and Prince Albert, with the Earl of Morley as commodore and Captain Bukeley as vice-commodore. There were 38 yachts enrolled, of from 10 to 142 tons each, and the club house was situate at the pretty Millbay Creek. The utilitarian demands of the Great Western Docks Company caused that admirable site to be destroyed, and yachts were from that time forward compelled to moor in the exposed harbour.

PLYMOUTH.

(From the Water Colour by J. W. M. Turner, R.A.)

Play ruled high at the Royal Western Yacht Club in 1846 in consequence of the admission of two blacklegs, who abused the institution and induced "pigeons" to visit their private lodgings. There they "plucked" them to the extent of hundreds of pounds in the course of a single night. Suspicion was excited by the practice of these men in betting on the turn-up card, and one who showed the king nine times managed to nett £1,000. On the eve of their exposure the gang gave ostentatious entertainments, and their houses were graced by the rank and fashion of the district. The bomb fell from the "Plymouth Journal," where Mr. Isaac Latimer accused one of the party of having undergone two years' imprisonment for marking cards in a saloon at Tours. It was also asserted that the men had been expelled from a club at Guernsey for similar conduct. When these revelations were made, the chief actors were expelled from the Royal Western Yacht Club, and one of them sued the "Plymouth Journal" for libel. The jury found for the proprietors on all pleas of justification, but gave the plaintiffs a farthing on a technical ground.

Aerial pretensions were not unknown in Plymouth, and there was an attempt in 1830 which narrowly escaped a tragic end. A man who had been travelling about the country taking "flying leaps," announced his intention of "flying" from Prince Rock to the opposite shore. In the presence of several thousand people, he commenced the preparations for his flight, his person secured by ropes around his breast and legs, which were fixed to ropes extended across the harbour and secured by rings. He had partly traversed the estuary when the rope relaxed and he fell in the water, and was only rescued with difficulty. Graham, the aeronaut, attempted to ascend from the Citadel, but his balloon was blown to pieces in a gale that anticipated the performance—much to the danger of a throng that was waiting to behold the achievement. In June, 1862, a crowd assembled at the Citadel to witness the performances of Blondin on a tight-rope, three hundred feet in length and from fifty to sixty feet high. The well-formed figure of the acrobat, his chest resplendent with medals, made three journeys, on one occasion partly enveloped by a sack, and on another with a bandage over his eyes. A multitude was drawn together in the same year by announcements that Signor Soldino would perform the "wonderful and hitherto unknown feat of flying from the Signal House on the Hoe across the water at a considerable elevation to the Devil's Point, where he will alight, and, after the lapse of a few minutes, fly back again and pitch on the Hoe. The public will be surprised to see the ingenious way in which the wings will be attached to the body in order to facilitate the aerial transit." Little doubting the good faith of the invitation, the public swarmed to the Hoe in such numbers that the town was nearly empty; and, when the Signor did not appear, the gulled sheepishly whispered one to another, "You're Sold-I-Know."

In 1860, Plymouth yachting was memorialised in a painting by Admiral Beechey, which includes portraits of such well-known patrons as Mr. W. F. Moore and Mr. W. V. Phillips; and vessels of local fame, such as Talisman, Edith, Falcon, and Cornish-Devil. Interest was enlivened in 1866 by the presence of a fleet of mosquito boats and racing cracks; and in 1870, yachting was more scientifically pursued. In 1876 the Royal Plymouth Corinthian Yacht Club was instituted, with a club house at the West Hoe Pier; and, amongst its boats, were Seagull, Amy, Quickstep, Mabel, Ripple and Daisy. Thence to 1899 the period was revolutionary, and the members erected a club-house under the Citadel, with Mr. E. A. Boolds as Vice-Commodore. Vanessa, Madge, Jullanar, Evolution and other boats were constructed from the designs of up-country yachtsmen. Maharanee and Chittywee were presented by Plymouth builders as types that could be built and comply with the measurement rules. The result was the construction of models radically differing in shape and form from the vessels that were formerly used as yachts. Rope shrouds, lanyards, dead eyes, stone and shifting ballast were consigned to a forgotten limbo, and thus made way for the speed that is cherished above all. The South Western Yacht Club, formed in 1890, secured the coveted symbols of Admiralty and Royal Warrants in the first and second years of its existence. Progress in pace and alteration of shape have been demonstrated by many visitors, of which the Prince of Wales's Britannia was the best all-round boat seen in the Port.

Racing, Hunting, &c., 1825-1899. Plymouth Races were inaugurated in 1825, and the scene was suggestive of "the early joys of Merrie England." Boys dived for six-pences into filthy depths ; larrikins raced on donkeys ; pigs with shaven and greasy tails were pursued to the mud and "shared" between their captors ; women ran for red cloaks and blind-folded drivers raced with wheelbarrows. Larrikins climbed for legs of mutton suspended from tallowed poles, and the ground resounded with the blare of trumpets, beat of drums and cries of contending showmen. The ears of "laughter-loving folks" were stunned by the shouts of glib quacks and Cheap Jacks, and their eyes were dazzled by the flare of nauseous lamps. Gaudily painted canvases invariably excited expectations that the interiors occasionally belied, and wonders of diverse character were grotesquely jumbled —equestrian heroes and learned pigs ; boa-constrictors and performing fleas ; dwarfs of forty pounds and fat people of four hundred ; rat-eating Indians and Chinese nondescripts. What freaks Nature did not evolve the ingenuity of the showmen improvised ; and, in 1827, children clad in sealskins were exhibited as savages who would only gnaw the bodies of vermin.

After three meetings at Crabtree, Chelson Meadow was adopted as the course in 1828, and gambling "hells" with flashy designations were conducted there by "showy women, unprincipled decoys and Satanic leaders." The uninitiated were inveigled by libations offered by harpies at the door, and "heaps of gold and silver" were swept into the coffers of confederates. Vice was clad in a hundred allurements ; and, as the "plucked pigeons" emerged, their woeful countenances evoked contemptuous laughter. The chief event in the first programme was a sweepstake of ten sovereigns, and Lord James Fitzroy, Mr. J. Bulteel, Mr. Charles Trelawney, Mr. H. Molyneaux, Mr. T. Lechmere and Colonel Gilbert were the leading gentlemen "mounts." At the meeting held in 1830, the morn broke beauti-fully, and it seemed as though the population had turned out to commemorate a jubilee. Streets, lanes and highways were alive, and every mode of conveyance was in requisition. Parties moved up Catwater to the sound of music, and all were prepared for the day's pleasure. After the first race, the clouds suddenly gathered, and the rain descended in torrents—thick, heavy and incessant. The crowd ran for shelter under hedges, trees, booths, umbrellas, or whatever offered refuge from the pitiless storm. This was endured for over an hour with fortitude, and then a panic seized all classes : horses, carriages, men and women rushed helter-skelter from the course, and the programme was practically con-cluded without spectators. The chief event on the second day was the Queen's Cup, of the value of 100 guineas ; but the field was left to Sir L. Glynn's Jenny Vertpyre and Mr. Radcliffe's old mare—Brownlock. The latter ran a stone and a half heavier than Jenny Vertpyre, but the struggle was one of the hardest ever witnessed in the west, Jenny only winning the first heat by barely half a length and the second by a length. For the handicap plate of 100 sovs., on the following day, the winner had to give way to Mr. Bigg's Whisk, but there was a dead-heat for second place, Jenny and Mr. Taunton's Coronet running neck-and-neck the whole length of the course and finishing in this form after a tremendous race. The meetings were continued from year to year and presented the same animated groupings—peers in their chariots of fours, with glittering outriders, booted grooms and powdered lacqueys; dashing equipages from contiguous country houses and barracks; the same outlandish bustle and confusion—neighing and trampling of steeds, rattling of carriages and donkey carts, lusty laughter and perpetual clamour. Captain Holloway, Rev. Courtenay Bulteel, Mr. J. R. Newcombe and Mr. Edwin Scoble remained for years the chief patrons of the sport; until, the Queen's Cup having been withheld, the glory of the festivity departed; and, one by one, the fine old gentlemen who were so long identified with its popularity dropped out of sight, to relate many a stirring reminiscence in their country seats.

Of other sports that appealed to the varying tastes of the local public, fox-hunting held the leading position, and no picture was more familiar in Plymouth than Charles Tre-lawney in his pink jacket, seated upon his speckled Grimaldi, with foxhounds filling in the background of the picture :

> 'Twas in Eighteen Hundred and Fifty-Two,
> You know Squire Trelawney (of course you all do) ;
> Well, 'twas Janry the Sixth, the wind S.S. West,
> That this meet Lyneham Inn, boasted some of the best.
> There were the Deacons, those huntsmen so stout,
> Harry Terrell and Harris, the man with the gout ;
> Scoble, Liscombe, Strode, Bishop, and Fearon so neat
> Courtenay Bulteel and Harris, too, honoured this meet.
> Warwick Hunt and his sons, two young hopefuls from Burleigh,
> Logan Downes and bold Sleeman, who sure must rise early !
> Young Woollcombe and Glanville completed the throng,
> For Glanville of Derriford's never far wrong !
> About twelve of the clock was the time of the day
> When a bold fox broke cover : cried Tom, " Gone away ! "
>
> Through Lockyer's estates like an arrow he passed
> And came to the fastness of the High Cliffs at last,
> Here he gallantly plunged himself into the sea,
> And said in his heart " Who'll dare follow me ? "
> But soon to his cost he perceived that no bounds
> Could stop the pursuit of Trelawney's fast hounds ;
> His policy here never served him a crack
> For Ringlet soon fastened her mouth in his back !
> To recover the shore now sure was his drift,
> But 'ere he could reach the top of the cliff
> Whoo—whoop ! Spite his speed and his courage alack
> He's worried and killed by the rest of the pack ! !

How often the inheritors of these traditions assembled on the lawn at Ivybridge, spic-and-span, with brand-new coats, tan boots, below the whitest and fullest of breeches, brown Napoleons and buckskins, top-hats and guards, spurs and hunting crops—the sun rising like a ball of fire, harbinger of heavy rain and bespattering mud. All the aristocracy of South Devon assembled, in stately barouche and stylish brougham, dog-carts drawn by dappled greys, with the master, Mr. William Coryton, extending a cheering greeting to all, and courtly receptions to the ladies—with their regulation hats or bewitching " bowlers "— including famous Dianas of the chase like Miss Turner, of Combe Royal, and Miss Pitt, mounted on a champion that allowed " the beauties " little lead. Many a time and oft did a southerly wind and a cloudy horizon proclaim these hunting mornings, away to Stowford Cleaves, then to the earth under Harford Rock, and, hey, for the wood at Flete, where sly Reynard made himself scarce. The same bright companies grouped around Master Major Green, Arthur the Huntsman, Johnny the Whip and " Miles's Boy," near the sluggish Erme, or lively Cherrybrook, Harford Bridge or Pyles Wood, to drive the otter to cave or drain, and record a thrilling "kill" or unsensational "blank."

Ratting, badger-baiting, bull-baiting and cock-fighting were much in favour throughout the West. The object of bull-baiting was to make the beef tender ; and, although the sport was discountenanced, the word went round whenever the performance was fixed. The last occasion on which a bull was baited at Plymouth was in 1830, when a large number of people assembled in a field in Gilbert's Lane, Milehouse, and the admission to the entertainment was a shilling. The bull was tethered to the ground, and dog after dog was let loose to worry it preparatory to the slaughter. By degrees the bull turned up the ground to find a refuge for its nose and mouth ; and, again and again, one dog was tossed, another was gored, a third was caught by the farmer's wife, who ran about holding her apron open, so that she might intercept the pets and break their falls. "Fresh dog—form a lane !" was the periodical cry as a new trainer came forward to gain experience for his animal and to prove its expertness.

There were not wanting hoary veterans who defended cock-fighting as giving quite as much pleasure to birds as spectators ; and, as a genuine silver spur was dug out of an old Roman wall near St. Keyne, in Cornwall, fanciers contended that mains must have been held in the West for generations. In later times, when the custom was forbidden, interest in the encounters increased, and there was a good deal of training in Plymouth, and regular encounters at different points. In 1828 a match between Devon and Cornwall was fought at Ridgway, for £4 a battle and £200 on the main. Skelton, the Devon feeder, won by seven battles on the main of 35 couples. At the next fight, in 1829, Pearce, of Cornwall, won the main by seven battles, much to the disappointment of "knowing coves" who had backed Skelton heavily. "The birds were in excellent condition, and the turns could not have been better." Local champions were often carried to London, Manchester, and other places, and occasionally met their match. The scent of the police was keen in the district, and a crowd of the fraternity was pounced upon in a barn at Egg Buckland. Some of the offenders were taken to Roborough, where sporting sympathisers on the Bench assisted to break down the evidence and release the defendants. On another occasion, a magistrate was seized near Newton, but he was acquitted on the plea that he was only a casual spectator. A local trainer once engaged in a fight on which heavy bets were laid ; and, after he and his opponent had killed two birds apiece, the visitor laid low four cocks in succession. This represented six to two, and the odds being enormous the excitement was acute. Such a disparity had rarely been known in an important event ; but, as the birds were weighed for the final encounter, the outsider's turned the scale. Although there were not three barleycorns between the rivals, the objection was fatal, and the stakes were claimed. The antagonist was furious, and his friends demanded that the scales should be tested. "They were tested this morning by a gentleman mutually agreed upon," said the umpire, "and there can be no going back." Suddenly there was an agonised shout that the disconcerted competitor was plucking out tail feathers from his bird, and as the freshly drawn evidence lay at his feet, the contest was ruled against him on the ground of fraudulent practice.

In more modern times, Football has held the field, and in 1898 the Devon County Rugby Team carried off the English County championship, with the leading players drawn from the Devonport Albion and Engineer Students clubs.

Plymouth Great November Fair was held in the large open spaces that encircled the Market within and without ; and the event supplied scenes of boisterous animation.   Never failing in their attractions were the music of the gong, the big drum, the cracked horn, the bell, and the oratory of the one-penny, two-penny and three-penny showmen.   No amusement was more popular with the dockyardsmen or " mateys," or with the soldiers and sailors who resorted nightly to this haunt with their wives, daughters and sweethearts, many of them radiant in the plaid cloaks of the period :

> You young men and maidens, give attention to my song,
> I'll tell you of the fashion now, and not detain you long ;
> The truth which I shall tell to you, I'll tell it as a joke,
> Every pretty girl in Devonport wears a fine Plaid Cloak.
>
> > With a fine Plaid Cloak,
> > What a show they cut in Devonport,
> > With a fine Plaid Cloak.
>
> There is Eliza Long and Miss Betsey Clark,
> They say unto their mammy, we must have a new Plaid Cloak ;
> Oh yes, my dear, their mammy says, there's plenty to be got,
> But what you shall have one, I'll go to the Pawnshop.
>
> 'Twas down North-Corner Street, one evening I did walk,
> When I met a pretty lass, and together we did talk ;
> I stepped up beside her, then she began to joke,
> I took a walk along with her, and she wore her fine Plaid Cloak.
>
> * * * * * * * *
>
> So now I will conclude—of my song I'll make an end,
> Here's success to the Plaids, and may they never want a friend ;
> So my pretty lasses drink a health, and now let us sing—
> Success to Plymouth Fair and God Save the King.

Here a throng assembled in front of Brown's Amphitheatre ; or, to quote the description, "Amphitheatro, ne grand Mercado de Plymouth." Within, a huge man, with debauched face, balanced swords, tobacco pipes and plates on his chin.   Glass-blowers were at work in an adjoining show, and the manufacture of silk was also in progress.   Another amphitheatre was a substantial building with front and side boxes, pit and gallery—the interior, like the exterior, coloured with gaudy paintwork.   There Mrs. Chaff rode at full speed, with and without saddle or bridle, and Mrs. Wells demonstrated her skill on the slack wire with a modesty of dress that was eulogised as a decorous pattern to more " respectable " places of amusement.   Mr. Bell proved in humour to be scarcely inferior to Joey Grimaldi ; a young Indian was quite at his ease on the flying rope, and ranked only second to Don Antonio, the double-jointed man who had astonished "the Londoners"; Mr. Furlong leapt over a gate whilst standing on the backs of two horses ; and there was a Grand Roman Entrée in which sixteen young and well-trained horses were introduced at the same time.   Wit, music and harmony mingled at Samuel's Theatre—and a tragedy, a comedy, a harlequinade and several songs were despatched, to the content of a packed audience, in less than an hour. Outside the Argascopia, the manager, whose ringlets bespoke the unoffending artiste, declared in dulcet tones : " The performance will shortly commence by my performing several popular tunes on the musical glasses, the first of which will be ' Oh, dear, what can the matter be?'"   The screech of an artiste hard by, who was advertising the woes of

Master Punch, sadly annoyed the musician ; and his rage when his intention was drowned in the hideous noise without, just as he had commenced to tune his instrument, was suggestive of Hogarth's frenzied violinist. The Argascopia furnished a magic-lantern entertainment ; and the Mimic Clown, Ike Taylor and the Cabbage, Death-on-a-Pale-Horse and the Stag Hunt were presented in perfection.   In adjacent tents were exhibited serpents which only fed once in six months, a giant boy, a lady with white hair and pink eyes, performing monkeys, a hairy man, and a mechanical theatre.   The Brutal Murder of Mr. Weare and the Tragedy of Maria Martin in the Red Barn were pourtrayed with gory episodes.   Gingerbread nuts, toys and sweetmeats were everywhere on sale ; a dozen table knives and forks could be purchased for eighteenpence ; and desperate bargains in pocket knives, scissors, pencil-cases and shoehorns were available.   There was a wild Indian who was prepared to eat rats, but was no less content to devour unboiled liver—an entertainment very popular and cheap at the price.   But the scarcity of vermin was a perennial source of chagrin to the more juvenile spectators.   Some compensation was found in the antics of Molly, who was on view in the open, a female monkey who nursed her baby, grimly attired as an old woman with a mob cap.   In fact, there were, in the garrulous description of the showmen :

> Roaring boys—Gilded toys,
> Lollipops—Shilling hops,
> Tumble in —Just begin.
> Wooden walls—*Brandy balls,*
> " Gin and bitters—Apple fritters,
> Pudding nice—Penny a slice,
> A bang up swing—Just the thing,"
> *Not for us— We hate the fuss,*
> *And cannot bear— To skim the air*
> *At such a rate !*

Little gamblers of all grades, from the game of Black and White Cock down to the rustic sport of " Throwing at the Boxes," roundabouts, swings and other amusements were in evidence.   Nothing compared, however, with " Vauxhall "—a dancing saloon that dazzled by its splendour, with a thousand lamps arranged in devices representative of balloons, crowns and anchors.   Eighteenpence was charged for admission, and hundreds of masked partners engaged in waltzes, quadrilles and country dances.   Sixpenny plates of veal, ham, tongue and chicken were to be obtained, and hot grog was sold at a shilling a glass.

"S. Polito," sole proprietor of the Royal Managerie, occupied the principal part of the area at the back of the Market—the site now bounded by Old Town and Drake Streets.   He appealed to "a generous and enlightened public," no less than the curious, and proclaimed, in the intervals permitted by his brassy band, that he had within a collection of "rare and remarkable living ·objects such as I flatter myself all Europe cannot produce."   "We have here," he declared, "the stupendous Rhinoceros or real Unicorn— the most singular and formidable of all Terrestrial Animals.   Its strength is not inferior to that of the Elephant, and in size it only appears less by the different formation of its body and shortness of its legs. It is covered with an impenetrable coat of mail or armour, capable of resisting the force of a musket ball, and armed with a formidable horn over its nose, with which it can tear up almost everything before it, but so gentle that it will suffer any person to touch it."   Satisfied with the impression created by this oratorical flight, "S. Polito" commended "the noble lion with the full mane, absolutely the only one travelling in this kingdom, whose majestic countenance justly entitles him to the ancient name of the King of Beasts." Then the showman paid a deserved tribute to the wonderful size, strength and sagacity of his male elephant. In all ages the elephant had been the admiration of mankind, "but the present seems to be one of the most scientific of the race, and by the command of his keeper will perform many tricks that will not only astonish and entertain you, but justly prove him a half-reasoning creature." Of the zebra the language was no less picturesque : " It is the most perfect, the finest and most beautiful that has been seen in this kingdom in the memory of man ; in which it seems as if the most exquisite works of art had been combined with nature in this wonderful production. In symmetry of shape and beauty of colour, it is the most elegant of all quadrupeds ; it unites the grace-

OLD PLYMOUTH MARKET.

(From a Painting by Colonel Whipple, 1890.)

(Reconstructed, 1895-1899.)

ful figure of a horse with the fleetness of a stag, and is beautifully striped with regular lines, black and white." And so Polito continued his oft-told story—of male and female royal tigers from Bengal ; of the spotted or laughing hyæna; of the striped hyæna " of whom so many absurd and fabulous accounts have been given in ancient and modern times, *particularly by other exhibitors of wild beasts* "; of ostriches, emus, cassowaries, and " that wonderful bird of ancient fame, the Pelican of the Wilderness." " We have also here two black swans—those rarities of the New World whose existence has been considered fabulous : *Rara avis in terra, nigroque simillima cygno.*" Whilst the crowd were gaping with surprise the final announcement was made : " And the price of admission is, for ladies and gentlemen 2s. ; tradespeople 1s. Walk up, walk up, we are just about to begin." The time flew merrily, and it was long after midnight that the Market was cleared and lights were extinguished.   And the spectators sang as they dispersed :

> I have been to Plymouth Fair,
> Where I have been before :
> All among the Hottentots,
>   A-capering on shore :
> A-capering, a-capering, a-capering,
>   A-capering on shore !

The dignity of some of the showmen could hardly have been surpassed by Macready or Kean.   The famous Bradley, after a visit to the Plymouth theatre, asked Mr. J. R. Newcombe, Mr. Henry Reed and Major Rendle to visit his show in the Market, and promised them a treat in Richard III.   They accepted the invitation, and were received with stately grace on ascending the plank that led to the platform.   The veteran lessee took out his purse to pay for the admission of the party, but Bradley--radiant in the ideal attire of the master of a Circus Ring—grandiloquently disabused him : "Certainly not, sir, we gentlemen in the profession can afford to be polite to one another.   George "— this to his son, who was installed at the ticket office—" Three seats for three friends of mine."   Bradley, however, was not always so considerate.   " Billy" Pike, subsequently the versatile scenic artist at the Theatre Royal, indicated his early passion for the drama by haunting the precincts of the Market during the show period ; and as a boy, spent a whole day in assisting to erect Bradley's show--in the hope that his efforts would be recognised by a complimentary passport.   Deferentially approaching the great man, the lad remarked " If you please, sir, I've been helping to build your show since six this morning."   Propelling him some distance with his foot, Bradley exclaimed " Get out of this, you young devil."   As we have seen, this marked ingratitude did not cure the embryonic amateur and painter of his passion for the stage.

CHAPTER XIV.—DEVELOPMENT AND MODERN HISTORY.

Commercial   The wars so inflated the prosperity of the Three Towns that the
Depression : 1815-1821   prescient dreaded the return of peace. When the merchants gambled
in prize agencies and contraband goods, fortunes were rapidly made. But the wealth
acquired was of little enduring value, for its recipients were demoralised by the ease with
which they made it, and the methods of rivals were subversive of legitimate trading.
Amid the growth of lax and predatory dispositions there were a few redeeming gleams.
Successful men were profuse in hospitalities ; useful institutions rose to prove the existence
of public spirit ; munificent support led to the erection of the Theatre Royal and adjacent
hotel ; Sutton Pool and Catwater were improved ; the Breakwater was inaugurated ;
"legal quays" were created and there were other symptoms of enterprise. It was not
immediately that the depression was felt, although the sagacious foresaw that it must come.
The overthrow of " the Usurper " was welcomed as a cause for congratulation ; but, in a
few months, money ceased to circulate with the old rapidity, and the port discovered that
it had lost its source of maintenance as an auction mart for prizes and cargoes. Escape
from paralysis was sought in the development of fisheries, and the arrival of vessels from

AFTER THE WAR : SCENE ON THE RIVER TAMAR.
(From a Sketch by Samuel Prout.)

France with wines, spirits and tobacco caused some slight revival. But, as the exportation of copper, tin, deals and preserved fish was unauthorised, the traders could not freight vessels in exchange, and the gloom was opaque. Instinctive anxiety to save the situation was quite unavailing. Depression settled like night over Plymouth and Dock, and thousands were plunged in unutterable misery. Retrenchment was so drastic that two hundred men-of-war were laid aside in a single month, and only 12,000 sailors and 500 marines were retained. From every department there were wholesale discharges, and minor officials were reduced to nominal wages. Thus the stream that had nurtured Plymouth suddenly dried up; every class was thrown upon its resources; mutilated warriors and unemployed artisans begged the necessaries of subsistence; and 7,000 paupers received doles at the church doors. A road around the Hoe was started to mitigate the destitution; droves of dockyardsmen, soldiers and sailors emigrated to America; sedition was rampant, and the King was stigmatised as "the destroyer of his people." The trading classes insisted that Plymouth and Dock should be as fully inhabited in times of peace as of war; but the cynics retaliated that so many scabby sheep had followed Hone and other "blasphemous and disloyal politicians," that officialism was justified in its rigour.

To the Lords of the Admiralty—from the young and Single Ladies of Plymouth, Stonehouse, and Devonport.

MY LORDS AND GENTLEMEN.—

The old adage says, "It is better to give than receive," and to alleviate the wants of all officers' widows in the Army or Navy is certainly an act of kindness, which this country will ever be admired for. But the *single Ladies* of Plymouth, Stonehouse, and Devonport, beg to combine their grateful sentiments towards the Right Hon. Board of Finance, for their intention of placing the Widows' pension on the plan of 1822—which enabled them to retain it only while Widows. The Ladies in the above towns feel confident that such a system will greatly accelerate their OWN HOPES of MATRIMONY which the continued allowance of pensions after marriage, too often lured away from them to the more fortunate *Widows;* for when men are led by the possession of property, HOWEVER small, but SURE, little or no address is required, and much less of sincerity: such men soon distinguish widows enjoying the bounty of so generous a country; and as our towns abound with needy BATCHELORS on the look out for 50 POUNDERS, we are from such alarming consideration emboldened to lay before the Right Hon. Gentlemen our sentiments and peculiar feelings of joy at such a drawback to our hopes being removed; and to submit the same to your Hon. Board's indulgent forgiveness.—Signed in the name and behalf of the single Ladies of Plymouth, Devonport, and Stonehouse.

PENELOPE CANDIDUS.

Superannuation Street, Dock, 1822.

The institution of an Exchange in Woolster Street brought the commercial classes into closer communion. Coals were imported direct, ships from other ports were severely left alone, and nothing was brought from afar that could be raised on the spot. It was only in grain that free trade was advocated, and upon the attempt to limit its importation so that the farmers might still pay excessive rentals, the authorities of Plymouth and Dock formally insisted that, with the return of peace, there should be an abridgment of the privileges of landowners and a reduction in the cost of necessaries. Out of the torpor a commercial spirit rekindled the West Indian and Newfoundland traffic; shipbuilding revived as an industry, and there was a general desire to unite interests. But the Customs' restrictions were vexatious; delicate goods were so ransacked that consignees refused to accept delivery; and, whilst hams were admitted without difficulty, sides of bacon were excluded because a special Act protected Irish produce.

The Dartmoor Railway: 1823. Attempts to find employment on a large scale were encouraged by the Prince Regent, who offered tracts on Dartmoor for experiments in cultivation. This was popularly construed as the gift of a white elephant, as the land produced "neither heather, weeds, whins, brooms, nettles or thistles," and was extremely unlikely, therefore, to satisfy starving workmen. It was maintained, however, that lime would redeem the moor from sterility; and Sir Thomas Tyrwhitt, one of the members for

Plymouth, recommended an iron railroad so that trucks drawn by horses might convey that ingredient from the quarries at Catdown. He put his theory to the test by raising "an excellent crop of flax" on this unpromising soil; and the first railroad laid in Devon —and designated "the pride of the county".—was accordingly opened in 1823. Within the warehouse he had erected on Roborough Down, Sir Thomas Tyrwhitt gave a public breakfast, and "every elegant species of viand" was provided for a company which "comprised the respectability, worth and value of the neighbourhood." The guests marched through the tunnel by the aid of candles, and several loads of granite were drawn towards Hoo Meavy, where the primitive train was saluted with petards. The South Devon Band sounded airs of welcome, a numerous calvacade escorted the phenomenon to Plymouth, and the undertaking was toasted at the Royal Hotel in the faith that granite would become "as universal in use as it is beautiful in appearance." It was this achievement that stimulated the idea of "a general iron railway throughout the kingdom." The boldness of the proposition, a pamphleteer admitted, "may cause astonishment; but, unless there be greater obstacles than the levelling of the line of road, the raising of arches across valleys, and bridges over rivers, I cannot conceive why it was not undertaken years ago." As the Dartmoor railroad had been carried some 1,400 feet above the sea, the critics were disposed to allow that the conveyance of inland mails and passengers might be effected at a trifling cost, "compared with the enormous expense of stage coaches."

The Breakwater and Great Storms: 1812-1880   To the construction of the Breakwater, more than to any other cause, did Plymouth owe its position as a place of maritime importance. Originally, the Admiralty projected a scheme for protecting Torbay, which Lord Howe was accustomed to say would one day prove the grave of the British Navy, so open and exposed was its situation and so ill the repute it bore amongst

PLYMOUTH BREAKWATIR, IN COURSE OF CONSTRUCTION.
(From an old Sketch.)

naval officers. When Mr. Whidbey submitted plans and estimates, Lord St. Vincent suggested that the same design should be effected at Plymouth, and a report so satisfactory as to be conclusive was submitted to Parliament in 1812. The one serious objection urged was the possible destruction of the anchorage by accumulated mud and silt. There was a farther theory that Catwater and Hamoaze would eventually fill up, but this was brushed aside as visionary. The Prince Regent ordered the starting of the work, and the Oreston Quarry was bought from the Duke of Bedford for £10,000. Wharves and docks were erected to ship the stone, iron rails were laid to the quays, and vessels were constructed to carry masses of several tons in weight. The boulders were put on trucks, these were run on rails to the ship, and tipped on the site by the aid of cranes. At the spot where the embankment was to rise, the mighty indraught of the Atlantic was only feebly checked by the Tinker Rock, and the masses of granite were thrown into the sea itself. The laying of the foundation stone was fixed for the Prince Regent's birthday in 1812, and the morning was ushered in with ringing of bells and firing of salutes. Sir Robert Calder, the Port Admiral, and his officers sailed into the Sound, and the massed bands played martial airs as they were received on board the surveying slips. When all was in readiness a stone seven tons in weight was deposited on the centre of the Shovel Rock, and, at a concerted signal, there was a general booming of guns, and fervour found its echoes from numberless throats. The work did not make much progress for some months; but, in March, 1813, the granite showed dry at low water, and half a million tons were deposited by December, 1814. Severe gales blew in the Sound during the ensuing Spring, but the resistance offered by "the colossal pier" enabled forty line of sail to anchor inside the bulwark, and 150 vessels of all rigs rode without damage in Catwater.

The undertaking was far from complete when the harbour was visited by an abnormal tide; and, in January, 1817, by a storm of extraordinary violence. Distress signals were fired from the Sound, but no assistance could be rendered; and Queen Anne's Battery was swept by waves that sent their spray several hundred yards inland. The Princess Mary drove ashore, and was shivered in pieces; officers, crew, and passengers of both sexes were tossed amid splinters and timbers, and not a soul survived. Two hours later the Jasper frigate and the schooner Telegraph were driven ashore—the former at Mount Batten, and the latter under the Hoe. Despairing men clung to the rigging as the ships were dashed against the rocks; wild cries mingled with the tempest; and both vessels went to pieces, ninety officers and men foundering with the wreck. The shore was strewn with the débris and corpses; masses of rock were shivered; a breach was made in the wall of the dockyard; the new road under the Hoe was destroyed, and stones of five tons in weight were tossed like feathers. Seaweed was swept up the Stonehouse Hill in masses; several houses in Cawsand Bay were demolished; and the head of a man was found on the beach as cleanly severed "as though it had been cut off with a axe." The Breakwater suffered huge damage, and pavement stones of twenty tons in weight were carried out to sea.

It was left to the great gale of November, 1824, to disturb engineering calculations. For days before "the dreadful hurricane," sharp flashes of lightning, angry clouds and unwonted tides betokened the imminence of exceptional disturbances. On the 21st the wind veered in convulsive gusts, a dark curtain veiled the earth, flocks of petrels shrieked and flew for shelter, and towering waves rolled into the Sound. As ships ran for safety, the sight was watched with tremulous anxiety, then a pall of Cimmerian darkness shut out the view, and the populace were left in suspense. At midnight the storm lulled for twenty minutes, when it recommenced with incredible fury. Screams and shrieks were heard in the intervals of deafening roars of wind and waves, and dwellers by the waterside

MORNING AFTER THE GREAT GALE, 1824.
(From a Sketch by N. Condy.)

witnessed the appalling devastation. Sixteen vessels were at anchor in the Sound ; and, as the westernmost drifted across the others, all was confusion. In Catwater a cluster of ships to windward ran foul of those leeward, and at daylight twenty-five merchantmen were under Mount Batten and the Hoe—some reduced to chips, others on their beam ends, a few with their bottoms out, and the remainder mere wrecks. In the lower parts of Plymouth people passed the night in the top storeys, expecting every minute to be involved

OFF CATDOWN—MORNING AFTER THE GREAT GALE, 1824.
(From a Sketch by N. Condy.)

in ruin. Along the coast the desolation was frightful. One vessel was blown into Mount Edgcumbe from Barnpool and a second was hurled into the Baths under Richmond Walk. Disaster overtook the preventive fleet, Bigbury and Bovisand Bay were desolated, and the destruction in house property was estimated at several thousands of pounds.

A vessel was driven on the western end of the Breakwater, and the massive stones penetrated the deck and held her firm. Over the huge masonry itself the waves rolled with resistless majesty: the machinery was swept away, and the blocks were scattered. The surface was uprooted, and stones of ten tons were carried from the outer and deposited on the inner slope—a distance of 138 feet. Two hundred thousand tons were thus shifted; and, as the deposits settled firmly, the conformation was readjusted to the currents. The south side was increased beyond the slope by additions above low-water mark, and a foreshore was created which broke the body of the sea before it reached the main work. The principle of dovetailing the boulders was then adopted, and thick iron plates were used at the links. As these swelled with the rust, the device was reluctantly abandoned. In the end, the predictions of croakers were condemned as "presumptuous and chimerical," and five million and a half tons of granite having been deposited, the bulwark stood undaunted and immovable :

> Bleak, Naked, Stationed in the very Van
> Of conflict, where the winds of Heav'n arise
> To battle with the World of Waters.

Subsequent storms may be conveniently here recalled. The coast in November, 1836, was strewn with wreckage, and four vessels which ran for the harbour, unable to secure their anchorage, broke up on the rocks. Devonport on this occasion was deprived of its surviving relics of rusticity—two immense elm trees, which had stood for generations in the middle of Fore Street, and under whose branches folk had gathered on hot days to discuss the affairs of town or country. In February, 1837, the Spanish schooner Alban was running for safety from the gale, when she missed stays and struck upon the Break-water. Her boat being washed away, it was impossible for those on board to leave the vessel, including the wife of the captain, whose daughter was only a few hours old, and had been born during the storm. To add to the horror of the situation the vessel took fire; and, although within gunshot of several battleships, it was impossible to pierce with the human voice the roar of the hurricane. Mother and infant were washed off the deck; and just as the survivors were becoming insane with despair, the flames shot up and broke the intense gloom. The desperate situation of the schooner was perceived, and boats from the neighbouring vessels effected the rescue of the survivors. The lower parts of Plymouth and Union Street were inundated in February, 1838, when those who were in bed were awakened by the sound of rushing waters. The Octagon was submerged to the extent of several inches; and, when the tide receded, fish were found in the houses and roadway. Boisterous weather recurred in November of the same year, and a pinnace which was running for the Breakwater under closely reefed lug-sail, shipped a heavy sea near the Cobbler buoy and foundered with twenty hands.

Plymouth was visited by a hurricane in November, 1855, in the course of which the Ocean Queen struck the Mewstone. Crew and passengers stripped themselves the better to reach the shore; but, at daybreak, fifteen bodies were washed into Wembury Bay, and all that remained of the ship were a few spars and a portion of the stern. In 1865, the Hiogo leapt over the Breakwater, and became transfixed on the boulders. The inhabitants of the Three Towns were startled from their midnight slumber in September, 1867, by unusual atmospheric disturbance. The firmament appeared in a blaze, and persons started from sleep under the impression that their dwellings were on fire. So varied in form, colour and intensity was the electricity, changing from white to pale blue in the sheet lightning to bright or dark red in the chain and the forked, that the spectacle was "indescribably sublime." As the dense rain clouds approached the combination of colours produced emerald and orange tints, and a veritable waterspout choked the gulleys with sand and flooded the streets. In their panic the population believed that the end of the world had arrived. Similar consternation prevailed in December, 1872, when daylight was suddenly obscured and there was an impression that an unexpected eclipse had taken place. Without a moment's warning, the phenomenon was followed by a hurricane and deluge. A dense and overspreading cloud enveloped everything in smoke, and houses rocked to such a degree that hysterical alarm was general during "those really terrible moments." Several wrecks occurred in the Sound, and the lifeboat was so battered that a steamer had to tow it to Millbay with a rescued crew. The barque R. H. Jones made for Plymouth during another eventful gale in October, 1877 ; and, just as the vessel was nearing the Sound, the captain sent a seaman named Blom aloft to report the Breakwater light. It was too late, for at that moment the vessel leapt over the huge mole itself, and went to pieces on the boulders, the captain and twenty officers and men being drowned. Inside the bulwark lay the Turquoise corvette, and her second anchor was being dropped when faint cries were heard from a piece of wreckage to windward. It was impossible to lower a boat in such a sea, but a captain's coxswain, John Emmanuel Barnes, volunteered to swim to the timbers with a line around his body. Although he was once hauled back exhausted, he made another effort when the cries were renewed and secured Blom, who was clinging to the top of the mast. Apart from the memorable blizzards which are noted in connection with the Plymouth water famines of 1881 and 1891, the fall of hail in 1897 was one of the most remarkable, the downpour lasting for half an hour, and stones as large as walnuts producing floods and accumulations sudden beyond precedent.

WRECK OF H.M.S. HIOGO ON THE EDDYSTONE REEF, 1865.
(SHOWING SMEATON'S LIGHTHOUSE.)

*New Victualling
Yard; Diving Bell;
and Launches :
1820-1828.*
The construction of the New Victualling Yard at Devil's Point was remarkable for the use that was made of the diving bell. The foundation-stone of the seawall was laid eleven feet below water mark by means of this "curious triumph of art," and, in a few months, with the same contrivance, several thousand tons of limestone were deposited and cemented together. From the genius of Smeaton the pursuit of submarine experiments had received many developments, and, in the hands of Rennie, the machine took a form alike simple and plain. The bell employed at Plymouth was made of cast iron; it was six feet long and four broad, and contained 120 cubic feet of air. Twelve convex lens at the top admitted the light, and air was driven through a leathern hose by means of a pump worked by four men. Rennie's machine was first utilised in constructing a wall at the Dockyard in 1826, and 4,000 cubic feet of stone were deposited in four years. The diving bell was also used for another purpose. As the Eden sloop was deteriorating from dry rot she was sunk in Barnpool to save her. The bed was first inspected to see if she could be filled with safety, and after a boulder had been removed, the warship was lowered for a few weeks and refloated without injury. Sir Alexander Hardy descended off Devil's Point, but suffered such pains in the ears that he could not remain below. His daughter, however, finished the voyage without inconvenience, and sent up an amusing bon-mot:

> From a belle, my dear, you've oft had a line,
> But not from a bell under water;
> Just now I can only assure you I'm thine,
> Your diving, affectionate daughter.

Returning to the scene of his adventures in 1827, the Duke of Clarence laid the coping stone of the seawall and spread the mortar with a silver trowel amid the cheers of the workmen. On the following day the population poured forth to welcome the Duchess and the Princess Carolath. Seated in a carriage drawn by four horses, the party were received in regal state, and, when the town was reached, the horses were taken from the shafts, and the visitors drawn by the crowd to "the toll gate in Union Street," the Dock Yeomanry Cavalry and garrison staff supplying a dashing escort. When the Duchess alighted at Government House to greet her consort enthusiasm was unbounded; and, after passing through an avenue of redcoats to the Admiral's barge, the way to Mount Edgcumbe became "a regular aquatic procession." Men-of-war were radiant with the flags of all nations, and the rainbow hues of the yachts contrasted with the greensward of the park. Whilst the flashing waters were thus instinct with life and movement, peals of cannon awakened the echoes, and there was a roar of acclaiming responses. Big battleships and small brigs were smothered in the smoke of salutes, and the darkened air was broken by flashes of red light, as though a naval engagement were in progress. Vivid streams of fire burst from the muzzles of the guns on Mount Wise, and the clouds rolled away in slowly dissolving volumes. At night their Royal Highnesses entertained 600 persons to a ball and supper, and the twin decks of the Meteor and the Royal Sovereign, lashed together for the occasion, were surmounted with canvas stretched over rafters. The interior was a blaze of flags and banners; the seats were furnished with silken cushions; fancifully-arranged bayonets, holding vari-coloured wax candles, composed the chandeliers; and the deck was chalked with artistic devices. The Duchess and Lord Valletort opened the dancing at eleven o'clock, and the play of movement was surveyed from Mount Wise. As the atmosphere was still and the waters tranquil, the surface of the harbour reflected the tapering lights of the yachts at anchor, and the scene was no faint image of a Venetian carnival. Transparencies and dazzling arrangements of coloured lights rendered the Admiral's House a fairy palace ; the Town Hall blazed with flambeaux ; and a tiara of quivering flame rose high above the Column. At midnight, a signal gun attracted all eyes towards the Britannia ; and that noble battleship, which a moment before could scarcely be distinguished from the dark waters that surrounded her, was suddenly bathed from stem to stern in azure light, and the sea shimmered with living flame. Then clusters of rockets burst from her decks, and the air was luminous with trains of red fire and clusters of swiftly-moving stars.

In a few months the Duke of Clarence again journeyed to the West to present new colours to the Royal Marines at Stonehouse. The troops in garrison assembled on parade, and the Lord High Admiral, in a speech of an hour and a half's duration, reviewed the rise and progress of the Royal Marines, and alluded " with much eloquence of feeling " to their invaluable services afloat and on shore. The rain fell with remarkable violence, but the Duke persisted " in a firm and manly voice " to the end of his address. Colonel Vinnicombe received the colours with an assurance that the memory of the day would animate the corps to future deeds of glory. In the evening the barracks were illuminated, each of the entrance gates displaying the Lord High Admiral's double anchor and cables, with the letters " W " and " A " surmounted by a coronet. Another transparency depicted Fame drawing aside a curtain and displaying to Britannia the new flag, surrounded with trophies of war. On this occasion the Plymouth Corporation were quite alive to their opportunity :

" We participate in common with the inhabitants of this populous district, in the general diffusion of joy, elicited by your Royal presence ; presiding at the head of that service, in which we are reminded that your youth was passed ; and, notwithstanding your illustrious birth, subjected to its dangers and vicissitudes.

" In the revival of these early associations, we have one peculiarly our own, arising from the reflection that we have been allowed the honour for so many years of enrolling your Royal Highness's name as a member of our Corporate body, and that we have, therefore, the additional honour of receiving your Royal Highness as a brother freeman.

" We rejoice at seeing your Royal attention directed to so important a branch of the public service as that of the naval department, in which we may be allowed to take even a larger share of interest than the other parts of the kingdom, though none can be insensible to the vast debt of gratitude we owe to the Navy of Great Britain, and we rely on your Royal Highness's pardoning our zeal in earnestly recommending to your Royal patronage the several great national works now constructing in our port, for the preservation, protection and perpetuity of that Navy.

In his response the Duke was alike sympathetic and genially reminiscent : " I assure you I feel a deep sense of satisfaction at the feeling manifested on this occasion by yourself and the inhabitants of Plymouth generally. In the former part of my life I had the pleasure of passing several years in this neighbourhood, and I may truly say that I look back on that period as composing some of the happiest moments of my existence. If it were only on this account I should have cause to rejoice that my late venerable father had marked out for me the profession of which I was then a member. I am also exceedingly proud to say, that Plymouth was the first borough of which I was made a freeman. I feel much gratified that my revered brother, our most gracious sovereign, has thought fit to appoint me to the high situation which I hold, inasmuch as I shall be enabled to manifest the deep interest which, as a freeman of your borough, and as an Englishman, I entertain for the construction and preservation of the great national works, now carrying on at Plymouth. While I continue in office, I shall use all possible exertions in favour of every measure calculated to advance the improvement of the navy ; and be assured, gentlemen, that I shall always attend to the promotion of those brave officers who have adorned, by their gallant exploits, the naval annals of the nation."

The Spirit of Recovery : 1828. Ordinarily the close Corporation limited their duties to the collection of tolls, dues and profits arising from the letting of the fish, fruit, vegetables and butchers' stalls ; to the acceptance of tenders from such persons as "are willing to undertake the sweeping and cleansing of the streets " ; and the sale of the dung, dirt, ashes and soil, "from which it is apprehended there will be a considerable profit." But their powers of initiative were much greater ; and, in 1811, the Market was re-erected, and a new hotel and theatre were contemplated " for the greater convenience, accommodation and amusement of persons resorting to this town." £20,000 was raised by the grant of annuities on lives nominated by subscribers ; the nominees were placed in ten classes of twenty years each, according to their ages ; and the annuities were paid, with benefit of survivorship, up to the death of the last, so that the subscriber on such last nominee received a nett income of £100. The annuities were secured by bonds under seal of the Corporation ; and, in the first year, the Mayor and Commonalty "presented a lottery ticket to each class of subscriber, thereby affording a chance of an immediate tenfold return of their moneys." The avidity with which the £20,000 was subscribed induced the Mayor and Commonalty to give an addition of ground, so that the proposed buildings might possess "an unity of elegant structure, taste, and convenience," and a further sum of £10,000 was thereupon raised. Foulston prepared plans for erecting the group on the site adjacent to the existing Devon and Cornwall Bank, on which a pile known as "The Island" was subsequently placed. But, when he surveyed this contracted area, the architect protested that a fine building would be lost in such a position, and that carriage approach would be impossible. The Corporation then wanted to place the new theatre upon the site of the old one, and to utilise the areas of adjacent houses in Bedford Street. As Admiral Manley's residence and garden were not available, every effort to carry out this alternative was baffled. In front of George Place was a large unoccupied space, but Mr. Foulston was reminded that it was isolated and on the outskirts of the town. " Isolated ! " he retorted : "let me raise the fabric, and you will soon see a vast addition of houses in that locality." The authorities were won by his enthusiasm, but sought to abridge the space in front of the portico, and if the architect had not been insistent, the street would have been one-half its present width. It was current talk, when the ground was being laid out, that some young sparks, who were returning from a social evening, pulled up the stakes, and promiscuously replanted them in the form that the architect adopted. Be this as it may, so great was the confidence in Foulston that, within three months, opulent inhabitants contributed £46,000 to effect improvements in the town and vicinity.

The acquaintance of the district with war grew more and more reminiscent, illumined by occasional personal flashes. In September, 1819, the Duke of Wellington surveyed the Plymouth fortifications, and he was presented at the Town Hall with the freedom of the borough which had been voted to him in 1815. The ceremony was witnessed by a brilliant assemblage, and Sir William Elford, the Recorder, addressed the Duke at length. Mr. George Eastlake, the Mayor, dwelt on the happiness brought to Europe in its release from the menace of an overbearing military system, and the Duke, amid vociferous cheering, expressed his gratitude for the "high consideration" bestowed upon him. For years the sentiment against war was strong ; and, when Mr. Canning proclaimed a "wise and enlightened neutrality in the Peninsula," he was invited to receive the freedom of Plymouth. In November, 1823, he accepted the patent in a box cut from a block of Breakwater marble, set in silver, with the arms inlaid with gold ; and, in replying, hoped that Plymouth would receive an ample share of the blessings of peace. " I trust the time is not far distant when that noble structure—that gigantic barrier against the fury of the waves which roll into your harbour, will protect a commercial marine not less considerable in its kind than the warlike marine of which your port has so long been so distinguished an asylum, and when the town of Plymouth will participate in the commercial prosperity as largely as it has hitherto done in the naval glories of England."

Education was not neglected, either in the lower or the higher branches. In 1809 the " Dock Public School for Boys " was established by subscription " to counteract the baneful effects of ignorance and evil example in the rising generation, and to promote the best interests of society." The method of education which met with the most favour was that successfully pursued in the town by Dr. Bell and Mr. Lancaster, by which it was "clearly proved that one master can educate a thousand boys in reading, writing and arithmetic as effectually, and with as little trouble, as twenty or thirty have ever been instructed by the usual modes of tuition ; and it appears that a hundred boys may be educated at an expense not exceeding one pound each, including the master's salary." At the instigation of Mr. Henry Woollcombe, the " Plymouth Public School " was established " for the education of poor children," and Mrs. Whitfeld was appointed the first mistress. The Plymouth Grey-Coat School was also instituted, with Mr. Samuel Whitfeld as the master. On the occasion of the first anniversary of the Dock Lancastrian School, all the children and officers marched to the parish church ; and "a select and excellent choir " was assisted by the band of the West York Regiment and several amateurs. After the service, the boys returned "two and two with hands united," each carrying a Prayer-book and sprig of laurel in his hat, and "their appearance and the decorum of their behaviour was highly gratifying to the spectators." Two silken banners were carried, the one displaying a portrait of " our venerable monarch encircled by a wreath," and inscribed " The patron of education and friend of the poor." The other exhibited the arms of Sir John St. Aubyn, " president of the Dock Public School." Assembling in the large room, the prizes were distributed ; and a hymn composed by the secretary, Mr. H. J. Johns, was sung with band accompaniment :

> How dreary once the path we trod,
> Nor guide nor light had we,
> To shew our wandering feet the road
> That leads, great God ! to thee.

> Till Charity, with Christian zeal,
> Proclaimed our hapless state,
> And roused a generous band to feel
> Compassion for our fate.

> And whilst His holy name we praise,
> And ask His fostering care,
> Friends of our youth ! for you we raise
> The supplicating prayer !

> Father of Mercies ! God of love !
> Our benefactors bless,
> Be *Thou* their strength—their refuge prove,
> Who succoured our distress.

After determining that the accounts should be published for the satisfaction of the public, the members of the society withdrew to Goude's Hotel, "where an excellent dinner was served in the best style to about fifty philanthropists, who enjoyed the flow of reason and the feast of soul." Harmony was preserved "by the well-known talents of the worthy chairman, Mr. Elford," and " Knowledge, the strength of nations and the glory of man," was the leading sentiment submitted. To the efforts of Mr. W. H. Hawker were due the establishment, a few years later, of "an Infant School for the Reception of the Children of the Labouring Poor of Plymouth." Meanwhile the "Corporation Free Grammar School, Plymouth ; founded by charter of Queen Elizabeth, A.D. 1561," continued the leading means of diffusing superior education :

" It is the grand aim of the Master of this School (the Rev. H. Borwell, 1824) to unite in his system the leading advantages of public and private tuition. He is anxious to pay the strictest attention to the moral and religious principles of those intrusted to his care ; and, by laying a solid foundation in the various branches of knowledge, which he professes to teach, to enable his pupils to adorn in after life the respective stations in which they may be placed.

"His course of instruction comprehends the Greek, Latin, and English Languages— Latin and English Composition—Ancient and Modern History—Geography, with the use of the Globes, and the projection of Maps—Writing, Arithmetic, &c., Algebra, Euclid's Elements of Geometry and Trigonometry.

"With regard to domestic comfort, every pupil is allowed a separate bed ; all are treated as members of the family ; the health of each is the object of particular attention ; and any indulgence which indisposition may call for, is readily granted.

"The French language, dancing and fencing," were taught by Monsieur Huet, both at Plymouth and at Dock :

" Monsieur Huet, teacher of the true principles of *La Danse de Sociète*, and systematic reformer of imperfect dancing, assures those parents who wish their children to be properly taught, that his mode of tuition has the advantages of imparting a correct, easy, chaste and elegant style, from which it is impossible for anyone ever after to deviate. It is so different from all others, that he challenges any teacher in existence to produce a more efficacious system ; and by the power of his scientific method, pupils ever so young can acquire a more extensive knowledge of dancing in three months than could be attained in twelve on a different principle under the ablest masters. He refers persons interested in that polite branch of education, to the peculiarly striking and numerous advantages of his unique system (being mathematically and geometrically demonstrated), which is the result of many years' incessant study and application."

Jealousies between schoolmasters occasionally took grotesque forms, especially if they happened to be close neighbours, like Mr. Philip Hill, who was a "private" teacher of mathematics and the "higher" branches of education, and Captain Bromley, who was a "public" teacher of spelling, arithmetic, singing, and the "lower" branches of education. Captain Bromley carried on his " Model School" in Princes Street, Devonport (1828), and Mr. Hill taught his pupils in a room adjoining, separated only by a cupboard with a wooden partition. Through this Mr. Hill's pupils bore sundry holes, and fastening pins to thin sticks, drove them into the backs of Captain Bromley's pupils, causing them ever and anon to howl with pain, and not sparing them when they were rendering sacred music. The captain retaliated by banging at the partition with his stick ; and, entering Mr. Hill's door, threatened him with personal chastisement. Bromley was charged before the magistrates with creating a riot, but the summons was dismissed.

PLYMOUTH.

(*From the Water Colour by J. W. M. Turner, R.A.*)

The spirit of recovery did not assert itself until 1824, when powers to light, pave and widen the thoroughfares of Plymouth were granted by Parliament. Whimple and Treville Streets were especially contracted, and the Commissioners spent large sums in making "elegant entrances to certain properties" in which it was said they were not remotely interested. It was argued that these transformations should be effected by subscription, and citizens volunteered £50 a-piece if they were made "free of the borough." This proposal to widen the basis of the franchise did not obtain the approval of the privileged. Under the new regulations, occupiers of garrets were prosecuted for hanging linen out of windows, and tenants of private houses were fined for exposing meat for sale and thus interfering with the municipal market. The watchmen were low and degraded characters, notoriously in collusion with brothels and tippling houses; but the effect of the new legislation was extremely beneficial. Foulston devised many improvements, laying out Union Street to a width that was considered extravagant, and designing Lockyer, Cambridge and other avenues with residential and commercial houses. To his classic taste Plymouth owes more than to any other man of his generation, and his broad thoroughfares gave the town a bright appearance by day, as general illuminations at night rendered it increasingly attractive. Equally encouraging was the report of an intelligent bookseller: "When I came to Plymouth," said he, "a board of a few inches square would hold the stock-in-trade of all our fraternity; and now our shops (there are several excellent ones) will speak for the improvement of the public taste." Thus, in the words of an unknown writer:

> The world is changed, e'en darkness disappears,
>   The good old borough shines in all her glory;
> Those who had deemed her stricken well in years
>   Must now recant and tell another story.
> They've lost the season of their merry jests,
>   The time is past when Plymouth's old and hoary:
> She's younger by a century or two
>   Than when I knew her twenty years ago.
>
> All things are changed from piety to plays,
>   From streets to walks, from business unto pleasure,
> Even manners seem to have shaken off their stays
>   And true refinement prospers in a measure.
> We've acts to strengthen all our crooked ways,
>   Which will accordingly be done at leisure;
> We've also schools where universal knowledge is
>   Taught by instructors from the learned colleges.

From "Plymouth-Dock to Devonport": 1820-1828. The one exercise of electoral right in which Dock indulged was the choice of churchwarden for the parish of Stoke. "A crucial contest" in 1813 was aimed at the pretensions of dockyardsmen as the controlling factor, and the crusade was led by Mr. D. G. Davie, of James Street. Although artificers and shipwrights were men in whose "unfettered and uncontrolled judgment" he readily trusted, he resented attempts to convert their rights into "an engine of power." A few individuals, through their instrumentality, were controlling "this extensive and populous parish," and it was time to curtail their influence, and make them pay rates in proportion to their salaries. By way of reply, Mr. John Clouter, a clerk in the Ordnance Department, was nominated as Mr. Davie's opponent. Repudiating the suggestion that State employment rendered his class incapable of independent judgment, he observed that, from time immemorial, those desirous of misleading the credulous had cried aloud against the injustice and corruption of Government officials. "Even Bonaparte," exclaimed Mr. Clouter, "pretends to be animated by the higher feelings, but it would be absurd to suppose, for a moment, that the world gives him credit for possessing such virtues. The Usurper likewise brands those whom he deprecates with every vice and weakness which may enflame the public against them." These retorts were too effective for Mr. Davie ; and, although the poll was kept open for three days, the numbers at the close were :- Clouter, 480 ; Davie, 436. Mr. Clouter was presented with a silver goblet, accompanied by an address of congratulation "on conduct equally distinguished by manliness and forbearance during an arduous yet successful struggle." Inscribed cups were also given to Mr. Richard Blackmore and Mr. Charles Fink, in the hope that they would "ever be ready to advance into action to oppose every base and corrupt principle which might endeavour to raise its ghastly head with a view to excite division in our parish, and to infringe upon those rights in which we, His Majesty's servants, with all our fellow subjects, are equally entitled to participate."

Thus culminated a period of irritation in which feeling was so strong that "the unlucky wight who dared to raise his voice against the opposition ran no inconsiderable risk of a broken crown." Indeed, there was a recourse to the "meanest arts of perversion and falsehood to which malignity could descend," and, in pursuit of food for this base appetite, "the partisans plunged and wriggled through every sink of infamy and sewer of vice, until they were so crammed and covered with scandal as to become unfit either for touch or smell, and loathsome to behold.' Dock swarmed with brothels 'of the most infamous description," and, spreading their baneful contagion through the town, these "flourished unchecked on the ruin of public morals." When enquiry took place such scenes of human depravity were witnessed as shocked and disgusted the justices. One reformer had a near relative "who owns a house of the most shameful notoriety that the town of Dock exhibits,' but, "as it produces a good round sum, it cannot be considered a nuisance." The better to pave, clean and watch streets and lanes, and to "prevent encroachments, nuisances and annoyances," an Act was obtained that relieved Dock of merely county supervision, and gave the ratepayers a direct voice in their own concerns. This measure created a body of 157 Commissioners, with a qualification of the yearly value of £50, or a personal estate of the value of £100 per annum. The poor being their special care, they forthwith erected a new workhouse.

After some years there was a disposition to allow vacancies on the Board to remain open ; and, goaded by those who were ambitious of serving, the parishoners insisted that the seats should be filled up. Their representations were ignored, and, proceedings being prosecuted in 1829, the judges held that the survivors had no discretionary power. Much excitement prevailed when the mandamus arrived, and "Johnny Vivian," the town crier, clad in blue cloth mantle and cocked hat, all decorated with gold lace- a uniform presented to him for the occasion- made formal announcement that 91 vacancies were to be forthwith filled up, so that the total number of Commissioners should be 157, as at the outset. A furious party spirit had already rendered the conduct of the board notorious ; but, after the new elections, men were admitted "whose first impulse was the gratification of their own unruly passions, and who only assumed the merit of public virtue in order to mask the bitterness of private malice.' The time of the Board was devoted to the "vilest personalities, the rancour of which is to be rarely matched, and teems with scandalous falsehoods.' The new members retaliated by holding an annual supper at which they trolled in lusty chorus the defiant stanzas.

Say, who would not be a Commissioner?
    A great man of Devonport Town,
To examine the weights and the measures
    To which they are perfectly known.

To examine the Butcher and Baker,
    To examine the nuisances made,
And strive to prevent the forestalling?
    But that is too much of their trade.

Then why should they quarrel 'bout riches
    To qualify?—parcel of stuff!
For all are elected by scratches,
    And the lawyer says that is enough.

Then fill up your glasses, and drink,
    Success to our Devonport Town,
And toast up the noble chairman
    Who declared for the ninety and one.

Down to 1820 the Town Hall in Devonport was a small building in Duke Street in immediate contact with the old workhouse, and the public business was conducted there at so much inconvenience that the leading inhabitants declared in a manifesto:

"The justices can no longer be expected to continue their arduous duties in a place so ill-suited to the purpose and to their personal accommodation. There is great reason therefore to apprehend, unless a more commodious building be provided, that they will *discontinue* their sitting in the town; a proceeding that would manifestly be attended with so great an expense to the parish, and with so much delay and obstruction to public business, that it becomes highly requisite to provide against a measure which threatens such serious inconvenience. The same want of accommodation is constantly experienced by the inhabitants at large, upon every occasion when they are called together on the business of Public Institutions, or other matters of general interest.

"The advantages which must result to the parish, from the appropriation of the present Town Hall and Prisons to the purposes of the Workhouse, thereby *avoiding the expense which otherwise will inevitably, at no distant period, be incurred for the enlargement of the latter,* suggest another consideration of still higher importance to the interests of the parish, and strongly urges the necessity of carrying the proposed measure into immediate effect.

"The inhabitants of the Town and Parish are respectfully assured that, whilst the *primary* object will be to erect a building suitable to all the *useful* and *necessary* purposes of public business, and their general accommodation, it is conceived to be perfectly compatible with the design, and with a due regard to economy, to effect it upon such a scale, and in such a situation, as shall render it at the same time *ornamental* and *beneficial* to the town."

Such was the appeal made for subscriptions towards a new building, and, a site having been given by the Lord of the Manor, Foulston's plans were accepted, and the Town Hall was forthwith erected in Ker-street. Filled with pride at this brand-new possession, a memorial was addressed to the King in 1828 begging that a new name might be given to "Plymouth-Dock." Its tone breathed alike a spirit of importance and conscious indignity. Immense naval operations had been conducted in the town, and its arsenal had contributed to the glory and majesty of the empire. Dock had hailed the proud trophies so often and gallantly won, and had eagerly testified its attachment to the institutions of the country. But, to protect their address to the King, the inhabitants deplored and keenly felt that, although they exceeded in population and extent "every other town in Devonshire, they were only recognised as "a mere offshoot of the borough of Plymouth, and as an unimportant adjunct of a national establishment of which they were ambitious of being considered the local guardians and protectors." From this "anomalous and most degrading situation" Dock asked to be extricated by the "King's bounty and condescension," so that it should take rank as "one of the principal towns of an empire rendered happy by your Majesty's paternal government." The place at this time possessed chapels of ease in addition to a parish church, a Town Hall "unrivalled as to architecture and commodiousness"; a public dispensary for the necessitous sick, two classical schools provided with masters "who are ministers of the Established Church"; and various edifices dedicated to worship and charity. Such was the community upon which the King was asked to confer the name of Devonport, and the people hoped that "your Majesty may not consider us unworthy of also participating in those political privileges which your Majesty has been pleased to confer upon other ports in your dominions."

"Devonport, the people with loud acclaim hail thy name!" This was the sentiment that filled the inhabitants of Plymouth-Dock, to be "Dock" no more, when the concession was vouchsafed.

WHITEHALL, 24th Dec., 1823.

GENTLEMEN, Having laid before the King your petition, praying, for the reasons therein stated, that the name of the town of Plymouth Dock might be changed, and that his Majesty would be pleased to confer on the said town the name of DEVONPORT, or such other name as to his Majesty should seem proper, I am commanded to acquaint you that his Majesty has been graciously pleased to comply with the prayer of the said petition, and to direct that, on and after the 1st day of January next, the town of Plymouth-Dock shall be called and known by the name of DEVONPORT, and a communication has been made to the several Public Departments accordingly.

I am, Gentlemen,

Your most obedient humble Servant,

ROBERT PEEL.

To the Parishioners and Inhabitants of the Town of Plymouth Dock, and Parish of Stoke Damerel.

On the day chosen for changing the name the proclamation was made with flourishes of trumpets and the health and happiness of George IV. were commended to the crowd amid further fanfares. Above the procession was borne the municipal flag, proclaiming the word "Devonport"; there was a gilded figure of Fame sounding a trumpet and attended on either side by instrumentalists; the beadles walked in gold-laced purple cloaks and cocked hats bearing in their hands staves inscribed with the new designation, and surmounted with carved and gilded crowns. The officials and commissioners walked two and two, carrying emblems decorated with laurel leaves, all over the town flags and arches uttered the momentous word, and the proclamation was recited from point to point by Mr. Rodd, the Town Clerk amid unceasing acclamations. A pillar bore the name "Devonport" in gilded characters in Cumberland Street, and a public dinner was held at the "Devonport" Royal Hotel. The town of "Devonport" was toasted; the "Devonport" march was played by the "Devonport Amateur Band," and "the ladies of Devonport" were complimented. "Devonport" porter was distributed at the Tamar Brewery; a schooner was launched to which the new name was given ; and the poor were liberally entertained. The "Sovereign" coach was decorated with ribbons and flags inscribed "Devonport"; and, as it passed on its way to London, the guard played "Oh, dear, what can the matter be !" On the return journey the same coach was drawn by eight horses, gaily caparisoned, and the box seat was embellished with flags and laurels. An anonymous humourist thus hit the situation :

> Says Dick to Joe : "'Tis very strange
> That things is given so to change,
> For every day that comes to view
> Is sure to turn up something new ;
> For instance, and to prove the same
> Why Dock has got another name.
> And Devonport, 'tis christened now,
> 'Tis queer enough, but you'll allow,
> 'Twixt you and I, and the Dockyard Bell,
> I think that Dock sounds quite as well ;
> But Plymouth's in a mighty bother
> To find her whelp desert her mother."

A device column was designed by Foulston as a monument of the loyalty of the town, and the foundation stone was laid on the royal birthday. A medal, of which a cast in gold was presented to the King, represented Neptune in his car, drawn by sea-horses, surveying the town and harbour, and proclaiming to the world that he had selected Devonport as his head-quarters. The Breakwater and Eddystone Lighthouse were seen in the distance, and a bust of George IV. intimated that the Ocean God takes England's monarch under his special protection. On the reverse side was inscribed : "In grateful commemoration of the condescension of His Most Gracious Majesty George IV., who conferred on the town formerly known as Plymouth-Dock, the name of Devonport, Anno. Dom. MDCCCXXIV." A replica in silver gilt was presented to the Duke of Clarence, then on a visit of inspection to the port, and the real author of the concession. The Sailor Prince was saluted in "the most affectionate manner" by a number of naval heroes, including some who took part in Lord Rodney's action and the Battle of Cape St. Vincent. To resume the quotation :

> Then some grand scheme they 'gan to ponder,
> To strike the gaping mob with wonder,
> The fine great project seemed to swell 'em,
> When all their brains hatched out a Column,
> A sort of funny second Babel,
> That's if their pockets make 'em able,
> On Windmill Hill to build the thing,
> And on the top to perch the King !
> Not George the Fourth of flesh and blood,
> But George the Fourth of stone and wood !
> To show his glory they've an eye on,
> They'll stick un up above Mount Zion.

An amusing story was told of a dockyardsman who ascended the tower with a party of friends and remained rapt in contemplation of the view after their descent. He was thus locked in, and it was only after hours of pantomimic evolutions that the spectators realised that he was a prisoner.

After the close of the Napoleonic wars it was the custom of the warriors who resided in the Three Towns to dine together on the occasion of glorious—and they were always "glorious"—anniversaries. The Plymouth Naval Club was thus called into existence, with the Royal Hotel as its headquarters, and a model of the foremast of the Victory, showing the shot-holes it received at Trafalgar, was always used as the table centrepiece. On the anniversary day of Lord Rodney's action of 1782, Sir James Saumarez, who commanded the Russell on that occasion, and who had just taken up his residence as Port Admiral, was amongst those present, with Captain Blamey, Rodney's aide-de-camp. "Our floating towers—our castles on the main," was proposed by Sir John Rogers "with classic eloquence," and the after proceedings generally were "brilliant." On the commemoration of San Domingo, Captain Pym, who was in charge of the Atlas in that decisive engagement, proposed the "Heroes of the Memorable Day," and the toast was greeted with sustained cheering. Mr. Edmund Lockyer, the septuagenarian Mayor of Plymouth, commended "cannon law" as the best bulwark of Britain, and his remarks evoked the heartiest endorsement. The anniversary of Lord Hood's action off Basse Terre, in 1782, was attended by Captain Rotheram, who had served in nearly every general action for forty years, and who glowed with cheery memories of deeds of dogged valour. As he was the only person present at that magnificent display of tactics, it fell to his lot to propose "The memory of Lord Hood," and the toast was acknowledged in a silent libation. It was at the dinner held in 1822 to commemorate "Nelson's last glorious victory" that Captain Rotheram, as commander of the Royal Sovereign, delivered the most eloquent of all his speeches in proposing "The Heroes of that Day." "Long," he said, "had the hero sighed for the crash which was now about to take place—long hunted the foe in the old world and in the new; and who can describe the fire of his eye—the ecstacy of his heart—when he beheld their double crescent formed to receive him? Confident of the tact with which his general spirit had inspired not only every captain, but every man in his little host, he threw out the emblem of the sublime emanation of his mind—'*England expects every man to do his duty.*' The fleets of our enemies had been often beaten separately, and in rotation, but here they mustered their forces together, and the hopes of France and Spain were in a few moments swallowed up in one common ruin! Their gorgeous crescent waned before its full, and glorious was the death of the Hero, whose soul fled to Heaven on the wings of Victory! Need I tell you that his heart was warm, and kind as it was brave? Forgive, forgive the tear for him who blended the hero with the friend; and permit me to say, I thank my God, that nothing can take from me the honour of having been one of those who placed an unfading laurel on Britannia's brow on the memorable day of Trafalgar."

The dinners continued until the survivors of historic conflicts gradually disappeared from the scene, and there were none remaining to testify to their personal contact with the immortals whom they had helped to uplift. It was, however, political discussion that caused the club to expire. The dinner in 1835 was attended by Lord Minto and his colleagues of the Admiralty, and it was asserted in a Plymouth paper that the proceedings were "as flat and cheerless" as they could possibly be. "His Majesty's Ministers" was received with as solemn a silence as "The Memory of Lord Nelson," and the toast remained without response although the First Lord was present. Cheering for "The Duke of Wellington and Heroes of Waterloo" was on the contrary vociferous, and the representatives of the Government who were guests so severely felt the contrast of the treatment that they withdrew. The officers of the club warmly resented the publicity given to the affair; and, at a meeting of the members, a series of resolutions were adopted for general publication that indicate the practice and procedure followed on these occasions.

"Resolved—That this meeting cannot sufficiently reprobate the attempt which has been made to convert a professional Club, established to promote harmony and conviviality amongst its members, and expressly on anti-political grounds, into an arena for the display of political feeling and controversy; and that it takes this opportunity of again declaring its determination to support and maintain the anti-political principles upon which it was originally founded and has hitherto been conducted.

"That during the earlier years of the Club, under Tory administrations, the toast of 'His Majesty's Ministers' was *not* on its toast-list, and since its introduction has *never* been placed among those directed to be cheered, cheering having been always confined to 'The Royal Family' and 'The Heroes of the Day.'

"That the toast of 'The Duke of Wellington and the Heroes of the Peninsula and Waterloo' was established in those express terms in October, 1821, a period antecedent to his Grace becoming a Minister of this Government. This toast, though never within the number permitted to be cheered, has *ever* been received with applause, and was drunk in the same terms, and in the same manner, at the late Dinner, *as at all previous ones*.

"That a Toast-list pointing out the Toasts to be cheered has always been circulated at the Club Dinners, and that printed lists have existed since the beginning of 1834. That the Club has twice invited the Board of Admiralty of Whig Administrations; though Lord Melville and his Board were never paid that compliment.

Navarino and After: Slowly the old order changed, giving place to the new, until it was
1827-1835. rather the reflection of war that was witnessed, and the theatre of interchange was far removed from English shores. The standard of ships degenerated, and several frigates were built on old French models, carrying eighteen-pounders only on the main deck, and limited as to room and stowage. Before the campaign against Turkey in 1827, Sir Robert Seppings evolved ingenious plans for supplying masts in 48 pieces, and the Genoa was the first of her class to be furnished from Devonport Dockyard with this expedient. Its value was demonstrated on that battleship's return from the battle of Navarino. Her mainmast was struck by eighteen large shot, many of which went quite through, and it stood staunch through the terrible fire of the Turkish forts. The Genoa suffered chiefly in the starboard quarter from the oblique elevated fire of the Turkish ships, their shot striking above the waterways of the main deck and cutting through the upper and poop decks. To this circumstance the heavy loss of life among the marines on the main poop was attributed; and the quarter deck was literally covered with the brains and blood of slaughtered seamen. Heavy was the sorrow in Devonport at the fate of a townsman, Captain Bathurst, who met his death from a grape-shot of four pounds that passed through the middle of his body and lodged on the quarter deck. A stone boulder, weighing nearly a hundredweight, was blown through the Genoa's lower deck, and left a gap that it puzzled the ship's carpenters to patch up.

The war was no less fruitful of anecdotes than its predecessors. The pursers of the ships made it a practice to serve out boiled corn to the men for breakfast; and, when one of the vessels returned to Devonport, this hard fare was supplemented by a watercress tea. "Make way there," exclaimed an indignant seaman, "and dash my eyes for the brutes! We fight like lions and feed like horses—corn for breakfast and grass at night." The monotony of this treatment was varied when the body of Captain Bathurst was brought to Devonport, embalmed in a puncheon of rum. As the sailors were averse to the conversion of their ships into floating hearses, the carrying of the corpse was kept a profound secret by the officers, although less care was taken of the puncheon than would otherwise have been observed. When it was removed to the Stonehouse Hospital, in order that the body might be exhumed for formal interment, it was discovered that the liquor was nearly exhausted. The laugh turned against the men, but one of them adroitly retaliated, " Well, we can all say that he returned to Devonport in the best of spirits." The paying-off scenes were scarcely less hilarious than those after Waterloo. To the accompaniment of fiddles and tambourines, the seamen whiled the hours with dance and song, in the vicinity of Mutton Cove and North Corner ; and, as the night darkened and the hours lengthened, the attempts of redcoats to intrude upon the privileges of the mariners involved taverns and town in the throes of a riot. Heated with drink, and irrflamed with jealousies, the sailors matched their fists against the side arms of the soldiers ; and, when mere muscle did not prevail as against cold steel, they seized pokers, shovels and tongs, and drove trespassers to the open. There, in the midst of an uproarious crowd, the fights were resumed ; but, when the watchmen were summoned by rattle, soldiers and sailors made common cause and battered the constables with their own staves and maces. It was only when detachments and picquets poured forth from the barracks that the disturbers dispersed through the " Cribs " and other familiar haunts.

Naval and military customs underwent little modification during this decade, and the period was no less prolific than its predecessors in anecdotal lore of a more or less briny order. When the Ocean was paid-off in 1827 two sailors rolled down North Corner "half-seas over," and one of them lurched through the window of a grocer's shop. He was at once held by the bystanders, and payment of half-a-crown was demanded to cover the damage. He tendered a crown, and, whilst the tradesman was fumbling for the change, dashed his elbow through a second pane, with the remark : " Never mind, my hearty, here goes ; you needn't trouble about the money."

This example of the grotesque only serves to cast a deeper shade over the blood-thirsty encounters in the streets. A crowd of the Monaghan Militia fell upon a party of the Duncan's crew in Pembroke Street, and fists prevailed against belts until reinforce-ments rushed from the St. George's Barracks on Mount Wise, and, with fixed bayonets, charged the seamen. The Monaghans were then confined by order of the colonel in command, but a hundred of them forced the gates the following night ; and, returning to Pembroke Street, demolished the windows and the bar of the Lord Nelson public-house. The town was reduced to such a panic by this rioting that the regiments were called out, and the militiamen were restored to their quarters under heavy escorts. An encounter of a no less desperate fashion originated in a public-house brawl in Castle Street, Plymouth, where a number of the South Devon Militia ejected Spanish sailors who were drinking with English girls. The foreigners mustered all their friends and stormed the house, knives in hand, only to find themselves confronted by unsheathed bayonets. In the hand-to-hand carnage that ensued two men were killed and several were hacked till they fell unconscious. Another such dispute in Frankfort Street arose from a rumour that two Mayo officers had been arrested for assaulting a Portuguese officer. The militiamen rushed from the Frankfort Barracks, bayonets in hand ; and, surrounding the watch-house, smashed the door and stabbed the town corporal. Hearing that their officers were con-fined within the Globe tavern, the madmen forced the gate, cut and battered those who resisted them, and broke the landlord's teeth with a sword thrust. It was not until the East Norfolk Regiment arrived from the Citadel that the riot was quelled.

During a revel held at Stoke, men and women were dancing in the Pear Tree Inn "with the utmost good humour," when a body of marines insisted upon choosing partners. After a struggle they were ejected ; but, returning in increased numbers, they cleared the room at the bayonet point. The majority escaped by jumping through the windows, but one petty officer was killed and several other persons were wounded. By the time the constables appeared the assailants had dispersed among the crowd, and identification was impossible. Something of the prowess of a Hercules was witnessed in the course of another outburst in Castle Street, where a body of English soldiers and sailors were fraternising in the Fountain Inn when the room was invaded by a number of Dutchmen who offered to fight the occupants one by one. A Brixham man, of the name of Memory, was the first to accept the challenge, and he felled eleven foreigners in succession with his bare fists. By way of varying the entertainment one of the intruders stabbed him in the groin, and bayonets and daggers clashed until some fell wounded and the uninjured were expelled. The Irish Fusiliers followed the usual course of com- memorating regimental departures by indiscriminate rioting. The Plymouth constables were called out ; but, regardless of their presence, the soldiers marched in double file past the Town Hall, their weapons at the ready, and then raced down Looe Street. Here the way was barred by the military picquets, and numbers were wounded in the fiendish struggle that ensued. A crowd of men of both services were drinking together in Pembroke Street when a corporal struck a woman, and a sailor drubbed him for "his lubberly trick." The fight became general, and the soldiers fatally stabbed the seaman who had punished their comrade. Another such scene was witnessed in James Street, where scores of soldiers and sailors, stripped to the waist, fought in the roadway, and many were stretched insensible in the gutters. The men were encouraged and directed by their officers ; and, when the watchmen came upon the scene, the combatants co-operated in overwhelming them. Companies of soldiery then appeared to suppress the riot, and two lieutenants and several sailors were carried face downwards to the Town Hall, where they answered to their names in the morning with black eyes, broken arms and bandaged heads. The officers compounded their offence and were released, but the men were sent to prison.

Visits of Don Miguel Don Miguel, "the hopeful child of tyranny and oppression," who *and Duke of Clarence:* was once detained as a prisoner of England on board the Windsor *1828.* Castle, as she lay in the Tagus, was "comfortably maintained" at Whiddon's Hotel in 1828. Excursions were organised in his honour, but, when the Portuguese Prince learnt that his former floating abode was lying in Hamoaze, "it was down helm and home again." He condescended, however, to visit the Breakwater and Britannia guardship, and embarked under royal salutes in boats manned by cheering crews. In the evening, Captain Hawker and his fellow volunteer officers entertained him at dinner ; and Don Miguel then visited the "At Home" given in his honour by Earl and Lady Northesk. On Sunday the Prince attended service at the Roman Catholic Chapel at Stonehouse, and dined at the Citadel with Major-General Sir John Cameron. The avenues were lined with soldiers carrying torches, and the "Portuguese March" was performed as Don Miguel passed on his way. A favoured few were invited to join a shooting party at Saltram, and "much havoc was committed amongst the hares and pheasants." At the balls "the British fair did not escape the Prince's peculiar atten- tions." George IV. sent him a beautiful horse as a present, and the animal was afterwards used "to drag carts through the streets of Lisbon and was ultimately tortured to death." Before his departure, Don Miguel witnessed a review upon the Hoe, and professed his pleasure at the discipline maintained. At the farewell dance at the Royal Hotel, a guard of honour lined the staircase, and a dazzling transparency showed the words "Viva Don Miguel" over the Portuguese Crown. Two years afterwards, Don Miguel usurped the throne of Portugal, and so terrorised the population that three thousand exiles took shelter in the town where so much hospitality had been shown him. The refugees were housed at Coxside until peremptory orders were received for their deportation to Brazil ; "a few love affairs amongst the female part of the community serve as a memento of their visit, as will be found in the parish records."

In 1828 the Duke and Duchess of Clarence re-visited Plymouth to witness a dual event—the sailing of the Britannia and the launch of the Royal Adelaide. The Britannia had been warped from her moorings to a buoy in the centre of Hamoaze; and, as she unfurled her sails, and "mov'd triumphant over the yielding seas," cannon resounded from every battery and battleship, her own thunders being answered from the Citadel as she passed, and by long continued discharges of musketry from the soldiers who were massed on the ramparts. Excitement about launches had declined with the erection of sheds over the slips, in consequence of the impossibility of accommodating the multitude. Interest was revived with the dedication of the Royal Adelaide: the shore seemed burthened with human beings, and boats, barges, trawlers, yachts and steamers—"who went with amazing velocity"—were brought into requisition. After being christened by the Duchess in her own name the new battleship glided off the stocks, "majestical and slow," amid deafening cheering. A few months after this function the artisans heard to their dismay that convicts were to be employed "cheek by jowl" with them. For a while the indignity was tolerated; but, when discharges became the order of administration, the Three Towns rose in remonstrance. A joint meeting of the parishioners of Stonehouse and Stoke-Damerel was held, and a memorial was drawn up expressing "pain and sorrow that hundreds of industrious mechanics" should be reduced to misery and want whilst convicts were comfortably and carefully housed and fed, with rewards on results as a premium upon crime. "For the sake of honesty and every moral virtue we earnestly implore your lordships to cause the convicts to be removed, so that they may no longer supplant the honest labourers, driven by want to even envy the lot of convicted felons." The agitation was eventually successful.

Approaches Gates and   Explanation has already been given of the methods in which traffic
Bridges : 1768-1835.   was conducted between Plymouth and Dock in the early days of
their joint necessity. After the supersession of the ferry that plied across Stonehouse Pool by the bridge which was built in 1768 at the expense of Lord Mount Edgcumbe and Sir John St. Aubyn, the toll was demanded by men who stood in the open way. Some years elapsed before the owners "dared" to outrage public sentiment by erecting a gate, and the scenes which this measure occasioned were not always amusing. The main roads between Plymouth and Dock were contracted and filthy—one by way of Stonehouse Lane and the other known as the road by Millbay, each sixteen feet wide "from hedge to hedge," and composed of wretched materials badly laid. The hill to Dock—Stonehouse Hill—was a "dreadful impediment," which it was assumed that nothing short of an earthquake would diminish, and the highway laws were so restrictive that it was taken for granted the roads could never be widened. There was one turnpike road from Brent Bridge, with a gate, stop-gate and weighing machine at Crabtree, the yield of which was £851 a year; and a second gate stood across the road at Ivybridge which produced £523. The tolls "on the New Road" yielded £1,204 a year, and they were partly raised at "Fanning's toll house and gate," and at "Arnold's Point House, Arnold's Quay and Efford Quay." The lessee had "the advantage of selling water to the shipping in the harbour, which can be drawn from the reservoir at Arnold's Point into the casks on board the boats lying alongside the quay by means of a pump." The Stonehouse turnpike trustees controlled the Stonehouse Lane Gate, the Millbay Gate, and the Stonehouse Hill Gate, and the annual yield of tolls was £652 (1800-1810). The road from Saltash Ferry to Plymouth was by way of Pennycomequick, and there was another into Cornwall from Mutton Cove across

to " Cremhill." The ferries were invariably rowed by women. Dreary and perilous were these routes--the water passages subject to storms which were often serious prior to the erection of the Breakwater, and the roadway continuations alike lonely and circuitous. Ferries plied between Dock and Torpoint ; but, notwithstanding the penalties under which " the ferry man is bound to keep in constant use a certain number of boats and able men," the service became more and more inefficient during the Napoleonic Wars " in conse- quence of the great increase of wages and the difficulty of procuring fit men." In 1809 the proprietors, with a view of improving the service, insisted, for the first time, upon exacting the full toll allowed by their Act from all persons travelling with horses and other animals : twopence for every horse, &c., and one penny for each person accompanying the same, *whether going or returning.*

The commemoration of the Jubilee of George III. witnessed considerable improve- ments in the means of approach. An old grievance of the Dockers at being deprived of their promenade within the lines found courteous compensation in the conversion of the coast under Mount Wise into " an agreeable promenade," and the name of " Richmond Walk " was bestowed by the authorities in honour of the nobleman through whose instru- mentality the concession was made—the Duke being then Master of Ordnance. A new coach road from the lower glacis of the Citadel, through Higher Mill Lane, by Mill Prison, over Stonehouse Hill and Saltash Passage, had just been completed. About the same

A VIEW OF THE LAIRA, FROM CRABTREE, TO THE HEAD OF CATWATER.

(From the Engraving by W. Hay, 1781, inscribed " To the Gentlemen of the Plymouth Independent Company of Volunteers.")

time, Lord Boringdon conceived the idea of enclosing Chelson Bay; and, although the practicability of devoting the reclaimed soil to agricultural purposes was derided by Mr. Vancouver and other experts, 175 acres of excellent meadow land were added to the Saltram estates at a cost of £9,000. Lord Boringdon also started a floating (cable) bridge to bring the opposite banks of Catwater into intercourse, and he promoted a company to construct an embankment along the Laira—thus providing another new road by whose means the distance from Yealmpton to Plymouth was diminished by seven miles. There was a reciprocal enterprise on the part of the Corporation, and the new thoroughfare was continued into the town at the public cost. It was dedicated by the name of "Jubilee" Street in 1809. The public rejoicings were inaugurated by the firing of fifty guns at sunrise on the day fixed for the commemoration. Plymouth poured out to Crabtree to meet the directors of the embankment, and a procession was formed, in which an imposing array of Russell's waggons played a prominent part, the horses being decorated with illuminated couplets of gratitude: "Sirs, for the road on Laira's banks, accept the wearied horses' thanks." There was a great display of cattle, corn and vegetables "raised on the land recovered from the sea, notwithstanding Mr. Vancouver's prediction that it would never be worth a farthing."

Amid the playing of bands and ringing of bells, a multitude repaired to the Hoe, to witness the roasting of a whole ox, and the carcase was spitted with ease and carved into "royal steaks." These were distributed amongst the poor with bread and beer. The Mayor and his brethren then dined at the King's Arms "according to the old English fashion—on roast beef and plum pudding," and, before returning to the Hoe to witness the blazing of bonfires on every headland, the sentiment was loudly cheered: "May the Jubilee be followed by increasing prosperity." A glee was also sung with a swinging chorus:

> Then fill high your glass, the bottle keep going,
> And sacred to Bacchus this hour we'll ordain;
> A Jubilee toast, boys, come set the wine flowing,
> Here's the Third George for Ever, the Lord of the Main!

The Millbridge was originally erected in 1525 by Sir Piers Edgcumbe, to whom the rights in the ferry and the road were transferred by the Wises, as lords of the manor of Stoke Damerel. No outside knowledge of this transaction survived early in the nineteenth century, and carts, carriages and horses plied over the bridge without let or hindrance. In 1807 the Edgcumbes introduced a gate for the first time within the memory of man, and the Mayor and Corporation of Plymouth, in the assumed vindication of public right, marched in state to the site, and, with the assistance of a body of carpenters, demolished the gate and threw the timbers into the stream. The miller, in his indignation, swore roundly at the Mayor, and his Worship fined him upon the spot for his rudeness. The popular impression was that the tenant of the mill was bound to keep the bridge in order, and that the public authorities on either side were similarly required to maintain the approaches. As it seemed rather late in the day to assert the right to levy tolls at Millbridge, and the Edgcumbes had a material interest in diverting the traffic to the Stonehouse Bridge, where the legal claim was admitted, the structure was permitted to lapse into a dilapidated and dangerous condition. The inhabitants of the Three Towns gradually inferred that the object was to drive the traffic to the Stonehouse Bridge, and parish meetings were held to organise joint proceedings. William Hayman, the miller, was accordingly indicted at the Devon Assizes in 1829, as tenant of the mill and bridge under the Edgcumbes, for failing to carry out his portion of the repairs. Serjeant Wilde, who was retained by the parishioners of Stoke Damerel and East Stonehouse, imputed collusion between the Earl and his tenant with the object of instituting a claim to toll ; but Serjeant Merewether, for the miller, repudiated any such sinister object. He confessed that the owners had been lax in enforcing their right, but insisted that it had been periodically asserted ; and, to the consternation of the prosecutors, produced the grant by the Wises, whose existence had not till that time been even suspected. The Lord Chief Justice at once stopped the case. There was evidence that the bridge and mill had been used for a very long time as a public highway, but the defendant had proved possession in the reign of Henry VIII., and the claim of the public to immemorial usage could not, therefore, be allowed. " I may be in the wrong," said his lordship, " but, if they think so, the prosecutors are at liberty to move the Court above for a new trial." This verdict estab-

DEVIL'S POINT, WITH THE FORT AND THE FERRY.

(From a Water Colour in the possession of Mr. Sydenham.)

lished the property of the bridge and mill in the Edgcumbe family, but the town authorities insisted that the judgment only affected the liability to repair, and that the right of passage to the public remained unchallenged. Another campaign was instituted to confirm this aspect of the case, but a compromise was suggested as a means of avoiding litigation—that foot passengers should be allowed to pass without payment, and that a charge should be made for horses and vehicles, the condition precedent being that the bridge should be forthwith reconstructed. An attempt was made to improve on these terms by stipulating that, when the cost of the work had been covered by income, payment of the toll at Millbridge should free the access to the Stonehouse Bridge ; but this proposal was ruled out on the ground that Sir John St. Aubyn, part owner of the Halfpenny Gate, had no interest in the Millbridge. Eventually the capitulation of the public was complete, and the Act sanctioning the reconstruction of the bridge and the levying of the tolls was passed without demur. The result was the reduction of a hill on the Devonport side of the bridge that had hitherto been too steep to admit of the ascent of animals : and Stoke, Newpassage and Plymouth were brought into easier communication.

The legality of the Cremyll ferry was then impeached on the ground that universal exaction of the toll had not been insisted upon, and that the original franchise was forfeited in the abandonment of Devil's Point as the scene of departure and the substitution of Mutton Cove. There was no conventional agreement between the Edgcumbes and the St. Aubyns in this case, but it was urged that the transfer from Devil's Point was made at the request of the lord of the manor of Stoke Damerel. "to meet the wants of the increasing population of his town." In the compromise it was agreed that those who used the ferry-boats should pay one penny in addition to the former toll, and that those who hired boats should pay "the accustomed and ancient toll of one penny."

There were important developments during the next few years. A new road was cut from St. Austell to Devonport in 1836, by way of Crafthole and St. John's Lake to the north of Torpoint. Thence a steam-bridge was started, "an ingenious contrivance" built from the design of Mr. Rendle. Over two thousand passengers were conveyed on the opening day, in addition to stage coaches, waggons and cattle. Jealous of this success, the Saltash authorities encouraged the formation of a similar company, to whom they leased their ferry rights on condition that the traffic was continuously maintained. The success of this second experiment was less pronounced, and, as the apparatus was allowed to remain idle for two years, the Corporation confiscated the plant by virtue of powers they had reserved. On the day of the seizure a general holiday was proclaimed ; and, flourishing their silver oars by way of asserting their privileges, the Mayor and his brethren assumed formal possession, and set horse and ferry boat in motion, despite the protests of the secretary of the company. Having thus restored ferry communication, the Corporation spent the rest of the week in perambulating the boundaries of the borough : from Penlee Point to Shag Rock, and from the Lynher to Oakle Tor Rock. On each day there were processions of decorated boats, and business was interspersed with pleasure. The aldermen and councillors feasted, their wives and daughters danced on the green, and the young men indulged in various sports.

One of the most valuable means of opening up the South Hams was forthcoming in the erection of Laira Bridge by Lord Boringdon in 1827, and the cutting of a new road to Exeter in connection therewith. In consequence of the depth of the river bed, the foundations of the structure were prepared with much care, the piles being driven several feet below the level of the river, and an artificial bottoming deposited which consolidated under water into a mass "as indestructible as soft rock." The principle of making the arches the segments of a circle was introduced to obviate the unpleasantness of the flat circular segments springing from straight sided piers. There was a good deal of objection to paying the tolls ; and, in 1828, Captain Bainbridge demanded free access as an officer of the King. The collector replied that he would not allow the King himself to pass without payment, but Bainbridge forced his way through on horseback, and when the collector seized the animal's head, he drew his sword and flourished it so actively that the man lost no time in diving out of reach. A summons was issued, and the officer was fined and compelled to apologise for brandishing his weapon. In 1832 the lessees of the Embankment sued a firm of millers, Shilson and another, for refusing to pay the tolls and for driving their waggons over the Plymouth and Dartmoor Railway, which ran parallel with the Embankment. The case was heard at the Devon Assizes, where it was argued that the

THE OLD FERRY HOUSE BY RICHMOND WALK, AND HALFPENNY GATE.

(From an old Sketch, re-drawn by W. D. Snell.)

railway could not stand if the embankment were abandoned, and that the company could not maintain the embankment if they were deprived of the means of support. The right to levy was upheld.

Stonehouse Hill was lowered in 1828, and ascent and descent were thus considerably facilitated. The remains of the Old Ferry House stood on the Devonport side of the bridge until 1830, and a picturesque object then disappeared. Aversion to the toll continued to be evinced in various forms. Two sailors, who were pulled up when "cruising" towards Plymouth in 1817, decided to "'bout ship" rather than satisfy the demand. A butcher, however, passed with a calf on his shoulder, and, on being assured by the collector that the man had only paid for himself, "Jack" slung his comrade in the same fashion, and promised that his mate should "stand treat" next time. A party of officers, who were returning from a ball in 1825, were making their way to Devonport, to the strains of "We pirates live a jolly, jolly life," when the toll was demanded. In a moment, the melody changed to discord, the roysterers tried to rush the gate, the collectors laid about with their stools, and the officers replied with swords. When the watchmen appeared the officers were without hats, the clothes of the collectors were torn in rags, and the lessee was being rolled in the mud. An indictment for rioting was preferred, but the offenders escaped with fines. For a while the collectors gave pedestrians a number to remember, and refused to allow them to pass without repayment, seizing articles of wearing apparel if they insisted upon going through without satisfying the claim. Lieutenant Toby came to the rescue of a marine in 1830, who had forgotten his number and had no coin in his pocket, and rating the lessee on his illegality, warned him that he would raise the subject in the Court. The lessee threatened Toby with violence, but, when the officer drew his sword, his assailant retreated to his office. The case was submitted to the magistrates, and they held that the lieutenant was justified. The introduction of tickets followed, but the expedient did not meet the difficulty with those who lost their passports. One of the watchmen found himself in this position in 1831, and the collector being no respector of persons demanded another halfpenny. A second wayfarer found himself in the same position, and, going to his assistance, the watchman sent the collector sprawling. Constable and civilian were summoned, but, as they produced their tickets from some obscure corner of their pockets, the complaints were dismissed. The watchman promptly revenged himself by arresting the collector as a deserter from the South Devon Militia. An Irishman named MacCooghan tried to force the pass in 1832, and his hat was seized. He retorted and made off with the hat of the collector, and, being overtaken, closed. In the struggle both hats were destroyed. An attempt to economise by issuing tickets only one way led to frequent broils, because of the natural refusal to trust to the recollection of the officials. One "brute" who seized the cap of a boy, and assaulted his mother for seeking to recover it, was heavily fined by the justices. The right to remain on the bridge without intending to use the gate was tested by James Smith, an Excise officer. He was leaning against the pier at midnight, and the collector ordered him to move on. Smith replied by threatening him with a pistol if he further advanced. The defendant explained that he was watching for smugglers; and that, as his mission required secrecy, he was not bound to disclose his reason for selecting the bridge for duty. The magistrates acquiesced in this view.

From Coach to Steam: In the early years of this century "The Royal Devonshire Cheap
1800-1840.   Coaches, with six horses," were in the habit of setting out from the
London Inn, Dock, every morning at six and eight o'clock (Sundays excepted), calling at the Globe Inn, Plymouth; Oxford Arms, Totnes; Golden Lion, Newton. They arrived at the New London Inn, Exeter, "where they meet the Royal Devonshire, Bath, and

London coaches every Tuesday, Thursday, and Saturday evenings at six o'clock." "Cheap and expeditious travelling" was offered by "the Royal Clarence Coach," which "sets out from the Prince George Inn, Dock; calls at the Commercial Inn, Plymouth; Seven Stars, Totnes; Globe Inn, Newton; and arrives at the Half Moon Inn, Exeter, at seven o'clock in the evening—Inside, 10s. 6d.; outside, 7s. 6d. Performed by H. Whitmarsh, J. Martin and Co." "Cheap travelling" was also placed within popular reach by "F. Goude, of the King's Arms Inn, Fore Street, Dock," whose "light balloon coach" left Dock for Exeter "every morning at six o'clock," the prices being the same. On the other hand, the route from Exeter was accomplished in "the entirely new and elegant Royal balloon mail coach, on a much improved principle, which sets out every morning to the King's Arms, Plymouth, and the King's Arms, Plymouth-Dock, arrives at half-past eight, and leaves at half-past five in the afternoon. Fare, 11s. 6d.; outside, 15s."

The main thoroughfare to Stonehouse, Stoke and Dock ran along the northern side of "the Globe," a little, squat, humble tavern, with thatched roof and dormer windows, by the side of the Frankfort Gate, whose demolition has been recorded elsewhere. A quaint signboard depicted a traveller on horseback, and a Boniface of rotund proportions handing him the stirrup cup with which it was the custom of landlords to bid their guests a safe journey. Underneath this frontispiece was the clearly written legend: "Huzza, my boys, for Doch-an-dorrach"—a whimsical suggestion of the parting drink at the door, and an intimation that the traveller was now bound for Dock. The Globe Tavern was reconstructed with the popularity of the coach, and it became so popular a resort that, after a proposal to use the large space in front for the purpose of erecting a new Town Hall in 1800, it was extended by the raising of a huge block. From that time "the Globe Tavern" became "the Globe Hotel"; one of the most famous of the coaching centres; as, in later times, it reigned as the political headquarters of the Conservative party.

A characteristic story of the perils which were run by travellers is told. A single footpad stopped one of the coaches on the way to Exeter. He had no weapon but a clasp knife, and this he thrust into the window of the coach with a threat to stab the one male inmate if he evinced the least hesitation in delivering his money. The gentleman gave the highwayman two five pound notes and four shillings. The lady passengers—three fair sisters from Plymouth—were in the greatest agitation lest the fellow should commit some atrocity, and held their money out, begging that he would take it and leave them. But he had no sooner done with the gentleman than he removed all apprehension by saying, "Now, ladies, don't be frightened; I never did the least injury to a woman in my life, nor never will, d—— me. As for your money, keep it to yourselves. All I ask from you is a kiss apiece. If you grudge me that I'm sure you're neither sensible nor good humoured." Having exacted the penalty, the rascal went on his way.

The humour and inconvenience of the coach were alike illustrated in the rhyme of the period:

> Having taken my place in the Plymouth stage,
> To visit a friend I had promised an age,
> I was rous'd in the morning before it was light,
> With the prospect of rumbling and tumbling till night.
> On mounting the coach 'twas my luck to be fix'd
> Two very fat elderly ladies betwixt;
> On the opposite seats were a brat and his nurse,
> A sergeant, whose joy was to swagger and curse,
> And between, *a la* bodkin, big, burly and staunch,
> Mine host, that of Falstaff, might rival the paunch,

THE FRANKFORT GATE, ADJOINING GLOBE TAVERN (HOTEL).

(Gate taken down in 1789; hotel demolished, 1899.)

We had scarce clear'd the stones, when the road growing hilly,
To and fro', like a ship, roll'd the merciless dilly :
At this my good patrons, who sat on each side,
Were provok'd, one to cough, and the other to chide ;
The soldier to swear, and with none to say " Fie,"
The landlord to snore, and the baby to cry :
If such be the charms of a stage, I'll take root ;
Or if ever I travel I'll travel a-foot.

"The Piece of Old Hat," a ballad composed by a naval officer at Dock, told how one of the sailors surprised his comrades on the occasion of a trip to London. Knowing the destitute condition to which naval excursionists were occasionally reduced on the return, the man adopted an experiment which enabled him to call for a drink at every stopping place on the homeward journey by merely twirling a piece of old hat when Boniface presented himself at the door. The other sailors could not understand the magic of this emblem :

He'd loudly to the landlords call
To bring them forth a drop,
For sailors feel their thirst begin
Whene'er the horses stop.

A Jew who travelled by the same coach was delighted at the exercise of these talismanic powers, and Jack assured him that he bought the rag of a wizard in Japan. Enchanted with the idea, the Jew offered a substantial sum for the relic, only to find that it wholly lost its power in his hands. The sailor had simply made a deposit at each house on the upward journey, and the twirling of the hat was to represent the means of identification.

Towards 1829 "expeditious travelling by water" came into favour as auxiliary to the coach. Steamers plied between the Three Towns and Portsmouth, and coaches waited at the latter port to carry passengers to London. The vessels left Millbay at 12.30 a.m., and arrived at Portsmouth at 4 p.m., enabling travellers to enter the metropolis at midnight. The entire journey was thus accomplished in "the incredibly short time of 23½ hours." This was a mighty revolution in locomotion : "What would our forefathers have said to this?" was asked in 1825—"those who rarely went to town without preparing their wills and were six or seven days in performing the journey?" A memorable advance was made when a coach was started to run "eleven miles an hour all the way to London." "Steady" was the motto of "the cove who handled the ribbons" and "all right was his vurship in the dickey." "Lush" was out of the question. "This is going it with a vengeance : if our ancestors had done such things, Jehus, steamers, prads and all would have been burnt as sorcerers !"

There were some changes towards 1830, but the plan of travelling was the same. The Subscription New Light Coach, conveying four inside and ten outside passengers, left at half-past three in the morning from Townshend's London Inn, Devonport ; W. Avent's Crown Inn, Stonehouse ; and Hannaford's Commercial Inn, Plymouth ; through Ridgway, Ivybridge, Buckfastleigh, Ashburton, and Chudleigh, arriving at the Half Moon Hotel, Exeter, at four o'clock in the afternoon. It proceeded at six through Ilminster, Wincanton and Salisbury, and arrived at the Bull and Mouth, London, at half-past three o'clock on the following afternoon. The same company ran coaches to Bristol, Bath and London, and to Birmingham, Manchester, Sheffield and Liverpool. Every accommodation was paid to passengers and luggage, and no racing was allowed. "The new and splendid Erin," of 500 tons burthen and 180-horse power, left Catwater for London, and dropped passengers up the Thames every Saturday, "taking goods and passengers, horses and carriages." The proprietors of this "fine vessel take the opportunity of informing the public that it is their intention *to continue her sailing throughout the winter,* and hope for a continuance of favours, particularly when it is considered with what certainty she performs the voyages."

So early as 1830 the germ of the Motor Car occurred to a Plymothian, Mr. John Lee Stevens, who advocated the application of steam to stage coaches so that transit between Plymouth and Devonport should be rapid and economical. Mr. Stevens's company did not float, but he found consolation in having first proposed this particular method of utilising "one of Mr. Gurney's engines." Coach proprietors did not yet realise that their extinction was impending, and their rivalries knew little compunction. So early as 1802 the attempt to run a coach in competition with the "Mail" led to the issue of a public remonstrance which was suggestive of the modern boycott. "For the express purpose of protecting and encouraging the proprietors of the Mail Coach, we hereby agree to use ourselves, and recommend all our acquaintances to use, no other coach whatsoever but the coach to and from Exeter and the towns of Plymouth and Dock." Time completely cured this objection to the development of traffic ; and so large was the number of proprietors in 1840 that return fares were temporarily reduced to a few shillings, and travellers embraced the gratuitous use of the Safety. They were provided with breakfast before starting ; lunch at the Seven Stars, Totnes ; and dinner with wines at Congdon's Hotel, Exeter—and no questions were raised as to payment ! The warfare ceased with a compromise, and the owners ran their vehicles in turn to avoid disastrous clashing. This arrangement induced another hotel-keeper to enter the field and claim a share of the mileage. His conveyance was seized at Bristol and impounded ; and, by way of reprisal, he seized the Bristol coach as it entered Devonport, and despatched a gang of labourers to the King's Arms Hotel to intercept another belonging to the same firm. Having accomplished this mission, the men were driven to Ermington, and there took possession of a third coach from Bristol. The attack was repelled by force of numbers, and a mounted messenger dashed into Devonport for fighting reinforcements. These were hurried to the scene in carts, and the third conveyance was stormed and conducted in triumph to the Dockyard gate. Fearing that their fourth coach would meet the same fate, the Bristolians hired a hundred Plymouth porters to escort it from Ermington to Fore Street. There was no further molestation, and the conveyance was guarded to the hostile house amid uproarious shouts. An exchange of "prizes" followed the "treaty of peace."

Visits of Victoria to Plymouth and Devonport : 1837-1856. The country was prepared for the death of George IV., and when, on a Sunday afternoon in June, 1830, the intimation was brought into Plymouth by the "Defiance" coach, it was received with "marked sorrow" by the inhabitants, who had always been conspicuous for their attachment to the House of Brunswick. "Appropriate psalms were sung without music" at the evening services, the flags were lowered to half-mast, and the warships fired sixty minute-guns. During the ensuing week the ceremony of proclaiming the new monarch was conducted. Attended by the Common Council and the freemen of the borough, the Herald (Mr. William Pridham), who was mounted on horseback, read the legal document outside the Town Hall, and "God Save the King" was played amid loud acclamations. Those in authority then moved through the town, and the proclamation was read in the Market Place, Bedford Street, George Street, on the Parade, and on Briton Side. At Devonport the ceremony was no less spectacular, and the officials were accompanied by mounted beadles and trumpeters. The document was in these terms :—

"Whereas it hath pleased Almighty God to call to his mercy, our late Sovereign Lord, King George the Fourth, of blessed memory, by whose decease the Imperial Crown of the United Kingdom of Great Britain and Ireland is solely and rightfully come to the high and mighty Prince William Henry, Duke of Clarence, I, therefore, on behalf of the commissioners, parishioners and inhabitants of this town and parish, do hereby publish and proclaim that the high and mighty Prince William Henry, Duke of Clarence, has now, by the death of the late Sovereign of happy memory, become our only lawful and rightful liege lord, William the Fourth, Defender of the Faith, to whom we do acknowledge all faith and constant obedience, with hearty and humble affection beseeching God, by whom Kings and Queens do reign, to bless the Royal Prince William the Fourth with long and happy years to reign over us. God Save the King."

The procession moved through the town to the Dockyard, and the flags at the Chapel Tower and Column were hoisted mast high. Drums beat the salute as the guards turned out and presented arms, and the mechanics encircled the group. On the sound of trumpet, Mr. Rodd again read the proclamation, and huzzas mingled with the National Anthem. At the North-eastern Barrier Gate, the Gun Wharf, Stoke Church, as well as the official residences of the Port Admiral and Commander-in Chief, similar functions were observed. On Mount Wise the troops in garrison commemorated the accession, salutes from the battery being taken up from Drake's Island and the Citadel, and thereafter by the fleet at anchor. As soon as the great guns had ceased, the troops fired a feu-de-joie, and then, for the rest of the week, the colours were again dropped at half-mast.

Colossal enthusiasm prevailed in the Three Towns when the Sailor Prince was enthroned. Banners floated from every window and roof, and houses were bright with garlands and laurel. Tables were laid in the streets for 4,000 poor people, and as many children joined the procession which the dockyardsmen organised. With cars, banners and models the shipwrights led the way, their favourite emblems inscribed "William, England's King and Briton's Glory," and "Adelaide, England's Queen and Briton's Pride." "The King and Our Excellent Constitution" admitted of displays of ingenious partisan feeling, the Constitution being depicted as a man-of-war, from which the mechanics were removing the decayed timbers—an idea which was claimed as in harmony with the new King's known antipathy to the dry rot! The sailmakers crowded a richly ornamented car, conspicuous amongst the occupants being the hoary centenarian, Watson, captain of the main top in the King's old frigate, Pegasus, who was supported by twelve boys dressed as sailors, and bearing aloft a canopy. A huge nautilus shell, with Neptune and Britannia occupying prominent positions, was drawn by six grey horses, and, on either side of the car, appeared the boasts : "Britannia Maintains Her Right" and "Neptune is Our Glory." As every workshop in the Dockyard was similarly represented, nearly an hour was occupied in passing the gates, and there were 2,000 persons in the procession. Without the lines it was reinforced by various Orders and Lodges of Accepted Freemasons, and the Knights Templars of St. John, with their insignia, added brilliancy to the scene. The drapers wore white satin sashes, tied with blue, and red and white silk sashes affected by their assistants. Mount Wise was entered though St. George's gate, and there the toast of the Monarch and Queen was drunk with "three times three." In the evening there were public dinners, at the chief of which the King was claimed as a Reformer. "The Bill, the whole Bill, and nothing but the Bill" was received with acclamation, and "Our Revered and Beloved Monarch" was toasted with "four times four." A vast quantity of showering rockets, "principally of Government manufacture," were set off.

On August 3rd, 1833, "the future Queen of England" paid her first visit to Plymouth. The force of the tide carried the Royal yacht, the Emerald, under a hulk, and the mainmast sprung in two places. Sail and gaff fell upon the deck and narrowly escaped the Princess and her mother. They were " immediately and respectfully hurried below," and, in considerable alarm, Victoria rushed to the embrace of the Duchess of Kent, " whom she tenderly fondled." After shedding some tears, she became composed and " evinced much firmness." On landing, the Princess held a reception at the Royal Hotel, Plymouth, where the Mayor and Aldermen appeared in their scarlet robes and the Councillors in their black silk gowns. The Corporation formally expressed their delight " at the opportunity afforded us of being presented to an illustrious princess whom high destiny may place at the head of our excellent Constitution, and to see her, under the guidance of her royal mother, familiarised with the institutions, manners and customs of the English people." The reply was delivered by the Duchess, who mentioned that her daughter wished to make the visit because " the sea is so congenial to the habits of the nation." As a matter of education, " I was anxious," she explained, " to bring her to this great arsenal, so associated with naval renown, and where we have found ourselves so cordially received by the inhabitants. The object of my life," she continued, " is to render the Princess worthy of the solicitude she inspires, and if it be the will of Providence that she should fill a higher station—I trust most fervently at a distant date—I shall be fully repaid for my anxious care if she is found competent to discharge a sacred trust. Communicating with all classes of society, as the Princess does, she cannot but perceive that the greater the diffusion of religion, knowledge, and love of freedom in a country, the more orderly, industrious and wealthy is its population. The desire to preserve the constitutional prerogatives of the Crown ought to be co-ordinate with the protection of the liberties of the people, and the hearty encouragement of that principle of progressive amelioration, the full development of which is not only the greatest source of advantage to the country, but of security to the Throne." On the conclusion of this " admirable reply," the Mayor presented such gentlemen " as were solicitous of the honour."

The Princess and her mother then witnessed the presentation of colours to the 89th Regiment, and from one extremity of the Hoe to the other the promenade was crowded with soldiery. A few rapid evolutions enclosed the royal party, and the Duchess, her arm embracing her daughter, read in her name an address to Sir Edward Milnes, the colonel, who remained on his right knee with his sword presented. In acceding to the wish that she might present the colours, the Princess " responded to the pride every Briton must feel in looking back on the splendid achievements of the military force of this country. They are indeed proud memorials of the past and best guarantee of the nation." The Duchess then delivered the colours into the hands of Victoria, who transferred them to the custody of the ensigns. Then the tattered trophies which had waved on many a battle-field in Egypt, Java and America, were enclosed in a case with other records of renown, and the regiment passed in review. In the afternoon the royal party were rowed around the ships in commission, and yards were manned, cannon fired, and cheers given. On the Sunday the Dockyard Chapel was crowded " by a fashionable congregation " in honour of the royal visit. After the service the party crossed to Mount Edgcumbe, and the air gave the Princess such an appetite that she asked for a crust of bread, and ate with " infinite relish the most modest fare the house had ever afforded." A visit to the Eddystone was made on the Monday, and the Dee steamer amused the guests by firing shot and shell on the way. Dancing was indulged on the deck in returning, and the commander of the frigate, although one of his legs was not too well adapted for such recreation, " displayed as much agility as the youngest man present." After inspecting the Breakwater, the royal frigate anchored in the Sound amid " three times three cheers."

"The melancholy intelligence" of the death of William IV. was promulgated at Plymouth on the arrival of the Brunswick steamer in June, 1837. Shops were closed, flags were lowered and the church bells tolled. The Royal Adelaide was draped black, and fired seventy-two minute guns to chronicle the number of years the King had lived. He had shared the glories and sorrows of a profession closely identified with the interests of the district, and weather-beaten tars recounted many an incident which they had witnessed in their naval youth. The Royal Standard was hoisted half-mast on the following day in honour of Victoria's accession, and salutes were fired from the ships in the harbour. In Plymouth and Devonport the municipal authorities paraded the streets, and the change was formally announced in the following terms:

"Whereas it has pleased Almighty God to call to His Mercy our late Sovereign Lord King William the Fourth, of blessed and glorious memory, by whose decease the Imperial Crown of the United Kingdom of Great Britain and Ireland is solely and rightfully come to the High and Mighty Princess Alexandrina Victoria, saving the rights of any issue of his late Majesty King William the Fourth which may be born of his late Majesty's Consort: I do hereby, on the part of the Inhabitants of this Town and Borough, publish and proclaim that the High and Mighty Princess Alexandrina Victoria is now by the death of our late Sovereign, of happy memory, become our only lawful and rightful Liege Lady Victoria, by the Grace of God, Queen of the United Kingdom of Great Britain and Ireland, Defender of the Faith, saving as aforesaid. To whom, saving as aforesaid, we do acknowledge all faith and constant obedience, with all hearty and humble affection, beseeching God, by whom Kings and Queens do reign, to bless the Royal Princess Victoria with long and happy years to reign over us. God save the Queen."

Public meetings were held in the Three Towns to formulate addresses of congratulation; and, at Devonport, a desire to "whisper into the ears of Her Majesty" on the subject of Reform led to tumult and recrimination. On Coronation Day, special services took place at the churches, triumphal arches spanned the thoroughfares, thousands of children assembled on the Hoe and Mount Wise, and mounted yeomen carried battleaxes of twisted and cut glass. Richly coloured medallions showed the Queen in her royal robes, with the Archbishop placing the crown on her head. The British Lion was also in much request, and transparencies of battleships depicted the crew acclaiming Victoria as she trod their decks. Devonport was so embellished as to be suggestive of "an enchanted garden," and a display of fireworks was witnessed in the evening from "the old Timber Pond outside the lines." Stonehouse was resplendent with a profusion of flags and arches; there were dinners, balls, and treats for the aged and children; and, for "the respectable tradesmen, who feasted at the Prince George Hotel, the luxury of turtle was provided."

In August, 1843, the Queen and Prince Albert included the port in their "marine excursion." Studious silence was preserved by the authorities as to their arrangements, but whispers of preparations escaped from the Dockyard. When the royal yacht approached Plymouth, the heights were swarmed by devoted subjects, and a flotilla of pleasure boats sailed out to accord the fair young monarch welcoming cheers. Peals of artillery awakened the echoes as the yacht passed towards Barnpool, and Victoria, who remained on deck, pleasantly acknowledged the salutations of her subjects. Simple indeed was her attire: a straw bonnet with pea green ribbons and a small rosette of flowers, and an apron trimmed with lilac satin thrown over a violet silk dress. Prince Albert wore a frock coat and grey trousers, and a gold lace band ornamented his cap. The Hindostan, a ship of ninety guns, then recently launched, was minutely inspected in the Dockyard, and the Prince was struck

LAUNCH OF H.M.S. HINDOSTAN AT DEVONPORT, 1841.

with astonishment at the panorama at "Bunker's Hill." Meanwhile the local authorities were hunting in all directions for the visitors ; and, when Lord Aberdeen undertook to convey their addresses, they were more than chagrined. By way of compensation, the Queen was persuaded to risk another of the crushes that had occasioned her so much discomfort elsewhere, and apprehensive, if elated, the Mayor issued an earnest

CAUTION.

It being very probable that Her Majesty will land to-morrow and proceed through this Town and Stonehouse into Plymouth, and great inconvenience having been caused during Her Majesty's visit to other places by the pressure of the crowd on Her Majesty's carriage ; all Persons are especially requested to abstain from such improper conduct, which has caused great personal annoyance to Her Majesty and is most discreditable to the Inhabitants. It is particularly requested that no one will attempt to run by or follow Her Majesty's Carriage, which will no doubt proceed at a moderate pace. The Mayor appeals with confidence to the Inhabitants for the entire preservation of order, and relies on their assistance in carrying out every regulation for Her Majesty's personal comfort.

The Queen was received on landing by the authorities of Devonport ; and, reinforced by the officers of the garrison and the Lords of the Admiralty, the cavalcade moved towards Stonehouse. There the Mayor of Plymouth extended a welcome, and Her Majesty was escorted through Union Street to the Citadel. The party returned through Hoe Gate to No Place and thence to Fore Street. It had been arranged that Prince Albert should be invested with the office of Lord High Steward, and a suite of rooms was prepared at the Royal Hotel for the purpose. But the day proved too exhausting, and the ceremony was observed on board the Victoria and Albert, where the Mayor gratefully recalled the visit of the girl Princess and her mother. "Whilst we acknowledge with thankfulness that all the promises of that springtime have been richly fulfilled, we rejoice that the change in your Majesty's domestic and personal relations has been productive of augmented happiness to yourself and given assurance, under Providence, of the continuance of a line deservedly dear to the British people." Devonport tendered its individual thanksgiving : "Since the period at which we were last honoured by the presence of Royalty, most eventful changes have occurred in the domestic annals of the Borough. Its importance as one of your Majesty's naval arsenals has been acknowledged by the favour of his late Majesty King George the Fourth, who bestowed upon it that name which now distinguishes it. The political changes which occurred in the reign of your Majesty's august predecessor have entitled us to address the legislature through representatives of our own election ; but we owe to your Majesty's especial grace that final boon which, by extending to us the benefit of municipal institutions, now enables us to express our loyalty and gratitude in a corporate capacity." As a reward for these compliments, the Queen sanctioned the substitution of the name of Devonport for Plymouth-Dock "in every bill, warrant, or quittance," and official letters were for the first time authorised to be addressed to " Devonport " instead of " Plymouth."

QUEEN VICTORIA PROCEEDING IN THE STATE BARGE TO LAND AT DEVONPORT DOCKYARD.
(From a Sketch by N. Condy.)

The Queen paid her next visit to Plymouth in April, 1846, and, on this occasion, she received the municipal authorities on the quarter-deck of her yacht—the more fully to convince them that she desired no public demonstration. The Prince of Wales and Princess Alice accompanied the royal pair, and "the children were allowed to amuse themselves in the park." During a journey up the Tamar, Saltash was pointed out as one of the boroughs from which two members were formerly drawn, and the liveliest interest was exhibited in "this gem of the old Constitution." The chief object of the visit was to inspect Cotehele, and, on landing from the Fairy steamer, the Queen was driven through the romantic drive of towering oaks and spreading chestnuts, and expressed her charm at the preservation in which armour, furniture and tapestries were found at the mansion. On sailing down Hamoaze, the Royal Standard was dipped three times by way of homage to the battleships there lying in repose, and a crowd of officials and citizens on the deck of the frigate Thetis, which had just been launched, gave three hearty cheers. These salutes were re-echoed from the fleet of boats that extended from Cremyll Beach to Mutton Cove. On returning to the anchorage, there were some presentations, which were meant to have been formal. The commandant of the marines, however, "much to the surprise of his brother officers," entered into a quiet chat with Her Majesty, asked as to her health, hoped the voyage had been agreeable, and enquired if she were a good sailor. The Queen did not resent these "familiarities," but replied "in her usual affable manner" that the trip had been very pleasant, although she had suffered from sickness, and could scarcely claim to be hardy upon the water. That night, as her yacht lay in the Sound, the lusty tars danced hornpipes, and rendered glee songs, in the presence of the Queen, and there was

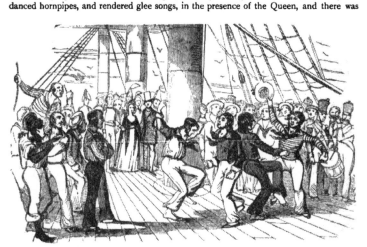

SAILORS DANCING ON BOARD THE ROYAL YACHT, PLYMOUTH SOUND, 1846.

no attempt to abridge freedom or damp pleasures. Prince Albert drove to Princetown to inspect some naphtha works which were being carried on in the abandoned war prison, and he allowed himself to be shut in the Black Hole, a detached building in which offenders against discipline were formerly incarcerated. The massive oak door, studded with iron spikes, was closed upon him so that he might appreciate the gloom and solitude of the chamber. The same afternoon the Queen visited Millbay and Sutton Pool, and the scene in Catwater was one of great animation, crowds assembling at Queen Anne's Battery and other points to cheer her as she was rowed in her cutter to Saltram.

Six years elapsed ere the Queen re-visited Plymouth, and a request was on this occasion conveyed that no popular displays should be made. Dissatisfied with this intimation, the Mayors of Plymouth and Devonport boarded the royal yacht to obtain a confirmation of the decree at the Queen's own hands. Her Majesty was not to be seen, and Mr. Alfred Rooker, on behalf of Plymouth, conveyed a wish to pay the customary compliments. Consent was given, but not in quite the manner desired. The Queen was assured by post that the lapse of time had only increased the local feeling of attachment, and the Mayors were informed by return that the Secretary of State would forward the usual acknowledgments. Each evening clusters of craft surrounded the yacht off Barnpool, and the varying hues constituted "a lovely scene" in the moonlight. The Queen's last visit to Plymouth was due to the accident of weather. She left Cowes in August, 1856, to make for Jersey, but the squadron was compelled by gales to stand down Channel to westward. Her Majesty's arrival in the Sound, although unexpected by the public, was anticipated by the officials, and the Victoria and Albert entered Hamoaze amid a bright panorama of dressed ships and manned yards. In the storm the royal yacht had rolled heavily, and the Queen suffered severely from sea sickness. Upon her recovery, she visited Mount Edgcumbe and Endsleigh and drove through Devonport to visit the "new steam factory." The troops were exercised on Mount Wise, but the artillery raised such clouds of dust that the review was abruptly curtailed. The Queen was then escorted to the Port Admiral's house and vehemently cheered on appearing at the balcony. At Saltram the royal party were the guests of Lord Morley, and the famous art collection was much admired. As the weather remained gusty, the Queen returned to Windsor by rail, and, although Millbay Station was crowded with municipal officials, no attempt was made to interfere with her freedom of action, "a consideration that Her Majesty evidently appreciated."

Advent of the Railway : 1845-1891. Expiring amid the romance of leafy lanes were those echoes of "The Merry Ploughboy" that had for so many generations stirred the population with familiar resonance, and which never failed to attract a beaming crowd as the equipages rattled from the east end of Plymouth to the Dockyard gates. The reality of the coach was passing into a picturesque dream, and the cheery horn and crisp whip were to be superseded by the snort and smoke of the iron horse. But the system was not to vanish without an experience alike suggestive and pathetic. Snow fell so heavily in February, 1841, that the Quicksilver mail was embedded between Ivybridge and Laira, and traffic was suspended until a gang of seventy labourers dug out the vehicle. After the letters had been conveyed to Ivybridge on saddled horses, a road was cut through the snow, and quite an array of obstructed coaches dispersed for London and Plymouth.

Soon the prevailing topic was the wonderful new machine for travelling without horses, which had a body of iron like a barrel, a furnace in the rear, and a perpendicular pipe ten feet high to carry off the smoke. At the first South Devon Railway meeting held in Plymouth, the engineer of the Great Western Company was chiefly concerned in dispelling the fears of the nervous. No accidents could occur—Mr. Price pointed out —if passengers kept their seats until the train came to a standstill, and the rails would be so protected that stage coaches could not possibly drive over them. These qualms settled, it was urged that there was not sufficient intercourse between Exeter and Plymouth to justify the experiment; but Mr. Rundle, the member for Tavistock, contended that the reduced cost of conveying passengers and stock would popularise travelling and lead to an increase of exchange. Hitherto farmers had been driving their cattle to London, impairing their strength and weight, whereas all produce would now be swiftly and economically carried. Emphasis was laid on the eminence of Plymouth as a port, and its possibilities of expansion, no less than on the facilities for carrying troops and stores. To this proviso George Stephenson attached the highest value, and there was a rush of railway projects aiming at the favour of the Three Towns. The "South Devon" held the field, and the prospectus presented the future of the port in such promising colours that the citizens of Exeter displayed "extraordinary uneasiness," and organised a depreciatory crusade. The capital was easily subscribed, without their assistance, and despite their disparagements. Brunel was entrusted with the work, and warmly recommended Eldad, "at the end of Five Fields," as the terminus, in order that an extension should be made into Cornwall "if this should be thought expedient." Mr. George Soltau warmly opposed the choice of "No Place" for the purpose, because persons would find their way to Devonport instead of Plymouth, and he advocated Friary as a more appropriate station site. Mr. Brunel laughed at the idea of conflicting interests. "Although," he said, "you speak of your Three Towns, we only know one long, straggling, scattered community." He held that no company would dream of approaching such a population at one extremity; but he so far yielded to pressure as to abandon his own idea and substitute land "at the back of the Octagon." This surrender aroused the fears of Devonport, whose citizens had subscribed on the understanding that a station would be placed near the North East Barrier Gate. Passionately protesting that "there is neither public landing-place nor population at Millbay," they insisted upon petitioning Parliament in favour of Devonport. Their Town Clerk, Mr. T. Woollcombe, as chairman of the company, "solemnly warned" them that they would not improve their position by this course; and, harsh though the hint sounded, it was justified in the event.

Whilst the South Devon Railway was in course of construction, the Duke of Wellington left London on an official visit. The line had only reached Teignmouth, and he resumed the journey to Plymouth by coach. At Ivybridge there was no fresh relay of horses in

DUKE OF WELLINGTON IN THE WEST OF ENGLAND, 1846.
(By permission from the ILLUSTRATED LONDON NEWS.)

readiness, and his Grace walked on to avoid mobbing. He was overtaken by the Tally-
Ho coach, and Hex, the guard, asked him to honour the conveyance by taking a seat.
" No, I thank you," was the prompt reply : "I am waiting for my carriage." Hex assured
the Duke that he would be greatly delayed, but the old soldier rejoined : "Never mind,
they'll find horses to take me on. Besides," he added, pointing to pedestrians with whom
he was discussing the scenery, "I have company." The baffled driver hastened on and set
Plymouth alive with the report that the veteran was tramping his way to the town.
Wellington, however, covered the last few miles in his conveyance, and a huge reception
awaited him as he drove to the Royal Hotel. The hostelry was soon besieged by Mayor and
Corporation, carrying an address that the Duke declined to accept ; and a lady tried to
secure an interview on the ground that she was " the little girl of Salamanca" whom
Wellington kissed when he entered that city. The Duke was not anxious to repeat the
performance, and the fair Spaniard was informed that his Grace had retired to bed! Dressed

DUKE OF WELLINGTON INSPECTING PLYMOUTH CITADEL.

in a blue frock coat, white vest and trousers, and wearing a star upon his breast, he
inspected the defences on the following day. On returning to town, he broke the journey
at the Seven Stars Hotel, Totnes, and an amusing colloquy indicated the excitement :

Enthusiast : My dear Mrs. Webb, is it true that the Duke of Wellington stopped at
your house to-day ?

Mrs. Webb : Oh, yes, sir, it is true, for I shook hands with him.

Enthusiast : My dear Mrs. Webb, have you shaken hands with anyone since ?

Mrs. Webb : No, indeed, sir, I have not.

Enthusiast : Then, my dear Mrs. Webb, pray do shake hands with me.

It was not until 1848 that the labour of years and anticipations of thousands were realised in the opening of the line to Laira. From this dawn of the new era all classes expected bright results, and the arrival of the first train was the signal for considerable rejoicings. The directors breakfasted at Totnes, and the progress to Laira was watched by wondering crowds :

> Aw, Johnny, aw Johnny, whatever es that
> A urning along like a hoss upon wheels ?
> 'Tes as bright as yer buttons and black as yer hat,
> An' jes hark to en, Johnny, an' yer how a' squeals.

The Inspector-General would not sanction a level crossing in Union Street, and one of the tradesmen objected to any deviation from the original scheme. After travelling from court to court a compromise was effected, and the line was completed to Millbay. The pioneer train was met at Plympton by the local authorities, and, on reaching Mutley, it was hailed by the band of the Royal Marines, who were seated in an open truck embowered with flags. The strains of " See the Conquering Hero Comes " were re-echoed by multitudes as the train made its way to Plymouth, municipal addresses were presented, and the Mayor of Devonport conveyed the habitual reminder of the unfulfilled pledge. Tempted by the prospect of colossal profits, the South Devon Company adopted the atmospheric system of traction. If Brunel was bewitched, so were the shareholders, and the appliances were laid the whole way from Exeter to Newton. Four atmospheric trains were set to work, but the pumping station could only be kept going by a horse power that rendered impossible a commercial return. The losses were ruinous, and the experiment was abandoned in time to avoid absolute financial catastrophe. The process had inspired hope in the early stage, for a luggage train of eight carriages ran twenty miles in fifty minutes, stoppages included, and the ease of the travelling was described as delightful. But, as week succeeded week, the fuel bill attained ghastly dimensions, the breakdowns were calamitous, and the atmospheric system was supplanted by steam. The patentees were offered the privilege of continuing at their own cost the trials they had made at the expense of the company, but they shrunk from the temptation.

Mr. Thomas Gill erected a pier and wharves at Millbay when the line approached completion, and the Plymouth Great Western Docks Company obtained powers in 1846 to effect large developments. A measure for deepening Millbay and lengthening the pier became law in 1848 ; and the various local railway companies subscribed towards the extensions. The Sutton Harbour Company then sought to raise £120,000 to connect their scheme with the railways, and yet another syndicate went to the public for half a million. Theirs was the most ambitious and far-seeing programme of all. They aimed at the purchase of the Halfpenny Gate and Millbridge, the conversion of Stonehouse Pool into docks, and the clearing of intervening property as far as the Five Fields, where the South Devon line was to be intersected. The order was too tall for the times, and the only contest was between Sutton Harbour and the Great Western Docks. There was no avowal of cross purposes—on the contrary, an expressed desire for mutual prosperity. The Millbay extensions were confirmed without difficulty, but the Admiralty vetoed the Sutton Harbour proposals. The South Western Railway Company thereupon projected a line which was disparaged as traversing "a desolate and moorland country." Their interests and those of Sutton Harbour forthwith became identical, but, although the way was opened to ultimate competition, the South Devon Company was empowered to connect with both harbours. They confined their attention to Millbay, however, and thus supplied their rivals with the necessary argument for obtaining further powers. Financial crash paralysed progress for a few years, and jubilations were general when operations were resumed at the Great Western Docks. Flags waved and arches spanned the roads, processions paraded the streets, and models of steamers were alive with sailor boys. At Millbay two barrows of rubble were placed on a specially constructed and flag-decorated staging, and the Mayor of Plymouth tipped one and the Mayor of Devonport the other— a harmony of arrangement which was welcomed as a harbinger of future prosperity. When the first mails were conveyed to the docks for despatch, bands played and banners were upheld, and the directors of the Screw Steam Navigation Company generously entertained the Mayor and Corporation.

There were several projects in the air when the first attempt was made to float the Tavistock Railway Company in 1844, but the more the rival plans were dissected, the more was the belief confirmed that some such scheme would be "highly remunerative." Three hundred guests from Plymouth attended the opening of the line in 1859, and they were welcomed by be-robed officials carrying silver-headed maces, and by scores of the inhabitants attired as monks of the Abbey. In the procession printing and mining operations, boiler making, foundry casting and granite blasting were in progress; peals as of "the music of bells" were produced by mimic quarrying; and Bishop Blaize, the patron saint of the woolcombers, posed in full canonicals. An open table was provided for visitors, and two tons of cake disappeared with the tea. A towering arch bore the motto, "Time is Money," and "Success to the Iron Road" was the prevailing sentiment.

When the Cornwall Railway was projected the desire was to carry the train across the Tamar at Torpoint by means of a floating bridge, but the Government refused the necesssary consent on the ground that it would obstruct the navigation of the river. In 1849 Brunel boldly counselled the erection of a bridge at Saltash that should be 100 feet high, 300 feet from pier to pier, and too lofty to interfere with the passage of the river. Under favourable conditions this was regarded as a stupendous undertaking, and the rapidity of the tide, rough weather, and uncertainty of foundation increased the spirit of doubt. Scientific men questioned the practicability of a proposal in which Brunel never lost faith, and, after some experiments, he supplied a public demonstration of his methods. Nothing short of solid rock would resist the pressure and vibration of an edifice that was

SALTASH BRIDGE IN COURSE OF CONSTRUCTION, 1858.

(By permission from the ILLUSTRATED LONDON NEWS.)

to resemble rather the massive columns of Egypt rather than the achievements of modern engineers.   Between Brunel and the bed lay seventy feet of water and twenty feet of mud, and in such a tideway, and at so great a depth, a coffer dam was out of the question.   The principle was nevertheless ingeniously applied, and all obstacles were vanquished.   An immense wrought-iron cylinder, 100 feet high, 37 feet in diameter, and 300 tons in weight, was sunk upon the spot from which the main tower was to rise, and the water was pumped out and the air forced in.   Then the men descended, and worked as in a gigantic diving bell at the bottom of the river.   Mud and gravel were thus exhausted until the solid rock was reached and levelled to give even support to the cylinder all round.   Powerful steam pumps supplied the labourers with air, and excavation was conducted at an atmospheric pressure of 35lbs. to the inch.   A large number of visitors, encased in waterproof jackets, descended the cylinder to witness the operations, and surprise was general and congratulation unrestrained.   The cylinder was subsequently moved 35 times, and after 175 borings had been taken, the rock was excavated to a depth at which its impervious nature could be ascertained.   To prevent irruption between cylinder and rock, a circle of small oak piles was driven downwards, and these were strengthened by an iron band on approaching the bottom.   The mud proved of a soft blue or black consistency for three feet, then it was mixed with shells, next it grew so compact that the pickaxe was required, a layer of large stones followed, and the bed was reached twelve feet below the surface of the mud.   The excavation of this hard dunstone was continued for three feet, and at this depth it was pronounced to be capable of sustaining any weight.   In the centre of the first deposit of hewn stone was placed a copper tablet, in an oaken box, with the inscription : " Cornwall Railway. Saltash Bridge. Trial Foundation of Central Pier. January, 1849. I. K. Brunel, engineer. William Glennie, resident ditto."

The shock sustained by railway enterprise caused a suspension of work until 1853, when tenders were invited and the contract was taken at £162,000 by Messrs. Mare and Co., of Blackwall.   The firm went into bankruptcy, and it was with difficulty that the first tube was completed and the more expensive part of the masonry raised.   The tube was floated between the piers destined to receive it in May, 1858, and a busy scene animated the river and its banks.   Stands, tents and marquees were provided for visitors ; the bells of Saltash rang out ; shows vied with refreshment booths ; fleets of steamers and yachts plied from Plymouth and Devonport ; and an endless array of carriages streamed along the road.   On turning Bull Point the tube was seen gliding like some silent monster towards the main tower.   Resting upon pontoons, each towed by naval tugs, it swung into position with the accuracy of clockwork.   As the tide fell, the pontoons sunk ; wedges and supports were knocked away ; and the tube, after reposing upon the piers, was raised by hydraulic pressure to the necessary elevation.   The second tube was launched in June, 1859, amid similar displays of interest, and the Royal Albert Bridge was then fairly on its way to completion—the columns raised on massive piles, and the metal casts of such dimensions as had scarcely been imagined.   The design combined the tubular with the suspension principle, the bridge was 2,200 feet in length, and the railroad hung by massive chains.   Each section of the bridge had been constructed on a temporary quay by the water's edge, and temporary docks admitted the pontoons at each end.   Before the spans were lifted they were tested with a strain, including their own weight, of 2,300 tons.   This load represented five and a-half tons per inch of section on the tubes and chains, and it deflected the entire span seven inches.   When the mass was removed the recovery was immediate.   The test of the Inspector was only a load of 400 tons ; and, under this, the deflection was little more than an inch.   The bridge was opened by the Prince Consort, and the royal train was met at Saltash by the Mayor, Mr. J. H. Cook, who rejoiced that the distinguished visitor had shown his encouragement of art by dedicating the Royal Albert Bridge : " that noble work of engineering skill which has united the important counties of Devon and Cornwall and made our borough the main entrance to the district of which it forms a part—a work destined to be a memento to generations yet unborn of your Royal Highness's name and memory, as also of the skill and perseverance evinced by the architect in the construction thereof." The Prince Consort hoped that " this work, which reflects so much credit on the enterprising men by whom it has been planned and executed, may be productive of increasing prosperity to your town and county." Amid salvoes of artillery the first train passed slowly forward to the Combe viaduct, where the visitors surveyed the entire structure, and, leaving the train, the Prince walked over the bridge, followed by acclamations from ashore and afloat. After the departure of the Prince from Saltash the Corporation of the borough assembled at the Guildhall, where they partook of a cold collation. The absence of the Mayor from the festivities was construed

OPENING OF SALTASH BRIDGE BY THE PRINCE CONSORT.
(By permission of the ILLUSTRATED LONDON NEWS.)

as discourteous, " and some inuendoes were thrown out suggestive of his worship being on a wild goose chase for a knighthood, which he is said to have long secretly coveted." When the sounds of rejoicing had died away, Brunel, fatally stricken by disease, travelled to Saltash to witness from a couch the embodiment of his superb, if costly, conception.

As the waste lands blossomed at Devonport, the sites of market gardens were converted into villas, and the mother church counted the spires of several stately daughters. The unpretending graving docks were supplemented by others of larger capacity, and the Admiralty enclosure extended below the westernmost landing-place at Mutton Cove. Then, as by a touch of the magician's wand, Keyham arose with its' docks, wharves and factories. It was in 1844 that the first spade was inserted, and Nasmyth's tilt hammer drove the piles that formed the coffer. The engine began its mighty task in 1845, to the wonder of spectators, and a dam of 1,600 feet, in which 800 loads of timber were used, was soon completed, the area of 74 acres being intersected with railways and the excavated soil thus early removed.   The one-storeyed huts in which the soldiers had been housed gave place to the Raglan and Granby Barracks, and the number of soldiery in the town increased with the growing armaments.   The absence of railway accommodation, and the restricted building facilities, rendered Devonport powerless to supplement the advantages conferred by the Government, but hope proved hardy in the parody with which the rafters of the Royal Hotel reverberated on the occasion of the Court Leet dinners :

A Railway Station in the town will alter its old face,
And rails, and trams, and 'busses for our welfare then will race,
And one thing more, I've been informed, is sure to be the case,
That we are likely soon to have a decent bathing place
            Say the Tenants of this Lord.

Devonport never ceased to lament the sacrifice of its interests by the South Devon Railway Company, and its irritation resulted in the introduction of the narrow gauge system. A line, wholly independent of the South Western Company, was projected by the Devon and Cornwall Company, with an important station near Albemarle Villas.   The House of Commons passed the Bill, but, when the Lords were reached, the Great Western and South Devon interests were combined for opposition, and the measure was thrown out. Indignation in Devonport found vent in a proposal to call upon the Town Clerk to resign his office.   Councillor Aunger was the author of the resolution, basing his action on the fact that Mr. Woollcombe had throughout been the chairman of the South Devon Railway Company, and that its board of directors had always been the enemy of Devonport. Mr. Aunger argued that this was the only way in which Parliament could be convinced that the Council was in earnest, and he declared that he had heard Mr. Woollcombe say that if he had to resign one of two positions it would be that of Town Clerk.   Mr. J. W. Ryder described the attack on the Town Clerk as contemptible, and oil was only poured on the troubled waters by the official announcement that, after the feeling manifested in the town at the rejection of the bill, the promoters had determined to renew the application.

Time made for certain progress, and, when the new company opened its line to Oke hampton, the West was united to the rest of the country without break of gauge.   Between Lydford and Okehampton the connection was soon continuous, and the advent of the narrow gauge to Devonport itself was passionately urged by Dr. May.   Investigation proved that the traffic was so large as to justify this accommodation, and the hitherto sceptical South Western Railway officials were convinced by the figures.   A Parliamentary Committee recommended free and equal access from Lydford to Devonport, and thence to the Great Western Docks and Sutton Pool, but the concession was not to be speedily realised.   The battle of the gauges was to be fought to the bitter end, and the South Western proposed to discard the South Devon by branching off at Marsh Mills, and travelling direct to Friary Green.   Here a station was to be provided for passengers and goods, and the line was to continue in a circuit to the Old Cattle Market in Tavistock Road, where the terminus was to be formed.   Thence the plan was to run to Devonport, with a branch across the Parsonage Fields, direct to Stonehouse Pool.   If the scheme had been completed in this way, not a foot of the South Devon line would have been used.   The final evidence in favour of the extension was irresistible ; and, as the outcome of a compromise, the narrow gauge rails were laid on the broad gauge system.   North Road Station was erected, with equal access to both companies, separate booking clerks, ticket collectors, and joint general management.   The Devon and Cornwall Railway were empowered to carry a loop line to Devonport, and from the terminal station near the Rectory Grounds a branch to Stonehouse

ENTRANCE TO FRIARY THROUGH SPARKE'S GATE: Site of South Western Railway
(Friary) Station.

(*From a Sketch by Samuel Prout.*)

Pool was effected. Running powers over a portion of the Cornish Railway admitted of an entrance to Keyham, as well as over the South Devon line into Sutton Pool. "Hail, all Hail! The Narrow Gauge Rail!" Thus Devonport attained, in May, 1876, much for which it had clamoured. All parts of the borough were decorated with flags and mottoes on the arrival of the first train, and the municipal procession and troopings of the guard were witnessed by delighted crowds. Eight hundred persons sat down to a banquet in the Goods' Shed, and several of the innkeepers closed their premises in the evening because their supplies of liquor were exhausted. The commemorative ode proclaimed :

> The town will no longer be left in the shade
> As the rail will be used both for pleasure and trade !
> All hail to our guests : those who strove in the past,
> To obtain us fair play, have secured it at last !

In 1891 the lingering aspiration of Devonport was realised in the grant of a wholly separate system—stations rose at Friary and Albemarle as previously projected, the local portion of the South Western ran parallel with the Great Western for many miles, and the Great Western abandoned the broad for the narrow gauge. Docks were started at Stonehouse Pool, but the pace was slow as the contractors had to remove 11,000 tons of mud and excavate 23,000 tons of hard material. Mr. May was also the moving spirit in this development.

Plymouth Mayoral Contests: 1802-1835. If the freemen were potential in matters Parliamentary before the Reform Bill extinguished their pretensions, they were no less mighty in local management until the Municipal Corporations Act deprived them of influence and privilege. They originally played a small part in the election of Mayor and then an appeal to the courts gave them a real voice. The custom of appointing a chief magistrate at the hands of a jury nominated by the retiring Mayor, consisting of two aldermen and two freemen, was discarded, and the freemen rejoiced for several years in the dignities and hospitalities with which they thus became endowed. The election of Mayor continued to take place on St. Lambert's Day, and its occasional fall upon the Sabbath did not dissuade the authorities from going through the traditional programme. Mayor, Recorder, Aldermen, Common Council and Commonalty assembled at the Guildhall ; and thence marched to the Church of St. Andrew's to hear an "excellent sermon" on brotherly love and the duty of magistrates. On their return to the Council Chamber the Bribery Act was read and the names of the freemen were called—"a most respectable list, beginning with their Royal Highnesses and descending many degrees to our local squires and gentlemen—some of the latter so dubbed to gratify their ambitions, since their gentility is far below the correct pitch." The nominations were made, a show of hands was taken, and a poll was demanded in the event of a contest. The books were closed at half-past two, the formal declaration was followed by appropriate speeches, and a "dinner of every delicacy of the season" wound-up "a day of much bustle and festivity." The circulation of the social glass was maintained till a late hour. On "Scarlet Day" (Michaelmas) all concerned again attended church, but, after a while, the glory of this function departed, aldermen discarded their fine gowns "and could not be distinguished from their fellow townsmen," and even the Mayor and Mayor-Elect walked with or without their robes as suited "their caprice or whims." The only attempt at display consisted in carrying the town colours, and the constables with their staffs "looked like so many dockyard warders."

Protracted litigation followed an attempt to elect a Mayor in 1802, the contest arising out of the unpopularity of Alderman Remmett, the nominee of the aldermen and capital

TO THE CURIOUS.

JUST arrived from the BANKS of the THAMES, and to be seen at the newly-erected Menagerie in Market-Place, Plymouth, the
WONDERFUL MAN-DAMUS.

This singular production is not described by Linnæus, or any other Naturalist, and is exceedingly rare, none having been exhibited in the Town since the Year 1728.

It measures from Head to Tail about Two Feet and a Half. The Skin is without Fur, or Hair, and is nearly similar in Texture to that of the Sheep; having for its Ground-Colour a Pale Yellow, variegated in all parts with numerous, moderately large, and somewhat roundish black Spots, and abrupt Lines.

Its disposition is changeable; being at this time so very gentle that the most timid Female need not be afraid of approaching it; but, from confinement, it is expected in a few Days to become Outrageous, and exhibit such surprising Feats of Strength, that the Keepers (though a powerful Body of Men) will not dare to oppose it, being at such Times particularly terrifying and commanding.

TERMS OF ADMISSION.

Ladies and Gentlemen, 1s. each—Servants and Children, 6d.

N.B.—The Exhibition will continue open but a short Time, and may be viewed from Nine o'Clock in the Morning till Dusk.

Dated Nov. 13, 1802.

was vested in the Mayor and Commonalty at large. The bye-law under which the election had been conducted was described as a piece of aldermanic usurpation which could not override common law, since it had been enacted by aldermen and capital burgesses without conference with the Common Councillors and freemen. Mr. Cleather was unable to prove that it had been properly adopted or exercised, and loud was the outcry when he resumed the proceedings on the lines pursued the day before. The election of assessors was conducted with the same form and the same result, the 36 freemen retired for twelve hours more, and yet again emerged to declare that they could not agree. Mr. Cleather thereupon dissolved the meeting, and intimated that a mandamus to authorise and enforce the election must be applied for. The opposing factions raced to reach the court with the first application, but the friends of Mr. Langmead triumphed, and the judges directed their mandamus to the Mayor and Commonalty at large. The writ itself was subject to considerable sarcastic comment, and when the Corporation was next summoned, Mr. Langmead was proposed and carried, without any reference to

burgesses. Alderman Langmead, the candidate of the Common Councillors and freemen, was honoured and esteemed, but the select portion of the Corporation insisted on continuing the system of rotation. On St. Lambert's Day, Mr. Cleather, the retiring Mayor, called upon the aldermen and capital burgesses to withdraw to an adjoining room and appoint two assessors. They returned and recorded the favourite names, and the Common Councillors and freemen were invited to choose two assessors to act on their behalf. The four assessors selected a jury of 36 Common Councillors and freemen, and these took the oath to elect a capital burgess who had not served as Mayor for eight years to act in that capacity. At noon they retired to a private apartment, and there wrangled until midnight, when they announced that they were equally divided. Mr. Cleather thereupon adjourned the proceedings, and when the meeting was resumed the following day, the protest was raised that the choice

MAN-DAMUS.

THE Public are hereby informed, that this Day is positively the last in which the MAN-DAMUS can be exhibited, as it is ordered to Town by the Fifth of December.

The Old Managers state they have been greatly disappointed in the Amount of the Receipts arising from the Show of the Man-damus, as it does not Amount to a Sum sufficient to clear the Expenses—a Circumstance which they attribute, in a great measure, to the surly Disposition of the Animal.

The New Managers intend to procure, as speedily as possible, another Animal of the same Species, called a PEREMPTORY MAN-DAMUS.

This Animal is of a much more Noble disposition, being very docile and obliging if dealt gently with; but, if roused, manifests a great Degree of Spirit.

The Abilities of this Animal are very much superior to the Man-damus; it excels in knowledge the Learned Pig; it will point out to any Persons in the Room who have lost their Rights or Charters; Books or Parchments; Money or Lands—a Method of Recovery.

It is expected that the Old Managers will oppose the Introduction of this Noble Animal into the Borough, from an Apprehension that it may deprive them of their Profits; but the Public are respectfully informed that it will come down by Royal Authority, and be exhibited Gratis.

N.B.—This Animal possesses no Physical Qualities, except a little Purging.

Monday, November 29, 1802.

assessors and jury. Mr. Cleather declined to admit the legality of the proceedings ; and, as the presiding officer and holder of the writ, insisted upon the appointment of more assessors and jurymen. These were sworn as before, but their withdrawal found them once more equally divided, and they were dismissed without arriving at any decision. Mr. Cleather refused to countenance Mr. Langmead's election, and filed a statement that no return had taken place. The new party was meanwhile denied the use of the Guild-hall in which to meet ; and they protested in a manifesto against "the highly unconstitutional and dishonourable interference which has taken place for the purpose of preventing us from exercising the undoubted right vested in us of assembling in Common Hall." They were desperately in earnest : "Shall this interference," they exclaimed, "so disgrace-ful both to its authors and abettors, be tamely submitted to ? Or shall it be deservedly and indignantly repelled ? Shall we suffer the free exercise of the rights vested in us to be invaded from any quarter ? No! Let us, by the firmness of our conduct, teach such as have dared to attempt the violation of those rights that we are freemen, not in name only, but in fact. Let us avail ourselves of he present opportunity—for if this be lost none may ever occur to us again—of rescuing our memories from the eternal infamy which will attach to us if we now quietly permit a death blow to be given to our just and ancient privileges." For a time, however, the freemen had to submit to humiliation, and they accordingly resorted to a small "eating and tippling" house which was known as "The Shoulder of Mutton." Another application for a mandamus was then submitted on behalf of Mr. Langmead, and the issues were sent down for trial at the Devon Assizes. There it was decreed that the election lay with the Mayor and Commonalty at large, and a mandamus, brief and peremptory in character, was despatched to Mr. Cleather ordering a Mayor to be chosen for the residue of the term. "We do command that you and everyone of you hav-ing a right to vote shall proceed to the election of a Mayor according to the custom and usage of the said borough." Those qualified to take part were specifically enumerated as "the late Mayor, Recorder, Aldermen or Capital Burgesses, Common Councilmen, and Freemen." There was a further order to communicate the result forthwith, "lest by your default complaint should be again made to us as to how you shall have executed this our writ." The aldermanic party capitulated, and in May, Mr. Langmead, who had resigned his seat as a capital burgess to show his contempt for his brethren, was adopted without further struggle. He signalised the victory of the freemen by presenting the town with a lifeboat, and a procession of the inhabitants marched to the Barbican, carrying flags and banners. Mr. Langmead was rowed into the pool from the dock in which his gift had been built, lifted out of his seat by a body of merchants, and carried shoulder high to the George Tavern, where wines were served. The humiliation of the aldermen was commemorated in another *jeu d'esprit*.

TO THE PUBLIC.

THE MAN-DAMUS which was exhibited a few months' since in the new Menagerie, not having given the general satisfaction promised by the Keepers (but which, on the contrary, proved to be a shameful Imposition on the Public), has induced some Persons celebrated for taming wild Animals, to procure, at a considerable Expense, a

MAN-DAMUS

of the real Breed.—This Animal, though Diminu-tive, is the most perfect of its kind ever seen, in which Particular it forms a striking contrast to that lately exhibited, which was generally allowed to be of a spurious Sort ; it is produced with Quills, somewhat like those of the Porcupine, which, how-ever, are dropped as soon as it arrives at Maturity, but the Marks are still visible on the Skin. Its Appearance, in other Respects, resembles the former, except that it has a Large Fiery Tail, and that its Aspect is better calculated to terrify its Enemies.

To convince the Public that the Keepers of this Animal have not procured it for the Sake of any Personal Benefit, it will be exhibited Gratis, in the new Menagerie, on Friday, the 20th instant.

N.B.—The Menagerie has been cleared of those Animals who, by their growling, rendered it so disagreeable to the Ladies during the last Exhibi-tion.   VIVANT REX ET REGINA.

Plymouth, May 16, 1803.

Upon achieving this victory, and asserting the co-equal authority of the freemen, Sir Warwick Hele Tonkin, as Town Clerk, was presented with a silver cup " for his indomitable spirit in beginning, his unwearied zeal in continuing, and his great exertions and abilities in carrying to a favourable issue a case which has restored to the freemen the right to vote for chief magistrate and other privileges that had been withheld from them for several centuries." To Mr. Joseph Pridham a similar cup was presented "for his zeal and ability in his conduct as the solicitor to the Commonalty in a case which has restored to them the right of voting for their chief magistrate and other privileges withheld for centuries." From that time forward the "Shoulder of Mutton" party founded a party club, and annually dined in the same house, a shoulder of mutton—the largest and finest that could be obtained—occupying "the first or chiefest place." During the dispute between the freemen and the freeholders in 1807, electioneering squibs were issued avowedly by "The Shoulder of Mutton Club"—an act of presumption to which the attention of the Prime Minister was called, as so many of the members were in the employ of the Government. The Admiralty Commissioner of the port was consulted, but neutrality was strictly observed.

At the Mayoralty election in 1810, Dr. Lockyer polled 84 freemen, as against 45 who supported Dr. Bellamy, and his Worship attended church, accompanied by "the respectable freemen and inhabitants," and preceded by the mace and standard bearers and the band of the North Devon Militia. The relative duties of magistrate and people were expounded by "our respected vicar, Mr. Gandy, with an energy and animation that could not fail to make a lively impression on the minds of the auditors." A witty commentator of the period vowed that the freemen, as usual, relieved the monotony of the service by praying that the dinner might be good! There was a closer fight for the Mayoralty in 1811, and Dr. Bellamy was elected by 68 freemen, 58 voting for Dr. Remmett, his Whig antagonist. This contest occurred on a Sunday, and no objection was raised to Dr. Bellamy until he presented himself to be sworn, when it was urged that he had not received the sacrament for twelve months. Challenged as to the truth of this impeachment, the new Mayor declined to answer, and, on the vicar of St. Andrew's refusing to administer the oath, his Worship, to the consternation of the townsfolk in attendance, declined to attend the service. The office was declared void, and then Dr. Bellamy took the sacrament, filled the office and finished his term. Still, the prejudice was not at an end, and a suit was instituted to determine whether his Worship could truly claim to be one of the "twenty-four." Three dissentient burgesses testified that the Mayor and twelve chief burgesses had usually filled up vacancies by "calling to them twenty-four of the free inhabitants." There were instances since 1803, it was admitted, in which the Commonalty had elected, as well as the Mayor and chief burgesses; but, prior to that, the privilege was restricted to the Mayor and chief burgesses, and they had uniformly protested against the interference of the Commonalty. Thus the old issue was revived in 1812, when there were two vacancies in the number of Common Councilmen. Only five of the chief burgesses attended the election, and the Commonalty adopted Dr. Bellamy and Dr. Lockyer after the accustomed protest had been offered. A rule was granted against Dr. Bellamy, but the matter being carried no further, he occupied his seat—not without attempts to disturb his peace of mind by the promise of a sure and speedy death. An anonymous letter, sent through the Plymouth Post-office, bore the hazy menace " Beware of your life, Bellamy, for you must inevitably die." The threat was taken seriously, and a reward of £500 was offered for information of "the man or woman " who had sent the document.

During the next three years there was much difficulty in persuading gentlemen to serve on account of the expense and "the infinite disquietude, embarrassment and perplexity in which the chief magistrate is thrown by means of dissensions unhappily prevailing." In 1813 Mr. Henry Woollcombe was persuaded to sit, and Sir Diggory Forrest accepted the position in 1814. In 1815 affairs reached a deadlock. The choice fell upon Mr. Hunt, a solicitor, whose position had been "materially improved by an appointment procured through the interest of one of the members of the borough." In spite of art exerted, and argument advanced, he was deaf to blandishments, declared the office distasteful, and declined to be put in nomination. The freemen would have chosen Mr. Hunt without his consent if he had not abstained from taking the Sacrament during the preceding twelve months; and, although importuned, steadfastly declined to comply with the ordinance. Counsel were consulted as to whether he could not be compelled to yield, but the answer was not satisfactory, and Mr. William Lockyer accepted the position. A large silver medal was struck to be worn by him and his successors "in honourable token of that inestimable branch of the British Constitution, Trial By Jury, by whose verdict the right of the freemen to elect a chief magistrate for the borough was restored, after having been unjustly withheld for three centuries." In 1816 the difficulty of obtaining a Mayor recurred. Captain Pym bolted when his name was mentioned, and he was brought back to the hall by the sergeants-at-mace. On the Sunday, when he was expected to attend church in state, he walked to Tamerton; and the service was postponed for his attendance. At the end of his year, he extenuated his failings in the characteristic remark : " If I have departed from your customs, remember I was a pressed man, and not a volunteer."

During the Mayoralty of Captain Arthur, in 1818, it was necessary to present a firm and united front to a more dangerous enemy than the aldermen—the Government itself, which claimed the ownership of the Hoe. For years the ceremony of beating the boundaries had been discarded on account of the rowdyism, leading to bloodshed, which accompanied the festival. The custom was now revived with the avowed object of resisting the trespass, and, accompanied by the inhabitants, the officials proceeded to the Hoe, where painted notices, signed " R. H. Crew, Secretary," which claimed the land as War Office property, were demolished amid vehement cheering. A map was produced to prove that a portion of the Hoe was given to Charles II. for the purpose of erecting the Citadel. The crowd perambulated the entire area and the boundaries of the town as well, and the close of the function was marked by drinking bouts and stubborn fights. 1820 was memorable for another conflict between the "Shoulder of Mutton Club" and the antagonists of the freemen, and the former carried Mr. Squire by a majority of four votes over Mr. Jacob, the candidate proposed by the Corporation. In 1823, Mr. Nicholas Lockyer revived Freedom Day, and the officials went over the boundaries on horseback. An amateur band led the procession, and the lads from Hele and Lanyon's Schools were once more turned adrift to plague the tradesmen. On reaching the Barbican, the Mayor lifted a youngster out of one of the boats that had been rowed from Catdown, in accordance with established custom, asked him various questions bearing upon the ceremony, and boxed him on the ears to impress the circumstance upon his memory. At Fisher's Nose another boy was taken out of a boat, subjected to the same discipline, rewarded with a sum of money, and pressed into public service. The object of this perambulation was to further emphasize the right of Plymouth in its Hoe, and two granite pillars and a gate were dedicated by Mr. Edmund Lockyer as a manifesto of municipal property. During the ensuing twelve months an Act was obtained which preserved inviolate the rights of the Corporation "over the whole of this delightful spot," and Mr. Kingdon, the owner of some contiguous fields, provided a road of forty feet in width, so that the public approach should be convenient. To this thoroughfare the name of Lockyer Street was given, in honour of the Mayor, "the father and general benefactor of the town." An attempt to bestow the freedom of the borough upon the donor in recognition of his generosity was thwarted by the selfishness of the men in possession ; but a grateful public drew Mr. Kingdon to the Hoe on Freedom Day, and the gate was opened and closed with every formality. Cakes and wine were distributed, and a substantial meal was provided for the Corporation in t·:e evening.

In 1824 the contest was between Mr. John Moore and Mr. H. Marshall, a leading advocate of Reform, and the voting gave the former 164 and the latter 91—a majority of 73 for Mr. Moore. Much acrimony developed during the contest and the new Mayor, in hoping that it would cease, observed that "we live in portentous times, when it is not only necessary for a man to be surrounded with friends, but also to know that they are friends." The complement to this philosophic comment was supplied by Mr. Marshall, who asserted that he should have refrained from the poll if he had not believed that a greater number would have supported him. "The Shoulder of Mutton" devotees sought to elect Dr. Bellamy, in 1825, only to find Mr. W. H. Hawke more powerful. In 1828, Dr. Bellamy once more "allowed himself" to be proposed by the "oppressed freemen," whose claims had been "so long and so often resisted." This attempt was also ineffectual, 63 votes being tendered for Captain Pridham and 30 for Dr. Bellamy. The outside freemen were attracted in 1829 by the prospect of another contested election. On the one side, the name of Captain Nicholas Lockyer was submitted, and, on the other, that of Mr. Richard Freeman. Dr. Bellamy protested with personal illustrations that the Mayoralty was now a simple matter of loaves and fishes, and Mr. Edmund Lockyer construed this remark into an imputation that he had betrayed the borough. "But," quoth he, "if Sir George Cockburn is the purchaser, he has not been very diligent in payment, for I have never yet received a farthing of the money." The show of hands was in favour of Mr. Freeman, who won with 70 votes, the number registered for Captain Lockyer being 63. The conflict in 1830 was preceded by a struggle as to whether time-expired apprentices were entitled to the freedom, and their claims to vote were successfully resisted. Dr. Bellamy, "amid immense cheering," protested that he was not against the men, but the manner of their introduc- tion. Citizens only asked now, "What will this bring to me or mine?" and the Mayors were invariably drawn from the "aristocratical party." Captain Wise was proposed by Mr. H. Woollcombe, and Captain Lockyer by Sir Manasseh Lopes. The votes recorded for the former were 75, and for the latter 73. Another trial of strength was anticipated in 1832 when Mr. Henry Marshall was brought out to oppose Captain Tozer. Mr. Baldly who issued an address pledging himself to protect the freemen, promptly withdrew in favour of Mr. Marshall. The latter was supported by several of the new freemen and by Liberals who resented a plumper that Captain Tozer gave against Reform at a previous election. Captain Tozer now pleaded that he had been the means of increasing the freemen, and that, although he voted against the popular parliamentary candidate, he was not opposed to Reform itself. Mr. Marshall thereupon withdrew and his opponent was elected. Captain Frazer was appointed custodian of the key of the "Common Coffer" and Mr. George Bayley "Warder of the Windows." The retiring Mayor, Captain Lockyer, "ac- cording to the usual privilege," nominated as freeman Sir Ralph Lopes," whose name was received with loud and reiterated cheering."

TO THE INDEPENDENT FREEMEN OF
    THE BOROUGH OF PLYMOUTH.

Gentlemen,—In consequence of the resignation of Dr. Baldy, and the numerous solicitations of my Brother Freemen, I beg to offer myself to your notice as a Candidate for the Office of Mayor for the year ensuing , and, as a native of the Town, and identified in all respects with its interests, I venture to hope for the honour of your support on the day of election.

I can with great truth assure you, that should I be so fortunate as to become the object of your choice, I will, most impartially and honestly, main- tain your Rights and Privileges, and endeavour to the utmost of my power to discharge the Duties of the Office so as to merit your approbation,

I have the honour to be, Gentlemen,
        Your obedient and faithful Servant,
                    HENRY MARSHALL.
Plymouth, September 15th, 1831.

During the months previous to the passing of the Reform Bill, some of the freemen called upon Mr. W. H. Hawker to establish his right to sit as an alderman. The judges had to determine whether Plymouth was a borough by prescription ; whether the Corporation existed from the time of Richard I. ; and whether, having existed from that time, it consisted of 13 aldermen and 24 councillors, with Mayor and aldermen elected from out of the Common Council. Mr. Serjeant Wilde contended that the election of aldermen had been legally practised, and that, in the three cases in which custom was violated, writs of ouster were obtained against two individuals, and the third only escaped that ignominy by dying. Mr. Justice Park was exasperated at having "such an oppressive job" as the settlement of this obscure argument introduced, and warmly censured the aldermen's party "for springing their worm-eaten charters upon him." Serjeant Wilde thereupon withdrew the case, much to the relief of his lordship and the disappointment of the spectators. These webs of legal subtleties were soon to be swept away by the broom of Municipal Reform. The election of Mr. John Moore in 1834 was the last under the Old Charter, and the form was observed of waiting from eleven until noon to see if the Prior of Plympton would appear to offer any objection. It was a long reach from the days when "the priest hath often been sore, sick and in great jeopardy of his life from travelling through the hail, rain, or snow " to assert authority in Sutton or give housel, or nayling, (holy unction), on the way. Now, however, that there was no pretence of hard travelling, the Prior, that "most ancient and reverent person" made no sign, and the function was pronounced complete. So that the Close Corporation expired with a jest upon its' lips. Its income at this time was £6,000 a year, including rent of market, £2,250 ; hotel, theatre and mills, £1,642 ; water, £2,030.

A curious custom that obtained before the Municipal Reform Bill was the election of a "Mayor" of Crabtree. The authors of this travestie met for social purposes at the Lamb Inn, in Treville Street, and, attired in huge cloaks trimmed with red braid facings, walked in state to the Crabtree Inn. Each individual bore a carved mace, with a cockle shell on the top of it, and the Ex-Mayor carried an enormous shell which had been elaborately gilded and decorated for the occasion. The "Town Clerk" was conspicuous with a monster bowl, in which the punch was subsequently brewed, and the "Recorder" was distinguished by carrying a similar emblem. The form of electing the various officers was duly observed, and the hospitalities were so prolonged that those who walked out on foot were only too glad to return in a waggon. Equally grotesque was the ceremony of "Mayor Choosing" at Cannwood : another excuse for a day's outing

"DREADFUL CATASTROPHE !

Whereas a fortnight ago a beautiful greyhound puppy answering to the name of H—— did in a fit of hydrophobia make his escape from Baron's Kennel. It has since been ascertained that the above Puppy has bit several who are now languishing in the most excruciating torment. Amongst those persons is His Royal Highness Jacques, the Mock Duke Aranza, the present Mayor of Cannwood. In order to prevent the said Puppy from doing any further mischief and to encourage those well-disposed persons who may be willing to assist us, We, the Justices and Corporation of Cannwood, offer a reward of two glasses of punch to any person who can cure the said 'Puppy,' and a further reward of the freedom of our borough, to be presented in a gold box, beautifully ornamented with the cranium of an Ass, to any gentleman who will undertake to restore the mental energies of our unfortunate Mayor. Done by order of the Court,
TOWN CLERK,
Codger's Hall, alias Battle's Kitchen, Cann Wood,"
1812.

and a night's orgie, which was arranged by the tavern wits with the same fantastic humour and extravagance of regalia. On these occasions the buglers of the Yeomanry awoke the glades with their echoes. Whenever the conduct of the Close Corporation occasioned discontent, "proclamations" were issued by the bogus bodies to represent the scorn of the general community, and criticisms were expressed with more force than decency, accompanied by thinly veiled imputations on morals and honour.

To anticipate the operation of Reform, the Close Corporation admitted 400 freemen at a fee of 25 guineas apiece, and as obligation was thus cancelled, the members of the Aldermanic and Lockyer party found a general disposition to repudiate them when the Municipal Reform Act was passed. Many who had hitherto dominated the destinies of the town accordingly retired in dudgeon from further participation in its affairs. On the morning of the first election the streets were in a bustle, peals of bells lent animation to the proceedings, and states of the poll were published hourly in every ward from nine o'clock till the closing at four. The voters who were "asked no questions," handed in papers bearing their signatures and a description of their property. The Guildhall was crowded to hear the declaration of the numbers ; and, amidst tumultuous cheering, the Mayor certified that everything had been " open, fair and honest," and then resigned " the important trust which has been reposed in me for the past fifteen months." The polling resulted in the return of Ultra-Tories, 5 ; Liberal-Tories, 6 ; Conservative-Whigs, 7 ; Whigs, 12 ; Radicals, 6 ; Total, 36. Mr. T. Gill was proposed as Mayor, and was unanimously elected "amid the loudest acclamations of the burgesses."

Challenged with favouritism in appointing the new magistrates, Lord John Russell replied that the Plymouth Bench ought to fairly represent both political parties. Thus encouraged, the Conservatives pointed out that they polled within twenty of the aggregate recorded for the Reform candidates, and yet the Plymouth Bench was exclusively Whig and Liberal. Lord John remitted this protest to the Town Clerk, and as the magistrates recommended the inclusion of some Conservatives, the Council at once met and protested against this interference on the plea that justices should be nominated by the "dominant political party " in their own body.

Apart from this attempt at usurpation, which was not entertained, there had been ridiculous competition between the Benches at Plymouth and Devonport for the honour or privilege of committing offenders, and persons were sent for trial on frivolous pretexts—an anxiety not unassociated with certain family relations between magistrates and clerks that had a material regard to fees. The county justices did not hesitate to say that the ratepayers paid for the rivalry, and there was an attempt to economise by asking the magistrates at Jump (Roborough) to work with those of Devonport. Social aversion rendered the understanding impossible, and the former refused to sit in the same court. " As nobody would meet them," the Devonport magistrates "did exactly as they pleased " ; and, to cut the Gordian knot, Plymouth and Devonport were "disjointed from the county " and the boroughs granted a common Recorder, with separate sittings.

The enfranchisement of Devonport was the prelude to the demand for municipal privileges. There was a prescient recommendation from the Boundary Commissioners that the Three Towns should be constituted one Corporation, and Devonport welcomed this proposal as pregnant with immediate and ulterior advantages. Then a section protested that interests, habits, prejudices and passions were opposed to the union, although it was admittted that expense would be saved by having one Court, one Recorder, one Chief Magistrate, and one Police Establishment. It was further argued that amalgamation would embroil Plymouth and Devonport in perpetual contests over precedence and choice of officers. Mr. Ramsay maintained that the combined Corporation would be the Corporation of Plymouth, that essential business would be conducted in the older borough, and all the important meetings held and municipal records preserved in its Townhall. These arrangements, he contended, would be unfair to Devonport, whose population was as large as that of Plymouth. Amalgamation was supported by the Commissioners, who were said to dread the creation of a more influential authority than their own in Devonport. Their patriotism was impeached at a vestry meeting, roundly denounced there, and stigmatised as being "highly censurable and insulting to the ratepayers." A joint committee of the parishioners and Commissioners sat for two months, and the majority eventually recommended the demand for a charter. Plymouth had debts—Devonport had none. Plymouth had corporate property—Devonport had none. Plymouth was an ancient and commercial town, whose interests, habits and peculiarities were distinct from those of Devonport, where people depended for their prosperity on the establishments and services. Whilst Devonport was thus anxious to secure independence, Plymouth was as little disposed to encourage union. At the eleventh hour there was a mood of reaction, for the probable cost of incorporation troubled many Devonport people, and an economist meeting was summoned. The Admiral-Superintendent granted the dockyardsmen two hours for dinner, instead of one, so that they might attend in force ; and, after tumultuous interruption, it was decided to defer judgment until a financial estimate of the cost of a charter was submitted. An assurance was received that it would not exceed £150, and by unanimous consent a petition was approved of which the principal clause ran :·

"Your petitioners beg leave most humbly to represent to your Most Gracious Majesty that the town of Devonport and parish of Stoke Damerel aforesaid, of which we are inhabitant householders, is not a town corporate, but your petitioners submit to your Majesty that it is expedient that the said town and parish of Stoke Damerel, of Devonport, should be incorporated. Your petitioners therefore most humbly pray that your Majesty will be pleased, under the above provision of the said Act, to grant to the inhabitants of the said town and parish of Stoke Damerel, of Devonport, a separate charter of incorporation ; and that your Majesty will also be pleased by such charter to extend to the said inhabitants, within such district as shall or may be set forth in your Royal Charter, the several powers and provisions in the said Act contained. And your Majesty's petitioners, as in duty bound, will ever pray, etc."

In compliance with this appeal the charter was granted :

"We, therefore, as well by virtue of the powers and authorities vested in us, as by virtue of the powers and authorities given to us by the said recited Act for the regulation of the Municipal Corporations in England and Wales, do hereby grant and declare that the inhabitants of the town of Devonport and the parish of Stoke Damerel, comprised within the district herein-before described, and their successors, shall be ever hereafter one body corporate and politic in deed, fact and manner, and that the said body corporate shall be called the Mayor, Aldermen and Burgesses of the Borough of Devonport in the County of Devon."

The number of electors for municipal purposes was less by nearly one hundred than that registered under the Parliamentary, or £10 franchise—a difference attributable to the three years' residential reservation, which was more operative in seaports than in inland communities. Attempts to avert the introduction of party politics in the first elections proved futile, and 22 Whigs, 3 Moderate Radicals, 7 Ultra-Radicals, and 6 Conservatives were returned. The first Mayor was Mr. Edward St. Aubyn, (in whose favour Mr. Glad-·stone subsequently restored the baronetcy that had lapsed), who, on his unexpected accession to the estate in 1864—when the Rev. W. J. St. Aubyn was ignored as the eldest son and the property conferred upon the youngest—presented the Corporation with the massive gold chain worn by subsequent Mayors. Mr. T. Woollcombe was chosen as first Town Clerk. Before the agitation had passed there was a feud between Mr. Ramsey and Mr. Elms, the leaders of the opposing parties. Mr. Elms charged Mr. Ramsey with destroying books and unsatisfactorily accounting for the parish funds, and explained that he indulged in this language because Mr. Ramsey had published anonymous aspersions on himself in journals which he financially controlled. Mr. Ramsey was unable to deny the authorship of these contributions, and, Mr. Justice Denman expressed regret at the trial that a magistrate "should have condescended to write such scurrilous and abusive letters." The jury gave only nominal damages, and the Judge refused to certify for costs.

Jealousy towards the new body found expression in December, 1838, when the Earl of Durham was formally received by the Mayor in the Town Hall. There the Commissioners had been formerly supreme, but, on this occasion, they were not admitted to the ceremony. Smarting under the snub, they met to consider the conduct of "those individuals" who had so promptly ignored their existence. A resolution of scathing censure was passed upon Mayor, Council and officials, and this "foreign interference with the rights of the rate-payers" was denounced as a "gross insult." An amendment was moved to omit the word "gross," but the majority adhered to it. In acknowledging this reproach, the Town Clerk explained that the idea of intentional unpleasantness "must be universally scouted and ridiculed."

Mayoral elections were characterised by much scheming. On one occasion, when the parties were closely balanced, the minority tried to turn the scale in the absence of a Councillor who was lying seriously ill in London. This gentleman was surreptitiously brought down, and concealed in the Mayor's Parlour; and, when the votes were called, he was escorted into the hall to the dismay of the antagonistic plotters. At a subsequent election there were four candidates, and the disorder was so deafening that Mr. John Beer urged that Devonport should be relieved of the incubus of Incorporation. The bye-play on such occasions was very free. One retiring Mayor, Mr. Billing, told Captain Somerville that, if he could depend on the wives, he could rely upon the Husbands, and that he would win in any case, since he had the best Ryder. The first act of another Mayor, on assuming the robes, was to accuse his opponent of being in his "dotage," and the Council loudly marked their disapprobation of this language. "The annual farce" was rehearsed at the house of the leader of the party in power, and there one aspirant slapped his breeches pocket and vowed: "I'm —— if I don't be Mayor." In the ballot he was "sold," and his chagrin was aggravated by the discovery that more papers were dropped in the box than there were Councillors present.

Business was embarrassed by disputes between the magistrates and the Watch Committee. The first altercation took place in May, 1839, when a fair was held in Morice Town, and the magistrates ordered the police to see that all public-houses were closed at the usual hour. By order of the Watch Committee the notices were disregarded, but heavy fines were inflicted on the defaulters. The magistrates also claimed the right of inspecting the police reports, and of authorising the issuing of summonses—to which the Watch Committee held that this limited their authority and abridged exclusive rights. The magistrates retorted that they were responsible for the peace of the town, and would be placed in an "awkward and dangerous position by assuming responsibilities without exercising corresponding powers." They also held that the law might be thwarted by the private feelings or interests of Councillors who desired to screen offenders. The question was submitted to the Home Secretary, by whom the opinion of the Law Officers of the Crown was taken in 1840, and communicated in the following terms:

"The Law Officers are of the opinion, that the Magistrates have no right to direct the Superintendent or Inspector of Police to submit the Reports of the Police (by which is understood to be meant the occurrence book) to the sitting Magistrates daily. That book is kept under the authority and for the information of the Watch Committee and the Magistrates do not appear to have any legitimate control over, or interference with it. But the Watch Committee does not possess any exclusive right of directing informations to be prosecuted before the Magistrates, in respect of offences which may become known to Police or to the Magistrates. Generally speaking, however, it is neither usual nor expedient that Magistrates should initiate proceedings before them in such cases as those referred to. Such a course must tend to render their decisions less satisfactory, and to lead to other practical inconveniences, and particularly in places having a Committee of the Town Council, on whom the duty of watching the conduct of the police seems to be especially cast. The Law Officers are of opinion, that persons apprehended for alleged offences, or bailed under the authority of the police, ought to be taken before the Magistrates, and the Watch Committee have no authority or jurisdiction over such persons."

Mr. John Bright visited the town in 1843, and the conflict of authority was revived. It was rumoured that there was a plot to create a riot, that the dockyardsmen had obtained leave to fan the flames, and that a gang of Chartists from Plymouth were "to be thrown as stinkpots or firebrands into the proceedings." Incitements to disorder were placarded on the walls, and, in the emergency, the magistrates instructed the Superintendent of Police, (Mr. Brockington), to distribute a sufficient force in the midst of the crowd. The Watch Committee had instructed him to hold the police in readiness, but not to introduce them into the hall, as their presence might precipitate a disturbance. Bewildered by the rival instructions, the Superintendent asked the Town Clerk what he was to do, pleading that if he obeyed the magistrates "the Watch Committee will discharge me." "You will disobey the magistrates at your peril," was the solacing answer. There was no real disorder at this Corn Law demonstration, and the Council challenged the Magistrates as to their right to interfere. With chilling courtesy, they replied : "With every disposition to treat enquiries proceeding from the Watch Committee with respect, we must decline to admit, by such a reply as the resolution requires, their right to question proceedings adopted by magistrates in the terms of their commission and on their magisterial responsibility. We have only, therefore, to state that, in the absence of the Chief Magistrate from the borough, on whom would more naturally have devolved the responsibility of taking precautions for the preservation of the public peace, we felt called on to issue the order in question, which we shall be fully prepared to justify, whenever required by competent authority so to do." A special meeting of the Council discussed the correspondence, and Mr. J. W. Ryder moved a vote of censure upon "this unnecessary and uncalled-for intervention." An amendment justifying the magistrates was supported with considerable heat by the Town Clerk, but the resolution was carried by 24 to 16. Upon this, it was protested that the "law-makers" of the Watch Committee were the "law-stretchers," and that the members of this "Modern Star Chamber" would soon become "law-breakers."

A fresh cause of scandal arose in 1848, when the Watch Committee complained that the magistrates were lax in discharging their duties, and that their connivance at breaches of the licensing laws was "disgraceful." One case was quoted in which a summons against a publican was dismissed, and a brewer who was the owner of the house sat on the Bench. It had now become impossible to secure convictions for licensing offences, justices encouraged the endowment of low houses, and dens of vice were established whose "outpourings polluted the neighbourhood in which they were situate." So that the balance of imputation was not uneven.

The subject was revived in 1891 when the Rev. W. Mantle gave evidence before the Royal Commission on Licensing, in which he imputed that the integrity of judgment of the Watch Committee could not be depended upon, and that suggestive scenes had been witnessed at meetings among the members. He also declared that it was common knowledge that certain licensed premises had been favoured, and that they were used by leading townsmen as clubs in violation of the law. The answer to these statements was given by Mr. Hornbrook, then chairman of the committee, who protested that the interests of the public were safer in the hands of a large body of men, of divided political opinions, than in the arbitrary discretion of a teetotal chief constable. The Council, at a special meeting, approved by a large majority the principle that the *status quo* should be preserved.

Cholera, Small Pox and Insanitation: 1827-1899. The Three Towns were periodically decimated by small-pox and the heaviness of the affliction was due to the persistence with which, in spite of the medical manifestoes, parents insisted upon inoculating their children. The disease made frightful ravages, every other person walking in the streets appeared to be disfigured, and the few ladies who escaped with their beauty unimpaired were more than ever admired. The small-pox outbreak was to be followed in 1831 by a more devastating visitor—the cholera, which stalked through the Three Towns like a scythe-armed spectre. Zealous advocacy on the part of the doctors led to the creation of a Local Board of Health, Plymouth and Devonport were mapped into districts, and empty buildings were hired as hospitals. Attempts to remove poor patients were attended with fanatical protests, and agonised creatures were rescued from the nurses and restored to their homes to expire of fright and exhaustion. This objection to removal was due to a suspicion—which disclaimers failed to eradicate—that the doctors desired subjects for dissection, and the prudential prohibition to admit to the mortuary the friends of those who expired lent colour to the superstition, and occasioned repeated riots. Heroic medical men were followed through squalid districts by women and children, who shouted insulting epithets, and a manifesto was placed on the walls contradicting "the false and malicious reports" in circulation, and assuring the public "that no post-mortem examinations" had been conducted without the consent of relatives. Every other person who was attacked suc-

DOCK.

THE undersigned Medical Gentlemen of this Town have seen with extreme concern, the late malignancy of the SMALL-POX, which, in several instances, has again swept away nearly whole families. They lament these effects of this destructive disease more at this time, *because they have immediately arisen from the introduction of it by Inoculation*—a practice which, from its commencement, has, by maintaining a source of perpetual circulation to this fatal poison, added considerably to its general mortality. Adverting to these irresistible facts, they have again consulted together, and, after the most deliberate re-consideration of all the existing circumstances connected with VACCINE INOCULATION, feel themselves *conscientiously* and *professionally* called upon to adhere to their former resolutions and reciprocal engagements, and have accordingly renewed their *determination* not to inoculate for the Small-pox, excepting after the inoculation for the Cow-pox; and that only in peculiar circumstances, where an experiment may be required to satisfy doubting parents; but in no instance can they *recommend* the exposure to so malignant a poison.

They judge the communication of these resolutions, coupled with the practice of inoculating *their own families with the Cow-pox exclusively*, the most decisive and satisfactory means of conveying to the public their perfect reliance on this mild preventive for protection against the Small-pox.

While the undersigned are industriously and disinterestedly endeavouring to remove *so pestilential a disease* from this town, it would give them the highest satisfaction to see the medical gentlemen in the neighbouring towns generally and unitedly engaged in adopting similar means to accomplish so desirable an end. In prosecuting, therefore, the attainment of a great public benefit, by a means sanctioned and recommended by the Legislature, they deem it no deviation from the strictest attention to *professional etiquette*, respectfully to solicit the co-operation of their medical brethren.

VAUGHAN MAY, M.D., ROBERT SARGENT (since dead), DANIEL LITTLE, RICHARD DUNNING, DIGORY MORRIS SPRY, JOHN SMITH, JOHN LOWER, JOHN PENKIVIL, JOHN BONE,
SURGEONS.
December 18, 1804.

In consequence of a recent melancholy termination of a case of *inoculated Small-pox* in this neighbourhood, we, the undersigned medical gentlemen of this town, feel it a duty incumbent on us to declare our *present sentiments* to the public on Vaccination, or Cow-pock Inoculation; which we conceive cannot be better done than by republishing, as above, our former resolutions, entered into on the 18th of December, 1804.

VAUGHAN MAY, M.D., RICHARD DUNNING, DIGORY MORRIS SPRY, JOHN J. SMITH, JOHN LOWER, JOHN PENKIVIL, JOHN BONE,
SURGEONS.
Dock, 6th May, 1809.

cumbed; and, for awhile, the doctors despaired of arresting the plague. Improved methods of treatment resulted in the reduction of the mortality to one-third, and eventually ignorant and prejudiced people were impressed by the devotion of the medical men, aided by private citizens, some of whom were attacked in the course of the work. The neigh-bourhood of "The Marsh" (Union Street) and Sutton Pool were festering scenes of squalor, and, alarmed by the reports of horrors witnessed in these districts, the wealthier classes left the town to reside in the moorland villages : only to find that every hamlet became contaminated and that they were just as safe in their own homes. Months passed before the disease spent itself, and the bereaved carried the corpses to the cemetery in unfinished coffins. Poor families were wholly swept away; and, in not a few instances, only one member—and that a child—lived to tell the tale. After the terror had ceased, a medal was struck in honour of much self-denial, and the medical men were presented with snuff-boxes bearing inscriptions that testified to their "humane and unceasing attention to the poor during the awful visitation of malignant cholera at Plymouth, A.D. 1832." A silver salver was also given to Captain William Furlong Wise, R.N., the hero of San Domingo in 1806, whose humane efforts during the epidemic were especially conspicuous.

In the early decade of the 19th century, a stray farm dwelling was to be seen in the Mutley or Mannamead district ; the Copperhouse Fields occupied the site of Ham Street ; there stood a solitary farmstead on the site of Five Fields, and pasture land stretched to the bottom of Cambridge Street. Tothill area was purely agricultural and the only dwellings at Woodside were the mansions occupied by the Bewes and Colomb families. There were a few detached residences in George Street, with large gardens in front and at the rear ; and, in one of these, Mr. Nicholas Lockyer tried the prisoners during his Mayoralty. A lake occupying the site of West Hoe Baths emptied itself into Sandy Cove, and the Millbay Soap Works were ultimately erected on this spot. Deep water ran up the Millbay Road, and the tide flowed along the course of the tram rails in Union Street. At the Plymouth end of this road, where the ground was solid, near the site of the Farley Hotel, a few substantial residences were enclosed by gardens. One of these, which existed on the site of Athenæum Lane, was occupied by the Pridhams, and thence to Barley House, the mansion of the Elliot family, the landscape was uninterrupted. Whenever the Pridhams and the Elliots desired each other's company at night they con-veyed the signal by waving a lamp from an upper window until the glimmer attracted attention. The Crescent, an old burial ground for the French prisoners, was levelled for farming purposes, and the first crop was a prolific yield of turnips. Down by the fore-shore, where Caroline Place stands, there was a quarry worked by a worthy of the name of Peter Simmons, who also hollowed out Battery Hill in the same vicinity. The old Victualling Yard was at Lambhay Point, and the site of the existing establishment was rocky foreshore. There were turnpike gates at Mutley, Union Street, Millbay Road and Stonehouse Lane.

Eldad, Stoke, and Morice Town were scattered hamlets, and there was no inn near Millbridge for the convenience of travellers, or for belated husbands to assure their wives that they had been "No Place." This particular road was avoided, because of the dread of footpads and "pitch-plasterers," and the most favoured thoroughfare to Devonport was via Millbay, the Marine Barracks and the Halfpenny Gate. Devonport itself was a dismal place after the wars, badly lit and lifeless. The existing Park was a wilderness known as the Brickfields, and the present Brickfields went by the name of Parsonage Fields. Entrance to the town was gained by a series of drawbridges, one at the top of Stonehouse Hill, another on Newpassage Hill, and a third at the entrance to Fore Street. Dilapidated huts were distributed over the area of the present Raglan Barracks, and in these the artillery and line regiments were accommodated. Blockhouses at Longroom and Stoke received the militia, and the married couples were housed in St. George's Barracks on Mount Wise. The site of Keyham Yard was agricultural land, and Navy Row—the present Albert Road—was the only pretence to a street in Morice Town. An official residence for the Port Admiral was in 1809 erected on the site of the old mansion at Mount Wise, and extensive fortifications and ramparts were being thrown around the town when the cessation of campaigning caused the officials to condemn the scheme as useless. It was completed a few years later with a view of giving work to the unemployed.

The cholera made its second appearance in Plymouth in 1850, and ten per cent. of the population were attacked. Nine hundred victims succumbed; but, as in the former outbreak, it was impossible to ascertain the full extent of the calamity. It was in Stonehouse Lane that the direst effects were experienced, for it was a separate town in itself, without streets or squares—a mere conglomeration of alleys, courts and backlets, all of them badly drained and unventilated, with "filthy rooms crammed with filthy people." The area was so overcrowded that medical men could make no headway, and a wooden hospital was erected on the site of the Five Fields. There the prejudice against removing the stricken again gave rise to rioting, and it was only by exercising a strong will that the authorities could mitigate the epidemic. Clearing each house in turn, the inspectors took charge of the bedding and burnt it, then the fire engine was brought into play, houses were saturated within and without, and premises were fumigated. Miss Sellon and her Sisters of Mercy moved about "like ministering angels," and the Rev. George Prynne, Mr. Thomas Morrish and Mr. Joseph Beer "literally stood between the living and the dead," consoling and ameliorating the lot of those who were deserted by their friends. Mr. Beer died before his services could be rewarded, but the heroism of Mr. Morrish was recognised by a public presentation. When the plague had exhausted itself, the Rev. J. Odgers and other philanthropists set forth in plain language the conditions that prevailed in the narrow, crooked and steep back streets of Plymouth, with their loosely-jointed pavements and dirty water-surface channels. Irregularly built, both as regards elevation and architecture, the former mansions of merchants of high degree were now the resort of the "improvident, vagrant, vicious and unfortunate." The quaint carving on the stonework looked out of place, the gables were shattered, and the surfaces were blotched by foul weather stains. Houses were divided and sub-divided on every floor, staircases were darkened and massive balusters broken, once firm handrails were ricketty, the stucco was blackened and in holes, and the laths dusty and rotten. On the landings, where the space was open, there were neither panes nor glass, and improvised doors led to make-shift tenements. Rude-looking poles from which clothes were hung to dry were extended at every window, and the play of air was thus obstructed. More especially filthy were Lambhay Hill, Looe Street, Castle Dyke Lane, Castle Rag or "Damnation Alley," Arches Row, Cambridge Lane West, Catte Street, and Stonehouse Lane. Without check or remonstrance, pigs and fowls were bred in cellars and gardens, most houses were without water, and there were no facilities for removing offal. White's Lane, Stoke's Lane, Pin's Lane, and Garrison Lane were thick with filthy accumulations; few of the backlets were provided with closets, washhouses or drying places; and drains were considered a doubtful luxury.

Improvement had been attempted at Devonport some years prior to the visitation, but the manorial system accustomed the inhabitants to look to the Lord of the Manor instead of trusting to their own efforts. The sites for the Town Hall, Public Library, Mechanics' Institute and various places of worship were invariably granted in answer to memorials requesting free gifts on public grounds; but streets remained unwidened, obstructions continued to exist, and slums were untouched. Plymouth had advanced so rapidly

THE CHOLERA PHOBIA.

" There is nothing like leather."—OLD FABLE.

A meeting took place on Tuesday at the Plymouth Town-hall, to consider plans for preventing cholera. Dr. ——— having consented to take the chair, recommended above all things that the public would bear in mind the proverb—" That he who is his own counsellor has a fool for his client," and apply the same to medicine—" He that is his own doctor has a fool for his patient." Dr. ——— begged them to prevent their friends administering any of their own nostrums, but on the appearance of the slightest symptoms send at once to — —street.

Messrs. ——— and ——— both observed, that any one staying at their establishments may consider themselves in perfect safety, as their *larders* and *cel'ars* present such means of keeping up the *vital action* so much spoken of, that they bid defiance to cholera or any other pestilence.

Mr. ——— considered that the vital energy was best promoted by the exclusion of *cold*, and recommended an inspection of his *"double-mill'd for G'eat Coats, Trowsers, &c,"* which he assured the meeting was "cholera-proof."

Hot flannel and blankets being particularly recommended by the Physicians, Mr. ——— hoped his advice would not be disregarded when he solicited an inspection to his *"real Welch, warranted not to shrink;"* likewise that their wives and daughters would not forget his stock of muffs and boas.

Mr. ——— begged to say, that though he had read that fable of Æsop's closing with the words "there's nothing like leather," yet he had nothing but the public weal at heart when he suggested his *"double-soled Wellingtons,"* likening the constitution to a building, the foundation of which, if allowed to get wet, the whole is soon in ruins.—A voice here exclaimed, " the roof should be kept dry also," and on looking round we discovered his neighbour, Mr. ———, the umbrella-maker.

Mr. ——— next addressed the meeting and said, that he was happy to find the recommendation of the Board of Health, respecting *brandy*, had not been overlooked; as the order-book of his firm had lately offered a specimen of the anxiety of the good folks of Plymouth to be provided in that particular, but he begged to add, that the Board did not forbid the moderate use of *Port, Sherry, Claret,* or any other of the "exhilarating liquids," with which their stock abounds.

One of the *Ladies* from the *Fish market* here popped her head in at the door, and entreated them to preserve their bodies by the purchase of "soles," and not to despair while there was a *ray* of hope left. After saying this she took to her (h) *eels.*

Mr. ———, solicitor, begged to remark, that in case " the worst came to the worst," how important it was that " *wills, deeds of gift, &c.*" should not be delayed 'till the last moment, and thought that a call at his office would not be unbecoming at the present period.

Just as the meeting was breaking up, in came that staunch reformer, Mr. Thomas Hynes, who stated that the cholera spared all troubled with the "*Caledonian Cremona,*" alias " *Scotch Fiddle,*" which habit had rendered " no trouble " to him, and that he would be happy to visit any family for the purpose of introducing that sure preventive. This speech was received with shouts of applause, and Mr. H. was overwhelmed with *invitations.*

to commercial success that the Court Leet jury at Devonport recommended the manor authorities to resume perpetual renewal and the commutation of existing leases. In the fear that this departure would involve "legal doubts and personal risks," owing to the " very peculiar circumstances in which the property is placed," the trustees declined to sanction so large a change. They offered, however, to encourage new houses "of a superior class" by conceding terms of from sixty to ninety years; and also undertook, where leases had been granted on three lives subsequent to 1842, that the lessee "may hereinafter renew within one year after the dropping off of each life, on payment of a fine, to be calculated with reference to the ages of the existing lives, according to tables which will be prepared and kept at the Manor-office and be open at all times to the inspection of the lessee." Whilst symptoms of comparative improvement were abroad, the second cholera visitation occurred, and found the purlieus of Quarry Lane in a "beastly state from end to end," the houses " being worse than the commonest privies." There were loathsome cesspits and temporary contrivances, improvised drains overflowed through dilapidations, and the effluvia was intolerable. Every room was crammed with "wretched, beastly and degraded creatures swarming with vermin and wallowing in filth"; tenants washed and dried their clothes in the rooms in which they ate, drank, slept and cooked; and "the fœtid and sickening smell arising from these abodes of wretchedness baffles all description, and is enough to produce the worst consequences." Quarry Court was a similar abode of misery, "calculated to sicken the heart and create abhorrence, disgust and pity." It swarmed with children "who border on a state of nudity," and the women and men were not much better clothed. Anæmic infants and adults laid on foul palliasses stretched on mud floors, and in the courts pools of stagnant water collected. Morice Town was "the haunt of every vice and misery of which human nature is capable"; every

FF

third house was an inn ; and children swarmed the lanes in "absolutely heathen ignorance." In his report, Mr. Rawlinson, the Local Government Board Inspector, declared that Plymouth and Devonport took rank with Warsaw—the most insanitary town on the Continent. These strictures were resented by the Plymouth Improvement Commissioners, who were rewarded for their neglect and remonstrances by an act that improved them out of existence. An attempt was made to relieve the overcrowding by erecting the Shaftesbury Cottages. Nothing was done in Devonport, however, until 1858, when Dr. Row impeached the manor authorities for allowing the abandoned workhouse in Duke Street to be colonised by 227 persons. A demand was raised for model dwellings, baths and washhouses, and a deputation was appointed to meet the ground-rent land-owner to promote these purposes. Difficulties arose as to the suitability of sites, and neither project was further prosecuted.

Plymouth complied with the spirit of Mr. Rawlinson's report as funds permitted. Two schemes of improvement were laid down—a main line through Old Town Street, Bedford Street, George Street and Union Street, and the clearing of the district around Sutton Pool. Old Town Street at this time was narrow, winding, and on an incline, and various properties were purchased to facilitate access. Notte Street and Woolster Street were also thrown back, and "Stone-in-Darns," a quaint group with time-worn pillars, was swept away. The Duke of Cornwall Hotel was built on Millbay Grove ; Five Fields gave place to North Road, with its avenues of terraces ; and the level sward of Ford Park and the slopes of Mannamead became dotted with villas. ˌCharles Place and South Devon Place were thrown out as the advance guard of that army of streets and houses which has ever since been growing, and the sea breezes of the Hoe played around the Esplanade and terraces that followed in its wake. The conversion of the Barley Estate opened the way between King Street and North Road, and St. Michael's Terrace having been finished, the fields behind Houndiscombe House were given over to the builders. Then the Greenbank Estate was admirably planned for villas and terraces, and Prison Lane, which ran through that property, became Greenbank Road. In 1862, the Corporation removed the old ruins that surrounded the graveyard of St. Andrew's Church, including the quaint houses which first moved Samuel Prout to his reverence for the antique. They then widened Westwell Street to three times its previous width, so that there should be another leading thoroughfare to the Hoe. The old Lyceum and Four-in-Hand public-house thus disappeared ; but an attempt was made by Mr. Hine and others to save the Hoe Gate, whose removal was commended as an essential feature of the scheme. Apart from the spirit of utilitarianism, decency was said to forbid its continued existence, and the relic was sold for £44, the proprietor reserving some of the architectural ornaments and "the crock of guineas buried in the basement." This gate was the one remaining evidence of the circumvallation, and its removal was deeply lamented when demolition was beyond recall. It was the property of Plymouth in 1657, and was then leased "on payment of an annual rent of two shillings" to Mr. Alsop, member for the borough, as "all that piece, lift, gate or gate house, then lately new erected and built by the said lessee, and commonly called Hoe Gate." In the room over this structure William Elford Leach, the distinguished naturalist, was born in 1790.

Streets, lanes and alleys in Devonport vanished during the next quarter of a century, and ghosts of the past would have searched in vain for their former haunts. Near the gate in Fore Street stood the Dockyard Inn, with its pictorial representation of the entrance and a man ringing the familiar bell. Opposite The Dog and Pot, whose emblem was so repeatedly stolen by frolicsome seamen, was The Golden Lion, a famous white-ale brewery, the resort of local characters, of whom one was known as "The Walking Ale Can" by reason of his huge girth and tippling propensities. The Prince George Inn was superseded by Franklyn's Bar, and close at hand were Heydon's Rooms. Here a party of young officers promised to exhibit a "cherry coloured cat," and caused much uproar by producing a domestic pet of irreproachable black. When Fore Street was first remodelled the houses facing the site of the Public Hall were recessed beyond the existing street line, and the old-fashioned Rising Sun stood at the corner of Andrew's Lane, the narrow thoroughfare that led to Cherry Garden Street. The site of the existing South Western Hotel and Temperance Hall was a piece of No Man's Land, and here travelling showmen, menageries, Cheap Jacks and others pitched their tents and caravans. A butcher's shop occupied the site of the Post Office, and the way to Chapel Street was through Coxworthy's Court, a group of ancient tenements where many a deal took place in smuggled goods. The Crown Hotel vanished, and the Workhouse in Duke Street was demolished. Keame (Keyham) House still remained with its weather-beaten masonries—a delightful old mansion with quaint rooms, rambling passages and antiquated stairways. Its windows were furnished with stone sills and mullions, leaded lights and diamond frames; its hall was paved with marbles, and the porches were overgrown with plants. In striking juxtaposition to this mansion of the De Albemarles, the Steam Factory and Joinery were threatening to overlap its spirit-traversed corridors. As the past of Keame House was enshrouded in superstitions, so was its later record not without interest. One of the tenants, Captain Gennys, was in the habit of driving an equipage with four ponies, named Thunder, Lightning, Storm and Tempest; and, on the death of one of them, he caused it to be stuffed and placed in the hall with the fantastic trimmings in which it had pranced through the streets.

Plymouth was revisited by small-pox in 1872, and hundreds of victims were mowed down. Panic was so widespread that the newspapers were prevailed upon not to publish the daily death roll, and vaccination was almost universally accepted as a preventative. When the epidemic spent itself, and sanitary suggestions were advanced, a pamphlet on "Overcrowded Plymouth" was published by Mr. H. Whitfeld, as the result of a visit to the slums. The borough stood third on the national black list for herding; and, although houses had augmented, a new race occupied the new dwellings. Families who swarmed in dirty hovels a dozen years before were festering in them yet—the rooms as miserable, the alleys and lanes more mouldy, and the atmosphere pervading them a little mustier. These remains were dens of fever and immorality, after the manner of those which were cleared as the result of Mr. Odgers's visitation, and the prevailing condition was one room to one family, the single apartment often accommodating two sets of tenants. In Granby Green, King Street, Bath Lane and Octagon Cottages, mire and moisture suggested the swamp on which these huts were erected; the rooms were small, dark, damp and dirty, and the occupants so debased that layers of straw on bare floors sufficed for sleeping purposes. A primitive water-closet, with no flushing apparatus, ordinarily sufficed for sixty or seventy persons. Disgusting as were even the scenes by day, a second community rendered the district hideous by night—a population of the destitute and dissolute, who inhaled their own pestilential odours, and vanished with the sunrise. Castle Street—or "The Rag," in which every house was formerly an inn and every inn a brothel—had mitigated its character as the result of the courageous interposition of the Rev. Francis Barnes, who more than once entered its Infernos when nude men and women were dancing—causing the furies to decamp before his stern rebuke, and some landlords to disappear without even removing their furniture. The former taverns were now tenanted by scores of families, and some houses accommodated sixty souls. Palace Court, in Catte Street, where John Painter received Catherine of Aragon, and which is said to have been the early residence of the Abbots of Plympton, still remained—a stately edifice of three storeys, with massive walls

PALACE COURT, ON THE EVE OF DEMOLITION.—Site of Palace Court Board Schools.

(From a Sketch by H. Snell, 1880.   Photo. by H. T. Radford.)

of dark limestone, pierced with doors and windows, picturesque enough even now with those granite mullions and dressings, smothered corbels, whitewashed carvings and rich ribbed roofings of oak.   It was the home of as many families as it contained apartments. There yet remained in New Street the survivals of mansions and merchant houses, and under the withered whitewash could be traced oaken panellings and glorious carvings. Affluent adventurers of the Elizabethan era had dwelt in those reeking tenements, so that, as some of the older haunts were swept away, overcrowding had intensified in others to which the evicted resorted.   Dust, rust and rot had claimed Looe Street for its own, and its dilapidated mansions yielded from £60 to £70 a year in rack rents.   In Higher, Lower and Middle Lanes were clusters of tottering retreats for the infamous, and How Street was none other than a scattered and monstrous rookery.   When the existence of these plague spots was revealed, meetings were convened by the Mayor, an Artisans' Dwellings Company was formed, and their blocks of model dwellings were supplemented by others raised by Sir Edward Bates and Mr. John Pethick.   The movement was further stimulated in 1890, when Mr. J. T. Bond, the Mayor, conducted a slumming tour which resulted in the condemnation of a large section of Looe Street.   Provision was made for the displaced population at Prince Rock, and the reconstructed area was opened in the Mayoralty of Alderman Pethick in 1898.

Before leases on lives were conceded at Devonport, every street contained insignificant and incongruous elevations, with windows of small diamond panes.   After the concession the town awoke from its lethargy, and the main streets exhibited marked improvements. Keyham Factory was finished, Raglan Barracks were completed, and the fleets were more often in evidence. The flush of prosperity caused reconstruction to be steadily prosecuted, and Weakley's Hotel passed away with its romantic roadside memories. A few doors west the Fountain Inn was cleared, business premises rose upon the ruins, and "The Modern Pompeii," as Devonport had been designated, emerged from desolation into day-light. Mount Edgcumbe Terrace offered invitations to residential classes, Osborne and Wingfield Villas followed, and then Collingwood, Nelson and Argaum. Thus the suburb of Stoke became charming to view, and Mannamead advanced to greet her sister with grace-ful movement. The old Brickfields, or Ordnance Fields, were conceded by the military authorities and converted by ready subscription into a Public Park ; and the upland was cleared at a cost of £1,000 and dedicated to the recreation of the inhabitants. Upon the sites of notorious rendezvous, churches and chapels were reared. St. Mary's, in James Street ; St. Stephen's, in Clowance Street ; and St. Paul's, in Morice Square, were all built on land formerly covered by disreputable dens. Hope Chapel, in Fore Street, extinguished another "loathsome by-way," and the Unitarian Chapel, in Duke Street, blotted out a most unsavoury haunt. The old search for the Post Office in Ker Street revealed the state of affairs in that district, socially and structurally. Virtuous ladies, eager for a line from their absent spouses, were compelled to take a circuit of half a mile in order to avoid the insults of *Billing's Row* and the annoyance of Pembroke Street. Parents and children wondered what road to select and the worst nuisances to avoid. Sailors unable to find the way, but not brooking to be "baffled in the chase," stormed the roof of the meeting house on Windmill Hill. Quixotic adventurers in another quarter dared the dreaded, though disarmed, wind-mill to stay them in their career ; and, to complete the scene, those directed to the place gave sixpence to a bell-man, or letter-purveyor, for his services. After the tottering dwelling and narrow passage that supplied the entrance to Chapel Street were demolished, a new Post Office was raised, and open access was provided to Fore Street. The barrier gates were condemned as incommodious, dangerous and "a nuisance," and removed without regrets.

In 1855 there were only three freehold patches of land in the borough of Devonport —one of 32 acres, the property of the Couch family, and situate at Ford ; Earl's Acre ; and a portion of the Swilley estate, consisting of 51 acres. The piece of freehold land outside the manorial rights, belonging to the Couches, then became available, and attracted the eye of a local syndicate—the Devon and Cornwall Freehold Land Society. Mr. G. H. Rundle was the moving spirit in its formation, and Mr. A. Norman designed dwellings with open spaces that were unfortunately much abridged. Ford sprang into existence, to meet that demand for workmen's houses to which an unappreciative ear had hitherto been turned. At the manor dinner in 1872, the steward announced having made "careful enquiry of the number of houses he had himself authorised to be built since 1862, on ground belonging to Sir Edward St. Aubyn, and the total was 192 in the ten years. That was an evidence of prosperity which he thought was not at all discouraging." The condition of "The Cribs" next arrested the attention of the authorities. These warrens threatened to tumble around the ears of their occupants—persons so repellent that no citizen could enter without certainty of insult. Bragg's Alley, an infamous spot, once tenanted by Admirals whom Nelson was accustomed to visit, was now abandoned to corpulency and cracks, and the visitor wandered from court to alley, from alley to square, and from square to passage, until he despaired of escape from these "infernal regions." Bragg's Alley and its "island" purlieus were extinguished under an Artizans' Dwelling Scheme, which found in Dr. May an ardent enthusiast. The original intention was for the Corporation to complete the work they inaugurated, but the manor authorities recovered the freehold by erecting the houses, and the town raised to a common level the pits that abounded. As the result thoroughfares were widened, but the alterations intensified the overcrowding by driving the population into districts no less dense. In 1882 the Lord of the Manor reported at the court-leet dinner that the amount of building during the year had been limited, and was "chiefly confined to completing works already begun. By not hurrying on unduly they avoided the danger of over-building. It was a bad thing when the desire to build was greater than the demand for houses, and houses became tenanted by a class of persons lower than those for whom they were intended." Nevertheless the Devonport Mercantile Association, especially through Mr. William Lamb and Mr. William Ford, as successive secretaries, continued to press upon the different authorities the need of increased accommodation for the working classes, and Mr. Josiah Clark gave evidence on behalf of the town at the Royal Commission on Leasehold Enfranchisement, showing how closely associated were the depression for which Devonport suffered, and the dilapidations and overcrowding complained of. Mr. Kearley, M.P. reiterated the complaints in the House of Commons.

SECTION OF BACK OF MORICE SQUARE, DEVONPORT, 1895.
(Ordnance Row Area.)

In 1895 "The Boy From the Back of Morice Square" was brought to the notice of the Devonport public in an open letter addressed by Mr. H. Whitfeld to "The Lady of the Manor." As the outcome of pathetic revelations made by this typical street gamin, the Dockyard Dwellings Company was inaugurated, and land was conceded at sixpence per foot—subsequently raised to one shilling per foot—to admit of building operations without the interposition of middle-man or rack-renter. Under the title of "The Curse of Devonport," the same writer published a pamphlet two years later, of which twelve thousand copies were sold in one day. An extract from the preface will explain the purpose of the author :

"Proceeding systematically through the borough slums, I could not fail to be impressed with those recurring views of ruined and collapsed houses which a casual visitor from a volcanic country might be excused for regarding as the evidences of a nineteenth century earthquake. Whilst Plymouth, indeed, has still its overcrowding evils, and is trying to cure them, the Manorial System of Devonport results in structural decay and public indifference. The sanitary aspect, in truth, is almost inferior to the commercial consequences of that Leasehold Curse which has so long hung over the borough like a depressing cloud. Without malice, and extenuating nothing, the facts have been set

SECTION OF JAMES STREET, DEVONPORT, 1895.—Portion of Site of Municipal Dwellings, 1899-1900.

forth, in the hope that revelation may be followed by reform so comprehensive and complete that Devonport may not only vie with Plymouth in the application of social remedies in the interest of the poor, but may prevail upon the Manor Authorities to loosen that uncommercial grasp on available sites which has for years been the cause of impoverishment to nearly every class of its community by giving to land in the borough a purely fictitious and arbitrary value."

One of the most interesting of the experiences was encountered at the back of Monument Street, where the cells of the old Devonport lock-up were being used as living—and dying—apartments. The ascent of "Jacob's Ladder," as the place was historically known, was treated by the author after this wise:

"As we mount this Jacob's Ladder by one flight of stone steps, and wind our way downwards by another flight of a similar kind—for the malefactors were introduced by one route and the officials by the other—we begin to speculate whether the Lord may not be in this place—this Jacob's Ladder at the back of Monument Street—for the purpose of bringing home to the consciences of men in authority some sense of their responsibility. What must be the state of affairs in Devonport, when cells, that passed muster in the days before prison reform became a phrase, are still used for the habitations of young children ?   Does not the existence of this ancient lock-up, does not this survival of the unfittest in this locality, point the moral of these disclosures, and demand that the note of human honour shall be loudly sounded in the borough ! Just think of that sewage sodden shillet, with those excrescences in the form of dwellings, shored up and buttressed to prevent their falling into the lane, tenants and all—for the sickening mass lurches forward every now and then, and supplies new cracks for escapement—and then put it to yourself whether we have not here idealised the Curse of Devonport."

As the result of these disclosures public opinion was aroused in the borough, and the author of the pamphlet was elected by the ratepayers of one of the most overcrowded wards—Clowance—to stimulate the movement.   Feeling ran painfully high and incidentally led to administrative changes in the Council, Mr A. B. Pilling being elected Town Clerk.   Mr. Venning, who resigned that office, was presented with his portrait by

SECTION OF BACK OF MORICE SQUARE, DEVONPORT, 1895.
(Ordnance Row Area.)

many members of the Corporation.   The Mayor, Mr. Thomas Waddon Martyn, a young man of exceptional gifts, threw himself into the work with passionate zeal, and the movement promised immediate realization when his untimely death occurred.   An overwhelming demonstration of sorrow ill atoned for a loss which much retarded progress.   Mr. Whitfeld was subsequently elected chairman of the Housing Committee ; and wild rendezvous for cats and rats in Clowance Lane, James Street, and other districts were cleared and reconstructed.   The Housing Committee then undertook what their opponents ridiculed as a "holiday trip" to ascertain the methods pursued by other municipalities, and, on returning, counselled the immediate utilization of a site acquired for street improvement purposes in James Street, as also the area known as the Back of Morice Square or Ordnance Row.   There were the accustomed delays interposed by the Local Government Board, but, in October, 1899, in the Mayoralty of Mr. W. Hornbrook, the

REAR OF SECTION OF JAMES STREET, DEVONPORT, 1895.

foundation stone of the new buildings was laid by Mr. Whitfeld. The effects of the agitation, however, had already been to induce the manor to throw their land upon a more open market ; the inclusion of the free-hold system of St. Budeaux within the borough kindled for the first time in the history of Devonport the instinct of competition ; and hundreds of houses were raised in advance of the achievement of the municipal programme itself.

A comprehensive scheme of street improvement was carried out in Plymouth after the inauguration of the municipal tram service. Old Town Street was widened so as to admit a double line of rails, and a similar extension was carried through Ebrington Street that brought the business centres into immediate contact with the new town, which had sprung mushroom-like into existence upon the sites of the battlefields at Lipson. The Laira Bridge and Embankment were also purchased to complete the municipal design. The introduction of electricity as a means of lighting was consummated in the Mayoralty of Alderman Pethick in 1899, with Alderman C. Radford as the chairman of the responsible committee, and it was immediately applied to the traction of the tram cars, to the joy of Alderman Bray, chairman of the much-abused Tramway Committee. In 1899 the debt of Plymouth on Sanitary Account was £737,000. The leading sources of revenue on Corporate Estate Account were: Water, £20,967 ; Markets and abattoirs, £6,993 ; Royal Hotel and Theatre, £2,524 ; mills, lands and houses, £483 ; Guildhall and Municipal Buildings, £867 ; Laira Bridge, £2,192. The liabilities on Borough Fund account were placed at £960,792 ; and the assets consisted of the Reservoirs, £450,000 ; Markets, £100,000 ; Hoe, £30,000 ; Municipal Buildings, £66,000 ; Asylum, £55,000 ; Tramways, £71,500 ; Hotel and Theatre, £100,000 ; Laira Bridge, £37,000.

Plymouth Water: Through the Courts to Burrator : 1830-1899.   In 1830 lively controversy prevailed in the Three Towns as to the right to the Plymouth water. Mr. Bird, a popular solicitor, led the case for the public, his contention being that the water was left as a charity, and that the authorities had seized the supply to defray their municipal expenses. As the Mayor and his brethren refused to allow their title to be inspected, the suspicion grew strong that they were abusing "a sacred trust." Mr. Bird set himself to destroy "this Moloch of the Close Corporation," and added to their disrepute by exposing efforts to induce him to desert the cause. In May, 1831, the Attorney-General applied for a mandamus compelling the authorities to restore certain conduits on the ground that they were trustees for the inhabitants and mariners entering the port. At the beginning of the century the pipes supplied twenty-seven conduits, all of which were freely accessible to the townsfolk without any charge. The Commonalty allowed these facilities to fall into disuse, and, having stopped up every one, deprived the general community of access, diverted the stream into various mills, and, by means of leaden pipes, into the houses of the rich. Without applying for an empowering bill, they imposed a tax of 16s. upon each householder thus accommodated, and the general and free use of the commodity was withheld from the poorer classes. The Attorney-General contended that this was a perversion of the Act of Elizabeth and the Judges suggested an indictment. A meeting was accordingly held at which the townsfolk determined to prosecute measures for the restoration "of the ancient rights of the inhabitants to a full and gratuitous enjoyment of the town's water." Surveys of each street were taken to show the houses that had been deprived, and maps were made of the leat with a view of tracing the progress of the "usurpation" from the period when Drake first "brought the water to Plymouth." On appealing to the Courts, the promoters were told that the claim to enjoy the privilege without contributing to the maintenance of leats and conduits was extremely questionable, and the Attorney-General thereupon abandoned the application. In despair, the agitators turned to the Charity Commissioners, urging that Sir Francis Drake executed the undertaking "at his own expense," with the exception of the cost of procuring the Act and purchase money of the land over which the leat flowed. These arguments were in vain, and the only modification secured was a sliding scale of charges. This reconciled the small consumers to the alteration of the system, but their champions turned the agitation to account at the first Reform election in a squib issued to promote the return of Mr. John Collier. In 1853 the Council promoted a Bill to increase their powers, and a heated controversy resulted in its defeat, and the penalising of each gentleman who voted to promote the measure in the sum of £65.

Plymouth's right to the free use of the water flowing through the leat was contested in 1868, and safeguarded by Mr. Charles Whiteford, the Town Clerk. It was the contention of Sir Massey Lopes that the Act of Elizabeth did not endow the town with absolute property in the water of the Meavy, and that power to deal with the stream was only conferred for three purposes—the scouring of the harbour, the supply of the navy and the prevention of fire. Originally, it was argued, the domestic use of the water was not intended, and it was an unopposed Act of George IV. that created rather than confirmed the power. That measure did not, however, confer on the Corporation the monopoly of the water to the injury of riparian ownership ; or justify an extension of the supply outside the boundaries of the borough, as was now contemplated. Counsel for Sir Massey Lopes argued that a larger quantity of water was being taken for a different purpose from that conferred, and that he was prejudiced in the agricultural development of his land by the rights bestowed in the Act just obtained. The authorities had been empowered to prevent the fouling of the feeders of the Meavy and these were accordingly rendered unavailable for working china clay. Other mining operations were out of the question and the estate to that extent had deteriorated. The issues were referred to arbitration, and Baron Pollock held, and his ruling was confirmed by Lord Chief Justice Bovill, that the Corporation were entitled to all the water that entered the leat and to devote it to any purpose they pleased in the interest of the town. Arrangements were thereupon made to furnish the inhabitants with a continuous supply, and to devote the surplus to the encouragement of manufactures.

A succession of dry summers next placed the authorities in increased difficulty, and the piping of the leat only conserved a very limited yield.

Early in 1881 an acute famine was occasioned by a fall of snow which overwhelmed the stream and rendered the inhabitants once more dependent upon the wells. Water was sold by the barrel, and the stoppage of factories threw hundreds out of employment. The demand for a storage reservoir was thereupon advanced, and Mr. Hawksley recommended the Head Weir, around which Councillors and friends had so often drunk : " May the descendants of him who brought us (for a time 'gave us') water never want wine." Thereupon commenced the " Battle of the Sites," and the controversy was maintained in various forms for ten years. Sir Massey Lopes refused to sell the land which Mr. Hawksley had selected, and the Surveyor of the Corporation (Mr. G. Bellamy) suggested the impounding of the Harter Brook, which lay farther up the valley. The alternative was resisted upon the ground that the catchment was too limited to guarantee a full summer supply, and on the plea that the smaller yield could not be kept wholesome in the event of prolonged drought. Mr. Hawksley replied that a reservoir at the spot would impound 300,000,000 gallons, and the Council agreed to buy the land from Sir Massey Lopes for £5,000. A Bill was accordingly promoted, and at many a conference held in the office of the " Western Daily Mercury," first with Mr. W. Digby, C.I.E., in the editorial chair, and then with Mr. H. Whitfeld, as his successor, a raking opposition was organised by Mr. R. N. Worth, Mr. A. Debnam, Mr. W. N. Elliott, Dr. Merrifield and Mr. Cornelius Boolds. Literature was freely distributed on each side ; but, at the statutory meeting held in the Guildhall, the proposal was rejected. The majority of the Council persevered with the scheme until Mr. John Bayly presented the town with the land on the left bank of the Head Weir. This made the public more than ever resolved to thwart a proposal which was regarded as veiling an effort to assert a claim already overruled. Sir Massey refused to sell the remainder of the land, and a " Water Rights Association" having been formed, with Mr. J. R. Lake as chairman, Mr. C. C. Boolds as treasurer, and Mr. R. N. Worth as secretary, hostility was vigorously propagated by speech and pamphlet. As the flood of controversy rose, angry feelings were aroused ; and, after months of bitter interchanges, Sir Massey Lopes consented to sell his portion of the Head Weir land. When the trial pits were sunk to a great depth, however, the coverted site was pronounced to be " bottomless," with a bed-rock so remote that the construction of a dam could not be recommended. On the one side this report was received with distrust ; and, on the other, as an excuse for resuscitating the Harter scheme. The Water Rights Association accordingly retained Mr. Inglis to advise them, and he urged the Burrator gorge as being the best of all the sites, thus breathing new life into the suggestion which had been advanced by Mr. Beardmore forty years previously. The opposition to Harter was so pronounced that the ratepayers decided against it by nearly three to one. Mr. J. T. Bond now joined the crusaders ; and, with the resignation of the old Water Committee upon their defeat at the poll, he was chosen to succeed Mr. James Moon as chairman. The first step of an invigorated regime was to appoint Mr. Sandeman as water engineer, and to substitute Mr. Mansergh for Mr. Hawksley as consulting expert. An elaborate report was prepared showing that a reservoir at Burrator would contain 700,000,000 gallons ; and, consent to proceed with the work having been obtained, the Corporation determined to employ its own staff, the better to guarantee the stability of the dam.

It was the blizzard of March, 1891, that precipitated arrangements for prosecuting this gigantic task. In one night the streets of the Three Towns were covered with snow to the depth of several inches, trees were uprooted within the town, houses were unroofed, and attempts at vehicular traffic were abandoned. To add to the terrors of the night, a fire broke out at Wingfield Villa, and the flames could be seen from all parts of the Three Towns. Thick flakes of snow dropped upon huge tongues of fire, the falling water froze into fantastic icicles on the angles of the building, and the hair of Mr. J. Burns, the captain of the Devonport brigade, and that of his colleagues, was rigid from the same cause. Crowds of persons endeavoured to reach the scene by way of Millbridge, but the force of the hurricane rendered it impossible to pass, and the waters of Stonehouse Pool could be heard dashing against the walls. At daybreak, Plymouth was isolated from the rest of the country. Trains had ceased to run, several were snowed in, a few came into collision with serious results to life and limb, and the telegraph wires were everywhere blown down. Huge drifts blocked the doors of hundreds of dwellings, windows were enveloped in frozen

CLOCK TOWER AND ROYAL HOTEL DURING THE BLIZZARD, 1891.

(From a Photo. by Heath & Co., Plymouth.)

snow, and novel and beautiful effects were presented at the Clock Tower, Royal Hotel and Theatre, and New Guildhall. The Plymouth and Devonport leats were so buried under masses of ice, that the water supplies ceased to flow. The stream over the Head Weir was solid, there were mountainous drifts at Clearbrook, and at Yannadon snow fourteen feet in depth extended for half a mile. At the request of Mr. J. T. Bond, the Mayor, a regiment of soldiers was told off to assist a crowd of labourers in hewing a way through this Arctic visitation. Four days passed and, as the blizzard periodically recurred, soldiers and labourers grew discontented, trains were blocked, food supplies failed, and the army of succour almost broke into open revolt. But the Mayor, Mr. G. R. Barrett, Mr. Samuel Roberts, and others inspirited the workers ; a passage of three feet was cut through the drifts at the end of the seventh day and the water was restored to motion by men who kicked along sluggish masses of ice and snow with their sea-boots.

The experience stilled the contending voices, and it was decided to throw a dam across the picturesque Burrator gorge that should resist the weight of four times the volume of water that the valley was calculated to hold. Shortly, the scheme was to spend £150,000 in the provision of a reservoir more than 100 acres in extent, and having a capacity of upwards of 650,000,000 gallons, by damming the Meavy with a masonry embankment and laying thence to the service reservoir at Roborough a conduit consisting of iron pipes 25 inches in diameter. To the timid the scheme came as a shock—its magnitude frightened and its cost appalled. But Mr. Sandeman convinced the Water Committee of its practicability, necessity and cheapness. Mr. James Mansergh and Mr. James Topley, the geologist, approved the recommendations ; and Water Committee, Council, and, finally, ratepayers sanctioned the plan. So general was the confidence that, when the judgment of the town was invited, not more than fifteen rows of seats in the Guildhall were occupied, and these were rather " packed " than filled by workmen in the employ of the Corporation, and personal friends of the public men who were identified with the movement. The Bill received the needful approval, and a free hand was given with regard to the inevitable Parliamentary contest.

The Corporation Bill was attacked by numerous petitioners, among them Sir Massey Lopes, Lord Morley, and, oddly enough, Sir Francis Drake. East Stonehouse tried to secure its own supply by promoting a separate Bill, and the Devonport Water Company sought to extend their limits so that they might supply customers, present and prospective, whom Plymouth claimed as hers. The three conflicting Bills were referred to the same committee. The policy of Plymouth, after taking precautions against drought and frost, was to obtain as many customers as possible, and to secure a monopoly in Stonehouse, to the exclusion of Devonport. It was equally the interest of Plymouth to define and curtail the Devonport limits of supply, and to prevent her company from selling in the area claimed by Plymouth. The contest in the House of Commons lasted six days. Every counsel of eminence was engaged, and the best known water engineers were also retained. The assault on the scheme was feeble, and the attack on the Stonehouse proposals as searching and damaging. In the result the Plymouth scheme was passed ; its Corporation, by arrangement with Stonehouse, secured the monopoly of supply in that district ; the Devonport limits were carefully defined, and her company debarred from competing or supplying in the Plymouth territory. The contest was not renewed in the House of Lords, and the Act received the Royal Assent on the 10th June, 1893. The vigour which had characterised the Corporation and its Town Clerk (Mr. Ellis) still attended their proceedings; and so rapidly was the work pushed forward that, on the very day the Royal Assent was given, the legal formalities that enabled the land to be entered for possession were completely arranged. All documents were prepared, the Royal Assent was communicated by telegram, the dates of the documents were filled in, and they were delivered the same day. The land required for the works was bought for less than the original estimate, and the business so conducted that in no single instance was progress hindered for an hour by reason of legal difficulty or adverse claim. The rights of owners were examined and firmly, fearlessly, yet fairly, dealt with ; land in large areas was bought for less than £50 an acre—of better quality and higher value than that for which the Corporation gave £200 an acre in the "tinkering days" referred to by Mr. R. Burnard in his "Dartmoor Pictorial Records."

THE LAST FISHING FEAST ON THE HEAD WEIR SITE, 1898.

(From a Photo. by W. Heath, Plymouth.)

The first block of stone was blasted in the presence of an unusual gathering of ladies and gentlemen in 1893, the electrical apparatus that fired the dynamite being switched on by Mr. William Law, who for three years hospitably dispensed the office of Mayor. Progress was apparently slow, but it was certain. The face and top of the dam were built of square blocks of granite, and the core of huge masses of granite, buried in concrete of a density equal to granite itself. Between each block on the resisting side of the dam the spaces were filled with slightly damp cement, wedged in by iron chisels, and thus impervious water-tight joints were achieved, so far as engineering precautions could calculate. In all some 60,000 tons of material were built into the dam, and, as the foundations were excavated to 53 feet below the bed of the river so as to reach solid rock or avoid suspicion of crevice, the height of the structure from the lowest point to top of parapet was 145 feet, and a storage of 650,000,000 gallons was guaranteed. For months the Meavy was diverted by a tunnel through the dam, and, when the river was impounded, the tunnel was filled with concrete, and an iron shield was placed over its entrance. Near Sheepstor a second dam prevented the overflow of the reservoir at a point where the land dipped, and to reach the solid rock it was necessary to excavate through decomposed granite to a wholly unexpected depth. A new drive from Mullicroft Barn to Burrator dam compensated for the loss of the Sheepstor Road, and similar facilities on the other side of the valley admitted of access to Sheepstor village. A weir pool was formed outside the dam, to receive the overflow and satisfy the statutory requirement of 400 gallons per minute, or 576,000 gallons per day into the Meavy. The work was completed in September, 1898, in the third Mayoralty of

Alderman J. T. Bond, and the event witnessed the reconciliation of Sir Massey Lopes and his neighbours. Mr. Bond entertained the inhabitants in the Guildhall, irrespective of class, creed and politics, and hundreds of the leading inhabitants became his guests at the most historical of all the "fishing feasts." Special trains ran the invited ladies and gentlemen to Yelverton and other conveyances to Yannadon; and a lovely morning attracted so many thousands that the roads were almost impassable for vehicles and bicycles At noon the Mayor, Councillors and visitors pledged themselves, for the last time on the Head Weir site, to the pious memory of Sir Francis Drake—first in a goblet of water and then in a goblet of wine. An hour later, at the point where the leat crossed Longstone Farm, the luncheon was attended by hundreds of both sexes—for the first occasion on record. At its conclusion, the Mayor laid the memorial stone testifying to the origin and completion of the structure, and closed the valve to intercept the flow of the river. "In the name of, as well as on behalf of, and for the service of the people of Plymouth," Mr. Bond declared the stone to be well and truly laid, and congratulated his fellow townsmen upon the consummation of such "a rich and priceless possession." Sir Massey Lopes then presented him with a silver loving cup, as an earnest of his desire to live on the best possible terms with Plymouth, and a bumper of water having been exchanged, the Mayor revealed the fact that Sir Massey Lopes had transferred without payment the land on which the dam stood. Four hundred citizens were entertained at a banquet in the Guildhall, and each guest was presented with a bronze medal, on one side of which was a view of the Reservoir, with the words : "Belongs to the People of Plymouth," and on the other the inscription :

THE BURRATOR RESERVOIR. — OPENED 1898.

(From a Photo. by W. Heath, Plymouth.)

"Plymouth, 21st September, 1898. The Burrator Reservoir, constructed to avert the danger and hardship to which the town was formerly liable, was this day completed. This medal was struck to commemorate the event, and is the gift of J. T. Bond, Mayor, 1891-1896-1898." The year following the completion of this work Plymouth was visited by a drought of unusual duration, and the inhabitants of Devonport were partly supplied from the reserves which their neighbours had been able to make—the supply taken by the company amounting on some days to a million gallons.

Devonport and Stonehouse Water: 1793-1899. The Act for supplying "'Dock, Stonehouse and the towns adjacent" with water came into operation in 1793. An attempt was made to dispute the rates demanded by the company, and complaisance was then general until 1822, when Mr. Ramsey contended that "we have for twenty years submitted to as barefaced an imposition as was ever practised on the inhabitants of any town." It was the depression of trade that caused interest in the subject to be rekindled, and it was then ascertained that the company had been charging in excess of the Plymouth rates—contrary to the express prohibition in their Act. There was no necessity to appeal to the Courts on the subject, for the company admitted their culpability, and submitted to a reduction of their income by £1,000 a year. This diminution was not to the satisfaction of the directors, and they specially exempted the licensed victuallers, bakers and other large consumers. Aggrieved at this, the persons prejudiced combined to resist the increased rate, and the company cut off their supplies, a deprivation which was checkmated by establishing surreptitious connections with the pipes of sympathetic neighbours. The company thereupon advertised rewards to those who would undertake to convict the offenders, and "threatened to cut off the water from the house or office of any persons" who helped them. Application was accordingly made in the Court of King's Bench, in 1823, by Mr. Follet, at the instance of Mr. Matthias Watts, hotel-keeper, of Devonport, and a rule was granted that compelled the company to supply "on the same terms as the inhabitants of Plymouth are charged."

Elm pipes were used as the means of distribution, but there was no attempt at storage until 1830, when a site for a reservoir to contain four days' supply was utilised at Stoke. Before it was completed the leat was blocked by a heavy snowstorm, and the inhabitants were dependent on wells. When these began to give out and distress was universal, the Plymouth Corporation, who had maintained a free current by employing detachments of labourers, offered their neighbours the entire use of the night supply. Just as the connections were being established at Brooklands the thermometer fell, and the snowstorm was so heavy that the work could not be completed. Water was thereupon carried from Plymouth to Dock in hogsheads, for which 1s. 3d. apiece was charged. A town's committee visited the rise of the stream at Blackabrook, and, on returning from what friends of the company described as their "holiday jaunt," they despatched gangs to the scene of obstruction, and the leat was cleared. Having regard to the negligence of the company, the inhabitants refused to pay the water rate, and the vestry insisted on being reimbursed the cost of clearing the source. The company agreed to pay for the labour, but repudiated the expense incurred in "the jaunt to the Moor." They also consented to allow one-seventh off the annual charge as compensation to those who had purchased other supplies.

Devonport was aroused to the peril of its public health in 1868 by the contiguity of Dartmoor Prisons to the company's leat. The stream passed across uncultivated land lying between Princetown and the settlement, and the village soil was carried over the "cut" in a wooden trough, and that of the prisons underneath by means of a dyke. These troughs were so saturated that more sewage passed into the leat than over or under it. For the purpose of irrigation and manuring, the adjacent land was also traversed by open drains, and thus the surface overflow was carried direct to the stream. A dyke running parallel conveyed the drainage to the various troughs, and the contents had found their way to the supply. The condition of the banks generally was so disgusting that Dr. Munroe was called in by the Council to report in detail, and Dr. Wilson testified that monstrous rats waxed fat and sported in the leat by scores. Loud were the calls for instant redress, but the company argued that the Government ought to remedy the difficulty. Application was made in 1876 for an Act conferring power to carry out filtering beds and other works. Resistance to increased charges was unavailing, and the rate, which then stood at 16s., with 8s. for water closet, on houses within the lines, and at 20s. a year, with 10s. for water closet, on houses without the lines, was raised in harmony with rentals, the highest being £3 10s. a year for houses not exceeding the annual value of £80.

In 1895 the claim of the company to raise their charges in proportion to rentals or poor law assessments caused the company to stop the supply of Mr. Shannon, a tradesman of Fore Street. Consequent litigation led to a demand for the purchase of the works by the municipality, and the principle of purchase was endorsed by the Council in 1898. The sudden death of the Mayor, Mr. T. W. Martyn, who had animated the dry bones of Devonport by his reforming zeal, dislocated the plans with which he was identified. Some months later, Mr. Whitfeld, as chairman of the Water Committee, reintroduced the subject, and showed that, on the basis of a compensation calculated at £320,000, with repayment extending over sixty years, a temporary increase of threepence or fourpence on the rates would meet the expense, and the natural increment of population would enable the authorities to make small profits until the completion of the transaction. The opposition was led by Dr. John Rolston, on the ground that the company was giving a good and pure supply, and that the information forthcoming was insufficient. The resolution to purchase was carried by a small majority of the Council, and a hostile agitation being set on foot, an antagonistic committee was formed. A statutory meeting, convened at the instance of the opponents, was attended by over 2,000 people. Amid considerable excitement an adjournment was carried, and the audience numbered nearly 3,000 on the next occasion. The resolution in favour of purchase was carried by an overwhelming majority and a poll of the town was demanded. In the meantime the opponents of the scheme actively asserted that the loss to the ratepayers would involve an eighteenpenny rate. The issue degenerated into a November faction fight, and, as the substantial unanimity of the ratepayers was vital to the success of a Parliamentary application, and both parties were afraid to jeopardise seats, Mr. Whitfeld resigned the chairmanship. Dr. Rolston then accepted the position, but the committee would neither proceed nor abandon the scheme, and, on reporting the *impasse* to the Council, were formally dissolved.

Some Disastrous Fires: 1810-1897. Fires were the occasion as a rule of serious panics, for buildings were so closely herded together, and the means of suppressing outbreaks so limited, that the worst was invariably feared. Whenever the alarm was raised guns were fired from the ramparts, the drums beat to arms, lines of soldiery and sailors surrounded the district, the parish engine rattled to the scene, generally to be discarded by reason of rust or want of sufficient force, and an unending stream of workers passed in procession from wells, waterside or conduits, singing in hoarse chorus :

> Fire, fire, fire down below
> Bring a bucket of water
> Fire down below ! !

GG

A dreadful outbreak laid waste to Pembroke Street in 1810. Pans, pitchers and vessels of every kind were requisitioned to keep the engine going, but all such efforts were unavailing, and it was only by destroying the roofs of several houses that the progress of the conflagration was checked. Five men fell with a dwelling that collapsed, but, "strange to relate," they emerged unscathed from the smoking ruins. The "parish engine" made its appearance at a fire in Catherine Street, Devonport, in 1828. When the outbreak first occurred not a soul was to be seen in the streets, and the watchman did not present himself with his rattle until the flames had extended to the adjoining premises. The whole district was threatened for some time, and the troops experienced the utmost difficulty in preventing the crowd from plundering the deserted shops. An outbreak at once tragic and pathetic destroyed the residence of Fort Major Watson in the Plymouth Citadel in 1836. The crackling of the flames in the early morning aroused a servant, who ran to the door to give the alarm to the gunner. Some of the inmates escaped by jumping from the windows through the flames, but the Major, a tall and heavy man, fell into the furnace within as he was preparing to jump. Two of his daughters were shrieking for help, when the floor collapsed and carried them with it. The remains of the officer and his children were found in a heap "as though they had been consumed in each other's arms." Early one morning in January, 1840, smoke was seen issuing from the cupola of the Royal Hotel, Devonport. The seat of the outbreak was a bedroom occupied by Colonel Horndon, of Callington, and the flooring dropped before he could be reached, carrying the aged occupant with it. Guests and servants lost their way in the corridors, and it was only the shouts of the rescuers that enabled them to escape, blackened and burnt, to the open air. Bursting through the roof the flames shed an illumination over the town, and, with the collapse of the walls, the parish engine was buried beneath the debris.

TALAVERA.   MINDEN.   IMOGENE.

CONFLAGRATION IN DEVONPORT DOCKYARD, 1840.

The Dockyard was devastated in September, 1840, by a fire which was little less than a national calamity, the destruction resulting in the loss of two line-of-battle ships and a frigate. It was at four o'clock on a Friday morning that policemen on duty near the three northern docks were suddenly alarmed by the appearance of smoke from the bows of the Talavera. This, with the Minden, another 74, was being fitted out for demonstration purposes; and, in close proximity, was the frigate Imogene, which had been prepared for commission. Cries and shouts induced the sentinels to fire their muskets in the air, and, in a few minutes, a large force of military and police was summoned. By this time the interior of Talavera was on fire and the flames illumined the surrounding workshops, docks, and jetties, and a number of battleships in addition to those just mentioned. The ringing of the yard bell, and the firing of guns, summoned the engines from the various stations in the Three Towns, but their combined efforts failed to stay the course of the conflagration.

FIRE IN DEVONPORT DOCKYARD, 1840.
(From the Painting by N. Condy. Photo. by H. Lamb.)

The hissing timbers of the Talavera strained and parted with explosive gusts, and all expectation of saving her was abandoned. Attempts were thereupon made to preserve the Adelaide gallery, which, with its wide-spreading sheds, rose in imposing tiers to the left and right, the intermediate openings being filled with deals and loose timber. In this "walk," as it was called, were stored the mementoes of many a hard-fought battle, and scores of figure-heads of ships that had borne the brunt of some of the most famous naval actions in British History. At one end hung the flag under which Nelson fought and died at Trafalgar; and, at the other, the banner which streamed from the poop of the Queen Charlotte during the bombardment of Algiers. Here, too, lay the capstan of the St. George, only just recovered at Spithead after it had lain buried for fifty years, and a Sphinx which had recently been rescued from the sands of Egypt and was supposed to be three thousand years old. All these relics of former times, after having passed the ordeal of fiery action and rushing tempest, were now doomed to destruction, including the decorative devices that had borne the flags of Rodney, Duncan, Howe, St. Vincent, Nelson and Collingwood! The flames from the Talavera darted from under the coping of the shed in terrific volumes, ran along the paper-covered top, and engulfed the entire range of the gallery with its combustible contents. Roaring like a furnace the fire shot into the air; and thick masses of smoke rolled over the yard, now brightened to a dull red colour, as some portion of the building crashed, and then settling like a funeral pall into the surrounding darkness. From the roof of the Adelaide gallery the flames spread to the covering of the south dock in which lay the Imogene. The frigate itself was ablaze, and the fire attained such dimensions that the safety of the entire yard was seriously questioned. In the near vicinity of the Talavera lay the Minden, and again and again the flames played across her bows. Water from a dozen engines was continuously poured upon her main-deck timbers and the planks of the forecastle; and, by superhuman efforts, the Minden was saved from the fate of her neighbour. Meanwhile the flames raged with the utmost violence on board the Talavera and the Imogene, and along the sheds and the Adelaide gallery. As the dock occupied by the Imogene was surrounded by timber, and the stacks communicated with the sail-loft and storehouses, desperate efforts were made to destroy the connections. In an hour and a-half from the alarm the conflagration reached its climax; and broad streaks of fiery light played on the dark waters of Hamoaze and imparted to the opposite coast a gleaming radiance. At times, the spectators looked as though they were standing on the banks of a lake of fire, and the thick flakes whirled aloft from the burning hulls glowed like meteors in the darkened air. Amid hoarse cries, stubborn shouts, and wild cheers, the work of battling with this volcano went forward. Shortly after six o'clock the Talavera and Imogene were burnt to the water's edge, the pyramids of fire settled down for want of fresh fuel, and bare and discoloured walls alone remained of the sheds and stores. The disaster was variously attributed to dockyard discontent, official parsimony, and the plot of a foreign power whose spies were "seen gloating" over the devastation. The view that finally obtained was that the presence of combustibles was sufficient to explain the calamity, and that the use of coal tar to prevent the Talavera's timbers from contracting dry-rot accounted for her sudden envelopment.

In March, 1843, the Theresa Collier belonging to Mr. Thomas Billing, caught fire as she lay off Mutton Cove; and, as the hose from the shore was insufficient, officers and men promptly abandoned her. One man was forgotten, and a boy only escaped by using a blazing ladder. The overturning of a lamp on board the barque Cambridge, as she lay by the slip in Mr. Gent's shipbuilding yard, resulted in such a blaze that she was scuttled to save other vessels. She settled on the mud and one mass of flame played from stem to stern until the returning tide passed over the remains. An explosion in a shop kept by Mr. Isaacs, on the Parade, Plymouth, was accompanied by fatal results in June, 1848. The house was rack-rented; and, as escape by the stairs was cut off by the flames, men, women and children implored assistance at every window. Several inmates were saved by means of a long ladder, but this in turn catching fire when a man was ascending, he dropped to the pavement mangled and two children simultaneously fell into the flames. Faning's Rope Walk, which ran for half a mile on the other side of South Devon Place, caught fire in the hemp department one night in March, 1853, and extended to a dwelling house that adjoined the turnpike gate. The tenant, a custom-house officer, named Macey, placed his wife and four children out of danger, and then returned to rescue another daughter. The floor of the bedroom collapsed; parent and child were buried with it; and their remains were charred beyond identification. The thatched roof of the rope-walk and a hundred barrels of tar caught fire, and the premises were utterly destroyed. Devonport enjoyed immunity from outbreaks until February, 1855, when Mr. Hudd's spirit stores in Fore Street ignited. It was impossible to work the parish engine in consequence of the want of water, and the flames reaching to the opposite side of the street, roofs and walls soon crashed there as well. A piercing wind blew in furious gusts, and the frost coated the hats of the firemen and icicles formed on the scorched timbers.

Much argument had been expended on the proposed reconstruction of the Higher Grist Mills in Tavistock Road, Plymouth; but in 1859 a fire converted the ruins into a charred and blackened mass. There was an abundance of water for use, but the hose was of insufficient length, and the firemen were dependent upon buckets which they filled from a tank in the tanyard. Ere the engines could play, the buildings collapsed. Fore Street, Devonport, was canopied by streaks as of golden sand, in May, 1863. Mr. Emmett, the proprietor of some oil stores in Princes Street, descended to his cellar, to obtain a supply from a large drum, when the vapour came into contact with a lighted candle he carried. The premises were ablaze on the instant, and the flames, now bright when the turpentine was being consumed, changed to deep orange or vivid blue as the sugar or tallows were reached. The powdered remains of Mr. Emmett were dug out from the cellars; and the "Commercial Rooms," which were built by Mr. Thomas Husband "for reading and conversation," disappeared for ever. The Plymouth tanyard, opposite Sherwell Chapel, was destroyed in 1855 by a fire that originated in Mr. Caleb Trotter's coach-house, and then devastated the wools and hides. An outbreak in Stonehouse Lane a few years later, swept away a large area, and claimed a local eccentric, "Billy Buttons," as a victim. Messrs. Snawdon's furniture premises in Union Street were found on fire by a street sweeper in July, 1873. The family and servants only escaped with their lives, for a hard and shifty wind blew the forked tongues hither and thither. Several houses were simultaneously blazing, and the flames extended to Battery Street and Union Place.

Loss of life resulted from a fire in Looe Street in the early hours of Sunday morning, December 12th, 1885. The many inmates of No. 3, the original publishing office of the "Plymouth Herald," had just retired to rest when the alarm rang out, and flames belched from every window. There were from sixty to seventy people living in the house; and, as the neighbourhood was thickly populated, consternation was general. The majority of the inmates escaped by jumping from the window nearest to the pavement; but others who were aroused too late hung from the sills until the heat caused them to relax their grip, and they dropped with dull thuds to the pavement. An infant was thrown by its father to the crowd, and caught without injury. In all twelve lives were lost, one woman and her seven children being suffocated in a single apartment. The Presbyterian Church, Eldad, was burnt to the ground in 1882. The heating apparatus had been used the previous Sunday evening, and a defect in the flue occasioned a fire which had so far developed that the edifice crashed in before the brigades arrived on the scene. Deeds of heroism were witnessed, in 1886, at a fire which gutted the building in Cobourg Street, formerly used as the Blind Institution. Let to rack-rent, the rooms accommodated sixty souls, and, as the fire took possession of the stairs, exciting escapes were witnessed. At the height of the conflagration a distracted mother discovered that one of her children had not been brought out; and a young tradesman, Peter Whitfeld, mounting the ladder, shambled along a narrow ledge of parapet with his back to the wall. Proceeding through the dense smoke he went from room to room and appeared with the unconscious infant at a lower window. He then made his way along another narrow ledge with the little one in his arms—the crowd breathless with fear lest the two should fall into the street before a shorter ladder had been procured and placed in position. When the rescue was complete there was an outburst of cheering ; but there was, after all, one fatality to deplore. Whitfeld was presented with the Royal Society's silver medal for his gallantry.

Another fire in the Dockyard in June, 1894, was attributed to the act of a workman in leaving an unextinguished pipe in his coat pocket. The scene was a large store opposite the quadrangle in which the authorities reside ; and, the alarm being raised at ten o'clock on a Saturday night, an unmanageable crowd gathered in a few minutes, and the precincts were impassable. The store was full of combustibles, and the flames shot to a great height. Excitement was unbounded because the workmen dreaded a catastrophe that would deprive them of employment. In two hours, however, the fire was suppressed, and the building was gutted. Coils of steel were twisted into all conceivable shapes. Mr. Lancaster's factory in Phœnix Street was suddenly reduced to ruins in 1897. The alarm was no sooner given than the building was a blazing mass from end to end. Mr. Sowerby, the captain of the Plymouth brigade ; Mr. W. Blight, the captain of the Stonehouse brigade (with the steam engine just presented by Mr. J. C. Wills) ; and Mr. J. Burns, as the captain of the Devonport brigade, rendered splendid service. The loss was heavy, but Mr. Lancaster heroically set to work to repair it.

From the Russian War   A generation passed after Navarino and then the attitude of
to Keyham   Russia towards Turkey united England and France in support of
Extension : 1853-1899.   "the sick man." Steam was slowly asserting itself as the real method of propulsion and iron as the only defence against devastating shell. These discoveries were not all made at once, however, and the launch of the Phœbe, a frigate of fifty guns, shortly after the declaration of hostilities, showed that the faith in wooden walls had yet to be abandoned. The Phœbe was in her way a noble addition to the British Navy, and, as the Nile quitted her moorings the same day, the occasion excited unbounded gratification. The Nile steamed down the harbour against wind and tide, at no very dashing rate, as it was considered imprudent to strain her engines to get under weigh, but, after rounding Devil's Point, the speed was increased, and naval men were satisfied that steam would soon be the indispensable motive power. An hour later, the Phœbe was despatched from the stocks, and glided into Hamoaze amid loud and sustained huzzas. Intense was the interest excited by the launch of the St. Jean D'Acre, the largest vessel yet constructed for the reception of a screw propeller, the invention which was rapidly revolu-tionising naval architecture. By the connoisseurs she was voted a masterpiece of strength, and a superb combination of skill and beauty. Soon the country had need of every ship and seaman it could command. Drive was the order of the day, past errors had to be rectified, and wondrous things were achieved in incredibly short periods. The completion of the Exmouth was urged, and, amid the drinking of wine and the crashing of the indis-pensable bottle, she advanced to meet the rushing waters. Verses were distributed in honour of the hero of Algiers, admonishing Britons to keep their guns in tune, and to mark their log with one glass of grog "for another first of June." A few weeks later, on an ideal summer's day, the Conqueror, a line-of-battle ship of larger dimensions, although of the same class as the St. Jean D'Acre, was consecrated to her purpose. As the dog shores were removed, creak, crack, bang and away she drove from the dock, the spray dashing against her sides in salute as she bowed to the river, and turned with graceful movement to the harbour.

Stirring were the scenes as the troops embarked for the Crimea, and the excitement overflowed as the Hussars pranced into Plymouth, accompanied by a bucolic escort that received accessions from every village that the regiment passed through on its way. The streets were thronged as the gallant fellows made their picturesque ride into Devonport ; and after being billeted in the various inns, they assembled in Fore Street in the morning to gratify the populace.   Men and horses alike were in splendid condition, and mighty cheers were raised when they moved towards the Dockyard gates, holding aloft the flashing sabres with which they proposed "to shave the Russians."   As they embarked upon the transports, volley upon volley of cheering rose from the clustered decks of the steamships, and the cries were re-echoed from the manned yards of the picturesque three-deckers.   Similar demonstrations marked the departure of the First Royals, and, as the regiment marched from the Citadel, a sinuous red line of a thousand men was seen coursing its way through the serried civilian mass.   The soldiers jauntily returned the farewells, and from thousands there rose the strains of "Cheer, Boys, Cheer!" to the thrilling accompaniment of the Royal Marine band.   And so the fervour of the Three Towns was rekindled by these patriotic displays, followed by moments of serious anxiety.   Suspense was broken by overwhelming rejoicings when the success on the Alma and the storming of the heights of Inkerman came over the telegraph.   The vessels in harbour were resplendent with flags, salutes were fired from battery to battleship and from battleship to battery, and the church bells testified to abounding pride and universal relief.   The landing of hundreds of Russian prisoners from successive transports left no doubt as to the reality of the successes in the bleak Crimea ; and the Millbay and other barracks once more overflowed with prisoners. So taxed was the accommodation in the Three Towns that, when the Dauntless put into the port with a horde of half-clad wretches, the order was given that they should be carried to France.   Officers and soldiers alike pleaded to be landed at Plymouth, but necessity was

RUSSIAN PRISONERS AT PLYMOUTH, 1855.

imperative, and, when the men were hauled out of the holes and corners to which they had resorted in the hope of avoiding transhipment, many of them wept piteously.

In the absence of the regulars, Plymouth was garrisoned by the South Devon Militia and mercenaries from various European states who were known as "The Jagers." When they were first embodied the militiamen were slovenly, uncouth, motley, and unpromising levies of whom the officers despaired. But the men submitted to discipline and trained with remarkable aptitude, and, when volunteers were called for at the Citadel, two hundred of them walked out from the ranks and enrolled in the crack regiments. Accompanied by the recruiting sergeants, the batches were escorted through the town by military bands and marched to the transports amidst approving shouts. Various devices were employed to stimulate the recruiting ardour of the district. General Sir Harry Smith held a great field-day on Roborough Down, and the road to the moor resembled Epsom approach on a Derby Day. Lady Morley presented colours to the South Devon Militia at the Citadel, and, "in a clear and firm voice," testified to the valour of the men who had embraced active service. The Jagers failed to add to the comfort or confidence of the community by repeatedly rioting in the streets and byeways of Plymouth. By way of punishment they were removed to Maker, and from that time Cawsand and Millbrook existed in perpetual alarm. They by no means confined their outrages to the villagers, and occasionally drew their knives upon each other. One of them, Hans Hansen, battered in the head of a German surgeon at Millbrook, and robbed him of a remittance he had just cashed. After this the mercenaries were subjected to sterner discipline, and disaffection developing into mutiny, they were removed to Bovisand. Here the grievances of the privates were championed by one of the sergeants, and, at his instigation, a whole company grounded their arms in disobedience of orders. Without loss of time the insubordinates were marched to the Citadel under an overpowering escort of militia and regular forces, and, as these made their way through the streets holding triangles and "cats" aloft in view of the populace, the apprehension could not be suppressed. As soon as the soldiery reached the Citadel, the gates were closed against civilians, marines and artillerymen lined the ramparts, ball cartridge was served out to every man on duty, and a square was formed within which the chief instigators were tried. Until ten at night the Court sat, and the troops were again under arms the following morning when the ringleaders were lashed to the triangle and flogged till they fainted. The war was rapidly drawing to a close; and, as the services of the auxiliaries were no longer required, the Three Towns were relieved of "these troublesome friends."

Thousands journeyed by road and rail in May, 1856, to witness the commemoration of the peace. Church bells pealed, ships fired salutes, troops were reviewed in the Brickfields, and the artillery thundered forth their rejoicing salvos. After dark the fleet burst into a blaze of light, on an arranged signal rockets formed variegated devices, and illuminations culminated in an allegorical device of "Peace." Sailors paraded the streets with characteristic light-heartedness, crowding waggons dressed to represent battleships, beer barrels in front and drummers behind, with white flags at the maintops bearing skulls and crosses to indicate the prevailing passion for "death or glory!" Visiting admiral and general by turn, a vociferating concourse kept them company, and the "captain," a pewter pot in one hand and glass in the other, extended the hospitality of the "ship" to those ready to receive it. With the cessation of the war followed rigorous retrenchment and depression. The Dockyard regulations became more rigid, workmen were overhauled on leaving the shops, and officers were detained if they could not give the watchword after nightfall. Employés were often subjected to a second search, and, if a whisp of oakum were found, they were summarily discharged. So that the few survivals of hoary prerogatives were suppressed with merciless hands. The close of the war was marked, however, by an increasing tendency to more humane punishment. Although examples of petty tyranny were to be met with, the disposition was less brutal. Thus a carpenter's mate who resented the goading tactics of a boatswain by cleaving his skull with an axe was tried in Hamoaze and sentenced to be hanged. When the prisoner heard the decree he fell to the deck, but the persecution was so clearly established that he was reprieved, and the boatswain was degraded to the ranks. Another survival was doomed in 1859. A seaman was flogged on the deck of the Cæsar as the dockyardsmen passed on their way to Keyham workshops. Forming in a crowd, they hooted during the punishment, and Captain Mason, crossing on shore, arrested the leading man for looking on. It was contended that it was illegal to flog in the presence of the workmen ; but the leading man was suspended, and various deprivations were visited upon others who were identified. Threatening letters were sent to the officers of the Cæsar, and the controversy prepared the public for the abolition of the " cat."

In 1858 attempts were made to displace the mass at the entrance to Hamoaze, which was known as the Vanguard Rock, because a ship of that name struck upon it. One of the huge cylinders that had been sent out to blow up the sunken fleet at Sebastopol, and had not been required, was filled with a ton of gunpowder and sunk so that the end rested in a cavity of the rock. Efforts to fire the explosive by galvanism and safety fuses were continued until successful, the cylinder eventually bursting within thirteen minutes after the ignition of the fuse, and throwing up a cone of spray one hundred feet in diameter at the base and forty feet in height. So tremendous was the effect upon the surrounding water that sand and seaweed were piled in masses, the shore vibrated as with an earthquake, thousands of fish jumped into the air, and a heavy ground swell followed as after a storm. Many tons of stone were detached, and the rest was so split and cracked that the application of grappling irons and haulage easily effected its removal.

Over forty years had now elapsed since a squadron of the fleet cast anchor in Cawsand Bay. In the early days of the century Nelson's three-deckers were clawing off the shore. In 1872 Admiral Hornby's flagship was flying the signal " Prepare to ram," and ironclads were propelled through the water in pursuit of "a powderless programme." The old salts conjectured what the admirals of the Napoleonic era would have thought if they could have watched the winches, compressors and other machinery by which the Sultan's 400 pounders were moved with as much ease as the carronades of the old frigates, with their 18 and 32 pounders ! The spectacle of such a fleet of ironclads was no less a revelation to the Three Towns, and the Hoe was crowded with spectators when it steamed to sea. The personnel of the Navy was experiencing a transition no less remarkable, and a local humourist not inaptly soliloquised on the change :

> Ships are all of iron now,
> Floating tubs with rams for bow ;
> Nelson's tars would stare to view
> What the Navy has come to !
> Seamen walk in private suits,
> Smart felt hats and patent boots ;
> And they're all teetotallers : Gracious ! Whew !
> What is the Navy coming to ?

The Zulu War revived impressions in 1879, when the marines and other troops were despatched from Plymouth. Several hundreds of the former were paraded at Stonehouse on the morning of their departure, and, to add to the gaiety of the occasion, each man wore a sprig of green in his cap. As this decoration was contrary to service regulations, the Colonel-Commandant ordered the removal of the emblem with the pleasantry : "You may wear your laurels, my lads, when you return." The troops made their way to the Dockyard through a tremendous crush, and amid a ringing fire of cheering which at times overpowered the strains of the massed bands. The embarkation of the soldiery was soon effected, and the Jumna steamship moved into the Sound amid the vociferations of thousands of artisans who crowded the jetty, and tens of thousands of visitors who swarmed the slopes of Mount Wise and the rocks at Devil's Point. And so the brave fellows embarked to the strains of a song specially written for the occasion :

> So cheer up, my lads, let us join hands
> Like Royal Marines in our brotherhood bands,
> God Save the Queen, our watchword shall be,
> Wives and sweethearts at home and Zululand free !

Local interest in the struggle was displayed not so much when the news of the reverse of Isandula came to hand, to excite a wave of humilation and sorrow, as when the inhabitants heard with immense relief and pride of the glorious stand which was subsequently made at Rorke's Drift, at the instance of a Plymouth Grammar School boy, Major Chard. Elated by their victory, the Zulus were over-running the country, and it would have been no discredit if Chard and his comrade, Bromhead, had fallen back, as there were so many thousands of savage warriors in eager pursuit. Resolving to stop an onrush which would have placed the colony at the mercy of the dusky warriors, Chard strengthened the small station at Rorke's Drift, of which he had been left in charge, and, from behind a barricade of biscuit tins and mealy bags, he and his devoted little band fought for many hours, brave fellows continually falling around, and the contiguous farmstead ablaze, with wounded comrades within. Exercising unwavering intrepidity, Chard wore down the Zulus, the horde withdrew discomfited, and the credit of Great Britain was preserved. An old schoolfellow of Major Chard's, Mr. Eliot Square, who subsequently met with a tragic end, organised a movement for presenting the hero with a sword of honour. The land rang with the skill, coolness and determination of the brave St. Budeaux lad ; and, on three different occasions, he dined at Court and repeated to Her Majesty the thrilling episodes of his memorable resistance. Before Major Chard journeyed to Plymouth, Cetewayo, the Zulu King, was brought to the port a prisoner of war, and he left for London with as much attire about his prodigious form as when he was driven at bay after the battle at Coomassie. When he returned to take his departure he wore an irreproachable frock coat and silk hat, and his gloved hand carried a silver-mounted walking stick presented by " my brother, the Prince of Wales." Major Chard received the Plymouth sword in the presence of over three thousand leading inhabitants, and, when he acknowledged the gift, as he did in a few modest remarks, the ovation was overpowering. His regret was that Bromhead was not present to describe the satisfaction with which they refreshed themselves with a bottle of beer when, begrimed and dishevelled, they at last saw the swarm of Zulus dispersing over the plain. Then he lamented that his old master, Mr. W. Bennett, could not witness the compliment paid to one of his pupils, and, finally, he wished that he had been worthy of so much distinction. But the men of Plymouth felt their hearts overflowing at the knowledge that this shy, retiring, gallant stripling was the author of an exploit which ranked with those of the Armada hero, who once knelt in the village church where Chard so often worshipped. Twelve months later the British troops emerged successfully from Tel-el-Kebir, and the Plymouth detachment of the Royal Marines and members of the Royal Naval Brigade serving in the port were entertained at the Devonport Public Hall, and thanksgiving services were held in the local churches and chapels.

With the introduction of steam a large class immediately became unsuited for modern warfare, and wooden ships that had never been to sea were sold, broken up, or sent to swell the procession in Hamoaze, which became known as " Rotten Row." The disposition of these vessels occasioned the Government a vast amount of difficulty ; for, whilst they were inevitably abandoned, it was necessary to prevent them from falling into the hands of a hostile country. Eventually they were broken up in the private yards, under the supervision of Government inspectors, the copper bolts being returned by arrangement. At this period much activity was displayed in strengthening the defences of Plymouth, and a fort was placed at the western end of the Breakwater. Others were raised at Tregantle, equally commanding the Channel and Hamoaze ; and Scraesdon, to prevent the approach of an enemy landing at Fowey. Staddon Heights, Picklecombe, Laira and other points were also rendered equally inaccessible. Ancient embrasures were removed from the Citadel, Armstrong guns were erected on concrete foundations, and a grand chain of communication around the Three Towns was thus effected. It was originally proposed to put a fort on the Breakwater itself, but eventually a site was found near and inside the mole for the purpose, and it was decided to erect the defence to low-water level. There was much difficulty in obtaining a solid foundation, and the exposed position and rough weather caused the work to be prosecuted with difficulty. In June, 1862, a quadrangular staging was laid around the site. Piles seventy feet deep were entirely submerged in the sea and fixed into the rock with iron shoes by means of a pile engine stationed on a vessel moored near the place. In the following August the whole of the work was swept away by a heavy sea from the west, and, to counteract the force of future gales, chain guys were fixed to the piles and secured by anchors to the sea or holdfasts to the Breakwater. An easterly gale occurred when the work was approaching completion, and, as there were no guys from the east to save it, those from the west aided the catastrophe by their massive weight. The stage collapsed with several of the workers, but they were all rescued uninjured. By September the work was replaced, and the last pile was driven within a month. An engine was then deposited on the staging to lift stones from the barges alongside, and travellers were fixed for their transportation to the spot required. The foundations were next prepared with the assistance of four diving bells supplied with air by means of steam power—the first ever used at the port—and, in course of four months, two feet of mud were thus removed from the bottom and the bed-rock was exposed. This was levelled by means of blasting, which was conducted with as much ease as in a quarry, the fuse being so ingeniously contrived as to burn after the diving bells had been hauled up and it was left in the water. The helmetted men who were engaged in clearing the bottom were often blown to the surface of the water, in consequence of the valves of the apparatus being choked with mud ; and, when boats were sent to catch these buoyant apparitions, they were so tossed about by the wash of the sea that the greatest difficulty was experienced in securing them. In March, 1863, the first stone of the foundation was laid, and the facing of the fort consisted of granite, backed by concrete blocks, of which 2,400 tons were placed in position each week. The concrete was raised to the height of 32 feet ; and, upon this, within granite facings, 14,000 tons of rubble masonry were thrown. Low water having thus been touched, the construction of the fort proper was commenced. The underground rooms were so devised as to be reached by winding staircases, and entrances were furnished to magazines that were calculated to hold 1,500 barrels of gunpowder. A fresh-water reservoir of adequate capacity was provided, as also were large stores for coal. On the roof there was a concrete platform, and, after fifteen guns had been let into walls fourteen feet thick, two additional floors admitted of a further armament of thirty guns. The work was carried out by Messrs. Henry Lee and Sons, of London.

Coincident with the development of Devonport, and the adaptation of its dock to the most ponderous types of battleships, was the appointment of Sir William White as Chief Constructor of the Navy. His genius had evolved more splendid examples of the ironclad than all other shipbuilders of the modern world, so that if Devonport failed to produce an admiral of enduring memory, its training school for young apprentices yielded the one man whom England required in her increasing struggle to maintain indisputable maritime supremacy. Devonport, which had hitherto been restricted to the construction of second or third class cruisers, was now admitted to the privilege of turning out leviathan iron-clads; and modern shipways were constructed to admit of their being successfully launched. The Ocean was the first of the class to be laid down, a vessel of 12,950 tons displacement, with engines of 13,500 indicated horse-power. She was christened in July, 1898, by the Princess Louise, in the presence of a brilliant throng of spectators, and launched amid a chorus of syrens and foghorns. Preparations were forthwith made for

LAUNCH OF H.M.S. IMPLACABLE, 1899.
CONSTRUCTED BY SIR W. WHITE, FIRST FREEMAN OF DEVONPORT.

building in the same space an even more gigantic battleship, the Implacable, an improved Majestic, of 14,900 tons displacement. She was launched in March, 1899, after being seven months on the slip, by Lady Ernestine Edgcumbe, gliding majestically to the waves, and so easily withal that scarcely a ripple disturbed the surface of Hamoaze. Thus Devonport was restored in an incredibly short space of time to one of the first of the national shipbuilding establishments, and £10,000 was paid every Friday in Dockyard wages. No sooner was the Implacable despatched than the Bulwark was laid down—the stateliest and most imposing ship of the trio. She was launched in September, 1899, when the port was once more throbbing with war sensations, departures of troops and preparations for meeting the challenge to the Boers for supremacy in the Transvaal. The suspense was less prolonged, though no less acute than of yore, for the telegraph was now at work ; but the enthusiasm was as high as ever as regiment after regiment marched to the railway stations, and fired their royal salutes from the carriage windows whilst the engines raised their first puffs towards Southampton, the chief port of embarkation. Once more Plymouth rejoiced over the thrilling charge up the almost inaccessible hill at Glencoe, which was led by its heroic and familiar neighbour, General Symons, of Hatt, near Saltash, and gloried in the achievements of the Devon Regiment at Elandslaagte. Further imposing naval additions and gigantic dock extensions at Keyham were simultaneously in progress. One hundred acres were enclosed within a huge dam by the contractor, Sir John Jackson, and forests of timber were imported for the purpose of carrying out a scheme admittedly destined to render Devonport the first naval rendezvous in the world. A huge tidal basin with a water area of over thirty-five acres, or four times the size of the largest basin in existence at Keyham, is the leading feature of this development, whilst a tidal caisson will admit of direct communication with Hamoaze. Three graving docks, to be connected with the basin, and an entrance lock, all in parallel lines, are to communicate at one end with the tidal basin, and at the other with an open basin, so that battleships of the largest class may

SALTASH IN 1899.
(*From a Sketch by H. Martin.*)

hereafter be docked at Devonport. When the millions sterling contemplated for the purpose have been expended, one long line of Government depots, docks and ships will extend from Devil's Point to Bull Point. To facilitate its command of the waters of the port the Admiralty in 1899 arranged with the Corporation of Saltash for the surrender of their historical fishing rights inside the Breakwater up to Laira Bridge, and in Hamoaze to the mouths of the Tavy and the Lynher. For the sum of £1,000 these time-honoured privileges were relinquished in 1899.

Recent Municipal Events: 1863-1899.   The rejoicings with which, in the Mayoralty of Mr. Charles Norrington, in 1863, the marriage of the Prince and Princess of Wales was commemorated were only surpassed in 1865, when the young couple visited Plymouth to inspect the exhibition of the Royal Agricultural Society, which was held at Pennycomequick. Attended by the Countess de Grey, the Earl of Mount Edgcumbe, and a guard of honour, the Prince and Princess drove from the Royal William Victualling Yard, where they had landed from their yacht, through streets that were filled with multitudes and spanned by triumphal arches. After lunching in the showyard, the royal pair and their suite went to Saltash Passage, and visited the warships of several nations that were then at anchor in the port. A ball of unusual splendour was held at the Victualling Yard, at which the Austrian and French officers were specially welcomed, and the Prince ascended a gilded throne to survey the scene. With flashing bayonets, military and naval uniforms, gas illuminations, and countless arrangements of flags, the ensemble was pronounced incomparable for effect. On the following day, the royal party visited Mount Edgcumbe, and in the evening the Prince entertained a party on board the Osborne. The vessel was a blaze of illuminations, and the movements of the guests were watched by thousands from the shore.

Overpowering enthusiasm was excited in 1874 by the announcement that Garibaldi intended to visit the West, in order to pass a few days with Colonel Peard at Penquite; and, on the day fixed for the journey, crowds surrounded the Millbay Railway Station for hours—bells pealing and bands playing. Unaware of the reception that awaited him, the Italian hero broke his journey in Somerset, and his Plymouth admirers thereupon reluctantly dispersed. Upon his arrival at midnight several thousand people reassembled, and, as "The Deliverer" emerged from his carriage—dressed in a loose grey coat, red shirt, and drab cloth trousers—he received a deafening welcome. After a short stay on the platform he resumed his journey, and, on the following day, Mr. Charles Norrington, Mayor of Plymouth, and Mr. T. Woollcombe, Town Clerk of Devonport, accompanied by aldermen and councillors of each borough, travelled to Penquite, where "Garibaldi's Fighting Englishman" arranged for the presentation of the various addresses that recognised in the Italian hero's efforts to emancipate his native country "the noblest vindication of national rights." In reply, Garibaldi declared that the nationalities were with England because England's heart was with the nationalities. He drove to Fowey a few days later to take his departure, and a triumphal arch upon the quay bore the words, "Long Live Garibaldi and His Englishman." An admiring lady attempted to kiss the patriot's hand, but he exclaimed, with a gesture of evident displeasure, "No, madam, pray." Garibaldi embarked under a salute of fifteen guns, given by the Volunteer Artillerymen, and was received on board the Ondine by the Duke of Sutherland, whose affectionate welcome moved him to tears. A visitor of another temperament, Louis Napoleon, the deposed Emperor of the French, visited Plymouth in 1871, in company with the Prince Imperial and Prince Murat. He visited the Hoe to inspect the scene of Bonaparte's sojourn in English waters, but the crowd was as persistent and effusive as that which gathered in 1815, and

From a photo. by Heath, Plymouth.

PLYMOUTH DURING THE TRANSVAAL WAR, 1900.

Presentation of the Maxim Gun to the 2nd Devon Volunteers upon the Hoe.

To face page 432.

OPENING OF PLYMOUTH GUILDHALL, 1873.—Procession, including the Prince of Wales.

(From a Photo. by Heath.)

the exile was glad to escape to Mount Edgcumbe, which the Earl had placed at his disposal.

The old Town Hall in Whimple Street was grotesque, ill-contrived and unsightly, and the authorities reserved the pleasure of superseding it whenever funds and site were available. In 1849 the Guardians erected a new workhouse, and the land in Catherine Street was acquired by the municipality ; other ground was purchased, and in 1869 a premium was offered for the best plans. Some drawings combined Municipal Offices and Guildhall in one architectural group, but the successful design provided for two buildings. Mr. Waterhouse was retained to advise the committee, and his choice, with appropriate coincidence, fell upon that which was identified as bearing the motto of Messrs. Norman and Hine, local architects. Mr. John Pethick was appointed to carry out the work, and the pile was opened in 1873, in the Mayoralty of Mr. Alfred Rooker, to whose brilliant advocacy the scheme was primarily due. Banks, business houses and Government establishments were closed on the day appointed for the ceremony, and, in honour of the visit of the Heir Apparent, the streets were planted with fir trees and draped with flags. When the Prince landed from his yacht, and drove through Union Street to the Council Chamber, trumpets proclaimed his progress, and thousands of coloured scarves waved in the Square as he walked to the main entrance. There Mr. Rooker begged his acceptance of a white wand as the emblem of his office as Lord High Steward of the Borough—carefully explaining that, although its origin could not be fixed with accuracy, the dignity had been accepted by a series of royal and illustrious personages. A silver key, bearing the borough arms, was then presented to the Prince. As he was unsuccessful in unlocking the one door he made an attempt upon the second ; and then, to the general amusement, they both flew open unassisted. The local authorities were sadly disconcerted, but the Prince laughed heartily and congratulated them on the result of so much local genius, perseverance, and energy as this stately pile evinced. A banquet followed, and illuminations and fireworks were general.

In 1880 a committee comprising the principal public men of the Three Towns was appointed to consider the expediency of purchasing the Halfpenny Gate. After many meetings, they reported that, whilst there was no indisposition on the part of the owners to sell, there was little evidence of earnestness in the intention of the local authorities to buy. An attempt to mould a statesmanlike frame of mind was made in 1887, when Mr. W. H. Alger, Mayor of Plymouth, projected a scheme of expropriation as a happy means of commemorating the Jubilee Year of Victoria's reign. Lord Mount Edgcumbe and Lord St. Levan, on being interviewed, admitted the unpleasant character of the holding ; and, after the Plymouth Council adopted the proposal in principle, the authorities of Stonehouse and Devonport nominated members to act on a Joint Committee. It was found that the tolls had been let from 1880 to 1888 at an average sum of £5,740 per annum—and that this amount did not represent the profit of middleman or cost of collection. The sum for which the owners were prepared to sell was £124,300, and it was calculated that, at 22½ years purchase, the revenue would fully meet repayment and interest. After much controversy, a conditional offer of £106,000 was submitted in the name of the three authorities. This proposal was definitely declined, and the Joint Committee was informed that the minimum price was a round sum of £120,000. This alternative the various Councils were earnestly admonished by the committee to accept, and it was insisted that, on such terms, at the current rate of interest, the bridge would be free to the general population at the end of forty years, and that no increased rate would fall upon the ratepayers in the interim. At this stage the Devonport authorities broke away from further negociations on the ground that the sum asked was too high, and, although their neighbours were most eager to complete the purchase, they rejected the scheme by 25 votes to 7, five members declining to take any part in the division. The unexpected defection of Devonport rendered united action out of the question, the scheme was crushed, and the owners forthwith disposed of their interest to the General Tolls Company for £124,000. With this change of proprietory, the Three Towns Tramway Company were called upon to pay £19 per week, instead of from £12 to £15, by way of agreed charges for the passage of their cars. The arrangement continued till 1894, when the compromise was terminated by notice. Sixpence was claimed for each car drawn by three horses, another penny in respect of each horse returning, and threepence in respect of such car returning—or tenpence for each car. The company refused to comply with this demand, and a horse was distrained in order that the issue might be raised. After going from Court to Court, the Tolls Company abandoned the charge of threepence for the return journey, and the judges held that a tramcar, as "a coach," should be embraced within the meaning of the concession to the original owners, although it was not the description of vehicle contemplated in the 18th century. They pronounced for a levy of sixpence upon each car drawn by three horses or more from Plymouth to Devonport, and one penny for each returning horse. This success of the Tolls Company in legally enhancing the value of the property induced a return of the hot fit at Devonport, and, in 1895, its Council evolved a proposal of their own to purchase the Bridge. Their invitation to the Plymouth Council to co-operate was lightly—almost contemptuously --regarded on the ground that it was useless to renew any negociations until Devonport had irrevocably committed itself. On this occasion the idea was thrown out of applying for power to throw a new bridge across the Creek--from Fore Street to Eldad-- but it was dismissed as infringing upon the vested interests of the Company, and as interfering with the military disposition of the Brickfields. Mr. Alger once more endeavoured to induce the Three Towns to face the real solution of the problem, but the controversy could not be quickened on account of the distrust engendered by previous breakdowns. As soon as Mr. Pilling appeared on the scene as Town Clerk of Devonport he renewed the negociations, and the Tolls Company then offered to sell for £170,000. Whilst the committee were endeavouring to secure better terms, the company broke away with the intimation that the latest returns showed such an increase in the pedestrian use of the bridge that the municipal hesitation to close must once more be regarded as fatal.

The character of the County Councils Bill in 1888 was so revolutionary that it almost took away the municipal breath. Devonshire was to be constituted a parliament for purposes of local government, and, instinctively jealous of Exeter as the capital, the Three Towns urged the responsible minister, Mr. Ritchie, so to divide the county that the Southern and Western representatives should assemble at Plymouth, and urged that such an authority would be powerful enough to kill many of the evils to which "cliques, cabals, and caucuses have too long been giving rise." As Mr. Ritchie nervously yielded before sundry persistent opponents the disposition in Plymouth was to contract the scope of reform by becoming a county of its own ; and, in Stonehouse, Dr. Christopher Bulteel earnestly commended the amalgamation of the Three Towns. Whilst Plymouth sought to preserve its integrity, Devonport grew apprehensive of absorption, and its representatives made desperate efforts to reduce the standard of population of the exempted boroughs so that it might also be constituted a County Council. Sir Henry Waring, as Mayor, waited upon Mr. Ritchie with the Plymouth memorial. It embodied various alternatives, each of them designed to disturb confidence in the original programme of ideal county government. The suggested division of Devon county into two shires —North and South—Mr. Ritchie dismissed as utterly impossible. "No Government," he remarked, "would overload an already heavily laden Bill with such a thorny proposal." Then it was urged that the Three Towns of Plymouth, Stonehouse and Devonport, "which are geographically one large town, and contain 140,000 innabitants, should be grouped together and constitute a county of themselves." "I tell you," Mr. Ritchie replied, "that it is no good to push such a question." Finally it was argued that Plymouth should be made a county of itself, the measure was emasculated to meet that and similar cases, the down grade continued to grow in favour, and Devonport was equally successful in continuing its identity, although it was just below the minimum limit of population. Soon afterwards an act was passed that abolished the scratching system of electing guardians, and the ballot was substituted in its stead. To complete the scheme of uniformity the Devonport Board of Commissioners were replaced by a more compact and regularly elected body of Poor-law representatives.

The available land in Plymouth was becoming so restricted, and the possibility of ratable increase so remote, that it was determined in 1894 to apply for powers to amalgamate the parishes of East Stonehouse, Compton, Egg Buckland and Laira. Plymouth was committed to a large expenditure on a sewerage scheme which would only effect a limited improvement if the outside districts were not included, and, as the large overflow population of Plymouth was settling in increasing numbers in the contiguous parishes, there was the certainty that outsiders would enjoy all the value of residence in Plymouth without contributing anything to its rates. The case for the inclusion of Compton and the districts that lay within the Parliamentary borough of Plymouth was not easily assailed, although the application was strenuously resisted; but the hostility of Stonehouse was the less disguised because of the unfortunate spirit in which the residents had been approached. Counsel for the borough contended that, although Stonehouse had always been a separate township it was practically a part of Plymouth, its streets being conterminous and its interests generally in common. Compton, so far as the Mannamead section was concerned, was due to the prosperity of Plymouth—the suburb to which merchants resorted, and whose residents enjoyed all the advantages of commercial and social contact. The prayer of the borough —with the exception of Stonehouse—was conceded on terms, but the battle was carried by Compton to the House of Lords. There a compromise was effected, involving a modification of the differential rate, which was finally settled at 4s. 3d. for the first five years, 4s. 6d. for the next ten years, and 6s. for a further period. The acreage of the borough was thus increased by 60 per cent., and the Millbay Docks were brought within the scope of the borough poor rate. To Councillor J. A. Bellamy, the chairman of the Extension Committee, the town mainly owed the success which crowned these efforts, and it was only party jealousy which withheld from him the honorary freedom of the borough. To the annoyance of the "Uitlanders" the extended bounds were beaten in advance by the Mayor, Alderman J. T. Bond, and a commemorative medal was struck in honour of the event. Alderman C. Radford was the first chief magistrate of "Greater Plymouth."

Redistribution accompanied extension, and, instead of six wards returning two members each, the borough was carved into fourteen divisions with three councillors apiece. As all the aldermen and councillors were required to throw up their seats and trust to the tender mercies of a general election, it was mutually agreed that inconvenient personal questions should be avoided by re-electing all the aldermen and by amicably dividing the seats of Councillors. This arrangement to defer the eventual struggle for supremacy was resolutely resisted by the young Conservatives, and the idea was abandoned. In the result their party was visited with crushing discomfiture, and the first Council of Greater Plymouth registered a clear majority of seven Liberals exclusive of Independents, the majority rising to fourteen after the aldermanic elections. Events made for speedy and sensational developments. At the instance of the Chamber of Commerce, opinion was sought as to the possibility of converting Cattewater into a harbour adapted to the develop-

ment of commerce and the necessities of ocean liners. Explorations of the bed conducted by
Sir Wolfe Barry and Mr. Bretherton disclosed a deposit capable of being removed to any
depth required, and the solitary obstacle to navigation of a substantial kind was "a patch
of rock " whose removal presented no engineering difficulties. As a part of the foreshore
had been acquired by the Corporation, the cost of obtaining the remainder, constructing
necessary wharves and docks, and lengthening the Batten Breakwater, was estimated at
£660,000. When the scheme was first unfolded by Mr. J. T. Bond, the Mayor, it was
welcomed with patriotic fervour, and Sir Wolfe Barry's eulogy of Cattewater—Catwater
had ceased to be the form of spelling—as possessing unrivalled capacity was accepted as a
sufficient basis for hoping that Plymouth would yet develop the finest natural harbour in
the world. The Council was so enamoured by the prospect that only one member voted
against the resolution, and the approval of the ratepayers was tempestuously accorded at the
Guildhall meeting. An opposition, at once subtle and formidable, was already formed and
the political parties were mutually rended. Prominent Conservatives like Alderman Pethick,
Councillor S. J. Page and Mr. William King cast their influence in favour of the scheme,
and Councillor Woollcombe, Mr. Paul Swain, and Mr. Wolferstan organised the opposition
committee. Temporary offices were engaged in George Street by the rival parties, subscription
lists were opened, and pamphlets on the subject were distributed broadcast. The real opposition emanated from frontagers, whose premises were to be scheduled ; and from proprietors
on the south side of the harbour who felt that the opposite bank would be developed to their
disadvantage. Sir Wolfe Barry's programme was satirised as ridiculously impracticable so far
as the expectation of attracting ocean liners was concerned, and Sir Alexander Rendel was
consulted by the opponents to demonstrate that more satisfactory suggestions might be
made. The fishermen were told that their industry would be imperilled, and the ratepayers
were bombarded with sinister suggestions that they were being exploited in the interest of
the owners of Queen Anne's Battery. The estimate of the Corporation experts was discounted, the project was denounced as rushed, and as certain to involve the town in
a heavy increase of rates. After a polemical warfare of unprecedented virulence, which
extended over several weeks, the town was polled, and the numbers recorded for the
proposed Bill were 8,778, and 5,933 against. With the declaration of the numbers, the
arrangements for the Parliamentary campaign began. Over a score of interests were
marshalled in direct hostility ; the Mayor's good faith was openly impeached, and he
publicly protested that he had really prevailed upon the owners of Queen Anne's Battery
to put their patriotism before their pockets. The actual veto was imposed by the Lords
of the Admiralty, who, claiming Plymouth as a naval port, blocked the scheme on the
ground that ocean liners in numbers would too largely draw upon the two deep water
channels that admit of entrance to the Sound. Opposition of this nature had not
been contemplated, and the announcement created a shock of surprise that amounted to
consternation. The First Lord, Mr. Goschen, was waited upon on behalf of the Council,
and he informed the Mayor that the commercial development of Plymouth was viewed
with the gravest concern, and that the conditions precedent to Admiralty sanction involved
the blowing up of the Mallard and the Winter shoals at the cost of the municipality. Such an
expenditure could not be entertained by the locality, and thus the first real attempt to utilise
Plymouth's harbour for the benefit of its people was limited to the utilization of its own
piece of foreshore for its strictly municipal conveniences.

The jubilation of the antagonists was stimulated to frenzy by a financial crisis in the
fortunes of the Corporation, which promply evoked the imputation that the scheme to convert
Cattewater was an ingenious device to raise a large loan with the object of concealing the
true situation by appropriating the funds that the scheme would have placed at the disposal of

the Corporation to the emergent requirements of various committees. By common consent a policy of municipal progress had been presented. A fish market had been erected on the Barbican ; the old market had given place to the new ; the yet irregular old Town Street was adapted to modern conditions ; the narrow Ebrington Street had been broadened ; the plant of a bankrupt tramway company had been acquired and access opened to Mannamead and the East End ; extensive and expensive sewage works had been carried out ; workmen's dwellings had been provided and unhealthy areas cleared ; and the fall of repayment of loans and interest rendered necessary an unprecedented appeal to the pockets of the inhabitants. Improvements had marched a little faster than increment arising from expansion, and the sudden loosening of the land in Devonport, in response to the insistent demand for workmen's homes, had caused a temporary pause in the Plymouth pace. Thus the inhabitants were required to pay, for the first time in their experience, a seven shilling rate ; and, although property had everywhere advanced in value, and wages were never higher or employment more remunerative, the tide of indignation rose and the flood overwhelmed the Progressives. Their majority was reduced in a day to two, and a situation was created which was reminiscent of the Mayoral struggles of the pre-Reform elections. Anticipating their defeat, the Progressives strongly urged the Conservatives to nominate a Mayor. When the reverse was an accomplished fact, and the Council was almost balanced, the Conservatives refused to accede to the request of their opponents unless it was agreed that they should rule through the chairmanships of the important spending committees. Interviews failed to reconcile the parties, and, on the ninth of November, 1898, the retiring Mayor, Mr. Bond, announced to 3,000 persons in the Guildhall that the Liberals could not find his successor, and that the Conservatives declined to do so. The proceedings were adjourned until the following morning ; and then, differences as to the equitable disposition of the chairmanships having been adjusted, Alderman John Pethick came to the rescue and accepted the office amid prolonged cheering. The "boom" in building, which had been checked by the awakening in Devonport, was, in the ensuing twelve months, more active than it had ever been in either borough, and the financial situation in Plymouth was so readjusted that the reactionary spirit was stayed and the financial outlook pronounced to be more than ever hopeful.

In 1897, with the advent of Mr. A. B. Pilling as Town Clerk, a scheme of borough extension, which had for a long time existed in a nebulous condition, became materialised at Devonport. There were many reasons for the desired annexations. The population of the old borough had overflowed into the outlying districts, and converted them into thickly populated areas, which, though urban in character, remained under rural government. So little had the District Council coped with the needs of these districts that the inhabitants applied for powers to transform St. Budeaux into an urban community. Another reason for the expansion was the necessity of safeguarding the health of Devonport by controlling these suburbs. Insanitary conditions prevailed that might easily become a general menace, and it was advisable to control the mudbanks, covered with water at high tide, known as Weston Mill Creek, which formed part of the northern boundary. Another important reason for amalgamation arose from the fact that land in the old borough was almost entirely within the disposition of the Lord of the Manor. The absence of free trade in building had made Devonport one of the most overcrowded towns in the country, and, by the enlargement of the borough, it was anticipated that a gradual dispersion of the inhabitants would take place, and the congestion be steadily relieved. As Devonport was bounded on the south and west by the waters of Hamoaze, and on the east by Plymouth and Stonehouse, the only possible direction of development was northwards. Application was accordngly made for a Provisional Order to include within the borough parts of the parishes of St.

Budeaux and Pennycross (Weston Peverel).   At the local enquiry the proposals of the Corporation met with vigorous opposition.   Mr. Pilling conducted the case for Devonport unaided, and he was opposed by Queen's counsel and others acting on behalf of Plymouth Corporation, Plympton St. Mary Rural District Council, Devon County Council, St. Budeaux Parish Council, Great Western Railway Company, and the Marchioness of North-ampton.   The Local Government Board eventually sanctioned the Order and introduced it in a Confirming Bill in 1898   Hostile petitions were presented, and the measure was referred to a Select Committee.   After a fight extending over five days, the Order was confirmed, with modifications.   When the Bill reached the House of Lords, the opposition was con-tinued by the Rural District Council, Guardians of the Poor for Plympton St. Mary, St. Budeaux Parish Council, and Great Western Railway Company.   After three days' hearing, the Confirming Bill passed the Committee, and the differential rate was fixed at 4s. in the £ for the first five years, and 4s. 6d. for the following five years.   The old borough consisted of 1,925 acres, with a population of 60,000 and a ratable value of £216,146.   The extended borough comprised 3,173 acres, with a population of 63,000 and a ratable value of £230,785.   The added areas were granted a representation on the Council of twelve members, and the number was thus raised from 48 to 60.   In one year, 1898, the ratable value of the added portion of St. Budeaux had grown, without the aid of increased assessments, from £10,995 to £13,129, an increase of 20 per cent.   The extension of the Devonport boundaries was followed by the investiture of Sir William White (the Chief Constructor of the Navy), Alderman J. W. Ryder and Alderman Joseph May with the freedom of the borough.   Each patent was enclosed in a silver casket, and the recipients were heartily cheered by a representative audience.   Mr. William Waycott was Mayor when the extension order was passed and confirmed.   The bounds of the extended boroughwere first beaten in the Mayoralty of Mr. William Hornbrook in 1899, and, before the end of his year of office, the first sod of an electric system of tramways connecting the added area with Devonport was cut at Camel's Head by Mr. William Waycott, chairman of the Municipal Committee, at the request of the directors of the two companies who had obtained the powers, enabling the Council to buy at the expiration of fifteen years.

CAMEL'S HEAD BRIDGE, 1899.

CHAPTER XV.—POLITICAL: BEFORE AND AFTER THE REFORM BILL.

Pre-Reform Plymouth Elections: 1792-1831. In Plymouth the choice of members was in the hands of the privileged few, and freedom of speech was often an ornamental phrase. The elections were select festivals with a social side, to which only the freemen were invited; and it was not customary to enter overmuch into politics. If there was actual popular discontent, a deal of courage was necessary to its expression in a borough where the power was held by Ministerial dependents, and treason was a word capable of considerable elasticity of meaning. An example of the real danger of plain speaking was forthcoming in 1792, when, taking advantage of the Fifth of November celebrations, the Rev. William Winterbotham, assistant preacher at the How's Lane Baptist Chapel, reviewed the times in two fearless sermons. Commenting upon the persecution of the Baptists at Birmingham, where a few "friends of freedom" were set upon by "banditti," who endangered their lives and plundered their property. to the familiar cry of "Church and King," Mr. Winterbotham declared that the moment a monarch subverted the Constitution, the people were entitled to "hurl the despot from the throne." Whilst lamenting the scenes that were "tarnishing" the French Revolution, he commended the attempt of "a great nation to recover that Liberty which is their inherent right," and quoted the deposition of James II. to prove that the people had full right to "cashier their governors for misconduct." Dealing with the prevailing heavy expenditure, Winterbotham charged Ministers of the Crown with overruling Magna Charta, asserted that individuals bought seats for corrupt purposes, and that independent citizens were prevented from serving the country on account of the enormous cost of political contests. Applying the local instance, Mr. Winterbotham proceeded: "The Bill of Rights declares that the election of members for Parliament ought to be free—yet the greater part are returned by aristocratic influence, Ministerial manoeuvres, and rotten Corporations. Few boroughs have more electors than Plymouth, and even here one hundred and sixty-three individuals, of whom it cannot be said that the odd sixty-three have any will of their own, are the spokesmen of twelve thousand inhabitants, leaving out of account Dock, Stoke, and Stonehouse, whose numbers are more than double." Mr. Winterbotham was subsequently assured by "one of the oldest and most respectable members of the Corporation of Plymouth" that he might have estimated the number of independent electors much lower, "for, of his own knowledge, he could assert that at no one election which had taken place for more than forty years had there ever been fifty persons who voted without restraint; "so very pure are the electors and so very free are the elections in this immaculate borough."

For thus discussing the grievance of the age, Mr. Winterbotham was reported to the Plymouth magistrates by Government employés who went to his "meeting-house" to hear the sermons delivered; and he was committed to take his trial for "maliciously and seditiously intending to disquiet, molest, and disturb the peace and common tranquillity of our Lord the King and of this Kingdom, to bring His Majesty and his Government into contempt, and to excite the subjects of the King to sedition against his Goverment." Mr. Serjeant Rooke opened the case for the Crown by arguing that, as power was derived from the Supreme Being, to upbraid the Government without just occasion was a crime, and to preach discontent "blasphemy against the Majesty of Heaven." He accused Winterbotham of betraying that gospel "which he pretends to preach"; pointed to the rebellion in France and the fate of Charles I. as illustrating the results of such teachings; and urged that "offenders of this sort" should receive no mercy from juries. After several witnesses had variously construed the phraseology used by defendant, Mr. Clapp was heard in his behalf, and the hostile manifestations in court rendered his task so difficult that he hinted he should despair of securing an acquittal if the verdict were given by the audience. Taking special care to impress the Court with the fact that the defendant, as a Baptist, belonged to a body more nearly in sympathy with the Church of England than any other sect, he expressed a confidence he evidently did not feel that the jury would never convict a man merely because he was a Dissenter. It was because some sects were supposed to entertain opinions concerning government that were "more obnoxious than others," that he explained Winterbotham's precise position " and thus set him strait." He then contended that the defendant simply discussed the Revolution of 1688, and shewed to what an extent the existing Government had abandoned the lessons of an event which it had been inviting the country to commemorate. Mr. Clapp, although he disclaimed any sympathy with the defendant, could not consent to apply the fire and faggot to everyone with whom he differed. "If you, gentlemen of the jury, have that feeling, much good may it do you." It was Reform for which Winterbotham contended, "and you, who have Cornwall before and Somerset behind you, must have heard of the corruption attending the election of members from others besides Mr. Winterbotham." Witnesses were called to argue that the extravagant construction placed on the sermons was due to failure of memory or defective historical knowledge. In his reply, Serjeant Rooke deepened the prejudice by declaring that a pulpit was a most improper place for debating politics, and that ministers were the least incapable of all men to conduct such discussions. He also urged that Winterbotham had not produced the manuscript of his sermon to the Mayor of Plymouth, and the defendant replied that he was prevented from showing that it contained no criminal language. The justice who sat with the Mayor was the "spring and motion" of the prosecution; the defendant was not suffered to confront the witnesses; nor was he invited to refute their evidence. The depositions were taken in the office of "Mr. Inquisitor-General Foot (alias Mr. Deputy Solicitor), there they were manufactured into form, and sworn before Mr. Mayor and Co." Mr. Winterbotham said he was sent for, not to vindicate himself, but to find security for his appearance in the sum of £800. All appeals on behalf of the defendant were unavailing. He was convicted by separate juries of delivering two different sermons with seditious intent, and was sentenced to "the very moderate and merciful penalty of four years' imprisonment and a pecuniary fine of £200." The costs amounted to hundreds of pounds, but the unswerving fidelity of his congregation enabled Winterbottom to satisfy his persecutors and renew his ministrations after his term had expired.

There was promise of a fiercely contested election in 1796, when Sir William Elford, a native of the town, resolved to try conclusions with Sir F. L. Rogers. Admiral Sir Alan Gardner was the third candidate, and, as he represented the Government, his return was beyond question, although he was then serving on a foreign station. Of the other two candidates, Rogers was "recommended by Government" and "Sir W. Elford "is by no means disapproved of by it." Herein lay the dilemma, and, in an electioneering appeal, " A Townsman " begged friends of the ministry to recollect that "they do not in any sense oppose Government, but are rather serving its truest interests in voting for Sir W. Elford." Sir Alan Gardner cut the Gordian knot by resolving to sit for Westminster, and there was a rapprochement between the forces of Rogers and Elford. In their exultation the friends of both aspirants issued a leaflet of thanksgiving : " Rejoice, oh Ye Mortals ! And again I say Rejoice ! I beg leave to congratulate you, my dear friends, on the present posture of affairs. Sir Alan Gardner, your worthy representative, stands for the City of Westminster, and your respectable candidate, Sir W. Elford, is patronized by Government to succeed him. Vote for him, my dear fellows, and thereby preserve the peace of your ancient borough." The arrangement proved mutually satisfactory, and there was no further appeal until 1802, when the election was memorable for the severity of the lampoons. Prior to the dissolution only one candidate presented himself—Sir Francis Glanville—who had filled the interval caused by the death of Sir F. L. Rogers. As he declined to stand again, it was inferred "that the pass-box containing the patronage of this ancient borough, instead of being seen rolling into the Treasury, as at the last election, has fairly rolled out of it, and has been by some strange neglect entirely lost " :

> God prosper long our noble King
>   Our lives and safeties all ;
> The election soon for Plymouth Town
>   Will surely on us fall ;
> Therefore another member get
>   Frank Glanville doth retire
> Whom Fame has sent to old Catchfrench
>   To be a Cornish squire.
> Sir William Elford he doth say
>   He will your member be ;
> Pray God the Colonel may succeed
>   For all should vote for he.
> He served his Country and his King
>   When ordered for to go
> To quell rebellious Irishmen,
>   The Englishmen also.
> Therefore, I pray you vote for him
>   Who is a Colonel bright ;
> Elect him then, and he'll serve you
>   By day as well as night.
>   God Save the King. *—Chevy Chase, 1802.*

Advertisements calling for a new candidate were invited in various squibs : " Oyer and Terminer," " Oyez, Oyez, Oyez, &c.," " None need apply whose characters will not bear the strictest scrutiny." Mr. P. Langmead, an old resident, who had never spared his means or courage, came forward, and the fun was fast and furious. In " Plymouth Election Races " excellent running was promised by " Quiz, Clerk of the Course." No thorough-breds were to start—only hacks and hunters—and the pedigrees of the three competitors promised good sport. " Sir Billy " had been kept in training by the " knowing ones," and was " got out of a famous blood mare by that handsome Arabian horse Bickham." " General Cartouch, aged, has won several plates, and is capable of enduring a severe contest ; he is from that strongly-built, bony horse Quebec by an Esquimaux mare." " Volunteer "—Mr. Langmead—was the favourite : " Although he has never started for a plate the odds are much in his favour ; he is said to be worth more than the famous Eclipse ; is sound at Bottom, and was got by Public Spirit out of that celebrated mare Independence." In a subsequent jeu d'esprit, " To the Amateurs of Sporting," the assurance was given that " Sir

Billy" looked remarkably well, showed much activity, evinced no inclination to bolt in going over the course, albeit the presence of certain "jockeys" in his company at first raised doubts as to whether he had been "physicked." "Volunteer" was sustaining his popularity and doing credit to his dam, and there was promise of noble sport. Ten to one was offered that General Cartouch would not go to the post, for he was now "stiff in the off fore leg," and, next, so overheated that he would not "bleed free." The licence with which personal peculiarities were discussed, induced Sir William Elford to publish a manifesto deprecating the issuing "of those papers which are known as election squibs, the purport of which is to depreciate one and to exalt others of the candidates, on grounds foreign to those of their respective merits and pretensions, of which the electors are perfectly competent to judge, and the effect of which is unnecessarily to inflame and irritate the minds of those engaged beyond what the necessities of the case would otherwise demand. He takes the liberty of expressing an earnest hope that this practice will not be continued, as he sincerely wishes to allay, instead of to excite, irritation, and to persevere in that perfect forbearance which he and his friends have hitherto observed." General Cartouch abandoned the contest, and Mr. Langmead, in acknowledging his unopposed return as the second member, announced to the world that the support "unequivocally pledged to me was of such weight, independence, and respectability as no influence could have shaken and no opposition could have overthrown."

Expectation turned to ashes in the mouth of Mr. Langmead, and he resigned his seat in 1806. Sir Thomas Tyrwhitt stepped into his shoes for the rest of the session. As soon as the dissolution was announced, "A Card" was issued, in which "the worthy and independent freemen of the Borough of Plymouth" were "respectfully entreated not to engage their votes for the next general election of members to represent this antient and loyal Borough in Parliament, as a character of high respectability and real weight intends to offer himself to their notice for that distinguished honour—not, however, in opposition to the truly respectable and highly approved gentleman whom the electors have lately, with such perfect unanimity, returned as one of their representatives." Sir C. M. Pole was chosen as Tyrwhitt's colleague, and Sir William Elford had to face the opposition arising from his refusal to play a submissive rôle. In his interest the "independent electors" were abjured to rise to a sense of their consequence : "You are in number near 300; ask your own hearts whether the majority of that number are Placemen or Pensioners? Upon what ground then does any Minister say that he will send you a member who shall represent you? Choose a gentleman of independent spirit and fortune (and you have such amongst you) who will insist on your rights, and feel, from affection to his native town, interested in asserting them. Don't permit yourselves to be dull'd and dragooned into servitude—if you do, you are no longer independent or free." The appeal was unavailing, and Elford was thrown out. Twelve months later he renewed the attack and won with Mr. T. Bewes. The freemen supported the retiring members, and the votes of the freeholders, the mainstay of Elford and Bewes, were upset on petition. Apprehensive that Elford might again present himself, the enraged freemen met and resolved to curb his pretensions. Elford had shewn himself "a determined opponent of the rights and franchises of the freemen of this borough, particularly in the late petition, by endeavouring to establish an unfounded right of voting in the freeholders, wholly destructive of the franchises of the freemen." The freemen accordingly appointed Mr. Langmead and Dr. Gasking to urge the King's Ministers "to withdraw their support (if any has been given) from Sir William Elford, and not endeavour to impose a representative on the freemen of this borough who is so deservedly obnoxious to their feelings." A compromise was effected. Elford ceased to obtrude as a candidate, and was appointed Recorder of Plymouth.

The modification of the privileges of the freemen cut into financial perquisites as well as public privileges. Every qualified elector was entitled to convey the freedom to apprentices who served him for seven years, and those in business had a great advantage over private individuals who possessed the vote. Parents preferred to apprentice their sons with those who could give them a title to the freedom, and paid larger premiums than was expected by those who had no such favours to transmit. These apprentices served with the more fidelity, so that the advantage was beneficial in proportion to the time each freeman carried on business. Such a privilege as this, "so conducive to the interests of the freemen and so well qualified to render them a numerous body," was viewed with "an evil eye" by those who desired to hold the reins and render the general body no less submissive and subservient to their purposes. Some of the freemen brought matters to a crisis by binding several apprentices, and under the pretence that this constituted an electoral inequality, a bye-law was passed providing that only first apprentices should be entitled to the freedom. Thus electors engaged in business were stripped "of by far the greater part of the benefits resulting from their ancient and valuable inheritance." The political consequences were serious enough, but the dispossessed contended that the practice had been really "instrumental in supplying this opulent and flourishing town with a proper number of freemen, and thereby prevented it from falling into a state of vassalage and dependence upon some wealthy peer and commoner, like many of the neighbouring boroughs in Cornwall." It had been the practice in Plymouth, the champions of apprentices admitted, to institute a difference between freemen who married and had sons, and those who remained single, for the former were considered industrious and deserving, and the latter as useless and pernicious members of the community. Devious were the devices now practised with a view of reducing the number of freemen. None could be admitted unless they made their claim within two years, and resolutions were passed to prevent the repeal of this encroachment. Strongly convinced that the franchise was being grossly narrowed and restricted, Mr. John Hawker called a meeting at the King's Arms, in September, 1809, to concert measures for restoring the rights of which he and many others had been "unjustly deprived." The framers of the new bye-laws outwitted him by attending in overwhelming force, and carried a resolution that there had been no violations of rights. Thus the "clique strengthened the chains by which every year they seek to hold the town in subjection." It was rising resentment that caused Plymouth to manifesto in 1812 in favour of "independent and unbiased members," and to protest against the connivance of official corruption of which Sir C. M. Pole and Sir T. Tyrwhitt were suspected. Although the former "luffed and raked" the opponents of the Government "like an experienced seaman," he gave little satisfaction to the unenfranchised in his own constituency :

His own thick Pole, held in derision,
Has proved, like Nature's pole, a vision !

Conscious that the freeholders and non-electors were powerless, the members disregarded all criticisms. In 1812 Tyrwhitt was appointed "Gentleman Usher of the Black Rod of the Most Noble Order of the Garter," and the election that ensued supplied an interesting record of political customs. The choice was made in the Guildhall, and Sir William Elford, the Recorder, "in an elegant and appropriate speech," proposed Colonel Bloomfield. His name having been adopted by acclamation, the new M.P. addressed the meeting in a "clear and impressive manner." There was a common bond between the freemen and himself—"the attachment and devotion of us all to the illustrious personage who lives in the hearts of the people." It had long been his happiness to serve that distinguished personage, "and this day has consummated my pride in devoting my services to you, who are amongst the most loyal and faithful of his subjects." The Mayor then moved that the freedom should be conferred on the new member, and the proposition was welcomed "with the most marked approbation." In the evening the freemen and their friends sat down to "an elegant dinner," and amongst the toasts were "Unanimity and Prosperity to the Town and Corporation of Plymouth," "Lord Wellington and our Brave Army in the Peninsula," "Lord Keith and the Channel Squadron" (for which his lordship returned thanks, expressing every confidence in his ships and men if an opportunity should offer of their meeting the enemy), "Sir Rowland Hill and the Invincible Troops Under His Command" (which was drunk with enthusiastic applause). "Mrs. Bloomfield and Her Charming Family" was rapturously toasted, and "The Pious Memory of Sir Francis Drake—may the descendants of him who gave us water never want wine," excited the usual enthusiasm. Then followed "The Ladies of Plymouth," a toast which, "as was justly observed," the single could drink "with gallant fervour, and the married with grateful love." "The Glorious Memory of Sir John Moore and the Heroes of Corunna" was observed "in solemn silence"; "The Pious Memory of the Immortal Nelson" followed; and then "The Agriculture of Plymouth, and may its meadows and pastures evince their prosperity in Bloom-fields." The toasts were intermixed with songs, and the company "parted at a late hour, highly gratified by the events of the day, but more particularly satisfied and pleased by the polite attention and conduct of their accomplished chairman and new representative." During the evening the deep-toned octave of St. Andrew's, "commonly called Old Church," contributed "beautiful peals."

Elucidation of "the present state of the borough" was contributed by Sir William Elford in February, 1818. Bloomfield had accepted the situation of Privy Purse, and the Recorder's denials that the freemen were to be bought or sold were very quaint. He explained to the new candidate, Sir William Congreve, that the electors were "numerous and respectable," and that, although a majority always supported the Government, there was a section above all influence. As for the idea that the freemen were under the thumb of some potential member of their own body, "nothing could be more erroneous or imply a greater insult to the freemen. If anything could induce them to oppose a candidate of their own opinions, it would be the apprehension that their support might be attributed to supposed extraneous influences. Nothing was more fallacious or delusive than that any one person possessed such influence, and he tendered the candidate an earnest recommendation not to assume that such was the case. Sir William would do well to correspond immediately and directly with all who had occasion to apply to him, and that without the intervention of any other channel of communication whatsoever." With a due sense of the fitness of things, Mr. Lockyer, one of the supposed controllers of party influence, added his hope that Sir William would act upon this advice, since each freeman had an equal right to address the member direct, and to receive a reply without interference. If any private individual pretended to govern the electors, or prevent a free exercise of their chartered rights, Sir William should utterly ignore him. In the absence of any other candidate, Congreve was elected, and he offered his "most solemn pledge" to act upon these adroit dissimulations. "I take the opportunity also," he sagaciously added, "of publicly requesting the company of all the freemen of Plymouth to a social board which I shall order to be spread at the Royal Hotel on Tuesday next. I do this lest, by accident, any of the cards which I shall direct to every freeman should not reach the intended destination." In harmony with this invitation the dinner took place; and "all who know this truly elegant house, and the very diligent and attentive possessors of it, will easily imagine what regularity and comfort prevailed throughout the day." Sir William spared no expense to make his friends happy. "The eatables were bountifully spread, the wines were choice and good, and the dessert such as the season afforded." The King was toasted with "every demonstration of regard and respect," but it was the Prince Regent whom Sir William particularly eulogised, because it was his noble example that had placed Bonaparte "as a supplicating prisoner on board a man-of-war in Plymouth Sound." As the Prince had recently presented the borough with his portrait—done in "Hoppner's most chaste style"—this reference was extremely opportune. Excellent songs were sung, "some by the member," in short, "so far as every effort of the perfect gentleman could go to make his friends happy," it was exercised. Subsequently "the merry dance was kept up with great spirit to a late hour, when time broke in upon inclination, and the scene of gaiety closed."

Whilst this junketing was in progress, Hynes, "the travelling nuisance," was arrested for hawking Hone's publications in Plymouth. Hynes, "Mad Tom Hynes" or "Noisy Tom" as he was variously described, was a most eccentric character. Born at Totnes in 1774, he left the farm in which he was engaged and, making his way to Plymouth, entered on board the Colloden. Thither his master pursued him, but, as lusty lads were in request, the captain refused to give him up. Hynes received severe wounds in active service, and was discharged with intellect impaired. He then served as a Plymouth watchman, and so continued until he was found hopelessly intoxicated at his post. Hynes then wandered about Devon and Cornwall selling Cobbett's Register, and, when times were dull, he conducted religious meetings at street corners. Having considerable facility of speech, he was in evidence during every political crisis, and the officers of the law were always at his heels. Friary Court had declined from its high estate to be the St. Giles of the West— the resort of professional beggars, itinerant match-sellers, tape-vendors, knife-grinders, purveyors of "full, true and particular accounts" of murders and confessions, blacking vendors, and "every variety of rogue and vagabond under the sun." Tom Hynes presided at the Saturday night revels held in Friary Court, and he was assisted by "The Lord of

FRIARY COURT IN 1831.

the Isles," " Billy Brown," " Charley Warn," " Nicky O'Flynn," and " Jack o' Diamonds " —individuals who were scarcely less notorious than himself. " Bruising matches " varied the pandemonium, and bundles of " last dying speeches and confessions " were used as missiles. It was for selling " seditious and slanderous " leaflets and pamphlets, which were composed by " a goose chick " and emanated from the tramps' printing press in this rendezvous, that Hynes was imprisoned. Orders were issued to confiscate the plant, but type and presses were already on their way to America, " that precious land of promise and depository of patriotic men." The " Western Luminary " nevertheless congratulated the Three Towns " on this extermination, root and branch, master and man, of the blasphemy, sedition and libel with which they have so long been polluted," and scornfully exclaimed : " How woefully various are the fates of Patriots !" A few lines from one of Hynes's " poems," as circulated in " Hell-Born-Town " (Dock), will afford some clue to their general characteristics :—

> Near Plymouth lives a wicked wight,
>   A very wicked wight is he, Sir ;
> He roams abroad late at night,
>   That nobody might see, Sir !
>
> He neither cares for sister, brother,
>   As I have oft been told, Sir !
> Uncle, father, wife or mother,
>   Or nephews, young or old, Sir !
>
> Your wife and you have settled here
>   Good company to meet, Sir !
> The sea you love and live thus near
>   'Cause your nephew's in the fleet, Sir !
>
> A charming retreat has this ———— made
> But no part of the purchase has ever been paid ;
> With his garden so large, which his gardener must stock,
> And ———— retails all his produce at Dock.

Plymouth was stirred profoundly by the divorce proceedings against Queen Caroline, and an indignation meeting was held at the New London Inn, in September, 1820, at which a petition was adopted demanding that the Bill of Pains and Penalties should be " thrown out " as a dangerous violation of the Constitution, inasmuch as it did not secure her Majesty " a fair and unbiassed trial." The petition was very outspoken :

" That, witnessing with sorrow the many attempts which have been made to degrade this Illustrious Personage in the eyes of the nation and the world, your Petitioners, the inhabitants of Plymouth, cannot contemplate, without serious apprehension and alarm, the Bill of Pains and Penalties now before that House—a course of proceeding never resorted to but in the worst of times, and for the worst of purposes—a Bill which, under the pretence of national expediency, opposes the principles of mercy and humanity, by treating her Majesty as guilty, even before conviction—and which is also subversive of the first principles of justice, by depriving her of those means of establishing her innocence, which are the birthright of every subject of this realm.

That should a period ever arrive (which God avert) when the Parliament of this country shall be debauched by the arts of corruption into a servile compliance with the designs of an arbitrary Prince, a Bill of Pains and Penalties may, under the pretext of state necessity, be perverted to the gratification of the worst passions of the human heart ; the barriers of justice (which in the social state neither King or subjects can burst with impunity) would be broken down, and the liberties of England perish, perhaps for ever.

That, whatever be the result of this investigation, your Petitioners consider it to be a dangerous violation of the Constitution of this country ; and, so far from being sanctioned by state necessity, appears to have been adopted in direct opposition to the feelings and wishes of the people ; so that, whether viewed in a political, moral, or judicial light, it is, in its course and its consequences ; evidently calculated to debase and destroy those correct principles which give value, dignity, and security to life, and may ultimately be productive of internal dissension, public calamity, and national dishonour.

Your Petitioners, therefore, most earnestly pray that should this ill-omened Bill be ever sent from the Lords to your Honourable House, you will, as the Constitutional Guardians of the People's Rights, throw it out, and not suffer the page of British History to be polluted by so injudicious and unjust a measure."

A counter meeting was convened to present the King with "an affectionate and manly address"; but, when the resolution was submitted, hostile cries prevented the promoters from claiming that it had been "unanimously" adopted. Mr. John Hawker thereupon appealed to the dissentients to withdraw, and, on their refusal to do so, he threatened to take the names of the disturbers—a course that evoked much indignation. Mr. Henry Gandy justified the support of the King, and denied being either servile or " a government man" because he did so. He also caused some excitement by accusing a portion of the local press of propagating "seditious, blasphemous and mischievous doctrines." Lord Exmouth, who had moved the loyal address, led the cheering for the King, and this caused an outburst of popular irritation, during which his effigy was carried through the Three Towns in a cart, and torn in pieces by the mob "in the excess of their wantonness." The carter was arrested, but so menacing were appearances that the Mayor released him, and the fragments of the make-up were then gathered together, carried with explanatory placards to a vacant spot, and burnt amid cheering. The insult was credited to dockyardsmen touched "with the Radical mania for sedition and infidelity," the result of the "black and filthy literature" on sale in the streets. In the local papers no reference was made to these doings of the " Dock Ingrate Society "; but incensed Tories at a distance declared "the guilt and baseness were not confined to the dirty actors," and that "whilst candle-headed fools, knaves and rogues stood tittering and sniggering at this demonstration of gross ingratitude, not one man was found with honest indignation and British energy enough in him to tear the scoundrels from the cart." In a passionate outburst the writer demanded : "Shall he whom you saw struggling in the waves at your own doors, to save the shipwrecked men of the Dutton, and who did save them ; shall Lord Exmouth above all men be selected to make sport for the dregs of your own town?" The incident was indignantly commemorated by an Exeter journalist, who was subsequently imprisoned at the instance of the King, for libelling the Queen before her guilt was established :

> At Dock was the "shame,"
> Where the Radical flame,
> Faced the Hero, the pride of our shore ;
> Even at Dock was it seen
> That the friends of the Q———,
> Were small tradefolk in league with the W———,

There was great sympathy with the Queen in Plymouth, and when the Italians who accused her of adultery, passed through on the way to Falmouth, they were assailed with execrations. On arriving at the port of departure, there was such an outburst that the officer in charge threatened to shoot the first man who threw a stone. The witnesses then took their leave in safety. Resentment was still more significantly shown at Plymouth, in 1821, when the Queen was excluded from the Coronation ceremony. There was a general abstinence from illuminations in honour of the King, and the commemoration was confined to military displays and charitable entertainments.

Elections came and passed, and the privileged classes in Plymouth were found in fierce and frothy opposition to Catholic emancipation. In March, 1827, the Mayor, Mr. Richard Arthur, the Rev. John Hatchard, Dr. Blackmore, Mr. W. H. Hawker, and Dr. Bellamy were the leading speakers at a public meeting, at which it urged that equality of treatment could only be granted at peril to the Constitution. The Rev. J. Worsley, Unitarian Minister, and Mr. John Bayly derided their fears, but the petition was adopted and the Townhall placed at the disposal of the opponents for promoting the organisation. The rising tide of Reform did not tempt the freemen to increase their number, and, in 1828, it was insisted that the town had only selfish interests to consider. Sir George Cockburn begged the electors to remember the public works in progress and insisted that "duty and gratitude" should direct them to choose "government men." Mr. Henry Woollcombe, in proposing his election, insisted that members should never be shackled by inconvenient pledges, and Dr. Bellamy, who suspected Sir George of leaning to the Catholic cause, withdrew from the Guildhall before the vote was taken—an act of "grace" which was suitably acknowledged. Sir George entertained over 150 freemen at the Royal Hotel, and, after dinner, he pledged himself that the best interests of the town and port should be his particular study. When he looked upon that great island which had sprung up as if by magic in the Sound, making that part of the harbour a roadstead of perfect safety, he saw that great things might be done for Plymouth ; and he trusted that there would be found amongst the inhabitants, men of public spirit, who would persevere to increase the commerce of the port, and make it equally as well famed as a commercial as it was as a naval station. It had been long his study to watch over the naval interests of this country in general, but it had now become his duty to attend to those of this port in particular, and it was a duty which he would never neglect. He should have it in his power to promote those interests at headquarters, and he would be always ready to assist the endeavours of those who laboured for the good of Plymouth. On the next day Sir George was chaired and subsequently left in a carriage for London.

Reform was really in the air, and Lord John Russell was inviting examples of genuine hardship. Dr. Woollcombe espoused the cause of the Plymouth freeholders, not so much to urge their special claims as to give momentum to the agitation, pointing out that, in the reign of Charles II., there were 300 voters with a population of 7,000, whilst there were now 21,000 residents, with 200 freemen only. Freeholders were excluded from a right which their predecessors enjoyed for ages, either exclusively or concurrently with the freemen, and they now earnestly maintained that they could not, "without a dereliction of a duty they owe to themselves, to their posterity, to the unrepresented inhabitants of the town, and to their country, abandon the prosecution of their claims, whenever an opportunity is afforded them of doing so with a prospect of success." Dr. Woollcombe pleaded for relief by inclusion, but Reform, when it arrived, was more embracing than either freemen or freeholders contemplated. Upon the accession of William IV., the storm rapidly gathered ; but the retiring members, Sir George Cockburn and Sir T. Byam Martin, merely expressed their gratitude for "uninterrupted confidence."

The agitation was pulsating the mass of the population ; but the members pursued their hostile course, and were hoist by their own petards through an amusing miscalculation. Anticipating that ministers would resign upon defeat, they voted against them, only to find that they sat tight. So that Plymouth " whose connection with the Government had been so close and long standing, now finds itself in the position of having two anti-Reformers out of office, and in opposition to the known sentiments of 19-20ths of the inhabitants." The probable fate of the Reform Bill was the only subject now discussed ; and, on the motion of Dr. Cookworthy, adopted a petition "imploring your right hon. House not to disappoint the hopes nor to endanger the safety of the nation by the rejection of the measure." Excitement was intensified by this unbending attitude and execrations were heard all through the West. A multitude gathered in front of the Royal Hotel, where hustings had been erected, draped with green baize and surmounted with flags. "That highly respected and staunch reformer, Mr. Thomas Bewes," was called to the chair, and sternly rebuked the peers for pronouncing a system of corruption "to be the only good form of Government." Another concourse assembled in the Devonport Town Hall, and, after similar speeches, "the people sang the National Anthem with indescribable effect. Nine times nine cheers were given for the King and his Ministers, and a most hideous yell for the Bishops." Petitions were despatched in which the inhabitants of Plymouth and Devonport ventured "at the unexampled crisis, to express our grief at the rejection, by the House of Lords, of the bill to amend the Representation of the people in England and Wales, especially after it had obtained the assent of a large majority of the House of Commons. We nevertheless repose, with unabated confidence, in your Majesty's paternal goodness to sanction such Constitutional but decisive means as may ensure the final success of the great and healing measure of Parliamentary Reform."

In 1831 the freemen of Plymouth became alarmed, and "in a spirit of acknowledged liberality," admitted a considerable addition to their ranks, but robbed the concession of its virtue by debarring the new electors from the right to take part in the approaching election. Alive to their influence, if not assured of their power, the latter issued a manifesto warning the old freemen that the re-election of "anti-Reformers" would be a misrepresentation in the "plain understanding of the term." To test the convictions of the enfranchised, the Hon. George Eliot presented himself as "a steady supporter of the general measure of Parliamentary Reform lately proposed by his Majesty's Ministers, convinced as I am that nothing can be so well calculated, in its consequences, to afford security to the throne, stability to our institutions, a full and free development of the resources of this empire, the extinguishment of discontent, and the happiness of all classes of his Majesty's subjects." Great excitement prevailed in the town, not only amongst members of the Corporation, but on the part of residents generally, and the possibility of anti-Reform members being returned by 150 freemen, when the sentiments of 30,000 were in favour of the Bill, threw the borough into deep anxiety. The old members found their holdings disputed after years of quiet possession, and such was the heat engendered that, although neither adverted in his address to the enthralling subject, Sir George Cockburn issued a statement expressing surprise that he had been reported as an enemy to every kind of Reform. "I hasten," he said, "to assure you that this assertion is wholly unfounded and untrue, and I will explain to you collectively, and individually, when I wait upon you, my reasons for opposing the Bill introduced by his Majesty's Government, and the sentiments I really entertain on this important subject." Sir Byam Martin disdained any conciliatory attitude, and only undertook to pay strict attention to local interests. The Hon. George Eliot was, meanwhile, cheered by spontaneous offers of encouragement, and the cauldron of feeling seethed until it overflowed.

II

Early on the morning of the first day's polling in April, 1831—the last and most eventful of the pre-Reform elections in Plymouth—the streets were crowded to excess, inflammatory incitements were passed from hand to hand, and it was evident the struggle would not pass without strong demonstrations of feeling. Shortly after the Mayor took his seat, Martin and Cockburn entered the Guildhall, and were received with a chilling silence that strangely contrasted with the roar that greeted Captain Eliot. The calcula tion had been that Cockburn would not stand against the decided feeling of the inhabi-tants, avowedly relying upon those members of the Corporation who had pledged them-selves in other times, and under different circumstances. When his determination to proceed was known, all orders of people, from highest to the lowest, were seized as with a mania. Dense masses paraded the streets, the populace was menacing, shops were closed, business was at a standstill, and nothing was discussed save the insults offered to the inhabitants in attempting to return one who voted in opposition to "a patriotic and popular King's wishes." Freemen who supported Cockburn were received with hisses and yells, but the friends of Eliot were greeted with cheering, and the candidate was loaded with favours. The ebullitions towards dusk were turbulent, uproar without was not more violent than clamour within the hall, and recurring struggles caused a suspension of the proceedings. The doors having been closed by order of the Mayor, the populace broke the windows, and the officials hesitated any longer to exclude them. But the uproar continued, and, although the Mayor threatened to close the poll if silence was not kept, every artifice was unavailing, and none could secure order until Captain Eliot rose. He requested the inhabitants to give every gentleman a fair and patient hearing, and implored them, if they had his interest at heart, to quietly allow the business to proceed. Whatever might be the result, he was satisfied that in Plymouth not one man in a hundred was other than a Reformer. This assurance was greeted with volleys of cheering, and then there was a lull in the storm. But there arose "the most dreadful yells" when the first day's polling gave Sir Byam Martin 94 votes, Sir George Cockburn 84, and the Hon. Captain Eliot 54. At night bands of music paraded the town, and uproar and bad feeling were intensified. An unbridled crowd surrounded the Royal Hotel early the next morning, and the air rang with the battle cries of Reform, as the popular candidate drove to the Guildhall in an open landau which was decorated with laurel. He was preceded by bands, and supporters carrying banners, on which were inscribed in gilded letters "The People's Choice." In his wake, twenty thousand persons rended the air with a hurricane of cheers. Hitherto the conduct of the populace, with one or two exceptions, had been tolerably restrained, but, "as will happen on all occasions of strong public excitement, a multitude of the lowest characters gave way to their natural ferocity." Cockburn and his friends, who were following, were suddenly enclosed by an infuriated multitude, who pelted them with stones, offal, and rubbish, and hooted and insulted them with opprobrious epithets. They reached the Town Hall with clothes torn and in miserable plight, and the crowd, finding the doors closed, broke the windows and clambered through. Nor was the scene in the Hall itself, where the Riot Act was twice read, much less violent, though no actual outrage was committed. Sir George thought it prudent to retire to another apartment; and, a representation being made that he could not leave the premises without an escort, his Worship sent to Devonport for an armed force.

Meanwhile acclamations announced the exit of Captain Eliot, and, entering his landau to create a diversion, he was drawn through the principal streets to the hustings, where he addressed "a multitude greater than was ever known to assemble in Plymouth." On the conclusion a cry was raised for Cockburn, and "a horde of desperate ruffians of the lowest class," armed with clubs and stones, instantly ran to reinforce the crowd that were still preventing Cockburn's escape in Whimple Street. He was enabled to leave under an escort of 120 soldiers, with the Mayor, magistrates, constables, and others as a body-guard. The party passed down Market Street, through Notte Street, towards the hotel; but the populace followed, uttering ferocious threats and imprecations, and "the cowardly wretches" discharged showers of missiles at the devoted band as they entered Lockyer Street. The limited number of troops left the party exposed to attack; missiles flew as thick as hails, many were repeatedly struck, and his defenders severely hurt. Sir George was cut through his hat by a brickbat, which caused the blood to flow profusely, and it was with difficulty he reached the hotel, his supporters carrying him in their arms, and battling their way to the entrance. After a contest marked by a display of feeling "which has never been witnessed in Plymouth," the poll was closed and the numbers were declared:—Martin, 101; Cockburn, 91; Eliot, 63; rejected votes, 11. The latter were tendered for Eliot, but rejected on the ground that they were second apprentices excluded by the bye-law just passed. Captain Eliot made a triumphal circuit, and, on taking leave at the outskirts of the town, said "he should not fail to acquaint his Majesty with the loyalty of the people of Plymouth."

Plymouth and the County Elections: 1790-1831. There were as many county voters in Plymouth as freemen, and the Three Towns usually took a keener interest in the elections for Devon and Cornwall than in those that passed in their midst. The procedure at these elections may be exemplified by rules observed at the election for Devon in 1790. Within two days of the receipt of the writ, the Sheriff caused proclamation to be made at the City of Exeter of "a special court to be holden there for the sole and express purpose of an election," not sooner than ten days and not later than sixteen from that day. When the freeholders duly assembled the Sheriff demanded silence and read aloud the Act "for the more effectual prevention of bribery and corruption." These forms complied with, the Sheriff took the oath and formally called for "a show of hands." But the contest could not be so determined, as a poll was intended, "which is always known and agreed upon between the contending candidates," and the Sheriff caused booths to be erected at the candidates' expense in "the most public and usual place" in the towns and villages appointed. The polling could not be continued "for more than fifteen days," Sundays excepted, and was kept open "for seven hours at the least between eight in the morning and eight in the evening." Each clerk entered in the poll book the name of the freeholder, his place of abode, the site of his freehold, of what it consisted, by whom it was occupied, and for whom he voted. At the close of each day, the sworn votes tendered were cast up. If any voter was rejected it was competent for him to present further evidence of his right, and it was expressly enjoined that the Sheriff should preserve his own consequence and not enter "into loud disputes with advocates. He should not raise his voice or get in a passion, but, if the advocates are noisy, sit down till they will give him a quiet hearing." It was not considered the duty of the Sheriff to deprive any voter of his qualification, and more especially he was recommended not to appear witty by asking gentlemen of fortune if their freeholds were worth 40s., or by pressing old men to declare they were 21 years of age. "Gentlemen are often displeased at these jokes, and they are often ill-naturedly misrepresented by the standers-by." These rules were drawn up for guidance at the Devon Election in 1790, and with the assistance of fifty special constables, no election was ever conducted "with greater regularity and decorum." The retiring members were Mr. John Rolle and Mr. J. P. Bastard. Sir Charles Bamfylde stood against them for three days, and then, despairing of success, resigned. In 1796 Mr. Rolle was created a peer, and Sir Lawrence Palk was chosen in his stead,

These gentlemen represented the county without opposition until 1812, when Palk resigned, and Sir Thomas Acland offered himself. Some premonition of the Reform controversy which was to convulse the country now pierced the ears of the privileged. No one had a stone to throw at Acland, and Bastard was described as "a sound spot in a sea of national corruption." At the last moment Mr. Graves, a naval officer for whom Lord St. Vincent refused to find a ship, issued a programme that included the abolition of tests, extension of votes, and purification of elections. All went peacefully enough at the hustings until the farmers heard the candidate advocate that the election dinner should be "stopped." Then there arose the "most foul-mouthed salutations" ever heard at a Devonshire contest. An "accident" caused the poll to be closed before "the sensation excited in Mr. Graves's favour" could reach the borders of the county, "but his indictment of those who caused the honourable stream of military promotion to be turned through the filthy channels of prostitution" was circulated far and wide. "The accident" lay in Graves's difficulty in procuring sufficient support to keep the poll open. On the first day he received four votes, on the second day eleven, on the third day four—a total of 19! He then refused to give "any further trouble," and the figures for the members were:— Bastard, 823; Acland, 400. The smallness of the poll was due to the fact that there was no time to inform the constituency a contest had been sprung.

Discontent, following the Peace, strengthened the hands of the Reformers in Devon, and Lord Ebrington took the field on the death of Mr. Bastard in April, 1816. A nephew of the deceased member entered the arena, and Roger Giles issued a sarcastic reminder to the Yeomanry:

"I don't know how you take it, but it looks rather odd to be canvassed by a Lord. It seems to me the Lords have got a house of their own. Do Lord Ebrington's friends really expect that the County of Devon will be represented by two members of the same family—the one the son of Lord Fortescue, the other his nephew by marriage, placing the whole of this influence in the hands of the Lord Lieutenant?"

Committees to watch the interests of the candidates were formed in Plymouth. "Economy, Ebrington, and England for Ever" was the battle cry of the Whigs, but it did not stir Devonshire to its depths. On the second day the Sheriff proposed to open more booths, but abandoned the idea when Lord Ebrington insisted that Mr. Bastard could overwhelm him as he had engaged the whole of the carriages and horses in the county. Mr. Bastard was 28 ahead when 300 of Ebrington's supporters entered Exeter on horseback and placed him in a majority of 94. On the fourth day the tide turned in Mr. Bastard's favour, and he led by 104 after a calvacade of carriages arrived from Totnes and Plymouth. The fifth day was no less disastrous for Ebrington, and it closed with a majority of 306 for his antagonist. On Saturday night the numbers for Bastard were 2,238, and for Ebrington 1,702, and the latter then electrified the crowd, whom it was customary to address at the close of each day's campaigning, by shouting: "I decline the contest. Only a small proportion of my supporters have recorded their votes, but at an expense which, I am not ashamed to confess, I cannot afford." Lord Ebrington "almost sobbed" in expressing his disappointment; and, in the effort to continue, tears ran down his cheek. Mr. Bastard was then girt with sword and spurs, "according to prescriptive usage," and escorted from the scene in a triumphal car, horns and trumpets playing. A body of sailors were no less conspicuous in the procession than the traditional "Blue Man," who, clad in velvet, and wearing a befitting helmet, rode in front of the new "knight of the shire."

Mr. Bastard was entertained at Plymouth, the principal toast being "The glorious majority of 623, and the thousands whom the close of the poll prevented from manifesting their zeal at the hustings in favour of Mr. Bastard." An intimation that Lord Ebrington meant to renew the struggle drew an interim address from Sir Thomas Acland, who trusted "that you wi'l not consider it as a premature or unnecessary interruption of the quiet of the peace of the county if I declare at this moment my firm determination of renewing to you the offer of my services." In a few weeks Lord Ebrington accepted a formal requisition and a " prophecy" was circulated to this effect :

> "Lord Ebrington may struggle for a second time to obtain the object of his ambition, but he will fail ! The chagrin of disappointment will then take hold of him. He will discover that he has estranged and alienated the best friends of his father's house. He will pass their mansions with a sigh, and their owners with the chilling bow of studied courtesy. O, melancholy rashness ! O, miserable result ! "

The campaign was forthwith inaugurated, pamphleteering was continuous, committees were formed in Plymouth and every other centre, lists of pledges were published on either side, and horse proprietors placed their coaches gratuitously at the disposal of their favourites. This excitement was sustained for two years, when, Ministers "having redeemed their pledges, went to the country in the consciousness that they had done their duty." Devon was flooded with skits. " Johnny Softhead " wanted to know how the son of a peer could be a Reformer, and " Veritas " enquired what Sir Thomas Acland could see in the Prince Regent "to warrant the flattery and adulation " he used in moving the " ever to be remembered address." The impression gained ground that Acland was the weak candidate, and efforts were made to rally support in his interest :

> Come on, ye Devonians, for loyalty famed,
> Be faithful and true as of old ;
> Of the stamp of your character be not ashamed—
> Come unbought, and you will not be sold.
>
> By party, by faction, by blusterings unawed,
> Exert, then, each noble endeavour ;
> Your King and your country, the Church of your God,
> Protect, and cry "Acland for Ever ! "

The better to ensure victory, Ebrington's coachmen were forbidden to carry any voters who did not pledge their "plumpers" before taking their seats. "Amid stunning uproar" the poll was declared: Ebrington, 4,090 ; Bastard, 3,829 ; Acland, 3,804. The streets of Exeter were crowded with the opponents of Ebrington, and the declaration came to them as a stupendous shock. Tradesmen hung out crape and closed their shops ; and cards were distributed calling for manifestations of "mourning."

BLACK DAYS:
July 1st and 2nd, 1818.

Sacred to the "Triumph in Devonshire of Fraud, Falsehood, and Ebrington ! "

Similar sentiments influenced the Tories of Plymouth, who met, to the number of 170, and protested against the "disgraceful treatment of Sir Thomas Acland."

> Let us vow from our country no faction shall sever,
> Our hearts to her cause and her patriots due,
> Let our shout then be Acland and Bastard for ever,
> Independence our motto, the Oak and True Blue.

Lord Ebrington's Plymouth friends commemorated his return with exuberant delight, but the opposition were contemptuous in their comments. Whilst they admitted that he was drawn into the town by the populace, "it was only by a hired mob"; and, although he was entertained at a dinner, "the Mobility of Plymouth were assembled together by art and contrivance, and those who could not incur the expense were subscribed for by some who could but ill afford to do so." The party consisted of 200 persons, "many of whom were not freeholders." One in particular, a limb of the law, "attempted to create a sort of O.P. row, and was actually kicked out of the room." Another person who attracted attention was "a converted son of Israel," who lost his snuff-box as he stood on a table to give out a sentiment. "Nor could this precious appendage to Emmanuel's pocket" be found until a constable appeared; and after searching some of the liberal and enlightened, he discovered the treasure —"O, shame!—in the pocket of a Patriot!" During this visit Charles Church was in course of repair, and there only remained a vane to be placed on the ball of the weathercock. Wishing to give Lord Ebrington a proof of his attachment, the contractor engraved his name, with the date of the victory, upon "the fickle engine," and he arranged with his son to place it upon the ball. His lordship was commencing the venison when the "patriotic artist" begged his lordship to repair immediately to the windows and witness the extraordinary feat, exclaiming: "At this moment, my lord, the weathercock of Charles Church is being placed upon the ball, and upon it is inscribed your

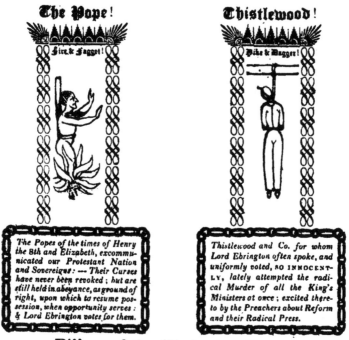

Pillars of the Ebrington Cause.

name!" This set the room in an uproar, cries of "Turn him out!" resounded from all quarters, and the engineer could not persuade the company that he meant to compliment the hero of the festivity. Messengers were despatched to intercept the intention, but "Young Stewart" had already descended, and "Lord Ebrington now rides triumphant for all time upon the cock of Charles Church, Plymouth."

The death of the King in 1820 led to the greatest fight on record. The Tories met to arrange for the return of "our late faithful, able, and excellent representative, Sir Thomas Acland," and Lord Ebrington was reviled by reason of his assumed sympathy with " Hone and the other blasphemers—those mischievous and contemptible curs who ought to be muzzled." At the dissolution his lordship made for Plymouth—not to canvass, "Oh, no; only to conciliate." Nothing was heard of Mr. Bastard's intentions, and a wail of alarm was raised:

"Freeholders of Devon, are you so fallen, so poor, so spiritless, that not a single voice can be heard to whisper 'No Popery?' For Heaven's sake, and your own, reflect seriously on the evils that will inevitably result to yourselves and your children if you yield up your hearts to apathy at a crisis so fearful as this! Let your rallying cry echo from parish to parish."

Thus abjured, Mr. Bastard re-entered the field, and the Tory centres resounded with cries of "Bastard and Protestantism," "Acland for Devon," "Down with the Assassins." At the nomination, cries of "How's Thistlewood?" saluted Lord Ebrington, followed by stormy shouts of "No Popery." When he secured the show of hands, his success was attributed to the "unwashed fingers of an insolent incursion of Apron men." The flames were fanned by the circulation of caricatures showing the allies by whom the Ebrington cause were supported. A significant endeavour to limit Whig expense resulted in this skit:

"L——— E———. Economy being the order of the day, it has been suggested to the committee appointed to carry into effect the wishes of a few extraordinary minds that, instead of using during the contest, any articles which are contributory to the Revenue, the inimitable Radical Breakfast Powder of Mr. Hunt should be substituted for tea. Powder made of Tom Paine's bones will be mixed with the flour of which the bread will be composed; and, as a further proof that the wishes of the committee are truly economical, some rare old fox-hunters, who have been turned out of the stables to refresh their constitutions with grass, are to be given as a voluntary substitute for beef by some odd-fellows. The public are respectfully informed that every kind of misrepresentation will again be got up to effectuate the return of our friend as one of the members for Devonshire.

"N.B.—Plenty of Radical Pop and old Smoked Jack for sale at the Radical shop that Hugh keeps, with a few barrels of powder unfortunately left on land in Cato Street, sent from our friends, Thistlewood and Co., for sale for Ready Money."

Another attack was in the form of verse:

> Our shallow friend (it almost makes me sick),
> To be thus hampered by an Heretick;
> Our Ebringtonian, witty Whig defender,
> Wished me my shield and armour to surrender,
> And, in the bond of peace, with Bastard's crew,
> To own their Hierarchy to be true.

> Blood of my ancestors ! How could I stand
> And, passively, my energies command,
> To serve a mere electioneering plan,
> When Pop'ry through my very vitals ran ?

Sir Thomas Acland found it necessary to repudiate rumours that he had told Lord Ebrington that Mr. Bastard's expenses were defrayed by private subscription. Upon this the division was placarded with :

"Victory ! Victory ! Acland and Truth ! Ebrington and his cause fallen together ! Lord Ebrington has asserted that a gentleman declared that which this individual, to his face, has publicly denied, and his lordship now produces, as proof, letters which contain nothing but anonymous opinion, and do not state that this gentleman ever uttered one syllable on the subject. March, 1820."

The other skit was just as outspoken :

"Died, on Saturday evening, by a blow from Sir Thomas Acland, a misunderstanding. Some of the common people gave her a shorter name. She is said to have been of very high birth, and to have lately visited some of the market towns in great company. The most praiseworthy exertions were made in the course of the evening to restore her to life by Mr. A———— U————, and some other gentlemen, but we are sorry they cannot claim a reward from the Royal Humane Society, as every sign of life was extinct, and the remains were absolutely offensive. Two severe wounds being found on her head, the Coroner's Jury gave a verdict of Justifiable Homicide in favour of Sir Thomas Acland."

The public were stirred to frenzy when Lord Ebrington asserted from the hustings that he had received the statement on high authority. The name of the Duke of Bedford went through the throng, and the clamour was deafening as the Whig champion added : "I was told that Mr. Hugh Hoare, the uncle of Sir Thomas Acland, was coming into the county to promote a subscription for Mr. Bastard." Upon this Mr. Hoare exclaimed : "I am here, and say that it is not true." Thereupon Lord Ebrington stood "silent and aghast," but, as the tumult subsided, he reiterated that the information was conveyed to him. "Groans," "various exclamations," "the lie direct," filled the air, and suggestions were made that Lord Ebrington had garbled the letter. Vehement cries of " Yes, its false," " It's infamously false," " It's fraud and falsehood throughout," rendered the din distracting. Lord Ebrington, "amid cries and execrations," then produced the document, and handed it to the High Sheriff and Mr. Hoare thereupon shouted : "I did not come here for the purpose expressed in that letter " :

> Aghast he stands ! deluded lord !
>   Thy fate will shortly be decided ;
> Thou hast the power of just one word
>   And that (no wonder) is derided.

> Too proud, too full : a heart like thine
>   May well with indignation throb ;
> For thou must, after all, resign,
>   The transient idol of a mob !

At the end of the first day's polling, Sir Thomas Acland and Mr. Bastard were buoyant. On the ensuing evening, Lord Ebrington announced that he had misinterpreted the point that had occasioned so much agitation and at once withdrew from the contest.

The poll then closed: Acland, 2,546; Bastard, 1,959; Ebrington, 1,793. The members accepted Lord Ebrington's withdrawal as "all that was wanting in reparation" and as a triumph of "personal and public honour." But the Tory poets had not done with his lordship:

> The faction has ceased, which awhile domineer'd,
> Like a comet it blazed, though the mischief we feared,
> From its tail of combustion in smoke disappeared !
> Sure ne'er was falsehood so promptly betrayed,
> And ne'er was truth in such beauty arrrayed !
> The close of the contest can ne'er be forgotten,
> Nor a cause ever thrive which at heart is so rotten.
> It existed a while, by unnatural means,
> With scarce any Devonshire blood in its veins ;
> Grew sickly and rank, at a few months of age,
> Like a wretched abortion it quitted the stage.

The day of the Reformers was to come. After another futile attempt in 1826, when Lord Ebrington retired after the poll had been opened three hours, the struggle for supremacy was protracted to the bitter end in 1829. Sir Thomas Acland and Mr. Bastard were more resolutely than ever confronted, and Plymouth was moved to its depths. There were many clever skits on either side :

> Protestants,—*Read*—*Meditate*—*Decide*—Catholic Annotations, approved of by the most Reverend Dr. Troy, Roman Catholic Archbishop of Dublin.—"The Church Service of England being in heresy and schism, therefore, not only unprofitable, but Damnable." *Annot. on Acts* x. 9.—"The prayer of a Protestant cannot be heard in Heaven." *Annot. on John* xv. 7.—"Their prayers and service are no better than the Howlings of Wolves." *Annot. on Mark* iii. 2.—"The Translators of the English Bible ought to be Abhorred to the Depths of Hell." *Annot. on Hebrews*, v. 9.—"A Christian (that is a Catholic) is bound to burn and deface all heretical books ; for example, the English Bible." *Annot. on* 1 *Thess.* ii.

Lord Ebrington was the local favourite, and the electorate were warned not to sleep at their posts, for the enemy was abroad. "The Cause : the Country's Cause," these placards proclaimed, "looks well. Remember that you have the King on your side—a Patriot King—the true monarch of the people. If the Cause is lost, you are lost, and the country is threatened with incalculable evils." Significant of the times was Sir Thomas Acland's protest against the financial penalties in which county candidates were involved, no less than his avowal that he no longer intended to incur unlimited and unnecessary expenditure. Having fought six contests in eighteen years, and realised the waste and ruin of the system, he should keep "within the bounds of prudence," and confine himself to the limits pre-scribed by Statute law. "That other class of electioneering, neither sanctioned by law nor capable of control, nor free from objections of a more serious kind, I must unequivocally and entirely decline !" At the nomination the excitement was terrific. A placard with the words "Charity for Ireland" was displayed by the Liberals. "Oh, no," exclaimed Lord Rolle, "Englishmen ought to remember that charity begins at home." Some of the crowd called for the hangman to burn the device, and three cheers were then given by the Protestants for the county motto, "No Surrender," with the words "No Popery" added. Then a placard was displayed from the hustings : "Freeholders of Devon, Who gave £20 to the Roman Catholic Rent in order to support the Popish Association? Lord Ebring-ton !" Lord Ebrington laughed as heartily at the taunt as the accusers howled. In spite of

THEATRICALS EXTRAORDINARY.

THEATRE-ROYAL, CASTLE, EXETER.

On Friday next, January 16, 1829, will be performed by particular desire of several gentlemen of distinction, the much admired Comedy of the

CONTEST,

Or Who Shall Win ?

The principal characters as under.

PAPISTS.

Try Me—*(A working man, but at present labour-ing under Popish delusion)*—Mr. Ac——d.

Mischief—*(A dear friend of Try Me's, and a Member of the Catholic Association)* — Mr. Eb——g · n.

Traitor—*(Likewise a Member of the Association)* —Mr. Patrick O'C——nn—ll. From the Theatre (not the Royal), Dublin, being his first appearance here.

Suavity—*(A Gentleman who is candidate for a Cardinal's hat)*—Mr. Ch—c—ll—r M—rt—n.

Prater—*(A violent disclaimer against rotten boroughs, but who represents one himself)*—Mr. R—ss—ll.

Dignity—*(A half-and-half friend of the Pope's)* Mr. M·—bl—y.

Eye Glass—*(A traveller in the gridiron line, from the Chudleigh manufactory)*—Mr. J. P. J—n—s.

Lath—Mr. T—rr—ll }
Moonshine——Mr. N—t—n } *Unitarians from*
Wall—Mr. K—nn—w—y } *the Exeter Theatre.*

Snug—*(A gentleman who says little but thinks more)*—Mr. Oliver.

Chorus of Radicals, Papists, &c., by the Members of the Devon County Club.

PROTESTANTS.

Sir E. Hearty, alias True Blue—*(A firm friend to his king and country)*—Mr. Bastard.

John Hearty—*(His brother possessed of the same sentiments)*—Mr. J. B—st—d.

Sam Sturdy—*(A fine scion of a true British Stock)* —Mr. S. K—ew—h.

Steadfast—*(A gentleman above all corruption)*— Mr. B——k.

Loyalty—Mr. B—ll—r.

Chairman—Mr. D——ke.

Anti-humbug—Mr. L<——te.

At the end of the Play God save the King will be sung, in full chorus, by the Gentlemen of the Cathedral, assisted by every true Protestant present.

In the course of the performance, Mr. Ac——d will favour the company with the following song, the words and music composed expressly for the occasion :—

"Alas, I well know I shall feel to my cost, From such company keeping, what friends I have lost ;
Believe me, I never had been here to-day,
But to tell you the truth, I could not keep away.
To have acted like this I must ever deplore,
Pray forgive me this time, and I'll do so no more."

☞ Ladies and Gentlemen desirous of witness-ing the performance are requested to attend early, as the fullest house ever known is expected.

L——G M———D ———Manager.

VIVAT REX.

---

the hostile reception he encountered on the hustings, he held the poll, day after day, and eventually headed the poll with 2,944. Acland was returned as his colleague with 2,764 ; but Bastard was rejected, "after twelve years of faithful service," with 2,174. The declaration was hailed with hilarious joy, and Lord Ebrington received a hearty invitation to visit Plymouth. An immense concourse assembled at the eastern entrance of the town to receive him, and in Jubilee Street the horses were taken from his carriage. He was drawn to the Royal Hotel, escorted by regimental bands and mounted yeomanry ; the streets were lined with spectators ; the fronts of houses were bright with flags, national and emblematical ; and, from the windows, his lordship received the greetings of the ladies. On reaching the Royal Hotel he addressed the people from a hustings, and afterwards received such of the freeholders as wished an "introduction." At six o'clock dinner was announced by the band striking up "The Roast Beef of Old England," and 120 persons, freeholders, and other support-ers sat down to tables "loaded with all that the heart could wish." The dinner was "a prettyish affair," and Lord Ebrington pleased the company by addressing them as "estim-able and virtuous," compliments that evoked a deal of cynical criticism. In 1831 Lord John Russell and Lord Ebrington were re-turned, without opposition, for the county— then, for the last time, called upon to return two members for the whole.

The Pocket Boroughs Around Plymouth : 1769-1831. The story of the pocket boroughs on either side of the Tamar reads like a chapter from the gro-tesque. It was no less strange than true that, whilst boiling a cabbage in some boroughs, and beating a lapstone in others, conferred the elective franchise upon the fortunate "potwolloper, or happy son of St. Crispin," merchants, though their ships formed fleets and manufacturers who employed battalions of work-people, were without any rights. Corruption dominated the pocket boroughs, and petitions were frequently presented against successful candidates. No less than seven cases were tried at the Cornwall Assizes in 1769 to recover damages for bribery, and "to have heard the evidence given as to the infamous practices used at the elections would make you shudder." Disappointed aspirants were awarded damages varying from £1,000 upwards, but, in an action brought by Mr. Cummins against a Mayor for corrupting eighteen voters, Judge Willes declared that bribery threatened the ruin of the nation, and intimated that if he had the authority to fine on his own account, he would award the full damages of £3,000. "The Judge gained much honour and praise in the county by his behaviour on that occasion."

The 1812 election cost the members for Camelford £8,000, and 24 freemen received £100 apiece. In 1818 five of the same voters met at the Allworthy Inn to exchange views with a divine, who was anxious to advise them as to their national obligations. Having no desire to thwart his patriotic purpose, the electors bargained for a substantial deposit as a guarantee of good faith. £6,000 was promised to a coterie known as "the bundle of sticks"; and, after the money had been paid, the word was given that the candidates might appear. Then "the bundle of sticks" fell to pieces, and the swindlers discovered wealthier men. At Penryn the voters estimated their privileges more modestly, and a candidate was assured that the distribution of £2,000 between 200 electors would carry the seat. A better-informed authority testified that the freemen expected £40 in notes under their breakfast plates on the morning of the poll, and that their support could not be relied upon for less. In 1818 Mr. Swann was sent to prison, and his seat was declared vacant, but the electors of Penryn again returned their hero, when he emerged from gaol, paraded the streets with bands, and "made every demonstration of loyalty and pleasure." Fireworks followed, and Mr. Swann was toasted "with the warmest marks of attachment." In truth, such was the reliance on the corrupt intentions of candidates that a dashing fellow, "calling himself the son of Admiral Harvey," drove into Liskeard "in style," and obtained £1,000 from one bank and £500 from another on production of a forged letter. At Falmouth he exchanged the notes for sovereigns, and embarked for France! The devices of some representatives to save their skins were not without interest. A. and B. were returned for Barnstaple. C., the defeated candidate, petitioned against their return. A. refused to buy off his pursuers. C. prosecuted him to conviction. B. took his seat as an honourable member.

In one of the Cornish boroughs the right of election was vested in seven leaseholders, and the lord of the fee selected persons advanced in years, so that he might hope for early vacancies in the event of defections. This was known as "The Old Man's Borough." The climax of comicality was reached at Plympton, where the freemen were either un-married, and liable by age to additional tax, or were without children although married. The depths sounded at Plympton may be gathered from James Northcote's indignant protest when his friend and master, Sir Joshua Reynolds, accepted the office of alderman in his birthplace. Regarding the "foul transactions of such a dirty borough" as alien to Sir Joshua's temperament, he could only believe that he had been so much absorbed in work that he had not taken stock of "the villainy and corruption" which prevailed there. "If ever," wrote Northcote, "the Devil should take it into his head to stand for the borough—which he has hitherto done by proxy—and outbids all the other applicants, the whole clan must vote with him." The mystery of selection at Plympton was made clear in the Journals of the House of Commons, where the privilege was declared to be "in the freemen and in sons of freemen who claimed their freedom." The sons of freemen were never noticed by the ruling powers, and, to avoid danger from rebellious offspring, the choice fell on those who were not likely to disturb calculations. Thus "deserted, doleful,

dilapidated Plympton, once the seat of industry and independence," became a veritable
"Bachelors' Borough." To be one of its freemen was regarded as a standing joke, and the
ceremony of installation was considered as equivalent to taking the veil and a devotion to
celibacy that placed a man beyond the pale of connubial hope.

Lord Cochrane determined to enter Parliament in 1805, and, as Honiton was open,
he started from Plymouth to woo its freemen. His opponent, Mr. Bradshaw, was in the
field, but Cochrane had amassed a huge sum in prize money, and it was supposed he would
spend it in sailorly fashion. It was only necessary to outbid Mr. Bradshaw to win the
seat, for, as one of the electors frankly confessed, "I always votes for Mr. Most." To the
general disgust, Cochrane stood as a political purist, and, as a number of freemen nevertheless voted for him, he decided to win Honiton without bribery the next time it was
vacant. As soon as the poll was declared, he sent round the bell-man and announced that
his adherents were to be paid ten guineas apiece. The novelty of rewarding the supporters
of an unsuccessful candidate caused unwonted speculation, for Cochrane's return might
have been ensured for less money, since feeling ran strongly in his favour, and "a little
judicious expenditure" would have easily turned the scale. When Mr. Bradshaw's friends
realised that ten guineas was the price for remaining honest, they considered they had
been easily bought at five guineas. The country was soon in the heat of electioneering
again, and Cochrane (then Lord Dundonald) left Plymouth in a vis-a-vis drawn by six
horses, followed by imposing equipages alive with officers and seamen of the Pallas.
Through Honiton the word rang that his gains were more than ever fabulous; but,
respecting his scruples, the electors refrained from inconvenient enquiries as to the rewards
they were to receive. Dundonald was triumphantly returned, and admiration for the hero
was gratifying indeed. The town-crier now made no announcement, the freemen exchanged

HONITON: OR, THE PICTURE OF A ROTTEN BOROUGH, 1805.

speculatory glances, and insinuating questions as to the remuneration were hazarded. These only evolved the curt reply : " Not one farthing !" " But, my lord," protested his agent, " you gave ten guineas apiece to the minority on the last occasion, and the majority ought to be much more generously treated now." " No doubt," replied his lordship, " but the former gift was a recognition of the disinterested conduct of my supporters in not taking the bribes offered by my opponent. To pay my present supporters would be a violation of my principles." His lordship was then importuned to console the freemen with a supper. " By all means," he responded ; " it will give me great satisfaction to know that so rational a display of patriotism has superseded a system of bribery that reflects less credit on the donor than the recipients." The supper expanded into a colossal treat for partisans and opponents ; for wives, friends, and children on both sides ; in short, for the whole town ! In 1807 Dundonald severed his connection with Honiton, pleading that the cry for places in Devonshire was so incessant that the member for a rotten borough could not feel of equal consequence with those who resented the profligacy of public expenditure. He was returned with Sir Francis Burdett for Westminster, and, as one who knew " the Plymouth Yard," exposed the scandals that embittered existence there, and denounced the corruption which disgraced the administration of the Stonehouse Naval Hospital. Dundonald paid the penalty of his candour, and was ordered to join Collingwood's fleet in the Mediterranean.

In March, 1808, Grampound witnessed " the most obstinate contest " that had occurred there since 1741. The Corporation candidates were Sir Robert Williams, jun., and Mr. John Teed ; and the freemen nominated the Hon. George Cochrane and Captain Holmes. Fourteen votes each were given by the freemen, and thirteen by the Corporation, and the judges held on petition that the vote was vested "in the Mayor and burgesses, and not in the Mayor, capital and free burgesses of the borough." Through successive elections the hardiest affection for bribery continued to prevail, and Sir Manasseh Lopes distributed £8,000 in "loans" in 1818. Twenty-four of the bribed were prosecuted to conviction ; and the member himself—who claimed to be a purist as contrasted with ministers—was fined and imprisoned. One of the convicted argued that bribery was a question of degree, and that the difference recognised was the imaginary line between wholesale and retail corruption. " The glory of Grampound," said Lord John Russell in moving its disfranchisement in 1820, "is about to depart. No more will benevolent baronets corrupt such constituencies under the guise of relieving their necessities, and not again will its freemen threaten to murder those who propound the Bribery Oath." Corruption at Grampound was so general that, after the Mayor had appropriated a large sum for his own use, several freemen were paid £35 apiece. One of the electors was acquitted because he took money in Devon and voted in Cornwall ; and the Judge was disposed to be lenient in his case because he was the only person who showed moral compunction. He withdrew from the room to avoid the formality of perjury, and the one man who took the oath had actually accepted a bribe although he possessed no qualification. Of the elections in Cornish boroughs few were more tenaciously fought than those at Fowey, and the contest in 1815 was characterised by such " inveterate fury " that sons threatened the lives of parents. Lord Valletort, " of the Blues," was confronted by Mr. Atwood, banker, of London, " of the Greys," and, after three days' polling, the numbers were declared : Atwood, 152 ; Valletort, 114. The latter declared that his opponent's triumph would be short-lived, and that, when the votes of Prince's Tenants and non-residents were disallowed, the seat would revert to himself. The forecast was justified, the next appeal was made to a more select franchise, and Lord Valletort and his colleague won "by a head." "Scot and lot" were equally divided, but the majority of " Prince's Tenants " cast the balance in favour of the heir to Mount Edgcumbe.

The "battle of Culloden" was one of the most significant of the Cornish electioneering episodes. Culloden was the name of a tenement in the borough of Camelford, and the owner devised it to his four sons, who were all under age when he died. The main portion of the territorial influence in Camelford was held by the Earl of Darlington, and, in the attempt to out-bid him, the Marquis of Hertford quietly acquired three fields from two of the sons on the day they attained their majority, so that he might erect sufficient houses to wrest the patronage of the borough from the opposition. A third son's share was captured by the Earl of Darlington when he arrived at man's estate, and the portion that belonged to the fourth was held on lease. In some unexplained way the tenant quitted possession and a Darlington nominee stepped in, to the chagrin and rage of the Hertfordites. Immediately arrangements were made to besiege and defend the house, and the riot that ensued was so serious that the Mayor read the Act, took the leading Hertfordians in custody, and left the Darlington faction in possession of the spoils. The prisoners were tried at the Cornwall Assizes for assault and conspiracy, but the Judge was indignant at being asked to adjudicate on the "miserable party broils of a pitiful borough," and the jury returned a verdict of acquittal.

The election at Callington in 1828 was fiercely conducted, and resulted in much mural literature. On the one side a "Freeholder of Callington" complained that the Portreeve acted with gross partiality by admitting illegal votes for Sir C. Robinson and Colonel Lygon, and rejecting the just claims of the opposite party. The answer to this was that the Portreeve refused to allow speculators to vote on fee farm rents, the highest of which did not amount to more than 4s. 6d. yearly, and that he considered himself justified in rejecting the franchises of 58 persons—locally designated "Broom-sticks"—who acquired their supposed privilege a few hours before they entered the room. In order to induce the Portreeve to countenance these "two-penny" votes, "unwarrantable and indecent threats" were used by the counsel who journeyed from London to represent the defeated candidates. The retort to this was that the Portreeve admitted freeholders, who had the right of franchise passed over to them by Lord Clinton on promising to pay a farthing at Christmas as "borough rent." Of the sixty-eight who voted for the members returned, thirty-eight were of this description. Most of them obtained possession of their deeds only a few hours before they came to the hall, and were unable to describe the property they tendered their votes for until slips of paper were put into their hands containing the particulars. Some of these, being incautiously dropped in the hall, were read aloud, to the amusement of the auditors. The purchase money for these freeholds ranged from twenty to forty shillings, and the holders no sooner tendered their votes than the legal adviser of the returned members prevented any questions calculated to elicit whether the vote was a just one or otherwise. The only reply to be obtained was, "I am legally advised to decline answering that question." The state of the poll was—Lygon, 68; Robinson, 68; Attwood, 51; Thompson, 51.

At St. Ives, in the same year, the proceedings were rendered grotesque by the gulling of the constituency, after expectations of a highly remunerative contest had been raised. The day before the election, whispers were circulated that another candidate was expected, and the friends of Mr. Arbuthnot were seen gliding like eels from house to house "secretly brushing up the memories of the immaculate." Scouts were sent out, who returned with the alarming news that there were certain indications of mischief, that expresses had arrived and departed again, and that consequently the enemy was near at hand. This exertion was continued all night, and by break of day, everything was considered to have been done that was practicable. Hopes and fears alternately preponderated, because Sir James Morrison's name had got wind, and, about three hours before the time arrived for going to the Town Hall, two carriages were seen descending the hill at a tremendous pace, and everyone was on the tip-toe of expectation. Freemen, Aldermen, and Mayor turned out, headed by their Patron, Sir Christopher, and posted themselves at the head of the street near Bennett's Hotel, each straining his eyes to catch the first glimpse of the strangers. It was "truly ludicrous" to witness this anxiety when a well-known "out-and-outer," as an agent for electioneering purposes, passed, followed by the known friends of Mr. Morrison. "It was immediately bubble and squeak, helter-skelter, orders and counter-orders, all bustle and confusion." Hogarth's pencil could not have done justice to the scene of mingled disappointment and delight when it was announced that Mr. Morrison was not to be proposed.

In 1830 attempts were made by outsiders to test the prerogatives of patrons. At St. Mawes, where the ceremony was usually very quiet, the proceedings were interrupted by tenants from adjoining manors, who claimed the right to vote. The candidates nominated in the interest of the Duke of Buckingham were Sir C. E. Carrington and Mr. G. W. Pigot, and the opposition was represented by Mr. W. Haldimand and Mr. R. W. Edgall. On the tender of the first name for the latter gentlemen, a legal argument was raised to the status of their supporters ; and ruling that only the tenants of the Duke could vote, the Mayor rejected the others, and declared his favourites duly elected. There was "a prodigious uproar" at Truro, and the hall was so crowded that Mr. Bird, of Plymouth, who represented the inhabitants, withdrew from the room because the Mayor would not adjourn to the open air. Lord Encombe and Mr. N. W. Peach were proposed by the councillors present, amounting to thirteen persons ; and Sir J. W. Lubbock and Mr. W. Tooke were supported by the burgesses at large. The former polled 14, and 146 votes were given for the latter. At Lostwithiel, the representatives of the patron, Lord Mount Edgcumbe, forcibly ejected from the room two strangers who were nominated as candidates, and they submissively left the town.

The Reform agitation reached "the ancient and loyal borough" of Beeralston, where a contest followed the elevation of Lord Lovaine to the peerage in 1829. As opposition was expected, there was a numerous assemblage of voters, and persons possessing property in the borough and parish of Beer Ferris. According to ancient custom, these grouped around a greenwood tree which stood in the centre of the village, and Mr. Kerswill, surgeon, of Devonport, the Portreeve, stood upon a stone at the trunk to conduct the ceremony, and there remained until the easterly wind drove him to the inn. After precept and Bribery Act had been read, Mr. Toll proposed Mr. John Atwood on behalf of the public, and Mr. W. Foot, of Devonport, nominated Mr. David Lyon, in the interest of the patron. The show of hands was in favour of Atwood, and, as neither candidate was present, Mr. Lyon's friends demanded a poll. Mr. Foot tendered the first burgage vote, and Mr. Snell, of Callington, contended, on behalf of the free burgesses, freeholders, and inhabitant householders, that the holders of such tenures had no exclusive privilege. When he questioned Mr. Foot as to whether he held the deeds and received the rents of the alleged holding, he declined to answer, and others followed his example. At the close of the poll, Mr. Snell urged the Portreeve to make a double return, but, after consulting with his assessor, Mr. Boger, Mr. Kerswill declared Lyon to be elected. Thirty-one burgesses, freeholders, and inhabitant householders had voted for Atwood, and Lyon was supported by seven non-resident burgage-holders, who had only just acquired their nominal interest. A petition was laid, but it was ruled that the right of election had been properly exercised by the holders of burgage tenure, under the Earl of Beverly, patron of the borough, and that the right had been bequeathed by his father, the Duke of Northumberland, with his estates in the district. The free burgesses, freeholders and inhabitant householders claimed an equal right to vote, but the House of Commons decided that the privilege was confined to freehold tenants holding burgage tenures, on their paying a minimum of threepence per annum as ancient burgage rent to the lord of the borough. In 1831 only two electors attended the election at Beeralston, and the proceedings were unique, even for the period. The Portreeve, Dr. Butter, of Plymouth, with his clerk, sat under the same greenwood tree ; and one of the voters handed him a card containing the names of two candidates, proposed by himself, and seconded by his friend. He was told by the clerk that he was too early. Before the reading was completed the other voter passed in a card corresponding with the former, and he was informed that he was too late. The Portreeve and his assistants then adjourned to the public-house, and filled in a return which was not signed by a voter.

The right at Saltash was vested in the Mayor and burgesses ; but it passed in 1807 to every person seized of an estate for life in an ancient burgage tenement, wheron an ancient dwelling-house then stood, or formerly stood, and in no other persons. In the reign of George III., Saltash was incapacitated by a series of accidents from continuing as a Corporation, and surrendered its charter. A petition for its restoration resulted in the grant of another patent. There was a higher tone at Saltash than in many rotten boroughs, but the absence of responsibility was evinced during one of the later elections, when the agent of a candidate called on a freeman with the remark : "You are aware, sir, there is a vacancy in your borough, and I am come to solicit your vote." "Yes, certainly," replied the freeman. After some bargaining, he observed : "By-the-bye, sir, I forgot to ask the name of the gentleman you wish me to support." "Oh," was the reply, "he's a banker in London ; but I am sorry to say I have for the time forgotten his name." And the pair parted without the elector knowing for whom he had promised or the agent being able to remember for whom he was acting. In 1827 Mr. William Russell, of Branspeth Castle, Durham, whose father had represented Saltash in three succeeding Parliaments, heralded his own candidature by "a most splendid dinner to the Mayor, Corporation, free burgesses and other friends." After a "jovial" evening the company separated "highly gratified with the unbounded liberality and elegance displayed. The evening was very 'stormy,' and the guests carried home a fair portion of 'the heavy wet.'" The following evening Mr. Russell entertained 200 guests at a ball and supper, the Assembly Rooms being decorated with variegated lamps, and, at intervals, rockets, portfires and other fire-works were displayed. The "urbanity and munificence" of the host were in the mouths of all when the hour for separation—5 a.m.--arrived. Influenced by the instinct of self-preservation, the freemen of Saltash posed as Reformers, with, however, a consistent anti-Catholic bias. The borough was held in the Whig interest, but "the Saltashers" would not "have a Papist-plus-Reformer" thrust down their throats. In 1830, the Earl of Darlington and Mr. John Gregson were returned, and a large company sat down to dinner and sustained the festivities "with much spirit till a very late hour." Mr. Crampton, Solicitor-General for Ireland, was the next candidate, and, on being asked if he was friendly "to the deservedly popular measure of Reform," Mr. James Buller, whose family exercised the political influence of the borough, replied that his friend had accepted office with that view. The freemen dined in the borough long room, and the evening passed with "hilarity and good humour." As a reward for its loyalty to Reform, an attempt was made to preserve the identity of Saltash by constituting the parish the area of the constituency. But the device was too transparent, and Ministers had to abandon it.

Cornwall was the scene of a conflict as memorable as that which resulted in Lord Ebrington's success for Devon. At the nomination rain fell in torrents ; but 5,000 persons remained around the hustings throughout the pitiless storm. A thousand Reformers entered

Bodmin, on horseback, headed by Sir Charles Lemon and Mr. Pendarves, and 700 more partook of breakfast at Sir William Molesworth's seat at Pencarrow. Never had there been witnessed such an array of county yeomanry, the laurel leaf of Reform was dominant, and Lemon and Pendarves were received with shouts "that made the welkin ring." Lord Valletort and Sir Richard Vyvyan were cheered by their friends, but the latter was

SALTASH APPROACHING ELECTION.

For SALE by PRIVATE CONTRACT, and on TERMS well worthy of attention, the FREEHOLD and Inheritance of, and in an excellent Messunge, DWELLING-HOUSE and PREMISES, situate in the centre of the Borough of Saltash, and fronting the main street thereof.

The above is an indisputable BURGAGE TENURE, and will confer on the Purchaser a right of Voting for Members both to represent that Borough and the County of Cornwall in Parliament : privileges capable of being exercised to great advantage. For particulars, and to treat for the purchase, apply (if by letter post-paid) to Mr. VEALE, Saltash.

19th July, 1830.

assailed by the Reformers with a storm of groans and cries of "Come again this day six months." Not a word could be heard from the hustings, and efforts to obtain silence were in vain. Lord Valletort was little better received, although he was in favour of limited Reform. Animated scenes were witnessed at Lostwithiel on the day of the polling. The Reform colours (rose and yellow) were displayed in the proportion of ten to one among the freeholders, and fifty to one in the crowd. Thousands of pedestrians plodded their way to the town, bodies of horsemen poured in from the country side, and vehicles decorated with favours, and crammed with voters, made for the rival head-quarters. At noon four stage coaches, and a large car, brought seventy freeholders from Plymouth and Devonport, and paraded the town flourishing the Union Jack. These were followed by a waterman's boat manned with Three-Towns' voters, who had hoisted a huge bottle of "Russell's Purge" as a figurehead. Through the day the chorus rang :

> We've scorned Corruption—scorn'd to bend
>   At Baal's Shrine the knee,
> We've dragged the monster from his Den
>   And shall we not be free ?
> Then Rise Reformers, One and All,
>   Stand forth ye tried and true,
> And show us, at your country's call,
>   What Cornishmen can do.

At the close of each day's excitement the declarations evoked "thunders of applause," and Lord Valletort announced that, when his antagonists polled one-half the freeholders, his colleague and himself would resign. The Reformers daily gained strength, and the numbers were declared :—Pendarves, 1,819 ; Lemon, 1,804 ; Vyvyan, 901 ; Valletort, 811. The statement was received with immense cheering, amid which the new knights of the shire came forward, wearing swords and spurs, and addressed the crowd. Tolerably effectual means were adopted by the Reform Committee to meet the wants of their supporters, and they bought the Old Palace and fitted it with grates and other essentials for cooking. Although the large dining-room would not hold more than three hundred "with comfort," four hundred crowded the tables from day to day. A cook and ten assistants were imported from Plymouth, and the huge joints were spitted in the open and turned by a wheel with cranks. Thirty bullocks were killed for the supply of the chief dining-room, and 130cwt. of beef was placed upon the table, in addition to 45cwt. of mutton. An enormous stock of liquids was laid in, and eight hogsheads of porter, eight hogsheads of cider, two pipes of wine, one hogshead of brandy, and one hogshead of rum were added each morning. In passing through Devonport on his way to London, Mr. Pendarves addressed a crowd from

KK

the balcony of the Royal Hotel, and apologised for the insufficiency of the entertainment. The ordinary houses of convenience "in the heart of our opponents' territory" were monopolised, and he and Sir Charles could only provide "good meat, good bread, and good drink for our friends." Gusts of feeling swept the Three Towns at the approaching triumph of Reform, and the popular song was everywhere shouted to the tune of '· Borough Bridge is Broken Down" :

> Callington is as good as gone ;
> Whitchurch is a church in peril ;
> Death has opened its jaws to swallow St. Mawes,
> And Saint Mic-hell has gone to the Devil.
>
> St. Germans' fate is not to win ;
> Lostwithiel is lost with its poll ;
> We have nothing to choose but lose both the Looes,
> And strike Plympton from off the Rolle.
>
> 'Tis plaguey bad fun for Okehampton,
> 'Tis agony in Tregony's bower ;
> Saltash looks not very sweet thereon,
> And Beer-alston has turned sour.
>
> Poor Bossiney now none will come nigh,
> Appleby none will taste ;
> Poor old Fowey has lost its joy,
> And Grampound is but a waste.

Plymouth's First Reformed Elections: 1832. Attempts to emasculate the Reform Bill united "the wealth, talent and respectability of the port" on Plymouth Hoe, and petitions were adopted by 30,000 people. Landowners, clergymen, merchants, bankers, traders, and artisans of every class were in attendance, and revolutionary emblems were displayed in the sight of the soldiers who swarmed the slopes of the Citadel. Afterwards the crowd marched in procession, and went free through the Halfpenny Gate, Lord Mount Edgcumbe waiving the toll, "an unexpected mark of liberality from his lordship, who is an anti-Reformer." When the Bill was again in peril, there was an expression of something like despair. Business was suspended, gloom spread through all ranks, groups assembled in anxious conversation, shops were closed, flags were displayed at half-mast, muffled bells were rung, and "every demonstration of public sorrow was exhibited." As soon as the measure escaped the last shoals and quicksands, and the pent-up anxiety was relieved, the authorities appointed a day of commemoration. At daybreak the population was astir; the streets were crowded with visitors; houses were bright with evergreens, flowers, banners and flags; triumphal arches were raised and garlands suspended; the bells rang merry peals, and congratulations were universal. The trades procession of emblems, devices and models extended a mile and a half in length; and the dresses and decorations "surpassed description." £5,000 was expended upon this spectacle, and thousands were engaged for weeks in preparing the set spectacles. "Sir Francis Drake and the Genius of Plymouth" were represented in one car, and a tableau of Neptune and Britannia was drawn in a boat by a dozen seamen. "Adam and Eve" were shown in the garden, as the first gatherers of fruit; "Justice" was conspicuous with the scales; "Bacchus" offered copious libations to himself; a shepherd and shepherdess, with sheep, sheltered within an arbour of evergreens; and ploughs were driven by teams of greys, with "ancient farmers" holding the reins. "A Country Shoemaker's Shop of the Olden Times" was in full working order, with the motto, "Reform Leather : Free from Corruption." The cobblers were busily employed, and Master Jobson was reading the paper as they worked. St. George, in glittering armour, was attended by his esquires, and a dying dragon "represented that unconstitutional monster so long near the throne, but greater than the throne itself." Captive Boroughmongers, clad in penitential linen, were guarded by watchmen carrying battle-axes ; and a barrister, in gown and wig, upheld a banner with the inscription : "The Last of the Borough Bridges." In Bilbury Street "the star of knowledge refracted its rays on the demons of corruption." A transparency of Lord Ebrington showed a scroll that bore the words : "Devonport is Now Free." In Queen Street there was a view of the Eddystone Lighthouse by moonlight, and a piece of wreckage bore the words :

> The ship is safe though lost a mast,
> Huzza, my boys, the Reform Bill's passed !
> May Trade and Commerce never fail,
> And honest industry, ever prevail !

Other devices represented Dr. Russell administering a purge to John Bull, and another depicted John Bull thanking Dr. Russell for the draught that had effected his recovery.

Wrapt in snug repose, the freemen had hitherto pledged their patrons, and it was enough that these served the Government. How mighty was the upheaval in Plymouth when the franchise was suddenly conferred upon 2,500 instead of 200 voters ! Alive to their newly-acquired privileges, the public asked two natives—"men of high honour and unsullied principle"—to stand. What course would the old members adopt ? Out of touch with the population, the opponents of the Bill for which the struggle had been strenuous—would they submit their names to the enlarged electorate ? The borough had not long to speculate, for his Majesty considerately nominated Sir George Cockburn to the command of a foreign station, and, as the latter naively explained, " It is, of course, out of my power to offer myself to you for the honour of representing you in Parliament." Sir Byam Martin also sang the song of the swan, but cheerfully looked forward to a period "when I may command the favour of the new voters as well as the freemen."

INHABITANTS OF PLYMOUTH.

When Counsellor Bird first entered the Freemasons' Hall alone to call the ' Mayor and Commonalty' to an account for the profligate appropriation of Drake's Pious Legacy to your Forefathers and their Descendants for ever, Inhabitants of this town.

Who was the first man that, Unsolicited, stepped forward to support him in the assertion of your valuable Rights? John Collier, Esq.!

Who was the second man that stood between the Poor Man and Oppression? Mr. John Edmonds!

How have your Corporate Guardians protected you? Read DRAKE'S Legacy and Old COLE'S Chronicles !

Have they shown more respect for your Lives than your Property? No ; for you must buy your own even to preserve you from Cholera !

Men of PLYMOUTH ! Verily I say unto you, let your cry be ' The Three C C C's,' Collier, Commerce, and the Constitution !

The first will restore your Rights, the second reward your Industry, and the third protect you in the enjoyment of them !

Who are now the Friends of Order ? ' The PEOPLE.'

I am proud to be One of that People.

July 2nd, 1832.

Mr. Collier received a requisition to stand for his native town, which was signed by 442 "of my friends and neighbours. This spontaneous call affords one the highest gratification, and, laying aside all private considerations, I do not hesitate to comply with such a flattering request." Reform in the Church, as respected the collection and distribution of its revenues, he regarded as a leading object of attention. He looked with abhorrence on slavery, and promised to do his best to extirpate it, and proclaimed himself a foe to lavish expenditure and unnecessary wars. " It only remains for me to express my hope that, whilst you retain a grateful remembrance that the Bill for which we have contended together is now the law of the land, you will not expect it to work miracles. It cannot all at once cure the defects of long misgovernment, but it will prevent misgovernment in future. Our political regeneration must be the work of time. You have now the power of choosing your own representatives, and it is your duty to elect such men as will attend to your interests, and in whose hands the transformation of the House of Commons will be a lever to relieve the many odious burthens which have pressed the industry and prosperity of this country to the earth."

Mr. Thomas Bewes, being no less earnestly solicited, did not hesitate to consent to sacrifice the little ease that was left to him : "Having participated with you so largely in the endeavour to render the cause of Parliamentary Reform triumphant, I presume that my political principles do not require that exposition which may be expected from a stranger; but that those principles should admit of no doubt, I here distinctly affirm them to be a sincere attachment to our excellent Constitution in Church and State, accompanied by an anxious desire to see removed those blemishes which now deform them, in order to render both more satisfactory to the just expectations of an enlightened age. I profess an equally strong attachment to the cause of civil and religious liberty. I look to a strictly economical expenditure of the money, and to a reduced taxation as far as may be consistent with the national security—to the abolition of all sinecures and unmerited pensions, which press heavily upon the energies of the country without having the redeeming virtue of services performed on its behalf—to the utter extinction of slavery, as soon as the safety of the negro himself can be assured, with the least injury to the West India proprietor and the white population—to a revision and settlement of the Corn Laws, whether by a modification of the existing Statutes, or by some new legislative measure relating to this important subject—anxiously desiring to give no preference to any particular interest, but to view the question solely as one affecting the general welfare of the country—and finally, to the preservation of peace so far as it shall be consistent with the honour and integrity of the empire."

The withdrawal of the old members left Messrs. Bewes and Collier without any opponents, and their election was unchallenged—a doleful anti-climax to all the excitement. Consolation was found, however, in the chairing ceremony, and, mounting their gorgeous seats, the new members were escorted through the town with bands, banners, and an interminable cavalcade.

Devonport's First Parliamentary Election: 1832. The earliest expression of a demand for the enfranchisement of Devonport as a Parliamentary borough was raised in 1827. Penryn had been stripped of her right, and the Dockyard householders claimed the reversion on the ground that the parish of Stoke Damerel contained some forty thousand inhabitants. It was not only without members, but had no voice at that time in the county elections. The memorial was not entertained, but the agitation thus inaugurated continued with warmth. On the occasion of the visit of the Duke of Clarence in 1828, strong representations were made to him : "How inferior it may be in political importance, Devonport, with its 40,000 inhabitants, has never been surpassed in loyalty, and the gracious condescension of our beloved Sovereign in conferring a name upon our town has excited feelings of veneration and gratitude which we shall ever devoutly cherish." The Duke was not insensible to the local desire : "I cannot undervalue the importance of Devonport with its forty thousand loyal inhabitants, and am sure the gracious condescension of our beloved Sovereign will ever be gratefully remembered for having conferred a name upon a town in which exists so important a naval arsenal. I must always," he added, "remember the many happy hours I have spent in this place, and I thank you most sincerely for your kind wishes." "As minister of this very large and populous parish," the Rev. John Hawker assured the Duke that the day would be recorded "in the archives of our town with triumph, and handed down for the information of our children," and the Prince gracefully conceded that the Dockyard, the Harbour, and the Breakwater made the port the finest in the world.

When the Reform agitation was at its height in 1831, "a numerous and highly respectable meeting, constituting the opinion of the town," declared that whilst the men of Devonport respected the claims of all, "we cannot but feel aggrieved and degraded by our present situation, where, in a large town and parish, containing nearly 40,000 souls, six only can be found legally qualified, by freeholds in the parish, to vote even for a county member, whatever their possessions in this parish might be or their payment of taxes." From this gathering emanated a memorial to Parliament, in which it was asserted that "without vote by ballot all reform will be useless," and the West was stigmatised as "the throne of the boroughmongers." The fate of Devonport trembled in the balance, and there was a suspicion that Plymouth people were exercising hostile influences. So far from this, however, the latter asserted that "the extent, population, and wealth of Devonport render it just that the franchise should be extended to its inhabitants, and your petitioners pray your honourable House to give them a separate representation, instead of annexing them to Plymouth." The Plymouth fear was that, as Devonport was an old manor, the lord would exercise unlimited influence over the voters; and that, as its population and ratable houses exceeded those of Plymouth, the representation of the Three Towns would thus be transferred to Sir John St. Aubyn. The leading inhabitants of Devonport retorted that Sir John had never interfered with the political judgment of the inhabitants, and had far less influence than was imagined with those who accepted his leases. They affirmed, indeed, that he possessed smaller political power than his tenantry, and that, if he had the desire, he could never exercise permanent command over such a numerous body of electors as would be created when the prayer of the parish was granted. Devonport further retaliated that there was no influence in the town analogous to that exercised by the Close Corporation of Plymouth, where a few leading families had always returned their pet nominees. Intrigues at the expense of Devonport were destined to defeat, and, in March, the borough and Stonehouse were combined for Parliamentary purposes :—"The Town of Devonport and Parish of Stoke Damerel and the Township of Stonehouse : Every male person of full age, and not subject to any legal incapacity, who shall have occupied, for six months previously, any house of the said towns of the clear yearly value of ten pounds, or bona-fide subject to the yearly rent of ten pounds, or which shall have been for the same rated to the relief of the poor, or to the duty assessed upon inhabited houses, at a sum not less than ten pounds, shall have a right to vote for the "election of members for such towns." Thus Devonport not only achieved its purpose, but was united to a people "who have long been intimately connected with the town, and who will find no difficulty in cordially and sincerely amalgamating with the inhabitants for the support of their common rights as Englishmen and good and loyal subjects." The number of householders enfranchised was 3,600 in Devonport and Stonehouse, and 2,500 in Plymouth. Thus 6,100 voters were created in the Three Towns, where, hitherto, two or three hundred had exercised the monopoly.

Although Ministers had consented to the new constituency, the victory had yet to be won in the Upper House. Lord Wynford opposed the clause on the ground that Devonport was a part of Plymouth, and should be associated with it. The united population of the Three Towns was 70,000 persons, and that was a great number. But there were more populous places with two members, and it was better that Devonport should be united to Plymouth, with which it was connected in interest and character. If, said Lord Wynford, the enfranchisement of Devonport was the means of creating another Government borough, he would waive his objections, for Ministers would soon require "every source of strength to stem the tide of democracy." The reply was tendered by the Earl of Morley, who contended that Plymouth and Devonport were by no means one and the same community. Plymouth had the smaller population, and was an ancient borough. Devonport had only existed for a short period, and to hamper Plymouth with the franchise of a manorial town would ruin the one and be unsatisfactory to both. The situation was saved by Earl Grey, who, as a former resident in Devonport, testified to its wealthy and populous characteristics, and maintained that, although the Government would exercise a definite interest, its authority would not be predominant. The clause that Devonport and Stonehouse stand part of the Bill was then agreed to.

Prejudice at Devonport ran strongly with Sir George Grey and Sir Edward Codrington, two moderate Liberals, but a third aspirant—Mr. Leach, a native of the town—entered the arena, at the request of 400 advanced Reformers, who thought him the "least Conservative of the trio." The town was daily paraded by rival bands, and each candidate retained a number of inns, which were variously distinguished by colours. Sir Edward Codrington further expressed his intention of giving a ball, and the ladies were all the more enthusiastic in displaying his favours. Grey, blue, and pink ribbons were profusely exhibited on the nomination day; and the population flocked to the hustings erected beneath the portico of the Town Hall. Sir George Grey drove up in a barouche and four, and his friends displayed blue banners. Mr. Leach was drawn by four greys, and his procession was headed by a band, whilst his supporters waved brilliant flags. Sir Edward Codrington arrived in a car that symbolised the stern and quarter-deck of the Asia, the ship in which he served at the Battle of Navarino. He was accompanied by several "jolly tars," in full sailing trim; and his flag was "nailed to the poll." Silence at the hustings was demanded by the beadle, and, the request having been complied with, the speeches were delivered, and the show of hands was taken. As it was in favour of Grey and Codrington, a poll was challenged by Mr. Leach. The candidates were early in the field the following morning, bands of music parading the streets, and committees and friends rallying their forces. Booths were erected in front of George Square, on a site near Granby Barracks, outside Tamar Terrace, and on Stonehouse Quay. The polling was maintained with wonderful spirit, until, doubting the probability of his success, Mr. Leach sent his resignation to the opposition committee, and, at noon the following day, Mr. Billing announced the numbers: Grey, 1,178; Codrington, 891; Leach, 575. The members were thereupon "chaired," and Sir Edward spoke "from the quarter-deck of his three-decker." Mr. Leach was consoled by a banquet, and, after asserting that Englishmen must look to the ballot for the preservation of their liberties, he denounced those who first solemnly pledged and then abandoned him as deserving the scorn, indignation and contempt of honest men. He then heartily toasted "The unbought, unsold, incorruptible and glorious minority of 575, and the unpolled Independent electors of the borough." A significant sentiment was proposed by Mr. Ramsay: "The People—may they know their rights, and, knowing, dare maintain them."

Arising out of the election, a criminal information for libel, tending to a "breach of the peace," was filed against Mr. Thomas Woollcombe, the partner of Mr. Leach. The provocation was a charge that Mr. Woollcombe departed from his declarations in favour of Sir Edward Codrington, by writing a letter charging that gentleman with being interested in a slave plantation. The correspondence fell into the hands of Sir Edward's Committee, and, aggrieved by the publicity which they gave to a private communication, Mr. Woollcombe demanded an explanation. At the Town Hall recriminatory language was used, and, in the absence of an apology, Mr. Woollcombe explained his position in a pamphlet. Sir Edward replied that the leading statements were unfounded, and, when Mr. Woollcombe demanded the withdrawal of that imputation on his word, Sir Edward declined to hold any further communication with him. Mr. Woollcombe thereupon sent his friend, Mr. Charles Trelawney, and threatened to "post" Sir Edward if he refused to accept the challenge. Sir Edward curtly replied : "Mr. Woollcombe may do as he pleases," and obtained permission to institute a criminal prosecution. Mr. Woollcombe pleaded guilty at the trial, and the Solicitor-General urged that he had been much provoked. Mr. Justice Parke delivered judgment in these words :—"The Court, looking at the circumstances of provocation under which you wrote, arising from the language used by Sir Edward Codrington in his letter, thinks there is some excuse for your conduct, but not any great excuse ; for, originally, you yourself gave offence by inserting in your pamphlet words which could not otherwise than be very offensive to the plaintiff. Under these circumstances, the duty of the Court is to pass upon you such a sentence as we think will be commensurate with the crime you have committed. The Court cannot help entertaining feelings of gratitude to Sir Edward Codrington, who, on this occasion, has shown himself possessed of high moral courage, by preferring an appeal to the laws of his country to the appeal you wished to provoke. Looking at all the circumstances of the case, the sentence of the Court is that, for this offence, you pay a fine of £100, that you be imprisoned in the custody of the Marshal for one calendar month, and that you be further imprisoned until the penalty be paid." This harsh sentence excited much indignation amongst Mr. Woollcombe's friends ; and he was subsequently entertained at a banquet, where he claimed to have received proofs of approbation such as rarely fell to the lot of private individuals. Sir Edward's committee retaliated by expressing indignation " at the infamous falsehoods and unblushing calumnies which, under the mask of sympathy for an offender against the laws of social life and moral dignity, have been circulated far and wide by the disappointed and degraded faction that drags out a miserable existence by fomenting discord."

Lord John Russell and South Devon : 1832. Lord John Russell was invited to contest the newly-created constituency of South Devon, and, on arriving at Plymouth, was met by a crowd of several thousands on Mutley Plain. There he ascended the "splendid car of the Devonport Drapers' Company," and passed amid enthusiastic cheering to the Royal Hotel, where Mr. Richard Bayly rejoiced that his efforts had been crowded with success, "in spite of the secret machinations of false friends and the open opposition of avowed enemies." These sentiments were endorsed by Mr. T. Bewes, who confessed his inability "to add to the glorious laurels which already so profusely adorn his lordship's brow." The gratitude of Devonport was expressed by Mr. Leach, and Mr. John Collier contrasted the realisation of hopes with the despair that swayed Plymothians when they protested on the Hoe against the triumph of corruption. Lord John, in his response, warned the country that it must not look to Reform to work miracles; only to stop the spring of abuses at its source. Mr. Bulteel joined him in the contest, and Mr. Yarde-Buller sustained the Conservative cause. But the vote was with the Whigs, and their champions were returned :— Russell, 3,782 ; Bulteel, 3,684 ; Buller, 3,217. Between Lord John Russell and Mr. Bulteel there were 3,102 split votes, and the Plymouth district yielded the following figures : Bulteel, 696 ; Russell, 520 ; Yarde-Buller, 275. In his address of thanks Lord John Russell observed :—"It is a matter of great satisfaction to me that the county of Devon has not changed its sentiments on the question of Reform. To reform safely is a far more difficult task than to retain obstinately or to overturn rashly. Yet it is by such a course alone that members of the new Parliament can faithfully obey public opinion."

"They have drained the juice and left us the *Peel*" was the Reformers' song in 1834. A dissolution followed the change of Ministry which brought Sir Robert Peel to the front in 1835, and the members for Plymouth were especially outspoken. Mr. Bewes thundered in his address: "The Tories, whom you have already repudiated as the unrelenting foe of civil and religious liberty, have once more obtained entrance to the Royal Councils, and would even persuade you of their conversion to sentiments which they have hitherto disclaimed in terms of unqualified abhorrence. To this desperate expedient of an appeal to the people, like the last throw of the unsuccessful gambler, our opponents have had recourse, thereby hoping to regain the power that they so long abused. Place no reliance on these dissembling Proselytes of Freedom!" Mr. Collier was quite as emphatic in his appeal: "From 1830 to 1832 you were all, or nearly all, Reformers. Knowing my political principles you elected me one of your representatives without any other pledge than to do my utmost for my constituents and my country. How faithfully and well I have performed my arduous and important duties remains for you to declare. The principles which in 1832 you and I held in common I hold still, and, if you restore me to my seat, by them I shall invariably be guided." Sir James Cockburn fought the Tory battle on behalf of his brother, Sir George, the old member, and the latter's popularity was evinced in a poll which justified Mr. Collier's instinct in anticipating that personal considerations would influence the conflict:—Collier, 714; Bewes, 682; Cockburn, 662.

At Devonport Sir George Grey and Sir E. Codrington were again the Liberal candidates—the former as an avowed enemy of the Tories, and the latter as a "True Reformer." Mr. Dawson, a member of the Peelite administration, came forward as a "Liberal-Conservative," and he was told by Admiral Codrington that the only respect in which he was a Conservative lay in his desire to "conserve corruption." At Mr. Dawson's meeting, which was held in the Town Hall, a resolution was passed declaring that he ought not to receive the suffrages of the electors, as he was member of an administration which had insulted the enfranchised by opposing the grant of the suffrage. Turned coats and rat-traps were the favourite emblems on the day of the nomination, and the show of hands, like the vote, went against Mr. Dawson :—Codrington, 1,114 ; Grey, 956 ; Dawson, 764. The chairing was a memorable affair. In a huge car, drawn by six horses, which embodied the idea of "John Bull's Castle," Sir Edward sat enthroned, attended by sailors who were armed with battleaxes. Sir George Grey was at home in a triumphal pavilion,

PLYMOUTH POLL ANALYSIS, 1835.

Description of Voters.	Bewes.	Collier.	Cockburn.
Baronets	1	1	—
Knights	1	—	1
Esquires	9	7	1
Physicians	4	3	2
Barristers	1	—	1
Clergymen	—	—	5
Solicitors	18	18	8
Surgeons	10	10	7
Merchants	48	44	10
Gentlemen	73	77	56
Gentlemen in receipt of Government pay	32	32	107
Old Freemen	21	21	77
Shipowners	5	4	3
Shipwrights	7	6	12
Tradesmen	374	400	244
Artists	2	2	1
Architects	3	2	1
Surveyors.	2	1	1
Dissenting Ministers	4	5	2
Innkeepers and Victuallers	22	28	58
Accountants	5	6	3
Clerks and Travellers	6	8	9
Musical Professors	3	4	1
Librarians	1	1	—
Schoolmasters	10	10	2
Dancing Masters	1	1	—
Mariners	5	7	16
Farmers	6	5	6
Parish Clerks	1	1	1
Fishermen	2	3	2
Millers	2	2	1
Sheriff's Officers	—	1	1
Journeymen	—	—	1
Labourers	3	4	19
Servants	—	—	1
Policemen	—	—	1
Pig Drovers	—	—	1
1835.	682	714	662

draped in festoons of silvery hue, and surmounted by a floral bower, of which a gilded crown formed the apex. Messrs. Collier and Bewes followed in an open chariot, decorated with laurels and flags of classic design; and drawn by six horses, with postilions who were resplendent in liveries of scarlet and gold. Hundreds of admirers on richly caparisoned steeds formed the escort, and pedestrians followed with waving branches of palm. Colonel Abernethie refused to allow the troops of the garrison to supply "the triumphal music," and, as soon as he took his seat, Sir Edward charged the local authorities with firing a salute in honour of the flag that Mr. Dawson suspended from his hotel window. Sir John Beresford retaliated that naval officers would never dream of honouring in this fashion any flag that Sir Edward had flourished from his hotel window, and, with this flout, the incident terminated.

Lord John Russell Rejected for South Devon: 1835. Lord John Russell's triumph was short-lived, for he had to seek re-election on accepting office in 1835. At a meeting held at the Mechanics' Institute, Dr. Cookworthy soundly rated the weak-kneed Liberals, and Lord John Russell rubbed in the salt by hinting that he was not disposed to trust men " whom he saw one day calling out for Reform, and the next day anxious for compromise." His prospects were not unattended with anxiety, for the new rural electors were under the dominion of their landlords, and the "independent" small farmers were alarmed at the prospect of legislation permitting the wholesale importation of foreign corn. Lord John Russell, at a meeting held in the Common Hall, at which he was invested with the freedom of Plymouth, disclaimed revolutionary projects. It was his leading aim to reduce the army and root out corruption and sinecures, and the uneasiness of his supporters increased with incessant cries of "The Church in Danger" and "No Popery." Lord John Russell's committee, of which Mr. Richard Bayly was chairman for the Plymouth district, issued a call-to-arms, and tried to encourage advocates of progress by claiming "a large accession to his lordship's friends from the electors who have recently registered themselves." Lord John was conscious of the penalty he had incurred by advocating Church and Municipal Reforms, but he philosophically argued that "even the Tories are obliged to confess reluctantly what they can no longer deny."

Mr. Edmund Parker was the Conservative champion, and "a distinguished Liberal nobleman of the neighbourhood" went to his assistance, as the Catholic question was trailing the scent. Mr. Parker was ready to "cut off every joint of O'Connell's tail," and Dr. Bellamy denounced the Irish agitator as a "dragon that required to be docked." Every hamlet, village, and town in the division was inundated with "No Popery" placards, the pulpits fulminated against "Rome," and anti-Catholic orators travelled from all parts of the country. Thousands of pounds were raised in the manufacturing centres to defray the cost of Lord John's return, and this innovation caused the Conservatives to call upon the electors of South Devon to assert their independence of these collections, "from a guinea to a penny." "Let us mark our sense of this new and foreign interference," exclaimed Sir Ralph Lopes, "and show that we are quite competent to judge and act for ourselves." Lord John could not obtain a hearing at the nomination, but the show of hands was nevertheless in his favour. There was intense feeling in Plymouth, where rats were exhibited from the lamp-posts. Whenever a "turncoat" appeared, the multitude directed his attention to the suspended rodents; and notorious "weathercocks" found dead vermin thrust in their pockets. For some hours the pioneer of Reform stood at the head of the poll in Plymouth, and then a cavalcade of three hundred of Mr. Parker's supporters arrived to vote. Their appearance greatly exasperated the multitude, as there were several former supporters of Lord John Russell in their midst, and the prospect of his defeat stirring the spectators to frenzy, abuse of no measured kind was lavished whenever clergymen were seen.

The first day's polling in Plymouth left Lord John thirteen votes in the rear, and there were ominous symptoms of disturbance on the morrow. Bright weather heralded the morn, and the town was "indescribably gay" as bodies of yeomen entered on horseback, flying their favourite colours and escorted by the rival brass bands. At nightfall it was announced that Mr. Parker was still twelve votes ahead, and reports from the South Hams were proportionately favourable. Uproar then intensified, and the Reformers carried about their "Tithe Cart," with pigs and fowls penned within. They also displayed placards bearing the inscriptions: "English Christianity towards the Irish," and "The Parsons' Motto: All's fish that comes to our hook." Around these rallying points free fights were waged, and the military were summoned to assist the police in clearing the streets. The final declaration was: Parker, 3,755; Russell, 3,267. In Plymouth and the district the numbers polled were: Parker, 456; Russell, 444.

"The contest for the representation of the Southern Division of the County of Devon has ended in my rejection," Lord John Russell wrote in his farewell address:

"It is a consolation to me to think that I have not in any way swerved from those principles which originally gave me a title to your support. It is likewise consolatory to acknowledge, which I do, with the warmest feelings of gratitude, that I have received the strongest proofs of zeal and regard from those friends on whose undisputed worth and sound understanding I set the highest value. It is to the effects of intimidation and undue influence, to temporary alarm in weak minds, caused by the revival of the cry of "No Popery," to the advantages gained by misrepresentations and slander, among the ill-informed, and, lastly, to the great industry displayed by my opponents in registering their friends and dependents, that my defeat is to be attributed. Still, when I compare the advantage thus obtained in a single election with the long, powerful and popular resistance which was made to the Roman Catholic Claims, I cannot but feel that the cause of liberality, toleration and truth, has gained ground; and I clearly foresee the day when the unconstitutional threat, the rooted prejudice, and the petty calumny which have been successful against me, will shrink before the advance of political freedom and the diffusion of religious charity."

Disappointment was profound in the Three Towns and an address from the free-

THE POOR VOTER'S SONG.

They knew that I was poor,
    And they thought that I was base ;
And would readily endure
    To be covered with disgrace ;—
They judged me of their tribe,
    Who on dirty mammon dote,
So they offered me a bribe
    For my vote, boys, vote !

O shame upon my *betters*,
    Who would my conscience buy ;
But shall I wear their fetters ?
    Not I, indeed, not I !

My vote ?—it is not mine
    To do with as I will ,
To cast, like pearls to swine,
    To these wallowers in ill ;
It is my country's due ;
    And I'll give it, while I can,
To the honest and the true,
    Like a man, boys, man !
        O shame, &c.

What though these men be rich,
    And what though I be poor ;
I would perish in a ditch
    Ere I'd listen to their lure ;
They may treat me as a prey,
    But their vengeance shall be braved,
I've a soul as well as they
    To be saved, boys, saved !
        O shame, &c.

Did I swallow down the hook
    That was baited by the base,
How could I dare to look
    My young ones in the face ?
Could I teach them "the right way,"
    While I heard a voice within
Reproach me night and day
    With my sin, boys, sin !
        O shame, &c.

No, no—I'll hold my vote
    As a treasure and a trust ;—
My dishonour none shall quote,
    When I'm mingled with the dust ;
And my children, when I'm gone,
    Shall be strengthen'd by the thought,
That their Father was not one
    To be bought, boys, bought !

O shame upon my *betters*,
    Who would my conscience buy !
But shall I wear their fetters ?
    Not I, indeed, not I !

            Plymouth, 1835.

holders was presented to Lord John Russell at Endsleigh, in which they expressed the warmest admiration of his services, together with an earnest wish "that your strength and spirit may long be preserved firm and unbroken." To this the Tories retaliated by sending the vanquished leader "an address" of biting scorn on the occasion of his return for Stroud, which almost immediately occurred:

TO LORD JOHN RUSSELL.

Sir,—We, the undersigned, beg to assure you of our perfect satisfaction that you are returned to Parliament for Colonel Fox's Borough of Stroud. We heartily congratulate that warm constituency on clothing you with their representation, after being thrust out of Devonshire so unexpectedly. In return for their goodwill to you, we hope you will not hesitate to reward these independent electors, by educating their children in the craft and subtility of Whiggery, and that for this purpose you will appropriate the revenues of the Church. And further, we hope that in the disposal of whatever good things may fall to your lot to distribute, you may remember you have a host of brothers, Russell by name, and that charity begins at home; that you may despise the whisper of a faction; that you may rule over the King, and become great in your own estimation, is our confident expectation; and that you will speedily pass an Act of Parliament making every man a gentleman, remitting all taxes, and thereby creating a fund, out of which every man may receive an independence, is the hope of your sincere friends, who here follow.—Dated, Devonport, 25th May, 1835.

Plymouth, Devonport and South Devon: 1837. Sir James Cockburn fought the next Plymouth election in his own name in 1837, and Captain Blackwood joined him in protesting against the "revolutionary doctrines" of the New Reformers. The "No Popery" spirit was loudly displayed on the nomination day, and oranges were thrown at the Liberal candidates. The latter were aghast to learn that their opponents had opened seventeen inns, but whether the ceremony of pumping was necessary in the morning does not transpire. Hourly statements were issued, and the retaliatory tactics of the Liberals were not ineffective: Collier, 780; Bewes, 772; Cockburn, 551; and Blackburn, 446.

Prior to this dissolution the Devonport Conservatives rallied their forces at a banquet, and the London "Sun" described the guests as being in that "peculiar state of excitement which, for politeness sake, we shall call hallucination." The "Times" retorted that the talent and spirit displayed were not inferior to those exhibited in the same town by the Liberal leaders. The banquet failed in its object, and, at the eleventh hour, Mr. Dawson left to wage another contest, and Lord Valletort declined to be nominated. Sir Edward Codrington passed from the scene in 1840, and Mr. Tufnell was nominated as his successor. "Vote by Ballot," "Justice to Ireland," "National Education," and "Abolition of the Corn Laws" were the Liberal battle cries; and Mr. Dawson, who had returned to the borough, gave preference to "Church and State" and "Purity of Election." Laurel leaves with blue and white ribbons were the favours affected by the Liberals, and variegated holly, adorned with purple and scarlet ribbons, obtained with the Conservatives. After days of exhilaration, equipages and excitement, Mr. Tufnell carried the show of hands, and the Mayor was chased by the crowd for declaring that it was in his favour. During the early hours the booths were monopolised by Mr. Dawson's supporters, and at ten o'clock they claimed to be 180 ahead. Dismayed at this boast, the Reformers retaliated with a statement which claimed for Mr. Tufnell a majority of 52. The Conservative ardour was not to be damped, and at noon their inns were placarded with the rejoinder: "Glorious news! Mr. Dawson is at the head of the poll by 134!!" This active rivalry in damp sheets and wet ink was due to the Liberal dread and the Conservative hope that the friends of Mr. Leach would sullenly refuse to take any part in the fight, but, after submitting the rivals to hours of mingled suspense and hope, they marched in a phalanx to the booths, and showed their importance and magnanimity by turning the scale: Tufnell, 974; Dawson, 750. The "chairing party" was accompanied by a turbulent multitude. In no wise dejected, Mr. Dawson reappeared in 1841, but his opponents were still too powerful. Thousands walked to Laira Bridge to welcome the Liberal candidates, and the coach in which they travelled from London was drawn by hand to Devonport. Very slight change had taken place in the opinions of individual electors : Tufnell, 976 ; Grey, 932 ; Dawson, 780.

An attempt was made in 1836 to put heart into the Liberals of South Devon by holding a banquet at Totnes. The largest hall in the town was selected for the feast, and the streets were bright with banners that claimed "The People, the Source of all Power." From one long streamer flourished the legend : "Behold the Voice of the People went forth and the Temples of Corruption were shaken !" "The Rising Star of Reform— Princess Victoria," was toasted, and then "The People, from whom is derived all Power, for whom is formed all Good Government, through whom is the Nation's Greatness." The function was successful so far as it went, but the Conservatives, not to be beaten at these tactics, erecting a special building to accommodate 500 electors, and every kind of conveyance, from coach and six to farmers' carts, drove from the remotest villages of the county. "For God, Our King and the People" was their favourite motto, and with such effect did they demonstrate and work during the poll week in 1837 that Mr. Parker threw up the sponge when these numbers had been reached: Buller, 4,971; Parker, 4,674; Bulteel, 3,744. This success was commemorated by a dinner in the Plymouth Theatre, which presented a scene of "rare enchantment." "A galaxy of beauty" beamed from the circle, and hundreds of guests were seated upon a flooring which had been raised to the level of the stage. During the speeches the emblematical "Crown" caught on fire, and the chairman found it necessary "to extinguish the Stars of Brunswick."

John Bright at Plymouth and Devonport: 1846. Claims of a domestic nature caused the old members for Plymouth to retire in 1841, and Mr. Gill, another honoured townsman, was now associated with the Hon. Hugh Fortescue in the Liberal interest. Mr. Johnson, of Laira House, once a Reformer, was "the selected pet of the Conservatives," but an acrimonious contest effected no material change in the strength of parties :—Gill, 821 ; Fortescue, 787 ; Johnson, 552. After the declaration, the Mayor was mobbed ; and, when he called upon Colonel Hill to suppress the riot, he laughed in his face and called him a coward. As the officer had otherwise indicated his prejudice by flying the Conservative colours from the ramparts of the Citadel, he was ordered by the Horse Guards to apologise to his Worship. The Corn Law agitation found the new members lukewarm, and Mr. John Bright travelled to Plymouth and condemned their hesitation at a monster meeting which was held at the Theatre Royal. An Anti-Corn Law demonstration was also arranged at Devonport, and inflammatory placards forecasted a stormy evening :—"We trust the Conservatives will prevent the lecturer from boasting of his visit as a triumph, for they have the power to do so if they choose to exert it." Apprehension of disorder intensified when the curate of Millbrook, Mr. Thomas, challenged Mr. Bright to a debate in the Town Hall, the rumour running that the Tory dockyardsmen intended to disturb the proceedings and that a gang of Chartists from Plymouth meant to be revenged if they did. The debate was conducted decently and in fair order. Mr. Thomas moved his Protectionist resolution in a speech of an hour's duration, and Mr. Bright delivered a luminous and argumentative reply. Towards the close, when he expressed his pleasure at travelling so far to promote this object, he was assailed with a cry of: " Yes, and well paid for it." Turning upon the interruptor, Mr. Bright replied : " If I were paid for my services it would not make me any the less regardful of the truth. If Mr. Thomas ministers, he is remunerated by somebody. But the only compensation I have the honour of receiving is the joy of spreading true principles amongst my fellow subjects." The amendment demanding the repeal of the Corn Laws was accepted with a few dissentients. The election in 1847 turned on the question, and the Conservatives of Devonport prepared for the contest by holding a banquet, which was satirised as " Sacred to the Memory of Broken Vows and Departed Worth, and a Thousand Disappointments." Many of the aldermen were said to have attended with their coats " turned inside out," and they were charged with joining the " Most Noble Order of Ratcatchers." A full length caricature was displayed showing Sir Robert Peel picking Lord John Russell's pocket of the tariff with the one hand, and cramming the income tax down John Bull's throat with the other. Sir John Romilly was associated with Mr. Tufnell, and Mr. Sanders espoused the Protectionist and anti-Catholic platform :—Tufnell, 1,133 ; Romilly, 1,018 ; Sanders, 852.

HUSTINGS SCENE AT PLYMOUTH ELECTION, 1847.
(Outside the Royal Hotel.)

Liberal Cohesion Broken at Plymouth and Devonport. 1847-1859.   Lord Ebrington (formerly Mr. Fortescue) made his peace with the Government, and accepted office. This did not satisfy the more advanced reformers of the borough, and, when he offered himself for re-election, he was opposed by Mr. Henry Vincent, an eloquent democrat whom crowds flocked to cheer although a charge was made for admission. " Absolute free trade and the abolition of all monopolies " stirred the enthusiasm of the masses, but the programme failed to captivate the enfranchised :—Ebrington, 714 ; Vincent, 187. Mr. Gill's retirement in 1847 attracted several aspirants to the borough, but Mr. Calmady was chosen to fight with Lord Ebrington. Mr. Roundell Palmer (Lord Selborne) entered the field " free from all party engagements and opposed to all rash and fundamental changes," and, as Mr. Calmady declined to canvass and trusted to his admitted popularity, a Liberal seat was lost :—Ebrington, 921 ; Palmer, 836 ; Calmady, 769. The banquet to celebrate Mr. Palmer's return was attended by supporters of both parties, and it was playfully designated "the wedding feast of Liberal-Conservatism "—the force to which the victor had especially appealed.

Sir John Romilly's action in advocating the closing of inns on polling days excited the keenest prejudice against him at the dissolution in 1847, and his opponents accentuated the feeling by accusing him, in spite of his professions, of opening a public-house in every ward in Devonport for committee purposes. Sir John heatedly protested that, if his agents had thus abused his instructions, he would leave the town at an hour's notice, and this passionate display of earnestness proved fatal :—Tufnell, 1,079 ; Berkeley, 1,056 ; Romilly, 1,046 ; Maxwell, 1,032. Thus the Conservatives won a seat, and "Jack's the Lad" (Berkeley) carried off "The Devonport Cup."

In 1852 Lord Ebrington left Plymouth to preserve the "family seat" at Barnstaple, and a fateful period for his old supporters approached. As Mr. Roundell Palmer did not share that aggressive antipathy to Tractarianism for which the borough was now notorious, he received the hint to withdraw. Mr. Robert Collier (Lord Monkswell), the son of Mr. John Collier, who was chosen by the Liberals, strongly resisted sacerdotal innovations, and made the inspection of convents a leading plank in his programme. Mr. Charles John Mare emerged unscathed from the Evangelical catechism, and he was promised the support of the Rev. John Hatchard as a faithful champion of Protestantism. Meanwhile other candidates appeared—Mr. Braine, "emphatically a Reformer, although not a Radical-Reformer," and Mr. B. Escott, who made no disguise of Chartist leanings. The Liberal trio refused to agree to a test ballot, but united in a proposal to forego processions, bands of music, coloured favours and party badges, as being incitements to disorder and corruption. Mr. Mare, when approached with the same object, said he had completed arrangements for an unusually grand show, but he offered to waive the advantage if his opponents would present £300 apiece to the local charities. This alternative was not entertained, and so the contest continued. It was characterised by unusual turbulence and intoxication, and represented an emphatic Conservative majority : Mare, 1,036 ; Collier, 1,004 ; Braine, 906 ; Escott, 372. A petition was filed against Mr. Mare, and evidence was given of treating without stint, of promises of place made to a large number of voters, of boasts by Mr. Mare's canvassers that the patronage of Lord Derby's Government was to be found in their pocket. It was also proved that Mr Stafford, Secretary of the Admiralty, was frequently seen in Mr. Mare's company, and that he gave several banquets to Dockyard employés. One prominent supporter of Mr. Mare's was also declared to have said from the hustings : "I don't know much about politics, but I do know that Mr. Mare's Queen of the South, now lying in Plymouth, is a very fine steamer." Serjeant Kinglake could not resist the evidence of a widespread expectation of favours and patronage, and the Committee of the House of Commons found that Mr. Mare and his agents had alike been guilty of bribery.

The Liberals of Devonport had by 1852 recovered from the depression in which Sir John Romilly's adherence to the purity policy had thrown them. Mr. Tufnell withdrew from the borough in 1854, and Sir John Maxwell found himself opposed by Sir E. Perry :

Our honoured Tufnell's cherished name :
His brightly marked career ;
Perry be thine to magnify :
Be ours to bless and cheer !!

The Liberal majority was again decisive : Perry, 1,091 ; Maxwell, 631.   General Berkeley's retirement early in 1857 found the Conservatives unprepared, and Mr. James Wilson and Sir Erskine Perry were returned unopposed.   The latter incurred the displeasure of Mr. Bernal Osborne by assisting to put Lord Palmerston in a minority of one, and he wagered that he would denounce Sir Erskine from the Devonport hustings at the next election. The impeached member thereupon threw up his seat, and called upon Mr. Bernal Osborne, as the Liberal Whip, to fulfil his threat.   No candidate could be found to oppose him, and the menace remained unfulfilled.   The incident provoked a skit, in which Mr. Bernal Osborne was made the subject of 'ridicule :

> " You've giv'n a vote 'gainst Ministers—
> A shocking sight to see ;
> Five hundred pounds at Devonport
> You'll not elected be !
> With fury all your friends are filled,
> Woollcombe has asked me down ;
> No hustings speaker you, I know,
> They'll pelt you from the town."

It was Mr. Braine who incurred the expense of unseating Mr. Mare, but, upon the issue of the new writ, Mr. Alfred Rooker, Mr. J. N. Bennett and others formed a "cave," on the plea that his domestic career was clouded.   Mr. Braine's friends insisted that he was the victim and not the cause of this unpleasantness, but Mr. Rooker and his friends would not withdraw their objections.   "The clique," as they were designated, united in a request to Mr. Roundell Palmer to stand again on a coalition platform, and the Liberal breach was thus complete : Palmer, 944 ; Braine, 876.   With Mr. Braine's retirement, Mr. Rooker abandoned Mr. Palmer, and the future Lord Chancellor bade the borough a final farewell.   The Liberals closed their ranks in 1857, when Mr James White joined Mr. Collier, and Mr. John Hardy accepted the Conservative invitation.   Bales of squibs and anti-Palmerstonian literature were distributed, but Mr. Hardy was hopelessly distanced : Collier, 1,167 ; White, 1,166 ; Hardy, 662.   "Reform or no Reform" was revived in 1859, when Mr. Collier and Mr. White again led the van for the Liberals.   Lord Valletort appeared as an opponent of "rash and extravagant innovations," but was so heckled that one chairman left the hall at the mercy of his disturbers.   Confusing clamour with electioneering, the Liberals took a jaunty view of Lord Valletort's chances, and, although warned of the peril of over-confidence, assured themselves that their cause was safe :

> Those Tory bells, those Tory bells,
> How many a tale their music tells,
> Of old but not forgotten time,
> When young we listened to their chime.
> Tory misrule has passed away,
> And many a freeman then so gay
> Within the tomb now darkly dwells,
> And hears no more those Tory bells !
>
> But still those bells awake their din :
> Derby is out !   Who shall come in ?
> Mount Edgcumbe's scion joins the cry
> The pluck of Plymouth men to try !

And Tory belles in crinoline,
Try all their arts a vote to win
For this young lord, whose plastic mind
Is Vall-a-tort and undefined.

Go Trevor, Tracey, Mennie, Moore,
Go Shipping Interest, Kohinoor,
Go mark the tale the Poll Booth tells
In requiem to your Tory Bells!
Liberals, remember Charles John Mare,
Corruption—Bribery—and declare
That never more your votes shall swell
Responsive to a Tory bell.

In the end the poll was declared : Valletort, 1,153 ; Collier, 1,086 ; White, 964. It was in vain that either of the successful candidates endeavoured to procure a hearing, but Mr. White was vehemently cheered when he derided popular representation as " a deplorable parody." Then came the turn of the Conservatives to rejoice in verse :

Not a sigh was heard, not a farewell note,
    As White to the Terminus hurried ;
Not a Radical offered to carry his coat,
    And he looked profoundly flurried.

He hurried off early, at morning light,
    Ere the little boys unfeeling
Could shout at his heel with all their might,
    "Yah! Yah! Go back to Ealing!"

Slowly and sadly he got on the 'bus,
    And he thought how they'd laugh at the story,
That after making an awful fuss
    He was utterly smashed by a Tory.

No stout Whig flunkeys around him pressed,
    Or gave him a cheer at the station :
He looked like a Radical blown from the West
    By Plymouth's indignation.

When sadly he sat in the carriage there,
    And the train from the platform started,
He could hear loud cheers that filled the air
    From the Tories merry-hearted.

Coldly they'll talk of the beaten buffoon,
    Whose cash being settled, they're jollier ;
And if an election should come again soon,
    They'll do the same business for Collier.

"Bully" Ferrand's   A gusty era in Devonport politics drew near with the approach
Devonport Fights.   of Mr. Bousfield Ferrand, who was destined to remain for years the
terror of the Liberals.   On arriving with Mr. Peel in 1857 he sprang into popularity, and
easily carried the show of hands.   Desperate efforts were made to counteract this advan-

tage, and the constituency was inundated with the effusions of " Josias Greensauce, Poet Laureate of Devonport," who expressed his opinion of Mr. Ferrand in incisive verse :

> He can fawn, and can flatter, and tell what fine things
>   For the poor men to do he is able ;
> Tho' he often has stood, and did all that he could,
>   To keep a Cheap Loaf from their table.
>
> He has sat with the " Commons " in years that have past,
>   And his value was understood fully ;
> He was shunn'd by them all, as a " Firebrand " should,
>   And by all he was voted a " Bully."
>
> And tho' he can rise, and with tears in his eyes,
>   Blubber out such a pitiful story,
> Of " the Babe in the Snow," that he saved long ago,
>   Yet we can't, nor we won't, have a " Tory."

A noisy crowd awaited the declaration, and the figures stood : Wilson, 1,216 ; Perry, 1,198 ; Ferrand, 1,079 ; Peel, 1,079. Sir Erskine took office and Sir Michael Seymour presented himself in the Liberal interest. Almost simultaneously Mr. James Wilson accepted a position of profit and the Chiltern Hundreds. Ministers contrived that the two contests should take place within a few days of each other, and the first round was unusually embittered. Assuming an expression of " almost undefinable fierceness and malignity," Mr. Ferrand denounced Sir Michael Seymour as "a cowardly assassin," and his supporters as "rascals " and "liars." The show of hands again went with the Conservatives ; periodical states of the poll aggravated the delirium ; and, when the doors of the Town Hall were thrown open to the public, the rush was as of a torrent. There was another discomfiture in store for the great " word thumper" : Seymour, 1,096 ; Ferrand, 1,047. No sooner was this fight over than electioneering was resumed with Sir Arthur Buller as Liberal candidate. Mr. Ferrand's energy was colossal. He knew no rest, nor was he ever weary, and no one could withstand his thunderous rhetoric. Anxiety settled on the Liberals as their majority once waned to vanishing point, but, at two o'clock, their reserves were brought into action, and this advantage they slowly improved upon : Buller, 1,189 ; Ferrand, 1,114. Deafening uproar followed the announcement of the figures, and insulting epithets were hurled broadcast. Mr. Ferrand accepted his defeat with " defiant hardihood," and was presented on the hustings with a copy of an "impromptu " to " The Thrice Defeated," of which thousands were cast to the crowd :

> Fare thee well, and if for ever,
>   Still for ever be the strain,
> Happy will it be if never
>   We thy face shall see again !
>
> If thy heart were bared before us
>   Ev'ry inmost thought would show,
> Like a plague you came to bore us—
>   As a plague, we bid you go.
>
> And thy heart by us glanced o'er,
>   Could it speak would now confess—
> Falsehood could not make thee lower,
>   Folly could not make thee less !

ʜʜ

Tell thy friends so sharp and knowing
That their tactics will not do ;
Tell the Carlton—money flowing—
Dev'nport likes nor them nor you.

Mr. Ferrand's superhuman efforts did not pass unrewarded, and he received at St. George's Hall a silver vase to which 2,559 persons had subscribed.   Insisting that Devonport was once a forlorn hope, he boasted having advanced to the citadel, and asserted that he would soon unlock the gate.   The banquet was marked with much hilarity, and Mr. Ferrand made an attack upon Mr. John Bright which evoked from "The Tribune" the merciless retort : "I am surprised that you should think it necessary to enquire into the correctness of anything said by the person in question.   Judging from the language used, I should suppose that the speaker must have been either drunk or mad."   One of the local rhymesters discussed with freedom some of the incidents :

They sent, in pink paper, a ticket to "Dizzy,"
But he wrote them an answer to say he was busy ;
And then that young "statesman" from over the water,
They said would attend the Conservative slaughter,
        And he might have been there,
        On the right of the chair,
        To have made them all stare
At the sight of so much aristocratic gentility,
        But his father said "No,
        Valletort, you shan't go,
        For that Ferrand is low,
        T'will be giving a blow,
And inflicting a slur upon our nobility."

The meeting had join'd in a Babel of talk,
And Ferrand was crowing as "Cock of the Walk,"
        While the gentry below
        Had been fuddling so,
And the wine in their craniums was making such ravages
That they ranted and roared like a legion of savages ;
One gentleman wish'd his opinions to show
By proposing three cheers for the "Babe in the Snow,'
And another friend hoped he might not be too soon
In suggesting three more for the "Man in the Moon."
        Still, the din was unceasing
        And riot increasing ;
In fact, matters now had becoming quite exciting ;
Half the people quite drunk, and the other half fighting.

For the crockery ware that was smash'd in the fray,
There's a little bill left of ten guineas to pay ;
And for years to come many a grumbling sinner
Will think of the famous Conservative Dinner.

In February, 1862, Sir Michael Seymour was restored to active duties, and his resignation brought Mr. Ferrand into Devonport once more.   He dashed through Fore Street

FORE STREET, DEVONPORT, SHOWING ROYAL HOTEL.

(By permission of Mr. W. WESTCOTT.)

in his carriage as the dockyardsmen were leaving the establishment for the day, and forthwith improved his opportunity : " Give my respects," he exclaimed, " to all the pretty Devonport girls " :

> And didn't that hero, whose fit never fails,
> Strut and swagger about like a cock with two tails !
> To the " brave sons of toil " their spirits to cheer
> Why didn't he forward a barrel of beer ?
> Or a nice drop of " short " just to make 'em " toddy,"
> And their wives a few blankets, or even some " shoddy."

Satirical literature was now of little avail, and Mr. Ferrand obtained the show of hands at the expense of Sir Frederick Grey. " It is time," he shouted from the platform, " that you had a change—that change you shall experience to-morrow." As the hustings were dispensed with on this occasion, the crush in the Guildhall was terrific, free fights were general, and the barriers which had been erected to keep the rival sections apart swayed with the attempts of frenzied Liberals and Conservatives to molest each other. Mr. Ferrand had not prophesied without knowing, and, before the poll closed, the Liberals were conscious of defeat : Ferrand, 1,234 ; Grey, 1,204. Amid a tempest of cheering, Mr. Ferrand claimed that he had rescued Devonport from Whig domination, and that it had ceased at last to be a Government pocket borough.

Sir A. Buller abandoned Devonport in favour of Liskeard in 1865, and Mr. Thomas Brassey, the Liberal nominee, professed to favour the " healthiest tendencies of the times." Mr. Fleming, who was brought down by Mr. Ferrand, supplied in his meekness an amusing antithesis to his friend's unsparing invective " and fierce loudness." In the first hour of the polling, from eight to nine, Mr. Brassey received 204, as against 165. The next hour yielded just as pleasant a story : Brassey, 595 ; Fleming, 535. After this the public anxiety was assuaged by half-hourly statements ; and, as the rivals drove about, their carriages were stopped by supporters, and forests of hands were outstretched in frantic greetings. After the declaration nothing could restrain the ebullitions of the Liberals : Brassey, 1,264 ; Fleming, 1,208. This contest had been fixed for the eve of the general election in order to ascertain if the constituency was wavering. Mr. Brassey was joined at the dissolution by Mr. Phinn, and Messrs. Ferrand and Fleming were again the Conservative choice. Unqualified control of the situation was now Mr. Ferrand's aim, and his party so crowded the polling booths on the morning of the fight that the Liberals were afraid to issue "a state." The eventual declaration justified their forebodings : Fleming, 1,307 ; Ferrand, 1,290 ; Brassey, 1,279 ; Phinn, 1,243. The announcement was followed by an outburst furious beyond precedent. Drunken men seized the reporters' tables at the hustings and used the wood as staves ; women and children were trampled upon, and infuriated Liberals stormed the Mayor's chair. Proceedings to unseat the members were instituted, and a Parliamentary Commission found that Messrs. Ferrand and Fleming had been guilty of bribery through their agents by paying dockyardsmen for loss of time in voting when they were allowed half-a-day's holiday and wages for the purpose. Mr. Disraeli moved in the House of Commons that the dockyardsmen should be disfranchised, and he derisively descanted on the conspiracy which was manifest within the gates of the establishment when attempts were made to serve the Speaker's warrant on the suspected. In a subsequent debate he pointed out that Mr. Stafford, a former Secretary of the Admiralty, stood at the Dockyard Gate as the men emerged, and that he entertained at dinner all the officials of influence and leading men. An agony of apprehension seized Devonport at the prospect of losing its representation, meetings were held and memorials despatched to

Parliament, and the clause in the new Reform Bill that omitted the Dockyard boroughs was finally abandoned. Lord Eliot and Mr. Montagu Chambers, the Liberal candidates for the two vacant seats, made effective use of Mr. Disraeli's desire to annihilate the Dockyard influence. Mr. Ferrand, prevented by the verdict from again contesting the constituency until the probationary period had expired, was thus hopelessly handicapped in his attempts to promote the return of Mr. Cecil Raikes and Mr. Reginald Abbot; and his personal reproaches, as to the conduct of the Liberals in unseating him, shrank into insig- nificance as contrasted with the attempt of his Parliamentary leaders to destroy the Dock- yard franchise. Gangs of roughs paraded the streets on the day of the poll, peaceful inhabitants were insulted, and the roughs did battle with the police. Favours were fairly divided, but the Conservative committee rooms were serenaded by itinerant vocalists who testified the Liberal confidence in expressive doggerel:

> The game is up, the bubble's burst,
> And Devonport, without a sigh,
> Can say, while cutting the connexion,
> Good-bye, Bousfield, good-bye!
> > Good-bye, Bousfield, good-bye!
> > We've closed a bargain badly made,
> > Good-bye, Bousfield, good-bye!

The statement of the figures was hailed with terrific cries: Eliot, 1275; Chambers, 1,269; Raikes, 1,216; Abbot, 1,215. Mr. Ferrand vanished unseen from the town, but he returned in 1868, when Lord Eliot gave offence by his Ritualistic proclivities and involved his party in the responsibility of a fresh selection. Mr. Montagu Chambers was colleagued by Mr. J. D. Lewis, and Major Palliser, of "chilled shot celebrity," joined the "irrepressible and never-to-be-abashed Bousfield Ferrand." A babel of confusion prevailed at the nomination, and the Conservatives held the lead at the poll until the supporters of the Permissive Bill marched in a body to the booth. Mr. Ferrand and Major Palliser then retired to their hotel to avoid too many expressions of sympathy or taunt, and the voice of the Mayor at the declaration was inaudible for oaths and curses: Lewis, 1,541; Chambers, 1,519; Ferrand, 1,370; Palliser, 1,365.

The Stuart Lane Episode at Plymouth: 1861-1868. Lord Valletort's election to the peerage in 1861 caused a vacancy at Plymouth, and the Liberal choice fell on Mr. Walter Morrison, who advocated "civil, religious and commercial liberty at home and abroad." Mr. C. Bewes abandoned the cause, to the consternation of the Liberals, and gave his support to Mr. Addington, the Conservative champion. Although free and open public-houses and processions were now forbidden, there were the old scenes of drunken violence in the streets. The show of hands was taken in the usual way at the hustings, and the majority went for Morrison. Mr. Addington's friends worked with such energy that the Liberals looked "blue" in the morning, and it was only with "the workmen's dinner hour" that the supporters of Mr. Morrison rallied. Each half-hour's statement of the poll was awaited with feverish impatience, and the Royal Hotel was surrounded at the close by a throng who smashed the seats and menaced the hustings with demolition. The numbers were with difficulty announced: Morrison, 1,179; Addington, 984. Salvoes of cheering proceeded from the multitude, "now swaying like the waves of the sea," and handkerchiefs fluttered by hundreds from the surrounding balconies. In June, 1865, another attempt to break down Liberal domination was made by Mr. Stuart Lane, and disagreeable recriminations followed Mr. Morrison's imputation that his opponent was resorting to bribery. The utmost exertions were made to capture the polling booths at daybreak, and "many birds left their nests" at six o'clock to secure a majority on the first hour's voting. Drunkenness and fighting were general until the declaration, and this was made amid a hurricane of conflicting cries: Collier, 1,299; Morrison, 1,218; Lane, 1,147. A carpet bag was held aloft bearing the inscription: "Mr. Stuart Lane, Passenger for Paddington," and, although Conservatives struggled desperately to secure it, "the luggage" was "carried in triumph."

Reform was once more in the air in 1868, and, at a demonstration on the Hoe, watermen were carried in boats, smiths worked at forges, bakers' exhibited big and little loaves, printers threw out freshly printed copies of the "Western Reform Times," and ploughs were drawn by stately teams. When Parliament was dissolved the local contest turned less on the franchise than on Mr. Stuart Lane's relations to the Credit Foncier Company, and, with a view of "refuting calumnies," he invited the electors to a meeting at St. James's Hall. There a hostile crowd forced the gates; shouts, screams and catcalls prevailed; and the gallery so creaked beneath struggling and fighting masses that, after a platform display in dumb show, lights were lowered and the proceedings abandoned. Horseplay and turbulence characterised the nomination; caps were thrown from the hustings; candidates were occupied in dodging lumps of mud and rotten eggs; and the hustings oscillated beneath the pressure. The result of the polling was: Collier, 2,086; Morrison, 2,065; Lane, 1,509.

Lord Amberley made a resolute attempt to wrest from the Conservatives their long control of South Devon, but his advanced views on the Malthusian question evoked ecclesiastical prejudice, and, on the day of the nomination, an indelicate drawing was hoisted within view of the hustings, and the framework was demolished in the free fight that ensued. Sir Massey Lopes and Mr. Kekewich were pelted with flour balls and rabbit skins, and, by the time their addresses were finished, they presented the appearance of "whited sepulchres." But they emerged safely enough from the poll: Lopes, 3,234; Kekewich, 3,233; Amberley, 2,694.

The Advent of Mr. Edward Bates (Plymouth): 1871-1874. Plymouth Liberals now moved towards division and disaster. In 1871 Sir Robert Collier passed through rapid promotions, and he was re-elected with sullen acquiescence from time to time until he accepted the Recordership of Bristol as well as the office of Attorney-General. He explained at a meeting of indignant constituents that he simply accepted the former position because so many distinguished lawyers had filled it, but a Radical amendment was carried depre-

"THE GREAT SEVEN-LEAGUER" (SIR R. COLLIER) JUMPING OVER THE HEADS OF THE JUDGES.

cating "the appearance of personal aggrandisement on the part of Her Majesty's legal advisers, whilst labourers are being discharged from the dockyards by Mr. Childers's policy of retrenchment." Shortly afterwards, Sir Robert Collier received a judicial appointment, and he terminated his connection with the borough in 1871. It was thus with a sense of impending disaster that the Liberals fought under the banner of Mr. Alfred Rooker. The more advanced did not forget that this gentleman assisted Mr. Roundell Palmer to defeat Mr. Braine, and they left the Albert Hall in high dudgeon when the Nonconformist vote rejected Sir George Young in favour of the eloquent local solicitor. Mr. Edward Bates was received with corresponding enthusiasm as the Conservative candidate, and the advocacy of Liverpool working men led to riotous scenes at the Drill Hall. Too ardent Liberals were thrown from the platform into the body of the hall, their hats were smashed and their coats torn to shreds. Mr. Rooker was opprobriously assailed at the nomination, flour balls were thrown in profusion, and cries of "Cant" were howled by opponents. The Liberal sense of dejection became intensified, and the party anticipated the reverse the ballot had in store: Bates, 1,753; Rooker, 1,511. At the declaration a large board was borne aloft, in which Mr. Rooker was depicted attired with bows of crape, and, exclamations of "Down with it" being raised, the caricature was trampled to shreds. Hats were smashed, scores were rolled in the mud, and pandemonium prevailed for hours. In February, 1874, Mr. Sampson Lloyd joined Mr. Bates, and Sir George Young became the colleague of Mr. Morrison. Mr. Bates made the commercial development of Plymouth his chief aspiration, and Mr. Sampson Lloyd advocated "every well-advised reform and the removal of every proved abuse." "Co-operation" was the cry raised against Mr. Morrison by the tradesmen, and licensed victuallers gave their support to the Conservatives. The heaviness of the blow was not expected by the Liberals, and they sang two nights before the polling:

> Our Bates he is gone and the Mighty One, too,
> Our Sampson is shorn of his tresses;
> For the Giant of York, with Sir George and his crew,
> Have won all the people's caresses.

When the poll was declared, the numbers were: Bates, 2,045; Lloyd, 2,000; Young, 1,714; Morrison, 1,700.

The Childers "Cheeseparing" at Devonport: 1874-1880 Dockyard reductions rendered hateful the name of Childers in Devonport, and Liberals were the more demoralised in 1874 because Mr. Chambers had so long insisted upon clinging to a borough which had "ceased to feel any attachment for him." There was a corresponding want of confidence on the part of the Conservatives, and they offered to allow Mr. J. D. Lewis to be returned unopposed with Mr. J. H. Puleston. The overtures were rejected, and Mr. Soltau-Symons was selected as the second Liberal candidate and Captain Price as Mr. Puleston's colleague. Liberal attempts to conduct the contest on political lines utterly failed, and the constituency rang with complaints of "the Childers Cheeseparing" and "the Collier Scandal." Messrs. Bates and Lloyd carried Plymouth the day before the Devonport poll, and Admiral Elliott journeyed from Chatham, fresh from his own success, to advise the dockyardsmen to ignore politics and vote in their own interests. The Conservative colours were predominant, and the figures were announced: Puleston, 1,525; Price, 1,483; Lewis, 1,327; Soltau-Symons, 1,250. In Morice, Clowance, St. Aubyn and St. John's wards the Liberals claimed majorities; but in Stoke and Tamar they commanded small followings. Remembrance of the Dockyard depletion was still keen when Mr. Gladstone led the Midlothian campaign, and Messrs. Puleston and Price were mainly concerned in advocating increased wages for Government employés. Mr. J. D. Lewis retaliated that his opponents would be unable to increase the rates of pay because their party would never have sufficient money to do so, and these retorts led to successive rowdy outbursts. Confidence in the old members remained unshaken : Puleston, 1,753 ; Price, 1,746 ; Lewis, 1,509 ; Sellar, 1,476. The connection was as closely maintained in 1885 : Price, 2,968 ; Puleston, 2,944 ; Medley, 2,653 ; Terrell, 2,636.

Plymouth and the Bates Petition : 1880.   The Plymouth Liberals entered upon the campaign of 1880 with surprising verve, and confidently counted upon returning Mr. Macliver and Sir George Young as exponents of the Midlothian programme.   The Conservatives preserved a "mysterious faith," which caused their opponents to feel "that they were walking upon mined ground," and the figures partly justified their misgivings : Bates, 2,442 ; Macliver, 2,406 ; Young, 2,402 ; Lloyd, 2,314. Passionately exasperated by this reverse, the Liberals petitioned against the return of Mr. Bates, and the case was heard in the Guildhall before Mr. Justice Lush and Mr. Justice Manisty in June, 1880. In 1874 the respondent sent £600 worth of clothing for distribution amongst the poor, and the Rev. Charles Wilson, a leading Congregationalist, refused to accept any tickets on the ground that such gifts were demoralising. In 1876 there was a large distribution of coals and blankets, and, whilst the clergy became almoners in their parishes, the Nonconformist ministers returned their share of the tickets. Later on, the Mayor, Mr. Joseph Wills, received a cheque from Mr. Bates for £250, with a request that he would use it to relieve the necessitous poor. Mr. William Derry joined the committee on the understanding that electors should not participate, but he discovered that this condition was not respected. On the eve of the contest, Mr. Bates purchased a leading interest in the Sugar Refinery, an industry then distressed by the operation of the foreign bounty system, and the capital he introduced enabled seventy electors to be re-engaged. These were the main allegations of the indictment, and Mr. Isaac Latimer, the petitioner, testified that feasts were held at the Workhouse and Hospital, on the occasion of a wedding in the family of Mr. Bates, and that the excessive indulgence of committee men occasioned scandal. It was further shown that seven fishermen were remunerated for their loss of time and expense in travelling from Penzance. Personal malice on Mr. Latimer's part was contended by the defence, and an article was read from his paper in which Mr. Bates was derided as "that big wooden-headed man." This expression he at once disclaimed, and attributed to the uninspired pen of his editor. In Mr. Bates's favour a letter was submitted, written upon the eve of one of the distributions, insisting that, in spite of misconceptions as to motive, the poor in Plymouth should rejoice with his friends and neighbours over the marriage of his son.

In pronouncing judgment, Mr. Justice Lush said the Court was asked to find that the "alleged sympathy of the respondent with the poor was a hypocritical sham and a mere pretext for veiling his real motive--a corrupt one for purchasing popularity. We unhesitatingly decline to draw any such inference. It is clear that Mr. Edward Bates is a man of large-hearted benevolence, and that his disposition is to share his abundant means with the poor of the place with which he is connected. We believe that in making these gifts he acted with a large sense of responsibility and duty." Nevertheless, the conduct of his agent in bringing several fishermen to Plymouth constituted an infraction of the law for which Mr. Bates was bound to be unseated. "With great regret" Mr. Justice Lush made that announcement, and Mr. Justice Manisty expressed his "profound personal sorrow" that the law left the Court with no alternative. "Through no fault of his own, but by the movement of petitioners, who have been actuated, I believe, by party spirit, not only the poor and needy, but all grades and denominations, religious and political, in Plymouth, and the people at large have been deprived of a kind friend and a generous benefactor, and the constituency of a member of whom they had just reason to be proud." As soon as the judgment was pronounced, Mr. Bates was followed by a multitude to the Globe Hotel, and, speaking from the balcony, he exclaimed : "I am now a free agent. I can do any-thing I like in Plymouth without being told that I am debauching you and your friends generally—and not only you, but some of the Liberal party and Liberal poor." Mr. Latimer's cab was stoned as he drove into the midst of a crowd that was awaiting him out-side the "Mercury" office, and appearances were so unpleasant that the driver whipped the horse and took refuge in flight. Mr. (now Sir) Edward Clarke, who had acted as one of the respondent's counsel, was chosen to fight the vacant seat for the Conservatives, and the tide of popular feeling ran strongly against the petitioning party : Clarke, 2,449 ; Young, 2,305.

Home Rule : Mr. Gladstone at Ply-mouth : 1885-1897.   The Liberals swept the country in 1885, but the reappearance of the hitherto disfranchised member, now Sir Edward Bates, preserved Plymouth from the influence of the popular wave. The Hon. Reginald Brett joined Mr. Macliver, and the fervour of Liberals ran high with the knowledge that the number of available electors had doubled. But the confidence of the Conservatives remained unshaken to the end : Bates, 4,354 ; Clarke, 4,240 ; Macliver, 4,132 ; Brett, 3,968. In a few months Mr. Gladstone launched his Home Rule manifesto, and his appeal found his Plymouth supporters so unprepared that they had to fight their battle with comparative strangers. After a visit by Lord Hartington, hundreds of Liberals resolved to support Sir Edward Bates and Sir Edward Clarke, and, in sore dismay, the resident Nationalists invited Mr. Parnell to visit Plymouth. When the Irish chief discovered that neither Liberal candidates nor the local official Liberals would appear upon his platform, he stormed, in the presence of the few who received him at the Duke of Cornwall Hotel, that he would never have visited the town as other than the guest of the Gladstonian leaders, and angrily declared that he would not attend the meeting in their absence. The Liberal candidates were sought out, but they refused to incur the risk of appearing in Mr. Parnell's company. In the meantime thousands of people were passing the window at which the Irish chief stood, on their way to the Drill Hall, where the demonstration was to be held, and Mr. Parnell yielded to appeals not to disappoint so vast a throng. When he reached the building and found the multitude upstanding, he passionately rebuked the organisers for having failed to spend £50 in seating the area for the occasion. "The money would have been forthcoming" he indignantly insisted whilst the audience was indulging in thunderous cheering. The speech itself was described by Irish journalists present as the most powerful Mr. Parnell had ever delivered—possibly the more vehement because of the annoyance to which he had been exposed. Answering Mr. Balfour's threat of twenty years of coercion, he asked in a scornful note : " What are twenty years in the life of a nation ?" His appeal was unavailing, and the declaration found the Plymouth Liberals hopelessly outdistanced : Clarke, 4,137 ; Bates, 4,133 ; Stephens, 3,255 ; Strachey, 3,175.

The Home Rule division in 1886 did not result in any increase in the Conservative strength at Devonport, but wholesale abstentions occasioned a large augmentation in the Conservative majority : Puleston, 2,954 ; Price, 2,943 ; Ford, 1,963 ; Showers, 1,918. Outside the Royal Hotel the grotesque spectacle was witnessed of the successful members and defeated candidates endeavouring to address their friends at the same time from different windows.

Mr. Gladstone paid a flitting visit to Plymouth in 1877, when he landed at the

BEDFORD STREET, PLYMOUTH.

Showing the old Globe Hotel at the entrance to Frankfort Street ; demolished, 1899.

(By permission of Mr. W. WESTCOTT.)

Millbay Docks and addressed, to a crowd of thousands, in a voice at its zenith for richness and resonance, his protest against the Bulgarian atrocities. The second occasion upon which he sought to " Awake the West " was in June, 1891, when he conducted a triumphal procession through Cornwall and Devon. Leaving his yacht at Falmouth, Mr. Gladstone travelled by road ; and, from every village and hamlet in the Mining Division, the popula- tion swarmed to the cross ways. The approaches to Redruth were densely thronged, and for two miles the horses could only proceed at a walking pace. In the main street of the town itself the carriages became jammed by the multitude, and swayed, creaked and almost collapsed with the pressure. Whilst Mr. Gladstone was addressing these thirty thousand people, cries of pain arose from the crowd near the wheels, and Colonel Fludyer, raising his stentorian voice, held aloft the quaint emblem of his authority—a huge stick, bearing the inscription "Conybeare for Ever." The pressure was relieved by withdrawals to adjacent avenues, and the "Grand Old Man" passed a panegyric on Mr. Conybeare as an honest man who had suffered imprisonment because, like other Englishmen who visited Ireland, he could not contemplate inequalities practised in the name of law. At Truro he broke into sunshiny banter : " The Liberalism of Cornwall—it pervades nearly the whole population. If I may say so, it is in the very air of the country. The atmosphere is Liberal. In this home of the old British race, more than perhaps in any other part of England, it is entitled to claim that honour." Mr. Layland Barratt welcomed the orator at St. Austell in the name of his fellow Cornishmen, and once more, in light and cheery vein, Mr. Gladstone rallied his hearers : "If I had Tory friends—and I have a few—I would advise them, in their own interests, not to come into the County of Cornwall, because, if they do, and stay there for a short time, they will infallibly become Liberal like the rest of the country." And then, as though the moors had breathed into him the breath of an optimistic mood, he remarked : "Our hearts bound with expectation, and our opponents are filled with dismay and "—this with a mirthful gleam—"the dismay will do them a great deal of good." At Tintagel the versatile artist taught the reporters that it was never safe to leave him out of sight, and he was unsuspectedly discovered discoursing on King Arthur and the Knights of the Round Table to the villagers at the mouth of a cave. He made his way via Launceston to Tavistock, and the scenes recalled the episodes of Midlothian. From station to station he was acclaimed until he reached Plymouth, where there were extended waving welcomes from every window and parapet. Exacting was the ordeal, and, when the Grand Hotel was reached, Mr. Gladstone at once withdrew. Whilst others banqueted, he embraced the balmy restorer, and, on entering the Drill Hall at eight o'clock, his mind was as serene and refreshed as though his eyes had just opened unto day. The speech itself was effortless—free from invective, throbbing with pathos, and disarming as to argument. The while that it was being delivered men fainted like women and were laid out on the grass to recover at their leisure from the heat. "Give Ireland Home Rule," Mr. Gladstone concluded : "give it to her for her own sake and give it to her for our own. Rely upon it that the effect of that measure will pour in a golden flood throughout the country." A far vaster multitude had gathered upon the Hoe—variously estimated at from sixty to a hundred thousand—and Mr. and Mrs. Glad- stone surveyed the serried mass, and the illuminations that played upon it, from the balcony of the Grand Hotel.

Mr. Gladstone's tour was followed by the dissolution of 1892, and Devonport replaced its Conservative with Home Rule members. Weary of Parliamentary work, Sir Edward Bates retired from Plymouth before Lord Salisbury went to the country, and a wealthy Conservative shipowner, in the person of Sir William Pearce, exercised the same fascina- tion over the Vintry Ward electorate. Serious divisions existed in the Liberal ranks as the result of Labour agitations, and Mr. Gladstone's majority received no accession from Plymouth : Clarke, 5,081 ; Pearce, 5,081 ; Harrison, 4,921 ; Lidgett, 4,861.   In 1895 a better understanding amongst Plymouth Liberals enabled them to reap the partial reward of their long unrequited efforts.   The withdrawal of Sir William Pearce weakened the Conservatives, and the appearance of Mr. Mendl endowed the Liberals with new hope : Clarke, 5,575 ;. Harrison, 5,482 ; Hubbard, 5,456 ; Mendl, 5,298.   Mr. Harrison's death in 1897 opened the way for a hand-to-hand struggle on a much increased constituency.   Mr. Mendl was the champion of the Liberals and the Hon. Ivor Guest represented the Conservatives. Plymouth was ablaze with rival colours, and the streets were paraded by the gayest of equipages.   The counting was awaited at midnight by a surging multitude that so overflowed from the Guildhall Square into Bedford Street that the façade of the Devon and Cornwall Bank collapsed, and a score of persons were precipitated into the area, and more or less seriously injured.   The result was hailed with booming cheers : Mendl, 5,966 ; Guest, 5,802.

In 1892 the Devonport constituency had grown to 7,629 electors, and the retirement of Mr. Puleston placed the Conservatives in considerable difficulty.   Captain Price was joined by Mr. R. Harvey, who found that a budget of Dockyard grievances had arisen which the former members had failed to redress.   The candidates chosen by the Liberals— Messrs. Kearley and Morton—interviewed every branch of the service, mastered hitherto inscrutable problems of classification, and job and task, and denounced the espionage with which the employés were pursued.   Mr. Kearley impeached the Admiralty as " The Champion Sweater," and the Dockyard electorate once more swung round as he and his colleague pronounced for Home Rule as well as a general re-adjustment of the laws affecting Labour—inside the Dockyards as well as without.   The news of the Plymouth reverse was flashed in red fire from the roof of the Liberal Club in Bedford Street just as the victory of Messrs. Kearley and Morton was conveyed in clouds of blue from their headquarters in Fore Street : Kearley, 3,354 ; Morton, 3,325 ; Price, 3,012 ; Harvey, 2,972. During the ensuing three years the Liberal First Lord made considerable concessions to the dockyardsmen, and the pensioners received further advantages.   Nevertheless, upon an augmented electorate, the Conservatives conducted in 1895 a better fight : Kearley, 3,570 ; Morton, 3,511 ; Pridham-Wippell, 3,303 ; Thynne, 3,262.

CHAPTER XVI.—CHURCH AND DISSENT IN MODERN TIMES.

Developments and Characteristics: 1759-1899.   The ecclesiastical history of Plymouth in the eighteenth century has been already dealt with, but Payne's description of the town in 1759 may be conveniently quoted as supplying some idea of the social, moral and religious advance which the lapse of 150 years has witnessed : " Plymouth contains as many souls as the city of Exeter, but we can't readily admit that its population is so large unless it be in its most flourishing wicked time of what some call a good red-hot war with France, when, indeed, 'tis too much overstocked with inhabitants new—come from Ireland, Cornwall, and other parts, and gathered flocks of females, charitably inclined to solace moneyed sailors in distress.   That they may do it honestly, and with a good conscience, they marry them extempore, possibly half a dozen successively in as many months ; their former husbands dying almost as soon as out of the Sound (in a double meaning).   The true Plymothians themselves are in the main allowed to be as polite, genteel, religious, and worthy a people as those enjoyed by any other place ; and the regulations and government are excellent.   But in the times aforesaid, through the vast resort of the necessitous, rapacious and lewd by land, and of the half-mad Jack Addles from the sea, the scenes are altered much, and very grievous to the best natives.   Then is (though but in common with other seaport towns) too much introduced sharping, tricking, debauchery, pride, insolence, profaneness, impurity with impudence ; and this in spite of strenuous endeavours of the magistrates and their officers to prevent it.   But, I say, such corruption (which defaces the town's right and natural appearance) is of foreign birth, and brought by the concourse from abroad."   In those days of strongly marked contrasts one of the leading divines of the town was Dr. Whitfeld, curate of Charles Church, who subsequently became the incumbent of St. Margaret's, Lothbury.   It was one of Dr. Whitfeld's sisters who married a Leach, and from this connection sprung the distinguished zoologist who was born over the Hoe Gate, and became the curator of the British Museum.

With the break-up of the old Presbyterian dominance in Plymouth and Dock, some became Unitarians, others Independents, and not a few Moderate Calvinists.   The Baptists divided themselves into Particular and Calvinistic sections, and High Calvinists were arrayed as Bryanites and Baringites, after those whom they followed.   Bryan, a Wesleyan living at Bodmin, longed for the passionate fervour of the pioneers, and Baring was another seceder who held narrower views than the majority favoured.   The Old Tabernacle was occupied by the orthodox Whitfieldites, and the New Tabernacle was supplied by ministers from Lady Huntingdon's College.   Many Methodists, disliking an appellation which was popularly an epithet of scorn, described themselves as Independent Calvinists.   According to Polwhele their internecine conflicts were unsparing.   Wesley declaimed against Whitfield " for the horrible blasphemies of his horrible doctrines," and the Moravians were denounced as " the worst of men in principle and practice."   The Arminian Methodists execrated the Calvinists of all grades, and the Calvinists gave back " every curse sevenfold into their bosom."   To add to the complexity in which seekers after truth found themselves in the district, Joanna Southcott, who was born at Gittisham, in Devonshire, excited the liveliest local controversy by the predictions she made during the later Napoleonic wars, and she was claimed as the woman who was to give birth to Shiloh and thus bruise the serpent's head.   Joanna, described by some as mad and by others as a sincere fanatic, persuaded many simple-minded ministers and others to believe in her as an inspired prophetess, and she secured a considerable following in the Three Towns. When, at the age of 65, she was brought to bed with the apparent symptoms of pregnancy, expectations were general amongst her believers that the supernatural was about to occur, and she was herself absolutely assured that she had been divinely chosen for the purpose. Her death, and the post-mortem examination conducted in the presence of medical devotees, although it satisfactorily disposed of the theory that she was about to give birth to a child, did not disillusion the belief of her followers that she would reappear, and so late as 1850 a few unshorn followers in Plymouth and Devonport still lingered and awaited her second coming.

St. Andrew's Church, 1840.   (Showing the Graveyard and Old Workhouse.)

Of the clergy who ministered early in the nineteenth century, pleasant types have been passed on for the reverence of posterity.   The Rev. John Gandy, for fifty-six years vicar of St. Andrew's, was " a beautiful example of the Christian pastor " ; and, in the words of the monument erected to his memory in St. Andrew's Church—representing Religion standing near a sarcophagus—" he exercised the endowment of a powerful mind in the spirit of one who knew that he was a steward and desired only to be found faithful."   Mr. Gandy was a man of ready wit, and, when a parishioner declared that he would rather make matches than lead such a life as one of his neighbours, he replied : "So would I, for making matches is quite in my line."   The desire of a bereaved family to hold an early funeral evoked the suggestion that their anxiety was to smuggle the corpse.   "Well, upon my word," the old Vicar rejoined, "it does look as if the spirit is not to be Duty-Paid."

Dr. Robert Hawker, Vicar of Charles, was known as "The Star of the West" by reason of his eloquence—impressive and earnest, with wealth of ordered imagery and chaste flow of diction.   He came from Exeter, where his father practised as a surgeon, and served his apprenticeship with Mr. White, at Briton Side. He married Miss Anna Rains, the daughter of a naval officer, and joined a battleship as assistant surgeon. On his return he rejoined his old regiment, which was stationed at Devonport, and he there caught the fervour of Evangelical appeals and quitted the service that he might enter the Church. His first appointment was to the curacy of Charles, of which Mr. Bedford was then vicar ; and, upon that gentleman's death, he became a candidate. His friends were canvassed, and among these Mr. White, his former master, was not only a member of the Corporation, but Mayor of the borough, and he actively espoused his cause. Though there was another candidate, so great was the majority in Mr. Hawker's favour that, on the day of election, there was but one dissentient voice. His presentation to the vicarage by the Mayor and Commonalty of Plymouth received the Bishop's seal in 1784, and thus a youth whose life was so full of levity that he once threw a squib into the midst of a Plymouth congregation, attained a position which in time rendered him the object of national controversy. Unrivalled as a textuary, the readiness with which he quoted in illustration always surprised and impressed his auditors. At an evening party, if a Bible were called for, that he might contribute his thoughts on some particular chapter, " when it was too early to order the candles and too dusky to see without them," he would repeat in full the extract under discussion, and interweave his own exposition as though the Book were open before him. One of his earliest achievements was the institution of a Sunday-school, and he personally conducted the service. As he started this building without the promise of a guinea, he gave it the name of " The Household of Faith." After a hymn had been sung, he regularly read the liturgy as far as the first lesson. Opposite his desk a select band of the best readers would sit uniformly clad in caps and tippets provided from the funds of the charity, and by a mere indication of the head Dr. Hawker directed the children to commence. As they read so he would enlarge and expound until the end of the chapter, and, after another hymn, congregation and children were dismissed with the Benediction. The building was used on week-days as a " school of industry."

Dr. Hawker's experience of the services rendered him extremely averse to the practice of flogging, and he was often the means of relieving a delinquent from punishment. He moved amongst the soldiery fearlessly whenever they were visited with pestilential sickness. During the retreat from Corunna several transports put into Plymouth, and the doctor was engaged for days in assisting to bring ashore hundreds who were afflicted with fever. They were temporarily deposited in a large barn to which the name of Friary Hospital was given ; and, within three months, more than 1,000 died. The corpses were carried in cart loads to the burial ground in St. Andrew's parish, and interred there in large trenches dug for the purpose. Over 300 inhabitants perished of the same contagion. " During the residence of the soldiers who survived the pestilence at Friary Hospital, one of them, by name Patrick O'Connor, had sold (perhaps to provide for some pressing occasion) a book of his. It was lying," wrote Dr. Hawker, " on an old bookstall, which lay in my way, when going to the burying ground. On the back of the title-page the poor man had written his name, and the state of his then misery, thus : ' Patrick O'Connor, once of the famous city of Limerick, in the county of Kilkenny, in the kingdom of Ireland ; but now dying of a broken heart in Friar's Hospital, Plymouth. ' " As deputy-chaplain of the garrison at Plymouth, it became Dr. Hawker's duty, although wholly unpaid, to visit the sick in the hospitals, both in the garrison at Plymouth, "and the military hospital at Stoke Village, which is somewhat two miles distant from the garrison. And in consequence of this appointment, I have once in every week, in summer's heat and winter's rain, discharged the duty of visiting those hospitals. In the execution of which, at the Stoke hospital particularly (while the sick troops continued in that temporary build-

MM

ing, and before the new hospital was opened near Stoke Church), I have performed divine service, in prayers and expounding the Scriptures, sometimes in the three distinct wards of that hospital, and always in two of them, when the other was not in use, amidst the floating miasma of typhus, and the effluvia of other disorders." It was his experience of the distresses which remained unheeded that induced Dr. Hawker to establish the Misericordia, a charitable institution for relieving the wants of forlorn and destitute strangers. For the benefit of unfortunate young girls he also inaugurated the Plymouth Asylum, and its purpose is pathetically described in some verses of his own poem :

The child of sin and woe,
  Ah ! whither shall I flee ?
To what kind bosom go
  To tell my misery ?
    For none will see
    But all agree
    To frown on me—
      A Magdalene !

Methinks I feel a ray
  Of hope arising round ;
Some angel points the way—
  ' Here's an asylum found ! '
    What's this I see ?
    And can it be
    Inviting me—
      A Magdalene !

Dr. Hawker, a man of wide toleration, did not hesitate to entertain at his table the Rev. John Wesley. In the first sermon he ever preached, which was addressed to the soldiers assembled on Roborough Down, he never mentioned the name of Christ, and incurred some criticism on that account. He soon demonstrated, however, that he was no Arian. Arian, if not Socinian doctrines, were preached "in an ancient meeting house in Charles parish" which was believed to have been originally a Presbyterian place of worship. Here a minister of ability industriously promulgated his Socinian sentiments, and Dr. Hawker thought it his duty " to prevent the minds of his congregation in particular, or parishioners in general, from being led away from the pure faith of the gospel, by the revival of opinions long since exploded or discountenanced in Plymouth, which seemed to be once more mingling with the fashionable doctrines of the times." With this apology, his volume of the Sermons on the Divinity of Christ was sent to press, at the close of the year 1790, and led to another discussion on local Unitarianism.

Not free from criticism on his own account, because of his tolerance of Methodists, Dr. Hawker was popularly regarded as "little better than a Wesleyan himself." During a visit to Cornwall, for the benefit of his health, he was invited to preach in several churches, and the presence of the famous Evangelical created so much interest that Dissenting ministers "shut up their conventicles" to enable congregations to attend the churches in which the divine held forth, and "turned their own edifices into meeting houses." "The fame of your preaching," wrote the Rev. R. Polwhele, "has reached me from the east and from the west ; it has been echoed from the heights of Maker, and re-echoed from the shores of the Lizard. There is a lying spirit gone forth from amongst the people, which has seduced them from the paths of truth into dark and dangerous ways. The mania of Methodism has seized the West of England, and of this mania, sir, you are represented as having taken an advantage for the purpose of disseminating doctrines which the sobriety of reason would reject as unscriptural. Let me ask you whether you think your credentials are such as will justify your conduct to your Diocesan or to any other than the mad enthusiast or the arrogant fanatic ? Many were drawn to you by the fascination of your eloquence who were on the point of deserting their proper churches, where, compared with yours, the preaching of their own pastors was spiritless." Polwhele called upon Hawker to discard " the whole tribe of enthusiasts," and more especially " those great fabricators of Methodism, Whitfield and Wesley," whose " blasphemies," in claiming the presence of the

Holy Spirit, were sufficient to make him "shudder," and whose prayers that they might be persecuted he compared to the superstitions of St. Francis. Polwhele was no mealy-mouthed controversialist. In his estimation Whitfield was a "hypocrite," ever prompted to dis-obedience by the Devil, and Wesley was not free from the same "infernal influence." The acme of Methodism "was a sinless perfection;" Wesley was "full of artifice;" and Hawker was one who had entered the very penetralia of their heresies by undertaking this "Quixotic Expedition."

Mr. Hawker lost no time in repudiating the reproach of itinerancy, but he retaliated upon the Vicar of Manaccan that he would not object to travel "if convenience and opportunity offered, without neglecting the duties of my own parish. Gladly would I go from parish to parish, and from one county to another, 'to seek for Christ's sheep,' (as the ordination service enjoins), that are dispersed abroad. And pardon me yet further, when I add, that of all places, did it come within my reach, Manaccan, with your permission, should be the favourite spot of my itinerancy. I should like above all things to take wing and alight on some perch near you, to warble, in the best manner I am able, the sweet notes of the gospel, though your and your friends might perhaps think, I do but chatter as a swallow." In a spirit of large toleration and tenderness he replied that he had done no more than take "sweet counsel" with fellow Christians, that he could not prosecute polemics with one who apparently forgot that it was his duty to "serve God for the promotion of his glory and the edifying of his people," and persistently refused to adopt a literal construction of the articles and liturgy of the Church of England.

So sorely did the Vicar of Manaccan resent Mr. Hawker's answer that he disclaimed further communication with him, and addressed a letter to the Bishop of Exeter on the Itinerancy and Nonconformity of the Vicar of Charles, and complained of his unfairness and subtlety in argument. "Dr. Hawker is fond," he said, "of discussing such questions as arise from the articles of Liturgy, that he may entangle his Church opponents in their talk. For his shield and his spear, he has recourse to the Church armoury, whence his antagonists profess to have borrowed theirs." For this resort to the Bishop, Mr. Polwhele was soundly trounced: "Mr. Polwhele," Dr. Hawker rejoined, "in calling his lordship's authority to his aid, acts like a school-boy, who skulks from behind to give the first blow, and, when he has been well beaten for his temerity and presumption, declares off to fight no more, and runs away to his master with the tale." The charge of Nonconformity formed, in his view, "a new dictionary in language, which the dullness of my apprehension prevents me from understanding, that it is become a crime to fill up the intermediate hours, which the public demands of my Church do not occupy, to the promotion of the same important purposes, by private visitations among the people. I confess, indeed, that, in all this, there is evidently a very strong Nonconformity to the conduct of writers of religious jest-books, and to men, who subscribe to doctrines, which they have the unblush-ing confidence to tell the world they do not believe." To his daughter the divine wrote in further explanation of this controversy: "It is not Dr. Hawker, Vicar of Charles, with whom they contend; for if I had preached only the dry system of morality and not the doctrine of the cross, never, no never would they have come forward against me, though I had got drunk and tumbled into the grave after the corpse. But it is Dr. Hawker, the preacher of vital godliness, they hate, and, therefore persecute."

Dr. Hawker was assailed from another standpoint. Under the pseudonym of Verax, which one of his reviewers urged should have been Mendax, the Rev. James Bidlake, of Ply-mouth, published a pamphlet, entitled, "The True Gospel of Dr. Hawker, shewn to be at variance with the gospel of Christ and his apostles, and therefore undeserving of its assumed appellation." In this pamphlet he controverted the Doctor's statements, and attempted to prove that salvation was unconditional; that to offer Christ to the congregation even indiscriminately was Scriptural; and that, by believing, a sinner became interested in Christ. After the lapse of several months, another pamphlet was published, entitled, " Truth Vindicated, or a Series of Remarks on some of the leading Doctrines of the Gospel, occasioned by Dr. Hawker's appendix to his True Gospel, by James Bidlake, alias Verax." This induced the Doctor to publish a criticism of this pamphlet, under the title of the " True Portrait of Antinomianism, being an Admonitory Letter to the Rev. James Bidlake." By way of rejoinder, Mr. Bidlake remarked : " Were I required to give a definition of ancient and modern Antinomianism in separate words, I should speak of it as an amalgam of irreligion, ignorance, conceit, pride, obstinacy, selfishness, and cowardice. It is moreover clamorous, morose, scornful, insolent, petulant, revengeful. It is the hot-bed of discord, and the most effectual promoter of religious feuds. It is a Diotrephes in the house of God, and a tyrant in the domestic circle. When it attaches to dispositions naturally amiable, it converts them into bad ones; and it makes those who are naturally bad intolerable." Joseph Cottle, the author of several poetical works, issued a tirade entitled " Some strictures on the Plymouth Antinomians," and the reader was asked to believe that the local Antinomians were sinners above all other Antinomians. " It would have been well," wrote the Rev. John Williams, Vicar of Stroud, and Hawker's other self, " if the mellowed relenting, which Mr. Cottle tells us he felt in publishing these strictures, had induced him to commit them to the flames. The Lord pardon him for the mischief he has done ! Dr. Hawker was a witness for God and His truth in this awful day of ours, when the sovereignty of God in the election of grace is not only called in question, if not a subject of derision and scorn. Mr. Cottle is evidently of the free-will school, if not a Pelagian !"

During the distress that prevailed in 1817, the parish of Charles, by voluntary contributions and collections every Sunday morning in the church, adopted the plan of selling a thousand sixpenny loaves of the best quality for threepence to each person. Dr. Hawker suggested this experiment, and improved the occasion by publishing a little tract, " Bread selling to the poor at half-price, a sweet memorial of the Bread of Life, which is given to the poor of the Lord's people without money and without price ! " As illustrating his humility it is related that he entered a baker's shop in Butcher's Lane and, paying for an eight-pound loaf, placed it under his arm. The tradesman begged that he might send it, but the minister replied : " No, I am going to take it to a starving family near—a man and his wife and eight children; and if you'll give me another loaf I'll carry that as well." On the instant, the baker supplied a second loaf, and Mr. Hawker placed a loaf of bread under each arm. The testimony borne after his death best conveys the homage in which he was held by his admirers : " The elegance yet simplicity of diction, the liveliness and brilliancy of imagination, the perspicuity and vigour of thought, the depth and compass of Christian knowledge and experience, with which he was talented and blest (though the living eloquence be now silent), are still extant in his sermons on the Divinity of Christ, and on the Divinity and operations of the Holy Ghost, in his Zion's Pilgrim and other numerous works of polemical, practical, and experimental Divinity ; but above all, in his poor man's commentary on the Bible; in which he richly dwells on God the Father's electing love, on God the Son's redeeming blood, and God the Spirit's regenerating grace, as the sole cause of all health and happiness to the Church of Christ." Contemporary with Dr. Hawker was the young parish apprentice, John Kitto, who, in spite of incurable deafness, the result of a fall from a ladder, so applied himself to Biblical studies that he qualified as Doctor of Divinity and published many standard theological works,

Intolerance reared its head in various forms in Plymouth and Dock after Whitfield and Wesley passed from the scene, and the " castigation " of congregations was regarded by naval officers as a chartered humour, and their military colleagues despatched regimental bands to disturb open-air preachers. Petty persecutions only deepened the determination of the faithful to worship in their own way, and, when the Congregationalists built the Princes Street Chapel, Devonport, in 1801, on the space where Whitfield had been accustomed to harangue crowds, and the Wesleyans erected in 1817 their Ebenezer

Chapel in Plymouth, the Dissenters so won respect that the magistrates were more than ever persuaded to put into operation the law that at least extended the semblance of civil and religious liberty. The services that had been previously held by the Wesleyans in Chapel Lane were systematically subjected to disorderly interruptions, and a gang of brawlers were pounced upon in 1812 by the more muscular members of the congregation and transferred to the custody

INTERIOR OF EBENEZER CHAPEL.

of the watchmen. These drastic measures imbued the disturbers with a contrite spirit, and they were released on publicly promising to abstain from such conduct in the future. To this the minister and officers of " the meeting house" agreed, and the delinquents published a humiliating apology for having made "a great noise, thereby disturbing and disquieting a congregation of people called the Methodists." They " humbly " begged the pardon of the offended for " the heinous offence we have committed," and sincerely pledged themselves " never to offend in like manner again." This document the Mayor of Plymouth supplemented with a manifesto, in which he pointed out that "the ministers and elders of the Dissenters and other tolerated sects" might rest assured

EXTERIOR OF EBENEZER CHAPEL.

that he would afford them "support and countenance" by appointing constables to attend at the doors of "their houses of divine worship," so that they might quietly enjoy the rights which the laws of the country had conferred.

St. Aubyn Chapel was erected, under an Act which was procured in 1769, at a cost of £248, and the measure provided that two of the pews could be let as freeholds, so that they might become legitimate property. The then Rector of Stoke Damerel strongly opposed the grant of a chapel-of-ease, and, as a compromise, was empowered to prevent marriages or baptisms from taking place there, and also to dismiss the incumbent if he transgressed any of the conditions. The chapel was further precluded from "claiming a district," and it was not until comparatively modern times that these impoverishing disabilities were removed. The edifice was built at a cost of £3,850, and a marble slab for the purposes of an altar-piece, which had been purchased in India at a cost of £400, was presented by the St. Aubyn family. The most attractive preacher in Dock was Dr. Jacobs, the incumbent of this chapel, and, during his ministrations, not a seat could be procured for " love or money." The Rev. Samuel Rundle, who succeeded to the incumbency in 1839, "truly an ambassador of Christ," was engaged in season and out of season in visiting the sick, and he promoted the educational work of the town with an earnestness that led all who were associated with him to utter his name with gratitude. The erection of the Military Chapel deprived Mr. Rundle of his stipend as chaplain of the troops, and he was compelled to seek another pulpit. Conspicuous among the Devonport worthies who attended the chapel was Mr. Nicholas May, a centenarian, who remembered when Dock consisted of a few scattered hamlets, and whose patriarchial mantle descended upon Dr. Joseph May, the nonogenarian alderman who was admitted to the freedom of the borough in 1899. The Rev. George Billing, subsequently incumbent of Louth, and General Nelson were also consistent attendants.

Philip Gibbs officiated as the pastor of the Plymouth Baptists for half a century, and Winterbotham resumed his ministrations after emerging from prison on the charge of preaching seditious sermons. Contention continued to disturb the brethren at Devonport with spasmodic revivals of energy and hope. The oldest Baptist chapel was in Pembroke Street, which was built in 1781 as a branch of the Church at Plymouth. It flourished so well that it attained distinct and separate importance, and the intense fervour that animated converts may be judged by an extract from an old MS. written by James Silk Buckingham, subsequently member for Flushing, whose repulsive experience of the navy is elsewhere on record :

"My repentance was most sincere. I determined to begin a new life, and applied myself with all practicable diligence to the abandonment of my old connections and the formation of new. I felt it my duty also to undergo the form of adult baptism, which was performed on me with other converts, by a very worthy minister, the Rev. Isaiah Birt, in the Baptist Chapel of Plymouth-Dock, on one of the coldest days of winter ; and never could the powerful influence of mental emotions to ward off physical danger be more manifested than in this case, where neither of the baptised individuals —some very old, and others of the most delicate constitutions—suffered not the least inconvenience from being immersed in the icy water, and standing in it for a consider- able time during which the ceremony lasted. For myself I can truly say I felt a holy glow inexpressibly agreeable, and thought that if religious duty demanded it, I could have borne a baptism of fire with the same equanimity. I could understand and appreciate by this the exultation and the joy of the martyrs. Soon after this an occasion arose in which a Calvinistic minister, Mr. Reece, a Welsh gentleman of great learning and eloquence, whose ministry I preferred to all others on account of its absolute and uncomprising predestinarianism, was taken suddenly ill, and he sent for me to take his place in the pulpit. I was then not sixteen, and had never anticipated such an event. Instead of being, however, in the least degree embarrassed, I considered this to be a distinct call from Heaven, or an occurrence decreed, like every other, from all eternity, or before the foundations of the world were laid, and that I had no power to resist it. I went without fear or hesitation and preached what was deemed and declared to be a most powerful and convincing extempore sermon."

Stoke Church Controversies : 1825-1837. Over the fabric of Stoke Church the Lord of the Manor, although patron of the living, had no control, and there were differences between the Rector's and People's Wardens which it only required a litigious disposition like that of the Rev. W. J. St. Aubyn to fan into flames. For thirty years prior to his appointment the Rev. John Hawker laboured in the church as curate, and it was assumed that he would continue in that position. Mr. St. Aubyn's first act, however, was to give Mr. Hawker notice to quit and vacate the house within six weeks. Mr. Hawker had especially commended himself to the esteem of the congregation ; and, when he announced from the pulpit that he had been dismissed from his livelihood and home, many of the worshippers were moved to tears. The evicted minister applied to Bishop Phillpotts for a small incumbency ; but, as he had strenuously denounced Tractarianism, his "supplication" was disregarded. A movement was thereupon inaugurated by a profoundly indignant public to provide Mr. Hawker with a chapel of his own, and the necessary fund was raised by subscription. The Lord of the Manor of Stoke Damerel refused, however, to sell the necessary site, and Mr. Hawker's friends were compelled to buy land in Plymouth. A building was constructed on the site of Wyndham Square, to which the name of "Eldad" was given to signify that the incumbent was "the favoured of God," but it was impossible to proceed because the Bishop required three months in which to consider whether he would consent to the ceremony of consecration. After the interval had expired, Dr. Phillpotts intimated his willingness to conduct the ceremony, contingent on conditions that proved his reluctance and prejudice. Date after date was suggested to meet his convenience, and then Mr. Hawker cut the Gordian knot by withdrawing from the Established Church and dispensing with his lordship's assistance. The increasing toleration of Ritualistic forms had been working a steady change in his mind, and he declared in his dedicatory sermon that he could best continue a faithful minister of the Church he loved by separating from "her greatest foes." His enemies might describe him as a Dissenter, "but I shall be faithful to the Church Services, and from these I shall neither dissent nor part, for I am fully satisfied with them." For a generation Mr. Hawker preached to large congregations, conspicuous amongst the Evangelists of the district for the skill with which he "united the fervour of Calvin with the reasoning power of Luther."

In 1810 the parishioners of Stoke Damerel, through Mr. Richard Rodd, their solicitor, negociated with the agents of Sir John St. Aubyn as "lord of the fee of all the land in the said parish" and patron of the living, for a site to be used as a burial ground, and the area having been purchased for £1,500, was enclosed and prepared for sepultural purposes. A conveyance of the land was executed by Sir John St. Aubyn, dated September 11th, 1811, in trust for the parish for ever, "as and for burying places for the use of the said parish of Stoke Damerel, and the inhabitants thereof, and for no other purpose whatever." The conveyance was "by some unaccountable means" lost, and Sir John St. Aubyn thereupon executed another deed, conveying the fee of the land upon the same conditions as it was originally granted. The Bishop of Exeter, however, under powers vested in him by an Act of George III., refused to revive the rights of the parishioners and required that the freehold should be vested in the Rector.   Upon the induction of the Rev. W. J. St. Aubyn he seized the fee of the parishioners, used the burial ground as his own freehold, and exacted "large and unaccustomed fees for interment." A memorial was sent to the House of Commons praying for restitution, but this remained unheeded, and the burial scandal of 1829 was thus brought about.   It was the custom to accept seven shillings for opening vaults at the Plymouth parish churches ; but, upon the death of his son, in 1828, Mr. Blackmore, a prominent resident of Devonport sent Mr. St. Aubyn a guinea and requested the necessary arrrngements to be made for the interment.   The Rector returned the money, with an intimation that his fee for opening a vault was £2 12s. 6d. This charge Mr. Blackmore repudiated and insisted upon interring his son in the family tomb. On the publication of the correspondence there was much indignation and crowds collected near the church upon the day of the funeral.   Mr. Blackmore's solicitor, standing by the coffin, demanded its admission to the vault, and the Rector refused to comply until the stipulated fee had been paid.   The mourners then walked towards the vault, and the gates were closed by Mr. St. Aubyn's order. Thereupon the party retraced their steps to Mr. Blackmore's house, where the coffin was enclosed in a lead shell, and deposited in a bedroom.   A mandamus to compel the Rector to bury was applied for, and the issue was then raised as to his right to demand unusual fees.   The Chancellor regretted that the Rector had pushed his claims, but held that by opening a grave he had shown his readiness to bury. Shortly after this decision a military officer, who was in charge of a funeral party, finding that the Rector was not present to conduct the service, read through the form of burial himself, gave the word for the body to be lowered and ordered the volley to be fired.

STOKE CHURCHYARD.
(From a Photo. by the Rev. E. A. Donaldson, 1899.)

The grave was partly filled when the Rector appeared on the scene, and having commanded the coffin to be disinterred, he caused the ceremony to be repeated by his curate.

Claims to particular pews and sittings also occasioned frequent disputes in Stoke Church. Doors of seats were locked by those whose ownership was challenged, and were forced open by rivals who were no less satisfied of the legality of their own claims. In some cases, after the service had commenced, persons who had taken possession were violently ejected ; and, when summonses were issued, the magistrates experienced much difficulty in deciding between the disputants. In 1831 Mr. Williams pushed Miss Cuming from her pew during the delivery of the first prayer ; but she established her right, and her assailant was fined 40s. Excitement was further aggravated by the Rector's resolve to levy Easter dues at the rate of twopence per head, but the custom was established to the satisfaction of the Bench before whom the delinquents were carried. Mr. Rundle revived the protest in 1831, and insisted that there was no law to justify the exaction and that there had been no pretence of proving one. Mr. Garland, who had been sexton for fifty years, testified that he regularly collected the dues, and the Rector produced an Act of William and Mary to prove prescriptive usage. The defendant was thereupon ordered to pay. Fresh odium was incurred by Mr. St. Aubyn during the year following, 1832, when he levelled the graves without consulting friends or relatives, on the ground that it was necessary to improve the surroundings of the church. He attributed the outburst of anger with which his conduct was assailed to his admitted want of popularity—a state of feeling no one regretted more than himself. Messrs. Blackmore, Clouter and others thereupon took the necessary measures for forming a Cemetery Company, but Dr Phillpotts refused to consecrate the site they bought for the purpose, and the promoters abandoned the project. At a parish meeting, however, the conduct of the Bishop was vehemently denounced in several resolutions, and his lordship issued a writ for libel against Mr. Clouter for having, as chairman, submitted them to the vote of the parishioners. After an explanation from the defendant that he deprecated the resolutions, the action was stayed.

A fracas arising out of the excessive pretensions of the churchwardens occurred on the occasion of a visit by the Bishop in 1834. A large crowd assembled at the doors, with a view of obtaining admission, but Mr. Lyne, one of the officers, kept the people at bay—admitting those whom he knew, and shutting the door against all save personal friends. Mr. John West Herring, in the assertion of his right, made his way to the chancel in the midst of a group of the favoured, but Mr. Lyne pursued and hustled him, and commanded him to leave the edifice. He flatly refused to do so, and the defendant then struck him in the chest and locked the pew at which he was demanding admittance. The Rector testified that he authorised Mr. Lyne to keep the middle aisle clear so that the Bishop might have a clear passage to the altar. The defendant argued that the aisle contained faculty seats, and to this the reply was made that the complainant was in the exercise of a common right, as all the seats in the centre were not held by prescriptive right. Defendant was fined 20s. for an assault which the justices thought had been committed under circumstances of "great palliation," and was to be attributed to the "bad blood" prevailing in the parish, a state of anarchy which would, they continued, lead to "more serious consequences than the present." Annoyed by the comment, Mr. St. Aubyn published a letter reflecting on the conduct of the magistrates, complaining of their improper treatment, and threatening to bring their conduct before the Privy Council. The justices replied by delivering a strong homily from the Bench on Mr. St. Aubyn's criticisms.

This want of harmony between the Rector and his parishioners diminished the maintenance fund, and the fabric became so dilapidated that Mr. St. Aubyn attempted in 1832 to raise a rate to cover the cost of restoration. Muttered discontent soon blazed into indignation, and Messrs. Elms, Towson and J. W. Ryder organised the Dissenters to resistance. Incensed at the success of their tactics, the Archdeacon of Plymouth advised the Rector to cite the mover and seconder of each resolution aiming at the evasion of the rate, and wear out the heart of the hostility by involving the leading recalcitrants in heavy costs. Mr. Towson urged the parishioners to defy these threats, and, as every attempt to enforce the rate was thwarted, the state of the edifice went from bad to worse. At Plymouth, although objection to the payment of Church rates was embodied in various memorials to Parliament, the sums voluntarily subscribed in rates and pew rents avoided the discord that distracted Stoke. At St. Andrew's, indeed, the service and vicar were so popular that, after paying £3,000, which was borrowed for restoring the fabric, the amount was paid in prompt instalments, and the wardens had a balance of " £400 or £500 a year, which they did not know what to do with." This affluence and amity at Plymouth did not tend to moderate Mr. St. Aubyn's exasperation at the refusal to comply with his demands. Irritation increased with each renewal of the controversy, and the periodical contests for wardens produced in the church the characteristics of a bear-garden. A supreme struggle between the factions occurred in 1837, and for three days a babel of confusion prevailed within the edifice. Handbills were showered broadcast containing " scandalous, false and unfounded statements " about the Rector, and retaliatory attacks on Messrs. Elms and Towson were denounced by lusty orators as " unmanly, unfounded, disgraceful and assassin-like." A crowd of " youths and idle persons " jumped about the seats, jostled the people in the aisles, and filled the church with " indecorous shouts." The Dissenting candidate, Mr. Willing, headed the poll for the first two days, and then there was a rally in favour of Mr. Abbot which gave him a majority of 140 on a poll of 1,100 parishioners. After six years of controversy, regular attendants and Dissenters raised £800 by subscription to repair the building, and the subsequent abolition of Church rates found all parties in harmony.

Sale of St. Andrew's and Charles' Advowsons : 1832.   If it was delightful for the Plymouth freemen to be entertained it was no less pleasant for them to confer their bits of patronage. The election of an incumbent of Charles Church in 1832 supplied the last opportunity of this kind which they were destined to enjoy, and there was a rush of candidates for the living vacated by Dr. Carne. Each gentleman issued an address to " the Mayor, Aldermen, Councillors and Freemen of the Borough of Plymouth," some objecting to canvassing on principle, and others personally soliciting and inducing their friends to appeal on their behalf. Each aspirant indulged in some " humble but sincere hope " that, by " energy, zeal and unwearied attention to parochial duties," a proof would be afforded " that your patronage was not unworthily bestowed." On the day the election was held, Captain Arthur created a diversion by proposing that the living should be sold and the funds divided among the creditors of " the embarrassed Corporation." This suggestion the Rev. John Hatchard denounced as savouring of simony, and he was loudly cheered when he urged that the disposal of next presentations should be rendered illegal. Manifestoes were circulated appealing to the freemen to " dam up the floodgates of miserable influence," and to evince by their choice their repugnance to the " corrupted currents " which were threatening the Protestant religion with " polluted streams." The Rev. Septimus Courtenay secured the incumbency with 108 votes, and other candidates obtained varying degrees of support. As a means of reconciling the contentions occasioned, the restoration of the church was suggested, and £1,500 was voluntarily raised by the congregation.

As soon as the Municipal Reform Act enabled local authorities to dispose of ecclesiastical endowments, the Plymouth Council applied for powers to realise the advowsons of St. Andrew's and Charles, and, as the Close Corporation had left a heavy debt to be discharged by their successors, no one revived the argument that such a course would be "degrading and irreligious." Advertisements were accordingly issued in 1836 inviting tenders for "all that advowson of the Vicarage of St. Andrew's, with the appendant chapelries of Saint Budeaux, East Stonehouse, and Weston Peverell or Pennycross," the revenues of which were estimated at £850 per annum, in addition to an "excellent house for residence, with a large walled garden in a complete repair." The advowson was commended as "peculiarly valuable from the extent of ecclesiastical patronage which it offers, the Vicar of St. Andrew's being also patron of St. Andrew's Chapel, Plymouth, and the minister of St. George's Chapel, Stonehouse, in the gift of the Vicar, also appoints to St. Paul's Chapel in the same parish." It was added that "the present incumbent is 43 years of age." The estimated income of the Vicarage of Charles was given at about £600 per annum, and the patronage of the Chapel of Charles devolved upon the incumbent of the Church. Each advowson was offered separately, and it was urged that the property derived "considerable importance from the extended limits and augmented population of the town of Plymouth, both of which are rapidly increasing under the influence of a prevalent spirit of commercial activity, and the vicarial revenues may be expected to be proportionately improved by these causes and the consequently augmented value of the agricultural produce of the vicinity." The age of the incumbent of Charles was given as 56 years.

There was an outburst of indignation on the part of the more devout, arising from the care with which every "pecuniary particular" was mentioned to induce persons to purchase, whilst the "numerical value" of the souls in each parish was passed over in silence. "So that amid all the reform and general diffusion of knowledge, souls, yes, never-dying souls, are to be sold at the highest marketable price, without any consideration whatever with the sellers concerning either the character or qualification of the purchaser." A suggestion was made that the sales should be deferred until vacancies occurred; but, although this alternative was not entertained, the absence of offers caused the property to hang on hands for some years. The living of Charles was eventually purchased at £2,030 by Mr. Hodge, of Pounds, for his son, who declined, however, to accept a ministerial career. Then the Rev. Edmond Holland, a wealthy clergyman, took over the responsibility and placed the advowson in the hands of the Church Patronage Society—not as is popularly supposed, in those of the Simeon Trustees. The living of St. Andrew's Church also fell to the gift of the Church Patronage Society, and three clergymen and two laymen were chosen as trustees. The advowson was purchased for £4,000, and Plymouth was thus further enriched by the sale of its Church property. The Vicar was, and is compelled, however, to pay the Corporation £8 per annum, and the churchwardens were, and are, entitled to receive the equivalent sum from the treasurer of the Corporation. The Bastards, of Kitley, secured the "great tithes"—of the annual value of £5—and became lay rectors of St. Andrew's and Pennycross. The latter parish was subsequently constituted a separate ecclesiastical district by arrangement with the Vicar of St. Andrew's.

· Evangelical Plymouth and Bishop Phillpotts: 1842-1845.   Plymouth's ecclesiastical tendency was rigidly Evangelical. The names of the Rev. John Hatchard and St. Andrew's Church were inseparable, and to speculate on the possibility of one without the other was an absurdity. Refusing to attach that significance to "holy places" on which his Tractarian brethren insisted, Mr. Hatchard's pride was in his church, and he viewed with real alarm the onward march of Ritualism. At Charles

Church the traditions were Calvinistic, and Dr. Carne, who was preferred to the living in 1827, was one of their most trusted exponents, uniting in his devotion to his sacred calling "the meekness of wisdom and watchfulness of the Christian pastor." During the cholera in 1832, Dr. Carne and his wife, "his zealous and affectionate helpmate," were taken within four days of each other, and a memorial of "respect and attachment" was erected by grateful parishioners and sorrowing friends. Esteem for the Rev. Septimus Courtenay, an advanced Evangelist, was so great that Charles Chapel was erected by subscription to prevent his departure from Plymouth, when the death of Dr. Hawker resulted in the appointment of another vicar. Mr. Courtenay, however, was elected to the living upon the death of Dr. Carne, and the Rev. D. A. Doudney became incumbent of the chapel, doing as much as any man of his generation to impress his contemporaries with ultra-Calvinistic views of New Testament doctrines. " Regarding the sacred Scriptures under the teaching of the Holy Ghost as the only source of truth, he made the glory of Christ and His Redemption the great subjects of his ministry, and while he laboured diligently in the public preaching of the gospel, he exemplified in his life the doctrines which he taught." Such was the testimony borne in the memorial that was erected, and after his death, the Rev. H. A. Greaves was selected as the vicar—"a grave and sound divine" with not the slightest suspicion of either " Tractarian leaven or Rationalistic tendencies." Thus the influence of leading clergymen was heavily cast into the Protestant scale, the community was alert to the most trifling changes, and detected disloyal and treacherous instincts in every sacerdotal departure.

Bishop Phillpotts made few attempts to disguise his antipathy to avowed Evangelicals, and the Rev. John Hatchard, Vicar of St. Andrew's, became one of his pet aversions. Trinity Church was erected in 1842, to attract the fishermen, as the outcome of Mr. Hatchard's importunities, and an offertory was suggested at the consecration service to please the Bishop. When the bags were carried round, however, he exclaimed, to the profound surprise of the congregation, "Stop the collection," and wardens and sidesmen returned abashed to their seats. The Bishop also treated Mr. Hatchard with "chilling coldness," although four of his children were lying at the point of death. "I feel compelled," Mr. Hatchard observed in an open letter, "to advert with deep pain to your lordship's exclamation in church, the truth of which can be confirmed by hundreds who have not hesitated to express their opinion that my theological views have thus rendered me the object of your lordship's severest reprehension." Mr. Hatchard's admirers did not forgive the Bishop for the anxiety he had occasioned their Vicar, and, at the confirmation service he conducted in St. Andrew's in 1844, they humiliated him by responding to his sermon with "a beggarly collection." This slight his lordship requited with an onslaught on the pew system and those who took advantage of it. The scene was a public meeting which was held the day after the service, and there he denounced the audience, chiefly consisting of ladies, for the poverty of their offerings at church, and for their conduct in monopolising the pews to the exclusion "of the ragged and naked." With rising heat the Bishop exclaimed: "I tell you in the presence of God that you have cheated and robbed the poor," and, after insisting that they had no such vested rights in the pews as they imagined, and that he would see the wrong redressed, he added: "I will not come to this place year after year and see the house of God stolen from the poor. You shall not shut yourselves in snug pews and cram the poor into the aisles—I'll see to that, at any rate."

Without loss of time, the Bishop commanded Mr. Hatchard to supply his legal representative with a statement of pew rents received during the past 11 years, but the Vicar contented himself with mildly deprecating his lordship's " strong language," " startling allusions," and

" emphatic gestures." By way of rejoinder, the Bishop authorised Chancellor Martin to examine the wardens on oath touching the monetary transactions of the Church, and, in a letter no less vehement than his address, he denounced the practice of defacing the walls of the edifice with offers of " Seats for hire." " This," he asserted, " is a very great abuse, illegal in all cases, but inexcusable in a parish containing 24,000 inhabitants, where many of the sittings are let to non-parishioners. It is most manifest that, as Bishop, I should depart from my duty if, the knowledge of such facts being forced upon me, I any longer tolerated them. I do, therefore, absolutely forbid the churchwardens of St. Andrew's from continuing the practice of affixing rents to the seats in the parish church, and I hereby require them to order the seats, according to law, in such manner as they shall on just consideration deem most suitable and convenient to all parishioners." The congregation were accordingly convened, and, after deprecating with pain and surprise the Bishop's letter, a resolution was moved describing his instruction as uncalled-for by necessity and as fraught with obvious and extensive mischief. The Rev. N. Howard, minister of St. Andrew's Chapel, argued that Churchmen were bound to obey their Bishop in all things lawful and canonical, and proposed, as an amendment, that no more pew rents should be levied in the parish. This policy of surrender was discountenanced, and the first clear note of defiance loudly sounded.

The pew system was nevertheless doomed. The long neglect of St. Andrew's Church imperatively called for restoration. Year after year the painter and plasterer had added another coat of whitewash and colour to the granite pillars and sculptured images, already buried in such accretions to the depth of an inch. It was confessed, to quote an inveterate punster, that "a scandalous system of Pew-seyism " prevailed at St. Andrew's, and that people who did not often visit Plymouth, and had only a remote connection with it, bought the seats as a speculation and re-leased them to parishioners. By these means they reaped substantial profits, and the Church was destitute of revenues to meet the

INTERIOR OF ST. ANDREW'S CHURCH, 1840.

deficiencies. In the scheme prepared by Mr. Foulson it was arranged that these illegal holdings should be abolished ; one hundred seats were set apart for the Corporation, five hundred more were thrown open to the poor, and the remainder were let at annual rentals. By pulling down the old galleries, erecting others, and enlarging the area of the edifice, the accommodation was doubled.   But the beauty of the interior was not enhanced.

The offertory question was raised in 1845 at St. John's, Devonport, where the Rev. J. Lampen refused to comply with the request of Mr. St. Aubyn, as patron of the living, to make a collection for a purpose the Rector had very much at heart. Mr. St. Aubyn thereupon visited the church in company with his wardens, and deposed Mr. Lampen from the service. A large portion of the congregation left the building before the Rector mounted the pulpit, and banged the doors of their pews as they went. As the Rector was withdrawing, at the conclusion of the sermon, an old lady waylaid him in the aisle, scolded him soundly, and shook her fist in his face. After some time Mr. Lampen modified his antagonism to the offertory system, and then his followers raged against him as a supporter of "Tractarian innovations," imploring him to reconsider his attitude on the plea that many clergymen who had resorted to the offertory had "since joined the Roman Catholic Church." He remained unconvinced, and the first time the obnoxious departure was made, worshippers "left their pews in disgust." In an open letter of explanation Mr. Lampen protested that "to connect the offertory with Popery or the essential errors of Tractarianism is to confound things which have no connection, and it has been the means in many cases of diverting the mind from the real errors of the sister systems."

Upon the issue of Dr. Phillpotts's Pastoral Letter ordering the use of the surplice, the Three Towns burst into a conflagration of passion at this "Romish innovation." Walls were alive with placards reviling the Bishop "and the solemn fops who now disgrace the Church of England," and the people were implored not to submit to the tyranny of "this Lord over God's heritage" by consenting to his "Modified Popery." As the flames of anger, strife and division were thus fed, the tocsin was sounded, and mighty were the Protestant remonstrances. "Assemble immediately," ran the bills in 1845, "there's not a moment to be lost." "The congregation of St. Andrew's" begged the Bishop to revoke the decree, but his lordship curtly informed them that they had assumed a designation unknown to law in Church or State, and that they had desecrated the House of God by assembling within the edifice to pass such resolutions as they had forwarded to him. To the request of such an assembly "I cannot pay any attention whatever." The storm of protest so raged that the Bishop considered it expedient to bend : "It has been represented to me by many of you in different parts of the diocese that the use of the surplice in preaching is far more repugnant to the feelings of the people, as being associated in their minds with Popish superstitions, than could reasonably have been anticipated. To these feelings, however erroneous, I deem it my duty to surrender what may be abandoned without the sacrifice of principle." The Tractarian crusade was nevertheless waged with strong feelings by the Bishop, and with as unflinching an hostility on the part of Evangelicals. When his lordship learnt that the incumbent of Turnchapel, Mr. Babb, had assured his congregation that they would imperil their souls by attending Ritualistic services in Plymouth, he deprived him of his license, and refused the prayer of a memorial from the Three Towns asking that he might be re-instated. "Is there to be any termination of the strife?" the Bishop was asked by a leading layman. "My mind's made up," was the laconic reply.

A quaint illustration of the dread of "Puseyism" was forthcoming in a parish close to Plymouth, where an admirer of Dr. Phillpotts was appointed as curate. Hitherto the psalmody had been supplied by the choir ; and, when this "reverend sprig" announced that he should henceforth give out the psalms himself, consternation was too deep for words. In vain did the clerk remonstrate. The curate was resolute. So was the clerk, and, when the fateful moment arrived, he left his desk and walked to the gallery to lead the choir in the accustomed fashion. As he passed the churchwardens' pew, the old-world functionary bent over and exclaimed, in an audible whisper : " He's a-going to do it, and damme if I know where it'll end." Upon reaching the gallery, the priest gave out the psalm. No music followed, the choristers were dumb, and the congregation looked on in amazement. Leaning over the front of the gallery, the aged clerk shouted across in triumph to the curate : " I told 'ee how 'twould be, measter ; I told 'ee how 'twould be. If it isn't as it was, they weant sing at all." Discomfited and exasperated, the curate informed the clerk at the end of the service that he should remove the singing gallery altogether. " No, measter, you weant," that worthy grimly responded ; "if so be as you was to try to, I wedn't answer for yer life for five minutes."

The Anti-Tractarian Outburst : 1845-1849. Mr. Hawker's death, in 1845, was the indirect cause of that anti-Tractarian outburst which continued for years to excite grave suspicions, giving emphasis to the lightest rumour, causing slander and scandal, and evoking remorseless recriminations. No clergyman could be found to fill the unconsecrated pulpit at Eldad which Mr. Hawker had occupied, and the trustees sold the building to the Church of England. The living fell to the patronage of the Bishop, who promptly uprooted the Calvinistic past by appointing the Rev. George Prynne as Mr. Hawker's successor. Rumours filled the town that the old worshippers would riot if changes were attempted, and a strong force of police was employed to prevent any rush on the part of the disorderly element. There were only moderate innovations at the consecration services, and although these filled the worshippers with amazement, the ceremony concluded without any ribald interruptions. The same afternoon Dr. Phillpotts laid the foundation-stone of the Orphans' Home—" a house of religion and charity for the Sisters of Mercy "—and thus were inaugurated the causes of more religious irritation than Plymouth had witnessed for generations. Restrained had been the public demeanour at the conversion of Eldad Chapel into St. Peter's Church. As soon as Mr. Prynne adopted the surplice and other unaccustomed forms, the congregation betrayed by restless movements their dislike of the alterations. The leaders waited upon the incumbent in the vestry, and he promised to take the opinion of the Bishop. When the reply of his lordship was published, the remonstrants were injured as well as outraged by its tone : " It is painful to see that there are any persons in your district who show themselves so insensible, as some of them are doing, to the value of that great blessing, which it has pleased God in His Mercy to give them, in now having a Church instead of a conventicle. That Church must not be a Church in name only, but in truth, and my prayers will not be wanting to your active endeavours to bring back a long-misled people to the service of Almighty God in His Church." The "innovations " of Mr. Hawker (the Bishop continued) had been superseded by "proper usage, and I will not encourage a lawless and presumptuous attempt on the part of a small portion, and surely not the most exemplary or religious portion, of the laity, to urge a clergyman to a violation of the laws of both Church and State." This letter brought upon the head of the Bishop a severe rebuke from Mr. T. H. Hawker, of Devonport :

" I could, if I thought proper, prove to the world that your arbitrary conduct was the means of preventing Eldad Chapel from being originally consecrated, although you were unable to prevent the late proprietor from using therein the ritual of the Established Church in all its integrity, and, also that in your diocese alone scandal is being brought upon the Church by your endeavours to introduce papistical forms and Godless ceremonies.

" It is with your unrighteous and uncharitable observations that I now wish to deal, and I have no hesitation in declaring they are highly discreditable to you, and tend to cast a stigma upon the sacred office which you hold, unfortunately for the welfare of the Protestant Church. The venom, however, which dictated such allusions will fall harmless on the memory of my father. Far better would it be for you to keep in view the declaration of our Saviour ' that blessed are the peacemakers.' There is, however, one hope left for us---the See of ' Rome ' is now vacant, and you have my earnest wishes for a speedy translation."

A memorial was now sent from a great meeting in Plymouth and addressed to the Archbishop of Canterbury (January, 1849) :

" Tractarian principles and practices have greatly increased within this diocese. It is within the knowledge of many of us that, whilst a large body of the clergy, chiefly young men, deeply committed to the Tractarian System, have freely obtained appointments, and are now ministering within the diocese, a considerable number of other clergymen of piety and learning, but not holding Tractarian views—some of them advanced in years—beneficed, and serving in this and the neighbouring county of Cornwall, have been from time to time rejected by the Bishop as unfit to receive institution or license ' by reason (as his Lordship has alleged) of their holding doctrines contrary to the true Christian faith.'

" This practice having been extensively pursued by the Bishop has been necessarily attended by the two-fold effect of attracting Tractarians to the diocese, and of deterring clergymen of opposite views from accepting appointments within it—so that patrons and incumbents of Evangelical sentiments can with difficulty procure ministers and curates whose doctrinal principles shall be congenial with their own. A great and crying evil has thus arisen. The ministerial care and oversight of large bodies of the people, especially in our populous town, have been committed to clergymen to whose teaching and ceremonial practices the people at large entertain a well grounded aversion, and who consequently withhold or withdraw attendance at their churches."

In the course of his reply the Archbishop wrote :—" In replying to the memorial which you have presented to me, as agreed upon at a recent public meeting, held at Plymouth, I will first allude to that part of it which I have read with great satisfaction. It cannot be otherwise than gratifying to one placed in the situation which I have been called to occupy, when he receives from a numerous, and, I doubt not, influential body of laymen, an assurance of their steadfast adherence to our Church, to her doctrine, and her constitution. Attached, too, as I am, not less by official duty than by private conviction, to the principles of the Reformation, I rejoice to find those principles sincerely professed and manfully upheld."

The Orphans' Home   Private characters were impeached, and rectitude of purpose was
Enquiry: 1849.   denied, as sensitive Protestant ears were distressed by stories of
mysterious rites performed by Sisters of Mercy at the Orphans' Home. So loud was the outcry that, with the consent of all parties, Bishop Phillpotts held an enquiry at the Mechanics' Institute. There were no accusers, although there were plenty of witnesses, and his lordship pointed out that he had no authority over Miss Sellon, the Lady Superior, but construed her readiness to answer questions as indicating her desire to meet the " grave charges which have been circulated." The case against the Sisters was that they indulged in ceremonies which were Romish in their tendency, that the children were called upon to attend " Laud," that the use of crosses in the institution was general, and that a picture of the Virgin was placed in the Oratory which bore the inscription : " Thou art beautiful,

ST. ANDREW'S CHURCH, FROM GUILDHALL SQUARE.

(By permission of Messrs. TREVOR & Co.)

NN

both Mother and Virgin." Airily enough his lordship treated these charges, and the complainants were more than ever convinced that he was party to a "subtle conspiracy against the Church." The use of Latin names, he said, was unfortunate, but they were not necessarily Romish, for they were adopted by the English Church "long before the corruptions of Rome were known." Hot passages-at-arms between Bishop and laity increased the excitement, and, when one of the clergy interposed with a remark that evinced some bias, and there was a cry that he should withdraw if he meant to give evidence, his lordship declared that he would not so insult his reverend brethren as to imagine that they would be biassed by anything they heard. It was next asserted that Dr. Pusey was in the habit of visiting the Home, and the Bishop, in one of those alert interpositions which incensed the Evangelicals, asserted that he knew nothing that divine had written which was not a cause of pride. When Mr. J. N. Bennett sought to explain the construction placed upon these visits, his lordship waved him aside : "If the gentleman wants to dissolve this meeting, I will at once say the meeting is at an end." Evidence was given by a child that the Sisters were in the habit of bowing to a cross on an altar. "This," said the Bishop, "would have been an offence if practised by a clergyman, but in the case of ladies it can only be considered an indiscretion." A suggestion was advanced that one of the favourite chapters was of a doubtful tendency. "For God's sake," Dr. Phillpotts drily observed, "if there is a chapter in the Bible that ought not to be read, let us have it." Amid laughter, it was urged that it was the improper interpretation that the complainants dreaded. His lordship's rejoinder was significant : "Let us get on ; remember there are only twelve hours in the day."

Miss Sellon declared that it was her devotion to the Home which induced her to bow to the altar, and Dr. Phillpotts thereupon observed : "I am pleasingly surprised to think that these ladies have found it in their hearts to act in the way they have. I was going to call them unfortunate, but I do not know who are fortunate if they are not." This eulogium provoked derisive laughter, which the Bishop ignored ; and, when Miss Sellon mentioned that her father was an officer, he described him as an honour to his profession, and deplored he was not present to defend his daughter. "But there," his lordship added, "you do not require the protection of an earthly father." Miss Sellon continued that she was not aware of illegalities, and only introduced the pictures of the Madonna to relieve the deadness of the walls. When the engravings were produced, his lordship was unreserved in their praise. "Look at the Romish inscription !" exclaimed Mr. Elworthy. "There is nothing Romish in the inscription," answered his lordship ; "the words are a beautiful Biblical extract—nothing more." The complainants could carry their indictment no further, and Miss Sellon, in persuasive language, contested the statements as to the management of the Home, asserting that they were as false as the practice was cruel of tempting young girls from her roof in order that they might betray their benefactress. Only ignorance could invest her methods with Popery, and she reprobated "the inquisitorial spirit," which made her the victim of insinuations "as painful and insulting as they are unjust." Warmly denying that she was public property because she worked for the poor, she deplored this hateful hostility. "There is One," she concluded with impressive gesture, "Who knoweth the secrets of hearts, and He, He alone, is my Judge. The morning may be gloomy, yea, the noonday may be clouded, but at eventide there shall be light. The Lord shall give strength to His people. The Lord shall give His people the benefit of peace. Oh, my God, I will give Thee Thanks for ever !"

In pronouncing judgment, the Bishop said he had journeyed to Plymouth with an impartial mind, albeit with a feeling of veneration for these young ladies. "I go from hence not knowing how to express my admiration of their conduct." If there were some things he wished they had not adopted, "they are absolutely overpowered by the graces and excellences by which the Sisters have been influenced." Clasping his hands together, his lordship said he knew he should be denounced as a Papist, but "I shall never cease to express my regard for that wise and virtuous and angelic woman." Overcome by his emotions, the Bishop paused, and his faltering was the signal for mocking laughter. Resuming without resenting this manifestation, he confessed that he regretted that the cross and the flowers had been placed on the altar, and this concession evoked a tempest of cheering. But his lordship was not slow to improve the occasion : "Strange things" had been done by Miss Sellon, no doubt, "but they are not so strange as those works of Mercy which I wish were not so strange as they are. Miss Sellon will go from this room not as a Sister of Mercy, but as a Martyr of Mercy. When she rises before us she makes us feel what poor, miserable things we are as compared with those with whom she works. I say that she will leave this room with the thanks and gratitude of all whose thanks and gratitude are worth having." Hisses and scornful laughter once more greeted the Bishop's words, and the indignation of "Anti-Puseyites" was at white heat. Evangelical clergymen and laymen forthwith met in public and accused the Bishop of duplicity, insinuating that, although he had saluted Miss Sellon as a stranger, he was seen to enter the Home on the morning of the enquiry, and that he had there rehearsed the proceedings. A protest was drawn up to the effect that the enquiry was "partial, unfair, and ill-calculated to command the confidence of the public," and to this the signatures of a large number of clergymen, magistrates, merchants and professional men were subscribed.

The Bishop's eulogy of Miss Sellon and the Sisters did not spare them every mark of obloquy that prejudice could suggest, and their daily visits to Stoke Church for the purpose of taking Communion gave rise to angry discussions as to the increase in the wine bill. At a meeting of the parishioners it was pointed out that the cost of administering the sacrament had risen from £3 to £11 a year, and a memorial was addressed to the Rector in these terms :

It is with the deepest regret that we feel ourselves called upon to notice officially a circumstance connected with the celebration of the services in our Church ; and the more so at the present time when there exists so great an excitement throughout the land by reason of the recent act of the Pope of Rome ; but at the same time as church-wardens, and knowing the feelings of the parishioners on the subject, we consider we are only performing our duty in so doing. The circumstance we allude to is the administration of the Holy Communion every morning to some ladies who, we believe, term themselves the Sisters of Mercy, residents in another parish, and whose extraordinary genuflexions and prostrations in the Church have called forth severe remarks on their Romish conduct, which are by no means pleasant to hear.

We have consulted the Rubric, and gather from it that three parishioners at least should be present at the administration of the Communion ; and feeling therefore it is improper the custom alluded to should be continued, we enter our protest against it, and we shall, with all due respect to yourself, decline to supply you with any more wine for the purpose ; leaving to you the responsibility of continuing the ceremony to persons not parishioners, and possessing to all outward appearances the most Romanising inclinations.

We trust you will believe us when we say that in requesting the discontinuance of the Communion to the Sisters of Mercy, we are not moved by any other than feelings of sorrow lest the large congregations which attend our Church should be offended by a continuance of a custom which we should be glad to see abolished without loss of time.

As the memorial was not heeded, the churchwardens stopped the supply of wine, and Miss Sellon thereupon sent the Rector a dozen bottles for the purpose. An appeal was made to the Bishop, and the services were eventually stopped on the plea that they compelled the workmen who were engaged in repairing the church to suspend their operations for an hour every day at the expense of the Restoration Fund.

Plymouth's Protest against the Diocesan Synod : 1851. The next stage in the campaign was reached in 1851, when the Bishop convened a Synod with the object of commanding submission to the Article of the Creed : " I acknowledge one Baptism for the remission of sins," which, it was alleged, had been "virtually denied" by the the Judicial Committee of the Privy Council. Demonstrations at Plymouth were addressed by Evangelical clergymen and dissenting ministers, and Dr. Cuming attended to impeach the Bishop. A large body of the clergy of the district refused to elect representatives to the Synod on the ground that it could only be productive of "great evil and mischief," that its decisions would be powerless in law, and that it would place the diocese in "unbecoming, injurious and schismatical opposition to the constituted authorities." This protest was signed by John Hatchard, Vicar of St. Andrew's ; H. A. Greaves, Vicar of Charles ; H. C. Smith, Vicar of Trinity ; R. Malone, Vicar of Christ Church ; G. Hadow, Vicar of St. Andrew's Chapel ; G. Bellamy, incumbent of Charles Chapel ; J. Tagert, curate of St. Mary's, Devonport ; R. Gardner, incumbent of St. Michael's ; Thomas Cave, incumbent of St. Mary's ; R. W. Needham, incumbent of St. Paul's, Stonehouse ; W. H. Nantes, incumbent of East Stonehouse, and others. Shortly afterwards the pulpit at Christ Church fell vacant, and Mr. Hatchard nominated the Rev. H. Gray to the living. The Bishop refused to endorse his appointment because his views on Baptismal Regeneration were unsatisfactory. Not to be vanquished, the Vicar of St. Andrew's nominated the Rev. T. G. Postlethwaite, whom Dr. Phillpotts had episcopally recognised a short time before, but his lordship maintained his opposition and placed "a Tractarian warming pan" in the pulpit. Mr. Hatchard vowed in the course of a sermon that he would never consent to nominate a man who was "not true to the principles of Evangelical truth," and his lordship abandoned the contest on discovering that the living was not vacant when he rejected Mr. Gray.

" Escapes " from the Orphans' Home : " The Confessor ": 1852. Prejudice against the Orphans' Home was sedulously fostered until 1852, when a bomb was cast to the public by Miss Geraldine Campbell, "a seceding Sister," whose story was received with jubilant consternation. She had entered the institution through the medium of "a confessor," and accused the Mother of wearing the cap of "an abbess" in the presence of the inmates. It was her "disclosures" as to penances that fired the public, for Miss Campbell testified that restless Sisters were enjoined to silence for days, and compelled to write their wishes on slates, that the more troublesome were condemned to lie on the floor with their arms outstretched in the form of a cross, and that, after submitting to this discipline for twenty minutes a day, they were undressed like infants and put to bed with arms crossed on their breasts. "Sister Geraldine" was so "distraught" by the shame and exhaustion occasioned by her own punishment, that she resolved to "escape," and, instead of waking the other Sisters at daybreak, according to custom, seized a shawl and bonnet, and made her exit through the lobby door. To add to the dementia which these statements occasioned, another Sister, Miss Bowering, of Bolton, also effected her "escape," and sought the "protection" of a policeman. The papers teemed with the "sensational disclosures" of these young ladies, and the Bishop removed his name from the list of patrons because the fundamental principle that enabled inmates to withdraw

when they pleased had been "virtually abandoned." Miss Sellon admitted that she had set up a standard of "holy obedience" and, although he professed undiminished admiration, his lordship warned her against "extravagance" of personal assumptions. "Be content, I implore you, to be a Sister in Christ, and the Sisters will then, I doubt not, honour and love you as a Mother. But so rigorous a submission of the understanding and the will of one human being to another cannot in my judgment be enforced without serious danger to the spiritual condition of her who governs, and of those who are governed." Miss Sellon denied that she had sought the title of "Spiritual Mother," but experience prevented her from saying it was an unreality. She thanked the Bishop with "a deep and earnest gratitude" for all his kindness, and thus ended his lordship's countenance of the Orphans' Home.

The storm now played around the Rev. George Prynne, "Confessor" at the Home, and the Evangelical clergy petitioned the Bishop to institute another enquiry. Dr. Phillpotts had arranged to hold a confirmation service at St. Peter's Church, and subscribers to institutions from which it was proposed to send children raised such protests that investigation was ordered. The Bishop decided that a limited number of the clergy should attend and an equal proportion of the laity, and journalists were admitted on promising that "nothing should be printed which was calculated to offend public decency." Impeachment of Mr. Prynne's methods was preferred by the Rev. W. H. Nantes, who argued that he had glorified Confession and Absolution. The case rested upon the evidence of a girl who had been discharged by the Sisters for misconduct, and it was urged that a revengeful feeling had induced her to "concoct her wicked statements." Heated and numerous were the interruptions, and the general argument was that children tender in years had been subjected after confession to degrading penances. The Bishop made short work of the accusations by replying that, if a girl was not too young to sin, she was not too young to confess, when confession was a means to forgiveness. Confession was not excluded from the practice of the Church, and he had no desire to be a better Protestant than Latimer, Ridley or Cramner. He therefore acquitted Mr. Prynne of so much as an indiscretion, and with surpassing solemnity of demeanour, commanded the clergy to attend the confirmation as arranged. Mr. Hatchard replied that he should certainly object to the presence of the children of the Royal Orphan Asylum, but, suppressing him with a gesture of impatience, the Bishop peremptorily added : "An investigation has been held into Mr. Prynne's conduct, It leaves him without blame, and I should be ashamed of myself as a man, as a Bishop, and as a Christian, if I committed the gross injustice of not holding the confirmation in his church."

The Three Towns were forthwith inundated with literature denouncing "Popish practices and mummeries," and at a monster meeting whose object it was to preserve the the Church "from the abyss," the Rev. H. A. Greaves stigmatised Mr. Prynne's Confessional as contrary to the doctrine and spirit of the Establishment. On seeing these outspoken expressions in print the Bishop requested Mr. Greaves to do Mr. Prynne the justice of taking the necessary measures to prove his contention, and hinted with keen irony that the magistrates and professional men who had joined him in this remonstrance would not be so insensible to their honour as to refuse to furnish the funds for instituting the suit. Mr. Greaves merely retorted that it was rather the duty of the Bishop than a clergyman to prosecute ecclesiastical offenders. Having failed to draw the Vicar of Charles, Dr. Phillpotts turned to Mr. Hatchard with a similar request. The Vicar of St. Andrew's tersely left the responsibility with his diocesan : "In case of any well-founded rumour reaching the ear of the Bishop regarding the misconduct of his clergy it is the duty of his lordship to take proceedings. If Mr. Prynne deems himself injured by statements made by me or any other persons, the courts of law are open for his vindication. If he will avail himself of that course, I shall be quite prepared to justify every charge which I have made." Mr. Prynne preferred to vindicate his actions in the columns of the "West of England Conservative," where his plea that the Church encouraged "the general habit of confession" at length brought him into conflict with the Bishop. As a matter of fact, wrote Dr. Phillpotts, "the Church discourages confession as a general habit," and he expressed his regret that, in quoting from his Pastoral Letter, Mr. Prynne "did not give equal weight to the passage condemning the habit of going to confession as a part of the ordinary discipline of a Christian life." After this interchange interest in the controversy waned, and the excitement of the Russian War took the sharp edge off the strife. The publication of some reminiscences of the controversy in a Church magazine induced Miss Sellon to reprobate the revival of such foolish and revolting stories : " I began working for the poor," she explained, "without imagining that my name would ever become public—the last penalty that a woman would willingly incur. For the rest, I can only say that the abhorrence I feel at the idea of such un-Christian conduct, and contemptible exercise of power as is imputed in these extracts, is only equalled by my astonishment at their invention."

The Bradlaugh Prosecution : 1860. Whilst the Tractarian controversy divided and distracted Churchmen, the Freethinkers became an organised force, and were frequently addressed by George Jacob Holyoake and Charles Bradlaugh. The latter was the more aggressive in his methods, and, in December, 1860, he gave notice of his intention to deliver five lectures in the Three Towns, the last of the series in the Devonport Park. At the time appointed a considerable number of people assembled, and Mr. Bradlaugh made an attempt to address them, when he was interrupted by the superintendent of police, who had been authorised by the Town Council to prevent such lectures and proceedings in a place created solely for the recreation of the public. Mr. Bradlaugh contended that temperance advocates used the Park unhindered, but the officials refused to argue the matter, and threatened that, if Bradlaugh proceeded, they would forthwith eject him. The agitator submitted, "with the determination to do better at some future time," and the experiment was accordingly the prologue. The real drama was to come, and the first act was played three months later. A space known as the "Parsonage Field," adjacent to Devonport Park, was hired for two lectures by the Plymouth and Devonport Secular Society, and, on the afternoon of Sunday, March 3rd, Mr. Bradlaugh went thither accompanied by his sympathisers. He was about to speak when he saw several inspectors and constables, and Mr. Edwards, the superintendent, warned him that, if he proceeded with his lecture, he was authorised to remove him from the field. Mr. Bradlaugh answered that he had given way in the Park because he was undecided as to his right, but, now that he had an agreement with the owner of the field, he intended to remain until he was removed. Turning to the crowd, he commenced his address with these words : "Friends, I am about to address you on the Bible." He was thereupon seized by six constables, and hustled outside the gate. An inspector told him to go about his business, and he replied, "My business here is to lecture. If you let me go I shall return to the field." Thereupon the superintendent determined to convey him to the station-house, and, after bail had twice been refused, he was confined in an underground cell "without fire, light or stool." In the morning he and a companion were brought up "like felons" through a trap-door into the dock. Their appearance was greeted by a hearty burst of cheers, and, after reciting the charge, Edwards said he had no desire to press it if the prisoners would promise "not again to make an attack upon public morals." The charge against Mr. Bradlaugh was subsequently dismissed without hearing the whole of the evidence for the defence, and notices were immediately issued by the War Department forbidding the use of the Park for lectures.

Mr. Bradlaugh, speaking in Plymouth, declared his intention of persisting, and bills were freely posted announcing that "Iconoclast" would attend near the Park Lodge to vindicate the right of free speech. Excitement in Plymouth was very great, and Mr. Bradlaugh was temporarily baffled by his desire not to bring his friends into collision with the police. After ascertaining that all the water was under the jurisdiction of the Saltash Corporation, he resolved to lecture from a boat in such a way that, whilst the audience were assembled within the borough of Devonport, the speaker should be outside its jurisdiction. So he embarked in Stonehouse Creek in a waterman's boat, on which was an improvised platform, and from this he delivered a short address with the Union Jack defiantly hoisted at the bow. The superintendent appeared with twenty-eight constables, and the Mayor was prepared to read the Riot Act. "But all their precautions were set at nought, and the right of open air propaganda was victoriously asserted." Legal proceedings were then commenced against Mr. Edwards for assault and false imprisonment, but these were unsuccessful. Mr. Bradlaugh attributed his want of success to his error in retaining Mr. Robert Collier to plead for him, instead of defending himself, for counsel apologised for his client's opinions by hoping that a young man of such undoubted talents would "return to the truth." This line, in the opinion of Mr. Bradlaugh, was a grave and irreparable blunder, and the "Western Morning News" hinted that Mr. Collier was "more anxious to assert his own orthodoxy than to establish his client's rights." From Mr. Baron Channel plaintiff received less consolation, for, in summing up, he observed that a person going about "diffusing such doctrines as Mr. Bradlaugh was calculated to produce the greatest possible evil." Thus the judge ruled that there was moral justification for the action of the police, and the jury awarded Bradlaugh a farthing damages. Application for a new trial was refused by Lord Chief Justice Erle, who held that "there are in law opinions which are a crime, and that the nominal wrong in this case has been abundantly compensated by the sum awarded." As Bradlaugh had to pay the costs, the debt hung around his neck like a millstone for the rest of his life.

Recent Activities and Down-to-date Differences: 1822-1899. Owing to the growth of membership "by the blessing of God on the labours of Mr. Birt," the chapel in Pembroke Street became too small for the Baptist Church and congregation; and, a vacant chapel in Morice Square being offered for sale, it was purchased with the intention of occupying both. Dr. Steadman co-operated for many years with Mr. Birt, and then it was found desirable for the congregations to work apart—Pembroke Street being retained by the former and Morice Square by the latter. The Church at Plymouth meanwhile outgrew the accommodation in the Pig Market; and, in 1789, removed to How Street, where the Rev. William Winterbotham was elected co-pastor with Mr. Gibbs. After his release from prison on the charge of preaching sedition, Winterbotham received a bank draft for £1,000, and, as he was strictly enjoined not to enquire as to the donor, it was assumed that one of his persecutors had forwarded the gift to relieve his conscience. He eventually removed to Shortwood, in Gloucestershire, and in 1808 the Rev. John Dyer became pastor. He was succeeded in 1815 by the Rev. George Gibbs; and, in 1825, the Church invited the Rev. Samuel Nicholson, who worshipped at Plymouth-Dock, where his father served as deacon, to accept the pastorate. His ministrations, extending over thirty-three years, were especially successful—high-toned and spiritual and remembered with loving esteem. During his pastorate the chapel in George Street was built, and the Rev. George Short was elected as his colleague when age advanced and physical

BAPTIST CHAPEL, ON MUTLEY PLAIN.

(By permission of Mr. J. L. Keys.)

infirmities set in. The Rev. T. C. Page became pastor in 1860, and the second chapel was erected at Mutley in 1869. The sum of £5,500 was raised before a stone was laid, and the opening day's services witnessed the discharge of the debt of £8,000. It was originally intended to have one Church, with two pastors and two congregations, and the Revs. John Aldis and Robert Lewis were elected to collaborate. Desire for independent administration once more asserted itself, and separate Churches were constituted. With the decay of Pembroke Street as a commercial centre, and of Morice Square as a residential resort, both congregations declined, and the former became dependent on its own off-spring. Mutley was the outskirt of Plymouth when the chapel was raised in 1869, but terraces and villas were soon disposed around that ornate building. At the outset, the congregation was so Puritanical in sentiment that it dispensed with all musical instruments, but the Rev. Benwill Bird, a broad-minded pastor who was destined to minister for a full generation, educated his followers to appreciate the charm of music, and an organ was introduced in 1877. In 1883 the Rev. Samuel Vincent was appointed to George Street, and he attained such distinction that he was elected president of the Baptist Union in 1898. In 1899 the interior of George Street Chapel was reconstructed, and Pembroke Street Chapel was furnished with a worthier elevation and otherwise much improved.

The story of Unitarianism in Plymouth may be resumed from the point when the death of Nathaniel Harding led to the election of Henry Moore as his successor—a result which was not effected without strong opposition on the part of those who were favourable to George Whitfield's doctrines. Moore was so pronounced an Arian that a number of the congregation took their departure and united with those who sat under Mr. Baron at the Batter Street Chapel. After his death the Rev. John Hanmer was appointed, but he developed such strong Arian views that he was removed at the instance of the congregation, who appealed to the Court of Queen's Bench in 1762, and the Rev. Christopher Mends was chosen to succeed him. The Unitarian pulpit was thereupon filled by Mr. Hanmer, and a succession of ministers, including the Rev. Thomas Porter, conducted an active propaganda until 1813, when the denomination for the first time enjoyed the benefit of the Toleration Act. Upon his retirement, the dilapidated old chapel was demolished and another erected on the site. It was opened in 1832, and the Rev. W. J. Odgers enshrined his name as a fearless investigator of local epidemics and a strenuous advocate of social reform. Mr. Freckleton succeeded him and then Mr. Sharman.

Whitfield's revival led to considerable activity amongst the Independents, subsequently Congregationalists, at Devonport towards the close of the eighteenth century, and the artificers assisted in extending the chapel in which the Rev. Andrew Kinsman officiated. "So soon as the bell rang, and they came off from working for an earthly King, they went to work with fresh ardour and built for the King of Kings." The labourers and smiths did such work as they could, and sang as they carried the material to the site: "Gilder and carver I am none, but I can carry lime and stone." "The Old Tabernacle" was then built at Briton Side, and "the New Tabernacle" in Norley Street followed. Further Congregational development took place in 1845, when a considerable number built Union Chapel, in Courtenay Street—from the plans of Mr. Wightwick—and worshipped under the Rev. C. T. Hine. It had been intended that the whole of the members should remove, but a section preferred to remain in Batter Street, under the Rev. W. Whittley. The congregation of Norley Chapel migrated in 1864 to a stately Gothic pile in Tavistock Road, to which the name of Sherwell was appropriately given. The foundation stone was laid by Mr. David Derry in 1862, and the building was dedicated to public worship two years afterwards. Sherwell Chapel owed its existence to the Rev. Charles Wilson, whose popularity at Norley crowded the little edifice. The Sherwell estate site

SHERWELL CHAPEL.
(By permission of Mr. W. WESTCOTT.)

became available after a fire had destroyed the old Corporation mills, and the munificent offers of Mr. Alfred Rooker, Mr. Alexander Hubbard, Mr. David Derry, Mr. Charles Fox, and others rendered the scheme immediately possible.

Plymouth Brethrenism derived its name from the town in which the society first took root, although members were alternately designated Darbyites, as followers of the local minister who supplied them with a home and habitation. Anthony Groves, a chemist who carried on business in Plymouth, and who was an intimate friend of Dr. Kitto, is said to have first enunciated the doctrines that gave rise to Brethrenism. Refusing to acknowledge that they were a sect, their practice differed materially from that of the Established Church. They met on the first day of the week to celebrate the Lord's Supper, and any brother was at liberty to speak for mutual edification or to occupy the desk which took the place of a pulpit. The prayer meetings were "reading meetings," and anyone was admitted who was believed to be "a child of God," after his or her name had been given out and no objection was raised by regular attendants. Sunday-school, Bible, Missionary and charitable enterprises were discouraged and discountenanced ; none of the preachers were paid ; and the faith of the brethren was "in God and not in the Church." The world was reserved for judgment, they contended, and it was contrary to Christian doctrine to take part in its government. They neither prayed for the pardon of sin, nor the presence or influence of the Spirit, disclaimed the amassing of wealth, denied more comfort than was necessary to simple existence, and repudiated medical aid in the event of illness. According to Rust, no sectaries were more sectarian or more exclusive in their assumptions than the Plymouth

Brethren. In their flourishing days, about 1830, the chapel in Ebrington Street was attended by crowded congregations, and it was even then a creed with well-to-do members to discard all luxuries and set aside mahogany furniture for plain deal. A merchant captain named Hall, who lived in Boon's Place, was one of the pillars of the faith, and his complacency caused cynics to dub the Plymouth Brethren as the " Hall-Rights."

Impatience of the condition in which he found St. Andrew's Church caused the Rev. C. T. Wilkinson to undertake its further restoration upon his appointment to the vicarage in 1875. The noble oaken screen which formed a prominent feature of the edifice had disappeared, the timbers of the roof were no longer open, and the rood staircase had became a disused relic. The first gallery was erected in 1595, and Foulston's transformation left the interior of the fabric cramped. The whitewash and decay manifest in the days of Mr. Hatchard, moreover, caused the architect to apply his Gothic art with little respect for antiquity, and he reduced the church to a mere shadow of itself. It was the object of Sir Gilbert Scott to restore the building to something like its original appearance, and, clearing away the galleries, he opened up the tower so that the view of the interior from one end to the other might be unbroken. The church was seated with open pews, and a handsome pulpit by Mr. Hine replaced the " old three-decker." The organ which was originally built in 1737 by Mr. J. Parsons was restored, and the mouldering walls of the burial ground were substituted by a handsome palisading. A determination to further improve the exterior resulted in the grant of a faculty to level the mound in which so many thousands

ST. ANDREW'S CROSS, PLYMOUTH.

(By permission of Mr. JOHN SMITH.)

Plymothians had slept through successive generations, and a stately cross was erected upon the site from the design of Mr. James Hine in 1897. The bell ringing laws of the Church may here be quoted :

"NOS RESONARE HIBET PIETAS MORS, ATQ. VOLUPTAS."

> " Let awfull Silence first proclaimed be,
> And praise unto the holy Trinity,
> Then honour give unto our Valiant King,
> So, with a blessing, raise this noble Ring,
> Hark how the chirping Treble rings most clear,
> And Covering Tom comes Rowling in the Rear.
> Now up an end at stay, come let us see
> What Laws are best to keep Sobriety.
> Then all agree and make this their decree,
> Who Swear or Curse or in an hasty mood
> Quarrell and Strikes altho' they draw no blood;
> Who wears his Hatt or Spurrs or turns a Bell
> Or by unskilfull handling marr's a peal,
> Let him pay Six pence for each single crime—
> 'Twill make him cautious 'gainst another time ;
> But if the Sexton's fault an hindrance be
> We call from him the double penalty.
> If any should our Parson disrespect
> Or Wardens' orders any time neglect
> Lett him be always held in foul disgrace
> And ever after banished this place.
> Now round lett goe with pleasure to the ear
> And peirce with eccho through the yielding air,
> And when the bells are ceas'd then lett us Sing,
> God bless our holy Church—God save the King.
>   1700."

Until comparatively recent times, Charles Church contained pews that were contrived to hold "a great number of people with no little comfort to themselves," and the pulpit towered to an elevation at which the preacher could detect inclinations to somnolence or irreverence on the part of worshippers. It was Mr. Greaves who discovered that the habit of erroneously describing the parish by the name of "Charles the Martyr" had been introduced through the caprice of one or more of the clerks. Investigation proved that the Act of 1640 provided that the new edifice should be called Charles Church, and this style remained unchanged and unchallenged for 190 years, the first misnomer occurring in 1837 and the last in 1854. In order that the misapprehension should be disposed of, a memorial was presented to the Poor Law Board in London in 1868 pointing out that the mistake had been revived in the returns of the Education Department, and asking that the original name of the parish should be substituted. The request was complied with, and a hope expressed that if people would insist after this in giving the parish "a wrong name" they would "grow wiser as they grow older." Like the other Churches Charles had its belfry statute :

Let awful silence first proclaimed be,
And praise unto the Holy Trinity,
Then Honour give unto our Gracious King,
So with a blessing, Raise this Noble Ring.
Hark how the chirping Treble sings most clear,
And cov'ring Tom comes rowling in the rear.
Now up an end, at stay, come lets agree
What Laws are best to keep Sobriety.
Who swears or cursth or in an hasty mood
Quarrells or strikes, although he draws no blood
Or wears his Hat, or Spurs, or turns a Bell
Or by unskilful handling mars a peal ;
Shall forfeit Sixpence for each Single crime --
'Twill make him cautious 'gainst another time
Or any should our Parson disrespect
Or Wardens orders any time neglect,
Let such till they relent be in disgrace
Nor dare to enter such a sacred place.
Now round lets go and when we've done let's sing
God bless our Holy Church, God save the King.
                    Amen.

Church Extension in the Three Towns was steadily maintained throughout the century. St. Andrew's Chapel, erected in granite upon Foulston's unpretending plans, was raised at a cost of over £5,000, and supplied with an altar piece by Ball—the hapless Plymouth artist, who, like Haydon, committed suicide. The severely simple chapel at Eldad was replaced by an edifice in the Perpendicular style designed by Mr. Fellowes Prynne, son of the Vicar, and the completion of the tower in 1899 commemorated the fiftieth year of the rev. gentleman's priesthood. St. Saviour's Church was built in 1845 from Mr. Wightwick's plans, and St. John the Evangelist from those of Mr. B. Ferry, who revived the taste for the ornate in local ecclesiastical architecture. Mr. Piers St. Aubyn followed with St. James's Church in 1861, and Emmanuel was built in 1870, from the elevation of Mr. Reid. All Saints', under the Rev. C. Chase, became the home of advanced Sacerdotalists. In Devonport the pace was proportionately maintained. St. Michael's, in Albert Road, was reared in 1845, and St. Paul's, in Morice Square, in 1850—by public subscription. St. Mary's Church, in James Street, owed its ex-

ST. PAUL'S CHURCH, MORICE SQUARE.
(By permission of Mr. A. H. Swiss.)

istence to the same means. Towards the cost of building the church of St. James the Great, in 1850, the Government subscribed £4,000, on condition that a sufficient proportion of seats was reserved for Dockyard employés. St. Stephen's Church, Devonport, was raised in 1852 ; and St. John's, Sutton-on-Plym, in 1856. St. Mark's, Ford, was erected in 1874 ; St. Saviour's, Lambhay Hill, in 1870 ; and St. James the Less in 1874. St. Matthias was built at the entire cost of Mrs. Watts. The intention of the donor was that the pulpit should be filled by an Evangelist Divine, but the first incumbent—the Rev. Philip Williams—developed a moderate Ritualistic bias, and, upon his withdrawal, a Low Churchman, the Rev. Russell Carey, was appointed—a step that led to the resignation of the choir and the exodus of many of the congregation. St. Barnabas, in Stuart Road,

ADMIRALTY HOUSE, DEVONPORT, SHOWING TOWER OF ST. STEPHEN'S CHURCH.

(By permission of Mr. W. WESTCOTT.)

became the hand-maiden of Stoke Church in 1897, and the appointment of the Rev. Gordon Ponsonby as Vicar of the mother church of Devonport, following the happy and beneficent ministrations of Prebendary W. St. Aubyn—the Good Vicar as he was styled to distinguish him from his contentious relative—so united the congregation that the construction of a new parish church became almost immediately possible.

Other developments included the erection of the Roman Catholic Cathedral at Plymouth in 1855. Previous to this, Mass had been celebrated at St. Mary's Chapel, a neat edifice near the Naval Hospital at Stonehouse, which was erected in 1806 at the instance of Mr. Guilbert, a French refugee. Dr. Errington was installed as first Bishop of Plymouth in 1851, and Dr. Vaughan, his successor, laid the foundation stone of the Cathedral, with its beautiful spire, and the Nunnery of the Little Sisters of the Poor, with schools adjoining for the children of Roman Catholic parents. Messrs. Hanson were the architects of the group, a cruciform structure in the early English style, and it is admittedly one of the finest in the district. The Wesleyans recovered their activity in 1864, when Mr. John Allen, a munificent contributor, laid the foundation stone of the King Street Chapel.

Later on two equally fine chapels were reared—Wesley, in Ham Street, and Mutley, on Mutley Plain. In 1899, during the recrudescence of the Ritualistic controversy the Rev. George Prynne was one of the earliest to abandon the use of incense, in obedience to the general appeal of the Archbishop of Canterbury, supported locally by the Diocesan of Exeter, Dr. Bickersteth. His curate, the Rev. H. H. Leeper, resigned his appointment by way of protest against this unexpected surrender.

WESLEY CHAPEL, HAM STREET.

General religious work was promoted at the premises of the Young Men's Christian Association, Bedford Street, Plymouth, and Public Hall, Devonport, mainly through the instrumentality of Dr. A. Hingston and Mr. J. P. Goldsmith. The Young Women's Christian Association met in Lockyer Street. Other sects carried on their regular services —Primitive Methodists, Ebrington Street ; Reform Methodists ; Bible Christians, Greenbank ; United Free Methodist Society, Stonehouse ; Catholic Apostolic or Irvingites, Princess Street ; Universalists, Henry Street ; Free Evangelicals, Portland Place ; Presbyterians, Wyndham Street ; Protestant Evangelicals (under the ministrations of the Rev. William Elliott), in Compton Street ; Spiritualists, Richmond Street ; Christadelphians, Octagon ; Salvation Army, Manor Street, periodically stimulated by the visits of "General" Booth.

CHAPTER XVII.—MEN, MOVEMENTS AND ENTERPRISES.

Plymouth and Devon-   The first printing press was set up in Plymouth by Jourdaine in
port Journalism :   1696, and, although there was an effort made in the eighteenth
1808-1899.   century to establish a newspaper, the "Plymouth Weekly Times"
did not long survive. It contained little other than news of the war, and, with the
exception of a local advertisement now and then, no reference to the town in which it was
published. It was not until 1808 that the first serious experiment was attempted, and
then insatiable anxiety to know how far Great Britain and her allies were thwarting the
military encroachments of Bonaparte led to the issue, in March, of the first number of
the "Plymouth Chronicle and General Advertiser for the West of England." A block of
Smeaton's Eddystone Lighthouse—with a flashlight illuminating the surface of the waters—
illustrated the title, and, in his opening address, the editor pointed out that the period was
calculated to make "every British heart feel the most lively interest in the concerns of his
country." Whilst the historian of the future would "exhibit in his brightest pages the
struggles which we support and the triumphs we obtain," the journalist would transmit to
posterity "the memorials of this eventful crisis."

There was a promise to combine with the records of the campaign "such varied
information of a private or public character, interesting or entertaining, as we are able to
collect. Whatever may be the fate of the future numbers of our work, its friends may
rest assured that in the heart of the editor the first impression of the 'Plymouth Chronicle'
will never be out of print." Thus was launched a newspaper destined to enjoy an
existence of some duration—a sheet of four pages, of five columns each, and sixteen
inches in length. Its price was sixpence, and this sum included the stamp duty of three-
halfpence per copy. R. Shields, the printer and publisher, carried on business at
New Market Street, Plymouth, "where advertisements will be received," and the paper
was to be obtained of Messrs. Haydon and Co., Market Place, Plymouth ; Mr. Philes,
Dock ; Mr. Gray, jun., Stonehouse ; and Messrs. Taylor and Newton, Warwick Square,
London.

The fortune of war or flaw of fate caused the first number of the "Plymouth and
Dock Telegraph, or Naval and Commercial Register," to appear one week later than its
contemporary, and its irritation at being out-manœuvred was ill-concealed. The proprietors
had resolved on the publication of the "Telegraph" twelve months previously, and orders
for type and other material were then despatched. "Strange to say, we did not receive
the most essential part of our plant until last Monday night, and, in the meantime, an
opponent has started up and entered into competition with us for the meed of public
favour." The editor undertook to present his readers with "an impartial statement of
facts, and to leave the public to make their own comments. This determination we
regard as the only one which will enable us to make the 'Plymouth and Dock Telegraph'
a useful and respectable vehicle of public information. For our own opinions and
principles we feel all natural regard and concern. With us they have their due weight and
influence ; with our readers they would probably have neither." · After this naive confession, the conductor reminded his readers that it had long been a matter of regret and
surprise that "this extensive and populous district," which now exceeded a total of 60,000,

exclusive of the navy and army, " should so long have been deprived of the advantage and amusement resulting from such an undertaking, and indebted to a distant retrograde source (" Flindell's Exeter Luminary ") for a knowledge of every interesting and incidental occurrence transpiring in its own immediate neighbourhood." And so was evolved the " Dock Telegraph," of the same dimensions and price as the " Chronicle." It was printed by L. Congdon at 52, Fore Street, Dock ; and published in addition by B. Haydon and P. Nettleton, Plymouth ; and T. Huss, Stonehouse.

From the outset the relations between the papers were suggestive of the spirit of rivalry that scorned fraternal relations : " We have received repeated complaints from distant advertising friends stating that their advertisements have not appeared in ' our paper ' as requested. The only answer we can make to these complaints is that we never received the orders alluded to. We are well aware that numerous mistakes have arisen from a supposition (particularly among persons residing at a distance, who are unacquainted with the local situation of this part of the country) that Plymouth and Dock are one and the same place ; whereas they are distinct towns, situated at two miles distance from each other. We have therefore to request that all orders and advertisements intended for the 'Plymouth and Dock Telegraph' may be addressed to L. Congdon, 52, Fore Street, Dock ; this being the only mode we can suggest to prevent a repetition of the numerous disappointments that have already taken place."

With despatch boats and men-of-war constantly touching the port, interest in the campaign was ever sustained at a thrilling point ; but dependence upon the coach for regular supplies of stamped newspaper sheets led to awkward consequences when the weather interrupted traffic. In January, 1809, the " Dock Telegraph " announced that the roads " between this place and the metropolis " were so inundated "as to preclude the travelling of waggons," and it was compelled to print " a part of this week's impression on blank paper—the duty for which will be accounted for on oath. We took every means in our power to guard against a recurrence of this unpleasant circumstance, having ordered a supply by coach which should have arrived on Wednesday, but it did not come to hand until our first side was nearly worked off." The following week the editor went to press without waiting to include general home news, and explained to his subscribers that it would be impossible to say when the "weekly mail " would reach the town, as the floods were so general and unprecedented that the water reached " above the traces of the horses " that travelled from Exeter for ordinary business purposes.

The indirect methods in which news of the first importance—such as the Battle of Leipzic—came to hand is not without interest : " After our last week's paper had been worked off we were favoured with the following extract of a letter from Heligoland which has been received by a merchant in Plymouth." In December, 1810, the Philomel brig put into Dock with despatches from Collingwood detailing the victory over the Toulon Squadron. The "joyful intelligence" was gratuitously communicated to the Dock public in "a Telegraph Extraordinary "—the progenitor of the modern " Special Edition." No supply was sent to Plymouth, lest the " Chronicle " should reproduce the same news, and, when the "Telegraph " had thus effectively advertised its enterprise, " our green-eyed contemporary," in his usual strain of malignancy, took the liberty of threatening the infliction of penalties which only exist in his shallow imagination." " The Chronicle " went further than mere threats ; and, thoroughly exasperated at having been forestalled " by the superior sources of information which enabled us to print and distribute these supplements, meanly stooped to the character of a base informer, and lodged information against us for printing supplements liable to the same duty as a newspaper. His Majesty's Commissioners of Stamp Duty, however, with their usual liberality, and seeing through the malignant views of the informer, have generously consented to remit the penalty attached to our unintentional violation of the revenue laws on our paying the duty for the supplements which we gave away. It is true that we have it in our power to retaliate on our adversary, but we scorn to sully our reputation by classing ourselves with a vile herd of informers." The "Chronicle" replied by calling its contemporary a "bully" and a "traducer," and thus gave the "Telegraph" another opportunity of expending its scathing invective : "In the publication of the supplements which have subjected us to the informa- tion, we had no other end or aim in view than that of contributing towards the gratification of the numerous readers of the 'Telegraph,' without the least design or wish to encroach on the very narrow and contracted sphere of our adversary's circulation. If we did not hold the character of an informer (in civil society) in utter abhorrence, we, too, might have entered into competition with our opponents for the meed of infamy by acquainting Government, that, within the short space of a few weeks, they have Five Times violated the law. This, though true, would justly have entitled us to the Informers' appellation of malignant ; for it would have irrevocably suppressed the publication of their papers. With respect to the epithets of bully and traducer, we beg leave to disavow all claim to their application, and leave them, with every deference, to our puissant and learned friends, to whose vocabulary of scurrility they will form a necessary appendage—assuring them, at the same time, that, while we have the grapes within our reach, we will not envy the sarcasms of the disappointed foxes ! "

Taking into consideration "the very heavy duties and small profits attached to the printing of newspapers," the Legislature passed an Act "allowing the proprietors to charge an additional halfpenny on each paper." The "Chronicle" and "Telegraph" were at once raised to 6½d. each copy, "which trifling increase we trust our friends will not deem unreasonable, especially when it is considered that the stamp duty on each copy sold is 5d., leaving only 1½d. on each paper to defray the expense of newsmen, journeymen's wages, wear of material, and other incidental and unavoidable charges." The crushing of Napoleon and the depression that followed the Peace proved fatal to the career of the "Chronicle," and, after having "floated for eight years," it was condemned by its enemies to be "sunk for the Dry Rot." The "Chronicle" and "Telegraph" were then incorporated under the title of "The Plymouth and Dock Telegraph and Chronicle," and the proprietors hoped that this step would be productive of advantage and convenience to their mutual friends by enabling them "to derive a greater extent of publicity for their advertisements and at less expense than each paper could before afford in its separate circulation." In a farewell address the owner of the "Plymouth Chronicle" confessed the obligations imposed on him since the commencement of his paper, "and the only return he can offer is the assurance of his sincere and indelible gratitude."

The field remained without a rival until 1819, when it occurred to a member of the renowned Flindell family at Exeter that "Plymouth has never yet possessed a newspaper worthy of her high character and congenial with her proper spirit and true interests." In the days of "the threatened subjugation of Britain," two journals made their appearance in "the double-headed port," but neither "evinced the wisdom of a Cecil," and, seduced by the Circe who should have counteracted, "nursed the canker-worm of infidelity in the heart of this great laboratory and fortress of national defence," and scattered through "our barracks, our dockyards and our wooden walls the doctrines of treason ! Will it be believed that 500 copies of the drugged 'Plymouth Chronicle' were smuggled in a week on board the fleet of Brest, and like a flight of blighting insects continued for years to blister our national defence and with vampire tooth extract its life blood ? " It was for this reason that the "Plymouth Gazette" was started in 1819, but its editor had no desire to over-colour the sins of the dead, as the guilt of the " Plymouth Chronicle " was not of the first order.   It had wielded neither the torch nor the dagger of Marat—it simply " drivelled in querulous sentimentality," and perished of its inherent tendency to dissolution.   The " Dock Telegraph " was the real criminal.   Having obtained " the carcase " of its contemporary, it wallowed " in its own slime, like the boa serpent with the horns of the beast it has absorbed protruding from its front."   It was really not the intention of the " Plymouth Gazette " " to pour a broadside " into the " Telegraph " on its " first cruise," but " Messrs. Docky-Cum-Chronic " were just then spreading the clouds of sedition, and no time was to be lost.

The Liberals of Plymouth had learnt of the intended advent of the " Gazette," and, on the first day of issue, there was launched " The Plymouth and Dock Weekly Journal and General Advertiser for Devon, Cornwall, Somerset and Dorset."   According to the " Gazette," it was run by a confederation of printers who had co-operated to assume a virtue they did not possess.   " You have started on our backs and watched our movements as the rule by which to regulate your own.   Proceed, emulate our career of true patriotism, and, in the name of God, Whom alone we fear, may the high prize of public favour be given to the worthiest."   The " Gazette," whose columns were wider and appearance brighter than any other local organ, was published at 31, Market Street, at 7d. per copy.   The same price was asked for the " Journal," which was issued from 57, Market Street by Nettleton and Son, and was destined to outlive its contemporaries, and to give birth to one of the daily newspapers.   Its inaugural address was couched in terms of grace and moderation, claiming that England owed to its Press its repute as a thinking nation, and hoping that the day was distant when the licentiousness of journalism would become " the grave of its freedom."   The proprietors of the " Journal " hastened to avow their attachment " to the constitution of this country in Church and State, an attachment arising from a conviction that, though in these establishments there may be something to censure, there is much more to admire."   An undertaking was given to respect the opinion of any individual who differed from the paper, " nor will such opinions be excluded when marked by that urbanity and moderation which is due from one Englishman, and more especially from one Christian, to another."   The " Plymouth Gazette " exhausted its resources and invective in fifteen months, and was then withdrawn from the scope of public criticism.

Within a month of its disappearance the " Patriot, or Palladium of British Liberty," entered upon the scene to advocate the advanced doctrines which the " Plymouth Gazette " had deprecated.   Civil, Religious and Political Liberty was the platform it espoused; together with the freedom of the Press, whose " uncorrupted channels " the Government were endeavouring to suppress, because journalists asserted that Queen Caroline was the victim of a conspiracy.   After an existence of eleven months, the proprietor of the " Patriot "—Mr. R. Bond, of Whimple Street—bade his readers a grateful farewell.   " There has never previously appeared a journal in this part of the country that has dared to utter those bold truths which lurked in the bosoms of the greater number of the community, but which mistaken prudence or natural timidity confined to their narrow habitations.   When the ' Patriot ' sprung the mine, a thousand voices re-echoed the honourable sound ; timidity was emboldened ; and trembling honesty, that had hitherto been confined for want of a proper medium through which to express its sentiments, came forward and was hailed by us and by the public with unfeigned demonstrations of unmixed pleasure."   The " Patriot " experienced an early resurrection as the " Devonshire Freeholder," and its removal to Exeter as a printing centre was ascribed to the ease with which news from London could be obtained in that city.   As there was "no locality in principle," Mr. Bond relied upon receiving the same support, "and it is with pleasure that we state that not one of our subscribers has intimated an intention of discontinuing the paper in consequence of the selection of a more convenient site for printing."

Changes in the ownership of the surviving journals took place in the course of a few years. Mr. Congdon retired from the "Dock Telegraph" in 1827, and his successors vowed "with willing hearts" to support King, Church and State, "though they will be guided only by the principles of equity and moderation. Having no particular interests to serve beyond those of the country at large, they are desirous of holding an even hand between the extremes of party zeal, not, however, to the sacrifice of one atom of their independence or of what may appear to them the true interests of their country." The purchaser was Mr. George Soper, editor of the "Plymouth Journal," and he held the proprietory until 1832, when Mr. William Richards, printer and bookseller, entered into a partnership. In 1823 the "Plymouth Journal" was sold to Mr. John Robins, solicitor, and, after some time, was acquired by Mr. Richard Webb, who passed it over to Mr. W. Gill, by whom it was transferred to Messrs. Daniel May and William Byers, with Mr. L. Jones as the editor. The "Dock Telegraph" continued to suit the taste and disposition of its patrons, and "from first to last sought to present its readers with an impartial statement of facts. Firmly attached to the institutions of the country and superior to every consideration of abstract party, it has been our study to conduct the 'Telegraph' upon those principles of loyalty, independence and integrity which, while consistent with such mild and temperate reforms as may be necessary in the progress of social improvement, are utterly repugnant to all violent and hasty change."

The enfranchisement of Devonport and extension of the suffrage in Plymouth led to the multiplication of "ephemerals" and "mushrooms." There were over thirty of such journals started between 1832 and 1836. The "Devonport Standard and Plymouth United Service Gazette" was run in the election interest of Mr. Dawson. Mr. George Hearle, a bookseller, was the publisher, but the paper had no acknowledged editor, and its printed matter was mainly supplied from London. Its second number was printed under the style of the "West Devon Standard," and it existed in this form for eight months. The "West of England Conservative" rose from its ashes with the avowed aim of rebutting "the unholy designs of the advocates of wild abstractions and Utopian theories, and to expose and deride the miserable sophistries by which it is sought to entangle the hearts and mystify the judgments of the unwary and uninformed." Warm in its attachment to the Church, the "West of England Conservative" pledged itself "never to impugn the sincerity of Dissenters," promising that, while it would be slow to offer insult, it would be quick to resent injury. It had, however, a keen desire to "hang upon the gibbet of scorn" all demagogues and political incendiaries, and nailed to the mast "unstained and unstainable the True Blue Motto, 'For God, the King, and the Constitution.'" Its directors were soon derided as "jackdaws in borrowed plumes, strutting about with great pomposity and turning up their noses at the Reformers as if they had never been expelled from the Liberal camp, and as though the inhabitants of Devonport were not aware of the hollowness of their pretensions." Mr. Rogers was the editor, and, after a six months' existence, the "West of England Conservative" was submitted to auction and bought by Mr. James Husband, solicitor, of Devonport. In 1840 it became the property of Mr. Ramsay, and his leader writer was stigmatised as the disseminator of "falsehood, calumny and vulgar insolence," and "the obedient tool who compounds the whispered words of the Mephistopheles behind the scenes." In its disgust the "Dock Telegraph" turned with loathing "from the sickening spectacle of the cauldron which has boiled over with the venom and

slime concocted from the poisonous fangs of the vile reptiles who run our contemporary."
The effect of journalistic competition was evidently not calculated to improve the morals
or mend the manners of its local exponents. " Rabble rash," " dirty work," " dirty tail,"
" chattering jackanapes," were familiar epithets, and remonstrances did not result in any
modifications of style.

Many " ephemerals " were of the catch-penny order, with "meanness and subserviency"
as the badge of the "miserable tribe." The "Devonport Independent," "Plymouth Herald,"
and " Plymouth Journal " were reared on more enduring foundations. The " Independent "
was started by the Liberals during the heat of an election contest, and continued on those
lines for some time. But the speculation was "the reverse of fortunate, and those who
founded it were glad to get it off their hands." Professional relations continued to be
marked by uncomplimentary exchanges, sometimes arising from disputes as to circulation,
or as the result of plagiarising news obtained by extraordinary individual effort. On the
occasion of an important Parliamentary division, which was challenged at three o'clock on
a Friday morning, the " Dock Telegraph " went to press with the numbers within twenty-
four hours, and, as the distance from London was 216 miles, this was an instance of despatch
"never equalled by any provincial paper." No sooner was the " Dock Telegraph " printed
than the " Devonport Independent " obtained an early copy, and "most unhandsomely "
reproduced the report "without the least acknowledgment of the source from which the
news was stolen." To add insult to injury, the " Independent " laughed at the complaint,
callously remarking that such acts were of "everyday occurrence." From that time forward
the " Independent " regularly published a second edition by "disgracefully plundering "
extracts from the " Telegraph," and the latter denounced this conduct as an evasion of the
Stamp Act. To introduce matter "relating to events that occur after the first edition has
gone to press is to publish a new paper and incur a fresh liability to duty." Undeterred
by exposure or threats, the " Independent " avowed its intention of defying the law, and
regularly appropriated the information which its contemporary received from London "at
much expense and trouble."

As no copy of a paper could be issued without a stamp, every artifice was employed to
impose ideas of booming circulation on the public, and interminable were the wrangles as
to whether proprietors purchased stamps for two or three years and included them in one
year's boast of subscribers. Vitriolic flood-gates were loosened when these returns were
published, and the " Independent " twitted its contemporary, the "Telegraph," with having
in the compass of eighty-six lines, used the word " scavenger" five times, and "dirt,"
" filth " and " mire " on eight different occasions. With withering indignation the " Independent " observed : " We might, did we choose, trace, with an unscrupulous disposition,
the antecedents of our contemporary ; we might pretend, with a vicious fabrication, to
scrutinise his motives of conduct and habits of thought, throughout long periods of his
life ; we might summon his family to bear the insolence of depraved innuendo ; we might
break through the sacred canons of a past friendship, to blazon the suspicion of a turpitude
we know to evolve a lie ; and we might convey it in language so gross as to outrage any
but those of a most depraved appetite and accustomed to feast on such garbage. But
there is one security against this : we must sink to the level of our contemporary first.
And here, undoubtedly, we speak of him in reference to his present unhappy declension,
and not as he once was regarded." The explanation of this effort of the " Independent "
to refrain from a due expression of its contempt for the " Telegraph " was the publication
of figures that aspired to prove that the former sold only 695 copies per week, and the
latter disposed of 1,269, "with a steadily increasing circulation."

Journalism in the Three Towns dropped several degrees lower than this in 1840 when a publication was launched by the name of "Paul Pry," in which "neither truth, worth nor innocence" was spared, and respectable people were libelled. To override the Stamp Act, the vendors "gave away" the copies of "Paul Pry," and sold a slip of writing paper. This colourable pretence did not save them, and proceedings were also instituted against the publisher. One issue was impounded, and the prisoner tendered an apology in open court and consented to destroy all the copies. "The South-Western Standard," another "ephemeral," was subjected to something like corrosive sublimate : "It is not often that we notice the attacks of our contemporaries, but we are especially unambitious of entering the lists with such a journal as the 'Standard,' which, pretending to be the organ of the Tory party in this neighbourhood, is in reality scouted by all honourable and high-minded Conservatives, who look upon their cause as disgraced by its advocacy. It is now in the hands of a few desperate turncoats, who use it as a convenient cloak for their servility, and a ready vehicle for their private malice. The public is not generally aware that five pages of this mock-Conservative journal are merely a reprint of that libellous London paper, the 'United Service Gazette,' all the articles in the 'Standard' being precisely the same as they appear in the 'Gazette' of the week previous, and the remaining three pages are a reprint from the local papers, with the exception of an occasional scurrilous article, aimed at men of any grade who may happen to be distinguished for public spirit, or liberal and enlightened views, which is the whole amount of its pretension to originality. This wholesale piracy of other journals may suit the easy consciences of men who have leaped with unblushing effrontery from the extreme of Radicalism to Ultra-Toryism ; but the moral influence of such a set of time-serving scribblers, must be anything but flattering or useful to their adopted party." The demise of the "Standard" was hailed with blithesome humour. It had but a short time to live, being "full of trouble" and "of chronic debility." "Deformed, unfinished, sent before its time into this breathing world, scarce half 'made-up,' its dissolution was daily looked for and proved, as the old women say—a happy release." The "Telegraph" doubled the number of its pages in 1851, when the "taxes upon knowledge" were reduced. The effort was too much for its resources, and it passed through a crisis that led to the temporary suspension of its issue. On resuming, the new proprietor objected to the assumptions of the priesthood, "whether Tractarian or otherwise," and this independence led to an increase of circulation that more than compensated for the loss sustained during "the interregnum." In 1854, the "Independent" passed from Mr. William Byers into the hands of Mr. Andrew Boolds, who at once intimated that he should refuse to imitate his contemporaries in their "love of fighting" or fondness "for the modified knavery of puffing."

The "Plymouth Mail" was started in 1853 in the interest of Mr. Charles Mare, and was edited for awhile by Mortimer Collins, a native of the town, a fine, handsome man, who was known as the "King of Bohemians" by reason of his indifference to the canons of social observances. The "Mail" covenanted with the public to eschew "all personality, coarseness, and vulgarity." Morality was its "pole-star," and "British and Protestant interests" its objective. Its staff was known as "The Swell Mob of the 'Mail,'" and the "Independent" followed up the disclosures made in the petition against Mr. Mare by attacking "the blacklegs" who had induced him to plunge into politics and journalism. Strongly drawn, the picture was strangely prophetic. "Gentle reader, have you ever ventured within the precincts of a gambling saloon—one of those hells where manhood is perilled, and fortune, honour and all that life holds dear is staked upon the throw of a dice, the turn-up of a card or the colour of a ball? Have you noticed a novice flushed with excitement plunge into the vortex of the game, unconscious that he is in the hands of sharpers by whom he is urged and tempted on to ruin? You see the simpleton confident in the plethora of his wealth—sometimes indifferent concerning the insignificant stakes he is playing—and after the victim is fairly cleaned out he is turned out of doors, either hopelessly lost or to become a wiser and a sadder man. We have only to change the arena and we have a very good illustration of the game that our keen-scented Blacklegs are attempting to practice on the infatuated Mare. He will not have," the writer concluded, " to plead that he was not apprised of the character of his company ! " From the office of the " Mail " emanated the emissaries of benevolence who rendered famous the Totnes elections. At the enquiry it transpired that the gold was passed by a gloved hand through a hole in the curtains that surrounded a bed in one of the rooms of the King's Arms Hotel. The identity of this " Man in the Moon " was never discovered, but, prior to the death of Mr. Aitken Davies, in 1899, he informed his family that he was the author of these mysterious distributions. Mr. Mare died penniless and abandoned in a London lodging-house in 1898, and a collection was made by Plymothians to prevent the expenses of his funeral from being borne by the parish !

Of the various newspapers the " Journal " was especially fearless. On one occasion a Mayor of Plymouth delivered a long homily to one of its reporters in open Court, touching certain comments which had been passed upon his conduct at a fire, and he concluded by exclaiming : " I will take care never to buy another copy of your paper." The assailed representative avenged himself by italicising the word " buy " and suggested that his Worship would "borrow." The rival organs did not stand on much ceremony if they were overtaken by mechanical difficulties. A breakdown in the night imperilled the publication of the " Mail," and Mr. Aitken Davies, breaking open the lock of the " Journal " office, carried the " formes " across the street (George Street), and, setting the machinery in motion, finished the printing of his issue. The manager of the " Journal " was in a towering passion when he learnt of the trespass. Eventful in connection with the Tractarian movement was the prosecution of Mr. Isaac Latimer, the editor of the "Mercury,"on a charge of libelling the Rev. George Prynne. The statements created a painful sensation, but defendant argued at the Assizes that the individual aimed at was not the incumbent of St. Peter's at all, but Burgess, a Latter Day Saint, who had caused excitement by preaching an amalgam of the doctrines of Joanna Southcott and the Mormons, and by suddenly and suggestively disappearing. Burgess had been drawing crowds to his chapel in Manor, and created quite a panic in Plymouth and Devonport by fixing the date of the end of the world. Mr. Prynne was unaware that Burgess had been holding his services "not one hundred miles from Eldad Chapel," and read the article embodying certain hints as intended for himself. So did many other people who were not conscious of the explanation. Mr. George Wightwick, Mr. R. G. Edmonds, Mr. Alfred Rooker and the Rev. John Hatchard testified that the public construed the reference as applying to Burgess, and the jury acquitted the defendant. Prosecutor and Mr. Latimer lived sufficiently long to hold each other in the highest personal estimation. Tractarian controversies induced the local reporters to visit the churches where innovations in service or sermon were introduced, and the verger of St. Stephen's Church grew so angry when he saw them taking notes that he jogged their elbows and muttered: " If you take the notes, you shan't carry them away with you." When the journalists left the church they were followed by the congregation, who shouted " Down with Latimer's reporters." The verger was summoned before the Devonport magistrates, and it was urged that the complainants did not attend the service for worship, but stared about and made unseemly observations. Extenuating the zeal of the verger. the Bench at once dismissed the summons.

Let each post his cash ; he need no further roam,
I'll supply him with doings abroad and at home.
I've the " Telegraph," always as true as the clock,
Which will please, though sometimes it may give you a shock!
There's another never fails in this town to appear—
'Tis the " Herald " which always comes punctually here.
I've the stout " Plymouth Mail," with its maximum news
And its maximum number, for all who may choose ;
Its motto " Our Queen and Fair Liberty's Tree,"
And with a coat of steel network 'tis armed cap-a-pie.
I've the bold " Plymouth Journal," the friend of our Church,
No Protestant true will it leave in the lurch,
To Puseyite capers it never will bend,
But the Church in its purity ever defend.
And yet with all this it will always amuse
By bringing you weekly a budget of news !
Should any disprove, I'll make them amendment,
And change it at once for a true " Independent !"
Now I hope that my friends will not gossiping go,
I'll supply all the news that 'tis right they should know ;
They may then stay at home and dispense with their labours,
Of seeking to know the affairs of their neighbours !

Such was Haydon's regular advertisement. Local journalism took a new and permanent departure in January, 1860, when the first " Western Morning News "—a small four-paged paper—was published by a syndicate, of whom Mr. Edward Spender and Mr. William Saunders were the moving spirits. " In matters of politics and religion we shall be strictly independent. We do not hold a brief for any party in Church or State. The journalist should aim at a higher office than that of the advocate retained to defend a client, or to blacken an opponent. If we have a right idea of his vocation, he will strive to be the impartial judge, rather than the ingenious but one-sided counsel. He will carefully seek to avoid the misrepresentations of motive and perversions of fact that too often disfigure the Press in its treatment of public men. But let it not be supposed that independence involves neutrality or silence. Although we have drawn up no confession of faith, we shall not be found wanting in the expression of opinions. Bound to no party, we shall have no hesitation in criticising any. We have set before ourselves a high standard. Being but human, we shall no doubt often fall short of it. Nevertheless, we believe that English men and women are always ready to forgive occasional failings, when they see the hearty desire manifested to serve the cause of truth with vigour and honesty."

Within six months the " Western Daily Mercury " was started " on independent and undeviating Liberal principles." It emanated from the office of the " Plymouth Journal," with " the greatest good of the greatest number," and " whole hearted and united action " as its creed. Under Mr. Spender the " Morning News " indicated high literary management, and his Liberal sympathies were obvious. The " Daily Mercury " attained no less rapid distinction, but differences between proprietor and editor led to the vacation of a position which was not easily supplied. Mr. Spender made London his journalistic centre of operations, and Mr. William Hunt took charge of the " Western Morning News" for a short time. Mr. Albert Groser was at this time engaged on the staff of the " Western Daily Mercury," and, upon Mr. Hunt's departure for Hull, he accepted the editorship of the opposition journal.   The existence of two daily papers soon told disastrously upon the weeklies.   In 1862 the "Plymouth Mail" was absorbed by the "Western Morning News," and, after a gallant struggle, the "Dock Telegraph" issued its last number in June, 1863.   Its funeral oration was pronounced by the "Devonport Independent," by whom its political and journalistic pretensions were absorbed.   "Ripe of years and of good repute," the "Telegraph" had announced "its approaching dissolution" with an absence of feeling that was "very creditable" to Mr. R. Clarkson Smith, its proprietor. Having submitted to its "last lock-up," it had experienced the process of "final distribution and wreck of matter."   "Bodily departed," the "Telegraph" bequeathed its militant "spirit" to the "Independent."   "We are sorry that it ran out of breath, but we must take these ordinations of the Press as they occur.   If we have been drawing from the former supporters of our late contemporary, whilst we accept the chief responsibility of our own increased vitality, we are guiltless of being intentionally accessory to its death."

Mr. Groser reconciled many Liberals by making temperance reform a plank on which Churchmen and Dissenters were able to unite, and Mr. Spender's brilliant London letters captivated Conservatives who were interested in ecclesiastical forms and theological disputes.   The general leaning of the "Western Morning News" was so pronounced that the Conservatives once more reverted to their ideal of a purely party organ.   Expecta- tion was strong when the "Western Daily Standard" was started in 1869, as the promoters had enlisted the support of influential partisans throughout the West of England. Its career was destined to be brief, and in less than a year, the proprietors confessed the utter futility of contending against their contemporaries.   In March, 1870, the last copy contained a philosophic farewell : "An hour or so more and our wheels and works stand still. They creak and complain for lack of oil, but the damage is not irreparable.   Clever work- men think our case most hopeful—time will show.   But now we see a hand which the reader cannot see that beckons us away ; we hear a voice you cannot hear that says we must not stay.   Let us first put up the shutters, draw our editorial chair to the fire, light a cigar, mix a tumbler of something stronger and more cheering than toast and water, Messieurs of the 'Western Morning News,' and thus snugly ensconced review the shadowy past. Then, the last inch smoked, the last drop drained to the health of all staunch and true Conservatives (would there were more of them), summon our satellites, printers' devil, and all, address them like Napoleon his guards at Fontainebleau, turn off the gas, lock our office door, haul down and furl for a while our broad 'Standard.'   Then let the worst betide, we are ready and can bear it ; and may be we shall soon rise up from sleep and enter invigorated on a longer and more prosperous career.   But if the end is now our rest will be the rest of those who, having laboured and striven against overwhelming difficulties, implacable foes, insufficient supplies and the rest, when at length overcome, fell fighting stoutly to the last."

"The Western Globe" represented another effort of the Conservatives to claim a political organ.   It was started in 1873, and the county court proceedings that followed its demise indicated that its mission was rather mercenary than political.   A prominent Conservative was sued for the recovery of £5, the price of an article which he instigated with the object of "touching up Jack," and "puffing" the candidature of Mr. Puleston. The proprietor failed to produce documentary evidence that he was to be remunerated, and the suit was dismissed.

The pathetic end of Mr. Spender, who was drowned with two of his sons whilst bathing in a treacherous cove in Whitsand Bay, left Mr. Groser the administrative force of the "Western Morning News" after 1878.   Telegraphic facilities were then only moderately developed, and he gave the paper a more than local reputation by organising despatches during the Zulu War which were invariably in advance of the official reports. This reputation was maintained during the editorship of Mr. Michie, and with Mr. Croft, as the successor of Mr. E. Hawkings as chief of the commercial department. Mr. Isaac Latimer, the proprietor of the "Western Daily Mercury," was a fighting journalist, imbued with the superstition that a libel action in a popular cause was a valuable investment. His battle with the Rev. George Prynne failed to add to his wealth, and his action in petitioning against the return of Sir Edward Bates did not increase the loyalty of leaders who realised his value, and that of his paper, when they desired to promote some personal purpose. They stood by him when he won, although indifferently then, and abandoned him the moment he incurred any obloquy. Editors passed in rapid succession in Mr. Latimer's office : one was too prosaic, the other too poetic ; one was too popular, the other too incisive ; one was too fond of discussing India and the other too fond of discussing Plymouth. Each in turn was warmly criticised by those who read the paper at the clubs, and the property, as well as the party, suffered from the lack of definite aim and continuity of policy. In 1891 the "Devonport Independent" passed to the editor-ship of Mr. Whitfeld, and as the "Western Independent" recovered immediate reputation- The reorganised organ, to quote the first article, "shall be the medium for ventilating and redressing grievances. It shall deprecate shams whatever their party paternity may be. It shall excite attention whenever the drum of hollowness is being sounded. It shall protect the weak and encourage the strong to be generous. The intolerable evil of the leasehold system it will not hesitate to impeach, and the axiom that property has its duties as well as its privileges we shall impress on Lords of Manors with such object lessons as may occur at our doors." In 1899 Councillor T. H. Gill, a Conservative, confessed in public that the campaign against overcrowding, which mainly inspired the propaganda of the "Western Independent," had led to the uprooting of the worst of the old manorial traditions of Devonport. The "Western Daily Mercury" was eventually sold to Mr. Owen, M.P., a wealthy paper manufacturer, and, at his death, it passed into the hands of the Western Newspaper Company, with Mr. Harry Jones as editor. For the first time in its existence the organ had been developed with ample working capital, and the proprietors suddenly launched the "Western Evening Herald," with Mr. R. Walling at the helm, to meet another manifest want. Up to this time, after mutually destructive experiments, half-heartedly conducted, the dailies had entered into a mutual arrangement to prevent the introduction of this particular form of competition. After the "Herald" had been running five years, the "Western Evening News" emerged from the office of its Unionist contemporary to divide the interest excited in the Transvaal War of 1899.

Professional and Commercial Worthies: 1800-1899.   Mr. William Burt was a solicitor of great commercial authority, and his knowledge of local maritime customs was unrivalled. At the close of the Napoleonic Wars, when business men were in despair, he wrote a series of letters, subsequently published in a volume, displaying grasp and originality of a highly practical order, encouraging the local merchants to adopt a cheerful view of the capacity of the port, and to depend with courage upon their own initiative. The first development of Millbay was due to Mr. Burt's suggestion. Mr. John Collier, chief of the wine and spirit house which had existed for two centuries, was an excellent example of the senator in municipal and Parliamentary life. Largely as he reaped the fruits of commercial activity, he dispensed with corresponding liberality the means which his opportunities provided. His devotion to business did not detach him from public concerns, and he heartily supported Wilberforce's agitation against the slave trade and zealously advocated every local reform. Stern and uncompromising in his opposition to all attempts at encroachment upon popular privilege, he regarded the old borough system with unmitigated aversion, and not only lived to see it crumble to pieces, but, with his fellow townsman, Mr. Thomas Bewes, he shared in the work of sweeping away in Parliament what remained of its corruptions and abuses.

To the initiative of Mr. Thomas Gill in 1818 was due the Millbay Soap Works, and the name of the article became a household word. The business was transferred to a company in 1856, with Mr. Gill as managing director. He also purchased the West Hoe and worked it for limestone, and, after erecting the Millbay Pier, sold it to the Great Western Railway Company. Mr. Gill also inaugurated a large iron foundry at Tavistock, and was generally regarded as one of the most enterprising men of his time. Mr. John Burnell was his contemporary—the head of the South Devon Shipping Company and a leading figure in the British and Irish Sugar Refinery Company. Credit for the inauguration of these works belonged to Mr. James Bryant, who reared, on the site of a vegetable garden and old tanyard, monumental buildings in which refining prospered until bounty-fed sugar crushed out the local industry. Mr. Bryant also promoted several candle works, and these were incorporated, with others in the town, by the New Patent Candle Company, who thereupon removed their works from Manor Street to Coxside.

Mr. Richard Derry came from Launceston to try his fortunes in Plymouth. An industrious and reverent lad, he turned aside into a quiet field and knelt down in prayer on the day he first entered the town. The stripling became a prosperous man of business, and was distinguished for his liberality. His eldest son, David, completed his education under the Rev. William Rooker, at Tavistock, and revived the Plymouth Sunday School. In 1829 he was chosen, with William Moore, Herbert Mends Gibson, William Hole Evens, John Edmonds and Charles Tanner, rising men of their generation, to serve on the Commission of Public Improvement. A financial crisis gave birth to the Devon and Cornwall Bank, and David Derry hepled to widen its operations from small beginnings, and assisted in developing local railway enterprise. The General Bank, privately conducted by Messrs. Hingston and Prideaux, was merged in the new company. Mr. Derry was once Mayor of Plymouth; and his son, Mr. William Derry, who occupied the position three times, was instrumental in the erection of the Clock Tower, and presented to the town the clock that it contains.

A notable figure was Herbert Mends Gibson, with his shrewd, sharp face and steady gait, eminent as a solicitor and the most noted political sphinx in the town—who claimed the men of 1832 for his heroes and Lord John Russell as his model. In the stirring times of Collier and Bewes, Gibson and John Edmonds made the breach and carried the trenches. They pleasantly belittled their young Liberals as pigmies compared with the giants who carried Reform. At their feet Alfred Rooker was accustomed to sit until he inherited the mantle, and then, cultured and eloquent alike, he shone as the most ornate orator that Plymouth has produced. He was not forgiven by his political foes for being a Noncon-formist, or by his political friends for setting aside party to satisfy personal compunctions. His ambition of sitting as member for his native town was never realised, but he witnessed as Mayor the opening of the New Guildhall, which his advocacy had rendered possible after the unavailing protests of half-a-century. His life's work was commemorated by the erection of a statue, the work of Stephens, but the sward at the entrance to Westwell Street was not granted without the exhibition of some sectarian jealousy.

William Moore saw Plymouth rise from a comparatively unimportant town to become the Metropolis of the West. He knew it well when the site of the Royal Hotel and all beyond it was a range of fields, witnessed the entrance of the first stage coach and heard the whistle of the first train to Millbay. He was a Tory of the old school, and, although he purchased his freedom, was a consistent advocate of Reform. In the early years of the nineteenth century the principal business of Plymouth, so far as its shipbuilders were concerned, consisted in repairing naval transports and merchantmen which made for the Sound as the first harbour of refuge from the storms of the Atlantic. After the Peace, shipbuilding, as distinct from ship-repairing, made considerable advance, and formed an important branch of the operations of the port. At first no attempt was made to turn out vessels of more than one hundred tons burthen, but, after the Russian War, several ships of over one thousand tons were launched, which were specially commended for their sailing qualities and finish. Plymouth-built pilots and fishing boats were eagerly purchased for Cowes, Hull and Grimsby, and the local shipyards were excellently appointed. Exquisite examples of form were produced by Mr. Joseph Moore, founder of the business in Sutton Pool. During the career of his son, Mr. John Moore, a solicitor of position, hundreds of broad acres of good wild-fowl shooting were marked out as sites for terraces. His grandson, William Foster Moore, who owned a patent slip and building slips at the Friary, was three times Mayor of Plymouth. Mr. Joseph Banks had extensive dry docks and building slips at Queen Anne's Battery; Messrs. R. Hill and Sons, a wet dock, patent slip and building slips at Cattedown; and similar facilities were possessed by Mr. Shilston and Mr. Gent at Coxside; Mr. Pope at Turnchapel; and by Mr. Ridley and Mr. Hocking at Whitehall Yard, Stonehouse.

The abolition of the "wooden walls" as the main line of national defence involved the cessation of Mr. Edred Marshall's shipbreaking Yard in Deadman's Bay. The proprietor sold the foreshore to Mr. E. Duke for wharves, and established in the neighbourhood a box-making factory which constituted one of the mechanical marvels of the town. Of the contractors who attained fame in the district Mr. John Pethick, "Honest John," has been notable as a builder of docks, bridges and railways in all parts of the country. Mr. A. R. Debnam was entrusted by the Lords of the Admiralty with the construction of the Naval Barracks at Keyham, and by the Co-operative Society with the rearing of their colossal premises in Frankfort Street. Mr. R. T. Relf replaced the oscillating wooden viaducts on the Cornwall Railway with massive stone bridges, in addition to laying down several new lines. Mr. Samuel Roberts, as the builder of the Municipal Artisans' Dwellings at Devonport; Mr. Shellabear, of the Royal Engineer Students' College; Mr. Anthony Lethbridge, of the palatial "Prudential" Offices; Mr. T. May, of the Devonport Technical Schools, and Plymouth Municipal Artisans' Dwellings, have likewise achieved enduring reputations.

In a room at the rear of a small shoemaker's shop which Mr. Charles Goodanew occupied in Tin Street (Vauxhall Street) six "cobblers," two carpenters, and one painter met in 1859 to discuss the formation of a Co-operative Society on the model suggested by Holyoake in his "History of the Rochdale Pioneers." The nine promoters were all Chartists, men who appreciated the democratic propaganda of Holyoake, Bradlaugh, and George Odgers—the latter a Plymothian, hard and square-headed, who spent his early life in making and mending boots at Roborough-—and the first of his class who aspired to sit as a working-man member in Parliament. These early Plymouth co-operators chose Mr. Charles Shovel as their chairman, Mr. John Webb as secretary, Mr. J. Adamson as treasurer. "In a small apartment in a back lane known as Catte Street," wrote Mr. Webb, "we established a shop, office, library, reading, meeting and committee room—the stock stored in a cupboard." Acting as their own buyers, carriers and salesmen, the pioneers, by the end of the quarter, had enrolled 72 members and achieved a profit of 1s. 2d. in the £. From these insignificant seeds were evolved a vast ramification. With increase of business the members removed to Kinterbury Street, where, again, so successful were their operations, that they soon found themselves cramped, cabined, and confined. Their removal to more commodious premises in Cornwall Street witnessed experimental efforts in building,

INTERIOR OF PLYMOUTH GUILDHALL.

(By permission of Mr. Westcott.)

baking, tailoring, drapery, coal supply and other enterprises.   The outcome was not always encouraging, but the members persisted, and 1899 found the Society installed in Frankfort Street in one of the most imposing blocks of business premises in the West of England, and with numerous educational and social branches throughout the Three Towns.   The membership then numbered 20,385 : the turnover was £351,384 ; and the yearly profits reached £54,577.

PLYMOUTH ELECTRICITY WORKS.—OPENED 1899.

(By permission of the " ELECTRICAL ENGINEER.")

Chemical works were instituted in 1854 by Messrs. Burnard and Alger, and their fine wharf in Cattewater suggested subsequent developments.   When the Admiralty thwarted the dock scheme of the Corporation, Messrs. Burnard and Alger materially improved their own Parliamentary right to levy dues and rates, and the Plymouth Corporation were restricted to the construction of wharves that were essential to their shipping purposes in connection with their Electricity Depôt.   Works for manufacturing artificial manure were also carried on by Messrs. Norrington, and others by Mr. Harvey, in Deadman's Bay, for the distillation of tar.   The first important biscuit factory was set up in Plymouth by George Frean, by whom the business was transferred to Mr. Robert Serpell.   In 1899 it was removed to Reading by Mr. Henry Serpell, the then proprietor, and the whole of his staff accompanied him.   The Victoria Soap Company was formed in 1858 by Mr. Thomas A. Morrish, with premises in the Millbay Road, and, in 1863, the shareholders absorbed Messrs. Bryant and Burnell's soap works in Sutton Road.   Works in the same district for manufacturing paper and glass disappeared before the requirements of the Great Western Dock Company.   In 1889 some down-to-date promoters purchased the chief local breweries, including that of Mr. Vosper at Stonehouse, which possessed an excellent and inexhaustible spring, and the Plymouth Breweries Company was the outcome of these operations.   Textile

PP

revivals resulted from the clothing enterprises of Messrs Tippets, at Millbay, and Mr. E. S. Lancaster, in Phœnix Street, each of whom employed hundreds of hands in producing specialities in local serges. The long-established maltsters' business of Messrs. Pitts and King was also incorporated, and the firm made, after the Council fiasco, an attempt to develop the south Cattewater bank. An insufficient response on the part of the public thwarted this second attempt to improve the facilities of the harbour. The premature death of Mr. Thomas Pitts, a member of the company and an enthusiastic volunteer officer, resulted in the resolve to erect a Memorial Hall in the parish, to whose interest he had devoted himself for years. Under the auspices of Mr. Henry Matthews—in the old Sugar Refinery in Mill Lane—jam manufacture became a local staple, and the yield of confectionery attained considerable dimensions in Tuckett's factory at Millbay.

Mr. Bryant carried on a starch factory previous to the erection of the Sugar Refinery, and the accumulation of discarded grain was so great that cattle were reared on the site, and the milk was gladly sold at a penny per gallon. Mr. Edward James became associated with Mr. Bryant and a lucifer match factory was instituted. Various experiments had been made by different local chemists, and the first matchwood was dipped in a bright red consistency. It was fired by contact with a white chemical liquid and blown into a flame by the breath. The next development was due to Mr. Fitz-Henry, a chemist in Market Street, whose match gradually ignited on being slowly drawn through folded sand-paper. Messrs. Bryant and James, who were joined by Mr. May, manufactured the first match that struck on the box. Their factory was destroyed by fire, and then Messrs. Bryant and May transferred the business to a more populous centre. In 1840, Mr. James established by the waterside of Sutton Pool a factory for the production of starch, blue, and blacklead, and thus founded a new family of Plymouth merchants. Almost simultaneously another line of Jameses, belonging to Cornwall, opened business in Old Town Street as oil, colour and lead merchants, and Mr. Edward James, the leading proprietor, proved in public life alike disinterested and courageous. The memorial window in the Council Chamber, containing several panel portraits of Devonshire and Cornish worthies by Fouracre, was placed there in 1899 by his children, one of whom, Alderman John James, was three times Mayor of Devonport, where he established a large business in addition to that conducted in Octagon Street.

Plymouth Volunteering assumed definite form in 1794, when the tradesmen enrolled themselves by way of example, under the command of Colonel John Hawker and Captain Edmund Lockyer. Both officers filled a large place in the politics of their day, and the former was on terms of visiting acquaintance with Prince William Henry, who stood as godfather to William Henry Hawker. The two companies of volunteers attired themselves in fine red cloth, with yellow facings, and their bear-skin helmets gave them a picturesque appearance. Artisans gradually displaced tradesmen in the ranks; and, as the six companies were officially required to do permanent duty in defending the port, they were clothed and remunerated out of the funds of the Imperial Exchequer. The Plymouth Foot corps, consisting of three companies, were constituted in 1797. The men wore blue coats with red collars, white waistcoats, and blue pantaloons, and maintained their own fife and drum band. Major Culme, Captain Robert Fuge, Captain Ben Fuge, and Captain A. Hill drilled and disciplined a body of 190 men, who considerably varied in bulk and height, and supplied the satirists with abundant references to their Davids and Goliaths. Captain Julian's Rangers were a more select corps. They affected the traditional Plymouth trained band uniform of green, boasted of their shooting, and made a fine show with their colours. Mr. Peter Langmead maintained a company of volunteers at his own cost. These mainly consisted of brewers who had lost nothing as to dimensions by reason of their occupation, and the critics did not spare exclamations of awe and admiration for their girth. A small force of yeomanry were supplied by the butchers. They possessed an artistic standard, and their uniform of red and yellow, surmounted by helmets, was highly popular. Captain Clements took charge of the Sea Fencibles—Custom-house officers and fishermen, remarkable adepts in the use of the pike and skilled in big gun exercise. Captain Pridham raised two companies of volunteers at Stonehouse, who clothed and armed themselves, and Captain Scoble formed on the same lines a company of his employés, who were known as "Barrack Artificers." After the peace these various forces were consolidated under the title of the Prince of Wales's Own Plymouth, and the historical uniform of green became general. Colonel Pawle formed at Dock a body of Volunteer Artillery, who were officially enrolled under the name of the Duke of York's Own. The Dock Infantry were another strong force, and the total volunteer reserve represented 2,000 men in the Three Towns. With the cessation of the danger the necessity of the service passed, but, during the Crimean War, Mr. W. H. Hawker resuscitated local interest, and Major Duperier instructed the 2nd Devon (Plymouth) Volunteer Rifle Corps. 150 persons of repute in professions and commerce purchased their own uniforms; green was revived as the dominant colour; and black kid gloves attested the respectability of the enrolled. Captain Bewes, Colonel Hutchinson and Colonel Fisk successively commanded, and, under the last-named—"a gallant and beloved old officer"—the corps attained its palmiest days. A body of cadets was thereupon organised; and, to assist in purchasing accoutrements, the "South Devon Lilies" gave a series of entertainments. The Drill Hall was erected, and, thanks to Mr. Kinton Bond's and Mr. C. Norrington's efforts, a rifle range was also acquired. Captain Elliott followed Colonel Fisk, and harmony resulted in a further increase of membership. Elliott's departure was a misfortune, for favouritism obtained and merit was ignored. Col. Spearman, V.D., Col. Pitts, V.D., Captain John Stevens, Captain F. B. Westlake, Captain George Browse, V.D., and Major Rendle, V.D., assisted to revive the popularity of the corps, and Lord Mount Edgcumbe, as Colonel Commandant, restored it to its original favour. The Devonport Corps was created by Mr. John Beer and Major St. Aubyn in 1859, and the Keyham Artillery Corps was established almost simultaneously.

A Group of Modern Artists. Of the artists whose names were household words in Plymouth during the first half of the nineteenth century, Samuel Prout won in architectural drawing a reputation no less immortal than that which Reynolds achieved in portraiture. Prout came of an old Devonshire stock, his mother being the daughter of Mr. Cater, an enterprising Plymouth shipping venturer. Delicate from his birth, the lad received, whilst nutting, a sunstroke which rendered him an invalid. His delicacy was the despair of his parents, the more so since he would indulge in no other form of occupation than that of drawing. It was Prout's instinct, however, that directed his genius, and, while he was yet a pupil of Bidlake's at the Grammar School, he became the associate and friend of Benjamin Haydon and Opie, and so impressed was the latter by his intelligence that he painted his portrait in a room of the old building where monks had ministered in distant ages. It was whilst he was aflame with the passion of his art, yet sensitive to the criticism of his own intuition, that Prout gained the friendship of Ambrose Bawden Johns. He, strange to say, had served his apprenticeship to Benjamin Haydon's father, only to abandon the selling of books for the painting of pictures. Johns had the advantage of Prout in point of years and experience, and he supplied his depressed young friend with counsel and encouragement which Prout was able, in a few years, to repay with tenfold authority. Prout's early aspirations were in the direction of landscapes and coast scenes, but his experiments were failures, and he told Johns, with tears in his eyes, that he should never succeed as an artist.   Noticing that his young friend excelled in presenting the types of houses with which Plymouth then abounded, Johns urged him to develop his gifts as an architectural artist.   "Thenceforth," to quote Ruskin, "Prout devoted himself to ivy-mantled bridges, mossy water-mills and rock-built cottages," and the neighbourhood yielded him a never-failing harvest of subjects.   His spirits towered above his physical infirmities, and merry were the meetings which he and his fellow Plymothians held in London in the heyday of their early promise—Haydon conscious of a skill that was destined to bring him fame, but no fortune ; and Eastlake, affluent as the outcome of his success in painting Napoleon when the Bellerophon lay in Plymouth Sound.   Prout now became lost to his native town, and abandoned the English capital in turn to spend happy years amongst the quaint survivals of Antwerp and other Continental cities that had been preserved from the hand of the restorer.   "There will never be any more Prout drawings." Ruskin sorrowfully said.   The subjects vanished with their interpreter.

Ambrose Bawden Johns, who, in his home at Devonport, had encouraged Prout to persevere, lived to receive the kindly criticisms of his friend.   He so increased his repute as a landscape artist that he was known as the "Turner of the West," and the one complaint Samuel Prout made of his works was that they resembled ancient masters.   "If you paint in this manner," he rallied him, "you will not put a stop to the sale of old pictures.   There are few collectors who purchase both ancient and modern works, and there is always a bias, which I pray may develop, in favour of the examples of living artists, so that we may be kept alive and employed."   Johns was on terms of intimacy with the great colourist, and his later manner developed so many characteristics of similitude that one gem of his was sold at Christie's as a Turner and engraved with that artist's name.   In spite of the struggle through which he passed in early life, Johns was alike a gentleman and a student by nature, and Turner, Wilkie, and others, found in his social qualities a never-failing delight.

Distressing is the story of Benjamin Haydon, the historical painter, who died in 1846.   Full of hope and enthusiasm, he left Plymouth to study at the Royal Academy, only to find his career one continual battle with difficulties.   Eminent in talent, devoted to his profession, temperate in habits, unwearying in industry, his labours never yielded him an unencumbered subsistence.   His "Judgment of Solomon" was regarded as such a triumph that the Mayor and Commonalty of Plymouth conferred on Haydon the freedom of the borough.   Young as he was, he had exhibited the highest genius, and presented an example of intense application and enduring perseverance.   William Eastlake quoted the name of Reynolds to illustrate the types of moral heroes to which the town had given birth, and the Mayor, Mr. Woollcombe, taking up the theme, declared that it was a reproach to Plymouth that, whilst the country sounded the merits of her gifted sons, the inhabitants suffered the men themselves to remain without notice or reward.   Haydon also contributed freely to periodical literature, but never accepted any remuneration ; and he declined a Government appointment lest it might interfere with the pursuit of the art to which he was so intensely devoted.   His masterpieces were completed in circumstances of privation and the most famous of all was painted in a debtor's prison.   It was when his pecuniary embarrassments were so acute that he completed six works to illustrate the laws, institutions and liberties of the country.   Just as his noble canvas of "Alfred Explaining Trial by Jury" was on the point of completion, his brave spirit succumbed and his mind gave way, and he was heard to say—before the most sad and tragic chapter of all—that he found it impossible, after all his toils, to commence the world afresh.   It was Haydon's habit to write comments on the pages of his books as he read them, and he recalled in some of these notes the interesting conversations he had held with distinguished men. In one of these he mentioned that the Duke of Wellington was told on the field of Waterloo that he was in command of "a wretched army." "I know it," confessed the Duke, "but we will win the battle yet." Shaw, the Lifeguardsman, was one of Haydon's favourite models. "I had five models who fought in the great battle—all of them were distinguished for their bravery; three of them were killed." In the judgment of some contemporaries, Haydon was an enthusiast, too haughty and too vain to succeed. His genius knew no fetters and wonders were always on the point of accomplishment. Wordsworth, however, justly interpreted the man and his works in the ode he dedicated to his memory:

> And, oh! when Nature smiles, as oft she may,
> Through long-lived pressure of obscure distress,
> Still to be strenuous for the bright reward,
> And in the soul admit of no decay;
> Brooks no continuance of weak-mindedness—
> Great is the glory, for the strife is hard!

Samuel Cook commenced his career by painting signs for inns and scenes for "peep shows." Born of poor parents at Camelford, he was apprenticed at a wool-combing factory, but spent his leisure and occasionally his busy moments in decorating the floor with a piece of chalk. "That boy will never be fit for anything but a limner," said his employer, and "Limner Cook" the lad was called until, on arriving at man's estate, he resolved to tramp to Plymouth. He carried his best boots in his handkerchief and wore his old ones till he reached Torpoint, where he tossed them away as having rendered him sufficient service. After serving as a house decorator, at moderate wages, Cook improvised scenes for the local theatres, and cultured and capable citizens were not slow to recognise a genius in the unassuming student. The friendship of Wightwick secured him the entrée to the charmed circle of which Hamilton Smith, William Jacobson, William Eastlake and Lady Morley were conspicuous ornaments, and, in the little house which existed on the site of the Guildhall Square, Cook painted his most effective examples. He triumphed where Prout had no sympathy, having, to quote the appreciation of Ruskin, "a great understanding of the sea." Delicate in health, attenuated in form and pallid of countenance, Cook was nevertheless endowed with infinite capacity for enjoyment, and the enchanting days he spent on the moors with Philip Mitchell, not the least among Plymouth artists, yielded many a reminiscence illustrating the reverence in which he was held—the more since his demeanour excited love rather than distrust and won respect instead of stimulating jealousy. His masterpiece—a view from Stonehouse Bridge—was suspended between the best examples of Turner and Prout at South Kensington Museum.

It was Haydon's inspiration that induced Charles Lock Eastlake to participate in the lottery of art, happily with successful results. He won fame with his first achievement "The raising of Jairus's Daughter," and his patron, Mr. Harman, sent him to Paris to study. Thence he returned to Plymouth, where he painted Napoleon at the gangway of the Bellerophon, and people journeyed from all parts of the country to inspect the work at a gallery in Frankfort Place. Eastlake became par excellence the student of Italian life and manners, and his erudition rendered him at home with the minutest characteristics of that school. His social circle included Elizabeth Barrett Browning and the leading disciples of English and American culture, but he was free from all affectation and pretence. It is said that he was deficient in courage, and that a little of Haydon's self-esteem would have done him no harm. Certainly his features, though fine, were "tinged by constitutional timidity" and lacked vigour of expression. He was knighted on being elected President of the Royal

Academy, and his discrimination as Director of the National Gallery secured valuable examples for that depository.

Born at Plymouth when Haydon was at the zenith of his career, Solomon Hart also caught the infection of his aims, and, like his ideal, was only indifferently supported. He delighted, with Haydon, in mighty canvases, and secured admission to the Royal Academy with "Lady Jane Grey at the Place of Execution." This majestic masterpiece lay unheeded in a roll for several years, and Hart then presented it to his native town. Samuel Hutchings Rogers was another of Bidlake's clever boys, and the doctor sent him to London and maintained him there until he was recognised as one of the leading marine and landscape artists of the day. Other artists whose persons and easels were familiar in Plymouth was Luny; Nicholas Condy, who settled down to painting in his native town after surviving the perils of the Peninsular War; Nicholas Matthew Condy, his son, whose representations of old battleships are still sought by collectors; Philip Mitchell, who was born at Devonport, and excelled as a landscape artist; W. Gibbons who rejoiced in the atmosphere of the Barbican; E. Opie whose works frequently hung at the Royal Academy; A. B. Brittan whose animal sketches were extremely powerful; and Lord Monkswell (Sir R. Collier), who attained high repute as an amateur painter of Alpine scenery. W. H. Pike (Oliver Paque) was equally facile with oil and water colours, a genius in black and white, and a welcome exhibitor at all the great galleries. Historic art in the West was indebted to J. T. Fouracre for many commemorative ideals, of which his "Siege Window" in the Plymouth Guildhall was the most characteristic. He devoted himself to works of a decorative character, and was the first in the West to make stained glass. Local sculpture owed much to Harry Hems, of Exeter, whose effigies decorated the Plymouth Guildhall—a man of many parts, with huge tomes of newspaper cuttings concerning his life and his work, the vast majority of them written by himself, as he once merrily confessed. John Barratt was a sympathetic interpreter of tors and streams; H. Martin—a gifted student of the surviving architectural characteristics that delighted Samuel Prout; and Arthur Collier, a moorland artist of subtle perceptions. The younger Brittan reproduced in his cattle sketches the cunning of his father's hand, and Arthur Shelly's Swiss scenes were marked by force.

Of the moderns Pike took rank as a scenic artist whilst yet a lad, and his bold and rapid execution of colossal conceptions was amazing. He achieved his first success during an Exeter pantomime, when the Fenian scare provided authors of librettos with jocose references to the searches for arms which were then being prosecuted. "Down with the house of everyone that in it has a pike," exclaimed the King. Quoth his liege:

> Your Majesty had better be careful what you doos
> We have a Pike in this house we would not like to lose.

Pike next painted the scenes at the Plymouth Theatre, and his landscape works were ever in request. On leaving for Venice he was publicly testimonialised and he was "discovered" in the City of Gondolas by Luke Fildes, who was attracted by his character sketches and his remarkable skill with the pencil. On taking up his residence in London Pike was at once recommended by Fildes and appointed as a leading artist of the "Daily Graphic." He did not neglect oils and colours, and his examples touched high water mark, leading to his election as member of the Society of Water Colours, R.B.A., and Royal Institute. He contributed to their galleries his best Venetian work and some dashing Langham sketches.

Philip Mitchell, tall, stately and courtly in every movement, was a delightful raconteur of stories in the Cornish and Devonshire dialect. He was travelling across country with a brother artist, impedimenta in hand, when the companions were accosted by a farmer. "Travellers, I spose, are 'ee?" Mitchell nodded in genial acquiescence. Hodge was confirmed in his judgment that the pedestrians were "packmen," and, reflectively nursing his scrubby chin, he asked "Got a good razzor, 'ave 'ee?" During an expedition to Brown Willy, Mitchell engaged a yokel to look to his gear, and, whilst at work, some children began harrying the cattle he was sketching. "Yur," the lad shouted in sympathetic protest, "You just *put down* they cows, will 'ee." Edward Opie was always in quest of subjects, and, impressed by the physique and rugged characteristics of a navvy he met in a lane, he asked him to sit to him as a model—"I'll pay you half-a-crown an hour." "Zur," was the rebuke of the outraged clodhopper, "I be a respectable man, I be."

Charitable, Social and Educational: 19th Century. Plymouth Public Dispensary was founded in 1798 at the old Mayoralty House in Woolster Street, and then transferred to How Street. Mr. Wightwick prepared plans in 1835 to enable the Charity to command its own home in Catherine Street. The consummation had long been desired and was rendered possible by Mr. Charles Yonge's bequest of £1,000, assisted by the munificence of Messrs. Fortescue, Seccombe, Fuge, W. Prance and Dr. Remmet. The institution was the forerunner of the South Devon and East Cornwall Hospital, and encouraged by the flow of funds, the governors of the charity acquired a site in Sussex Place. Further plans were prepared by Mr. Wightwick, and the foundation stone was laid by the Rev. John Hatchard "in grateful acknowledgment of the divine favour, through which we have been enabled to begin the building, and in humble reliance on the blessing of God in our endeavours to carry the charitable objects of the institution into full effect." The Hospital was thrown open to patients in 1840, and additional wings were added in a few years. Intermittent outbreaks of erysipelas convinced the governors in 1875 that the sanitary arrangements could no longer be relied upon, and that the

SOUTH DEVON AND EAST CORNWALL HOSPITAL, 1899.
(By permission of Mr. A. H. SWISS.)

establishment was otherwise inadequate to increasing demands. The Hospital Sunday and Saturday movements augmented the resources of the exchequer, and leading citizens and county residents handsomely contributed. A site on the Seven Trees Estate, bounded by Clifton Place on the one side and Woodland Terrace on the other, was selected, and six blocks were constructed on the best known principles of hospital sanitation, at a cost of about £40,000. In view of the more conspicuous benefactions, the wards were named in honour of the donors—Lopes, Maristowe, Gill, Rooker, Prance, Radford, Bewes, Dawson, Mount Edgcumbe, and John Hayes. Throughout the reconstruction the duties of honorary treasurer were discharged by Mr. W. H. Alger, and those of honorary secretary by Mr. Walter Wilson, and, at the opening in 1885, special tributes were paid to their services. In 1892 Mr. E. A. Pearn, of Compton Leigh, conveyed the mansion in which he lived, together with over four acres of pleasure ground surrounding it, and twenty acres of land contiguous, so that a Convalescent Home for patients might there be established. During the brief interval preceding his death, Mr. Pearn paid the committee a rental for the house, and his reason for thus passing over the estate was due to a desire to surmount the difficulty of conveying landed property under the Mortmain Act. Mr. Pearn, moreover, invested the necessary funds for endowing for all time this noble addition to the hospital. Sir Massey Lopes continued to make princely gifts to the Hospital from time to time, and his generosity was especially recognised.

THE BLIND INSTITUTION, NORTH HILL.
(By permission of Mr. JOHN SMITH.)

Dr. Gale, who had been deprived of his own sight in the course of scientific experiments, suggested the Institution for the Blind in 1859. Premises were erected in Cobourg Street, from which the committee removed to North Hill with the increase of applications and augmentation of legacies. The new building was designed by Mr. H. J. Snell. Mr. E. Henley was a staunch supporter of the institution in its earlier, and Mr. William Derry and Mr. Greek Wills in its more recent operations. Local charities of all denominations found a princely supporter in Mr. Jacob Nathan, who bequeathed at his death £4,000 for a Jewish School to bear his name, and £1,000 to maintain the Plymouth Synagogue. In a scheme of benefactions that embraced every leading charity in the country, those of the Three Towns received their generous proportion.

Dr. Butter was held in honoured estimation as physician to the Eye Infirmary. Originally located in Cornwall Street, the staff removed to Westwell Street, and a substantial building was eventually erected at Millbay. Here, in the course of thirty-two years, Dr. Butter relieved or cured 32,000 persons—a memorial to his benevolence which led to the presentation of his portrait and a salver in 1854. In 1899 it was decided to abandon the old establishment, and, at the instance of Mr. William Law, a fund was formed in honour of the Diamond Jubilee of Queen Victoria, and a spacious and desirable building was reared and fitted at Mutley at a cost of £15,000. Up to the eve of its removal some 80,000 patients had been treated, the vast majority of them successfully, and the honourable roll of surgeons included the names of Edward Moore, J. H. Luscombe, William Square, J. Eliot Square, C. E. Russel Rendle and John R. Rolston.

Few Plymouth doctors were more gratefully or strikingly remembered by the poor than John Budd, and his cures were so extraordinary, and withal so simple, that his reputation was great whilst yet he was young. During his residence in George Street, Devonport, young officers made frequent attempts to invo've him in some episode that they might tell against him, but the doctor was always equal to the emergency. He was the original of the story in which some sparks pretended that a friend was suffering torments through swallowing a fly. Dr. Budd went to his outhouse, and, on returning, placed a fat spider before the astonished group, with the remark, " Tell your friend to swallow that." On another occasion some officers whom he had served invited him to mess, and when he replied that he never dined out, they asked leave to entertain him at home. Budd replied that he should have no objection, and he subsequently declared that he had never fared better under his own roof. On his removal to Plymouth, his cottage in Westwell Street became the daily Mecca of the poor, despite the fact that he never stood on the order of treatment. One young man, who was speechless from lock-jaw, he kicked over the stairs. " Oh, doctor," he exclaimed, " you have broken my arm." " Never mind your arm now that I have loosened your tongue." An old lady with a tumour in the throat he asked to see him the following day. She did so, and, as she took her seat, a dish of boiled dumplings was placed upon the table. Without a moment's notice the doctor pelted his assistant with these missiles, the assistant retaliated, and the pair cut such sorry figures that the aged sufferer was seized with a fit of uncontrollable laughter and burst the abscess.

The provision of a Hospital for Devonport was due to Mr. Thomas Woollcombe, Mr. Alfred Norman—by whom the plans were prepared—and Miss Florence Nightingale, who arranged the chief wards. The memorial stone was laid in 1862 by Lord Mount Edgcumbe, who placed the promoters of this, and indeed every other local charity, under recurring obligations by giving permission for his park to be used for fetes and garden parties to swell subscription funds. The inaugural ceremony was conducted with elaborate Masonic honours. An address was delivered by the Rev. John Huyshe, Grand Chaplain of England, and Corinthian, Doric and Ionic lights were displayed by the brethren. The Government granted £3,500 towards the Lock Wards, then first instituted for the treatment of unfortunate women, but the exercise of the Act which legitimatised compulsory examination resulted in occasional abuses, and repeal was advocated on the ground that the liberty of the subject was violated and the statute law rendered ethically indefensible. Devonport was the active centre of the propaganda, and prosecutions were instituted against the constabulary for molesting virtuous females. Indignation meetings were held after each fresh attempt to convict the metropolitan police of excess of duty, and refractory displays were the invariable rule. Mr. T. Woollcombe was the staunchest defender of the Act, and, on one occasion, when the supporters of Repeal monopolised the speaking until ten o'clock, he resumed the argument and continued it for two hours. The friends of Repeal had returned to their homes, but their opponents remained cheering until midnight, when an amendment was carried with ease. Public opinion was too strong for the compulsory principle, and it was abandoned by Mr. Gladstone's Government. After its Repeal women voluntarily tendered themselves for treatment when their case was desperate.

ROYAL ALBERT HOSPITAL, DEVONPORT.

(By permission of Mr. A. H. Swiss.)

Anxiety for the fatherless was the absorbing care of Mrs. Tripe, wife of Dr. Tripe, an old Devonport resident, and the grandfather of Mr. L. P. Metham. Her efforts were not too warmly received, but, after some years she enlisted sufficient support to witness the inauguration, in 1834, of the Devon and Cornwall Female Asylum in Lockyer Street. The plans were provided by Mr. Wightwick, and the foundation stone was laid by the Earl of Morley. So numerous were the bereaved of sailors and soldiers, and so urgent their claims, that Mrs. Tripe came to the conclusion that an institution ought to be erected in Devonport to provide for the class, and the Royal British Female Orphan Asylum was established with the expressed sympathy and financial support of Queen Victoria. A house was rented as a temporary asylum until 1845, when the foundation stone of the new building was laid with Masonic ritual, in the presence of thirty thousand people. The building was completed at a cost of £5,000, and it was occupied by twenty orphans on the anniversary of Waterloo in 1846. As time went on the numbers largely increased, and the cholera epidemic of 1849, the pestilence of the Eclair, the destruction of the Amazon by fire, the wreck of the Avenger, and the foundering of the Birkenhead found the doors open to many destitute children. The Crimean War and Indian Mutiny next taxed available resources, and Mr. Metham, who continued the work of Mrs. Tripe, issued eloquent appeals to the nation, and the orphaned were furnished with timely shelter. In 1872 national depression resulted in famine prices, and the home grew so overcrowded that extension was imperative. The Admiralty set aside £4,000 a year for the support of 200 girls, and this particular asylum received fifty of the number. The committee then made provision for a hundred more children at a cost of £6,000, and the Duke of Edinburgh laid the memorial stone of the new wings in 1874. Of the amount required £1,500 was subscribed by the Freemasons of Devon and Cornwall, and the Prince of Wales followed the Prince Consort's example by accepting a life governorship. The loss of the Eurydice, Atalanta, Serpent and Victoria, with their chapters of harrowing grief for so many Devonport families, found the Asylum prompt in offers of relief, and the Afghan, Zulu and Egyptian Wars evoked the same merciful consideration and corresponding public benevolence. In 1889, the fiftieth anniversary of Mr. Metham's unbroken association as honorary secretary, witnessed the presentation to that gentleman of his own portrait, those of the Queen and Prince Consort (sent by Her Majesty), and others of the Duke and Duchess of Edinburgh (forwarded by themselves.) A silver salver was given by the subscribers to the Home, and a piece of plate was contributed by "old girls," full of gratitude for the past. A gold Jubilee medal was also given to Mrs. Metham. Mr. Metham died in the act of preparing the report of the sixtieth anniversary of his secretariat—overcome at the intimation that twenty orphans were to be elected to commemorate his diamond jubilee of honorary service.

For establishing the Sailors' Rest thousands of gallant fellows owed an irredeemable debt to Miss Agnes Weston, who not only provided for their care on shore, but championed the interests of their wives and children. This noble woman, by offering a home to the seamen was instrumental, more than any one person of her generation, in changing the habits of the service by preserving thousands from the perils of "paying off," and sending them to their wives and families flush of funds. In emergencies caused by such disasters as the loss of the Eurydice, Serpent and Victoria the same lady stepped into the breach of immediate want. When Devonport was inconsolable for the loss of brave sons, and the Patriotic Commissioners jealously hoarded their accumulated stores, she sprung to the help of the bereaved with immediate relief. Chilling indifference and niggardly allowances were so clearly exposed by Miss Weston and Mr. Kearley, M.P. for the borough, that the basis of administration was revised by Parliament. Miss Weston celebrated the Silver Wedding of her work in 1899 by completing the Sailors' Rest to its original design. The want of confidence in the administration of public subscriptions by the Patriotic Commissioners induced the "Western Morning News" to promote in 1899 an independent fund for the relief of the widows and orphans of the brave fellows who were falling in the Transvaal. The garrison was then depleted of troops. Regiment upon regiment had marched to the railway station amid scenes of thrilling enthusiasm, and spectators mingled with the warriors, carrying their rifles and their knapsacks—"Tommy Atkins" and civilians deliriously singing "The Soldiers of the Queen," and enjoining each other in hoarse chorus to "Remember Majuba." Times had changed indeed. There was now no daily arrival of prizes and waste of treasure desperately won. War no longer brought immediate wealth in its train for the Three Towns, but commercial depression for all classes. And yet, in spite of all this, the "Western Morning News" raised several thousand pounds from its readers, and took care that the money should be promptly disbursed in a district that yielded the splendid fellows who composed the "Devons" and the Duke of Cornwall's Light Infantry ; that sent from the Royal Marine Barracks at Stonehouse, the indomitable Britons who scaled the heights of Enslin when the bullets rained as in a sand storm ; that filled the gap vacated by the heroic death of General Symons with the fine figure of Colonel Pole-Carew ; and which gave, in the person of that magnificent general, Sir Redvers Buller, a Commander-in-Chief to the British forces.

ROYAL MARINE BARRACKS, STONEHOUSE.
(By permission of Mr. JOHN SMITH)

Literary, Scientific, Educational: 19th Century. From out the group of literary and educational worthies of the nineteenth century the name of Nicholas Tom Carrington stands foremost. The son of a dockyardsman, he was a self-taught genius. At the age of fifteen he entered the establishment as an apprentice, but, instead of attending to his duties, he was invariably absorbed in poetic dreamlands. In the rough pastimes of his fellows he refused to participate, and he was often reproved by the overseers for being discovered with a book in some retired corner. " I was totally unfit," he remarked, ''for the work of a measurer, to which I was apprenticed. Mild and meek by nature, fond of literary pursuits, and inordinately attached to reading, it is strange that a mechanical profession should have been chosen for me. It was, however, partly my own fault, as the popular prejudice was in favour of the yard, and I was carried away by the prevailing mania." Complaints of his inattention to work were conveyed to his parents, and, to avoid their reproaches, Carrington ran from home and joined a battleship as a common sailor. In this capacity he was present at more than one engagement, and he participated in the victory of Cape St. Vincent. The revolting scenes he witnessed in fighting caused him to write a poem with which the captain was so impressed that, realising Carrington's refined and sensitive temperament, he gave him his discharge. The young man started as a schoolmaster in the neighbourhood of Morice Square, and Dr. Joseph May was one of his pupils. Reserved in temperament and impassive of demeanour, Carrington developed an impatience of teaching, which left no particularly affectionate memories with pupils who were unconscious of deserving heavy chastisement. It was this morose irritability that induced him to abandon the profession. After contributing articles and studies to the newspapers, he published his " Dartmoor," " Banks of the Tamar," and other compositions indicating his love for vast solitudes and pensive moods. Dartmoor was the ideal of his imagination. It was the " wild and wondrous region " that possessed his childhood's affections—his mind was absorbed in its hill mysteries, in the dialect of '' its half-savage peasants," and its storm-swept wilds :

                                                            I love to tread
                    Thy central wastes when not a sound intrudes
                    Upon the ear, but rush of wing or leap
                    Of the hoarse waterfall.   And oh, 'tis sweet
                    To list the music of thy torrent-streams ;
                    For thou, too, hast thy minstrelsies for him
                    Who from their liberal mountain-urn delights
                    To trace thy waters, as from source to sea
                    They rush tumultuous.   Yet for other fields
                    Thy bounty flows eternal.   From thy sides
                    Devonia's rivers flow ; a thousand brooks
                    Roll o'er thy rugged slopes ;--'tis but to cheer
                    Yon Austral meads unrivalled, fair as aught
                    That bards have sung, or Fancy has conceived
                    'Mid all her rich imaginings : whilst thou,
                    The source of half their beauty, wearest still
                    Through centuries upon thy blasted brow,
                    The curse of barrenness.

In " My Native Village" and other poems, Carrington showed how truly his soul
was possesed of sentiment—the pride of birth, simple though the hamlet of Harewood
was, and of affection for Hamoaze and the battleships which reposed on its bosom.   Thus
he wrote of a frigate as it lay under Mount Edgcumbe :

                    Is she not beautiful ? "reposing there
                      On her own shadow," with her white wings furled ;
                    Moveless, as in the sleepy, sunny air,
                      Rests the meek swan in her own quiet world.

H.M.S. IMPREGNABLE IN HAMOAZE, 1899.
(By permission of Mr. JOHN SMITH.)

Is she not beautiful? her graceful bow
  Triumphant rising o'er the enamoured tides
That, glittering in the noon-day sunbeam, now
  Just leap and die along her polished sides.

And on the stern magnificent, recline
  Old forms that many a classic eye regale;
From fair and fabled lands, and streams divine,
  The sculptor's hand pourtrays a classic tale.

There is nor voice nor murmur on the land;
  Still fiercer glows the ray on tower and tree;
There is nor surge nor ripple on the strand,
  And not an air is stealing o'er the sea.

A thousand eyes are on her; for she floats
  Confessed a queen upon the subject main;
And hark! as from her decks delicious notes
  Breathe, softly breathe, a soul-entrancing strain.

MORWELLHAM, ON THE TAMAR.
(By permission of Mr. JOHN SMITH.)

His picture of the scene at Morwellham, as given in his "Banks of the Tamar," was
boldly drawn:

Ye rise ye noble rocks with grandeur, but ye have
An air of loveliness, for Summer throws
Unnumber'd wreaths around you. Not thus break
Upon the view, the hideous crags which edge
The eternal Ocean, beetling o'er the deep
With most terrific aspect, huge and wild

And bleak and desolate, by Nature set
To battle with the world of waters.   Here
Arise not fearful sounds from roaring cliffs
And howling caverns—voices strange and deep
That terrify the ear, and refluent force
The life-blood's purple current.   Nothing here
Is heard but the soft murmur of the stream,
Or lute of voyager, or gush of song,
From brake, and bower, and sky.   Devonia lifts
Her rocks sublimely, but they wear a crown—
A verdurous crown, and have a graceful zone
Of flowers and foliage, while around their feet
The frequent grove uprushes—majesty,
And strength, and beauty !

Carrington bitterly felt the neglect of his townsmen.   "How am I crucified by the upstarts," he exclaimed after publishing his "Dartmoor."   "One subscriber sends me back my book because esquire is not added to his name ; another because M.D. is not attached ; and these are men of the highest respectability in the slang of modern refinement !   And, what do you think, a dignified officer of the Plymouth Corporation has returned his copy, observing that he will not pay more than half a guinea, and, if I will remove the plates, he will then take the book."   In the words of Doran, a minor poet of Bath, who was a great admirer of Carrington, his general treatment was pathetic :

Alas, such meed the world is us'd
Upon the gifted few to shed,
Was flung to him,—('twas not abus'd)
It gave him praise who wanted bread.
'Twas all he car'd for, all he sought ;
· Fame, honest fame, was his, alone,—
Fame and the sunlit dreams of thought
He could at least claim for his own.

A man of generous impulses and wide appreciations, Dr. Bidlake, head-master of Plymouth Grammar School at the opening of the nineteenth century, gave a practical bent to the gifts of the brilliant lads who gathered around him.   Poetry, music and painting he could alike discuss and illustrate with a sympathetic pen, he seemed to weep as he wrote his elegies, and a tearful note ran through his protests against the wanton sacrifice of the songsters and the dumb.   He made no affectations of modesty in publishing his poems, disdained to pretend that he had been implored by friends to do so, or that he had been encouraged by eulogies which were bestowed upon copies circulated without authority.   "Ingenuously confessing a desire of obtaining praise, if I should be thought to deserve any, I rely upon the candour of just criticism ; and am too faithful to myself to employ any artificial means of procuring commendation."   The same impulses guided Bidlake in all that he wrote : "Publication requires no apology.   It is a lottery in which all but the immodest and the profane have an equal right to adventure.   The world is at liberty to receive or reject every book.   Some may be raised into temporary fame on the momentary whirl of popularity.   Some may get into notice by venal praise.   But when there is no intrinsic merit the glittering meteor will vanish into mortifying neglect and irretrievable oblivion."   The close of Bidlake's life was clouded by affliction and poverty, for he was seized with blindness arising from a brain affection, and, compelled to resign his living at Stonehouse, was thrown upon the charity of his friends. Extracts from his "Verses written at Mount Edgcumbe" will indicate the quality of his poetry:

What groves on groves ascending grow !
How green the crystal waves below !
And there the fishers ply their trade,
And round the circling nets are spread ;
And as the barks approaching close,
The ardent work more busy grows,
The struggling shoals, in glitt'ring strife,
Are robb'd of liberty and life.
Beneath the still umbrageous wood
The simple cottage crowns the flood,
Where oft, with pomp fatigued, the great
For meditation find retreat.

Amidst the woods, the trembling deer
Impetuous rush, all wild with fear ;
Oft turn to gaze with jealous eye,
As from destructive man they fly ;
And from the dark wood to the lawn
Lead off in troops the bounding fawn.

The raptur'd eye now wanders round
The circling stretch of distant ground,
Where fading mountains crown the scene,
With many a fertile vale between ;

VIEW OF MOUNT EDGCUMBE.
(By permission of Mr. JOHN SMITH.)

THE DEWERSTONE, NEAR PLYMOUTH.

(From a photo. by Heath.)

(By permission of Mr. J. H. Keys.)

Where, sporting with the solar beams,
Fam'd Tamar winds his wanton streams;
And deck'd with villas, forts, and towns,
With woods and pastures, hills and downs,
With docks and navies, England's pride,
And lighter barks that swiftly glide;
With islands, shores, and caverns deep,
In hours of calm where tempests sleep.

Of the brilliant crowd who were accustomed to assemble at the Plymouth Institution, the first place must be given to Henry Woollcombe, a man of easy address and polished bearing, mild cheerfulness and gentle sympathy, with a touch of the old school in his carriage. He was the soul of beneficent movements, and no one was in more frequent request as president of meetings—a post for which he was peculiarly adapted. To his efforts were due the formation of the Plymouth Institution, and he retained its presidency until his health failed. William IV. visited the Athenæum during his long period of office and many honoured Plymothians were present on the occasion. Woollcombe made the first serious effort to compile Plymouth History, and, although his manuscript was never published, it proved the indispensible study of every subsequent aspirant. Amongst the scholars and students who surrounded Mr. Woollcombe at the Plymouth Institution were Byrth and Macaulay, alike dialectical and felicitous in expression; Luney, the orator of the lecture hall; Collier and Cookworthy, the former luminous, and the latter with the capacity of the great chemist from whom he descended; George Wightwick, architect and dramatist, the welcome guest at every country house party; Colonel Hamilton Smith, a man of marvellous research and facile pencil; Dr. William Elford Leach, the supreme authority on zoology; John Prideaux, who was to become professor of chemistry in the Cornish Mining School; Samuel Rowe, the zealous antiquarian; A. B. Johns, the local Turner—and many others, including Snow Harris and Jonathan Hearder.

No less familiar at educational and artistic functions was the presence of William Cotton, the authority on prints, paintings and works of art. Mr. Cotton's father married the sister and heiress of Charles Rogers, and thus he inherited the literary and other treasures of the most trustworthy connoisseur of the nineteenth century. The collection was bequeathèd by Cotton to the Public Library in Cornwall Street, whose proprietors built a not too commodious room for its reception and custody. One of the most diligent students of local archæology was Mr. James C. Bellamy, who wrote the "Natural History of South Devon," and compiled in chronological sequence "A Thousand Facts" relating to the development of the Western Counties.

Sir William Snow Harris and Dr. Hearder were alike distinguished for their scientific researches, and worked on such intimate terms that doubt arose as to the actual authorship of the electrical inventions with which the collaboration was associated. The application of conductors to guard ships from the effects of lightning was proposed after they were fixed to buildings, but scientific men were only slightly acquainted with naval architecture, and the methods proposed proved inadequate. The conductors supplied to British ships-of-war were moveable chains, and the idea was to continue them from the topgallant-mast head, down the back-stay, over the channels, into the water. The difficulty of fixing these conductors limited their use, and serious injuries from lightning were common from the absence of necessary precautions. It was the fixing of conductors to masts with which the name of Sir W. S. Harris was enduringly associated. This invention maintained a continuous line of conductors, as useful when the masts were lowered as when raised. Strips of copper sheeting in layers were let into the after part of the masts which were connected by means of copper inserted in caps. Preference was given to copper sheet rather than to copper rods, because of the greater extent of surface obtained, as the electric fluid was found to be transmitted along the surfaces of conductors, and these only required sufficient thickness to prevent fusion. The extent of conducting surface was given greater than the best electricians had found by experiment to be necessary under the severest explosions. A metal rod was fixed on the truck, which could be refixed at the head of the topmast when the topgallant-mast was struck. The continuity was maintained from the heel of the lower masts into the water by copper bolts driven through the keelson and meeting horizontal bolts which were driven transversely through the keel. This disposition was adopted to prevent the bolts from passing through the false keel. To prevent the possibility of a false keel when the topmast was lowered, arising from the diameter of the upper part of the topmast being considerably less than the hole in the cap, a small plate was secured to the upper side of the cap, having a metal drop attached to it by a hinge which allowed it always to fall against the copper in the mainmast. Thus the effectual application of conductors was first ensured, and disasters at sea due to lightning were soon diminished.

Dr. Jonathan Hearder, who was born in 1809, was devoted all his life to chemical and electrical enquiry, and his name and work attained general reputation amongst leading physicists. He pursued his studies and experiments with enthusiasm to the end, although, almost at the outset of his career, a calamity befell him which would have disheartened a less courageous and resolute lover of knowledge. Whilst testing a fulminating compound he lost his sight by explosion, and it was subsequently to this that he achieved his most valuable discoveries in connection with the induction coil and the therapeutic appliance of electricity. Dr. Hearder was one of the earliest to perceive that a telegraph cable across the oceanic track was not only important but practicable, and the cable he invented was, with slight modifications, ultimately adopted for Atlantic telegraphy. He also invented a thermometer for ascertaining by pressure the depth of water to which the lead had actually sunk. There was no more popular lecturer in the West than Dr. Hearder. Endowed with a marvellous memory, he was never at a loss for a fact or a date, and he was most successful as an experimenter. His attainments were not exclusively scientific. He was one of the best all-round men who participated in the debates at the Plymouth Institution, and, in his early days, was associated with his brother, Mr. George Hearder, in the production of "The South Devon Museum," a work which was rich in historical and antiquarian lore. Dr. Hearder tested electricity in order to ascertain its value for nocturnal military operations, and, in 1835, exhibited an incandescent electric light in the course of a lecture at Liskeard.

The group of scholarly worthies just discussed was succeeded by another of equal merit—William Prance, J. N. Bennett and Alfred Rooker, who each contributed instalments to the History of Plymouth; Dr. Peter Holmes, for many years master of the Mannamead Grammar School; Dr. Spence Bate, whose remarks on Crustacea were embodied in the report of the Challenger Expedition; J. Brooking Rowe, who catalogued the fauna of Devon; and Mr. James Hine, to whom, more than to any other explorer, Plymouth is indebted for preserving the old architectural memories of the town. At the same time Devonport rejoiced in the fame attained by Mr. John Towson, who, although he was not the originator of great circle sailing, invented a set of tables that simplified the system. The Liverpool merchants presented him with £2,000 in recognition of his services in devising composite sailing. William Byers, another man of distinct individuality, developed, in spite of many discouragements, an extensive business as publisher, and played an active part in local affairs. Bishop Colenso received his early education at the Devonport Classical and Mathematical School, and the promising Cornish lad there delivered many a prize speech from the Classics.

Plymouth contributed a president to the Institution of Civil Engineers in the person of Mr. J. M. Rendel, a man of untiring energy, clear perception and accurate judgment. In his youth he was selected by that acute observer of scientific genius, Mr. Telford, to lay out and construct considerable lengths of turnpike roads in Devon and Cornwall, and the difficulties he overcame endowed him with the self-reliance of his subsequent career. At the age of 22, he suggested and constructed the Laira Bridge, and then planned and executed steam ferries at Dartmouth, Devonport, Saltash and elsewhere. His advice was in such request by railway promoters that he removed to London, and, as a witness at the Parliamentary enquiries in 1832, stepped into foremost rank. Harbours of refuge at Port-

land and Holyhead he conceived with broad views and executed with consummate rapidity, and the Government regarded him as its most reliable expert in engineering enterprises.

Mr. R. N. Worth and Mr. L. Jewitt raced for the distinction of publishing the first " History of Plymouth." The latter was earlier in the field, but the former first emerged from the press. Mr. Llewellyn Jewitt's prospectus was openly circulated, and his book was going through the press, when, " much to my surprise another so-called History of Plymouth " was issued. Worth's was a cheaper publication, and seriously interfered with the sale of the other work, involving Mr. W. H. Luke, the proprietor, in considerable pecuniary loss. " On the total disregard of literary etiquette," wrote Mr. Llewellyn Jewitt in his preface, " it is not *Worth* my while to remark." The members of the Plymouth Institution, who had encouraged this production, expressed themselves with more force than temper. Mr. Llewellyn Jewitt's book, however, was little better than a hap-hazard compilation, and Mr. Worth atoned for the hurry which characterised the original edition of his own History by producing a few years later a volume of ample proportions, which was a monument of research and devotion to the task. An enthusiastic antiquarian, the author was one of the first authorities on scientific, artistic, and geological investigations in a circle that embraced gifted and patient students like Brooking Rowe, Baring-Gould, Spence-Bate and F. Brent. Henry Holman Drake (Red Dragon), a Devonport man, was directly descended from one of the leading Commissioners whose maiden sisters and aunts were accounted the only persons in the town who lived on their own means. Their property passed into the hands of the St. Aubyns, whose arms Dr. Drake quartered as a landless representative. As a descendant of the great circumnavigator, Dr. Drake vehemently contested Worth's argument that he was paid for bringing the water into Plymouth, and the controversy became so embittered that the former charged the latter with garbling quotations from the municipal archives in order to establish his argument. The Rev. Erskine Risk also published a pamphlet, "Drake Rehabilitated." In his masterly edition of "Hasted's History of Kent" Dr. Drake set himself the task of discovering how Sir Francis and his brethren became Kentishmen. Admiral Sir John Hawkins, of Deptford, was the cousin of John Trelawny and of Sir Francis Drake. It was militant Protestantism that took the Drake family into Kent and Sir Francis devised his estates to his younger brother Thomas, a Kentishman by birth.

The loftier heights of poetic fame were won by Robert Stephen Hawker, for many years Vicar of Morwenstow. He left a legacy of envenomed theological dispute, but achieved an undying reputation for literary work, whose merit is never likely to occasion controversy. Hawker was grandson of the famous Calvinistic Vicar of Charles. Born at Stoke in 1804, he became the direct antithesis in doctrine of his ancestor. Ready of wit, genial in disposition, ripe of scholarship, and manly of appearance, he made a host of friends at Oxford, and the Tractarian pioneers, who were revolutionising thought in that University, persuaded him to discard the gloomy ecclesiastical traditions of the family. Hawker soon attracted the attention of Dr. Phillpotts, and received the preferment of Morwenstow. He set over the door of the residence that he there erected the beautiful lines:

> A house, a glebe, a pound a day,
> A pleasant place to watch and pray;
> Be true to the Church, and kind to the poor,
> O Minister for evermore!

The church, according to Dr. Lee, was a dusty desolation and the churchyard a wilderness. "Dissenters, who called themselves Bryanites, were alone active in the parish," and "certain emasculated Wesleyans" divided what "little religious enthusiasm had managed to exist." Hawker determined to lead "the pagans and barbarians of the wild coasts of Cornwall to the fount of regeneration," and made little disguise of his stand-point when he shrunk "with horror from the false fame of that double-dyed thief of other men's brains—John Milton, the Puritan." Hawker had witnessed enough of black surplice to detest it utterly, and he walked along the iron-bound coasts, its downs and headlands, attired in a broad-brimmed hat of dark brown velvet, and a brown cassock with red buttons—a costume at once "canonical, becoming and picturesque." "Mine," he wrote, "was a perilous warfare. If I had not, like the Apostle, to fight with wild beasts at Ephesus, I had to soothe the wrecker, to persuade the smuggler, and to handle serpents in my intercourse with adversaries of many a kind." In his seaside home Hawker produced poems that elicited the admiration of Tennyson, and the ballad relating to the imprisonment of the Seven Bishops, which he first published anonymously in the Plymouth papers, was reproduced by Dickens in "Household Words" as a work of genuine antiquity:

THE SONG OF THE WESTERN MEN.

> A good sword and a trusty hand!
> A merry heart and true!
> King James's men shall understand
> What Cornish lads can do.
>
> And have they fixed the where and when?
> And shall Trelawny die?
> Here's twenty thousand Cornish men
> Will know the reason why!

Out spake their captain brave and bold,
  A merry wight was he ;
' If London Tower were Michael's hold,
  We'll set Trelawny free !

' We'll cross the Tamar land to land,
  The Severn is no stay,
With " one and all," and hand in hand,
  And who shall bid us nay ?

' And when we come to London Wall,
  A pleasant sight to view,
Come forth, come forth, ye cowards all,
  Here's men as good as you !

' Trelawny he's in keep and hold,
  Trelawny he may die ;
But here's twenty thousand Cornish bold
  Will know the reason why !'

Lord Macaulay and Sir Walter Scott welcomed and commented upon the poem in the same faith, and, after enjoying the *obiter dicta* of his contemporaries, Hawker put them to confusion by revealing the fact that he was the author, with the exception of the choral lines :

And shall Trelawny die ?
Here's twenty thousand Cornishmen
Will know the reason why.

A man of generous emotions, Hawker's heart bled with genuine sympathy for "the Sisters of Mercy at the Tamar Mouth," and he addressed to " Lydia, their Lady in the Faith whose heart the Lord opened," his pathetic picture of the spiritual " desolation " that reigned in contemporary Plymouth :

O city, where my birthplace stands,
How art thou fallen amid the lands !
Thy daughters bold, thy sons unblest,
A wither'd Salem of the West !
Hark ! from yon hill, what tones arise,
Thy peace is hidden from thine eyes !

Daughter ! my spirit turns to thee :
Here by the lonely Severn sea,
I too have borne, years fierce and long,
All hatred and rebuke and wrong ;
And now thy truth shall soothe the sigh—
The life I live—the death I die.

It was the passing of the Public Worship Act that determined Hawker to sever himself from " a Church which had neither authority nor doctrine," and which had " made Dr. Temple a Bishop." His second wife afterwards suggested that for " thirty years at least my dear husband has been at heart a Roman Catholic. No one converted him, as no human being influenced him in the slightest degree. He quietly read himself into his convictions, embraced all the tenets of the Roman Catholic faith, and his heart yearned for communion with it." Holy Unction was administered by Canon Mansfield as he lay upon his death-bed at Plymouth, and his avowed wish to pass a night in the Cathedral was consulted, for his coffin rested there on the eve of interment. The change, which came as a shock, if not as a surprise to Tractarian friends, excited a tumult of passion in Evangelical centres. Yet, with lapse of years, Robert Stephen Hawker will be increasingly reverenced by the tolerant for his imperishable lyrics, his quaint humour, and his hereditary sympathy for the poor.

Another poet of Plymouth birth --Austin Dobson—although not of Plymouth lineage, richly flavoured his stirring compositions with the historic brine of the port. Charming hymns, breathing the spirit of hope, emanated from the mellowed pen of the Rev. George Prynne, and passed into standard collections. Ernest William Radford also wrote many dainty poems, and his brother, George Radford, evinced in mellifluous verse a similar devotion to Nature and appreciation of her methods. Other local authors did admirable work. A Plymouth lad, descendant of one of its honoured families, and educated at its Grammar School, became the first specialist in the industrial arts of India. Sir George Birdwood mastered the literature of the world, and it was his duty to diffuse a general knowledge of the native trade products of our Eastern Empire. His appointment at the India Office he laughingly described as "An Idle Fellowship for the Endowment of Irrelevant Research," but the benefits he conferred on the Hindoos by developing their commerce were so conspicuous that there was no name more honoured by the Queen's dusky subjects. To the literature of Dartmoor Mr. William Crossing freely contributed. Mr. J. Hine treasured the characteristics of many old buildings of Plymouth, and Mr. W. H. K. Wright pursued local research with the same unsatisfied and unselfish spirit.

What Carrington was in poetry, Samuel Rowe was in prose—the worshipper of Dartmoor, its moods, its mysteries, its wastes, its weird antiquities. A bookseller at the outset of his career, Rowe abandoned business to enter the Church, for which his culture and reverential spirit especially adapted him. He first indicated how the moor had taken possession of his imaginative soul by reading a charming essay before the Plymouth Institution, and his diction was so chaste and artistic that he was urged by sympathetic and learned colleagues to continue in his delightful and absorbing speculations. Rowe also wrote of the scenery of Dartmoor with a majesty of phrase and felicity of illustration that indicated the master hand. "Nature is the engineer that fortified these heights thousands of years ago, hers are the massive walls, hers the mighty bastions, hers the granite glacis, scarped down to the roaring torrent below, hers the hand that raised those stupendous citadels which fables might have garrisoned with demigods and beleagured with Titans; whilst, in the recumbent mass that guards the approach (Vixen Tor), imagination, with scarcely an effort, might design an archetype of the mystic Sphynx in kindred porphyry, of proportions more colossal, and of date more ancient than that which still looks forth in serene and lovely grandeur over the sands of the Memphian desert." With the instinctive jealousy of a devoted antiquarian, Rowe saw that the hand of the spoiler would one day be laid on the verdure that he loved, and he raised his first protest against the desecration and destruction of the vast expanse when it was proposed to reclaim a part of it for agricultural and manufacturing purposes: "If Dartmoor," he pleaded, "could be ploughed to its very crest, and a scanty and precarious crop raised from corn patches two thousand feet above sea level, who will venture to affirm that there would be no counter balance to the dearly-bought benefit? How much of health is now wafted from the mountain's brow over the circumjacent towns and villages." The piecemeal confiscation of Commons' land that Samuel Rowe foresaw led to the establishment of the Dartmoor Preservation Society and to a revival of interest that was responsible for valuable contributions to the literature of the subject by J. Brooking Rowe,

VIXEN TOR, DARTMOOR.

(From a photo. by Heath.)

(By permission of Mr. J. H. KEYS.)

Baring-Gould, Robert Burnard, and R. Hansford Worth. These authorities engaged in periodical conferences amid the tors, and individual and collective discoveries were made. Mr. Brooking Rowe's amplification and commentary on Samuel Rowe's " Perambulations " was really a masterpiece of disinterested application. He touched with reverential hand his ancestor's picturesque theories, toning them only when they were demonstrably open to doubt, and then in the spirit of one who declined to dogmatise. In a field of pre-historic knowledge which was too wide to justify iconoclastic interference with pretty conceits and roaming fancies, Brooking Rowe, despite the powerful scepticism of other students, preferred to remain in the faith that only the fringe of enquiry had been reached, and that even the disputed Druid ministered within the hut circles with which "the wild and wondrous region " of the moor abounded.

Mr. Burnard, in his "Dartmoor Pictorial Records," assisted to unseal many of the mysteries of the hut circles, the smelting furnaces, the kistvaens and the cairns, and to throw light on hitherto unsuspected archæological treasure-trove. Whilst he did not permit the passion for the antique to escape him, Mr. Burnard, no less than Samuel Rowe, revelled in the sweet superstitions and seductive legends of the moor. In one of his volumes he recalled the story of Elford's flight from Cromwell's forces and his resort to the Pixies' Cave at Sheepstor. The adventurous tourists who climb the clitter of boulders that furnish the access to this gloomy retreat will look in vain for traces of those paintings on the walls with which it is said that the refugee passed the heavy hours of his concealment. Affection for the moor was also sustained by the Plymouth Pedestrian Club, of which Mr. Kinton Bond was the first president. The initial condition of member-ship was the traditional walk to Cranmere Pool.

Education owed much to John Bidlake, who was himself instructed in the Grammar School of which he became master, and who helped to mould many inspiring careers. During his generation the most respectable lads were slovenly in habits, indifferent in dress, and inattentive to cleanliness. They held everything in contempt with the exception of their sports, and those who refrained from rough recreations were despised as milk-sops. It was a crime to use a sponge to clean a slate, and corduroy trousers always indicated at the knees a familiarity with the gravel of the playground. From Bidlake to Jago was a far-cry. The latter accomplished great work in the cause of voluntary education at the Public School in Cobourg Street, and his career found its real memorial in successes achieved and distinctions gained by old boys in all parts of the world. The honour attained by Mr. Henry Duke, Q.C., in winning a proud position at the Western Bar and the Recorder-ship of Plymouth, was a tribute to Mr. Webb's tuition in George Street. Mr. E. Brown and Mr. T. Nicholson worked with unceasing assiduity in the interest of the poor, and organised the means by which the Ragged Schools in Catte Street were maintained until the Education Act was passed. At the outset of the operations of the School Board in Plymouth the majority adopted the Conscience Clause, and Mr. R. C. Serpell thereupon resigned the chairmanship. A test election to fill the vacancy resulted in the return of Mr. Samuel Eliot, one of the few who refused to pay the School Board-rate on the ground that it was partly devoted to denominational education. Subsequently Professor Anthony held the chairmanship for many years, and the conduct of affairs was mainly in the hands of Nonconformists. Professor Anthony contributed towards the cause of Higher Educa-tion in Plymouth and Dr. May in Devonport. Major Chard was a pupil of the Rev. William Bennett M.A. at the Plymouth Grammar School, and Major Scott-Turner, who fell gallantly fighting in a sortie from Kimberley in December, 1899, was educated in the same institution by Mr. John Bennett, M.A. Under the long-continued regime of Mr. J. Kinton Bond, M.A., the establishment maintained its historic reputation.

The erection of the Plymouth College at Ford Park, with Mr. F. H. Colson, M.A., as the head-master, and of the High School for Girls at North Hill were further evidences of educational development of the first order.   The Western College was the outcome of the Congregational activity which was displayed in 1845, and, in 1860, increasing prosperity led to its permanent establishment in the locality and the erection of an imposing building at Mutley.   Professor Charlton was appointed president of the College, and Professor Anthony officiated as his colleague.   The dedication in 1861 was memorable for the readiness with which those present cleared the entire debt before the close of the opening day's proceedings.   Education owed much to the efforts of the local Freemasons, and the success of Mr. F. B. Westlake in raising splendid sums for this purpose was rewarded in 1899 by his appointment as Past-Deputy Grand Director of Ceremonies in the Grand Lodge of England, and as the London representative for Devonshire on the Great Masonic Charities.   Mr. Westlake was also one of the pillars of the Plymouth Club, social institution originally formed by Mr. William Harvey, Mr. John Pethick, and the brothers Densham, who went to London and founded the Mazawattee Tea Company.

Towards the better education and general culture of the skilled artisan class the original Plymouth Mechanics' Institute appreciably contributed.   It was raised in 1827 "at the expense of a Society of Mechanics," assisted by a liberal donation from Mr. Charles Greaves, and the foundation stone was laid by Mr. Edmund Lockyer, the president.   In 1850 the old building was nearly demolished, and the re-opening incidents were witnessed by a few survivors of the original ceremony.   The south front of the building by Foulston, was retained, and the extensions were directed by Messrs. Wightwick and Damant, of whom the former was president for the year.   Membership rapidly increased from 270 to 750, and the Institute fulfilled its mission until 1899, when the committee reluctantly confessed that it had outlived its programme.   The trustees transferred their library, together with a surplus of £2,000, to the Athenæum, and special reading accommodation was added to the Institution, which, at that time, was in a somewhat languishing state itself.   Devonport Mechanics' Institute was constituted on similar lines.   It owed its inception to the advocacy of Mr. Towson, but succumbed, a few years before its con temporary, to the competition of free libraries and cheap musical evenings.   The Old Townhall in Whimple Street was converted into a Free Library in the Mayoralty of Mr. R. C. Serpell, and the Devonport Mechanics' Institute was purchased by the Corporation to meet a similar demand for free literature.

Research received an important impetus when the Marine Biological Association built their laboratory at Plymouth.   The object was to increase accurate knowledge concerning the life conditions and habits of British food fishes and molluscs.   As the fauna and flora of Plymouth were representative, the association readily accepted the site under the Citadel which was offered by the War Department for the purpose of their aquarium, and direct salt-water communication with Cattewater was mechanically maintained.   The laboratory was opened by Professor Flower in 1888, and the ceremony was attended by Sir James Clarke Lawrence, Prime Warden of the Fishmongers' Company, by whom a distinguished party of scientists was entertained in honour of the event.   At this pierod there were 80 trawlers, averaging 43 tons, engaged in fishing at Plymouth, and many of these were owned by their own skippers.   There were a few larger boats, but the impression prevailed that the smaller sized trawls were preferable, as they were less susceptible to changes of wind, and were therefore in more regular occupation.   In favourable weather the process of hauling in the trawl occupied about an hour, and three tons of fish was no uncommon result of a single operation.   Experience proved that night was the best time for securing soles, and that the round fish rose in time for morning catches.   The effect of

SHEEPSTOR AND SHEEPSTOR CHURCH.

(From a photo. by Heath.)

(By permission of Mr. J. H. Keys.)

Of the breeding habits of fish along the Plymouth coast little was known, save that Whitsand Bay was full of small young flatfish from June to October, and was apparently a nursery for them. The mackerel fishery varied in time and supply, and was invariably productive, but the harvest of herrings showed symptoms of declension. The pilchard was uncertain in habit and uncertain as to yield. Early in the 19th century several mill-ponds that communicated with Hamoaze by means of gates were used as mulletries. The fish entered the ponds with the tide, the gates were closed, and the hauls were landed by means of seines. "The Mulletry" at Weston Mill Lake was cut off from the tide except by a sluice, and in recent years it was used for storing mullet. These were caught in Hamoaze with a seine and deposited in the pond until required for market. Start Point was the favourite haunt for crabs and lobsters, but pots were also laid in the deep water outside the Breakwater. Oyster beds long existed in Cattewater, opposite Queen Anne's Battery, but they were desolated by excessive dredging.

Movements for paying tardy tribute to the more historical worthies resulted in an unwonted diffusion of historical literature. John Colbourne, Field Marshal Seaton, one of the Devonshire heroes who fought at Waterloo, was memorialised by a statue executed by Mr. G. G. Adams, of London. There were strongly expressed objections to the proposal to put it upon Plymouth Hoe, and, as "it was difficult to find a spot suitable to its display without diminishing its proportions by contrast," Mount Wise was selected as the site. The work was unveiled in the presence of the massed troops in November, 1886. The Tercentenary of Sir Francis Drake was celebrated by a similar movement, and the advocacy of Mr. C. F. Burnard, as chairman of the Plymouth committee, was unremitting. There was not much enthusiasm evinced on the part of the public; and, as the subscriptions fell short of early promise, Mr. Burnard prevailed upon the Duke of Bedford to grant the committee a replica of Boehm's original statue, set up outside the Fitzford Gate at Tavistock. This was unveiled in 1884, and Mr. Burnard's services were recognised by a public

THE DRAKE STATUE, BY BOEHM.

(By permission of Mr. JOHN SMITH.)

banquet. Unsatisfied with this record of the hero's lifework, Mr. W. H. K. Wright advocated a National Commemoration of the Tercentenary of the Defeat of the Spanish Armada, and he travelled with Mr. Burnard from town to town to awaken public interest. It was hard work, but the funds were forthcoming, and the design of Herbert Gribble, the Plymothian who planned the Brompton Oratory, was accepted. The memorial was unveiled by the Duke of Edinburgh amid picturesque military and social surroundings, and the Prince and his suite were entertained at a banquet by Mr. J. T. Bond, the Mayor. When the Smeaton Lighthouse was doomed by the Brethren of Trinity House —in consequence of the decay of the ledge of rock on which it was reared—Mr. F. J. Webb suggested that the famous beacon should be re-erected upon the Hoe on the original lines. The consent of the authorities concerned having been obtained to the removal of the tower itself, Mr. John Pethick completed the practicability of the proposal by supplying the granite with which it was necessary to substitute the basement that it was impossible to wrench from the reef. The memorial stone of the new lighthouse was laid by the Prince of Wales, who was then on a visit to the port, and Sir James Douglas raised, by the side of the stump on the Eddystone, an edifice more commodious and lofty than Smeaton devised. The new lighthouse was solemnly dedicated in the presence of the Duke of Edinburgh in 1882, and the Smeaton Tower was opened by the Deputy-Master of Trinity House, at the request of the then Mayor, Mr. Greenway. Charming accessories of martial music and prismatic groupings were not wanting to render the spectacle memorable.

Queen Victoria's Jubilee year was the more heartily welcomed in 1887 as the opportunity for projecting the Plymouth Technical Schools in Tavistock Road. Mr. H. J. Snell furnished the plans, the memorial stone was laid by Sir Henry Waring, in the third year of his Mayoralty, and the institution was opened by Mr. John Shelly, then chief magistrate. The Diamond Jubilee celebrations were similarly seized as opportune for proposing the institution of a Museum and Art Gallery for Plymouth. Mr. C. Radford, the Mayor, launched the suggestion, and the site of the Old Town Mills was granted for the purpose by the municipality. As Beaumont Park had been just acquired for a public recreation ground, the mansion of the Bewes family forthwith became the depository of a promising collection. In 1899 Beaumont Museum was thrown open on Sundays, not without protest from the Rev. Samuel Vincent and others, so that the working classes might view the pictures and curiosities. On the Diamond Jubilee day, the foundation stone of the Devonport Technical Schools, a handsome building, also from the design of Mr. H. J. Snell, was laid by Mr. W. Waycott, the Mayor. A fine peal of bells was placed in the tower at the expense of Alderman James, and a stained glass window by Fouracre, representative of art and science, and the development of maritime architecture within the career of Sir William White, the Keyham student who became Chief Constructor of the Navy, was fixed in the hall as the contribution of Mr. Hornbrook, during whose Mayoralty, in 1899, the building was formally opened. A pleasant reminiscence of the Diamond Jubilee Celebration at Devonport was the almost phenomenal activity then exhibited by Alderman John Ryder. He was elected as a member of the Corporation in the first year of Queen Victoria's Accession, when the borough was granted its charter, and continued to sit uninterruptedly either as Councillor or Alderman, and nine times as Mayor, during the development of Her Majesty's illustrious reign. Mr. Ryder was serving in a representative capacity at the age of 90 whilst the Queen was yet seated on the throne—an experience probably unique in the national experience, and not the least agreeable in the history of the Three Towns.

APPENDIX.

Topographical Significations, Street Nomenclature, &c.

[In response to a general wish, an attempt has been here made to identify and delineate in alphabetical order topographical significations, and to trace the nomenclature of the old streets of the Three Towns and District. The author does not profess to have exhausted the subject, and the explanations are given as collated from a variety of sources. Many notes not easily introduced into the ordinary text are here included with a view of rendering the work as complete as possible.]

Abbey in Winchelsea Street: "This inn is called the Mitre, from its being of a Papistical foundation, once a very respectable tavern; but now (1810) ye whole of ye building is lett out to as many persons as there are rooms. It extends from the front back into Seven Stars Lane." (Harris.) Mr. Hellyer, the then owner, sold the property to the Rev. Thomas Madge, son of Mr. Matthew Madge, cabinet-maker, of Broad Street, and £1,900 was obtained for it on re-disposal.

Albemarle Villas (Devonport): After the D'Albemarles, formerly the site of the "Cake Houses"—the only dwellings between Dock and Stoke Church.

Amphitheatre: Formerly in Clowance Street, Devonport, a "pitch" for circuses, &c.

Arch Street, Frankfort Street, Plymouth: Opposite to the "Mercury" office, built 1793-1812.

Arthur's Place: In Notte Street.

Back of Morice Square or Ordnance Street Area (Devonport): The area known as the Ordnance Street Area was bounded on the Northern and Western sides by the Gun Wharf; on the Eastern side by Morice Square, and the Southern side by Ordnance Street. The area was intersected by Ordnance Row and Ordnance Court, by which access was gained to dwelling houses and stores.

Barbican: The Little House on the Round Barbican, built in 1528. Called the Governor's House (1809). The Barbican Stairs, built 1584. The conduit, built by the Barbican, 1602. Barbican was rebuilt 1678, after being partly washed away in 1672. The Barbican House and Gateway was taken away in 1830. The Old Fish House served as a Breakwater for Sutton Pool, and occupied two-thirds of the site of the western pier, and the other third was the tidal way nearest the old Barbican, where vessels of large burden could enter. It was washed down in a dreadful storm in 1703. A small house, "old, neatly paved and kept very clean," was on the Round Barbican—"and this was the place to hear the news of the day, and much resorted to some years ago." (Harris, 1810.)

Barley House Estate: Site of King Street Chapel, Plymouth, adjoining the Barley Sheaf and bounded by a low hedge.

I

Barrack Street : Russell Street.

Bilbury Lane : An original locality for bilberries or whortleberries.   Billabiri Street, 1342 ;
      Byllebury Street, 1440.   Lower Broad Street.   Now lower part of Treville
      Street.

Billet Lane : Now White Lane.

Blackfriars Lane : Temporarily altered to Pelter's Lane.

Bloody Field : Site of Plymouth Market.

Bloody Roma's Cave : Said to exist under the Eastern Hoe, of which weird tales were told.

Boon's Place : Henry Boon, Mayor, 1414.   Boon, builder, 1825.

Bowling Green House (Plymouth) : Supposed to have been situate on the outskirts of the
      town towards Tavistock.   (Early 19th century.)
            "A letter addressed by John Chamberlain, to Sir Dudley Carletown (afterwards
            Viscount Dorchester), at the Embassy in Paris, dated June 27, 1602,
            contains the following passage : " Our fleet comes away to convoy home
            the carraque they have taken within the mouth of the river of Lisbone
            . . . Fulke Grivell is gon down post to Plimmouth, and so to the sea, to
            meet her and kepe her from comming into that pilfering town (as they
            terme it), but to bringe her alonge to Portsmouthe."

Brickfields : Site of clay pits and bricks manufactured.   Upper part known as Brickfields
      and lower as Parsonage Fields—now all Brickfields.

Briton Side : Breton Side, scene of the French devastations—abandoned in favour of
      Exeter Street when the new road was opened for traffic.   Breton Side was
      revived a few years ago.   Subsequently altered back and still retained.

Broad-Hoe Lane : Hoegate Street with the widening and to commemorate the Hoe-Gate.
      Hoe Lane, 1765 ; Broad Hoe Lane, 1778-1812 ; Hoe Gate Street, 1883.

Buckwell Street : Notorious as a place where the women bucked—or washed their clothes
      in the water that came from the well.   Otherwise Higher Broad Street.

Bull Hill (top of High Street, adjacent to Free Library) : Scene of burning the Pope's
      Bull.   Otherwise Market Street and scene of bull-baits.

Bull Ring (under the Hoe—opposite to Pier entrance) : Scene of the bull-baits.

"Burton Boys " : The residence of the Burton Boys was from Martin's Gate eastwards.
      Now (1809) from St. Martin's Gate eastward still bears the name of Briton Side.
      (Harris.)   In 1604 Walter Matthews, " the Maior, buylded a newe conditt by
      the great tree at Brittayne side at his own cost and charges."

Butcher's Lane : Treville Street.   At the bottom was the Butchers' Arms, a great resort for
      farmers of inordinate drinking capacity.

Cambers Court : Lambhay Street.

Castle Dyke Lane : Contiguous to the old Castle, of which one gateway now survives.
      There appears to be no mention of the Castle after the erection of the Citadel
      until 1804, when only one tower remained—30 feet in diameter—and this so
      decomposed that it was pulled down for safety.   The quadrangular space was
      used as a garden.

Castle Rag, alias Damnation Alley, alias Silver Street—the last named representing an
      unsuccessful attempt to disguise its tattered morality.

Catch-French Lane: The point where the French incursions were arrested. (?) French Lane, 1812.

Catdown (Cattedown): A pamphlet purporting to give the life and adventures of Captain John Avery, a Plymouth pirate, was printed and sold by J. Baker, at the Black Boy, in Paternoster Row, in 1709, gives this reference to Catdown:

> "His father is described as a mariner residing "at a place call'd Cat-Down, a sort of an eminence overlooking an Arm of the Sea, which, by various Mœanders and Windings, runs several miles into the Country, and takes its Name from a Mountain or Down, which at once swells above, and defends it from the Insults of tempestuous Weather."

Catherine Street: The approach to the fair chapel of St. Catherine on the Hoe (1); in honour of the visit of Catherine of Aragon (2).

Catte Street: After the "Catte of Hingstone." As the temporary home of Cat-herine of Aragon—a suggestion by the wags. Cat Street, 1765. Subsequently Stillman Street.

PLYMOUTH CASTLE.—Remains of Entrance, now used as a Dwelling (1899).

Catwater : The "chateau" at the mouth of the Plym. (Brewer). "Chat" (cat), "eau" (water). "The Cattegatt to Henstone" (1440).

"The Chapel" Wine and Spirit stores : Devonport (corner of George Street and Ker Street). Originally the Unitarian Chapel. "This quaint old building, situate at the corner of Duke and George Streets, Devonport, was originally built for the Unitarians in the year A.D. 1790, and was opened as a place for worship 1791. The congregation of the chapel decayed in consequence of its being understood that Commissioner Fanshawe intimated that all dockyardsmen who attended the new chapel would be discharged as disloyal subjects. The French Revolution was then in full operation, and the Unitarians were the most ardent admirers of that movement in Great Britain. Three of that sect were executed as ring-leaders in a most disgraceful riot in Birmingham, on the 14th July, 1791. Ten years afterwards, in 1801, the chapel was converted, the conversion being so wide apart from its original purpose as could be imagined. The chapel became a Temple of Bacchus, dedicated to the sale of wines and spirits. Thus the change from the Spiritual to the spirituous. The old building still retains remnants of its ecclesiastical character, and a chaplain is still attached, who performs certain duties with zeal and punctuality."

Chapel Lane (Plymouth) : Now Chapel Street.

Charles Church : King Charles's Church (Baron) ; Charles the Martyr (unauthorised) ; New Church.

Cherry Garden Street (Devonport) : Formerly Back Street, now York Street (altered to meet the objections of sailors who did not care to let their comrades know that their wives resided in the locality).

Church Alley : Entered from Whimple Street.

Church Hill : Churcherhull (Domesday). Site of St. Andrew's Church.

Citadel Terrace : Hoe Place.

Clowance Street (Devonport) : After the St. Aubyn family estate.

Cock and Bottle Lane : Altered to Good Street, 1778, and then Holy-Cross Lane, 1883.

Colmer's Lane : So called after Abraham Colmer ; altered to Canterbury Street.

Commercial Hotel : Old Town Street. "Capital family and travellers' house (1824)." Site of Chubb's Hotel.

Compton : The old Contone, manor held by Judhel in succession to the Saxons Godwin and Alwin.

Copperhouse Lane : Leading to Copperhouse fields (Regent Street).

Coxside : Existence of cockle-shells in abundance. Here Cockside Prison.

Coxside Nunnery (Plymouth) : Early in the seventeenth century Mrs. Mary Ward entered a French convent of Poor Clares at St. Omer, and she very soon became anxious to establish a house of English Poor Clares. Her zeal, however, was not rewarded until some time after, when, hearing that some land had recently been devised for religious purposes, she succeeded in obtaining it—the Bishop of St. Omer, the Abbot of St. Bertins, and the Austrian Archduke giving the requisite authorities. With the help of the Rev. John Genning, a Monk of the Franciscan Recollects, and with the approbation of the Pope, who in a brief directed the Bishop to afford every assistance to those who had the project in view, the Monastery was founded at Gravelines. Mary Gough was chosen the Superior, and on the 14th September, 1609, the new house was taken possession of by the Superior, and two other professed nuns, and two lay sisters. The community prospered, and two years later it was necessary to enlarge the convent, and in 1624 there were sixty-five ladies in the house who by their labours of charity had won the love and gratitude of all in their neighbourhood. All went on happily until the Revolution. In October, 1793, the convent was surrounded by soldiers, and the property of the inhabitants seized. At this time there were only thirty-five nuns in the house. Shortly after, the sisters from Dunkirk were brought prisoners to Gravelines, and there were then seventy-seven ladies shut up with the Poor Clares. A few days after the Commissioners arrived—it reads like what happened in England in the time of Henry VIII. and Thomas Cromwell —who, having securing the sacred vessels, vestments, and ornaments—this is always the first thing to be done in dealing with anybody or anything connected with religion—tore down and obliterated all pictures and tokens of piety, or royalty, or nobility, inside and out, and shut and locked up the church and sacristy, to prevent any religious services being performed there longer. For eighteen months the nuns of Gravelines and Dunkirk suffered together; but little food was allowed them, and no fuel, and the rigours of a severe winter compelled the poor prisoners to use not only such wood as they could obtain by cutting down the trees in the garden, but also the doors and wainscotting of the house. At length they were told they were free, and they immediately applied for passports for England, and reached London 3rd May, 1795. At first they settled at Gosfield, in Essex, but soon came to Plymouth, some time in 1796, where they remained until 1836 or thereabouts, when they removed, and were amalgamated with the community at Clare Lodge, Catterick, Yorkshire.— *J. Brooking Rowe.*

The whole of the Nunnery building was in existence prior to the erection of the present factory (1891), and remained standing for several years after the older portion of the factory was built. The house and beautiful garden was occupied by our family for some years, and I can well remember as a child the four magnificent elm trees and an unusually large pink thorn (quite 40 feet across) under whose spreading branches the mounds over the graves of several nuns could be seen. The house ceased to be a residence in 1859. A portion of it was then removed, and that part of the site, as well as the garden, built over, including the apartment used as a chapel. The remaining part (about half) is still in existence, and is now used as offices. Its first use as a private residence, as I know, was by a Mr. Shepherd, who carried on the business of a tanner, on a portion of the site occupied by the present factory, and whose celebrated dream connected with the Assizes, then held at Launceston, made some stir at the time. The next tenants were the nuns of the order of St. Clare, who gave the place the name of "Clare House." I am unable to find the date of their arrival, but I believe they originally came from France. They were, I fancy, rather a needy Sisterhood, not very numerous (probably about ten or twelve), and a large proportion of them French. My late mother when very young visited them once or twice, introduced by their confessor, the Abbé de la Greselle, who was her French master at the time. Lady visitors were permitted in this way to see the Sisters and so present them with little delicacies, not included in the Convent fare. The nuns expressed themselves as very contented and happy, but this feeling was evidently not universal, for my mother used to relate that a carpenter

who was employed by some of her family was passing along Sutton Road early
one morning on his way to work and witnessed the elopement of one of the
ladies. His attention was attracted by a figure, closely wrapped in a cloak,
running along on the top of the garden wall, which then extended to the southern
end of Shepherd's Lane. Here a gentleman met her with a carriage, into which
they stepped and drove off at a rapid pace. The Lady Superior was "Mother
Jubilarian." She was a "merry, chatty old lady." The Sisterhood left
Plymouth, I think, soon after 1820 and went to live at Gravelines, in France,
believing that they could sustain themselves more cheaply there than in England.
The occupant who succeeded the nuns and preceded our family was Sir William
Parker, whose family is connected by marriage with one or more of the leading
Plymouth descents.—*W. Collier James, Plymouth, 1891.*

Cremyll Point (now Devil's Point): Cremhill Point, Crem-ble-ill (Carew-Crymell); the hill
(aill Gaellic) of Crom Beal; sharp-edged (crimp) hill (Bannister).

The Cribs (Devonport): The site on which Willis Street, Northbrook Street, Corry Street
and part of Duncan Street (then James's Street Ope) now stand. The district
was known as The Cribs' or Doidge's Well. It consisted of a number of alleys
and courts such as Braggs' Alley, Francis Alley, and Trafalgar Court. It was
reconstructed from James Street to Dockwall Street (now Edinburgh Road) in
1878. Site opposite the Devonport Municipal Dwellings, James Street.

Crosse Downe (1561): Site of land adjoining present Plymouth Workhouse.

Deadlake: Dedlake, the old Stoke Damerel flete. Filled in and converted into Victoria
Park, 1870-1899.

Denham's Lane: Frier's Lane, 1765; Denham's Lane, 1778; Friar's Lane, 1883.

Denham's Stairs: In 1753. Two rows of trees, planted by the King's Engineer, from
the top of Little Hoe Lane, to the end of the walk on the Hoe; and a single
row, from the same place, to Denham's Stairs. (Baron.)

Devonport Gas Company's Works: Keyham; first established in 1845.

Devonport: Defennport (Devon-port), the name given by the Danes who entered the
Sound, A.D. 924.

Hewn out of a Rock
Our matchless Naval Arsenal and Dock:
Without whose Walls, first Christened of the same,
The only Town in England of that Name;
Until, without a Sirname to acknowledge,
She sought another from the Heralds' College:
And this she did by way of a Refresher,
Letters mis-sent to Davenport in Cheshire.
On Thursday's New Year, Eighteen twenty four, 't
Was "Glory be to Plymouth Devon Port!"
As 'twas in the Beginning; on a Rock,
Is now, and ever shall be: Plymouth Dock.*—*Baron.*

*An Old Boniface, at the corner of Pembroke Street, refused to newly-christen
his measures, on the score that he got all his money by Dock, and was likely
to lose it by Devon Port.

Devil's Point : After Duval, a French Hugenot, who settled there. Popularly the point where the Devil touched when he jumped across from Cornwall. Formerly Cremyll Point.

> These Towns Three,
> And many other Suburbs you may see,
> Have sprung like Scions, from the Parent Tree.
> Its length and breadth, with little to disjoint,
> To Monsieur Duval's, called "The Devil's Point."—*Baron.*

Dirty Alley : Altered to Peacock Lane.

Dock Theatre : Site of Cumberland Gardens, Devonport.

Doidge's Well (Devonport) : On the farm belonging to Mr. Doidge.

Drake's Place Monument : "Sir Francis Drake first brought the water into Plymouth in 1591. This conduit was new built in the Maioralty of William Cotton, merchant, 1671." The stone carvings were part of the old public conduit erected from the head of Old Town Street in 1834, William Hole Evens, Mayor. The wall and carvings were re-erected in the second Mayoralty of Alfred Rooker in 1874, James King, Chairman of the Water Committee. The trough was part of one of the channels by which the water was distributed through the town. The south reservoir was made in the third Mayoralty of Edmund Lockyer, 1825 ; and the north reservoir during the Mayoralty of Richard Pridham, 1828.

Drake's Street : Built 1812.

Duck Hunting Pond : Near Tothill House, formerly the residence of the Colombs. Said to be bottomless. An extensive rookery was contiguous.

Duck's Lane, 1765 ; altered to Week's Street 1778.

Dung Quay Lane : Near Briton Side, tipping station for refuse.

Eales's Market Place : Site of Plymouth Market, 1807. "As fine a market as any in or out of the metropolis" :

> A Tuesday's Child is full of Grace ;
>   A Tuesday's Mayor is full of Grease :
> Hereafter Eales's Market Place
>   And Kethrick's Pie shall never cease.
>
> The inexhaustible Supply
> Of Eales's Market Place, the Pie
> Of Kethrick's Feast, shall ne'er go by ;
> For Poets' Verses never die.—*Baron.*

East Cross Street : Old street intersecting Looe Street.

East Gate at Cockside : Built 1589. Removed.

Eddystone : Ed (again) and Ea water (Anglo-Saxon), Edystone (Smeaton), Edestone or Iddistone.

Fine Well : In Finewell Street, in the middle of a garden belonging to the Abbey (Harris), Fownes-well (Wright).

Fisher's Nose : Fyshe Tor, the present Lambhay Point.

Fish Cage : Whimple Street, Plymouth, and site of Guard House.

Five Field Lane and Four Field Lane : Now North Road.

Fountain Inn, Fore Street, Devonport: A letter written by Collingwood, in 1801, is of
    interest:
        "It gave me much concern, to hear an opinion expressed by some that our
          friend, Lord Nelson, had not borne his elevation with the temperance of a
          wise man. But surely more was said about it than the matter warranted.
          He was at Plymouth when I was there, a fortnight since, and I could not
          observe the slightest difference in his manner. . . . How surprised you
          would have been to have dropped into the "Fountain Inn," and seen Lord
          Nelson, my wife, and myself, sitting over the fireside *cozing*, and little Sarah
          teaching Phyllis, her dog, to dance."

Foxhole Street: Vauxhall Street.

Foynes Lane: So called after the Fownses. Altered to Woolster Street.

Frank Ford Square: Russell Street (site of Mare's Foundry and Frankfort Square
    Barracks).

Frankfort Gate, or West Gate: Removed 1783. Frankfort Row, 1812.

Freedom Fields: Site of Freedom Park (scene of Sabbath Day Fight).
    At three o'Clock in the Afternoon of Freedom Eve the Freedom Boys used to
    assemble for the purpose of "Knocking Down the Glove" set up over the
    Guildhall door, having been allowed a little latitude during the remainder
    of that, and the entire of the following, day:

        In days of yore, had Freedom Boys French Leave
        Of "Knocking Down the Glove" of Freedom Eve;
        And pilfered Tradesmen used, thereon, to say
        That Freedom Eve itself was Freedom Day.

    After partaking of an illigant Breakfast on Freedom Day, at the Royal Hotel, or
    Mayor Elect's House, the Corporation and Freedom Boys, with Ducking
    Horns, &c., escort the Mayor Elect on Horseback, round the bounds of the
    Borough, and to Freedom Field. Returning, and dismounting on the
    Parade, they proceed to take the Freedom Boys out of the boat, at the
    Barbican and Fisher's Nose, giving each a lick in the Head, by way of a
    Remembrancer, and a little Silver Ointment to cure it:

        In this respect, we are not speaking fables;
        Many a Mayor Elect has turned the tables:
        So boxed and cured his ear that no one pities un,
        Remember this and be a sober Citizen!—*Baron.*

French Church (Stonehouse): A letter from Pentecost Barker in May, 1762, of Plymouth,
    to the Rev. Samuel Merivale, of Tavistock, contains some interesting allusions:
        "The French Parson seems to be decaying. Should he die, as he must some
          time or other, I take it *that* church will be void, as most of the *now* French
          were born here or at Stonehouse. Those, of whom I remember many
          scores, who came from France in 1685-6, &c., are mostly dead; and their
          offspring are more English than French, and will go to the English Church,
          though some few may come to us. What an alteration Time makes! There
          was (when I was such another as Mr. John ——) a French Calvinist
          Church, and a Church of England French Church here, besides a Church
          at Stonehouse. Many women in wooden shoes—very poor, but very
          industrious—living on limpets, snails, garlick and mushrooms. I'll make

you laugh. A Gentleman employed a gardener to pick snails from the walls, and then, coming into the garden behind his back, heard him, in killing the snails, say '—— take the French ! When they came here first, they would not suffer a snail to live ; but they are now grown so proud, that we are overrun with them.' When I went to Rochelle, in the year 1713, I brought over several pair of *sabots de bois* (so they call them) for some at Stonehouse. But they are all dead and gone."

(From a note in the handwriting of J. H. Merivale.)

" The Will [of Pentecost Barker], which was proved at Doctors' Commons, Oct. 20, 1762, and bears date 17th Nov., 1758, commences in the following characteristic strain. 'I resign and commend my Soul or Mind to the Eternal Mind, the Great God, the Fountain of Light, Life, and Love, hoping for every good thing in an after state from the inconceivable Benignity or infinite Goodness of the Divine Nature, as divulged in the Gospel of Jesus Christ.' He then directs his body to be buried in the Upper Churchyard of St. Andrew's, Plymouth, and eight poor inhabitants to carry him to the grave, and wishes his funeral to be performed ' in as public a manner as possible.' He gives all his estates in Devon, Cornwall, Kent, or elsewhere, together with all the residue of his personal property, to Tristram Avent, of Plymouth, William Phelp, of St. Kew, and Abraham Brown, of Endallion, Gentleman, &c., whom he also appoints his Executors, on trust to pay the rents, interest, &c., ' to his dear Wife Jane Barker, or as by some called Jane Mills, during her life,' and afterwards to several persons as his residuary legatees therein named ; and the Will is proved by Avent and Brown, two of the executors, the third having died in the interim.

" To sum up all that I have, besides, been able to discover with relation to this eccentric personage, as well as to the unhappy disputes in the Plymouth congregations in which he bore so active a part, I have only to refer the reader to the reported Case of ' The King against Barker and others,' in the 3rd volume of Burrowes's Reports, p. 1265, from which it appears that on the 10th of June, 1761, the Court of K.B. was moved by Norton for a mandamus to the surviving trustees, &c. . . ."

Friary in New Street : " This building was once situate on the south side of New Street and was exactly opposite the lane now called Crooked Billet Lane. Before it and on the opposite side of the street were two very old houses, which have lately been taken down and large warehouses erected on the site. During the last twenty years scarce anything or part of the said Friary was standing except the two arch gateways, but they were walled up and in the wall which was in the line with the street." (Harris, 1810.)

Friary in Southside Street : " Site of the Black Friars' retreat and giving rise to Black Friar's Lane. The principal front in Southside Street, said to have been used as the Old Guildhall before its removal to Whimple Street and High Street. The King's Arms were placed over the Tower Entrance Door." (Harris.)

Friary Gate : Removed 1763. Friary Green, 1634-1812. Friary Street, 1765-1812.

Gascoyne Cottages : Upper North Street. Gascoyne Place, top of Gasking Street.

Gascoyne Street : Gasking Street, after Dr. Gasking, to whose memory a mural tablet exists in Charles Churchyard. Formerly Northgate Street.

Gasking Gate: Or North Gate, removed 1768. Close at hand was Gascoyne's Gate, which was also taken down to widen the street. ("By order of the Mayor and Commonalty, 1813.")

George Square, Devonport: Site of the Military Chapel, built in 1856.

Gibbet Pond: Portion of the Stonehouse Lake, near the Military Hospital, where the Millbridge murderers were hanged in chains.

Gibbons Street: Site of Gibbons's Field, a favourite evening resort ; and, judging from the skeletons unearthed, the scene of heavy fighting in the days of the siege. Gibbons was the name of the miller and owner.

Globe Inn: Frankfort Place, "a tavern and eating house much resorted to by commercial travellers," 1824. Subsequently Globe Hotel. Site of Prudential offices.

Gooseberry Lane: Opposite the old Eye Infirmary (portion of new G.W.R. offices).

Govett's Lane: Off Buckwell Street.

Granby Cellars, Devonport: The site of the Classical and Mathematical Schools.

Great George Street: George Street, Plymouth.

Greenbank Lane: Afterwards Prison Road, now Greenbank Road, was for a short interval named Cheltenham Road. There was a peculiar echo in the lane, so that by whispering against the east wall you could converse with anyone at the other end.

Green Market: "On the south side of Whimple Street, where the street is narrowest." The Old Green Market was in front of the vicar's garden, which the town sold off in parcels for building.

Grey Coat School: At the rear of Hampton Buildings. Erected in 1814.

Gunwharf (Devonport): Situate along the margin of Hamoaze, north of the Dockyard, divided by the street leading to North Corner landing-place. Constructed in the heavy form peculiar to Sir John Vanburgh, and, according to Rowe: This massive style gave rise to the well known epitaph on the architect :

> Lie heavy on him earth, for he
> Laid many a heavy load on thee.

Guy's Quays, 1812-1823: Off Woolster Street.

Hamoaze: Water border (Bannister); Wet, oozy habitation, circuit or enclosure (Borlase); Amus—protection or safety; Hamaux—hamlets (French); oozing of the adjacent "hams"; Ham-ouze (Defoe); Hamo's Port, after a crafty Roman (Geoffrey of Monmouth).

Hampton Shute or Park: Anciently Gilwil Park, site of part of Charles Church. (Worth.) "There is a traditionary account that from Martin's Gate up the whole of Green Street was the ancient wall of the town as far as that street goes. There are no remains left (1810). Above the street a wall or very ancient hedge is shown as the remains. This hedge was the western boundary of Hampton Shute House Fields, and was sold in parcels, when all the higher part of it was dug up to the foundations, except the part taken down the lowest, in possession of Dr. Hawker. He built his wall on the old one, and it was so strong that it separated with the greatest reluctance." (Harris.)

Ham Street: So called after the property of the Trelawneys, Ham, near St. Budeaux.

The Hawe at Plymouth (high-hill); Hoe: Formerly the hyll called the Windrygge.

> Speak not of Italy—she cannot show
> A brighter scene than this.
>
> Lines written on this spot by Stevens—a native poet.

"The Hoe in mediæval days was looked upon as distinctly exterior to the town, but as its most important adjunct. Close adjoining was the town barn, which may have been that originally of the Priory. On its ridge was the fire-beacon, always well stored with furze, wherewith to signal the approach of danger, while a strict look out was kept in the fifteenth and sixteenth centuries by a watchman at Rame. A watch-house was erected by the beacon in the reign of Elizabeth. Not far from the beacon was a windmill, associated at almost the very earliest date of special mention with the ominous name—for a miller—of Michael Prigge; and it is in connection with this windmill that we find the first attempt made to provide for the comfort of the Hoe public by the 'Hoe Committee' of that day. This was the erection of a 'bench' or seat round the windmill. They had no lack of amusements of various kinds. On the Hoe were the butts for the practice of archery, which came to very frequent reparation, and so must have been much in use. There the townsfolk gathered when 'John the Drummer,' or one of his colleagues, summoned them to arms on the approach of a threatening sail. There most of the capital punishments of the town took place. The entries of the charges for erecting 'gibbets on the Hawe' are unpleasantly numerous in the earlier records of Plymouth. Most memorable, however, was the execution of a poor wretch who took part in the western rebellion for the restoration of Roman Catholicism, a nameless 'traytor of Cornewalle,' who was dragged thither on a hurdle, and hung, drawn, and quartered at considerable expense in money or wine."

"Ye How. (1590.) The place where this forte is to be builte is called the *Howe*, which commandeth the towne and Harborowe: The manner after what sorte in their opinions, they doe humblie thinck fittest to haue it donne, they haue set downe in a plot which shall be imediatelie sent up with one to attend yor good lordships': honorable pleasures. There is nowe some 13 peeces of Ordinance placed on the How parte of which they haue borrowed of sondrie persons, to serue this present action, if neede so require: And uppon the Castle towers which is of no strength they haue placed fowre. The haue besids in St. Nicholas Islande about 23 peeces of Ordinance, the greater parte whereof are likewise borrowed. If the borrowed peeces were restored, the places would be lefte verie bare. So that they doe likewise become humble suitors, that her Matie would be pleased to bestowe 8 or 10 brasse peeces out of her stoare, the rest they themselues would furnish. This forte beinge once erected, the towne and whole contrie should be more resolute and safe, which would be a great incouragement to the Realme, and the ennemy knowinge the Artillerie to be out of danger would with lesse boldness enterprise that waie: Nowe the Harborowe lyinge without anie defence to make longe resistance, the towne uppon this late reporte was strucken with such feare, that some of them had convaied their goods out of the towne, and others no doubt would haue followed, if they had not ben stopped by the cominge of Sr. ffr. Drake, who the more to assure them brought his wife, and familie thither : So that if the ennemy had made his approch in his absence he had assurdlie taken the town without anie resistuance, and carried awaie their Ordinance."

"St. Nicholas Islande.   They haue of late (1590) at their owne charge fortified St. Nicholas Islande with a wall where the entraunce was lowest and easiest to be made of 20 foote in height and 150 in length, ·which hath made that place of the Islande, equall in Strength with the rest.   Within the Islande they haue arms (as calivers, muskets, and piks) for the arminge of 350 men. Besids they haue brought thither 50 barrels of pitch, 40 barrels of tarre, 10,000 weight of hearth pitch, as manie of brimstone, to be in a readines, to be prepared for fire works uppon anie occacion.   Uppon May daie laste (as their custome is every yeare) they made shewe uppon the How of at leaste 1,300 men well appointed, which were there all the morning mustered. ffrom that daie and hereafter Sr. ffr: Drake hath taken order that there shall be watch and warde euery night kept in the towne no lesse than if it were a towne of garrison.   Of which watch euery Master in his torne as Capten is to haue the charge, and to watch with them himselfe untill midnight, and then to be releeued by his deputie, who shall likewise be a man of good substance and truste.   This watch did Sr. ffr: himselfe beginne on friday laste."

Hawk Street : Altered to Higher Street, 1778-1812.

Hicks's Lane : Between Looe Street and How Street, with a room overhead as a square. head, 1765.

High Street (Plymouth) : Before 1765 ; Market Street, 1778 ; High Street, 1825.

Hill Street : Off Ham Street ; formerly Frenchman's Lane.

Hoe Gate : Removed 1863.

Holiwell : Near site of Plymouth Prison.

Holman's Buildings (Devonport) : Near North Corner, after name of builder.

Horse Pond : Without the Frankfort Gate.

Horse Pool Lane.

Hospital Burying Ground : The Crescent :

"Dr. Yonge built the Crescent ; and the Corporation, with the concurrence of the Navy Board, granted the Land in front, hitherto used as a Burial Ground, to him, to enclose with iron rails and form it into a Shrubbery, with Walks : in consideration of his having given up, to the Publick, a wide road, running north and south to the Hoe."   (Baron, 1823.)

The place that is now called the Crescent was formerly the burial ground for the prisoners of war who died at Millbay prison.   I have witnessed the burial of many of them.   They were taken from the prison gates to the grave in a cart made for the purpose, drawn by a donkey belonging to old Samuel Fuge, who had the contract for the work.   The upper part of the grounds was separated by a hedge from Dunsterville's rope·walk that was between the ground and Mill Prison Lane, now "Citadel Road."   A boy was in the burial ground one morning for the purpose of catching birds with bird lime on a thorn-bush.   Seeing a grave not filled in, he got down on the coffin to hide himself from the birds ; hearing a noise in the coffin he was soon out again, and ran away, quite alarmed and frightened, down to the entrance gate that stood near, where the Athenæum now stands. Some persons who were passing, seeing the poor boy, asked him what was the matter, when he kept crying out, "A man buried alive." Several persons went up to the grave, when they found the boy's story was true. The lid of the coffin being raised, the poor French prisoner was soon taken up, and immediately conveyed to the prison infirmary. After a few months he got quite convalescent, and was sent home to France—one of the exchanged prisoners. After his arrival home, he wrote to the Rev. Herbert Mends, minister of Batter Street Chapel, Plymouth, asking if he would be kind enough to find the boy who was the means of saving his life. Mr. Mends, after making inquiries, was fortunate enough to discover who the boy was, and replied to the letter by giving particulars respecting him. In the course of a few days he received another letter from France, with an enclosure for five pounds, asking him if he would kindly hand it over to the boy, also stating that he (the Frenchman) would forward him the same amount yearly so long as he lived. The money was duly received for four or five years, when Mr. Mends received an account of the Frenchman's death.— *Western Antiquary.*

Household of Faith : Situate in Vennel Street (south of Charles Church).

How Street : Formerly Howe's Lane.

Huer's Row, 1778 : Hewer's Row, 1812 ; top of North Street.

The Island (Catherine Street, Devonport) : Bounded on the north by Catherine Street, by about forty feet ; on the west by the narrow portion of Catherine Street ; of twelve feet wide ; on the north by Fore Street ; and on the east by Stafford's Hill.

The Island (Plymouth) : An irregular block of buildings that existed in Bedford Street, bounded by the site of the Liberal Club, the Devon and Cornwall Bank, the Young Men's Christian Association and contiguous buildings. It was a comparatively modern excrescence, but rendered the approaches so narrow that it was removed.

James Street Area (Devonport) : The area known as the James Street Area was bounded on the northern side by Duke Street ; on the southern side by Duncan Street ; on the eastern side by courtlages of Monument Street, Duncan Street and Duke Street.

Jew Wood, Radford : Scene of murder of Little Isaacs, the Jew.

Jory's Alm's Houses, Coxside : "They were twelve in number and built in a line. Each had two rooms, one below and another on top, so as to be quite independent of each other, with small plots of garden ground before each. The intention of the founder was that it should for ever be for none but the widows of deceased ship masters." (Harris, 1810.) Over the doorway in a triangular space was the inscription : "These twelve charity houses, with an endowment for ever for the support of twelve widows, are the sole gift of Joseph Jory, Esq., native of Plymouth, Anno 1703.

Jump : Now Roborough, formerly "The Jump," or variously Trenaman's or Treliman's Jump.

"Towards the latter end of August, or beginning of September, the Water Committee breakfast at Jump, or Castle Farm ; and proceed to the Head Weir of the Leat, where they drink a glass of *aqua pura* to the pious memory of Sir Francis Drake, and return (with what sport they can) to Castle Farm, to dine. After dinner the first name toasted is significantly intended to be that of His Worship's Successor." (Baron, 1824.)

Keame : Keyham, after Keame House ; Kaime Place Creek (1540).

King's Arms Hotel : Briton Side.

King's Inner Boundary Wall (Devonport) : Wall separating the barracks and the fortifi-
          cations; commenced in 1787 and completed in 1795, to the displeasure of the
          inhabitants, whose rights of way were violated. (Worth.)

King's Mills : Rowe Street, Plymouth (now demolished), contiguous to Technical Schools.
          Two fine plane trees grew in the space opposite the Harvest Home Hotel.

Kinterbury Powder Mills : Nearly opposite Saltash.

Knockershole : Knackersnowle, now Crown Hill.

The Laboratory (Mount Wise) : "The Laboratory consists of twenty-one detached buildings,
          inclosed by a high wall, and forming an oblong square. These buildings are
          designed to be used as workshops, for smiths, joiners, harness makers, and other
          tradesmen employed in the manufactory of stores requisite for an equipment of
          a military expedition. Neat houses for officers are erected on the eastern side,
          where the entrance is also situated." (Rowe, 1824.)

Ladywell Buildings : 1812. Site of Lady-well, possibly of the hermitage of our lady at
          Quarry well, near Gascoyne Cottages.

Laira : From larus, a gull ; therefore Lary, a place resorted to by gulls. (Rowe.)

Lambert's Ope (Devonport) : From Fore Street to Princes Street ; after the name of the
          builder.

Lambhay : Existence of contiguous hedge for enclosure purpose.

Lewis Jones's Turnpike Gate : At south end Mutley Plain. Lewis Jones's Lane, 1812.

Liberty Fields : Site of Pembroke Street (Devonport).

Linam Lane, 1765 : Altered to Middle Lane 1778-1883.

Lipson : The old Lulyett's Fea, or long lost Leuricestone, Lisistone, Lypstone. (Worth.)

Little Church Alley : Leading from Treville Street to Charles Church Graveyard. Little
          Church Lane, 1778 ; New Church Lane, 1812.

Little Hoe Lane : Hoe Street.

Loader's Lane, 1778 ; altered to Higher Lane, 1883.

Longroom : Formerly a fashionable resort at Stonehouse. Now used for drilling troops.

Looe Street ; Afterwards Pike Street and now Looe Street again.

Looe Street Area (Plymouth) : Bounded by Looe Street and How Street, and intersected
          by Looe Lane and a number of courts and alleys with no special designations.
          Looe Lane was broadened, and the courts and alleys were blotted out.

Love Lane or Green Lane : Now Greenbank Avenue.

Love Lane, 1765 : With a grove of trees formerly known as Burying Place Lane, 1778 ;
          and now Westwell Street.

Love Street : The site of Basket Street, 1778 ; site of Plymouth Municipal Offices.

Lower Lane : Altered to Patrick Street.

Maker : From the Cornish Macreton.

Marine Road : Under the Hoe, commonly called "Under the Hoe," constructed by the
          poor and paid for by public subscription.

Market Street : Thus the humour of Baron, the so-called Corporate Poet, of Plymouth :
"On Easter Thursday, April 24, 1794, at 1 a.m., the Poet Corporate born—
apropos, of the Mayoralty, of Andrew Hill, in the Parish of Saint *Andrew*, and
upon a *Hill*; formerly High Street, then Market Street, now again High Street.

> As the Knights of the Garter were ceasing to gorge
> The Feast of their Tutelar Patron, Saint George ;
> From out of the Womb of my Mother unfurled ;
> At One in the Morning I entered the World ;
> In my own Parish Saint, and Steep street, I fulfil
> The Name of the Time Being's Mayor, *Andrew Hill*."—*Baron.*

Marrow-Bone Slip : Mary-le-Bone, or Marybone. Accumulation of marrow bones at the
foot-oil factory there.

Martin's Gate : Removed 1789. One arch led up Green Street and the other up Bilberry
Street. Conduit here built 1718 and demolished 1763.

Mayoralty House : Woolster Street (now the Mayoralty Stores). "The Mayor's Feast
is annually held on the same day that the Mayor is chosen. It is given by the
Old Mayor on his leaving office to the Corporation freeman and friends. Before
the war with France in 1793 most of the freemen took a friend with them, but
latterly they have not. The feast before the building of the new Guildhall,
1801, was held at the Mayoralty House." (Harris.) Supposed scene of the murder
of Master Page.

The Rev. Baring-Gould quotes in "A Book of the West," a letter by Daniel
Lysons, author of Magna Britannia, in 1827, which may be regarded as assisting
the literature on the murder of Master Page. Mr. Baring-Gould holds that it is
possible that Judge Glanville was a brother of Eulalia, but maintains that he was
not present at the trial, but that on the authority of Philip Wyot, then town
clerk of Barnstaple, the presiding judge was Lord Anderson. Lyson's letter is
as follows :

"The Judge's daughter was attached to George Stanwich, a young man of
Tavistock, lieutenant of a man-of-war, whose letters, the father disapproving of
the attachment, were intercepted. An old miser of Plymouth, of the name of
Page, wishing to have an heir to disappoint his relatives, who perhaps were too
confident in calculating upon sharing his wealth, availed himself of this apparent
neglect of the young sailor, and settling on her a good jointure, obtained her
hand. She took with her a maidservant from Tavistock, but her husband was so
penurious that he dismissed all the other servants, and caused his wife and her
maid to do all the work themselves. On an interview subsequently taking place
between her and Stanwich, she accused him of neglecting to write to her, and
then discovered that his letters had been intercepted. The maid advised them
to get rid of the old gentleman, and Stanwich, with great reluctance, at length,
consented to their putting an end to him. Page lived in what was afterwards
the Mayoralty House (at Plymouth), and a woman who lived opposite, hearing
at night some sand thrown against a window, thinking it was her, own arose, and,
looking out, saw a young gentleman near Page's window, and heard him say,
'For God's sake stay your hand!' A female replied, ''Tis too late; the deed is
done !' On the following morning it was given out that Page had died suddenly
in the night, and as soon as possible he was buried. On the testimony, however,

of his neighbour, the body was taken up again, and, it appearing that he had been strangled, his wife, Stanwich, and the maid were tried and executed. It is current among the common people here that Judge Glanville, her own father, pronounced the sentence."

May's Cross : At the head of Pennycomequick Hill, 1812 ; juncture of Cobourg Street and North Road.

Mew-stone : The home of the mew.

Military Hospital : Near Stoke Church, commenced 1797.

Millbay Grove : Site of Duke of Cornwall Hotel.

Millbay Prison : Millbay Barracks. Here was witnessed the last execution in Plymouth, 1807. Cajetono Canado, a Spanish prisoner of war, quarrelled with a comrade in misfortune over some bread and cheese, and in his passion stabbed him. The gallows were erected on a piece of ground adjoining the Millbay Soap Works.

Millbridge : The bridge by the mill across the upper part of Stonehouse Creek or Stoke Damarle Flete. Rebuilt in 1830, and a table of tolls first set up in 1832. The mill abuts on the western side of the bridge, almost close to the northern shore of the creek, and is now in a ruinous condition. (1899.)

Moon's Lane, 1765. Moon Street.

Morice Square : After the Morice family.

MILLBRIDGE.—Showing mill and portion of the bridge towards the Naval Hospital.
(*Photo. by J. A. Boolds, 1899.*)

Morice Town Ferry (Newpassage): "The road to the ferry at Morice Town is defended by the North Barrier Gate and a drawbridge over the ditch, which is in this place excavated in the rock to a considerable depth. Near the gate is a guardhouse, which with the other erections in this quarter have been recently constructed." (Rowe, 1824.)

Mount Edgcumbe: Piers Edgcomb (Caualeiro Execom) was visited at Mount Edgcomb in 1580 by Don Antonio. "To the Governour of Mount Edgcomb House"— a letter demanding the delivery of the same for the use of the Parliament (1644):

> This Mount all the mounts of Great Britain surpasses,
> 'Tis the haunt of the Muses, the mount of Parnassus;
> Fame lies—'tis not Stratford, this, this is the spot
> Where Genius on Nature our Shakespeare begot;
> This only the birth-place of Shakespeare could be,
> Whose wonders can e'en make a poet of me.—*Garrick.*

Mount Pleasant: Site of Blockhouse, Devonport.

Mount Wise: After Sir Thomas Wise, "who hath built there a fair house for his pleasure and named it Mount Wise" (Pole, 1635), by whom the barton was sold to Sir William Morice. A large Tudor edifice, rebuilt in 1809.

Mud Street, 1765; Holy Cross Lane, 1768; Chapel Lane—Higher Broad Street, 1812; Meeting Lane, 1828; Buckwell Lane, 1883.

Mutley: Mod lei; Mud-ley; Maudlyn or Lepers' House. The Maudlyn-house ("neere Plymouth—1648"). Maudlyn Fort, site of Blind Institution:
Thus Baron: The town applied to have fresh Water brought into it, and gave £200 in hand to Sir Francis Drake. In December, he began on the Leat, and brought it into the Town (25 Miles) on Saturday the 24th of April following, when the Corporation, attired in full Civick Costume, and attended with a Band of Musick, went out to "*Motte Leigh*" to meet it; and the Worthy Baronet, turning round, said—"Now, Gentlemen! I have brought it thus far; I leave it to *you* to carry it into Town." The Corporation, however, had not the sense "to wind it round the Hill"; and, for a length of time, it ran to waste down into Dead Lake.

Mutton Cove: By reason of the leg-of-mutton formation of the creek.

Navy Row (Devonport): Albert Road, formerly the only houses between Devonport and Morice Town.

New Church Twelves: King Charles's Alms Houses. (Baron.) Built by Lanyon; Lanyon's Charity. "Over the door at the entrance on a stone fixed is this inscription: 'John Lanyon, merchant, deceased, and some time Mayor of this town, was the first benefactor to this house, and gave £300 towards the building, 1679, for the poor of this parish." On another stone was inscribed "John Gubbs, Esq., late of Plymouth, deceased, gave to the poor of Plymouth £100, which Robert Gubbs, his executor, of Exon, hath apply'd and given to these almhouses."

New or Coal Quay, 1765; Parade, 1778; New Quay, 1812; Parade, 1828.

New Street, Plymouth, 1765: Top of Pins Lane, an important street at the beginning of the century. Site of the town house of the Colliers, and still presenting some of the best architectural survivals, used as bonded stores.

2

New Town : Richmond Hill and then York Street.

"No Place" : "Where have you been all the day?"   "No Place !"   Signboard of inn.

Norley Street : Formerly Norley Lane.

North Corner : Now Cornwall Street.

Notte Street : Formerly Nut Street, site of clumps of hazel bushes.

Old Betheseda Chapel : Park Street, Plymouth.

Old Church Twelves : The almshouse of Plymouth, by the side of the Church in Catherine
     Street, and now part of site of east end of Municipal Buildings. Hospital
     House. (Leland.)

Old Custom House : Removed from its former mean and inconvenient situation in Custom-
     House Lane to a newly-erected building in 1820. "The new custom-house
     fronts the Parade or coal quay, and the warehouses and cellars behind extend
     into Foyne's Lane. The front is built of granite, with a colonnade of five arches,
     supported by rusticated piers of the same material. On the ground floor are the
     offices of the principal surveyor, tide surveyor, landing waiter, searcher, &c."
     (Rowe, 1824.)

Old Devonport Barracks : Racket Court Barracks, at the back of Clowance Street, were
     not used for troops. They were private dwellings, purchased by Government
     for barracks in a case of emergency, but were not calculated for the purpose.
     A court for playing the game of tennis, formerly on this spot, gave name
     to the building. (Rowe, 1824.)

   George Square Barracks adjoined the entrance to Dock from Plymouth, at the
       South Barrier Gate, where troops were constantly on duty at the guardrooms.
       (Rowe, 1824.)

   The Horse Artillery Barracks were a range of buildings on the north of the road
       from Plymouth. On the opposite side was a row of houses for the officers.
       Adjoining these barracks were the Cumberland Squares, situated within each
       other ; both of which were occupied by regiments of infantry. (Rowe, 1824.)

   Ligonier Square : Occupied by the Royal Artillery, adjoined Cumberland Square
       to the north. Beyond was Frederick Square, in which the Royal Engineers
       and artificers were stationed.

   Old and new Granby Squares were on the north of Fore Street. These were
       infantry barracks.

   Marlborough Square also contained barracks for infantry, and was situated at
       the head of Marlborough Street.

Old Four Castles : Old Town Street, site of Ruse's furniture factory.

Old Grammar School or Volunteer Depôt, Plymouth :

   "The grammar school, with the residence of the master, Rev. Wm. Williams, is
       situated in St. Catherine Street. The schoolroom, a narrow, gloomy apart-
       ment, contains forms for seven classes. The playground and garden for the
       master is adjoining." (Rowe, 1824.)

Old Naval Watering Place : "At Staddon Point a quay was erected as a landing-place for
     the accommodation of boats taking in water for vessels in the Sound. This
     reservoir (which was constructed in a hollow between two hills) was supplied
     from an excellent stream, and was capable of containing from ten to twelve

thousand tons; a sufficient quantity to water fifty sail of the 'line. From this spot the water was carried down in iron pipes to the landing-place, which were furnished with every convenience for conveying the water on board the ships." (Rowe, 1824.)

Old Nunnery: Site of James's Starch Works.

Old Penny Lane: Whitecross Street now.

Old Powder Magazine: Keyham Point, commenced 1784.

Old Presbyterian Chapel: Batter Street, Plymouth.

Old Town Gate: At the head of Old Town Street, close below the junction with Drake's Street. Rebuilt 1759. Removed 1809.

Old Town Without, or Old Town Street Without: At the Old Town Street end of Drake's Street, site of a public conduit, with a may-tree in the immediate neighbourhood. "The strainer and pool at the head of the town was made in 1593 to the great conduitts at Old Town Gate. The water flows through a tunnel or covered trough, and the remainder flows open to the sea at Millbay." (Harris, 1810.)

Old Tabernacle: Opposite the Exeter Street Hall (Treville Street).

Old Unitarian Chapel: Broad Street, Plymouth.

Old Victualling Office: "The establishment for supplying the navy with provisions was situated below the eastern rampart of the Citadel, and extended from the pier at Sutton Pool to the mouth of Catwater Harbour. The entrance from the town, with the warder's lodge, was on Lambhay Hill; and at a short distance were the offices of the agent victualler, storekeeper, and clerk of the cheque. On the left were granaries sufficiently capacious to contain immense quantities of corn; to these succeed the cellars, in which were deposited wine and spirits; storehouses for beef, pork, butter and cheese; and extensive lofts filled with biscuit. There were two bakehouses, each containing four ovens, where the biscuit was baked." Remains now used for stores.

Old Workhouse (Plymouth): In October, 1888, the Rev. Charles H. Pope, of Kennabankport, Me., contributed to the New England Historical and Genealogical Record a note on the old Plymouth workhouse, formerly standing in Catherine Street, some time known as Hospital of the Poor's Portion:

"We are able to present on the opposite page a picture of the very building where 'Divers Godly Persons' of the counties of Devon, Dorset, and Somerset met to organize, some time in March, 1629-30. The building was the 'New Hospital in Plymouth,' an almshouse,' not quite finished, and therefore unoccupied. Two months later it was formally occupied by the town authorities, and was known for a century and a quarter as 'The Hospital of Poor's Portion.' The building was demolished about 1859 (?1869). But as we look upon this picture we can easily imagine ourselves mingling with the company on their solemn day of 'Fasting and Prayer'; we hear 'Patriarch White' of Dorchester, in Dorset, preach 'in the fore part of the day,' and we watch with great interest while, in the 'latter part of the day,' the band 'did solemnly make choice of and call those godly Ministers the Rev. Mr. John Warham and Mr. John Maverick to be their officers, and they did accept thereof and expressed the same.' Over the main doorway of the building this motto was chiselled:—

'BY GODS HELPE THROVGH CHRIST.'

In that faith the devout party sailed, March 29th, 1630, and founded
Dorchester, the oldest portion of our present Boston. On board the *Mary
& John*, and in their New England home, the pastors, so installed, fulfilled
their office together nearly six years. Then the younger (Warham) with a
portion of the colony, went to found Windsor, Conn.; while the older
Maverick, with the remainder, continued by the 'Bay' till called to the
eternal home."

The Hospital of Orphan's Aid, commonly called the "Green School," was
founded by Thomas and Nicholas Sherwell, early in the 17th century,
for the education of poor boys. It was formerly located in Catherine
Street, near the Hospital of Poor's Portion (the workhouse) and the
Grammar School. It is at present, and has been for many years, carried
on in a private dwelling-house in Regent Street. In a copy of the " Rules and
constitutions to be observed by the Tutor and Governor of 'Orphan's Aid,'"
the 7th clause of this interesting document runs thus : " As we would have
especial care taken that the Sabbath day be duly observed generally in all
religious exercises, so more particularly for perpetual remembrance of God's
mercy to this land and His whole Church, more especially manifested to
this place in that great deliverance, A.D. 1588, we desire that yearly on the
Sabbath day next before the 25th July there be read by them the prophecy
of Joel, which was preached on and particularly applied to that invasion

INTERIOR OF OLD PLYMOUTH WORKHOUSE.—Portion of site of existing Plymouth Guildhall.

and deliverance in the church about that time, and in part accomplished in our sight, and further, that there be sung at the same time either the 46th or 124th Psalm, or some other to like purpose."

Osen (Oreston): Ozen.

In 1817, the men, in quarrying Oreston for the use of the Breakwater, came to a cavern in the solid face of the rock 160 feet from the original face, at the edge of Catwater, and 60 feet from the superincumbent soil. It was fifteen feet wide, twelve high, and forty-five long, filled, or nearly so, with a body of solid clay, in which were embedded the teeth and bones of the rhinoceros. In 1820, a smaller cavern was discovered of one foot high, eighteen feet wide, and twenty long, containing clay or mud, in which were embedded teeth and bones belonging to the rhinoceros, deer, and a species of bear. It was stated by Mr. Whidbey, and confirmed by the workmen, that neither of these caverns bore the appearance of ever having had an opening to the surface, or any communication with it whatever, but that they were closed all round with the same compact substance as that which forms the body of the rock ; that in many caverns of the same rock stalactite was found, but none in either of these.

A third cave, or rather a series of caves and galleries were discovered at Oreston, running in various directions through the compact limestone rock, in which were found a vast quantity of bones, horns, skulls, and teeth, some covered with mud and clay, others adhering to the sides of the caverns, lying on projecting ledges of rock, at various elevations, or crammed into crevices or fissures. They consisted of the remains of oxen, horses, deer, and various other animals, with a small proportion of the jaws and teeth of the hyæna. Among them were also found horns of various kinds, and in one cavity was a number of shells mixed with sand.

It was ascertained that some of these caverns, if not all of them, had a communication with the upper surface of the rock, but that they were firmly closed by the solid limestone on the side next to Cattewater, which was that on which the quarrying was carried on ; consequently on the first opening of one of these caverns, it had all the appearance of being a separate and detached chamber in the midst of the solid rock, and to this circumstance was owing the mistake of their being described as such in the Philosophical Transactions. Mr. Whidbey, however, anxious to ascertain the real state of the case, subsequently traced an internal communication between them, by means of galleries, or narrow passages, running in oblique directions through the very heart of the rock, in angles of about 45° with the horizon ; sometimes ascending and then descending. From the principal and lowest cavern, which was about thirty-five feet above the high-water of spring tides, and 600 feet from the original face of the quarry, one of these slanting galleries led upwards into a second cavern, from which another gallery continued in the same direction to a part of the rock near the surface, consisting of separate masses of limestone, intermixed with clay, but so compact and indurated, that it required to be blasted with gunpowder to effect a passage through it. The width of this seam was from ten to twelve feet, and on examination it was found to continue of the same nature to the surface of the country, a height of about fifteen feet. From this shaft (if it may be so-called) another gallery branched off still deeper into the rock, at the extremity of which was another large chamber, and in this too were found several teeth and bones. Another narrow gallery, not of sufficient width to admit the body of a man, proceeded apparently in the same direction out of this chamber. The sides of the caverns, passages and galleries were, for the most part, solid limestone ; occasionally, however, they were partially covered with clay, and in some places with stalactite.

> Barber, barber, bo'sun,
> Cut off his head and roast'un ;
> Put un in a bisky bag
> And send un over to Osun.—*Halliwell.*

Oxford Row (Plymouth) : Now Claremont Street.

Palace Court : Site of Palace Court Road Schools.

Peacock Lane : Leading from the top of Looe Street (then Pike Street) to Catte Street, and the site of the Pope's Head, a famous resort for actors and commercial men.

Pennycomequick : Pen-y-cwm-cuick or valley at the head of the creek (Worth) ; existence of quag in the hollow : Penny-corn-quick (Stuart period). Little Pennycome-quick Works ; site of Houndiscombe House.

Philadelphian District Baptist Chapel : Willow Street, Plymouth.

Pig Market : Site of old Plymouth Theatre (now Lipton's), and Frankfort Place, now a part of Bedford Street.

Pins Lane : Temporarily Lucknow Street.

Plymouth-Dock Workhouse : Duke Street, Devonport.

Plymouth : From Pelyn (head of the lake), then Plin-mouth ; and "Sutton villa supera costera portus de Plymouth." (Edward II.) (Worth.) "Sutton, now caullid Plimmouth." (Leland.)

> Plym christeneth that Town which bears her noble name.
> Upon the British coast what Ship yet ever came
> That not of Plymouth hears, where those brave Navies lie,
> From Cannons thund'ring flote, that all the world defy ;
> Which, to evasive spoil, when th' English list to draw,
> Have checked Hiberia's pride ; and kept her, still, in awe :
> Oft furnishing our Dames with India's rare devices ;
> And lent us gold as pearl ; with Silk, and dainty Spices ?—*Drayton.*

The following description of Plymouth in 1652 by Richard Peeke, of Tavistock, when questioned by the Spaniards, who took him prisoner, will interest and amuse some Plymouth readers :—

"'Of what strength,' quoth another Duke, 'is the fort at Plymouth ?' I answered 'Very strong.' 'What ordnance in it ?' 'Fifty,' said I. 'That is not so,' said he, 'there are but 17.' 'How many soldiers are there in the fort ?' I answered 'Two hundred.' 'That is not so,' quoth a Conde, 'there are but twenty.'

"The Marquis Alquenez asked me, 'Of what strength the little island [*i.e.*, Drake's Island] was before Plymouth ?'

" I told him 'I know not.'

" 'Then,' quoth he, 'we do.'

" ' Is Plymouth a walled town ?'

" 'Yes, my Lords.'

" ' And a good wall ?'

" 'Yes,' said I, ' a very good wall.'

" ' True,' says a Duke, ' to leap over with a staff.'

" ' And hath the Town,' said the Duke of Medina, ' strong gates ?'

" ' Yes.'

" ' But,' quoth he, ' there was neither wood nor iron to those gates, but two days before your fleet came away.' "

" ' Then,' quoth one of the [Spanish] Earls, ' When thou meetest me in Plymouth wilt thou bid me welcome ?' I modestly told him, ' I could wish they would not too hastily come to Plymouth ; for they would find it another manner of place than as now they slighted it.' "

Plymouth Ducking Stool (site of): The last person who went through the ignominy of being dipped at Plymouth was Nancy Clark, an aged fishwoman (a great drunkard), for an assault on Kitty Ware, in the same line of business ; also for cursing, swearing, and using obscene language. The stool was lowered slowly down into the water at high tide, by a crane which stood on the Barbican, for many years opposite the " North Country Pink " Inn.

Plymouth Haven or Plymouth Road : An Act of Anne is entitled :

" An Act for clearing, preserving, and maintaining the harbour of Catwater, lying near Plymouth, in the county of Devon ; and for the cleansing and keeping clean the pool, commony called Sutton Pool, lying in Plymouth aforesaid."

Plymouth Public Subscription School : In Old Town Without (now Cobourg Street). Erected 1814 : " The situation is open and healthy, and a spacious playground is attached to the building." (Rowe, 1824.) About the time of the erection of this school Brunswick Terrace, Gascoigne Terrace, Tavistock Street, Park Street, George Street, Portland Square, Frankfort Street, and Cornwall Street were the most modern additions to the town. They were followed by Cobourg Street, James Street, Union Street and Terrace, Queen Street, King Street, Princess Square, the Crescent, St. Andrew's Terrace, Charles's Place, Fareham Place (near the existing Gas Works at Coxside) and Woodside.

Plymouth Sound :

Where Plym and Thamar with embraces meet.—

—That spacious Sound, within whose arms

I have those vessels seen, whose hot alarms

Have made Iberia tremble. —*Browne's Britannia's Pastorals.*

Plymouth Stocks (site of) : The stocks were placed near the centre of the market, close to where the old boot stalls were located, and the culprit retained his awkward seat for about two hours, being exposed all the time to the jeers of the passers-by, and possibly to rougher treatment than mere words.

Plymouth Road or Haven : Catwater.

Pomeroy or Public Conduit Street : Lower and Higher Batter Street, and site of a Public conduit.

Pontey's Nursery: Gardens in which the Barley House formerly stood. Site of King Gardens, &c.

Pound Street: Adjoining unoccupied land by side of Technical Schools, in continuation with Cobourg Street. Site of Cattle Pound, 1850. John Pound, Mayor, 1513.

Prestyn House: The Abbey in Finewell Street. (Worth.)

Princes' Street (Devonport): So called because the princes lodged there. Corrupted into Princes Street.

Quarry Street (Devonport): Altered to Stanley Street to assist in purging it of disagreeable associations.

Radford House: The seat of the Harris family, and the scene of the discovery of valuable plate in 1827:

"In the reign of Elizabeth the estate was in the possession of Sir Christopher Harris, who represented Plymouth in Parliament. He was the personal friend of Sir Francis Drake, and stored at Radford some of the 'Gold and Silver in Blocks,' which that daring seaman brought home with him from the South Seas. At Radford Sir Christopher Harris entertained Drake and Raleigh, Howard, Hawkins, and the other captains who fought the Armada; and there, in 1618, as Vice-Admiral of Devon, he held Raleigh for a while in custody, on his return from the fatal expedition after the Golden City of Manoa. To Sir Christopher, who died in 1625, the plate originally belonged. He was succeeded at Radford by his great-nephew, John Harris, who represented Liskeard in the Long Parliament, and eventually threw in his lot with the king. Plymouth declared for the Parliament, and its Siege by the Cavaliers, which lasted just four years, was the chief event of the Civil War in the West of England. John Harris garrisoned Radford in the Royalist interest, and became a major-general of infantry in the besieging army. This position he held when, on the 18th of February, 1645, a rally of the Puritan Garrison drove the Cavaliers from their quarters at Mount Stamford, a short distance from Radford, and chased them a considerable way. Radford, was assailed, and either then, or at some similar time of imminent peril, the family plate disappeared; and whether it had been carefully hidden and the secret lost, or whether it had fallen into the hands of some lucky Roundhead, remained a mystery for nearly two centuries. At length, however, a man engaged in ploughing a field at Brixton, which is about two miles from Radford, on the 6th of December, 1827, found these twenty-three pieces of silver plate. It was perfectly clear that they had been intentionally hidden, and as they bore the Harris Arms, there was no moral doubt as to their ownership. The legal point was settled by the verdict of a jury specially empanelled to try the question. The plain inference was that the plate had been hidden by the Steward, in whose charge it had been placed, and by his death, probably during the February foray, the secret of its burial-place was lost. The plate, therefore, was assigned to John Harris, Esq., of Radford, the descendant of its former owner. The plate sold for £1,255, and was subsequently disposed of for £1,900 to Mr. Albemarle Cator, of Woodbastwich, Norfolk, who had married into the Mohun-Harris family."

Rehoboth Chapel: Buckwell Lane, site of Britannia Clothing Works.

Richmond Walk : After the Duke of Richmond in 1809.

Royal Naval Hospital (Stonehouse) : Opened 1762.

Royal Union Baths in Union Street : At entrance to Goods Yard.

Lady Rogers's School : " In a salubrious situation on the Tavistock turnpike." (1824.) Opposite the Drake's Reservoir ; since demolished.

Ryder's Cherry Garden : Situate at the bottom of Catherine Street and junction of Notte Street, Plymouth. "To accommodate His Majesty's Navy, landing at Barbican Stairs, a Road was cut through Ryder's Cherry Garden, which induced the Poet Corporate to give it the name of Cherry Garden Theatre ; or the Theatre Royal, Cherry Garden." (Baron.) There were several cherry gardens in the neighbourhood. 1810.

Saffron Row : Sarcastically applied to a row in Plymouth Market where the farmers daughters were extravagantly attired and people paid the more for their wares. Saffron being an expensive commodity.

Salem Chapel : Situate in Navy Row, Devonport.

Saltash : Vill of Ayshe.

Saltram : Saltham, because the "hams" of the Laira were washed there.

Sausage Lane : Leading from the Parade to Southside Street.

Scammel's Row : Situate above Ham Street, 1778-1812.

Searle's Lane : Finewell Street.

Seven Stars Lane : Birthplace of Dr. Kitto. Altered to Stillman Street.

Shambles or Pig Market : Bedford Street (from Spooner's Corner to the Bedford Inn).

Shambles, Bedford Street : The granite columns at the Belvedere on the Hoe and those at Drake's Place were formerly in the Shambles and subsequently in the Market before recent reconstruction.

Shakespeare Tavern : Corner of Westwell and Basket Street (the tramway route). Another resort for musicians and actors.

Sherwell House : After the Bros. Sherwell, who flourished in the 17th century.

"Shoulder of Mutton" : A famous "tippling" house where malcontent Plymouth freemen resorted :

> In days of yore, and be it ours to rhyme
> A Reminiscence of the olden time ;
> Knights of Saint Patrick whom we used to dub
> "The Members of the Should'r of Mutton Club,"
> Were, in the welfare of the Borough, warm ;
> Themselves achieved Municipal Reform :
> And met, without His Holiness's leave,
> Their Candidate upon Saint Lambert's Eve.—*Baron.*

Smart's Quay : 1812.

"Some Place" : Part of Tothill, in contradistinction to "No Place."

Soure Poole Mille : Millbay. Ralph de Valletort (1370) mentions a way to Sourepoolemylle, by the corner of his garden of Sutton "anglo gardina mei de Suthona." (Worth.)

South Gate : At the Barbican. Built 1602. Removed 1831.

Southside Street : Street south of the creek. Formerly Southside. Southside Quay or Barbican Quay, 1812.

Stafford's Hill (Devonport) : Led from Cherry Garden (York) Street to Fore Street. Lipton's Corner was built over a portion of the old site.

St. Andrew's Well : On the Horse road to Catdown Old Ferry Road. (Harris.) It possessed great ideal qualities in the days of papal obscurity, and was much resorted to by the devotees, and to seek the protection and blessing of that saint. It is an exceedingly old well, and there was a venerable fig tree that used to overshadow it. In the memory of some ancients the stumps and roots were to to be seen fifty years ago. (1810.)

St. George's Barracks or the Laboratory : Mount Wise.

St. Nicholas Island : Formerly Island of St. Michael, later Drake's Island.

St. Nicholas Island : " Old Nick's Island—a very appropriate place for confining rebels." (Baron.)

Stone-in-Darns : Ancient house in Notte Street in which tobacco was manufactured. Low doorway of massive granite.

Stonehouse : After Joel de Stanhust.

Stoke Damerel : (Stokedameron—Speed.) From Robert of Albermarle, who succeeded to the manor after the Saxon Brismar. (Worth.)

Strawberry Lane : Beginning of Stonehouse Lane.

Sutton : South Town. Sutton Valletort, Vaward or Vawtier (on the north) ; Sutton Prior (on the south) ; Sutton Raf, Rauff or Ralf, later Radcliff (on the east of the town). (Worth.) "Sutton Prior, now the greatest part of Plymouth." (Henry II.)

> Ere by the Name of Plymouth, handed down ;
> The Borough of this Penunited Town :
> On Lambhay Hill ; or e'er its Lamb was Mutton ;
> Southerly, Southern, South Town ; *vulgo*, Sutton.—*Baron*.

Sutton Pill or Pool : Commonly called the Prince of Wales's Cream Pot. (Baron) : Sutton Pool Harbour was nearly surrounded by the buildings of different parts of old Plymouth, and was divided at its entrance from Catwater by two piers of solid masonry, projecting from the Barbican and Teat's Hill. These were constructed in the years 1791 and 1799, by means of grants obtained from the legislature for that purpose. " This harbour, with Smart's quay, part of the New quay, and of Foxhole quay, Tin quay, and Dung quay, and various private quays and warehouses, was the property of the Duke of Cornwall, who claimed the products arising from the several dues which were paid by all ships entering the Pool, and occupying the quays for the purpose of landing or shipping merchandize. These dues, with the other property of the duchy above-mentioned, were leased out to the Sutton Pool Company, by whose exertions great improvements were effected in the harbour. The Barbican quay, part of Foxhole quay, and the New quay belong to the Mayor and commonalty, who let the dues arising from them, with the town water at the Barbican steps, and the use of the crane on the quay, to a yearly tenant. Part of Foxhole quay and Guy's quay are private property." (Rowe, 1824.) The property of the harbour was claimed by the Corporation of Plymouth, as far as an imaginary boundary line drawn from the

SUTTON POOL.

From a picture by W. Gibbons (1894), in the possession of Mr. John Greenway.

Bear's Head at Catdown to the Fish's Nose at the old Victualling-office point. The jurisdiction of their coroner was bounded by this line. The Corporation of Saltash was entitled to certain dues, collected from ships entering Catwater, and the Lord of the Manor of Plympton enjoyed the right of fishing in the northern parts of the harbour.

Sutton Vautort : Vautordis Park atte Pole, leased by James Vautort, lord of Sutton.

Tamar : River of Ptolemy's "Tamara"; "River of Saltash" (Charles II.) :

> The raptur'd eye now wanders round
> The circling stretch of distant ground,
> Where fading mountains crown the scene
> With many a fertile vale between—
> Where sporting with the solar beam
> Fam'd Tamar winds his wanton stream ;
> And deck'd with villas, forts and towns,
> With woods and pastures, hills and downs ;
> With docks and navies—England's pride—
> And lighter barks, that swiftly glide.—*Bidlake*.
> On Tamar's wave—
> Where its expanding waters proudly bear
> Their noblest freight, and navies own their care.— *Woodley*.

Tamarworth : Island at the mouth of the Tamar, Phœnician name for Plymouth.

Tavistock Street Improvement (Devonport) : Of this area Sydney Street was formerly Market Lane, and led from Tavistock Street to Crosse Street. Tavistock Street in 1884 consisted of a portion of the street from Market Street to Sydney Street, 24 feet in width, and from that point to Cherry Garden Street was only a narrow lane of the width of 12 feet. The Corporation then acquired the whole block of buildings bounded by Tavistock Street, Cherry Garden (York) Street, Sydney Street and Catherine Street, and made a regular width of 40 feet from Market Street to Cherry Garden (York) Street. The remainder of the land was sold by public auction, and the Metropole Theatre and other buildings stand on a portion of the site. The scheme cost the town £12,000.

Tin Street, 1765 : Now Vauxhall Street.

Tothill : William Totwell, Prior's Portreeve of Sutton (Wright). Or from the word "tote"—to spy a watch, apparently an outpost. Tothill Lane, formerly White Friars Lane. Now Tothill Avenue.

Towards the Ponds (Devonport) : Houses near the site of the pond (existing Market), of which "Young's Folly" were the more famous.

Town Square, Dock : Morice Square, Devonport.

Trelawney's Conduit, built in 1598 by Sir John Trelawney: "The building, which is square at Old Town Without, was very conveniently situated at the time it was built. Scarcely a house above it. Ye building and re-building are both preserved on a slate stone in the centre of the front, on one side of which are the Town Arms and Sir Francis Drake's, and over it the King's Arms, all neatly done in Portland stone, ornamented and surmounted by neat battlements all around. In 1812 the building underwent a thorough repair. Instead of the battlements being replaced, there were some old stones brought from the higher part of the lake, on which is the inscription raised on the stone: 'Made in the Mayoralty of John Trelawnye, 1598.' This was placed on the top of the conduit in front, and to raise the wall around they used the old trough stones taken up in this year from the conduit to the factory, and the remainder of the troughs or gutter stones were placed on the curb of the raised footway over the leat adjoining. The stone in the centre was taken from the water house above, where the water in a body is turned on to the town by night above ground or in case of fire. Before the building was repaired many wished to have it taken down, and it was but a few voices saved it (or a small minority). Dr. Bellamy was its greatest friend. All the stone work, after it was done, he had restored in one colour." (Harris.)

Treville Street: After two brothers who were local merchants in the 17th century.

Turnstile Slip: Leading out of Southside Street.

Turk's Head: Top of St. Andrew Street, almost opposite the Abbey.

Union Road, through the Marshes: Union Street.

United Gas Company Works: Millbay, established 1826. Stoke Church first lit with gas, 1831. (Worth.)

Venar Ward: After the Venours, subsequently portion of Vintry Ward.

Vinegar Hill, Plymouth: Mount and Prospect Streets district—so-called after the name of the builder, and applied by way of a jest as a speculation likely to involve him in a wry face.

Warren: The new Baptist burial ground south side of George Street.

Water House, Plymouth: Adjoining the Higher Mills; site of Sherwell Chapel and Drake's Pleasure Grounds.

Water-Lane (south of Pembroke Street, Devonport): From a pool of water in the old quarry workings below Mount Wise (Worth). Water Lane (Plymouth), 1765; Jory Street, 1828; part of Exeter Street.

Weakley's Hotel: Fore Street, Devonport, 1824.

West-well: In Burying Place Lane, in a field leading to the Hoe. Lately filled up. (Harris, 1810.)

Whitsand: White-sand.

Whimple Street: Famous for the sale of whimples or women's hoods. At one time the Booksellers' Row of Plymouth, and the birthplace of Benjamin Haydon.

White Cross Street: Now south end of North Street.

White Friars Lane: Now Beaumont Road, Plymouth.

White Hart Hotel: Adjoining Chubb's Hotel, a celebrated commercial house kept by Peter Yeo in 1840. Part of Spooner and Co.'s establishment.

Whiting Lane: Intersecting Bedford Street and East Street; now the property of Spooner and Co.

Windmill Street and Bowling Green: Site of old windmill (now part of Monument Street), adjoining the mount on which Devonport Column is erected, and partly the site of the Wesleyan Chapel.

White Lion Inn (Plymouth) : Opposite the Noah's Ark in Old Town Street. Near the site a number of skulls and human remains were dug up on the demolition of the house. Possibly burial ground without the Old Town Gate.

Workhouse Alms Houses : " These are quite hid from the public eye, and in general are hardly known to exist. They are situate in the Court of St. Andrew's Almhouses, adjoining the Old Church, on the North of the Grammar School, Catherine Street." (Harris, 1810.)

Workhouse Lane (otherwise Catherine Street, Plymouth) : Used as a convenient address to the Hospital of the Poor's Portion, or the Old Workhouse.

Zion Street (Plymouth) : Formerly Cherry Garden Street.

LIST OF SUBSCRIBERS.

Alger, W. H., The Manor House, Stoke Damerel.
Arber, W. H., 25, Sackville Street, Piccadilly, London.   (Five copies.)
Athenæum, Plymouth.
Atwill, Mrs. J., 3, Buckland Terrace, Yelverton.

Barber, R., Avondale Terrace, Plymouth.
Barratt, Francis Layland, 68, Cadogan Square, London.   (Two copies.)
Barrett, George R., Drakesleigh, Plymouth.
Bayly, R., Torr, Plymouth.   (Two copies.)
Bellamy, George D., Burrow Lodge, Lipson Road, Plymouth.
Bellamy, J. A., Hartley, Plymouth.
Bennett, John, M.A., 15, Woodland Terrace, Plymouth.
Bewes, Cecil E., Hillside, Plympton.
Bewes, Mrs. Reginald, Braeside, Mannamead.
Bickle, John W., 9, Queen's Gate, Plymouth.
Bird-Davis, C. H., Lipson, Plymouth.
Birdwood, Sir George, India Office, London.
Birdwood, H., care of Col. Bayly, Stoborough Grange, Littledown Road, Bournemouth.
Birdwood, H.M., care of Messrs. H. S. King and Co., 45, Pall Mall, London, S.W.
Birmingham, W., 9, Whimple Street, Plymouth.
Blanchard, John, 33, Bedford Street, Plymouth.
Blandford, Mrs., 22, Elmsdale Road, Tyndall's Park, Bristol.
Blight, W. W., 73, Durnford Street, Stonehouse.
Blundell, C. W., Whiteford Road, Mannamead, Plymouth.
Bond, J. Kinton, 13, The Crescent, Plymouth.   (Six copies.)
Bond, J. T., Plymouth.   (Two copies.)
Bond, P. G., M.R.C.V.S., 105, Union Street, Plymouth.
Boolds, Andrew W., 42, Portland Road, Stoke, Devonport.
Boolds, C.C., 1, Queen Anne's Gate, Plymouth.
Boolds, E. A., Albemarle Villas, Stoke, Devonport.
Bowden, C. H., 59, St. Aubyn Street, Devonport.
Bowen, Alderman, St. Budeaux.
Bowering and Co., Messrs., George Street, Plymouth.
Brooks, C. J., 3, Sussex Street, Plymouth.   (Two copies.)
Brooming, S. D., St. Stephen's School, Devonport.
Brown, J. P., 2, Houndiscombe Villas, Plymouth.
Bulteel, Thomas, Naval Bank, Plymouth.
Burnard, Robert, F.S.A., 3, Hillsborough, Plymouth.
Burnard, Charles F., Chatsworth Lodge, Plymouth.
Burns, John F., 6, Argaum Villas, Stoke, Devonport.

3

Campbell, Mrs., 1, Donegal Terrace, Stoke, Devonport.
Carr, Rear-Admiral, H.M. Dockyard, Devonport.
Carlton, Arthur, Metropole Theatre, Devonport.
Chapple, Edwin, George Street, Plymouth.   (Two copies.)
Cheves, Dr. J. T., Anderton, Plymouth.
Clarke, Sir Edward, 37, Russell Square, London.
Cocks, James, 8, Edgcumbe Street, Stonehouse.
Coles, A. N., South Lipson Terrace, Plymouth.
Collins, George, 8, Windsor Terrace, Plymouth.
Co-operative Library, 4, Radford Place, Market, Plymouth.
Cornish, J. E., 16, St. Ann's Square, Manchester.
Crealock, John James, 45, Torrington Place, Plymouth.
Cummings, Samuel, 9, Werter Road, Putney, S.W.

Darke, R., 15, Cranborne Avenue West, Plymouth.
Davies, E. Aitken, Walker Terrace, Plymouth.
Davy, Albert J., 23, Fleet Street, Torquay.
Dawe, W. H., 17, Clifton Place, Plymouth.
Debnam, A. R., St. James Villa, Plymouth.
Debnam, A. W., Surveyor, East Stonehouse.
Derry, W., Houndiscombe House, Plymouth.
Doidge, Messrs, Union Street, Plymouth.   (Two Copies.)
Down, John, 8, Limerick Place, Plymouth.
Drake, H. H., 43, St. George's Avenue, Tufnell Park, N.
Duke, H. E., 1, Paper Buildings, Temple, London.
Duke of Cornwall Hotel Company, Plymouth, per F. B. Westlake (Chairman).

Earwaker, Edwin, 11, Grimstone Terrace, Plymouth.
Ede, Henry, 5, Revelstoke Terrace, Beaumont Road, Plymouth.
Ellis, J. H., Woodhaye, Ivybridge.

Faull, Arthur C., Albemarle House, North Road, Plymouth.
Firks, George, 10, Old Town Street, Plymouth.
Fisher, Miss, Lindores, Glasgow.
Foot, Isaac, 10, Notte Street, Plymouth.
Ford, William, 3, Tamar Terrace, Stoke, Devonport.   (Three copies.)
Foster, Richard, Lanwithan, Lostwithiel.
Fouracre, John T., 16, Portland Square, Plymouth.
Fox, Charles A., Bank Chambers, Plymouth.
Fuge, Mrs. E. P., 3, Earl's Acre, Plymouth.
Full, W., Ker Street, Devonport.

Gameson, J. Herbert, Solicitor, Bodmin.
Gardner, R. H., 46, Chapel Street, Devonport.
Geake, T. H., 6, Athenæum Terrace, Plymouth.
Genoni, A., Swiss Café, Plymouth.
Goodman, Charles, 1, Fitzroy Terrace, Stoke, Devonport.
Goodhart, MacCormick.
Green, M., Market Arcade, Plymouth.

Greenway, John, 2, Shaftesbury Villa, Ford Park, Plymouth.
Grigg, G., Cann House, Tamerton.

Hand, Thomas W., City Librarian, Free Public Libraries, Leeds.
Harris, A. Saunders, 5, Gascoyne Place, Plymouth.
Harvey, T. H., Cattedown, Plymouth.
Hedger, Edwin Henry, 8, Saltash Street, Plymouth. (Six copies.)
Hedley, Captain, Newcastle-on-Tyne.
Helson, George, 11, Salisbury Place, Plymouth.
Hems, Harry, Fair Park, Exeter.
Hill, H. S., "Western Morning News," Plymouth.
Hill, W. A., 8, Beyrout Place, Stoke, Devonport.
Hine, James, F.R.I.B.A., Lockyer Street, Plymouth.
Hingston, C. Albert, M.D., 3, Sussex Terrace, Plymouth.
Hocking, C. F., 117, Fore Street, Devonport.
Holloway, Elphinstone, Major, Worsley Lodge, Southsea.
Holman, R. C., D. and C. Bank, Mutley, Plymouth.
Hornbrook, W., Garfield Villa, Devonport. (Two copies.)
Hosking, W. O., Commercial Rooms, Plymouth.
Hunt, F. W., Librarian, Devonport Free Library.
Hurrell, John S., The Manor House, Kingsbridge.

Inskip, George H., Captain R.N., 22, Torrington Place, Plymouth.

Jackman, W., Caprera Terrace, Plymouth.
Jago, Chas. S., Public School, Cobourg Street, Plymouth.
James, C. Hamilton, Woodside Cottage, Plymouth.
James, John B., Holland House, Plymouth. (Twenty copies).
Jarvis, H., Marlborough Street, Devonport.
Jeffery, Arthur W., F.R. Met. Soc., etc., Board of Trade Office, Glasgow.
Jewson, E. M., Duke of Cornwall Buildings, Plymouth.
Jillard, George, Truro.
Jolliffe, 6, Clarendon Terrace, Devonport.
Jones, Harry, Leigham Terrace, Plymouth.

Kearley, Hudson E., M.P., 41, Grosvenor Place, S.W.
Kegan Paul, French, Trubner and Co., Limited, Paternoster House, London.
Keily, M. D., 16, Caprera Terrace, Plymouth.
Keys, W., Whimple Street, Plymouth.
King, Wm., 59, Southside Street, Plymouth.
Kirton, M. A., Stoke, Devonport.

Layland-Barratt, Francis, D.L., 68, Cadogan Square, S.W. (Two copies.)
Lamble, J. A., 44, Portland Road, Stoke, Devonport.
Lancaster, Edward S., 1, Windsor Terrace, Plymouth.
Lane and Cottier, 8, Frankfort Street, Plymouth. (Two copies.)
Lemann, F. C., Blackfriars' House, Plymouth.
Levy, Asher, 190, Union Street, Plymouth.
Ley, H. F., 38, Springfield Terrace, Plymouth.
Littleton, W., Morice Town, Devonport.

Lockie, John, Stonehall, Stonehouse, Devon.
Luff, Henry George, 64, Chapel Street, Devonport.
Luke, Chas., 8, Bedford Street, Plymouth. (Two copies.)

MacCormick-Goodhart, F. E., 2, Clifton Crescent, Folkestone.
Madge, Mrs., Leigham Street, Plymouth.
Martin, John, (late Hon. Sec. Devonians in London), 11, Thorngate Road, W.
Martin, W., 6, Windsor Terrace, Plymouth. (Two copies.)
Mason, J.. Librarian, St. Martin's Public Library, 115, St. Martin's Lane, London.
Maton, T., 63, George Street, Plymouth.
Matthews, Henry, 11 and 12, Bedford Street, Plymouth.
May, T., 33, Cobourg Street, Plymouth.
McArthur, W. A., M.P., 4, Third Avenue, Hove, Sussex.
Mc Donald, C., 23, Abingdon Road, Plymouth.
Moon, James, Brixton House, Brixton.
Morton, Miss H. C., Herrn Hut, Boscombe, Hants. (Two copies.)
Mountsteven, Francis Hander, Major, 3rd Devon Regt., Craythorne House, S.E.
Mudge, Arthur T., Sydney, Plympton.

Newcombe, A., Thomas's Hotel, Devonport. (Two Copies.)
Nicholls, Walter J., Tregarne Terrace, St. Austell
Norrington, C., Abbotsfield, Mannamead.
Northey, E. A., Auctioneer, Plymouth.

Olver, T. R. Ellis, 7, Portland Villas, Plymouth.
Organ, Charles, 16, Victoria Terrace, St. Budeaux.
Organ, Charles Alfred, B.A., Froebel House, Stoke, Devonport.

Page, James H., 20, Portland Villas, Plymouth.
Page, S. J., 42, Woolster Street, Plymouth.
Park, Chas. J., M.P.S., Mutley Plain, Plymouth.
Parkhouse, Edward, Old Town Street, Plymouth.
Pawley, W. H., St. James Place, Plymouth.
Pearce, Percy T., Princess Square, Plymouth.
Penberthy, R. H., 20, Marlborough Street, Devonport.
Penny, Edward L., Rev., D.D., R.N., Coryton, Pentillie Road, Plymouth.
Perkins, George, 33, Emma Place, Stonehouse.
Pethick, John, Down Park, Yelverton. (Two copies.)
Phillipps-Treby, P.W., Major-General, Goodamoor, Plympton.
Phillips, Frank, 7, West Hoe Terrace, Plymouth.
Phillips, Sydney H., Mannamead, Plymouth.
Phillips, W. W. H., Westwell Street, Plymouth.
Pike, W. H., 66, Park Hill Road, Haverstock Hill, N.W
Pilling, A. B., Hopwood, Devonport.
Piper, F. J., "Merivale," Yelverton. (Eight copies.)
Pitcher, R. W., 6, Marlborough Street, Devonport.
Plimsaul, F., 37, St. Mary Axe, London.
Plymouth Library, Cornwall Street.
Plymouth County Council (for Muniment Room).

Pocock, Henry, London, E.C. (Twelve copies.)
Ponsonby, S. G., Rev., Stoke, Devonport.
Pope, Horace K., 7, Gloucester Square, Southampton.
Popplestone, R. W., 37, Bedford Street, Plymouth.
Pote, W. H., 47, Fore Street, Devonport.
Prance, William Henry, 12, The Crescent, Plymouth.
Pridham, Edmund, 4, Balmoral Place, Plymouth.
Pryor, W., Westwell Street, Plymouth.

Quinn, J. Henry, Chelsea Public Libraries, S.W.

Radford, C. H., 2, Queen's Gate Villas, Plymouth.
Radford, John Heynes, Uppaton, Buckland Monachorum.
Ray, C. H., St. Michael's Terrace, Plymouth.
Rider, Alonzo J., High School, Devonport.
Risdon, Geo., 35, Marlborough Street, Devonport.
Roberts, A. G , St. Aubyn Street, Devonport.
Roberts, Harold, Caroline Place, Stonehouse.
Roberts, Samuel, sen., Mount Pleasant, Plymouth.
Roberts, S., jun.. Mount Pleasant, Plymouth.
Rodd, R. Robinson, 81, Durnford Street, East Stonehouse.
Rodda, R. C. T., 2, Carlisle Terrace, Plymouth.
Rowe, J. Brooking, Castle Barbican, Plympton.
Rowbotham, Albert E., Glenside, Clayton Bridge, Manchester.
Roy, David, 5, Windsor Villas, Plymouth.
Royal Western Yacht Club, Plymouth.
Ryder, J. W., Tamar Terrace, Devonport.

Sale, David, Fore Street, Devonport.
Sanders, William Sedgwick, Moor View Lodge, Exeter.
Sansom, Louis, 5, Houndiscombe Villas, Plymouth. (Two copies.)
Scott-Tucker, H., Belvedere, Mannamead.
Seale-Hayne, C., M.P., Pill House, Chudleigh.
Shannon, Alfred, 18, St. Hilary Terrace, Stoke, Devonport.
Shannon, Hugh, 21, Fore Street, Devonport.
Shellabear and Son, 27, Mutley Plain, Plymouth.
Shellabear, George, Chubb's Hotel, Plymouth. (Three copies.)
Shepherd, D. Davies, Ford, Devonport.
Sleep, Fred, L.D.S., Queen Anne Terrace, Plymouth.
Snawdon, J., Trafalgar House, Plymouth.
Snell, H. J., 6, Grimstone Villas, Plymouth.
Sowerby, J. D., Chief Constable, Plymouth.
Spooner, Edwin Chas., Raventor, Bridestowe.
Spry, W. J. J., (late H.M. Royal Yacht Alberta), 66, St. Andrew's Road, Southsea.
Square, J. Eliott, 22, Portland Square, Plymouth.
Stanbury, C. H., Outlands, Devonport.
Stanbury, G., 30, Woolstone Road, Catford, London, S.E
Stanbury, H., 13, Hobart Terrace, Plymouth.
Stancombe, R., Athenæum Hotel, Plymouth.

Stephens, R. W., 34, Catherine Street, Devonport.
Sydenham, E. Dickerson, R.N., Malta.
Sydenham, F. W., R.N., Malta.
Sydenham, L. G., 4, Portland Villas, Plymouth.
Sydenham, L. J., Portland Villas, Plymouth.　(Two copies.)

Tangye, Richard, Sir, Gilbertstone, Kingston Vale, Putney, London, S.W.
Tattersall, Thomas, Municipal Offices, Devonport.
Tozer, J. C., Mount Edgcumbe Terrace, Devonport.
Trelawny, J. Jago, Major-General, Coldrenick, Liskeard.
Trist, G. S., Secretary London Anti-Vivisection Society.
Tucker, Henry, Belvedore, Mannamead, Plymouth.

Varnier, Alex. H., 1, Whiteford Road, Mannamead, Plymouth.

Wade, W. Cecil, Victoria Chambers, Plymouth.
Wakeling, H. H., 26, Wyndham Square, Plymouth.
Walford, Colonel, Warlegh, Tamerton Foliott.
Ward, John, St. Aubyn Street, Devonport.
Ward, Miss Marion, 3, Buckland Terrace, Yelverton.
Watkins, A., 2, South Lipson Terrace, Plymouth.
Watson, G. F., 14, Smeaton Terrace, Plymouth.
Watts, John W., Seaton Place, Ford, Devonport.
Watts, R. I., Princess Square, Plymouth.
Waycott, William J., Clarendon Terrace, Stoke, Devonport.
Westlake, F. B., George Street Chambers, Plymouth.
Westlake, W. C., Oakenhayes, Tavistock.
White, Sir William H., K.C.B., 39, Roland Gardens, London, S.W.
Willcocks, H. S., 32, Wyndham Square, Plymouth.
Wildman, A. C., Cornishman Office, Parade Street, Penzance.
Williams, Richard S. J., " Noah's Ark," Plymouth.
Williams, Thomas H., 1, Gibbons Street, Plymouth.
Willoughby, Joseph, Central Foundry, Plymouth.　(Two copies.)
Willoughby, Samuel, 63, Finsbury Pavement, London.
Wilson, James, Hutton House, Birmingham.
Winnicott, J. F., Rockville, Mannamead.
Wood, Charles, Carlton House, St. Lawrence Road, Plymouth.
Woodley, Jno. L. C., Plymouth Proprietary Library, Cornwall Street, Plymouth.
Woods, W. Herbert, 50, Bedford Street, Plymouth.
Woolley, Samuel, Devon and Cornwall Bank, Devonport.
Wright, W. H. K., Public Library, Plymouth.

Yeo, H. R., 68, Lisson Groove, Mutley, Plymouth.
Yeo, A., Sticklepath House, Plymouth.

INDEX.

Strode, Henry, Member for Plympton, reports Tinners to the King, 30.

Stuarts: James I. and Plymouth, 77; Fatal flaw in character, 77; Rising hatred of the, 91; Acclaimed by Plymouth at the Restoration, 116; Fall of the Stuarts, 144; The Citadel delivered to Prince of Orange supporters, 144; Jacobite disaffection and uprising, 144.

Superstitions: Bideford Witches, etc., 137; "Boat-Ahoy," 287; Baker the Wizard, 286; Suspected Fowl at Hooe, 290; Miracles Wrought at Sutton, 11; Ominous Clouds of Ravens, 115; "Old Witch of Plymouth," 123; Roger Reope, fisherman, condemned to weave ropes of sand, 6; "Screeching Dolly," 291; "Susan's Overthrow," 288; Tallant's Ghost, 287; Admiral Duckworth's Ghost, 287; "Plymouth Tragedy," 288; Ghosts on Dartmoor, 5.

Sugar Refinery in Mill Lane, 536.

Printed by HIORNS & MILLER, 107 Fore Street, Devonport.